CATALOGUE

OF BOOKS IN

The Roxbury Branch Library

OF THE

BOSTON PUBLIC LIBRARY,

INCLUDING

THE COLLECTION OF THE FELLOWES ATHENÆUM,

TOGETHER

WITH NOTES FOR READERS UNDER SUBJECT-REFERENCES.

SECOND EDITION, AUGUST, 1876.

BOSTON:
ISSUED BY THE LIBRARY.
ROCKWELL AND CHURCHILL, CITY PRINTERS.
1876.

NOTE.

The first edition, 1,000 copies, of this Catalogue, 140 pages, was issued October, 1873, when the collection contained about 5,000 volumes, over 1,000 of the more costly of which belonged to the Fellowes Athenæum. The present edition, 2,000 copies, shows about 11,000 volumes, and of this number about 3,600 volumes are the property of the Fellowes Athenæum.

PREFACE.

THE present Catalogue of the Roxbury Branch of the Public Library of Boston has some distinctive features, which are introduced because of the success attending the employment of them in the printed catalogues of the popular department of the Central Library. These consist of helps to readers by descriptive interpolations in connection with titles; and by notes for longer elucidations, where it seemed desirable to guide to more or less extended study of subjects. Similar notes were first employed in 1873 in the Catalogue of History, Biography, and Travel, which pertained chiefly to the collection in the Lower Hall in Boylston street, and they produced marked good effects on the character of the books read from that collection. These features were copied in part in the catalogues of a few of the small libraries in Massachusetts; but nowhere was this principle so well carried out as in the Catalogue of the Public Library of Quincy, issued in 1875, and it is understood that the excellent development of the notes in that catalogue was largely due to the labors of the President of the Trustees of that library, Mr. Charles Francis Adams, jr. In the analysis of books and in references to magazine and review articles, somewhat similar work is now going forward, to a large extent, in the new Catalogue of the Brooklyn Mercantile Library; and by the favor of the librarian, Mr. S. B. Noyes, the sheets, so far as printed, have been put to service as a check-list in the preparation of the notes in this Catalogue. A like use has been made of the Quincy Catalogue, though the chief dependence has been upon the Lower Hall Catalogue, already named, and upon the additions which have been made to it, in anticipation of a new edition. The accuracy of the work is largely due to the supervision of the Library proof-reader, Mr. William H. Foster, and to the careful attention of the proof-reader in the office of the City Printers.

As a list of books, the present Catalogue has acquired something like rounded proportions through the favor of the Trustees of the Fellowes Athenæum, who have freely purchased the necessary books to fill in the gaps which the final revision disclosed. As this work of expansion has gone on with the progress of the Catalogue through the press, it has occasioned the considerable list of addenda, and has caused the mention of some titles, without shelf-numbers, in the notes, when the orders for them were not answered in sufficient season to make the record of their accession complete. Some of these titles will be found in the addenda; others of the books are not yet received.

JUSTIN WINSOR, *Superintendent.*

BOSTON PUBLIC LIBRARY, CENTRAL DEPARTMENT,
August 1, 1876.

PUBLIC LIBRARY OF THE CITY OF BOSTON.

ROXBURY BRANCH,

INCLUDING THE FELLOWES ATHENÆUM.

SECOND EDITION.

*** *Friends of the Public Library will confer a favor, if they will kindly communicate to the Superintendent the correction of any error they may discover in this List, or the authorship of any works treated as anonymous, or the name of any person entered only under initials or under a pseudonymn.*

*** *The entries below are usually of sufficient length for comparison of editions; but in cases of juvenile and popular books, the titles are often only given at such length as may be necessary for finding purposes.*

Shelf. No.

A., A. A. All for greed ... 311.24
— Love the avenger ... 312.2
ABADDON, the spirit of destruction: poem. Fairfield, S. L. New York, 1830. 8° ... 1623.4
ABANDONED. [Fiction.] Verne, J. ... 733.11
ABAUZIT, Firmin. Essays. (*In* Sparks, J. Collection of essays and tracts in theology) ... 1918.9.1
ABBÉ Tigrane, The. Fabre, F. ... 715.19
ABBOT, Ezra. Bibliography of the doctrine of a future life. *See* ALGER, William Rounseville .. 5831.3
ABBOT, The. Scott, *Sir* W. Boston ... 523.10
— *Same.* Leipzig ... 324.10
ABBOTSFORD. Irving, W. London, 1853. 16° ... 715.5
ABBOTT, Edwin Abbott. A Shakespearian grammar. An attempt to illustrate some of the differences between Elizabethan and modern English. New edition. London, 1872. xxiv, 511 pp. 16° ... 5617.7
— and SEELEY, John Robert. English lessons for English people. London, 1871. xxiv, 292 pp. Sm. 8° ... 1535.1
ABBOTT, Jacob. The August stories. August and Elvie ... 923.1
— — Granville valley ... 923.4
— — Hunter and Tom ... 923.2
— — The schooner Mary Ann ... 923.3
— [Franconia stories.] Agnes ... 914.10
— — Beechnut ... 914.14
— — Caroline ... 914.7
— — Ellen Linn ... 914.13
— — Malleville ... 914.15
— — Mary Bell ... 914.16
— — Mary Erskine ... 914.8
— — Rodolphus ... 914.9
— — Stuyvesant ... 914.12
— — Wallace ... 914.11
— Harper's story books ... 936.1

Contents.—Vol. I. Bruno; Willie and the mortgage; The strait gate. II. Little Louvre; Prank; Emma. III. Virginia; Timboo and Joliba; Timboo and Fanny. IV. Harper establishment; Franklin; The studio. V. Story of ancient history; Story of English history; Story of American history. VI. John True; Elfred; The museum. VII. The engineer; Rambles among the Alps; Three gold dollars. VIII. The Gibraltar gallery; The alcove; Dialogues. IX. The great elm; Aunt Margaret; Vernon. X. Carl and Jocko; Lapstone; Orkney. XI. Judge Justin; Minigo; Jasper. XII. Congo; Viola and Arno; Little Paul.

— History of Alexander the great ... 915.3
— History of Alfred of England ... 914.34
— History of Charles I of England ... 914.26
— History of Charles II of England ... 914.28

Shelf. No.

ABBOTT, Jacob, *continued.*
— History of Cleopatra, queen of Egypt ... 915.11
— History of Cyrus the great ... 915.8
— History of Elizabeth ... 915.10
— History of Genghis Khan ... 914.36
— History of Hannibal the Carthaginian ... 914.22
— History of Julius Cæsar ... 914.23
— History of Margaret of Anjou ... 914.29
— History of Mary queen of Scots ... 915.7
— History of Nero ... 914.27
— History of Peter the great, emperor of Russia ... 915.4
— History of Pyrrhus ... 915.12
— History of Richard I of England ... 915.13
— History of Richard II of England ... 915.6
— History of Richard III of England ... 915.5
— History of William the conqueror ... 914.24
— Marco Paul's voyages and travels. [Marco Paul at the] Springfield armory ... 914.4
— — [Marco Paul in] Boston ... 914.5
— — [Marco Paul in] New York ... 914.6
— — [Marco Paul in the forests of] Maine ... 914.3
— — [Marco Paul in] Vermont ... 914.2
— — [Marco Paul on the] Erie canal ... 914.1
— The Rollo series. Rollo at play ... 917.6
— — Rollo at school ... 917.11
— — Rollo at work ... 917.3
— — Rollo learning to read ... 917.15
— — Rollo learning to talk ... 917.8
— — Rollo's correspondence ... 917.5
— — Rollo's experiments ... 917.12
— — Rollo's museum ... 917.4
— — Rollo's philosophy. Air ... 917.14
— — — Fire ... 917.10
— — — Sky ... 917.9
— — — Water ... 917.13
— — Rollo's travels ... 917.7
— — Rollo's vacation ... 917.2
— The Rollo story books. The apple gathering ... 917.28
— — Blueberrying ... 917.27
— — Causey building ... 917.26
— — The freshet ... 917.34
— — Georgie ... 917.35
— — The halo round the moon ... 917.29
— — Labor lost ... 917.31
— — Rollo in the woods ... 917.30
— — Rollo's garden ... 917.32
— — The steeple trap ... 917.33
— — Trouble on the mountain ... 917.37
— — The two wheelbarrows ... 917.36

Shelf. No.

ABBOTT, Jacob, *continued.*
— Rollo's tour in Europe. Rollo in Geneva 917.18
— – Rollo in Holland 917.21
— – Rollo in London 917.20
— – Rollo in Naples 917.24
— – Rollo in Paris 917.22
— – Rollo in Rome 915.14
— – Rollo in Scotland 917.19
— – Rollo in Switzerland 917.23
— – Rollo on the Atlantic 917.16
— – Rollo on the Rhine 917.17
— Science for the young. Heat 912.5
— – Light 912.4
— – Water and land 912.3
— Stories of Rainbow and Lucky. [Handie] 914.21
— – [Rainbow's journey] 914.19
— – [Selling Lucky] 914.20
— – [The three pines] 914.17
— – [Up the river] 914.18
— A summer in Scotland. With engravings. New York, 1848. 331 pp. 12° 425.11
— The way to do good. Boston, 1836. 348 pp. 12°. 5836.4
ABBOTT, John Stevens Cabot. American pioneers and patriots. The adventures of the chevalier de La Salle and his companions, in their explorations of the new world, two hundred years ago. Illustrated. New York [1875]. 384 pp. 12°. 1014.13
— – Captain William Kidd, and others of the pirates who ravaged America two hundred years ago. Illustrated. New York, 1874. 373+ pp. 12°. 1014.11
— – Christopher Carson. Familiarly known as Kit Carson. With illustrations. New York, 1873. 342+ pp. Portrait. 12° 1014.8
— – Daniel Boone the pioneer of Kentucky. Illustrated. New York, 1872. 331 pp. 12° 1014.4
— – David Crockett: his life and adventures. Illustrated. New York, 1874. 350+ pp. 12° .. 1014.10
— – Ferdinand de Soto, the discoverer of the Mississippi. Illustrated. New York, 1873. 351 pp. Portrait. 12° 923.34
— – George Washington; or, life in America one hundred years ago. Illustrated. New York [1875]. 360 pp. 12° 1014.16
— – Life and adventures of rear-admiral John Paul Jones, commonly called Paul Jones. Illustrated. New York [1874]. 359 pp. Portrait. 12° ... 1014.12
— – Life of Christopher Columbus. Illustrated. New York [1875]. 345 pp. Portrait. 12° ... 1014.15
— – Miles Standish, the puritan captain. Illustrated. New York, 1872. 372+ pp. Map. 12°. 1014.6
— – Peter Stuyvesant, the last Dutch governor of New Amsterdam. Illustrated. New York, 1873. 362+ pp. Portrait. 12° 1014.14
— The French revolution of 1789 as viewed in the light of republican institutions. With engravings. New York, 1859. 439 [435] pp. 8° ... 821.2
— History of Frederick II, the great. With illustrations. New York, 1871. 584 pp. Portrait. Maps. 8° 1021.3
— History of Henry IV, king of France and Navarre. 915.2
— History of Hernando Cortez 915.1
— History of Hortense, queen of Holland 914.32
— History of Joseph Bonaparte, king of Naples and of Italy 914.33
— History of Josephine 914.30
— History of King Philip, of the Wampanoags. Including the early history of the settlers of New England 914.31
— History of Madame Roland 915.9
— History of Maine, from the earliest discovery to the present time. Illustrated. Boston, 1875. 556 pp. Portrait. 8° 813.16
— History of Maria Antoinette 914.25
— History of Napoleon Bonaparte. With maps and illustrations. New York, 1870. 2 v. Portraits. 8° 1021.1
— History of Napoleon III, emperor of the French. Including a narrative of the most important events in Europe since the fall of Napoleon I. With illustrations. Boston, 1870. 690 pp. Portrait. 8° 1021.2

ABBOTT, John Stevens Cabot, *continued.*
— Italy, and the war for Italian independence. Including a biographical sketch of Pius IX. Boston, 1871. 638 pp. Illustrated. Map. Portraits. 12° 824.15
— The monarchies of continental Europe. The empire of Austria. New York, 1859. 520 pp. Portrait. 12° 825.1
— Romance of Spanish history. With illustrations. New York, 1869. 462 pp. 12° 824.3
ABBOTT, Lyman. A dictionary of religious knowledge. With maps and illustrations. Edited by L. Abbott, assisted by T. J. Conant. New York, 1875. xv, 1074 pp. 8° 6320.2
ABBOTT, Rosa. *See* PARKER, Rosa Abbott.
ABDEL KADER, Life of. Churchill, C. H. London, 1867. Sm. 8° 5934.4
A'BECKETT, Gilbert Abbott. The comic history of England. With 20 coloured etchings, and two hundred woodcuts. London, N. D. xviii, 804 pp. 8° 823.6
ABEL, C. D. Elementary principles of machinery. 2d edition. London, 1868. xvi, 189+ pp. 12°. 6428.2
ABERCROMBIE, John. Inquiries concerning the intellectual powers, and the investigation of truth. New York, 1857. 376 pp. 12° 1529.4
ABERDEEN, *Earl of. See* GORDON, George Hamilton.
ABINGTON, *Mass.*, Historical sketch of. Hobart, A. Boston, 1839. 8° 812.1
ABODE, The, of snow. [Himalayas.] Wilson, A. New York, 1875. Sm. 8° 5933.10
ABOUT, Edmond (François Valentin). Handbook of social economy; or, the worker's A B C. Translated from the last French edition. New York, 1873. xx, 284 pp. 12° 1528.9
— L'homme à l'oreille cassée. 3e édition. Paris, 1862. 277+ pp. 16° 2016.7
— The man with a broken ear. Translated from the French by H. Holt 517.20
— Le progrès. 3e édition. Paris, 1865. 440+ pp. 18° 5536.3
— Le roi des montagnes. 6e édition. Paris, 1863. 301+ pp. 18° 5536.13

Note.—Brigandage in Greece.

ABÚ BECR MOHAMMED IBN ZACARÍYÁ AR-RÁZÍ (*commonly called* RHAZES). Treatise on small-pox and measles. Translated from the Arabic by W. A. Greenhill. London, 1848. vii, 212 pp. 8°. 6013.10
ABYSSINIA, The Nile tributaries of. Baker, *Sir* S. W. London, 1871. Sm. 8° 425.3
— *Same.* With supplement. Hartford, 1871. 8°. 5932.1

See also Africa, Magdala, Nile.

ACADEMY, The. A weekly review of literature, science, and art. Vol. 5-8. London, 1874, 75. 4 v. 4° 6721.1
ACCESSIBLE field sports. Gilmore, P. London, 1869. Sm. 8° 1514.10
ACHILLES fillias. Sue, M. J. Pest, 1852. 16° 2027.4
ACOUSTICS. Lees, W. Elements of. New York [Glasgow], 1873. 16° 1717.10
— Radau, R. Wonders of. New York, 1870. 16°. 1714.11
— Smith, T. R. Acoustics in relation to architecture and building. London, N. D. 12° 1715.1
ACROSS America and Asia. Pumpelly, R. New York, 1871. 8° 5916.2
ACROSS the continent. Bowles, S. Springfield, 1868. 16° 417.6
ACTON, William. The functions and disorders of the reproductive organs in childhood, youth, adult age, and advanced life considered in their physiological, social, and moral relations. Philadelphia, 1865. 269 pp. 8° 6022.6
ACTORS and acting. Lewes, G. H. On actors and the art of acting. Leipzig, 1875. Sq. 16° 1638.1
— *Same.* London, 1875. Sm. 8° 5428.20
— Mathews, L. E. Anecdotes of actors. London, 1844. 8° 5623.7
— Russell, W. C. Representative actors. London [187-]. Sm. 8° 5427.4

See also English stage.

Shelf. No.

ADAM, William. The law and custom of slavery in British India, in a series of letters to Thomas Fowell Buxton. Boston, 1840. 279 pp. 12°.. 1915.4
ADAM Bede. Lewes, M.......................... 310.25
ADAMS, Andrew Leith. Field and forest rambles, with notes and observations on the natural history of eastern Canada. London, 1873. xvi, 333 pp. Illustrated. Map. 8° 6613.11
ADAMS, Charles Francis, *joint author*. Life of John Adams. *See* ADAMS, John Quincy 5026.1
— Remarks upon [his] memorial address on the late W. H. Seward. Welles, G. New York, 1874. 12°.5027.10
ADAMS, Charles Francis, *jr.* A chapter of Erie. Boston, 1869. iv, 152 pp. 12° 1916.1
ADAMS, F. Colburn. The story of a trooper. With much of interest concerning the campaign on the peninsula, not before written. New York, 1865. 616+ pp. 12° 816.10
ADAMS, Francis Ottiwell. History of Japan from the earliest period to the present time. Vol. I. To 1864. London, 1874. Folded map. 8° ... 5911.6
ADAMS, Hannah. An abridgement of the history of New-England. Boston, 1805. iv, 185 pp. 12°. 818.7
— Dictionary of all religions and religious denominations, ancient and modern. 4th edition. Boston, 1817. 376+ pp. 8°.................. 5812.3
— History of the Jews from the destruction of Jerusalem to the 19th century. Boston, 1812. 2 v. in 1. 12° 828.12
— A view of religions. Collected from the best authors, ancient and modern. 3d edition. Boston, 1801. 504 pp. 8°............1530.4 and 5814.7
ADAMS, Henry G. Beautiful shells; their nature, structure, and uses; with directions for collecting, cleaning, and arranging them, and descriptions of the most remarkable species. Illustrated. London, 1871. 156+ pp. 16° 6636.1
ADAMS, John. Adams, J. Q. and C. F. Life of. Philadelphia, 1871. 2 v. 12° 5026.1
— Parker, T. Historic Americans. Boston, 1871. Sm. 8°.. 5025.4
— Selection of patriotic addresses to the president. With his answers. Boston, 1798. 12° 1917.4

Note. — Admirable material exists in the Diary, Autobiography, and the other writings and correspondence [see Bates Hall catalogues] for a study of his character. A life was begun by John Quincy Adams and continued to 1770, and completed by Charles Francis Adams, and since published separate from his works, as above. See the accounts in Bancroft [vol. viii, ch. 60, for his character], Hildreth (who takes in his presidency), and other general historians. Eulogies on his death may be found in the first volume of Webster's and Everett's Orations. Theodore Parker's Historic Americans gives a sharp, incisive characterization. Lives of his contemporaries, like Irving's Washington [1211.2, etc.] and Parton's Jefferson [1215.1], throw much side-light on his career. See also the North American review, vols. 85 and 113.

ADAMS, John Quincy. Letters on the masonic institution. Boston, 1847. 284+ pp. 8°........ 5822.2
— Memoirs, comprising portions of his diary from 1795 to 1848. Edited by Charles Francis Adams. Vol. I–IX. Philadelphia, 1874–76. 9 v. Portraits. 8°..........................5021.10
— and Charles Francis. Life of John Adams. Revised and corrected. Philadelphia, 1871. 2 v. 12°.................................... 5026.1

Note. — The principal life is that by C. F. Adams, which is too voluminous to be popular, and is not yet finished. Among the eulogies at his death, note Everett's Orations [1921.1.2]. See W. Everett's paper in the Atlantic, Aug., 1875. An account of his administration will be found in Hildreth's United States [5011.11 3]; in Benton's "Thirty years' view" [812.2]; and Parton's Jackson [1212.1].

ADAMS, Nehemiah. A south-side view of slavery; or, three months at the South, in 1854. Boston, 1854. 214+ pp. 16° 817.8
— Memorial volume to commemorate the 25th anniversary of [his] installation. *See* BOSTON, *Mass. Essex Street church and society*........1914.10
ADAMS, Samuel, Life of. Wells, W. V. Boston, 1865. 3 v. 8° 5021.7

Note. — Wells's Life is extensive and authoritative, based chiefly on what is left of the patriot's papers, now in the possession of Bancroft, whose later volumes display his character in a manner that party feeling had earlier obscured or perverted. See also the histories of New England, Massachusetts, and Boston.

Shelf. No.

ADAMS, Thomas. *See* PAGE, H. A. Noble workers. London, 1875. Sm. 8°.................... 5936.3
ADAMS, William. Sacred allegories. [With a memoir of the author.] Leipzig, 1864. 282+ pp. Illustrated. Sq. 16° 311.23
ADAMS, William Henry Davenport. Animal life throughout the globe. An illustrated book of natural history. London, 1876. 704 pp. Sm. 8°.1523.25
— The buried cities of Campania; or, Pompeii and Herculaneum. Boston, 1870. 282 pp. Illustrated. 16°................................ 437.5
— The monsters of the deep: and curiosities of ocean life. A book of anecdotes, traditions, and legends. London, 1875. 325 pp. Illustrated. Sm. 8°.. 6617.1

Note. — "The present volume is founded on M. Armand Landrin's 'Les monstres marins.' To the particulars accumulated by M. Landrin, the translator has added numerous facts and details gathered in the course of his own reading." — *Preface.*

— The queen of the Adriatic; or, Venice past and present. Boston, 1869. 376+ pp. Illustrated. 16° 227.4
ADAMS, William T. (*Oliver Optic.*) [Army and navy series.] Brave old salt.................. 924.3
— – Fighting Joe.............................. 924.6
— – The sailor boy........................... 924.4
— – The soldier boy. A story of the great rebellion. 924.5
— – The Yankee middy......................... 924.1
— – The young lieutenant...................... 924.2
— [Boat club series.] All aboard............... 924.17
— – The boat club 924.15
— – Little by little.......................... 924.18
— – Now or never.............................. 924.13
— – Poor and proud............................ 924.16
— – Try again................................. 924.14
— The Great Western series. Going West 938.9
— In doors and out............................ 714.37
— Lake shore series. Bear and forbear.......... 925.18
— – Brake up 925.17
— – Lightning express 925.19
— – On time 925.15
— – Switch off................................ 925.20
— – Through by daylight....................... 925.16
— Our standard-bearer; or, the life of General Ulysses S. Grant. Illustrated. Boston, 1868. 348 pp. 16°.................................. 916.14
— The Riverdale books. The birthday party...... 918.8
— – Careless Kate............................. 918.4
— – The Christmas gift........................ 918.12
— – Dolly and I............................... 918.13
— – The Do-somethings......................... 939.2
— – The gold thimble 918.11
— – The little merchant 918.9
— – The picnic party.......................... 918.6
— – Proud and lazy............................ 918.10
— – Robinson Crusoe, jr....................... 918.7
— – Uncle Ben 918.5
— – The young voyagers........................ 918.3
— Starry flag series. Breaking away............ 924.24
— – Down the river 924.21
— – Freaks of fortune 924.22
— – Make or break 924.20
— – Seek and find 924.19
— – The starry flag 924.23
— Upward and onward series. Bivouac and battle.. 924.10
— – Cringle and cross-tree 924.11
— – Desk and debit............................ 924.7
— – Field and forest.......................... 924.8
— – Plane and plank........................... 924.12
— – Sea and shore 924.9
— Woodville series. Haste and waste 925.2
— – Hope and have 925.6
— – In school and out 925.1
— – Rich and humble 925.5
— – Watch and wait............................ 925.3
— – Work and win.............................. 925.4
— Yacht club series. The coming wave 923.19
— – The Dorcas club 924.26
— – Little Bobtail 923.18
— – Money-maker 923.17
— – Ocean-born; or, the cruise of the clubs.... 923.20
— – The yacht club 923.16

Shelf. No.

Adams, William T., *continued.*

— Young America abroad. Cross and crescent; or, Young America in Turkey and Greece. Boston, 1874. 347 pp. Illustrated. 16° 925.11

— – Dikes and ditches; or, Young America in Holland and Belgium. Boston, 1873. 346 pp. Illustrated. 16° 925.9

— – Down the Rhine; or, Young America in Germany. [Title-page missing.] Boston, 1873. 341 pp. Illustrated. 16° 916.16

— – Northern lands; or, Young America in Russia and Prussia. Boston, 1872. 360 pp. 16° 925.7

— – Outward bound; or, Young America afloat. Boston, 1873. 336 pp. Illustrated. 16° 925.13

— – Palace and cottage; or, Young America in France and Switzerland. Boston, 1873. 348 pp. Illustrated. 16° 925.10

— – Red cross; or, Young America in England and Wales. Boston, 1871. 336 pp. Illustrated. 16°. 91 .18

— – Shamrock and thistle; or, Young America in Ireland and Scotland. Boston, 1871. 343 pp. Illustrated. 16° 916.17

— – Sunny shores; or, Young America in Italy and Austria. Boston, 1875. 409 pp. Illustrated. 16° 925.12

— – Up the Baltic; or, Young America in Norway, Sweden, and Denmark. Boston, 1873. 368 pp. Illustrated. 16° 925.8

— *editor.* Our boys and girls album 911.1

Note. — Vol. 9 of Our boys and girls, with a special title-page.

— and others. The great bonanza. Illustrated narrative of adventure and discovery in gold mining, silver mining, among the raftsmen in the oil regions, whaling, hunting, fishing, and fighting. With illustrations. Boston, 1876. 261 pp. 8°. 910.3

Adams-Reilly, A., *joint author.* Life and letters of J. D. Forbes. *See* Shairp, John Campbell 5332.4

Adams family. Thayer, E. Family memorial. Hingham, 1835. 8° 611.2

Addison, Joseph, Biography of. Spalding, J. (*In* Macaulay, T. B., *lord,* and others. New biographies of illustrious men) 5428.4

See also Spectator, The.

Adela Cathcart. MacDonald, G. 725.23

Adèle. Kavanagh, J. 319.1

Adeler, Max, *pseud.* *See* Clark, Charles Heber.

Adirondacks. Headley, J. T. The Adirondack. New York, 1875. 12° 816.8

— Murray, W. H. H. Adventures in the wilderness; or, camp-life in the. Boston, 1869. 12° 414.13

Adlard, George. Amye Robsart and the earl of Leycester. History of Kenilworth castle; with memoirs and correspondence of Sir Robert Dudley, son of the earl of Leycester. London, 1870. xi, 244+ pp. Illustrated. Portrait. 8°.... 5423.5

Adler, George J. Dictionary of the German and English languages. New York, 1873. xvi, 522 pp. 8° ................................*R.R., D.3.8

— A progressive German reader. New York, 1852. xii, 308 pp. 12° 2025.2

Admiral Levacher, Der. Sue, M. J. Pest, 1852. 16°. 2027.7

Adulteration. Food: its adulterations, and the methods for their detection. Hassell, A. H. London, 1876. Sm. 8° 6035.8

Adventures in the land of the Behemoth. Verne, J. Boston, 1874. 8° 713.3

Adventures, The, of a brownie. Craik, D. (M.) . 927.23

Adventures of a young naturalist. Biart, L...... 912.9

Adventures of Caleb Williams. Godwin, W. Boston 521.22

— *Same.* New York. 2 v. 536.5

Adventures, The, of Captain Blake. Maxwell, W. H. 518.8

Adventures of Dick Onslow among the red skins. Kingston, W. H. G. 935.26

Adventures, The, of Johnny Ironsides. Girardin, J. 1114.1

Adventures, The, of Mr. Verdant Green. Bradley, E. 715.1

Adventures, The, of Peregrine Pickle. Smollett, T. (G.) 315.17

Shelf. No

Adventures, The, of Philip. Thackeray, W. M. Leipzig 335.5

— *Same.* (*In his* Works.) London 513.1.6

— *Same.* New York 1820.2

Adventures, The, of Roderick Random. Smollett, T. (G.) Leipzig 315.16

— *Same.* London 513.13

Adventures on the great hunting grounds of the world. Meunier, V. (A.) New York, 1872. 16°. 1714.7

Advertising, History of. Sampson, H. London, 1874. Sm. 8° 6136.12

Advocate's, The, wedding-day. Crowe, C. (*In* Johnson, (E.) R. Little classics) 529.4.8

Aerial world, The. Hartwig, G. London, 1874. 8°. 6832.3

— *Same.* New York, 1875. 8° 1520.5

Aëronautics. Pettigrew, J. B. Dissertation on. New York, 1874. 12° 6436.14

— Wise, J. Through the air: a narrative of forty years experience as an aëronaut. Philadelphia, 1873. 8° 1520.3

See also Balloon ascents.

Æschylus. [Opera] ex novissima recensione Frederici A. Paley. Accessit verborum quae praecipue notanda sunt et nominum index. New York, 1860. viii, 272 pp. [Harper's Greek and Latin texts.] 16° 6118.12

— Tragedies. Literally translated. With notes, and an introduction, by T. A. Buckley. London, 1871. xx, 234 pp. Portrait. Sm. 8° 6115.14

Contents. — Prometheus chained; The seven against Thebes; The Persians; Agamemnon; The choephori; The furies; The suppliants.

— Æschylus [outlined and explained]. Copleston, R. S. Edinburgh, 1870. 16° 6115.8

Æsopus. Fables. With a life of the author. Illustrated. New York, 1872. xiii, 311 pp. 16°.. 6118.8

Æsthetics, The science of. Day, H. N. New Haven, 1872. 12° 6226.4

Afloat and ashore. Cooper, J. F. 525.15

Africa. Baker, *Sir* S. W. Ismailïa. A narrative of the expedition to Central Africa for the suppression of the slave trade. New York, 1875. 8°. 5933.5

— Baldwin, W. C. African hunting from Natal to the Zambesi, from 1852 to 1860. New York, 1863. 12° 224.2

— Boyle, F. To the Cape for diamonds. A story of digging experiences in South Africa. London, 1873. Sm. 8° 5934.6

— Burton, R. F. Two trips to Gorilla land and the cataracts of the Congo. London, 1876. 2 v. 8°. 5933.12

— Cumming, R. G. The lion hunter of South Africa. Five years' adventures in the far interior. London, 1870. Sm. 8° 5934.11

— Du Chaillu, P. B. Explorations and adventures in equatorial Africa. New York, 1861. 8°.... 423.4

— – Wild life under the equator. New York, 1872. 12° 933.3

— Kingston, W. H. G. The wilds of. London, 1872. Sm. 8° 921.2

— Livingstone, D. Last journals in Central Africa, from 1865 to his death. New York, 1875. 8°. 421.10 and 5921.3

— – Livingstone and his African explorations. New York, 1872. 12° 5915.2

— – Missionary travels and researches in South Africa; including a sketch of sixteen years' residence in the interior of. New York, 1858. 8° 422.9

— – Perilous adventures and discoveries in the interior of, together with the success and important results of the Herald-Stanley expedition, as furnished by H. M. Stanley. Philadelphia [*cop.* 1872]. 16° 5915.5

— Marryat, F. The mission: or, scenes in. [Fiction] 337.13

— Morse, J., and Parish, E. New gazetteer of the Eastern continent. Charlestown, 1802. 8°.... 432.4

— Murray, H. Historical account of discoveries and travels in. Edinburgh, 1818. 8° 423.3

— Reade, (W.) W. The African sketch book. London, 1873. 2 v. 8° 5925.4

Shelf. No.

AFRICA, *continued.*

— Schweinfurth, G. The heart of. London, 1874. 2 v. 8° 5911.12

— Stanley, H. M. How I found Livingstone: travels, adventures and discoveries in Central Africa. New York, 1872. 8° .... 422.24 and 5931.5

— Taylor, (J.) B. Journey to Central Africa. New York, 1857. 12° 425.8

— – The lake regions of Central Africa. New York, 1873. 12° 224.9

— – Travels in South Africa. New York, 1872. Sm. 8° 224.1

— Verne, J. Five weeks in a balloon; or, journeys and discoveries in. [Burlesque.] New York, 1869. 8° 735.26

— – Meridiana: the adventures of three Englishmen and three Russians in South Africa. [Fiction.] London, 1873. Sm. 4° 713.1

See also Abyssinia, Algeria, Apingi, Ashantee, Behemoth, Carthage, Dahomy, Egypt, Gorilla country, Nile, Nubia, Sahara, Zulu land.

Note.—For a synopsis of the literature of African exploration, see p. 9 of the Lower Hall Catalogue of history, etc., with the supplemental note in the Bulletin, vol. II, p. 264.

Baker's Ismailïa chronicles one of the most important expeditions of our day. The books by Livingstone are among the most significant. Schweinfurth was a German naturalist, who made noteworthy investigations, and his narrative is epitomized in Harper's monthly, May, 1874, and in connection with Ismailïa in the Edinburgh review, 1875. Cumming was simply a sportsman. Du Chaillu's testimony, though suspected of sensationalism, has not been successfully called in question. Bayard Taylor's books are popular narratives. Verne's are a compound of burlesque and fiction.

W. W. Reade has also a paper on the heroes of Central Africa in the Atlantic monthly, vol. 19. Stanley writes on the great African explorers in Scribner's monthly, May, 1873.

For the natives in their ethnological relations, see Wood's Uncivilized races [6610.2; 6610.3].

AFRICAINE, L'. Meyerbeer, G. (*In* Ditson, O., and co. Standard opera librettos) 6233.3.4

AFTER dark. Collins, (W.) W. 326.11

AFTER life. Sewell, E. M. 314.18

AFTER years. Bradley, W. I. 913.12

AFTERMATH. [Poems.] Longfellow, H. W. Boston, 1873. 16° 1615.23

AGAINST the stream. Charles, E. Leipzig. 2 v. .. 329.12

— *Same.* New York 737.17

AGAINST the world. Hadermann, J. R. 528.3

AGASSIZ, Elizabeth Cary, *joint author.* Journey in Brazil. *See* AGASSIZ, Louis (John Rudolphe) .. 422.8

AGASSIZ, Louis (John Rudolphe). Geological sketches. Boston, 1871. iv, 314 pp. Illustrated. 16° 1525.13

— Methods of study in natural history. Boston, 1873. viii, 319 pp. Illustrated. 12° 1525.11

— Agassiz and spiritualism. Putnam, A. Boston [1874]. 16° 1538.12

— and Elizabeth Cary. Journey in Brazil. Boston, 1868. xix, 540 pp. Illustrated. 8° 422.8

AGATHA'S husband. Craik, D. (M.) 323.19

AGE of chivalry. Bulfinch, T. Boston, 1871. 12°. 924.1

AGE of fable. [Mythology.] Bulfinch, T. Boston, 1871. 12° 1523.3

AGINCOURT. [Historical fiction.] James, G. P. R. .. 327.12

AGNES. Abbott, J. 914.10

AGNES. Oliphant, M. (O. W.) 328.5

AGNES Grey. Brontë, A. 321.24

AGNES Hopetoun's schools and holidays. Oliphant, M. (O. W.) 936.27

AGNES of Sorrento. [Savonarola, etc.] Stowe, H. (E.) B. 527.16

AGRICOLA, Cnæus Julius, Life of. Tacitus, C. C. Philadelphia, 1849. Sm. 12° 6118.6

AGRICULTURAL chemistry. Nash, J. H. The progressive farmer: a scientific treatise on. New York, 1856. Sm. 8° 1524.10

— Stoeckhardt, J. A. Chemical field lectures. New York, 1854. 12° 1525.29

AGRICULTURE. Andrews, G. H. Rudimentary treatise on agricultural engineering. London, 1852. 3 v. in 1. 12° 1715.15

— Buel, J. The farmer's companion. Boston, 1839. 12° 1527.13

— Burn, R. S. Outlines of modern farming. London, 1865, 71, 72. 5 v. 12° 6417.1

Shelf. No.

AGRICULTURE, *continued.*

— Colman, H. European agriculture and rural economy. Boston, 1849. 2 v. 8° 1521.7

— Greeley, H. What I know of farming. New York, 1871. 12° 1515.16

— Lavergne, L. (G. L. G.) de. L'agriculture et la population. Paris, 1865. 18° 5827.1

— Morris, E. Farming for boys. Boston, 1872. Sm. 4° 932.1

— Norton, J. P. Elements of scientific agriculture. New York, 1855. 12° 1524.17

— Waring, G. E., *jr.* Elements of. New York, 1854. 12° 1527.19

See also America, Botany, Cattle, Flowers, Fruit, Gardening, Insects, Landscape gardening, United States, Vegetation.

AGUILAR, Grace. The days of Bruce; a story from Scottish history. 2 v. 533.19

— Home influence 313.1

— Home scenes and heart studies 533.18

— The mother's recompense; a sequel to Home influence 313.2

— The vale of cedars. [Fifteenth century, in Spain]. 533.17

— Woman's friendship 533.16

— The women of Israel. New York, 1872. 2 v. Illustrated. 12° 1226.19

AHN, (Johann) Franz. New practical and easy method of learning the Italian language. 1st and 2d course. London, 1861. iv, 198 pp. 12° 2037.1

AHNEN, Die. Freytag, G. Leipzig, 1874. 2 v. 16°. 5733.3

AIDÉ, Hamilton. Carr of Carrlyon 328.25

— In that state of life 328.24

— The Marstons 328.26

— Mr. and Mrs. Faulconbridge 720.14

— Morals and mysteries 328.27

— A nine-days' wonder. Boston 720.27

— *Same.* Leipzig 331.15

— Penruddocke 329.2

— Rita: an autobiography 311.19

AIDS to reflection. Coleridge, S. T. London, 1867. 16° 5818.11

AIKIN, John. Geographical delineations, or a compendious view of the natural and political state of all parts of the globe. Corrected and enlarged. Philadelphia, 1807. 416+ pp. 1 plate. 8° 232.1

— Calendar of nature. *See* HOWITT, Mary 1934.12

AIKIN, Lucy. Memoirs of the court of Elizabeth, queen of England. From the last edition. New York, 1870. 532 pp. 16° 5415.4

— Correspondence. *See* CHANNING, William Ellery. 5616.9

AILEEN Ferrers. Morley, S. 710.30

AIMWELL, Walter, *pseud.* *See* SIMONDS, Walter.

AIMWELL stories. *See* SIMONDS, Walter.

AINSLIE, Herbert. Higher law. A romance 737.25

— The pilgrim and the shrine; or, passages from [his] life and correspondence. London, 1871. 467+ pp. 8° 5626.8

AINSWORTH, William Harrison. Boscobel; or, the royal oak. [Charles I's time] 339.10

— Cardinal Pole: or, the days of Philip and Mary. An historical romance 322.19

— The constable de Bourbon. [Francis I, of France]. 322.21

— The constable of the tower. An historical romance 322.8

— The flitch of bacon: or, the custom of Dunmow . 322.25

— The goldsmith's wife. A tale 330.11

— The good old times. [Rebellion, 1745.] 2 v. .. 329.11

— Hilary St. Ives 322.24

— John Law, the projector. [Queen Anne's time] .. 322.14

— The Lancashire witches 339.2

— The Lord mayor of London. [George II's time] .. 322.17

— Merry England: or, nobles and serfs. [Fiction]. 319.18

— Mervyn Clitheroe 322.22

— Mervyn Clitheroe's Leben und Abenteuer. Deutsch von E. Steinmann. Pest, 1859. 4 v. in 1. 16° 2026.2

— The miser's daughter. [George II's time] 721.22

— Myddleton Pomfret 322.16

— Old court 322.26

Shelf. No.

AINSWORTH, William Harrison, *continued.*
— Old Saint Paul's: a tale of the plague and the fire. [London, 1664–66] 712.6
— Ovingdean grange. A tale of the South Downs. 322.13
— Preston fight; or, the insurrection of 1715. A tale 331.16
— Rookwood. A romance 712.9
— Saint James's; or, the court of Queen Anne..... 322.18
— The South-sea bubble. A tale of the year 1720. 322.20
— The Spanish match: or, Charles Stuart at Madrid. 322.23
— The spendthrift............................... 322.15
— The star-chamber. [James I's time] 322.9
— Talbot Harland. A tale of the days of Charles II. 322.10
— Tower hill. [Henry VIII's time] 322.12
— Windsor castle. [Henry VIII's time]........... 322.11
AIRS of Palestine. A poem. Pierpont, J. Baltimore, 1816. 8°........................ 1611.3
AÏSSÉ, Charlotte Élisabeth. Lettres. *See* DAYDIE, Blaise Marie, *chevalier*........................5527.13
ALABAMA claims. Argument of the United States at Geneva, June 15, 1872. Paris, 1872. 560+ pp. 8°..5010.10
— The case of the United States, to be laid before the tribunal of arbitration, to be convened at Geneva. Washington, 1872. 204 pp. 8°..... 5010.6
— Correspondence concerning claims against Great Britain. *See* UNITED STATES. *Department of state*.. 6911.1
— The counter case of Great Britain as laid before the tribunal of arbitration, convened at Geneva. Washington, 1872. 1105 pp. 8°............. 5011.9
— *Same.* 3 v. 8°.................................. 5011.2
— The treaty of Washington. Cushing, C. New York, 1873. Sm. 8° 816.1
ALASKA. Dall, W. H. Alaska and its resources. Boston, 1870. L. 8° 5031.1
— Whymper, F. Travels and adventures in. New York, 1869. 8° 5035.1
ALBERT [Francis Albert Augustus Charles Emanuel], *prince consort.* Principal speeches and addresses. With an introduction, giving some outlines of his character. Leipzig, 1866. viii, 246 pp. Portrait. Sq. 16°..................... 1928.1
— Martin, T. Life of the prince consort. Vol. I. New York, 1875. 12° 1022.3
— Victoria, A., *queen of England.* The early years of. New York, 1867. 12°.................1224.13
— *Same.* New York, 1868. 12° 1022.5
ALBERTSEN, Frank, *pseud.* The four-footed lovers. 910.4

Contents. — Bossy and Bonny; Squirrel mischief; Bunn's adventures; Squirrel wooing.

ALBOIZE DU PUJOL, Édouard, *joint author.* Histoire de la Bastille. *See* ARNOULD, Auguste........ 2010.1
ALCESTIS. [Leisure hour series]................. 518.23
ALCHEMY, The, of happiness. Ghazzali, A. H. M. B. M. A. Albany, 1873. 8° 1531.9
ALCOHOL. Carpenter, W. B. Use and abuse of alcoholic liquors. Boston, 1861. 12° 6036.9
— Forbes, *Sir* J. Physiological effects of alcoholic drinks. Boston, 1848. 12° 1527.15
ALCOTT, Amos Bronson. Concord days. Boston, 1872. 276+ pp. 12°.......................... 5217.1
— Record of Mr. Alcott's school, exemplifying the principles and methods of moral culture. Peabody, E. P. Boston, 1874. 16°.............. 1937.3
ALCOTT, Louisa May. Aunt Jo's scrap-bag. 3 v.... 926.15

Contents. — Vol. I. My boys, etc. II. Shawl-straps. III. Cupid and Chow-chow, etc.

— Eight cousins; or, the aunt-hill 1117.1
— Hospital sketches, and Camp and fireside stories.. 926.13
— Little men 926.14
— Little women 926.12
— Moods 517.3
— Morning-glories, and other stories 926.10
— An old-fashioned girl........................... 926.9
— Three proverb stories 935.20

Contents. — Kitty's class-day; Aunt Kipp; Psyche's art.

— Work.. 918.28
ALCOVE, The. Abbott, J. Harper's story books ... 936.1.8

Shelf. No.

ALDEN, Henry M., *joint author.* Harper's pictorial history of the great rebellion. *See* GUERNSEY, Alfred H. ................................*R.R. Desk
ALDEN, Joseph. The science of government in connection with American institutions. New York [*cop.* 1866]. 295 pp. 12°.................. 6336.1
ALDEN family. Thayer, E. Family memorial. Hingham, 1835. 8°............................... 611.
ALDINE, The, a typographic art journal. Vol. 6–8. New York, 1873–75. 3 v. F°............... 6520.1
ALDINE edition of British poets. *Namely:* —
— Chaucer, G. Poetical works. London [1872]. 6 v. Sm. 8° 5628.1
ALDRICH, Thomas Bailey. Marjorie Daw and other people.. 735.27
— Prudence Palfrey 738.13
— Story of a bad boy. [Fiction] 923.23
ALEC Forbes of Howglen. MacDonald, G. Leipzig. 328.3
— *Same.* New York 720.26
ALESSANDRO Stradella. Polko, E................. 731.31
"ALEX," *pseud.* As it should be. Philadelphia, 1874. 274 pp. 16°........................ 1736.5

Note. — An essay on the condition of women.

— As she would have it. Philadelphia, 1873. 105 pp. 16°.. 1736.6

Note. — An essay on woman's rights.

ALEXANDER I, *pope.* *See* HIPPOLYTUS, *St.*
ALEXANDER, *Mrs.* —. Leisure hour series. Her dearest foe 517.21
— – Ralph Wilton's weird.......................... 518.26
— – Which shall it be?............................ 732.12
— – The wooing o't................................ 518.18
ALEXANDER the great, History of. Abbott, J. 915.3
ALEXANDRE le grand: tragédie. Racine, J. de. Théâtre complet. Paris, 1870. 12° 5537.3
ALEXANDRIA, Tyre and. Tarbox, I. N. Boston [*cop.* 1865]. 16° 426.5
ALEXANDRIAN, The: a republication of valuable literary and scientific works. Vol. II. New York, 1835. 8° 1910.4

Contents. — Vol. II. Foster, J.: Essays, in a series of letters. 133 pp. — Macnish, R.: Philosophy of sleep; Anatomy of drunkenness. 96 pp. — Staël-Holstein, A. L. G. Necker, *baronne* de: Influence of literature upon society; Prefixed life of the author; Reflections on suicide. 112+ pp. — Mason, J.: Treatise on self-knowledge. Added life of the author. 41+ pp.

ALEXIS the runaway. Parker, R. A. 933.14
ALFORD, Fanny, *editor.* Life, journals and letters of Henry Alford. Edited by his widow. 2d edition. London, 1873. vii, 551+ pp. Illustrated. Portrait. 8°.................................... 5421.1
ALFORD, Henry. Alford, F. Life, journals and letters of. London, 1873. 8°.................. 5421.1
— Page, H. A. Noble workers. London, 1875. Sm. 8° 5936.3
ALFRED the great. Abbott, J. History of 914.34
— Hughes, T. Life of. Boston, 1871. 12° 1025.7
— Pauli, R. Life of. Appended Alfred's Anglo-Saxon version of Orosius. London, 1857. Sm. 8°... 5427.5

See also Note under England, Saxon period.

ALFRED; an epic poem. Cottle, J. Newburyport, 1814. 24°.................................... 5619.1
ALGER, Horatio, *jr.* Brave and bold series. Brave and bold 933.4
— – Jack's ward 1117.2
— Campaign series. Charlie Codman's cruise...... 934.28
— – Frank's campaign............................. 925.14
— – Paul Prescott's charge....................... 924.25
— Helen Ford 1115.5
— Luck and pluck series. Bound to rise.......... 935.29
— – Herbert Carter's legacy......................1115.10
— – Luck and pluck............................... 935.7
— – Risen from the ranks 935.32
— – Sink or swim 935.8
— – Strive and succeed 935.28
— – Strong and steady............................ 935.9
— – Try and trust................................ 928.3
— Ragged Dick series. Ben, the luggage boy..... 934.11
— – Fame and fortune............................. 934.12

Shelf. No.

ALGER, Horatio, *jr.* Ragged Dick series, *continued.*
— – Mark, the match-boy 934.16
— – Ragged Dick 934.13
— – Rough and ready 934.15
— – Rufus and Rose 934.14
— Tattered Tom series. Julius; or the street boy out West 934.32
— – Paul, the peddler 934.10
— – Phil, the fiddler 934.30
— – Slow and sure 934.31
— – Tattered Tom 934.9
— – The young outlaw 933.12
— and CHENEY, O. Augusta. Seeking his fortune, and other dialogues. Boston [1875]. 270 pp. 16°. 1518.11
ALGER, William Rounseville. Critical history of the doctrine of a future life. And a complete bibliography of the subject, by Ezra Abbot. New York, 1871. x, 914 [912]+ pp. 8° 5831.3
— The friendships of women. Boston, 1872. xvi, 416 pp. 16° 1535.20
— The solitudes of nature and of man. Boston, 1871. 412 [408] pp. 16° 1535.22
ALGERIA. Gaskell, G. Algeria as it is. London, 1875. Sm. 8° 5935.4
— Gérard, (C.) J. (B.) Lion hunting and sporting life in. London, 1857. 16° 427.4
— Herbert, *Lady* M. E. A search after sunshine; or, Algeria in 1871. London, 1872. 8° 5911.2
ALHAMBRA, The. Irving, W. London, 1853. 16° .. 715.7
— *Same.* Philadelphia, 1872. Sm. 8° 1815.15

Note. — A semi-fictitious chronicle of its history.

ALHAMBRA, The, and the Kremlin. [Travels.] Prime, S. I. New York [1873]. 8° 5914.6
ALICE. Bulwer-Lytton, E. (G. E.) L. 336.10
ALICE Brand. Riddle, A. G. 713.6
ALICE Franklin. Howitt, M. 937.6
ALICE Lorraine. Blackmore, R. D. Leipzig 331.10
— *Same.* New York 711.35
ALICE'S adventures in Wonderland. Dodgson, C. L. 912.20
ALICIA Warlock. Collins, (W.) W. 711.33
ALISON, *Sir* Archibald. History of Europe, 1789–1815. New York, 1871. 4 v. 8° 5913.6
— – 1815–52. New York, 1868, 70, 71. 4 v. 8°. 5913.5
— Miscellaneous essays. New York, 1871. 390 pp. Portrait. 8° 1531.7
ALL aboard. Adams, W. T. 924.17
ALL for greed. A., A. A. 311.24
ALL for love. Dupuy, E. A. 716.7
ALL the year round. Conducted by Charles Dickens. New series. Vol. 6. London, 1871. 8°. 1334.1
ALLEGORIES, Sacred. Adams, W. Leipzig, 1864. Sq. 16° 311.23
ALLEN, C. Bruce. Cottage building. With notes and additions by J. Weale. 6th edition, with illustrations. London, 1870. viii, 133 pp. 12° .. 1715.28
ALLEN, David Oliver. India, ancient and modern. 2d edition. Boston, 1856. xii, 618 pp. 8° .. 5921.1
ALLEN, Ethan, Life of. Sparks, J. (*In* Sparks, J. Library of American biography) 5028.1.1
ALLEN, John Fisk. Practical treatise on the culture and treatment of the grape vine. 3d edition. New York, 1856. 330 pp. Illustrated. 12° .. 6425.4
ALLEN, Joseph. Battles of the British navy. New edition. London, 1868. 2 v. Sm. 8° 5417.5
ALLEN, Joseph Henry. Manual of devotions for families and Sunday schools. Boston, 1852. xi, 163 pp. 12° 5818.8
ALLEN, Myron O. History of Wenham, from 1639 to 1860. Boston, 1860. 220+ pp. 12° 816.4
ALLEN, Rowland Hussey. The New-England tragedies in prose. Boston, 1869. 156 pp. 12° .. 817.4

Contents. — The coming of the quakers; The witchcraft delusion.

Note. — This is written in elucidation of Longfellow's "New-England tragedies."

ALLEN, S. M. Fibrilia: a substitute for cotton. With illustrations. Boston, 1861. x, 182 pp. 12°. 6435.1
ALLEN, William. American biographical and historical dictionary. 2d edition. Boston, 1832. viii, 800 pp. 8° .... *R.R., D.3.2

Shelf. No.

ALLIBONE, Samuel Austin. Critical dictionary of English literature and British and American authors. Philadelphia, 1871. 3 v. 8° .. *R.R., A.3.6
ALLWORTH abbey. Southworth, E. D. E. N. 727.5
ALMANACH de Gotha. Annuaire diplomatique et statistique pour l'année 1863. 100e année. Gotha [1862]. Portraits. 1, 984+ pp. 24° .. 2019.4
ALMANACS. American almanac and repository of useful knowledge. Vol. 1–32. Boston, 1830–61. 32 v. 12° 1728.1
— The banker's almanac and register. New York, 1854–56, 59–61, 65–75. 17 v. 8° 5820.1
— Boston almanac, 1838, 40–42, 44–72. Boston [1838–72]. 33 v. 16° 5017.6
— Hone, W. Every day book. London [1871]. 2 v. L. 8° 5621.5
— Nast, T. Illustrated almanac for 1873. New York, 1872. 8° 1816.2
ALONE. Terhune, M. V. 724.3
ALPS. Abbott, J. Rambles among the 926.1.7
— Baedeker, C. Handbook for travellers in the Eastern Alps. Coblenz, 1871. 16° 5718.2
— Ball, J. Alpine guides. Pennine Alps, including Mont Blanc and Monte Rosa. London, 1873. 16° 5926.6
— – Peaks, passes and glaciers. A series of excursions by members of the Alpine club. London, 1860. Sm. 8° 5717.1
— Murray, J. Knapsack guide for travellers in the Eastern Alps. London, 1867. 16° 5527.8
— Tyndall, J. Hours of exercise in the. New York, 1873. 12° 223.1
— Whymper, E. Scrambles amongst the, 1860–69. Philadelphia, 1873. 8° 5932.3

See also Switzerland.

ALPS, The, of Arabia. Maughan, W. C. London, 1873. 8° 5932.10
ALROY. Disraeli, B. 324.22
ALTAR, The, at home. Miles, H. A. Boston, 1855. 16° 6327.8
— *Same.* Boston, 1859. 16° 6327.19
ALTON Locke. Kingsley, C. 326.18
ALTON sermons, The. Hare, A. W. London, 1874. Sm. 8° 6325.18
ALWYN'S first wife. Craik, D. (M.) 323.27
AMANTS magnifique, Les: comédie-ballet. Molière, J. B. P. Œuvres. Paris, 1869. 12° 5537.2.3
AMATEUR drama series. *See* BAKER, George Melville.
AMATEUR dramas. Baker, G. M. Boston, 1873. 16° 1635.22
AMATEUR'S, The, rose book. Hibbard, S. London, 1874. Sm. 8° 6625.3
AMATEURS and actors: a farce. Peake, R. B. New York, N. D. 12° 1635.5
AMATOR VIRTUTIS, *pseud.*, *compiler.* The youth's companion; or a safe guide to eminence. Andover, 1820. 159+ pp. Sm. 12° 1919.1

Contents. — Sermon on Christian magnanimity, and an address to his senior class, by Dr. Witherspoon; Oration on the death of Dr. Dwight, by Dr. Spring; Analysis and index.

AMAZON, The. Dingelstedt, F. (F. F.) 526.4
AMAZON, *river.* Bates, H. W. The naturalist on the river Amazons. London, 1873. Sm. 8° .. 5935.2
— Kingston, W. H. G. On the banks of the. London, 1872. Sm. 8° 921.6
— Orton, J. The Andes and the. New York, 1871. 16° 5933.13

See also Brazil.

AMBER gods, The. Spofford, H. E. 538.3
AMBROSE Gwinett: a melo-drama. Jerrold, D. (W.) New York, N. D. 12° 1635.4
AMENITIES of literature. Disraeli, I. New York, 1871. 2 v. Sm. 8° 1533.13
AMERICA. Abbott, J. S. C. The adventures of the chevalier de La Salle and his companions, in their explorations of the new world, two hundred years ago. New York [1875]. 12° 1014.13
— Baldwin, J. D. Ancient America. New York, 1872. 12° 5027.5

Shelf. No.

AMERICA, *continued*.

— Bishop, N. H. The Pampas and Andes. A thousand miles' walk across South America. Boston, 1872. 16° 934.1
— Browne, D. J. The trees of. New York, 1846. L. 8° 6621.1
— Bryant, W. C. Letters of a traveller; or, notes of things seen in. New York, 1870. 12° 5915.9
— Butler, W. F. The wild North land: the story of a winter journey, with dogs, across northern North America. London, 1874. 8° 5032.3
— Franchere, G. Narrative of a voyage to the northwest coast of, 1811-14. New York, 1854. 12° 414.10
— Gasparin, A. (É.), *comte* de. America before Europe. New York, 1862. 12° 414.2
— Greenhow, R. The history of Oregon and California and the other territories on the northwest coast of North America. Boston, 1845. 8°. 810.2
— Hall, B. Travels in North America, in 1827, 28. Philadelphia, 1829. 2 v. 12° 417.14
— Helps, *Sir* A. The Spanish conquest in. New York, 1856. 4 v. 12° 816.6
— Humboldt, (F. H.) A. Personal narrative of travels to the equinoctial regions of. London, 1872. 3 v. Sm. 8° 5036.4
— Kingston, W. H. G. The Western world. Picturesque sketches of nature and natural history in North and South America. London, 1874. 8°. 434.1
— Leland, C. G., *editor*. Fusang, or the discovery of America by Chinese Buddhist priests in the 5th century. London, 1875. 8° 5925.6
— Macgillivray, W. Travels and researches of A. von Humboldt in the equinoctial regions of. New York, 1855. 18° 438.1
— Map of the United States, the British provinces, Mexico, the West Indies and Central America, with a part of New Granada and Venezuela. New York, 1849. Size, 2 ft. 4 in. × 3 ft. 3 in. 5032.4
— Marcoy, P. Travels in South America from the Pacific to the Atlantic ocean. London, 1875. 2 v. L. 8° 5030.5
— Michaud, A. Flora Boreali-Americana. Paris, 1803. 2 v. 8° 6624.2
— Mitchell, S. L. Observations on the geology of North America. New York, 1818. 8° 6633.1
— Orton, J. The Andes and the Amazon; or, across the continent of South America. New York, 1871. 16° 5933.13
— Paez, R. Travels and adventures in South and Central America. New York, 1868. 12° 427.8
— Parkman, F., *jr*. The Jesuits in North America in the 17th century. Boston, 1872. 12° 5015.5.2
— Pumpelly, R. Across America and Asia. New York, 1871. 8° 5916.2
— Robertson, W. History of. London, 1840. 8°. 5610.1
— Rogers, H. D., and Johnston, A. K. Atlas. London, 1857. F° 5030.1
— Schele de Vere, M. Romance of American history. New York, 1872. 12° 5016.1
— Snowden, R. History of North and South America, from its discovery to the death of Washington. Philadelphia, 1818. 2 v. in 1. 12°. 818.8
— Stephens, J. L. Incidents of travel in Central America. New York, 1856. 2 v. 8° 422.5
— Stevenson, D. Sketch of civil engineering in. London, 1859. 12° 6428.3
— Tuckerman, H. T. America and her commentators. New York, 1864. 8° 5033.5

See also the various divisions under their several names, as Brazil, Canada, Mexico, Peru, United States, etc.

Note. — A synopsis of the literature of the history of America will be found in the Lower Hall Catalogue for history, etc., p. 12; and for all matters relating to the early history and antiquities of the Pacific slope, Mexico, Central America, and Peru, Bancroft's "Native Races" [5920.4] will afford the latest summary, with ample references for verification. Tuckerman's "America and her commentators" surveys the successive European observers from the earliest visitors. For Pre-Columbian America, see the note in Bulletin no. 37. The subject of the mound builders is popularly examined in Baldwin, who also pictures the old civilizations of Mexico and Peru, but careful statements on this point will be found in the introduction to Prescott's Mexico [5014.2] and Peru [5014.3]. Brinton's "Myths of the New World" covers the

Shelf. N

AMERICA, *continued*.

religious views and mythological beliefs of these earlier inhabitants. For the Spanish conquest, the work of the English historian Robertson is a well sustained narrative; but the American reader will naturally prefer the later researches of Prescott, in the works already referred to; while Helps's Spanish conquest covers much the same ground, and aims to show in connection how slavery took its rise. Bancroft's first volume of his "United States" [5012.3] traces the beginnings of the colonizations that grew into the American republic; but Parkman's series of books [5015.5] best traces the progress of the struggle of England and France for the possession of North America.

AMERICAN academy of arts and sciences, *Boston*. Memoir of Sir Benjamin Thompson, count Rumford. By G. E. Ellis. Philadelphia [1871]. xvi, 680 pp. Portraits, illustrations, and facsimile. 8° ..... 5022.
AMERICAN agriculturist, The. Vol. 31, 32. New York, 1872, 73. 2 v. in 1. 4° ..... 1432.
AMERICAN almanac and repository of useful knowledge. Vol. 1-32. Boston, 1830-61. 12° ..... 1728.
AMERICAN and foreign Sabbath union. Permanent Sabbath documents. Boston, 1851. 12° ..... 1536.
AMERICAN annual cyclopædia and register of important events. 1861-72. New York. 1872. 12 v. Illustrated. Portraits. 8° ..... *R.R., C.3.
AMERICAN baron, The. De Mille, J. 511.1
AMERICAN board of commissioners for foreign missions. Anderson, R. History of the missions in India. Boston, 1874. 8° ..... 5812.
— — History of the missions to the Oriental churches. Boston, 1872. 8° ..... 5812.
— — History of the Sandwich Islands mission. Boston, 1870. 8° 5812.1
AMERICAN colleges and the American public. Porter, N. New Haven, 1870. 12° ..... 1934.
AMERICAN colonization society. Memorial of the semi-centennial anniversary, at Washington, January 15, 1867. With documents concerning Liberia. Washington, 1867. 191+ pp. 8° .. 5222.
AMERICAN educational annual, The. A cyclopædia, or reference book for all matters pertaining to education. Vol. I. New York, 1875. 8° ..... 1932.
AMERICAN family, An, in Germany. Browne, J. R. New York, 1871. 12° 424.1
AMERICAN family, An, in Paris. With illustrations. New York, 1870. xii, 319 pp. 16° ..... 911.
AMERICAN game in its seasons. Herbert, H. W. New York, 1873. 12° 1516.1
AMERICAN girl, An, abroad. Trafton, A. Boston, 1873. 16° 736.1
AMERICAN homes series. *Namely:* —
— Eggleston, E. The schoolmaster's stories 921.1
— Hall, T. G. Her mother's Fancy 921.1
AMERICAN Hoyle, The. Dick, W. B. New York [*cop*. 1864]. 12° ..... 1516.

Note. — Rules for games of cards, etc.

AMERICAN liberties and American slavery. Treadwell, S. B. New York, 1838. 12° 817.1
AMERICAN literature. *See* UNITED STATES.
AMERICAN naturalist, The, an illustrated magazine of natural history. Vol. 4, 7-9. Salem, 1871-75. 4 v. 8° ..... 6523.
AMERICAN note-books, Passages from the. Hawthorne, N. Boston, 1872. 2 v. in 1. 12° ..... 1813.
AMERICAN notes. [Travels.] Dickens, C. (J. H.) Leipzig, 1842. Sq. 16° ..... 418.
— *Same*. Boston, 1874. 16° 1824.1
— *Same*. Philadelphia, N. D. 8° 732.3
AMERICAN pioneers and patriots. *See* ABBOTT, John Stevens Cabot.
AMERICAN protestant magazine, The. Vol. 1-4. New York [1845-48]. 4 v. 8° ..... 1336.
AMERICAN publisher's circular and literary gazette. Vol. 1-4. Philadelphia, 1863-65. 4 v. in 2. 8°. 1422.
AMERICAN religion. Weiss, J. Boston, 1871. 12°. 1537.
AMERICAN revolution. *See* UNITED STATES.
AMERICAN social science association. Free lending libraries. A paper read before the association, at New York, May 22, 1874. By William W. Greenough. Cambridge, 1874. 10 pp. 8° ..... 1932.
AMERICAN temperance society. Permanent temperance documents. Boston, 1835. 12° ..... 5834.

Shelf. No.

AMERICANISMS. Pickering, J. A vocabulary, or collection of words and phrases peculiar to the United States. Boston, 1816. 8° 6121.1
— Schele de Vere, M. Americanisms; the English of the New World. New York, 1872. 12°..... 6124.1

See also Note under English language.

AMES, Azel, *jr.* Sex in industry: a plea for the working-girl. Boston, 1875. 158 pp. 16°.... 1937.5
AMES, Fisher. Works. Prefixed, notices on his life and character [by J. T. Kirkland]. Boston, 1809. xxxi, 519+ pp. Portrait. 8° 1530.5
AMES, Mary Clemmer. Eirene; or, a woman's right. 711.17
— His two wives 724.25
— A memorial of Alice and Phœbe Cary, with some of their later poems. Portraits. New York, 1873. xii, 351 pp. Sm. 8°.................. 1014.5
— Ten years in Washington. Life and scenes in the national capital, as a woman sees them. Illustrations. Portrait. Hartford, 1875. 587 pp. 8°.. 612.8
AMMONIUM, Physiological action of. Amory, R. (*In* Massachusetts medical society. Publications).. 6021.4
AMONG my books. [Essays.] Lowell, J. R. Boston, 1873, 76. 2 v. 16° 1934.8
AMONG the brigands. De Mille, J.................. 932.44
AMONG the pines. [North Carolina.] Gilmore, J. R. New York, 1862. 12°.................... 916.3
AMORY, Robert. Physiological action of bromide of potassium and ammonium. (*In* Massachusetts medical society. Publications) 6021.4
AMOS, Sheldon. International scientific series. The science of law. New York, 1874. xx, 417 pp. Folded sheet. 12°.......................... 6316.3
AMOUR, L', médecin: comédie-ballet. Molière, J. B. P. Œuvres. Paris, 1869. 12° 5537.2.2
AMOUROUX, Jules. The practical draughtman's book of industrial design, etc. *See* JOHNSON, William 6620.2
AMPÈRE, Jean Jacques (Antoine). *See* MÉRIMÉE, P. Portraits historiques et littéraires. Paris, 1874. 12°..................................5527.14
AMPHITRUO. Plautus, T. M. Philadelphiæ [*cop.* 1842]. Sm. 12°................................ 6118.4
AMPHITRYON: comédie. Molière, J. B. P. Œuvres. Paris, 1869. 12°.............................5537.2.2
AMUSEMENTS. *See* RECREATIVE arts.
ANABASIS, The. Xenophon. London, 1872. Sm. 8°.6115.12
ANACREON. Odes. *See* MOORE, Thomas. Poetical works 1614.9.1
ANALECTIC magazine, The, containing selections from foreign reviews and magazines. Vol. 1-4. Philadelphia, 1813, 14. 4 v. 8°............. 1336.1
ANALYSIS of ornament. Wornum, R. N. London, 1873. 8°...................................... 6211.9
ANATOMY. Cutter, C. Anatomy and physiology. Boston, 1847. 12°............................. 6037.3
— Edwards, H. W. Outlines of. Boston, 1841. 8°.6021.15
— Huxley, T. H. Manual of the anatomy of vertebrated animals. New York, 1872. 12°.......1523.12
— Jackson, J. B. S. Anatomical museum of the Boston society for medical improvement. Boston, 1847. 8°...................................... 6022.3
— Koelliker, A. Manual of human microscopical anatomy. Philadelphia, 1854. 8°............ 6032.3

See also Bones.

ANCIENT city, The. Fustel de Coulanges, W. D. Boston, 1874. 16°......................... 5923.6

Note. — A study of the religion, laws, etc., of Greece and Rome.

ANCIENT classics for English readers. *See* COLLINS, William Lucas, *editor.*
ANCIENT harmony revived, being a selection of choice music for divine worship, taken from old and approved authors. 5th edition. Boston, 1857. 280 pp. Oblong 8° 1518.7
ANCIENT lyre, The. Zeuner, C. Boston, 1840. Oblong 8°.. 1518.5
ANCIENT states and empires. Lord, J. New York, 1869. 8°....................................... 815.8

ANDERDON, William Henry. Antoine de Bonneval: a tale of Paris, in the days of St. Vincent de Paul. 716.17
ANDERSEN, Hans Christian. The improvisatore. [A tale of Italian life.] Translated from the Danish by Mary Howitt 714.25
— O. T. A Danish romance 524.14
— Only a fiddler. A Danish romance 524.13
— Pictures of travel in Sweden, among the Hartz mountains, and in Switzerland, with a visit at Charles Dickens's house. Author's edition. New York, 1871. vi, 293 pp. Sm. 8° 426.17
— A poet's bazaar. Pictures of travel in Germany, Italy, Greece, and the Orient. Author's edition. New York, 1871. v, 343 pp. Sm. 8°......... 426.18
— In Spain and a visit to Portugal. Author's edition. New York, 1870. vii, 288 pp. Sm. 8°.. 426.16
— Stories and tales 923.25
— The story of my life.........................1225.18
— The two baronesses.......................... 524.15
— Wonder stories told for children 923.24
ANDERSON, James. Memorable women of the puritan times. London, 1872. 2 v. Sm. 8°...... 5427.6

Contents. — Vol. I. Mary Tracy, wife of H. Vere, baron of Tilbury; Brilliana Conway, wife of Sir Robert Harley; Margaret Tindall, wife of John Winthrop; Anne Dudley, wife of Simon Bradstreet; Anne Marbury, wife of William Hutchinson; Mary Dyer; Anne Vere, wife of Thomas, third lord Fairfax, and her daughter Mary, duchess of Buckingham; Elizabeth Steward, mother of Oliver Cromwell; Elizabeth Bourchier, wife of Oliver Cromwell; Mary Love; Bridget Cromwell, Elizabeth Cromwell, daughter[s] of Oliver Cromwell. II. Mary Cromwell, Frances Cromwell, daughter[s] of Oliver Cromwell; Lucy Apsley, wife of colonel Hutchinson; Katharine Boyle, wife of Arthur Jones, viscount Ranelagh; Margaret Charlton, wife of Richard Baxter; Elizabeth, wife of John Bunyan; Agnes Beaumont; Katharine Matthews, wife of Philip Henry; Rachel Wriothesley, wife of lord William Russell; Alice Beconsaw, wife of lord John Lisle; Elizabeth Gaunt; Hannah Hewling, wife of major Richard Cromwell; Bridget Ireton, wife of Thomas Bendish.

ANDERSON, Robert Patrick. Victories and defeats. An attempt to explain the causes which have led to them. London, 1873. xii, 353 pp. 8°.5922.10
ANDERSON, Rufus. Foreign missions: their relations and claims. 3d edition, revised. New York, 1869. xiv, 373 pp. 8° 5812.16
— History of the missions of the American board of commissioners for foreign missions in India. Boston, 1874. xvi, 443 pp. Maps. 8° 5812.4
— History of the Sandwich Islands mission. Boston, 1870. xxiv, 408 pp. Portrait. Map. 8° 5812.15
— Republication of the Gospel in Bible lands. History of the missions of the American board of commissioners for foreign missions to the Oriental churches. Boston, 1872. 2 v. Portrait. Map. 8° 5812.1
ANDERSON, William. The London commercial dictionary, and sea-port gazetteer. [With appendix.] New edition. London, 1826. viii, 848, 44+ pp. Plate. 8° 6434.4
ANDES, The, and the Amazon. Orton, J. New York, 1871. 16 ....5933.13
ANDRÉ, *Major* John, Life and career of. Sargent, W. Boston, 1861. Sm. 8° 5426.9

Note. — The best special life of André; but illustrative matter will be found in general histories of the United States, like Bancroft; the lives of Washington, and in Lossing's Pictorial field-book of the revolution.

ANDRÉ del Sarto: drame. Musset, (L. C.) A. de. Comédies et proverbes. Paris, 1867. 12° 5534.4.1
ANDREAS Hofer. [Fiction.] Mundt, C. (M.)......531.37
ANDRÉE de Taverney. Dumas, A. (D.) 510.9
ANDREW, Jane. The seven little sisters who live on the round ball that floats in the air............ 928.5
ANDREWS, C. C. Hints to company officers on their military duties. New York, 1863. 68 pp. 24°. 6927.7
— Minnesota and Dacotah, in 1856. Washington, 1857. 215 pp. 12°.............................. 415.3
ANDREWS, Ethan Allen. First lessons in Latin; or, an introduction to Andrews and Stoddard's Latin grammar. 8th edition. Boston, 1846. 216 pp. Sm. 12° 1939.4
— *editor.* A copious and critical Latin-English lexicon, founded on the larger Latin-German lexicon of William Freund: with additions and corrections. New York, 1872. xxv, 1663 pp. 8°. *R.R., D.3.5

Shelf. No.

ANDREWS, G. H. Rudimentary treatise on agricultural engineering. With illustrations. London, 1852. 3 v. in 1. 12° 1715.15

ANDREWS, J. N. Sermons on the Sabbath and law. 2d edition. Battle Creek, 1870. Irregularly paged. 16° 6328.2

ANDROMAQUE: tragédie. Racine, J. de. Théâtre complet. Paris, 1870. 12° 5537.3

ANECDOTES. Baring-Gould, S. Yorkshire oddities, incidents and strange events. London, 1875. 2 v. Sm. 8° 5616.17

— Boyd, M. Social gleanings. London, 1875. Sm. 8° 5613.7

— Byerley, T., and Robertson, J. C. The Percy [and] American anecdotes. New York, 1858. 2 v. in 1. 8° 1231.3

— Forney, J. W. Anecdotes of public men. New York, 1873. 12° 1015.2

— Mathews, L. E. Anecdotes of actors. London, 1844. 8° 5623.7

— Newcomb, H. Anecdotes for boys. Boston, 1869. 12° 918.21

— — Anecdotes for girls. Boston, 1870. 12° 918.18

ANGEL, Henry. Practical plane and solid geometry. New York [Glasgow], 1873. 182 pp. 16° 1717.4

ANGEL, The, in the house. [Poem.] Patmore, C. (K. D.) Boston, 1856. 2 v. 16° 1612.10

ANGEL-VOICES; or, words of counsel for overcoming the world. After the mode of Richter's "Best hours." Boston [*cop.* 1846]. 96 pp. 16° 5818.12

ANGELINA Gushington's thoughts on men and things. Gushington, A. New York, 1872. 12° 1916.4

ANGÉLIQUE JACQUELINE MARIE ANGÉLIQUE DE SAINTE MADELEINE ARNAULD D'ANDILLY, *abbess of Port Royal, called Mère.* Martin, F. Angelique Arnauld, abbess of Port Royal. London, 1873. Sm. 8° 5937.11

ANGLO-AMERICAN colonization, The first records of. Thornton, J. W. Boston, 1859. 8° 612.5

ANICETUS, *pseud.* *See* CLARK, William Adolphus.

ANIMAL and vegetable parasites of the human body. Kuechenmeister, F. London, 1857. 8° 6021.17

ANIMAL locomotion. Pettigrew, J. B. New York, 1874. 12° 6436.14

ANIMAL mechanics, Principles of. Haughton, S. London, 1873. 8° 6613.4

ANIMAL mechanism. Marey, É. J. New York, 1874. 12° 6436.11

ANIMALS. Adams, W. H. D. Animal life throughout the globe. London, 1876. Sm. 8° 1523.25

— Hamerton, P. G. Chapters on. Boston [London], 1874. 16° 6614.9

— Haney, J. Art of training animals. New York [*cop.* 1869]. 12° 1713.3

— Helps, *Sir* A. Some talks about animals and their masters. London, 1873. Sm. 8° 6617.5

— Kirby, W. Power, wisdom and goodness of God, as manifested in the creation of animals, and in their history, habits and instincts. Philadelphia, 1836. 8° 6613.8

— Menault, E. The intelligence of. New York, 1872. 16° 1714.5

— Wolf, J. The life and habits of wild animals. London, 1874. 4° 6610.6

See also Dairy cows, Natural history, Zoology.

ANJOU, *France.* The life and times of Margaret of Anjou. With memoirs of the houses of Anjou. Hookham, M. A. London, 1872. 8° 5522.10

ANNA Bolena. Donizetti, G. (*In* Ditson, O., and co. Standard opera librettos) 6233.3.2

ANNALS of a fortress. Viollet-le-Duc, E. E. Boston, 1876. 8° 6223.4

Note. — A popular history of military engineering.

ANNALS of a quiet neighbourhood. MacDonald, G. .. 328.1

ANNALS of the English stage. Doran, J. W. New York, 1865. 2 v. L. 12° 1532.2

ANNALS of the parish. [Scottish life.] Galt, J. 515.11

ANNAPOLIS, *Maryland.* Ridgeley, D. Annals of. Baltimore, 1841. 12° 817.15

— Taylor, O. M. History of. Baltimore, 1872. 8°. 813.9

ANNAPOLIS, *Maryland, continued.*

— *Naval academy.* *See* UNITED STATES. *Department of the navy* .... 816.

ANNE BOLEYN, *or* BULLEN. Dixon, W. H. History of two queens. Leipzig, 1873, 74. 6 v. in 4. Sq. 16° 1238.2

— *Same.* London, 1873–74. 4 v. 8° .... 5414.

See also Anna Bolena.

ANNE Hereford. Wood, E. P. .... 333.

ANNE Judge, spinster. Robinson, F. W. 731.2

ANNE of Geierstein. Scott, *Sir* W. Boston .... 533.

— *Same.* Leipzig .... 324.

ANNUAIRE des deux mondes. Histoire générale des divers états. 1862–67. Paris, 1864–68. 3 v. 8°. 5316.

ANNUAL of scientific discovery: or, year-book of facts in science and art, 1850–59. Edited by D. A. Wells and G. Bliss, jr. Boston, 1850–59. 10 v. Portraits. 12° .... 1524.

ANNUS Domini: a prayer for each day of the year. Rossetti, C. G. Oxford, 1874. Sq. 16° 5819.1

ANOTHER chapter of Erie. Crough, G. New York, 1869. 12° .... 1916.

ANSELM, *St., archbishop of Canterbury.* Church, R. W. Saint Anselm. [London] 1870. Sm. 8° ... 5937.

ANSWERS to prayer; or, Dorothea Trüdel. An account of the wonderful healing of sick persons in answer to special prayer, at Mannedorf, Switzerland. Boston, N. D. 198 pp. 12° .... 1026.

ANTARCTIC regions, Summer in the. Tomlinson, C. London [1872]. Sm. 8° .... 5915.

ANTE-NICENE Christian library: translation of the writings of the Fathers down to A. D. 325. Edited by A. Roberts and J. Donaldson. Edinburgh, 1867–72. 24 v. 8°. *Namely:* —

— Arnobius *Afer.* The seven books of Adversus gentes 6322.4.19

— Bible. *Apocryphal New Testament.* Gospels, etc. 6322.4.16

— Clemens, T. F. Writings .... Vol. 4, 12 of 6322.4

— Clementine homilies, The 6322.4.17

— Cyprianus, T. C., and others. Writings. Vol. 8, 13 of 6322.4

— Donaldson, J., *editor.* The apostolical constitutions 6322.4.17

— Gregorius *Thaumaturgus,* and others. Works .. 6322.4.20

— Hippolytus, *St.* Writings .... Vol. 6, 9 of 6322.4

— Irenæus, *St.* Writings .... Vol. 5, 9 of 6322.4

— Justinus *Martyr,* and Athenagoras. Writings. 6322.4.2

— Lactantius, L. C. F. Works .... Vol. 21, 22 of 6322.4

— Liturgies and other documents 6322.4.24

— Methodius, *bishop of Tyre,* and others. Writings. 6322.4.14

— Origines. Writings .... Vol. 10, 23 of 6322.4

— Syriac documents attributed to the first three centuries 6322.4.20

— Tatianus, and others. Writings 6322.4.3

— Tertullianus, Q. S. F. Writings. Vol. 11, 15, 18 of 6322.4

— — The five books against Marcion 6322.4.7

— Testaments, The, of the twelve patriarchs, and Fragments of the second and third centuries .. 6322.4.22

— The writings of the apostolic fathers 6322.4.1

ANTEFIX papers. *See* MASSACHUSETTS art teachers' association. Boston, 1875. 8° 6212.3

ANTERIUS, *pope.* *See* HIPPOLYTUS, *St.*

ANTEROS. [Fiction.] Lawrence, G. A. 315.25

ANTHONY, Henry Bowen. Memorial addresses, on several occasions; delivered in the senate of the United States. Providence, 1875. Engraved title-page. 52 pp. Portraits. 8° 5221.1

ANTHRACITE fires. An inquiry into [their] influence upon health. Derby, G. Boston, 1868. 12° .. 1526.15

ANTHROPOLOGY, Manual of. Bray, C. London, 1871. Sm. 8° 6616.7

ANTIQUARY, The. Scott, *Sir* W. Boston 523.17

— *Same.* Leipzig 324.4

ANTIQUITIES. Chambers, R. The book of days. A miscellany of popular antiquities. London, N. D. 2 v. 8° .... *R.R., A.3.7

— Mueller, F. M. Chips from a German workshop. New York, 1872. Sm. 8° 5616.1.3

Shelf. No.

ANTIQUITIES, *continued.*
— Smith, W. Dictionary of Greek and Roman antiquities. London, 1872. 8°............*R.R., E.3.5

See also Archæology.

Note. — See also the histories of countries, like America, etc.

ANTI-SLAVERY and reform papers. Thoreau, H. D. Boston, 1872. 12°...................... 225.2
ANTI-SLAVERY examiner. No. 10. American slavery as it is: testimony of a thousand witnesses. New York, 1839. 8°...................... 812.10
ANTOINE de Bonneval. Anderdon, W. H. 716.17
ANTONIA. Dudevant, A. L. A. D.................. 526.23
ANTONINA; or, the fall of Rome. Collins, (W.) W. 326.4
ANTONINUS, Marcus Aurelius. Thoughts. Translated by G. Long. 2d edition. Revised and corrected. London, 1869. 210+ pp. Sm. 8°.6115.16
— *See* FARRAR, F. W. Seekers after God. London, 1875. Sm. 8°...................... 5937.7
ANTONY Brade. Lowell, R. T. S.................. 714.5
ANTONY Waymouth. Kingston, W. H. G. 935.27
ANTWERP, The siege of. Schiller, (J.) F. (C.) von. New York, 1847. 12°...................... 826.5
— *Same.* New York, 1872. Sm. 8° 827.26
APACHE country, Adventures in the. Browne, J. R. New York, 1871. 12° 415.13
APELLES and his contemporaries. Greenough, H. Boston, 1860. 342 pp. Sm. 8° 536.10
APES, Man and. Mivart, St. G. New York, 1874. 16°...................................... 6617.6
APINGI country. My Apingi kingdom. [Africa.] Du Chaillu, P. B. New York, 1872. 12°..... 933.2
APOCALYPSE, The, revealed. Swedenborg, E. New York, 1873. 2 v. 8°...................... 6323.3
APOCRYPHAL New Testament. *See* ANTE-NICENE Christian library.........................6322.15.16
APOSTLES, The. Renan, (J.) E. London, 1869. 8°. 5812.8
APOSTLES of mediæval Europe. Maclear, G. F. [London, 1869.] Sm. 8° 5937.5
APOSTOLICAL constitutions. Donaldson, J. Edinburgh, 1870. 8°...........................6322.16
APPERLEY, Charles James. Life of John Mytton. With his hunting, racing, shooting, driving, and extravagant exploits. By Nimrod [*pseud.*]. New edition. With a memoir of Nimrod. London [1871]. xi, 235 pp. Sm. 8°............ 5427.2
APPLE gathering, The. Abbott, J................ 917.28
APPLEDORE cook book, The. Parloa, M. Boston [1873]. 8°.............................. 6426.2
APPLETON, Daniel, and co. Dictionary of machines, mechanics, engine-work, and engineering. Illustrated. New edition, with appendix. New York, 1869. 2 v. Portraits. L. 8°.....*R.R., D.3.3
— Hand-book of American travel. Northern and eastern tour. With maps. Revised for 1872, with appendix. New York, 1872. viii, 292 pp. 12°...................................... 425.17
— — Southern tour. *See* JONES, Charles H........ 413.5
— Journal of literature, science, and art. Vol. 9–13. New York, 1873–75. 5 v. 4° 1332.1
— Juvenile annual. For 1871. With illustrations. New York, 1871. 382+ pp. 12° 933.8
APPLETON, Nathan. Introduction of the power loom, and origin of Lowell. Lowell, 1858. 36 pp. 8°................................ 6434.3
APPLETON, Thomas Gold. A sheaf of papers. By T. G. A. Boston, 1875. 362 pp. 12°........1537.23
ARABELLA Stuart. James, G. P. R............... 327.13
ARABESQUES. [Fiction.] Greenough, S. D........1516.12
ARABIA. 'Ilâm-en-nâs. Historical tales and anecdotes of the time of the early Khalîfahs. London, 1873. Sm. 8° 5927.6
— Jessup, H. H. The women of the Arabs. New York [1873]. 16°.......................... 5916.6
— Maughan, W. C. The Alps of Arabia. Travels in Egypt, Sinai, Arabia and the Holy Land. London, 1873. 8° 5932.10
— Palmer, E. H. The desert of the Exodus. New York, 1872. Sm. 8° 222.2
— Palgrave, W. G. A year's journey through central and eastern Arabia. London, 1871. Sm. 8°. 5916.7

Shelf. No.

ARABIA, *continued.*
— Robinson, E., and Smith, E. Biblical researches in Arabia Petræa. Boston, 1841. 8°......... 5810.5
— Taylor, (J.) B. Travels in. New York, 1872. 12°. 224.6

Note. — Sections of books of travel in Asia and the East often pertain in part to Arabia; and, as the original centre of Mahometanism, lives of the prophet and histories of that faith largely concern Arabia.

ARABIAN days' entertainments. Hauff, W. 533.6
ARABIAN nights' entertainments 928.14
ARATRA pentilici. Ruskin, J. New York, 1872. 12°. 6236.2
ARBLAY, Frances d', *formerly Miss Burney.* Evelina. 311.28
ARC, Joan of. *See* DARC, Jeanne.
ARCHÆOLOGY. Fairholt, F. W. Rambles of an archæologist among old books and in old places. London, 1871. Sm. 4° 6232.3
— Stevens, E. T. Flint chips. A guide to prehistoric archæology. London, 1870. 8° 5913.6

See also Antiquities.

ARCHELAUS, *bishop of Mesopotamia.* *See* GREGORIUS *Thaumaturgus, or, Neo-Cæsariensis, St.*
ARCHER, E. M., *pseud.* Christina North. A novel. 711.18
— Under the lines.............................. 713.11
ARCHES, Experimental essays on the principles of construction in. Bland, W. London, 1867. 12°. 1716.6
ARCHIBALD, A. K. Poems. Boston, 1848. 200 pp. Engraving. 16°............................1616.17
ARCHIE Lovell. Edwards, A. B. 312.15
ARCHITECTS. Clement, C. E. Architects, and their works. New York, 1874. 16°..............1513.17
— Vasari, G. Lives of the most eminent architects. London, 1855. 5 v. Sm. 8° 6215.6
ARCHITECTURAL modelling in paper, Art of. Richardson, T. A. London, 1859. 12° 1716.5
ARCHITECTURE. Allen, C. B. Cottage building. London, 1870. 12° 1715.28
— Bardwell, W. What a house should be. London [1873]. 8° 6221.4
— Bicknell, A. J. Wooden and brick buildings with details. New York, 1875. 2 v. F°..... 6220.7
— Brown, R. Domestic architecture. London [1842]. 4° 6220.3
— Burn, R. S. Self-aid cyclopedia. London, N. D. 8°. 6223.2
— Bury, T. T. Rudimentary architecture. London, 1867. 12°.................................1716.21
— Downing, A. J. Architecture of country houses. New York, 1866. 8°......................... 1511.2
— — Cottage residences. New York, 1844. 8°.... 1511.7
— — *Same.* New York, 1873. Sm. 4° 6221.3
— Eastlake, *Sir* C. L. History of the Gothic revival. London, 1872. Sm. 4°................ 6221.2
— Fergusson, J. History of architecture in all countries, from the earliest times to the present day. London, 1874. 2 v. 8°.....................6222.3
— — History of the modern styles of. London, 1873. 8°...................................... 6212.3
— Garbett, E. L. Rudimentary treatise on the principles of design in. London, 1867. 12°...1715.24
— Gardner, E. C. Illustrated homes. Boston, 1875. Sq. 16°............................. 6227.3
— Gordon, G. H. An inquiry into the principles of beauty in Grecian architecture. London, 1860. 12°.......................................1716.18
— Horton, C. W. Architecture for general students. New York, 1874. 16°....................... 6227.2
— Hussey, E. C. National cottage architecture. New York, 1874. 4°........................ 6220.2
— Lakey, C. D. Village and country houses. New York, 1875. 8° 6220.8
— Leeds, W. H. Rudimentary architecture. London, 1871. 12°................................1716.22
— Lefèvre, A. Wonders of. New York, 1872. 12°. 1714.2
— Morris, T. A house for the suburbs. London, 1870. 16°................................ 6223.1
— Ruskin, J. Inquiry into some of the conditions at present affecting "the study of architecture" in our schools. New York, 1872. 12°.......6236.12
— — Lectures on. New York, 1872. 12°.........6236.12
— — The poetry of. New York, 1873. 12°.......6236.19
— — The seven lamps of. New York, 1871. 12° .. 6236.3
— Springer, A. H. Handbuch der Kunstgeschichte. Stuttgart, 1855. 8°........................ 1513.1

Shelf. No.

ARCHITECTURE, *continued.*
— Vaux, C. Villas and cottages. New York, 1872. 8°.......... 6221.1
— Viollet-le-Duc, E. E. Discourses on. Boston, 1875. 8°.......... 6220.9
— - The story of a house. Boston, 1874. 8°..... 1513.3
— Wheeler, G. Rural homes; or, sketches of houses suited to American country life. New York, 1852. 12°.......... 1513.2

See also Building, Church architecture, Drawing, Dwelling houses.

Note.—An extensive survey of the literature of architecture is given in Bulletin no. 35, p. 429. Fergusson's is the best general history in English.

ARCTIC regions. Arctic geography and ethnology. *See* ROYAL geographical society, *London.* London, 1875. 8°.......... 5923.9
— Blake, E. V. Arctic experiences. New York, 1874. 8°..........5911.15
— English explorers, The. With chapter on Arctic explorations. London, 1875. Sm. 8°......... 5927.9
— Hall, C. F. Arctic researches and life among the Esquimaux, 1860-62. New York, 1865. 8°. 422.4
— Hartwig, G. The polar and tropical worlds. Springfield, 1874. 8°.......... 1520.7
— Hayes, I. I. An Arctic boat journey, in the autumn of 1854. Boston, 1860. 12°......... 226.1
— Koldewey, C. The German arctic expedition of 1869-70. London, 1874. L. 8°.......... 5722.3
— Markham, A. H. A whaling cruise to Baffin's bay and the gulf of Boothia. London, 1874. 8°. 5912.11
— Realm, The, of the ice king. London [1874]. Sq. 16°..........5934.12
— Sargent, E. Arctic adventure by sea and land. Boston, 1857. 12°.......... 426.10
— Tomlinson, C. Winter in the. London [1872]. Sm. 8°.......... 5915.3
— Verne, J. The English at the north pole. [Fiction.] London, 1875. Sm. 8°.......... 724.27
— - The fur country. [Fiction.] Boston, 1874. 8°. 713.2
— Wells, J. C. The gateway to the Polynia. A voyage to Spitzbergen. London, 1873. 8°....5911.14

See also Franklin, *Sir* John, Polar sea, Repulse bay.

Note.—A full summary of the literature of Arctic explorations is given in the Lower Hall Catalogue for history, etc., p. 15, with supplemental notes in the Bulletin, vol. II, pp. 239, 305.

ARENA, The, and the throne. Townsend, L. T. Boston, 1874. 16°..........1527.14
ARETÆUS, the Cappadocian. Extant works. [Greek and English.] Edited and translated by F. Adams. London, 1856. xx, 510 pp. 8°......6013.20
ARGYLL, George Douglas Campbell, *Duke of.* *See* CAMPBELL, George Douglas.
ARISTOPHANES. Birds. With notes and a metrical table, by C. C. Felton. Cambridge, 1849. xv, 228 pp. 12°.......... 6115.2
— Comedies. A new and literal translation, from the revised text of Dindorf. By W. J. Hickie. London, 1872, 73. 2 v. Portrait. Sm. 8°.... 6115.6

Contents.—Vol. I. The Acharnians; The knights; The clouds; The wasps; Peace; The Birds. II. Lysistrata; The Thesmophoriazusæ; The frogs; The Ecclesiazusæ; Plutus.

— Aristophanes [outlined and explained]. Collins, W. L. Edinburgh, 1872. 16°..........6116.14
ARISTOTELES. Grote, G. London, 1872. 2 v. 8°. 6112.1
ARITHMETIC. Pike, N. New and complete system of. Boston, 1809. 12°..........1933.16
— Walsh, M. A new system of mercantile arithmetic. Newburyport, 1803. 12°..........1933.17
ARIZONA. Browne, J. R. A tour through Arizona. New York, 1871. 12°.......... 415.13
— Cozzens, S. W. The marvellous country; or, three years in. Boston, 1873. 8°.......... 412.1
ARK, The, of Elm island. Kellogg, E.......... 922.16
ARMADALE. Collins, (W.) W.......... 326.5
ARMAND: a play. Ritchie, A. C. Boston, 1855. 12°. 1635.3
ARME Therese! Foudras, T. L. A., *marquis* de. Pest, 1852. 2 v. in 1. 16°.......... 2027.6
ARMENGAUD, Charles. The practical draughtsman's book of industrial design, etc. *See* JOHNSON, William.......... 6420.2

Shelf. No.

ARMENGAUD, Jacques Eugene. The practical draughtsman's book of industrial design, etc. *See* JOHNSON, William.......... 6420.2
ARMITAGE, George. The horseowner and stableman's companion. London [1871]. xii, 237 pp. 1 plate. Sm. 8°.......... 6616.5
ARMOUR, James. Iron and heat. With illustrations. London, 1871. 163+ pp. 12°..........1716.40
— Power in motion. Horse power, wheel gearing, driving bands, and angular forces. With illustrations. London, 1871. iv, 188 pp. 12°....1716.41
ARMS and armour in antiquity and the middle ages. Lacombe, M. (J.) P. New York, 1871. 16°..1714.15
ARMSTRONG, Francis Claudius. The young middy; or the perilous adventures of a boy-officer. 931.8
ARMSTRONG, John. Life of Anthony Wayne. (*In* Sparks, J. Library of American biography)..5028.1.4
— Life of Richard Montgomery. (*In* Sparks, J. Library of American biography)..........5028.1.1
ARMY and navy official gazette. Vol. 1. 1863-64. Washington, 1864. 4°.......... 6910.4
ARMY and navy series. *See* ADAMS, William T.
ARMY life in a black regiment. Higginson, T. W. Boston, 1870. 12°.......... 416.5
ARMY life on the border, Thirty years of. Marcy, R. B. New York, 1866. 12°.......... 415.16
ARMY reunion, The: with reports of the meetings of the societies of the army of the Cumberland; the army of the Tennessee; the army of the Ohio; and the army of Georgia. Chicago, 1868. Chicago, 1869. 339 pp. Portraits. 8°.......... 5013.9
ARNAULD, Angélique. *See* ANGÉLIQUE, etc.
ARNE. Björnson, B.......... 735.25
ARNOBIUS *Afer.* The seven books of Arnobius adversus gentes. Translated by Archd. Hamilton Bryce and Hugh Campbell. Edinburgh, 1871. xix, 386 pp. [Ante-Nicene Christian library.] 8°..........6322.4.19
ARNOLD, Benedict, Life of. Sparks, J. (*In* Sparks, J. Library of American biography).........5028.1.3
ARNOLD, Frederick. Our bishops and deans. London, 1875. 2 v. 8°.......... 5810.6
— Oxford and Cambridge: their colleges, memories, and associations. With engravings. London [1874]. viii, 400 pp. Sm. 4°.......... 5433.2
— Turning-points in life. New York, 1873. 364 pp. 12°..........1536.12
ARNOLD, Howard Payson. European mosaic. [Travels.] Boston, 1864. vii, 339 pp. 16°........ 435.1
ARNOLD, Matthew. Culture and anarchy: an essay in political and social criticism. London, 1869. lx, 272 pp. 8°.......... 5613.2
— God and the Bible. A review of objections to "Literature and dogma." Boston, 1876. 329 pp. 12°.......... 5815.5
— Essays in criticism. Boston, 1873. xv, 506+ pp. 12°..........5617.10
— Higher schools and universities in Germany. [2d edition.] London, 1874. lxxxvii, 270 pp. Sm. 8°.......... 5836.6
— Literature and dogma. An essay towards a better apprehension of the Bible. 3d edition. London, 1873. xxxvi, 388 pp. Sm. 8°.......... 5815.6
— St. Paul and protestantism; with an essay on puritanism and the church of England. 2d edition. London, 1870. xxxix, 182 pp. Sm. 8°.5815.24
ARNOLD, Thomas, *D. D.* History of Rome. From the last London edition. New York, 1872. xvi, 670 pp. 8°.......... 821.5
— Introductory lectures on modern history, with the inaugural lecture. 6th edition. London, 1871. xi, 315 pp. 8°.......... 5912.5
— Life of Hannibal. New York, 1870. 320 pp. 16°. 1028.7
— Life and correspondence of. Stanley, A. P. Boston, 1872. 12°..........1225.14
ARNOLD, Thomas, *A. M.* Chaucer to Wordsworth. A short history of English literature, from the earliest times to the present day. London [1873]. xv, 454 pp. Sm. 8°.......... 5628.2
ARNOLD family. Thayer, E. Family memorial. Hingham, 1835. 8°.......... 611.2

Shelf. No.

ARNOULD, Auguste, ALBOIZE DU PUJOL, Édouard, and MAQUET, Auguste. Histoire de la Bastille. [Suivie par Le donjon de Vincennes. Par É. Alboize du Pujol et A. Maquet.] Illustrée de gravures. Paris, 1845, 51, 53. 8 v. 8°.... 2010.1

Contents. — Vol. I-VI. Histoire de la Bastille. VII, VIII. Le donjon de Vincennes.

ARNOULD, *Sir* Joseph. Memoir of Thomas, first lord Denman. London, 1873. 2 v. Portraits. 8°. 5332.1
ARNOULT, Émile, *joint author*. French grammar. *See* PINNEY, Norman.......................... 2013.1
AROUND a spring. Droz, G..................... 511.23
AROUND the world. Prime, E. D. G. New York, 1873. 8°......... 233.1
AROUND the world in eighty days. [Fiction.] Verne, J.................................. 725.27
ARRAH Neil. James, G. P. R.................. 327.11
ARSENNE, Louis Charles. Manuel du peintre et du sculpteur. Paris, 1833. 2 v. Folded plates. 24°. [Manuel Roret]........................ 6219.1
ART. Brande, W. T., and Cox, G. W. Dictionary of. London, 1872. 3 v. 8°............*R.R., E.3.6
— Cherbuliez, V. Études de littérature et d'art. Paris, 1873. 16°.............................. 5536.7
— Chorley, H. F. Recent art and society, as described in [his] autobiography. New York, 1874. 12°..................................5616.14
— Clement, C. E. Handbook of legendary and mythological art. New York, 1872. Sm. 8°..1513.15
— Fairholt, F. W. Rambles of an archæologist among old books and in old places: papers on. London, 1871. Sm. 4°........................ 6232.3
— Field, G. Grammar of colouring. London, N. D. 12°.. 1715.3
— Hamerton, P. G. Thoughts about art. Boston, 1871. 16°.. 1515.3
— Hulme, F. E., and others. Art-studies from nature, as applied to design. London, 1872. Sm. 4°.. 6222.2
— Jameson, A. (M.) Sketches of art, literature, and character. Boston, 1866. 16°........... 5618.3
— Keddie, *Miss* —. The old masters and their pictures. London, 1873. Sm. 8°..............1516.21
— *Same*. Boston, 1874. 16°.................. 6216.3
— Knight, C. Arts and sciences; or, fourth division of "The English cyclopædia." London, 1866–68. 8 v. 4°..........................*R.R.,F.2.1
— Long, S. P. Art: its laws, and the reasons for them. Boston, 1871. Sm. 8°................ 1513.7
— Luebke, W. History of. London, 1869. 2 v. 8°. 6210.4
— Rio, A. F. Poetry of Christian art. London, 1854. 12°.. 6234.1
— Ruskin, J. The eagle's nest. Ten lectures on the relation of natural science to. New York, 1873. 12°.. 6236.5
— – Lectures on. New York, 1872. 12°.........6236.13
— – The political economy of. New York, 1866. 12°.. 6236.8
— – Sesame and lilies. New York, 1872. 12°....6236.15
— – The two paths: being lectures on. New York, 1866. 12°.. 6236.8
— Smith, W. Art education. Boston, 1872. 8°.. 6211.3
— Taine, H. A. The philosophy of. Art in Greece. New York, 1872. 12°............................. 6217.2
— – – Art in the Netherlands. New York, 1871. 16°.. 6217.1
— Timbs, J. The year-book of facts in science and art. London, 1866. Sm. 8°..................1527.12
— Tyrwhitt, R. St. J. Christian art and symbolism, with some hints on the study of landscape. London, 1872. 16° ....1514.14 and 6235.1
— Urbino, L. B., Day, H., and others. Art recreations. Boston, 1873. 12°.................... 1515.9
— Viardot, L. Wonders of European art. New York, 1871. 16°.................................. 1714.1
— – Wonders of Italian art. New York, 1871. 12°.1714.23
— Wagner, (W.) R. Art life and theories. New York, 1875. 12°................................ 6234.3
— Winckelmann, J. (J.) History of ancient art. Boston, 1872, 73. 4 v. L. 8°................ 6211.1

Shelf. No.

ART, *continued*.
— Wright, T. History of caricature and grotesque in. London [1864]. Sm. 4°.................. 5923.4

See also Artists, Decorative art, Domestic arts, Drawing, Europe, Fine arts, Great Britain, Music, Ornament, Painters, Painting, Perspective, Recreative arts, Sculpture, Useful arts.

Note. — Histories of various countries and epochs often contain chapters on the arts of that country or epoch. See also the lives of artists, like Allston, Michel-Angelo, Raphael, etc., and the lives of patrons of art, like Roscoe's Lorenzo de' Medici and Leo X. Nearly all of Mrs. Jameson's books are of interest to the student of art. Luebke's is one of the latest and best general histories. Ruskin's earlier books are mentioned under Architecture and Painting, but his later views are at variance with them. Taine represents a modern school of writers.

ART, The, of dining; or, gastronomy and gastronomers. New edition. London, 1853. vi, 137 pp. 16°.. 6428.6
ART education. *See* MASSACHUSETTS art teachers' association. The Antefix papers. Papers on art educational subjects. Boston, 1875. 8°.... 6212.3
ART-JOURNAL, The. New series. Vol. 12, 13. London, 1873, 74. 2 v. 4°.......................... 6521.1
ARTHUR, Timothy Shay. Cast adrift.............. 921.8
ARTHUR Bonnicastle. Holland, J. G.............. 536.17
ARTHUR Brown. Kellogg, E......................... 922.8
ARTHUR O'Leary. Lever, C. (J.) Leipzig........ 332.27
— *Same*. London.................................. 516.21
ARTIST'S [Dürer's] married life. Schefer, L. New York, 1871. 16°.................................. 1027.3
ARTISTE. Grant, M. M.............................. 731.16
ARTISTS. Fairholt, F. W. Homes, works, and shrines of English artists. London, 1873. Sm. 4°.... 6213.6
— Tuckerman, H. T. Book of the artists. [American.] New York, 1870. 8°........................ 1511.6

See also Architects, Musicians, Painters, Sculptors.

ARTOIS, Vallet d'. Manuel du fabricant de gants. 2e édition. Paris, 1835. 549+ pp. Folded plates. 24°. [Manuel Roret].................. 6439.2
ARTS, Dictionary of. Ure, A. London, 1872. 3 v. 8°. 6422.3
ARUNDELL, John Francis, *baron of Wardour*. Tradition, principally with reference to mythology and the law of nations. London, 1872. ix–xxix, 431+ pp. 8°...................................... 6333.1
As it should be. ALEX, *pseud*. Philadelphia, 1874. 16°.. 1736.5
As she would have it. ALEX, *pseud*. Philadelphia, 1873. 16°...................................... 1736.6
ASBURY twins, The. Clarke, R. S. 1115.17
ASCOGH, Anne. *See* ASKEW, Anne.
ASH, John. New and complete dictionary of the English language. Prefixed a grammar. London, 1775. 2 v. 8°........................*R.R., F.3.12
ASHANTEE, *Africa*. Brackenbury, H. The Ashanti war. Edinburgh, 1874. 2 v. 8°...........5911.16
— Stanley, H. M. Coomassie and Magdala: the story of two British campaigns in Africa. New York, 1874. 8°......................................5931.14
ASHER, J. R., and Adams, G. H., *publishers*. New commercial, topographical, and statistical atlas and gazetteer of the United States: with maps showing the Dominion of Canada, Europe and the world. New York [1873]. 284 pp. F°. *R.R.Desk
ASHWELL, Samuel. A practical treatise on the diseases peculiar to women, illustrated by cases. Boston, 1843. 312 pp. 8°..................6021.11
ASIA. Hellwald, F. von. The Russians in Central Asia. A critical examination down to the present time of the geography and history of Central Asia. London, 1874. Sm. 8°........... 5914.9
— Morse, J., and Parish, E. New gazetteer of the Eastern continent. Charlestown, 1802. 8°.... 432.4
— Polo, M. The book of Ser Marco Polo. London, 1875. 2 v. 8°...................................... 5933.7
— Pumpelly, R. Across America and Asia. New York, 1871. 8°...................................... 5916.2
— Rawlinson, *Sir* H. (C.) England and Russia in the East. A series of papers on the political and geographical condition of Central Asia. London, 1875. 8°...................................... 5921.5

See also Arabia, Asia Minor, Assyria, Babylon, Bokhara, Burmah, China, East (The), India, Japan, Palestine, Persia, Russia, Syria, Turkey

Shelf. No.

ASIA MINOR. Taylor, (J.) B. The lands of the Saracen; or, pictures of. New York, 1857. 12°. 424.13
— Willis, N. P. Pencillings by the way. New York, 1844. L. 8° 430.2
ASKEW, *or* ASCOGH, Anne. Passages in the life of the Faire gospeller. Manning, A. New York, 1867. 12° 517.19
ASLAUGA's knight. La Motte Fouqué, F. (H. C.), *Freiherr* de 313.7
ASPASIE de Milet. Becq de Fouquières, L. Paris, 1872. 18° 6116.1
ASPEN court. Brooks, (C.) S. 538.7
ASPENDALE. Preston, H. W. 718.3
ASSAYING. Metallurgy of copper. Lamborn, C. London, 1868. 12° 1715.16
ASSYRIA. Rawlinson, G. The five great monarchies of the ancient Eastern world; or, the history, geography, and antiquities of. London, 1871. 3 v. 8° 5922.3
— Rollin, C. Ancient history of the Assyrians. Boston, 1807. Vol. 1-4, 6-8. 7 v. 8° 5913.1
— Smith, G. Assyrian discoveries; an account of explorations and discoveries on the site of Nineveh, 1873, 74. London, 1875. 8° 5932.12

See also Asia, Babylon, Nineveh, and History (ancient).

Note. — The art of Assyria is illustrated in Layard's Nineveh [5912.2 and 9], and in the section on Assyria in Fergusson's History of architecture [6222.3].

ASTERIUS, Urbanus, *St.* *See* HIPPOLYTUS, *St.*
ASTOR, John Jacob. *See* PARTON, J. Famous Americans of recent times. Boston, 1871. 8° 1214.14
ASTORIA. Irving, W. London, 1850. 16° 417.1
— *Same.* Philadelphia, 1871. Sm. 8° 1814.1
ASTRONOMY. Burritt, E. H. The geography of the heavens. New York, 1854. 12° 6818.1
— Chalmers, T. Selections of discourses on the Christian revelation viewed in connection with modern astronomy. Hartford, 1818. 16° 5819.17
— Denison, E. B. Astronomy without mathematics. New York, 1871. 12° 6817.1
— Farrar, J. Elementary treatise on. Cambridge, 1827. 8° 6433.2
— Flammarion, C. The wonders of the heavens. New York, 1871. 16° 1714.13
— Kiepert, H. Grosser Hand-Atlas des Himmels und der Erde. Thüringer, 1873. F° ......*R.R.Desk
— Lewis, *Sir* G. C. An historical survey of the astronomy of the ancients. London, 1862. 8°. 6813.5
— Main, R. Rudimentary astronomy. London, 1869. 12° 17:6.38
— Mitchell, O. M. The planetary and stellar worlds. London [1860]. 16° 1526.14
— Plummer, J. I. Introduction to. New York [Glasgow], 1873. 16° 1717.6
— Proctor, R. A. Essays on. London, 1872. 8°. 1521.4 and 6813.1
— - The expanse of heaven. London, 1873. Sm. 8°. 6815.1
— - Other worlds than ours. New York, 1871. 12°. 1527.4
— - Our place among infinities. London, 1875. Sm. 8° 6815.2
— - Recent solar researches. (*In* Estes, D. Half-hour recreations in popular science) 6813.7
— - The universe and the coming transits. London, 1874. 8° 6813.4
— Rambosson, J. Astronomy. London, 1875. 8°. 6812.1
— Whewell, W. Astronomy and general physics considered with reference to natural theology. Philadelphia, 1833. 12° 6438.5

See also Earth, Moon, Nautical astronomy, Optics, Planetary and stellar worlds, Stars, Sun.

AT Capri. Bauer, K. Philadelphia [1875]. 16°.. 714.19
AT her mercy. Payn, J. Leipzig 319.19
— *Same.* New York 732.30
AT his gates. Oliphant, M. (O. W.) 510.5
AT home and abroad. Taylor, (J.) B. New York, 1870, 72. 2 v. 12° 234.1
AT last: a Christmas in the West Indies. Kingsley, C. Leipzig, 1871. 2 v. in 1. Sq. 16° 326.17
AT odds. Tautphoeus, J. M., *baroness* von 317.22
AT the altar. Werner, E. 727.34

AT the back of the north wind. MacDonald, G. 915.16
AT the sign of the silver flagon. Farjeon, B. L. 711.3
ATHALIE: tragédie. Racine, J. de. Théâtre complet. Paris, 1870. 12° 5537.3
ATHANASIA. Sears, E. H. Boston, 1858. 12° 5816.16
ATHANASIUS, *St.* Orations against the Arians, according to the Benedictine text. With an account of his life by W. Bright. Oxford, 1873. xcviii, 258+ pp. Sm. 8° 6325.5
ATHENÆUM, The. Vol. 1-6. London, 1873-75. 6 v. 4° 6732.1
ATHENAGORAS. Writings. *See* JUSTINUS *Martyr*..6322.4.2
ATHENIA of Damascus: a tragedy. Dawes, R. New York, 1839. 12° 5217.4
ATHENS. Bulwer-Lytton, E. (G. E.) L. Athens: its rise and fall. Leipzig, 1843. 2 v. in 1. Sq. 16° 828.10
— Phillips, J. L. T. Site and antiquities of. (*In* Many lands and many people) 431.3

Note. — Histories of Greece and of the ancient world necessarily cover the history more or less particularly of Athens.

ATHERSTONE priory. Comyn, L. N. 728.3
ATKINSON, Charles Follen, *joint author.* Cotton culture and the South considered with reference to emigration. *See* LORING, Francis William..... 6435.3
ATKINSON, J. Beavington. An art tour to northern capitals of Europe. London, 1873. xii, 455 pp. 8° 6213.4
ATKINSON, William Parsons. Classical and scientific studies, and the great schools of England: a lecture. Cambridge, 1865. 117 pp. 8° 1912.3
ATLANTIC, Rollo on the. Abbott, J. 917.16
ATLANTIC essays. Higginson, T. W. Boston, 1871. 12° 1915.2
ATLANTIC monthly. Vol. 1-36. Boston, 1857-75. 36 v. 8° 1425.1
ATLANTIC tales 524.10

Contents. — Hale, E. E., My double, and how he undid me; O'Brien, F. J., The diamond lens; Davis, R. B., Life in the iron mills; Dodge, M. A., The pursuit of knowledge under difficulties; Lowell, R. T. S., A raft that no man made; Arnold, G., Why Thomas was discharged; Chesebro', C., Victor and Jacqueline; Nordhoff, C., Elkanah Brewster's temptation; Hale, L. P., The queen of the red chessmen; Terry, R., Miss Lucinda; Whelpley, J. D., The Denslow palace; Taylor, (J.) B., Friend Eli's daughter; Appleton, E. H., A half-life and half a life; Hale, E. E., The man without a country.

ATLANTIC, The, to the Pacific. Lester, J. E. Boston, 1873. 12° 417.12
— *Same.* London, 1873. Sm. 8° 417.13
ATLAS. Asher, J. R., and Adams, G. H., *publishers.* New commercial, topographical, and statistical atlas and gazetteer of the United States: with maps showing the Dominion of Canada, Europe and the world. New York [1873]. F° ....*R.R.Desk
— Black, A. and C. General atlas of the world. Edinburgh, 1871. F° ..................*R.R.Desk
— Bradford, T. G. A comprehensive atlas. Boston [*cop.* 1835]. 4° 5030.2
— Complete historical, chronological, and geographical American atlas. Philadelphia, 1822. F° .. 5030.8
— Kiepert, H. Grosser Hand-Atlas des Himmels und der Erde. Thüringer, 1873. F° ......*R.R.Desk
— Las Cases, M. J. E. A. D. Genealogical, historical, chronological, and geographical atlas. Philadelphia, 1821. F° 5030.7
— Philip, G., and son. Philip's atlas of the counties of England, reduced from the ordnance survey. By E. Weller. London, 1875. F°...*R.R.Desk
— Smith, W. An atlas of ancient geography, biblical and classical. London, 1874. F° ......*R.R.Desk
Spruner, C. von. Atlas antiquus. Gothae, 1865. 4° ....*R.R.Desk
ATMOSPHERE. Flammarion, C. The atmosphere. London, 1873. L. 8° 6832.2
— Hartwig, G. The aerial world: a popular account of the phenomena and life of the. London, 1874. 8° 6832.3
— *Same.* New York, 1875. 8° 1520.5
— Reclus, (J. J.) É. The ocean, atmosphere, and life. New York, 1873. 8° 6632.2
ATONEMENT. The Scripture doctrine of atonement examined. Taylor, J. Boston, 1809. 12° ... 6328.1

Shelf. No.

ATTERBURY, Francis. Macaulay, T. B., *lord*. Leipzig, 1860. Sq. 16° 1238.18

— *Same*. (*In his* New biographies of illustrious men) 5428.4

ATTIC philosopher, An, in Paris. Souvestre, É. New York, 1873. 12° 532.9

ATTILA. Histoire d'Attila. Thierry, A. (S. D.) Paris, 1856. 2 v. 8° 2012.1

AUBER, Daniel François Esprit. Fra diavolo; Masaniello. (*In* Ditson, O., and co. Standard opera librettos) 6233.3.3

AUBREY. Marsh-Caldwell, A. 313.28

AUDUBON, John James. Audubon, *Mrs.* J. J. Life of. New York, 1871. 12° 5026.3

— Buchanan, R. Life and adventures of. London, 1869. 8° 5023.7

Note. — A life prepared by his widow was subjected by the English publishers, under the editing of Robert Buchanan, to a curtailment of four-fifths of its bulk, which publication was reissued in this country by the widow, "with some additions and omissions of objectionable passages." There is a brief biographical sketch by Smiles [1024.13].

AUDUBON, *Mrs.* John James. Life of John James Audubon, the naturalist. With an introduction by J. G. Wilson. New York, 1871. 443 pp. Portrait. 12° 5026.3

AUER, Adelheid von. It is the fashion. From the German 533.21

AUERBACH, Berthold. Romane. Stuttgart, 1871. 12 v. in 4. Sq. 16° 5735.12

Contents. — Vol. [I.] 1. Spinoza. 2. Dichter und Kaufmann. [II.] 3, 4. Neues Leben. [III.] 5-8. Auf der Höhe. [IV.] 9-12. Das Landhaus am Rhein.

— Sämmtliche Schwarzwälder Dorfgeschichten. Stuttgart, 1871. 8 v. in 3. Sq. 16° 5735.13

Contents. — Vol [I.] 1. Der Tolpatsch; Die Kriegspfeife; Des Schlossbauers Vefele; Tonele mit der gebissenen Wange; Befehlerles; Die feindlichen Brüder; Ivo, der Hajrle. 2. Florian und Creszenz; Der Lauterbacher; Sträflinge; Erdmuthe. [II.] 3. Die Frau Professorin; Lucifer. 4. Die Geschichte des Diethelm von Buchenberg; Hopfen und Gerste. 5. Der Lehnhold; Der Viereckig oder die amerikanische Kiste. [III.] 6. Ein eigen Haus; Barfüssele. 7. Joseph im Schnee; Brosi und Moni. 8. Edelweiss.

— Black forest village stories. Translated by C. Goepp 926.27

— Edelweiss. Translated by E. Frothingham 517.4

— German tales. With an introduction by C. C. Shackford 918.14

— On the heights. Translated by F. E. Bunnètt. Boston 517.2

— *Same*. Leipzig 311.22

— Villa Eden. Translated by C. C. Shackford 511.20

— Waldfried. A novel. Translated by S. A. Stern. 734.24

AUERSPERG, Anton Alexander, *Graf* von. The last knight, a romance-garland. From the German of Anastasius Grün [*pseud.*]. Translated, with notes, by J. O. Sargent. New York, 1871. ix, 200 pp. Sm. 4° 5738.5

AUGUST and Elvie. Abbott, J. 923.1

AUGUST stories. *See* ABBOTT, Jacob.

AUGUSTINUS, Aurelius, *St.*, *bishop of Hippo*. The city of God. Translated by M. Dods. Edinburgh, 1872. 2 v. 8° 5811.11

AULULARIA. Plautus, T. M. Philadelphiæ [*cop.* 1842]. Sm. 12° 6118.4

AUMALE, Henri (Eugène Philippe Louis) d'Orléans, *duc* d'. History of the princes de Condé in the XVIth and XVIIth centuries. Translated from the French by R. B. Borthwick. London, 1872. 2 v. Portrait. Folded map. 8° 5522.9

AUNT JANE'S hero. Prentiss, E. 737.2

AUNT Jo's scrap-bag. Alcott, L. M. 3 v. 926.5

AUNT Kipp. Alcott, L. M. 935.20

AUNT Madge's story. Clarke, R. S. 927.8

AUNT Margaret. Abbott, J. Harper's story books.. 936.1.9

AUNT Patty's scrap-bag. Hentz, C. L. 935.15

AURELIAN. Ware, W. New York, 1869. 12° 512.14

Note. — Originally published under the title of Probus.

AURICULAR confesssion and popish nunneries. Hogan, W. Boston, 1845. 12° 1538.17

AURORA borealis. Strange discoveries respecting the aurora. Proctor, R. A. (*In* Estes, D. Half-hour recreations in popular science) 6813.7

Shelf. No.

AURORA Floyd. Braddon, M. E. 325.2

AURORA Leigh. [Poem.] Browning, E. B. Leipzig, 1872. Sq. 16° 1614.15

— *Same*. (*In her* Poems.) New York, 1862. 16°. 1612.4.3

AUSTEN, Jane. Emma 524.12

— Mansfield park 325.25

— Northanger abbey, and Persuasion 325.24

— Pride and prejudice 325.23

— Sense and sensibility. Leipzig 325.22

— *Same*. And Persuasion. Boston 515.5

Note. — These novels are healthy in tone, and excellent pictures of English middle life and of the country gentry, as they existed at the beginning of this century.

— Memoir of. Austen-Leigh, J. E. London, 1870. 8° 1221.6

AUSTEN-LEIGH, James Edward. Memoir of Jane Austen. London, 1870. v, 326+ pp. Illustrated. Portrait. 8° 1221.6

AUSTIN, George Lowell. History of Massachusetts, from the landing of the pilgrims to the present time. Boston, 1876. xix, 578 pp. Wood-cut. Portraits. 8° 813.19

— Life of Franz Schubert. Boston, 1873. 163 pp. Portrait. 12° 1228.7

AUSTIN, James Trecothie. Life of Elbridge Gerry. With contemporary letters, to the close of the American revolution. Boston, 1828. xvi, 520 pp. Portrait. 8° 1011.3

AUSTIN, Jane Goodwin. Cipher: a romance 711.7

— Moonfolk. A true account of the home of the fairy tales 912.22

— The shadow of Moloch mountain 511.1

AUSTIN Elliot. Kingsley, H. Boston 724.4

— *Same*. Leipzig 326.24

AUSTRALIA. Braim, T. H. New homes: the rise, progress, present position, and future prospects of the Australian colonies. London, 1870. 12°. 5934.10

— Powell, G. S. B. New homes for the old country. A personal experience of. London, 1872. 8°.. 5931.6

— Thomes, W. H. The gold hunter's adventures; or, life in. Boston, 1873. 12° 735.3

— Trollope, A. Australia and New Zealand. Leipzig, 1873. 3 v. in 1. Sq. 16° 418.5

— Vincent, F., *jr.* Thirty thousand miles of travel in. New York, 1876. 12° 436.8

AUSTRIA. Abbott, J. S. C. The monarchies of continental Europe. The empire of. New York, 1859. 12° 825.1

— Adams, W. T. Sunny shores; or, Young America in. Boston, 1875. 16° 925.12

— Baedeker, C. Handbook for travellers. Coblenz, 1871. 16° 5718.2

— Coxe, W. History of the house of Austria, 1218–1848. London, 1864–72. 4 v. 16° 5715.1

— Map of Austria and the German empire. [Also plan of Vienna and its exhibition. 4¾ in. × 4 in.] London, 1873. 30 in. × 18 in. 5730.3

— *Exhibitions of industry and art. Vienna exhibition. See* MASSACHUSETTS. *Legislative documents. Journals, reports, etc.* 6911.3

See also Germany.

AUSTRO-HUNGARIAN monarchy. L'Autriche-Hongrie, ses institutions et ses nationalités. Lévy, D. Paris, 1871. 18° 627.2

AUTHORITY. Recherches historiques du juste et de l'autorité. Philosophie appliquée. Mailfer, H. C. Paris, 1873. 2 v. 8° 6332.1

AUTHORS, Quarrels of. Disraeli, I. New York, 1814. 2 v. 12° 1537.17

AUTHORSHIP, Aspects of. Jacox, F. London, 1872. 16° 6136.6

AUTOBIOGRAPHIC sketches. De Quincey, T. Boston, 1869. 16° 1825.7

AUTOBIOGRAPHY of an actress. Ritchie, A. C. Boston, 1854. Sm. 8° 1216.6

AUTOCRAT, The, of the breakfast-table. Holmes, O. W. Boston, 1872. 12° 1934.3

AUTUMNAL catarrh. Wyman, M. New York, 1872. Sm. 8° 6012.7

AVARE, L': comédie. Molière, J. B. P. Œuvres. Paris, 1869. 12° 5537.2.3

Shelf. No.

AVELING, S. T. Heraldry: ancient and modern. Including Boutell's Heraldry, revised, with additions. With illustrations. London [1873]. xx, 430 pp. Sm. 4° 5415.7
AVENGER, The. De Quincey, T. 715.10
AXEL and Anna. Bremer, F. 511.5
AYERS, George B. How to paint photographs in water colors. Philadelphia, 1870. 148 [146] pp. 12° 6217.8
AYRSHIRE cattle. The dairy cow. A monograph on the Ayrshire breed of cattle. Sturtevant, E. L. and J. N. Boston, 1875. 12° 1522.12
AYRSHIRE legatees, The. Galt, J. 515.11
AYTON, Richard. The rendezvous: an operetta. New York, N. D. 28 pp. 1 plate. 12° 1635.3
AZARIAN. Spofford, H. E. 728.1
AZEGLIO, (Giuseppe Maria Girolama Raffaele) Massimo Taparelli, *marquis* d'. Recollections. Translated, with notes and an introduction by Count Maffei. London, 1868. 2 v. Portrait. Sm. 8° 5525.8

"B. O. W. C.," The. De Mille, J. 935.18
BABES, The, in the wood. De Mille, J. 710.22
BABOLAIN. Droz, G. 518.15
BABYLON. Layard, A. H. Discoveries in the ruins of. London, 1853. 8° 5912.9
— Rawlinson, G. The five great monarchies of the ancient Eastern world; or, the history, geography, and antiquities of. London, 1871. 3 v. 8° 5922.3
— Rollin, C. Ancient history of the Babylonians. Vol. 1-4, 6-8. Boston, 1807. 7 v. 8° 5913.1

See also Assyria.

Note. — The general reader will find a summary of the history, antiquities and identification of sites in McClintock and Strong's Cyclopædia, under Babylon, Babylonia, and Chaldæa; and a popular paper on the history, by Jacob Abbott, in Harper's monthly, vol. 36. The closer student will follow history in the original sources of Herodotus, particularly in Rawlinson's edition with his appended essays [6112.2]. Among the modern authorities of importance is that portion of George Rawlinson's Five ancient monarchies, devoted to Babylon, and for parallel reading Grote's History of Greece [5926.1].

BACH, Johann Sebastian. Bach and Beethoven. Barnard, C. F., *jr.* Boston, 1861. 16° 926.21

See also the note on Music in the Bulletin for Jan., 1876, p. 34.

BACHE, Alexander Dallas. Report on education in Europe, to the trustees of the Girard college for orphans. Philadelphia, 1839. xiii, 666+ pp. 8° 5834.3
BACHELDER, John B. Illustrated tourist's guide of the United States. Popular resorts, and how to reach them. Including Gettysburg. Boston, 1873. viii, 148+ pp. Sm. 8° 413.10
BACHELOR, The, of the Albany. Savage, M. W. 535.19
BACHELOR'S, A, revery. Mitchell, D. G. (*In* Johnson, (E.) R. Little classics) 529.4.4
BACKLOG studies. Warner, C. D. 928.1
BACKWOODSMAN, The. Wraxall, *Sir* (F. C.) L. 735.39
BACON, Albert M. Manual of gesture. Chicago, 1873. 260+ pp. 12° 1736.2
BACON, George Blagden. Illustrated library of travel, exploration, and adventure. Siam, as it was and is. New York, 1873. viii, 347 pp. Illustrated. 1 map. 12° 224.10
BACON, Francis, *lord*. Essays, with annotations by R. Whately, and notes and a glossarial index by F. F. Heard. Boston, 1873. xlix, 641 [639] pp. 8° 5615.2
— Dixon, W. H. Personal history of. Leipzig, 1861. Sq. 16° 1238.17
— Rémusat, C. (F. M.), *comte* de. Bacon, sa vie, son temps, sa philosophie, et de son influence jusqu'à nos jours. Paris, 1858. 18° 2016.9

Note. — See Lodge's Portraits [5337.6.3]; Macaulay's Essays [1918.4]; and the histories of England covering Queen Elizabeth's reign.

BACON, Leonard. The genesis of the New England churches. With illustrations. New York, 1874. 485 pp. 8° 5812.13

Note. — Dr. Bacon, using well-known authorities, and making no effort at new research, aims to show how the idea of voluntary churches — as distinct from a national church — began in England, and was developed in the churches of New England, pointing out the distinction between the puritans (who sought to reform within the church, and who guided the Massachusetts colony under Endicott) and the separatists, who gathered the church at Scrooby, were exiled to Holland, and came to Plymouth, and there founded the system of voluntary churches. The record is brought down to 1629.

BADDECK, and that sort of thing. [Nova Scotia.] Warner, C. D. Boston, 1874. 16° 418.8
BADEAU, Adam. Military history of Ulysses S. Grant. Vol. I. New York, 1868. xiii, 683+ pp. Portrait. Maps. 8° 5021.8

Note. — No more published.

BADEN, Frances Henshaw. The Christmas guest. *See* SOUTHWORTH, Emma Dorothy Eliza Nevitte. 522.9
BADEN-POWELL, George Smyth. *See* POWELL, George Smyth Baden.
BADEN-POWELL, Warington. *See* POWELL, Warington Baden.
BAEDEKER, Carl. Belgium and Holland. Handbook for travellers. With maps and plans. 2d edition, revised. Coblenz, 1871. xxviii, 328 pp. 16° 5728.5
— Italy. Handbook for travellers. With maps and plans. 2d edition, revised. Coblenz, 1870, 72. 2 v. 16° 5528.2

Contents. — Vol. I. Northern Italy and Corsica. II. Central Italy and Rome.

— Paris and Northern France. Handbook for travellers. With maps and plans. 3d edition, revised and augmented. Coblenz, 1872. xxxii, 320 pp. 16° 5527.7
— The Rhine and Northern Germany. Handbook for travellers. With maps and plans. 4th edition, revised and augmented. Coblenz, 1870. xxii, 444 pp. 16° 5718.3
— Southern Germany and Austria, including the Eastern Alps. Handbook for travellers. With maps and plans. 2d edition, revised. Coblenz, 1871. xxii, 380 pp. 16° 5718.2
— Switzerland, and the adjacent portions of Italy, Savoy, and the Tyrol. Handbook for travellers. With maps, plans, and panoramas. 5th edition, revised. Coblenz, 1872. xliv, 418 pp. 16° 5718.4
— Traveller's manual of conversation in English, French, German, Italian. With vocabulary, short questions, etc. 20th edition. Coblenz, 1870. ix, 331+ pp. 12° 6127.1
BAGEHOT, Walter. Lombard street: a description of the [English] money market. New York, 1873. viii, 359 pp. 12° 5435.8
— Physics and politics. London, 1872. 224+ pp. Sm. 8° 1526.25
— *Same.* New York, 1873. 224+ pp. 12° 6436.2
BAILE, J. Wonders of electricity. Translated from the French. Edited, with additions, by John W. Armstrong. With illustrations. New York, 1872. viii, 335+ pp. [Illustrated library of wonders.] 12° 1714.30
BAILEY, James M. Life in Danbury. Boston, 1873. 303 pp. Illustrated. 16° 538.1
BAILEY, Rufus William. The scholar's companion; containing exercises in the orthography, derivation, and classification of English words. New edition. Philadelphia, 1844. 299 pp. 12° 1933.10
BAILEY, Samuel. Essays on the pursuit of truth, on the progress of knowledge, and on the fundamental principle of all evidence and expectation. Philadelphia, 1831. 233 pp. 12° 5837.1
— *See* RIBOT, T. English psychology. New York, 1874. 8° 5835.5
BAILEY, Samuel W., *compiler*. Homage of eminent persons to the Book. New York, 1870. 128 pp. 16° 5819.14
BAILY, William L. Our own birds. A familiar natural history of the birds of the United States. Revised and edited by E. D. Cope. Philadelphia, 1869. 265 pp. Illustrated. 12° 913.25
BAIN, Alexander. Critical remarks on [the] intellectual character, writings and speeches [of George Grote]. *See* GROTE, George 5633.2

Shelf. No.

BAIN, Alexander, *continued.*
— Mind and body. The theories of their relation. New York, 1873. 196+ pp. Illustrated. [International scientific series.] 12° 6035.2
— *See* RIBOT, T. English psychology. New York, 1874. 8° 5835.5
BAIRD, Spencer Fullerton, BREWER, Thomas Mayo, and RIDGWAY, R. History of North American birds. Vol. I, II. Illustrated. Boston, 1874. 2 v. L. 8° 6611.1

Contents. — Vol. I, II. Land birds.

BAIREUTH, *Bavaria.* Art life and theories. With drawings of the Bayreuth opera house. Wagner, (W.) R. New York, 1875. 12° 6234.3
BAJAZET: tragédie. Racine, J. de. Théâtre complet. Paris, 1870. 12° 5537.3
BAKER, George Melville. Amateur drama series. The exhibition drama. Illustrated. Boston, 1875. 248 pp. 12° 1635.6
— Amateur dramas. Boston, 1873. 252 pp. Illustrated. 16° 1635.22
— A baker's dozen. Original humorous dialogues. Boston, 1874. 137 pp. 16° 1517.6
— The drawing-room stage: original dramas, comedies, farces [etc.] for amateur theatricals and school exhibitions. Illustrated. Boston, 1873. 274 pp. 16° 1516.9
— The maidenhood series. Running to waste...... 927.28
— The mimic stage. Boston, 1871. 290 pp. Illustrated. 12° 1635.23
— *editor.* Ballads of beauty. With illustrations. Boston, 1875. 3–166 pp. Sm. 4° 1623.5
— — The reading club and handy speaker. Selections in prose and poetry, for readings and recitations. Boston, 1875, 76. 3 v. 16° 1538.13
BAKER, Harriet Newell (Woods). (*Mrs. Madeline Leslie.*) Cora and the doctor 524.7
— I'll try 934.6
— The Leslie stories. Never give up 926.5
— — The secret of success 926.6
— — Up the ladder 926.8
— — Worth and wealth 926.7
— Little Agnes 934.5
— Play and study 935.6
— The two homes 926.4
BAKER, James L. Men and things; or, short essays on various subjects, including free trade. Boston, 1858. 287 pp. 12° 5216.4
BAKER, *Sir* Samuel White. The Albert N'yanza great basin of the Nile, and explorations of the Nile sources. With map and illustrations. New edition. London, 1872. xxvii, 499 pp. Sm. 8° 5936.4
— Ismailia. A narrative of the expedition to Central Africa for the suppression of the slave trade. Organized by Ismail, khedive of Egypt. With maps, portraits, and illustrations. New York, 1875. 542 pp. 8° 5933.5
— The Nile tributaries of Abyssinia, and the sword hunters of the Hamran Arabs. 4th edition, with illustrations and maps. London, 1871, xix, 413 pp. Sm. 8° 425.3
— *Same.* With a supplement, By W. L. Gage. Illustrated. Hartford, 1871. xx, 624+ pp. Maps. 8° 5932.1
— The rifle and the hound in Ceylon. With illustrations. Philadelphia, 1871, 305 pp. 16°.. 1515.2
BAKER, Sarah. Christian effort. New York, 1850. 271 pp. 16° 5819.6
BAKER, Thomas. Elements of practical mechanism and machine tools. With remarks on tools and machinery by James Nasmyth. With illustrations. 4th edition. London, 1871. xii, 240 pp. 1 folded plate. 12° 1716.14
— Mathematical theory of the steam engine. New edition, revised. London, 1870. vi, 118 pp. Illustrated. 12° 1716.1
BAKER, William Munford. Carter Quarterman..... 530.17
— Mose Evans 726.23
— The new Timothy 535.1

Shelf. No.

BAKER'S, A, dozen. Original humorous dialogues. Baker, G. M. Boston, 1874. 16° 1517.6
BALDWIN, John Denison. Ancient America. With illustrations. New York, 1872. 299 pp. 12°. 5027.5
— Pre-historic nations. New York, 1872. 414 pp. 12° 824.7
BALDWIN, Thomas, *joint author.* Lippincott's pronouncing gazetteer. *See* THOMAS, Joseph. *R.R., B.3.2
BALDWIN, William Charles. African hunting from Natal to the Zambesi, from 1852 to 1860. With illustrations. New York, 1863. 397 pp. Map. Portrait. 12° 224.2
BALFE, Michael William. Bohemian girl; Rose of Castile. (*In* Ditson, O., and co. Standard opera librettos) 6233.3.3
BALL, Benjamin West. Elfin land: and other poems. Boston, 1851. 150+ pp. 12° 1616.12
BALL, John. Alpine guides. Pennine Alps, including Mont Blanc and Monte Rosa. London, 1873. 181–378 pp. 4 maps. 16° 5936.6
— *editor.* Peaks, passes and glaciers. A series of excursions by members of the Alpine club. 5th edition. London, 1860. xiii, 328+ pp. Maps. Sm. 8° 5717.1
BALLADS. Baker, G. M. Ballads of beauty. Boston, 1875. Sm. 4° 1623.5
— Lockhart, J. G. Ancient Spanish ballads. Boston, 1861. 16° 1616.5
— MacCarthy, D. F. Book of Irish ballads. New York, 1873. 16° 5626.3
— Murray, J. C. Ballads and songs of Scotland. London, 1874. 8° 5626.5

See also Note under English literature.

BALLANTYNE, Robert Michael. Black ivory; a tale of adventure among the slavers of East Africa.. 538.9
— The coral island 934.18
— Deep down. A tale of the Cornish mines....... 935.10
— The dog Crusoe. A tale of the Western prairies. 935.30
— The dog Crusoe and his master 935.31
— Erling the bold. A tale of the Norse sea-kings. 935.11
— Fighting the flames. [London fire brigade]..... 935.12
— The floating light of Goodwin sands............ 935.16
— Freaks on the fells 923.9
— Gascoyne the sandal-wood trader............... 923.11
The gorilla hunters 913.26
— The lifeboat 934.17
— Man on the ocean. A book about boats and ships. 1715.30
— Martin Rattler; or, a boy's adventures in the forests of Brazil 923.10
— The Norseman in the West; or, America before Columbus 914.37
— The pirate city. An Algerine tale............... 927.30
— Rivers of ice. A tale illustrative of Alpine adventure and glacier action 931.11
— Shifting winds 926.33
— Silver lake 935.14
— Tales of adventure; or, wild work in strange places 933.25

Contents. — Away in the wilderness; The pioneers; Hunting the lions; Up in the clouds.

— Tales of adventure on the coast................ 1115.4

Contents. — The story of the rock; Wrecked but not ruined; Saved by the lifeboat; Chasing the sun.

— Ungava: a tale of Esquimaux-land............. 923.12
— The wild man of the West. A tale of the Rocky mountains 926.32
BALLOON ascents. Glaisher, J., Flammarion, C., Fonvielle, W. de, and Tissandier, G. Travels in the air. Philadelphia [London], 1871. 8°.... 5911.1
— Marion, F. Wonderful balloon ascents. New York, 1871. 16° 1714.18

See also Aëronautics.

BALLOU, Hosea, Life of. Whittemore, T. Boston, 1854. 2 v. 12° 5026.6
BALLOU, Maturin Murray. History of Cuba; or, notes of a traveller in the tropics. Illustrated. Boston, 1854. 230 pp. 12° 825.9
— Treasury of thought. Forming an encyclopædia of quotations from ancient and modern authors. Boston, 1873. xii, 579 pp. 8° .... *R.R., E.2.4

Shelf. No.

BALLOU'S monthly magazine. Vol. 36-40. Boston [1872-74]. 5 v. Illustrated. 8°........... 1433.2
BALLSTON, *New York*, An analysis of the mineral waters of. Steel, J. H. Saratoga Springs, 1838. 12°............................... 817.14
BALTIC sea. Canoe travelling: log of a cruise on the Baltic. Powell, W. B. London, 1871. Sm. 8°. 5934.8
BALZAC, Honoré de. *See* STEPHEN, L. Hours in a library. New York, 1874. 12°............. 6136.9
BANCROFT, Aaron. Essay on the life of George Washington. Worcester, 1807. vii, 552 pp. Portrait. 8°................................ 5024.2
BANCROFT, George. History of the colonization of the United States. Abridged by the author. Boston, 1841. Illustrated. Map. 16°.......5016.11
— History of the United States, from the discovery of the continent. 24th edition. Boston, 1872-74. 10 v. Portraits. Maps. 8°............ 5012.3
— – General index. [Boston, 1875.] 595-741 pp. 8°.. 811.16
— – *See* PRESCOTT, W. H. Biographical and critical essays.........................1537.8 and 5237.5
— *Same.* Vol. I, II. Revised edition. Boston, 1876. 2 v. [Centenary edition.] 8°........ 815.4
— Memorial address on the life and character of Abraham Lincoln. Washington, 1866. 69 pp. 8°.. 1212.8
BANCROFT, Hubert Howe. The native races of the Pacific states of North America. New York, 1874-76. Maps. Illustrations. 5 v. 8°..... 5920.4

Contents. — Vol. I. Wild tribes. Also list of 1,200 authorities quoted. II. Civilized nations. III. Myths and languages. IV. Antiquities. V. Primitive history.

BANIM, John. The Boyne water.................. 517.6
— The peep o' day; or, John Doe. And The last baron of Crana 517.5
— The rival dreamers. (*In* Johnson, (E.) R. Little classics).....................................529.4.12
BANISHED son, The. Hentz, C. L. 534.12
BANKER'S, The, almanac and register. New York, 1854-56, 59-61, 65-75. Illustrated. 17 v. 8°.. 5820.1

Note. — Changes in the title at various times.

BANKS, Nathaniel Prentiss. The bobbin boy. Thayer, W. M. Boston, 1860. 16°........... 916.8
BANKS, History of. Hildreth, R. Boston, 1837. 12°.. 5828.2
BARBARA's history. Edwards, A. B. 314.25
BARBAULD, Anna Lætitia. Thoughts on public worship. (*In* Sparks, J. Collection of essays and tracts in theology)..............................1918.9.4
— Memoir of. Ellis, G. A. Boston, 1874. 2 v. 12° 5426.15
BARBE-BLEUE. Offenbach, J. (*In* Ditson, O., and co. Standard opera librettos)...................6233.3.5
BARBER, John Warner, and HOWE, Henry. The loyal West in the times of the rebellion; also, before and since. Illustrated. Cincinnati, 1865. 764 pp. Maps. 8° 5033.4
BARBERINE. Musset, (L. C.) A. de. Comédies et proverbes. Paris, 1867. 12°...............5534.4.1
BARBIERE di Siviglia. Rossini, G. (*In* Ditson, O., and co. Standard opera librettos)...........6233.3.3
BARBIERI, Giuseppe. Orazioni quaresimali ed altre nuove opere. Milano, 1836, 37. 2 v. 12°.... 2038.2
BARCHESTER towers. Trollope, A................. 334.10
BARCLAY, George Lippard. Little Cuba; or, circumstantial evidence 710.36
BARDS, The, of the Bible. Gilfillan, G. New York, 1869. 12°.................................... 1523.8
BARDWELL, William. What a house should be, *versus* death in the house. A companion book to "Healthy homes, and how to make them." Illustrated. London [1873]. viii, 95+ pp. 8°. 6221.4
BARHAM, Richard Harris. (*Thomas Ingoldsby.*) The Ingoldsby legends. [Humorous poems.] Globe edition. With Cruikshanks's illustrations. New York, 1872. 2 v. in 1. 12° 524.9
— Jerry Jarvis's wig. (*In* Johnson, (E.) R. Little classics).......................................529.4.4

Shelf. No.

BARHAM, Richard Harris, *continued.*
— Personal reminiscences. (*In* Stoddard, R. H. Bric-à-brac series)............................ 1828.4
— Life and letters of. Barham, R. H. D. London, 1870. 2 v. Sm. 8°........................... 1224.3
BARHAM, Richard Harris D. Life and letters of Richard Harris Barham: with a selection from his miscellaneous poems. London, 1870. 2 v. Portrait. Sm. 8°.............................. 1224.3
BARING-GOULD, Sabine. Curious myths of the middle ages. London, 1872. [New edition.] x, 660 pp. Illustrated. 16°....................... 716.2
— Gabrielle André. An historical novel.......... 710.39

Note. — The English edition of this book is entitled "In exitu Israel."

— Legends of the patriarchs and prophets, and other Old Testament characters. New York, 1872. 380 pp. Sm. 8°.................................. 5814.5
— The lives of the saints. 2d edition. London, 1872, 73. 5 v. 5 plates. 8°................. 5937.1

Contents. — Vol. I. January. II. February. III. March. IV. April. V. May.

— Yorkshire oddities, incidents and strange events. 2d edition. London, 1875. 2 v. Sm. 8° 5616.17
BARKER, George Frederick. A text-book of elementary chemistry, theoretical and inorganic. Louisville, Ky. [*cop.* 1870]. vi, 342+ pp. 12°. 6437.5
BARKER, Mary Anne, *lady.* [Mrs. Frederick Napier Broome.] Houses and housekeeping. A fireside gossip upon home and its comforts. London, 1876. 170+ pp. Sm. 8°................. 6428.8
— Station amusements in New Zealand. Leipzig, 1874. 288 pp. Sq. 16°............................ 319.15
— Station life in New Zealand. Leipzig, 1874. 229 pp. Sq. 16°.................................. 438.4
BARNABY Rudge. Dickens, C. (J. H.) 2 v........ 1824.5
BARNARD, Charles Francis, *jr.* (*Jane Kingsford.*) The tone masters. Bach and Beethoven. Illustrated. Boston, 1871. 243 pp. 16° 926.21
— – Handel and Haydn. Illustrated. Boston, 1871. 223 pp. 16° 926.22
— – Mozart and Mendelssohn. Illustrated. Boston, 1870. 193 pp. 16° 926.23
BARNARD, Jonathan G. The C. S. A. and the battle of Bull Run. With 5 maps. New York, 1862. 124 pp. 8° 6924.3
— and BARRY, William Farquhar. Engineer and artillery operations of the army of the Potomac, to the close of the peninsular campaign. Illustrated. New York, 1863. 230 pp. 8° 6924.2
BARNES, Albert. Notes on the Acts and the Epistles. *See* BIBLE. *New Testament* 6327.1.20-22
BARNEVELDT, Jan van Olden, Life and death of. Motley, J. L. London, 1874. 2 v. 8°......... 5713.3
BARNEY Brady's goose. Carleton, W............... 518.5
BARNEY O'Reirdon the navigator. Lover, S. (*In* Johnson, (E.) R. Little classics) 529.4.9
BARREN honour. Lawrence, G. A. 315.21
BARRIERS burned away. Roe, E. P................. 724.21
BARRINGTON. Lever, C. (J.) Leipzig............ 332.7
— *Same.* London 516.1
BARROW, *Sir* John. Life of Peter the great. New York, 1856. 320 pp. 16°......................... 1228.8
— Life, voyages, and exploits of Sir Francis Drake. New edition. London, 1861. xii, 187 pp. Sm. 8°.. 5428.5
BARROWS, William. The general; or, twelve nights in the hunters' camp 934.2
BARRY, Charles A. How to draw. Boston, 1871. 57 pp. Illustrated. 12° 1516.5
BARRY, John Stetson. History of Massachusetts. Boston, 1855, 57. 3 v. 8°.......................... 812.5

Contents. — Vol. I. The colonial period. II. The provincial period. III. The commonwealth period.

BARRY, Michael Joseph, *editor.* The songs of Ireland. New York, 1873. 232 [228] pp. 12° .. 5626.4
BARRY, P. Fruit garden. Revised. Illustrated. New York [*cop.* 1872]. 491 pp. 12° 6625.2
BARRY, William. History of Framingham, Mass. Boston, 1847. iv, 456 pp. 8° 5011.6

Shelf. No.

BARRY, William Farquhar, *joint author*. Engineer and artillery operations of the army of the Potomac. *See* BARNARD, Jonathan G. 6924.2
BARTHÉLEMY DE BEAUREGARD, (Emmanuel) Justin. Histoire de Jeanne d'Arc. Ornée de gravures. Paris, 1847. 2 v. 8° 5523.1
BARTHOLOMEW fair, Memoirs of. Morley, H. London [1874]. Sm. 8° 5418.8
BARTLETT, George Bradford. Parlor amusements for the young folks. Boston, 1875. 80 pp. 16°. 1517.5
BARTLETT, John, *editor*. Familiar quotations: being an attempt to trace to their source passages and phrases in common use. 6th edition. Boston, 1874. xii, 778 pp. 16° .... *R.R., F.3.8
— *Same*. 7th edition. Boston, 1875. xvi, 864 pp. 16° .... *R.R., F.3.10
BARTLETT, William Henry. The pilgrim fathers; or, the founders of New England in the reign of James I. With illustrations. London, 1853. 240+ pp. 8° 5021.4
BARTOL, Cyrus Augustus. Discourses on the Christian spirit and life. Boston, 1850. iv, 344 pp. 12° ....5815.19 and 6325.14
— Pictures of Europe, framed in ideas. Boston, 1855. 407+ pp. 12° 214.2
— Radical problems. Boston, 1873. 407+ pp. 16°. 1525.14
— The rising faith. Boston, 1874. 386+ pp. 16°. 5817.12
— The word of the Spirit to the church. Boston, 1859. 86 pp. 16° 6321.1
BARTOLI, Daniele, and MAFFEI, Giovanni Pietro. Life of St. Francis Xavier. With a preface by Dr. Faber. 6th American from the last London edition. Baltimore, 1872. 653 pp. 12°.. 5526.9
BARTON, Bernard. Poems. New edition. Boston, 1832. 378 pp. 12° 1628.1
BASCHAT, Armand. Le duc de Saint-Simon, son cabinet et l'historique de ses manuscrits. Paris, 1874. xlviii, 520 pp. Heliotype. 8°, l. p.... 5531.2
BASCOM, John. Philosophy of English literature. A course of lectures delivered in the Lowell institute. New York, 1874. 318+ pp. 12°.. 5216.8
— Philosophy of rhetoric. Boston, 1870. 251 pp. 12° 1535.12
BASHAN, The giant cities of. Porter, J. L. New York, 1871. 12° 5915.7
BASIL. [Fiction.] Collins, (W.) W. 326.7
BASIL Godfrey's caprice. Parr, H. 314.1
BASKERVILLE, Alfred, *translator*. The poetry of Germany. Translated into English verse with the original text on the opposite page. 9th edition. Philadelphia, 1872. 332 [664] pp. 16°. 1625.4
BASKET, A, of chips. Brougham, J. New York, 1855. 12° 1522.13
BASS family. Thayer, E. Family memorial. Hingham, 1835. 8° 611.2
BASTÉ, Eugène Pierre (*Eugène Grangé*), and MONTEPIN, Xavier Aymon de. The Corsican brothers: a dramatic romance, adapted from Dumas. New York, N. D. 60 pp. 12° 1635.3
BASTIAT, Frédéric. [People's edition.] Essays on political economy. [Translated from the French.] London, 1872. viii [vi], 48, 72, 56, 68 pp. 16° 5828.1

Contents.— Capital and interest; That which is seen, and that which is not seen; Government; What is money? The law.

— *Same*. 4th edition. London [1875]. 16° 5828.3

Note.— Only one of the essays in this collection was given in Horace White's edition. The views of Bastiat have been adopted by Perry in his Political economy and by Amasa Walker in his Science of wealth.

BASTILE. Histoire de la Bastille. Arnould, A., Alboize du Pujol, É., and Maquet, A. Paris, 1845, 51, 53. 8 v. 8° 2010.1
BATCHELDER, Samuel. Introduction and early progress of the cotton manufacture in the United States. Boston, 1863. iv, 108 pp. 16° 6435.4
BATES, *Mrs*. D. B. Incidents on land and water, or four years on the Pacific coast. 4th edition. Boston, 1858. 336 pp. Illustrated. 12° 235.1

Shelf. No.

BATES, Henry Walter. The naturalist on the river Amazons. 3d edition. With illustrations. London, 1873. x, 394 pp. Sm. 8° 5935.2
BATES, Joseph. Autobiography. And a brief account of the great advent movement of 1840-44. Battle Creek, 1868. 306 pp. Portrait. 16° .. 1218.2
BATES, Joshua, Memorial of. *See* BOSTON, *Mass*. .. 5031.4
BATES, William, *D.D.* Essay on divine meditation. *See* BURDER, George. Village sermons 6327.7.4
BATES, *Prof*. William, *editor*. Gallery of illustrious literary characters (1830-38). Drawn by D. Maclise. Accompanied by notices chiefly by W. Maginn. London [1873]. 239+ pp. 4°.. 5632.2
BATKINS, Jefferson Scattering, *pseud*. *See* JONES, Joseph S.
BATTLE of Dorking, The. Chesney, G. New York, 1871. 12° 5617.2

Note.— An imaginary conflict following a supposed invasion of England by the Germans.

BATTLE, The, of life. Dickens, C. (J. H.) 338.6
BATTLE of the books, The. Swift, J. Works. London, 1856. 8° 5611.2.1
BATTLE-PIECES and aspects of the war. 1861-66. [Poems.] Melville, H. New York, 1866. 12°. 1624.3
BATTLE summer, A. [Fiction.] Terhune, M. V.... 727.31
BATTLES of the British navy. Allen, J. London, 1868. 2 v. Sm. 8° 5417.5
BATTLES of the world, The fifteen decisive. Creasy, *Sir* E. S. New York, 1872. 12° 824.6
BAUER, Karoline. (*Carl Detlef*.) At Capri. A story of Italian life. By Clara Bauer. Translated from the German by MS. [International series] 714.19
— Dead to the world; or, sin and atonement. From the German. Translated by MS. 716.15
— Valentine, the countess; or, between father and son. Translated from the German by MS. 723.4
BAUER, Louis. Lectures on orthopædic surgery. 2d edition, revised, with illustrations. New York, 1868. 336 [332] pp. 8° 6022.13
BAUERMAN, H. Treatise on the metallurgy of iron. 3d edition, revised. Illustrated. London, 1872. xii, 455 pp. 12° 1716.42
BAVARIAN highlands, The. Schmid, H., and Stiller, C. London, 1874. 8° 5720.1
BAXTER, Richard. A call to the unconverted. New York, 1831. v, 144 pp. Sm. 12° 5818.15
BAY state democrat, The. August 24—Nov. 9, 1838. Boston, 1838. 4° 6730.38
BAYER, Carl Robert. The struggle for existence. A romance. After the German of Robert Byr [*pseud*.]. By Auber Forestier [*pseud*. of A. A. Woodward] 728.7
BAYLE-MOUILLARD, Elizabeth. (*Elizabeth Celnart*.) Manuel des dames, ou l'art de l'elegance. 2e édition, revue, corrigée, et ornée de figures. Paris, 1833. 262+ pp. 24°. [Manuel Roret]. 6229.1
— Nouveau manuel d'economie domestique. 3e édition. Ornée de figures. Paris, 1837. 266+ pp. 24°. [Manuel Roret] 6429.6
BAYLEY, Jonathan. Great truths on great subjects. Six lectures. London, 1874. 216 pp. Sm. 8°. 6328.17
BAYNE, Peter. The days of Jezebel, an historical drama. Boston, 1872. 240 pp. 12° 1636.4
— Essays in biography and criticism. Boston, 1857. 2 v. 12° 1226.15
— Life and letters of Hugh Miller. Boston, 1871. 2 v. Portraits. 12° 1225.16
BAYNES, Robert H., *editor*. Lyra Anglicana. Hymns and sacred songs. Leipzig, 1868. xvi, 297 pp. Sq. 16° 1613.8
BAY-PATH, The. Holland, J. G. 536.3

Note.— Fiction, early history of Massachusetts.

BAZAR book, The, of health. Tomes, R. New York, 1873. 16° 1538.5
BAZAR book, The, of the household. Tomes, R. New York, 1875. 16° 1518.9
BEACH, Charles A. Pitzmaroon; or, the magic hammer 912.12
BEALE, Anne. Simplicity and fascination 535.4

Shelf. No.

BEALE, Lionel Smith. Bioplasm: an introduction to the study of physiology and medicine. With illustrations. London, 1872. xvi, 345 pp. 16°. 6037.2
— Disease germs; their supposed nature. Coloured illustrations. London, 1870. 82+ pp. Sm. 8°. 6036.2
— How to work with the microscope. 4th edition. [With] illustrations. London, 1868. xix, 383 pp. 8° 6822.1
— On life and vital action in health and disease. London, 1875. 110+ pp. Sm. 8° 6036.14
BEAR and forbear. Adams, W. T. 925.18
BEATEN paths. Thompson, E. W. Boston, 1874. 16°. 437.6
BEATRICE. Kavanagh, J. 323.8
BEATRICE: or, the unknown relatives. Sinclair, C.. 714.29
BEATRICE Cenci. [Fiction.] Guerrazzi, F. D...... 716.5
BEAUCHAMP. James, G. P. R. 327.1
BEAUCHAMPE. Simms, W. G. 725.18
BEAUMONT, Averil. Thornicroft's model 319.26
BEAUMONT, Francis, and FLETCHER, John. Works. With an introduction by G. Darley. New edition. London, 1872. 2 v. Portraits. 8° 5621.2
BEAUTIFUL fiend, A. Southworth, E. D. E. N. 726.19
BEAUTIFUL, The, Miss Barrington. Parr, H....... 315.28
BEAUTIFYING country homes. Weidenmann, J. New York [*cop.* 1870]. 4° 6220.1
BEAUTY and the beast. Willis, N. P. (*In* Johnson, (E.) R. Little classics) 529.4.4
BEAUVOIR, Ludovic, *comte* de. Pekin, Jeddo, and San Francisco. Conclusion of a voyage round the world. Translated from the French by A. and H. Stephenson. With engravings. London, 1872. x, 291+ pp. 16° 5935.11
BÉBÉE, or two little wooden shoes. Rame, L. de la.. 913.30
BECK, John Brolhead. Lectures on materia medica and therapeutics. Prepared for the press by C. R. Gilman. New York, 1851. 581 pp. L. 12°. 6022.18
BECKER, Bernard H. Scientific London. London, 1874. viii, 340 pp. Sm. 8° 5616.16
BECKER, Carl Ferdinand. Lehrbuch des deutschen Stiles. Herausgegeben von T. Becker. Frankfurt am Main, 1850. viii, 336 pp. 8° 5735.7
BECKET, Thomas à. *See* THOMAS À BECKET.
BECKFORD, William. Vathek. [Eastern romance.] New York, 1869. viii, 189+ pp. Portrait. Sq. 16° 518.3
BECKMANN, John. History of inventions, discoveries, and origins. Translated by W. Johnston. 4th edition, revised and enlarged by W. F. and J. W. Griffith. London, 1846. 2 v. Portraits. 16°. 1526.7 and 6425.1
BECKONING series, The. *See* COBDEN, Paul, *pseud.*
BECKWITH, John Charles. General Beckwith. Meille, J. P. London, 1873. 16° 5338.1
BECQ DE FOUQUIÈRES, L. Aspasie de Milet. Paris, 1872. viii, 366+ pp. 18° 6116.1
BED-TIME stories. Moulton, L. C. 927.24
BEDE, Cuthbert, *pseud.* *See* BRADLEY, Edward.
BEDE's charity. Smith, H. 737.34
BEECHCROFT. Yonge, C. M. 736.4
BEECHER, Catharine Esther. Housekeeper and healthkeeper. New York, 1873. 482 pp. Illustrated. 12° 1725.1
— Letters to the people on health and happiness. New York, 1855. 192, 29+ pp. 16° 1918.11
— Physiology and calisthenics. New York, 1858. 193, 58 pp. 16° 6038.2
— Treatise on domestic economy. Revised edition, with additions and engravings. New York, 1858. 369+ pp. 12° 1524.8
— and STOWE, Harriet (Elizabeth) Beecher. The new housekeeper's manual: embracing a new revised edition of The American woman's home, with The handy cook-book, by C. E. Beecher. Illustrated. New York, 1873. xvii, 591 [581]+ pp. 8° 1723.8
BEECHER, Edward. The conflict of ages; or, the moral relations of God and man. 5th edition. Boston, 1854. xii, 552 pp. 12° 1524.21
BEECHER, Eunice W. Motherly talks with young housekeepers. New York, 1873. xx, 492 pp. Portrait. 12° 1515.13

Shelf. No.

BEECHER, Henry Ward. Lectures to young men. New edition, with additional lectures. New York, 1873. xvii, 280 pp. 12° 1914.6
— Life of Jesus, the Christ. New York, 1871. xii, 510 pp. Map and illustrations. 8° 1021.4
— Life thoughts, gathered from [his] extemporaneous discourses by one of his congregation. Boston, 1858. xviii, 299 pp. 12° 5815.9
— *Same.* New York, 1871. xviii, 299 pp. 12° .. 1533.11
— Norwood. [Fiction.] 40th edition. New York, 1868. xi, 549 pp. 12° 524.5
— Plain and pleasant talk about fruits, flowers and farming. New York, 1859. 420 pp. 12° 1514.22
— Star papers; or, experiences of art and nature. New York, 1855. 359 pp. 12° 1924.2
— *Same.* New edition, with additional articles. New York, 1873. 447+ pp. 12° 1924.4
— A summer parish: Sabbath discourses and service of prayer, at the "Twin mountain house," White mountains, 1874. New York, 1875. vi, 231 pp. Portrait. 8° 6325.8
— Yale lectures on preaching. New York, 1872. xii, 263 pp. 12° 1914.7
— *See* PARTON, J. Famous Americans of recent times. Boston, 1871. 8° 1214.14
BEECHER, Lyman. Autobiography, correspondence, etc. Edited by C. Beecher. With illustrations. New York, 1871. 2 v. Portrait. 12° 1214.13
— Views in theology. 2d edition. Cincinnati, 1836. 240 pp. 12° 6328.20
BEECHNUT. Abbott, J. 914.14
BEECHY, Henry William. Memoir of Joshua Reynolds; with remarks on his professional character; illustrative of his principles and practice. *See* REYNOLDS, *Sir* Joshua. Literary works 6215.8
BEES. The cottage bee keeper. New York, 1854. Sm. 8° 1524.15
— The honey bee. London, 1852. 16° 6619.3
— Pettigrew, A. The handy book of bees. Edinburgh, 1875. Sm. 8° 6619.4
— Weeks, J. M. A manual: or, an easy method of managing bees. New York, 1855. 12° 1524.14
BEETHOVEN, Ludwig van. Fidelio. (*In* Ditson, O., and co. Standard opera librettos) 6233.3.3
— Letters. (1790–1826.) Translated by Lady Wallace. With portrait and fac-simile. Boston [1866?]. 2 v. in 1. 16° 1026.1
— Barnard, C. F., *jr.* Bach and Beethoven. Boston, 1871. 16° 926.21
— Elterlein, E. von. Beethoven's pianoforte sonatas explained. London, 1875. Sm. 8° 6237.4
— Haweis, H. R. Music and morals. New York, 1872. 12° 1513.16

Note. — See Note in Bulletin no. 36, p. 35.

BEETON, S. O., *editor.* Great book of poetry: selection[s]. London [1871]. Unpaged. 8° 5631.1
BEGGAR girl, The, of the Pont des arts. Hauff, W. 312.21
BEHEMOTH, Adventures in the land of the. Verne, J. Boston, 1874. Sm. 4° 713.3
BEHIND the counter. Hacklaender, F. W. 311.11
BELCHER, *Lady* Diana. The mutineers of the Bounty and their descendants in Pitcairn and Norfolk islands. With map and illustrations. London, 1870. x, 420+ pp. Sm. 8° 1224.4
— *Same.* New York, 1871. 377 pp. 12° 435.2
BELDEN, Lemuel Whittelsey. Account of Jane C. Rider, the Springfield somnambulist. Springfield, 1834. 134 pp. 12° 1928.4
BELGIUM. Adams, W. T. Dikes and ditches; or, Young America in. Boston, 1873. 16° 925.9
— Baedeker, C. Handbook for travellers. Coblenz, 1871. 16° 5728.5
— Kampen, N. G. van. History and topography of. London, N. D. 8° 5931.19
— Murray, J. Handbook for travellers on the continent: being a guide to. London, 1871. 12°. 5915.1
BELKNAP, Jeremy. The foresters, an American tale: being a sequel to the history of John Bull the clothier. In a series of letters to a friend. 2d edition, revised and enlarged. Boston, 1796. 240 pp. 16° 529.9

Shelf. No.

BELKNAP, Jeremy, *continued.*
— Life. With selections from his correspondence and other writings. Collected and arranged by his grand-daughter. New York, 1847. 253+ pp. Portrait. 16° 5027.4
BELL, Acton, *pseud.* *See* BRONTÉ, Anne.
BELL, Benjamin. A system of surgery. Illustrated. 7th edition, corrected and enlarged. Edinburgh, 1801. 7 v. 12° 6023.6
BELL, *Sir* Charles. Expression: its anatomy and philosophy. With notes and illustrations. New and enlarged edition. New York, 1873. 200+ pp. 12° 1527.10
— The hand, its mechanism and vital endowments, as evincing design. New edition. Philadelphia, 1835. 213 pp. Illustrated. 12° 6036.6
— Letters, selected from his correspondence with his brother, George Joseph Bell. London, 1870. xiii, 434+ pp. Illustrated. Portrait. Sm. 8°. 5433.9
BELL, Currer, *pseud.* *See* BRONTÉ, Charlotte.
BELL, Ellis, *pseud.* *See* BRONTÉ, Emily (Jane).
BELL, Henry Glassford. Life of Mary queen of Scots. New York, 1855. 2 v. Portrait. 12° 1228.1
BELL, Luther V. [Boylston prize dissertation.] *See* HOLMES, Oliver Wendell 6023.17
BELL-TOWER, The. Melville, H. (*In* Johnson, (E.) R. Little classics) 529.4.3
BELLAH. Feuillet, O. 714.12
BELLAMY, *Mrs.* E. W. The little Joanna. By Kamba Thorpe [*pseud.*] 721.21
BELLAMY, Joseph. Works. With a memoir of his life and character. Boston, 1850. 2 v. 8° 5813.12
BELLE Brittan on a tour, at Newport, and here and there. Fuller, H. New York, 1858. 12° 413.7
BELLE Hélène, La. Offenbach, J. (*In* Ditson, O., and co. Standard opera librettos) 6233.3.5
BELLE, The, of the family. Grey, *Mrs.* 521.26
BELLE Powers' locket. Mathews, J. H. 1117.16
BELLEHOOD and bondage. Stephens, A. S. (W.) 734.11
BELLES-lettres, Lectures on. Blair, H. Brooklyn, 1807. 2 v. 8° 1533.16
BELLEW, Frank. The art of amusing. A collection of games, tricks, puzzles, and charades. With illustrations. London, N. D. 299 pp. Sm. 8°. 1518.10
BELLINI, Vincenzio. Norma; Il pirata; La sonnambula. (Ditson, O., and co. Standard opera librettos) 6233.3.4
— I puritani. (Ditson, O., and co. Standard opera librettos) 6233.3.3
BELLOWS, Albert J. The philosophy of eating. 7th edition. New York, 1872. 426 pp. 16° 1523.4
BELLOWS, Henry Whitney. The old world in its new face. Impressions of Europe in 1867, 68. New York, 1870. 2 v. 12° 423.6
BELLS, Rudimentary treatise on. Denison, E. B. London, 1868. 12° 1716.12
BELTON estate, The. Trollope, A. 334.16
BEMENT, C. N. The rabbit fancier. New York, 1855. 101 pp. Illustrated. 12° 1524.3
BEMIS, George. Report of the case of John W. Webster, indicted for the murder of George Parkman. [With] appendix. Boston, 1850. xi, 628 pp. 1 plate. 8° 1530.1
BEN, the luggage boy. Alger, H., *jr.* 934.11
BEN Brace. [Sea novel.] Chamier, F. 521.24
BEN Burton. Kingston, W. H. G. 1118.3
BENCH and bar. [Anecdotes.] Bigelow, L. J. New York, 1871. 8° 1532.1
BENEDICITE; illustrations of the power, wisdom, and goodness of God, as manifested in his works. Child, G. C. New York, 1872. 16° 6615.4
BENEDICT, Frank Lee. John Worthington's name. 731.30
— Miss Dorothy's charge 731.9
— Miss Van Kortland 710.5
— Mr. Vaughan's heir 721.4
— My daughter Elinor 710.4
— St. Simon's niece 720.39
BENEDICTUS, *St., of Monte-Cassino.* The mission of St. Benedict; The Benedictine schools. Newman, J. H. Historical sketches. London, 1873. Sm. 8° 5925.5.3

Shelf. No.

BENGER, Elizabeth Ogilvy. Life of Mary queen of Scots, with anecdotes of the court of Henry II during her residence in France. From the 2d London edition. Philadelphia, 1852. 2 v. Portrait. Fac-simile. 12° 1224.11
BENJAMIN, Park, *editor.* Wrinkles and recipes, compiled from the Scientific American. A collection of practical suggestions, processes and directions for the mechanic, the engineer, the farmer, and the housekeeper. Illustrated. New York [1875]. 252 pp. 16° 1717.12
BENNET, James Henry. Winter and spring on the shores of the Mediterranean: or, the Genoese Rivieras, Italy, Spain, Corfu, Greece [etc.] as winter climates. 5th edition. London, 1875. Maps. Illustrations. xvi, 655 pp. Sm. 8° 436.3
BENNETT, James Gordon. *See* PARTON, J. Famous Americans of recent times. Boston, 1871. 8°. 1214.14
BENNETT, Joseph. Billiards. With illustrations. Edited by Cavendish [*pseud.* for Henry Jones]. London, 1873. viii, 483 pp. 8° 6413.1
BENSON, George. Essay on the belief of things above reason. (*In* Sparks, J. Collection of essays and tracts in theology) 1918.9.4
BENTON, J. G. Instruction in ordnance and gunnery. 2d edition. New York, 1862. 550 pp. Illustrated. 8° 6924.1
BENTON, Thomas Hart. Thirty years' view; or, a history of the American government, 1820–50. New York, 1854, 56. 2 v. Portrait. 1 plate. 8°. 812.2
BÉRANGER, Pierre Jean de. Chansons. Précédées d'une notice sur l'auteur et d'un essai sur ses poésies par P. F. Tissot. Paris, 1829. 4 v. Portrait. Illustrated. 16° 5538.1
BERBER, The. Mayo, W. S. 532.13
BÉRÉNICE: tragédie. Racine, J. de. Théâtre complet. Paris, 1870. 12° 5537.3
BERGER, E., *pseud.* *See* SHEPPARD, Elizabeth Sara.
BERKELEY men, The, *pseud.* *See* LESTER, Charles Edwards.
BERLIN and Sans-souci. [Historical fiction.] Mundt, C. (M.) 531 15
BERLIN und seine Umgebungen im neunzehnten Jahrhundert. Eine Sammlung in Stahl gestochener Ansichten von Mauch, Gärtner, Biermann und Hintze, nebst topographisch-historischen Erläuterungen von S. H. Spiker. [No. 1–19.] Berlin, 1833. 122+ pp. 74 plates. 4°. 5910.4
BERNARD, *St.*, Life and times of. Morison, J. C. London, 1868. Sm. 8° 5525.9
BERNARD, Frédéric. Wonderful escapes. Revised from the French and original chapters added by R. Whiteing. With plates. New York, 1871. vi, 308 pp. 16° 1714.20
BERNARDIN DE SAINT-PIERRE, Jacques Henri. *See* SAINT-PIERRE, Jacques Henri Bernardin de.
BERNICE, the farmer's daughter. Kelly, C. E. 928.20
BERTHA'S engagement. Stephens, A. S. (W.) 522.17
BERTHOUD, Henry. Stories of bird life: a book of facts and anecdotes. With illustrations. London, 1875. 320 pp. Sm. 8° 6617.9
BERTRAM family, The. Charles, E. 723.29
BERTRAMS, The. Trollope, A. 334.14
BESANT, Walter. The French humourists from the 12th to the 19th century. London, 1873. vi, 447+ pp. 8° 5532.2
— and PALMER, E. H. Jerusalem, the city of Herod and Saladin. London, 1871. viii, 492 pp. 1 plate. Sm. 8° 5924.3
BESSEMER process in the United States. By L. Smith. *See* GRUENER, L. (E.) New York, 1872. 8° 6631.4
BESSIE among the mountains. Mathews, J. H. 1117.23
BESSIE and her friends. Mathews, J. H. 1117.22
BESSIE at school. Mathews, J. H. 1117.24
BESSIE at the sea-side. Mathews, J. H. 1117.20
BESSIE in the city. Mathews, J. H. 1117.21
BESSIE on her travels. Mathews, J. H. 1117.25
BESSIE Brown. Denison, M. A. 928.16
BESSIE Fairfax, The vicissitudes of. Parr, H. 726.26
BESSIE'S trials at boarding-school. Perry, N. 1115.18

Shelf. No.

BESSY Rane. Wood, E. P. 333.2
BEST of husbands, The. Payn, J. Leipzig 319.27
— *Same.* New York 731.35
BEST reading, The. Putnam, G. P. New York, 1872. 12° ..........................*R.R., F.3.5

Note. — A classified list of books on various subjects, which are easily procurable. Topics arranged alphabetically.

BETROTHAL, The. [Poem.] Patmore, C. (K. D.).1612.10.1
BETROTHED, The. Scott, *Sir* W.................. 523.19
BETTER self, The: essays for home-life. Friswell, J. H. Philadelphia [1875]. 16°...............1536.21
BETTERTON, Thomas. History of the English stage. Revised with additional notes, by C. L. Coles. Boston, 1814. 148, 60 pp. 8°............. 813.3
BETTINE. Musset, (L. C.) A. de. Comédies et proverbes. Paris, 1867. 12° ....5534.4.2.
BETTY's bright idea. Stowe, H. (E.) B............ 715.24
BEULAH. Wilson, A. J......................... 737.32
BEWICK, William. Life and letters. Edited by T. Landseer. London, 1871. 2 v. Portrait. Sm. 8°. 5423.8
BEYLE, (Marie) Henri, *called* Stendhal. *See* MÉRIMÉE, P. Portraits historiques et littéraires. Paris, 1874. 12° 5527.14
BÉZE, Théodore, *joint author.* Les pseaumes de David. *See* MAROT, Clement..................5819.12
BIART, Lucien. Adventures of a young naturalist. Edited and adapted by P. Gillmore. With illustrations. New York, 1872. 12°............ 912.9
BIBLE. The Holy Bible. London, 1871. Unpaged. 8° ....*R.R., B.2.3
— Commentary on the Holy Scriptures. By J. P. Lange [and others]. Translated from the German, and edited, with additions, by P. Schaff [and others]. New York, 1873, 74. 15 v. 8°. *R.R., B.2.1
— Abbott, L. A dictionary of religious knowledge. New York, 1875. 8°........................ 6320.2
— Arnold, M. Literature and dogma. An essay towards a better apprehension of the Bible. London, 1873. Sm. 8° 5815.6
— Bailey, S. W. Homage of eminent persons to the Book. New York, 1870. 16° 5819.14
— Baring-Gould, S. Legends of the patriarchs and prophets, and other Old Testament characters. New York, 1872. Sm. 8°.................... 5814.5
— Bissell, E. C. The historic origin of the Bible. New York [1873]. Sm. 8°...................1536.14
— Borrow, G. The Bible in Spain. New York, 1869. 8°..................................5931.13
— Clark, R. W. New serial question books on the heroes of the Bible. 4th series. Boston [*cop.* 1864]. 16° 5819.17
— Conway, M. D. The sacred anthology. London, 1874. 8° 5813.14
— Cruden, A. Complete concordance to the Holy Scriptures. New York, 1872. L. 8°.....*R.R., A.2.1
— Doctrines of Scripture. Boston, 1857. 16° 5819.3
— Gilfillan, G. The bards of the Bible. New York, 1869. 12° 1523.8
— Jacox, F. Bible music. Boston, 1872. 16° ... 6234.2
— Jowett, B. On the interpretation of Scripture. (*In* Essays and reviews) 1538.3
— *Same.* (*In* Hedge, F. H. Recent inquiries in theology).....................1526.24 and 5814.15
— Kitto, J. Popular cyclopædia of biblical literature. Boston, 1871. L. 8°............*R.R., A.2.2
— MacClintock, J., and Strong, J. Cyclopædia of biblical, theological, and ecclesiastical literature. New York, 1871–73. 5 v. 8° .........*R.R., A.2.3
— Mayo, A. D., and Vickers, T. The Bible in the public schools. New York, 1870. 24°........ 5819.2
— Miner, A. A. Bible exercises. Boston, 1863. 12°......................................1538.10
— Observations on the Bible. Boston, 1842. 12°..5818.20
— Palfrey, J. G. Academical lectures on the Jewish Scriptures. Vol. I. Boston, 1838. 8°........ 5811.8
— Palmer, E. H. The desert of the Exodus. New York, 1872. Sm. 8° 222.2
— Putnam, A. Bible marvel workers. Boston, 1873. 16°.....................1536.18 and 5815.25

Shelf. No.

BIBLE, *continued.*
— Scripture lessons; being a selection from the Old and New Testaments, for the use of schools. Boston, 1823. 12°.........................1537.16
— Smith, W. Dictionary of the Bible. New York, 1872. 4 v. 8°........................*R.R., B.2.2
— Walden, T. Our English Bible and its ancestors. Philadelphia [*cop.* 1871]. 16° 5818.13
— *Pentateuch*, Lectures on the. Colenso, J. W. London, 1873. 8° 5811.5
— *Genesis.* Davies, T. A. Genesis disclosed: proving the error that all men have descended from Adam and Eve [etc.]. New York, 1874. 12°. 6327.11
— – Smith, G. The Chaldean account of Genesis. New York [London], 1876. 8°.............. 6320.4
— *Psalms.* Les pseaumes de David. Marot, C., and Béze, T. [No title-page.] 16°..........5819.12
— *Daniel*, Complete and truthful exposition of the visions of. Snow, S. S. New York, 1863. 12°. 1524.9
— *New Testament.* The New Testament. [French and English.] London, 1840. Unpaged. 12°. 6328.9
— – The New Testament: the authorized English version; with introduction, and various readings from the three most celebrated manuscripts of the original Greek text. By C. Tischendorf. Tauchnitz edition. Leipzig, 1869. xvi, 414+ pp. Sq. 16° 1528.2
— – The revision of the English version of the New Testament. Lightfoot, J. B., Trench, R. C., Ellicott, C. J., and Schaff, P. [Various publications.] New York, 1873. 8° 5814.11
— – A translation of the New Testament. [With notes.] By Gilbert Wakefield. From the 2d London edition. Cambridge, 1820. xii, 450, 163 pp. 8° 5810.4
— – An exposition of the historical writings of the New Testament. Kenrick, T. Boston, 1828. 3 v. 8° 6324.2
— – *Gospels.* Comprehensive commentary; containing the text, and nearly all that is valuable in Henry, Scott, and Doddridge. Edited by W. Jenks. [Vol. IV.] Matthew—John. Brattleboro', 1834. Portraits, engravings, maps, and wood-cuts. L. 8°......................... 6320.3
— – – Formby, H. The life, passion, death, and resurrection of our Lord Jesus Christ. Being an abridged harmony of the four gospels in the words of the sacred text. London [1874]. Sq. 16°..6328.22
— – – Furness, W. H. Remarks on the four gospels. Philadelphia, 1836. 12° 5815.14
— – – *Same.* Revised with additions. Philadelphia, 1838. L. 8° 5811.7
— – – Livermore, A. A. The four gospels, with a commentary. Vol. 2, Mark, Luke, and John. New edition. Boston, 1858. 12° 1534.6
— – *Acts.* Notes. By A. Barnes. 20th edition. New York, 1860. 356 pp. Map. 12°........ 6327.1
— – *Romans.* Critical and exegetical commentary on the New Testament. Part IV. Romans. Meyer, H. A. W. Edinburgh, 1873. 8°...... 5810.2
— – *Epistles of St. Paul*, A paraphrase and notes on the. Locke, J. Cambridge, 1832. 8°..... 6322.1
— – *Ephesians, Philippians, and Colossians.* Notes. By A. Barnes. New York, 1845. 331 pp. Illustrated. 12° 6327.22
— – *Thessalonians, Timothy, Titus, and Philemon.* Notes. By A. Barnes. New York, 1845. 355 pp. 12° 6327.20
— – *Hebrews.* Notes. By A. Barnes. New York, 1843. 335 pp. 12° 6327.21
— – *Revelation.* Cumming, J. Lectures on the book of. 1st series. Philadelphia, 1854. 12°. 6326.2
— – – Snow, S. S. Complete and truthful exposition of. New York, 1863. 12° 1524.9
— – – Swedenborg, E. The Apocalypse revealed. New York, 1873. 2 v. 8°.................. 6323.3
— *Apocryphal New Testament.* Apocryphal Gospels, Acts, and Revelations. Translated by Alexander Walker. Edinburgh, 1870. xxiv, 547 pp. [Ante-Nicene Christian library.] 8°........6322.4.1

Shelf. No.

BIBLIOGRAPHICA genealogica Americana. Durrie, D. S. Albany, 1868. 8° 5022.8
BIBLIOGRAPHY. Dibdin, T. F. Bibliomania; or, book-madness. London, 1876. 8° 6131.3
— Hazard, W. P. The library; or, some hints about what books to read, and how to buy them. Philadelphia [*cop.* 1870]. 12° 1537.1
— Jacox, F. Aspects of authorship: or, book marks and book makers. London, 1872. 16° 6136.6
— Putnam, G. P. The best reading. With a classified bibliography for easy reference. New York, 1875. 12° 6136.10

Note. — See the Handbook for readers published by the Library.

BIBLIOTHECA sacra, and theological eclectic. Vol. 30, 31. Andover, 1873, 74. 2 v. 8° 6736.1
BICHAT, (Marie François) Xavier. Physiological researches upon life and death. Translated by T. Watkins. Philadelphia, 1809. xx, 300 pp. 8° 6023.10
BICKERSTETH, Edward Henry. The rock of ages. With an introduction by F. D. Huntington. Boston, 1860. 214 pp. 12° 1524.7
BICKMORE, Albert Smith. Travels in the East Indian archipelago. With maps and illustrations. London, 1868. 555 pp. 8° 422.7
— *Same.* New York, 1869. 8° 5932.4
BICKNELL, A. J., *editor.* Wooden and brick buildings with details, containing 160 plates. Also, descriptive letterpress, specifications [etc.]. New York, 1875. 2 v. F° 6220.7
BIG brother, The. Eggleston, G. C. 714.35
BIGELOW, Henry Jacob. Manual of orthopedic surgery. A dissertation which obtained the Boylston prize for 1844. Boston, 1845. viii, 211+ pp. Plates. 8° 6011.10
BIGELOW, Jacob. Brief expositions of rational medicine: prefixed, The paradise of doctors, a fable. Boston, 1868. 69+ pp. 12° 6037.1
— Modern inquiries: classical, professional, and miscellaneous. [Essays.] Boston, 1870. xi, 379 pp. Sm. 8° 5216.1
— Remarks on classical and utilitarian studies. Boston, 1867. 57 pp. 16° 1526.18
— The useful arts, considered in connexion with the applications of science. With engravings. New York, 1851. 2 v. Folded plates. 12° 1514.1
BIGELOW, L. J. Bench and bar. With portraits and illustrations. New York, 1871. 532 pp. 8°. 1532.1
BIGLOW papers, The. Lowell, J. R. Boston, 1872, 73. 2 v. 16° 5227.1

Note. — Satires on politics, etc., in the Yankee dialect, with notes, etc.

BILLARD, Charles Michel. Treatise on the diseases of infants. With appendix by J. Stewart. New York, 1839. viii, 620 pp. 8° 6022.10
BILLIARDS. Bennett, J. London, 1873. 8° 6413.1
BILLINGS, Josh, *pseud.* *See* SHAW, Henry W.
BILLINGS family. Thayer, E. Family memorial. Hingham, 1835. 8° 611.2
BILLY Grimes' favorite. Nowell, H. P. H. 936.26
BINNEY, C. J. F. History and genealogy of the Prentice or Prentiss family. Boston, 1852. iv, 272 pp. 8° 612.2
BIOGRAPHIA literaria. Coleridge, S. T. Philadelphia, N. D. 8° 1611.5
BIOGRAPHY. Allen, W. American biographical dictionary. Boston, 1832. 8° .........*R.R., D.3.2
— Allibone, S. A. Critical dictionary of English literature and British and American authors. Philadelphia, 1871. 3 v. 8° ...........*R.R., A.3.6
— Bayne, P. Essays in biography. Boston, 1857. 12° 1226.15
— Cates, W. L. R. Dictionary of general biography. London, 1875. 8° ...................*R.R., E.2.11
— De Quincey, T. Biographical essays. Boston, 1870. 12° 1825.6
— Drake, F. S. Dictionary of American biography. Boston, 1872. 8° .....................*R.R., E.3.1
— Edgar, J. G. Footprints of famous men. New York, 1872. 16° 913.13

BIOGRAPHY, *continued.*
— Emerson, R. W. Representative men. Boston, 1875. 12° 1916.6
— Field, M. B. Memories of many men, and of some women. Boston, 1874. 12° 1036.1
— Godwin, P. Cyclopædia of biography. New York, 1872. 12° ........................*R.R., F.3.4
— Hall, S. C. Book of memories of great men and women of the age, from personal acquaintance. London, 1871. 4° 1231.1
— Harvard memorial biographies. Cambridge, 1867. 2 v. 8° 5025.12
— Hole, C. Brief biographical dictionary. New York, 1866. 16° .....................*R.R., F.3.9
— Horne, R. H. A new spirit of the age. New York, 1844. 18° 1038.1
— Irving, W. Biographies and miscellanies. Philadelphia, 1871. Sm. 8° 1815.4
— Jerdan, W. Men I have known. London, 1866. Sm. 8° 5423.11
— Johnson, (E.) R. Little classics. Authors. Boston, 1875. Sq. 16° 529.4.16
— Knight, C. Biography; or, third division of "The English cyclopædia." London, 1866–68. 6 v. 4° ..................................*R.R., F.2.1
— Lamartine, A. (M. L.) de. Memoirs of celebrated characters. New York, 1854. 3 v. 12°. 1025.10
— Macaulay, T. B., Rogers, H., Martin, T., and others. New biographies of illustrious men. Boston, 1857. 12° 5428.4
— MacCarthy, J. Modern leaders. New York, 1872. 8° 5930.2
— Martin, F. Handbook of contemporary biography. London, 1870. 16° .............*R.R., F.3.7
— Mueller, F. M. Chips from a German workshop. New York, 1872. Sm. 8° 5616.1.3
— Page, H. A. Noble workers. London, 1875. Sm. 8° 5936.3
— Phillips, L. B. Dictionary of biographical reference. London, 1871. 8° ...............*R.R., E.3.2
— Prescott, W. H. Biographical and critical essays. London, 1856. 16° 1537.8
— – Biographical and critical miscellanies. Philadelphia, 1875. 12° 5231.3
— Smiles, S. Brief biographies. Boston, 1873. 16°. 1024.13
— Smith, W. Dictionary of Greek and Roman biography. London, 1870. 3 v. 8° ....*R.R., E.3.3
— Thomas, J. Universal pronouncing dictionary of biography. Philadelphia, 1871. 2 v. 8°.*R.R., A.3.5
— Thomson, K. and J. C. The queens of society. New York, 1861. 12° 1216.17
— – The wits and beaux of society. New York, 1861. 12° 1216.18
— Vapereau, G. Dictionnaire universel des contemporains. Paris, 1870, 73. L. 8° ....*R.R., E.2.10

See also America, Architects, Artists, Bible, Christ, Engineers, England, Europe, France, Germany, Great Britain, Greece, Heroes, Indians, Inventors, Ireland, Italy, Jews, Knights, Military biography, Missions, New England, New York, Novelists, Painters, Philosophers, Poets, Popes, Roman catholic church, Rome, Sculptors, Statesmen, Women, United States.

Note. — For universal biography the most convenient reference book is Thomas, who gives authorities for further investigation. For Americans only, Drake's is the best. For English and American writers, use Allibone in the first instance.

BIOLOGY. Spencer, H. Principles of. New York, 1868, 73. 2 v. 12° 6635.2
— Stevenson, S. H. Boys and girls in. New York, 1875. 12° 1527.17
BION. Idylls. *See* THEOCRITUS 6115.17
BIOPLASM. Beale, L. S. London, 1872. 16° 6037.2
BIRD, Harriet, Recollections of. Taber, S. W. Boston, 1857. Sm. 12° 5819.20
BIRD, Joseph. Protection against fire, and the best means of putting out fires in cities, towns, and villages. New York, 1873. iv, 278 pp. Sm. 8°. 1726.1
BIRD, Robert Montgomery. Nick of the woods 536.4
BIRD, The, and the bell, with other poems. Cranch, C. P. Boston, 1875. 12° 1617.15
BIRD-KEEPING. A practical guide for the management of cage birds. Illustrated. London, [1868]. iv, 156 pp. 16° 6618.1

Shelf. No.

BIRDS. Baily, W. L. Our own birds. Philadelphia, 1869. 12° 913.25
— Berthoud, H. Stories of bird life. London, 1875. Sm. 8° 6617.9
— Burroughs, J. Wake-robin. New York, 1871. 16°. 1525.12
— Elliott, A. A chapter on feathered pets. London, 1872. 16° 916.19
— Figuier, (G.) L. Reptiles and birds. London [1869]. 8° 1521.3
— Flagg, W. The birds and seasons of New England. Boston, 1875. 8° 6614.11
— Holden, C. F. Holden's book on. New York, 1873. 12° 1519.6
— Michelet, J. The bird. London, 1870. 8° 6612.5
— Ruskin, J. Loves meinie. Lectures on Greek and English birds. New York, 1873. 12° 6236.20
— Samuels, E. A. The birds of New England and adjacent states. Boston, 1872. 8° 6612.4
— Synopsis of the birds of the United States. New York, 1828. 8° 6614.1

See also Canary bird.

Note. — See note in Bulletin, vol. II, p. 232.

BIRDS of a feather. Bradley, M. 936.30
BIRKS, Thomas Rawson. First principles of moral science. London, 1873. vii, 320 pp. Sm. 8° .. 5836.2
BIRTH and education. Schwartz, M. S. 531.6
BIRTHDAY party, The. Adams, W. T. 918.8
BIRTHMARK, The. Hawthorne, N. (*In* Johnson, (E.) R. Little classics) 529.4.8
BISHOP, Nathaniel H. The Pampas and Andes. A thousand miles' walk across South America. With an introduction by E. A. Samuels. 3d edition. Illustrated. Boston, 1872. 310+ pp. 16°. 934.1
BISMARCK-SCHOENHAUSEN, Otto (Eduard Leopold), *Prinz* von, Life of. Hesekiel, J. G. L. London, 1870. 8° 1221.8
— *Same.* New York, 1870. 8° 1021.5
BISSELL, Edwin Cone. The historic origin of the Bible. With an introduction by R. D. Hitchcock. New York [1873]. xxiii, 432 pp. Sm. 8° 1536.14
BITS of talk about home matters. Hunt, H. (M.) Boston, 1873. Sq. 16° 1939.2
BITS of travel. Hunt, H. (M.) Boston, 1872. Sq. 16°. 428.10
BITTER-SWEET. A poem. Holland, J. G. New York, 1872. 12° 1615.18
— *Same.* (*In his* Garnered sheaves.) New York, 1873. Sq. 16° 1617.2
BIVOUAC, The; or, stories of the peninsular war. Maxwell, W. H. 518.6
BIVOUAC and battle. Adams, W. T. 924.10
BJÖRNSON, Björnstjerne. Arne: a sketch of Norwegian country life. Translated by A. Plesner and S. Rugeley-Powers 735.25
— The happy boy: a tale of Norwegian peasant life. Translated by H. R. G. 735.25
BLACK, Adam and Charles. General atlas of the world. American edition. Edinburgh, 1871. F°. *R.R.Desk
— Picturesque tourist of Ireland. Illustrated by a map of Ireland, charts and plans. Edinburgh, 1855. vii, 310 pp. Wood-cuts. Sm. 8° 229.2
BLACK, Charles Christopher. Essay on L. da Vinci's scientific and literary works. *See* HEATON, Mary M. 6211.5
— Michael Angelo Buonarroti. Sculptor, painter, architect. The story of his life and labours. London, 1875. xiv, 262+ pp. Portrait. Photographs. 8° 6211.7
BLACK, William. A daughter of Heth 311.26
— Kilmeny 319.16
— Love or marriage? 720.18
— The maid of Killeena and other stories. Leipzig. 330.12

Contents. — The maid of Killeena; Queen Tita's wager; A fight for a wife; The true legend of a billiard club; A sequel to that.

— *Same.* New York 711.9

Contents. — The maid of Killeena; Queen Tita's wager; A fight for a wife; The true legend of a billiard club; A sequel to that; The man who was like Shakspeare.

— The marriage of Moira Fergus 720.38
— The monarch of Mincing-Lane 720.13

Shelf. No.

BLACK, William, *continued.*
— A princess of Thule. Leipzig 328.28
— *Same.* New York 732.10
— In silk attire 330.24
— The strange adventures of a phaeton 319.6
— Three feathers. Leipzig 331.9
— *Same.* New York 720.2
BLACK baronet, The. Carleton, W. 524.1
BLACK diamonds gathered in the darkey homes of the South. Pollard, E. A. New York, 1859. 12°. 1915.8
BLACK dwarf, The. Scott, *Sir* W. Boston 523.15
— *Same.* Leipzig 324.11
BLACK forest village stories. Auerbach, B. 926.27
BLACK hills, *Dakota*, Report of a reconnaissance of the. *See* UNITED STATES. *Department of war* .. 630.1
BLACK ivory; a tale of adventure among the slavers of East Africa. Ballantyne, R. M. 538.9
BLACK panther, The. Wraxall, *Sir* (F. C.) L. 931.10
BLACK sea, Travels on the. Cunynghame, *Sir* A. T. London, 1872. 8° 5931.8
BLACK sheep. Yates, E. 318.22
BLACK tulip, The. Dumas, A. (D.) 510.7
BLACKBURN, Henry. The Harz mountains: a tour in the toy country. With illustrations. London, 1873. 184 pp. Sm. 4° 5733.3
— Normandy picturesque. With illustrations. 1st American from 2d London edition. Boston, 1873. 291 pp. Map. Sq. 16° 5528.3
— The Pyrenees: a description of summer life at French watering places. With illustrations by G. Doré, and a map. London, 1867. xvi, 326 pp. 8° 5522.3
BLACKBURNE, Francis. Confessions of faith. (*In* Sparks, J. Collection of essays and tracts in theology) 1918.9.1
— *Same.* Also Selection from Benjamin Hoadly's works. Boston, 1823. [No title-page.] 169–344 pp. 12° 6327.11
BLACKIE, John Stuart. Biography of Homer. (*In* Macaulay, T. B., *lord*, and others. New biographies of illustrious men) 5428.4
— Horæ Hellenicæ: essays and discussions on some important points of Greek philology and antiquity. London, 1874. xii, 394 pp. 8° 6113.4
— On self-culture. 3d edition. Edinburgh, 1874. 91 pp. 16° 5838.5
BLACKMORE, Richard Doddridge. Alice Lorraine. A tale of the South downs. Leipzig 331.10
— *Same.* New York 711.35
— Lorna Doone 710.16
— The maid of Sker 711.20
BLACKSTONE, *Sir* William. Commentaries on the laws of England. With notes, and a life of the author, by G. Sharswood. Philadelphia, 1872. 2 v. Portrait. 8° 6311.1
BLACKWELL, Antoinette Brown. The sexes throughout nature. New York, 1875. 240 pp. 12° .. 5837.5
BLACKWOOD, Frederick Temple, *lord Dufferin.* Letters from high latitudes; voyage to Iceland, Jan Mayen, and Spitzbergen, in 1856. Boston, 1859. 406 pp. 12° 225.3
BLADE-O'-GRASS. Farjeon, B. L. 521.7
BLAGDEN, George Washington. Pastor's memorial. Twenty-fifth anniversary of [his] installation. *See* BOSTON, *Mass. Old South church and society* 5817.3
BLAGDEN, Isa. The woman I loved, and the woman who loved me: a Tuscan wedding 339.5
BLAINE, Delabere Pritchett. An encyclopædia of rural sports. New edition, revised and corrected. Illustrated. London, 1870. xiii, 1246 pp. 8°. 6412.2
BLAIR, David. A grammar of natural and experimental philosophy. With engravings. 20th edition from the 12th London edition. Hartford, 1824. 214 pp. 12° 1538.22
BLAIR, Hugh. An abridgment of lectures on rhetoric. Revised and corrected. Windsor, 1809. 291 pp. 12° 1918.6
— Lectures on rhetoric and belles lettres. 4th American edition. Brooklyn, 1807. 2 v. 8°. 1912.2
— Sermons. 8th edition. London, 1783. 2 v. 8°. 5814.1

Shelf. No.

BLAKE, *Lady* —. Ruth Maxwell 731.4
BLAKE, E. Vale, *editor*. Arctic experiences: containing Capt. G. E. Tyson's wonderful drift on the ice-floe, a history of the Polaris expedition, the cruise of the Tigress, and rescue of the Polaris survivors. Added a general Arctic chronology. New York, 1874. 486 pp. Illustrated. Portraits. 8° 5911.15
BLAKE, John Lauris. Conversations on natural philosophy. Illustrated. Boston, 1837. 276 pp. 12°...................................1526.30
BLAKE, Lillie Devereux. Fettered for life......... 734.23
BLAKE, Louisa. Poems. Boston, 1832. vii, 138 pp. 12°.................................... 5218.3
BLAKE, Sophia Jex. A visit to some American schools and colleges. London, 1867. xii, 250 pp. Sm. 8°................................. 1736.7
BLAKE, William, Life of. Gilchrist, A. London, 1863. 2 v. 8°................................ 6213.9
BLANC, (Auguste Alexander Philippe) Charles. Grammar of painting and engraving. Translated from the French by Kate Newell Doggett. With the original illustrations. New York, 1874. xx, 330 pp. 1 colored plate. L. 8°.... 6212.2
BLANC, (Jean Joseph) Louis. History of ten years [in France], 1830–40. London, 1844, 45. 2 v. 8°. 5517.4
BLANCHE Seymour. By the author of "Erma's engagement"...................................... 732.1
BLAND, William. Experimental essays on the principles of construction in arches, piers, buttresses, etc. With illustrations. 3d edition. London, 1867. vi, 138 pp. 12° 1716.6
— Forms of ships and boats. With illustrations. 5th edition, revised. London, 1868. viii, 97+ pp. 12°.....................................1715.10
BLEAK house. Dickens, C. (J. H.) Boston. 2 v...1824.11
— *Same*. Leipzig. 4 v. in 2........................ 338.19
BLEEDING. *See* EPILEPSY.
BLESSINGTON, *Countess of*. *See* GARDINER, Margaret.
BLIND people: their works and ways. Johns, B. G. London, 1867. Sm. 8° 5428.7
BLITHEDALE romance, The. Hawthorne, N. Boston, 1871. 16° 1813.8
— *Same*. Boston, 1873. 16° 1813.11

Note. — Supposed to picture the Brook farm experiment.

BLOCKADE, The, of Phalsburg. [Fiction.] Erckmann, É., and Chatrian, A. London, 1870. 16°. 715.12
— *Same*. New York, 1871. 12° 913.21
BLOCKADE runners, The. Verne, J. 713.4
BLOODLETTING, Researches on the effects of. Louis, P. C. A. Boston, 1836. 8°...................... 6014.4
BLOOMFIELD. Robert. Rural tales, ballads, and songs. 2d edition. London, 1802. ix, 119+ pp. Illustrated. Portrait. 16° 1628.3
BLOSSOMING, The, of an aloe. Hoey, *Mrs*. C. 711.15
BLOT, Pierre. Hand-book of practical cookery. New York, 1873. 478 pp. Illustrated. 12°.. 1515.5
BLOWPIPE, A system of instruction in the practical use of the. Plympton, G. W. New York, 1868. 12°...................................... 6436.3
BLUE ribbon, The. Tabor, E. 732.19
BLUEBEARD's ghost. Thackeray, W. M. (*In* Johnson, (E.) R. Little classics).................529.4.9
BLUEBEARD's keys. Thackeray, A. I. Leipzig.... 330.20
— *Same*. New York 720.11
BLUEBERRYING. Abbott, J........................... 917.27
BLUNDERER, The: a comedy. Molière, J. B. P. Dramatic works. Edinburgh, 1875. 8°......5530.3.1
BOARDING-SCHOOL days. Gordon, C............... 915.22
BOARDMAN, William E. The higher Christian life. Boston, 1858. 330+ pp. 12°....1536.10 and 6325.10
BOAT club. Adams, W. T. 924.15
BOAT club series. *See* ADAMS, William T.
BOAT life in Egypt and Nubia. Prime, W. C. New York, 1858. 12° 424.6
BOATS. Ballantyne, R. M. Man on the ocean. A book about boats and ships.....................1715.30
— Kingston, W. H. G. The boy's own book of boats, with instructions how to make sailing models 1718.1

Shelf. No.

BOBBIN boy, The. N. P. Banks. Thayer, W. M. Boston, 1860. 16°.................................. 916.8
BÔCHER, Fedinand, *editor*. College series of French plays. Boston, 1867. 12° 2015.2

Contents. — Les petits oiseaux; Mlle. de la Seiglière; Le Roman d'un jeune homme pauvre; Les doigts de fée.

BODILY strength and skill, Wonders of. Depping, G. New York, 1872. 16° 1714.12
BODY and mind. Maudsley, H. London, 1873. 8°..6036.15
BOGART, William H. Daniel Boone, and the hunters of Kentucky. Illustrated. Boston, 1874 [*cop*. 1854]. 464 pp. 12° 5025.9
BOGEN, F. W. The German in America. [German and English.] 2d edition. Boston, 1851. 177 pp. 12°.. 1939.3
BOHEMIAN girl. Balfe, M. W. (*In* Ditson, O., and co. Standard opera librettos) 6233.3.3
BOIELDIEU, François André. La dame blanche. (*In* Ditson, O., and co. Standard opera librettos) 6233.3.5
BOITARD, Pierre. Nouveau manuel du cordier. Paris, 1839. 294+ pp. 24°. [Manuel Roret]. 6429.8
BOKHARA, *Asia*, Narrative of a mission to. Wolff, J. New York, 1845. 8° 821.4
BOLEYN, Anne. *See* ANNE BOLEYN.
BOMBAUGH, Charles C. The literature of kissing, gleaned from history, poetry, fiction and anecdote. Philadelphia, 1876. 382 pp. 12°...... 5924.5
BONAPARTE, Jérôme. Lettres et documents inédits 1837 à 1848. *See* THIERS, Louis Adolphe 5515.2
BONAPARTE, Joseph. *See* JOSEPH BONAPARTE.
BONAPARTE, Louis Napoléon. *See* NAPOLÉON III.
BONAPARTE, Napoléon. *See* NAPOLÉON I.
BONAPARTE family. The Napoleon dynasty. A history of the Bonaparte family. Lester, C. E. New York, 1873. 12° 825.17
BONAPARTE-PATTERSON marriage in 1803, The. Saffell, W. T. R. Philadelphia, 1873. Sm. 8°. 825.4
BOND, John James. Handy-book of rules and tables for verifying dates with the Christian era; giving an account of the chief eras, and systems used by various nations; with easy methods for determining the corresponding dates; with regnal years of English sovereigns, 1066–1874. London, 1875. xlii, 465 pp. Sm. 8° 5627.2
BOND, Robert. Handbook of the telegraph. 3d edition, revised and enlarged, with illustrations. London, 1870. 114+ pp. Folded plates. 12°. 1715.4
BONER, Charles. Memoirs and letters. With letters of Mary Russell Mitford to him during ten years. Edited by R. M. Kettle. London, 1871. 2 v. Sm. 8° 5426.2
BONES. Dupuytren, G., *baron*. Injuries and diseases of. London, 1847. 8° 6013.7
— Wagner, A. Process of repair after resection and extirpation of. London, 1859. 8°........ 6023.1
BONIFACIUS, (Winifrid), *St., archbishop of Mentz*. S. Bonifaco and the conversion of Germany. Hope, *Mrs*. —. London, 1872. 16°.......... 5735.6
BONNER, John. Child's history of Greece. With illustrations. New York, 1871. 2 v. 16°.... 926.2
— Child's history of Rome. New York, 1870. 2 v. Illustrated. 16° 926.1
— Child's history of the United States. With engravings. New York, 1870. 3 v. 16°...... 926.3
BONNET, Charles. Philosophical and critical inquiries concerning Christianity. Translated by J. L. Boissier. Philadelphia, 1803. 304 pp. Portrait. 16° 1918.10
BONNEVILLE, Captain, Adventures of. Irving, W. London, 1854. 12° 826.3
— *Same*. Philadelphia, 1871. Sm. 8°...........1815.14
BONNIE Scotland. Lippincott, S. J. Boston, 1872. 16° 933.29
BONSTETTIN, Charles Victor de. The man of the North, and the man of the South; or the influence of climate. Translated from the French. New York, 1864. 200 pp. 12° 1938.2
BONWICK, James. Mike Howe, the bushranger of Van Dieman's land.................................. 725.28

Shelf. No.

Book, A, about boys. Moncrieff, A. R. H. Boston, 1869. 16°.............................. 926.34
Book, A, about doctors. Jeaffreson, J. C. Leipzig, 1870. 2 v. in 1. Sq. 16°....................1238.16
Book about dominies. Moncrieff, A. R. H. Boston, 1869. 16°.............................. 1535.9
Book-keeping. Marsh, C. C. Theory and practise of bank book-keeping. New York, 1864. L. 4°.............................. 1720.1
— Trémery, F. Nouveau manuel complet du teneur de livres. Paris, n. d. 24°.................. 6819.1
Book, The, of adventure and peril. Bruce, C. London, 1875. Sm. 8°.......................... 426.23
Book, The, of days. Chambers, R. London, n. d. 2 v. 8°.............................*R.R., A.3.7
Book, A, of golden deeds. Yonge, C. M. London, 1870. 16°.............................. 1939.1
Book of memories. Hall, S. C. London, 1871. 4°. 1231.1
Book, The, of snobs. Thackeray, W. M. (*In his* Miscellanies)..............................335.13.1
— *Same.* (*In his* Works)........................ 513.1.9
Book, The, of the seasons. Howitt, W. Philadelphia, 1831. 12°.............................. 1838.3
Books and reading. Porter, N. Books and reading; or, what books shall I read and how shall I read them? New York, 1873. Sm. 8°...... 6134.1
— Putnam, G. P. The best reading. Hints on the selection of books. New York, 1875. 12°.....6136.10
— Van Rhyn, G. A. F. What and how to read. New York, 1875. 12°......................6136.11
Booksellers. History of booksellers, the old and the new. Curwen, H. London [1873]. 12° ..5426.16

See also Note in Bulletin, Vol. II, p. 234.

Boone, Daniel. Abbott, J. S. C. Daniel Boone the pioneer of Kentucky. New York, 1872. 12°.. 1014.4
— Bogart, W. H. Daniel Boone, and the hunters of Kentucky. Boston, 1874 [*cop.* 1854]. 16°. 5025.9
Borbstædt, A., and Dwyer, F. The Franco-German war to the catastrophe of Sedan and the fall of Strassburg. With strategical maps, tabular views of marches, plans of battles [etc.]. London, 1873. viii, 701 pp. 8°............. 5713.2
Border and Bastille. Lawrence, G. A............ 315.26
Border beagles. Simms, W. G.................. 716.27
Border lines of knowledge in some provinces of medical science. Holmes, O. W. Boston, 1862. 12°..1522.14
Border reminiscences. Marcy, R. B............ 413.3
Borderland, The, of science. Proctor, R. A. London, 1873. 8°.............................. 6814.3
Bores, The: a comedy. Molière, J. B. P. Dramatic works. Edinburgh, 1875. 8°..........5530.3.2
Borgia, Lucrezia, *duchess of Ferrara.* Gilbert, W. Lucrezia Borgia. A biography. London, 1869. 2 v. Sm. 8°.............................. 5526.7
— Gregorovius, F. Lucrezia Borgia. Stuttgart, 1874. 8°.............................. 5733.6
Borrow, George. The Bible in Spain. 13th edition. New York, 1869. 232 pp. 8°.........5931.13
— Lavengro; the scholar — the gipsy — the priest. New York, 1857. 198 pp. 8°.............. 511.4
— Romany Rye; a sequel to "Lavengro." New York, 1867. 141 pp. 8°.................... 511.21
— Wild Wales: its people, language, and scenery. 3d edition. London, 1872. viii, 347 pp. Sm. 8°. 5438.6
— The Zincali; or, an account of the gypsies of Spain. New York, 1869. 148 pp. 8°........5931.13
Boscobel; or, the royal oak. [Historical fiction.] Ainsworth, W. H.............................. 339.10
Bossuet, Jacques Bénigne. Bossuet and his contemporaries. Farrar, H. S. London, 1874. Sm. 8°..5526.14
Boston, *Mass. Auditor.* Annual report of the receipts and expenditures of the city of Boston and the county of Suffolk, 1867–75. Boston, 1868–75. 6 v. 8°.............................. 6923.1
— *Board of health.* The sanitary condition of Boston. Report of a medical commission appointed to investigate the sanitary condition of the city. Boston, 1875. 199 pp. Charts. 8°.......... 6913.6

Shelf. No.

Boston, *Mass., continued.*
— Celebration of the centennial anniversary of the battle of Bunker hill [prepared by James M. Bugbee]. With an appendix containing a survey of the literature of the battle, its antecedents and results [by Justin Winsor]. Boston, 1875. Illustrated. 174 pp. L. 8°................. 810.10
— History of the introduction of pure water into Boston, with a description of its Cochituate water works. Compiled by [N. J. Bradlee]. Illustrated. Boston, 1868. xxi, 299+ pp. 8°. 610.2 and 5010.18
— Inaugural address of S. C. Cobb, mayor, Jan. 5, 1874. Boston, 1874. 34 pp. 8°............6923.11
— *Same.* Jan. 4, 1875. Boston, 1875. 30 pp. 8°.6923.13
— Memorial of Abraham Lincoln. Boston, 1865. 153 pp. L. 8°.............................. 5020.4
— Memorial of Daniel Webster. Boston, 1853. viii, 270 pp. Portrait. 1 plate. 8°.......... 1011.4
— Memorial of Edward Everett. Boston, 1865. 315 pp. Portraits. L. 8°.................... 810.9
— Memorial of Joshua Bates. Boston, 1865. 58 pp. Portrait. 1 plate. L. 8°.................... 5031.1
— Memorial of Samuel F. B. Morse. [Boston] 1872. 103+ pp. 8°..............1211.5 and 5023.3
— Memorial of the inauguration of the statue of Franklin. Boston, 1857. 412 pp. 1 plate. 8°. 1211.6
— Municipal register for 1873. Boston, 1873. 278 pp. 8°.............................. 1210.1
— Ordinances of the city and acts of the legislature of Massachusetts on municipal subjects passed 1873. Boston, 1874. 251–334 pp. L. 8°..... 810.4
— Proceedings, April 17, 1865, on occasion of the death of Abraham Lincoln. Boston, 1865. 35 pp. 8°.............................. 5020.6
— *Primary schools.* Annals of the primary school committee, 1818–55. Compiled by J. M. Wightman. Boston, 1860. 8°.................... 5010.3
— *Public library.* Bulletins. Vol. I, II. No. 1 to 35. Oct., 1867, to Oct., 1875. [Appended to vol. I, The Tosti engravings. Portraits.] Boston, 1871, 75. 2 v. L. 8°..............*R.R., D.2.5
— – Catalogue. Boston, 1854. iv, 180 pp. 8°.*R.R., D.2.8
— – A chronological index to historical fiction; including prose fiction, plays and poems. 2d and enlarged edition. Boston, 1875. iv, 32 pp. L. 8°. *Desk
— – Historical fiction. Novels, plays, poems. [Boston, 1871.] 9 pp. L. 8°...........*R.R., D.2.4
— – Index to the catalogue of books in the Bates Hall. Boston, 1861. vii, 902+ pp. L. 8°..*R.R., D.2.2
— – – First supplement. Boston, 1866. iv, 718, 21+ pp. L. 8°........................*R.R., D.2.3
— – Index to the catalogue of [books] in the Lower Hall. Boston, 1858. iv, 204 pp. L. 8°. *R.R., D.2.1
— – Lower Hall. Catalogue of books in the classes of history, biography, and travel, with notes for readers under subject-references. 2d, or consolidated edition. Boston, 1873. 304 pp. L. 8°.*R.R., D.2.16
— – – Class list for English prose fiction, including translations and juvenile fiction [and some juvenile works not fiction]. 5th edition. [Boston, 1871.] 76 pp. L. 8°..............*R.R., D.2.4
— – – Class list for poetry, the drama, rhetoric, elocution, collections, periodicals, and miscellaneous works. [Boston, 1870.] 128 pp. L. 8°. *R.R., D.2.4
— – – Class list for works in the arts and sciences. 2d edition. [Boston, 1871.] 71+ pp. L. 8°. *R.R., D.2.4
— – – Finding list for French, German, and Italian books. [Boston, 1867.] 45 pp. L. 8°.*R.R., D.2.4
— – – Foreign languages. Books arranged by authors, titles, and subjects. 2d edition. [Boston, 1876.] 68 pp. L. 8°. ............*R.R., D.2.20
— – Miscellaneous documents. Boston, 1851–72. Sm. 8°.......................................*R.R., D.2.14
— – Nineteenth annual report of the trustees. Boston, 1871. 77 pp. 8°...................*R.R., D.2.9
— – Periodicals currently received; and Works of reference in the Reading Room and at the Desk in Bates Hall. [Boston, 1870.] 31 pp. L. 8°. *R.R., D.2.4

Shelf. No.

BOSTON, *Mass. Public library, continued.*

— – Points to be considered in cataloguing, revising, and proof-reading. [Boston, 1870.] 8 pp. L. 8°. .... *R.R., D.2.4

— – Presentation of a bust and portrait of Joshua Bates, by his daughter, Mrs. Elizabeth van de Weyer. Boston, 1866. 19 pp. L. 8°.... *R.R., D.2.4

— – The Prince library. A catalogue of the books and manuscripts [of] T. Prince, bequeathed to the Old South church, and now deposited in the Public library. Boston, 1870. xvi, 159+ pp. L. 8° .... *R.R., D.2.6

— – Proceedings at the dedication of the building. Boston, 1858. 194 pp. Illustrated. 8°. 5012.8 and *R.R., D.2.11

— – Second — nineteenth annual report of the trustees. Boston, 1852–71. 8° .... *R.R., D.2.15

— – The Tosti engravings. [Complete.] Boston, 1873. L. 8° .... *R.R., D.2.17

— – – Portraits. [Boston, 1871.] 24 pp. L. 8°. *R.R., D.2.4 and 7

— – Twentieth annual report of the trustees. Boston, 1872. 8° .... *R.R., D.2.10

— – *East Boston branch.* List of books, arranged by authors, titles, and subjects. [Boston, 1871.] 92 pp. 8° .... *R.R., D.2.4

— – *Roxbury branch.* [Documents relating to the establishment of the Roxbury branch and its union with the Fellowes Athenæum. Boston, 1872, 73.] 8° .... 5010.17 and *R.R., D.2.18

— – *South Boston branch.* List of books, arranged by authors, titles, and subjects. [Boston, 1872.] 72 pp. 8° .... *R.R., D.2.4

— – – Proceedings at [its] dedication, May 16, 1872. [Boston, 1872.] 22 pp. 8° ..... *R.R., D.2.13

Note. — The best material for the history of the Boston public library is in the series of annual reports, with the Proceedings at the dedication of the Central building. A chapter in the life of George Ticknor [1012.5 2; 5023.10.2, ch. 15] throws light upon the history of its formation, and an article in Scribner's monthly [1438.1.3] epitomizes its history and its methods.

— *The railroad jubilee.* Account of the celebration commemorative of the opening of railroad communication between Boston and Canada, Sept. 17–19, 1851. Boston, 1852. 288+ pp. Map. 8°. 811.5 and 6923.3

— Reception and entertainment of the Chinese embassy. Boston, 1868. 77 pp. 8° 831.2

— Report by the commission appointed to investigate the subject of the annexation of certain neighboring cities and towns to the city of Boston. [Boston, 1873.] 131 pp. Map. 8° 5010.19

— Report of the commissioners appointed to investigate the cause and management of the great fire. Boston, 1873. xxiv, 662 pp. 8° 813.6

— *School committee.* Annual report, 1857–64, 66–74. Boston, 1858–74. Illustrated. 17 v. L. 8° ... 6924.10

— – Report on drawing. Boston, 1874. 20 pp. 41 plates. 8° 6213.11

— – *Same.* Boston, 1875. 50 pp. 40 plates. 8°. 1511.9

— *Superintendent of public schools.* Twenty-ninth semi-annual report. Boston, 1874. 236+ pp. 8°. 6924.6

— Abbott, J. Marco Paul in Boston 914.5

— Description of the Boston water works. Boston, 1848. Sm. 12° 819.3

— Drake, S. A. Old landmarks and historic personages of. Boston, 1873. 12° 5035.3

— Drake, S. G. History and antiquities of, 1630–1770. Boston, 1856. L. 8° 5010.11

— Frothingham, R. History of the siege of. Boston, 1851. 8° 812.6

— Hales, J. G. Survey of Boston and its vicinity. Boston, 1821. 12° 424.21

— Hamilton, J. W. Memorial of Jesse Lee and the old elm. Boston, 1875. 12° 617.2

— Kidder, F. History of the Boston massacre, March 5, 1870. Albany, 1870. 8° 5011.4

— Lander, S. W. Spectacles for young eyes 922.20

— Lawrence, W. R. History of the Boston dispensary. Boston, 1859. 8° 6032.1

Shelf. No.

BOSTON, *Mass., continued.*

— Loring, J. S. The hundred Boston orators, from 1770 to 1852. Boston, 1853. 8° 5022.9

Note. — Accounts of those who have publicly delivered orations; with an introduction, chiefly on the Boston massacre.

— Martin, J. G. Twenty-one years in the Boston stock market. Boston, 1856. 8° 1711.1

— Nason, E. Sir Charles Henry Frankland, baronet: or Boston in the colonial times. Albany, 1865. 8° 5013.15

— Quincy, J. Municipal history of. Boston, 1852. 8° 5011.5

— Savage, E. H. Chronological history of the Boston watch and police, 1861–65; with recollections of a Boston police officer. Boston, 1865. 12°. 5010.7

— – Police records and recollections; or, Boston by daylight and gaslight for two hundred and forty years. Boston, 1873. 8° 5013.8

— Shurtleff, N. B. Topographical and historical description of. Boston, 1871. 8° 5010.1

— Warren, J. C. The great tree on the common. Boston, 1855. 8° 411.1

— Wheildon, W. W. Siege and evacuation of. Boston, 1876. 8° 811.19

— Whiting, W. Destruction of Boston harbor. Speech against an application for leave to fill up flats in Mystic river. Boston, 1851. 8° 6923.2

See also Bunker hill, Charlestown, Copp's hill burial ground, Roxbury.

Note. — See the Lower Hall Catalogue of history, etc., p. 32, for a survey of the literature of the history of Boston.

Drake's History is the most elaborate, but it comes down only to 1770. Frothingham's Life of Joseph Warren [1010.6] and his "Siege of Boston" [812.6] will continue the story into the beginning of the revolutionary period; and a full account of the authorities for the interval 1761–76 will be found in the Bulletin for July, 1875. Lossing's Pictorial field-book of the revolution [810.17] has interest for this period, subsequent to which, the reader will best depend upon the histories of Massachusetts, like Barry's [812.5]. Quincy's Municipal history of Boston covers 1630–1830. Schouler's Massachusetts in the civil war [5012.2.2] shows Boston's part.

For the associations and history of localities, Shurtleff's description is full for the points covered; but Drake's Old landmarks covers a wider area, and is more popularly written.

— *Church of the Disciples.* Service book. Boston, 1844. vi, 183+ pp. 16° 6328.16

— – The disciples' hymn book: a collection of hymns and chants. Boston, 1844. Unpaged. 16° 6328.16

— *City hospital.* First medical and surgical report. Edited by J. N. Borland [and] D. W. Cheever. Boston, 1870. 688 pp. Illustrated. 8° 6012.24

— *English high school.* Semi-centennial anniversary. Boston, 1871. 112+ pp. Illustrated. 8° 5832.3

— *Essex Street church and society.* Memorial volume to commemorate the twenty-fifth anniversary of the installation of N. Adams. Boston, 1860. 128 pp. Portraits. 16° 1014.10

— *Female anti-slavery society.* Report, with a concise statement of events, previous and subsequent to the annual meeting of 1835. Boston, 1836. 108 pp. 12° 818.9

— *Female asylum,* Reminiscences of the. Wales, A. L. Boston, 1844. 16° 5835.6

— *Old South church and society.* Pastor's memorial. Twenty-fifth anniversary of the installation of G. W. Blagden. Boston, 1862. 118 pp. 12° ... 5817.3

— *Second church.* Our pastors' offering. A compilation from the writings of the pastors. Boston, 1845. 126+ pp. 16° 5819.11

— *Social law library.* Catalogue. 2d edition. Boston, 1849. xii, 197 pp. 8° 6135.2

— *Society for medical improvement.* Descriptive catalogue of the anatomical museum. Jackson, J. B. S. Boston, 1847. 8° 6022.3

— *Society of natural history,* Address to the. Warren, J. C. Boston, 1853. 8° 6613.9

BOSTON almanac. 1838, 40–42, 44–72. Boston [1838–72]. 33 v. 16° 5017.6

BOSTON athenæum, History of the. Quincy, J. Cambridge, 1851. 8° 811.4

BOSTON book, The. Being specimens of metropolitan literature. Boston, 1841. 352 pp. 12° 5217.2

Shelf. No.

BOSTON directory for 1872-75. Boston [1872-75]. 4 v. 8°....*R.R., E.2.5

BOSTON directory, supplement. Containing the names of persons who have made changes in business since July last. Also a list of all persons carrying on business in Charlestown, West Roxbury, Brighton, November, 1873. Boston [1873]. 178+ pp. 8°....*R.R., E.2.8

BOSTON illustrated. [Boston] 1872. 132 pp. [No title-page.] 8°.... 814.1

— *Same.* [Revised edition, with additions. Title on cover.] Boston [1875]. 136 pp. 2 maps. Sm. 4°.... 814.8

BOSTON lectures, 1872. Christianity and scepticism. Boston [1872]. vi, 291 pp. 16°.... 5816.4

BOSTON musical education society's collection of church music. Edited by B. F. Baker and I. B. Wood. 8th edition. Boston, 1845. 304 pp. Oblong 8°.... 1518.4

BOSTON pearl, The, and galaxy. Vol. 21. Boston, 1838. F°....6730.34

Note. — No. 1-12, 13-16, 17-20, 22-25, 39-41, 42-52, missing.

BOSWELL, James. Life of Samuel Johnson. Including a journal of a tour to the Hebrides. New edition with additions and notes, by J. W. Croker. London, 1831. 5 v. Portraits. Map. 8°. 5423.7

— *Same.* London, N. D. 4 v. Illustrated. 16°..1225.12

BOTANY. Burbidge, F. W. The art of botanical drawing. London [1873]. Sq. 16°.... 6217.7

— Figuier, (G.) L. The vegetable world. London, 1868. 8°.... 1521.6

— Gray, A. How plants behave. New York, 1874. Sm. 4°....1523.24

— – How plants grow; with a popular flora. New York, 1874. Sm. 4°.... 6626.7

— Grindon, L. H. Phenomena of plant life. Boston, 1866. 12°....1523.13

— Phelps, A. H. L. Botany for beginners. Hartford, 1833. 12°.... 6627.3

— *Same.* New York, 1838. 12°.... 1528.5

— Wakefield, P. An introduction to. Philadelphia, 1818. Sm. 8°.... 6626.8

See also Flowers, Medical botany, Vegetation.

BOTH sides of the street. Walker, M. S.... 913.28

BOTTA, Carlo (Giuseppe Guglielmo). Lettere. Torino, 1841. xix, 192+ pp. 16°.... 2037.2

BOTTOM of the sea, The. Sonrel, L. New York, 1872. 16°.... 1714.9

BOUCICAULT, Dion (L.), *joint author.* Foul play. *See* READE, Charles.... 724.18

BOUDOIR cabal, The. Murray, G. 3 v. in 2.... 314.11

BOUILLET, Adolphe. L'armée d'Henri V. Les bourgeois-gentilshommes de 1871. Paris, 1872. xxiv, 258+ pp. 18°.... 5526.1

BOUILLY, Jean Nicolas. Les encouragemens de la jeunesse. Paris [1830]. 2 v. Illustrated. 12°. 5537.6

BOULTON, Matthew, Life of. Smiles, S. London, 1865. 8°.... 5421.5

BOUND to rise. Alger, H., *jr*.... 935.29

BOUNTY, *ship*. Belcher, *Lady* D. The mutineers of the. London, 1870. Sm. 8°.... 1224.4

— *Same.* New York, 1871. 12°.... 435.2

— Herbert, D. Great historical mutinies. London, 1876. Sm. 8°.... 5924.2

BOURDALOUE, Louis. The preacher and the king; or, Bourdaloue in the court of Louis XIV. Bungener, L. F. Boston, 1855. 12°.... 716.4

BOURGEOIS gentilhomme, Le: comédie-ballet. Molière, J. B. P. Œuvres. Paris, 1869. 12°...5537.2.3

BOURGOIN, J. Théorie de l'ornement. Accompagné de 330 motifs d'ornements. Paris, 1873. xi, 366+ pp. 8°.... 6220.4

BOURNE, John. Catechism of the steam engine. New edition. New York, 1854. 288 pp. 12°.1526.13

BOUTWELL, George Sewall. Manual of the direct and excise tax system of the United States. Washington, 1863. x, 500 pp. 8°.... 6923.5

BOW, The, in the cloud: discourses. Briggs, G. W. Boston, 1846. 12°.... 5818.9

BOWDITCH, Henry Ingersoll. Memoir of Amos Twitchell. With an appendix, containing his addresses, etc. Boston, 1851. v, 212 pp. Portrait. 12°....1216.13

— Nat the navigator. Life of Nathaniel Bowditch. Boston, 1870. 192 pp. Illustrated. 16°.... 913.20

BOWDITCH, Nathaniel. Bowditch, H. I. Nat the navigator. Life of. Boston, 1870. 16°.... 913.20

— Bowditch, N. I. Memoir of. Boston, 1840. 4°. 1010.2

BOWDITCH, Nathaniel Ingersoll. History of the Massachusetts general hospital. Boston, 1851. xi, 442 pp. 1 plate. 8°....6012.25

— Memoir of Nathaniel Bowditch. 2d edition. Boston, 1840. 172 pp. Portraits. 4°.... 1010.2

— Suffolk surnames. Boston, 1857. 108 pp. 8°..5022.11

— *Same.* 2d edition, enlarged. Boston, 1858. xv, 383 pp. 8°....5022.17

BOWEN, Francis. Life of Baron Steuben. (*In* Sparks, J. Library of American biography)..5028.1.9

— Life of Sir William Phips. (*In* Sparks, J. Library of American biography)....5028.1.7

BOWLES, Emily. In the Camargue. [Fiction].... 723.6

BOWLES, Samuel. Across the continent: a summer's journey to the Rocky mountains, the Mormons, and the Pacific states. Springfield, 1868. xx, 452 pp. Map. 16°.... 417.6

BOWMAN, Anne. The young exiles; or, the wild tribes of the North. A tale of adventures....1118.5

BOWRING, John. Poetry of the Magyars, preceded by a sketch of the language and literature of Hungary and Transylvania. London, 1830. xvi, lxxxiii, 312+ pp. 8°.... 1622.1

BOX and Cox: a comedy. Morton, J. M. New York, N. D. 12°....1635.24

BOX tunnel, The. Reade, C. (*In* Johnson, (E.) R. Little classics).... 529.4.9

BOY farmers, The, of Elm island. Kellogg, E.... 922.12

BOY hunters, The. Reid, M.... 932.14

BOY joiner, The. Davidson, E. A. London [1874]. 4°. 1512.3

BOY slaves, The. Reid, M.... 931.1

BOY tar, The. Reid, M.... 923.26

BOY'S, The, book about Indians. Tuttle, E. B.... 915.20

BOY'S, A, kingdom; or, four years in a cave.... 933.23

BOY'S own book: a complete encyclopædia of outdoor and indoor exercises and diversions.... 916.5

BOY'S, The, own book of boats. Kingston, W. H. G. 1718.1

BOY'S, The, own volume of fact, fancy, history, and adventure. Christmas, 1863. Illustrated. Edited by the publisher [S. O. Beeton].... 912.1

BOY'S, The, playbook of science. Pepper, J. H....1524.18

BOYCE, Allen P., *joint author.* The art of lettering, and sign painter's manual. *See* LYFORD, Thomas J.... 6210.1

BOYD, Andrew Kennedy Hutchinson. Recreations of a country parson. [Essays.] Boston, 1862. 2 v. 16°....1535.16

BOYD, Mark. Social gleanings. London, 1875. xv, 340 pp. Sm. 8°.... 5613.7

BOYDELL, John. The gallery of illustrations for Shakespeare's dramatic works, reduced and re-engraved by the heliotype process. With selections from the text. Edited by J. Parker Norris. Philadelphia, 1874. 100 plates. 4°.. 5620.2

BOYER, —. Nouveau manuel complet du porcelainier, du faïencier, du potier de terre, du briquetier, du tuilier. Orné de 224 figures. Paris, 1846. 2 v. 24°. [Manuel Roret].... 6439.8

BOYER, Abel. Le dictionnaire royal, françois-anglois, et anglois-françois. Nouvelle édition, par Louis Du Mitand. Londres, 1816. 2 v. in 1. 4°....*R.R., D.3.9

BOYESEN, Hjalmar Hjorth. Gunner: a tale of Norse life.... 529.3

— A Norseman's pilgrimage.... 728.12

BOYHOOD, The, of great men. Edgar, J. G. New York, 1872. 16°.... 913.14

BOYLE, Frederick. To the Cape for diamonds. A story of digging experiences in South Africa. London, 1873. xix, 415 pp. Map. Sm. 8°... 5934.6

BOYLSTON prize dissertations. Parsons, U. Boston, 1839. 8°....6011.12

Shelf. No.

BOYNE water, The. Banim, J. 517.6
BOYNTON, Charles Brandon. History of the navy during the rebellion. Illustrated. New York, 1867. 2 v. Portraits. 8° 5012.1
BOYNTON, Henry Van Ness. Sherman's historical raid. The memoirs in the light of the record. A review based upon compilations from the war office. Cincinnati, 1875. 276 pp. 8° 5024.5
BOYS and girls in biology. Stevenson, S. H. New York, 1875. 12° 1527.17
BOYS at Chequasset. Whitney, A. D. T. 932.23
BOYS, The, at Dr. Murray's. Bradley, W. I. 934.3
BOYS, The, of Grand Pré school. De Mille, J. 932.43
BRACE, Charles Loring. The dangerous classes of New York, and twenty years' work among them. New York, 1872. iii, 448+ pp. Illustrated. 12°. 5824.1
— Home-life in Germany. New York, 1853. 443 pp. 12° 425.19
— The Norse-folk; or, a visit to the homes of Norway and Sweden. New York, 1857. 516 pp. Illustrated. 12° 426.21
— The races of the old world. New York, 1870. 540+ pp. 12° 1523.1
BRACEBRIDGE hall. Irving, W. London, 1850. 16°. 715.5
— *Same.* Philadelphia, 1871. Sm. 8° 1814.2

Note. — Sketches of a phase of English country life, two or three generations ago.

BRACHET, August. Dictionnaire étymologique de la langue française. Préface par E. Egger. 5e édition. Paris [1868]. cvii, 560+ pp. 12°.. 5537.4
BRACKENBURY, Henry. The Ashanti war. A narrative prepared from official documents. With maps and plans [etc.], by H. Cooper. Edinburgh, 1874. 2 v. 8° 5911.16
BRACKETT, Albert G. History of the United States cavalry. New York, 1865. 337 pp. Illustrated. 12° 816.5
BRADDON, Mary Elizabeth. Aurora Floyd 325.2
— Dead-sea fruit 325.11
— The doctor's wife 325.3
— Eleanor's victory 325.12
— Fenton's quest 325.14
— Henry Dunbar 325.4
— Hostages to fortune. Leipzig 316.15
— *Same.* New York 521.35
— John Marchmont's legacy 325.9
— Lady Audley's secret 325.10
— The lady's mile 325.13
— Lost for love. Leipzig 330.8
— *Same.* New York 710.35
— The Lovels of Arden 325.7
— Lucius Davoren; or, publicans and sinners. 3 v. in 2 .... 329.13
— Only a clod 325.1
— Publicans and sinners 732.13
— Run to earth 325.6
— Rupert Godwin 325.8
— Sir Jasper's tenant 325.5
— A strange world. Leipzig 330.18
— *Same.* New York 711.11
— Strangers and pilgrims. Leipzig 330.13
— *Same.* New York 731.7
— Taken at the flood. Leipzig 329.25
— *Same.* New York 731.34
— To the bitter end 532.10
BRADFORD, Alden. Biographical notices of distinguished men in New England. Boston, 1842. 464 pp. 12° 1015.3
— History of Massachusetts, 1775–89. Boston, 1825. 376 pp. 8° 811.2
— History of the federal government, for fifty years: from March, 1789, to March, 1839. Boston, 1840. 480 pp. 8° 5010.13
— New England chronology: from [its] discovery, by Cabot, in 1497, to 1820. Boston, 1843. 202 pp. 12° 817.6
BRADFORD, Samuel Dexter. Works. Boston, 1858. xii, 427 pp. Portrait. 8° 5232.1
BRADFORD, Thomas Gamaliel. A comprehensive atlas, geographical, historical and commercial. Boston [*cop.* 1835]. Illustrated. 180 pp. 4°. 5030.2

Shelf. No.

BRADLEE, Nathaniel J., *compiler.* History of the introduction of pure water into Boston. With a description of its Cochituate water works. Illustrated by maps and plans. Boston, 1868. xxi, 299+ pp. 8° .... 610.2 and 5010.18
BRADLEY, Edward. The adventures of Mr. Verdant Green, an Oxford freshman. By Cuthbert Bede [*pseud.*] 715.1
BRADLEY, Mary. The proverb series. Birds of a feather 936.30
— – Handsome is that handsome does 935.5
— – A wrong confessed is half redressed 934.4
BRADLEY, Warren Ives. (*Glance Gaylord.*) After years. A sequel to Culm rock 913.12
— The boys at Dr. Murray's 934.3
— Culm rock 913.11
— Donald Deane, and his cross 913.9
— Gay cottage 918.29
— Mr. Pendleton's cup 913.10
— Patience Hathaway 913.8
— Rainford series. Gilbert Starr and his lessons... 913.4
— – Gilbert's last summer at Rainford, and what it taught 913.6
— – Jack Arcombe 913.5
— – Will Rood's friendship 913.7
BRAGELONNE; the son of Athos. Dumas, A. (D.).. 511.8
BRAGGADOCIO. Tuthill, L. C. 915.24
BRAIM, Thomas Henry. New homes: the rise, progress, present position, and future prospects of the Australian colonies and New Zealand. Illustrated. London, 1870. 411 pp. 12° 5934.10
BRAIN. Clarke, E. H. The building of a. Boston, 1874. 16° 5837.4
— Carpenter, W. B. Unconscious action of the. (*In* Estes, D. Half-hour recreations in popular science) 6813.7
BRAINERD, David, Life of. Peabody, W. B. O. (*In* Sparks, J. Library of American biography)..5028.1.8
BRAITHWAITE, William and John, *editors.* Retrospect of practical medicine and surgery. Part 1–4, 6–54, 63–66. New York, 1813–73. 33 v. 8°. 6010.2
BRAKE up. Adams, W. T. 925.17
BRAKESPEARE. A novel. Lawrence, G. A. 711.6
BRAMLEIGHS, The, of Bishop's folly. Lever, C. (J.). 332.14
BRANDE, William Thomas, and Cox, George William, *editors.* Dictionary of science, literature, and art. New edition. London, 1872. 3 v. 8°....*R.R., E.3.6
BRANDT, Joseph (*Thayendanegea*), Life of. Stone, W. L. Albany, 1865. 2 v. 8° 5022.4
BRANTÔME, Pierre de Bourdeilles, *seigneur* de. *See* MÉRIMÉE, P. Portraits historiques et littéraires. Paris, 1874. 18° 5527.14
BRASSEY, Thomas. Work and wages practically illustrated. 2d edition. London, 1872. xvi, 296 pp. Sm. 8° 6413.2
— *Same.* New York, 1872. Sm. 8° 5823.1
— Life and labours of. Helps, *Sir* A. London, 1872. Sm. 8° 5426.6
BRASSFOUNDER'S, The, manual. Graham, W. London, 1870. 12° 1716.2
BRAUN, Julius. On the curative effects of baths and waters, being a handbook to the Spas of Europe. Including a chapter on the treatment of phthisis by baths and climate by Dr. Rohden. An abridged translation [by Miss F. E. Bunnètt], with notes edited by H. Weber. London, 1875. xvi, 658 pp. 8° 6032.4
BRAUT, Die, von Messina. Schiller, (J. C.) F. von. Werke. Stuttgart, 1865. 8° 5734.1.6
BRAVE and bold. Alger, H., *jr.* 933.4
BRAVE and bold series. *See* ALGER, Horatio, *jr.*
BRAVE lady, A. Craik, D. (M.) 323.20
BRAVE old salt. Adams, W. T. 924.3
BRAVO, The. Cooper, J. F. 525.30
BRAY, Anna Eliza. Life of Thomas Stothard. With illustrations. London, 1851. xxiv, 246 pp. Portrait. 4° 6213.8
BRAY, Charles. Manual of anthropology, or science of man, based on modern research. London, 1871. xxiii [xxi], 358 pp. Sm. 8° 6616.7

Shelf. No.

BRAZIL. Agassiz, L. (J. R.) and E. C. Journey in. Boston, 1868. 8° 422.8

— Codman, J. Ten months in. New York, 1872. 16° 5916.4

— Hartt, C. F. Geology and physical geography of. Boston, 1870. 8° 5033.1

— Fletcher, J. C., and Kidder, D. P. Brazil and the Brazilians. Boston, 1868. 8° 411.5

— Stewart, C. S. Brazil and La Plata: the personal record of a cruise. New York, 1856. 12° 425.18

Note. — The most noteworthy scientific travels of recent years have been Agassiz's general account of the Thayer expedition of 1865-66, reviewed in Atlantic monthly, March, 1868; in Saturday review, or Living age, no. 1242. See also preliminary papers on the Amazonian region in the Atlantic monthly, March and July, 1866. Hartt's book is a special treatise on the geology and physical geography as observed by that expedition.

Another exploration was conducted in 1867, under the auspices of the Smithsonian institution, and Prof. Orton has furnished an account of their descent of the Amazon from its sources in his "Andes and the Amazon" [5933.13], and the Messrs. Myers, another of their explorations of the northern tributary, the Rio Negro, in their "Life and nature under the tropics."

The more important English travellers of late have been Wallace on the Amazon, 1852, and his companion, Bates, who after a much longer sojourn, published, in 1863, his excellent Naturalist on the Amazons [5935 2].

The most popular comprehensive book on Brazil is perhaps that by Fletcher and Kidder, both protestant missionaries. Codman's book is of use chiefly upon the commercial character of the country, and disagrees with the conclusions of Fletcher and Kidder.

See also popular papers in Harper's monthly, vols. 7, 10, 11 and 39, and Hours at home, Aug., 1867.

BREAD-AND-CHEESE and kisses. Farjeon, B. L. 531.26

BREAD and oranges. Warner, S. 1117.4

BREAD upon the waters. Craik, D. (M.) 330.20

BREAKFAST, luncheon and tea. [Cook book.] Terhune, M. V. New York, 1875. 12° 1533.2

BREAKING a butterfly. Lawrence, G. A. 315.20

BREAKING away. Adams, W. T. 924.24

BREAST, Treatise on the diseases of the. Velpeau, A. A. L. M. London, 1856. 8° 6013.21

BREMEN lectures, The, on fundamental, living, religious questions. By various eminent European divines. Translated from the original German, by D. Heagle. With an introduction, by A. Hovey. Boston, 1871. 308 pp. 12° 1536.11

BREMER, Fredrika. Father and daughter. Translated by Mary Howitt 524.26

— The H— family: Trälinnan; Axel and Anna; and other tales. Translated by Mary Howitt 511.5

— Hertha. Translated by Mary Howitt 536.8

— The homes of the New World; impressions of America. Translated by Mary Howitt. New York, 1853. 2 v. 12° 414.24

— Life in Sweden. The president's daughters. Translated by Mary Howitt. New York, 1870. 2 v. in 1. 8° 511.3

— The neighbours. And other tales. Translated by Mary Howitt 716.3

Note. — The novels give hearty genial representations of the well-to-do and professional classes in the social life of Sweden.

BRENDA, *pseud.* "Nothing to nobody" 1118.2

BRESCIANI, Antonio. Lionello. A sequel to The Jew of Verona 714.21

BRESSANT. Hawthorne, J. 737.13

BREWER, Ebenezer Cobham. Dictionary of phrase and fable. 3d edition. London [1875]. xii, 983 pp. 8° .... *R.R., F.3.13

BREWER, Thomas Mayo, *joint author.* History of North American birds. *See* BAIRD, Spencer Fullerton 6611.1

BREWSTER, Anne M. H. Compensation or always a future 716.34

BREWSTER, *Sir* David. The kaleidoscope, its history, theory, and construction. 3d edition. With engravings and plate. London, 1870. vi, 189 pp. Portrait. Sm. 8° 6816.1

— Letters on natural magic. New York, 1870. 314 [308] pp. Illustrated. 16° 1519.4

— Life of Sir Isaac Newton. New York [1831]. 323 pp. Portrait. 16° 1028.1

— Nouveau manuel de magie naturelle et amusante. Orné de figures. Paris, 1839. 286+ pp. 24°. [Manuel Roret] 6419.2

BREWSTER, Osmyn. *See* CROCKER, Uriel.

BRIC-À-BRAC hunter, The. Hall, H. B. Philadelphia [London], 1875. Sm. 8° 6214.4

BRIC-À-BRAC series. *See* STODDARD, Richard Henry, *editor.*

BRICKS. Boyer, —. Nouveau manuel complet du briquetier. Paris, 1846. 2 v. 24° 6439.8

— Dobson, E. Treatise on the manufacture of. London, 1868. 12° 1716.25

BRIDAL eve, The. Southworth, E. D. E. N. 727.10

BRIDE, The, of Lammermoor. Scott, *Sir* W. Boston. 523.12

— *Same.* Leipzig 324.16

BRIDE, The, of Lewellyn. Southworth, E. D. E. N. 727.2

BRIDE'S, The, fate. Southworth, E. D. E. N. 727.16

BRIDES and bridals. [Wedding customs of different times.] Jeaffreson, J. C. London, 1872. 2 v. 8°. 5822.6

BRIDGES, Rudimentary treatise on tubular and other iron girder. Dempsey, G. D. London, 1865. 12° 1716.17

BRIDGMAN, Thomas, *compiler.* Epitaphs from Copp's hill burial ground, Boston. With notes. Boston, 1851. xxiii, 252+ pp. Illustrated. 12°. 5016.5

— Inscriptions on the grave stones of Northampton, and other towns in the valley of the Connecticut. With brief annals of Northampton. With portraits. Northampton, 1850. 227 pp. Illustrated. 12° 5016.6

BRIEF biographies of European public men. *See* HIGGINSON, Thomas Wentworth, *editor.*

BRIGADIER Frederick. A novel. Erckmann, É., and Chatrian, A. 721.13

BRIGAND, The: a drama. Planché, J. R. New York, N. D. 12° 1635.4

BRIGGS, George Ware. The bow in the cloud. Fifteen discourses. 2d edition. Boston, 1846. 216 pp. 12° 5818.9

BRIGHAM, Charles Brooks. Diabetes mellitus. Boston, 1868. 55 pp. 8° 6023.20

BRIGHAM, William Tufts. Cast catalogue of antique sculpture. With an introduction to the study of ornament. Boston, 1874. iv, 200 pp. Photographs. 4° 6210.7

BRIGHT, Matilda A. (*Lyndon.*) Oxley 528.4

BRILL, Francis. Farm-gardening and seed-growing. New York [*cop.* 1872]. 151 pp. 12° 6226.6

BRINDLEY, James, Life of. Smiles, S. Lives of the engineers. London, 1874. Sm. 8° 5421.4.1

BRINLEY, Francis. Life of William T. Porter. New York, 1860. vii, 273 pp. 12° 1215.2

BRINTON, Daniel Garrison. The myths of the new world. A treatise on the symbolism and mythology of the red race of America. 2d edition revised. New York, 1876. viii, 331+ pp. 8°. 5924.7

BRISTED, Charles Astor. Five years in an English university [Cambridge]. 3d edition, revised. New York, 1873. 572 [570] pp. 12° 5835.1

BRITANNICUS: tragédie. Racine, J. de. Théâtre complet. Paris, 1870. 12° 5537.3

BRITISH AMERICA. Saskatchewan and the Rocky mountains. Carnegie, J., *earl of Southesk.* Edinburgh, 1875. 8° 5931.16

BRITISH constitution, The. Brougham, H., *lord.* Works. Edinburgh, 1872. 16° 5614.4.11

BRITISH museum, *London.* Catalogue of prints and drawings in the museum. Division I. Political and personal satires. Vol. II. June, 1689–1733. [London] 1873. 8° 6131.1

— Roman medallions in the British museum. By Herbert A. Grueber. Edited by Reginald Stuart Poole. London, 1874. 66 plates. [Catalogues of the Roman coins in the British museum.] 8°. 6131.2

— Cowtan, R. Memories of the. London, 1872. 8°. 6133.2

— Edwards, E. Lives of the founders of the. London, 1870. 8° 6133.1

— Nichols, T. Handbook for readers at the. London, 1866. 16° 6136.4

BRITISH poets, The. *See* CHILD, Francis James, *editor.* 5628.5

BRITISH rural sports. Walsh, J. H. London, 1872. Sq. 16° 6414.1

BRITTANY, *France.* A farmer's vacation. Waring, G. E., *jr.* Boston, 1876. 8° 5933.11

Shelf. No.

BROCK, *Mrs.* Carey. Sunday echoes in weekday hours. A tale illustrative of the church catechism. London, 1868. viii, 413 pp. Sm. 8°.. 911.2
BROCK, Sallie A. Kenneth, my king. A novel.... 735.15
BROCK, William. Biographical sketch of Sir Henry Havelock. Leipzig, 1858. xii, 282 pp. Map. Sq. 16°.............................. 1237.3
BRODIE, *Sir* Benjamin Collins. Autobiography. 2d edition. London, 1865. 187+ pp. 16° 5428.3
— Observations on the diseases of the joints. With alterations and additions. From the 4th London edition. Boston, 1842. 343 pp. 8°..........6023.16
BRODRIBB, William Jackson, *joint author.* Pliny's letters. *See* CHURCH, Alfred................6116.12
BROKEN chains. Werner, E.................... 732.36
BROKEN lights: an inquiry into the present condition and future prospects of religious faith. Cobbe, F. P. Boston, 1864. 16°.................. 1526.8
BROKEN to harness. Yates, E.................. 318.19
BROMIDE of potassium, Physiological action of. Amory, H. (*In* Massachusetts medical society. Publications)........................... 6021.4
BRONCHITIS. Green, H. Treatise on. New York, 1846. L. 8°............................. 6021.2
— Slade, D. D. Bronchitis and its consequences. (*In* Massachusetts medical society. Publications)................................ 6021.4
BRONTÉ, Anne. (*Acton Bell.*) Agnes Grey. *See* BRONTÉ, Emily (Jane)................ 321.24
— The tenant of Wildfell hall................. 738.9
BRONTÉ, Charlotte. (*Currer Bell.*) Jane Eyre. Leipzig.................................. 321.23
— *Same.* New York.......................... 735.29
— The professor............................. 321.20
— Shirley. Leipzig.......................... 321.22
— *Same.* London........................... 728.8
— Villette.................................. 321.21
— Life of. Gaskell, E. C. Leipzig, 1857. 2 v. in 1. Sq. 16°.............................1238.11
— *Same.* New York, 1857. 2 v. 12°..........1225.29
— *Same.* London, 1871. 16°................. 1225.9
BRONTÉ, Emily (Jane). (*Ellis Bell.*) Wuthering heights. And Agnes Grey. By Acton Bell ... 321.24

Note.—For an account of the Bronté novels, besides Mrs. Gaskell's Life, see Peter Bayne's Essays [1226.15.2].

BROOKE, Stopford Augustus. Christ in modern life. Sermons. New York, 1872. viii, 408 pp. Sm. 8°.................................. 5814.9
— Freedom in the church of England. Sermons suggested by the Voysey judgment. 2d edition. London, 1871. vi, 109+ pp. 16°........... 5816.9
— Life and letters of Frederick W. Robertson. Boston, 1865. 2 v. Portrait. 12°.......... 1225.7
— Sermons preached in St. James's chapel, York street, London. Boston, 1869. viii, 323 pp. Sm. 8°..................................... 5815.4
BROOKES, The, of Bridlemere. Melville, G. J. W. 321.19
BROOKLINE, *Mass.* Proceedings at the dedication of the town hall, Feb. 22, 1873. Brookline, 1873. 64 pp. L. 8°.......................5011.12
BROOKLINE, Jamaica Plain, and West Roxbury directory for 1873-74. Boston, 1873. 174+ pp. Map. 8°............................*R.R., E.2.9
BROOKS, Charles. Family prayer book, and private manual: added forms for religious societies and schools. With a collection of hymns. New edition. Boston, 1853. 268 [366] pp. 12°...5815.18
— History of Medford, Mass., 1630-1855. Boston, 1855. viii, 576 pp. Illustrated. Portrait. 8°.5013.16
BROOKS, (Charles) Shirley. Aspen court....... 538.7
— The silver cord 310.6
— Sooner or later............................ 310.5
BROOKS, Frederick. Sermons. Boston, 1876. v, 299 pp. Portrait. 16°.......................6325.16
BROOKS, James. A seven months' run, up, and down, and around the world. New York, 1872. xiv, 375 pp. Map. Sm. 8°........... 423.12
BROOKS, Maria Gowen. Zóphiël; or, the bride of seven. [Poem.] Boston, 1833. viii, 261 pp. 16°.................................... 1618.3

Shelf. No.

BROOKSVILLE, *Maine*, History of. Wheeler, G. A. Bangor, 1875. 8°.......................... 813.2
BROUGHAM, Henry, *lord.* Works. Edinburgh, 1872. 11 v. 2 plates. Portrait. Fac-simile. 16°... 5614.4

Contents.—Vol. I. Lives of philosophers of the time of George III. II. Men of letters of the time of George III. III-V. Statesmen of the time of George III and IV. VI. Natural theology; Dialogues on instinct; Observations on the structure of the cells of bees; Fossil osteology. VII. Dissertations and addresses—rhetorical and literary. VIII. Dissertations—historical and political. IX, X. Speeches. XI. The British constitution.

— Life and times, written by himself. New York, 1871, 72. 3 v. Fac-simile. 12°............ 5425.2
BROUGHAM, John. A basket of chips. New York, 1855. 408 pp. Wood-cut. 12°.............1522.13
— The great tragic revival: [a drama]. New York, N. D. 10 pp. 12°.................... 1635.5
— The musard ball: an extravaganza. New York, N. D. 12 pp. 12°......................... 1635.5
— Neptune's defeat: [a comedy]. New York, N. D. 24 pp. 12°.............................. 1635.5
— Shakespeare's dream: an historic pageant. New York, N. D. 7 pp. 12°.................. 1635.5
— Take care of little Charley: a farce. New York, N. D. 14 pp. 12°........................ 1635.5
BROUGHT to the front. Kellogg, E............... 938.10
BROUGHTON, Rhoda. Cometh up as a flower. An autobiography.............................. 311.30
— Nancy. Leipzig. 2 v. 329.14
— *Same.* New York........................... 725.34
— Not wisely, but too well 310.2
— Red as a rose is she 310.1
— Tales for Christmas eve...................... 319.8
BROWN, Charles Brockden. Prescott, W. H. Biographical and critical essays. London, 1856. 16°.. 1537.8
— *Same.* Philadelphia, 1875. 12°..............5237.3
— Sparks, J. Library of American biography....5028.1.1

Note.—See Allibone and the paper on early American novelists in the Atlantic monthly, April, 1876.

BROWN, Henry T. Five hundred and seven mechanical movements, including many never before published, and several which have only recently come into use. New York, 1871. 122 pp. Illustrated. Sm. 4°..........................1525.16
BROWN, John. The Northern courts; containing memoirs of the sovereigns of Sweden and Denmark, since 1766. London, 1818. 2 v. Portrait. 8°................................. 5713.1
BROWN, John, *M. D.* Horæ subsecivæ. Rab and his friends and other papers. Leipzig, 1862. vii, 340+ pp. Sq. 16°.................... 311.29
— Marjorie Fleming. Boston, 1864. 47 pp. 12°. 916.32
— *Same.* (*In* Johnson, (E.) R. Little classics)..529.4.10
— Rab and his friends. (*In* Johnson, (E.) R. Little classics)....................................529.4.4
— Spare hours. Boston, 1873. 2 v. Portrait and illustrations. Sm. 8°......................... 537.5

Note.—"Spare hours" contains nearly the same matter as "Horæ subsecivæ."

BROWN, Richard. Domestic architecture. 63 plates. London [1842]. xii, 342 pp. Portrait. 4°... 6220.3
BROWN, Samuel Gilman. Life of Rufus Choate. 2d edition. Boston, 1870. xvi, 468 pp. Portrait. Sm. 8°..................................... 5025.1
BROWN, Thomas. On the credibility of miracles. (*In* Noyes, G. R. Collection of theological essays)....................................6325.12
BROWN, William Wells. The rising son; or the antecedents and advancement of the colored race. Boston, 1874. 552+ pp. Portrait. 8°...... 814.6
BROWN-SÉQUARD, Charles Édouard. Lectures on the physiology and pathology of the central nervous system. Philadelphia, 1860. xii, 276 pp. 8°.......................................6022.14
BROWNE, Charles Farrar. The genial showman. Reminiscences of Artemus Ward. Hingston, E. P. New York, 1870. 8°.................... 1211.9
BROWNE, Daniel Jay. The trees of America, native and foreign. Illustrated. New York, 1846. xii, 520 pp. L. 8°........................... 6621.1

Shelf. No.

BROWNE, John Ross. Adventures in the Apache country: a tour through Arizona and Sonora, with notes on the silver regions of Nevada. Illustrated. New York, 1871. 535 pp. 12° .. 415.13

— An American family in Germany. Illustrated. New York, 1871. 381 pp. 12° 424.18

— Crusoe's island: a ramble in the footsteps of Alexander Selkirk. With sketches of adventure in California and Washoe. New York, 1872. 436 pp. Map and illustrations. 12° 415.12

— The land of Thor. Illustrated. New York, 1870. 542 pp. 12° 424.17

— Report on the mineral resources of the states and territories west of the Rocky mountains. *See* UNITED STATES. *Department of the treasury* ... 6631.6

BROWNE, *Sir* Thomas. Religio medici and other papers. Boston, 1872. xviii, 440 pp. Portrait. 16° 5617.16

BROWNING, Elizabeth Barrett. Poems. From the last London edition, corrected by the author. New York, 1862. 4 v. 16° 1612.4

Contents. — Vol. I. A drama of exile; The seraphim; Prometheus bound, from the Greek of Æschylus; Lament for Adonis, from the Greek of Bion; Vision of poets; The poet's vow; The romaunt of Margret; Isobel's child; The romaunt of the page; The lay of the brown rosary; Romance of the Ganges; Rhyme of the duchess May; Miscellaneous. II. Miscellaneous; Sonnets; Casa Guida windows. III. Aurora Leigh; Miscellaneous. IV. Memorial, by T. Tilton; Last poems; Translations.

— Aurora Leigh. [Poem.] Leipzig, 1872. 334 pp. Sq. 16° 1614.15

— A selection from [her] poetry. Copyright edition. Leipzig, 1872. 318 pp. Sq. 16° 1613.21

Note. — See Stedman's Victorian poets [1837.1]; Smiles's Brief biographies [1024.13]; Bayne's Essays [1226.15.1]; Chorley's Reminiscences in the Bric-à-brac series [1828.2]; Kate Field's paper on English authors in Florence, in the Atlantic monthly, Dec., 1864; Allibone's Dictionary, etc.

BROWNING, Robert. Poetical works. With portrait. Leipzig, 1872. 2 v. in 1. Sq. 16° 1613.13

Contents. — A soul's tragedy; Luria; Christmas-eve and Easter-day; Men and women; In a balcony; Dramatis personæ; Dramatic romances.

— Fifine at the fair, and other poems. Boston, 1872. 280+ pp. 16° 1615.22

— Red cotton night-cap country; or, turf and towers. [Poems.] Boston, 1873. 220 pp. 12° 1617.4

Note. — See Smiles's Brief biographies [1024.13]; Stedman's Victorian poets [1837.1]; Allibone's Dictionary, etc.

BROWNLOW, William Gannaway. Sketches of the rise, progress, and decline of secession. Philadelphia, 1862. 458 pp. Portrait. 12° 815.3

BROWNLOWS. Oliphant, M. (O. W.) 531.27

BRUCE, Charles, *editor.* The book of adventure and peril: a record of heroism and endurance on sea and land. Illustrated. London, 1875. vii, 600 pp. Sm. 8° 426.23

BRUCE, James, *earl of Elgin.* Narrative of [his] mission to China and Japan. Oliphant, L. New York, 1860. 8° 421.2

BRUCE, James, *Scottish traveller.* Travels. *See* ENGLISH explorers. London, 1875. Sm. 8° 5927.9

BRUHNS, Carl, *editor.* Life of Alexander von Humboldt. Compiled by J. Löwenberg, R. Avé-Lallemant, and A. Dove. Translated from the German by J. and C. Lassell. With portrait[s]. London, 1873. 2 v. 8° 5723.1

BRUIN: the grand bear hunt. Reid, M............ 037.22

BRUN, Friederike (Sophie Christiana). Römisches Leben. Leipzig, 1833. 2 v. 2 plates. 16° .. 2027.2

BRUNEL, Isambard. Life of Isambard Kingdom Brunel, civil engineer. London, 1870. xxviii, 568 pp. Portrait. 8° ....1221.7 and 5422.7

BRUNEL, Isambard Kingdom, Life of. Brunel, I. London, 1870. 8° ....1221.7 and 5422.7

BRUNO. Abbott, J. Harper's story books......... 936.1.1

BRUSH, George Jarvis, *joint author.* A system of mineralogy. *See* DANA, James Dwight........ 6630.2

BRUYÈRE, Jean de la. Les caractères [de Théophraste, avec les mœurs de ce siècle]. Paris, 1816. 3 v. Portrait. 12° 5537.7

Shelf. No

BRYANT, William Cullen. Letters from the East. New York, 1869. 256 pp. Illustrated. 12° .. 424.9

— Letters of a traveller; or, notes of things seen in Europe and America. New York, 1870. 442 pp. Portrait. 12° .... 5915.

— Orations and addresses. New York, 1873. 393+ pp. Portrait. 12° .... 1926.

— Poems. New York, 1871. 363 pp. Sm. 12° ... 1616.

— *editor.* Picturesque America; or, the land we live in. New York [*cop.* 1872, 73]. 2 v. 4° 5030.9

— *translator.* The Iliad of Homer. Translated into English blank verse. *See* HOMERUS 6111.3

— — The Odyssey of Homer. Translated into English blank verse. *See* HOMERUS 6111.1

BRYCE, James. The holy Roman empire. 4th edition. London, 1873. xxvii, 479 pp. Sm. 8° ..5814.1

BUBBLES from the Brunnen of Nassau. Head, *Sir* F. B. London, 1866. 12° .... 425.

BUCCANEER, The. Hall, A. M. 727.2

BUCHAN, William. Domestic medicine. Boston, 1809. 629+ pp. 8° .... 6034.

BUCHANAN, Claudius, Life and writings of. Pearson, H. Boston, 1818. 12° 1227.8

BUCHANAN, James. Mr. Buchanan's administration on the eve of the rebellion. New York, 1866. 296 pp. 8° 813.8

BUCHANAN, Robert. The land of Lorne, including the cruise of the "Tern" to the outer Hebrides. London, 1871. 2 v. 12° 424.1

— Life and adventures of John James Audubon, the naturalist. From materials supplied by his widow. 3d edition. London, 1869. viii, 366 pp. Portraits. 8° .... 5023.

— Master-spirits. London, 1873. 349+ pp. 8° .. 6134.

BUCHHEIM, Charles A. Deutsche Lyrik. With notes and a literary introduction. London, 1875. xx, 415 pp. Portrait. Sm. 8° .... 2028.

BÜCHNER, (Friedrich Carl Christian) Ludwig. *See* BUECHNER, (Friedrich Carl Christian) Ludwig.

BUCKINGHAM, Joseph Tinker. Annals of the Massachusetts charitable mechanic association. 432 pp. Boston, 1853. 8° .... 6914.

— Specimens of newspaper literature: with personal memoirs, anecdotes, and reminiscences. Boston, 1850. 2 v. Portraits. 12° .... 1913.

BUCKLAND, Frank. Log-book of a fisherman and zoologist. Illustrated. London, 1875. xiv, 407+ pp. 8° 6614.1

BUCKLE, Henry Thomas. Essays. With a biographical sketch of the author. New York, 1869. 209 pp. 12° 1915.3

— Miscellaneous and posthumous works. Edited with a biographical notice by H. Taylor. London, 1872. 3 v. 8° .... 5633.

Contents. — Vol. I. Miscellaneous works published during the author's lifetime. II, III. Common-place books.

— History of civilization in England. New edition. London, 1872. 3 v. 16° .... 5417.

BUCKMINSTER, Joseph, Memoirs of. Lee, E. B. Boston, 1849. 12° 5025.1

— *Same.* 2d edition. Boston, 1851. 12° .... 1213.

BUCKMINSTER, Joseph Stevens. Sermons. Boston, 1829. 358 pp. 8° 6322.3

— Works; with memoirs of his life [by S. C. Thacher]. Boston, 1839. 2 v. 12°. 5814.16 and 6325.1

— Memoirs of. Lee, E. B. Boston, 1849. 12° ...5025.1

— *Same.* 2d edition. Boston, 1851. 12° .... 1213.

BUDDHISM. Eitel, E. J. Buddhism: its historical, theoretical and popular aspects. London, 1873. 8° .... 5613.

— Mueller, (F.) M. Lectures on the science of religion; with a paper on Buddhist nihilism, and a translation of the Dhammapada or "Path of virtue." New York, 1872. Sm. 8° .... 5616.

Note. — See also Clarke's "Ten great religions" [1523.2], and histories of India in general.

BUECHNER, (Friedrich Carl Christian) Ludwig. Man in the past, present and future. From the German, by W. S. Dallas. London, 1872. xv, 363 pp. 8° .... 6613.

Shelf. No.

BUEL, Jesse. The farmer's companion. Boston, 1839. 303 pp. 12° ... 1527.13
BUFFALO land. Webb, W. E. Cincinnati, 1872. 8°. 5032.2
BUFFETS. Doe, C. H. Boston, 1875. 8° ... 721.9
BUGBEE, James M. Account of the battle of Bunker hill. *See* HOLMES, O. W., and others. Memorial. Bunker hill ... 810.8
— Celebration of the centennial anniversary of Bunker hill. *See* BOSTON, *Mass*. ... 810.10
— Fires and fire departments. Reprinted from "The North American review" for July, 1873. Boston, 1873. 44 pp. 8° ... 1711.2
BUILDING. Allen, C. B. Cottage building. London, 1870. 12° ... 1715.28
— Burn, R. S. Building construction; showing the employment of timber, lead, and iron work. New York [Glasgow, 1874]. 2 v. 16° ... 6228.1
— Dobson, E. Rudiments of the art of. London, 1871. 12° ... 1716.26
— Monckton, J. H. The national builder. New York [*cop.* 1872]. 4° ... 6620.1
— Richardson, C. J. House-building. New York, 1873. Sm. 8° ... 6226.3
— Skillings, D. N., and Flint, D. B. Illustrated catalogue of portable sectional buildings. New York [*cop.* 1862]. 4° ... 6222.1

See also Architecture, Dwelling-houses.

BULFINCH, Thomas. Age of chivalry; or legends of King Arthur. Boston, 1871. 414 [412] pp. Illustrated. 12° ... 824.1
— Age of fable; or beauties of mythology. Boston, 1871. 488 pp. Illustrated. 12° ... 1523.3
— The boy inventor; a memoir of Matthew Edwards. Boston, 1860. 109 pp. 1 plate. Portrait. 12°. 1226.13
— Legends of Charlemagne; or romance of the middle ages. Boston, 1871. xx, 373 pp. Illustrated. Sm. 8° ... 824.2
BULKLEY, C. H. A. Niagara. A poem. New York, 1848. 191+ pp. 12° ... 1625.14
BULLEN, Anne. *See* ANNE BOLEYN.
BULWER, *Sir* Henry Lytton (Earle). Historical characters: Talleyrand; Cobbett; Mackintosh; Canning. Leipzig, 1868. 2 v. in 1. Sq. 16°. 1238.14
— Life of Henry John Temple, viscount Palmerston: with selections from his diaries and correspondence. Leipzig, 1871, 74. 3 v. in 2. Sq. 16°. 1238.15
BULWER-LYTTON, Edward (George Earle) Lytton, *lord Lytton*. Dramatic works. Leipzig, 1860. 2 v. in 1. Sq. 16° ... 1614.5

Contents. — Richelieu; Money; The duchess de la Vallière; The lady of Lyons; Not so bad as we seem.

— Miscellaneous prose works. Leipzig, 1868. 4 v. in 2. Sq. 16° ... 336.5

Contents. — Vol. I. The reign of terror: its causes and results; Oliver Goldsmith; Charles Lamb and some of his companions; Gray's works; Sir Thomas Browne; Pitt and Fox; Pym *versus* Falkland; Life of Schiller. II. Essays written in youth; The influence of love upon literature and real life.

— Alice ... 336.10

Note. — A continuation of "Ernest Maltravers."

— Athens: its rise and fall. [A history.] Leipzig, 1843. 2 v. in 1. Sq. 16° ... 828.10
— Calderon, the courtier. A tale ... 5618.5
— Caxtoniana: a series of essays on life, literature, and manners. Leipzig, 1864. 2 v. in 1. Sq. 16°. 1918.2
— The Caxtons ... 336.16
— The coming race. Leipzig ... 329.8
— *Same.* New York ... 5617.13

Note. — A fiction concerning a people inhabiting the interior of the globe, forming a satire on current views on politics and science.

— Devereux ... 336.3

Note. — Bolingbroke and others of Queen Anne's time.

— The disowned ... 336.11
— Ernest Maltravers ... 336.18

Note. — The story is continued in "Alice."

— Eugene Aram ... 336.9

Note. — A tale founded on the career of a remarkable man of this name, executed in England for murder in 1759. Compare Hood's poem [1627.1].

5

Shelf. No.

BULWER-LYTTON, Edward (G. E.) L., *continued.*
— Eva; The ill-omened marriage, other tales and poems; and The pilgrims of the Rhine ... 336.15
— Godolphin and Falkland ... 336.4
— Harold, the last of the Saxon kings ... 336.19

Note. — An historical romance of William the conqueror's time. Kingsley's "Hereward the Wake" [326.15] can be read in connection.

— The house and the brain. (*In* Johnson, (E.) R. Little classics) ... 529.4.2
— Kenelm Chillingly. Leipzig. 4 v. in 2 ... 319.10
— *Same.* New York ... 5633.3
— King Arthur. [Poem.] Leipzig, 1849. 2 v. in 1. Sq. 16° ... 1614.8
— The lady of Lyons. [Drama.] New York, N. D. 61 [57] pp. 12° ... 1635.21
— The last days of Pompeii. [Historical fiction]. 336.13
— The last of the barons ... 336.20

Note. — An historical tale concerning Warwick the king-maker, in the reigns of Henry VI and Edward IV, fifteenth century.

— Leila; or, the siege of Granada ... 532.11
— The lost tales of Miletus. [Poems.] Leipzig, 1866. xiv, 264+ pp. Sq. 16° ... 1614.7
— Lucretia: or, the children of night ... 336.14
— The maid of Malines. (*In* Johnson, (E.) R. Little classics) ... 529.4.6
— My novel. 4 v. in 2 ... 336.17
— The new Timon. A poetical romance. And St. Stephen's. A poem. Leipzig, 1860. 298+ pp. Sq. 16° ... 1614.6

Note. — The new Timon is a satire in part on contemporaries.

— Night and morning ... 336.8
— The odes and epodes of Horace. A metrical translation, with introduction and commentaries. *See* HORATIUS FLACCUS, Quintus ... 1613.7
— The Parisians. Leipzig. 4 v. in 2 ... 329.21
— *Same.* New York ... 734.16 and 5533.1
— Paul Clifford ... 336.2
— Pausanias the Spartan. An unfinished historical romance. Edited by his son. Leipzig ... 336.20
— *Same.* New York ... 733.19
— Pelham ... 336.7
— Rienzi. Leipzig ... 336.1
— *Same.* New York ... 5536.11

Note. — Italian history, fourteenth century.

— Speeches, now first collected. With some of his political writings hitherto unpublished, and a prefatory memoir by his son. Edinburgh, 1874. 2 v. 8° ... 5633.3
— A strange story ... 336.12
— What will he do with it? 4 v. in 2 ... 336.21
— Zanoni ... 336.6

Note. — Time of first French revolution.

BULWER-LYTTON, (Edward) Robert, *lord Lytton*. (*Owen Meredith.*) Fables in song. Boston, 1874. 332 pp. 16° ... 1617.8
— *Same.* Leipzig, 1874. 2 v. in 1. Sq. 16° ... 1614.16
— Poems. Selected and revised by the author. Leipzig, 1869. 2 v. in 1. Sq. 16° ... 1613.3
— Lucile. Boston, 1872. iv, 251 pp. Sq. 16° ... 1616.2
BUMSTEAD, Freeman Josiah. The pathology and treatment of venereal diseases: including the results of recent investigations upon the subject. With illustrations. Philadelphia, 1861. xii, 686 [670] pp. 8° ... 6022.7
BUMSTEAD, John. On the wing. A book for sportsmen. With illustrations. Boston, 1871. 274 pp. 16° ... 1516.4
BUNGAY, George W. Crayon sketches and off-hand takings, of distinguished American statesmen, orators, divines, essayists, editors, poets, and philanthropists. Boston, 1852. 156 pp. 16°. 1516.24
BUNGENER, Laurence Louis Felix. Louis XV and his times; or, the priest and the Huguenot. From the French. Boston, 1874. 308 [298] pp. 1 plate. [Historical series.] 12° ... 627.4

Shelf. No.

BUNGENER, Laurence Louis Felix, *continued.*
— The preacher and the king; or, Bourdaloue in the court of Louis XIV. From the French. With an introduction, by G. Potts. New edition, with a likeness and a biographical sketch of the author. Boston, 1855. 338 pp. 12° 716.4
BUNKER hill, Battle of. Celebration of the centennial anniversary of the. *See* BOSTON, *Mass.*... 810.10
— Coolidge, G. A. Brochure of Bunker hill. Boston, 1875. Oblong 16° 819.5
— Drake, S. A. Bunker hill. Boston, 1875. 8°.. 811.13
— – General Israel Putnam, the commander at Bunker hill. Boston, 1875. 8° 1011.8
— Ellis, G. E. History of the battle of Bunker's hill. Boston, 1875. 8°.................... 811.1
— Frothingham, R. The centennial: battle of Bunker hill. Boston, 1875. 16° 618.3
— – History of the battle, and an account of the monument. Boston, 1851. 8°.............. 812.6
— Holmes, O. W., and others. Memorial. Bunker hill. June 17, 1775, 1875. Boston [1875]. L. 8°...................................... 810.8
— Wheildon, W. W. New history of the. Boston, 1875. 8°.................................. 811.17

Note. — For the literature of Bunker hill, see the appendix in the Memorial above [810.10], and the Library Bulletin for July, 1875. See also the orations by Everett and Webster.

BUNKER-HILL monument association. Inauguration of the statue of Warren, June 17, 1857. Boston, 1858. 8°............................ 1211.3
BUNSEN, Christian Carl Josias, *Freiherr* von. Egypt's place in universal history. Translated from the German, by C. H. Cottrell. [Vol. v, with additions by S. Birch.] London, 1854–67. 5 v. Illustrated. Maps. 8° 5912.12
— God in history. Translated from the German by S. Winkworth. With a preface by A. P. Stanley. London, 1868, 70. 3 v. 8°...........5813.13
— Memoir. Drawn chiefly from family papers by Francis, baroness Bunsen. Philadelphia, 1868. 2 v. Portrait. 8°......................... 5723.2
— Bunsen's Biblical researches. Williams, R. (*In* Essays and reviews)........................ 1538.3
— *Same.* (*In* Hedge, F. H. Recent inquiries in theology)......................1526.24 and 5814.15
BUNYAN, John. The pilgrim's progress from this world to that which is to come. Leipzig, 1855. xviii, 364 pp. Sq. 16° 315.18
— Macaulay, T. B., *lord.* Biography of. (*In his* New biographies of illustrious men) 5428.4
— Southey, R. Life of. London, 1861. Sm. 8° .. 5428.6

Note. — The most popular life is by Southey, which gave occasion to Scott's review in his "Miscellanies," and to Macaulay's eulogistic essay, originally in Edinburgh review, Dec., 1830, the views in which he repeated in his contribution to the Encyclopædia Britannica, and in his History of England [838.1]. See also Macaulay, quoted in Harper's monthly, vol. 14. The views of Hallam [1531.2] are less eulogistic, and he thinks Bunyan over-estimated. For critical estimates, see Dunlop's History of fiction [6136.3]; Kingsley's New miscellanies [1533.8]; and the references in Allibone, McClintock and Strong, etc. Whittier has a sketch in his Old portraits [1937.1.1].

BUONARROTI, Michelangelo, *or* Michel Agnolo. Black, C. C. Michael Angelo Buonarroti. Sculptor, painter, architect. The story of his life and labours. London, 1875. 8°.......... 6211.7
— Duppa, R. Life and works of. London, 1870. 16°...................................... 6217.3
— Grimm, H. Life of. Boston, 1871. 2 v. Sm. 8°. 1022.2

Note. — Grimm's Life is the most recent, and most voluminous, offering some new matter, and viewing its subject in his relations to his times, presenting, on p. 66, vol. 1, a review of the principal authorities. Consult also Vasari's "Lives of eminent painters," etc. [6215.6]; Lanzi's "History of painting in Italy" [6215.4], and the authorities named in the note under Painting; also Roscoe's Lorenzo de' Medici [5525.1] and Leo x [55266]. Duppa's is the best of the briefer accounts. Mrs. Jameson's memoir, in her Early Italian painters [6228.2], is short, and see also her Loves of the poets [5618.2]. Black's is the most recent study. For critical opinions, see Reynolds's Discourses [6230.1]; Ruskin's Modern painters [6236.18.2]; and Alison's Essays [1531.7]. See also Histories of sculpture.

BURBIDGE, F. W. The art of botanical drawing. With engravings. London [1873]. 63 pp. Sq. 16°...................................... 6217.7
BURCKETT, Florence. Wildmoor. A novel 552.2

Shelf. No.

BURCKHARDT, Jacob. The Cicerone: or, art guide to painting in Italy. Edited by A. von Zahn. Translated from the German by Mrs. A. H. Clough. London, 1873. viii, 291 pp. Sm. 8°. 6216.1

Note. — A translation of that part of Burckhardt's Cicerone which is devoted to painting. The arrangement is by artists and schools, with an index to the places where the paintings are to be found.

BURCLIFF. Trowbridge, J. T.................... 929.1
BURDER, George. Village sermons. Added, collects, or short prayers, [and] An essay on divine meditation, by William Bates. Philadelphia, 1821. 4 v. 12° 6327.7
BURGESS, Ebenezer, *compiler.* Dedham pulpit; or, sermons by the pastors of the First church in Dedham, in the XVIIth and XVIIIth centuries; with a centennial discourse by the present pastor [Ebenezer Burgess]. Boston, 1840. viii, 517 pp. 8°...............................5813.11

Contents. — Sermons by John Allin, 1671; William Adams, 1678, 85; Joseph Belcher, 1698, 1701, 10, 22; Samuel Dexter, 1728, 38; Jason Haven, 1758, 61, 64, 69, 70, 71, 74, 83, 92, 96; Ebenezer Burgess, 1838.

BURGOMASTER'S, The, family. Walrée, E. C. W.... 731.20
BURGOYNE, *Sir* John Fox. Remarks on the maintenance of macadamized roads. *See* MALLET, Robert 1716.16
— Treatise on the blasting and quarrying of stone. To which is added some remarks on the blowing up of bridges. New edition. London, N. D. vii, 138 pp. Illustrated. 12°..................1716.15
— Life and correspondence of. Wrottesley, G. London, 1873. 2 v. 8°.................... 5333.2
BURIED alone. By a new writer................. 311.25
BURIED cities, The, of Campania. Adams, W. H. D. Boston, 1870. 16°......................... 437.5
BURKE, Edmund. Works. Boston, 1826, 27. 7 v. 8°. 5634.1

Contents. — Vol. I. A vindication of natural society; Inquiry into the origin of our ideas of the sublime and beautiful; Short account of a late short administration; Observations on a publication, intituled The present state of the nation; Thoughts on the cause of the present discontents; Speech on American taxation. II. Speeches and letters. III. Speeches; Reflections on the revolution in France; Letters; Appeal from the new to the old whigs. IV. Hints for a memorial to be delivered to M. de M. M.; Thoughts on French affairs; Heads for consideration on the present state of affairs; Remarks on the policy of the allies with respect to France; Observations on the conduct of the minority, particularly in the last session of parliament, 1793; Preface to the address of M. Brissot to his constituents; Letters; Thoughts and details on scarcity. V. Letters; Tracts, relative to the laws against popery in Ireland; Fragments and notes of speeches in parliament; Hints for an essay on the drama; Essay towards an abridgement of the English history. VI. Ninth report of the select committee of the house of commons on the affairs of India, 1783; Articles of charge of high crimes and misdemeanors against Warren Hastings. VII. Speeches on the impeachment of Warren Hastings; Report in relation to proceedings on the trial of Warren Hastings, 1794.

— *Same.* 4th edition. Boston, 1871. 12 v. Portrait. Sm. 8°............................. 5635.1

Contents. — Vol. I. A vindication of natural society; Inquiry into the origin of our ideas of the sublime and beautiful; Short account of a late short administration; Observations on a publication, intituled "The present state of the nation"; Thoughts on the cause of the present discontents. II. Speeches and letters. III. Speeches; Reflections on the revolution in France. IV. Letters; Appeal from the new to the old whigs; Hints for a memorial to be delivered to M. de M. M.; Thoughts on French affairs; Heads for consideration on the present state of affairs; Remarks on the policy of the allies with respect to France. V. Observations on the conduct of the minority, particularly in the last session of parliament, 1793; Preface to the address of M. Brissot to his constituents; Letters; Thoughts and details on scarcity. VI. Letters; Fragments of a tract relative to the laws against popery in Ireland. VII. Fragments and notes of speeches in parliament; Hints for an essay on the drama: Essay towards an abridgement of the English history. VIII. Ninth report of the select committee of the house of commons on the affairs of India, 1783. VIII, IX. Articles of charge of high crimes and misdemeanors against Warren Hastings. IX, X. Speeches on the impeachment of Warren Hastings. XI. Report in relation to proceedings on the trial of Warren Hastings, 1794. XI, XII. Speeches in the impeachment of Warren Hastings.

— Morley, J. Edmund Burke: a historical study. London, 1867. 8° 5613.3
— Prior, J. Life and character of. Philadelphia, 1825. 8°.................................. 5424.6

Note. — Prior's Life makes the earliest use of extensive original matter, and in the later editions [see Bates Hall catalogues] he had the advantage of Burke's correspondence first published in 1844; as did Macknight, whose work presents Burke more fully in his political career. The most recent study of his character is by Morley. For his public character, see Brougham's Statesmen [5614.4.3]; Sir James Mackin-

Shelf. No.

BURKE, Edmund, *continued*.

tosh's life; Goldwin Smith's "Three statesmen" [5425.1, under Pitt]. The biographers and partisans of Fox [see Fox] are generally unjust to Burke, in the opinion of his admirers. As an orator, see Macaulay's Essay on Hastings [1918.4]; De Quincey, on rhetoric, in Historical essays [1825.3.2]. Rogers's Recollections gives specimens of his table-talk. See Thackeray, quoted in Harper's monthly, vol. 21; and Miss Mitford's account of his home, in Harper's monthly, vol. 2. There is an analytical account of Burke in Buckle's Civilization, chap. vii [5417.1]. See further references in Thomas and Allibone.

BURKE, *Sir* (John) Bernard. A genealogical and heraldic dictionary of the peerage and baronetage of the British empire. 37th edition. London, 1875. xcvi, 1366 pp. Illustrated. L. 8° 5410.3

— The rise of great families, other essays, and stories. London, 1873. iv, 371 pp. Sm. 8° 5611.8

BURKE, Thomas Nicholas. English misrule in Ireland. A course of lectures, delivered in reply to Froude. With an appendix, containing a review of the so-called "bull" of Adrian IV. By P. H. Moran. And "An analysis of the rebellion of 1631," by Mathew Carey. New York, 1873. 324 pp. Portrait. 12° 827.6

— Lectures and sermons. New York, 1872. 644 pp. Portrait. 8° 1910.1

BURLESQUES. Thackeray, W. M. Works. London, 1872. Sm. 8° 513.1.8

BURMAH. Gouger, H. A personal narrative of two years' imprisonment in. London, 1860. 12° .. 425.21

— Vincent, F., *jr.* The land of the white elephant. New York, 1874. 8° 5923.7

BURN, Robert Scott. Outlines of modern farming. With illustrations. London, 1865, 71, 72. 5 v. Vol. 1–3, 2d edition. 12° 6417.1

Contents. — Vol. I. Soils, manures, and crops. II. Notes, historical and practical, on farming and farming economy. III. Stock: cattle, sheep, and horses. IV. The dairy — pigs — poultry, with notes on the diseases of stock. V. Utilization of town sewage; Irrigation; Reclamation of waste land.

— Putnam's elementary science series. Building construction; showing the employment of timber, lead, and iron work in the practical construction of buildings. New York [Glasgow, 1874]. 2 v. 16° 6228.1

Contents. — Vol. I. Text. II. Plates.

— Self-aid cyclopædia for self-taught students: comprising general drawing, architectural, mechanical, and engineering drawing, ornamental, drawing and design, mechanics and mechanism, the steam engine. Illustrat[ed]. London, N. D. 8°. 6223.2

BURNAND, Francis Cowley. Happy-thought hall ... 533.20

BURNAP, George Washington. Discourses on the rectitude of human nature. Boston, 1850. x, 409+ pp. 12° 1522.7

BURNELL, George R. Rudimentary treatise on limes, cements, mortars, concretes, mastics, plastering, etc. 9th edition, with appendices. London, 1872. xviii, 136 pp. 12° 1716.11

— Rudiments of hydraulic engineering. New edition, with illustrations. London, 1868. x, 283 pp. Folded plate. 12° 1716.10

BURNET, Gilbert, *bishop of Salisbury*. History of his own time: from the restoration of Charles II to the treaty of peace at Utrecht, in the reign of Queen Anne. New edition, with historical and biographical notes. London, 1857. xx, 949+ pp. 8° 5410.4

— *See* LAWRENCE, E. Lives of the British historians. New York, 1855. 12° 1224.7.1

BURNEY, Frances. *See* ARBLAY, Frances d'.

BURNS, Robert. Poetical works. With life and portrait of the author. Leipzig, 1845. xxiv, 366 pp. Sq. 16° 1613.18

— Life and works of. Chambers, R. New York, 1852, 54. 4 v. Sm. 8° 1225.4

Note. — Chambers's Life makes the latest elaborate use of all the scattered biographical material. See Harper's monthly, vol. 1, by E. Elliott; vol. 7, on Burns's last days; vol. 22, by H. T. Tuckerman; and vol. 36, by Shanks. See also Kingsley on Burns and his school [1223.5]; Wilson's "Hour's talk about poetry" [1531.7]; "Haunts of Burns" in Atlantic monthly, Oct., 1860. See additional references in the Lower Hall Catalogue for history, etc., p. 41.

Shelf. No.

BURR, Aaron, Life and times of. Parton, J. New York, 1861. 12° 1223.10

Note. — Parton presents Burr in as favorable a light as he can, and his biography is the best general narrative. See Lossing's account of Burr's conspiracy, in Harper's monthly, vol. 25. See also Atlantic monthly, vol. 1; and Benton's Thirty years' view [812.2], and Hildreth's United States [5011.11.1].

BURR, Enoch Fitch. Pater mundi. Boston, 1872, 73. Vol. 1, 5th edition. 2 v. Sm. 8° 1527.11

Contents. — Vol. I. Modern science testifying to the Heavenly Father. II. Doctrine of evolution.

BURR, Theodosia. *See* PARTON, J. Famous Americans of recent times. Boston, 1871. 8° 1214.14

BURRITT, Elihu. Ten-minute talks on all sorts of topics. With autobiography of the author. Boston, 1874. 360 pp. Sq. 16° 5238.1

— A walk from London to Land's end and back, with notes by the way. With illustrations. 2d edition. London, 1868. vii, 350 pp. Sq. 16°. 5438.4

BURRITT, Elijah Hinsdale. The geography of the heavens, and class-book of astronomy. New edition. Revised and illustrated. By H. Mattison. New York, 1854. 324 pp. 12° 6818.1

BURROUGHS, John. Wake-robin. New York, 1871. iv, 231 pp. 16° 1525.12

BÜRSTENBINDER, Emilie. A hero of the pen. By E. Werner [*pseud.*]. Translated by Frances A. Shaw 521.19

BURT, Nathaniel C. The land and its story; or, the sacred historical geography of Palestine. Illustrated with maps and engravings. New York, 1869. 381 pp. Sm. 4° 421.8

BURTON, Richard Francis. The city of the saints [Great Salt Lake city, Utah], and across the Rocky mountains to California. With illustrations. New York, 1862. xii, 574+ pp. Map. 8° 412.2

— Personal narrative of a pilgrimage to El-Medinah and Meccah. With introduction by Bayard Taylor. With map and illustrations. 2d American edition. Boston, 1858. 492 pp. 12° 423.14

— *Same.* Leipzig, 1874. 3 v. in 1. Map. Sq. 16°. 428.5

— Two trips to Gorilla land and the cataracts of the Congo. London, 1876. Folded maps. Illustrations. 2 v. 8° 5933.12

— and DRAKE, Charles F. Tyrwhitt. Unexplored Syria. London, 1872. 2 v. Illustrated. Maps and plate. 8° 5933.3

BURTON, Warren. Helps to education in the homes of our country. Boston, 1863. viii, 368 pp. 16° 1933.18

BURY, T. Talbot. Rudimentary architecture. 5th edition, with illustrations. London, 1867. viii, 208 pp. 12° 1716.21

BUSH, (Annie) Forbes. Memoirs of the queens of France. From the 2d London edition. Philadelphia, 1854. 2 v. 12° 1224.10

BUSH, George. Statement of reasons for embracing the doctrines and disclosures of Emanuel Swedenborg. With a biographical sketch of the author. New York, 1875. xxiv, 120+ pp. Portrait. 12° 6328.18

BUSH-BOYS, The. Reid, M. 923.27

BUSHNELL, Horace. Views of Christian nurture, and of subjects adjacent thereto. Hartford, 1847. 251 pp. 12° 5817.8

BUSHRANGERS, The. Thomes, W. H. 735.5

BUSINESS forms. Hill, T. E. Manual of social and business forms. Chicago, 1876. 4° 5821.3

— New clerk's magazine; containing all the most useful forms which occur in business transactions. By a member of the Massachusetts bar. Boston, 1832. 12° 1727.1

BUTLER, Benjamin Franklin. General Butler in New Orleans. Parton, J. New York, 1864. 12° .. 815.2

BUTLER, Charles. Historical outline of the controversy respecting the text of the three heavenly witnesses. (*In* Sparks, J. Collection of essays and tracts in theology) 1918.9.2

BUTLER, Frances (Anne). *See* KEMBLE, Frances (Anne).

Shelf. No.

BUTLER, Frederick. Complete history of the United States to 1820. Hartford, 1821. 3 v. Portraits. 8° 812.9

— Sketches of universal history. 3d edition. Hartford, 1821. 407 pp. Illustrated. 12° 817.9

BUTLER, Joseph, Biography of. Rogers, H. (*In* Macaulay, T. B., *lord*, and others. New biographies of illustrious men) 5428.4

BUTLER, Samuel. Poetical works. Boston, 1873. 2 v. Portrait. [The British poets.] 16° 5628.6

BUTLER, W. F. The wild north land: being the story of a winter journey, with dogs, across North America. With illustrations and route map. London, 1874. x, 358+pp. Portrait. 8°. 5032.3

BUTLER, William. The land of the Veda; together with the incidents of the great Sepoy rebellion. With a map, 42 illustrations, tables of Christian missions, and a glossary of Indian terms. New York, 1872. 550 pp. 8° 5931.1

BUTLER, William Allen. Mrs. Limber's raffle; or, a church fair and its victims 718.5

BUTTERFLY hunters, The. Conant, H. S. 933.1

BUTTRESSES, Experimental essays on the principles of construction in. Bland, W. London, 1867. 12°. 1716.6

BY and by. Maitland, E. 737.22

BY still waters. Mayo, I. F. 724.8

BYERLEY, Thomas, and ROBERTSON, James Craigie. (*Sholto and Reuben Percy.*) The Percy anecdotes. Revised edition. Added, American anecdotes. Illustrated with portraits. New York, 1858. 2 v. in 1. 8° 1231.3

BYR, Robert, *pseud.* *See* BAYER, Carl Robert.

BYRNE, Oliver. Spons' dictionary of engineering, civil, mechanical, military, and naval; with technical terms in French, German, Italian, and Spanish. London, 1869–71. 6 v. L. 8°..*R.R., E.2.1

BYRON, George Gordon Noel, *lord*. Works. 2d edition. With portrait. Leipzig, 1866. 5 v. Sq. 16° 1614.12

Contents. — Vol. I. Don Juan. II. Childe Harold's pilgrimage; The giaour; The corsair; Lara; The siege of Corinth; Parisina; The prisoner of Chillon; Mazeppa; Beppo. III. The bride of Abydos; The island; Hours of idleness; English bards and Scotch reviewers; The age of bronze; Hints from Horace; The curse of Minerva; The waltz; The lament of Tasso; Ode on Venice; The prophecy of Dante; Ode to Napoleon Buonaparte; Monody on the death of R. B. Sheridan; The dream; The vision of judgment; The Morgante Maggiore of Pulci; Francesca of Rimini; The blues. IV. Hebrew melodies; Domestic pieces; Occasional pieces; Manfred; Cain; The deformed transformed; Heaven and earth. V. Marino Faliero; The two Foscari; Sardanapalus; Werner; A fragment; Parliamentary speeches.

— English bards and Scotch reviewers; a satire. Added, An ode to Bonaparte. Boston, 1814. 72 pp. 12° 1619.2

— The giaour, a fragment of a Turkish tale. Philadelphia, 1813. 53 pp. 12° 1619.1

— Letters and journals: with notices of his life. By Thomas Moore. New York, 1868. 2 v. 8° ... 5631.4

— Lord Byron. A biography. Elze, C. (F.) London, 1872. Sm. 8° 5423.3

Note. — Moore's Life is the chief authoritative one, and it gave rise to Macaulay's essay [1918.4]. Recollections by George Ticknor and Edward Everett are given in Allibone. His English home is described in Irving's Newstead abbey [715.5]; in the Atlantic monthly, by Mrs. Waterston, Feb., 1864; and in Harper's monthly, vol. 21. See recollections by Leigh Hunt, in Harper's monthly, vol. 1; also see vol. 3; and by J. H. Siddons, in vol. 26. In Allibone and in Poole's Index will be found references to contemporary criticism, for which see also Jeffrey's essays [5610.8]; Whipple's Essays [1936.2.1]; and Kingsley's New miscellanies [1533.8]. There is a French estimate in Taine's English literature [5613.1.2]. The life by Elze is a German view, based on latest information.

See illustrative matter in H. C. Robinson's Diary [5425.3]; in George Ticknor's Life [1012.5; 5023.10]; and in the lives of his contemporaries Shelley, Southey, Moore, Wordsworth, Irving, etc.

BY-WAYS of Europe. Taylor, (J.) B. New York, 1872. Sm. 8° 224.4

CABIN, The, on the prairie. Pearson, C. H. 937.18

CABOT, Sebastian, Life of. Hayward, C. (*In* Sparks, J. Library of American biography) .. 5028.1.9

CÆSAR, Caius Julius. Commentaries on the Gallic and civil wars. Literally translated. London, 1872. iv, 572 pp. Portrait. Sm. 8° 6115.5

— The commentaries of Cæsar [outlined and explained]. Trollope, A. Edinburgh, 1870. 16°. 6116.5

Shelf. No.

CÆSAR, Caius Julius, *continued.*

— Quæ extant. Interpretatione et notis illustravit Johannes Godvinus. Novi Eboraci, 1820. v, 421 pp. 8° 6114.1

— Abbott, J. History of 914.23

— Napoléon III. History of. New York, 1866. 2 v. 8° 5521.1

Note. — The life by the late emperor of the French, though presenting new information, particularly of the ancient topography of Gaul, is considered rather a laudation and exposition of *Cæsarism* than a wholly trustworthy life of the Roman conqueror. It ends with the passage of the Rubicon. Abbott's account is a popular one. See also Plutarch's Lives [5932.5]. On the question of the blame of Cæsar or Brutus, see Seeley's Roman imperialism [5616.3]. See Rome, *note*, and particularly Mommsen's History of Rome [5516.1], and Merivale's History of the Romans [5515.3, vol. 1 and 2].

CÆSARS, The. De Quincey, T. Boston, 1873. 12°. 1825.10

CAGED lion, The. Yonge, C. M. 318.12

CAGNONI, Antonio. Don Bucefalo. (*In* Ditson, O., and co. Standard opera librettos) 6233.3.1

CAIUS, *a presbyter of Rome.* *See* HIPPOLYTUS, *St.*

CALDERON DE LA BARCA, Frances Erskine. Life in Mexico, reviewed. Prescott, W. H. Biographical and critical essays. London, 1856. 16° ... 1537.8

— *Same.* Philadelphia, 1875. 12° 5237.3

CALDERON, the courtier. A tale. Bulwer-Lytton, E. (G. E.) L. 5618.5

CALDERWOOD secret, The. Johnson, V. W. 721.6

CALDOR, M. T. Social charades, and parlor operas. Boston, 1873. 169 [167] pp. 16° 1516.10

CALDWELL, Charles. Discourse on the genius and character of Horace Holley. With appendix. Boston, 1828. viii, 294 pp. Portrait. 8° 1530.3

CALEB Krinkle. Coffin, C. C. 733.1

CALEB Williams, Adventures of. Godwin, W. Boston 521.22

— *Same.* New York. 2 v. 536.5

CALHOUN, John Caldwell. *See* PARTON, J. Famous Americans of recent times. Boston, 1871. 8°. 1214.14

CALIBAN: the missing link. Wilson, D. London, 1873. 8° 1533.15

CALIFORNIA. Geological survey. [By] J. D. Whitney. The Yosemite guide-book. With maps. [Cambridge], 1871. 133 pp. 16° 5039.1

— Browne, J. R. Crusoe's island. With sketches of adventure in. New York, 1872. 12° 415.12

— Burton, R. F. The city of the saints, and across the Rocky mountains to. New York, 1862. 8°. 412.2

— Colton, W. Three years in. New York, 1851. 12°. 414.16

— Cronise, T. F. The natural wealth of. San Francisco, 1868. L. 8° 5031.5

— Dunbar, E. E. The romance of the age; or, the discovery of gold in. New York, 1867. 12° ... 815.9

— Frémont, J. C. Exploring expedition to. Auburn, 1854. 12° 414.14

— Greenhow, R. History of. Boston, 1845. 8° .. 810.2

— Howland, E. With the Count de Beauvoir in. (*In* Many lands and many people) 431.3

— Lippincott, S. J. New life in new lands: notes of travel. New York, 1873. 12° 214.1

— Marcy, R. B. The prairie traveler. A handbook for overland expeditions. New York, 1859. 16°. 417.7

— Mitchell, S. A. Map, etc., of. Philadelphia, 1846. Sm. 12° 418.7

— Marryat, F. Narrative of the travels and adventures of Monsieur Viollet in. [Fiction] 337.7

— Nordhoff, C. California: for health, pleasure, and residence. New York, 1873. 4° 5031.2

— – Northern California, Oregon, and the Sandwich Islands. New York, 1874. 8° 432.5

— Patterson, L. B. Twelve years in the mines of. Cambridge, 1862. 12° 417.3

— Soulé, F., Gihon, J. H., and Nisbet, J. Annals of San Francisco; containing a summary of the history of. New York, 1855. 8° 810.3

— Taylor, (J.) B. Eldorado; or, adventures in the path of empire. New York, 1864. 12° 425.6

— Wise, H. A. Los Gringos; or, an inside view of. New York, 1849. 12° 435.4

Note. — For the early history, see Greenhow, 1844, and Soulé's Annals of San Francisco. See also Dana's Two years before the mast [918.1; 5037.1].

For resources, see Cronise, etc.; articles on wine-making in Atlantic monthly, May, 1864, and Harper's monthly, vol. 29,

Shelf. No.

CALIFORNIA, *continued.*

and the State geological survey [see Bates Hall catalogues], out of which grew King's Mountaineering in the Sierra Nevada [413.1].

For description, the most popular book is, perhaps, Nordhoff's; see also Harper's monthly, vol. 44; but see also chapters in Whymper's Alaska [5035.1]; Ludlow's Heart of the continent [413.4]; Carleton's New way [433.1]; Prime's Round the world [233.1]; Revere's Keel and saddle [5914.3]; and papers in Harper's monthly, vol. 11; vol. 20 (on gold); vol. 21 (J. T. Headley, Overland to California); vols. 23, 24 and 27; vols. 37 and 38 (J. Ross Browne); and vol. 45.

For the period of the gold discovery, see Frémont's report as epitomized in Upham's Life of Frémont [1214.6], and General Sherman's experiences, 1846–57, in his Memoirs [1212.3.1; 5024.5.1].

For the aboriginal period, see the summarized knowledge of Bancroft's Native races of the Pacific states [5920.4].

CALISTHENICS, Physiology and. Beecher, C. E. New York, 1858. 16° 6038.2

CALIXTUS, *or* CALLISTUS, *pope.* *See* HIPPOLYTUS, *St.*

CALKINS, Marshall. Trichina spiralis in Springfield. (*In* Massachusetts medical society. Publications) 6021.4

CALKINS, N. A. Primary object lessons for a graduated course of development. With lessons for the proper training of the faculties of children. 4th edition. New York, 1862. 362+ pp. Illustrated. 12° 1535.4

CALL, A, to the unconverted. Baxter, R. New York, 1831. Sm. 12° 5818.15

CALLED to account. Cudlip, A. 317.15

CALLISTA. [Historical fiction.] Newman, J. H. 319.9

CALORIC. Metcalfe, S. L. Philadelphia, 1869. 2 v. 8° 5832.1

CALVERLY, C. S. Leisure hour series. Fly leaves. [Poems.] New York, 1872. vi, 233 pp. 16°. 1617.3

CALVERT, George Henry. Goethe: his life and works. Boston, 1872. 276 pp. 16° 1027.2

CALVIN, *or* CAUVIN, Jean. Dyer, T. H. Life of. London, 1850. 8° 5812.12

— Guizot, F. (P. G.) Great Christians of France. [London, 1869.] Sm. 8° 5937.6

CAMBODIA, *Asia.* The land of the white elephant. Vincent, F., *jr.* New York, 1874. 8° 5923.7

CAMBRIDGE, *England.* Oxford and Cambridge: their colleges, memories, and associations. Arnold, F. London [1874]. Sm. 4° 5433.2

— *University.* Five years in an English university. Bristed, C. A. New York, 1873. 12° 5835.1

CAMBRIDGE, *Mass.*, Poetic localities of. Stillman, W. J. Boston, 1876. Sm. 4° 5231.1

See also Harvard college.

CAMDEN, William. *See* LAWRENCE, E. Lives of the British historians. New York, 1855. 12° 1224.7.1

CAMEOS from English history. Yonge, C. M. London, 1869. 2 v. 16° 826.12

CAMERON, Charles A. The chemistry of food in relation to the breeding and feeding of live stock. London, 1868. viii, 253+ pp. 1 plate. 16°. . 6437.1

CAMERON pride, The. Holmes, M. J. 534.9

CAMILLE; or, the fate of a coquette. Dumas, A., *the younger* 733.15

CAMP and fireside stories. Alcott, L. M. 926.13

CAMP-FIRES of the revolution. Watson, H. C. New York, 1869. 8° 811.4

CAMPAIGN series. *See* ALGER, Horatio, *jr.*

CAMPAIGNS, The, of Napoleon Buonaparte, from the siege of Toulon to his death. [Also] an account of the French revolution. Compiled from distinguished authors. By an American. With engravings. Boston, 1840. 422, x pp. 8° ... 825.7

CAMPBELL, George. The philosophy of rhetoric. New edition, with the author's last additions and corrections. New York, 1868. 435 pp. 12° 1533.5

CAMPBELL, George Douglas, *duke of Argyll.* Iona. London, 1870. 141+ pp. Illustrated. Sm. 8°. 427.9

— Primeval man. London, 1869. ix, 200 pp. Folded plate. 16° 5916.5

— The reign of law. 2d American from the 5th London edition. New York [1869]. xxvii, 462 pp. 16° 1525.15

CAMPBELL, Hugh. Nervous exhaustion and the diseases induced by it. With observations on the origin and nature of nervous force. London, 1873. viii, 195 pp. Sm. 8° 6036.8

Shelf. No.

CAMPBELL, John, *lord.* Lives of the lord chancellors and keepers of the great seal of England, from the earliest times till the reign of George IV. 5th edition. London, 1868. 10 v. Sm. 8° 5427.9

CAMPBELL, John. Negro-mania: being an examination of the falsely assumed equality of the various races of men. Philadelphia, 1851. 549 pp. 12° 6614.7

CAMPBELL, Thomas. Life and letters. Edited by W. Beattie. 2d edition. London, 1850. 3 v. Portraits. Fac-simile. Sm. 8° 5622.3

— Poetical works. New edition, with illustrations. Boston, 1873. viii, 260 pp. 16° 1615.12

— Personal recollections of. Stoddard, R. H. Bric-à-brac series 1828.9

— Review of [his] "Lectures on Greek poetry." *See* REVIEWS, etc. 1536.23

CAMPING-OUT, The, series. *See* STEVENS, Charles Asbury.

CAN wrong be right? Hall, A. M. 311.8

CAN you forgive her? Trollope, A. 330.7

CANADA. Adams, A. L. Field and forest rambles, with notes and observations on the natural history of eastern Canada. London, 1873. 8° ... 6613.11

— Medley, J. G. An autumn tour in the United States and Canada. London, 1873. Sm. 8° ... 5036.6

— Moodie, S. (S.) Life in the clearings versus the bush. New York [1853]. 12° 414.8

— – Roughing it in the bush; or, life in. New York, 1852. 2 v. 12° 414.12

— – *Same.* 2 v. in 1 .... 414.9

— Parkman, F., *jr.* The old régime in. Boston, 1874. 12° 5015.5.4

— Thoreau, H. D. A Yankee in. Boston, 1872. 12° 225.2

CANARY bird fancier, The. By a fancier. With directions for the care of native and exotic songsters. 8th American edition. New York, 1846. 72 pp. 12° 1519.5

CANCELLED will, The. Dupuy, E. A. 522.16

CANDLE, Chemical history of a. Faraday, M. New York, 1861. 16° 1717.1

CANDLISH, Robert Smith. Sermons. With a biographical preface. New York, 1874. xxiii, 315 pp. 16° 6326.23

CANNING, George. *See* BULWER, *Sir* H. L. (E.) Historical characters. Leipzig, 1868. Sq. 16°. 1238.14

CANOE, The, and the saddle. Winthrop, S. Boston, 1873. 12° 537.19

CANOE travelling. Powell, W. B. London, 1871. Sm. 8° 5934.8

CANWRIGHT, D. M. History of the doctrine of the immortality of the soul. Battle Creek, 1871. 184 pp. 12° 6328.11

CAPE COD. [Descriptive essays.] Thoreau, H. D. Boston, 1873. 16° 215.2

CAPE COD and all along shore. Nordhoff, C. New York, 1868. 12° 536.27

CAPE OF GOOD HOPE. Last letters from Egypt. Added letters from the Cape. Gordon, L. A., *lady* Duff. London, 1875. Sm. 8° 436.5

CAPEN, Nahum. History of democracy: or, political progress, historically illustrated, from the earliest to the latest periods. With portraits. Vol. I. Hartford, 1874. 8° 6332.3

CAPEN family. Thayer, E. Family memorial. Hingham, 1835. 8° 611.2

CAPRICE, Un. Musset, (L. C.) A. de. Comédies et proverbes. Paris, 1867. 12° 5534.4.2

CAPRICES, Les, de Marianne. Musset, (L. C.) A. de. Comédies et proverbes. Paris, 1867. 12°. 5534.4.1

CAPTAIN Brand of the "Centipede." Wise, H. A. .. 720.6

CAPTAIN Horace. Clarke, R. S. 927.1

CAPTAIN Jack. MacKnight, C. 923.5

CAPTAIN'S, The, not a-miss: a farce. Wilks, T. E. New York, N. D. 12° 1635.5

CAPTAIN'S, The, story. Davis, R. H. (*In* Johnson, (E.) R. Little classics) 529.4.2

CARDELLI, —, *pseud.* *See* DUVAL, Henri.

CARDINAL Pole: or, the days of Philip and Mary. An historical romance. Ainsworth, W. H. 322.19

Shelf. No.

CARDS. Frickell, G. One thousand tricks with cards. New York [*cop.* 1869]. 12° 1515.15
— Parlor tricks with cards. New York [*cop.* 1863]. 16° 1516.23
CARE, Henry, *compiler*. English liberties, or the free-born subject's inheritance. With additions, by W. N. 5th edition. Boston, 1721. 288+ pp. 12° 828.4
CARELESS Kate. Adams, W. T. 918.4
CAREY, Annie. Threads of knowledge, drawn from a cambric handkerchief; a Brussels carpet; a print dress; a kid glove; a sheet of paper. London [1872]. 166+ pp. Illustrated. Sq. 16°. 6438.1
CAREY, Rosa Nouchette. Wooed and married 733.17
CAREY's library of choice literature. The literary chronicle. Part 1, 2. Philadelphia, 1836. 2 v. in 1. 8° 6730.42
CARICATURE and grotesque in literature and art, History of. Wright, T. London [1864]. Sm. 4°. 5923.4
CARICATURE history of the Georges. Wright, T. London [1867]. Sm. 8° 5415.5
CARION, Carl Stellwag von. Treatise on the diseases of the eye. Translated from the 3d German edition and edited by C. E. Hackley and D. B. St. J. Roosa. With appendix. Illustrated. 2d American edition. New York, 1868. xiv, 774 pp. 8° 6022.12
CARL and Jocko. Abbott, J. Harper's story books. 936.1.10
CARLÉN, Emilia Flygare. Ivar. From the original Swedish, by A. L. Krause 521.16
— "Lavinia;" or, one year. From the original Swedish, by A. L. Krause and E. Perce 533.9
CARLETON, Will. Farm ballads. Illustrated. New York, 1873. 108 pp. 8° 1621.1
— Farm legends. [Poems.] Illustrated. New York, 1876. 131 pp. 8° 1621.3
CARLETON, William. The black baronet 524.1
— The evil eye 524.2
— Neal Malone. (*In* Johnson, (E.) R. Little classics) 529.4.5
— Parra Sastha; or, the history of Paddy Go-easy and his wife Nancy 518.4
— Redmond, count O'Hanlon, the Irish rapparee. [Also] Barney Brady's goose 518.5
— Selection from. *See* HALF hours with Irish authors. New York, 1873. 12° 737.9
— Traits and stories of the Irish peasantry. New edition. With the author's latest corrections, an introduction, and explanatory notes 524.17
— Willy Reilly, and his dear Coleen bawn 524.3

Note. — A popular novelist of Irish life and manners.

"CARLETON," *pseud.* *See* COFFIN, Charles Carleton.
CARLISLE, *Earl of.* *See* HOWARD, George William Frederick.
CARLOS, Don. Schiller, (J. C.) F. von. Werke. Stuttgart, 1865. 8° 5734.1.3
CARLYLE, Thomas. Critical and miscellaneous essays. New edition. New York, 1876. Portrait. 568 pp. [Modern British essayists.] 8° 5610.7
— The early kings of Norway: also An essay on the portraits of John Knox. New York, 1875. 257 pp. Portraits. 12° 627.3
— The French revolution: a history. Leipzig, 1851. 3 v. in 1. Sq. 16° 838.10
— *Same.* London, 1871. 3 v. in 1. Sq. 16° 827.1
— Heroes, hero-worship and the heroic in history. London, 1872. 235+ pp. Sq. 16° 1535.19
— History of Friedrich II of Prussia, called Frederick the great. Leipzig, 1858–65. 13 v. in 7. Sq. 16° 1237.1
— Latter-day pamphlets. [1850.] New York, 1872. 299+ pp. Sq. 16° 1535.18
— Life of Friedrich Schiller: comprehending an examination of his works. Leipzig, 1869. 344 pp. Sq. 16° 1238.19
— Oliver Cromwell's letters and speeches. Leipzig, 1861. 4 v. in 2. Sq. 16° 1238.1
— Sartor resartus. London [1831]. 228+ pp. Portrait. Sm. 8° 5838.6
CARMEN's inheritance. Fisher, F. C. 520.4
CARMOSINE. Musset, (L. C.) A. de. Comédies et proverbes. Paris, 1867. 12° 5534.2
CARNÉ, Louis de. Travels in Indo-China and the Chinese empire. From the French. With a notice of the author by Count de Carné. London, 1872. xxi, 365 pp. Map. Illustrations. 8° 5931.9
CARNEGIE, James, *earl of Southesk.* Saskatchewan and the Rocky mountains. A diary and narrative of travel, sport, and adventure, during a journey through the Hudson's bay company's territories, in 1859 and 1860. With maps and illustrations. Edinburgh, 1875. xxx, 448 pp. 8° 5931.16

Note. — Contains, in an appendix, remarks on several of Shakespeare's plays, etc.

CARNIVAL of Venice. Petrella, E. (*In* Ditson, O., and co. Standard opera librettos) 6233.3.6
CAROLINE. Abbott, J. 914.7
CAROLL, Martha. How Marjory helped 915.23
CARPATHIAN mountains. Try Cracow and the Carpathians. Hutchinson, A. H. New York [London, 1872]. Sm. 8° 5936.2
CARPENTER, Francis B. The inner life of Abraham Lincoln. Six months at the White house. New York, 1870. 359 pp. 16° 1216.9
CARPENTER, William Benjamin. Epidemic delusions. (*In* Estes, D. Half-hour recreations in popular science) 6813.7
— The microscope and its revelations. 4th edition. Illustrated. London, 1868. xxviii, 796 pp. 16° 6827.1
— Principles of human physiology. New American from the last London edition. With illustrations. Edited, with additions, by F. G. Smith. Philadelphia, 1868. 902 pp. 8° 6012.6
— Unconscious action of the brain. (*In* Estes, D. Half-hour recreations in popular science) 6813.7
— Use and abuse of alcoholic liquors, in health and disease. Boston, 1861. xxviii, 264 pp. 12° 6036.9
— Zoology. New edition, thoroughly revised, by W. S. Dallas. London, 1857. 2 v. 16° 6616.1
CARPENTRY. The boy joiner. Davidson, E. A. London [1874]. 4° 1512.3
CARR of Carrlyon. Aïdé, H. 328.25
CARROLL, Lewis, *pseud.* *See* DODGSON, Charles Lutwidge.
CARRUTHERS, Robert. Abbotsford notanda. *See* CHAMBERS, Robert 5425.9
CARRY's confession. Robinson, F. W. 731.18
CARSON, Christopher. Familiarly known as Kit Carson. Abbott, J. S. C. New York, 1874. 12° 1014.8
CARTER, Robert. A summer cruise on the coast of New England. Boston [*cop.* 1864]. viii, 261 pp. 12° 415.15
CARTER Quarterman. [Fiction.] Baker, W. M. ... 530.17
CARTHAGE. Davis, N. Carthage and her remains. London, 1861. 8° 422.1
— Rollin, C. Ancient history of the Carthaginians. Vol. 1–4, 6–8. Boston, 1807. 7 v. 8° 5913.1

Note. — Davis's explorations were begun in 1856, under the auspices of the British government, and he is thought to confound Punic with Roman remains. There is a popular account of the ruins in Harper's monthly, vol. 22.
All histories of the ancient world, of Rome, and of Hannibal cover the history of Carthage in good part; but see particularly Philip Smith's Ancient history [5916.14]; Mommsen's History of Rome [5516.1.2] for a comparison of Rome and Carthage, and Grote's History of Greece [5006.1.3, ch. 21].

CARY, Alice, A memorial of. Ames, M. C. New York, 1873. Sm. 8° 1014.5
CARY, Phœbe, A memorial of. Ames, M. C. New York, 1873. Sm. 8° 1014.5
CARY, Thomas Greaves. Memoir of Thomas Handasyd Perkins; containing extracts from his diaries and letters. With an appendix. Boston, 1856. 304+ pp. Portrait. 8° 5021.12
CASEY, Silas. Infantry tactics. New York, 1862. 3 v. Illustrated. Folded plates. Sm. 12° 1529.1

Shelf. No.

CASIMIR Maremma. Helps, *Sir* A. Boston, 1870. 16° 518.12
CASPIAN sea, Travels on the. Cunynghame, *Sir* A. T. London, 1872. 8° 5931.8
CASSAL, Charles, and KARCHER, Théodore, *editors*. The graduated course of translation from English into French. Part I. The junior course. With a vocabulary of idioms and difficulties. London, 1875. xii, 140 pp. Sm. 8° 5534.7
CASSELL'S technical manuals. *Namely:* —
— Davidson, E. A. Linear drawing and orthographic and isometrical projection 6218.2
CASSELL'S History of the United States. Ollier, E. London [1875]. L. 8° 810.11
CAST adrift. Arthur, T. S. 921.8
CAST away in the cold. [Arctic story.] Hayes, I. I. Boston, 1872. Sm. 4° 933.7
CASTAWAY. Yates, E. 318.24
CASTAWAYS, The. Reid, M. 937.23
CASTELAR, Emilio. Old Rome and new Italy. (Recuerdos de Italia.) Translated by Mrs. A. Arnold. New York, 1873. 301 pp. 12° 824.11
CASTILIAN days. Hay, J. Boston, 1871. 12° 227.2
CASTINE, *Maine*, History of. Wheeler, G. A. Bangor, 1875. 8° 813.2
CASTLE Avon. Marsh-Caldwell, A. 313.26
CASTLE Daly. Keary, A. Leipzig 321.25
— *Same*. Philadelphia 714.36
CASTLE Dangerous. Scott, *Sir* W. 533.5
CASTLE of Ehrenstein. James, G. P. R. 327.3
CASTLE Richmond. Trollope, A. 334.8
CASTLEMON, Harry, *pseud.* *See* FOSDICK, Charles A.
CASTLES in the air. Gore, C. G. F. 311.1
CATARRH. *See* AUTUMNAL catarrh.
CATES, William L. R. Dictionary of general biography. 2d edition, with a supplement. London, 1875. 1297, 161 pp. 8° .... *R.R., E.2.11
— *joint author*. Encyclopædia of chronology. *See* WOODWARD, Bernard Bolingbroke .... *R.R., E.3.7
CATHARINE, *of Aragon*. Dixon, W. H. History of two queens. Leipzig, 1873, 74. 6 v. in 4. Sq. 16° 1238.21
— *Same*. London, 1873, 74. 4 v. 8° 5414.3
CATHAY and the way thither. Yule, H. London, 1866. 8° 5923.10
CATHERINE, *St., of Sienna*. Die Wunder der Katharina von Siena. Hagen, (E.) A. Künstler-Geschichten. Leipzig, 1840. 12° 2026.1.2
CATHERINE. Thackeray, W. M. Leipzig 335.8
— *Same*. (*In his* Works.) London 513.1.11
CATHOLIC, The. Derby, E. H. Boston, 1856. 12° 1524.22
CATHOLIC world, The. A monthly magazine of general literature and science. Vol. 16–21. New York, 1873–75. 6 v. 8° 6715.1
CATLIN, Jacob. A compendium of the system of divine truth. 3d edition. Boston, 1851. viii, 302 pp. 12° 5817.9
CATSKILL fairies, The. Johnson, V. W. 910.2
CATTLE. Dadd, G. H. The nature and treatment of the diseases of. Boston, 1859. 12° 1522.15
— Quincy, J. Essays on the soiling of. Boston, 1859. 8° 6614.4
— Report of the commissioner of agriculture on the diseases of. *See* UNITED STATES. *Department of agriculture* 6610.1

See also Ayrshire cattle, Chemistry, Food.

CAUCASUS. Cunynghame, *Sir* A. T. Travels in the Eastern Caucasus. London, 1872. 8° 5931.8
— Mounsey, A. H. Journey through the. London, 1872. 8° 5931.7
CAUSERIES avec mes élèves. Sauveur, L. Boston, 1874. 16° 2015.5
CAUSERIES du lundi. Sainte-Beuve, C. A. Paris [1873]. 15 v. 12° 5538.4
CAUSEY building. Abbott, J. 917.26
CAVALCASELLE, G. B., *joint author*. The early Flemish painters. *See* CROWE, J. A. 6215.3
— History of painting in Italy. *See* CROWE, J. A. 6213.2
— History of painting in North Italy. *See* CROWE, J. A. 6213.1

Shelf. No.

CAVALIER, The, dismounted. Whitmore, W. H. Salem, 1864. 8° 5014.6
CAVALLO, Tiberius. Essay on the theory and practice of medical electricity. London, 1781. 124 pp. Folded plate. 8° 6014.3
CAVÉ, Marie Elisabeth. The Cavé method for learning to draw from memory. Translated from the 4th Paris edition. New York, 1871. 134 pp. 12° 1516.6
CAVENDISH, *Sir* William, *earl of Ogle and duke of Newcastle*. The cavalier and his lady. Selections from the works of the first duke and duchess of Newcastle. Edited with an introductory essay by E. Jenkins. London, 1872. 287+ pp. 16° 5638.1
CAVENDISH, *pseud.* *See* JONES, Henry.
CAVES. Cave hunting, researches on the evidences of caves respecting the early inhabitants of Europe. Dawkins, W. B. London, 1874. 8° 6632.5
CAXTON, Laura, *pseud.* *See* COMINS, Lizzie B.
CAXTONIANA: a series of essays on life, literature, and manners. Bulwer-Lytton, E. (G. E.) L. Leipzig, 1864. 2 v. in 1. Sq. 16° 1918.2
CAXTONS, The. Bulwer-Lytton, E. (G. E.) L. 336.16
CAYUGA lake, *N. Y.*, Scenery of the head waters of the. Spencer, S. Ithaca, 1866. 16° 417.4
CAZEAU, Paulin. Theoretical and practical treatise on midwifery. 4th American from the 6th French edition by W. R. Bullock. With illustrations. Philadelphia, 1866. 987 pp. 8° 6012.23
CAZIN, Achille. Phenomena and laws of heat. Translated and edited by E. Rich. New York, 1872. xi, 265+ pp. Illustrated. 16° 1714.6
CECIL Castlemaine's gage. Rame, L. de la 331.5
CECIL Dreeme. Winthrop, T. 736.7
CECIL'S tryst. Payn, J. 310.10
CELEBRATED characters, Memoirs of. Lamartine, A. (M. L.) de. New York, 1854. 3 v. 12° 1025.10
CELLARIUS, *pseud.* Drawing-room dances. New York, 1858. 105 pp. Illustrated. 16° 1514.4
CELLINI, Benvenuto. Memoirs, written by himself: containing a variety of information respecting the arts, and the history of the 16th century. Translated by T. Roscoe. London, 1871. viii, 504 pp. Portrait. Sm. 8° 1225.17
CELNART, Elizabeth, *pseud.* *See* BAYLE-MOUILLARD, Elizabeth.
CEMENTS, Rudimentary treatise on. Burnell, G. R. London, 1872. 12° 1716.11
CENSUS of the United States. *See* UNITED STATES. *Department of the interior.*
CENTENNIALS. Celebration of the centennial anniversary of the battle of Bunker hill. *See* BOSTON, *Mass.* 810.10
— Frothingham, R. The centennial: battle of Bunker hill. Boston, 1875. 16° 810.3
— Hale, E. E. One hundred years ago. Boston, 1875. 8° 811.15
— Wheildon, W. W. Siege and evacuation of Boston and Charlestown. Boston, 1876. 8° 811.19
CENTURY club, *New York city*. Twelfth night at the Century club, Jan. 6, 1858. New York, 1858. 93 pp. 4° 817.1
CERAMIC art. *See* POTTERY.
CEREBRO-SPINAL meningitis in Massachusetts, Report on. Parks, L. (*In* Massachusetts medical society. Publications) 6021.4
CERISE. Melville, G. J. W. 321.10
CERVANTES-SAAVEDRA, Miguel de. History of Don Quixote of La Mancha. From the Spanish by Motteux. With notes; and an essay on the life and writings of Cervantes, by J. G. Lockhart. Boston, 1870. 4 v. 16° 5927.4
— Mérimée, P. Portraits historiques et littéraires. Paris, 1874. 18° 5527.14
— Prescott, W. H. Biographical and critical essays. London, 1856. 16° 1537.8
— — Biographical and critical miscellanies. Philadelphia, 1875. 12° 5237.3

Note.—See also Ticknor's History of Spanish literature [5922.2].

Shelf. No.

CESARINE Dietrich. Dudevant, A. L. A. D........ 511.15
CEYLON, The rifle and the hound in. Baker, *Sir* S. W. Philadelphia, 1871. 16° 1515.2
CHADBOURNE, Paul Ansel. Lowell lectures: 1871. Instinct: its office in the animal kingdom, and its relation to the higher powers in man. New York, 1872. 307 pp. Sm. 8°............... 6617.4
CHADWICK, William. Life and times of Daniel De Foe. London, 1859. viii, 464 pp. Portrait. 8°. 5422.6
CHAINBEARER, The. Cooper, J. F................. 525.18
CHALDEAN account of Genesis. Smith, G. New York [London], 1876. 8°.................. 6320.4
CHALLICE, A. E. Illustrious women of France. 1790–1873. With illustrations. London, 1873. xii, 352+ pp. 7 portraits. Sm. 8° 5525.7

Contents. — Madame Tallien; Empress Joséphine; Queen Hortense; Caroline Bonaparte; Duchesse d'Angoulême; Duchesse de Berry; Queen Marie Amélie; Duchesse d'Orléans; Empress Eugénie; Princess Mathilde.

CHALLIS, F. My wife's husband: a farce. New York, N. D. 33 pp. 12° 1635.3
CHALMERS, Thomas. Works. Hartford, 1822. 3 v. 12°...6328.12

Contents. — Vol. I. Evidences; Discourses. II. Sermons. III. Discourses; Occasional sermons.

— The power, wisdom, and goodness of God, as manifested in the adaptation of external nature to the moral and intellectual constitution of man. New edition. Philadelphia, 1835. 308 pp. 12°.................................. 6618.2
— Selection of discourses on the Christian revelation viewed in connexion with modern astronomy. And occasional sermons. Hartford, 1818. 322 pp. 16°..............................5819.17
CHAMBERS, Robert, *Edinburgh bookseller and author, b.* 1802, *d.* 1870. The book of days. A miscellany of popular antiquities. London, N. D. 2 v. Illustrated. 8°........................*R.R., A.3.7
— Cyclopædia of English literature. Philadelphia, 1872. 2 v. Illustrated. Portraits. 8°..*R.R., C.2.3
— Life and works of Robert Burns. New York, 1852, 54. 4 v. Sm. 8° 1225.4
— Life of Sir Walter Scott. With Abbotsford notanda by R. Carruthers. Edited by W. Chambers. Edinburgh, 1871. 196+ pp. 16°..... 5425.9
— The songs of Scotland prior to Burns. With the tunes. Edinburgh [1873]. 462 pp. Illustrated. Sq. 16° 5637.1
— Vestiges of the natural history of creation. 4th edition. New York, 1846. vi, 353 pp. 12°..1515.17
— Chambers, W. Memoir of. New York, 1872. Sm. 8°.....................................1225.15
— Page, H. A. Noble workers. London, 1875. Sm. 8°...................................... 5936.3
CHAMBERS, Robert. Index to heirs-at-law, next to kin, legatees, missing friends, encumbrancers, and creditors or their representatives in chancery suits, who have been advertised during the last 150 years. 3d edition, revised by E. Preston. London, 1872. 411+ pp. 8° 5415.3
CHAMBERS, William. Memoir of Robert Chambers, with autobiographic reminiscences of W. Chambers. New York, 1872. 313 pp. Sm. 8°.....1225.15
— and Robert. Chambers's encyclopædia. A dictionary of universal knowledge for the people. Illustrated with maps and engravings. London, 1868. 10 v. L. 8° ....................*R.R., D.3.1
— – Information for the people. Philadelphia, N. D. Illustrated. 2 v. 8° ....................*R.R., C.2.4
CHAMIER, F. Ben Brace 521.24
CHANCE, A, for himself. Trowbridge, J. T......... 925.27
CHANCE acquaintance, A. Howells, W. D.......... 529.1
CHANCE child, A. Mayo, I. F. (*In* Johnson, (E.) R. Little classics)............................ 529.4.9
CHANDELIER, Le. Musset, (L. C.) A. de. Comédies et proverbes. Paris, 1867. 12° 5534.4.2
CHANDOS. Rame, L. de la 327.21
CHANEY, George Leonard. F. Grant and co.; or, partnerships. A story for the boys who "mean business"................................. 928.15
CHANGED brides, The. Southworth, E. D. E. N. ... 727.4

Shelf. No.

CHANGING base. Everett, W. 935.2
CHANNEL islands. A farmer's vacation. Waring, G. E., *jr.* Boston, 1876. 8°....................5933.11
CHANNING, Edward Tyrrel. Life of William Ellery. (*In* Sparks, J. Library of American biography).......................................5028.1.6
CHANNING, Walter. A physician's vacation; or, a summer in Europe. Boston, 1856. iv, 564 pp. 12°.. 422.2
CHANNING, William Ellery, *D.D.* Works. 8th edition, with an introduction. Boston, 1848. 6 v. 12° 1525.1

Contents. — Vol. I. Introductory remarks; Character and writings of Milton; Life of Napoleon Bonaparte; Character and writings of Fenelon; Moral argument against Calvinism; National literature; Associations; The union; Education.
II. Slavery; The abolitionists; Annexation of Texas to the United States; Letter on catholicism; The creeds; Address on temperance; Address on self-culture.
III, IV. Discourses; Evidences of Christianity.
V. Remarks on the slavery question; Lecture on war; Lectures on the elevation of the laboring classes; Death of Dr. Follen, a discourse; Charges at the ordinations of C. Barnard and F. T. Gray, R. C. Waterston, and J. S. Dwight; Miscellanies; Appendix.
VI. Emancipation, 1840; Discourse on J. Tuckerman; Address on the present age; The church; Duty of the free states; Address on the anniversary of emancipation in the British West Indies.

— Address on temperance. Boston, 1837. 119 pp. 12° 5834.5
— Discourses, reviews, and miscellanies. Boston, 1834. ix, 603 pp. 8° 1910.2
— Slavery. Boston, 1835. 167 pp. 16°......... 818.5
— Memoir of. Channing, W. H. Boston, 1868. 3 v. 12° 1214.12
— and AIKIN, Lucy. Correspondence, from 1826 to 1842. Edited by Anna Letitia Le Breton. Boston, 1874. xx, 426 pp. 12°................. 5616.9

Note. — See note in Lower Hall Catalogue for history, etc., p. 50.

CHANNING, William Ellery, *of Concord.* Thoreau; the poet-naturalist. With memorial verses. Boston, 1873. xii, 357 pp. 12° ....1227.7 and 5027.8
CHANNING, William Henry. Memoir of William Ellery Channing, with extracts from his correspondence and manuscripts. 9th edition. Boston, 1868. 3 v. Portraits. 12°.............1214.12
— *joint editor. See* OSSOLI, Margaret Fuller, *marchesa* d'. Memoirs......................... 1215.4
CHANNINGS, The. Wood, E. P...................... 333.1
CHAPIN, Edwin Hubbell. The crown of thorns. A token for the sorrowing. Boston, 1860. 256 pp. 16°.. 1526.7
CHAPLAINS and clergy of the revolution. Headley, J. T. New York, 1864. 12°................ 1014.1
CHAPLET of pearls, The. Yonge, C. M. Leipzig... 318.4
— *Same.* New York 531.20
CHAPPAQUA, *N. Y.* The story of a summer [at Horace Greeley's home]; or, journal leaves from Chappaqua. Cleveland, C. New York, 1874. Sq. 16° 539.8
CHAPPELL, William. The history of music. (Art and science.) Vol. I. From the earliest records to the fall of the Roman empire. With explanations of ancient systems of music, musical instruments, and of the true physiological basis for the science of music, whether ancient or modern. London [1874]. lxxxix, 403+ pp. Illustrated. 8° 6232.5
CHAPTER, A, of Erie. Adams, C. F., *jr.* Boston, 1869. 12°...................................... 1916.1
CHARACTER. Bruyère, J. de la. Les caractères [de Théophraste, avec les mœurs de ce siècle]. Paris, 1816. 3 v. 12°......................... 5537.7
— Fernald, W. M. First causes of. Boston, 1865. 12°.. 5837.3
— Jameson, A. (M.) Sketches of. Boston, 1866. 16°.. 5618.3
— Smiles, S. Character. New York, 1872. 12° ..1935.41
— Whipple, E. P. Character and characteristic men. Boston, 1871. 12°............................ 1936.3
CHARADES, Social. Caldor, M. T. Boston, 1873. 16°..1516.10
CHARETTE: a tale "of lovers' sorrows and their tangled sin" 714.30

Shelf. No.

CHARICLES: a dramatic poem. Quincy, J. P. Boston, 1856. 16° ... 1615.17
CHARITY: comedy. Gilbert, W. S. Original plays. New York, 1876. 12° ... 1634.1
CHARLEMAGNE. Bulfinch, T. Legends of. Boston, 1871. Sm. 8° ... 824.2
— James, G. P. R. History of. New York, 1860. Sm. 12° ... 5528.9
CHARLEMONT. Simms, W. G. ... 725.19
CHARLES I, *of England*, History of. Abbott, J. ... 914.26
CHARLES II, *of England*, History of. Abbott, J. ... 914.28
CHARLES V, *of Germany*. Robertson, W. History of the reign of. London, 1840. 8° ... 5610.1
— *Same*. With life after his abdication, by W. H. Prescott. London, 1857. 2 v. 16° ... 1226.9
— Stirling, W. Cloister life of. Boston, 1853. 12°. 1223.6

Note.— Prescott's continuation of Robertson is based on material gathered by himself, in the use of which he was forestalled by Stirling. Prescott, in his edition of Robertson, vol. 3, p. 327, and his Philip II, end of book 1 [1222.1], reviews the authorities on his later years. See Motley's Rise of the Dutch republic (822.2]; Doran's Monarchs retired from business [1223.1]; the histories of the Reformation, and the notes under Spain and Germany. See also Harper's monthly, vol. 14.

Compare also Froude's History of England [826.8], and Guizot's History of France [5510.2].

CHARLES *the bold, duke of Burgundy*, Life of. Kirk, J. F. Philadelphia, 1864. 3 v. 8° ... 5511.1

See also France, *note*.

CHARLES EDWARD STUART, *prince, the young pretender*. Letters. *See* STANHOPE, Philip Henry, *5th earl Stanhope*. The "forty-five" ... 5418.7
CHARLES, Elizabeth. Against the stream. The story of a heroic age in England. [Napoleonic period.] Leipzig ... 329.12
— *Same*. New York ... 737.17
— The Bertram family ... 723.29
— Chronicles of the Schönberg-Cotta family ... 321.3

Note. — Luther and the reformation.

— Conquering and to conquer. [Early Christians]. 723.8
— The cottage by the cathedral, and other parables.. 321.2
— Diary of Mrs. Kitty Trevylyan ... 321.4

Note. — Whitefield and the Wesleys.

— The Draytons and the Davenents ... 321.1

Note. — Period of the English commonwealth.

— The early dawn; or, sketches of Christian life in England in the olden time. With introduction by H. B. Smith. New York, 1864. 397 pp. 12°. 725.40
— On both sides of the sea ... 321.7

Note. — Sequel to The Draytons and the Davenents.

— The victory of the vanquished ... 321.6
— Winifred Bertram ... 321.5
CHARLES Auchester. Sheppard, E. S. ... 532.1
CHARLES O'Malley. Lever, C. (J.) Leipzig ... 332.1
— *Same*. London ... 516.13
CHARLESTOWN, *Mass*. Catalogue [and supplement] of the public library. Charlestown, 1862, 72. 2 v. in 1. 8° ... 6132.4
— Siege and evacuation of Boston and Charlestown. Wheildon, W. W. Boston, 1876. 8° ... 811.19

See also Boston, *Mass*.

CHARLEY and Eva Roberts' home in the West. Thurston, L. M. ... 1117.9
CHARLEY Laurel. Kingston, W. H. G. ... 933.24
CHARLEY Roberts series. *See* THURSTON, Louise M.
CHARLIE Bell. Kellogg, E. ... 922.14
CHARLIE Codman's cruise. Alger, H., *jr*. ... 934.28
CHARLOTTE AUGUSTA, *princess of Wales*, Memoir of. Weigall, R., *lady*. London, 1874. Sm. 8° ... 5427.7
CHARMS and counter-charms. MacIntosh, M. J. ... 726.32
CHASTE as ice, pure as snow. Despard, *Mrs*. M. C. 714.3
CHATEAUBRIAND, François René, *vicomte* de. Œuvres complètes. Nouvelle édition; précédée d'une étude littéraire sur Chateaubriand, par M. Sainte-Beuve. Vignettes et gravées. Paris, N. D. 12 v. Portraits. 8° ... 5532.3

Contents.— Vol. I. Étude sur Chateaubriand; Essai sur les révolutions anciennes et modernes. II. Génie du christianisme. III. Atala; René; Le dernier Abencerage; Les Natchez; Poésies. IV. Les martyrs. V. Itinéraire de Paris à Jérusalem. VI. Voyages en Amérique, en Italie, en Mont-Blanc; Mélanges littéraires. VII. Mélanges politiques; Polémique. VIII. Polémique (fin.); Opinions et discours politiques; Fragments divers. IX. Études historiques. X. Histoire de France; Les quatre Stuarts; Vie de Rancé. XI. Le paradis perdu; Essai sur la littérature anglaise. XII. Le congrès de Vérone; Guerre d'Espagne; Table générale et analytique.

CHATEAUBRIAND, François René, *vicomte* de, *continued*.

— English literature, reviewed. Prescott, W. H. Biographical and critical essays. London, 1856. 16° ... 1537.8
— *Same*. Philadelphia, 1875. 12° ... 5237.3
CHATRIAN, Alexander, *joint author*. *See* ERCKMANN, Émile.
CHATTERTON, Thomas. Poetical works. With an essay on the Rowley poems by W. W. Skeat, and a memoir by E. Bell. London, 1872. 2 v. Sm. 8° ... 5615.5
— Masson, D. Chatterton: a story of the year 1770. London, 1874. Sm. 8° ... 5636.5
— Wilson, D. Chatterton; a biographical study. London, 1869. Sm. 8° ... 5425.6

Note. — See Note in the Lower Hall Catalogue for history, etc., p. 51.

CHATTO, W. A., *joint author*. Treatise on wood engraving. *See* JACKSON, John ... 6211.10
CHAUCER, Geoffrey. [Aldine edition of the British poets.] Poetical works. Edited by Richard Morris. With memoir by Sir Harris Nicolas. New and revised edition. London [1872]. 6 v. Sm. 8°. 5628.1

Contents. — Vol. I. Life; Essay on the language and versification of Chaucer; Introductory discourse to the Canterbury tales; Chaucer's pronunciation; On the genuineness of The romaunt of the rose; Scheme of the order of the Canterbury tales; Glossary. II, III. Canterbury tales. IV. The court of love; The parlement of briddes, or the assembly of foules; The boke of cupide, god of love, or the cuckow and the nightingale; The flower and the leaf; Troylus and Cryseyde, book 1-4. V. Troylus and Cryseyde, book 5; Chauceres A. B. C.; Chaucer's dream; The boke of the duchesse; Of quene Anelyda and false Arcyte; The house of fame; The legende of goode women. VI. The romaunt of the rose; The compleynte of a loveres lyfe; The complaynt of Mars and Venus; A goodly ballade of Chaucer; A praise of women; Minor poems; Appendix.

— Chaucer to Wordsworth. Arnold, T. London [1873]. 16° ... 5628.2
CHAUNCEY family. Memorials of the Chaunceys, including President Chauncy, his ancestors and descendants. Fowler, W. C. Boston, 1858. 8°. 610.3
CHAUNCY, Charles. A compleat view of episcopacy. Boston, 1771. x, 474 pp. 8° ... 1922.2
— Seasonable thoughts on the state of religion in New England. Boston, 1743. xxx, 424 pp. 8°. 1926.3
— Twelve sermons. Boston, 1765. iv, 344+ pp. 8°. 1922.3
CHAUVIN, Victor, *joint author*. The true Robinson Crusoes. *See* DENIS, (Jean) Ferdinand ... 938.8
CHEADLE, Walter Butler, *joint author*. The North-west passage by land. *See* FITZWILLIAM, William Wentworth, *viscount Milton* ... 5931.15
CHEEVER, William M. Practical evangelism. Boston, 1856. ix, 113 pp. 12° ... 1536.15
CHEMICAL technology, Handbook of. Wagner, R. (J.) New York, 1872. 8° ... 6431.2
CHEMISTRY. Barker, G. F. A text-book of elementary chemistry, theoretical and inorganic. Louisville, Ky. [*cop*. 1870]. 12° ... 6437.5
— Cameron, C. A. The chemistry of food in relation to the breeding and feeding of live stock. London, 1868. 16° ... 6437.1
— Cooke, J. P., *jr*. The new chemistry. New York, 1874. 12° ... 6436.15
— — Principles of chemical philosophy. Boston, 1874. 8° ... 6435.5
— Eliot, C. W., and Storer, F. H. A compendious manual of qualitative chemical analysis. New York, 1873. 12° ... 6436.4
— — A manual of inorganic chemistry. New York, 1875 [*cop*. 1866]. 8° ... 6435.6
— Fownes, G. Rudimentary chemistry. London, 1872. 12° ... 1715.25
— Grund, F. J. Elements of. Boston, 1838. 12°. 1717.11
— Hooker, W. Chemistry. New York, 1874. 12°. 6437.4
— Johnston, J. F. W. The chemistry of common life. New York, 1871. 2 v. 12° ... 1526.27
— Liebig, J. von. Animal chemistry. Cambridge, 1842. 12° ... 6035.3
— — Familiar letters on. New York, 1856. 12° .. 1525.3

Shelf. No.

CHEMISTRY, *continued.*
— Miller, W. A. Elements of. London, 1868-72. 3 v. 8° 6432.2
— Morfit, C., and Mucklé, A. Chemical and pharmaceutic manipulations. Philadelphia, 1849. 12° 6433.3
— Prout, W. Chemistry considered with reference to natural theology. London, 1855. Sm. 8° .. 6436.10
— Vogel, H. The chemistry of light and photography. New York, 1875. 12° 6436.16
— Watts, H. Dictionary of. London, 1868-72. 6 v. 8° .... *R.R., C.2.1

See also Agricultural chemistry, Heat.

CHENEY, Ednah D. The child of the tide 937.29
— Sally Williams, the mountain girl 915.21
CHENEY, O. Augusta, *joint author.* Seeking his fortune, and other dialogues. *See* ALGER, Horatio, *jr.* 1518.11
CHERBULIEZ, Victor. Étude de littérature et d'art. Paris, 1873. 334+ pp. 16° 5536.7

Contents. — Études sur l'Allemagne; Lettres sur le salon de 1872.

— Leisure hour series. Count Kostia. From the French by O. D. Ashley 518.13
— Miss Rovel. Translated by Frances A. Shaw.... 711.32
— Pauli Méré. Paris, 1865. 352+ pp. 18° 5536.16
— The romance of an honest woman 768.11
CHERPILLOUD, J. Book of versions; or, guide to French translation; with notes, for the use of schools. New edition. Revised by A. Gombert. Philadelphia, 1829. 252 pp. 12° 5538.3
CHERRY, J. L. Life and remains of John Clare, the "Northamptonshire peasant poet." With illustrations by Birket Foster. London, 1873. xiii, 349+ pp. Portraits. Sm. 8° 5625.1
CHESNEY, Charles Cornwallis. Essays in modern military biography. London, 1874. viii, 414+ pp. 8° 5922.8
— Waterloo lectures: a study of the campaign of 1815. 3d edition. London, 1874. xii, 266+ pp. 8° 5513.3
CHESNEY, George. The fall of England? The battle of Dorking. New York, 1871. 66 pp. 12°. 5617.2
CHESS. Edge, F. M. The exploits and triumphs, in Europe, of Paul Morphy, the chess champion. New York, 1859. 12° 1516.25
— Staunton, H. The chess-player's handbook. London, 1858. 16° 1514.3
CHEST, A treatise on the diseases of the. Swett, J. A. New York, 1852. 8° 6021.14
CHESTERFIELD, *Earl of.* *See* STANHOPE, Philip Dormer.
CHEVALIER, The. Dumas, A. (D.) 732.16
CHEVALLIER, E., *joint author.* The student's manual of oriental history. *See* LENORMANT, François. 5927.8
CHIAPAS, Incidents of travel in. Stephens, J. L. New York, 1856. 2 v. 8° 422.5
CHICAGO, *Ill.* *See* LIPPINCOTT, S. J. New life in new lands: notes of travel. New York, 1873. 12° 214.1
CHICKERING, Jonas, A tribute to the life and character of. Parker, R. G. Boston, 1854. 12° 1016.3
CHILD, George Chaplin. The great architect. Benedicite; illustrations of the power, wisdom, and goodness of God, as manifested in his works. New York, 1872. 375+ pp. 8° 6615.4
CHILD, Francis James, *editor.* English and Scottish ballads. Boston, 1871. 8 v. [The British poets.] 16° 5628.5
CHILD, Lydia Maria. The family nurse; or companion of the frugal housewife. Revised by a member of the Massachusetts medical society. Boston, 1837. 156 pp. 16° 1525.31
— Isaac T. Hopper: a true life. Boston, 1854. xv, 493 pp. Portrait. 12° 1214.3
— Philothea. [A novel.] Boston, 1836. 284+ pp. 12° 515.1
— A romance of the republic. Boston, 1871. 442+ pp. 12° 526.7

Shelf. No.

CHILD, The. Dupanloup, F. A. P. Boston, 1875. 12°. 1915.10
CHILD life: a collection of poems. Whittier, J. G., *editor.* Boston, 1875. Sm. 4° 1624.4
CHILD-LIFE in Italy. Watson, E. H. Boston, 1866. 16° 931.5
CHILD life in prose. Whittier, J. G., *editor.* Boston, 1874. Sm. 4° 912.10
CHILD life of Tom and Mary. Eyster, N. 938.5
CHILD, The, of the island glen. Kellogg, E. 914.42
CHILD, The, of the tide. Cheney, E. D. 937.29
CHILD wife, The. Reid, M. 527.5
CHILD's, A, dream of a star. Dickens, C. (J. H.) (*In* Johnson, (E.) R. Little classics) 529.4.10
CHILDE Harold's pilgrimage: a romaunt. Byron, G. G. N., *lord.* Works. Leipzig, 1866. Sq. 16°. 1614.13.2
CHILDHOOD, The, of religions. Clodd, E. London, 1875. Sm. 8° 6328.21
CHILDREN. Evanson, R. T., and Maunsell, H. Practical treatise on the management and diseases of. Boston, 1848. 8° 6012.11
— Underwood, M. Treatise on the diseases of. Philadelphia, 1842. 8° 6023.13
CHILDREN, The, in the wood: an opera. Morton, T. New York, N. D. 12° 1635.3
CHILDREN, The, of Amity court. Thurston, L. M... 1117.12
CHILDREN, The, of the abbey. Roche, M. R. 527.15
CHILDREN, The, of the New forest. Marryat, F.... 337.8
CHILDREN, The, of the public. Hale, E. E. (*In* Johnson, (E.) R. Little classics) 529.4.12
CHILDREN's, The, crusade. Gray, G. Z. New York, 1871. Sq. 16° 824.10

Note. — An interesting study of a curious episode of the crusade period.

CHILDREN's, The, voyage. Cupples, A. J. 912.19
CHILE con carne; or, the camp and the field. Smith, S. C. New York, 1857. 12° 515.2
CHILI, Los Gringos; or, wanderings in. Wise, H. A. New York, 1849. 12° 435.4
CHIMES, The. Dickens, C. (J. H.) 338.10
CHIMNEY-CORNER, The. Stowe, H. (E.) B. 1535.15
CHINA. Carné, L. de. Travels in Indo-China and the Chinese empire. London, 1872. 8° 5931.9
— Confucius (*or* Kong-Fu-Tse), and Mencius. Chinese classics: a translation by J. Legge. New York, 1870. 8° 5923.2
— Feudge, F. R. A tour in the China seas. (*In* Many lands and many people) 431.3
— Gutzlaff, C. Journal of two voyages along the coast of, 1831, 32. New York, 1833. 12° 426.13
— Hawks, F. L. Narrative of the expedition of an American squadron to the China seas, 1852-54. New York, 1856. 8° 421.1
— Huc, É. R. A journey through the Chinese empire. New York, 1855. 12° 5934.9
— Meadows, T. T. The Chinese and their rebellions. London, 1856. 8° 5921.13
— Medhurst, W. H. The foreigner in far Cathay. New York, 1873. 12° 424.19
— Miscellaneous pieces relating to the Chinese. London, 1762. 2 v. 16° 5938.1
— Nevius, J. L. China and the Chinese. New York, 1872. 12° 423.15
— Oliphant, L. Narrative of the Earl of Elgin's mission to, 1857-59. New York, 1860. 8° 421.2
— Taylor, (J.) B. Visit to, in 1853. New York, 1864. 12° 425.7
— Thomson, J. The straits of Malacca, Indo-China, and China. New York, 1875. 8° 5921.4
— Yule, H. Cathay and the way thither; being a collection of medieval notices of. London, 1866. 8° 5923.10

Note. — See Harper's monthly, vols. 11, 29, 31, 37, and 39.

CHINA-WARE. The bric-à-brac hunter; or chapters on chinamania. Hall, H. B. Philadelphia [London], 1875. Sm. 8° 6214.4
CHINCAPIN Charlie. Eyster, N. 938.4
CHINESE embassy, Reception and entertainment of the. *See* BOSTON, *Mass.* 831.2
CHIPS from a German workshop. Mueller, (F.) M. New York, 1871-76. 4 v. Sm. 8° 5616.1

Shelf. No.

CHIVALRY, Age of. [Charlemagne period.] Bulfinch, T. Boston, 1871. 12° ... 824.1

CHOATE, Rufus, Life of. Brown, S. G. Boston, 1870. Sm. 8° ... 5025.1

CHOICE, The, of a dwelling. Wheeler, G. London, 1872. Sm. 8° ... 6226.2

CHOICE receipts. Woodman, M. S. Boston, 1875. 12° ... 6427.2

CHOISY. Story, J. P. ... 521.20

CHOPIN, Frederick. Haweis, H. R. Music and morals. New York, 1872. 12° ... 1513.16

— Liszt, F. Life of. Boston, N. D. 16° ... 1227.2

CHOPIN, Jean Marie. Danemark. *See* EYRIÈS, Jean Baptiste Benoît ... 5911.11

CHOPS the dwarf. Dickens, C. (J. H.) (*In* Johnson, (E.) R. Little classics) ... 529.4.2

CHORLEY, Henry Fothergill. Modern German music. London [1854]. xvi, 418+ pp. Sm. 8° ... 6235.2

— Personal reminiscences. (*In* Stoddard, R. H. Bric-à-brac series) ... 1828.2

— Recent art and society as described in [his] autobiography and memoirs. Compiled from the edition of Henry G. Hewitt by C. H. Jones. New York, 1874. x, 317 pp. 12° ... 5616.14

CHOULES, John Overton. The cruise of the steam yacht North Star; a narrative of the excursion of Mr. Vanderbilt's party to England, Russia, Denmark, France, Spain, Italy, Malta, Turkey, Madeira, etc. Boston, 1854. 353 pp. Illustrated. Portraits. 12° ... 425.10

CHOUQUET, Gustave. First lessons in learning French. 7th edition. New York, 1849. 128 pp. Sq. 16° ... 2018.3

CHRIS and Otho. Smith, J. P. ... 727.26

CHRIST. Beecher, H. W. Life of Jesus, the Christ. New York, 1871. 8° ... 1021.4

— Brooke, S. A. Christ in modern life. New York, 1872. Sm. 8° ... 5814.9

— Cohen, J. The deicides. Analysis of the life of Jesus. Baltimore, 1873. 12° ... 5817.13

— Farrar, F. W. The life of Christ. New York [1874]. 2 v. 8° ... 5810.3

— Formby, H. The life, passion, death, and resurrection of our Lord Jesus Christ. London [1874]. Sq. 16° ... 6328.22

— Fox, W. J. Christ and Christianity. Sermons on the mission, character, and doctrine, of Jesus of Nazareth. Boston, 1833. 2 v. 12° ... 5815.12

— Furness, W. H. History of Jesus. Boston, 1850. 12° ... 5815.15

— – Jesus and his biographers. Philadelphia, 1838. 8° ... 5811.7

— – Thoughts on Jesus of Nazareth. Boston, 1859. 12° ... 5816.18

— Hudson, C. F. Christ our life. Boston, 1860. 12°. 6326.1

— Miller, W. Evidence from Scripture and history of the second coming of Christ, about 1843. Boston, 1842. 12° ... 5818.11

— Newcome, W. Observations on our Lord's conduct as a divine instructor. Charlestown, 1810. 8°. 5813.1

— Parker, J. Ecce Deus: essays on the life and doctrine of Jesus Christ. Boston, 1867. 12° ... 1526.4

— Renan, (J.) E. Life of Jesus. New York, 1865. 12° ... 1525.2

— Scenes in the life of Jesus. Boston, 1858. 16°. 918.2

— Sears, E. H. The fourth gospel the heart of Christ. Boston, 1872. Sm. 8° ... 6326.9

— Seeley, J. R. Ecce Homo: a survey of the life and work of Jesus Christ. Boston, 1866. 12°. 1526.5

— Thomas à Kempis. Imitation of Christ. London, N. D. 16° ... 5819.1

— *Same.* New York [1851]. 12° ... 1536.16

— Uhlhorn, G. The modern representations of the life of Jesus. Boston, 1868. 16° ... 6328.7

— Ware, H., *jr.* Discourses on the life and character of Jesus Christ. Boston, 1825. Sm. 8° ... 5814.2

Note.—The modern reaction from the orthodox views began with Strauss, who maintained what is called the "mythical theory," pronouncing miracles impossible, and the gospels a collection of fabulous accounts of Jesus, not deliberate fictions, but founded principally on traditions and popular notions concerning the expected Messiah. See "Apostolic age" and "Tübingen school" in McClintock and Strong's

Shelf. No.

CHRIST, *continued.*

Cyclopædia. The lead in refutation was taken by Neander, whose life is a grouping by events historically similar. At a later day, Renan, placing more reliance than Strauss on the historic proofs, gave rise to what is called the "legendary hypothesis," and has been chiefly combated by Pressensé. Prof. Seeley's "Ecce Homo" presents a striking view of Christ as the great inspirer of "the enthusiasm of humanity," the subject of "Christ as the creator of modern theology and religion" being reserved for another volume, not yet published. The object of "Ecce Deus," by Dr. Joseph Parker, is to supplement, and in part to controvert, the views presented in "Ecce Homo." The views of Dr. Furness, while he admits the essential authenticity of the gospels, are peculiarly naturalistic, and somewhat in sympathy with Dr. Schenkel's. Beecher's Life, which is not yet completed, is evangelical with broad sympathies. Farrar's Life is evangelical, non-controversial, and embodies recent researches. See also Milman's History of Christianity [5817.1.1]. The catalogues of the Bates Hall must be searched for several of the indicative lives named above. See the Note in the Lower Hall Catalogue for history, etc., p. 53.

CHRISTENDOM and the drink curse. Burns, D. London, 1875. 8° ... 1912.9

CHRISTIAN art. Tyrwhitt, R. St. J. The art teaching of the primitive church. London [1875]. Sm. 8° ... 6234.6

— – Christian art and symbolism. London, 1872. 16° ... 1514.14 and 6235.1

CHRISTIAN believing and living. Huntington, F. D. Boston, 1860. 12° ... 6325.11

CHRISTIAN character, On the formation of the. Ware, H., *jr.* Cambridge, 1831. 12° ... 5819.13

CHRISTIAN days and thoughts. Peabody, E. Boston, 1858. 16° ... 6328.13

CHRISTIAN disciple. Vol. 1–4; new series, v. 1, 2. Boston, 1813–20. 6 v. 8° ... 6324.3

CHRISTIAN doctrine, Lectures on. Peabody, A. P. Boston, 1844. 12° ... 5815.20

CHRISTIAN effort. Baker, S. New York, 1850. 16°. 5819.6

CHRISTIAN examiner and theological review. Vol. 36–41. Boston, 1844–46. 6 v. in 3. 8° ... 6324.4

CHRISTIAN layman, The. Parsons, B. Mobile, 1840. 12° ... 5815.16

CHRISTIAN life. Bartol, C. A. Discourses on the Christian spirit and life. Boston, 1850. 12°. 5815.19 and 6325.14

— Boardman, W. E. The higher Christian life. Boston, 1858. 12° ... 1536.10 and 6325.10

— Fernald, W. M. The true Christian life and how to attain it. Boston, 1874. 16° ... 6327.14

CHRISTIAN monitor, The. Vol. 1–10. Boston, 1806–11. 10 v. 12° ... 1327.1

CHRISTIAN morality. Fox, W. J. Boston, 1833. 16°. 5815.13

CHRISTIAN nurture, Views of. Bushnell, H. Hartford, 1847. 12° ... 5817.8

CHRISTIAN views. Parsons, B. Boston, 1848. 12°. 1524.16

CHRISTIAN year, The. Thoughts in verse for the Sundays and holidays throughout the year. Keble, J. New York, 1873. 12° ... 1616.6

CHRISTIAN'S mistake. Craik, D. (M.) ... 323.23

CHRISTIANITY. Bonnet, C. Philosophical and critical inquiries concerning Christianity. Philadelphia, 1803. 16° ... 1918.10

— Chalmers, T. Selection of discourses on the Christian revelation viewed in connexion with modern astronomy. Hartford, 1818. 16° ... 5819.17

— Christianity and scepticism. *See* BOSTON lectures. Boston, 1872. 16° ... 5816.4

— Cocker, B. F. Christianity and Greek philosophy. New York, 1872. Sm. 8° ... 5814.5

— Eaton, J. R. T. The permanence of. London, 1873. 8° ... 6324.1

— Fisher, G. P. Essays on the supernatural origin of. New York, 1866. 8° ... 6324.6

— Jaeger, A. Mind and heart in religion; or, Judaism and Christianity. New York, 1873. Sq. 16° ... 6326.22

— Kavanagh, J. Women of. New York, 1860. 12°. 1225.6

— Milman, H. H. History of. London, 1867. 3 v. 16° ... 5817.1

— Peabody, A. P. Christianity and science. New York, 1874. 12° ... 6326.17

— Pressensé, E. de. The early years of. New York, 1871. 12° ... 5816.2

— – Heresy and Christian doctrine. London, 1873. 8° ... 5813.8

Shelf. No.

CHRISTIANITY, *continued.*

— Priestley, J. Views of Christian truth, piety, and morality, selected from [his] writings. Cambridge, 1834. Sm. 8° ... 6326.6

— Pullen, H. W. Modern Christianity, a civilized heathenism. Boston, 1875. 12° ... 6325.6

— Russell, J., *earl.* Essays on the history of the Christian religion. London, 1873. 16° ... 6328.8

— Watson, R. An apology for Christianity. Providence, 1794. Sm. 8° ... 1925.2

See also Christ, Church, Ecclesiastical history, Evidences, Missions, Theology.

Note. — See Note in the Lower Hall Catalogue for history, etc., p. 53. Clarke's Ten great religions [1523.2] compares Christianity with other creeds. Gibbon's Roman empire [824.9] necessarily covers the rise and formation of the Christian church, but he is accused of hostility.

CHRISTIE Johnstone. Reade, C. Boston ... 527.3

— *Same.* Leipzig ... 339.23

CHRISTIE Redfern's troubles ... 717.10

CHRISTIE'S faith. Robinson, F. W. ... 716.8

CHRISTINA North. Archer, E. M. ... 711.18

CHRISTMAS books. Dickens, C. (J. H.) ... 1824.3

CHRISTMAS books. Thackeray, W. M. Works ... 513.1.12

CHRISTMAS carol, A. Dickens, C. (J. H.) ... 338.10

— *Same.* (*In* Johnson, (E.) R. Little classics) ... 529.4.5

CHRISTMAS gift, The. Adams, W. T. ... 918.12

CHRISTMAS guest, The. Southworth, E. D. E. N., and Baden, F. H. ... 522.9

CHRISTMAS locket, The. A holiday number of Old and new ... 1426.2

CHRISTMAS stories. Dickens, C. (J. H.), and others. 338.3

CHRISTOPHER NORTH, *pseud.* *See* WILSON, John.

CHRISTOPHERS, S. W. Homes of old English writers. London [1874]. Illustrated. vii, 284 pp. Sm. 8° ... 5428.16

Note. — Sketches of Hugh Latimer, John Donne, George Hakewill, John Hackett, Thomas Fuller, John Horn, John Howe, John Flavel.

— Hymn-writers and their hymns. London [1866]. xii, 378 pp. 16° ... 5626.2

CHRISTUS victor. Boston, 1855. 28 pp. Sq. 16° .. 1612.13

CHRONICLES of Carlingford. Oliphant, M. (O. W.) . 521.40

CHRONICLES of the Canongate. Scott, *Sir* W. ... 523.19

CHRONICLES of Wolfert's Roost. Irving, W. Leipzig, 1855. Sq. 16° ... 311.14

CHRONOLOGY. Bond, J. J. Handy-book of rules and tables for verifying dates with the Christian era. London, 1875. Sm. 8° ... 5627.2

— Woodward, B. B., and Cates, W. L. R. Encyclopædia of. London, 1872. 8° ... *R.R., E.3.7

CHRYSOSTOMUS, Joannes, *St.* Newman, J. H. Historical sketches. London, 1873. Sm. 8° ... 5925.5.3

— Stephens, W. R. W. Life and times of. London, 1872. 8° ... 5813.6

CHURCH, Alfred, and BRODRIBB, William Jackson. Pliny's letters [outlined and explained]. Edinburgh, 1872. 170+ pp. 16°. [Ancient classics for English readers] ... 6116.12

CHURCH, Florence, *formerly Miss Marryat.* The confessions of Gerald Estcourt ... 337.18

— Fighting the air ... 331.17

— For ever and ever ... 337.17

— Her lord and master ... 337.21

— Life and letters of Captain Marryat. Leipzig, 1872. 327 pp. Sq. 16° ... 1228.5

— *Same.* London, 1872. 2 v. Sm. 8° ... 5025.6

— Love's conflict ... 337.16

— A lucky disappointment ... 718.6

— Mad Dumaresq. 2 v. ... 329.19

— Nelly Brooke ... 337.14

— No intentions ... 310.28

— Open! Sesame! ... 720.35

— Petronel ... 337.15

— The prey of the gods ... 337.20

— Véronique ... 337.19

— A star and a heart. To which is added An utter impossibility ... 334.7

— Woman against woman ... 710.21

CHURCH, Richard William. Saint Anselm. [London] 1870. xii, 303 pp. Wood-cut. [Sunday library.] Sm. 8° ... 5937.3

CHURCH architecture. Stones of the temple; or, lessons from the fabric and furniture of the church. Field, W. New York, 1873. Sm. 8° ... 5815.7

CHURCH music. Boston musical education society's collection of church music. Edited by B. F. Baker and I. B. Woodbury. Boston, 1845. Oblong 8° ... 1518.4

— Zeuner, C. The ancient lyre, a collection of church music. Boston, 1840. Oblong 8° ... 1518.5

CHURCHILL, Charles Henry. Life of Abdel Kader, ex-sultan of the Arabs of Algeria; written from his own dictation, and compiled from other authentic sources. London, 1867. xiv, 331+ pp. Sm. 8° ... 5934.4

CHURCHILL, Fleetwood. The diseases of females. New edition, revised. With the notes of R. M. Huston. Philadelphia, 1850. 632 [624] pp. 8°. 6012.4

— Essays on the puerperal fever and other diseases peculiar to women. Selected from the writings of British authors previous to the close of the eighteenth century. London, 1849. viii, 552 pp. 8° ... 5013.13

— Theory and practice of midwifery. With notes and additions, by D. F. Condie. With illustrations. Philadelphia, 1855. xviii, 510 [478] pp. 8° ... 6022.17

CHURCHILL, John, *duke of Marlborough,* Life of. Coxe, W. London, 1847. 3 v. Sm. 8° ... 5426.10

CHYNOWETH, W. Harris. The fall of Maximilian, late emperor of Mexico. 2d edition. London, 1872. xviii, 277+ pp. 1 plate. Map. 8° .. 5013.2

CICERO, Marcus Tullius. Life and letters. London, 1875. Engraved title-page. xix, 829+ pp. Portrait. 8° ... 6111.5

Contents. — Life, by C. Middleton; Letters to his friends, translated by W. Melmoth; Letters to Atticus, translated by W. Heberden.

— De officiis libri tres. Ex editionibus Oliveti et Ernesti. Accedunt notæ Anglicæ. Cura C. K. Dillaway. Philadelphia, 1850. 283 pp. Sm. 12° ... 6118.2

— La république. Traduite d'après le texte découvert par M. Mai, avec un discours préliminaire et des suppléments historiques par [A. F.] Villemain. Nouvelle édition. Paris, 1864. xcii, 403 pp. 12° ... 5537.16

— Tusculanarum quæstionum libri quinque. Ex editionibus Oliveti et Ernesti. Accedunt notæ Anglicæ. Cura C. K. Dillaway. Philadelphia, 1849. 2 v. Sm. 12° ... 6118.3

— Collins, W. L. Cicero [outlined and explained]. Edinburgh, 1871. 16° ... 6116.10

— Forsyth, W. Life of. London, 1869. 8° ... 5932.8

— Middleton, C. Life of. London, 1837. 8° ... 5521.2

— Newman, J. H. Historical sketches. London, 1872. Sm. 8° ... 5925.5

CINDERELLA. Rossini, G. (*In* Ditson, O., and co. Standard opera librettos) ... 6233.3.3

CINQ-MARS ou une conjuration sous Louis XIII. Vigny, A. (V.), *comte* de. Paris, 1873. 18° ... 5536.19

CINQ-MARS: or a conspiracy under Louis XIII. Vigny, A. (V.), *comte* de. London, 1860. Sm. 8° ... 537.21

CIPHER: a romance. Austin, J. G. ... 711.7

CIRCUIT rider, The. Eggleston, E. ... 726.20

CIRCUMSTANTIAL evidence, Famous cases of. Phillips, S. M. Boston, 1873. 8° ... 6313.2

CITOYENNE Jacqueline. Keddie, *Miss* —. London, 1865. 16° ... 736.14

CITY, The: its sins and sorrows. Guthrie, T. New York, 1873. 12° ... 6327.16

CITY, The, of God. Augustinus, A., *St., bishop of Hippo.* Edinburgh, 1872. 2 v. 8° ... 5811.11

CITY, The, of the saints. [Mormonism.] Burton, R. F. New York, 1862. 8° ... 412.2

CITY road chapel, London, and its associations. Stevenson, G. J. London [1872]. 8° ... 5414.1

CIVIL engineering. Law, H. Civil engineering. London, 1869. 4 v. in 2. 12° ... 1716.37

— Stevenson, D. Sketch of civil engineering in North America. London, 1859. 12° ... 6428.3

Shelf. No.

CIVIL or Roman law. Hadley, J. Introduction to Roman law. New York, 1874. Sm. 8° 6316.2
— Justinianus I, *emperor.* The Institutes of Justinian. 5th edition. London, 1874. 8° 6314.1
CIVILIZATION. Baldwin, J. D. Pre-historic nations. New York, 1872. 12° 824.7
— Guizot, F. (P. G.) History of, from the fall of the Roman empire to the French revolution. 4 v. in 2. 12° 5924.8
— Lubbock, *Sir* J. The origin of. New York, 1871. 12° 1527.1
— Meadows, T. T. The Chinese and their rebellions. Added, an essay on. London, 1856. 8° 5921.13
— Tylor, E. B. Researches into the early history of mankind and the development of. London, 1870. 8° 5912.8
— Wilson, D. Prehistoric man. Researches into the origin of civilisation in the old and new world. London, 1876. 2 v. 8° 6613.13

Note. — See Note in the Lower Hall Catalogue for history, etc., p. 55.

CLANDESTINE marriage, The. Dupuy, E. A. 522.7
CLARE, John, Life and remains of. Cherry, J. L. London, 1873. Sm. 8° 5625.1
CLARENDON, *Earl of.* *See* HYDE, Edward.
CLARISSA [Harlowe]. Richardson, S. Leipzig. 4 v. in 2 .... 316.21
— *Same.* New York 518.27
CLARK, Charles Heber. Out of the hurly-burly; or, life in an odd corner. By Max Adeler [*pseud.*]. 723.5
CLARK, Daniel Kinnear. An elementary treatise on steam and the steam-engine, stationary and portable. With illustrations. London, 1875. xvi, 344 pp. [Weale's rudimentary series.] 12°. 6428.7
CLARK, Henry Alden, *joint compiler.* The Harvard book. *See* VAILLE, Frederic Ozni 5230.1
CLARK, Rufus Wheelwright. New serial question books on the heroes of the Bible. 4th series. For adults. Boston [*cop.* 1864]. 106 pp. 16°. 5819.17
CLARK, Thomas March. John Whopper the newsboy 926.2
CLARK, William Adolphus. Hard knocks; or, Who is first? A satire. By Anicetus [*pseud.*]. Boston, 1872. 118 pp. Illustrated. 16° 5216.5
CLARKE, Charles and Mary Cowden. "Many happy returns of the day!" A birth-day book. New edition. With engravings. London [1859]. viii, 355 pp. 16° 912.8
CLARKE, Edward Hammond. The building of a brain. Boston, 1874. 153 pp. 16° 5837.4
— Sex in education. Boston, 1874. 181 pp. 16°. 1937.2 and 5838.1
— — A reply to. *See* HOWE, Julia Ward 1937.4
CLARKE, James Freeman. Common-sense in religion. Boston, 1874. 443 pp. 12° 5817.7
— The hour which cometh and now is: sermons. Boston, 1864. vi, 348 pp. 16° 6326.3
— Ten great religions: an essay in comparative theology. Boston, 1872. x, 528 pp. 1 plate. 8°. 1523.2
— *joint editor.* *See* OSSOLI, Margaret Fuller, *marchesa* d'. Memoirs 1215.4
— and Lilian. Exotics: attempts to domesticate them. [Poems.] By J. F. C. and L. C. Boston, 1875. 141 pp. Sq. 16° 1627.3
CLARKE, John. Sermons. Boston, 1799. 501+ pp. Portrait. 8° 5814.3
CLARKE, Marcus. His natural life. A novel 721.24
CLARKE, Mary Cowden. The complete concordance to Shakspere. New and revised edition. Boston [London], 1873. vii, 860+ pp. 8° 5611.5
— The iron cousin 725.39
— A rambling story 718.1
CLARKE, Rebecca Sophia. (*Sophie May.*) The doctor's daughter 934.19
— Dotty Dimple stories. Dotty Dimple at her grandmother's 927.10
— — Dotty Dimple at home 927.12
— — Dotty Dimple at play 927.13
— — Dotty Dimple at school 927.15
— — Dotty Dimple out West 927.11
— — Dotty Dimple's Flyaway 927.14

CLARKE, Rebecca Sophia, *continued.*
— Little Prudy series. Captain Horace 927.1
— — Cousin Grace 927.3
— — Dotty Dimple 927.2
— — Fairy book 927.4
— — Little Prudy 927.6
— — Sister Susy 927.5
— Little Prudy's Flyaway series. Aunt Madge's story. 927.8
— — Little folks astray 927.9
— — Little grandfather 939.3
— — Miss Thistledown 927.26
— — Prudy keeping house 927.7
— The maidenhood series. The Asbury twins 1115.17
— — Our Helen 933.10
CLARKE, Richard H. Lives of the deceased bishops of the catholic church in the United States. With appendix and an analytical index. New York, 1872. 2 v. Portraits. 8° 5811.1
CLASSICAL and scientific studies, and the great schools of England: a lecture. Atkinson, W. P. Cambridge, 1865. 8° 1912.3
CLASSICAL and utilitarian studies, Remarks on. Bigelow, J. Boston, 1867. 16° 1526.18
CLASSICAL learning, The claims of, examined and refuted. Rumford, *pseud.* Boston, 1824. 8°. 5834.7
CLAUDIA. Douglas, A. M. 535.7
CLAVERINGS, The. Trollope, A. 334.1
CLAY, Henry. *See* PARTON, J. Famous Americans of recent times. Boston, 1871. 8° 1214.14
CLAYTON, Ellen Creathorne. Queens of song: being memoirs of some of the most celebrated female vocalists. Added a chronological list of all the operas that have been performed in Europe. With portraits. London, 1863. 2 v. 8° 1221.4
CLAYTON, Robert. Speech before the Irish house of lords on subscription to articles and creeds. (*In* Sparks, J. Collection of essays and tracts in theology) 1918.9.6
CLEMENCY Franklyn. Keary, A. 727.33
CLEMENS, Samuel Langhorne. (*Mark Twain.*) The innocents abroad. [Humorous travels.] With illustrations. Hartford, 1872. 651 pp. 8° ... 421.6
— Mark Twain's (burlesque) autobiography and first romance. New York [*cop.* 1871]. 47 pp. 12° 535.20
— Mark Twain's sketches, new and old. Hartford, 1875. 320 pp. Illustrated. Sm. 4° 712.8
— Roughing it. Illustrated. Hartford, 1872. 591+ pp. 8° 212.2
— and WARNER, Charles Dudley. The gilded age. Illustrated. Hartford, 1874. 574+ pp. 8°.. 712.1
CLEMENS, Titus Flavius, *of Alexandria.* Writings. Translated by William Wilson. Edinburgh, 1867, 69. 2 v. [Ante-Nicene Christian library.] 8° .... Vol. 4, 12 of 6322.4
CLEMENT, Clara Erskine. Handbook of legendary and mythological art. With illustrations. 4th edition. New York, 1872. x, 510 pp. Sm. 8°. 1513.15
— Painters, sculptors, architects, engravers, and their works. With illustrations and monograms. 2d edition. New York, 1874. xii, 661 pp. 16°. 1513.17
CLEMENTINE homilies, The. Edinburgh, 1870. 340+ pp. [Ante-Nicene Christian library.] 8°... 6322.4.17

Note. — Books 1-5, are translated by Thomas Smith; books 6-12, by Peter Peterson; and books 13-20, by James Donaldson.

CLEOPATRA, History of. Abbott, J. 915.11
CLERGYMAN'S, The, wife. Ritchie, A. C. 723.30
CLERK, Alice M., *translator.* Historical tales and anecdotes of the time of the early Khalîfahs. *See* 'ILÂM-EN-NÂS 5927.6
CLERK'S magazine, New; containing all the most useful forms, which occur in business transactions between man and man. By a member of the Massachusetts bar. Boston, 1832. 327 pp. 12° 1727.1
CLEVE hall. Sewell, E. M. 532.6
CLEVELAND, Cecelia. Story of a summer [at Horace Greeley's home]; or, journal leaves from Chappaqua. New York, 1874. 274 pp. Illustrated. Sq. 16° 1019.2

Shelf. No.

CLEVELAND, Charles. Ninetieth birthday gathering. Pease, G. Boston, 1862. 16° ... 1016.1
CLEVELAND, Charles Dexter. A compendium of English literature, chronologically arranged. Philadelphia [*cop.* 1848]. 776 pp. 12° ... 1534.7
CLEVELAND, Henry Russell. Life of Henry Hudson. (*In* Sparks, J. Library of American biography) ... 5028.1.10
CLEVER woman, The, of the family. Yonge, C. M. 318.9
CLIFF-CLIMBERS, The. Reid, M. ... 923.31
CLIFFORD, Frank S. A romance of perfume lands, or, the search for Capt. Jacob Cole. With facts about perfumes and articles used in the toilet. (Illustrated.) Boston, 1875. iv, 295 pp. 16°. 733.13
CLIMATE, The man of the North, and the man of the South; or the influence of. Bonstetten, C. V. de. New York, 1864. 12° ... 1938.2
CLIMBING plants, The movements and habits of. Darwin, C. (R.) London, 1875. Sm. 8° ... 6625.4
CLIMBING the rope. Nowell, H. P. H. ... 936.21
CLINTON. Simonds, W. ... 932.29
CLIQUE, The, of gold. Gaboriau, E. ... 710.7
CLIVE, Caroline. Paul Ferroll ... 310.7
— Why Paul Ferroll killed his wife ... 310.8
— Year after year ... 310.9
CLIVE, Robert, 1*st lord Clive*, Life of. Gleig, G. R. London, 1848. Sm. 8° ... 5428.8
CLOCK, The, struck three. Watson, S. ... 6325.17
CLOCKMAKER, The. Haliburton, T. C. ... 535.12
CLOCKS, Rudimentary treatise on. Denison, E. B. London, 1868. 12° ... 1716.12
CLODD, Edward. The childhood of religions: embracing a simple account of the birth and growth of myths and legends. London, 1875. viii, 288 pp. Sm. 8° ... 6328.21
CLOISTER, The, and the hearth. Reade, C. ... 316.24
CLOUD, The, on the heart. Roe, A. S. ... 723.31
CLOUD-PICTURES. Underwood, F. H. ... 537.18
CLUBS. Fairfield, F. G. The clubs of New York. New York, 1873. 12° ... 5036.1
— Timbs, J. Clubs and club life in London. London [1872]. Sm. 8° ... 5417.3
COAL. Hunt, R. Coal as a reservoir of power. (*In* Estes, D. Half-hour recreations in popular science) ... 6813.7
— Williams C. W. Treatise on the combustion of. London, 1858. 12° ... 1715.19
COAL-MINERS, Lawrence's adventures among the. Trowbridge, J. T. ... 932.20
COBB, Samuel C. Inaugural addresses. *See* BOSTON, *Mass.* ... 6923.11,13
COBB, Sophia Dickinson. Hillsboro' farms ... 716.9
COBBE, Frances Power. Broken lights: an inquiry into the present condition and future prospects of religious faith. Boston, 1864. 242 pp. 16°. 1526.8
COBBETT, Richard Stuteley. Memorials of Twickenham: parochial and topographical. London, 1872. xvi, 428 pp. 8° ... 5424.1
COBBETT, William. The American gardener. New York, 1852. 230 pp. Illustrated. 12° ... 1528.6
— *See* BULWER, H. L. (E.) Historical characters. Leipzig, 1868. Sq. 16° ... 1238.14
COBDEN, Paul, *pseud.* The beckoning series. Going on a mission ... 1115.1
— - Good luck ... 926.35
— - Take a peep ... 934.35
— - The turning wheel ... 1115.2
— - Who will win? ... 934.36
COBDEN, Richard. Russia and the Eastern question. Boston, 1854. 156 pp. 12° ... 027.3
COBDEN club, *London.* Essays, 2d series, 1871–2. 2d edition. London, 1872. vii, 556 pp. 8° ... 5822.1
— Free trade and free enterprise. Report of the proceedings at the dinner, June 28, 1873. Speech of D. A. Wells. With preface by Sir Louis Mallett, and list of members. London, 1873. 132 pp. 16° ... 5828.6
— Free trade and the European treaties of commerce; being report of proceedings at the dinner, July 17, 1875. With an introduction, etc. London, 1875. 175 pp. 16° ... 5828.8
COBDEN club, *London, continued.*
— Report of the proceedings at the dinner, July 11, 1874. With the report of the committee, and a list of members. London, 1874. 112 pp. 16°. 5828.7
— Second report of the commissioners appointed to revise the laws for the assessment and collection of taxes in New York, 1872. Reprinted by permission. London [1872]. 107+ pp. 16° ... 5828.5
COCHIN-CHINA. The land of the white elephant. Vincent, F., *jr.* New York, 1874. 8° ... 5923.7
COCHRANE, Thomas. Home mission work: its duties, difficulties, and encouragements. With prefatory note by William Hanna. Edinburgh, 1873. 95 pp. 16° ... 5819.16
COCKBURN, Henry Thomas, *lord.* [Works.] Edinburgh, 1872. 2 v. Portraits. Plate. Sm. 8°. 5635.2

Contents.—Vol. I. Life of Francis Jeffrey. II. Memorials of his time.

— Journal: being a continuation of memorials of his time, 1831–54. Edinburgh, 1874. 2 v. 8°. 5623.4
COCKER, B. F. Christianity and Greek philosophy. New York, 1872. 531 pp. Sm. 8° ... 5814.4
COCKTON, Henry. George Julian ... 717.7
— Life and adventures of Valentine Vox the ventriloquist ... 712.2
— Stanley Thorn ... 717.4
— Sylvester Sound; the somnambulist ... 521.41
CODMAN, John, *D. D.* Sermons, with addresses. Boston, 1834. 436+ pp. Portrait. 8° ... 5813.9
CODMAN, John. Ten months in Brazil: with notes on the Paraguayan war. 2d edition. New York, 1872. 218 pp. Illustrated. 16° ... 5916.4
CODRINGTON, *Sir* Edward. Memoir of [his] life. With selections from his correspondence. Edited by his daughter, Lady Bourchier. With portraits and illustrations. London, 1873. 2 v. 8°. 5332.2
COFFEE: its history, cultivation, and uses. Hewitt, R., *jr.* New York, 1872. 12° ... 6626.1
COFFIN, Charles Carleton. (*"Carleton."*) Caleb Krinkle. A story of American life ... 733.1
— Following the flag. From August, 1861, to November, 1862, with the army of the Potomac. Boston, 1865. vi, 336+ pp. Illustrated. 12°. 913.17
— Four years of fighting, from the battle of Bull Run to the fall of Richmond. Boston, 1866. xv, 558 pp. Portrait. 8° ... 813.7
— My days and nights on the battle-field. Boston, 1872. viii, 312 pp. Illustrated. 12° ... 913.18
— Our new way round the world. Illustrated. Boston [*cop.* 1869]. xviii, 524 pp. Maps. 8° ... 433.1
— The seat of empire. Boston, 1870. viii, 232 pp. Illustrated. 12° ... 425.15
— Winning his way ... 929.8
COFFIN, Robert Barry. My married life at Hillside. 726.29
— Out of town. A rural episode. By Barry Gray [*pseud.*] ... 724.29
COGAN, Thomas. Letters to Wilberforce on total depravity. (*In* Sparks, J. Collection of essays and tracts in theology) ... 1918.9.3
COHEN, Joseph. The deicides. Analysis of the life of Jesus, and of the several phases of the Christian church in their relation to Judaism. Translated by Anna Maria Goldsmid. Baltimore, 1873. vii, xliv, 283+ pp. 12° ... 5817.13
COLBURN, Zerah. Memoir. Written by himself. With his peculiar methods of calculation. Springfield, 1833. 104 pp. Portrait. 16° ... 1218.1
COLD heart, The. Hauff, W. ... 312.21
COLE, John William. Life and theatrical times of Charles Kean. Including a summary of the English stage for the last fifty years, and a detailed account of the management of the Princess's theatre, from 1850 to 1859. London, 1859. 2 v. Sm. 8° ... 5426.3
COLE, Miriam. *See* HARRIS, Miriam.
COLEMAN, Lyman. Genealogy of the Lyman family of Great Britain and America. Albany, 1872. 533+ pp. 1 plate. Chart. 8° ... 1211.4
COLENSO, John William. Lectures on the Pentateuch and the Moabite stone. 2d edition. London, 1873. viii, 436+ pp. 1 plate. 8° ... 5811.5

Shelf. No.

COLERIDGE, *Sir* John Taylor. Memoir of John Keble. 2d edition, with corrections and additions. New York, 1869. 2 v. 1 plate. Portrait. 16° 5426.4

COLERIDGE, Samuel Taylor. Works, prose and verse. Philadelphia, N. D. xvi, 546 pp. Portrait. 8°. 1611.5

Contents. — Juvenile poems; Sibylline leaves; Rime of the ancient mariner; Christabel; Miscellaneous poems; Remorse; Zapolya; The Piccolomini, translated from Schiller; Death of Wallenstein, translated from Schiller; The fall of Robespierre; Miscellaneous poems; Biographia literaria; The friend.

— Poems. Edited by D. and S. Coleridge. With a biographical memoir by F. Freiligrath. Leipzig, 1860. xlv, 344+ pp. Sq. 16° 1613.20

Contents. — Memoir; Poems written in youth; Poems written in early manhood, and middle life; Rime of the ancient mariner; Christabel; Sibylline leaves; Poems written in later life.

— Aids to reflection. Edited by D. Coleridge. 12th edition. London, 1867. xx, 352 pp. 16° 5818.11

— Specimens of [his] table talk. New edition. London, 1870. xxxii [xxx], 351 pp. 16° 5617.1

Note. — Coleridge's own "Biographia literaria," though called "Biographical sketches of his literary life and opinions," is chiefly a series of essays upon views held by him at different times. See also chapters in De Quincey's "Literary reminiscences" [1226.1].

For further biographical detail, see S. C. Hall, in Atlantic monthly, Feb., 1865; De Quincey's paper on Coleridge and opium-eating [1825.1.2]; and Day's Opium habit [1525.17]. Also Talfourd's Lamb [1813.5; 5615.1]; Hunt's Autobiography [1225.20]; Carlyle's Sterling; Wordsworth's Memoirs; and the preface to his Table talk.

For critical estimates, see Talfourd [1931.1]; Wilson's Hour's talk [1531.7]; Bayne's Essays [1226.15.2]; Shairp's Studies [1535.14]; M. D. Conway, in Harper's monthly, vols. 14 and 39. For his theological opinions, see references in McClintock and Strong's Cyclopædia. As a philosophical critic, see Whipple's Essays [1936.2.1].

COLERIDGE, Sara. Memoir and letters. Edited by her daughter. 3d edition. London, 1873. 2 v. 8°. 5424.8

COLFAX, Schuyler, Sketch of. Richardson, A. D. A personal history of U. S. Grant. Hartford, 1868. 8° 1210.2

COLLEGE, The, the market, and the court. Dall, C. H. (W.) Boston, 1867. 8° 1733.1

COLLEGIANS, The. Griffin, G..................... 517.7

COLLINS, Charles Allston. A cruise upon wheels: the chronicle of some autumn wanderings among the deserted post-roads of France. Leipzig, 1874. 2 v. in 1. Sq. 16° 428.6

COLLINS, Clifton Wilbraham. Plato [outlined and explained]. Philadelphia, 1874. 197+ pp. 16°. [Ancient classics for English readers]....6116.20

— Sophocles [outlined and explained]. Edinburgh, 1871. 181+ pp. 16°. [Ancient classics for English readers]..........................6116.11

COLLINS, J. H. The first book of mineralogy. New York [Glasgow], 1873. 160 pp. Illustrated. 16° 1717.8

COLLINS, Mortimer. Sweet and twenty........... 331.21

COLLINS, Robert. Practical treatise on midwifery. Boston, 1841. 320 pp. 8° 6023.15

COLLINS, T. Wharton. Humanics. New York, 1860. 358+ pp. Folded sheet. 8° 1734.2

COLLINS, William Lucas. Aristophanes [outlined and explained]. Edinburgh, 1872. 172+ pp. 16°. [Ancient classics for English readers] 6116.14

— Cicero [outlined and explained]. Edinburgh, 1871. 197+ pp. 16°. [Ancient classics for English readers]..........................6116.10

— Homer. The Iliad [outlined and explained]. Edinburgh, 1871. viii, 148+ pp. 16°. [Ancient classics for English readers]................. 6116.2

— — The Odyssey [outlined and explained]. Edinburgh, 1870. 136+ pp. 16°. [Ancient classics for English readers]........................ 6116.3

— Lucian [outlined and explained]. Edinburgh, 1872. 180+ pp. 16°. [Ancient classics for English readers]..........................6116.19

— Plautus and Terence [outlined and explained]. Edinburgh, 1873. 155+ pp. 16°. [Ancient classics for English readers]....................6116.17

— Virgil [outlined and explained]. Edinburgh, 1870. 190+ pp. 16°. [Ancient classics for English readers]........................ 6116.6

Shelf. No.

COLLINS, William Lucas, *continued.*

— *editor.* Ancient classics [outlined and explained] for English readers. Edinburgh, 1870–74. 20 v. 16°. *Namely:* —

— — Church, A., and Brodribb, W. J. Pliny's letters 6116.12

— — Collins, C. W. Plato........................6116.20

— — — Sophocles................................6116.11

— — Collins, W. L. Aristophanes.................6116.14

— — — Cicero 6116.10

— — — Homer. The Iliad......................... 6116.2

— — — — The Odyssey 6116.3

— — — Lucian 6116.19

— — — Plautus and Terence.......................6116.17

— — — Virgil 6116.6

— — Copleston, R. S. Æschylus................. 6116.8

— — Davies, J. Hesiod, and Theognis 6116.16

— — Donne, W. B. Euripides.....................6116.13

— — — Tacitus 6116.18

— — Grant, *Sir* A. Xenophon.................... 6116.9

— — Martin, T. Horace........................... 6116.7

— — Neaves, C., *lord Neaves.* The Greek anthology.6116.21

— — Swayne, G. C. Herodotus..................... 6116.4

— — Trollope, A. The commentaries of Cæsar.... 6116.5

— — Walford, E. Juvenal.........................6116.15

COLLINS, (William) Wilkie. After dark 326.11

— Alicia Warlock, (a mystery,) and other stories.. 711.33

— Antonina; or, the fall of Rome. [Fifth century]. 326.4

— Armadale....................................... 326.5

— Basil 326.7

— The dead alive 717.3

— The dead secret................................ 724.20

— The frozen deep. Boston........................ 726.30

— The frozen deep; and other stories. Readings and writings in America. Leipzig............ 319.25

Contents. — The frozen deep; The dream-woman; John Jago's ghost; or, the dead alive.

— Hide and seek 326.1

— The law and the lady. Leipzig 330.17

— *Same.* New York................................ 733.2

— Mad Monkton; and other tales.................. 511.25

— Man and wife 326.2

— Miss or Mrs?................................... 326.9

— The moonstone 326.10

— The new Magdalen. Leipzig 339.18

— *Same.* New York................................ 731.2

— No name.. 326.3

— A plot in private life and other tales 326.8

— Poor Miss Finch................................ 326.6

— The queen of hearts............................ 524.8

— The queen's revenge; and other stories......... 511.2

— Sights a-foot 511.24

— The woman in white............................. 326.12

— *joint author.* No thoroughfare. *See* DICKENS, Charles (John Huffam)................338.17 and 730.1

Note. — Wilkie Collins's books are the best modern representatives of the novel of plot, which is often mysterious. His "Woman in white" is accounted his best, and it is a story of Italian refugees in England. "The Moonstone" turns on the theft of an enormous diamond, which was the eye of an eastern idol. "The law and the lady" concerns women's rights under the English law. "Hide and seek" pictures recent artist life in England. "The new Magdalen" is a story of nursing in the Franco-Prussian war. "Armadale" is an English social mystery, turning on the similarity of two men. "The dead alive" is a short judicial mystery founded on the Boorn murder case.

COLLYER, Robert. Nature and life: sermons. 10th edition. Boston, 1872. 313+ pp. 12° 1537.4

COLMAN, Henry. European agriculture and rural economy. 2d edition, with additions. Boston, 1849. 2 v. Illustrated. 8° 1521.7

— European life and manners. Boston, 1849. 2 v. 12° 423.1

COLONNA, Vittoria, *marchesa di Pescara.* Her life and poems. Roscoe, *Mrs.* H. London, 1868. Sm. 8°...5525.11

COLOR-GUARD, The: a corporal's notes of military service in the nineteenth army corps. Hosmer, J. K. Boston, 1864. 12°....................... 826.1

COLORADO. *See* LIPPINCOTT, S. J. New life in new lands: notes of travel. New York, 1873. 12°. 214.1

Shelf. No.

COLORADO river. Exploration of the Colorado river of the West. *See* SMITHSONIAN institution, *Washington, D. C.* 230.1
COLTON, Calvin. Thoughts on the religious state of the country; with reasons for preferring episcopacy. New York, 1836. 208 pp. 12° 6326.13
COLTON, Charles Caleb. Lacon; or many things in few words: addressed to those who think. Revised edition, with a life of the author. New York, 1866. xvi, 504 pp. 12° 1533.12
COLTON, G. Woolworth. General atlas, containing 180 maps and plans. [With] letter-press descriptions, by R. S. Fisher. New York, 1873. Unpaged. F° .............................*R.R.Desk
COLTON, Walter. Ship and shore, in Madeira, Lisbon, and the Mediterranean. Revised by H. T. Cheever. New York, 1856. 313 pp. 1 plate. 12° 425.16
— Three years in California. With illustrations. New York, 1851. 456 pp. Map. Portraits. 12°. 414.16
COLUMBUS, Christopher. Abbott, J. S. C. Life of. New York [1875]. 12° 1014.15
— Irving, W. Life and voyages of. London, 1850. 2 v. 12° 1226.7
— *Same.* Added those of his companions. Philadelphia, 1871. 3 v. Sm. 8° 1815.2

Note. — Irving's is the best single life; but his career is necessarily covered in Prescott's Ferdinand and Isabella [5922.5] and in Help's Spanish conquest of America [816.6]. See note in Bulletin no. 33, p. 340.

COMBE, Andrew. The physiology of digestion considered with relation to the principles of dietetics. Boston, 1836. xvii, 328+ pp. 12°...6036.10
— The principles of physiology applied to the preservation of health, and to the improvement of physical and mental education. With woodcuts. New York, 1855. 396+ pp. 16° 1718.2
COMBE, George. The constitution of man, considered in relation to external objects. Illustrated. 20th edition, revised and enlarged. New York, 1872. xx, 436 pp. Portrait. 12° 1525.10
— Moral philosophy. New York, 1844. xii, 25-372 pp. Sm. 12° 1529.5
COMEDY of terrors, A. De Mille, J. 531.22
COMETH up as a flower. Broughton, R. 311.30
COMFORT, George F. A German course. New York, 1870. viii, 498 pp. 12° 1933.7
— A German reader. New York, 1871. xvi, 432 pp. 12° 1933.4
COMFORT for small incomes. Warren, E. Boston, 1866. 12° 1533.16
COMIC metamorphoses. Valentine, W. New York [*cop.* 1856]. 12° 1516.18
COMIN' thro' the rye. A novel 730.2
COMING race, The. [Fiction.] Bulwer-Lytton, E. (G. E.) L. Leipzig 329.8
— *Same.* New York 5617.13
COMING wave, The. Adams, W. T. 923.19
COMINS, Lizzie B. (*Laura Caxton.*) The Hartwell farm 912.14
— Marion Berkley: a story for girls 912.15
COMME on fait son lit on se couche. Souvestre, É. Théâtre de la jeunesse. Paris, 1860. 12°.....5536.15
COMMERCE. Anderson, W. The London commercial dictionary, and sea-port gazetteer. London, 1826. 8° 6434.4
— Cobden club, *London.* Free trade and the European treaties of. London, 1875. Sm. 8°......5418.13
— Yeats, J. Growth and vicissitudes of, from B. C. 1500 to A. D. 1789. London, 1872. 16°.. 6437.3
— – Manual of recent and existing commerce from 1789 to 1872. London, 1872. 16° 6437.2
COMMON-PLACE book. [Extracts.] Southey, R. London, 1850. 4 v. 8° 5624.1
COMMON school journal. Edited by H. Mann. Vol. 1-6, 8-11. Boston, 1839-49. 10 v. 8° 1335.1
COMMON sense. Newby, C. J. 314.10
COMMON-SENSE in religion. Clarke, J. F. Boston, 1874. 12° 5817.7
COMMON sense in the household. [Receipts, etc.] Terhune, M. V. New York, 1871. 12° 1533.6

Shelf. No

COMMON sense in the household series. *See* TERHUNE, Mary Virginia.
COMMUNISTIC societies, The, of the United States. Nordhoff, C. New York, 1875. 8° 5821.2
COMPANIONS of my solitude. Helps, *Sir* A. Boston, 1870. 16° 1914.3
COMPARATIVE anatomy and physiology. The cranial affinities of man and the ape. Virchow, R. (*In* Estes, D. Half-hour recreations in popular science) 6813.7
COMPENSATION. Brewster, A. M. H. 716.34
COMPLETE historical, chronological, and geographical American atlas. Philadelphia, 1822. Unpaged. 53 maps. F° 5030.8
COMPROMISE, On. Morley, J. London, 1874. 8°.. 5823.4
COMTESSE, La, d'Escarbagnas: comédie. Molière, J. B. P. Œuvres. Paris, 1869. 12° 5537.4.3
COMYN, L. N. Atherstone priory 728.3
— Elena. An Italian tale 727.30
CON Cregan, Confessions of. Lever, C. (J.) Leipzig. 332.24
— *Same.* London 516.8
CONANT, Caleb A. Grandmother's scrap-book 916.12
CONANT, Helen S. The butterfly hunters 933.1
CONANT, Thomas Jefferson, *assistant editor.* A dictionary of religious knowledge. *See* ABBOTT, Lyman 6320.2
CONCHOLOGY. A conchological manual. Sowerby, G. B. London, 1852. 8° 6632.4

See also Mollusca, Shells.

CONCORD, *Mass.* Corinthian lodge of ancient, free and accepted masons. By-laws, charter [etc.]. Added an historical sketch of masonry. By L. A. Surette. Concord, 1859. 191 pp. Portraits. 12° 817.13
— History of the battle of. Frothingham, R. Boston, 1851. 8° 812.6

Note. — For the fight in 1775, see Bulletin no. 34, p. 384.

CONCORD days. Alcott, A. B. Boston, 1872. 12°.. 5217.1
CONCORD river, *Mass.*, A week on the. Thoreau, H. D. Boston, 1868. 12° 215.1
CONCRETE works, Foundations and. Dobson, E. London, 1867. 12° 1716.27
CONDÉ, Louis II, *de Bourbon, prince of,* Life of. Stanhope, P. H., *5th earl Stanhope.* London, 1861. Sm. 8° 5527.10
CONDÉ, *Princes of,* History of the. Aumale, H. (E. P. L.) d'Orléans, *duc* d'. London, 1872. 2 v. 8°. 5522.9
CONDENSED novels. Harte, (F.) B. Boston, 1871. 16°. 524.22

Note. — Burlesque imitations of famous novelists.

CONFECTIONER. Manuel du confiseur. Duval, H. Paris, 1851. 24° 6429.7
CONFESSION; or, the blind heart. Simms, W. G.... 716.25
CONFESSIONS of an English opium-eater. De Quincey, T. Boston, 1872. 16° 1825.5
CONFESSIONS of Con Cregan. Lever, C. (J.) Leipzig. 332.24
— *Same.* London 516.8
CONFESSIONS of Gerald Estcourt. Church, F. 337.18
CONFIDENTIAL disclosures. Lamartine, A. (M. L.) de. New York, 1849. 12° 5536.10
CONFLICT of ages, The. [Eternal punishment.] Beecher, E. Boston, 1854. 12° 1524.21
CONFUCIUS (*or* Kong-Fu-Tse), and MENCIUS. The Chinese classics: a translation by James Legge. New York, 1870. 2 v. in 1. 8° 5923.2
CONGO. Abbott, J. Harper's story books 936.1.12
CONGO river. Two trips to Gorilla land and the cataracts of the Congo. Burton, R. F. London, 1876. 2 v. 8° 5933.12
CONGREGATIONAL history, 1200-1700. Waddington, J. London, 1869, 74. 2 v. 8° 5810.1
CONGREGATIONAL quarterly. Vol. 15-17. Boston, 1873-75. 3 v. 8° 6716.1
CONGRESSIONAL globe. *See* UNITED STATES. *Miscellaneous* .... Case 65
CONGREVE, William. Dramatic works. *See* WYCHERLEY, William 5611.6
CONINGSBY. [English political life.] Disraeli, B... 324.23
CONJUGIAL love. Swedenborg, E. New York, 1871. 8° 6323.4

Shelf. No.

CONNECTICUT, Genealogical notes of. Goodwin, N. Hartford, 1856. 8° ... 5011.8
CONQUERING and to conquer. Charles, E. ... 723.8
CONQUEST and self-conquest. MacIntosh, M. J. ... 718.4
CONQUEST, The, of the sea. Siebe, H. London [1874]. Sm. 8° ... 6418.4
CONSCIENCE, Hendrik *or* Henri. The demon of gold. 717.6
— Scènes de la vie flamande. Traduction de L. Wocquier. Première série. Nouvelle édition. Paris, 1864. 302 pp. 18° ... 5536.12

Contents. — Ce que peut souffrir une mère; Le conscrit; Le gentilhomme pauvre.

CONSCRIPT, The: a story of the French war of 1813. Erckmann, É., and Chatrian, A. ... 913.22
CONSIDERATIONS on some recent social theories. Boston, 1853. 158+ pp. 16° ... 5827.3
CONSOLATION in affliction. Greenwood, F. W. P. Sermons of consolation. Boston, 1844. Sm. 8°. 5817.10
— Macduff, J. R. Wells of Baca; or, solaces of the Christian mourner. Boston, 1854. 16° ... 5819.9
— Parkman, F., and others. An offering of sympathy to parents bereaved of their children and to others under affliction. Boston, 1830. 12°. 1538.4 and 5819.19
CONSOLATIONS in travel. Davy, *Sir* H. Boston, 1870. 16° ... 5617.5
CONSTABLE, Archibald. Personal reminiscences. (*In* Stoddard, R. H. Bric-à-brac series) ... 1828.10
— Archibald Constable and his literary correspondents. Constable, T. Edinburgh, 1873. 3 v. 8°. 5424.10

Note. — Constable was an Edinburgh publisher, and these books show his relations with eminent writers, the third volume of the latter being given to Sir Walter Scott wholly.

CONSTABLE, Thomas. Archibald Constable and his literary correspondents. A memorial. Edinburgh, 1873. 3 v. Portrait. 8° ... 5424.10
CONSTABLE de Bourbon, The. Ainsworth, W. H. ... 322.21
CONSTABLE of the tower, The. Ainsworth, W. H. ... 322.8
CONSTANCE Sherwood. Fullerton, *Lady* G. ... 325.21
CONSTANTIN, Léopold Auguste. *See* HESSE, Léopold Auguste Constantin.
CONSTANTINOPLE. Gautier, T. Constantinople. New York, 1875. 12° ... 824.12
— Holland, F. W. Constantinople. (*In* Many lands and many people) ... 431.3
CONSTITUTION of man, The, considered in relation to external objects. Combe, G. New York, 1872. 12° ... 1525.10
CONSTITUTION, The, of Massachusetts, and the United States; the declaration of independence, with Washington's farewell address. Northampton, 1806. 119 pp. 12° ... 618.1
CONSTITUTIONS, The, of the sixteen states which compose the confederated republic of America. Prefixed, the declaration of independence; articles of confederation; the definitive treaty of peace with Great Britain; and the constitution of the United States. Boston, 1797. 300 pp. 12° ... 818.3
CONSUELO. Dudevant, A. L. A. D. Paris ... 2018.2
— *Same.* Philadelphia ... 535.2
CONSUMPTION, Pulmonary. Fitch, S. S. New York, 1847. 12° ... 6327.1
CONTARINI Fleming. Disraeli, B. ... 324.18
CONTEMPORARY review, The. Vol. 22-26. London, 1873-75. 5 v. 8° ... 6511.1
CONTRABAND. Melville, G. J. W. ... 321.18
CONUNDRUMS and riddles, Book of. Howard, C. J. New York [1869]. 16° ... 1518.3
CONVICT, The. James, G. P. R. ... 327.8
CONWAY, J. D. Complete poems: or, hours of recreation. Lawrence, 1875. 200 pp. 16° ... 1625.15
CONWAY, Moncure Daniel. The earthward pilgrimage. London, 1870. 406 [402] pp. Sm. 8° ... 6326.18
— *editor.* The sacred anthology: a book of ethnical scriptures. London, 1874. viii, 479 pp. 8°. 5813.14
CONYNGHAM, D. P. The Irish brigade and its campaigns. Boston, 1869. 599 pp. 12° ... 824.4
— Sarsfield; or, the last great struggle for Ireland. Boston, 1871. ix, 224 pp. Portrait. Sq. 16°. 828.7
COOK, *Capt.* James: his life, voyages, and discoveries. Kingston, W. H. G. [London, 1871.] Sq. 16°. 215.3

Shelf. No.

COOKE, John Esten. Doctor Vandyke. [Virginia life about 1750] ... 510.2
— Henry St. John, gentleman. A tale of 1774-75. [Virginia life] ... 524.6
— Her majesty the queen. A novel ... 737.15

Note. — Time of Charles I of England and Henrietta of France.

— Leather stocking and silk. [Valley of Virginia about 1800] ... 524.16
— Life of Gen. Robert E. Lee. With illustrations, portraits, and maps. New York, 1871. vi, 577 pp. 8° ... 5022.2
— Pretty Mrs. Gaston, and other stories ... 736.29
— Stonewall Jackson: a military biography. With portrait and maps. New York, 1866. 470 pp. Sm. 8° ... 1214.11
COOKE, Josiah Parsons, *jr.* International scientific series. The new chemistry. New York, 1874. 326 pp. Illustrated. 12° ... 6436.15
— Principles of chemical philosophy. 3d edition. Boston, 1874. viii, 576, xii+ pp. 8° ... 6435.5
COOKE, M. C. A fern book for everybody. Containing all the British ferns. With the foreign species suitable for a fernery. London [1867]. 124+ pp. Illustrated. 16° ... 6619.1
— International scientific series. Fungi: their nature and uses. Edited by M. J. Berkeley. New York, 1875. xii, 299 pp. Illustrated. 12° ... 6436.13
COOKERY. Blot, P. Hand-book of practical cookery. New York, 1873. 12° ... 1515.5
— Kitchiner, W. The cook's oracle. Boston, 1822. 12° ... 1516.20
— Miller, E. S. In the kitchen. Boston, 1875. Sm. 4° ... 1532.8
— Parloa, M. The Appledore cook book. Boston [1873]. 8° ... 6426.2
— Terhune, M. V. Breakfast, luncheon and tea. New York, 1875. 12° ... 1533.2
— — Common sense in the household: a manual of practical housewifery. New York, 1871. 12°. 1533.6

See also Receipts.

COOLEY, Arnold James. Cyclopædia of practical receipts and collateral information in the arts, manufactures, professions, and trades. 5th edition, revised and partly rewritten by R. V. Tuson. London, 1872. xii, 1201+ pp. 8° ... 6423.1
— Hand-book of perfumes, cosmetics and other toilet articles. Philadelphia, 1873. 804 [418] pp. Sm. 8° ... 1514.13
— The toilet in ancient and modern times. Philadelphia, 1873. viii, 388 pp. Sm. 8° ... 1514.12
COOLIDGE, George A. Brochure of Bunker hill. [With heliotype views.] Boston, 1875. 32 pp. Oblong 16° ... 819.5
COOLIDGE, Susan, *pseud.* *See* WOOLSEY, Sarah Chauncey.
COOMASSIE, *Guinea.* Coomassie and Magdala. Stanley, H. M. New York, 1874. 8° ... 5931.14
COOPER, *Sir* Astley (Paston). Treatise on dislocations and fractures of the joints. New edition. Edited by B. P. Cooper. Boston, 1844. xliii, 499 pp. Illustrations. Portrait. 8° ... 6021.3
COOPER, Elizabeth. Life of Thomas Wentworth, earl of Strafford. London, 1874. 2 v. 8° ... 5313.5
COOPER, James Fenimore. Afloat and ashore. [Sea story] ... 525.15
— The bravo. [Venice] ... 525.30
— The chainbearer ... 525.18

Note. — Revolutionary period.

— The crater. [Volcanic Pacific island] ... 525.1
— The headsman ... 525.25

Note. — Switzerland and Italy — time of Calvin.

— The Heidenmauer ... 525.31

Note. — Scene in the Vosges mountains in the middle ages.

— History of the navy of the United States, [1607] to 1853. New York, 1853. With portraits and maps. 3 v. in 1. 8° ... 813.4
— — Continued to 1860. New York, 1866. 3 v. in 1. Portrait. 8° ... 813.5

Shelf. No.

COOPER, James Fenimore, *continued.*
— Home as found 525.20
— Homeward bound 525.27

Note. — These two novels made the author offensive to some of his countrymen, by his satire on the American character.

— The Jack o' Lantern 310.12

Note. — Same as Wing-and-wing.

— Jack Tier. [Sea adventures, West Indies] 525.8
— [Leather stocking tales.] The deerslayer 525.7
— – The last of the Mohicans 525.10
— – The pathfinder 525.5
— – The pioneers 525.28
— – The prairie 525.22

Note. — The Leather stocking tales trace the history of Natty Bumppo, a backwoodsman, and associate of the Indians, during the last century, and covering, particularly in The last of the Mohicans, the period of the old French war.

— Lionel Lincoln 525.9

Note. — Bunker hill and Boston in 1775.

— Mercedes of Castile 525.14

Note. — Spain and Columbus.

— Miles Wallingford 525.17

Note. — Sea story, sequel to Afloat and ashore.

— The Monikins. [Satire on American politics] ... 525.21
— The oak-openings. [Michigan early days] 525.19
— The pilot 525.29

Note. — Paul Jones figures.

— Precaution 525.32

Note. — A society novel, and Cooper's earliest.

— The Red Rover 525.24

Note. — Old French war — Newport and slavers.

— The redskins 525.2

Note. — Anti-rent troubles in New York state.

— Satanstoe 525.6

Note. — Westchester county, New York, middle of the last century.

— The sea lions 525.11

Note. — Sealers in the Southern ocean.

— The spy. Leipzig 310.11
— *Same.* New York 525.26

Note. — The revolutionary period on the Hudson. Washington figures, 1780.

— Stories of the prairie, and other adventures of the border 515.13
— Stories of the sea 515.12
— Stories of the woods 515.14

Note. — These three collections of "Stories" are selections from his novels.

— The travelling bachelor; or, notions of the Americans 536.7
— The two admirals. Leipzig 310.13
— *Same.* New York 525.16

Note. — English naval service, old French war.

— The Water-witch 525.23

Note. — Subsequent to the defeat of the Dutch in New York.

— The ways of the hour 525.13

Note. — Defects in courts of justice.

— The wept of Wish-ton-Wish 525.12

Note. — King Philip's war, 1675.

— The Wing-and-wing 525.3

Note. — Mediterranean — during the Napoleonic wars.

— Wyandotte. [Revolutionary frontier warfare] .. 525.4

Note. — See Allibone, Duyckinck, etc.; the estimates in Bryant's Orations [1926.1]; Atlantic monthly, Jan., 1862; Putnam's monthly, Feb, 1868 (his diary), and Oct., 1859; and Poe's literati [1934 2.3]. The article "Haunted lake" by Cooper's daughter, in Harper's monthly, vol. 44. is a description of Cooper's home and of the scene of The deerslayer. See also the lives of his literary contemporaries, Halleck, Irving, etc.

COOPER, T. T. The Mishmee hills. An account of a journey made in an attempt to penetrate Thibet from Assam to open new routes for commerce. Illustrated. London, 1873. 270 pp. Map. Sm. 8° 5933.6

Shelf. No.

COOPER, William. Yachts and yachting, by Vanderdecken [*pseud.*], being a treatise on building, sparring, canvassing, sailing, and the general management of yachts, with remarks on storms, tides, etc. London, 1873. viii, 391 pp. Plates. 8° 6412.5
— The yacht sailor: a treatise on practical yachtmanship, cruising and racing. By Vanderdecken [*pseud.*]. 4th edition. London, 1874. viii, 165 pp. 2 folded plates. 8° 6412.3
CO-OPERATION, The history of, in England. Vol. I. Holyoake, G. J. London, 1875. Sm. 8° 5826.9
COOPERS, The. Haven, A. B. 524.20
COPELAND family. Thayer, E. Family memorial. Hingham, 1835. 12° 611.2
COPLESTON, Reginald Stephen. Æschylus [outlined and explained]. Edinburgh, 1870. 196+ pp. 16°. [Ancient classics for English readers] 6116.8
COPP'S hill burial ground, Boston, Epitaphs from. Bridgman, T. Boston, 1851. 12° 5016.5
COPPÉE, Henry. English literature, considered as an interpreter of English history. Philadelphia, 1873. xiv, 488 pp. Sm. 8° 5614.6
— *editor.* The field manual of evolutions of the line, arranged for the use of officers of the U. S. infantry. Translated, with adaptation to the U. S. service, from the latest French authorities. Philadelphia, 1862. 144 pp. Sm. 12° 1529.8
COPPER, Metallurgy of. Tomlinson, C. London, 1868. 12° 1715.16
COPPERSMITH. Nouveau manuel complet du chaudronnier. Jullien, C. E., and Valerio, O. Paris, 1846. 24° 6439.3
CORA and the doctor. Baker, H. N. (W.) 524.7
CORAL island, The. Ballantyne, R. M. 934.18
CORAL reefs, The structure and distribution of. Darwin, C. (R.) London, 1874. Sm. 8° 6634.1
CORALS and the coral islands. Dana, J. D. New York, 1872. 8° 6630.3
— *Same.* (*In* Estes, D. Half-hour recreations in popular science) 6813.7
CORD and creese. De Mille, J. 521.14
CORINNE; or, Italy. Staël-Holstein, A. L. G. N., *baronne* de. New York, 1873. 12° 527.17
CORINNE, ou l'Italie. Staël-Holstein, A. L. G. N., *baronne* de. New York, 1873. 12° 2015.3
CORNEILLE, Pierre. Œuvres. Précédées d'une étude par [C. A.] Sainte-Beuve. Paris, 1866. 2 v. in 1. 16° 5534.5
CORNELL, S. S. Intermediate geography. New York, 1859. 88 pp. Illustrated. Maps. 4°. 5030.3
CORNHILL magazine. Vol. 1-32. London, 1860-75. 32 v. 8° 6534.1
CORRELATION, The, and conservation of forces. Grove, W. R. New York, 1873. 12° 1524.26
CORSE de Leon: or, the brigand. A romance. James, G. P. R. 722.6
CORSICA, Handbook for. Murray, J. London, 1868. 12° 5917.3
CORSICAN brothers, The. Dumas, A. (D.) 511.32
CORSICAN brothers: a dramatic romance, adapted from Dumas. Basté, E. P., and Montepin, X. de. New York, N. D. 12° 1635.3
CORTÉS, Hernando. Abbott, J. S. C. History of... 915.1
— Helps, *Sir* A. Life of. New York, 1871. Sm. 8° 1025.12

Note. — Helps's Life is drawn from his History of the Spanish conquest [816.6]; Prescott's Conquest of Mexico [5014.2] of course covers his exploits.

CORVIN, Otto. In France with the Germans. London, 1872. 2 v. Sm. 8° 5715.2
COSMETICS, Hand-book of. Cooley, A. J. Philadelphia, 1873. Sm. 8° 1514.13
COSMIC philosophy, Outlines of. Fiske, J. Boston, 1875. 2 v. 8° 5824.2
COSMOS. Humboldt, (F. H.) A., *baron* von. New York, 1872. 5 v. 12° 1523.7
COTTAGE, The, bee keeper. By a country curate. New York, 1854. xii, 119 pp. Illustrated. Sm. 8° 1524.15
COTTAGE, The, by the cathedral. Charles, E. 321.2

Shelf. No.

COTTAGE residences. Downing, A. J. New York, 1844. 8° 1511.7
— *Same.* New York, 1873. Sm. 4° 6221.3
COTTAGERS, The, of Glenburnie. Hamilton, E. 539.5
COTTIN, Sophie Ristaud. Elizabeth; or, the exiles of Siberia. New York, 1867. 127 pp. 1 plate. 32° 539.2
COTTING, Benjamin Eddy. Medical addresses. Boston, 1875. vi, 123+ pp. 12° 6015.5
COTTLE, Joseph. Alfred; an epic poem. Newburyport, 1814. 2 v. in 1. 24° 5619.1
COTTON, Charles, *joint author.* The complete angler. *See* WALTON, Izaak 6416.2
COTTON culture and the South considered with reference to emigration. Loring, F. W., and Atkinson, C. F. Boston, 1869. 16° 6435.3
COTTON manufacture in the United States. Batchelder, S. Boston, 1863. 16° 6435.4
COUES, Elliott. Field ornithology. Comprising a manual of instruction for procuring, preparing and preserving birds, and a check list of North American birds. Salem, 1874. iv, 116, 137 pp. 8° 6613.12
COULANGES, Numa Denis Fustel de. *See* FUSTEL DE COULANGES, Numa Denis.
COULSON, J. G. A. Harwood 720.30
— The Lacy diamonds 721.12
— The odd trump 720.1
COUNT Kostia. Cherbuliez, V. 518.13
COUNT of Monte-Cristo, The. Dumas, A. (D.) 511.30
COUNT Robert of Paris. Scott, *Sir* W. 533.4
COUNTERPARTS. [Psychological and musical.] Sheppard, E. S. 531.19
COUNTESS Gisela, The. John, E. 537.7
COUNTESS of Charny, The. Dumas, A. (D.) 511.7
COUNTESS of Rudolstadt, The. Dudevant, A. L. A. D. 726.18
COUNTRY living and country thinking. Dodge, M. A. Boston, 1863. 16° 715.8
COUNTRY quarters. Gardiner, M. 319.2
COUPON bonds. Trowbridge, J. T. 522.2
COURSES of reading. The best reading. Hints on the selection of books; courses of reading, etc. Putnam, G. P. New York, 1872. 12° .... *R.R., F.3.5
— *Same.* New York, 1875. 12° 6136.10
COURT, The, and camp of Bonaparte. New York, 1832. 389 pp. Folded sheet. 16° 1028.4
COURTING and farming. Smith, J. P. 724.32
COURTSHIP and marriage. Hentz, C. L. 534.13
COURTSHIP, The, of Miles Standish. Longfellow, H. W. Leipzig, 1856. Sq. 16° 1614.1
— *Same.* Boston, 1859. 12° 1612.3
COUSIN, Victor, and OTHERS. Jacqueline Pascal; or a glimpse at convent life at Port Royal. Translated by H. N. With an introduction, by W. R. Williams. New York, 1854. 318 [314] pp. 12°. 1226.10
COUSIN, The, from India. Craik, G. M. 937.28
COUSIN Clara. Wise, D. 932.26
COUSIN Grace. Clarke, R. S. 927.3
COUSIN Harry. Grey, *Mrs.* 534.22
COUSIN Maude. Holmes, M. J. 534.2
COUSIN Pierre, Le. Souvestre, É. Théâtre de la jeunesse. Paris, 1860. 12° 5536.15
COUSIN Phillis and other tales. Gaskell, E. C. 328.18
COWPER, William. Works. Comprising his poems, correspondence, and translations. With a life by the editor, Robert Southey. Illustrated. London, 1853–55. Portraits. Engraved title-page. 8 v. Sm. 8° 5627.4

Contents. — Vol. I-IV. Life and correspondence, with general index. V, VI. Poetical works, with index to the Task. VII. The Iliad of Homer. VIII. The Odyssey of Homer.

— *See* SAINTE-BEUVE, C. A. English portraits. New York, 1875. 16° 1025.3
COWTAN, Robert. Memories of the British museum. London, 1872. vii, 428 pp. Portrait. 8° 6133.2
COX, David, Memoir of. Solly, N. N. London, 1873. L. 8° 5420.3
COX, George William. The crusades. With a map. New York, 1874. xx, 220 pp. [Morris, E. E., *editor.* Epochs of history.] 16° 628.1

Shelf. No.

COX, George William, *continued.*
— General history of Greece, from the earliest period to the death of Alexander the great. With a sketch of the subsequent history to the present time. London, 1876. xxxi, 709+ pp. Maps. Sm. 8° 5916.13
— History of Greece. London, 1874. 2 v. Maps. 8°. 5911.5

Contents. — Vol. I. From the earliest period to the end of the Persian war. II. From the formation of the confederacy at Delos to the close of the Peloponnesian war.

— *joint author.* Dictionary of science, literature, and art. *See* BRANDE, William Thomas .. *R.R., E.3.6
COX, Samuel Sullivan. Why we laugh. New York, 1876. 387 pp. 12° 1837.2
COXE, William. History of the house of Austria, 1218–1848. 4th edition. London, 1864–72. 4 v. Portraits. 16° 5715.1

Contents. — Vol. I. 1218-1562. II. 1562-1705. III. 1705-92. IV. From the accession of Francis I to the revolution of 1848.

— Memoirs of [John Churchill] the duke of Marlborough, with his correspondence. New edition, revised by J. Wade. London, 1847. 3 v. Portraits. Sm. 8° 5426.10
COZZENS, Samuel Woodworth. The marvellous country; or, three years in Arizona and New Mexico. Illustrated. Boston, 1873. 532 pp. 8° 412.1
CRABB, George. Dictionary of general knowledge; or, an explanation of words and things connected with all the arts and sciences. Illustrated. London, 1830. 364+ pp. 12° 1513.6
— English synonymes explained in alphabetical order. Boston, 1819. 1006+ pp. 8° 6122.1
CRABBE, George. Life and poetical works. By his son. New edition. With portrait and engravings. London, 1861. viii, 584 pp. 8° 5631.2
CRACOW. Try Cracow and the Carpathians. Hutchinson, A. H. New York [London, 1872]. Sm. 8°. 5936.2
CRAIK, Dinah (Maria), *formerly Miss Muloch.* The adventures of a brownie 927.23
— Agatha's husband 323.19
— A brave lady 323.20
— Bread upon the waters; A family in love; A low marriage; The double house 330.22
— Christian's mistake 323.23
— Domestic stories 323.13
— Fair France. Impressions of a traveller. Leipzig, 1872. 296 pp. Sq. 16° 323.14
— *Same.* New York, 1871. 238 pp. 12° 424.20
— Hannah. [Marrying a wife's sister] 330.2
— The head of the family 323.12
— John Halifax, gentleman 330.1

Note. — This is generally thought her best novel.

— A life for a life 323.24
— The little lame prince and his travelling cloak .. 310.29
— Lord Erlistoun; Alwyn's first wife; The water cure; The last house in C—— st. 323.27
— Mistress and maid 323.11
— My mother and I. Leipzig 310.18
— *Same.* New York 726.22
— A noble life 323.15
— The Ogilvies 323.17
— Olive 323.18
— Poems. Leipzig, 1868. xii, 315 pp. Sq. 16° .. 1613.16
— Romantic tales 323.25
— The Rosicrucian. (*In* Johnson, (E.) R. Little classics) 529.4.7
— Sermons out of church. Leipzig, 1875. 271 pp. Sq. 16° 1928.5
— *Same.* New York, 1875. 217 pp. 12° 6327.15
— Studies from life 323.16
— Two marriages 323.21
— The unkind word and other stories 323.22
— The woman's kingdom 323.28
— A woman's thoughts about women. Leipzig 323.26
— *Same.* New York 1535.13
CRAIK, George Lillie. The English of Shakespeare; illustrated in a philological commentary on his Julius Cæsar. Edited from the 3d revised London edition by W. J. Rolfe. Boston, 1871. xiv, 381+ pp. 16° 5626.1

Shelf. No.

CRAIK, George Lillie, *continued.*
— Manual of English literature, and of the history of the English language, from the Norman conquest; with specimens. Leipzig, 1874. 2 v. in 1. Sq. 16° 1738.1
— The pursuit of knowledge under difficulties. Illustrated by anecdotes. Revised edition, with preface and notes, by F. Wayland. New York, 1868. 2 v. 12° 1013.2
CRAIK, Georgiana M. The cousin from India 937.28
— Esther Hill's secret 322.5
— Faith Unwin's ordeal 322.3
— Hero Trevelyan 322.4
— Leslie Tyrrell 322.6
— Lost and won 322.7
— Mildred 322.1
— Miss Moore. A tale for girls 937.26
— Only a butterfly and other stories 319.13
— Sylvia's choice. New York 710.15
— *Same.* [And] Theresa. Leipzig 335.17
— Winifred's wooing and other tales 332.2
— Without kith or kin. 2 v. 331.4
CRANCH, Christopher Pearse. The bird and the bell, with other poems. Boston, 1875. x, 317+ pp. 12° 1617.15
CRANFORD. Gaskell, E. C. 328.21
CRAPSEY, Edward. The nether side of New York. New York, 1872. 185 pp. 8° 5013.6
CRATER, The. Cooper, J. F. 525.1
CRAVEN, Pauline, *formerly M'lle de La Ferronnays.* Jettatrice; or, the veil withdrawn 720.15
— Leisure hour series. Fleurange. From the French. Translated by M. M. R. 518.17
CRAYON, Geoffrey, *pseud.* *See* IRVING, Washington.
CRAYON, Porte, *pseud.* *See* STROTHER, David H.
CRAYON miscellany, The. Irving, W. Philadelphia, 1872. Sm. 8° 1814.3
CRAYON sketches and off-hand takings, of distinguished American statesmen [etc.]. Bungay, G. W. Boston, 1852. 16° 1516.24
CREAGH, James. A scamper to Sebastopol and Jerusalem in 1867. London, 1873. 429+ pp. 8° 5931.10
CREASY, *Sir* Edward Shepherd. The fifteen decisive battles of the world; from Marathon to Waterloo. New York, 1872. 364 pp. 12° 824.6
CREATION. Chambers, R. Vestiges of the natural history of. New York, 1846. 12° 1515.17
— Haeckel, E. H. History of creation: or the development of the earth and its inhabitants by the action of natural causes. New York, 1876. 2 v. 12° 6615.5
— Powell, W. B. Philosophy of. London, 1856. Sm. 8° 6836.1
— Winchell, A. Sketches of. New York, 1874. 12° 1523.23
CREDO. [Theological essays.] Townsend, L. T. Boston, 1875 [*cop.* 1869]. 16° 1917.6
CREEDS. Greg, W. R. The creed of Christendom. London, 1874. 2 v. Sm. 8° 5816.21
— Lumby, J. R. The history of the creeds. Cambridge, 1873. Sm. 8° 6326.10
CREMER, W. H. The secret out: or, one thousand tricks in drawing-room or white magic. With illustrations. London, N. D. iv, 307 pp. 16° 1516.11
CRESCENT, The, and the cross; or, romance and realities of Eastern travel. Warburton, E. (B. G.) Leipzig, 1852. 2 v. in 1. Sq. 16° 317.8
CRIB and Fly: a tale of two terriers 928.22
CRICHTON, James, Biography of. Irving, D. (*In* Macaulay, T. B., *lord*, and others. New biographies of illustrious men) 5428.4
CRICHTON. [Fiction.] Ainsworth, W. H. 722.13
CRICKET. Wickets in the West; or, the twelve in America. Fitzgerald, R. A. London, 1873. Sm. 8° 5035.6
CRICKET, The, on the hearth. Dickens, C. (J. H.). 338.10
CRIMEA, The invasion of the. Vol. I-III. Kinglake, A. W. New York, 1875. 3 v. 8° 5924.9
CRINGLE and cross-tree. Adams, W. T. 924.11
CRISPINO e la comare. Ricci, F. and L. (*In* Ditson, O., and co. Standard opera librettos) 6233.3.1

Shelf. No.

CRITIC, The. [Farce.] Sheridan, B. R. Dramatic works. Leipzig, 1869. Sq. 16° 1614.11
— *Same.* London, 1848. 16° 1635.2
— *Same.* London, 1875. Sm. 8° 5626.9
CRITICISM. Arnold, M. Essays in. Boston, 1873. 12° 5617.10
— Homes, H., *lord Kames.* Elements of. Boston, 1796. 2 v. 8° 5834.4
— Pope, A. Essay on. [Poem.] London, 1871. 8°. 5612.2.2
CRITIQUE, La, de l'école des femmes: comédie. Molière, J. B. P. Œuvres. Paris, 1869. 12°. 5537.2.1
CROCKER, Uriel, and BREWSTER, Osmyn. Fiftieth anniversary of [their] copartnership, Nov. 1, 1868. Boston, 1869. 32 pp. 16° 1538.24
CROCKERY. Nouveau manuel complet du faiencier. Boyer, —. Paris, 1846. 2 v. 24° 6439.8
CROCKETT, David, Life and adventures of. Abbott, J. S. C. New York, 1874. 12° 1014.10
CROFFUT, W. A., *joint author.* A helping hand for town and country. *See* DRAPER, Lyman C. 1511.4 and 6422.1
CROKER, John Wilson. History of the guillotine. London, 1853. viii, 88 pp. Illustrated. 16°. 5528.6
CROLY, George. Salathiel, the immortal. New edition, revised. London [1858]. iv, 444 pp. 16°. 517.13
CROLY, Jennie Cunningham. For better or worse. A book for some men and all women. Boston, 1875. 237 pp. 16° 1537.22
CROMWELL, Oliver. Letters and speeches. With elucidations by T. Carlyle. Leipzig, 1861. 4 v. in 2. Sq. 16° 1238.1
— Russell, M. Life of. New York, 1856. 2 v. 12°. 1228.2
— Smith, G. Three English statesmen. New York, 1867. 12° 5425.1
— Southey, R. Life of. London, 1861. Sm. 8° .. 5428.6

Note. — The opinion held by Hume that Cromwell was a "fanatical hypocrite," was commonly accepted by the biographers of the last century. Southey's brief memoir arrives at the conclusion that Cromwell was penitent for his career. Russell's is a popular balancing of testimonies. Forster, in his lives of the statesmen, advanced a belief in Cromwell's essential hypocrisy, without indiscriminate denunciation of him; but in his later essay he somewhat changed his views in favor of a higher estimate. Carlyle's book introduces "elucidations," in which the author takes the decided ground of a champion; and his position has greatly influenced the more recent opinions. See also Carlyle's "Heroes and hero-worship" [1535.19]. Lamartine has embraced this belief in Cromwell's sincerity. Merle d'Aubigné has vindicated him. Guizot, while admiring his genius and sympathizing with his courage, does not wholly accept the sincerity theory. Goldwin Smith's lecture views him simply as a ruler. Macaulay's estimate will be found in vol. I of his History of England. See Campbell's "Lives of the chancellors" [5427.9]; Evelyn's Diary [5426.7]; Lodge's Portraits [5337.6.5]; an essay by Bayne in Contemporary review, Feb., 1873; Malcom's Index, and the references in Thomas, Oettinger, Hoefer, Michaud, etc. Several of the books named in this note must be searched for in the Bates Hall catalogues.

CRONISE, Titus Fey. The natural wealth of California. San Francisco, 1868. xvi, 696 pp. Illustrated. L. 8° 5031.5
CROSS and crescent; or, Young America in Turkey and Greece. Adams, W. T. Boston, 1874. 16°. 925.11
CROSS, The, of Berny. Girardin, D. G. de, and others 725.30
CROUCH, Julia. Three successful girls 714.23
CROUGH, George. Another chapter of Erie. New York, 1869. 48 pp. 12° 1916.2
CROWE, Catherine. The advocate's wedding-day. (*In* Johnson, (E.) R. Little classics) 529.4.8
CROWE, Eyre Evans. History of France. New York, 1840. 3 v. 12° 828.2
CROWE, J. A., and CAVALCASELLE, G. B. The early Flemish painters: notices of their lives and works. 2d edition. London, 1872. viii, 383 pp. Illustrated. Sm. 8° 6213.3
— History of painting in Italy, from the second to the fourteenth century. London, 1864. 3 v. Illustrated. 8° 6213.2
— History of painting in North Italy. With illustrations. London, 1871. 2 v. 8° 6213.1
See also Painting, *note.*
CROWFIELD, Christopher, *pseud.* *See* STOWE, Harriet (Elizabeth) Beecher.
CROWN, A, from the spear. Hamilton, C. V. 511.28
CROWN, The, of thorns. Chapin, E. H. Boston, 1860. 16° 1526.9

Shelf. No.

CROWN, The, of wild olive. Ruskin, J. New York, 1872. 12° 6236.6
CRUDEN, Alexander. Complete concordance to the Holy Scriptures. To which is added a concordance to the books called Apocrypha. With a life of the author. New York, 1872. 856+ pp. Portrait. L. 8° .... *R.R., A.2.1
CRUEL as the grave. Southworth, E. D. E. N. 726.10
CRUISE, The, of the Casco. Kellogg, E. 922.7
CRUISE, The, of the Dashaway. Nowell, H. P. H... 936.22
CRUISE, The, of the Frolic. Kingston, W. H. G.... 737.10
CRUISE, The, of the steam yacht North Star. Choules, J. O. Boston, 1854. 12° 425.10
CRUISE, A, upon wheels. Collins, C. A. Leipzig, 1874. 2 v. in 1. Sq. 16° 428.6
CRUSADES, The. Cox, G. W. London, 1874. Sq. 16° 628.1

See also Europe, History.

CRUSOE'S island: a ramble in the footsteps of Alexander Selkirk. Browne, J. R. New York, 1872. 12° 415.12
CRUST, Christie, *pseud.* *See* DENISON, Eliza Freeman.
CRYPTOGRAM, The. De Mille, J. 521.15
CRYSTALLISATION. Ethics of the dust. Ten lectures to little housewives on the elements of crystallisation. Ruskin, J. New York, 1866. 12°. 6236.4
CUBA. Ballou, M. M. History of. Boston, 1854. 12° 825.9
— Dana, R. H., *jr.* To Cuba and back. Boston, 1859. 12° 414.22
— Howe, J. W. A trip to. Boston, 1860. 12° ... 413.9
— Townshend, F. T. Wild life in Florida, with a visit to. London, 1875. 8° 5932.14
CUDJO'S cave. Trowbridge, J. T. 735.22
CUDLIP, Annie, *formerly Miss Thomas.* Called to account 317.15
— Denis Donne 317.14
— No alternative 714.10
— On guard 317.17
— Only herself 317.16
— A narrow escape 317.23
— Played out 317.13
— Walter Goring 317.18
CULLEY, R. S. A handbook of practical telegraphy. 5th edition, revised and enlarged. London, 1871. xvi, 408 pp. Plates and illustrations. 8° 6813.2
CULLIS, Charles. *See* PAGE, H. A. Noble workers. London, 1875. Sm. 8° 5936.3
CULM rock. Bradley, W. I. 913.11
CULTURE. Arnold, M. Culture and anarchy: an essay in political and social criticism. London, 1869. 8° 5613.2
— Shairp, J. C. Culture and religion in some of their relations. New York, 1872. 16° 5617.3
— Tylor, E. B. Primitive culture. London, 1871. 2 v. 8° 5922.6
— Youmans, E. L. The culture demanded by modern life. New York, 1872. 12° 5835.4

See also Self-culture.

CUMMING, John. Lectures on the book of Revelation. 1st series. Philadelphia, 1854. 512 pp. 12°. 6326.2
CUMMING, Roualeyn Gordon. The lion hunter of South Africa. Five years' adventures in the far interior of South Africa. 6th edition. With illustrations. London, 1870. x, 373 pp. Sm. 8°. 5934.11
CUMMING, (W.) Gordon. Wild men and wild beasts; or, scenes in camp and jungle 423.8
CUMMINGS, Jacob Abbot. Introduction to ancient and modern geography, on the plan of Goldsmith and Guy; comprising rules for projecting maps. 5th edition. Boston, 1818. xx, 316 pp. 12° 438.2
CUMMINS, Maria Susanna. El Fureidis 322.29
— Haunted hearts 322.30
— The lamplighter 322.28
— Mabel Vaughan. Boston 724.7
— *Same.* Leipzig 322.31

Note.—Miss Cummins's reputation was made by the realistic descriptions of homely life in The lamplighter, and was not added to by her subsequent novels.

CUNEIFORM inscriptions, The Chaldean account of Genesis, from the. Smith, G. New York [London], 1876. 8° 6320.4
CUNNINGHAM, Allan. The haunted ships. (*In* Johnson, (E.) R. Little classics) 529.4.8
— The king of the peak. (*In* Johnson, (E.) R. Little classics) 529.4.7
CUNNINGHAM, John William. A world without souls. 4th American, from the 2d London edition. Baltimore, 1810. 144 pp. 12° 1538.11
CUNYNGHAME, *Sir* Arthur Thurlow. Travels in the Eastern Caucasus, on the Caspian and Black seas, especially in Daghestan, and on the frontiers of Persia and Turkey, 1871. Illustrated. With maps. London, 1872. xvi, 367 pp. 8°. 5931.8
CUPID and Chow-chow. Alcott, L. M. Aunt Jo's scrap-bag 926.15.3
CUPPLES, Ann Jane. The children's voyage 912.19
— Driven to sea 923.8
— Singular creatures, and how they were found 913.19
CUPPLES, George. The deserted ship 915.19
CUPPLES, *Mrs.* George. *See* CUPPLES, Ann Jane.
CURATE, The, in charge. Oliphant, M. (O. W.) 721.25
CURIOSITIES of law reporters. Heard, F. F. Boston, 1871. 16° 6317.1
CURIOUS myths of the middle ages. Baring-Gould, S. London, 1872. 16° 716.2
CURLING, Henry. Love at first sight 710.14
CURRENCY or money. Hooper, S. Boston, 1855. 8°. 5822.4
CURRIE, James. The principles and practice of early and infant school-education. With an appendix of infant-school hymns and songs with appropriate melodies. New edition. London, N. D. xvi, 310 pp. Sm. 8° 5837.6
CURSE, The, of Clifton. Southworth, E. D. E. N... 527.8
CURSE, The, of gold. Stephens, A. S. (W.) 726.11
CURTEIS, George Herbert. Dissent, in its relation to the church of England. 2d edition. London, 1873. xxxii, 448 pp. 16° 5816.11
CURTIS, George Ticknor. Life of Daniel Webster. 4th edition. New York, 1872. 2 v. Portraits. 8° 1225.3
CURTIS, George William. The howadji in Syria. [Travels.] New York, 1856. viii, 350+ pp. 12° 452.12
— Lotus-eating: a summer book. Illustrated. New York, 1868. 206 pp. 12° 415.14
— My châteaux. (*In* Johnson, (E.) R. Little classics) 529.4.4
— Nile notes of a howadji. [Travels.] New York, 1857. x, 362 pp. 12° 424.15
— Potiphar papers. [Lively satire on New York society] 526.2
— Prue and I 526.1
— Trumps 524.11
CURTIUS, Ernst. History of Greece. Translated by A. W. Ward. New York, 1874, 75. 5 v. 12°. 5924.10
CURWEN, Henry. History of booksellers, the old and the new. With portraits and illustrations. London [1873]. 483 pp. 12° 5426.16
CUSACK, Mary Frances (*religious name Mary Frances Clare*). Illustrated history of Ireland: from the earliest period. 5th edition. London, 1872. 671+ pp. Maps. 8° 5412.1
— The liberator [Daniel O'Connell], his life and times. London, 1872. xlviii, 803 pp. Illustrated. Portraits. 4° 5420.1
— The life of Saint Patrick, apostle of Ireland. New York, 1870. 656+ pp. Illustrated. 4°. 5420.2
— The patriot's history of Ireland. New York, 1869. 320 pp. 16° 5418.4
CUSHING, Caleb. The treaty of Washington: its negotiation, execution, and the discussions relating thereto. New York, 1873. 280 pp. Sm. 8° .. 816.1
CUSHING, Luther Stearns. Manual of parliamentary practice. Rules of proceeding and debate in deliberative assemblies. Boston, 1848. 189 pp. 16° 1929.1
CUSHIONS and corners. Greene, R. J. 926.30
CUSHMAN, Pauline, Life of. Sarmiento, F. L. Philadelphia [*cop.* 1865]. 16° 1015.6

Shelf. No.

CUSTER, George A. My life on the plains. Or, personal experiences with Indians. New York, 1874. 256 pp. Illustrated. 8° 412.3

CUSTIS, George Washington Parke. Recollections and private memoirs of Washington, with a memoir of the author, by his daughter; and notes, by B. J. Lossing. With illustrations. Philadelphia [*cop.* 1859]. 644 pp. Portrait. Facsimiles. 8° 1011.6

CUTLERY. Manuel du coutelier. Landrin, H. Paris, 1835. 24° 6429.13

CUTTER, Calvin. Anatomy and physiology. Boston, 1847. 342 pp. Illustrated. 12° 6037.3

CUTTS, Edward L. Scenes and characters of the middle ages. With illustrations. London, 1872. xiii, 546 pp. Sm. 4° 5913.7

CUVIER, Georges Léopold Chrétien Frédéric Dagobert, *baron*. Essay on the theory of the earth. With mineralogical notes, and an account of Cuvier's geological discoveries by [R.] Jameson. Added, observations on the geology of North America. By S. L. Mitchell. New York, 1818. 431 pp. Illustrated. 8° 6633.1

CYCLOPÆDIAS. American annual cyclopædia and register of important events. 1861–72. New York, 1872. 12 v. 8° .... *R.R., B.3.1

— Burn, R. S. Self-aid cyclopædia for self-taught students. London, N. D. 8° 6223.2

— Chambers, R. Cyclopædia of English literature. Philadelphia, 1872. 2 v. 8° .... *R.R., C.2.3

— Chambers, W. and R. Chambers's encyclopædia. A dictionary of universal knowledge for the people. London, 1868. 10 v. L. 8° .... *R.R., D.3.1

— Cooley, A. J. Cyclopædia of practical receipts, etc. 5th edition, revised and partly rewritten by R. V. Tuson. London, 1872. 8° 6423.1

— Duyckinck, E. A. and G. L. Cyclopædia of American literature. Philadelphia, 1875. 2 v. 4° .... *R.R., D.3.11

— Godwin, P. Cyclopædia of biography. New York, 1872. 12° .... *R.R., F.3.4

— Dickens, C. (J. H.) Cyclopædia of [his] best thoughts. Compiled by F. G. De Fontaine. New York, 1873. L. 8° 1930.1

— Kitto, J. Popular cyclopædia of biblical literature condensed. Boston, 1871. 8° .... *R.R., A.2.2

— Knight, C., *editor*. English cyclopædia. London, 1866–69. 24 v. 4° .... *R.R., F.2.1

— MacClintock, J., and Strong, J. Cyclopædia of biblical, theological, and ecclesiastical literature. New York, 1871–73. 5 v. 8° .... *R.R., A.2.3

— Moore, J. W. Complete encyclopædia of music. Boston [*cop.* 1852]. L. 8° .... *R.R., E.2.3

— New American cyclopædia. New York, 1872. 16 v. 8° .... *R.R., B.3.1

— The penny cyclopædia. Vol. I–V. *See* SOCIETY for the diffusion of useful knowledge, *London*. London, 1833–36. 5 v. L. 8° .... *R.R., F.2.2

— Ringwalt, J. L. American encyclopædia of printing. Philadelphia, 1871. L. 8° .... *R.R., A.3.4

— Tomlinson, C. Cyclopædia of useful arts. London, 1868. 3 v. 8° .... *R.R., A.3.3

— Woodward, B. B., and Cates, W. L. R. Encyclopædia of chronology, historical and biographical. London, 1872. 8° .... *R.R., E.3.7

Note.—The New American cyclopædia, with its annual supplements, first mentioned above, is otherwise known as Appleton's, and is the best of the American *general encyclopædias*, but will be superseded by the new edition of it, to which illustrations are added, when the publication of the latter is completed. The ninth edition of the Encyclopædia Britannica, the most considerable of the English works, is not yet completed, and it can be found in the Central Library. Of the other English publications, Chambers's, in ten volumes, is the best for ordinary use. The English cyclopædia is a classified arrangement, with additions, etc., of the matter which originally constituted the Penny cyclopædia.

CYPRIANUS, Thascius Cæcilius, *St.*, and OTHERS. Writings. Translated by Robert Ernest Wallis. Edinburgh, 1868, 69. 2 v. [Ante-Nicene Christian library.] 8° .... Vol. 8, 13 of 6322.4

Contents. — Vol. I. Epistles; Treatises. II. Treatises; Writings of Novatian, Minucius Felix, etc.

CYRILLA. Tautphoeus, J. M., *baronin* von 317.20

CYRUS the great, History of. Abbott, J. 915.8

CZECHOWSKI, Michael B. Thrilling and instructive developments: an experience of fifteen years as Roman catholic clergyman and priest. Boston, 1862. 286 pp. 12° 1226.11

DACOTAH. Andrews, C. C. Minnesota and Dacotah. Washington, 1857. 12° 415.3

— Report of a reconnaissance of the Black hills of Dakota. *See* UNITED STATES. *Department of war.* 630.1

DADD, George H. The nature and treatment of the diseases of cattle, with descriptions and illustrations of various organs and functions of the animal economy. Boston, 1859. 395 pp. 12°. 1522.15

DAGHESTAN, *Russia*, Travels in. Cunynghame, *Sir* A. T. London, 1872. 8° 5931.8

DAHOMEY, *Africa*, History of. Dalzel, A. London, 1793. 4° 5910.1

DAIRY cow, The. Sturtevant, E. L. and J. N. Boston, 1875. 12° 1522.12

DAISY Brentwell. [Fiction.] Widdemer, I. 723.36

DAISY Burns. Kavanagh, J. 323.10

DAISY chain, The. Yonge, C. M. 318.6

DAISY Deane. Davis, C. E. 928.21

DAKIN, Celia V. *See* HAMILTON, Celia V.

DALL, Caroline (Wells) Healey. The college, the market, and the court; or, woman's relation to education, labor, and law. Boston, 1867. xxxv, 498 pp. 8° 1733.1

— Essays and sketches. Boston, 1849. 116 pp. 16°. 1917.3

— The romance of the association; or, one last glimpse of Charlotte Temple and Eliza Wharton. A curiosity of literature and life. [With supplement.] Cambridge, 1875. xii, 514 pp. 16°. 1534.11

— "Woman's right to labor;" or, low wages and hard work: lectures. Boston, 1860. xv, 184 pp. 16° 1737.1

DALL, William H. Alaska and its resources. Boston, 1870. xii, 627 pp. Map. Illustrated. 8°. 5031.1

DALTON, John Call, Memorial of. Green, J. O. Cambridge, 1864. 8° 5023.4

DALTONS, The. Lever, C. (J.) Leipzig. 4 v. in 2. 332.28

— *Same.* London 516.9

DALZEL, Archibald. History of Dahomey, an inland kingdom of Africa. With an introduction and notes. London, 1793. xxxi, xxvi, 230+ pp. Illustrated. Map. 4° 5910.1

DAME blanche, La. Boieldieu, F. A. (*In* Ditson, O., and co. Standard opera librettos) 6233.3.5

DANA, Charles Anderson, *editor*. The household book of poetry. 11th edition, revised and enlarged. With illustrations. New York, 1873. xxvii, 816 pp. 8° 1610.2

DANA, James Dwight. Corals and the coral islands. New York, 1872. 398 [394] pp. Illustrated. 8° 6630.3

— - *See* ESTES, H. Half-hour recreations in popular science. Boston [1874]. 8° 6813.7

— and BRUSH, George Jarvis. A system of mineralogy. Descriptive mineralogy. 5th edition, enlarged and illustrated. (6th sub-edition, with two appendixes and corrections.) New York, 1875. xlviii, 827, iv, 19+, x, 64 pp. 8° 6630.2

DANA, Richard Henry, *jr.* To Cuba and back. Boston, 1859. 288 pp. 12° 414.22

— Two years before the mast. New York, 1840. 483 pp. 12° .... 918.1 and 5037.1

Note.—The last of these books first gave Mr. Dana a literary reputation nearly forty years ago. It is the sea experience of a young graduate of Harvard, round the Horn, to the California coast after hides, and contains most graphic descriptions of sailors' duties and Pacific coast life before the gold discovery.

DANBURY, Life in. Bailey, J. M. Boston, 1873. 16°. 538.1

DANCE, Charles, *joint author*. High, low, Jack, and the game: a burletta. *See* PLANCHÉ, James Robinson 1635.5

DANCING. Drawing-room dances. Cellarius, *pseud.* New York, 1858. 16° 1514.4

DANDI, Sri. [Dasa Kumara Charitra.] Hindoo tales, or adventures of ten princes. Freely translated from the Sanscrit by P. W. Jacob. London, 1873. ix, 376+ pp. 8° 5936.5

Shelf. No.

DANGEROUS classes, The, of New York. Brace, C. L. New York, 1872. 12° 5824.1

DANGEROUS game, A. Yates, E. 731.32

DANIEL, George. Merrie England in the olden time. With illustrations. New edition. London [1841]. 422 pp. Sm. 8° 5617.14

DANIEL, William Barker. Rural sports. [London, 1801.] 2 v. in 3. Illustrated. 8° 6412.1

DANTE ALIGHIERI. The divine comedy. Translated by H. W. Longfellow. Leipzig, 1867. 3 v. in 1. Sq. 16° 1614.4

— *Same.* Boston, 1871. viii, 760 pp. 8° 5534.1

— The vision; or, hell, purgatory, and paradise. Translated by H. F. Cary. With life of Dante, notes and index. Illustrated. New York, 1853. Portrait. 587 pp. 16° 1615.3

— *See* LOWELL, J. R. Among my books. Boston, 1876. 16° 1934.8.2

Note. — See note in Lower Hall Catalogue of history, etc., p. 67.

DANVERS, Henry. A fascinating individual: a farce. New York, N. D. 22 pp. 12° 1635.5

DANVERS, *Mass.* Centennial celebration, June 16, 1852. [Together with the proceedings of the town in relation to the donation of George Peabody.] Boston, 1852. 208 pp. Portraits. Illustrations. 8° 5222.2

Contents. — Address by J. W. Proctor; Poem, by A. Nichols; Centennial celebration.

— Proceedings at the reception and dinner in honor of George Peabody, Oct. 9, 1856. Appended an historical sketch of the Peabody institute. Boston, 1856. vi, 195+ pp. Portrait. Illustrations. 8° 612.6

DANVERS papers, The. Yonge, C. M. 318.7

D'ARBLAY, Frances. *See* ARBLAY, Frances d'.

DARBY, William. Tour from the city of New York to Detroit, in the Michigan territory. With map[s]. New York, 1819. 228, lxxii+ pp. 8°. 411.1

DARC, Jeanne (*Joan of Arc, maid of Orleans*). Barthelemy de Beauregard, (E.) J. Histoire de Jeanne d'Arc. Paris, 1847. 2 v. 8° 5523.1

— Michelet, J. Jeanne d'Arc. Paris, 1873. Sm. 8°. 2016.8

— - Joan of Arc; or, the maid of Orleans. New York, 1870. 16° 1029.2

— Parr, H. Life and death of. London, 1866. 2 v. Sm. 8° 1225.8

Note. — Joan of Arc has been the subject of a large number of books, and those published before 1847 are enumerated in Barthélemy de Beauregard's life of her, which is a standard life. The publication of late years of the documentary records of her trial [see Bates Hall Index, under "Joan of Arc"] has enabled the most recent biographers to comprehend her character better. Michelet has written a reputable life, which is drawn from his History of France [811.7]. The most recent life in English is Harriet Parr's, based upon the documents referred to above, and on the whole is the best for the English reader, of the extended accounts. See also De Quincey's "Miscellaneous essays" [1825.2]; Gurney's Chapters from French history [5517.2]; Guizot's History of France [5010.2.3]; and Doran's Knights and their days [822.4].

The most noteworthy delineation in fiction for the English reader are Shakespeare's Henry VI; Southey's poem; and Schiller's drama, the latter, however, not being in very close accordance with the historical recitals. See also note in Bulletin, no. 34, p. 363.

DARIEN. Warburton, E. (B. G.) 317.7

DARIEN, Isthmus of. Reports of explorations and surveys to ascertain the practicability of a ship-canal between the Atlantic and Pacific oceans. *See* UNITED STATES. *Department of the navy* ... 5030.6

DARK night's, A, work. Gaskell, E. C. 328.22

DARK secret, The. Fleming, M. A. 720.3

DARKNESS and daylight. Holmes, M. J. 535.9

DARLEY, Felix O. C. Sketches abroad with pen and pencil. New York, 1869. viii, 192 pp. Sm. 4°. 433.2

DARNELL, Elias. Journal containing an account of those Kentucky volunteers and regulars, commanded by General Winchester, 1812–13. Also, narratives by [T. Mallary and J. Davenport]. Philadelphia, 1854. 98+ pp. Sm. 12° 819.6

DARNLEY: or, the field of the cloth of gold. James, G. P. R. Leipzig, 1847. Sq. 16° 327.16

DARTMOUTH college, *Hanover, N. H.* Report of the case of the trustees against W. H. Woodward. Farrar, T. Portsmouth, N. H. [*cop.* 1819]. 406+ pp. 8°. 6314.2

Shelf. No.

DARWIN, Charles (Robert). The descent of man and selection in relation to sex. With illustrations. New York, 1872. 2 v. 12° 1523.5

— The expression of the emotions of man and animals. With illustrations. New York, 1873. v, 374+ pp. 16° 6615.2

— Insectivorous plants. With illustrations. New York, 1875. x, 462 pp. 12° 6614.13

— Journal of researches into the natural history and geology of the countries visited during the voyage of [the] Beagle round the world. New York, 1871. 2 v. 16° 1526.11

— The movements and habits of climbing plants. 2d edition, revised. With illustrations. London, 1875. viii, 208 pp. Sm. 8° 6625.4

— Origin of species by means of natural selection. New edition, with additions and corrections. New York, 1873. xxi, 458 pp. 12° 1523.6

— The structure and distribution of coral reefs. With [woodcuts and] three plates. 2d edition, revised. London, 1874. xx, 278 pp. Sm. 8° . 6634.1

Note. — "The first edition of this book appeared in 1842, and since then only one important work on the same subject has appeared, namely, in 1872, by Professor Dana, on Corals and coral-reefs. In the present edition I have added some new facts and have revised the whole book; the latter chapters having been almost re-written." — *Preface.*

See also Darwinism, *note.*

DARWIN, Erasmus. Zoonomia; or, the laws of organic life. London, 1801. 2 v. 8° 6614.2

DARWINISM. Hodge, C. What is Darwinism? New York, 1874. 16° 6616.8

— Schmidt, (E.) O. The doctrine of descent and Darwinism. New York, 1875. 12° 6616.10

— Wallace, A. R. Contributions to the theory of natural selection. London, 1871. 16° 6616.4

Note. — In an historical introduction to his Origin of species, Darwin, in tracing the history of opinion on this subject, names thirty-four authors, who, previous to the publication of his book in 1859, had expressed views tending to prepare the way for his theory of natural selection, of which the book that most popularly affected contemporary views was probably the "Vestiges of creation" [1515.17] of an anonymous writer, which in Darwin's opinion removed prejudices, and prepared the way for the reception of analogous views. Tyndall epitomized the history of the idea in Nature, 1874, which was reprinted in no. 1581 of Living age. During the ten years subsequent to Darwin's promulgation of his theory, the change from a disbelief in it to a championship of it, is, according to Huxley, well shown in articles that appeared in the Quarterly review in July, 1860, and July, 1871. Wallace is allowed to have reached Darwin's conclusions independently; but the latter had the priority of publication; but Wallace's assistance in support of Darwin has been rendered in the Quarterly journal of science, Oct., 1867, and also in his Contributions to the theory of natural selection [6516.4; 6836.1], published as a book. Of the older scientists, most held to conservative views, but the most remarkable change was in the case of Sir Charles Lyell, in the 10th and subsequent editions of his "Principles of geology" [6631.7]. Agassiz was not ready to accept the theory, and his views would have been fully explained had he lived to complete the series of articles in the Atlantic monthly, which was begun in Jan., 1874. John Fiske combatted Agassiz's views, in the North American review, Oct., 1873; but see also Fiske's "Cosmic philosophy" [5824.2].

The success of his first announcement of the theory led Darwin to publish, in his lifetime, what he had intended for a posthumous work, as his fears had been that a too early application of his belief in detail to the question of the origin and descent of man would incite prejudices against the question in its purely scientific bearing. His "Descent of man" was consequently a logical outgo of the theory, and to answer the physiological objection that man has certain muscles not in the brute, given him to express his emotions, thus inferring a different origin, he was led to his other work named above on that subject. Darwin acknowledges that had he known the work of the German naturalist, Haeckel, "Natürliche Schöpfungsgeschichte," of which there is an English rendering, History of creation [6615.5], to have been in progress, there would have been no occasion for his effort.

Some of the most determined opposition to Darwinism has appeared in Mivart's "Genesis of species" [1536.5], which is reviewed in the North American review [5117.1.113]. Huxley took up Darwin's defence, in the Contemporary review, vol. 18 (see also his Lay sermons, etc., 1922.1). Mivart answered Huxley in the Contemporary review, vol. 19.

Other discussions of the question will be found in Lewes's "History of philosophy" [6832.1.2, — see also Fortnightly review, July, 1867; April, 1868; June, 1868; July, 1868]; in the Duke of Argyle's Reign of law [1525.15, ch. v, in opposition]; in Spencer's "Principles of biology" [6625.2]; in Burr's "Doctrine of evolution" [1527.11.2]; beside the works of Hodge and Schmidt above named.

See the following articles in periodicals, — Contemporary review, by Sir Alexander Grant, vol. 17; Popular science monthly, 1873 and 1874 (by Asa Gray); Atlantic monthly, July, 1860, Oct., 1860, Oct., 1866, July, 1868; North American review, April, 1870; Harper's monthly, Dec., 1867; Scribner's monthly, vol. 6; Old and new (against), vol. 8.

See the literature of the subject considered in Van Rhyn's "What and how to read" [6136.11], under the heads of Biology, Evolution, Species, and Zoology.

Shelf. No.

DASA KUMARA CHARITRA. *See* DANDI, Sri.

DATES. Bond, J. J. Handy-book of rules and tables for verifying dates with the Christian era. London, 1875. Sm. 8° 5627.2

— Haydn, J. Dictionary of. New York, 1870. 8° ....*R.R., E.3.8

DAUGHTER, The, of an empress. Mundt, C. (M.) .. 531.3

DAUGHTER, A, of Bohemia. Fisher, F. C. 732.23

DAUGHTER, A, of Heth. Black, W. 311.26

DAUGHTER'S, The, own book; or, practical hints from a father to his daughter. Boston, 1833. 240 pp. 1 plate. 16° 1538.21

DAUNT, W. J. O'N. Ireland and her agitators. New edition, revised. Dublin, 1867. xiv, 312 [310] pp. 12° 5417.4

DAURIGNAC, J. M. S., *pseud.* *See* ORLIAC, *Mme.* J. M. S.

DAVAULT'S mills. A novel. Jones, C. H. 722.4

DAVENPORT, John. Narrative. *See* DARNELL, Elias 819.6

DAVENPORT Dunn. Lever, C. (J.) Leipzig 332.4

— *Same.* London 516.7

DAVID Copperfield. Dickens, C. (J. H.) Boston. 2 v. 1824.7

— *Same.* Leipzig 338.14

DAVID Elginbrod. MacDonald, G. 328.2

DAVID Swan: a fantasy. (*In* Johnson, (E.) R. Little classics) 529.4.4

DAVIDSON, Ellis A. The boy joiner and model maker. With illustrations. London [1874]. 211 pp. 4° 1512.3

— Cassell's technical manuals. [Linear drawing and projection. London, 1868–75.] 2 v. in 1. Illustrated. Sm. 8° 6218.2

Contents. — Linear drawing; Orthographic and isometrical projection.

DAVIDSON, Lucretia Maria, Memoir of. Sedgwick, C. M. (*In* Sparks, J. Library of American biography) 5028.1.7

DAVIDSON, Margaret Miller, Biography and poetical remains of. Irving, W. Philadelphia, 1841. 12° 1217.2

DAVIES, Charles Maurice. Unorthodox London: or phases of religious life in the metropolis. London, 1873. viii, 448 pp. 8° 5811.4

DAVIES, G. Christopher. Rambles and adventures of our school field-club. With illustrations. London, 1875. x, 284+ pp. Sm. 8° 1115.15

DAVIES, James. Hesiod, and Theognis [outlined and explained]. Edinburgh, 1873. vii, 166+ pp. 16°. [Ancient classics for English readers].6116.16

DAVIES, Theodore. Losing to win 714.8

DAVIES, Thomas A. Genesis disclosed: proving the error that all men have descended from Adam and Eve [etc.]. New York, 1874. 222 pp. 12° 6327.12

DAVILLIER, (Jean) Charles, *baron.* L'Espagne. Illustrée par G. Doré. Paris, 1874. 799+ pp. L. 4° 5910.5

DAVIS, Caroline E., *formerly Miss Kelly.* Daisy Deane 928.21

— Matty Frost. A story for girls 1118.1

DAVIS, Eliza B. Edith; or, the light of home 733.3

DAVIS, Jefferson, Life of. Pollard, E. A. Philadelphia [*cop.* 1869]. 8° 5013.3

DAVIS, Nathan. Carthage and her remains: being an account of the excavations and researches on the site of the Phœnician metropolis in Africa, and other adjacent places. London, 1861. xvi, 631 pp. Illustrated. Maps. 8° 422.1

DAVIS, Rebecca Harding. The captain's story. (*In* Johnson, (E.) R. Little classics) 529.4.2

— A faded leaf of history. (*In* Johnson, (E.) R. Little classics) 529.4.10

— John Andross 737.33

— Kitty's choice. A story of Berrytown 731.10

— Margret Howth 715.20

DAVIS, *Mrs.* Stephen M. Life and times of Sir Philip Sidney. Boston, 1859. 281+ pp. Portrait. Plate. Fac-simile. 16° 1225.11

— *Same.* New edition. New York, 1875. 286+ pp. Portrait. Plate. Fac-simile. 16° 5337.4

Shelf. No.

DAVIS, William M. Nimrod of the sea 726.28

DAVY, *Sir* Humphry. Consolations in travel. With illustrations. Boston, 1870. iv, 297 pp. 16°. 5617.5

— Salmonia; or, days of fly fishing. With illustrations. Boston, 1870. xvi, 305 pp. 16° 1515.4

— Forbes, J. D. Biography of. (*In* Macaulay, T. B., *lord*, and others. New biographies of illustrious men) 5428.4

— Mayhew, H. The wonders of science; or, young Humphry Davy. New York, 1870. 16° 936.34

DAWES, Rufus. Geraldine, Athenia of Damascus, and miscellaneous poems. New York, 1839. 343 pp. Portrait. 12° 5217.4

DAWKINS, William Boyd. Cave hunting, researches on the evidence of caves respecting the early inhabitants of Europe. Illustrated. London, 1874. xxiv, 455 pp. 8° 6632.5

DAWSON, Henry B. The sons of liberty in New York. A paper read before the New York historical society. [New York] 1859. 118 pp. 8°. 811.12

DAWSON, John William. The story of the earth and man. New York, 1873. xiii, 403+ pp. Illustrated. 12° 1523.22

DAY, B. H. American ready reckoner. New York [*cop.* 1866]. 192 pp. 16° 1938.1

DAY, Henry, *joint author.* Art recreations. *See* URBINO, Lavinia Buoncore 1515.9

DAY, Henry Noble. The science of æsthetics. New Haven, 1872. xvii, 434 pp. Illustrated. 12°. 6226.4

DAY, Horace. The opium habit, with suggestions as to the remedy. New York, 1868. 335 pp. 12° 1525.17

DAY, Thomas. History of Sandford and Merton. Corrected and revised by C. Hartley. New edition. London [1850]. vii, 462 pp. Illustrated. 16° 935.4

DAY after the fair: a burletta. Somerset, G. A. New York, N. D. 12° 1635.3

DAY, The, after the holidays. Moncrieff, A. R. H. . 1115.8

DAY, A, by the fire. Hunt, (J. H.) L. Boston, 1870. 12° 5618.4

DAY'S, A, ride. Lever, C. (J.) Leipzig 332.8

— *Same.* London 516.4

DAYBREAK in Spain. Wylie, J. A. London [1870]. Sm. 8° 227.1

DAYDIE, Blaise Maria, *chevalier.* Correspondance inédite, faisant suite aux lettres de Mademoiselle Aissé. Publié sur les manuscrits autographes originaux, avec introduction et notes par Honoré Bonhomme. Paris, 1874. 335+ pp. 18° 5527.13

DAYS, The, of Bruce. [Scottish historical fiction.] Aguilar, G. 2 v. 533.19

DAYS, The, of Jezebel. Bayne, P. Boston, 1872. 12° 1636.4

Note. — Poetical drama, — Elijah the prophet, etc.

DAYS, The, of my life. An autobiography. Oliphant, M. (O. W.). New York, 1868. 12° ... 512.7

DAYS of yore. Keddie, *Miss* —. London, 1868. 16°. 736.17

DE officiis libri tres. Cicero, M. T. Philadelphia, 1850. Sm. 12° 6118.2

DEACONS. Murray, W. H. H. Boston, 1875. Sq. 12° 724.26

DEAD alive, The. Collins, (W.) W. 717.3

DEAD lake, The. Heyse, P. (J. L.) 311.9

DEAD men's shoes. Hadermann, J. R. 533.15

DEAD-SEA fruit. Braddon, M. E. 325.11

DEAD secret, The. Collins, (W.) W. 724.20

DEAD sin, The. Mayo, I. F. 524.18

DEAD to the world. Bauer, K. 716.15

DEALINGS with the dead. Sargent, L. M. Boston, 1856. 2 v. 12° 1816.1

DEALINGS with the fairies. MacDonald, G. 939.1

DEAN'S, The, daughter. Gore, C. G. F. 311.5

DEANE, William Reed. A genealogical memoir of the Leonard family. Boston, 1851. 23+ pp. 8° 612.4

DEAR Lady Disdain. MacCarthy, J. 721.23

DEARBORN, Henry Alexander Scammel, Address on the life and character of. Putnam, G. Roxbury, 1851. 8° 1932.1

Shelf. No.

DEARBORN, Nathaniel S. Guide through Mount Auburn, with engravings, [and] a plan of the cemetery. 11th edition. Boston, 1857. 55 pp. 12° 413.8

DEATH and life. Ware, M. G. (C.) Boston, 1864. 12° 1526.10

DEBATABLE land, The, between this world and the next. [Spiritualism.] Owen, R. D. New York, 1872. 12° 1526.28

DEBENHAM'S vow. Edwards, A. B. 312.12

DEBIT and credit. [Novel.] Freytag, G. 533.8

DEBORAH'S diary. Manning, A. 738.4

DECAISNE, Joseph, and NAUDIN, Charles Victor. Handbook of hardy trees, shrubs, and herbaceous plants. *See* HEMSLEY, W. B. 6624.1

DECOMPOSITION, The dependence of life on. Freke, H. Dublin, 1871. 8° 1528.12

DECORATIVE arts. Dresser, C. Principles of decorative design. London [1873]. 4° 6210.8

— Eastlake, *Sir* C. L. Hints on household taste in furniture, upholstery, and other details. Boston, 1872. Sm. 8° 6212.1

DE CRESSY. By the author of "Still waters" 310.16

DEDHAM, *Mass.* Burgess, E. Dedham pulpit. Boston, 1840. 8° 5813.11

— Worthington, E. History of. Boston, 1827. 8°. 811.18

DEEP down. A tale of the Cornish mines. Ballantyne, R. M. 935.10

DEEP waters. Drury, A. H. 720.9

DEERBROOK. Martineau, H. 737.21

DEERINGS, The, of Medbury. Townsend, V. F. 711.24

DEERSLAYER, The. Cooper, J. F. 625.7

DE FOE, Daniel. Robinson Crusoe. Leipzig, 1845. 495+ pp. Sq. 16° 310.14

— *Same.* With illustrations. New York, 1874. 356+ pp. 16° 733.9

— *Same.* Edited after the original editions. With a biographical introduction by H. Kingsley. London, 1868. xxxi, 607 pp. Sq. 16° 916.13

— Chadwick, W. Life and times of. London, 1859. 8° 5422.6

— Lee, W. Daniel De Foe: his life and newly discovered writings. London, 1869. 3 v. 8° ... 5422.5

— Stephen, L. De Foe's novels. (*In his* Hours in a library) 6136.9

Note. — Chadwick's book is discursively written. Lee made some recently discovered writings the occasion of a new biography in 1869. Of the briefer memoirs, Forster's Life [in his Biographical essays, — also Edinburgh review, Oct., 1845] is thorough enough for most readers.

DE FOREST, John William. The Lauson tragedy. (*In* Johnson, (E.) R. Little classics) 529.4.3

— Miss Ravenel's conversion from secession to loyalty 535.5

— Overland 531.24

— Playing the mischief 720.29

— The Wetherell affair 732.8

DEGERANDO, Joseph Marie, *baron.* *See* GERANDO, Joseph Marie, *baron* de.

DEICIDES, The. Cohen, J. Baltimore, 1873. 12° .. 5817.13

DEISM. Short method with deists. Leslie, C. Andover, 1823. 12° 5819.4

DE KROYFT, S. Helen. Little Jakey. (*In* Johnson, (E.) R. Little classics) 529.4.10

— A place in thy memory. New York, 1851. 191 pp. Plate. Portrait. 12° 5218.7

DELACOUR, Alfred (Charlemagne Lartigue), *joint author.* Les petits oiseaux: comédie. *See* LABICHE, Eugène (Marin) 2015.2

DELAFIELD, Richard. Report on the art of war in Europe in 1854–56. *See* UNITED STATES. *Department of war* 5910.3

DELAMOTTE, Philip H. A progressive drawing book for beginners. 2d edition. London, 1874. x, 122+ pp. Illustrated. Sm. 8° 6217.10

DELANO, Amasa. Narrative of voyages and travels, in the northern and southern hemispheres: comprising three voyages round the world; with a voyage in the Pacific ocean and oriental islands. Boston, 1817. 598+ pp. Map [imperfect]. Portraits. 8° 432.6

Shelf. No.

DELESDERNIER, Emily Pierpont. Fannie St. John. A romantic incident of the American revolution. New York, 1874. 63+ pp. Sq. 16° 5216.7

Note. — "My main purpose has been to make known the rare goodness of heart of my grandfather Gustavus Fellowes [brother of Caleb Fellowes, founder of the Fellowes Athenæum]." — *Preface.*

DE LIEFDE, J. B. Galama: or, the beggars. (The founders of the Dutch republic.) New York [1873.] 166 pp. 8° 520.3

Note. — Originally published in England in 1869, under the title of The beggars (Les gueux).

DELUSIONS, Epidemic. Carpenter, W. B. (*In* Estes, D. Half-hour recreations in popular science) .. 6813.7

DE MILLE, James. The American baron. With illustrations 511.19

— The babes in the wood. A story of the Italian revolution of 1848 .... 710.22

— [The "B. O. W. C." series.] The "B. O. W. C." [*i. e.* Brethren of the White Cross] 935.18

— – The boys of Grand Pré school 932.43

— – Fire in the woods 934.20

— – Lost in the fog 934.21

— – Picked up adrift 914.39

— – The treasure of the seas 928.6

— A comedy of terrors 531.22

— Cord and creese 521.14

— The cryptogram 521.15

— The Dodge club 511.22

— The lady of the ice 521.1

— The lily and the cross. A tale of Acadia 724.12

— The living link 710.2

— An open question 520.1

— The young Dodge club [series]. Among the brigands 932.44

— – The seven hills [*i. e.* Rome] 914.41

DEMOCRACY. Capen, N. History of. Vol. I. Hartford, 1874. 8° 6332.3

— Tocqueville, A. (C. H. C.) de. Democracy in America. Boston, 1873. 2 v. Sm. 8° 5015.1

DEMON, The, of gold. Conscience, H. 717.6

DE MORGAN, C. From matter to spirit. The result of ten years' experience in spirit manifestations. Intended as a guide to enquirers. With a preface by A. B. London, 1863. xlv, 388+ pp. Sm. 8° .6325.19

DEMOSTHENES. The Olynthiac and other public orations. Translated, with notes, by C. R. Kennedy. London, 1871. 312 pp. Sm. 8° 6115.19

— Orations against Leptines, Midias, Androtion, and Aristocrates. Translated, with notes, by C. R. Kennedy. London, 1856. 407+ pp. Sm. 8°. 6115.9

— Orations against Macartatus, Leochares, Stephanus I, Stephanus II, Euergus and Mnesibulus, Olympiodorus, Timotheus, Polycles, Callippus, Nicostratus, Conon, Callicles, Dionysodorus, Eubulides, Theocrines, Neæra, and for the naval crown; the funeral oration; the erotic oration, or panegyric upon Epicrates; exordia; the epistles. Translated by C. R. Kennedy. London, 1863. 401+ pp. Sm. 8° 6115.11

— Orations against Timocrates, Aristogiton, Aphobus, Onetor, Zenothemis, Apaturius, Phormio, Lacritus, Pantænetus, Nausimachus, Bœotus, Spudias, Phænippus, and for Phormio. Translated, with notes and appendices, by C. R. Kennedy. London, 1872. 420 pp. Sm. 8° 6115.10

— Orations on the crown, and on the embassy. Translated, with notes, by C. R. Kennedy. London, 1872. 401+ pp. Sm. 8° 6115.18

DEMPSEY, G. Drysdale. Rudimentary treatise on the locomotive engine. With illustrative diagrams. 3d edition. London, 1866. 152+ pp. 12° 1716.7

— Rudimentary treatise [on] tubular and other iron girder bridges. 3d edition. With engravings. London, 1865. viii, 136 pp. 12° 1716.17

DENE hollow. Wood, E. P. 333.16

DENIS, (Jean) Ferdinand. Portugal. Paris, 1846. 439+ pp. 32 plates. 8°. [L'Univers] 5911.10

— and CHAUVIN, Victor. The true Robinson Crusoes. Stories of adventure. Abridged from the French, by C. Russell 938.8

Shelf. No.

DENIS Donne. Cudlip, A. 317.14

DENIS Duval. Thackeray, W. M. Leipzig.......... 335.1

— *Same.* (*In his* Works.) London..........513.1.11

DENISE. By the author of "Mademoiselle Mori".. 310.17

DENISON, Edmund Beckett. Astronomy without mathematics. From the 4th London edition. Edited with corrections and notes by P. E. Chase. New York, 1871. 357 pp. Illustrated. 12° 6817.1

— Rudimentary treatise on clocks, watches, and bells. With illustrations. 5th edition. With appendix, and index. London, 1868. 424+ pp. Folded plate. 12° 1716.12

DENISON, Eliza Freeman. Autumn leaves. [Juvenile.] By Christie Crust [*pseud.*].......... 938.12

DENISON, Mary Andrews. Bessie Brown, the soldier's daughter 928.16

— The Denison series. A noble sister 1117.27

— Opposite the jail.......... 926.20

— Orphan Anne.......... 928.18

— Out of prison 1118.4

— Ruth Margerie: a romance of the revolt of 1689. 539.9

DENMAN, Thomas, *lord*, Memoir of. Arnould, *Sir* J. London, 1873. 2 v. 8°.......... 5332.1

DENMARK. Adams, W. T. Up the Baltic; or, Young America in. Boston, 1873. 16° 925.8

— Brown, J. The Northern courts; containing memoirs of the sovereigns of, since 1766. London, 1818. 2 v. 8° 5713.1

— Murray, J. Handbook for. London, 1871. 12°. 5716.3

— Philojuvenis, *pseud.* Edda; or, the tales of a grandmother. History of Denmark to 1448. London, 1875. L. 8° 5712.2

— Taylor, (J.) B. Northern travel: summer and winter pictures of. New York, 1858. 12° 426.3

DENON, (Dominique) Vivant, *baron.* Travels in upper and lower Egypt, during the campaigns of Bonaparte in that country. Translated from the French. Prefixed, an historical account of the invasion of Egypt by the French. By Arthur Aikin. With engravings. New York, 1803. 2 v. Map. Folded plates. 8°........ 222.3

DÉPIT amoureux, Le; comédie. Molière, J. B. P. Œuvres. Paris, 1869. 12° 5537.2.1

DEPPING, Guillaume. Wonders of bodily strength and skill. Translated by C. Russell. With illustrations. New York, 1872. 338 pp. 16°.1714.12

DEPTHS of the sea, The. Thomson, C. W. London, 1873. 8°.......... 6632.3

DE QUINCEY, Thomas. Autobiographic sketches. Boston, 1869. 383 pp. 16° 1825.7

— The avenger; and other papers. Boston, 1859. 327 pp. 12°.......... 715.10

— Biographical essays. Boston, 1870. 286 pp. 12°. 1825.6

— The Cæsars. Boston, 1873. 288 pp. 12° 1825.10

— The confessions of an English opium-eater, and Suspiria de profundis. Boston, 1872. 288 pp. Portrait. 16°.......... 1825.5

— Essays on the poets, and other English writers. Boston, 1871. 298 pp. 16°. 1825.4

— Flight of a Tartar tribe. (*In* Johnson, (E.) R. Little classics)..........529.4.1

— Historical and critical essays. Boston, 1866. 2 v. 12° 1825.3

— Literary reminiscences. Boston, 1851. 2 v. 12°. 1226.1

— Memorials, and other papers. Boston, 1868. 2 v. 12° 1825.8

— Miscellaneous essays. Boston, 1872. 288 [284] pp. 12°.......... 1825.2

— Murder, considered as one of the fine arts. (*In* Johnson, (E.) R. Little classics).......... 529.4.2

— Narrative and miscellaneous papers. Boston, 1871. 2 v. 12° 1825.1

— The vision of sudden death. (*In* Johnson, (E.) R. Little classics).......... 529.4.3

— *See* STEPHEN, L. Hours in a library. London, 1874. 16°.......... 6136.9

Note. — De Quincey's own writings are largely illustrative of his own life, particularly his Confessions of an opium-eater; see also Day's Opium habit [1525.17]; Literary reminiscences; Autobiographic sketches; Memorials, etc. See Harper's monthly, vol. 1; also see vol. 2; and references in Allibone.

Shelf. No.

DERBY, Elias Haskett. The catholic. Letters addressed by a jurist to a young kinsman proposing to join the church of Rome. Boston, 1856. xii, 293 pp. 12° 1524.22

DERBY, George. An inquiry into the influence of anthracite fires upon health; with remarks upon artificial moisture, and the best modes of warming houses. 2d edition, enlarged. Boston, 1868. 76 pp. 12° 1526.15

— Lessons of the war to the medical profession. (*In* Massachusetts medical society. Publications). 6021.4

— and OTHERS. Papers from the Second annual report of the Massachusetts board of health. Boston, 1871. Map. 8° 6023.18

Contents. — The causes of typhoid fever in Massachusetts, Health of towns, Trichina disease in Massachusetts, by G. Derby; Health of minors employed in manufactories of cotton, woollen, silk, flax, and jute, Mortality of Boston in 1870, by G. Derby and F. W. Draper; Air, and its impurities, by G. Derby and others.

DERBY, George Horatio. Phœnixiana; or, sketches and burlesques by John Phœnix. 12th edition. New York, 1869. 274 pp. 1 plate. 12° 535.14

DERRICK, Francis, *pseud.* *See* NOTLEY, *Mrs.* —.

DESCENT of man, The. Darwin, C. (R.) New York, 1872. 2 v. 12° 1523.5

See also Darwinism, *note.*

DESCRIPTION of the Boston water works. With maps and illustrations. Boston, 1848. 46 pp. Sm. 12°.......... 819.3

DESERT home, The. Reid, M. 937.21

DESERT, The, of the Exodus. Palmer, E. H. New York, 1872. Sm. 8° 222.2

DESERTED ship, The. Cupples, G.......... 915.19

DESERTED village, The. [Poem.] Goldsmith, O. Works. Leipzig, 1842. Sq. 16° 312.23

— *Same.* London, 1854. 8° 5612.1.1

DESERTED wife, The. Southworth, E. D. E. N. 527.10

DESK and debit. Adams, W. T. 924.7

DESMARRES, Louis Auguste. Traité théorique et pratique des maladies des yeux. Avec 78 figures. Paris, 1847. viii, 904 pp. 8°..........6021.16

DESPARD, *Mrs.* M. C. Chaste as ice, pure as snow. 714.3

DESPERATE remedies. Hardy, T.......... 518.22

DESPOTISM in America. Hildreth, R. Boston, 1840. 12°.......... 816.2

DESSERT book, The: a complete manual from the best authorities. With original recipes. By a Boston lady. Boston, 1872. 202 pp. 12° 6426.1

DESTINY. Ferrier, S. E. 518.20

DESTINY, The, of man. Erwin, W. New York, 1872. 12° 5817.4

DETHRONED heiress, The. Dupuy, E. A. 735.33

DETLEF, Carl, *pseud.* *See* BAUER, Karoline.

DEUTSCH, Emanuel (Oscar Menahem). Literary remains. With a memoir. New York, 1874. xx, 465 pp. 8° 5733.7

Contents. — Memoir; The Talmud; Islam; Semitic palæography; Semitic culture; Egypt, ancient and modern; Hermes Trismegistus; Judæo-Arabic metaphysics; Les apôtres; Five letters on the œcumenical council; Apostolicæ sedis; The Roman passion drama; On Semitic languages; On the Targums; On the Samaritan Pentateuch; The book of Jasher; Early Arabic poetry; Arabic poetry in Spain and Sicily.

— Islam. *See* SMITH, R. B. Mohammed and Mohammedanism 5816.23

DEUTSCHE Pioniere. Spielhagen, F. Berlin, 1871. 16°..........5735.10

DEUTSCHE Rundschau. Vol. 1–4. Berlin, 1874, 75. 4 v. 8° 1422.5

Note. — A literary and political review upon the model of the "Revue des deux mondes."

DEUTSCHES Leben in Lieb' und Treue. Bremen [1873]. 187+ pp. With illuminated plates. L. 4° 5730.4

Note. — A collection of German poetry by various authors.

DEUTSCHES Leben in Liedern. 2te Auflage. Bremen [1873]. 291+ pp. With illuminated plates. L. 4° 5730.5

DEVEREUX. Bulwer-Lytton, E. (G. E.) L......... 336.3

DEVIL, The. Where are my horns? Lepper, A. H. Boston, 1873. 16°.......... 6326.8

Shelf. No.

DE VOE, Thomas F. The market assistant, containing a brief description of every article of human food sold in the public markets. New York, 1867. 455 pp. Illustrated. Sm. 8° 1513.14
DEVOTION. Allen, J. H. Manual of devotions for families and Sunday schools. Boston, 1852. 12°. 5818.8
— Johnson, E. Exercises for private devotion. Boston, 1845. 16° 5819.7
DEVRIENT, (Philipp) Eduard. My recollections of Felix Mendelssohn-Bartholdy, and his letters to me. From the German by N. Macfarren. London, 1869. vii, 307 pp. Portrait. 8° 5727.2
DEWEY, Mary E., *editor*. Life and letters of Catherine M. Sedgwick. *See* SEDGWICK, Catherine Maria 1224.12
DEWEY, Orville. Discourses on human nature, human life, and the nature of religion. New York, 1847. 3 v. 12° 5237.2
— Discourses on various subjects. New York, 1835. 299 pp. 12° 5815.26
DE WITT, Henriette Guizot. *See* WITT, Henriette de.
DE WITT, Pauline Guizot. *See* WITT, Pauline de.
DEXTER SMITH'S musical, literary, dramatic and art paper. Vol. 3-6. Boston, 1873, 74. 4 v. in 2. 4°. 1331.1
DIABETES mellitus. Brigham, C. B. Boston, 1868. 8°. 6023.20
DIALOGUES. Abbott, J. Dialogues 936.1.8
— Alger, H., *jr.*, and Cheney, O. A. Seeking his fortune, and other dialogues. Boston [1875]. 16°. 1518.11
— Baker, G. M. A baker's dozen. Original humorous dialogues. Boston, 1874. 16° 1517.6
DIAMOND cut diamond. Trollope, T. A. 725.36
DIAMONDS and precious stones. Emanuel, H. New York [London], 1873. Sm. 8° 6635.3
DIANA Carew. Forrester, *Mrs.* — 722.8
DIANA of Meridor. Dumas, A. (D.) 510.14
DIANE. [Fiction.] Macquoid, K. S. 337.4
DIARY and notes of Horace Templeton. Lever, C. (J.) 332.9
DIARY in Turkish and Greek waters. Howard, G. W. F., *earl of Carlisle*. Boston, 1855. 12° 825.5
DIARY of a late physician, Passages from the. [Fiction.] Warren, S. 317.3
DIARY of a poor young lady. Nathusius, M. 314.12
DIARY of an ennuyée. [Fiction.] Jameson, A. (M.). 427.3
DIARY of an idle woman in Italy. Elliot, F. Leipzig, 1872. 2 v. in 1. Sq. 16° 228.3
DIARY of Mrs. Kitty Trevylyan. [Fiction.] Charles, E. 321.4
DIAZ, Abby Morton. A domestic problem. Work and culture in the household. Boston, 1875. 120 pp. 12° 1537.24
— Lucy Maria 916.29
— The schoolmaster's trunk, containing papers on home-life in Tweenit 714.4
— A story-book for the children 1115.9
— William Henry and his friends 935.19
— The William Henry letters 935.1
DIBDEN, Thomas. The lady of the lake: a melodramatic romance. From Sir W. Scott. New York, N. D. 24 pp. 12° 1635.4
DIBDIN, Thomas Frognall. Bibliomania; or, book-madness; a bibliographical romance. Illustrated. New and improved edition, added preliminary observations, and a supplement including a key to the assumed characters in the drama. London, 1876. xviii, 618, xxxiv pp. Portraits. Photographs. Fac-similes. Woodcuts. 8° 6131.3

Note. — Almost a fac-simile reprint of Bohn's edition of 1842.

DICK, William Brisbane. The American Hoyle; or, gentleman's hand-book of games. By "Trumps" [*pseud.*]. Illustrated. 9th edition. New York [*cop.* 1864]. 516+ pp. 12° 1516.1
— FROST, Sarah Annie, and TAYLOR, William. What shall we do to-night? or social amusements for evening parties. By Leger D. Mayne [*pseud.*]. New York [1873]. 366 pp. Illustrated. 12° 1516.19
DICK Duncan. Wise, D. 933.33
DICK Travers abroad. *See* SAMUELS, Adelaide F.

Shelf. No.

DICKENS, Charles (John Huffam). Works. Library edition. Boston, 1871-74. With illustrations. 29 v. 16°. *Namely:* —
— — I, II. Pickwick papers. [Debtor's prisons, etc.] 1824.1
— — III, IV. Nicholas Nickleby. [Yorkshire boarding schools and provincial theatres] 1824.2
— — V, VI. Martin Chuzzlewit. [American life]. 1824.3
— — VII. The old curiosity shop. Vol. I 1824.4.1
— — VIII. The old curiosity shop. Vol. II. Reprinted pieces 1824.4.2
— — IX. Barnaby Rudge. [Lord Gordon riots, 1780.] Vol. I 1824.5.1
— — X. Barnaby Rudge. Vol. II. Hard times. [English operative life] 1824.5.2
— — XI. Sketches 1824.6
— — XII. Oliver Twist. [Workhouse abuses and London low-life] 1824.7
— — XIII, XIV. Dombey and son 1824.8
— — XV, XVI. David Copperfield. [Supposed to have some reference to Dickens's own early life]. 1824.9
— — XVII. Pictures from Italy; American notes. [Travels] 1824.10
— — XVIII, XIX. Bleak house. [Delays in the Courts of chancery, etc.] 1824.11
— — XX, XXI. Little Dorrit. [Circumlocution office, etc.] 1824.12
— — XXII. Christmas books 1824.13
— — XXIII. A tale of two cities. [Paris and London in the time of the French revolution, 1780] 1824.14
— — XXIV. Great expectations 1824.15
— — XXV, XXVI. Our mutual friend 1824.16
— — XXVII. The uncommercial traveller, etc. ... 1824.17
— — XXVIII. The mystery of Edwin Drood, and other stories 1824.18
— — XXIX. A child's history of England: also a Holiday romance, and other pieces 1824.19
— American notes. [Travels.] Leipzig, 1842. viii, 310 pp. Sq. 16° 418.2
— *Same.* Philadelphia, N. D. 93 pp. 8° 732.37
— The battle of life; and The haunted man 338.6
— Bleak house. 4 v. in 2 .... 338.19
— A child's dream of a star. (*In* Johnson, (E.) R. Little classics) 529.4.10
— A child's history of England. Boston, 1854. 2 v. 16° 928.13

Contents. — Vol. I. From ancient times, to the reign of Henry V. II. Henry VI to Victoria.

— Chops, the dwarf. (*In* Johnson, (E.) R. Little classics) 529.4.2
— A Christmas carol. (*In* Johnson, (E.) R. Little classics) 529.4.5
— A Christmas carol in prose; The chimes; The cricket on the hearth 338.10
— Cyclopedia of [his] best thoughts. Compiled by F. G. De Fontaine. New York, 1873. 564 pp. L. 8° 1930.1
— David Copperfield 338.14
— Dombey and son 338.12
— Great expectations 338.15
— Hard times 338.7
— Hunted down; The uncommercial traveller 338.21
— Little Dorrit. 4 v. in 2 .... 338.16
— Martin Chuzzlewit 338.11
— Master's Humphrey's clock 330.3
— The mystery of Edwin Drood 338.5
— *Same.* [*Added*, Part second. By the spirit-pen of C. Dickens, through a medium, Thomas P. James] 732.21
— Nicholas Nickleby 338.4
— Oliver Twist 338.8
— Our mutual friend. Leipzig. 4 v. in 2 .... 338.13
— *Same.* New York. 2 v. 731.27
— Pickwick papers 338.1
— Pictures from Italy. Leipzig, 1846. 263+ pp. Sq. 16° 338.18
— The signal-man. (*In* Johnson, (E.) R. Little classics) 529.4.8
— Sketches 338.22
— A tale of two cities 338.20

Shelf. No.

DICKENS, Charles (John Huffam), *continued.*
- — Fields, J. T. Yesterdays with authors. Boston, 1875 [*cop.* 1871]. 12° 6136.13
- — Forster, J. Life of. Leipzig, 1872. 4 v. in 2. Sq. 16° 1238.4
- — Jerrold, (W.) B. The best of all good company. A day with Charles Dickens. Boston, 1873. 16°. 1215.3
- — Pierce, G. A. The Dickens dictionary. Boston, 1872. 12° .... *R.R., F.3.3
- — Stoddard, R. H. Anecdote biography of. New York, 1874. Sq. 16° 1828.3

Note. — The life by Forster is the latest and most authoritative, the writer having been Mr. Dickens's life-long friend and his literary executor. Field's Yesterdays with authors, also in Atlantic monthly, vol. 26, consists chiefly of personal reminiscences and of letters. See the estimates in Taine's English literature [5613.1]; in Poe's literati [1934.2.3]; and by B. Jerrold [1215.3]. See references in Allibone, Thomas, and in the Index to Harper's monthly.

His secretary's account of Dickens's visit to America in 1842 is given in the Atlantic monthly, vol. 26. See also Harper's monthly, vol. 12; Bayne's Essays [1226.15.1]; Whipple's Success and its conditions [1936.4], Literature and life [1936.6], and Lectures; Chorley's autobiography, etc. [5616.4]; Madden's Lady Blessington [1223.2]; Macready's Reminiscences [5623.6], etc. The Dickens dictionary is a key to the characters in his novels.

- — and COLLINS, (William) Wilkie. No thoroughfare. Boston 730.1
- — *Same.* Leipzig 338.17
- — and OTHERS. Christmas stories 338.3

Contents. — The haunted house; A message from the sea; Tom Tiddler's ground.

Note. — Neither of the above are thought to have been written by Dickens.

- — — Doctor Marigold's prescriptions; Mugby junction 338.9
- — — Somebody's luggage; Mrs. Lirriper's lodgings; Mrs. Lirriper's legacy 338.2

DICKINSON, Anna Elizabeth. What answer? 515.8

DICKSON, Walter. Japan: being a sketch of the history, government and officers of the empire. Edinburgh, 1869. vi, 489 pp. 1 plate. 8° ... 5931.2

DICTIONARY, A, of religious knowledge. Abbott, L. New York, 1875. 8° 6320.2

DICTIONNAIRE des sciences médicales. [Rédigé par Chaumetou et Mérat. Appendices et tables.] Paris, 1812–22. 60 v. Plates. 8° 6026.1

DIDAY, P. Treatise on syphilis in new-born children and infants at the breast. Translated by G. Whitley. London, 1859. xii, 272 pp. 8° 6023.3

DIET, Lectures on. Willich, A. F. M. Boston, 1800. 2 v. 12° 6015.1

DIETETICS, The, of the soul. Feuchtersleben, E., *Freiherr* von. New York, 1854. 12° 1527.18

DIGBY Grand. Melville, G. J. W 321.14

DIGBY Heathcote. Kingston, W. H. G. 929.7

DIGESTION. Combe, A. The physiology of digestion considered with relation to the principles of dietetics. Boston, 1836. 12° 6036.10
- — Fordyce, G. Treatise on the digestion of food. London, 1791. 12° 6034.1
- — Leared, A. The causes and treatment of imperfect digestion. London, 1875. Sm. 8° 6036.17
- — Lewis, D. Our digestion. Philadelphia, 1872. 12°. 1522.4
- Macé, J. History of a mouthful of bread. New York, 1872. 12° 1527.7
- — Prout, W. The function of digestion considered with reference to natural theology. London, 1855. Sm. 8° 6436.10
- — Scudamore, C. Treatise on the nature and cure of gout and rheumatism, including general considerations on morbid states of the digestive organs. Philadelphia, 1819. 8° 6023.14
- — Sweetser, W. Treatise on. Boston, 1837. 16°. 1525.5

DIKES and ditches; or, Young America in Holland and Belgium. Adams, W. T. Boston, 1873. 16°. 925.9

DILKE, Charles Wentworth. Greater Britain: a record of travel in English-speaking countries, during 1866 and 1867. With maps and illustrations. New York, 1869. 561 pp. 12°. 423.13 and 5935.7

DILLAWAY, Charles Knapp. History of the grammar school, or, "The free schoole of 1645 in Roxburie." With biographical sketches. Roxbury, 1860. 202 [204] pp. Fac-simile. 12° 5016.10

Shelf. No.

DINGLESTEDT, Franz (Ferdinand Friedrich). The amazon. Translated by J. M. Hart 526.4

DINING, The art of. London, 1853. 16° 6428.6

"DINKS," *pseud.* The sportsman's vade mecum. *See* HERBERT, Henry William 1522.3

DINORAH. Meyerbeer, G. (*In* Ditson, O., and co. Standard opera librettos) 6233.3.4

DIONYSIUS, *of Alexandria, St. See* GREGORIUS *Thaumaturgus, or Neo-Cæsariensis, St.*

DIPHTHERIA, Memoirs on. From the writings of Bretonneau, and others. Semple, R. H. London, 1859. 8° 6023.5

DISCARDED daughter, The. Southworth, E. D. E. N. 727.3

DISCARDED wife, The. Dupuy, E. A. 522.12

DISCOVERIES. Beckmann, J. History of. London, 1846. 2 v. 16° .... 1526.7 and 6425.1
- — Routledge, R. Discoveries and inventions of the 19th century. London, 1876. Sm. 8° 6425.8

DISEASE germs. Beale, L. S. London, 1870. Sm. 8°. 6036.2

DISLOCATIONS and fractures of the joints, Treatise on. Cooper, *Sir* A. (P.) Boston, 1844. 8° 6021.3

DISOWNED, The. Bulwer-Lytton, E. (G. E.) L. 336.11

DISRAELI, Benjamin. Alroy 324.22
- — Coningsby 324.23
- — Contarini Fleming 324.18
- — Henrietta Temple 324.25
- — Lothair. Leipzig 324.19
- — *Same.* New York 721.3
- — The rise of Iskander. (*In* Johnson, (E.) R. Little classics) 529.4.6
- — Sybil 324.24
- — Venetia 324.20
- — Vivian Grey 324,21
- — The young duke 721.18

Note. — These novels mostly depict fashionable and political life during the author's early public career, himself and his opponents appearing in "Vivian Grey;" Croker and others in "Coningsby;" while Byron and others figure in "Venetia." His "Lothair," however, is a picture of the catholic reaction of later times.

DISRAELI, Isaac. Amenities of literature, consisting of sketches and characters of English literature. New edition, edited by B. Disraeli. New York, 1871. 2 v. 16° 1533.13
- — Curiosities of literature. With a view of the life and writings of the author, by B. Disraeli. From the 14th corrected London edition. New York, 1872. 4 v. Portrait. 16° 5626.6
- — The literary character; or the history of men of genius. Literary miscellanies: and an inquiry into the character of James I. Edited by B. Disraeli. New York, 1868. 592 pp. Portrait. 16° 1533.14
- — Quarrels of authors. New York, 1814. 2 v. 12°. 1537.17
- — Romances. New York, 1803. Irregularly paged. 1 plate. 12° 1918.8

DISTINGUISHED persons in Russian society. From the German by F. E. Bunnètt. London, 1873. vi, 307+ pp. Sm. 8° 5924.4

DISTURNELL, J., *compiler.* United States register, or blue book for 1862. New York [1861]. 94+ pp. 12° 6927.3

DITSON, Oliver, and co. Standard opera librettos. With English and Italian words. Boston, N. D. 6 v. Sm. 4° 6233.3

Contents. — Vol. I. Thomas, (C.) A.: Mignon; Herold, L. J. F.: Zampa; Mercadante, S.: Il giuramento; Pacini, G.: Saffo; Ricci, F. and L.: Crispino e la comare; Ronger, F., called Hervé: Fleur-de-thé; Weber, C. M. F. E. von: Der Freyschutz; Cagnoni, A.: Don Bucefalo; Halévy, J. F. F. E.: The Jewess; Gounod, C.: Faust, Romeo and Juliet. II. Donizetti, G.: Anna Bolena, Don Pasquale, L'elisire d'amore, La favorita, La fille du régiment, Linda di Chamounix, Lucia di Lammermoor, Lucrezia Borgia, Maria di Rohan, I martiri; Mozart, J. C. W. A.: Marriage of Figaro, Don Giovanni, Il flauto magico. III. Rossini, G.: Semiramide, Otello, Il barbiere di Siviglia, William Tell, La gazza ladra, Cinderella; Auber, D. F. E.: Fra diavolo, Masaniello; Balfe, M. W.: Bohemian girl, Rose of Castile; Beethoven, L. van: Fidelio; Bellini, V.: I puritani. IV. Bellini, V.: Norma, La sonnambula, Il pirata; Meyerbeer, G.: Le prophète, L'étoile du nord, Robert le diable, L'Africaine, Les Huguenots, Dinorah. V. Offenbach, J.: Barbe-bleue, "Orpheus," Geneviève de Brabant, La perichole, Grand duchess of Gerolstein, La belle Hélène; Boieldieu, F. A.: La dame blanche; Flotow, F. F. A. von: Martha; Wallace, W. V.: Maritana. VI. Verdi, G.: Don Carlos, Rigoletto, Il trovatore, Sicilian vespers, I Lombardi, La traviata, Luisa Miller, Ernani, The masked ball; Petrella, E.: Ione, Carnival of Venice.

Shelf. No.

DIVINE comedy, The. Dante Alighieri. Leipzig, 1867. 3 v. in 1. Sq. 16° 1614.4
— *Same*. Boston, 1871. 8° 5534.1
DIVINE government, Illustrations of. Smith, T. S. Boston, 1831. 12°.......................5814.13
DIVINE love and wisdom. Swedenborg, E. New York, 1872. 8°........................ 6323.9
DIVINE providence. Swedenborg, E. New York, 1873. 8°..............................6323.10
DIVINE tragedy, The. [Drama on life of Christ.] Longfellow, H. W. Leipzig, 1872. Sq. 16°... 1614.3
DIVING. The conquest of the sea. A book about divers and diving. Siebe, H. London [1874]. Sm. 8°.................................. 6418.4
DIX, John Homer. Treatise upon the nature and treatment of morbid sensibility of the retina, or weakness of sight. Boston, 1849. vi, 146+ pp. 12°.............................. 6015.7
DIXON, William Hepworth. Biography of John Howard. (*In* Macaulay, T. B., *lord*, and others. New biographies of illustrious men) 5428.4
— Free Russia. [Emancipation of serfs.] New York, 1870. 359 pp. Sm. 8°.............. 422.22
— Her majesty's tower. [Historical associations.] Leipzig, 1869. 4 v. in 2. Sq. 16°........... 838.4
— History of two queens. Catharine of Aragon. Anne Boleyn. Leipzig, 1873, 74. 6 v. in 4. Sq. 16°....................................1238.21
— *Same*. London, 1873, 74. 4 v. 8°.......... 5414.3
— The Holy Land. Leipzig, 1865. 2 v. in 1. Sq. 16°.. 428.1
— New America. [Beyond the Mississippi.] Leipzig, 1867. 2 v. in 1. Sq. 16° 418.1
— Personal history of Lord Bacon. Leipzig, 1861. xiv, 422 pp. Sq. 16° 1238.17
— Spiritual wives. [Socialisms, etc.] Leipzig, 1868. 2 v. in 1. Sq. 16°.................. 1538.2
— The Switzers. London, 1872. x, 364 pp. 8° .. 5931.3
— White conquest. Leipzig, 1876. 2 v. in 1. Sq. 16°.. 439.4

Note. — Sketches of travel in the United States in 1875.

DOBELL, Horace. Tuberculosis: its nature, cause, and treatment. With notes on pancreatic juice. 2d edition. [London] 1866. xii, 84 pp. 16°. 6015.4
DOBSON, Edward. Foundations and concrete works. New edition, revised by G. Dodd. Illustrated. London, 1867. iv, 120+ pp. 12° 1716.27
— Rudiments of masonry and stonecutting. Illustrated. 6th edition. With an appendix on the causes of decay and the preservation of stone. London, 1870. viii, 146+ pp. Folded plates. 12° 1716.24
— Rudiments of the art of building. With illustrations. 8th edition. London, 1871. xvi, 168 pp. 12°....................................1716.26
— Treatise on the manufacture of bricks and tiles. Revised by C. Tomlinson. 4th edition, with additions by R. Mallet. With illustrations. London, 1868. xiv, 276 pp. 12° 1716.25
DOCTOR, The. Southey, R. New York, 1860. 2 v. in 1. 12° 1534.10
— *Same*. New York, 1872. 2 v. in 1. 12° 5617.9

Note. — A learned but somewhat fantastic conglomeration of excerpts, etc.

DOCTOR Antonio. [Italian life.] Ruffini, G. 316.17
DR. Howell's family. Goodwin, *Mrs*. H. B......... 734.13
DOCTOR Marigold's prescriptions. Dickens, C. (J. H.), and others............................. 338.9
DOCTOR Ox. Verne, J.............................. 529.2
DOCTOR Thorne. Trollope, A. 334.5
DOCTOR Vandyke. Cooke, J. E.................... 510.2
DR. Wainwright's patient. Yates, E................ 318.20
DOCTOR'S, The, daughter. Clarke, R. S. 934.19
DOCTOR'S, The, dilemma. Smith, H................ 530.6
DOCTOR'S, The, wife. Braddon, M. E. 325.3
DOCTORS, A book about. Jeaffreson, J. C. Leipzig, 1870. 2 v. in 1. Sq. 16° 1238.16
DOCTRINES of Scripture. Boston, 1857. 108 pp. 16° 5819.3

Shelf. No.

DOD, —. The laboring classes of England. By an Englishman. Also, A voice from the factories, a poem. Boston, 1847. 168 pp. 12° 5418.1
DODD family, The, abroad. Lever, C. (J.) Leipzig... 332.22
— *Same*. London.................................. 516.18
DODDRIDGE, Philip. The rise and progress of religion in the soul. Exeter, 1794. 390+ pp. 12° 6327.9
DODGE, Mary Abigail. (*Gail Hamilton.*) Country living and country thinking. Boston, 1863. vi, 461 pp. 16° 715.8
— Gala-days. Boston, 1863. 436+ pp. 16° 517.1
— Little folk life. New York, 1873. 219 pp. 16°.. 927.21
— Sermons to the clergy. Boston, 1876. 3-425 pp. 12° 1926.4
— Twelve miles from a lemon. New York, 1874. 320 pp. 12° 1536.19
— Woman's wrongs: a counter-irritant. Boston, 1868. 212 pp. 16° 1535.10
DODGE, Mary E. A few friends and how they amused themselves. Philadelphia, 1869. 182 pp. 12°. 526.10
DODGE, Nathaniel Shatswell. Stories of a grandfather about American history. Boston, 1874. 176 pp. Illustrated. Sq. 16°................ 913.29
DODGE club, The. De Mille, J. 511.22
DODGSON, Charles Lutwidge. (*Lewis Carroll.*) Alice's adventures in Wonderland 912.20
— Through the looking-glass, and what Alice found there 912.21
DODS, John Bovee. Spirit manifestations examined and explained. Judge Edmonds refuted. New York [*cop*. 1854]. 252 pp. 12°............. 1926.2
DOE, Charles H. Buffets. [Originally published in "The Boston courier."] Boston, 1875. 143 pp. 8° 721.9
DOELLINGER, Johann Joseph Ignaz von. Fables respecting the popes of the middle ages. Translated, with introduction and appendices by A. Plummer. London, 1871. lxiv, 302 pp. 8°.. 5813.5
— *Same*. With [his] Essay on the prophetic spirit and the prophecies of the Christian era, translated by H. B. Smith. New York, 1872. xxiv, 463+ pp. 12°............................5816.10
— The first age of Christianity and the church. Translated by H. N. Oxenham. 2d edition. London, 1867. xxiv, 439 pp. 8°............ 5813.4
— Lectures on the reunion of the churches. Translated with preface by H. N. Oxenham. New York, 1872. xliv, 165 pp. 16° 5816.6
DOESTICKS, Q. K. Philander, *pseud*. *See* THOMSON, Mortimer.
DOG, A, of Flanders. Rame, L. de la. (*In* Johnson, (E.) R. Little classics) 529.4.10
DOG Crusoe, The. Ballantyne, R. M.............. 935.30
DOG Crusoe, The, and his master. Ballantyne, R. M. 935.31
DOGS. Herbert, H. W. The dog. New York [*cop*. 1857]. L. 12° 1522.3
— Walsh, J. H. The dog. London, 1872. 8° 6614.3
DOIGTS, Les, de fée: comédie. Scribe, (A.) E., and Legouvé, (G. J. B.) E. (W.) Boston, 1867. 12° 2015.2
DOING and dreaming. [Fiction.] Mayo, I. F...... 714.22
DOING his best. Trowbridge, J. T. 916.27
DOINGS of the Bodley family. Scudder, H. E...... 910.1
DOLLARS and cents. Warner, A. B. 736.9
DÖLLINGER, Johann Joseph Ignaz von. *See* DOELLINGER, Johann Joseph Ignaz von.
DOLLY and I. Adams, W. T. 918.13
DOLOMITES, Untrodden peaks and unfrequented valleys: a midsummer ramble in the. Edwards, A. B. Leipzig, 1873. Sq. 16°................ 329.21
DOLORES. Forrester, *Mrs*. —. 724.30
DOMBEY and son. Dickens, C. (J. H.) Boston. 2 v.. 1824.6
— *Same*. Leipzig 338.12
DOMESTIC architecture. The habitations of man in all ages. Viollet-le-Duc, E. E. Boston, 1876. 8° 6223.5

Shelf. No.

DOMESTIC arts. Home arts for old and young. Smith, C. L. Boston, 1873. 12°............. 1517.3
DOMESTIC economy. Barker, M. A., *lady*. Houses and housekeeping. London, 1876. Sm. 8°.... 6428.8
— Bayle-Moullard, E. Nouveau manuel d'économie domestique. Paris, 1837. 24°.............. 6429.6
— Beecher, C. E. Housekeeper and healthkeeper. New York, 1873. 12°.......................... 1725.1
— – Treatise on. New York, 1858. 12°......... 1524.8
— – and Stowe, H. (E.) B. The new housekeeper's manual. New York, 1873. 8°.............. 1723.8
— Beecher, E. W. Motherly talks with young housekeepers. New York, 1873. 12°........1515.13
— Dessert book, The. By a Boston lady. Boston, 1872. 12°.............................. 6426.1
— De Voe, T. F. The market assistant. New York, 1867. Sm. 8°...........................1513.14
— Diaz, A. M. A domestic problem. Work and culture in the household. Boston, 1875. 12°..1537.24
— Draper, L. C., and Croffut, W. A. A helping hand for town and country. Cincinnati, 1870. 8°..............................511.4 and 6422.1
— Jeaffreson, J. C. A book about the table. London, 1875. 2 v. 8°...................... 6432.3
— Terhune, M. V. Breakfast, luncheon and tea. New York, 1875. 12°..................... 1533.2
— – Common sense in the household: a manual of practical housewifery. New York, 1871. 12°. 1533.6
— Tomes, R. The bazar book of the household. New York, 1875. 16°...................... 1518.9
— Warren, E. Comfort for small incomes. Boston, 1866. 12°...............................1533.16
— – How I managed my house on £200 a year. Boston, 1866. 12°......................... 1533.1

See also Cookery, Receipts.

DOMESTIC stories. Craik, D. (M.)................ 323.13
DOMESTICATED trout. How to breed and grow them. Stone, L. Boston, 1872. 16°............... 6616.3
DOMINIES, Book about. Moncrieff, A. R. H. Boston, 1869. 16°.............................. 1535.9
DON Bucefalo. Cagnoni, A. (*In* Ditson, O., and co. Standard opera librettos)...............6233.3.1
DON Carlos. Schiller, (J. C.) F. von. Werke. Stuttgart, 1865. 8°.........................5734.1.3
DON Carlos. Verdi, G. (*In* Ditson, O., and co. Standard opera librettos)......................6233.3.6
DON Garcie de Navarre: comédie. Molière, J. B. P. Œuvres. Paris, 1869. 12°.................5537.2.1
DON Garcie of Navarre: a comedy. Molière, J. B. P. Dramatic works. Edinburgh, 1875. 8°..5530.3.1
DON Giovanni. Mozart, J. C. W. A. (*In* Ditson, O., and co. Standard opera librettos)........6233.3.2
DON Juan. Byron, G. G. N., *lord*. Works. Leipzig, 1866. Sq. 16°.........................1614.13.1
DON Juan; or, the feast with the statue: a comedy. Molière, J. B. P. Dramatic works. Edinburgh, 1876. 8°...........................5530.3.3
DON Juan, ou le festin de Pierre: comédie. Molière, J. B. P. Œuvres. Paris, 1869. 12°........5537.2.2
DON Pasquale. Donizetti, G. (*In* Ditson, O., and co. Standard opera librettos)...............6233.3.2
DON Quixote, History of. Cervantes-Saavedra, M. de. Boston, 1870. 4 v. 16°.................. 5927.4
DONALD Deane, and his cross. Bradley, W. I...... 913.9
DONALDSON, James, *editor*. The apostolical constitutions. With notes. Edinburgh, 1870. 280 pp. [*With* CLEMENTINE homilies. Ante-Nicene Christian library.] 8°........................6322.4.17
DONALDSON, John William. History of the literature of ancient Greece. *See* MUELLER, Carl Otfried.................................. 6113.3
DONIZETTI, Gætano. Anna Bolena; Don Pasquale; L'elisire d'amore; La favorita; La fille du régiment; Linda di Chamounix; Lucia di Lammermoor; Lucrezia Borgia; Maria di Rohan; I martiri. (*In* Ditson, O., and co. Standard opera librettos)............................6233.3.2
DONNE, John. Christophers, S. W. Homes of old English writers. London [1874]. Sm. 8°.....5428.16
— Walton, I. Life of. London, 1866. 16°...... 5428.2
DONNE, William Bodham. Euripides [outlined and explained]. Edinburgh, 1872. vi, 204+ pp. 16°. [Ancient classics for English readers]....6116.13
— Tacitus [outlined and explained]. Philadelphia, 1873. vi, 194+ pp. 16°. [Ancient classics for English readers].........................6116.18
DORA. Kavanagh, J.............................. 323.4
DORA Deane. Holmes, M. J....................... 534.3
DORA's motto. Mathews, J. H....................1117.17
DORAN, John Wilberforce. Habits and men, with remnants of record touching the makers of both. New York, 1865. 402 pp. 12°.............. 1532.3
— Knights and their days. New York, 1864. 479 pp. Sm. 8°.................................. 822.4
— A lady of the last century (Mrs. Elizabeth Montagu): illustrated in her unpublished letters; collected and arranged with a biographical sketch, and a chapter on blue stockings. 2d edition. London, 1873. xvi, 372 pp. 8°.....5422.11
— Monarchs retired from business. New York, 1865. 2 v. 12°............................ 1223.1
— Table traits with something on them. New York, 1865. 489 pp. L. 12°...................... 1532.4
— "Their majesties' servants." Annals of the English stage, from Thomas Betterton to Edmund Kean. New York, 1865. 2 v. L. 12°....... 1532.2
DORCAS club, The. Adams, W. T.................. 924.26
DORCHESTER, *Mass.*, in 1630, 1776, and 1855. Everett, E. Boston, 1855. 158+ pp. 8°........ 5012.6
DORÉ, (Paul) Gustave. The Doré gallery: containing 250 engravings from the Doré Bible, Milton, Dante, etc. With memoir of Doré, critical essay, and descriptive letterpress, by Edmund Ollier. London [1871]. xxiv, 180 [178] pp. L. 4°...6210.11
DOROTHY. By the author of "Still waters"....... 310.15
DOROTHY Fox. Parr, L.......................... 314.13
DORR, Julia C. R. Expiation..................... 737.30
DO-SOMETHINGS, The. Adams, W. T................ 939.2
DOTTY Dimple. Clarke, R. S...................... 927.2
DOTTY Dimple at her grandmother's. Clarke, R. S.. 927.10
DOTTY Dimple at home. Clarke, R. S............. 927.12
DOTTY Dimple at play. Clarke, R. S............. 927.13
DOTTY Dimple at school. Clarke, R. S........... 927.15
DOTTY Dimple out West. Clarke, R. S............ 927.11
DOTTY Dimple's Flyaway. Clarke, R. S........... 927.14
DOUAI, Adolf. The Kindergarten. With plates. New York, 1871. 136+ pp. 12°.............1933.11
DOUBLE house, The. Craik, D. (M.).............. 330.22
DOUBLE play. Everett, W........................ 935.3
DOUBLE story, A. MacDonald, G................... 539.8
DOUBLE wedding, A. Warfield, C. A.............. 723.18
DOUBLY false. Stephens, A. S. (W.)............. 726.13
DOUGLAS, Amanda M. Claudia..................... 535.7
— Drifted asunder............................... 715.25
— Home nook.................................... 725.32
— In trust...................................... 535.6
— Kathie's stories. In the ranks................ 934.25
— – Kathie's aunt Ruth.......................... 934.24
— – Kathie's harvest days....................... 934.23
— – Kathie's soldiers........................... 934.22
— – Kathie's summer at Cedarwood................ 934.26
— – Kathie's three wishes....................... 934.27
— Lucia: her problem............................ 533.13
— Maidenhood series. Seven daughters........... 913.32
— The old woman who lived in a shoe............ 933.9
— Santa Claus land.............................. 928.12
— Stephen Dane.................................. 533.14
— Sydnie Adriance............................... 726.16
— With fate against him......................... 735.31
DOUGLAS, John Christie. A manual of telegraph construction: the mechanical elements of electric telegraph engineering. With diagrams. London, 1875. xxiii, 421 pp. Sm. 8°.......... 6826.5
D'OUTRE mort. Prescott, H. E. (*In* Johnson, (E.) R. Little classics)........................ 529.4.2
DOVE, Heinrich Wilhelm. The circulation of the waters on the surface of the earth. (*In* Estes, D. Half-hour recreations in popular science).. 6813.7
DOVE, The, in the eagle's nest. Yonge, C. M..... 318.17
DOWN in Tennessee. Gilmore, J. R. New York, 1864. 12°.................................. 716.19

Shelf. No.

DOWN the Rhine; or, Young America in Germany. Adams, W. T. Boston, 1873. 16° 916.16
DOWN the river. Adams, W. T. 924.21
DOWNING, Andrew Jackson. Architecture of country houses. With illustrations. New York, 1866. x, 484 | pp. 8° 1511.2
— Cottage residences; or a series of designs for rural cottages and cottage villas, and their gardens and grounds. Adapted to North America. Part I. Illustrated. 2d edition. New York, 1844. 187 pp. 8° 1511.7
— *Same.* New edition. Revised by H. W. Sargent and C. Downing. Illustrated. Edited by G. E. Harney. New York, 1873. xvi, 261 pp. Sm. 4° 6221.3
— Treatise on the theory and practice of landscape gardening, adapted to North America. 2d edition, enlarged, revised, and newly illustrated. New York, 1844. 497+ pp. 8° 1511.8
— *Same.* 8th edition. With a supplement. By H. W. Sargent. New York [*cop.* 1859]. 567 pp. Portrait. 8° 1511.3
DOWNING, Charles. Selected fruits: including their culture, propagation, and management in the garden and orchard. Illustrated. New York, 1871. x, 679 pp. 16° 6625.1
DOYLE, John Andrew. History of the United States. With maps illustrative of the acquisition of territory and the increase of population, by Francis A. Walker. New York, 1876. xix, 404+ pp. [Freeman, E. A., *editor.* Historical course for schools.] 16° 618.4
DRAINAGE. The practical land drainer. Munn, B. New York, 1855. 12° 1524.23
DRAKE, Benjamin. Tales and sketches from the Queen city. Cincinnati, 1838. 180 pp. 12° .. 5218.6
DRAKE, Charles F. Tyrwhitt, *joint author.* Unexplored Syria. *See* BURTON, Richard Francis... 5933.3
DRAKE, *Sir* Francis, Life, voyages, and exploits of. Barrow, *Sir* J. London, 1861. Sm. 8° 5428.5
DRAKE, Francis Samuel. Dictionary of American biography, including men of the time. Boston, 1872. viii, 1019+ pp. 8° ............*R.R., E.3.1
DRAKE, Samuel Adams. General Israel Putnam, the commander at Bunker hill. Boston, 1875. 24 pp. 8° 1011.8
— Historic fields and mansions of Middlesex [county, Massachusetts]. Illustrated. Boston, 1874. xiv, 442 pp. Fac-simile map. 8° 814.4
— Nooks and corners of the New England coast. With illustrations. New York, 1875. 459 pp. Sq. 8° 411.4
— Old landmarks and historic personages of Boston. Illustrated. Boston, 1873. xvii, 484 pp. 12° 5035.3
— *editor.* Bunker hill: the story told in letters from the battle field by British officers engaged. With an introduction and sketch of the battle. Boston, 1875. 76 pp. Heliotype. 8° 811.13
DRAKE, Samuel Gardner. History and antiquities of Boston, 1630–1770. Also, an introductory history of the discovery and settlement of New England. Boston, 1856. x, 840 pp. Illustrated. Folded plates. Portraits. L. 8° 5010.11
DRAMAS. Baker, G. M. Amateur dramas. Boston, 1873. 16° 1635.22
— – The drawing-room stage: original dramas, etc. Boston, 1873. 16° 1516.9
— – The exhibition drama. Boston, 1875. 12°... 1635.6
— – The social stage: original dramas, etc. Boston, 1875 [*cop.* 1870]. 16° 1635.7
— Gilbert, W. S. Original plays. New York, 1876. 12° 1634.1

See also Stage.

DRAMAS, Collection of. 3 v. New York, N. D. 12°. *Namely:* —
— The Corsican brothers, from the romance of Dumas, by E. Grangé and X. de Montépin; The children in the wood, by T. Morton; Winning a husband, by Macfarren; Day after the fair, by G. A. Somerset; Make your wills, by E. Mayhew and G. Smith; The rendezvous, by R. Ayton; My wife's husband, by F. Challis; Monsieur Tonson, by W. T. Moncrieff; The illustrious stranger, by F. Kenney 1635.3
— Young New York, by E. G. P. Wilkins; Victims, by T. Taylor; Romance after marriage, by F. B. Goodrich and F. L. Warden; The brigand, by J. R. Planché; The poor of New York; Ambrose Gwinett, by D. Jerrold; Raymond and Agnes, by M. G. Lewis; The gambler's fate, by H. M. Milner; The young scamp, by E. Stirling; The stage-struck Yankee, by O. E. Durivage; Box and Cox, by J. M. Morton; The lady of the lake, from Sir W. Scott, by T. Dibden 1635.4
— The musard ball, by J. Brougham; The great tragic revival, by J. Brougham; High, low, Jack, and the game, by J. R. Planché and C. Dance; A gentleman from Ireland, by F. O'Brien; Tom and Jerry, by W. T. Moncrieff; The village lawyer; The captain's not a-miss, by T. E. Wilks; Amateurs and actors, by R. B. Peake; Promotion, by J. R. Planché; A fascinating individual, by H. Danvers; Mrs. Caudle's curtain lecture [dramatized from D. Jerrold] by E. Stirling; Shakespeare's dream, by J. Brougham; Neptune's defeat, by J. Brougham; The lady of the bed-chamber; Take care of little Charlie, by J. Brougham; The Irish widow, by D. Garrick. 1635.5
DRAMATIC art and literature, Lectures on. Schlegel, A. W. London, 1871. 16° 6136.2
DRAMATIC poems. Read, H. F. Boston, 1848. 8°. 1631.1
DRAPER, Frank W. Papers from the Second annual report of the Massachusetts board of health. *See* DERBY, George 6023.18
DRAPER, John C., *editor.* Year-book of nature and popular science for 1872. New York, 1873. v, 333+ pp. 12° 1525.21
DRAPER, John William. History of the American civil war. New York, 1868, 70. 3 v. Maps. 8°. 811.6
— History of the intellectual development of Europe. New York, 1872. 5th edition. xii, 631+ pp. 8° 5921.2
— International scientific series. History of the conflict between science and religion. New York, 1875. xxii, 373 pp. 12° 5826.4
DRAPER, Lyman C., and CROFFUT, W. A. A helping hand for town and country. Introduction by H. Greeley. Illustrations. Cincinnati, 1870. 821 pp. 8° ....1511.4 and 6422.1
DRAPIER'S, The, letters. Swift, J. Works. London, 1856. 8° 5611.2.2
DRAWING. Barry, C. A. How to draw. Boston, 1871. 12° 1516.5
— Burn, R. S. Self-aid cyclopædia. London, N. D. 8° 6223.2
— Cavé, M. E. The Cavé method for learning to draw from memory. New York, 1871. 12°.... 1516.6
— Davidson, E. A. Linear drawing and projection. London [1868]. Sm. 8° 6218.2
— Delamotte, P. H. A progressive drawing book. London, 1874. Sm. 8° 6217.10
— Foster, V. Drawing copy books. London, N. D. 4 v. Oblong 8° 6217.6
— Johnson, W. The practical draughtsman's book of industrial science. Philadelphia, 1873. 4°. 6620.2
— Minifie, W. A text book of geometrical drawing for the use of mechanics and schools. New York, 1873. L. 8° 6420.3
— Pyne, G. Perspective for beginners. London, 1870. 12° 1716.29
— Ruskin, J. Elements of. New York, 1872. 12°.6236.11
— Smith, W. Teachers' manual of free-hand drawing and designing, and guide to self-instruction. Boston, 1873. L. 8° 6210.6
— *Same.* Boston, 1875. 8° 6210.12
— Turner, M. The young ladies' assistant in. Cincinnati, 1833. 16° 1517.4

See also Sketching.

Shelf. No.

DRAWING-ROOM dances. Cellarius, *pseud.* New York, 1858. 16° 1514.4

DRAWING-ROOM stage, The. Baker, G. M. Boston, 1873. 16° 1516.9

DRAYTON, Daniel. Personal memoir. Including a narrative of the voyage and capture of the schooner Pearl. Boston, 1853. 122 pp. Portrait. 12° 1216.4

DRAYTONS, The, and the Davenants. Charles, E. .. 321.1

DREAM children. [Imaginative stories for children.] Scudder, H. E. 938.1

DREAM life. Mitchell, D. G. New York, 1872. 12° 1934.10

DREAM-WOMAN, The. Collins, (W.) W. 319.25

DREAMS, Beadle's dime book of. Beadle, E. F. New York [*cop.* 1863]. 12° 1518.14

DREAMTHORP. Smith, A. (*In* Johnson, (E.) R. Little classics) 529.4.4

DRED. Stowe, H. (E.) B. 314.23

Note. — This novel of slavery was known later as "Nina Gordon."

DRESS-REFORM. Woolson, A. G. Boston, 1874. 16°. 1537.19

DRESSER, Christopher. Principles of decorative design. London [1873]. vi, 167+ pp. Illustrated. 4° 6210.8

DRIFTED asunder. Douglas, A. M. 715.25

DRIVEN to sea. Cupples, A. J. 923.8

DRIVER, John. Letters from Madeira. With an appendix. 2d edition. London, 1838. xi, 85, xxx+ pp. 16° 427.1

DROYSEN, Johann Gustav. Friedrich I. König von Preussen. Leipzig, 1867. vi, 434 pp. 8° 5733.3

DROZ, Gustave. Around a spring. From the French by M. S. 511.23

— Leisure hour series. Babolain. From the French by M. S. 518.15

DRUGS. Manuel des falsifications des drogues simples et composées. Pédroni, P. M. Paris, 1848. 24° 6439.6

DRUMMER boy, The. Trowbridge, J. T. 931.4

DRUMMOND, Robert Blackley. Erasmus, his life and character as shown in his correspondence and works. With portrait. London, 1873. 2 v. Sm. 8° 5726.2

DRUNKENNESS, Anatomy of. Macnish, R. (*In* The Alexandrian) 1910.4.2

DRURY, Anna Harriet. Deep waters 720.9

DRYDEN, John. Critical and miscellaneous prose works, with notes and illustrations; an account of the life and writings of the author, and a collection of his letters. By E. Malone. London, 1800. 4 v. Sm. 8° 5613.4

— *See* LOWELL, J. R. Among my books. Boston, 1873. 16° 1934.8.1

DRYSDALE, John (James), and HAYWARD, John Williams. Health and comfort in house building. London, 1872. vii, 114 pp. Plates. 8°. 6223.3

DUBLIN, *N. H.*, History of. Leonard, L. W. Boston, 1855. 8° 5011.3

DUBLIN review. New series. Vol. 20–25. London, 1873–75. 6 v. 8° 6517.1

DUBLIN university magazine. Vol. 81–86. Dublin, 1873–75. 6 v. 8° 6537.1

DU BOISGOBEY, Fortune. The golden tress. Translated from the French 532.14

DU CHAILLU, Paul Belloni. Explorations and adventures in equatorial Africa. With illustrations. New York, 1861. 528 [526] pp. 8° 423.4

— Lost in the jungle. With engravings. New York, 1872. 260 pp. 12° 933.6

— My Apingi kingdom: with life in the great Sahara, and sketches of the chase of the ostrich, hyena, etc. [With] engravings. New York, 1872. 254 pp. 12° 933.2

— Stories of the gorilla country. With illustrations. New York, 1870. 292 pp. 12° 933.5

— Wild life under the equator. With engravings. New York, 1872. 231 pp. 12° 933.3

Note. — These books all relate to the author's African experiences.

DUCHESS de la Vallière, The. Bulwer-Lytton, E. (G. E.) L. Dramatic works. Leipzig, 1860. Sq. 16° 1614.5

DUDEVANT, Amantine Lucile Aurore Dupin. (*George Sand*). Antonio. Translated by V. Vaughan. [Added The novels of George Sand, by M. J. M. Sweat; and George Sand, by J. McCarthy] 526.23

— Cesarine Dietrich. Translated by E. Stanwood. 511.15

— Consuelo. Nouvelle édition. Paris, 1869. 3 v. in 1. 12° 2018.2

— *Same.* Translated by F. Robinson 535.2

— The countess of Rudolstadt. From the French by F. Robinson 726.18

— Fanchon the cricket 536.2

— Handsome Lawrence. Translated by C. Owen ... 511.17

— Indiana. With a life of Madame Dudevant; and translated by G. W. Richards 535.3

— Les maîtres mosaïstes. Nouvelle édition. Paris, 1864. vii, 238+ pp. 18° 2016.5

— The marquis de Villemer. Translated by R. Keeler 511.18

— Mauprat. Translated by V. Vaughan 526.22

— The miller of Angibault. Translated by M. E. Dewey 526.5

— Monsieur Sylvestre. Translated by F. G. Shaw. 526.3

— My sister Jeannie. From the French by S. R. Crocker 717.5

— Recollections. (*In* Stoddard, R. H. Bric-à-brac series) 1828.1

— A rolling stone. Translated by C. Owen 511.16

— The snow man. Translated by V. Vaughan 526.6

DUDLEY, Robert, *earl of Leicester*, Amye Robsart and. Adlard, G. London, 1870. 8° 5423.5

DUDLEY, *Sir* Robert, *son of the preceding*, Memoirs and correspondence of. Adlard, G. London, 1870. 8° 5423.5

DUDLEY observatory, *Albany, N. Y.* Reply to the "Statement of the trustees." Gould, B. A., *jr.* Albany, 1859. 8° 1912.4

DUENNA, The. Sheridan, R. B. Dramatic works. London, 1848. 16° 1635.2

— *Same.* Leipzig, 1869. Sq. 16° 1614.11

— *Same.* London, 1875. Sm. 8° 5626.9

DUERER, Albrecht. Heaton, M. M. Life of. London, 1870. 8° 6210.5

— Schefer, L. The artist's married life. New York, 1871. 16° 1027.3

— Scott, W. B. Albert Durer: his life and works. London, 1869. 8° 6213.10

Note. — There are two recent English lives by Heaton and by W. B. Scott. Schefer's "Artist's married life," under the guise of fiction, is a well-known portrayal of Dürer's domestic life, and the English translation has a brief memoir by R. C. Waterston. Prime's "I go a-fishing" [6413.3] defends Dürer's wife. Also see Harper's monthly, vol. 40. See Kurz [5730.2] and other histories of German literature; Kugler's Handbook of German painting and other references under Painting; and Jackson's [6211.10] and other histories of engraving. For Dürer's associations with Nuremberg, see Mrs. Jameson's sketches. See further in Ruskin's Modern painters [6236.18.5]; Tyrwhitt's Christian art [1514.14; 6235.1]; Keddie's or Miss Tytler's Old masters [1516.21; 6216.3]. Also the article "Old books in New York" in Harper's monthly, vol. 44.

DUFEU, A. Découverte de l'âge et de la véritable destination des quatre pyramides de Gizeh, principalement de la grande pyramide. Paris, 1873. lxviii, 324+ pp. 8° 5932.11

DUFFERIN, *Lord.* *See* BLACKWOOD, Frederick Temple.

DUFIEF, Nicholas Gouin. Nature displayed in her mode of teaching language to man. Adapted to the French. [*Containing also*, Le lecteur français. Première partie.] 6th edition. Vol. I. New York, 1825. 2 v. in 1. 8° 2012.2

DU GRAIL DE LA VILLETTE, Charles Bernard, *called* Charles de Bernard. L'écueil. Nouvelle édition. Paris, 1864. 322+ pp. 12° 2016.10

DUHAMEL DU MONCEAU, Henri Louis. Traité des arbres fruitiers. Paris, 1768. 2 v. Illustrated. F° 6620.1

DUKE, The, and the cousin. Grey, *Mrs.* 530.5

DUKE, The, of Monmouth. [Historical fiction.] Griffin, G. 517.8

DUMAS, Alexandre, *the younger.* Camille; or, the fate of a coquette 733.15

Shelf. No.

DUMAS, Alexandre (Davy). The black tulip. [Scene at the Hague, 1672] 510.7
— The Corsican brothers 511.32
— The count of Monte-Cristo. [The Hundred days, Marseilles, 1815] 511.30
— Diana of Meridor; or, the lady of Monsoreau... 510.14
— Edmond Dantes. Sequel to The count of Monte-Cristo. [Causes of the revolution of 1848] 511.29
— The iron hand 510.10
— The forty-five guardsmen. [Time of Henry III, sixteenth century] 510.6
— The Garibaldians in Sicily. Translated by E. Routledge. London, 1861. 186+ pp. 16°... 828.1
— Madame de Chamblay 510.8
— [Memoirs of a physician series.] Memoirs of a physician. [France, 1770–74; death of the king]. 511.11
— - The queen's necklace. [Court life in France, 1784, etc.] 511.6
— - Six years later. [Bastile, 1789, etc.] Translated by T. Williams 511.14
— - The countess of Charny. [Champ de Mars, French revolution] 511.7
— - Andrée de Taverney 510.9

Note. — French revolution, July, 1791, to death of the king, Jan. 2, 1793.

— - The chevalier 732.16
— [The three guardsmen series.] The three guardsmen 511.10

Note. — *Sometimes called* The three musketeers; scene, 1625-28, siege of La Rochelle.

— - Twenty years after. [Mazarin, 1645, etc.] ... 511.31
— - Bragelonne; the son of Athos. [Revolution in England, 1688, etc.] 511.8
— - The iron mask 511.9

Note. — Louis XIV and the prisoner in the iron mask.

— - Louise la Valliere 511.12

Note. — Historical tale; La Valliere died, 1710; may be compared with Bulwer's drama of same name.

— The twin lieutenants; or, the soldier's bride 511.26
— Life and adventures of. Fitzgerald, P. London, 1873. 2 v. 8° 5522.5
DU MESNIL-MARIGNY, Jules. Histoire de l'économie politique des anciens peuples de l'Inde, de l'Égypte, de la Judée et de la Grèce. Paris, 1872. 2 v. 8° 5823.2
DUNBAR, Edward E. The romance of the age; or, the discovery of gold in California. New York, 1867. 134 pp. 1 plate. Portrait. 12° 815.9
DUNGLISON, Robley. A dictionary of medical science. New edition, revised by R. J. Dunglison. Philadelphia, 1874. 1131+ pp. 8° 6021.13
DUNLAVY, John. The manifesto, or a declaration of the doctrine and practice of the church of Christ. New York, 1847. viii, 486 pp. 8° 5813.3
DUNLOP, John. History of fiction. 2d London edition. Philadelphia, 1842. 2 v. Sm. 8° ... 6136.3
DUPANLOUP, Félix Antoine Philippe. The child. Translated by Kate Anderson. Boston, 1875. 294 pp. 12° 1915.10
DUPLESSIS, Georges Gratet. The wonders of engraving. New York, 1871. 338 pp. Illustrated. 16° 1714.16
DUPPA, Richard, and QUATREMÈRE DE QUINCY, Antoine Chrysostome. Lives and works of Michael Angelo and Raphael. Illustrated. London, 1870. 474+ pp. 16° 6217.3
DUPUY, Eliza A. All for love 716.7
— The cancelled will 522.16
— The clandestine marriage 522.7
— The dethroned heiress 735.33
— The discarded wife 522.12
— The hidden sin. Sequel to "The dethroned heiress" 735.38
— Michael Rudolph. "The bravest of the brave." 522.20
— The mysterious guest 522.5
— A new way to win a fortune 522.19
— Who shall be victor? A sequel to "The cancelled will" 522.15
— Why did he marry her? 522.14

DUPUYTREN, Guillaume, *baron*. Injuries and diseases of bones. Translated and edited by F. Le Gros Clark. London, 1847. xx, 459 pp. 8°.. 6013.7
— Lesions of the vascular system, diseases of the rectum, and other surgical complaints. Translated and edited by F. Le Gros Clark. London, 1854. 8° 6013.17
DÜRER, Albert. *See* DUERER, Albrecht.
DURIVAGE, O. E. The stage-struck Yankee: a farce. New York, N. D. 16 pp. 12° 1635.4
DURNTON abbey. Trollope, T. A. 711.16
DURRIE, Daniel Steele. Bibliographica genealogica Americana: an alphabetical index to American genealogies and pedigrees. Albany, 1868. xii, 296 [292] pp. 8° 5022.8
DU SOMMERARD, Alexandre. *See* MÉRIMÉE, P. Portraits historiques et littéraires. Paris, 1874. 12° 5527.14
DUTCH republic, The rise of the. Motley, J. L. New York, 1856. 3 v. 8° 822.2
DUVAL, Henri, and OTHERS. (*Cardelli.*) Manuel du limonadier du glacier, du chocolatier et du confiseur. Ornée de figures. Paris, 1851. vi, 516 pp. 24°. [Manuel Roret] 6429.7
DUYCKINCK, Evert Augustus and George Long. Cyclopædia of American literature: embracing personal and critical notices of authors, and selections from their writings, from the earliest period to the present day; with portraits, autographs, and other illustrations. Edited by M. Laird Simons. Philadelphia, 1875. 2 v. 4°..*R.R., D.3.11
DWELLING-HOUSES. Eassie, W. Healthy houses. A handbook of the history, defects, and remedies of drainage, ventilation, warming, and kindred subjects. New York, 1872. 12°....1525.6 and 6215.2
— Wheeler, G. The choice of a dwelling. A practical handbook of useful information on all points connected with hiring, buying, or building a house. London, 1872. Sm. 8° 6226.2
DYER, Thomas Henry. Life of John Calvin. With portrait. London, 1850. xii, 560 pp. 8° 5812.12
— Pompeii. Its history, buildings, and antiquities. Illustrated. Map, and plan of the forum. 3d edition. London, 1871. xvi, 579 pp. 8°..... 5513.1
DYNEVOR terrace. Yonge, C. M. 318.11
DYSPEPSY forestalled and resisted. Hitchcock, E. Amherst, 1831. 12° 6036.7

See also Digestion.

EAR, Treatise on the diseases of the. Troeltsch, A. von. New York, 1869. 8° 6022.11
EARL'S, The, daughter. Sewell, E. M. 738.10
EARL'S, The, promise. Riddell, J. H. 329.5
EARLOM, Richard. *See* GELÉE, Claude.
EARLY choice, The. Tweedie, W. K. London, 1856. 16° 916.7
EARLY dawn, The; or, sketches of Christian life in England in the olden time. New York, 1864. 12° 725.40
EARLY piety; or, recollections of Harriet Bird. Taber, S. W. Boston, 1857. Sm. 12° 5819.20
EARNEST words on true success in life. Palmer, R. New York, 1873. 8° 6136.7
EARTH. Cuvier, G. L. C. F. D. Essay on the theory of the. New York, 1818. 8° 6633.1
— Dawson, J. W. The story of the earth and man. New York, 1873. 12° 1523.22
— Figuier, (G.) L. Earth and sea. London, 1870. 8° 6631.3
— Guyot, A. The earth and man. Boston, 1872. 12° 1523.15
— Marsh, G. P. The earth as modified by human action. New York, 1874. 8° 6831.2
— Reclus, (J. J.) É. The earth. New York, 1872. 8° 6632.1

See also Geography, Geology.

EARTHLY paradise, The: a poem. Morris, W. Boston, 1871. 3 v. Sm. 8° 1625.3

Note. — A series of poems on mythological and other subjects, told in turn by bards at a convocation of wanderers.

Shelf. No.

EARTHS, The, in our solar system, and the earths in the starry heavens. Swedenborg, E. Boston, 1851. 8° 6831.1

EARTHWARD pilgrimage, The. Conway, M. D. London, 1870. Sm. 8° 6326.18

EASSIE, William. Healthy houses. A handbook of the history, defects, and remedies of drainage, ventilation, warming, and kindred subjects. With illustrations. New York, 1872. viii, 228 pp. 12° .... 1525.6 and 6226.7

EAST, The. Bryant, W. C. Letters from the East. New York, 1869. 12° 424.9

— Fetridge, W. P. Harper's hand-book for travellers in the East. New York, 1872. 12° 5935.1

— Kinglake, A. W. Eothen. Leipzig, 1846. Sq. 16° 228.1

— Lamartine, A. (M. L.) de. Souvenirs, impressions, pensées et paysages pendant un voyage en Orient 1832-33. Paris, 1859. 2 v. 12° 2016.12

— Lenormant, F., and Chevallier, E. A manual of the ancient history of the East. London, 1869, 70. 2 v. Sm. 8° 5927.8

— Martineau, H. Eastern life, present and past. Philadelphia, 1848. 8° 232.2

— Osgood, J. F. Notes of travel. Salem, 1854. 12° 5915.8

— Rawlinson, G. The five great monarchies of the ancient Eastern world. London, 1871. 3 v. 8° 5922.3

— — The sixth great oriental monarchy. London, 1873. 8° 5932.6

— Sketches of Eastern travel. (*In* Many lands and many people) 431.3

— Smith, P. Ancient history of the East. From the earliest times to the conquest by Alexander the great. London, 1871. 12° 5916.14

See also the names of Eastern countries, like Egypt, Syria, etc.

EAST and West poems. Harte, (F.) B. Boston, 1871. 12° 1615.13

EASTERN question. Cobden, R. Russia and the. Boston, 1854. 12° 827.3

— Palgrave, W. G. Essays on Eastern questions. London, 1872. 8° 6135.1

See also Crimea.

EASTERN seas, In the. Kingston, W. H. G. [Juvenile] 921.3

EASTERN states, Letters on the. Tudor, W. New York, 1820. 12° 1915.5

EASTERN yacht club. Constitution, by-laws, sailing regulations, etc. 1873. Boston, 1873. 65 pp. Folded plate. 16° 6419.1

EAST INDIAN archipelago. Bickmore, A. S. Travels in the. London, 1868. 8° 422.7

— *Same.* New York, 1869. 8° 5932.4

— Gibson, W. M. Glance at the. New York, 1868. 12° 424.3

EAST INDIES, Life in the. Thomes, W. H. Boston, 1873. Sm. 8° 535.15

EASTLAKE, *Sir* Charles Lock. Contributions to the literature of the fine arts. With a memoir compiled by Lady Eastlake. London, 1870. v, 346 pp. 8° 6232.1

— Hints on household taste in furniture, upholstery, and other details. Edited, with notes, by C. C. Perkins. From the revised London edition. Boston, 1872. xxxiv, 300+ pp. Illustrated. Sm. 8° 6212.1

— History of the Gothic revival. London, 1872. xvi, 427+ pp. Illustrated. Sm. 4° 6221.2

EASTLAKE, *Lady* Elizabeth Rigby, *editor.* Life of John Gibson. London, 1870. ix, 255 pp. Portrait. 8° 5423.13

EAST Lynne. Wood, E. P. Leipzig 333.4

— *Same.* New York 521.36

EASTMAN, Luke. Masonick melodies. Boston, 1818. 204+ pp. 8° 1623.1

EASTON, Alexander. Practical treatise on street or horse-power railways. Philadelphia, 1859. 139+ pp. Plates. 8° 6923.7

Shelf. No.

EASTWICK, Edward Backhouse. Autobiography of Lutfullah, a Mohamedan gentleman; and his transactions with his fellow-creatures. Leipzig, 1857. xiv, 342 pp. Sq. 16° 1238.7

— Handbook for India. With map and plans of towns. London, 1859. 2 v. 12° 5917.7

Contents. — Vol. I. Madras. II. Bombay.

EATING, The philosophy of. Bellows, A. J. New York, 1872. Sm. 8° 1523.4

EATON, Charlotte A. Rome in the 19th century. 5th edition. Added a complete index and illustrations. London, 1860. 2 v. Sm. 8° 5516.6

EATON, John Richard Turner. The permanence of Christianity. London, 1873. xix, 387 pp. 8° 6324.1

EATON, William, Life of. Felton, C. C. (*In* Sparks, J. Library of American biography) 5028.1.9

EBB-TIDE and other stories. Fisher, F. C. 711.28

EBERS, Georg. An Egyptian princess. From the German by E. Grove. Leipzig, 1870. 2 v. in 1. Sq. 16° 310.20

ECCE Deus. Parker, J. Boston, 1867. 12° 1526.4

ECCE Homo. Seeley, J. R. Boston, 1866. 12° 1526.5

See also Note under Christ.

ECCLESIASTICAL biography. Tableau de l'éloquence chrétienne au IVe siècle. Villemain, A. F. Paris, 1865. 12° 5537.14

ECCLESIASTICAL history. Abbott, L. A dictionary of religious knowledge. New York, 1875. 8° 6320.2

— Cohen, J. The deicides. Analysis of the life of Jesus, and of the several phases of the church in their relations to Judaism. Baltimore, 1873. 12° 5817.13

— Doellinger, J. J. I. von. The first age of Christianity and the church. London, 1867. 8° 5813.4

— — Lectures on the reunion of the churches. New York, 1872. 16° 5816.6

— Felt, J. B. Ecclesiastical history of New England. Boston, 1855. 2 v. 8° 5811.2

— Hardwick, C. History of the Christian church. Middle age. London, 1874. Sm. 8° 6326.21

— — History of the Christian church during the reformation. London, 1874. Sm. 8° 6326.20

— Hope, *Mrs.* —. Conversion of the Teutonic race. Conversion of the Franks and the English. London, 1872. 16° 5735.5

— — Sequel to the Conversion of the Teutonic race. S. Boniface and the conversion of Germany. London, 1872. 16° 5735.6

— Milman, H. H. History of Latin Christianity. London, 1867. 9 v. Sm. 8° 5817.11

— Newton, J. Review of. London [1770]. 12° 1538.7

— Robertson, J. C. History of the Christian church from the apostolic age to the reformation. London, 1874. 4 v. Sm. 8° 6327.10

— Socrates Scholasticus. Ecclesiastical history. London, 1853. 16° 5815.3

— Stephens, W. R. W. Saint Chrysostom: his life and times. London, 1872. 8° 5813.6

See also Christianity, Church, Missions, Popes, Reformation, and the names of the various denominations; and of various countries for their ecclesiastical history.

ECCLESIASTICAL literature, Cyclopædia of. MacClintock, J., and Strong, J. New York, 1871-73. 5 v. 8° .... *R.R., A.2.3

ECCLESIASTICAL polity. The apostolical constitutions. Donaldson, J. Edinburgh, 1870. 8° 6322.16

ECHOES of infant voices. [Poetical selections.] Boston, 1849. 144 pp. 12° 5218.4

ECHOES of the foot-hills. Harte, (F.) B. Boston, 1875. 12° 1615.8

ECKERMANN, Johann Peter, Conversations of Goethe with. *See* GOETHE, Johann Wolfgang von 5735.1

ECKLEY, Sophia May. The oldest of the old world. London, 1860. xii, 300 pp. 12° 224.7

ECLECTIC magazine of foreign literature, science, and art. New series. Vol. 16-22. New York, 1872-75. 7 v. With portraits. 8° .... 1314.

ÉCOLE, L', des femmes: comédie. Molière, J. B. P. Œuvres. Paris, 1869. 12° .... 5537.2.

Shelf. No.

ÉCOLE, L', des maris: comédie. Molière, J. B. P. Œuvres. Paris, 1869. 12° ... 5537.2.1

ÉCUEIL, L'. Du Grail de la Villette, C. B. Paris, 1864. 12° ... 2016.10

EDDA; or, the tales of a grandmother. Philojuvenis, *pseud.* London, 1875. L. 8° ... 5712.2

EDELWEISS. Auerbach, B. ... 517.4

EDEN, Charles H. Ralph Somerville; or, a midshipman's adventures in the Pacific ocean ... 1115.19

EDEN, Frederic. The Nile without a dragoman. 2d edition. London, 1871. viii, 312 pp. Sm. 8°. 5934.3

EDES, Robert Thaxter. Formation and significance of renal casts. (*In* Massachusetts medical society. Publications) ... 6021.4

— HIBBARD, James F., and SPARE, John. Dissertations on the part performed by nature and time in the cure of diseases. Boston, 1868. 155+ pp. 8° ... 6021.5

EDGAR, John George. The boyhood of great men. With illustrations. New York, 1872. 385 pp. 16° ... 913.14

— Footprints of famous men. With illustrations. New York, 1872. 369 pp. 16° ... 913.13

— Sea-kings and naval heroes. New York, 1868. 421 pp. Illustrated. 16° ... 913.16

— The wars of the roses; or, stories of the struggle of York and Lancaster. With illustrations. New York, 1859. 470 pp. 16° ... 913.15

EDGE, Frederick Milnes. The exploits and triumphs, in Europe, of Paul Morphy, the chess champion. New York, 1859. viii, 203 pp. Portraits. 12°. 1516.25

EDGEWORTH, Maria. Tales and novels. New York, 1860. 20 v. in 10. Illustrated. 12° ... 514.1

Contents. — Vol. I [1, 2]. Castle Rackrent; Essay on Irish bulls; Self-justification; Forester; The Prussian vase; The good aunt. II [3, 4]. Angelina; The good French governess; Mademoiselle Panache; The knapsack; Lame Jervas; The will; The Limerick gloves; Out of debt out of danger; The lottery; Rosanna. III [5, 6]. Murad the unlucky; The manufacturers; The contrast; The grateful negro; To-morrow; Ennui; The dun. IV [7, 8]. Manœuvring; Almeria; Vivian. V [9, 10]. The absentee; Madame de Fleury; Emilie de Coulanges; The modern Griselda. VI [11, 12]. Belinda. VII, VIII [13-15]. Leonora; Patronage. VIII [16]. Love and law; The rose, thistle, and shamrock. IX [17, 18]. Harrington; Thoughts on bores; Ormond. X [19, 20]. Helen.

— Early lessons. Boston [1851]. 4 v. Illustrated. 12° ... 939.6

Contents. — Vol. I. Little dog Trusty; Orange man; Cherry orchard; Harry and Lucy; Frank. II. Sequel to Frank. III, IV. Harry and Lucy, concluded.

— Murad the unlucky. (*In* Johnson, (E.) R. Little classics) ... 529.4.12

EDINBURGH review, for July and October, 1845. New York, 1845. 8° ... 1422.1

EDITH; or, the light of home. Davis, E. B. ... 733.3

EDITH'S ministry. MacKeever, H. B. ... 713.13

EDMOND Dantes. Dumas, A. (D.) ... 511.29

EDMONDS, S. Emma E. Nurse and spy in the union army. With illustrations. Hartford, 1865. 384 pp. 8° ... 813.1

EDNA Browning. Holmes, M. J. ... 535.18

EDSON, N. I. Silent Tom ... 928.4

EDUCATION. The American education annual. New York, 1875. 8° ... 1932.3

— Bache, A. D. Report on education in Europe. Philadelphia, 1839. 8° ... 5834.3

— Burton, W. Helps to education in the homes of our country. Boston, 1863. Sm. 8° ... 1933.18

— Clarke, E. H. The building of a brain. Boston, 1874. 16° ... 5837.4

— — Sex in education. Boston, 1874. 16°. 1937.2 and 5838.1

— Currie, J. The principles and practice of early and infant school-education. London, N. D. Sm. 8° ... 5837.6

— Dupanloup, F. A. P. The child. Boston, 1875. 12° ... 1915.10

— Eggleston, G. C. How to educate yourself. New York, 1872. 12° ... 1933.9

— Howe, J. W. Sex and education. Boston, 1874. 16° ... 1937.4

— Kingsley, C. Health and education. London, 1874. Sm. 8° ... 5836.10

Shelf. No.

EDUCATION, *continued.*

— Locke, J. Some thoughts concerning education. Boston, 1830. 16° ... 1737.3

— Lowell, A. C. Thoughts on the education of girls. Boston, 1853. 16° ... 1738.2

— Mayo, A. D., and Vickers, T. The Bible in the public schools. New York, 1870. 24° ... 5819.2

— Milton, J. A treatise of. Boston, 1830. 16° .. 1737.3

— Rousseau, J. J. Émile, ou de l'éducation. La Haye, 1762. 4 v. 8° ... 5535.6

— Spencer, H. Education: intellectual, moral, and physical. New York, 1873. 12° ... 5835.3

— Stetson, C. B. Technical education: what it is, and what American public schools should teach. Boston, 1874. 16° ... 5837.2

— Temple, F. The education of the world. (*In* essays and reviews) ... 1538.3

— *Same.* (*In* Hedge, F. H. Recent inquiries in theology) ... 1526.24 and 5814.15

— Wells, W. H. A graded course of instruction for public schools. New York, 1862. 12° ... 1535.11

See also Self-education.

EDWARD III, *of England.* Warburton, W. P. London, 1875. 16° ... 628.6

EDWARDS, Amelia Blandford. Barbara's history ... 314.25

— Debenham's vow ... 312.12

— The four-fifteen express. (*In* Johnson, (E.) R. Little classics) ... 529.4.8

— Half a million of money ... 312.13

— Hand and glove ... 312.14

— In the days of my youth ... 339.11

— Miss Carew ... 312.11

— A night on the borders of the Black forest [and other stories] ... 329.20

— Philip Earnscliffe ... 520.2

— Untrodden peaks and unfrequented valleys; a midsummer ramble in the Dolomites. Leipzig, 1873. 302 pp. Sq. 16° ... 329.1

EDWARDS, Annie. Archie Lovell ... 312.15

— Estelle ... 714.11

— Leah: a woman of fashion. Leipzig ... 329.28

— *Same.* New York ... 721.14

— Miss Forrester ... 732.2

— The ordeal for wives ... 724.28

— Ought we to visit her? ... 312.17

— Steven Lawrence, yeoman ... 312.16

— Susan Fielding ... 710.37

— A vagabond heroine. Leipzig ... 319.11

— *Same.* New York ... 725.29

EDWARDS, Charles. Pleasantries about courts and lawyers of the state of New York. New York, 1867. 528 pp. Portrait. 8° ... 5023.1

EDWARDS, Edward. Free town libraries, their formation, management, and history; in Britain, France, Germany, and America. Together with brief notices of book-collectors. New York, 1869. xiv, 262 pp. Folded sheets. 8° ... 6132.2

— Lives of the founders of the British museum; with notices of its chief augmenters and other benefactors. 1570–1870. London, 1870. x, 780+ pp. Illustrated. 8° ... 6133.1

EDWARDS, H. Sutherland. Life of Rossini. London, 1869. viii, 344 pp. Portrait. 8° ... 5522.4

EDWARDS, Henri Milne. Outlines of anatomy and physiology, translated from the French. By J. F. W. Lane. Boston, 1841. xii, 312 pp. 8° ... 6021.15

EDWARDS, Jonathan. Works. With an essay on his genius and writings, by H. Rogers: and a memoir by S. E. Dwight, revised and corrected by E. Hickman. 10th edition. London, 1871. 2 v. Portrait. L. 8° ... 5810.7

— Doctrine of original sin defended. Worcester [1757]. 370 pp. 8° ... 6325.1

— Enquiry into the modern prevailing notions of that freedom of will which is essential to moral agency. Boston, 1754. vi, 294+ pp. 16° ... 1524.12

Life of. Miller, S. (*In* Sparks, J. Library of American biography) ... 5028.1.8

EDWARDS, Justin. The temperance manual. New York [1847]. 90 pp. 16° ... 1919.2

Shelf. No.

EDWARDS, Matilda de Betham. Felicia 331.14

— The Sylvestres 312.27

EDWARDS, Matthew, The boy inventor; a memoir of. Bulfinch, T. Boston, 1860. 12° 1226.13

EDWIN Brothertoft. Winthrop, T. 736.8

EDWIN Drood, The mystery of. Dickens, C. (J. H.) Boston 1824.22

— *Same.* Leipzig 338.5

EGGLESTON, Edward. The circuit rider: a tale of the heroic age 726.20

— The end of the world. A love story 736.18

— The Hoosier school-master. A novel 535.17

— The mystery of Metropolisville 528.5

— The schoolmaster's stories, for boys and girls. [American homes series] 921.13

EGGLESTON, George Cary. The big brother. A story of Indian war 714.35

— How to educate yourself. New York, 1872. viii, 151 pp. 12° 1933.9

— How to make a living. Suggestions upon the art of making, saving, and using money. New York, 1875. 127 pp. [Putnam's handy-book series.] 12° 1536.20

— A man of honor 726.17

— A rebel's recollections. New York, 1875. vi, 260 pp. 16° 5016.15

EGLANTINE. Tabor, E. 720.37

EGMONT: a tragedy. Goethe, J. W. von. Oxford, 1869. 16° 2027.1

— *Same.* Boston, 1871. 16° 1646.3

EGYPT. Baker, *Sir* S. W. Ismailia: a narrative of the expedition to Central Africa for the suppression of the slave trade. Organized by Ismail, khedive of Egypt. New York, 1875. 8° 5933.5

— Bunsen, C. C. J. von. Egypt's place in universal history. London, 1854–67. 5 v. 8° 5912.12

— Denon, (D.) V., *baron.* Travels in upper and lower Egypt, during the campaigns of Bonaparte in that country. New York, 1803. 2 v. 8°. 222.3

— Gordon, L. A., *lady Duff.* Last letters from Egypt. London, 1875. Sm. 8° 436.5

— Lane, E. W. Account of the manners and customs of the modern Egyptians. London, 1871. 2 v. 16° 5926.2

— Lepsius, (C.) R. Discoveries in. London, 1853. 8° 5931.12

— Maughan, W. E. The Alps of Arabia. Travels in Egypt, Sinai, Arabia, and the Holy Land. London, 1873. 8° 5932.10

— Murray, J. Handbook for. London, 1873. 12°. 5917.8

— Prime, W. C. Boat life in. New York, 1858. 12° 424.6

Note. — Also in Harper's monthly, vol. 12, 13, and 14.

— Rollin, C. Ancient history of the Egyptians. Boston, 1807. 8° 5913.1.1

— Taylor, (J.) B. Egypt and Iceland in 1874. New York, 1874. 16° 436.2

— Tugnot de Lanoye, F. Rameses the great; or, Egypt 3300 years ago. [Popular.] New York, 1872. 16° 1714.3

— Wilkinson, J. G. Popular account of the ancient Egyptians. London, 1871. 2 v. Sm. 8° 5926.3

— Zincke, F. B. Egypt of the Pharaohs and of the Khedivé. London, 1873. 8° 5911.13

See also Africa, Fayoum, Nile.

Note. — Herodotus gives the earliest connected account, edited by Rawlinson [6112.2], whose edition is of particular value. Baldwin, in his "Pre-historic nations" [824.7], gives a popular summary of what is known of the time before Menes. Sir Gardner Wilkinson's books are of the highest authority, and his "Popular account" is sufficiently elaborate for the general reader. His book on Thebes and Egypt, 1835, was afterwards the basis of Murray's Handbook, which is, perhaps, the most convenient manual of all for Egyptian history, topography, manners, etc., ancient and modern. His elaborated summary, "Manners and customs," is to be found in Bates Hall. See Philip Smith's "History of the world"; Grote's "History of Greece" [5926.1.3, ch. 20]. Bunsen and Lepsius have independently worked out the chronology of ancient Egypt, and Bunsen has drawn out opposition to such views as are antagonistic to the old opinions regarding biblical chronology. Bunsen's chronological system is explained in the Christian examiner, Nov., 1867, where his adverse reviewers of the Journal of sacred literature, Oct., 1859, of the Dublin review, Feb., 1860, of the Quarterly review, 1859, and of Smith's Bible dictionary [B.2.2] are considered. Canon Cook, in the Speaker's commentary [in Central Library], has

EGYPT, *continued.*

an essay on the bearing of Egyptian history on the Pentateuch. See Plutarch's "Morals" [6113.1.4] for the old religion. Draper, in his "Intellectual development of Europe" [5921.2], traces the effects of Egyptian civilization. Lepsius had the advantage of the support of the Prussian government in pursuing his archæological researches, 1842–46. His Letters are popular. The advanced student can find in the Central Library Lepsius's splendid results in his "Chronologie"; in his "Denkmäler"; and in his "Königsbuch;" and can also consult the Bates Hall catalogues for the important results of the expedition authorized by Napoleon [see Lanfrey's Napoleon 5522.1.1, ch. x], and for the works of the Champollions, Leibnitz, Belzoni, Heeren, and others; and the recent works on the great pyramid by John Taylor, who aims to establish a connection between the dimensions and a universal system of measures; and of Piozzi Smyth, who throws light on the ancient Egyptian learning, etc., taking views against Bunsen on the chronology; and indulging in some fanciful theories. For popular accounts of the *pyramids*, see chapters in many of the above books, and also in Warburton's "Crescent and cross" [317.8], etc.

The general subject of *Egyptian art* will be found treated in comprehensive treatises on the history of architecture, painting, sculpture, etc. (which see); in Winckelmann [6211.1]; and in Wornum's "Epochs of painting" [6213.3].

On the *modern Egyptians*, Lane is the best authority; and for other editions of some of the above travels and descriptions, and for many others, see the Bates Hall catalogues. Wilkinson recommends Lady Duff Gordon's Letters.

For other modern descriptions, etc., see in addition, chapters in such general travels in the East as Warburton's [317.8]; Bryant's Letters [424.9]; Bellows's "The old world in its new face" [423.6]. Baker's "Ismailïa" is an account of an expedition sent with the protection of the khedive to suppress the slave trade on the upper Nile. Emanuel Deutsch's "Literary remains" [5733.7] has an essay on Ancient and modern Egypt.

See authorities cited in Smith's Bible dictionary, edition of Hackett and Abbot; also in the full account in McClintock and Strong.

See the note in the Lower Hall Catalogue of history, etc., p. 79.

EGYPTIAN princess, An. Ebers, G. 310.20

EIGHT cousins. Alcott, L. M. 1117.1

EIGHTH commandment, The. Reade, C. 716.6

EILOART, *Mrs.* C. J. The love that lived 711.12

EIRENE; or, a woman's right. Ames, M. C. 711.17

EITEL, Ernest J. Buddhism: its historical, theoretical and popular aspects. 2d edition. London, 1873. 122+ pp. 8° 5613.5

EKKEHARD. Scheffel, J. V. 315.9

EKKOES from Kentucky, by Petroleum V. Nasby. Locke, D. R. Boston, 1868. 12° 536.13

ELAM, Charles. A physician's problems. [Essays.] Boston, 1869. vi, 400 pp. 12° 425.6

ELDORADO; or, adventures in the path of empire. Taylor, (J.) B. New York, 1864. 12° 425.6

Note. — This book has no connection with the search for El Dorado undertaken by the early Spanish explorers in South America; but pertains to California, etc.

ELEANOR's victory. Braddon, M. E. 325.12

ELEANOR's visit. Mathews, J. H. 1117.13

ELECTRIC telegraph. *See* TELEGRAPH.

ELECTRICITY. Baile, J. Wonders of. New York, 1872. 12° 1714.30

— Farrar, J. Elements of. Cambridge, 1826. 8°. 6433.1

— Garratt, A. C. Electro-physiology and electrotherapeutics; showing the best methods for the medical uses of. Boston, 1860. 8° 6011.1

— Harris, *Sir* W. S. General principles of animal and voltaic electricity. London, 1869. 12° ... 1715.29

— – Rudimentary electricity. London, 1872. 12°. 1716.20

— Jenkin, F. Electricity and magnetism. London, 1873. Sm. 8° 6438.4

— Tyndall, J. Light and electricity. New York, 1873. 12° 1523.20

See also Electro-magnetism, Electro-metallurgy, Galvinism, Magnetism, Medical electricity, Telegraph.

ELECTRO-MAGNETISM, Elements of. Farrar, J. Cambridge, 1826. 8° 6433.1

ELECTRO-METALLURGY. Valicourt, E. de. Manuel de dorure et d'argenture par la méthode électro-chimique, et par simple immersion. Paris, 1845. 24° 6429.10

— Watt, A. Electro-metallurgy. London, 1871. 12° 1715.18

ELENA. Comyn, L. N. 727.30

ELFIN land. Ball, B. W. Boston, 1851. 12° 1616.12

ELFRED. Abbott, J. Harper's story books 936.1.6

EL FUREIDIS. Cummins, M. S. 332.29

ELGIN, *Earl of.* *See* BRUCE, James.

ELI Perkins (at large). Landon, M. D. New York, 1875. 12° 1536.25

Shelf. No.

ELIA, Essays of. Lamb, C. New York, 1835. L. 8°. 1911.4
— *Same.* (*In his* Works.) New York, 1872. 12°. 1813.5 and 5615.1.2
ELIA and Eliana, Essays of. Lamb, C. Leipzig, 1869. Sq. 16° 1918.3

Note. — The Eliana are essays by Lamb recovered of late from the magazines in which they were originally printed.

ELIAS, The voice of. Snow, S. S. New York, 1863. 12° 1524.9
ELIOT, Charles William, and STORER, Francis Humphreys. A compendious manual of qualitative chemical analysis. Revised by W. R. Nichols. 2d revised edition. New York, 1873. vi, 126, li pp. 12° 6436.4
— A manual of inorganic chemistry, arranged to facilitate the experimental demonstration of the facts and principles of the science. With appendix. New York, 1875 [*cop.* 1866]. xvi, 605, lxiii pp. Illustrated. 8° 6435.6
ELIOT, George, *pseud.* *See* LEWES, Marian.
ELIOT, John, Life of. Francis, C. (*In* Sparks, J. Library of American biography) 5028.1.5
ELIOT, Samuel Atkins. Sketch of the history of Harvard college, and of its present state. Boston, 1848. xiii, 190+ pp. Folded plan. 16°. 818.4
ELIOT, William Greenleaf. Lectures to young women. 3d edition. Boston, 1854. 196 pp. 16° .. 1917.5
ELISIRE d'amore. Donizetti, G. (*In* Ditson, O., and co. Standard opera librettos) 6233.3.2
ELIZABETH, *of England.* Abbott, J. History of... 915.10
— Aikin, L. Memoirs of the court of. New York, 1870. 16° 5415.4
— Raumer, F. (L. G.) von. Die Königinnen Elisabeth und Maria Stuart. Leipzig, 1836. 12° .. 2026.3

Note. — See Lower Hall Catalogue of history, etc.

ELIZABETH; or, the exiles of Siberia. Cottin, S. R. New York, 1867. 32° 539.2
ELLA. Simonds, W. 932.39
ELLEN Clinton. [Fiction.] W., H. 532.18
ELLEN Linn. Abbott, J. 914.13
ELLEN Middleton. Fullerton, *Lady* G. 325.17
ELLENBOROUGH, *First earl.* *See* LAW, Edward.
ELLERY, William, Life of. Channing, E. T. (*In* Sparks, J. Library of American biography) .. 5028.1.6
ELLICE, Edward. *See* MÉRIMÉE, P. Portraits historiques et littéraires. Paris, 1874. 12° 5527.14
ELLICOTT, Charles John. The revision of the English version of the New Testament. *See* LIGHTFOOT, Joseph Baber 5814.11
ELLIOT, Frances. Diary of an idle woman in Italy. Leipzig, 1872. 2 v. in 1. Sq. 16° 228.3
— The Italians. [Fiction.] Leipzig 330.16
— *Same.* New York 716.20
— Old court life in France. Leipzig, 1873. 2 v. in 1. Sq. 16° 320.4
— Romance of old court-life in France. With illustrations. New York, 1874. 254+ pp. L. 8°. 5510.1
ELLIOT, *Sir* Gilbert, 1*st earl of Minto.* Life and letters from 1751 to 1806. Edited by the countess of Minto. London, 1874. 3 v. 8° 5625.3
ELLIOTT, Alfred. Out-of-doors: a handbook of games for the playground. London, 1872. 225 pp. Illustrated. 12° 1517.8
— Within-doors: a book of games and pastimes for the drawing-room. With a chapter on feathered pets. London, 1872. 205 pp. Illustrated. 16°. 916.19
ELLIOTT, J. W. National nursery rhymes and nursery songs. Set to original music. With illustrations. London, 1872. 110+ pp. L. 8° ... 1510.1
ELLIS, Daniel. Thrilling adventures of the great union guide of east Tennessee during the southern rebellion. By himself. With illustrations. New York, 1867. 430 pp. Portrait. 12° 816.7
ELLIS, George Edward. History of the battle of Bunker's [Breed's] hill, on June 17, 1775, from authentic sources in print and manuscript. With a map of the battle-ground. Boston, 1875. 69 pp. 8° 811.1
— Memoir of Sir Benjamin Thompson, count Rumford. *See* AMERICAN academy of arts and sciences 5022.3

Shelf. No.

ELLIS, Grace Atkinson. Memoir of Anna Lætitia Barbauld, with many of her letters. Boston, 1874. 2 v. Portrait. 12° 5426.15
ELLIS, John Eimeo. Life of William Ellis, missionary to the South seas and to Madagascar. With an estimate of his character and work by H. Allon. With portrait. London, 1873. xxiv, 310 pp. 8° 5422.12
ELLIS, Sarah (Stickney). The wives of England. New York, 1843. 268 [264] pp. 12° 1935.6
ELLIS, William, Life of. Ellis, J. E. London, 1873. 8° 5422.12
EL-MEDINAH, Personal narrative of a pilgrimage to. Burton, R. F. Boston, 1858. 12° 423.14
— *Same.* Leipzig, 1874. 3 v. in 1. Sq. 16° 428.5
ELM island stories. *See* KELLOGG, Elijah.
ELOCUTION. Baker, G. M., *editor.* The reading club and handy speaker. Boston, 1875, 76. 3 v. 12° 1538.13
— Monroe, L. B., *editor.* Public and parlor readings. Humorous. Boston, 1874. 12° 1515.18
— — Miscellaneous. Boston, 1875. 12° 1515.14
— Sargent, E. The standard speaker. Philadelphia, 1873. 8° 1933.12
ELSIE Dinsmore. Finley, M. 926.16
ELSIE Venner. Holmes, O. W. Boston, 1872. 2 v. in 1. Sm. 8° 526.20
ELSIE's girlhood. Finley, M. 926.18
ELSIE's Santa Claus. Mathews, J. H. 1117.5
ELSIE's womanhood. Finley, M. 1117.3
ELSTER's folly. Wood, E. P. 333.18
ELTERLEIN, Ernst von. Beethoven's pianoforte sonatas explained. Translated from the German by Emily Hill. With a preface by E. Pauer. London, 1875. 120 pp. Sm. 8° 6237.4
ELZE, Carl (Friedrich). Essays on Shakespeare. Translated with the author's sanction by L. Dora Schmitz. London, 1874. 379+ pp. 8°. 5623.5
— Lord Byron. A biography. Translated, and edited with notes. Portrait and fac-simile. London, 1872. xxii, 516 pp. 8° 5423.3
EMANUEL, Harry. Diamonds and precious stones: their history, value, and distinguishing characteristics. With tests for their identification. 2d edition. New York [London], 1873. xxii, 266 pp. Illustrated. Sm. 8° 6635.3
EMERALD, The. Sargent, E. Boston, 1866. 12° .. 715.14
ÉMERIC-DAVID, Toussaint Bernard. *See* SANTI, *or* SANZIO, Rafaello (Raphael), da Urbino. A series of studies. Boston, 1875. L. 4° 6210.10
EMERSON, George Barrell. A report on the trees and shrubs growing naturally in the forests of Massachusetts. 2d edition. Boston, 1875. 2 v. Plates. 8° 6621.2
EMERSON, Ralph Waldo. Prose works. New and revised edition. Boston, 1873. 2 v. 12° 1934.6

Contents. — Vol. I. Miscellanies; Essays. II. Representative men; English traits; Conduct of life.

— English traits. [Characteristics of the English people.] Boston, 1856. 312 pp. 12° 425.4
— Letters and social aims. Boston, 1876. 314+ pp. 12° 1817.1
— May day and other pieces. [Poems.] Boston, 1874. iv, 205 pp. 16° 1616.15
— Nature. Boston, 1836. 95 pp. 12° 5218.5
— Poems. Boston, 1872. 251 pp. Portrait. 16°. 1616.11
— Representative men: seven lectures. Boston, 1875. 285 pp. 12° 1916.6

Contents. — Uses of great men; Plato; Swedenborg; Montaigne; Shakespeare; Napoleon; Goethe.

— Society and solitude. Boston, 1875. 300+ pp. 16° 1537.21
— *editor.* Parnassus. [Poems by various authors.] Boston, 1875. xlii, 534 pp. 8° 5214.5
— *joint editor.* *See* OSSOLI, Margaret Fuller, *marchesa* d'. Memoirs 1215.4
EMERSON's magazine and Putnam's monthly. *See* PUTNAM's magazine 5127.1
EMERY, Eliza B. Queens 931.3

Shelf. No.

EMERY, Mining and manufacture of. *See* WELLINGTON mills, *London* 1711.4

EMIGRANT'S story, The, and other poems. Trowbridge, J. T. Boston, 1875. 12° 1615.25

ÉMILE, ou de l'éducation. Rousseau, J. J. La Haye, 1762. 4 v. 8° 5535.6

EMILIA Galotti: a tragedy. Lessing, G. E. Leipzig, 1868. Sq. 16° 1613.6

EMILIA Wyndham. Marsh-Caldwell, A. 2 v. 330.23

EMLYN, Thomas. Humble inquiry into the Scripture account of Jesus Christ. (*In* Sparks, J. Collection of essays and tracts in theology) 1918.9.4

EMMA. Abbott, J. Harper's story books 936.1.2

EMMA. Austen, J. 524.12

EMMONS, Richard. The Fredoniad: or, independence preserved. An epick poem on the late war of 1812. Boston, 1827. 4 v. 12° 1611.1

EMMONS, William. The battle of Bunker hill. An historic poem in four cantos. 6th edition. Boston, 1856. 144 pp. Portrait. 12° 1615.11

EMOTIONS. The expression of the emotions in man and animals. Darwin, C. (R.) New York, 1873. Sm. 8° 6615.2

EMPEROR'S, The, picture. Hauff, W. 312.21

EMPRESS Josephine, The. [Historical fiction.] Mundt, C. (M.) 531.11

ENAMELLING, Art of. Gessert, M. A. London, 1857. 12° 1715.5

ÉNAULT, Louis. Histoire d'une femme. Paris, 1872. 472+ pp. 16° 5536.6

— The woman of honor; or, false friendships in society. Translated from the French, by Rebecca L. Tutt. Philadelphia [1875]. 19–205 pp. 8°. 721.1

ENCOURAGEMENS, Les, de la jeunesse. Bouilly, J. N. Paris [1830]. 2 v. 12° 5537.6

ENCYCLOPÆDIAS. *See* CYCLOPÆDIAS.

END of the world, The. A love story. Eggleston, E. 736.18

ENERGY, The conservation of. Stewart, B. New York, 1874. 12° 6436.7

ENGINEER, The. Abbott, J. Harper's story books. 936.1.7

ENGINEERING. Andrews, G. H. Rudimentary treatise on agricultural engineering. London, 1852. 3 v. in 1. 12° 1715.15

— Appleton, D., and co. Dictionary of. New York, 1869. 2 v. 8° .... *R.R., D.3.3

— Burnell, G. R. Rudiments of hydraulic engineering. London, 1868. 12° 1716.10

— Byrne, O. Spons' dictionary of. London, 1869. 6 v. L. 8° .... *R.R., 3.2.1

— Haswell, C. H. Engineers' and mechanics' pocket-book. New York, 1873. 12° 6428.1

— Maxton, J. The workman's manual of engineering drawing. London, 1871. 12° 1716.28

— Shelley, C. P. B. Workshop appliances. New York [London], 1873. Sm. 8° 6427.1

See also Civil engineering, Drawing, Railroads, Steam-engine, Telegraph engineering.

ENGINEERS, Lives of the. Smiles, S. London, 1861. 2 v. 8° 5421.4

ENGLAND. Abbott, J. Story of English history. 936.1.5

— A'Beckett, G. A. The comic history of. London, N. D. 8° 823.6

— Adams, W. T. Red cross; or, Young America in. Boston, 1871. 16° 916.18

— Aikin, L. Memoirs of the court of Elizabeth. New York, 1870. 16° 5415.4

— Blackstone, *Sir* W. Commentaries on the laws of. Philadelphia, 1872. 2 v. 8° 6311.1

— Buckle, H. T. History of civilization in. London, 1872. 3 v. 16° 5417.1

— Burke, E. Essay towards an abridgement of the English history. [A. D. 43–1215.] Boston, 1826. 8° 5634.1.5

— *Same.* Boston, 1871. Sm. 8° 5635.1.7

— Burnet, G., *bishop.* History of his own time: from the restoration of Charles II to the treaty of peace at Utrecht, in the reign of Queen Anne. London, 1857. 8° 5410.4

— Burritt, E. A walk from London to Land's end and back, with notes by the way. London, 1868. Sq. 16° 5438.4

ENGLAND, *continued.*

— Campbell, J., *lord.* Lives of the lord chancellors and keepers of the great seal of, till the reign of George IV. London, 1868. 10 v. Sm. 8° .. 5427.9

— Care, H. English liberties, or the free-born subject's inheritance. Boston, 1721. 12° 828.4

— Coppée, H. English literature, considered as an interpreter of English history. Philadelphia, 1873. Sm. 8° 5614.6

— Daniel, G. Merrie England in olden time. London [1841]. Sm. 8° 5617.14

— Dickens, C. (J. H.) A child's history of. Boston, 1854. 2 v. 16° 928.13

— *Same.* Boston, 1871. 16° 1824.19

— Dod, —. The laboring classes of. Boston, 1847. 12° 5418.1

— Edgar, J. G. The wars of the roses; or, stories of the struggle of York and Lancaster. [A. D. 1421–86; for youths.] New York, 1859. 16°. 913.15

— Ellis, S. (S.) The wives of. New York, 1843. 12° 1935.6

— Fox, C. J. History of the early part of the reign of James II. Philadelphia, 1808. 8° 823.1

— Freeman, E. A. The growth of the English constitution. Leipzig, 1872. Sq. 16° 838.2

— – History of the Norman conquest in. Oxford, 1869. 4 v. 8° 5014.4

— – Old English history. London, 1873. Sm. 8° .. 5418.11

— Froissart, *Sir* J. Chronicles of. London, 1868. 2 v. L. 8° 5920.2

— Froude, J. A. History of, from the fall of Wolsey to the death of Elizabeth. New York, 1873. 12 v. Sm. 8° 826.9

— Galibert, L., and Pellé, C. Angleterre. Paris, 1844. 8° 5911.7

— Hack, M. Stories from English history. London, 1872. 16° 5418.2

— Hallam, H. Constitutional history of, from the accession of Henry VII to the death of George II. New York, 1872. 3 v. Sm. 8° 5416.1

— Hamerton, P. G. A painter's camp in. Boston, 1871. 16° 426.19

— Hawthorne, N. Our old home: a series of English sketches. Boston, 1876 [*cop.* 1863]. Sq. 16°. 5439.1

— – Passages from his English note-books. Boston, 1871. 2 v. in 1. 12° 1813.4

— *Same.* Leipzig, 1871. 2 v. in 1. Sq. 16° 428.3

— Hope, *Mrs.* —. Conversion of the Franks and the English. London, 1872. 16° 5735.5

— Hume, D. History of, from the invasion of Julius Cæsar to the revolution in 1688. Boston, 1868. 6 v. 8° 5413.2

— Hyde, E., *earl of Clarendon.* History of the rebellion and civil wars in. Boston, 1827. 6 v. 8° 5412.4

— Jesse, J. H. Memoirs of the pretenders. London, 1860. Sm. 8° 5426.14

— Jewitt, L., and Hall, S. C. The stately homes of. London, 1874. 4° 5434.2

— Knight, C. History of. [Popular.] London [1862]. 8 v. 8° 5413.1

— Lingard, J. History of, from the first invasion by the Romans to 1688. London, 1855. 10 v. Sm. 8° 5417.8

— Lippincott, S. J. Merrie England. Boston, 1868. 16° 922.26

— Macaulay, T. B., *lord.* History of, from the accession of James II. Leipzig, 1849–61. 10 v. in 5. Sq. 16° 838.1

— Martineau, H. History of the peace: being a history of, from 1816 to 1854. Boston, 1865. 4 v. Sm. 8° 5416.2

— May, *Sir* T. E. Constitutional history of, 1760–1860. London, 1871. 3 v. 16° 5415.2

— Miller, H. First impressions of England and its people. Boston, 1853. 12° 425.13

— Molesworth, W. N. History of, from 1830. London, 1871. 3 v. 8° 5413.3

— *Same.* 2d edition. London, 1874. 3 v. Sm. 8°. 5415.1

— Neele, H. The romance of history. London, N. D. 16° 827.27

Shelf. No.

ENGLAND, *continued.*

— Paris, L. P. d'Orleans, *comte* de. Les associations ouvrières en Angleterre. Paris, 1869. 12°. 5827.2

— Pattison, M. Tendencies of religious thought in, 1688–1750. (*In* Essays and reviews)......... 1538.3

— *Same.* (*In* Hedge, F. H. Recent inquiries in theology).......................1526.24 and 5814.15

— Philip, G., and son. Philip's atlas of the counties of, reduced from the ordnance survey. By E. Weller. London, 1875. F°............*R.R.Desk

— Pike, L. O. History of crime in. London, 1873. 8°. 5412.2

— Rae, W. F. Wilkes, Sheridan, Fox: the opposition under George III. New York, 1874. Sm. 8°. 5415.8

— Smiles, S. The Huguenots: their settlements, churches, and industries in. New York, 1868. Sm. 8°.. 5514.1

— Smith, G. Three English statesmen [Pym, Cromwell, Pitt]: lectures on the political history of. New York, 1867. 12°...................... 5425.1

— Smith, P. V. History of English institutions. Philadelphia, 1874. 16°.................... 5418.5

— Stanhope, P. H., *earl, formerly lord Mahon.* "The forty-five." Being the narrative of the [Scottish] insurrection of 1745. London, 1869. Sm. 8°.. 5418.7

— – History of, comprising the reign of Queen Anne, until the peace of Utrecht, 1701–13. London, 1872. 2 v. Sm. 8°................. 5418.3

— – History of, from the peace of Utrecht to the peace of Versailles. [1713–83.] Leipzig, 1853. 7 v. in 4. Sq. 16°......................... 838.3

— Taine, H. A. Notes on. New York, 1874. 8°. 5435.7

— Thierry, (J. N.) A. History of the conquest of England by the Normans. London, 1869. 2 v. Sm. 8°.. 5417.2

— Timbs, J. Abbeys, castles, and ancient halls of. London [1870]. 3 v. 16°.................. 5438.1

— Wallace, *Mrs.* E. D. A woman's experiences in. New York, 1872. 12°.......................... 423.11

— Walpole, H. Anecdotes of painting in. London, 1871. 16°.................................. 6215.7

— Warburton, W. P. Edward III. London, 1875. Sm. 8°.. 628.6

— Willis, N. P. Pencillings by the way. New York, 1844. L. 8°........................... 430.2

— Wordsworth, C. Social life at the English universities in the 18th century. Cambridge, 1874. Sm. 8°.. 5835.7

— Wraxall, *Sir* N. W. Historical memoirs of my own time. Philadelphia, 1836, 37. 2 v. 8°.. 5812.7

— Wright, T. Caricature history of the Georges. London [1867]. Sm. 8°...................... 5415.5

— – The homes of other days. A history of domestic manners and sentiments in. London, 1871. L. 8°.. 5410.1

— Yonge, C. M. Cameos from English history. London, 1869. 2 v. 16°....................... 826.12

See also Great Britain, London, Selborne, Waterloo.

Note. — Catalogue notes on English history have been prepared separately, and can be seen at this library.

ENGLAND, Church of. Arnold, F. Our bishops and deans. London, 1875. 2 v. 8°............ 5810.6

— Arnold, M. Essay on puritanism and the. London, 1870. Sm. 8°...........................5815.24

— Brooke, S. A. Freedom in the. London, 1871. 16°.. 5816.9

— Curteis, G. H. Dissent, in its relation to the. London, 1873. 16°..........................5816.11

ENGLAND'S antiphon. MacDonald, G. [London, 1868.] Sm. 8°................................ 5937.8

ENGLISH, The, at the north pole. Verne, J. London, 1875. Sm. 8°.......................... 724.27

ENGLISH, The, in Ireland in the 18th century. Froude, J. A. London, 1872, 74. 3 v. 8°.... 5414.5

ENGLISH cyclopædia. Knight, C...............*R.R., F.2.1

ENGLISH explorers, The; comprising details of the more famous travels of Mandeville, Bruce, Park and Livingstone. With a chapter on Arctic explorations. Map and portraits. London, 1875. 639 pp. Sm. 8°.......................... 5927.9

ENGLISH family Robinson, The. Reid, M.......... 937.21

Shelf. No.

ENGLISH governess, The, at the Siamese court. Leonowens, A. H. Boston, 1873. Sm. 8°........ 222.1

ENGLISH language. Abbott, E. A. A Shakespearian grammar. An attempt to illustrate some of the differences between Elizabethan and modern English. London, 1872. 16°................. 5617.7

— Ash, J. New and complete dictionary of the. London, 1775. 2 v. 8°................*R.R., F.3.12

— Bailey, R. W. The scholar's companion; containing exercises in the orthography, derivation, and classification of English words. Philadelphia, 1844. 12°...............................1933.10

— Crabb, G. English synonymes explained in alphabetical order. Boston, 1819. 8°.......... 6122.1

— Craik, G. L. Manual of the history of the. Leipzig, 1874. Sq. 16°..................... 1738.1

— Gould, E. S. Good English; or, popular errors in language. New York, 1870. 16°.......... 1736.1

— Hotten, J. C. The slang dictionary, etymological, historical, and anecdotal. London, 1874. Sm. 8°.. 6126.6

— Marsh, G. P. Lectures on the. New York, 1872. Sm. 8°................................ 6123.2

— – Origin and history of the. New York, 1871. Sm. 8°.. 6123.1

— Millhouse, J. New English-Italian and Italian-English dictionary. London, 1874. 2 v. Sm. 8°..*R.R., F.3.11

— Sargent, E. The standard fourth reader. Boston, 1861. 12°.............................. 1735.4

— Schele de Vere, M. Americanisms; the English of the New World. New York, 1872. 12°.... 6124.1

— – Studies in English; or, glimpses of the inner life of our language. New York, 1868. Sm. 8°. 1533.4

— Soule, R. Dictionary of English synonymes. Boston, 1871. 16°....................*R.R., F.3.2

— Spalding, W. Outline of the origin and growth of the. Edinburgh, 1873. Sm. 8°........... 6127.2

— Spiers, A., and Surenne, G. French and English [and English and French] pronouncing dictionary. New York, 1872. 8°.............*R.R., D.3.2

— Stearns, E. J. A practical guide to English pronunciation. Boston, 1857. 12°.............. 1737.2

— Tauchnitz, (C.) B., *baron* von. Five centuries of the. Leipzig, 1860. Sq. 16°................ 1918.1

— Trench, R. C. English, past and present. New York, 1871. 12°.............................. 1735.3

— – On the study of words. New York [1851]. 12°..1735.2

— Webster, N. American dictionary of the. Springfield, 1873. 4°.......................*R.R., A.3.1

— *Same.* Counting-house edition. New York, 1872. Sm. 4°............................*R.R., A.2.5

— Wedgwood, H. A dictionary of English etymology. London, 1872. 8°.......................... 6121.2

— White, R. G. Words and their uses, past and present. New York, 1870. Sm. 8°.......... 1735.5

— *Same.* New York, 1872. Sm. 8°............ 1735.1

— Whitney, W. D. Language and the study of language. New York, 1872. Sm. 8°......... 6126.3

— Wilson, J. Treatise on English punctuation. Boston, 1850. 12°.......................... 1736.4

— Worcester, J. E. Dictionary of the. Boston, 1873. 4°...............................*R.R., A.3.2

— Zachos, J. C. Phonic primer and reader. Boston, 1864. 12°................................ 1736.3

Note. — Craik's history treats the subject only incidentally in connection with the history of the literature. Spalding's is a convenient outline. Prof. Hadley has an excellent, concise, and comprehensive account prefixed to the unabridged edition of Webster's dictionary, and there is a historical sketch of English dictionaries prefixed to Worcester's quarto dictionary. The Quarterly review, 1873. has a paper on modern English dictionaries. There is a paper on the origin of the language in Disraeli's "Amenities of literature" [1533.13]. Marsh's "Lectures on the English language" and his "Origin and history of the English language" are fitted for the general reader.

A large class of works (not all of which are very highly esteemed by linguistic scholars), which are represented by Dean Trench's "English, past and present," have of late years been published.

For accounts of the *English language in America*, see Schele de Vere's "Americanisms;" lecture 30 in Marsh's Lectures; Lowell's preface to the "Biglow papers" [5227.1]; chapter 3d of Grant White's "Words and their uses."

Craik's "English of Shakespeare," edited by Rolfe [5623.1], and Abbott's Shakespearian grammar [5617.7] concern an

Shelf. No.

ENGLISH language, *continued.*

important epoch in the development of the language. The English of Milton's day is examined in vol. 1 of Masson's Milton [5422.2].

On this subject of *words*, see Whipple's Essay [1936.2]; F. D. Maurice, in "The friendship of books" [6135.8]; and a review of Dean Alford's book, "The Queen's English," can be found in W. D. Whitney's "Oriental and linguistic studies" [6126.2]. Hotten's is the best gathering of its class.

ENGLISH lessons for English people. Abbott, E. A., and Seeley, J. R. London, 1871. Sm. 8°.... 1535.1

ENGLISH literature. Arnold, T. Chaucer to Wordsworth. A short history of, from the earliest times to the present day. London [1873]. 16°. 5628.2

— Bascom, J. Philosophy of. New York, 1874. 318+ pp. 12°.......................... 5216.8

— Brougham, H., *lord.* Men of letters of the time of George III. Edinburgh, 1872. 16° 5614.4.2

— Byron, G. G. N., *lord.* English bards and Scotch reviewers. Boston, 1814. 12°.............. 1619.2

Note. — A satire in verse on his critics.

— Chambers, R. Cyclopædia of. Philadelphia, 1872. 2 v. 8°......................*R.R., C.2.3

— Christophers, S. W. Homes of old English writers. London [1874]. Sm. 8°...............5428.16

— Cleveland, C. D. A compendium of, chronologically arranged. Philadelphia [*cop.* 1848]. 12°.................................... 1534.7

— Coppée, H. English literature, considered as an interpreter of English history. Philadelphia, 1873. Sm. 8°............................ 5614.6

— Craik, G. L. Manual of. Leipzig, 1874. 2 v. in 1. Sq. 16°............................ 1738.1

— Dibdin, T. F. Bibliomania; or, book-madness. London, 1876. 8°.......................... 6131.3

Note. — Accounts of rare books.

— Disraeli, I. Amenities of literature, consisting of sketches and characters of. New York, 1871. 2 v. Sm. 8°...............................1533.13

— Hazlitt, W. Lectures on the English poets. London, 1819. 8°.......................... 5610.6

— - Lectures on the English poets [and comic writers]. London, 1870. 2 v. in 1. Sm. 8°... 5616.5

— Johnson, S. Lives of the English poets. Leipzig, 1858. 2 v. in 1. Sq. 16°...............1238.20

— Kavanagh, J. English women of letters. Leipzig, 1862. Sq. 16°.......................... 1238.2

— MacDonald, G. England's antiphon. [London, 1868.] Sm. 8°............................ 5937.8

— Morley, H. English writers. Vol. I, II, part 1. London, 1867. 2 v. in 3. 8°............... 5622.1

— Palgrave, F. T. The golden treasury of songs and lyrical poems in the English language. London, 1874. Sm. 8°...................... 1627.4

— Parton, J. The humorous poetry of the English language, from Chaucer to Saxe. [A collection of such.] Boston, 1872. L. 12°............1612.31

— Russell, W. C. The book of authors. London [1871]. Sm. 8°.......................... 5638.2

— Spalding, W. History of. Edinburgh, 1875. Sm. 8°.................................. 6127.2

— Spencer, J. A. A course of English reading. New York, 1873. Sm. 8°..................1537.13

— Taine, H. A. History of. New York, 1872. 2 v. 8°.................................. 5613.1

— *Same.* Abridged. New York, 1872. Sm. 8°.. 5614.7

— Tauchnitz, (C.) B., *baron* von. Five centuries of. [Specimens.] Leipzig, 1860. Sq. 16°.... 1918.1

— Thackeray, W. M. The English humourists of the eighteenth century. Leipzig, 1853. Sq. 16°... 1238.8

— Trench, R. C. A household book of English poetry. London, 1870. Sq. 16°............. 5616.4

— Underwood, F. H. Hand-book of. British authors. Boston, 1875. Sm. 8°..................... 5613.6

— Van Rhyn, G. A. F. What and how to read; containing a list of the best books published in England during the past five years. New York, 1875. 12°..............................6136.11

— Villemain, A. F. Tableau de la littérature au moyen âge en Angleterre. Paris, 1871. 2 v. 12°...................................5537.11

ENGLISH literature, *continued.*

— Ward, A. W. A history of English dramatic literature. London, 1875. 8°.............. 5624.3

— Whipple, E. P. The literature of the age of Elizabeth. Boston, 1871. 12°............. 1936.5

— Whitelaw, A. The republic of letters, a selection, in poetry and prose, from the works of the most eminent writers, with many original pieces. Vol. 2-4. Glasgow, 1833. 3 v. 16°......... 5618.6

— Yonge, C. D. Three centuries of. New York, 1872. 12°.................................. 1536.1

Note. — An elaborate general history of English literature has not been written in English; but Taine, in pursuance of a theory of climatic and ethnological influences, has written a brilliant "History of English literature" [5613.1], which may not, however, always command assent from English readers. It has been abridged in English by Fiske [5614.7]. Morley's "English writers" is a work to be referred to. Craik's studies in this field have been of importance. His first work, "Sketches of the history of literature and learning," was the basis of his contributions to the chapters on the literature in the "Pictorial history of England," and was again enlarged into his "Compendious history," which may rank as the best native general history of the literature since the Norman conquest, and it is accompanied by specimens. Chambers's "Cyclopædia of English literature" is a very good selection of extracts, with sufficient commentary for the ordinary reader, but is very meagre for recent times. Underwood's is of similar character but less extensive. F. D. Maurice, in his "Friendship of books" [6136.8], aptly characterizes the chief English writers down to Cowper.

Of the briefer compendious manuals. — Spalding is compact; T. Arnold is judicious; C. D. Yonge's "Three centuries of English literature" gives extracts from the principal writers of each age, but is considered inexact; and Tauchnitz's "Five centuries" is a series of selections from eight principal writers from Wycliffe to Gray. The introduction to Allibone gives a summary of the earliest literature with a tabular statement of the writers from the 6th to the 19th century. Jeffrey briefly summarizes, in his review of Ford in his "Essays" [5610.8], the changes in the history of the literature.

Southey's Cowper [5627.4] sketches the English poets from Chaucer down. Landor's "Conversation on Southey and Porson" pertains to the poets. An account of the poets laureate can be found in Disraeli's "Curiosities of literature" [5626.6], and in the Atlantic monthly, 1858.

For the period covered, 15th, 16th and 17th centuries, the chapters on English literature in Hallam's "Introduction to the literature of Europe" [1531.2] will be found characteristically just and comprehensive; and Warton's "History of English poetry," for its period, 1100–1600, is learned, but not engaging, while a recent editor, W. C. Hazlitt, has much improved it. Whipple's "Literature of the age of Elizabeth" is the work of an acute critic and popular writer. Masson, in his Milton [5422 2], surveys the field during the time preceding the Commonwealth.

For the Queen Anne period, see particularly the last chapter of Stanhope's History [5418.3], and the lives of Swift, Addison, Steele, etc.

For the first half of this century, see chapters in Alison's Europe, 1815-52 [5913.6]. There are many biographies necessary to the full understanding of the literature of this century in connection with its literary society, like those of Scott, Byron. Leigh Hunt, Southey, Thomas Moore, Miss Mitford, Crabbe Robinson. Chorley, Hood, Landor. Lamb, Dickens. etc. See also Brougham's "Men of letters of the reign of George III" [5614.4 2].

There are monographs on the novelists, like Scott [5914.2] and Forsyth [6136.1]; on the historians. like Lawrence [1224.7]; on the comic writers, like Hazlitt, etc. George MacDonald's "England's antiphon" is a popular sketch of the religious poetry, with specimens.

For old songs and ballads, see the essay to Percy's "Reliques" [1613.12], and Scott's introduction to his "Border minstrelsy."

Johnson's Lives must always remain a noteworthy book, though given to the recording of some poets, now wholly forgotten; and the reader must always make allowance for his prejudices regarding Milton and Gray.

Stedman's "Victorian poets" [1837 1] is a marked characterization of the poetic representatives of our day.

See also Coppée's "English literature considered as an interpreter of English history," and the chapters on literature in Emerson's "English traits" [425.4].

The sketches in Knight's "Popular history of England" [5113.1] are only sufficient to illustrate the condition of the people; but in the appendix to vol. V there is a chronological table of writers.

For the English literature of America, see United States, literature, *note.* For accounts of individual writers, both English and American, the most convenient first researches can always be made in Allibone's "Dictionary of authors;" the accounts of those occurring in the alphabet before the letter O are, however, brought down no later than about 1858.

For the history of the *drama*, so far as it may have been treated independent of its connection with the general literature of England, the fullest narrative down to the death of Queen Anne is by Ward.

For the history of *newspapers*, see the note in the Bulletin for Oct., 1875, p. 427. The growth and progress of magazine literature is touched upon in Curwen's "History of booksellers" [5426.16].

ENGLISH orphans, The. Holmes, M. J............. 534.4

ENGLISH portraits. Sainte-Beuve, C. A. New York, 1875. 16°................................ 1025.3

ENGLISH radical leaders. Hinton, R. J. New York, 1875. 16°................................ 628.8

ENGLISH stage. Betterton, T. History of the. Boston, 1814. 8°............................ 813.3

— Cole, J. W. Summary of the English stage for the last fifty years. London, 1859. 2 v. Sm. 8°. 5426.3

Shelf. No.

ENGLISH stage, *continued.*
— Doran, J. W. "Their majesties' servants." Annals of the English stage, from Thomas Betterton to Edmund Kean. New York, 1865. 2 v. L. 12° ... 1532.2
— Fitzgerald, P. The romance of the. London, 1874. 2 v. 8° ... 5622.4
— Genest, J. Some account of the English stage, from the restoration in 1660 to 1830. Bath, 1832. 10 v. 8° ... 5622.2

Note. — Dr. Doran's book is much the best comprehensive history of the English stage, being recent and entertaining. Genest is a voluminous record down to 1830 of the presentations of the various seasons on the metropolitan and provincial stages, with little interest, however, to the general reader. In Percy's "Reliques" [1613.12] will be found an essay on the origin of the stage; and a paper on the first tragedy and the first comedy is given in Disraeli's "Amenities of literature" [1533.13]. Warton's "History of English poetry" also covers the earlier period. In connection with the lives of Shakespeare by his principal editors there are usual histories of the stage preceding and during his time, as in Knight, White, Hudson, etc. See also the biographies of Shakespeare, Betterton, Quin, Colley Cibber, Garrick, Macklin, Foote, Siddons, Kemble, Kean, Young, Cooke, Mathews, — which in this order constitute of themselves a consecutive history of the stage to nearly our time. Much of interest apropos of the stage can be found for their respective periods in the lives of Dryden, Pope, Addison, Steele, Sheridan, Byron, Scott, Planché, Dickens, etc.

Charles Reade's "Peg Woffington" [316.23; 327.3] is a brilliant novelette on this famous actress of the early part of the last century.

ENGLISH traits. Emerson, R. W. Boston, 1856. 12°. 425.4
ENGLISH travelers and Italian brigands. Moens, W. J. C. New York, 1866. 12° ... 423.16
ENGLISH universities, Social life at the. Wordsworth, C. Cambridge, 1874. Sm. 8° ... 5835.7
ENGLISHWOMAN'S domestic magazine. Vol. 15–17. London [1873, 74]. 3 v. 4° ... 6532.1
ENGRAVERS, and their works. Clement, C. E. New York, 1874. 16° ... 1513.17
ENGRAVING. Blanc, (A. A. P.) C. Grammar of. New York, 1874. 4° ... 6212.2
— Duplessis, G. G. The wonders of. New York, 1871. 16° ... 1714.16
— Perrot, A. M. Manuel du graveur. Paris, 1844. 24° ... 6439.4

See also Note in Bulletin, vol. II, p. 267.

ENIGMAS of life. Greg, W. R. Boston, 1873. 16°. 1534.2 and 6136.5
ENOCH Arden. Tennyson, A. Boston, 1864. 12° .. 1612.8
— *Same.* (*In his* Poetical works.) Leipzig, 1860. Sq. 16° ... 1614.10.5
ENTAIL, The. Galt, J. ... 515.9
ENTOMOLOGY. *See* INSECTS.
EOLINE. Hentz, C. L. Philadelphia [*cop.* 1869]. 12°. 534.14
EOTHEN. Kinglake, A. W. Leipzig, 1846. Sq. 16°. 228.1

Note. — Travels in the East.

EPICTETUS. *See* FARRAR, F. W. Seekers after God. London, 1875. Sm. 8° ... 5937.7
EPICUREAN, The. [A romance.] Moore, T. Poetical works. Leipzig, 1842. Sq. 16° ... 1614.9.5
EPIDEMIC delusions. Carpenter, W. B. (*In* Estes, D. Half-hour recreations in popular science) ... 6813.7
EPIDEMICS of the middle ages. Hecker, J. F. C. London, 1846. 8° ... 6013.4
EPILEPSY. Kussmaul, A., and Tenner, A. Nature and origin of epileptiform convulsions caused by profuse bleeding. London, 1859. 8° ... 6023.1
— Schroeder van der Kolk, J. L. C. Proximate cause and rational treatment of. London, 1859. 8°. 6023.2
EPISCOPACY. Chauncy, C. A compleat view of. Boston, 1771. 8° ... 1922.2
— Cotton, C. Thoughts on the religious state of the country, with reasons for preferring episcopacy. New York, 1836. 12° ... 6326.13
EPITAPHS. Bridgman, T. Epitaphs from Copp's hill burial ground, Boston. Boston, 1851. 12°. 5016.5
— — Inscriptions on the gravestones of Northampton, and other towns in the valley of the Connecticut. Northampton, 1850. 12° ... 5016.6
— Northend, C. A book of. New York, 1873. 12°. 1535.2
EPOCHS of history. *See* MORRIS, Edward E., *editor.*
ERASMUS, Desiderius. Drummond, R. B. Erasmus, his life and character as shown in his correspondence and works. London, 1873. 2 v. Sm. 8° .. 5726.2

Shelf. No.

ERASMUS, Desiderius, *continued.*
— Pennington, A. R. Life and character of. London, 1875. 8° ... 5726.3
— Seebohm, F. The Oxford reformers. London, 1869. 8° ... 5811.12

Note. — See Note in Bulletin, vol. II, p. 338.

ERCKMANN, Émile, and CHATRIAN, Alexandre. The blockade of Phalsburg. [Historical novel.] From the French. With illustrations. London, 1870. 272+ pp. 16° ... 715.12
— *Same.* New York, 1871. 308+ pp. Portraits and illustrations. 12° ... 913.21
— Brigadier Frederick. A novel. [*Also,* The dean's watch, and The invisible eye.] New York, 1875. 90+ pp. Portraits. 8° ... 721.13
— The conscript: a story of the French war of 1813. From the 20th Paris edition. With illustrations. New York, 1872. 330 pp. 16° ... 913.22
— Histoire du plébiscite. Paris, 1872. 341+ pp. 18° ... 5516.4
— Histoire d'un paysan. 1re–4e partie. Paris, 1873. 4 v. 18° ... 5536.14

Contents. — Vol. I. 1789. II. 1792. III. 1793. IV. 1794–1815.

— The invasion of France in 1814. [Historical fiction.] From the French. With a memoir of the authors. New York, 1871. 369 pp. Illustrated. 12° ... 913.23
— Madame Thérèse; or, the volunteers of '92. Translated from the 13th edition. With illustrations. New York, 1869. 289+ pp. 12° .. 524.4
— A man of the people. A tale of 1848. From the French. London, 1871. 2 v. 16° ... 736.23
— The outbreak of the great French revolution. Related by a peasant of Lorraine. Translated by Mrs. C. Hoey. London, 1871. 3 v. 16° .. 825.2
— The story of the plébiscite. From the French. With illustrations. London, 1872. 323+ pp. 16°. 524.25
— Waterloo. [Historical fiction.] From the French. With illustrations. New York, 1872. 368 pp. 12° ... 913.24
ERIC, or little by little. A tale of Roslyn school. Farrar, F. W. Edinburgh, 1875. Sm. 8° ... 938.11
ERICHSEN, John. The science and art of surgery. Edited by J. H. Brinton. Illustrated. Philadelphia, 1854. 908 [892] pp. 8° ... 6022.15
ERIE canal, Marco Paul on the. Abbott, J. ... 914.1
ERIE railway. Adams, C. F., *jr.* A chapter of Erie. Boston, 1869. 12° ... 1916.1
— Crough, G. Another chapter of Erie. New York, 1869. 12° ... 1916.2
ERLING the bold. Ballantyne, R. M. ... 935.11
ERMA'S engagement. By the author of "Blanche Seymour" ... 731.21
ERNANI. Verdi, G. (*In* Ditson, O., and co. Standard opera librettos) ... 6233.3.6
ERNEST Carroll, or artist-life in Italy. Greenough, H. Boston, 1858. 344 pp. 16° ... 737.28
ERNEST Linwood. Hentz, C. L. ... 536.12
ERNEST Maltravers. Bulwer-Lytton, E. (G. E.) L. 336.18
ERNST, Herzog von Schwaben. Uhland, J. L. Gedichte und Dramen. Stuttgart, 1863. 16° .. 5738.1.3
ERSILIA. [Fiction.] Poynter, *Miss* —. Leipzig .. 331.25
— *Same.* New York ... 517.23
ERSKINE, Thomas. Remarks on the internal evidence for the truth of revealed religion. And [Charles] Leslie's Short method with deists. Andover, 1823. 156, 64 pp. 12° ... 5819.4
ERSKINE, *Mrs.* Thomas. Leisure hour series. Wyncote ... 518.2
ERWIN, William. The destiny of man. New York, 1872. 312 pp. 12° ... 5817.4
ESPOUSALS, The. [Poem.] Patmore, C. (K. D.) Boston, 1856. 16° ... 1612.10.2
ESSAY on criticism. [Poem.] Pope, A. Works. Leipzig, 1848. Sq. 16° ... 1613.10
— *Same.* London, 1871. 8° ... 5612.2.2
ESSAY on man. [Poem.] Pope, A. Works. Leipzig, 1848. Sq. 16° ... 1613.10
— *Same.* London, 1871. 8° ... 5612.2.2
ESSAYIST, The. Vol. II. Boston, 1830. 4° ... 6730.39

Shelf. No.

ESSAYS of Elia. Lamb, C. Works. New York, 1872. 12° ...... 1813.5.2 and 5615.1.2

ESSAYS of Elia and Eliana. Lamb, C. Leipzig, 1869. Sq. 16° 1918.3

ESSAYS and reviews. Leipzig, 1862. 374+ pp. Sq. 16° 1538.3

Contents.— Temple, F.: The education of the world; Williams, R.; Bunsen's Biblical researches; Powell, B.: The study of the evidences of Christianity; Wilson, H. B.; The national church; Goodwin, C. W.: On the Mosaic cosmogony; Pattison, M.: Religious thought in England, 1688-1750; Jowett, B.: On the interpretation of Scripture; Note on Bunsen's Biblical researches.

— *Same.* *See* HEDGE, F. H. Recent inquiries in theology ...... 1526.24 and 5814.15

ESTELLE. Edwards, A. 714.11

ESTELLE Russell 312.18

ESTES, Dana, *editor*. Half-hour recreations in popular science. 1st series. Boston [1874]. xvi, 478 pp. Illustrated. 8° 6813.7

Contents.— Strange discoveries respecting the aurora, by R. A. Proctor; Recent solar researches, by R. A. Proctor; The cranial affinities of man and the ape, by R. Virchow; Spectrum analysis explained, and its uses to science illustrated, by Schellen, Roscoe, and Huggins; Spectrum analysis discoveries, by Schellen, Young, Roscoe, Lockyer, Huggins, and others; Nebulæ, comets, meteoric showers, by H. Schellen and others; Corals and coral islands, by J. D. Dana; Unconscious action of the brain, by W. B. Carpenter; Epidemic delusions, by W. B. Carpenter; Scientific miscellany; Geology of the stars, by A. Winchell; On yeast, by T. H. Huxley; Relations between matter and force, by J. H. Tice; The stone age, past and present, by E. B. Tylor; Theory of nervous ether, by Dr. Richardson; Toads in the hole; Origin of metalliferous deposits, by T. S. Hunt; Rotundity of the earth; The phenomena of sleep, by Dr. Richardson; Animal life at great depths in the sea; Russian metallurgical works; Coal as a reservoir of power, by R. Hunt; Hot springs in New Zealand, by H. Meade; Atoms, by Prof. Clifford; The circulation of the waters on the surface of the earth, by H. W. Dove; What is actinism?

ESTHER: tragédie. Racine, J. de. Théâtre complet. Paris, 1870. 12° 5537.3

ESTHER Hill's secret. Craik, G. M. 322.5

ETCHING and etchers. Hamerton, P. G. Boston, 1876. 8° 6233.1

ETHAN Brand. Hawthorne, N. (*In* Johnson, (E.) R. Little classics) 529.4.1

ETHELYN's mistake. Holmes, M. J. 534.5

ETHERIZATION. Rice, N. P. Trials of a public benefactor as illustrated in the discovery of. New York, 1859. 12° 6826.1

— Warren, J. C. Etherization. Boston, 1848. 12°. 6036.3

ETHICS and moral philosophy. Combe, G. Moral philosophy. New York, 1844. Sm. 12° 1529.5

— Follen, C. (T. C.) Lectures on moral philosophy. Boston, 1842. 12° 5735.4.3

— Kant, I. The metaphysics of ethics. Edinburgh, 1871. Sm. 8° 5836.3

— Maurice, (J.) F. D. Social morality. London, 1869. 8° 5833.5

— Paine, M. Physiology of the soul and instinct, as distinguished from materialism. New York, 1872. 8° 5831.1

— Paley, W. Principles of moral philosophy. Boston, 1830. 2 v. Sm. 12° 1538.6

— Parkhurst, J. L. Elements of moral philosophy. Boston, 1832. 12° 1537.14

— Ware, J. Hints to young men, on the true relation of the sexes. Boston, 1850. 16° 1528.1

— Wayland, F. Elements of moral science. Boston, 1836. 12° 5826.7

— *Same.* Abridged. Boston, 1850. Sm. 12° 1528.7

ETHICS of the dust, The. Ten lectures to little housewives on the elements of crystallisation. Ruskin, J. New York, 1866. 12° 6236.4

ETHIOPIA, Discoveries in. Lepsius, (C.) R. London, 1873. 8° 5931.12

ETHNOLOGY. Types of mankind; or, ethnological researches. Nott, J. C., and Gliddon, G. R. Philadelphia, 1854. 8° 6610.7

See also Man. Races.

ÉTOILE du nord. Meyerbeer, G. (*In* Ditson, O., and co. Standard opera librettos) 6233.3.4

ÉTOURDI, L': comédie. Molière, J. B. P. Œuvres. Paris, 1869. 12° 5537.2.1

ETRURIA. Etruscan researches. Taylor, I. London, 1874. 8° 6124.2

Shelf. No.

EUGENE Aram. Bulwer-Lytton, E. (G. E.) L. 336.9

EURIPIDES. Tragedies. Literally translated, with critical and explanatory notes, by T. A. Buckley. London, 1871. 2 v. Portrait. Sm. 8° 6115.3

Contents.— Vol. I. Hecuba; Orestes; Phœnissæ; Medea; Hippolytus; Alcestis; Bacchæ; Heraclidæ; Iphigenia in Aulide; Iphigenia in Tauris. II. Hercules furens; The Troades; Ion; Andromache; Suppliants; Helen; Electra; Cyclops; Rhesus.

— Donne, W. B. Euripides [outlined and explained]. Edinburgh, 1872. Sm. 8° 6116.13

— Schiller, (J. C.) von. Scenen aus den Phönizierinnen 5734.1.7

EUROPE. Alison, *Sir* A. History of, 1789–1815. New York, 1871. 4 v. 8° 5913.6

— – 1815-52. New York, 1868, 70, 71. 4 v. 8°. 5913.5

— Arnold, H. P. European mosaic. [Travels.] Boston, 1864. 16° 435.1

— Atkinson, J. B. An art tour to northern capitals of. London, 1873. 8° 6213.4

— Bache, A. D. Report on education in. Philadelphia, 1839. 8° 5834.3

— Bartol, C. A. Pictures of, framed in ideas. Boston, 1855. 12° 214.2

— Bellows, H. W. The old world in its new face. Impressions of, in 1867, 68. New York, 1870. 2 v. 12° 423.6

— Bryant, W. C. Letters of a traveller; or, notes of things seen in. New York, 1870. 12° 5915.9

— Channing, W. A physician's vacation; or, a summer in. Boston, 1856. 12° 422.21

— Colman, H. European agriculture and rural economy. Boston, 1849. 2 v. 8° 1521.7

— – European life and manners. Boston, 1849. 2 v. 12° 423.1

— Darley, F. O. C. Sketches abroad with pen and pencil. New York, 1869. Sm. 4° 433.2

— Delafield, R. Report on the art of war in Europe in 1854–56. *See* UNITED STATES 5910.3

— Draper, J. W. History of the intellectual development of. New York, 1872. 8° 5921.2

— Fetridge, W. P. Harper's hand-book for travellers in. New York, 1872. 12° 5935.1

— Flint, R. The philosophy of history in. Vol. I. Edinburgh, 1874. 8° 5921.7

— Gramont, A. A. A., *duc* de. Passé et présent, étude d'histoire contemporaine. Paris, 1875. 16° 5534.6

— Hallam, H. Introduction to the literature of Europe in the 15th, 16th, and 17th centuries. New York, 1854. 2 v. 8° 1531.2

— – View of the state of Europe during the middle ages. New York, 1872. 3 v. Sm. 8° 5916.1

— Howe, J. W. From the oak to the olive. [Travels.] Boston, 1868. 16° 437.2

— James, H., *jr.* Transatlantic sketches. Boston, 1875. 12° 436.4

— Kirkland, C. M. Holidays abroad; or, Europe from the West. New York, 1873. 2 v. in 1. 12° 427.6

— Lecky, W. E. H. History of European morals from Augustus to Charlemagne. New York, 1873. 2 v. 8° 5914.1

— – History of the rise and progress of rationalism in. New York, 1872. 2 v. 8° 5933.5

— Lippincott, S. J. Haps and mishaps of a tour in. Boston, 1854. 12° 424.4

— Longfellow, H. W. The poets and poetry of. Philadelphia, 1871. L. 8° 5922.1

— Macgregor, J. A thousand miles in the Rob Roy canoe on rivers and lakes of. Boston, 1871. 16° 428.11

— Morse, J., and Parish, E. New gazetteer of the Eastern continent. Charlestown, 1802. 8° 432.4

— Prime, S. I. The Alhambra and the Kremlin. [Spain and Russia.] New York [1873]. 8° 5914.6

— Russell, W. History of modern Europe. London, 1850. 4 v. 8° 5913.3

— Sachel guide for the vacation tourist in. New York, 1872. 16° 427.2

— Sewell, E. M., and Yonge, C. M. European history. London, 1872, 73. 2 v. Sm. 8° 5927.7

Shelf. No.

EUROPE, *continued.*

— Simonde de Sismondi, J. C. L. Historical view of the literature of the south of. London, 1872. 2 v. Sm. 8° 5927.10
— Stephen, L. The playground of. [Switzerland.] London, 1871. 16° 5935.8
— Sweetser, M. F. Europe for $2 a day. Boston, 1875. Sq. 16° 428.8
— Taylor, (J.) B. By-ways of. New York, 1872. Sm. 8° 224.4
— — Views a-foot; or, Europe seen with knapsack and staff. New York, 1856. 12° 425.22
— Thomes, W. H. The gold hunters in. Boston, 1873. Sm. 8° 735.4
— Viardot, L. Wonders of European art. New York, 1871. 16° 1714.1
— Wallace, *Mrs.* E. D. A woman's experiences in. New York, 1872. 12° 423.11
— Ward, R. Foundation and history of the law of nations in. Dublin, 1795. 8° 6315.2
— Ware, W. Sketches of European capitals. [London, Naples, Rome, etc.] Boston, 1851. 12°. 236.1

See also the various divisions under their several heads.

Note. — Evidences of prehistoric man in Europe are traced in Dawkins's "Cave hunting" [6632.5], but see further in the note in Bulletin, vol. II, p. 298. For Europe during the period of the Roman sway, histories of Rome, Gaul, etc., must be consulted.

The best introduction to the *general history* of modern Europe is Gibbon's "Decline and fall of the Roman empire" [824.9], which may be followed by Hallam on the Middle ages [5916.1], an able work, written in an enlightened spirit. The accounts which make up the history by the Misses Sewell and Yonge cover the interval from the 11th to the 13th century. For the 14th century, Froissart [5920.2] fills an important gap. Guizot, in the 11th lecture of his "History of civilization" [5924.8], makes it the marking line between the middle ages and the modern time. Kirk's "Charles the bold" [5511.1] embraces much of the 15th century. For the period of the *Reformation*, a central study is Robertson's "Charles the fifth" [12:6.9], wherein his "Progress of society" from the fall of the Roman empire is an able review. See also under "Reformation," "Luther," etc. Fisher's "Reformation" [5813.7, appendix 2] gives a list of authorities on the general history of this period. Motley's histories come in here, and there is a paper in the Quarterly review, 1874, on his tendency to put the Netherlands for all Europe. Schiller's clear and brilliant monograph on the "Thirty years' war" [826.2] will partly bridge the gap before the French revolution finally embraced all Europe. Alison's History is voluminous, but if his ultra conservative views are understood, it offers the best English account; and he did not add to his reputation by his continuation of the record to 1852. Writers like Buckle speak scornfully of Alison.

Russell's "Modern Europe" is a concise review, written in the form of letters, addressed by a nobleman to his son, of the period beginning with the decline of the Roman empire and closing originally in 1763; but it has been continued to 1837.

Castelar's papers on "The republican movement in Europe in late years" will be found in Harper's magazine, vols. 45–50.

The "Epochs of history" series of condensed monographs on salient points of European history promises to be when finished a valuable aid to popular study. Smyth's "Lectures on modern history" [5012.10; 5925.7] is a useful guide.

Literary history.

The beginnings of European literature are traced in Guizot's History of "civilization" [5924.8] and in Milman's "Latin Christianity" [5817.11].

There is nothing better for the period it covers than Hallam's excellent criticism and condensed narrative [1531.2]. Longfellow, who was assisted by Prof. Felton and others, gives a brief sketch of the different literatures, followed by accounts of the poets belonging to each, with citations. The strength of Sismondi's book is in its account of Italian literature, his account of the Spanish literature being superseded by Ticknor's book [5922.2]

Interesting accounts of literary society in Europe in this century are found in such books as the lives of Irving, Prescott, and Ticknor. See also the literatures of different countries.

Travels.

Beside the travels named above, see Andersen's "Poet's bazaar" [426.18]; Clemens's "Innocents abroad" [421.6]; Keeler's "Vagabond adventures" [1216.3]; Longfellow's "Outremer" [1838.4.1]; Mrs. Stowe's "Sunny memories" [426.6]; and Miss Trafton's "American girl abroad" [736.12].

EUROPEAN life, legend, and landscape. By an artist. Philadelphia, 1859. 154 pp. 1 plate. 12° ... 424.2
EUSTACE diamonds, The. Trollope, A. 720.33
EUTAW. [Historical fiction.] Simms, W. G. 716.29
EUTHANASY. Mountford, W. Boston, 1874. 16°. 5836.7
EVA. Bulwer-Lytton, E. (G. E.) L. 336.15
EVANGELINE. Longfellow, H. W. Poetical works. Leipzig, 1856. Sq. 16° 1614.1
— *Same.* (*In his* Poems.) Boston, 1858. 2 v. 16°. 1612.1.2

Note. — This poem, the most successful in the language in hexameters, is based on the forced removal of the French settlers in Nova Scotia, by order of the British government in 1755, which was carried out by General Winslow, of Massachusetts. See Whittier's notice [1937.1.2].

Shelf. No.

EVANS, Augusta J. *See* WILSON, Augusta J.
EVANS, Frederick W. Shakers. Compendium of the origin, history, principles, and doctrines of the United society of believers in Christ's second appearing. With biographies of Ann Lee [and others]. New York, 1859. 189 pp. 12° 5818.19
EVANS, Marian. *See* LEWES, Marian.
EVANS, Warren F. The mental-cure, illustrating the influence of the mind on the body, both in health and disease, and the psychological method of treatment. 2d edition. Boston [*cop.* 1869]. 364 pp. 12° 1525.8
EVANSON, R. T., and MAUNSELL, Henry. Practical treatise on the management and diseases of children. From the 5th Dublin edition. Boston, 1848. 430 [428] pp. 8° 6012.11
EVELINA. Arblay, F. d' 311.28
EVELYN, John. Diary and correspondence. Edited from the original MSS. at Wotten by W. Bray. New edition. London, 1862. 4 v. Portraits. Sm. 8° 5426.7
EVELYN Marston. Marsh-Caldwell, A. 313.27
EVERETT, Alexander Hill. Life of Joseph Warren. (*In* Sparks, J. Library of American biography) 5028.1.10
EVERETT, Edward. Dorchester in 1630, 1776, and 1855. An oration. Boston, 1855. 158+ pp. 8° 5012.6
— Life of George Washington. New York, 1860. 348 pp. Portrait. 12° 1214.7
— Life of John Stark. (*In* Sparks, J. Library of American biography) 5028.1.1
— Orations and speeches. 8th edition. Boston, 1870. 4 v. Portrait. 8° 1921.1
— Memorial of. *See* BOSTON, *Mass.* 810.9
EVERETT, William. Changing base 935.2
— Double play 935.3
EVERGREENS, Hedges and. Warder, J. A. New York, 1858. 12° 6626.3
EVERS, Henry. Steam and the locomotive engine. New York [Glasgow], 1873. 160 pp. Illustrated. 16° 1717.3
— Steam and the steam engine: land and marine. New York [Glasgow], 1873. 160 pp. Illustrated. 16° 1717.5
EVERY boy's annual. Routledge, E. 930.1
EVERY boy's book: a complete encyclopædia of sports and amusements With illustrations. New edition. London, 1863. 630+ pp. 16° 916.4
EVERY boy's book. Routledge, E. 6414.2
EVERY horse owner's cyclopedia. McClure, R. Philadelphia, 1872. 8° 6613.1
EVERY Saturday. New series. Vol. 1–4. Boston, 1873, 74. 4 v. 4° 1313.1
EVIDENCES of a revelation. Erskine, T. Remarks on the internal evidence for the truth of revealed religion. Andover, 1823. 12° 5019.4
— Hopkins, M. Lectures on the evidences of Christianity. Boston, 1846. 8° 1921.3
— *Same.* Boston, 1861. 12° 1532.7
— Paley, W. View of the evidences of Christianity. Hallowell, 1826. 12° 5816.8
— Powell, B. The study of the evidences of Christianity. (*In* Essays and reviews) 1538.3
— *Same.* (*In* Hedge, F. H. Recent inquiries in theology) .... 1526.24 and 5814.15
— Supernatural religion. 3d edition. London, 1874. 2 v. 8° 5812.14
EVIL eye, The. Carleton, W. 524.2
EVOLUTION. Burr, E. F. Doctrine of. Boston, 1873. Sm. 8° 1527.11.2
— Fiske, J. Outlines of cosmic philosophy, based on the doctrine of. Boston, 1875. 2 v. 8° ... 5824.2
— Haeckell, E. H. History of creation; or the development of the earth and its inhabitants by the action of natural causes. A popular exposition of the doctrine of. New York, 1876. 2 v. 12° 6615.5
— Henslow, G. The theory of evolution of living things, and the application of the principles of evolution to religion. London, 1873. Sm. 8°. 5814.18

Shelf. No.

EVOLUTION, *continued*.
— Winchell, A. The doctrine of. New York, 1874. 12° ... 6836.3

See also Note under Darwinism.

EWALD, Alexander Charles. Life and times of Algernon Sydney, 1622–83. London, 1873. 2 v. Portrait. Folded sheet. 8° ... 5422.10
EWALD, (Georg) Heinrich (August). History of Israel. From the German by J. E. Carpenter. Edited by R. Martineau. Vol. 1, 2, 2d edition. London, 1869–74. 5 v. 8° ... 5813.15
EWBANK, Thomas. A descriptive and historical account of hydraulic and other machines for raising water, ancient and modern; with observations on the mechanic arts [and] the steam engine. Illustrated. 16th edition. With additional matter. New York, 1876 [*cop.* 1863]. viii, 612 pp. 8° ... 6422.7
EWING, Juliana Horatia. A flat iron for a farthing; or, some passages in the life of an only son. With illustrations. 3d edition. London, 1875. xi, 290+ pp. Sm. 8° ... 1117.30
— Six to sixteen. A story for girls ... 1117.10
EXCURSIONS. Thoreau, H. D. Boston, 1866. 16°. 417.9
EXHIBITION drama, The. Baker, G. M. Boston, 1875. 12° ... 1635.6
EXILES of Florida, The. Giddings, J. R. Columbus, 1858. 16° ... 825.8
EXOTICS. [Poems, translations.] Clarke, J. F. and L. Boston, 1875. Sq. 16° ... 1627.3
EXPANSE of heaven, The. Proctor, R. A. London, 1873. Sm. 8° ... 6815.1
EXPERIENCE, The, of life. Sewell, E. M. ... 319.23
EXPERIENCES of a diplomatist. Ward, J. London, 1872. 8° ... 5714.6
EXPERIMENTAL essays. Tomlinson, C. London, 1863. 12° ... 1716.31
EXPIATED. By the author of "Behind the veil" ... 339.8
EXPIATION. Dorr, J. C. R. ... 737.30
EXPLOSIONS of steam boilers. Robinson, J. R. Boston, 1870. 12° ... 1713.4
EXPRESSION. Bell, *Sir* C. Expression: its anatomy and philosophy. New York, 1873. 12° ... 1527.10
— Darwin, C. (R.) The expression of the emotions in man and animals. New York, 1873. Sm. 8°. 6615.2
EXTRA globe, The. Vol. 6, 7. Washington, 1840, 41. 2 v. 4° ... 6730.40

Note. — No. 18 of vol. 7 is missing.

EYE. Carion, C. S. von. Treatise on the diseases of the. New York, 1868. 8° ... 6022.12
— Desmarres, L. A. Traité théorique et pratique des maladies des yeux. Paris, 1847. 8° ... 6021.16
— Dix, J. H. Treatise upon the nature and morbid sensibility of the retina, or weakness of sight. Boston, 1849. 12° ... 6015.7
— Mackenzie, W. Practical treatise on the diseases of the. Boston, 1833. 8° ... 6011.2
— Williams, H. W. A practical guide to the study of the diseases of the. Boston, 1862. 8° ... 6015.5
EYRIÈS, Jean Baptiste Benoît. Danemark. Continué par M. Chopin. Paris, 1846. 415+ pp. 24 plates. [L'Univers.] 8° ... 5911.11
EYSTER, Nellie. Sunny hour stories. Child life of Tom and Mary ... 938.5
— — Chincapin Charlie ... 938.4
— — On the wing ... 938.3
— — Tom Harding and his friends ... 938.2

F. Grant and co.; or, partnerships. Chaney, G. L. 928.10
FABER, Frederick William. Spiritual conferences. 10th edition. Baltimore, N. D. 17–476 pp. 12°. 6327.17
FABIAN, *pope*. *See* HIPPOLYTUS, *St.*
FABIOLA. [Fiction. Church of the catacombs.] Wiseman, N. (P. S.) New York, 1872. Sm. 8°. 736.19
FABLE, A, for critics. Lowell, J. R. [New York], 1848. 12° ... 1622.2

Note. — A poetical satire on literary contemporaries.

FABLES. Æsopus. Fables. New York, 1872. 16°. 6118.8
— La Fontaine, J. de. Fables. Paris, 1868. 2 v. 16° ... 5538.2

FABLES in song. Bulwer-Lytton, (E.) R. Boston, 1874. 16° ... 1617.8
— *Same.* Leipzig, 1874. Sq. 16° ... 1614.16
FABLES respecting the popes of the middle ages. Doellinger, J. J. I. von. London, 1871. 8° .. 5813.5
FABRE, Ferdinand. The abbé Tigrane. Candidate for the papal chair. [Fiction.] Translated by L. W. Bacon ... 715.19
FÂCHEUX, Les: comédie. Molière, J. B. P. Œuvres. Paris, 1869. 12° ... 5537.2.1
FACTS and fancies for school-day reading. Sedgwick, C. M. New York, 1873. Sq. 16° ... 929.6
FADED, A, leaf of history. Davis, R. H. (*In* Johnson, (E.) R. Little classics) ... 529.4.10
FAERIE queene, The. Spenser, E. Poetical works. Boston, 1871. 16° ... Vol. 1–4 of 5628.4
FAGGOT, A, of French sticks. [Descriptions of French life, etc.] Head, *Sir* F. B. London, 1855. 2 v. 12° ... 5526.11
FAIR France. Craik, D. (M.) New York, 1871. 12°. 424.20
— *Same.* Leipzig, 1872. Sq. 16° ... 323.14
FAIR god, The; or, the last of the 'tzins. [Fiction. Aztec history.] Wallace, L. Boston, 1873. 12°. 737.16 and 5014.10
FAIR Harvard: a story of American college life. Washburn, W. T. ... 533.12
FAIR maid, The, of Perth. Scott, *Sir* W. Boston. 533.2
— *Same.* Leipzig ... 324.14
FAIR play. Southworth, E. D. E. N. ... 737.6
FAIR puritan, The. Herbert, H. W. ... 716.1
FAIR Saxon, A. MacCarthy, J. ... 734.8
FAIR women. Forrester, *Mrs.* — ... 710.24
FAIRCHILD, Joy Hamlet. Remarkable incidents in [his] life. Compiled by himself. With portrait. Boston, 1857. xix, 464 pp. 12° ... 1014.9
FAIRE gospeller, Passages in the life of the. Manning, A. New York, 1867. 12° ... 517.19
FAIRFIELD, Francis Gerry. The clubs of New York. New York, 1873. 349 pp. 12° ... 5036.1
FAIRFIELD, Sumner Lincoln. Abaddon, the spirit of destruction; and other poems. New York, 1830. 157+ pp. 8° ... 1623.4
FAIRHOLT, Frederick William. Homes, works, and shrines of English artists. Added Rambles in Rome. Illustrated. London, 1873. x, 182 pp. Sm. 4° ... 6213.6
— Rambles of an archæologist among old books and old places: being papers on art. Illustrated. London, 1871. 259 pp. Sm. 4° ... 6232.3
— Tobacco: its history and associations. Including an account of the plant and its manufacture; with its modes of use in all ages and countries. With 100 illustrations. London, 1876. vi, 332+ pp. Sm. 8° ... 6425.6
FAIRIES of our garden. Watson, E. H. ... 931.6
FAIRY-FINDER, The. Lover, S. (*In* Johnson, (E.) R. Little classics) ... 529.4.12
FAIRY fingers. Ritchie, A. C. ... 723.19
FAIRY tales. Arabian nights' entertainments ... 928.14
— Clarke, R. S. Fairy book ... 927.4
— Hugessen, E. H. K. Queer folk ... 916.30
— Johnson, V. W. The Catskill fairies ... 910.2
— Kingsley, C. The heroes; or, Greek fairy tales. 935.25
— Laboulaye, É. (R. L.) Fairy tales of all nations. 921.5
— Macé, J. Home fairy tales ... 933.13
— Maguire, J. F. Young prince Marigold, and other fairy stories ... 928.11
— Milles et une nuits. Paris, 1842. 2 v. Sm. 8°. 5537.5
FAITH. Blackburne, F. Confessions of. Boston, 1823. 12° ... 0327.11
— *Same.* (*In* Sparks, J. Collection of essays and tracts in theology) ... 1918.9.1
— Murphy, S. J. The scientific bases of. London, 1873. 8° ... 5812.5
— Newman, F. W. Phases of. London, 1853. 12°. 1526.29
FAITH Gartney's girlhood. Whitney, A. D. T. ... 735.9
FAITH Unwin's ordeal. Craik, G. M. ... 322.3
FAITHFUL, Emily. A reed shaken with the wind ... 737.12
FALKNER Lyle. Lemon, M. ... 312.9
FALL, The, of the house of Usher. Poe, E. A. (*In* Johnson, (E.) R. Little classics) ... 529.4.2

Shelf. No.

FALLEN pride. Southworth, E. D. E. N. 727.1
FALLOUX, Frédéric Alfred Pierre, *vicomte* de, *editor*. Life and letters of Madame Swetchine. Translated by H. W. Preston. Boston, 1868. xv, 369 pp. 16° 1226.2
FALSE heir, The. James, G. P. R. 327.2
FALSTAFF, Revised text of. Lemon, M. *See* HATTON, Joseph 5425.7
FAME and fortune. Alger, H., *jr.* 934.12
FAMILIAR quotations. Bartlett, J. 6th edition. Boston, 1874. 12° .... *R.R., F.3.8
— *Same.* 7th edition. Boston, 1875. 12° .*R.R., F.3.10

Note. — The best collection of the kind. It differs from ordinary collections of quotations, in that it contains only those which have currency in writing or conversation.

FAMILY, A, in love. Craik, D. (M.) 330.22
FAMILY doom, The. Southworth, E. D. E. N. 734.25
FAMILY nurse, The. Child, L. M. Boston, 1837. 16°. 1525.31
FAMINES. The history of the great Irish famine of 1847, with notices of earlier Irish famines. O'Rourke, J. Dublin, 1875. Sm. 8° 5418.12
FANCHON the cricket. Dudevant, A. L. A. D. 536.2
FANCY work, Ladies'. Jones, *Mrs.* C. S., and Williams, H. T. New York, 1876. 8° 1512.6
FANNIE St. John. [Biography.] Delesdernier, E. P. New York, 1874. Sq. 16° 5216.7
FANNY'S birthday gift. Mathews, J. H. 1115.11
FANTASIO. Musset, (L. C.) A. de. Comédies et proverbes. Paris, 1867. 12° 5534.4.1
FAR above rubies. Riddell, J. H. 316.3
FAR from the madding crowd. Hardy, T. 518.24
FARADAY, Michael. Lectures on the chemical history of a candle: added a lecture on platinum. With illustrations. New York, 1861. 223 pp. 16° 1717.1
— Lectures on the various forces of matter, and their relations to each other. Edited by W. Crookes. With illustrations. New York, 1868. 198 pp. 16° 1528.8
— Gladstone, J. H. Michael Faraday. New York, 1872. 16° 5428.1
— Jones, (H.) B. Life and letters of. Philadelphia, 1870. 2 v. 8° 5423.4
— Tyndall, J. Faraday as a discoverer. New York, 1868. 12° 1224.14
— *Same.* New York, 1873. 12° 1523.21
FARJEON, B. L. At the sign of the silver flagon.... 711.3
— Blade-o'-grass 521.7
— Bread-and-cheese and kisses 531.26
— Golden grain 732.7
— An island pearl 530.11
— Jessie Trim 710.33
— Grif 521.8
— Joshua Marvel 521.9
— The king of no-land 710.27
— Love's victory 711.26
FARLEY, Stephen. Discourses and essays on theological and speculative topics. Boston, 1851. iv, 400+ pp. 12° 5815.23
FARM ballads. Carleton, W. New York, 1873. 8°. 1621.1
FARM legends. [Poems.] Carleton, W. New York, 1876. 8° 1621.3
FARMER, John, and MOORE, Jacob Bailey, *editors*. Collections, historical and miscellaneous; and monthly literary journal. Vol. 3. Concord [N. H.], 1824. 388, 88+ pp. 8° 1912.5
— Collections, topographical, historical and biographical, relating principally to New-Hampshire. Vol. 1, 2. Concord, 1822, 23. 2 v. 8°. 612.1
FARMER'S, A, vacation. [Travels in the Channel islands.] Waring, G. E., *jr.* Boston, 1876. 8°.5933.11
FARMING. *See* AGRICULTURE.
FARQUHAR, George. Dramatic works. *See* WYCHERLEY, William 5611.6
FARQUHARSON, Martha, *pseud.* *See* FINLEY, Martha.
FARRAGUT, David Glascoe. Farragut and our naval commanders. Headley, J. T. New York, 1867. 8° 5012.4
FARRAR, Adam Storey. Critical history of free thought in reference to the Christian religion. New York, 1863. xlvi, 487 pp. 12° 1522.2

Shelf. No.

FARRAR, Eliza Ware. Recollections of seventy years. Boston, 1866. viii, 331 pp. 12° 1225.2
FARRAR, Frederic William. Chapters on language. London, 1873. xx, 276 pp. Sm. 8° 6127.3
— Eric, or little by little. A tale of Roslyn school. 15th edition. Edinburgh, 1875. xiv, 393 pp. Illustrated. Sm. 8° 938.11
— The life of Christ. New York [1874]. 2 v. Illustrated. 8° 5810.3
— Seekers after God. New edition. London, 1875. xiii, 336+ pp. Illustrated. [Sunday library.] Sm. 8° 5937.7

Contents. — Seneca; Epictetus; Marcus Aurelius.

FARRAR, John. Elementary treatise on astronomy. Cambridge, 1827. vii, 320 pp. Folded plate. 8°. 6433.2
— Elements of electricity, magnetism, and electro-magnetism. Cambridge, 1826. vii, 395 pp. 8°. 6433.1
FARRAR, Timothy. Report of the case of the trustees of Dartmouth college against W. H. Woodward. Portsmouth, N. H. [*cop.* 1819]. 406+ pp. 8° 6314.2
FARRER, Henrietta Louisa. Bossuet and his contemporaries. London, 1874. xvi, 601 pp. Sm. 8°.5526.14
— The fathers of the church. 2d edition. London, 1875. 3 v. Sm. 8° 6328.25

Contents. — Vol. I. The church militant; Clement of Rome; Ignatius; Polycarp; Justin; Irenæus; Tertullian; Clement of Alexandria; Origen. II. Cyprian; Gregory Thaumaturgus; Dionysius; Athanasius; Basil the great; Gregory Nazianzen. III. Chrysostom; Jerome; Ambrose; Augustine; Cyril; Ephrem.

FASCINATING individual, A: a farce. Danvers, H. New York, N. D. 12° 1635.5
FASHION: a comedy. Ritchie, A. C. Boston, 1855. 12° 1635.1
FASHION and famine. Stephens, A. S. (W.) 726.5
FAST friends. Trowbridge, J. T. 921.10
FAST life, A, on the modern highway. Taylor, J. New York, 1874. 12° 735.35
FATAL marriage, The. Southworth, E. D. E. N. ... 727.21
FATED to be free. Ingelow, J. Boston 717.8
— *Same.* Leipzig 331.19
FATHER and daughter. Bremer, F. 524.26
FATHER Brighthopes. Trowbridge, J. T. 929.2
FATHER Tom and the pope. Ferguson, S. (*In* Johnson, (E.) R. Little classics) 529.4.9
FATHERS, The, of the church. Farrer, H. L. London, 1875. 3 v. Sm. 8° 6328.25
FAUST. [Dramatic poem.] Goethe, J. W. von. Leipzig, 1867. Sq. 16° 1613.21
— *Same.* Boston, 1871, 73. 2 v. 4° 5730.1
FAUST. Gounod, C. (*In* Ditson, O., and co. Standard opera librettos) 6233.3.1
FAVORITA, La. Donizetti, G. (*In* Ditson, O., and co. Standard opera librettos) 6233.3.2
FAWCETT, Henry. Speeches on some current [English] political questions. London, 1873. vi, 278 pp. 8° 5822.11
FAWCETT, Millicent Garrett. Tales in political economy. London, 1874. 104+ pp. Sm. 8° . 5827.4
FAYOUM, Le. Lernoir, P. Paris, 1872. 18° 5935.10
FAYRER, Joseph. The royal tiger of Bengal, his life and death. London, 1875. 99+ pp. Sm. 8°. 5935.9
FEATHERS from a moulting muse. [Poems.] Sargent, H. J. Boston, 1854. 16° 1615.4
FEDERAL government, History of. Freeman, E. A. Vol. I. London, 1863. 8° 5921.11
FELICIA. Edwards, M. de B. 331.14
FELIX Holt. Lewes, M. 310.24
FELLOWES, Gustavus. *See* DELESDERNIER, E. P. Fannie St. John. New York, 1874. Sq. 16°... 5216.7
FELT, Joseph Barlow. Annals of Salem. 2d edition. Salem, 1845, 49. 2 v. Illustrated. Portrait. Sm. 8° 5016.7
— Ecclesiastical history of New England. Boston, 1855. 2 v. 8° 5811.2
— Memorials of William Smith Shaw. Boston, 1852. 346+ pp. 12° 5027.7
FELTON, Cornelius Conway. Life of William Eaton. (*In* Sparks, J. Library of American biography). 5028.1.9
— *editor.* A memorial of J. S. Popkin. *See* POPKIN, John Snelling 6326.4

Shelf. No.

FEMMES savantes, Les: comédie. Molière, J. B. P. Œuvres. Paris, 1869. 12° 5537.2.3

FÉNELON, François (de Salignac de La Mothe). Adventures of Telemachus. Translated by Dr. Hawkesworth. With a life of Fénelon by Lamartine; an essay on his genius and character by Villemain; critical and bibliographical notices, etc. Edited by O. W. Wight. New York, 1872. 559 pp. 12° 1534.8

— Aventures de Télémaque. Suivies du recueil des fables. Paris, 1853. 538+ pp. Portrait. 12°. 2016.6

— *Same.* Paris, 1873. 538+ pp. Portrait. 12°.5526.10

— Selections from [his] writings. With an appendix containing a memoir. Boston, 1829. 283+ pp. 12° 1916.5

FENN, George Manville. The treasure hunters...... 710.28

— *editor.* The world of wit and humour. London [1872]. xv, 480 pp. Illustrated. L. 8° 5212.4

FENTON'S quest. Braddon, M. E. 325.14

FERDINAND and Isabella, History of the reign of. Prescott, W. H. Philadelphia, 1873. 3 v. 8°. 5922.5

FERGUSON, James. The story of the peasant-boy philosopher. Mayhew, H. New York, 1870. 16° 937.15

FERGUSON, Samuel Father Tom and the pope. (*In* Johnson, (E.) R. Little classics) 529.4.9

FERGUSSON, James. History of architecture in all countries, from the earliest times to the present day. 2d edition. London, 1874. Illustrated. 2 v. 8° 6222.3

— History of the modern styles of architecture. 2d edition. With engravings. London, 1873. xix, 584 pp. 8° 6212.3

— The Persian palace of Mashita. (*In* Tristram, H. B. The land of Moab) 5933.4

FERMENTED liquors. Feuchtwanger, L. New York, 1858. 12° 6826.2

FERN, Fanny, *pseud.* *See* PARTON, Sara Payson.

FERN book, A, for everybody. Cooke, M. C. London [1867]. 16° 6619.1

FERNALD, Woodbury M. A new age for the New church. Boston, 1860. 85+ pp. 8° 1530.6

— The true Christian life and how to attain it. Essays. Boston, 1874. iv, 309+ pp. Portrait. 16° 6327.14

— A view at the foundations: or, first causes of character. Boston, 1865. 210 pp. 12° 5837.3

FERRIER, Susan Edmonston. Destiny 518.20

— The inheritance 518.19

— Marriage 521.21

FESSENDEN, Thomas Green. The American kitchen gardener; containing directions for the culture of vegetables. Also, garden fruits. New York, 1855. 120 pp. 12° 1524.11

FETRIDGE, William Pembroke. Harper's hand-book for travellers in Europe and the East. With maps and plans of cities. New York, 1872. 763+ pp. 12° 5935.1

— Rise and fall of the Paris commune in 1871. Illustrated with map and portraits. New York, 1871. 516 pp. 12° 824.8

FETTERED for life. Blake. L. D. 734.23

FEUCHTERSLEBEN, Ernst, *Freiherr* von. The dietetics of the soul. From the 7th edition. New York, 1854. 12° 1527.18

— Principles of medical psychology. From the German by H. E. Lloyd. Revised and edited by B. G. Babington. London, 1847. xx, 392 pp. 8° 6013.8

FEUCHTWANGER, Lewis. Fermented liquors: a treatise on brewing, distilling, rectifying, and manufacturing of sugars, wines, spirits, and all known liquors. With wood-cuts. New York, 1858. 215 pp. 12° 6826.2

FEUDGE, Fannie R. A tour in the China seas. (*In* Many lands and many people) 431.3

FEUILLET, Octave. Led astray; or, "La petite comtesse." The sphinx; or, "Julia de Trecœur." "Bellah." Translated by O. Vibeur 714.12

— A marriage in high life. From the French. By Celia Logan. [International series] 722.2

Shelf. No

FEUILLET, Octave, *continued.*

— Le roman d'un jeune homme pauvre: comédie. With English notes. By F. Bôcher. Boston, 1867. 100 pp. 12° 2015.2

FEVER. Smith, S. Treatise on. Boston, 1831. 8°. 6011.9

— Tweedie, A. Clinical illustrations of. Boston, 1831. 8° 6011.9

FEW friends, A, and how they amused themselves. [Games, etc.] Dodge, M. E. Philadelphia, 1869. 12° 526.10

FEYDEAU, Ernest (Aimé). L'Allemagne en 1871. Paris, 1872. 274+ pp. 18° 5726.1

— Consolation. Paris, 1872. 205+ pp. Portrait. 18° 5536.3

FIBRILIA: a substitute for cotton. Allen, S. M. Boston, 1861. 12° 6435.1

FICHTE, Johann Gottlieb. New exposition of the science of knowledge. Translated from the German by A. E. Kroeger. St. Louis, 1869. iv, 182+ pp. 8° 1932.4

— Popular works. With a memoir by W. Smith. London, 1873. 564+ pp. 8° 5723.4

Contents. — The nature of the scholar; The vocation of man; The doctrine of religion.

FICTION. Dunlop, J. History of. Philadelphia, 1842. 2 v. Sm. 8° 6136.3

— Wheeler, W. A. Dictionary of the noted names of. Boston, 1872. 16° ..................*R.R., F.3.6

See also Novels, Poetry, and the sections on fiction under the different literatures.

FIDELIO. Beethoven, L. van. (*In* Ditson, O., and co. Standard opera librettos) 6233.3.3

FIELD, George. Grammar of colouring, applicable to house painting, decorative architecture, and the arts. With illustrations. New edition, with additions. London, N. D. viii, 180 pp. 12° .. 1715.3

FIELD, Kate. Hap-hazard. Boston, 1873. 253 pp. Sq. 16° 439.1

— Ten days in Spain. Illustrated. Boston, 1875. 277 pp. Sq. 16° 428.7

FIELD, Henrietta M., *wife of Rev. Henry M. Field.* Home sketches in France, and other papers. With some notices of her life and character. New York, 1875. 256 pp. Portrait. 12° 837.1

FIELD, Maunsell Bradhurst. Memories of many men and of some women: being personal recollections. New York, 1874. 339 pp. 12° 1036.1

FIELD, Walter. Stories of the temple; or, lessons from the fabric and furniture of the church. London, 1873. 318+ pp. Illustrated. Sm. 8°. 5815.7

FIELD and forest. Adams, W. T. 924.8

FIELD and forest rambles. Adams, A. L. London, 1873. 8° 6613.1

FIELD of ice, The. Verne, J. London, 1875. 8°. 733.5

FIELDING, Henry. Works. With memoir. By T. Roscoe. New edition, illustrated by G. Cruikshank. London, 1856. xxviii, 1116 pp. Portrait. 8° 5611.7

— History of Tom Jones, a foundling. Leipzig, 1844. 2 v. in 1. Sq. 16° 312.20

See also Allibone, Chambers's Cyclopædia, Forsyth's Novelists [6136.1], and other works on English literature of the last century.

FIELDS, James Thomas. Yesterdays with authors. 11th edition. Boston, 1875 [*cop.* 1871]. 352+ pp. 12° 6136.1

Contents. — Thackeray; Hawthorne; Dickens; Wordsworth; Miss Mitford.

FIFINE at the fair. [Poem.] Browning, R. Boston, 1872. 16° 1615.2

FIFTEEN decisive battles of the world, The. Creasy, *Sir* E. S. New York, 1872. 12° .... 824.

FIFTEEN years. Robinson, T. A. L. von J. [*Talvi.*] New York, 1871. 12° 714.2

FIGHT, A, for a wife. Black, W. Leipzig 330.1

— *Same.* New York .... 711.

FIGHTING Joe. Adams, W. T. .... 924.

FIGHTING the air. Church, F. 331.1

FIGHTING the flames. [London fire brigade.] Ballantyne, R. M. 935.1

Shelf. No.

FIGUIER, (Guillaume) Louis. Earth and sea. Translated, edited, and enlarged by W. H. D. Adams. Illustrated. London, 1870. 715 pp. 8°...... 6631.3
— The human race. Illustrated. New York, 1872. xvi, 548 pp. 8°........................ 6613.2
— The insect world; being a popular account of the orders of insects. Revised and corrected by E. W. Janson. With illustrations. London, 1869. 519+ pp. 8°........................ 1521.8
— *Same.* New edition, revised by P. M. Duncan. With illustrations. London [1872]. 538+ pp. Sm. 8°........................ 6615.1
— Mammalia. Their various orders and habits popularly illustrated by typical species. With engravings. London, 1870. xi, 606 pp. 8°.. 1521.2
— The ocean world: being a description of the sea, and its living inhabitants. Illustrated. London, 1869. xii, 615 pp. 8°........................ 1521.5
— Primitive man. Revised translation. Illustrated. London, 1870. xix, 348 pp. 8°............ 5912.3
— Reptiles and birds. Edited by P. Gillmore. With illustrations. London [1869]. xiii, 648+ pp. 8°........................ 1521.3
— The to-morrow of death; or, the future life according to science. Translated by S. R. Crocker. Boston, 1872. viii, 395 pp. Illustrated. 12°. 5816.3
— The vegetable world; being a history of plants, with their botanical descriptions and peculiar properties. New edition. Illustrated. London, 1868. viii, 576 pp. 8°........................ 1521.6
— The world before the deluge. The geological portion revised and much new matter added, by H. W. Bristow. With illustrations. London [1866]. viii, 449 pp. 8°..........1521.1 and 6617.2

Note. — Figuier's books are in low repute with scientists; but their somewhat imaginative details render them attractive to the popular sense.

FILE no. 113. Gaboriau, É........................ 710.40
FILLE, La, du régiment. Donizetti, G. (*In* Ditson, O., and co. Standard opera librettos)........6233.3.2
FINE arts. Eastlake, *Sir* C. L. Contributions to the literature of the. London, 1870. 8°......... 6232.1
— Hamerton, P. G. Etching and etchers. Boston, 1876. 8°........................ 6233.1
— Jameson, A. (M.) Legends of the monastic orders, as represented in the. Boston, 1866. 16°. 1517.7
— Keddie, *Miss* —. Modern painters and their paintings. Boston, 1874. 16°............ 6216.4
— Lossing, B. J. Outline history of the. New York, 1857. 12°........................ 1517.1
— Reynolds, *Sir* J. Discourses. London, 1842. 4°. 6230.1
— Ruskin, J. Frondes agrestes. Readings in 'modern painters.' Orpington, Kent., 1875. Sm. 8°........................6236.21
— Torrey, J. A theory of fine art. New York, 1874. 16°........................ 6237.1
— Tyrwhitt, R. St. J. A handbook of pictorial art. Oxford, 1875. 8°........................6213.12
— Wyatt, M. D. Fine art. A sketch of its history, theory, practice, and application to industry. London, 1870. 8°........................ 6232.2
— *Collections of engravings, photographs, etc.* Doré, (P.) G. The Doré gallery. London [1871]. L. 4°........................ 6220.6
— — Gelée, C. Liber veritatis. London, 1872. 3 v. F°........................ 6220.6

See also Architecture, Music, Painting, Sculpture.

FINE feathers do not make fine birds. Neily, K. J. 936.28
FINLAND, Handbook for. Murray, J. London, 1868. 12°........................ 5917.5
FINLEY, Martha. (*Martha Farquharson.*) An old-fashioned boy........................ 926.24
Elsie Dinsmore........................ 926.16
Elsie's girlhood........................ 926.18
Elsie's womanhood: a sequel to "Elsie's girlhood"........................ 1117.3
Holidays at Roselands........................ 926.17
Our Fred; or, seminary life at Thurston. Sequel to An "Old-fashioned boy"................ 926.19
Wanted — a pedigree........................ 736.27

FIOR d'Aliza. Lamartine, A. (M. L.) de. New York, 1868. 16°........................ 517.14
FIRE. Bird, J. Protection against fire. New York, 1873. Sm. 8°........................ 1726.1
— Tobey, E. S. The Boston hydraulic protection against fire. Boston, 1873. 12°............ 1712.1
FIRE in the woods. De Mille, J................. 934.20
FIRES and fire departments. Bugbee, J. M. Boston, 1873. 8°........................ 1711.2
FIRES, fire engines, and fire brigades. Young, C. F. T. London, 1866. 8°..................1521.10
FIRESIDE science. [Every day phenomena.] Nichols, J. R. New York, 1872. Sm. 8°........ 1525.9
FIRESIDE saints. Jerrold, D. (W.) Boston, 1873. 16°. 728.6
FIRESIDE travels. [Essays, etc., on places.] Lowell, J. R. Boston, 1864. 12°................ 426.4
FIRST fam'lies of the Sierras. [Fiction.] Miller, C. H. 717.12
FISH and fishing. Davy, *Sir* H. Salmonia; or, days of fly fishing. Boston, 1870. 16°............ 1515.4
— Hallock, C. The fishing tourist: angler's guide and reference book. New York, 1873. 16°...1515.12
— Herbert, H. W. Fish and fishing of the United States and British provinces. New York, 1866. L. 12°........................ 1512.1
— Holdsworth, E. W. H. Deep-sea fishing and fishing boats. London, 1874. 8°.............5932.13
— Norris, T. The American angler's book. Philadelphia, 1865. 8°........................ 1511.5
— Prime, W. C. I go a-fishing. New York, 1873. Sm. 8°........................ 6413.3
— Scott, G. C. Fishing in American waters. New York, 1875. 539 pp. 8°.................... 6412.4
— Walton, I., and Cotton, C. The complete angler. London, 1861. Sm. 8°........................ 6416.2

See also Salmon, Trout.

FISHER, Frances C. (*Christian Reid.*) Carmen's inheritance........................ 520.4
— A daughter of Bohemia........................ 732.23
— Ebb-tide and other stories........................ 711.28
— Hearts and hands. A story........................ 711.8
— Mabel Lee. A novel........................ 711.29
— Morton house........................ 711.30
— Nina's atonement, and other stories............ 732.3
— A question of honor. A novel................ 713.8
— Valerie Aylmer. A novel........................ 711.31
FISHER, George Park. Essays on the supernatural origin of Christianity, with special reference to the theories of Renan, Strauss, and the Tübingen school. New York, 1866. xii, 586 pp. 8°. 6324.6
— The reformation. New York, 1873. xxxiv, 620 pp. 8°........................ 5813.7
FISHER, Theodore Willis. Plain talk about insanity. With remarks on hospitals and asylums, and the medico-legal aspect of insanity. Boston, 1872. 97 pp. Illustrated. 8°........................ 6033.1
FISHER boys, The, of Pleasant cove. Kellogg, E... 922.31
FISKE, John. Myths and myth-makers: old tales and superstitions interpreted by comparative mythology. Boston, 1873. vi, 251+ pp. 16°. 5924.1
— Outlines of cosmic philosophy, based on the doctrine of evolution, with criticisms on the positive philosophy. Boston, 1875. 2 v. 8°..... 5824.2
— The unseen world, and other essays. Boston, 1876. 349+ pp. 12°........................ 5836.1
FITCH, Samuel Sheldon. Six lectures on the uses of the lungs; and [on] pulmonary consumption [etc.]. With illustrations. New York, 1847. 324 pp. 12°........................ 6027.1
FITTON, James. Sketches of the establishment of the church in New England. Boston, 1872. 346 pp. 1 plate. Portraits. Sm. 8°......... 5816.5

Note. — An account of the establishment, and the subsequent history, of the Roman catholic church in New England.

FITZGERALD, Percy. Charles Lamb; his friends, his haunts, and his books. 2d edition. London, 1866. vii, 229 pp. Portraits. Sq. 16°....... 5425.8
— The Kembles, including the lives of Mrs. Siddons, and her brother J. P. Kemble. London [1871]. 2 v. Sm. 8°........................5425.22
— Life and adventures of Alexander Dumas. London, 1873. 2 v. Portrait. 8°............... 5522.5

Shelf. No.

FITZGERALD, Percy, *continued.*
— Life of David Garrick. London, 1868. 2 v. Portraits. 8° 5422.8
— Life of Laurence Sterne. With illustrations. London, 1864. 2 v. Portrait. 1 folded sheet. Sm. 8° 1224.1
— The romance of the English stage. London, 1874. 2 v. 8° 5622.4
FITZGERALD, R. A. Wickets in the West; or, the twelve in America. London, 1873. ix, 335 pp. Illustrated. Sm. 8° 5035.6
FITZMAURICE, Edmond (George), *lord.* Life of William, earl of Shelburne, afterwards first marquess of Lansdowne. With extracts from his papers and correspondence. Vol. I. London, 1875. 8° 5333.4

Contents. — Vol. I. 1737–66.

FITZMAURICE, William Petty, *earl of Shelburne, 1st marquis of Lansdowne,* Life of. Fitzmaurice, E. (G.), *lord.* Vol. I. London, 1875. 8° 5333.4
FITZWILLIAM, William Wentworth, *viscount Milton,* and CHEADLE, Walter Butler. The North-west passage by land. Narrative of an expedition from the Atlantic to the Pacific, through British territory, by one of the northern passes in the Rocky mountains. 6th edition. London, 1866. xxiii, 400+ pp. Illustrations. Map. 8° 5931.15
FIVAS, V. de. New grammar of French grammars: comprising the substance of all the most approved French grammars extant. New York, 1868. 290 pp. 12° 2016.3
FIVE centuries of the English language and literature. Tauchnitz, (C.) B., *baron* von. Leipzig, 1860. Sq. 16° 1918.1
FIVE, The, great monarchies of the ancient Eastern world. Rawlinson, G. London, 1871. 3 v. 8°. 5922.3
FIVE hundred majority; or, the days of Tammany. Niles, W. New York, 1872. 8° 521.12
FIVE-MINUTE chats with young women. Lewis, D. New York, 1874. 12° 1522.9
FIVE old friends. Thackeray, A. I. Leipzig 331.7
— *Same.* (*In her* Works.) London 512.1.3
FIVE weeks in a balloon. [Burlesque on African travel.] Verne, J. New York, 1869. 8° 735.26
FLAG, The, of distress: a tale of the South sea. Reid, M. 921.18
FLAGG, Wilson. The birds and seasons of New England. With illustrations. Boston, 1875. vi, 457+ pp. 8° 6614.11
— The woods and by-ways of New England. With illustrations. Boston, 1872. xviii, 442 pp. Sm. 8° 5035.2
FLAMMARION, Camille. The atmosphere. From the French. Edited by J. Glaisher. With chromolithographs and woodcuts. London, 1873. xix, 505 pp. L. 8° 6832.2
— Stories of infinity. From the French by S. R. Crocker. Boston, 1873. 287 pp. 16° 6837.1

Contents. — Lumen; History of a comet; In infinity.

— The wonders of the heavens. From the French by Mrs. N. Lockyer. With illustrations. New York, 1871. iv, 289 pp. 16° 1714.13
— *joint author.* Travels in the air. *See* GLAISHER, James 5911.1
FLANDERS. Conscience, H. Scènes de la vie flamande. Première série. Paris, 1864. 18° ... 5536.12
— Stephens, F. G. Flemish and French pictures. London, 1875. 4° 6211.8
FLAT iron, A, for a farthing. [Fiction.] Ewing, J. H. 1117.30
FLAUTO magico, Il. Mozart, J. C. W. A. (*In* Ditson, O., and co. Standard opera librettos) 6233.3.2
FLAVEL, John. *See* CHRISTOPHERS, S. W. Homes of old English writers. London [1874]. Sm. 8°. 5428.16
FLAXMAN, John. Lectures on sculpture. With an introductory lecture and two addresses on the death of Thomas Banks and of Antonio Canova, and an address on the death of Flaxman by Sir Richard Westmacott. With 53 plates. New edition. London, 1865. xv, 308 pp. Portrait. Sm. 8° 6215.5

Shelf. No.

FLEMING, G. Practical horseshoeing. With illustrations. New York, 1872. 108 pp. 12° 1515.11
FLEMING, May Agnes. The dark secret; or, the mystery of Fontelle hall 720.3
— Guy Earlscourt's wife 522.6
— A mad marriage 724.31
— Norine's revenge, and Sir Noel's heir 723.22
— One night's mystery 733.37
— A terrible secret 724.19
— A wonderful woman 737.19
FLETCHER, Eliza Dawson. Autobiography, with letters and other family memorials. Edited by the survivor of her family [Lady Mary Richardson]. Boston, 1876. viii, 376 pp. Portraits. 16° .. 1022.6
FLETCHER, James Cooley, and KIDDER, Daniel Parish. Brazil and the Brazilians. Illustrated. 8th edition. Revised and enlarged. Boston, 1868. xii, 640 pp. Portrait. Maps. 8° 411.5
FLETCHER, John. Works. *See* BEAUMONT, Francis. London, 1872. 2 v. 8° 5621.2
FLEUR-DE-THÉ. Ronger, F. (*In* Ditson, O., and co. Standard opera librettos) 6233.3.1
FLEURANGE. Craven, P. 518.17
FLIGHT of a Tartar tribe. De Quincey, T. (*In* Johnson, (E.) R. Little classics) 529.4.1
FLINT, Austin. Practical treatise on the diagnosis, pathology, and treatment of diseases of the heart. Philadelphia, 1859. 473 pp. 1 plate. 8° 6022.4
— Treatise on the principles and practice of medicine. Philadelphia, 1866. 867 pp. 8° 6021.1
FLINT, Austin, *jr.* Experimental researches into a new excretory function of the liver. [No title-page. From the American journal of the medical sciences for Oct., 1862.] 61 pp. 8° 6023.19
— The physiology of man. New York, 1873. 4 v. 8° 6011.4

Contents. — Vol. I. Introduction; The blood; Circulation; Respiration. II. Alimentation; Digestion; Absorption; Lymph and chyle. III. Secretion; Excretion; Ductless glands; Nutrition; Animal heat; Movements; Voice and speech. IV. Nervous system.

— Recherches expérimentales sur une nouvelle fonction du foie. Paris, 1868. 122 pp. 8° 6023.19
FLINT, Robert. The philosophy of history in Europe. Vol. I. Edinburgh, 1874. 8° 5921.7
FLINT chips. [Pre-historic archæology.] Stevens, E. T. London, 1870. 8° 5913.7
FLIRT, The. Grey, *Mrs.* 521.32
FLITCH, The, of bacon. Ainsworth, W. H. 322.25
FLOATING city, A. Verne, J. New York, 1874. 8°. 713.4
FLOATING light, The, of Goodwin sands. Ballantyne, R. M. 935.16
FLOOD, Henry. *See* LECKY, W. E. H. Leaders of public opinion in Ireland. New York, 1872. 12° 1025.9
FLORA'S interpreter, and fortuna flora. Hale, S. J. Boston [*cop.* 1843]. 12° 1625.10
FLORAL decorations for the dwelling house. Hassard, A. London, 1875. Sm. 8° 6625.5
FLORENCE, *Italy.* Machiavelli, N. History of. London, 1871. Sm. 8° 5516.8
— Napier, H. E. Florentine history. London, 1846, 47. 6 v. 16° 5516.2
— Trollope, T. A. History of the commonwealth of. London, 1865. 4 v. 8° 5512.3

Note. — Napier's "Florentine history," coming down to 1824, is the best modern English narrative of her history; but see also the general histories of Italy; and for the period of the Commonwealth, Trollope's "History."

The Florence of the past is described in the lives of her principal citizens, like Dante, Michel Angelo, Galileo, etc.; see also Everett's oration on "The uses of astronomy" [1921.1.3]; and of a more recent day in the letters of Gray, of Shelley, and in Leigh Hunt's "Autobiography" [1225.20].

Murray's "Handbook" [5527.4] will map out the description of the modern city; but beside Taine, the general travels in Italy, of Hillard [426.8]; of Hawthorne, in his "French and Italian note books" [1839.3]; of Dickens [338.18], etc., will afford illustrative matter. See also Harper's monthly, vol. 8, by Jarves; Jameson's "Diary of an ennuyée" [427.3], etc. Also Motley's articles on her historical and other associations in Atlantic monthly, Nov. and Dec., 1857.

For the literary associations of Florence, see De Staël's "Corinne" [527.17]; Rogers's "Italy"; Byron's "Childe Harold" [1614.13.2] and "Prophecy of Dante" [1614.13.3]; and George Eliot's "Romola" [310.23].

There is an article in the Atlantic monthly, Dec., 1864, on English authors in Florence; see also lives of Landor, Mrs. Browning, etc.

Shelf. No.

FLORIAN, Jean Pierre Claris de. Guillaume Tell, ou la Suisse libre. Boston, 1849. 92 pp. Sm. 12°. 2019.2
— Numa Pompilius, second roi de Rome. Paris, 1812. 332 pp. Illustrated. Sm. 12° 2019.1
FLORIDA. Giddings, J. R. The exiles of. Columbus, 1858. 16° 825.8
— Irving, T. The conquest of. London, 1850. 16°. 826.3
— Townshend, F. F. Wild life in. London, 1875. 8° 5932.14
FLORUS, Lucius Annæus. [Works.] *See* SALLUSTIUS CRISPUS, Caius. London, 1872. Sm. 8°.... 6117.7
FLOTOW, Friedrich Ferdinand Adolf von. Martha. (*In* Ditson, O., and co. Standard opera librettos) 6233.3.5
FLOWER, The, of the family. Prentiss, E.......... 728.10
FLOWER people, The. Mann, M.................. 931.8
FLOWERS. Beecher, H. W. Plain and pleasant talk about fruits, flowers and farming. New York, 1859. 12° 1514.22
— Hassard, A. Floral decorations for the dwelling house. London, 1875. Sm. 8° 6625.5
— Rand, E. S., *jr.* Flowers for the parlor and garden. Boston, 1870. 12° 1515.6
— — Popular flowers, and how to cultivate them. Boston, 1873. Sm. 4° 1516.17
— Robinson, W. Hardy flowers. Descriptions and directions for their arrangement, culture, etc. London, 1872. Sq. 16° 6626.2
— Williams, H. T. Window gardening. Devoted specially to the culture of flowers and ornamental plants, for in door and parlor decoration. New York, 1876. 8° 1512.5

See also Gardening.

FLOWER, fruit and thorn pieces. Richter, J. P. F. (*Jean Paul.*) Leipzig, 1871. 2 v. in 1. Sq. 16° 316.8
FLOYD, Cornelia. Mice at play. A story for the whole family. By Neil Forest [*pseud.*].......1117.11
FLY leaves. [Society verses.] Calverly, C. S...... 1617.3
FOGGY night, The, at Offord. Wood, E. P. 333.13
FOLLE-FARINE. Ramo, L. de la.................. 327.22
FOLLEN, Charles (Theodore Christian). Works, with a memoir of his life. Boston, 1842. 5 v. Portrait. 12° 5735.4

Contents.—Vol. I. Life. II. Sermons. III. Lectures on moral philosophy; Fragment of a work on psychology. IV. Schiller's life and dramas. V. Miscellaneous.

FOLLOWING the flag. From August, 1861, to November, 1862, with the army of the Potomac. Coffin, C. C. Boston, 1865. 12° 913.17
FOLLY as it flies; hit at. Parton, S. P. New York, 1872. 12° 524.19
FONBLANQUE, Albany, *jr.* A tangled skein........ 720.8
FONTAINE, James. Memoirs of a Huguenot family; translated and compiled from [his] autobiography, and family manuscripts, comprising an original journal of travels in Virginia, New York, etc., in 1715 and 1716. By Ann Maury. With an appendix. New York, 1872. 512 pp. 12° 5525.3
FONTENELLE, Julia de. Manuel du bijoutier, du joaillier, de l'orfèvre, du graveur sur métaux et du changeur. Paris, 1832. 2 v. 24°. [Manuel Roret] 6219.2
— Nouveau manuel complet de physique amusante. Nouvelle édition, revue, corrigée et ornée de planches. Par F. Malepeyre. Paris, 1850. x, 430 pp. 24°. [Manuel Roret] 6439.5
FONVIELLE, Wilfrid de. Thunder and lightning. Translated from the French, and edited by T. L. Phipson. Illustrated. New York, 1872. 285 [283] pp. 16° 1714.22
— *joint author.* Travels in the air. *See* GLAISHER, James.. 5911.1
FOOD. Cameron, C. A. The chemistry of food in relation to the breeding and feeding of live stock. London, 1868. 16° 6437.1
— Hassall, A. H. Food: its adulterations, and the methods for their detection. London, 1876. Sm. 8° 6035.8

Shelf. No.

FOOD, *continued.*
— Smith, E. Foods. New York, 1873. 12° 6436.6
— Thomson, R. D. Experimental researches on the food of animals. New York, 1856. 12° 1524.13

See also Eating.

FOOTE, Andrew Hull, Life of. Hoppin, J. M. New York, 1874. 8° 1012.3
FOOTFALLS on the boundary of another world. [Spiritualistic.] Owen, R. D. Philadelphia, 1872. 12° 1533.7
FOOT-PRINTS of the Creator. [Geology.] Miller, H. Boston, 1859. 12° 1526.16
FOOTPRINTS of famous men. Edgar, J. G. New York, 1872. 16° 913.13
FOR a woman's sake. Phillips, W.........721.5 and 731.6
FOR better or worse. Croly, J. C. Boston, 1875. 16°. 1537.22
FOR ever and ever. Church, F. 337.17
FOR love and life. Oliphant, M. (O. W.) Leipzig. 328.30
— *Same.* New York.............................. 731.36
FOR richer, for poorer. Parr, H. 315.29
FOR the king's dues. Macdonell, A............... 532.12
FORAYERS, The. Simms, W. G.................... 716.26
FORBES, Archibald. Soldiering and scribbling. A series of sketches. Leipzig, 1872. 286 pp. Sq. 16° 319.7
FORBES, James David. Biography of Sir Humphry Davy. (*In* Macaulay, T. B., *lord*, and others. New biographies of illustrious men) 5428.4
— Page, H. A. Noble workers. London, 1875. Sm. 8° 5936.3
— Shairp, J. C., Tait, P. G., and Adams-Reilly, A. Life and letters of. London, 1873. 8° 5332.4
FORBES, *Sir* John. A physician's holiday; or, a month in Switzerland in the summer of 1848. With a map and illustrations. London, 1849. xii, 520 pp. 12° 226.2
— Physiological effects of alcoholic drinks. *See* MASSACHUSETTS temperance society..........1527.15
FORBES, Robert B. Shipwreck by lightning. Papers relative to Harris's lightning conductors. Boston, 1853. ix, 86+ pp. 8° 1711.3
— Voyage of the Jamestown on her errand of mercy [to Ireland]. Boston, 1847. ix, 27 [21], cliv pp. 1 plate. 8° 421.4
FORCE. Faraday, M. Lectures on the various forces of matter, and their relations to each other. New York, 1868. 16° 1528.8
— Grove, W. R., and others. The correlation and conservation of forces. New York, 1873. 12°.1524.22
— Guillemin, A. The forces of nature. London, 1872. L. 8° 1520.1
— Tice, J. H. The relations between matter and force. (*In* Estes, D. Half hour recreations in popular science) 6813.7
FORCED marriage, The: a comedy. Molière, J. B. P. Dramatic works. Edinburgh, 1875. 8°......5530.3.2
FORD, John. Dramatic works. *See* MASSINGER, Philip. London, 1869. 8° 5611.9
FORD, Richard. Handbook for Spain. 4th edition. With maps and plans. London, 1869. 2 v. 16°. 5917.1
FORDYCE, George. Treatise on the digestion of food. 2d edition. London, 1791. x, 204+ pp. 12°. 6034.1
FOREGONE conclusion, A. Howells, W. D......... 724.23
FOREIGN reminiscences. Vassal-Fox, H. R., 3*d lord Holland*. London, 1851. Sm. 8° 5435.6
FOREIGNER, The, in far Cathay. [China.] Medhurst, W. H. New York, 1873. 12° 424.19
FORENSIC oratory. Hortensius: an historical essay on the office and duties of an advocate. Forsyth, W. London, 1874. 8° 6314.3
FOREST, Neil, *pseud.* *See* FLOYD, Cornelia.
FOREST days. James, G. P. R.................... 327.14
FOREST exiles, The. Reid, M.................... 937.20
FOREST glen series. *See* KELLOGG, Elijah.
FOREST HILLS cemetery, *Boston*. Its establishment, progress, scenery, monuments, etc. With illustrations. Roxbury, 1855. iv, 237+ pp. 12°.5016.12
FOREST voices. Putlitz, G. (H. G.) zu. Albany, 1866. 16° 1538.23
FORESTER, Frank, *pseud.* *See* HERBERT, Henry William.

Shelf. No.

FORESTERS, The, an American tale. Belknap, J. Boston, 1796. 16° ... 529.9
FORGIVEN at last. Hadermann, J. R. ... 528.10
FORLORN hope, The. Yates, E. ... 318.23
FORMBY, Henry, *editor*. The pictorial Bible and church-history stories. Part IV, and vol. II. The life, passion, death, and resurrection of our Lord Jesus Christ. Being an abridged harmony of the four gospels in the words of the sacred text. With engravings on wood. London [1874]. viii, 182+ pp. Sq. 16° ... 6328.22
FORMOSA, *China*. The straits of Malacca, Indo-China, and China. Thomson, J. New York, 1875. 8° ... 5921.4
FORNEY, John Weiss. Anecdotes of public men. New York, 1873. 444 pp. 12° ... 1015.2
FORREST, George. Handbook of gymnastics. London, 1864. 64 pp. Illustrated. 16° ... 1519.3
— Handbook of swimming and skating. London, 1863. 61 pp. Illustrated. 16° ... 1519.1
FORRESTER, *Mrs.* —. Diana Carew ... 722.8
— Dolores ... 724.30
— Fair women ... 710.24
— From Olympus to Hades ... 710.23
FORRESTER, Francis, *pseud.* *See* WISE, Daniel.
FORS clavigera. [Essays.] Ruskin, J. New York, 1871, 72. 2 v. 12° ... 6236.10
FORSTER, John. Life and times of Oliver Goldsmith. Leipzig, 1873. 2 v. Sq. 16° ... 1028.2
— *Same.* 5th edition: illustrated. 2 v. London, 1871. 8° ... 1022.1
— Life of Charles Dickens. Leipzig, 1872, 73. 4 v. in 2. Portraits. Sq. 16° ... 1238.4
— Life of Jonathan Swift. Vol. I. New York, 1876. Portrait. Fac-similes. 8° ... 5333.6

Contents. — Vol. I. 1667–1711.

— Walter Savage Lander. A biography. Boston, 1869. v, 691+ pp. Portrait. 1 plate. 8° .. 5423.1
FORSYTH, Joseph. Remarks on antiquities, arts, and letters, during an excursion in Italy, in the years 1802 and 1803. From the 2d London edition. Boston, 1818. 443 pp. 8° ... 421.3
FORSYTH, William. Hortensius: an historical essay on the office and duties of an advocate. 2d edition. With illustrations. London, 1874. xviii, 412+ pp. 8° ... 6314.3
— Life of Marcus Tullius Cicero. 3d edition. With illustrations. London, 1869. xiv, 557+ pp. Portrait. 8° ... 5932.8
— The novels and novelists of the eighteenth century, in illustration of the manners and morals of the age. London, 1871. viii, 347 pp. Sm. 8°. 6136.1
FORTIFICATION. Annals of a fortress. Viollet-le-Duc, E. E. Boston, 1876. 8° ... 6223.4
FORTNIGHTLY review. New series. Vol. 13–16. London, 1873, 74. 4 v. 8° ... 6713.1
FORTUNE seeker, The. Southworth, E. D. E. N. ... 727.6
FORTUNES, The, of Glencore. Lever, C. (J.) Leipzig. 332.12
— *Same.* London ... 516.15
FORTUNES, The, of Nigel. Scott, *Sir* W. Boston .. 523.2
— *Same.* Leipzig ... 324.12
"FORTY-FIVE, The." Stanhope, P. H., *earl.* London, 1869. Sm. 8° ... 5418.7
FORTY-FIVE guardsmen, The. Dumas, A. (D.) ... 510.6
FORTY-SEVEN Rônins, The. Mitford, A. B. (*In* Johnson, (E.) R. Little classics) ... 529.4.11
FOSDICK, Charles A. (*Harry Castlemon.*) Go-ahead series. Go-ahead ... 934.7
— – No moss ... 934.8
— – Tom Newcombe ... 923.7
— The gun-boat series. Frank before Vicksburg ... 925.26
— – Frank in the woods ... 925.24
— – Frank on a gun-boat ... 925.25
— – Frank on the lower Mississippi ... 925.22
— – Frank on the prairie ... 925.23
— – Frank the young naturalist ... 925.21
— The Rocky mountain series. Frank among the rancheros ... 913.2
— – Frank at Don Carlos' rancho ... 913.1
— – Frank in the mountains ... 913.3

Shelf. No.

FOSDICK, Charles A., *continued.*
— The sportsman's club afloat ... 913.34
— The sportsman's club series. The sportsman's club among the trappers ... 913.36
— – The sportsman's club in the saddle ... 913.35
FOSS, Edward. Memories of Westminster hall. A collection of incidents and historical sketches, relating to Westminster hall, its famous judges and lawyers and its great trials, with an historical introduction. New York, 1874. 2 v. Illustrated. Fac-simile. 8° ... 5421.2
FOSTER, James. The death of Christ, considered as a sacrifice. (*In* Noyes, G. R. Collection of theological essays) ... 6325.12
— Essays. (*In* Sparks, J. Collection of essays and tracts in theology) ... 1918.9.5
FOSTER, John. Critical essays contributed to the Eclectic review. Edited by G. E. Ryland. London, 1871. 2 v. Sm. 8° ... 5614.3
— Essay on the evils of popular ignorance: and a discourse on the communication of Christianity to the people of Hindoostan. New edition, revised and enlarged. London, 1865. xx, 394+ ppp. 16° ... 5614.2
— Essay on the importance of considering the subject of religion. 2d American edition. Boston, 1828. 172 pp. 12° ... 1916.8
— Essays, in a series of letters. London, 1870. xvi, 342 pp. 16° ... 5614.1

Contents. — On a man's writing memoirs of himself; On decision of character; On the application of the epithet romantic; Causes by which evangelical religion has been rendered unacceptable to persons of cultivated taste.

— *Same.* (*In* The Alexandrian) ... 1910.4.2

Contents. — On a man's writing memoirs of himself; On decision of character; On the application of the epithet romantic; Causes by which evangelical religion has been rendered unacceptable to persons of cultivated taste; On popular ignorance.

— Life and correspondence. Edited by J. E. Ryland. London, 1861. Portrait. 2 v. 16° ... 5426.5
— The philosophy of popular ignorance. Revised. Boston, 1841. 318+ pp. 12° ... 1539.3
FOSTER, Vere. Drawing copy book[s]. London, N. D. 4 v. Obl. 8° ... 6217.6
FOTHERGILL, Jessie. Healey. A romance ... 721.11
FOTHERGILL, John Milner. The maintenance of health. A medical work for lay readers. New York, 1875. 366+ pp. 8° ... 6035.7
FOUDRAS, Théodore Louis Auguste, *marquis* de. Arme Therese! Uebersetzt von G. F. W. Rödiger. Pest, 1852. 2 v. in 1. 16° ... 2027.6
FOUL play. Reade, C., and Boucicault, D. (L.) Boston, 1874. 12° ... 724.18
FOUND dead. Payn, J. ... 312.19
FOUNDATIONS and concrete works. Dobson, E. London, 1867. 12° ... 1716.27
FOUQUÉ, Friedrich (Heinrich Carl), *Freiherr* de. *See* LA MOTTE FOUQUÉ.
FOUQUEAU DE PUSSY, J. J. Le grand-père et ses quatre petits-fils. Livre de lecture, à l'usage des écoles. Carefully prepared for American schools, and furnished with notes, by F. S. Williams. Boston, 1854. xii, 420 pp. 12° ... 2014.3
FOUR-FIFTEEN express, The. Edwards, A. B. (*In* Johnson, (E.) R. Little classics) ... 529.4.8
FOUR-FOOTED lovers, The. Albertsen, F., *pseud.* ... 910.4
FOUR years of fighting, from the battle of Bull Run to the fall of Richmond. Coffin, C. C. Boston, 1866. 8° ... 813.7
FOUR years in the saddle. [Confederate raider.] Gilmor, H. New York, 1866. 12° ... 817.17
FOURBERIES, Les, de Scapin: comédie. Molière, J. B. P. Œuvres. Paris, 1869. 12° ... 5537.2.3
FOWLER, William Chauncey. Memorials of the Chaunceys, including President Chauncy, his ancestors and descendants. Boston, 1858, vii, 304 pp. Portrait. Folded sheet. 8° ... 610.3
FOWNES, George. Rudimentary chemistry. With an appendix on the application of chemistry to agriculture. New edition. London, 1872. vi, 116+ pp. 12° ... 1715.25

Shelf. No.

Fox, Charles. Portrait of George Washington, from an original drawing, as he appeared while reviewing the continental army on Boston common, in 1776; a history of the portrait, and documentary evidence in proof of the correctness of the likeness. Boston, 1851. Portrait. 37 pp. L. 8° 1010.1

Fox, Charles James. History of the early part of the reign of James II; with an introductory chapter. Added, an appendix. Philadelphia, 1808. xxxii, 201, cci pp. 8° 823.1

— Lawrence, E. Lives of the British historians. New York, 1855. 12° 1224.7.2

— Rae, W. F. Wilkes, Sheridan, Fox: the opposition under George III. New York, 1874. 16° .. 5415.8

— Russell, J., *earl*. Life and times of. London, 1866. 3 v. Sm. 8° 5337.1

Fox, Cornelius B. Ozone and antozone, their history and nature. When, where, why, how is ozone observed in the atmosphere? Illustrated. London, 1873. xvi, 329 pp. 8° 6433.8

Fox, Henry Richard (Vassal), 3*d lord Holland*. *See* Vassal-Fox, Henry Richard, 3*d lord Holland*.

Fox, Gustavus Vasa, Narrative of the mission to Russia, in 1866, of. Loubat, J. F. New York, 1873. 8° 5911.3

Fox, William Johnson. Christ and Christianity. Sermons on the mission, character, and doctrine, of Jesus of Nazareth. Boston, 1833. 2 v. 12°. 5815.12

— Christian morality. Sermons. Boston, 1833. 391 pp. 12° 5815.13

Fox-hunting. Stevens, C. A. 927.25

Fra diavolo. Auber, D. F. E. (*In* Ditson, O., and co. Standard opera librettos) 6233.3.3

Fractures of the joints, Treatise on. Cooper, *Sir* A. (P.) Boston, 1844. 8° 6021.3

Framingham, *Mass.*, History of. Barry, W. Boston, 1847. 8° 5011.6

Framly parsonage. Trollope, A. 334.12

France. *Exhibition of industry and art*. Commission impériale sur l'exposition universelle de 1867. Œuvres d'art. Groupe I. Classes 1–5. Paris [1867]. 240+ pp. 18° 1737.5

Biography.

— Aumale, H. (E. P. L.) d'Orléans, *duc* d'. History of the princes de Condé in the XVIth and XVIIth centuries. London, 1872. 2 v. 8° 5522.9

— Bush, (A.) F. Memoirs of the queens of. Philadelphia, 1854. 2 v. 12° 1224.10

— Challice, A. E. Illustrious women of. 1790–1873. London, 1873. Sm. 8° 5525.7

— Kavanagh, J. French women of letters: biographical sketches. Leipzig, 1862. Sq. 16° ... 1238.3

— The men of the third republic; or, the present leaders of France. Philadelphia, 1873. Sm. 8°. 5517.1

— Sainte-Beuve, C. A. Portraits of celebrated women. Boston, 1868. 16° 1226.5

— – Portraits contemporains. Paris, 1870. 5 v. 12°. 5538.7

— – Portraits de femmes. Paris, 1870. 12° 5538.17

Geography, description, travel, etc.

— Adams, W. T. Palace and cottage; or, Young America in. Boston, 1873. 16° 925.10

— Baedeker, C. Handbook for travellers [in] Northern France. Coblenz, 1872. 16° 5527.7

— Collins, C. A. A cruise upon wheels: the chronicle of some autumn wanderings among the deserted post-roads of. Leipzig, 1874. 2 v. in 1. Sq. 16°. 428.6

— Craik, D. (M.) Fair France. Impressions of a traveller. New York, 1871. 12° 424.20

— *Same*. Leipzig, 1872. Sq. 16° 323.14

— Field, H. M. Home sketches in. New York, 1875. 12° 837.1

— Gautier, H. Les curiosités de l'exposition universelle de 1867. Paris, 1867. 18° 1518.13

— Head, *Sir* F. B. A faggot of French sticks; containing a series of descriptive sketches of the principal public institutions of Paris, and of the system of instruction of the French army. London, 1855. 2 v. 12° 5526.11

France. *Geography, description, travel, etc., continued.*

— Hamerton, P. G. A painter's camp in. Boston, 1871. 16° 426.19

— – Round my house; notes of rural life in France in peace and war. Boston, 1876. 16° 5527.10

— Hawthorne, N. Passages from [his] French notebooks. Boston, 1876. 2 v. 16° 1839.3

— Hézecques, C. A. F. F., *comte* d', *baron de Mailly*. Recollections of a page at the court of Louis XVI. London, 1873. 8° 5524.4

— Rhodes, A. The French at home. New York [1875]. Sq. 16° 5528.8

— Stephens, F. G. Flemish and French pictures. London, 1875. 4° 6211.8

— Taine, H. A. Notes on. New York, 1875. 12°. 5533.2

— Wallace, *Mrs.* E. D. A woman's experiences in. New York, 1872. 12° 423.11

— Willis, N. P. Pencillings by the way. New York, 1844. L. 8° 430.2

History, etc.

— Adams, C. K. Democracy and monarchy in France from the inception of the great revolution to the overthrow of the second empire. New York, 1875. 12° 5515.4

— Blanc, (J. J.) L. History of ten years, 1830–40. London, 1844, 45. 2 v. 8° 5514.7

— Bouillet, A. L'armée d'Henry V. Les bourgeois-gentilshommes de 1871. Paris, 1872. 18° 5526.1

— Crowe, E. E. History of. New York, 1840. 3 v. 12° 828.2

— Elliot, F. Old court life in. Leipzig, 1873. 2 v. in 1. Sq. 16° 329.4

— – Romance of old court-life in. New York, 1874. L. 8° 5510.1

— Erckmann, É., and Chatrian, A. Histoire d'un paysan. 1re–4e partie. [Fiction.] Paris, 1873. 4 v. 18° 5536.14

— – The invasion of France in 1814. [Fiction.] New York, 1871. 12° 913.23

— Froissart, *Sir* J. Chronicles of. London, 1868. 2 v. L. 8° 5920.2

— Gairdner, J. The houses of Lancaster and York, with the conquest and loss of. London, 1874. Sq. 16° 628.4

— Guizot, F. (P. G.) L'histoire de France, depuis les temps les plus reculés jusqu'en 1789. Paris, 1873–75. 4 v. L. 8° 5530.2

— – History of, from the earliest times to 1789. London, 1872. 3 v. 8° 5510.2

— Gurney, J. H. Chapters from French history. London, 1870. 16° 5517.2

— Hooper, G. Waterloo: the downfall of the first Napoleon: a history of the campaign of 1815. London, 1862. 8° 5511.2

— Hope, *Mrs.* —. Conversion of the Franks and the English. London, 1872. 16° 5735.5

— Jervis, H. W. History of. From the earliest times to the establishment of the second empire in 1852. New York, 1872 [1862]. 12° 824.13

— Jervis, W. H. The Gallican church. A history of the church of, from the concordat of Bologna, 1516, to the revolution. London, 1872. 2 v. 8°. 1531.8

— Jouy, V. J. E. de. L'hermite de la chaussée-d'Antin, ou, observations sur les mœurs et les usages français au commencement du XIXe siècle. Paris, 1815–18. 5 v. 12° 5518.2

— – L'hermite en province, ou observations sur les mœurs et les usages français au commencement du XIXe siècle. Paris, 1818. 3 v. 12° 5518.4

— Lamartine, A. (M. L.) de. History of the restoration of monarchy in. London, 1865. 4 v. Sm. 8° 5517.5

— Michelet, J. History of. New York, 1869. 2 v. 8°. 811.7

— Moreau, H. La politique française en Amérique, 1861–64. Paris, 1864. 8° 831.1

— Parkman, F., *jr*. Pioneers of France in the New World. Boston, 1872. 12° 5015.5.1

— Ritchie, L. The romance of history. London, N. D. 16° 828.11

— Ségur, P. P., *comte* de. Histoire et mémoires. Paris, 1873. 7 v. 8° 5513.4

Shelf. No.

France. *History, etc., continued.*

— Stephen, *Sir* J. Lectures on the history of. London, 1857. 2 v. 8°.................... 5514.8

— Thierry, (J. N.) A. The formation and progress of the tiers état, or third estate in France. London, 1859. 2 v. in 1. Sm. 8°............. 5517.9

— Whitehurst, F. M. Court and social life in France under Napoleon III. London, 1873. 2 v. 8°.. 5514.4

Revolution of 1789, *etc.*

— Abbott, J. S. C. The French revolution of 1789 as viewed in the light of republican institutions. New York, 1859. 8° 821.2

— Burke, E. Reflections on the revolution in. Boston, 1826. 8°..........................5634.1.3

— *Same.* Boston, 1871. Sm. 8°...............5635.1.3

— Carlyle, T. The French revolution: a history. Leipzig, 1851. 3 v. in 1. Sq. 16°........... 838.10

— *Same.* London, 1871. 3 v. in 1. Sq. 16°..... 827.1

— Erckmann, É., and Chatrian, A. The outbreak of the great French revolution. [Fiction.] London, 1871. 3 v. 16°.................. 825.2

— Héricault, C. d'. Thermidor, Paris en 1794. Paris, 1872. 12°............................ 5516.3

— Lamartine, A. (M. L.) de. Histoire des Girondins. Paris, 1848. 8 v. 8°................ 2011.1

— – History of the Girondists. New York, 1868. 3 v. 12°................................ 827.25

— Michelet, J. Historical view of the French revolution. London, 1864. Sm. 8°............... 5517.3

— – The women of the French revolution. Philadelphia, 1855. 12°......................... 1226.3

— Mignet, F. A. (M.) History of the French revolution, 1789–1814. London, 1868. Sm. 8°.... 5517.4

— Morris, W. O'C. The French revolution and first empire. New York [1875]. Sq. 16° 628.5

— Smyth, W. Lectures on the history of the French revolution. London, 1860. 2 v. Sm. 8°.....5517.10

Shelf. No.

France. *Revolution of* 1789, *etc., continued.*

— Somerville, W. C. Letters from Paris on the causes and consequences of the French revolution. Baltimore, 1822. 8°................. 5512.1

— Sybel, H. (C. L.) von. History of the French revolution. London, 1867, 69. 4 v. 8°...... 5514.2

— Thiers, (L.) A. History of the French revolution. New York, 1874. 4 v. in 2. 8°........ 5511.3

— Tocqueville, A. (C. H. C.) de. On the state of society in France before the revolution of 1789, and on the causes which led to that event. London, 1873. 8°.......................... 5514.9

Revolution of 1848.

— Lamartine, A. (M. L.) de. History of the French revolution of 1848. London, 1870. Sm. 8° ... 827.24

Franco-German war, 1870, 71.

— Borbstædt, A., and Dwyer, F. The Franco-German war to the catastrophe at Sedan and the fall of Strassburg. London, 1873. 8°........ 5713.2

— Corvin, O. In France with the Germans. London, 1872. 2 v. Sm. 8°.................. 5715.2

— Erckmann, É., and Chatrian, A. Histoire du plébiscite. [Fiction.] Paris, 1872. 18°...... 5516.4

— Hazen, W. B. The school and the army in Germany and France, with a diary of siege life at Versailles. New York, 1872. 8°............ 5714.5

— Hugo, V. (M.), *vicomte.* Actes et paroles, 1870–72. Paris, 1872. 18°...................... 5536.5

— Niemann, A. The French campaign, 1870–71. London, 1872. 8°.......................... 5515.1

— Sheppard, N. Shut up in Paris. Leipzig, 1871. Sq. 16°................................ 315.13

— Wartensleben, H. (L. W. C. A. F.), *Graf* von. Operations of the south army in January and February, 1871. London, 1872. Sm. 8°...... 5514.3

See also Bastile, Girondists, Paris, Peninsula war, Pyrenees, Waterloo.

NOTE ON FRANCE.

General and comprehensive works.

The latest history, and for the general reader perhaps the best, because less extensive, though still elaborate, is Martin's, for the period previous to the first revolution, digesting as it does the labors of Sismondi, Guizot, Thierry, and Barante. It has, however, been only in part translated into English, and upon it is based "The student's France," above named, a brief compendious account. Crowe's, covering 1465–1795 [828.2], is a concise popular account. Sir James Stephen's Lectures [5514.8] are of high repute, and De Tocqueville says of them that they show a "clear comprehension of our ideas, laws and habits." The chapters on French history in Smyth's "Lectures on modern history" [5012.10; 5925.7] are of importance to the general reader seeking to know the character of the books to be read. E. A. Freeman's essay on "The Franks and the Gauls" [5913.4] is a rapid survey of French history from the earliest times to our day.

The ingenious, brilliant, poetic Michelet, though without method and regularity in his eloquent narrative, by combining graphic descriptions with a tone of philosophy, and by praises of liberty and virtue, and as the adversary of the Jesuits, has always been popular in France. See Flint, "Philosophy of history" [5921.7], on Michelet and the democratic school of historians. Catholic writers, like Bishop Dupanloup, regret his impiety, and think he degenerates into pamphleteering. There is an English translation of the first section of his history, covering the interval to A. D. 1483 [811.7]; but the reader can find the entire sequence *in French* in the Bates Hall. Michelet is reviewed in J. S. Mill's Dissertations [5824.4] and in Alison's Essays [1531.7].

From political grounds the opposite to Michelet's, Capefigue reviews French history in a voluminous series of works, which are in some respects anomalous and eccentric. He is a staunch royalist, a defender of the papacy, believes the reformation an impious innovation, but he has great research, is brilliant and imaginative in style, and, where not influenced by political views, impartial. He constantly takes issue with Guizot, Thierry, Michelet, Thiers, and Mignet. The series in French is in Bates Hall, but they have not been translated into English.

The rise of the modern schools of French historians, which add a purpose beyond mere narrative, and have sought illustrations beyond battles and the life of courts, is largely due to Augustin Thierry's "Letters on the history of France;" and he illustrated his idea in his monograph on the history of the middle class (tiers état) [5517.9].

The highest repute acquired by a French historian probably belongs to Guizot, for his "History of civilization from the fall of the Roman empire to the revolution" [5924.8]. With a dignified style, he is able in analysis, in generalization, takes great range, is impartial, and of protestant views. Guizot is examined in Flint [5921.7]; in Alison's Essays [1531.7], etc. A history of France, which Guizot originally prepared for youths, and which he lived only to bring down to 1789 [5510.2, etc.], may be considered the best of the general histories for popular use.

By periods.— Ancient Gaul.

Besides Cæsar's "Commentaries" [6116.5], see Merivale's "Roman empire" [5515.3, vol. 1, ch. 5]; the "History of Cæsar" by Napoleon III [5521.1]; and other general works on the Roman empire. The summary in Guizot's France [5510.2] is the most accessible narrative in English.

Merovingian period, A. D. 420–752.

The picturesque and animated work of Augustin Thierry, written with the modern appreciation of the value of antiquarian lore, is of the highest importance. See also Montalembert's "Monks of the West" [5514.5].

Chapter 38th of Gibbon [824.9] is given to the founding of the French monarchy. The important battles of Chalons, A. D. 451, and Tours, A. D. 732, are described in Creasy's "Decisive battles" [824.6]. Hallam's "Middle ages" [5916.1] begins A. D. 486. Guizot's France [5510.2] affords a summary.

Carlovingian period, A. D. 752–987.

Guizot's 19th lecture of his "History of civilization" [5924.8], concerns the transition from the Merovingian period; lecture 20th is given to Charlemagne, and the 24th to the dismemberment of his empire. Palgrave's Normandy begins with the death of Charlemagne, goes to Charles the simple in vol. 1, and to William the conqueror in vol. 3. Hallam's "Middle ages" [5916.1] covers this period; and Guizot's France [5510.2] may be consulted for a summary.

On *Charlemagne*, beside the above authorities, see the history of him by G. P. R. James [5528.9]; Milman's "Latin Christianity" [5817.11.2]; Gibbon's Rome [824.9, chap. 49]; and Bulfinch's "Legends of Charlemagne" [824.2].

The Capets, A. D. 987–1328.

See the 8th chapter of Guizot's "History of civilization" [5924.8] for an excellent account of the crusades. Guizot considers the civilization in France to begin in this period. Michelet [811.7] and Hallam's "Middle ages" [5916.1] should be consulted. For fiction read James's "Philip Augustus" [722.7]; E. E. Hale's "In His name" [732.28] for the Waldenses; and Miss Yonge's "Richard the fearless" [927.20].

House of Valois, A. D. 1328–1589.

Follow first the general histories like Guizot's History [5510.2] and his "History of civilization" [5924.8]; and Hallam's "Middle ages" [5916.1].

Of the prominent characters of this period Louis IX, or *Saint Louis*, is portrayed in Guizot's "Great Christians of France" [5937.6]. English history mates with French history in the invasion under Edward III and the Black prince; and of the battle of *Cressy*, A. D. 1346, there is an account in Creasy's "Decisive battles" [824.6], as also of the later conflict, A. D. 1356, at *Poictiers*. There is a life of the Black prince by James; an account of Edward III's reign by Longman, and illustrative matter can be found in Strickland's "Queens of England" [5416.4.2], in Froissart [5920.2], and in Miss Yonge's "Cameos" [826.12]. Under Du Guesclin the French succeeded in driving the English from the country, A. D. 1370, etc., and the accounts in the general histories may be supplemented by Dumas's "Knight of Mauleon." For the Peasants' revolt in 1358, see James's "Jacquerie" [722.5]. Of Henry V's victory at *Agincourt*, A. D. 1415, the English as well as French histories must be consulted, and illustrative fiction will be found in James's "Agincourt" [327.12] and in Miss Yonge's "Lances of Lynwood" [737.8]. Shakespeare's plays of Henry V and Henry VI come in collaterally, and carry the progress of events along the English occupancy, and by the episode of *Joan of Arc*, for whom see the note under Darc, Jeanne. Within this period also falls James's "Agnes Sorel" [730.6]. The conquest and loss of France to the English crown is followed in Gairdner's "Lancaster and York" [628.4].

The reign of *Louis XI* extended 1461–83, and in this time the modern kingdom was consolidated. Michelet is translated [811.7] for this period, and there is a summary in Guizot's last history [5510.2]; and for Louis's relations to the church history, see Milman's "Latin Christianity" [5817.11], and the references in McClintock and Strong's Cyclopædia. Also see Gurney's "Chapters from French history" [5517.2]; and illustrative fiction can be found in Scott's "Quentin Durward" [324.2; 523.4]; and in Victor Hugo's "Hunchback of Notre-Dame" [511.27; 2016.2].

Contemporary with Louis was *Charles the bold*, duke of Burgundy, and his relations to the history of Louis's reign is traced in Kirk's "Life of Charles the bold" [5511.1]. Charles figures in Scott's "Anne of Geierstein" [324.1; 533.1]; in Charles Reade's "Cloister and hearth" [316.24]; in Scott's "Quentin Durward" [324.2; 523.4]; and in James's "Mary of Burgundy" [722.11].

See also Herz's drama of "King René's daughter" [1615.15] for Provence at this time.

The old chronicler Froissart [5920.2] covers the early part, 1326–1400, of this Valois period.

The summary on *Louis XII's* reign in Guizot's France [5510.2] will suffice the general reader before passing on to the period of *Francis I*, whose life and court are described by Pardoe [1223.11]; a summary of whose reign will be found in Guizot [5510.2], and whose relations to general European politics can be studied in Robertson's "Charles V" [1226.9]. The famous Field of the cloth of gold is depicted in James's "Darnley" [327.16]; and Ainsworth's "Constable de Bourbon" [322.21] falls within his time.

The historical narratives concerning the following reigns of this house may be illustrated by James's "Henry of Guise" [722.12], and Yonge's "Chaplet of pearls" [318.4] for Henry II's reign, 1547–59. Dumas's "Margaret of Valois" answers for Charles XII's period, 1560–74. Within this period falls the *massacre of St. Bartholomew*, A. D. 1572, upon which there is a special monograph by White, a chapter in Elliot's "Old court life" [329.4], an account in Motley's "Dutch republic" [822.2], and an "apology" in Disraeli's "Curiosities of literature" [5626.6]. There is much variance between protestant and catholic historians on this event, and Lingard in his "History of England" [5417.8], and others on the catholic side, hold views that need to be weighed while reading their opponents. All histories of the reformation and of the Huguenots necessarily cover this and other events of this contentious period.

For Henry III's reign, 1574–89, the histories may be paralleled with the novelists, Ainsworth in his "Crichton" [722.13]; James in his "Henry of Guise" [722.12]; and Dumas in his "Chicot" [718.8] and "Forty-five guardsmen" [510.6].

The manners of the 16th century are depicted in James's "Leonora d'Orco" [730.5] and "Corse de Leon" [5526.7]; in Manning's "Madame Palissy," and in Dumas's "Countess of Charny" [511.7].

Buckle, in his 8th chapter [5417.1], traces the changes in French intellect from this time to the age of Louis XIV.

The Bourbons, A. D. 1589–1793.

Henry IV, the founder of the line, ruled from 1589 to 1610; and a full note on the literature pertaining to him and his reign will be found in the Bulletin for July, 1875, p. 369.

There is a regular biography by James [5525.12]. His connection with Netherlandish history is covered in Motley's "United Netherlands" [5912.1] and in his "John of Barneveld" [5713.3]. See also Gurney's "Chapters from French history" [5517.2]. The wars of the League array historians by their protestant or catholic sympathies. Guizot, both in his "History of civilization" [5924.8] and in his "History" [5510.2], must be read as a protestant, though of broad sympathies. See also the Duc d'Aumale's "Lives of the Condés" [5522.9]; Thierry's "History of the tiers état" [5517.9]; Smiles's "Huguenots" [5514.1]; White's "Saint Bartholomew;" and Elliot's "Old court life" [329.4].

Illustrative fiction can be found in James's "Henry of Guise" [722.12]; his "Gowrie" [730.8]; his "Rose d'Albret" [730.7]; Ainsworth's "Crichton" [722.13]; and for poetic treatment, in Macaulay's "Ballad of Ivry" [1614.17].

Louis XIII, — 1610–43. — The most accessible full account is the section of Martin's History which has been translated into English. Buckle's 8th chapter in his Civilization [5417.1] gives a clear outline of the progress of events. The first chapter of James's "Reign of Louis XIV" [5526.5] summarizes this period, and notes the chief references for fuller study. James's novel of "Richelieu" gives some of the dramatic aspects of the time, and their rendering in this novel can be compared with Bulwer's delineation in his play of "Richelieu" [1614.5], and De Vigny's working up of the same period in his excellent novel "Cinq-Mars" [537.21]. See also Dumas's "Three guardsmen" [511.10], where the siege of La Rochelle is particularly described.

Louis XIV, — 1643–1715. — See the note in the Catalogue of history, etc., of the Lower Hall, p. 171, and p. 97 for references for closer study than the Branch library admits of. Martin's "Age of Louis XIV" is temperate in character and the fullest of the monographs. The English reader will find a good survey in chapters of Russell's Europe [5913.3]; and in James's "Life and times of Louis XIV" [5526.5] all that will ordinarily be needed.

For his military success, see Duc d'Aumale's "Lives of the Condés" [5522.9].

Voltaire neglected to give due prominence to the literary influences of this age; but the English reader will find this influence amply set forth by Hallam [1531.2], and popularly by Astié. See also the lives of Pascal, Corneille, Racine, Molière, Boileau, La Fontaine, Fénelon, etc. Bungener's "Preacher and the king" [716.4] has a slight thread of fiction, but it is in effect a treatise on Bourdaloue and the other sacred orators of the court. See also Farrer's "Bossuet and his contemporaries" [5526.14]. Buckle [5417.1, chap. 11] contends that the literary reputation of this reign was in spite of the king, not because of him.

Of the court and private life of the king, Miss Pardoe's book [1233.11] is the best for the English reader. There are estimates of Louis in Buckle's 11th chapter [5417.1] and in Guizot's 14th lecture of his "History of civilization" [5924.8]. See also J. C. Morrison, in the Fortnightly review, 1874.

For the religious aspects of the reign, and the results of the Revocation of the Edict of Nantes, see Smiles's "Huguenots" [5514.1]; and for illustrative fiction, James's "Huguenots" [722.10] and Mrs. Manning's "Jacques Bonneval" [738.6]. The catholic historians need, however, to be closely compared with the protestant.

Dumas has a series of novels covering this period, — "The three guardsmen" [511.10]; "Twenty years after" [511.31] for Mazarin, etc.; "Bragelonne" [511.8], for Louis' connection with the revolution in England; "The iron mask" [511.9]; and "Louise la Vallière" [511.12], which may be compared with Bulwer's play of the same name [1614.5].

Louis XV, — 1715–74.

The Count de Tocqueville, in 1846, complained of the paucity of historical treatises upon this reign, which he thought of so much interest as covering the great change of manners and ideas that led to the French revolution, which change the reader will also find portrayed in the early part of Carlyle's "French revolution" [827.1]. Buckle's 12th chapter [5417.1] is on the preparation for the revolution. The fullest treatment will be found in Martin's "Decline of the monarchy." An article by De Tocqueville on "France before the revolution" is given in his "Memoirs." Carlyle's "French revolution" [827.1] has a chapter on Louis XV's last days.

Illustrative fiction will be found in Dumas' "Memoirs of a physician" [511.11]; in James's "Ancient régime" [722.14]; in White-Melville's "Cerise" [321.10]; in Ainsworth's "John Law" [322.14], for the financial Mississippi bubble; and Bungener's "Priest and the Huguenot" [627.4].

See Germany, Seven years' war, for France's relation to European history.

Louis XVI, — 1774–89.

The histories of the French revolution necessarily begin with going over the *causes of the revolution* as developed in this reign. The chapter in Sybel [5514.2] is valuable. Carlyle enumerates them in a characteristic way [838.10]. The most recent showing of the smouldering fires of the coming revolution is in Taine's "Ancient régime." The economic conditions as portrayed in Young's Travels, one of the best authorities, are well summarized in Alison's Europe [5913.6.1]. Buckle [5417.1] is erudite and suggestive. See also Morley's "Rousseau" [5523.3] and his "Voltaire" [5523.2]; and Marmontel's Memoirs. See further in the note under Louis XVI in the Lower Hall Catalogue of history, etc.

Bancroft's view of Louis and his cabinet, in relation to the American revolution, is taken in his "United States" [5012.3.7, ch. 7, and 8, ch. 61].

Dumas has a series of novels illustrating this period, — "Memoirs of a physician" [511.11]; "The queen's necklace" [511.6, — see also Carlyle's Essays on "The diamond necklace," and "Count Cagliostro"]; "Six years later" (taking of the Bastile, etc.) [511.14]; "Countess of Charny" [511.7]; "Andrée de Taverney" [510.9], to the death of Louis XVI; and "The conspirators" [718.7].

For manners, see George Sand's "Mauprat" [526.22].

The French revolution, A. D. 1789–99.

Alison [5913.6] prefixes a list of authorities, and in his preface characterizes the contemporary records and journals. President White, of Cornell, adds a bibliography with characterizations to Morris's condensed history of the revolution [628.5].

Among the *histories of considerable extent*, the latest of them, that of Sybel [5514.2], which covers 1789–95, and extends the survey over all Europe, is on some grounds the best yet written, though somewhat heavy. It enjoys great reputation in Germany, elucidates particularly the German policy of that period, and the author was allowed access to the French, Prussian, and Neapolitan archives, and uses material never before brought forward.

Among the *French histories*, that by Thiers [5511.3] is a complete, highly-finished, voluminous plea in defence of the revolution, which later he would hardly have made, but which is in great favor with the liberals. In the early chapters, however, he is thought to be given to a loose pamphleteering spirit. Mignet (like Thiers, of the fatalist school) believes in the inevitable evil of the revolution, and his book [5517.4] has been very successful. He is rapid and concise in survey, selects few but apposite details, and characterizes with precision. He also has since somewhat modified his views. Michelet's "Historical view" has been translated into English [5517.3], but it is considered somewhat one-sided.

Bailly's "Mémoires" and Madame De Staël's work on the revolution, are the occasion of Jeffrey's enunciation of the average views of the English people of that day, in his Essays [5610.8].

Of the *English histories*, Carlyle's is the most famous, but its unquestioned ability is much marred to many by its strained melodramatic effects and jerky succession of pictures. In his essay he enumerates the chief authorities in vogue forty years ago, for an understanding of this period. Alison takes the aristocratic view [5913.6]; and Scott's toryism was clear in his "Life of Napoleon" [1221.5]. Burke and Mackintosh took respectively the conservative and liberal side at the time. Smyth's Lectures [5517.10] are in good repute. See also Brougham's Statesmen [5614.4.3].

The politics and philosophy of the French revolution make a chapter in C. K. Adams's "Democracy and monarchy in France" [5515.4]. The constitution of 1790–91 is discussed in Sybel [5514.2], and in Burke's "Reflections" [5634.1.3; 5635.1.3].

Of episodical monographs, Lamartine's on the *Girondists* [827.25] is probably of most repute, though he is accused of inaccuracy and copies the ancients in assigning imaginary speeches to the actors; and he surprised the public by his democratic sympathies and laudatory view.

On the *Reign of terror*, 1792–94, see Alison's Essay [1531.7]; Bulwer's [336.5.1]; Macaulay's Essays on Barère and Mirabeau [1238.13]; and Carlyle's Essay on Mirabeau. Mignet and Thiers may be considered the principal writers on the side of the revolution. See also Lamartine's Girondists [827.25]. The defeat of the Prussians at Valmy, 1792, forms one of Creasy's "Decisive battles" [824.6].

On *La Vendée*, see Fosteriana, and Jeffrey's Essays [5610.8].

On the *Assembly*, see Thiers; Mackintosh's Essays; and Sybel [5514.2] on its Communistic tendencies; Burke's "Reflections" is a commentary on their action.

For illustrative fiction, see Bulwer's "Zanoni" [336.6]; Dickens's "Two cities" [338.20; 1824.14]; Victor Hugo's "Ninety-three" [734.18]; Baring-Gould's "Gabrielle André" [710.39]; Dumas's "Love and liberty;" Schwartz's "Birth and education" [531.6]; C. Tucker's "Lady of Provence;" Muehlbach's "Marie Antoinette" [531.32]; Keddie's "Citoyenne Jacqueline" [736.14]; Erckmann-Chatrian's "Madame Thérèse" [524.4]; and "On the edge of the storm" [315.19].

Napoleonic period, A. D. 1799–1814.

The consulate extended from 1799 to 1804, when the empire began.

The principal English writers are the tory Scott [1221.5] and the aristocratic Alison [5913.5; 5913.6]. Thiers, for his "Consulate and empire," holds the very highest rank, and is of great popularity. His views are modified from those in his "History of the revolution;" but he is accused of concealing the emperor's bad traits. Bishop Dupanloup thinks that, in the close of the last volume, he has hit what will be the abiding estimate of Napoleon. Since the publication of Napoleon's "Correspondance" [see account in Parton's "Topics of the times," 1935.3], Lanfrey [5522.1] has begun the publication of a life of Napoleon, which is written so ably and with such new developments, that it has taken high rank, and may be considered as representing the reaction from Thiers. Lanfrey is reviewed in A. Hayward's Essays [5833.3.3]. Abbott's Napoleon [1021.1] is a popular and highly eulogistic account.

Of the *military histories*, Jomini holds the highest rank; though for a special monograph, Col. Napier's "History of the war in the peninsula" [5920.1] is unsurpassed. The military history of this period is told critically and concisely in Hamley's "Operations of war." See a full note on the Waterloo campaign in the Bulletin for Oct., 1875. The best summary of all is perhaps in Hooper's "Waterloo" [5511.2].

For Napoleon's sojourn at Elba, see Lamartine's "History of the restoration" [5517.5]; Madam Michelet's "Childhood;" and Harper's monthly, vol. 43.

See some personal recollections of the "Hundred days" in Paris, in the Atlantic monthly, April and May, 1858; and a chapter in vol. 3 of the Memoirs of John Quincy Adams [5021.10].

Estimates of the character of Napoleon will be found in Carlyle's "Heroes and hero-worship" [1535.19]; in Channing's Works [1525.2.1], who is deprecatory; in Emerson's "Representative men" [1916.6; 1934.6.2], who views him as a man of the world; in Bayne's "Essays" [1226.15]; and in Brougham's "Statesmen of the time of George III" [5614.4.5].

Lamartine, in the first volume of his "History of the restoration" [5517.5], makes an eloquent imprecation against Napoleon. Some traits of his private life can be gleaned from Alison's review of the memoirs of the Duchess D'Abrantes.

The Napoleonic period is illustrated largely in fiction, — Dumas's "Conscript;" Julia Kavanagh's "Madeleine;" Lever's "Tom Burke of Ours" [332.10; 516.19; 5627.3] and "Charles O'Malley" [332.1; 516.13] for the peninsular war; Chamier's "Ben Brace" [521.24] for the sea conflicts; Miss Yonge's "Kenneth" for the retreat from Moscow; Erckmann-Chatrian's "Conscript of 1813" [913.22], "Blockade of Phalsburg" [715.12; 913.21], and "Invasion of France in 1814" [913.23]. The Waterloo campaign and the Hundred days offer themselves as topics to Dumas, incidentally, in his "Count of Monte-Cristo" [511.30]; to Hugo, in his "Les misérables" [710.19]; to Lever, in his "Charles O'Malley" [332.1; 516.13]; to Thackeray, in his "Vanity fair" [335.7; 1820.1]; to Erckmann-Chatrian, in their "Waterloo" [913.24]; and Byron's third canto of his "Childe Harold" [1614.12.2], and Scott's "Field of Waterloo," commemorate the defeat of Napoleon.

Several of the Muehlbach novels cover the events of this period, but they must be read with caution.

Restoration of the Bourbons.

Lamartine [5517.5] is the most accessible authority in English.

Everett, in his "Mount Vernon papers," gives a sketch of the court in 1818. See Harper's monthly, vol. 43.

There is an account of the modern constitutions of France in Lippincott's magazine, May and August, 1875.

Revolution of 1830.

Louis Blanc [5514.7] covers the following decade. Guizot's Memoirs form a necessary commentary, though rather egotistical, and given to special pleading; but they throw little light on the secret history of the period. See Alison's "Essay on the revolution of 1830" and the last chapter of Brougham's Autobiography [5425.2].

See personal memoirs of the Orleans family in Harper's monthly, vol. 10.

Revolution of 1848.

Lamartine and Guizot were both observers of the events.

See also C. K. Adams's "Democracy and monarchy in France" [5515.4], and B. Jerrold's "Life of Napoleon III" [5522.3].

The causes of the revolution are delineated in Dumas's novel of "Edmond Dantes" [511.29]. See also Erckmann-Chatrian's "Man of the people" [736.23].

Louis Napoleon's period.

The late emperor has a popular champion in Abbott, and a favorable view is taken by R. B. Kimball, in the Galaxy, April, 1873. See also McCarthy's "Modern leaders" [5930.2], and Everett's "Mount Vernon papers." Kinglake in his "Invasion of the Crimea" [5924.9] takes an unfavorable view.

See also C. K. Adams's "Democracy and monarchy in France" [5515.4]; B. Jerrold's "Life of Napoleon III" [5522.3]; and Whitehurst on the "Court and social life" [5517.5].

See Murray's "Member for Paris" [316.7], and Erckmann-Chatrian's "Story of the plébiscite" [524.25] for fiction.

The Franco-German war, the Commune, etc.

Few publications on this period have yet acquired standing; but a large number of contemporary contributions to the history can be found in the Bates Hall.

See Mazzini, in the Contemporary review, vol. 17.

An epitome of events in the Franco-German war is given in Blackwood's magazine, 1875, or no. 1647 of Living age; and its events have been illustrated in Bulwer's "Parisians" [329 21; 734.16; 5533.1]; in De Mille's "Comedy of errors" [531.22]; in Henry Kingsley's "Valentin" [339.9]; and in Schucking's "Powder and gold" [538.3].

Ecclesiastical history.

For the *Reformation period*, see the summary in Fisher [5813.7, chapter 8, with a list of books, p. 579]. On the history of the protestant exiles and Huguenots, there is Smiles's most recent account.

Guizot's "History of civilization" affords much guidance in studying the relations of the church and state throughout.

See the epitomized "Church history of France," with references in McClintock and Strong's Cyclopædia under "France."

Shelf. No.

FRANCE, *continued.*

Language.

— Boyer, A. Le dictionnaire royal, françois-anglois, et anglois-françois. London, 1816. 2 v. in 1. 4° .... *R.R., D.3.9
— Brachet, A. Dictionnaire étymologique de la langue française. Paris [1868]. 12° 5537.4
— Cassal, C., and Karcher, T., *editors.* The graduated course of translation from English into French. Part I. The junior course. London, 1875. Sm. 8° 5534.7
— Cherpilloud, J. Book of versions; or, guide to French translation. Philadelphia, 1829. 12° .. 5538.3
— Chouquet, G. First lessons in learning French. New York, 1849. Sq. 16° 2018.3
— Dufief, N. G. Nature displayed in her mode of teaching language to man. Adapted to the French. New York, 1825. 8° 2012.2
— Fivas, V. de. New grammar of French grammars: comprising the substance of all the most approved French grammars extant. New York, 1868. 12° 2016.3
— Ladreyt, E. M. Conversational French reader. Boston, 1864. 16° 2015.1
— Magill, E. H. A French grammar. Boston, 1867. 12° 2014.2
— — Introductory French reader. Boston, 1868. 12°. 2014.1
— Pinney, N., and Arnoult, É. French grammar. New York, 1861. 12° 2013.1
— Prendergast, T. The mastery series. New York, 1868. 12° 1933.2
— Sauveur, L. Causeries avec mes élèves. Boston, 1874. Sm. 8° 2015.5
— Smith, L., Hamilton, H., and Legros, E. The International English and French dictionary. London, 1873. 2 v. 8° .... *R.R., D.3.14
— Spiers, A., and Surenne, G. French and English [and English and French] pronouncing dictionary. New York, 1872. 8° .... *R.R., D.3.12
— Williams, F. S. English into French. New York [*cop.* 1860]. Sm. 8° 2015.6

Literature.

— Besant, W. The French humourists from the 12th to the 19th century. London, 1873. 8°. 5532.2
— Louandre, C. (L.) Chefs d'œuvres des conteurs français. Paris, 1874. 2 v. 18° 5534.3
— Sainte-Beuve, C. A. Tableau historique et critique de la poésie française et du théâtre français au XVIe siècle. Paris, 1869. 12° 5538.15
— Soleinne, — de. Bibliothèque dramatique. T. I. Paris, 1843. 8° 5532.1
— Villemain, A. F. Cours de littérature française. Tableau de la littérature au moyen âge en France. Paris, 1871. 2 v. 8° 5537.11
— — Tableau de la littérature au XVIIIe siècle. Paris, 1873. 4 v. 12° 5537.10
— — Souvenirs contemporains d'histoire et de littérature. Paris, 1874. 2 v. 18° 5537.18

Shelf. No.

FRANCE. *Literature, continued.*

— Vinet, A. (R.) History of French literature in the 18th century. Edinburgh, 1854. 8° 6132.3

Note. — A brief general survey of French literature will be found in Longfellow's "Poets and poetry of Europe" [5922.1]; and much illustrative of the course of the literary history of France will appear from Buckle's "History of civilization in England" [5417.1], and Guizot's "History of civilization" [5924.8]. For the humorists, Besant is the best source. Hallam [1531.2] covers the 15th, 16th, and 17th centuries. The titles above explain the scope of their respective authors. Particularly for Louis XIV's time, see Martin's "Age of Louis XIV;" Guizot's "History of France" [5510.2.4], and for the drama of that period, see Macmillan's magazine, April, 1875; and the lives of Molière, Racine, Corneille, etc. For the last century, see Carlyle's essay on Diderot, and the lives of Voltaire [1221.2; 5523.4] and Rousseau [5523.3] by Morley. There is a paper on French fiction in Lippincott's magazine, Feb., 1874; and others on the history of the French newspaper press in A. Hayward's Essays [5833.3.2], and Cornhill magazine, 1873–74.

FRANCES Hildyard. Wood, E. P. 720.16
FRANCESCO, St., d'Assisi. (*Giovanni Francesco Bernardone.*) St. Francis of Assisi. Oliphant, M. (O. W.) [London, 1871.] Sm. 8° 5937.10
FRANCHERE, Gabriel. Narrative of a voyage to the northwest coast of America, 1811–14, or the first American settlement on the Pacific. Translated and edited by J. V. Huntington. New York, 1854. 376 pp. Illustrated. 12° 414.10
FRANCILLON, Robert Edward. Zelda's fortune 731.28
FRANCIS, *St.* *See* FRANCESCO, St., d'Assisi.
FRANCIS, Convers. Historical sketch of Watertown, Mass. Cambridge, 1830. 151 pp. 12° 5014.5
— Life of John Eliot. (*In* Sparks, J. Library of American biography) 5028.1.5
FRANCO-GERMAN war, 1870, 71. *See* FRANCE, *Franco-German war.*
FRANCONIA stories. *See* ABBOTT, Jacob.
FRANK. Edgeworth, M. Early lessons 939.6.1
FRANK among the rancheros. Fosdick, C. A. 913.2
FRANK at Don Carlos' rancho. Fosdick, C. A. 913.1
FRANK before Vicksburg. Fosdick, C. A. 925.26
FRANK in the mountains. Fosdick, C. A. 913.3
FRANK in the woods. Fosdick, C. A. 925.24
FRANK on a gun-boat. Fosdick, C. A. 925.25
FRANK on the lower Mississippi. Fosdick, C. A. 925.22
FRANK on the prairie. Fosdick, C. A. 925.23
FRANK the young naturalist. Fosdick, C. A. 925.21
FRANK Fairlegh. Smedley, F. E. 315.11
FRANK Warrington. Harris, M. 724.11
FRANK Wildman's adventures on land and water. Gerstaecker, F. 932.42
FRANK's campaign. Alger, H., *jr.* 925.14
FRANKLAND, *Sir* Charles Henry. Sir Charles Henry Frankland: or, Boston in the colonial times. Nason, E. Albany, 1865. 8° 5013.15
FRANKLIN, Benjamin. Autobiography. Edited, with notes and an introduction, by J. Bigelow. Philadelphia, 1872. 409 pp. Portrait. 12° 1013.3
— Life, written by himself. Now first edited from original manuscripts and from his printed correspondence and other writings, by John Bigelow. Philadelphia, 1874. 3 v. Portrait. 8° 5025.13
— *Same.* Philadelphia, 1875. 3 v. Portrait. 12°. 1213.3

Shelf. No.

FRANKLIN, Benjamin, *continued.*
— Abbott, J. Franklin 936.1.4
— Mayhew, H. Young Benjamin Franklin. London [1860]. Sm. 8° 916.2
— Memorial of the inauguration of the statue of. [With R. C. Winthrop's oration.] *See* BOSTON, *Mass.* 1211.6
— Parker, T. Historic Americans. Boston, 1871. Sm. 8° 5025.4
— Parton, J. Life and times of. New York, 1864. 2 v. 12° 1212.2
— Sainte-Beuve, C. A. English portraits. New York, 1875. 16° 1025.3

Note.—Franklin's Autobiography comes down only to 1758, and was originally printed from a somewhat imperfect copy of his manuscript. The autobiography in this form has been repeatedly printed, in the most authoritative form with Sparks's continuation, prefixed to his edition of Franklin's Works, to be found in the Bates Hall. Mr. Bigelow a few years since discovered the original manuscript, which corrected some parts of the usual copies, and added a few sentences at the end, and in his edition [1013.3] has added the letters of authentication, preserved with the original draft. The Life [1213.3; 5025.13], called "written by himself," is a joinery of extracts from his autobiography, his letters, and whatever else of his writings capable of being worked in. Parton's is the most extensive regular life.

See also Abbott, on his public life, in Harper's monthly, vol. 4; Brougham's "Statesmen of the time of George III" [5614.4.5]; Everett's oration on his youth [1921.1.2]; Foster's "Critical essays" [5614.3.2], etc.

FRANKLIN, *Sir* John. Hall, C. F. Arctic researches and life among the Esquimaux: being the narrative of an expedition in search of, 1860–62. New York, 1865. 8° 422.4
— Kane, E. K. Arctic explorations: the second Grinnell expedition in search of, 1853–65. Philadelphia, 1856. 2 v. 8° 422.2
— *Same.* Hartford, 1871. 8° 5912.4
— MacClintock, *Sir* F. L. The voyage of the "Fox" in the Arctic seas. Narrative of the discovery of the fate of. Boston, 1860. 8° 424.7
— Richardson, *Sir* J. Biography of. (*In* Macaulay, T. B., *lord,* and others. New biographies of illustrious men) 5428.4
— Sargent, E. Arctic adventure by sea and land, from the earliest date to the last expedition in search of. Boston, 1857. 12° 426.10

See also Note under Arctic regions.

FRASER–TYTLER, Christina C. *See* TYTLER, Christina C. Fraser.
FRASER'S magazine. Vol. 7–12. London, 1873–75. 6 v. 8° 6718.1
FRASERIAN papers, The. Maginn, W. New York, 1857. Sm. 8° 1935.5
FREAKS of fortune. Adams, W. T. 924.22
FREAKS on the fells. Ballantyne, R. M. 923.9
FRED, and Maria, and me. Prentiss, E. 717.2
FRED Markham in Russia. Kingston, W. H. G. 936.20
FREDERIC I, *king of Prussia.* Friedrich I, König von Preussen. Droysen, J. G. Leipzig, 1867. 8°. 5733.3
FREDERIC II, *the great, king of Prussia.* Abbott, J. S. C. History of. New York, 1871. 8° 1021.3
— Carlyle, T. History of. Leipzig, 1858–65. 13 v. in 7. Sq. 16° 1237.1

Note.—The most elaborate English biography is Carlyle's, but it is voluminous, and is reviewed by J. R. Lowell in North American review, April, 1866. Abbott's is the best summary for the general reader, and its chapters originally appeared in Harper's monthly, vol. 40. Macaulay's sketch [1238.13] is rapid and brilliant. See also Brougham's sketch in his "Statesmen" [5614.4.3]. There is a side view of the king in Kurd von Schlözer's "Chasot," reviewed in Max Müller's "Chips" [5616.1.3]. Stahr's "Lessing" [1022.7] and the lives of Voltaire, and the literary histories of Germany for the last century, may be consulted for his literary character and associations. See also papers in Harper's monthly, vols. 18 and 25.

Histories of Prussia, Germany, and the Seven years' war all necessarily cover the career of Frederic.

Several of the Muehlbach novels concern Frederic the great, like "Frederick the great and his family" [510.4], and "His court" [531.16]; "Berlin and Sans-souci" [531.15], etc., but they must not be trusted without the corrective influences of the regular histories.

FREDERICK the great and his court. [Fiction.] Mundt, C. (M.) 531.16
FREDERICK the great and his family. [Fiction.] Mundt, C. (M.) 510.4

FREDONIAD, The: or, independence preserved. An epick poem on the late war of 1812. Emmons, R. Boston, 1827. 4 v. 12° 1611.1
FREE lending libraries. Greenough, W. W. *See* AMERICAN social science association 1932.2
FREE masonry. Letters on the masonic institution. Adams, J. Q. Boston, 1847. 8° 5822.2
FREE Russia. [Travels, etc.] Dixon, W. H. New York, 1870. Sm. 8° 422.22
FREE trade. Free trade and the European treaties of commerce. *See* COBDEN club, *London* 5418.13
— Phillips, W. Propositions concerning protection and free trade. Boston, 1850. 12° 6435.2
FREE, yet forging their own chains. [Fiction.] Cornwall, C. M. 722.16
FREEMAN, Edward Augustus. Comparative politics. The unity of history. Lectures. London, 1873. vii, 522+ pp. 8° 5822.10
— Freeman's historical course for schools. Outlines of history. Adapted for American schools. New York, 1873. ix, 366 pp. 16° 828.8
— The growth of the English constitution. Leipzig, 1872. 287 pp. Sq. 16° 838.2
— Historical essays. London, 1872, 73. 2 v. 8° ... 5913.4
— History of federal government, from the foundation of the Achaian league to the disruption of the United States. Vol. I. London, 1875. 8°. 5921.11

Contents.—Vol. I. General introduction; History of the Greek federations.

— History of the Norman conquest in England. Oxford, 1869. 4 v. 8° 5014.4
— Old-English history. With maps. 3d edition. London, 1873. xxxiii, 371+ pp. Sm. 8° 5418.11
— Select historical essays. Leipzig, 1873. 334 pp. Sq. 16° 828.9
— *editor.* Historical course for schools. *Namely:*—
— – Doyle, J. A. History of the United States. New York, 1876. 16° 618.4
— – Freeman, E. A. Outlines of history. New York, 1873. 16° 828.8
FREEMAN, Samuel. The probate directory. Being the laws of the commonwealth of Massachusetts respecting the estates of testators, intestates, and wards. 2d edition. Boston, 1803. xi, 228 pp. 12° 6317.2
FREETHINKING. Farrar, A. S. Critical history of free thought in reference to the Christian religion. New York, 1863. 12° 1522.2
— Stephen, L. Essays on freethinking and plain-speaking. London, 1873. Sm. 8° 5838.3
FREILIGRATH, Ferdinand. Poems from the German. Edited by his daughter. 2d edition, enlarged. xviii, 260 pp. Sq. 16° 1613.17
FREKE, Henry. The dependence of life on decomposition. Dublin, 1871. 55 pp. Folded sheet. 8°. 1528.12
FRÉMONT, Jessie Benton. The story of the guard: a chronicle of the [civil] war. Boston, 1863. 233+ pp. 16° 815.5
FRÉMONT, John Charles. The exploring expedition to the Rocky mountains, Oregon and California. Auburn, 1854. 456 pp. Portrait. 12° 414.14
— Life of. Upham, C. W. Boston, 1856. 12° 1214.6
FRENCH family. Thayer, E. Family memorial. Hingham, 1835. 8° 611.2
FRENCH home life. London, 1873. 349+ pp. 8°. 5523.4
FRENCH plays, College series of. Bôcher, F. Boston, 1867. 12° 2015.2
FRERE, John Hookham. Works. With memoir by W. E. and B. Frere. London, 1872. 2 v. Portraits. 8° 5422.4

Contents.—Vol. I. Memoir; Contributions to The microcosm; Miscellanies (1785-92); Contributions to The anti-jacobin; Miscellanies. II. Translations from Aristophanes; Theognis restitutus; Translations from "The poem of the Cid;" Miscellaneous translations.

FRESHET, The. Abbott, J. 917.34
FRET cutting, Manual of. Seaton, *Sir* T. London, 1875. Sm. 8° 6425.7
FRET–SAWING. Sawyer, G. A. Boston, 1875. Sm. 4°. 1515.19
FREUND, Wilhelm. Latin-English lexicon. *See* ANDREWS, Ethan Allen .... *R.R., D.3.5

Shelf. No.

FREY, Joseph Samuel Christian Frederick. Judah and Israel: or, the restoration and conversion of the Jews and the ten tribes. 3d edition. Prefixed the author's narrative and portrait. New York, 1840. 310 pp. 12° 6327.2
FREYSCHÜTZ, Der. Weber, C. M. F. E. von. (*In* Ditson, O., and co. Standard opera librettos)..6233.3.1
FREYTAG, Gustav. Die Ahnen. Vol. 1, 4te Auflage; Vol. 2, 3te Auflage. Leipzig, 1873, 74. 2 v. 16° 5733.5

Contents.—Vol. I. Ingo und Ingraban. II. Das Nest der Zaunkönige.

— Debit and credit. Translated by L. C. C. With preface by C. C. J. Bunsen.................. 533.8
— Leisure hour series. Ingraban. 2d novel of a series entitled Our forefathers. From the German by Mrs. Malcolm....................... 538.6
— The lost manuscript. Translated by Mrs. Malcolm 521.4
— Soll und Haben. 19te Auflage. Leipzig, 1874. 2 v. Sq. 16°............................ 5738.3
— Die verlorene Handschrift. 7te Auflage. Leipzig, 1873. 505 pp. 8°...................... 5733.4
FRICKELL, G. Magic no mystery: conjuring tricks with cards, balls, and dice; magic writing, performing animals, etc. Edited by W. H. Cremer. With illustrations. London, 1876. 333 pp. Sm. 8°...................................1515.20
— The magician's own book, or the whole art of conjuring. Illustrated. New York [*cop.* 1857]. xi, 362 pp. Sm. 8° 1514.18
— *Same.* New York, 1870. xi, 162 pp. 12°.....1514.23
— The secret out; or, one thousand tricks with cards, and other recreations. New York [*cop.* 1869]. Illustrated. 398 pp. 12° 1515.15
— The sociable; or, 1001 home amusements. Illustrated. New York [*cop.* 1858]. 375 pp. 12°. 1514.6
FRIEDRICH. For names of sovereigns, *see* FREDERIC.
FRIEND, The. [Essays.] Coleridge, S. T. Works. Philadelphia, N. D. 8°..................... 1611.5
FRIENDS in council. [Conversational discussions.] Helps, *Sir* A. New York [*cop.* 1861]. 2 v. 12° 1914.2
— *Same.* Leipzig, 1873. 2 v. in 1. Sq. 16° 1538.14
FRIENDSHIP, The, of books. [Essays.] Maurice, (J.) F. D. London, 1874. Sm. 8°........... 6136.8
FRIENDSHIPS, The, of women. Alger, W. R. Boston, 1872. 16°..............................1535.20
FRISI, Paul. Treatise on rivers and torrents. Added, an essay on navigable canals. Translated by J. Garstin. New edition, corrected. London, N. D. xxiv, 226 pp. Maps. 12° 1715.20
FRISWELL, James Hain. The better self: essays for home-life. Philadelphia [1875]. xii, 300 pp. 16° 1536.21
FROISSART, *Sir* John. Chronicles of England, France, Spain, and adjoining countries, from the latter part of the reign of Edward II to the coronation of Henry IV. Translated from the French, with variations and additions from many MSS. By Thomas Johnes. Prefixed, a life of the author, an essay on his works, and a criticism on his history. London, 1868. 2 v. Illustrated. L. 8°. 5920.2
— *See* MÉRIMÉE, P. Portraits historiques et littéraires. Paris, 1874. 12° 5527.14
FROM everglade to cañon with the 2d dragoons (2d U. S. cavalry). Rodenbough, T. T. New York, 1875. 8°.................................. 5032.6
FROM fourteen to fourscore. Jewett, *Mrs.* S. W..... 714.26
FROM jest to earnest. Roe, E. P. 723.20
FROM my youth up. Terhune, M. V................ 724.22
FROM Olympus to Hades. Forrester, *Mrs.* —...... 710.23
FROM the earth to the moon. Verne, J. New York, 1874. 8°.................................. 734.15
FROM the oak to the olive. [Travels.] Howe, J. W. Boston, 1868. 16°........................ 437.2
FROMBERG, Emanuel Otto. Rudimentary essay on the art of painting on glass. From the German. 3d edition. London, 1857. 110+ pp. 12°...1716.23
FRONDES agrestes. Ruskin, J. Orpington, Kent., 1875. Sm. 8°.................................6236.21

Shelf. No.

FRONTIER series. *Namely:* —
— Barrows, W. The general; or, twelve nights in the hunters' camp........................... 934.2
— Pearson, C. H. The cabin on the prairie 937.18
— – The young pioneers of the North-west........ 937.17
FROST, Sarah Annie. The book of tableaux and shadow pantomimes. New York [*cop.* 1869]. 180 pp. 12° 1518.1
FROTHINGHAM, Nathaniel Langdon. The crossed swords. *See* HOLMES, O. W., and OTHERS. Memorial. Bunker hill 810.8
— Sermons, in the order of a twelvemonth. Boston, 1852. vi, 363 pp. 12°......................... 1525.7
FROTHINGHAM, Octavius Brooks. The religion of humanity. New York, 1873. 338 pp. 12°... 1537.6
— Theodore Parker: a biography. Boston, 1874. viii, 588 pp. Portrait. 12°.................5025.11
FROTHINGHAM, Richard. The centennial: battle of Bunker hill. With a view of Charlestown in 1775, Page's plan of the action, Romans' exact view of the battle, and other illustrations. Boston, 1875. 136+ pp. 16°.................. 618.3

Note. — Drawn mostly from the History of the siege of Boston.

— History of the siege of Boston, and of the battles of Lexington, Concord, and Bunker hill. Also, an account of Bunker hill monument. With illustrative documents. 2d edition. Boston, 1851. ix, 420 pp. 8° 812.6
— Life and times of Joseph Warren. Boston, 1865. xix, 558 pp. Portrait. 8°................. 1010.6
— The rise of the republic of the United States. Boston, 1872. xxii, 640 pp. 8°............. 5010.5
— A tribute to Thomas Starr King. Boston, 1865. 247 pp. 16° 1537.10

Note. — For the position of Frothingham's books among the histories of the revolutionary period, see the note on Centennial reading in the Bulletin for July, 1875, or the Bibliography [810.10].

FROUDE, James Anthony. The English in Ireland in the eighteenth century. New York, 1872, 74. 3 v. 8° 5414.5
— History of England from the fall of Wolsey to the death of Elizabeth. New York, 1873. 12 v. Sm. 8° 826.9
— Short studies on great subjects. New York, 1872, 73. 2 v. Sm. 8° 1914.5

Note. — Froude as a historian is graphic and readable; but his opinions are often dogmatically given, and his championship of Henry VIII, and defamation of the Queen of Scots, have drawn out adversaries, who criticise him severely. His views on Ireland and its connection with English history are not satisfactory to Irish critics.

FROZEN deep, The. Collins, (W.) W. Boston..... 726.30
— *Same.* Leipzig 319.25
FRUITS. Barry, P. Fruit garden. New York [*cop.* 1872]. 12° 6625.2
— Beecher, H. W. Plain and pleasant talk about fruits, flowers and farming. New York, 1859. 12° 1514.22
— Downing, C. Selected fruits: including their culture, propagation, and management in the garden and orchard. New York, 1871. 16°... 6625.1
— Duhamel du Monceau, H. L. Traité des arbres fruitiers. Paris, 1768. 2 v. F°............ 6620.1
— Thomson, D. Handy book of fruit culture under glass. Edinburgh, 1873. Sm. 8° 6625.6

See also Grape culture.

FUDGE family, The, in Paris. Moore, T. Poetical works. Leipzig, 1842. Sq. 16° 1614.9.4
FUDGES, The, in England. Moore, T. Poetical works. Leipzig, 1842. Sq. 16° 1614.9.5
FUEL. Percy, J. Metallurgy: the art of extracting metals from their ores. Introduction, refractory materials, and fuel. London, 1875. 8° 6631.10
— Prideaux, T. S. Economy of. London, N. D. 12°.1715.13
FULLER, Hiram. Belle Brittan on a tour, at Newport, and here and there. New York, 1858. 359 pp. 12° 413.7
FULLER, Martha. Righted at last 521.10
FULLER, Thomas. *See* CHRISTOPHERS, S. W. Homes of old English writers. London [1874]. Sm. 8°. 5428.16

Shelf. No.

FULLERTON, *Lady* Georgiana. Constance Sherwood. 325.21
— Ellen Middleton 325.17
— Grantley manor 325.19
— Lady-bird 325.20
— Mrs. Gerald's niece 325.15
— A stormy life 325.16
— Too strange not to be true 325.18

Note. — Lady Fullerton was converted to catholicism in 1852, and her stories published since that time have more or less relation to her faith. "Ellen Middleton" is a domestic story of earlier production. "Grantley manor" bears on the war of creeds.

FULTON, Robert, Life of. Renwick, J. (*In* Sparks, J. Library of American biography) 5028.1.10
FUNGI: their nature and uses. Cooke, M. C. New York, 1875. 12° 6436.13
FUR country, The. Verne, J. Boston, 1874. 8°.. 713.2
FURNACES, Reverberatory. Prideaux, T. S. London, N. D. 12° 1715.13
FURNESS, William Henry. History of Jesus. Boston, 1850. 291 pp. 12° 5815.15
— Jesus and his biographers. Philadelphia, 1838. viii, 450+ pp. L. 8° 5811.7
— Remarks on the four gospels. Philadelphia, 1836. 340 pp. 12° 5815.14
— Thoughts on Jesus of Nazareth. Boston, 1859. 311 pp. 12° 5816.18
FURNISHED apartments. Y., H. A. New York, [*cop.* 1870]. 16° 1636.1
FURNITURE. Eastlake, *Sir* C. L. Hints on household taste in. Boston, 1872. Sm. 8° 6212.1
— Pollen, J. H. Ancient and modern furniture. [London, 1875.] 8° 6214.5
FUSANG, or the discovery of America by Chinese Buddhist priests in the fifth century. Leland, C. G. London, 1875. 8° 5925.6
FUSTEL DE COULANGES, Muna Denis. The ancient city: a study on the religion, laws, and institutions of Greece and Rome. From the latest French edition by Willard Small. Boston, 1874. 529 pp. Sm. 8° 5923.6
FUTURE, The: a political essay. Throop, M. H. New York, 1864. 12° 1914.9
FUTURE life. Alger, W. R. Critical history of the doctrine of a. New York, 1871. 8° 5831.3
— Erwin, W. The destiny of man. New York, 1872. 12° 5817.4
— Figuier, (G.) L. The to-morrow of death; or, the future life according to science. Boston, 1872. 12° 5816.3
— Goodwin, T. A. The mode of man's immortality: or, the when, where, and how, of the. New York, 1874. 12° 6326.11
— Smith, W. The state of the dead and the destiny of the wicked. Battle Creek, 1873. 16° 6327.6

GABORIAU, Émile. The clique of gold. From the French 710.7
— File no. 113. From the French 710.40
— Other people's money. From the French 711.4
— The widow Lerouge. Translated by F. Williams and G. A. O. Ernst 530.7
— Within an inch of his life. From the French ... 732.35
GABRIEL, a story of the Jews in Prague. From the German by A. Milman. Leipzig, 1869. 267+ pp. Sq. 16° 313.19
GABRIELLE André. An historical novel. [French revolution.] Baring-Gould, S. 710.39
GAGE, William Leonard. Life of Carl Ritter. New York, 1867. viii, 242+ pp. Sm. 8° 1024.8
GAIL HAMILTON, *pseud.* *See* DODGE, Mary Abigail.
GAIN, The, of a loss. Yonge, C. M. 318.15
GAIRDNER, James. The houses of Lancaster and York; with the conquest and loss of France. With 5 maps. London, 1874. xiii, 252 pp. [Morris, E. E., *editor*. Epochs of history.] 16°. 628.4
GALA-DAYS. Dodge, M. A. Boston, 1863. 16°... 517.1
GALAMA; or, the beggars. De Liefde, J. B. New York [1873]. 8° 520.3
GALAXY, The. Vol. 1, 2, 5–12, 14–20. New York, 1866–75. 17 v. 8° 1428.1

Shelf. No.

GALIBERT, Léon, and PELLÉ, Clément. Angleterre, Écosse et Irlande. Paris, 1844. T. 4. 574+ pp. 69 plates. Maps. [L'Univers.] 8° 5911.7
GALILEI, Galileo. The private life of Galileo. London, 1870. xi, 307 pp. Portrait. Folded plate. 16° .... 5525.
GALLICAN church. *See* FRANCE. *History, etc.*
GALT, John. Annals of the parish, and The Ayrshire legatees. With memoir of the author 515.1
— The entail 515.9
— Haddad-Ben-Ahab the traveller. (*In* Johnson, (E.) R. Little classics) 529.4.9
— The provost, and other tales 526.24
— Sir Andrew Wylie of that ilk 515.10

Note. — Galt's novels pertain mostly to middle-class Scotch life.

GALTON, Francis. The art of travel. 4th edition, enlarged. With woodcuts. London, 1867. vi, 360 pp. 16° 5918.1
GALVANISM, Rudimentary treatise on. Harris, *Sir* W. S. London, 1869. 12° 1715.29
GAMBLER'S, The, fate: a drama. Milner, H. M. New York, N. D. 12° 1635.4
GAMES. Dick, W. B. The American Hoyle. New York [*cop.* 1864]. 12° 1516.1
— Elliott, A. Out-of-doors: a handbook of games for the playground. London, 1872. 12° ...... 1517.
— – Within-doors: a book of games and pastimes for the drawing-room. London, 1872. 16° 1517.9
— Smith, C. L. Home games for old and young. Boston, 1873. 12° .... 1517.

See also Cards, Whist.

GANGOOLY, Joguth Chunder. Life and religion of the Hindoos. With a sketch of my life and experience. Boston, 1860. xxx, 306 pp. Plate. 12° ....1025.13 and 5937.
GANNETT, Ezra Stiles. A memoir. Gannett, W. C. Boston, 1875. 8° 5025.14
GANNETT, William Channing. Ezra Stiles Gannett. Unitarian minister in Boston, 1824–1871. A memoir. Boston, 1875. xv, 9–572 pp. Portrait. Illustrated. 8° 5025.14
GARBETT, Edward Lacy. Rudimentary treatise on the principles of design in architecture. 3d edition. London, 1867. viii, 247 pp. Illustrated. 12° 1715.24
GARDENING. Brill, F. Farm-gardening and seed-growing. New York [*cop.* 1872]. 12° 6226.6
— Cobbett, W. The American gardener. New York, 1852. 12° 1528.6
— Fessenden, T. G. The American kitchen gardener. New York, 1855. 12° 1524.11
— Henderson, P. Gardening for profit. New York [*cop.* 1867]. 12° 1514.17
— Hole, S. R. The six of spades: a book about the garden and the gardener. Edinburgh, 1872. Sm. 4° 6226.5
— Karr, (J. B.) A. A tour round my garden. London [1874]. 4° 6626.4
— Loudon, J. W. Gardening for ladies. New York, 1847. 12° 6626.9
— Rand, E. S., *jr.* The window gardener. Boston, 1872. 16° 6626.5
— Roe, E. P. Play and profit in my garden. New York [*cop.* 1873]. Sm. 8° 1516.13
— Warner, A. B. Gardening by myself. New York, 1872. 12° .... 6627.
— – Miss Tiller's vegetable garden and the money she made by it. New York [*cop.* 1873]. 12° .. 1518.

See also Agriculture, Evergreens, Flowers, Fruits, Hedges, Landscape gardening, Vegetation.

GARDINER, Margaret, *formerly Miss Power, countess of Blessington.* Country quarters .... 319.
— Marmaduke Herbert 310.3
— Memoirs of a femme de chambre 310.4
— Meredith 330.2
Strathern 330.2
— Madden, R. R. Literary life and correspondence of. New York, 1855. 2 v. 12° .... 1223.

Shelf. No.

GARDINER, Margaret, *continued.*
— Stoddard, R. H. Personal recollections of. New York, 1875. Sq. 16° 1828.9

Note.— Lady Blessington's tales are society-novels of inferior merit; but as a leader of society herself, she forms a prominent figure in accounts of the social and literary life of the first half of this century. See Hall's "Book of memories" [1231.1]; Chorley's Memoirs [5616.14]; and Willis's "Pencillings by the way" [430.2]. See also the paper on Lady Blessington and Count D'Orsay in Harper's monthly, vol. 10.

GARDINER, Samuel Rawson. The thirty years' war. 1618–48. London, 1874. xxv, 233 pp. Folded map. [Morris, E. E., *editor.* Epochs of history.] 16° 628.2
GARDNER, Celia E. Rich Medway's two loves 714.24
— Stolen waters. [Poem.] New York, 1875. 326 pp. 12° 1625.12
— Tested 714.7
GARDNER, Eugene C. Homes and how to make them. Illustrated. Boston, 1874. 314 pp. Sq. 16° 1518.6
— Illustrated homes: a series of papers describing real houses and real people. With illustrations. Boston, 1875. 287 pp. Sq. 16° 6227.3
GARDNER, Franklin B. How to paint. For the use of the tradesman, mechanic, farmer [etc.]. New York, 1872. 127 pp. 16° 6429.1
GARDNER, John. Longevity: the means of prolonging life after middle age. 3d edition, revised and enlarged. Boston, 1875. 191 pp. 12° ... 6037.4
GARETH and Lynette. [Poem.] Tennyson, A. Boston, 1872. 16° 5617.6
— *Same.* (*In his* Poetical works.) Leipzig, 1872. Sq. 16° 1614.10.7
GARIBALDI, Giuseppe. The rule of the monk; or, Rome in the nineteenth century. [Fiction.] New York, 1870. 105 pp. 8° 521.18
GARIBALDIANS, The, in Sicily. Dumas, A. (D.) London, 1861. 16° 828.1
GARLAND of poetry, The. Kirkland, C. M. New York, 1872. 2 v. in 1. 12° 921.1
GARNERED sheaves. Holland, J. G. New York, 1873. Sq. 16° 1617.2
GARNIER, Pierre. Dictionnaire annuel des progrès des sciences et institutiones médicales. Précédé d'une introduction par A. Latour. Troisième année, 1866. Paris, 1867. xviii, 523+ pp. 12° 6016.1
GARRATT, Alfred C. Electro-psychology and electro-therapeutics; showing the best methods for the medical uses of electricity. Boston, 1860. 708+ pp. 8° 6011.1
— Medical electricity. 3d edition, revised and illustrated. Philadelphia, 1866. 1103 pp. 8°. 6012.2
GARRETT, Edward, *pseud.* *See* MAYO, Isabella Fivy.
GARRICK, David. The Irish widow: a farce. New York, N. D. 24 pp. 12° 1635.5
— Life of. Fitzgerald, P. London, 1868. 2 v. 8°. 5422.8

Note.— The life by Fitzgerald is extended and entertaining, and though carelessly put together, it embodies much new material, and is the best, as well as the latest, and is epitomized in Harper's monthly, vol. 37. A chapter in Forster's "Life of Goldsmith" [1022.1] first made public much matter concerning Garrick's early career. A sufficient account for the general reader is in Doran's "Their majesties' servants" [1532.2].

GARRISON, William Lloyd. Sonnets and other poems. Boston, 1843. 96 pp. 12° 1617.6
GARSTANGS, The, of Garstang grange. Trollope, T. A. 334.21
GARTENLAUBE, Die. 1873. Leipzig, 1873. Illustrated. L. 4° 1330.2
GAS. Hughes, S. Treatise on gas works. London, 1871. 12° 6438.2
— Magnier, M. D. Manuel de l'éclairage au gaz. Paris, 1849. 24° 6439.7
GAS-CONSUMER'S guide, The: a hand-book of instruction on the proper management and economical use of gas. With a full description of gas-metres, etc. Boston, 1871. 148 [146] pp. 16°. 6438.3
GASCOYNE the sandal-wood trader. Ballantyne, R. M. 923.11
GASKELL, Elizabeth Cleghorn. Cousin Phillis and other tales 328.18

Contents.— Cousin Phillis; Six weeks at Heppenheim; Curious, if true; Right at last; The Manchester marriage.

Shelf. No.

GASKELL, Elizabeth Cleghorn, *continued.*
— Cranford 328.21
— A dark night's work 328.22
— Lizzie Leigh; and other tales 328.17
— Life of Charlotte Brontë. Leipzig, 1857. 2 v. in 1. Sq. 16° 1238.11
— *Same.* New York, 1857. 2 v. 1 plate. Portrait. 12° 1225.29
— *Same.* London, 1871. viii, 441 pp. 16° 1225.9
— Lois the witch and other tales 328.14

Contents.— Lois the witch; The grey woman; The doom of the Griffiths; The half-brothers; The crooked branch.

— Mary Barton 328.23
— The moorland cottage 526.13
— My lady Ludlow 521.17
— North and South. Leipzig, 1855. 428+ pp. Sq. 16° 328.16
— Right at last, and other tales 736.26
— Ruth 328.15
— Sylvia's lovers 328.20
— Wives and daughters 328.19

Note.— Mrs. Gaskell's novels are examined in the Cornhill magazine, 1874, or no. 1555 of Living age.

GASKELL, George. Algeria as it is. London, 1875. xxviii, 327 pp. Sm. 8° 5935.4
GASPARIN, Agénor (Étienne), *comte* de. America before Europe. Translated by M. L. Booth. 3d edition. New York, 1862. xi, 419 pp. 12° .. 414.2
— The uprising of a great people: the United States in 1861. Abridged from the French. With appendices. London, 1861. vi, 82 pp. Sm. 8° 817.5
GASSENDI, Pierre Gassend, Biography of. Rogers, H. (*In* Macaulay, T. B., *lord,* and others. New biographies of illustrious men) 5428.4
GASTRONOMY. A book about the table. Jeaffreson, J. C. London, 1875. 2 v. 8° 6432.3
GATES ajar, The. Phelps, E. S. 537.9
GATLING guns. Report of the board of officers on Gatling guns of large calibre for flank defence. *See* UNITED STATES. *Department of war. Ordnance department.* Washington, 1874. 4° 6910.7
GAUTIER, Hippolyte. Les curiosités de l'exposition universelle de 1867. Avec 6 plans. Paris, 1867. 186+ pp. 16° 1518.13
GAUTIER, Théophile. Constantinople. From the French, by R. H. Gould. American edition revised. New York, 1875. 363+ pp. 12° 824.12
— Jean et Jeannette. Paris, 1863. 319+ pp. 18°. 5536.2
— A winter in Russia. From the French, by M. M. Ripley. New York, 1874. 348+ pp. 12°. 824.5 and 5915.10
— *joint author.* The cross of Berny. *See* GIRARDIN, Delphine Gay de 725.30
GAVIN, Antonio. The great red dragon; or the master-key to popery. Boston, 1854. 408 pp. 1 plate. 12° 1226.21
GAY cottage. Bradley, W. I. 918.29
GAYLORD, Glance, *pseud.* *See* BRADLEY, Warren Ives.
GAYWORTHYS, The. Whitney, A. D. T. 735.8
GAZETTEERS. Morse, J., and Parish, E. New gazetteer of the Eastern continent. Charlestown, 1802. 8° 432.4
— Thomas, J., and Baldwin, T. Lippincott's pronouncing gazetteer. Philadelphia, 1873. 8°. *R.R., B.3.2
GAZZA, La, ladra. Rossini, G. (*In* Ditson, O., and co. Standard opera librettos) 6233.3.3
GEBEL Teir. Tudor, W. 532.4
GEIER-WALLY. [Fiction.] Hillern, W. von 521.33
GEIKIE, Archibald. Life of Sir Roderick I. Murchison. Based on his journals and letters. With notices of his scientific contemporaries and a sketch of the rise and growth of palæozoic geology in Britain. Illustrated with portraits and woodcuts. London, 1875. 2 v. 8° 5333.3
GEIKIE, James. The great ice age, and its relations to the antiquity of man. London, 1874. xxiii, 575 pp. Illustrated. Maps. 8° 6633.2

Note.— "A systematic account of the glacial epoch, with special reference to its changes of climate." — *Preface.*

Shelf. No.

GELÉE, Claude, *called Claude Lorrain.* Liber veritatis. Reproduced in autotype from selected etchings by Richard Earlom, after the original drawings by Claude Lorraine. London, 1872. 2 v. F° 6220.6

Contents. — [Vol. I.] Marine subjects. [II.] Landscapes. [III.] Pastoral subjects.

GEM series. *See* SARGENT, Epes.
GENEALOGIES. Deane, W. R. A genealogical memoir of the Leonard family. Boston, 1851. 8°. 612.4
— Fowler, W. C. Memorials of the Chaunceys, including President Chauncy, his ancestors and descendants. Boston, 1858. 8° 610.3
— Shattuck, L. Memorials of the descendants of William Shattuck. Boston, 1855. 8° 612.7
GENERAL, The. Barrows, W. 934.2
GENERATIVE organs. The functions and disorders of the reproductive organs. Acton, W. Philadelphia, 1865. 8° 6022.6
GENESIS disclosed. Davies, T. A. New York, 1874. 12° 6327.12
GENESIS of species, On the. Mivart, St. G. London, 1871. Sm. 8° 1536.5
GENESIS, The, of the New England churches. Bacon, L. New York, 1874. 8° 5812.13
GENEST, John. Some account of the English stage, from the restoration in 1660 to 1830. Bath, 1832. 10 v. 8° 5622.2
GENEVA. Abbott, J. Rollo in 917.18
— Tribunal of arbitration. *See* ALABAMA claims.
— Wilson, H. B. Séances historiques de Genève. The national church. (*In* Essays and reviews). 1538.3
— *Same.* (*In* Hedge, F. H. Recent inquiries in theology) .... 1526.24 and 5814.15
GENEVIÈVE. Lamartine, A. (M. L.) de. New York, 1871. 8° 531.25
GENEVIÈVE de Brabant. Offenbach, J. (*In* Ditson, O., and co. Standard opera librettos) 6233.3.5
GENGHIS KHAN, History of. Abbott, J. 914.36
GENNESARETH, The Rob Roy on the. Macgregor, J. New York, 1870. Sm. 8° 423.17
GENTIANELLA. Randolph, *Mrs.* — 714.9
GENTLEMAN, A, from Ireland: a comedy. O'Brien, F. New York, N. D. 12° 1635.5
GEOFFRY Hamlyn. Kingsley, H. 326.23
GEOGRAPHY. Aiken, J. Geographical delineations, or a compendious view of the natural and political state of all parts of the globe. Philadelphia, 1807. 8° 232.1
— Colton, G. W. General atlas, containing 180 maps and plans. [With] letter-press descriptions, by R. S. Fisher. New York, 1873. F°. *R.R. Desk
— Cornell, S. S. Intermediate geography. New York, 1859. 4° 5030.3
— Cummings, J. A. Introduction to ancient and modern geography. Boston, 1818. 12° 438.2
— Hale, N. An epitome of universal geography. Boston, 1830. 12° 437.3
— Kiepert, H. Grosser Hand-Atlas des Himmels und der Erde. Thüringer, 1873. F° .... *R.R. Desk
— Knight, C. Geography; or, first division of "The English cyclopædia." London, 1866–69. 4 v. and supplement. 4° .... *R.R., F.2.1
— Mitchell, S. A. A system of modern geography. Philadelphia, 1846. 16° 437.4
— Morse, J. American universal geography. Boston, 1805. 2 v. 8° 437.2
— Smith, W. Dictionary of Greek and Roman geography. London, 1872. 2 v. 8° .... *R.R., E.3.4
— Thomas, J., and Baldwin, T. Lippincott's pronouncing gazetteer. Philadelphia, 1873. 8°. *R.R., B.3.2

See also Glaciers, Physical geography.

GEOLOGY. Agassiz, L. (J. R.) Geological sketches. Boston, 1871. 16° 1525.13
— Darwin, C. (R.) Journal of researches into the geology of the countries visited during the voyage of [the] Beagle round the world. New York, 1871. 2 v. 16° 1526.11

Shelf. No.

GEOLOGY, *continued.*
— Geikie, A. Life of Sir Roderick I. Murchison. With a sketch of the rise and growth of palæozoic geology in Britain. London, 1875. 2 v. 8°. 5333.3
— Hartt, C. F. Geology of Brazil. Boston, 1870. 8° 5033.1
— Hooker, W. Geology. New York, 1872. 12° .. 6636.3
— Kingsley, C. Town geology. London, 1872. Sm. 8° .... 1526.3 and 6636.2
— Lyell, *Sir* C. Geological evidences of the antiquity of man. With an outline of glacial and post-tertiary geology. London, 1873. 8° 6613.7
— – Principles of. New York, 1873. 2 v. 8° 6631.7
— Miller, H. The foot-prints of the Creator. Boston, 1859. 12° 1526.16
— – The old red sandstone. Boston, 1857. 12° .. 1524.20
— – Popular geology. Boston, 1859. 12° 1524.19
— – The testimony of the rocks. Boston, 1872. 12°. 1527.2
— Mitchell, S. L. Observations on the geology of North America. New York, 1818. 8° 6633.1
— Owen, R. Key to the geology of the globe. Boston, 1857. 8° 6631.9
— Portlock, J. E. Rudiments of. London, N. D. 12° 1716.3
— Tate, R. Rudimentary treatise on. London, 1871. 2 v. 12° 1715.7
— Taylor, J. E. Geological stories. London, 1873. 16° 6637.2

See also Earth, Physical geography.

Note. — On the connection of geology with prehistoric archæology, see Bulletin, vol. II, p. 298.

GEOMETRY, Practical plane and solid. Angel, H. New York [Glasgow], 1873. 16° 1717.4
GEORGE II, *king of England,* Historical sketches of the reign of. Oliphant, M. (O. W.) Boston, N. D. 8° 1032.1
GEORGE III, *king of England.* Brougham, H., *lord.* Lives of philosophers of the time of. Edinburgh, 1872. 16° 5614.4.1
— – Men of letters of the time of. Edinburgh, 1872. 16° 5614.4.2
— – Statesmen of the time of. Edinburgh, 1872. 16° .... Vol. 3–5 of 5614.4
GEORGE IV, *king of England,* Statesmen of the time of. Brougham, H., *lord.* Edinburgh, 1872. 16°. Vol. 3–5 of 5614.4

See also for George II, George III, and George IV, the Catalogue notes on English history, printed separately.

GEORGE Canterbury's will. Wood, E. P. 333.3
GEORGE Dandin: comédie. Molière, J. B. P. Œuvres. Paris, 1869. 12° 5537.2.2
GEORGE Geith of Fen court. Riddell, J. H. 316.1
GEORGE Julian. Cockton, H. 717.7
GEORGES, The four, *of England.* Thackeray, W. M. Leipzig, 1861. Sq. 16° 335.3

Note. — A graphic and caustic narrative of the court life of these reigns.

GEORGIE. Abbott, J. 917.35
GERALD Fitzgerald, "the chevalier." Lever, C. (J.). 730.4
GERALDINE. [Poem.] Dawes, R. New York, 1839. 12° 5217.4
GERANDO, Joseph Marie, *baron* de. Self-education; or the means and art of moral progress. From the French by Elizabeth P. Peabody. Boston, 1860. xv, 468 pp. 16° 1536.13
GÉRARD, (Cécile) Jules (Basile). Lion hunting and sporting life in Algeria. 4th edition. London, 1857. 224 pp. Illustrated. Portrait. 16° .. 427.4
GERDA; or, the children of work. Schwartz, M. S. 735.3[illegible]
GERMAN music, Modern. Chorley, H. F. London [1854]. Sm. 8° .... 6235.[illegible]
GERMAN poets. Gostwick, J. New York [1874]. 8°. 5723.[illegible]
GERMAN universities. Hart, J. M. New York, 1874. 12° .... 5836.1[illegible]
GERMAN tales. Auerbach, B. .... 918.1[illegible]
GERMANY. *Geography, description, travel, etc.*
— Adams, W. T. Down the Rhine; or, Young America in. Boston, 1873. 16° .... 916.1[illegible]
— Arnold, M. Higher schools and universities in. London, 1874. Sm. 8° .... 5836.[illegible]

Shelf. No.

GERMANY. *Geography, description, travel, etc., cont'd.*

— Baedeker, C. Handbook for travellers [in Northern Germany]. Coblenz, 1870. 16° 5718.3
— – Handbook for travellers [in Southern Germany]. Coblenz, 1871. 16° 5718.2
— Brace, C. L. Home-life in. New York, 1853. 12°. 425.19

Note. — A series of papers on home-life in Germany appeared in Fraser's magazine, 1875.

— Browne, J. R. An American family in. New York, 1871. 12° 424.18

Note. — Also in Harper's monthly, vol. 27.

— Gostwick, J. German poets. A series of memoirs and translations. New York [1874]. 8° 5723.5
— Hawthorne, J. Saxon studies. [Descriptions of Dresden, etc.] Boston, 1876. 12° 424.5
— Head, *Sir* F. B. Bubbles from the Brunnen of Nassau. London, 1866. 12° 425.2
— Hope, *Mrs.* —. S. Boniface and the conversion of. London, 1872. 16° 5735.6
— Johnson, A. C. Peasant life in. New York, 1859. 12° 827.9
— Kroeger, A. E. The minnesinger of. New York, 1873. 16° 5735.1
— Mansfield, R. B. The log of the Water lily. During two cruises in the summers of 1851–52, on the Rhine, Neckar, Main, Moselle, Danube and other streams of. Leipzig, 1854. Sq. 16°. 313.20
— Map of Austria and the German empire. London, 1873. 30 in. × 18 in. 5730.3
— Murray, J. Handbook for Northern Germany. London, 1871. 12° 5915.1
— – Handbook for Southern Germany. London, 1871. 12° 5716.2
— Shinn, E. The new Hyperion. Philadelphia, 1875. 8° 5722.4
— Spencer, E. Sketches of Germany and the Germans. London, 1836. 2 v. 8° 422.6
— Staël-Holstein, A. L. G. N., *baronne* de. De l'Allemagne. Paris, 1869. 18° 5536.21
— – Germany. New York, 1871. 2 v. in 1. 12°. 5726.1
— Wallace, *Mrs.* E. D. A woman's experiences in. New York, 1872. 12° 423.11
— Ward, J. Experiences of a diplomatist, being recollections of, 1840–70. London, 1872. 8° .. 5714.6

See also Austria, Prussia, Rhine, etc.

Note. — See Andersen's "Poet's bazaar" [426.18]; and a paper on the Harz mountains in Harper's monthly, vol. 47, and on the gambling spas in vol. 45.

History, etc.

— Bryce, J. The holy Roman empire. London, 1873. Sm. 8° 5814.19
— Feydeau, E. (A.) L'Allemagne en 1871. Paris, 1872. 18° 5726.1
— Gardiner, S. R. The thirty years' war, 1618–48. London, 1874. Sq. 16° 628.2
— Hozier, H. M. The seven weeks' war. Philadelphia, 1867. 2 v. 8° 5922.4
— Kohlrausch, H. F. T. History of; from the earliest period to the present time. New York, 1874. 8° 5712.3
— Menzel, W. History of. London, 1871. 3 v. 8°. 5715.3
— Moltke, H. C. B. von. Histoire de la campagne de 1866. Paris, 1868. 8° 5712.1
— Motley, J. L. Life and death of John of Barneveld. With the primary causes of the thirty years' war. London, 1874. 2 v. 8° 5713.3
— Schiller, (J. C.) F. von. Geschichte des dreissigjährigen Krieg. Stuttgart, 1867. 12° 5734.1.9
— – History of the thirty years' war. New York, 1846. 12° 826.6
— Tacitus, C. C. Germania. Philadelphia, 1849. Sm. 12° 6118.6
— Trench, R. C. Gustavus Adolphus in Germany, and other lectures on the thirty years' war. London, 1872. Sm. 8° 5717.2

Note. — The most popularly written *general* history, for the period it covers, is Kohlrausch's [5712.3]; but Menzel's [5715.3] is an honest, readable book, of good reputation, and comes down to 1814. See also Bryce's "Holy Roman empire" [5814.10] and Coxe's "History of the house of Austria" [5715.1], which covers an extended period, 1218–1792, and has been continued. See the general histories of Europe, and those of Austria, Prussia, etc.

Shelf. No.

GERMANY. *History, etc., continued.*

For the *Roman period*, see Cæsar's "Commentaries" [6115.5]; Tacitus's "Germania" [6118.6]; Gibbon's 9th chapter of his History [824.9]; and Merivale's "Roman empire" [5515.3]. The victory of Arminius is told in Creasy's "Decisive battles" [824.6].

For the period *before the reformation*, beside the general histories, see Mrs. Hope's "St. Boniface and the conversion of the Germans" [5735.6]; and Hallam's "Middle ages" [5916.1]. Also the note on Charlemagne and his period, under France.

In fiction, Meinhold's "Sidonia the sorceress" [531.1] is a picture of mediæval life. James's "Mary of Burgundy" [722.11] covers the period of Maximilian I. There are illustrations of the Vehm gerichte in Scott's "Anne of Geierstein" [324.1; 533.1].

For the *sixteenth century*, the most considerable English contribution is Robertson's "Charles the fifth," [1226.9]. See Reformation, *note*.

Gardiner's "*Thirty years' war*" [628.2] is an approved summary of the most recent German authorities on the history of that struggle for German unity, in the seventeenth century, known as the Thirty years' war between the Protestant and Catholic forces of Europe, 1618–48. A still more condensed review, without, however, the advantage of the latest researches, will be found in Dr. Smyth's well-known "Lectures on modern history" [5012.10; 5925.7]; and general views in connection with contemporary European history will be gained from the more comprehensive histories of Europe, Germany, Austria, Prussia, Sweden, etc. Schiller is unfavorable to Wallenstein, but his readable monograph has popularly the most extended reputation of any on the war.

The causes of the war have been elaborately traced in Motley's "John of Barneveld" [5713.3]. See Trench's lecture on Gustavus Adolphus in Germany [5717.2]; J. K. Hosmer's paper on Lützen, in the Atlantic monthly, April, 1876, and the note in the Bulletin, vol. II, p. 277.

For historical fiction on this period, see James's "Heidelberg," 1619–22 [327.7]; De Foe's "Memoirs of a cavalier" (Gustavus and Tilly); Schiller's drama of Wallenstein [827.26, etc.]. For baronial life, see Miss Yonge's "Dove in the eagle's nest" [318.17].

For the *Seven years' war*, A. D. 1756–63, the most elaborate account in English will be found in Carlyle's "Frederick the great" [1237.1]. The relations of Germany with England are recounted in Stanhope's "History of England" [838.3, ch. 32].

For the *Napoleonic wars*, see France.

For the *Seven weeks' war*, 1866, the most useful book for the English reader is Hozier [5922.4].

For the *Franco-German war*, 1870-71, see France.

The English reader will find great benefit from the commentaries on the different periods of German history, with criticisms on the authorities, in Smyth's "Lectures on modern history" [5012.10; 5925.7]. See Chesney's article on the military future of Germany, in Macmillan's magazine, Sept., 1875; and a paper on German parliaments, in Scribner's monthly, April, 1875.

Language.

— Adler, G. J. Dictionary of the German and English languages. New York, 1873. 8°. *R.R., D.3.8
— – A progressive German reader. New York, 1852. 12° 2025.2
— Becker, C. F. Lehrbuch der deutschen Stiles. Frankfurt am Main, 1850. 8° 5735.7
— Comfort, G. F. A German course. New York, 1870. 12° 1933.7
— – A German reader. New York, 1871. 12° ... 1933.4
— Heness, T. Introduction to the Leitfaden. Boston, 1874. 12° 2025.1
— Noehden, G. H. Grammar of the German language. Andover, 1842. 12° 1933.8
— Ollendorff, H. G. New method of learning the German language. New York, 1852. 12° 2025.3
— Otto, É. German conversation-grammar. New York, 1868. Sm. 8° 1933.5
— Prendergast, T. The mastery series. New York, 1868. 12° 1933.3
— Whitney, W. D. A compendious German grammar. New York, 1869. 12° 1933.6

Literature.

— Baskerville, A. The poetry of Germany. Philadelphia, 1872. 16° 1625.4
— Buchheim, C. A. Deutsche Lyrik. London, 1875. Sm. 8° 2028.7
— Carlyle, T. German romance: specimens of its chief authors. Boston, 1841. 2 v. in 1. 12°. 5725.2
— Cherbuliez, V. Étude de littérature et d'art. Paris, 1873. 16° 5536.7
— Deutsches Leben in Lieb' und Treue. Bremen [1873]. With illuminated plates. L. 4° 5730.4
— Deutsches Leben in Liedern. Bremen [1873]. With illuminated plates. L. 4° 5730.5
— Gostwick, J. German poets. A series of memoirs and translations. New York [1874]. 8°. 5723.5
— – and Harrison, R. Outlines of German literature. New York, 1873. Sm. 8° 5835.2
— Haym, R. Die romantische Schule. Berlin, 1870. 8° 5733.2

Shelf. No.

GERMANY. *Literature, continued.*
— Hedge, F. H. Prose writers of Germany. Philadelphia [*cop.* 1847]. 8° 5732.1
— Kurz, H. Geschichte der deutschen Literatur. Leipzig, 1873. 4 v. 8° 5730.2
— Vilmar, A. F. C. Geschichte der deutschen National-Literatur. Marburg, 1873. 8° 5733.1

Note. — General histories in English. Carlyle gave the first important impulse to the study of German literature in England, and his Essays [5610.7] contain much in elucidation. The subject, however, is presented compendiously in Gostwick's "Outlines" [5835.2]; while Max Müller furnishes a brief summary to his selection of the classics from the 4th to the 19th century, in his "Chips" [5616.1.3]. See Coleridge's essay in "The friend" [2611.5]. Also Mackintosh's review of Madame de Staël, in his Essays.

General histories in German. Kurz [5730.2], who follows the plan of Chambers and Duyckinck for English and American literatures, is the most convenient. The work of Dr. Vilmar [in German, 5733.1], coming down to 1832, though generally too laudatory in its estimates, deserves the reputation it has, and, not being overburdened with details, forms an excellent summary.

Early periods. For the Nibelungen period, see Carlyle's Essays, where is also to be found a review of the literature of the 14th and 15th centuries. See Kroeger, on "The minnesinger" [5735.1]; also Max Müller's "Chips" [5616.1.3]. See also Hallam [1531.2] for the 15th, 16th, and 17th centuries.

Eighteenth century. The English reader will find an able compact summary in some chapters in Lewes's "Life of Goethe" [5724.1], and he will also consult the "Life of Lessing," by Stahr [1022.7]; and of Schiller, by Carlyle [1238.19]. Madame de Staël [5726.1; in French, 5536.21] first disclosed to the rest of Europe the modern development of German literature; and she was thought to have been influenced by A. W. Schlegel in her bias towards the Romantic school, which Heine [see his "Prose miscellanies"] sought to counteract. See the paper on the Romantic school in the Atlantic monthly, Dec., 1875.

Nineteenth century. Beside the general histories, see Carlyle's Essays [5610.7].

Prose. This department has been specially cultivated in English by Carlyle in his "German romance" [5725.2], who gives memoirs of the writers, and reviews of their works, from Musäus to Goethe. Dr. Hedge's book [5732.1] gives the same treatment, with more extensive scope.

Poetry. The English reader will consult the section in Longfellow's "Poets and poetry of Europe" [5922.1], and the authorities there named. Baskerville's book [1625.4] is an anthology, with brief memoranda, with German and English text.

In German, Gervinus's History is extremely elaborated, marked by great industry and patience, but it has not been translated.

Drama. The section in the translation of Schlegel's Lectures [6136.2] is the best brief summary in English. See Lady Pollock, on the German and French drama, in the Contemporary review, Feb., 1873; and Carlyle, on German playwrights, in his Essays [5610.7].

Education. The reader must go to the Bates Hall catalogues for the history and development of education in Germany. Howitt's "Student life in Germany" is an amusing account of the students' ways of living. See, in this connection, articles on the German universities in Putnam's magazine, Oct., 1868, and Atlantic monthly, vol. 7. See also Matthew Arnold's "Schools and universities on the continent" [5836.6], and a chapter in Ross Browne's "American family in Germany" [424.18].

GÉRÔME, Jean Léon. In a caravan with Gérôme the painter. (*In* Many lands and many people) ... 431.3
GERRY, Elbridge, Life of. Austin, J. T. Boston, 1828. 8° 1011.3
GERSTAECKER, Friedrich. Frank Wildman's adventures on land and water. Translated and revised by L. Wraxall 932.42
— How a bride was won. Translated by F. Jordan. 521.3
— Wild sports in the far West. Translated from the German. With eight crayon drawings. Boston, 1861. xi, 396 pp. 12° 415.1
GERTRUDE. Sewell, E. M. 527.21
GERVINUS, Georg Gottfried. Introduction to the history of the nineteenth century. From the German. With a brief notice of the author. London, 1866. xx, 137 pp. 16° 836.2
— Shakespeare commentaries. Translated under the author's superintendence by F. E. Bunnètt. New edition, revised by the translator. London, 1875. l, 941 pp. 8° 5610.5
GESSERT, M. A. Rudimentary treatise on the art of painting on glass. From the German. Added an appendix on the art of enamelling, etc. 3d edition. London, 1857. iv, 92 pp. 12° 1715.5
GESTURE. Bacon, A. M. Manual of. Chicago, 1873. 12° 1736.2
— Russell, W. Rudiments of. Boston, 1830. 12°. 1517.9
GETTING on in the world; or, hints on success in life. Mathews, W. Chicago, 1874. 12° 5836.8
GHAZZALI, Abu Hamid Mohammed Ben Mohammed Al. The alchemy of happiness. Translated from the Turkish, by Henry A. Homes. Albany, 1873. 120 pp. 8° 1531.9

Shelf. No.

GHIBERTI, Lorenzo. Die Chronik seiner Vaterstadt. (*In* Hagen, (E.) A. Künstler-Geschichten) ... 2026.1.1
GHOST, The. O'Connor, W. D. (*In* Johnson, (E.) R. Little classics) 529.4.8
GIAOUR, The. [Poem.] Byron, G. G. N., *lord.* Philadelphia, 1813. 12° 1619.1
GIBBON, Charles. In honor bound 710.34
GIBBON, Edward. Autobiography and correspondence. London, 1869. 356 [354] pp. Sm. 8° 1024.5
— History of the decline and fall of the Roman empire. With notes, by H. H. Milman. New edition. Philadelphia [1845]. 6 v. Portrait. 12°. 824.9
— Lawrence, E. Lives of the British historians. New York, 1855. 12° 1224.7.2
— Rogers, H. Biography of. (*In* Macaulay, T. B., *lord,* and others. New biographies of illustrious men) 5428.4
— Sainte-Beuve, C. A. English portraits. New York, 1875. 16° 1025.3
GIBRALTAR gallery, The. Abbott, J. Harper's story books 936.1.8
GIBSON, John, Life of. Eastlake, *Lady* E. R. London, 1870. 8° 5423.13
GIBSON, Walter M. The prison of Weltevreden; and a glance at the East Indian archipelago. Illustrated. New York, 1855. xiv, 495 pp. 12°. 424.3
GIDDINGS, Joshua Reed. The exiles of Florida. Columbus, 1858. viii, 338 pp. Illustrated. 16°. 825.8
GIDEON'S rock. Saunders, K. 339.24
GIFT, Theo, *pseud.* Leisure hour series. Pretty Miss Bellew. A tale of home life 529.10
GIHON, John H., *joint author.* Annals of San Francisco. *See* SOULÉ, Frank 810.3
GILBERT, William. Lucretia Borgia, duchess of Ferrara. A biography. London, 1869. 2 v. Portrait. Sm. 8° 5526.7
GILBERT, William Schwenck. Original plays. New York, 1876. 366 pp. 12° 1634.1

Contents. — The wicked world; Pygmalion and Galatea; Charity; The princess; The palace of truth; Trial by jury.

GILBERT Starr and his lessons. Bradley, W. I. 913.4
GILBERT'S last summer at Rainford, and what it taught. Bradley, W. I. 913.6
GIL BLAS. Le Sage, A. R. The adventures of. London [1867]. Sq. 16° 517.18
— — Histoire de. Paris, 1872. 18° 5536.17
GILCHRIST, Alexander. Life of William Blake, with selections from his poems and other writings. Illustrated from Blake's own works. London, 1863. 2 v. Portrait. 8° 6213.9
GILDED age, The. Clemens, S. L., and Warner, C. D. Hartford, 1874. 8° 712.1
GILDER, Richard Watson. The new day. A poem in songs and sonnets. New York, 1876. 112 pp. Sq. 16° 1617.16
GILES's minority. O'Reilly, E. G. 928.10
GILFILLAN, George. The bards of the Bible. New York, 1869. 378 pp. 12° 1523.8
GILFILLAN, James. The Sabbath viewed in the light of reason, of revelation, and history, with sketches of its literature. New York [1862]. xii, 635 pp. 16° 1534.3
GILLET, Joseph Antony, *joint author.* Natural philosophy. *See* ROLFE, William James 6436.9
GILLIES, Robert Pearse. Personal reminiscences. (*In* Stoddard, R. H. Bric-à-brac series) 1828.10
GILLRAY, James. Works. *See* WRIGHT, Thomas... 5632.1
GILMAN, Arthur. Seven historic ages. [Juvenile]. 918.30
GILMAN, Samuel. Memoirs of a New England village choir. By a member. Boston, 1829. 149+ pp. Sm. 12° 1238.22
GILMOR, Harry. Four years in the saddle. [Civil war, 1861-65.] New York, 1866. 291 pp. 1 plate. 12° 817.17
GILMORE, James Roberts. (*Edmund Kirke.*) Among the pines: or, South in secession-time. New York, 1862. 310 pp. 12° 916.3
— Down in Tennessee, and back by way of Richmond. New York, 1864. 282 pp. 12° 716.19
— My Southern friends. New York, 1863. 308 pp. 12° 715.21

Shelf. No.

GILMORE, John. Storm warriors; or, life-boat work on the Goodwin sands. London, 1875. xvi, 358 pp. Wood-cut. Sm. 8° 5935.6
GILMORE, Parker. (*Ubique.*) Accessible field sports. London, 1869. xii, 336 pp. Illustrated. Sm. 8°. 1514.10
— Gun, rod, and saddle. Personal experiences. London, 1869. viii, 295 pp. Sm. 8° 1514.11
— Prairie and forest: a description of the game of North America, with personal adventures in their pursuit. New York, 1874. 378 pp. Illustrated. 12° 6415.1
GINX's baby. [Satire on English poor laws.] Jenkins, E. 311.21
GIPSIES. *See* GYPSIES.
GIPSY, The. James, G. P. R. 327.17
GIPSY's, The, daughter. Grey, *Mrs.* 521.27
GIPSY's, The, prophecy. Southworth, E. D. E. N. . 527.11
GIRARD, Stephen. *See* PARTON, J. Famous Americans of recent times. Boston, 1871. 8° 1214.14
GIRARDIN, Delphine Gay de, GAUTIER, Théophile, SANDEAU, (Léonard Sylvain) Jules, and MÉRY, Joseph. The cross of Berny. A novel 725.30
GIRARDIN, J. The adventures of Johnny Ironsides. A tale. Translated by Henry Frith 1114.1
GIRL'S, A, romance. Robinson, F. W. 731.37
GIRONDISTS. Lamartine, A. (M. L.) de. Histoire des Girondins. Paris, 1848. 8 v. 8° 2011.1
— - History of the. New York, 1868. 3 v. 12°. 827.25
GIURAMENTO, Il. Mercadante, S. (*In* Ditson, O., and co. Standard opera librettos) 6233.3.1
GLACIERS. Geikie, J. The great ice age, and its relations to the antiquity of man. London, 1874. 8° 6633.2
— Wonders of the physical world: the glacier, etc. London, 1875. Sm. 8° 1714.31
GLADIATORS, The. [Fiction.] Melville, G. J. W.. 321.15
GLADSTONE, John Hall. Michael Faraday. New York, 1872. 223 pp. Portrait. 16° 5428.1
GLADSTONE, William Ewart. Homeric synchronism: an enquiry into the time and place of Homer. London, 1876. 284+ pp. Sm. 8° 6117.5
— Juventus mundi. The gods and men of the heroic age. [Homeric period.] Boston, 1869. xxvii, 554 pp. 1 folded plate. Sm. 8° 1523.9
— Rome and the newest fashions in religion. Three tracts. The Vatican decrees. Vaticanism. Speeches of the pope. Leipzig, 1875. 287 pp. Sq. 16° 1918.12
— Speeches of pope Pius IX. [From the Quarterly review, Jan., 1875.] New York, 1875. 44 pp. 8° 1911.3
— The Vatican decrees in their bearing on civil allegiance. Added: a history of the Vatican council; with the Latin and English text of the papal syllabus and the Vatican decrees. By Philip Schaff. New York, 1875. 168 [166] pp. 8° 1911.1
— Vaticanism: an answer to Reproofs and replies. New York, 1875. 96 pp. 8° 1911.2
GLAISHER, James, FLAMMARION, Camille, FONVIELLE, Wilfrid de, and TISSANDIER, Gaston. Travels in the air. Edited by J. Glaisher. With illustrations. Philadelphia [London], 1871. xxix, 398+ pp. 8° 5911.1
GLANCE GAYLORD, *pseud.* *See* BRADLEY, Warren Ives.
GLANCES and glimpses. Hunt, H. K. Boston, 1856. 12° 1214.5
GLASS. Gessert, M. A. Rudimentary treatise on the art of painting on. London, 1857. 12° ... 1715.5
— Jarves, D. Reminiscences of glass-making. New York, 1865. 8° 6425.2
— Sauzay, A. Marvels of glass-making. London [1869]. Sm. 8° 6425.3
— - Wonders of glass-making in all ages. New York, 1871. 16° 1714.24
— Trowbridge, J. T. Lawrence's adventures among the glass-makers 932.20
GLEIG, George Robert. Life of Arthur, duke of Wellington. Revised, with additions. London, 1871. xvi, 501+ pp. Portrait. Sm. 8° 5426.13

Shelf. No.

GLEIG, George Robert, *continued.*
— Life of Robert, first lord Clive. London, 1848. vi, 314 pp. Sm. 8° 5428.8
— Story of the battle of Waterloo. New edition. London, 1861. vi, 330 pp. Sm. 8° 5927.5
GLEN Morris stories. *See* WISE, Daniel.
GLIDDON, George R., *joint author.* Types of mankind. *See* NOTT, Josiah Clark 6610.7
GLIMPSE, A, of the world. Sewell, E. M. 314.17
GLIMPSES of life in Victoria. By a resident. Edinburgh, 1872. xi, 428+ pp. 8° 5931.11
GLOVER, Mary Baker. Science and health. Boston, 1875. 456 pp. 12° 1733.3
GLOVES. Manuel du fabricant de gants. Artois, V. d'. Paris, 1835. 24° 6439.2
GLUCK, Christophe Willibald Ritter von. *See* HAWEIS, H. R. Music and morals. New York, 1872. 12°. 1513.16
GO-AHEAD. Fosdick, C. A. 934.7
GO-AHEAD series. *See* FOSDICK, Charles A.
GOAKS and tears. Lewis, C. B. 713.9
GOD and the Bible. Arnold, M. Boston, 1876. 12°. 5815.5
GOD in history. Bunsen, C. C. J. von. London, 1868, 70. 3 v. 8° 5813.13
GODDARD, J. T. The velocipede; its history, varieties, and practice. With illustrations. New York, 1869. 107 pp. 16° 1514.5
GODEY's lady's book. Vol. 85–91. Philadelphia, 1872–75. 7 v. 8° 1412.1
GODKIN, James. The religious history of Ireland, primitive, papal, and protestant. London, 1873. viii, 313 pp. 8° 5412.3
GODOLPHIN and Falkland. Bulwer-Lytton, E. (G. E.) L. 336.4
GODWIN, Parke. Cyclopædia of biography: a record of the lives of eminent persons. New edition. With Supplement, by G. Sheppard. New York, 1872. 825, 128+ pp. 12° .............*R.R., F.3.4
GODWIN, William. Adventures of Caleb Williams. Boston 521.22
— *Same.* New York. 2 v. 536.5
GOETHE, Johann Wolfgang von. Werke. Stuttgart, 1868. 36 v. in 18. 8° 5737.1

Contents. — Vol. [I.] 1, 2. Goethe's Leben; Gedichte. [II.] 3. Hermann und Dorothea; Achilleïs; Reineke Fuchs. 4. Götz von Berlichingen mit der eisernen Hand; Egmont; Clavigo. [III.] 5. Faust. 6. Iphigenie auf Tauris; Torquato Tasso; Die natürliche Tochter; Elpenor. [IV.] 7. Leiden des jungen Werthers; Briefe aus der Schweiz; Brief eines Landgeistlichen; Zwo biblische Fragen; Die Wahlverwandtschaften. 8. Wilhelm Meisters Lehrjahre. [V.] 9, 10. Wilhelm Meisters Wanderjahre. 10. Reise der Söhne Megaprazons; Die guten Weiber; Novelle. [VI.] 11, 12. Aus meinem Leben; Wahrheit und Dichtung.

[VII.] 13. Sprüche in Reimen; Sprüche in Prosa; Ethisches. 14. West-östlicher Divan. [VIII]. 15. Alles an Personen und zu festlichen Gelegenheiten gedichtete enthaltend. 16. Lustspiele und Farcen. [IX.] 17. Singspiele. 18. Schauspiele; Zeitstücke. [X.] 19. Italienische Reise. 20. Italien. [XI.] 21. Campagne in Frankreich; Belagerung von Mainz; Unterhaltungen deutscher Ausgewanderten. 22. Schweizerreise; Rhein, Main und Neckar. [XII.] 23. Annalen oder Tag- und Jahreshefte von 1749, bis Ende 1822; Biographische Einzelnheiten. 24. Benvenuto Cellini, B. 1–3.

[XIII.] 25. Benvenuto Cellini, B. 4; Anhang; Rameau's Neffe; Diderots Versuch über die Malerei. 26. Winckelmann; Philipp Hackert; Einleitung in die Propyläen; Ueber Laokoon; Der Sammler und die Seinigen; Ueber Wahrheit und Wahrscheinlichkeit der Kunstwerke; Philostrat's Gemälde; Antik und Modern; Nachträgliches. [XIV.] 27. Ferneres über Kunst. 28. Deutsche Literatur. [XV.] 29. Auswärtige Literatur und Volkspoesie. 30. Jugenddramen; Entwürfe.

[XVI.] 31. Götz von Berlichingen mit der eisernen Hand, für die Bühne; Die Wette; Mahomet, nach Voltaire; Tancred, nach Voltaire; Theater und dramatische Poesie. 32. Morphologie. [XVII.] 33. Zur Farbenlehre, didaktischer Theil. 34. Zur Farbenlehre, polemischer Theil. [XVIII.] 35. Materialen zur Geschichte der Farbenlehre. 36. Naturwissenschaftliche Einzelnheiten; Mineralogie; Geologie; Meteorologie; Zur Naturwissenschaft im Allgemeinen; Chronologie der Entstehung Goethescher Schriften.

— Auto-biography. Also Letters from Switzerland, and Travels in Italy. Translated by J. Oxenford and A. J. W. Morrison. London, 1872. 2 v. Portrait. Sm. 8° 1025.5
— Conversations with Eckermann and Soret. From the German by J. Oxenford. New edition. London, 1874. xxvii, 583 pp. Sm. 8° 5735.11
— Correspondence with a child. Boston, 1872. 504 pp. Portrait. Sm. 8° 533.10
— Egmont: a tragedy. From the German by F. Boott. Boston, 1871. 150 pp. 16° 1636.3
— *Same.* With English notes, etc. by C. A. Buchheim. Oxford, 1868. xlviii, 199 pp. 16° 2027.1

Shelf. No.

GOETHE, Johann Wolfgang von, *continued.*

— Faust. From the German by J. Anster. Leipzig, 1867. xiv, 295+ pp. Sq. 16° 1613.21

— *Same.* Translated, in the original metres, by Bayard Taylor. Boston, 1871, 73. 2 v. 4° .. 5730.1

— Hermann and Dorothea. Translated by E. Frothingham. With illustrations. Boston, 1870. 165+ pp. 16° 1615.16

— Wilhelm Meister's apprenticeship. From the German by E. Grove. Leipzig, 1873. 2 v. in 1. Sq. 16° 329.9

— Wilhelm Meister's apprenticeship and travels. From the German, by T. Carlyle. New edition, revised. Boston, 1871. 2 v. Portrait. Sm. 8°. 515.4

— Calvert, G. H. Goethe: his life and works. Boston, 1872. 16° 1027.2

— Lewes, G. H. The story of Goethe's life. London, 1873. 8° 5724.1

— Mendelssohn-Bartholdy, C. Goethe and Mendelssohn. (1821–31.) London, 1874. Sm. 8°. 5726.4

Note. — The story of his life by Lewes is a condensation of his large and excellent biography. Goethe's "Auto-biography," though interesting to the student, hardly supplies the place of a proper biographical narrative. See Longfellow's "Poets and poetry of Europe" [5922.1]. Goethe's "Correspondence with a child" is fictitious, but see Atlantic monthly, Feb., 1873, for a "Curiosity of literature." Calvert presents different phases of Goethe's life, with a chronological summary of events at the end.

See additional essays by Emerson, in his "Representative men" [1916.6; 1934.6.2]; by Hedge, in his "Prose writers of Germany" [5732.1]; by Carlyle, in his Essays [5610.7]; by De Quincey, in his "Biographical essays" [1825.6]; by Longfellow, in his "Hyperion" [1838.4.2]; by Mrs. Jameson, in her "Studies" [1916.3]; and by Jeffrey [5610.8].

Eckermann's "Conversations" [5735.11] is valuable as disclosing Goethe's opinions.

Goethe figures in two of the Muehlbach novels, "Old Fritz and the new era" and "Goethe and Schiller."

See the histories of German literature, and Gostwick's "Outlines of German literature" [5835.2].

GOING on a mission. Cobden, P. 1115.1

GOING West. Adams, W. T. 938.9

GOLD and dross. Mayo, I. F. 734.17

GOLD and name. Schwartz, M. S. Boston 531.10

— *Same.* New York. 2 v. 2028.3

GOLD brick, The. Stephens, A. S. (W.) 726.12

GOLD-BUG, The. Poe, E. A. (*In* Johnson, (E.) R. Little classics) 529.4.12

GOLD Elsie. John, E. 517.17

GOLD-FOIL, hammered from popular proverbs. Holland, J. G. New York, 1859. 12° 1535.5

GOLD hunter's, The, library. *See* THOMES, William H.

GOLD hunters, The, in Europe. Thomes, W. H. Boston, 1873. Sm. 8° 735.4

GOLD hunters', The, adventures. Thomes, W. H. Boston, 1873. 12° 735.3

GOLD thimble, The. Adams, W. T. 918.11

GOLDEN fetters. Lemon, M. 312.6

GOLDEN grain. Farjeon, B. L. 732.7

GOLDEN legend, The. [Dramatic poem.] Longfellow, H. W. Leipzig, 1856. Sq. 16° 1614.1

GOLDEN lion, The, of Grandpere. Trollope, A. 334.19

GOLDEN sorrow, A. Hoey, *Mrs.* C. 330.21

GOLDEN treasury, The. [An anthology.] Palgrave, F. T., *editor* 1627.4

GOLDEN treasury series. *Namely:* —

— Buchheim, C. A. Deutsche Lyrik 2028.7

GOLDEN tress, The. Du Boisgobey, F. 532.14

GOLDSMITH, Oliver. Works. Edited by P. Cunningham. London, 1854. 4 v. Illustrated. Portrait. 8° 5612.1

Contents. — Vol. I. Poetical works: The traveller; Edwin and Angelina; The deserted village; The haunch of venison; The captivity; Retaliation; Threnodia Augustalis; Miscellaneous poems; Dramas: The good-natured man; She stoops to conquer; Scene from the grumbler; The vicar of Wakefield. II. Enquiry into the present state of polite learning; The citizen of the world. III. The bee; Essays; Unacknowledged essays; Prefaces, introductions, etc. IV. Biographies; Reviews; Animated nature; Cock lane ghost; Vida's game of chess; Letters.

— Select works. With portrait. Leipzig, 1842. 399+ pp. Sq. 16° 312.23

Contents. — The vicar of Wakefield; The traveller; The hermit; The deserted village; The haunch of venison; The captivity; Retaliation; Miscellaneous pieces; The good-natured man; She stoops to conquer; Scene from the grumbler.

GOLDSMITH, Oliver, *continued.*

— The vicar of Wakefield. With illustrations printed in oil colours. London, N. D. xxxii, 286 pp. Sm. 4° 515.3

— Forster, J. Life and times of. London, 1871. 2 v. 8° 1022.1

— *Same.* Leipzig, 1873. 2 v. Sq. 16° 1028.2

— Irving, W. Oliver Goldsmith: a biography. Leipzig, 1850. Sq. 16° 1238.6

— *Same.* London, 1850. 16° 715.6

— *Same.* Philadelphia, 1871. Sm. 8° 1815.13

— Lawrence, E. Lives of the British historians. New York, 1855. 12° 1224.7.2

— Macaulay, T. B., *lord.* Biography of. (*In his* New biographies of illustrious men) 5428.4

Note. — Forster's "Life and times" makes what is in some respects the best literary biography produced in our day, and an excellent picture of literary England in the last century; and it furnished the material which Irving has gracefully worked up in his sketchy life. Macaulay's is a spirited sketch. See also Bulwer's essay [336.5]; Scott's "Lives of the novelists" [5914.2]; De Quincey's "Essays on the poets" [1825.4]; Howitt's "Homes and haunts" [1225.5]; Thackeray's "Humourists" [1238.8]; Forsyth's "Novels and novelists" [6136.1]; and Harper's monthly, vols. 14 and 48.

GOLDSMITH's wife, The. Ainsworth, W. H. 330.11

GONDI, Jean François Paul de, *cardinal de Retz.* Mémoires du cardinal de Retz, de Guy-Joli, et de la duchesse de Nemours. Nouvelle édition. Paris, 1817. 6 v. Portrait. 12° 5528.4

GOOCH, Benjamin. On some of the most important diseases peculiar to women; with other papers. Prefatory essay by R. Ferguson. London, 1859. lv, 235+ pp. 8° 6023.4

GOOD, John Mason. The book of nature. Boston, 1826. 2 v. 8° 6833.1

GOOD English; or, popular errors in language. Gould, E. S. New York, 1870. 16° 1736.1

GOOD fight, A. Reade, C. 538.2

GOOD for nothing. Melville, G. J. W. 321.11

GOOD luck. Cobden, P. 926.35

"GOOD luck!" Werner, E. 731.29

GOOD match, A. Perrier, A. 725.31

GOOD-NATURED man, The: a comedy. Goldsmith, O. Works. Leipzig, 1842. Sq. 16° 312.23

— *Same.* London, 1854. 8° 5612.1.1

GOOD old times, The. [Historical novel.] Ainsworth, W. H. 2 v. 329.11

GOOD society. Grey, *Mrs.* 521.28

GOOD time coming, The. Hale, E. E. 529.7

GOOD words. Vol. 14, 15. London, 1873, 74. 2 v. 8°. 1338.1

GOODEVE, T. M. Elements of mechanism. 2d edition. London, 1871. viii, 269 pp. Illustrated. 16° 6817.2

GOODRICH, Charles Augustus. History of the United States. 17th edition. Boston, 1827. 296, 20 pp. 12° 818.6

— Lives of the signers of the declaration of independence. 4th edition. Boston, 1834. 460 pp. 12° 1014.7

GOODRICH, Frank Boot. Remarkable voyages; or, man upon the sea: a history of maritime adventure, exploration and discovery, from the earliest ages to the present time. With illustrations. Philadelphia, 1873. 560 pp. 8° 421.7

— and WARDEN, Frank L. Romance after marriage: a comedy. New York, N. D. 28 pp. 12° 1635.4

GOODWIN, Charles Wycliffe. On the Mosaic cosmogony. (*In* Essays and reviews) 1538.3

— *Same.* (*In* Hedge, F. H. Recent inquiries in theology) .... 1526.24 and 5814.15

GOODWIN, Ezra Shaw. Sermons. With a memoir. Boston, 1834. 268 pp. 12° 5816.1

GOODWIN, *Mrs.* H. B. Dr. Howell's family 734.1

GOODWIN, Nathaniel. Genealogical notes, or contributions to the family history of some of the first settlers of Connecticut and Massachusetts. Hartford, 1856. xx, 362 pp. 8° .... 5011.

GOODWIN, T. A. The mode of man's immortality: or, the when, where, and how, of the future life. New York, 1874. 238 pp. 12° 6326.1

GOODWIN sands, Storm warriors; or, life-boat work on the. Gilmore, J. London, 1875. Sm. 8° .. 5935.

Shelf. No.

GOODY Gracious! and the forget-me-not. Neal, J. (*In* Johnson, (E.) R. Little classics) 529.4.10
GOODYEAR, Charles. *See* PARTON, J. Famous Americans of recent times. Boston, 1871. 8°. 1214.14
GORDON, Clarence. (*Vieux Moustache.*) Boarding-school days 915.22
— That good old time 916.24
GORDON, George Hamilton, *earl of Aberdeen.* An inquiry into the principles of beauty in Grecian architecture; with an historical view of the rise and progress of art in Greece. Extracted from Wilkins's translation of Vitruvius, to which this work is an introduction. London, 1860. viii [vi], 110 pp. 12° 1716.18
GORDON, Lucy Austin, *lady Duff.* Last letters from Egypt. Added letters from the Cape. With a memoir by her daughter, Mrs. Ross. London, 1875. xi, 346 pp. Portrait. Sm. 8° 436.5
GORDON, Mary. 'Christopher North,' a memoir of John Wilson; compiled from family papers and other sources. With an introduction by R. S. Mackenzie. New York, 1866. xi, 484+ pp. Illustrated. Portrait. 12° 1024.7
GORE, Catherine Grace Frances. Castles in the air. 311.1
— The dean's daughter 311.5
— Heckington 312.25
— A life's lessons 311.2
— Mammon 311.3
— New year's day, a winter's tale 938.7
— Progress and prejudice 311.4
— The two aristocracies 312.26

Note. — Mrs. Gore's novels are mostly descriptive of fashionable English life.

GORILLA country, Stories of the. [Africa.] Du Chaillu, P. B. New York, 1870. 12° 933.5
GORILLA hunters, The. Ballantyne, R. M. 913.26
GOSAU smithy, The. Parr, L. 335.18
GOSSE, Philip Henry. Evenings at the microscope; or, researches among the minuter organs and forms of animal life. New York, 1872. xii, 480 pp. 12° 1523.11
— The romance of natural history. [Popular science.] With illustrations. Boston [1860]. xiv, 372 pp. Sm. 8° 1523.14
GOSTWICK, Joseph. German poets. A series of memoirs and translations. With portraits by C. Jäger. New York [1874]. 265+ pp. 8°. 5723.5

Contents. — The poets of the Hohenstaufen time; The master-singers and their times; Klopstock; Wieland; Lessing; Herder; Goethe; Schiller; Jean Paul; Körner; Chamisso; Rückert; Uhland; Heine.

— and HARRISON, Robert. Outlines of German literature. New York, 1873. xii, 588 pp. Sm. 8°. 5835.2
GOTHIC revival, History of the. Eastlake, *Sir* C. L. London, 1872. Sm. 4° 6221.2

See also Architecture.

GOUGER, Henry. Personal narrative of two years' imprisonment in Burmah, 1824–26. With illustrations. London, 1860. xii, 327 pp. 12° 425.21
GOUGH, John B. Speech in Boston, Sept. 17, 1860. *See* MASSACHUSETTS temperance society 1524.2
GOULD, Augustus Addison. Report on the invertebrata of Massachusetts. *See* MASSACHUSETTS. 6631.8
GOULD, Benjamin Apthorp, *jr.* Reply to the "Statement of the trustees" of the Dudley observatory. Albany, 1859. v, 366+ pp. 8° 1912.4
GOULD, Edward S. Good English; or, popular errors in language. 4th edition, revised. New York, 1870. v, 228+ pp. 16° 1736.1
GOULD, Jeanie T. Marjorie's quest 723.2
GOULD, S. Baring. *See* BARING-GOULD, Sabine.
GOULDING, F. R. Marooner's island 926.31
GOUNOD, Charles. Faust; Romeo and Juliet. (*In* Ditson, O., and co. Standard opera librettos) .. 6233.3.1
GOUT, Treatise on the nature and cure of. Scudamore, C. Philadelphia, 1819. 8° 6023.14
GOVERNMENT. Alden, J. The science of government in connection with American institutions. New York [cop. 1866]. 12° 6336.1
— Helps, *Sir* A. Thoughts upon government. London, 1874. Sm. 8° 6333.2

Shelf. No.

GOVERNMENT, *continued.*
— Mailfer, H. C. Recherches historiques du juste et de l'autorité. Philosophie appliquée. Paris, 1873. 2 v. 8° 6332.1
— Sidney, A. Discourses on government. New York, 1805. 3 v. 8° 1923.1
GOWRIE; or, the king's plot. James, G. P. R. 730.8
GRACE Lee. Kavanagh, J. 323.2
GRAEFE, A. von. Three memoirs on iridectomy in certain forms of iritis, choroiditis and glaucoma. Translated by T. Windsor. London, 1859. viii, 380+ pp. 8° 6023.1
GRAESSE, Johann Georg Theodor. Lehrbuch einer allgemeinen Literärgeschichte aller bekannten Völker der Welt. Dresden, 1838. 13 v. 8° .. 6132.1
GRAHAM, Ennis. Not without thorns 731.5
— Tell me a story. [Juvenile] 1117.28
GRAHAM, James J. Elementary history of the progress of the art of war. London, 1858. xvi, 336 pp. 12° 6927.2
GRAHAM, John, *of Claverhouse, viscount Dundee,* Memorials and letters illustrative of the life and times of. Napier, M. Edinburgh, 1859, 62. 3 v. 8° 5331.2
GRAHAM, Walter. The brassfounder's manual. 3d edition, with illustrations. London, 1870. viii, 141 pp. 12° 1716.2
GRAMMAR. Hermes or a philosophical inqviry concerning vniversal grammar. Harris, J. London, 1786. 8° 1734.1

See also Language.

GRAMMONT, Philibert, *comte* de, Mémoires du. Hamilton, A. T. I. Paris, 1823. 32° 5528.5
GRAMONT, Antoine Agénor Alfred, *duc* de. Memor [*pseud.*]. Passé et présent, étude d'histoire contemporaine. 2e édition. Paris, 1875. 192+ pp. 16° 5534.6
GRANADA, Chronicle of the conquest of. Irving, W. London, 1850. Sm. 8° 826.4
— *Same.* Philadelphia, 1871. Sm. 8° 1815.6
GRAND duchess of Gerolstein. Offenbach, J. (*In* Ditson, O., and co. Standard opera librettos). 6233.3.5
GRANDMOTHER's money. Robinson, F. W. 731.23
GRANDMOTHER's scrap-book. Conant, C. A. 916.12
GRANDMOTHER's story of Bunker-hill battle. [A ballad.] Holmes, O. W. Memorial. Bunker hill. Boston [1875]. L. 8° 810.8
GRAND-PÈRE, Le, et ses quatre petits-fils. Fouqueau de Pussy, J. J. Boston, 1854. 12° 2014.3
GRANGÉ, Eugène, *pseud.* *See* BASTÉ, Eugène Pierre.
GRANT, *Miss* —. Victor Lescar 331.18
GRANT, *Sir* Alexander. Xenophon [outlined and explained]. Edinburgh, 1871. 180+ pp. Map. 16°. [Ancient classics for English readers] 6116.9
GRANT, Anne, *formerly Miss MacVicar.* Letters from the mountains, 1773–1807. 1st American edition. Boston, 1809. 2 v. 12° 1910.5
GRANT, *Sir* Hope. Incidents in the Sepoy war, 1857, 58. With some explanatory chapters by H. Knollys. Edinburgh, 1873. xiv, 380+ pp. Map. Sm. 8° 5924.6
GRANT, James. The great metropolis [London]. Vol. 1, 3d edition; v. 2, 2d edition. New York, 1837. 2 v. in 1. 12° 827.2
— The yellow frigate 517.12
GRANT, Maria M. Artiste 731.16
GRANT, Ulysses Simpson. Adams, W. T. Our standard-bearer; or, the life of. Boston, 1868. 16° 916.14
— Badeau, A. Military history of. Vol. I. New York, 1868. 8° 5021.8
— Richardson, A. D. A personal history of. Hartford, 1868. 8° 1210.2

Note. — Of the popular lives of Grant, among the most considerable in extent is that by Richardson, who was a war correspondent with his army. Of the exclusively military lives Badeau's is the best; only the first volume, however, is as yet published, bringing the record down to the early part of 1864; but the author, as a member of Grant's military household, had great advantages. See the works on the civil war, under the United States. Also Harper's monthly, vols. 30, 31, 35 and 39, and Atlantic monthly, vol. 23.

Shelf. No.

GRANTLEY manor. Fullerton, *Lady* G. 325.19
GRANVILLE valley. Abbott, J. 923.4
GRAPE culture. A practical treatise on the culture and treatment of the grape vine. Allen, J. F. New York, 1856. 12° 6425.4
GRAPES and thorns. Tincker, M. A. 720.12
GRAPHIC, The. Illustrated. Vol. 8–12. London, 1873–75. 5 v. F° 6710.1
GRATET-DUPLESSIS, Georges. *See* DUPLESSIS, Georges Gratet.
GRATTAN, Henry. *See* LECKY, W. E. H. Leaders of public opinion in Ireland. New York, 1872. 12° 1025.9

Note. — See Brougham's Statesmen [5614.4.3]; Foster's Essays [5614.2]; Rogers's Table-talk; Memoirs of Thomas Moore, Sir James Mackintosh, etc.

GRAY, Asa. Botany for young people. [Part I.] How plants grow. With a popular flora. Illustrated. New York, 1874. 233+ pp. Sm. 4°. 6626.7
— — Part II. How plants behave, how they move, climb, employ insects to work for them, etc. New York, 1874. 46 pp. Illustrated. Sm. 4°. 1523.24
GRAY, Barry, *pseud.* *See* COFFIN, Robert Barry.
GRAY, George Zabriskie. The children's crusade: an episode of the thirteenth century. New York, 1871. xiii, 240 pp. Sq. 16° 824.10
GRAY, O. W., *joint compiler.* Official topographical atlas of Massachusetts. *See* WALLING, H. F. *R.R., Desk
GRAY, Thomas. Poetical works. With memoir. Boston, 1871. cxviii, 223 pp. Portrait. 16°.. 1616.4

Note. — See also essay by Bulwer [336.5]; Hazlitt's "Lectures on the English poets" [5610.6; 5616.5]; Walpole's Letters, *passim;* Howitt's "Homes and haunts" [1225.5]; Johnson's "Lives of the poets" [1238.20]; and Jesse's "Etonians."
See Allibone and references, and the histories of English literature.

GREAT army, The. Sketches of life and character in a Thames-side district [London]. By the Riverside visitor. [2d edition.] London, 1876. vi, 533+ pp. Sm. 8° 1838.2
GREAT bonanza, The. Adams, W. T., and others. Boston, 1876. 8° 910.3
GREAT BRITAIN. The case of Great Britain, as laid before the tribunal of arbitration, convened at Geneva. Washington, 1872. 3 v. 8° 5011.2
— The counter case of Great Britain as laid before the tribunal of arbitration, convened at Geneva. Washington, 1872. 1105 pp. 8° 5011.9
— Correspondence concerning claims against Great Britain. *See* UNITED STATES. *Department of state.* 6911.1
— Allen, J. Battles of the British navy. London, 1868. 2 v. Sm. 8° 5417.5
— Bagehot, W. Lombard street: a description of the money market. New York, 1873. 12° 5435.8
— Brougham, H., *lord.* The British constitution. Edinburgh, 1872. 16° 5614.4.11
— Burke, *Sir* (J.) B. A genealogical and heraldic dictionary of the peerage and baronetage of the British empire. London, 1875. L. 8° 5410.3
— Fawcett, H. Speeches on some current political questions. London, 1873. 8° 5822.11
— Gairdner, J. The houses of Lancaster and York. London, 1874. Sq. 16° 628.4
— Green, J. R. A short history of the English people. London, 1874. Sm. 8° 5418.10
— Greg, W. R. Rocks ahead; or, the warnings of Cassandra. London, 1874. Sm. 8° 5826.6
— *Same.* Boston, 1875. 16° 1534.12
— Greville, C. C. F. The Greville memoirs. A journal of the reigns of king George IV and king William IV. London, 1875. 3 v. 8° 5414.6
— *Same.* (*In* Stoddard, R. H. Bric-à-brac series). 1828.5
— Higginson, T. W. English statesmen. New York, 1875. 16° 628.7
— Hinton, R. J. English radical leaders. New York, 1875. 16° 628.8
— Holdsworth, E. W. H. Deep-sea fishing and fishing boats. An account of the practical working of the various fisheries around the British islands. London, 1874. 8° 5932.13
— Holyoake, G. J. The history of co-operation in England. Vol. I. London, 1875. Sm. 8° 5826.9

Shelf. No.

GREAT BRITAIN, *continued.*
— Houghton, W. Sketches of British insects. London, 1875. Sm. 8° 6616.13
— Howitt, W. Homes and haunts of the most eminent British poets. New York, 1851. 2 v. 12° 1225.5
— Law, E., *first earl Ellenborough.* History of the Indian administration of Lord Ellenborough, in his correspondence with the duke of Wellington. London, 1874. 8° 5412.5
— Lodge, E. Portraits of illustrious personages of Great Britain. London, 1849, 50. 8 v. Sm. 8°. 5337.6
— Mills, A. The literature and the literary men of Great Britain and Ireland. New York, 1870. 2 v. 8° 1021.6
— Morley, H. Memoirs of Bartholomew fair. London [1874]. Sm. 8° 5418.8
— Napier, *Sir* W. F. P. English battles and sieges in the peninsula. London, 1873. Sm. 8° 5916.9
— Planché, J. R. History of British costume. London, 1874. Sm. 8° 6235.3
— Ranke, (F.) L. von. A history of England. Oxford, 1875. 6 v. 8° 5412.6
— Rawlinson, *Sir* H. (C.) England and Russia in the East. London, 1875. 8° 5921.5
— Sargent, F. W. England, the United States, and the Southern confederacy. London, 1864. 8°.. 812.7
— Smiles, S. Lives of the engineers. Comprising also a history of inland communication in Britain. London, 1861. 2 v. 8° 5421.4
— Smith, P. V. History of the English institutions. Philadelphia, 1874. 16° 5418.5
— Strutt, J. The sports and pastimes of the people of England. London, 1876. Sm. 8° 6414.4
— Thompson, T. Annals of influenza; or, catarrhal fever in Great Britain from 1510 to 1837. London, 1852. 8° 6013.14
— Thornbury, W. British artists, from Hogarth to Turner. London, 1861. 2 v. Sm. 8° 6214.3
— Wright, T. Our new masters. London, 1873. 8°. 5415.9
— Yonge, C. D. History of the British navy, from the earliest period to the present time. London, 1866. 8° 5412.7

See also England, Royal institute, Ireland, Scotland, Wales, and the "Catalogue notes on English history," printed separately.

GREAT elm, The. Abbott, J. Harper's story books. 936.1.9
GREAT expectations. Dickens, C. (J. H.) Boston. 1824.5
— *Same.* Leipzig 338.15
GREAT Hoggarty diamond, The. Thackeray, W. M. (*In his* Miscellanies.) Leipzig 335.13.1
— *Same.* (*In his* Works.) London 513.1.8
GREAT ice age, The. [Geology.] Geikie, J. London, 1874. 8° 6633.2
GREAT march [Sherman's to the sea], Story of the. Nichols, G. W. New York, 1866. 12° 815.7
GREAT red dragon, The. Gavin, A. Boston, 1854. 12° 1226.21
GREAT SALT LAKE CITY, *Utah.* The city of the saints. Burton, R. F. New York, 1862. 8°.. 412.2

See also Mormonism, Utah.

GREAT South, The. [Southern United States, with illustrations.] King, E. Hartford, 1875. 8°. 5031.6
GREAT tragic revival, The: a drama. Brougham, J. New York, N. D. 12° 1635.5
GREAT truths on great subjects. Bayley, J. London, 1874. Sm. 8° 6328.17
GREAT Western series, The. *See* ADAMS, William T.
GREATER Britain: a record of travel in English-speaking countries, during 1866 and 1867. [United States and Australia.] Dilke, C. W. New York, 1869. 12° .... 423.13 and 5935.7
GREECE. Adams, W. T. Cross and crescent; or, Young America in. Boston, 1874. 16° 925.11
— Blackie, J. S. Horæ Hellenicæ: essays and discussions on some important points of Greek philology and antiquity. London, 1874. 8° 6113.4
— Bonner, J. Child's history of. New York, 1871. 2 v. 16° 926.2
— Cocker, B. F. Christianity and Greek philosophy. New York, 1872. Sm. 8° 5814.4

Shelf. No.

GREECE, *continued.*
— Cox, G. W. General history of Greece, from the earliest period to the death of Alexander the great. London, 1876. Sm. 8°............5916.13
— – History of. London, 1874. 2 v. 8°........ 5911.5
— Curtius, E. History of. New York, 1874, 75. 5 v. 12°....................................5924.10
— Fustel de Coulanges, N. D. The ancient city: a study on the religion, laws, and institutions of. Boston, 1874. 16°. 5923.6
— Gordon, G. H. An inquiry into the principles of beauty in Grecian architecture; with an historical view of the rise and progress of art in. London, 1860. 12°........................1716.18
— Grote, G. History of. London, 1869. 12 v. 16°. 5926.1
— Guhl, E., and Koner, W. The life of the Greeks and Romans, described from antique monuments. New York [London], 1875. 8°.............. 5921.9
— Howard, G. W. F., *earl of Carlisle.* Diary in Turkish and Greek waters. Boston, 1855. 12°. 825.5
— Howe, S. G. Historical sketch of the Greek revolution. New York, 1828. 8°............ 821.1
— Kingsley, C. Greek fairy tales. London, 1868. 16°.. 935.25
— Liddell, H. G., and Scott, R. A Greek-English lexicon. Oxford, 1869. 4°.............*R.R., D.3.6
— Lloyd, W. W. The age of Pericles. A history of the politics and arts of Greece from the Persian to the Peloponnesian war. London, 1875. 2 v. 8°......................................5921.12
— Mahaffy, J. P. Social life in Greece from Homer to Menander. London, 1874. Sm. 8°........ 5925.1
— Mueller, C. O. History of the literature of ancient Greece. Continued after the author's death, by J. W. Donaldson. London [1858]. 3 v. 8°.................................. 6113.3

Shelf. No.

GREECE, *continued.*
— Mure, W. Critical history of the language and literature of antient Greece. London, 1854–67. 5 v. 8°.. 6113.5
— Murray, J. Handbook for. London, 1872. 12°.5917.10
— Pouqueville, F. C. H. L. Grèce. Paris, 1843. 8°. 5911.8
— Rollin, C. Ancient history of the Grecians. Vol. 1–4, 6–8. Boston, 1807. 8°............ 5913.1
— Ruskin, J. The queen of the air: a study of the Greek myths of cloud and storm. New York, 1872. 12°..................................6236.17
— Sewell, E. M. A first history of. New York, 1869. 12°.................................. 828.13
— Smith, W. Dictionary of Greek and Roman antiquities. London, 1872. 8°.........*R.R., E.3.5
— – Dictionary of Greek and Roman biography and mythology. London, 1870. 3 v. 8°....*R.R., E.3.3
— – Dictionary of Greek and Roman geography. London, 1872. 2 v. 8°...............*R.R., E.3.4
— – History of. New York, 1875. 12°..........5916.11
— Soleinne, — de. Bibliothèque dramatique. T. I. Paris, 1843. 8°.............................. 5532.1
— Sophocles, E. A. A glossary of later and Byzantine Greek. [Cambridge, 1860. Title-page missing.] 4°.............................. 6110.2
— Taine, H. A. The philosophy of art in. New York, 1872. 12°.......................... 6217.2
— Taylor, (J.) B. Travels in. New York, 1872. 12°.. 224.3
— Willis, N. P. Pencillings by the way. New York, 1844. L. 8°.......................... 430.2
— Wyse, *Sir* T. Impressions of. London, 1871. 8°. 5931.4
— Xenophon. The Hellenics, or Grecian history. London, 1872. Sm. 8°...................... 6115.4

See also Athens, Peloponnessus.

Note.— Dr. William Smith considers Grote's contributions to historical science the most valuable that have been made within the present generation, and Grote's History, notwithstanding the author's tendency to theorizing, is commonly esteemed the most valuable of all for the student, and except for its voluminousness for the ordinary reader. He presents the early legendary history, but begins to write in the modern critical spirit when he reaches B. C. 776, and continues the narrative to the close of Alexander's generation, B. C. 300. Grote undertook his work to correct the errors of Mitford, and to counteract the effects following upon Mitford's illiberal views of the popular institutions of the Greeks, which were also controverted in Bulwer's "Athens" [828.10], which comes down only to B. C. 429, and is reviewed from Mitford's stand-point in Alison's Essays [1531.7].

The modern critical and philosophical manner of writing history has thrown somewhat into disrepute the heroic and exaggerating method of Plutarch, many of whose Lives [5932.5] trace the progress of Grecian history which was copied by Rollin in his "Ancient history" [5913.1].

For the *legendary history*, see Max Müller's "Chips" [5616.1]; and the manuals mentioned in the note under Mythology. The 2d chapter of Mure's "Critical history" [6113.5] discusses the historic value of the mythical legends.

The most *popular* of the German histories is that of Curtius, which is to come down to B. C. 404, but it is not yet completed; but an English translation is in progress. In some respects he is more learned than Grote. Less extensive scope will be found in Cox's History [5911.5], and still less in Cox's smaller work [5916.3], coming down to the death of Alexander the great, and in Sewell's "First history" [828.13]. Philip Smith gives a good summarized narrative in his "History of the world." Important episodes with their bearing on the sequence of events are given in Creasy's "Decisive battles" [824.6]. Newman has an essay on the striving of ancient Greece for unity, in Fraser's magazine, 1874. Other illustrative matter will be found in Freeman's "Essays" [5913.4] and in his "History of federal government" [5921.11].

Those who wish to go to Herodotus as an original authority, will find much help from Rawlinson's notes in his edition [6112.2], and will follow it with Lloyd's "Age of Pericles" [5921.12], before going on to a later period with Thucydides [6115.8]. The view taken by Herodotus of Greek history is controverted in Plutarch's "Morals" [6113.1.4].

On the *life and manners* of the ancient Greeks, Grote is still the best, while Becker's Charicles, though a novel, embodies the critical researches of German scholarship, accompanied with illustrative notes; and Barthélemy's Anacharsis is a book of imaginary travels in the ripest times of ancient Greece. In this connection the books above named by Fustel de Coulanges, Guhl and Koner, and Mahaffy deserve examination.

On the *mythology*, see Clarke's "Ten great religions" [1523.2]; Max Müller's "Chips" [5616.1.1 and 2], an article on the relations of the religion of ancient Greece to her mythology, in the North American review, July, 1869; and Higginson's essay on the goddesses [1915.2; also in the Atlantic monthly, July, 1869]. See a chapter in Müller on religion. See De Quincey on Pagan oracles in his "Memorials" [1825.8], and an examination of De Quincey's views on the religion of the Greeks in the Christian examiner, March, 1866. There is an account of the oracles in Plutarch's "Morals" [6113.1.4]. See also Cocker's "Christianity and Greek philosophy" [5814.4].

Felton's Lectures, as the work of a genial writer and the foremost of American Greek scholars, and as embodying personal observations of travel, are of great usefulness to the general reader. Smith's Dictionaries, named above, embody the latest erudition and are of great excellence.

Emerson says, "An excellent popular book is J. A. St. John's Ancient Greece; the life and letters of Niebuhr, even more than his lectures, furnish leading views. The secret of the recent histories in German and in English is the discovery, owed first to Wolff and later to Boeckh, that the sincere Greek history of that period must be drawn from Demosthenes, especially from the business orations, and from the comic poets."

For the period of the Trojan war, Homer's poem, which Gladstone holds to be substantial fact, and has illustrated in his "Juventus mundi" [1523.9], may be compared with Shakespeare's treatment in his "Troilus and Cressida."

History, — middle period.

Gibbon's Rome [824.9] may be consulted for the "middle period" of Greek history.

On the war for independence begun in 1821, beside Howe, see Felton's Lectures and Mr. Everett's elegant essay in the North American review for October, 1823 [also in his works], and Mr. Webster's speech in congress [in his works, 5013.1] for the recognition of Greek independence.

For *description and travel*, beside the books named above, see W. C. Prime's paper in Harper's monthly, vol. 17.

Literature, etc.

For the general history of Greek literature, the English reader will find compendious accounts in some of the lectures of Felton's Greece; while Grote's view of the literature is as valuable as his history is in other sections. And similar side treatment will be found in Curtius; in Bulwer's "Athens" [828.10]; and in Lloyd's "Age of Pericles" [5921.12]. Mueller, who died in 1840, left incomplete what promised to be a most valuable history, but it has been continued by Donaldson [6113.3]. The work of Col. Mure [6113.5] is, however, the most elaborate monograph in English. See also De Quincey's article on "style" in his "Historical and critical essays" [1825.3].

On the *lyrical poetry*, see Felton's Lectures, and Grote [5926.1.4].

On the *Greek drama*, see Schlegel's "Lectures on the dramatic art and literature" [6136.2]; chapters in Grote [5926.1]; Book v of Bulwer's "Athens" [828.10]; Felton's Greece; Froude's "Sea studies" in Fraser's magazine, 1875; and De Quincey's theory of Greek tragedy in his Letters, etc.

Art.

See Dr. Lodge's translation of Winckelmann's well-known history of art among the Greeks [6211.1; also Atlantic monthly, April, 1873]. Taine's book is written in pursuance of his favorite theory of ethnological and climatic influences. The English reader will find the history of Greek art treated in general histories of art, of sculpture, and of painting; and special chapters in the books already referred to, by Grote, Felton, Lloyd, etc. See also Foster's "Critical essays" [5614.3.2].

There is a popular account in Viardot's "Wonders of sculpture" [1714.28].

Also Van Brunt's papers on the principles of Greek art in the Atlantic monthly, June, 1861, etc., and Ruskin on Greek landscape in vol. 3 of his "Modern painters" [6236.18]. Their architecture has ample treatment in the general works of Fergusson [6222.3] and Lübke [6210.4]; and with much sympathy in Rosengarten's "Architectural styles."

Shelf. No.

GREEK anthology, The [outlined and explained]. Neaves, C., *lord Neaves*. Philadelphia, 1874. 16°. 6116.21

GREEK church. The Eastern liturgy. London, 1866. 81+ pp. 32° 5818.18

— The great catechism. From the Greek edition, by J. T. S. London, 1867. 58+ pp. 32° 5818.17

— The holy canons of the seven œcumenic synods. From the original Greek. London, 1867. iv, 56+ pp. 32° 5818.16

— The pope of Rome and the popes of the oriental orthodox church. Tondini, C. London, 1871. Sm. 8° 5816.1

GREELEY, Horace. The American conflict, 1860–65. Illustrated. Hartford, 1865, 67. 2 v. 8° 810.1

— Essays designed to elucidate the science of political economy. Boston, 1871. 384 pp. 12° 1525.18

— Recollections of a busy life. A new edition, with a memoir of [his] later years and death. New York, 1873. 624, lxxxiii pp. Portraits. Facsimile. 8° 5023.8

— What I know of farming. New York, 1871. 335 pp. 12° 1515.16

— Cleveland, C. Story of a summer [at Horace Greeley's home]; or, journal leaves from Chappaqua. New York, 1874. Sq. 16° 1019.2

— Parton, J. Life of. Boston, 1869. 12° 5023.6

— and OTHERS. The great industries of the United States. With illustrations. Hartford, 1872. 1304 pp. 8° 1511.1

GREEN, Horace. Surgical treatment of polypi of the larynx, and œdema of the glottis. New York, 1852. 121+ pp. Illustrated. 8° 6023.12

— Treatise on diseases of the air passages, bronchitis, etc. New York, 1846. xv, 276 pp. 7 plates. 8° 6021.2

GREEN, John Orne. Memorial of John C. Dalton. An address, April 27, 1864. Cambridge, 1864. 35 pp. 8° 5023.4

GREEN, John Rich. A short history of the English people. With maps and tables. London, 1874. xxxix, 847 pp. Sm. 8° 5418.10

GREEN, Jonathan. Practical compendium of the diseases of the skin, including a particular consideration of the more frequent and intractable forms of these affections; with cases. From the 2d London edition. Boston, 1839. xii, 252 pp. 8° 6012.9

GREEN, Thomas Henry. An introduction to pathology and morbid anatomy. Illustrated. Philadelphia, 1871. 260 [256] pp. 8° 6021.9

GREEN gate, The. Wichert, E. 714.16

GREEN mountain boys, The: a historical tale of the early settlement of Vermont. Thompson, D. P. 734.1

GREENE, George Washington. Life of Nathanael Greene. New York, 1871. 3 v. Portrait. Map. 8° 5023.2

GREENE, Nathanael, Life of. Greene, G. W. New York, 1871. 3 v. 8° 5023.2

GREENE, R. J. Cushions and corners 926.30

— A winter and summer at Burton hall 926.29

GREENE, Robert, and PEELE, George. Dramatic and poetical works. With memoirs and notes by A. Dyce. London, 1861. vi, 624+ pp. 8°. 5621.4

GREENHOW, Robert. History of Oregon and California, and the other territories on the north-west coast of North America. 2d edition. Boston, 1845. xviii, 492+ pp. 8° 810.2

Shelf. No.

GREENLAND, The land of desolation: being a personal narrative of observation and adventure in. Hayes, I. I. New York, 1872. 12° 423.9

GREENOUGH, Henry. Apelles and his contemporaries. Boston, 1860. 342 pp. Sm. 8° 536.10

— Ernest Carroll, or artist-life in Italy. Boston, 1858. 344 pp. 16° 737.28

GREENOUGH, *Mrs.* Richard Saltonstall. *See* GREENOUGH, Sarah D.

GREENOUGH, Sarah D. Arabesques 1516.12

— In extremis 736.20

— Treason at home 522.3

GREENOUGH, Sarah L. Lilian 716.16

GREENOUGH, William Whitwell. Free lending libraries. *See* AMERICAN social science association. 1932.2

GREENWELL, Dora. The patience of hope 1535.7

GREENWOOD, Francis William Pitt. Sermons of consolation. 2d edition. Boston, 1844. viii, 312 pp. 16° 5817.10

GREENWOOD, Grace, *pseud.* *See* LIPPINCOTT, Sara Jane.

GREENWOOD, James. The London vocabulary, English and Latin. 1st American from the 25th London edition. Cambridge, 1816. x, 132 pp. Sm. 12° 6128.1

— A night in a workhouse. (*In* Johnson, (E.) R. Little classics) 529.4.1

— Rudimentary treatise on navigation: Part 1. How to keep the log and work it off. 2. On finding the latitude and longitude. With illustrations. 9th edition. London, 1870. viii, 167 pp. 12° 1715.11

— The true history of a little ragamuffin. New York, 1867. iv, 138 pp. 8° 521.5

— Wild sports of the world: a book of natural history and adventure. With illustrations. New York, 1870. 474+ pp. 8° 1514.21

GREG, William Rathbone. The creed of Christendom: its foundations contrasted with its superstructure. 3d edition. London, 1874. 2 v. Sm. 8° 5816.21

— Enigmas of life. [Essays.] Boston, 1873. 322 pp. 16° .... 1534.2 and 6136.5

— Literary and social judgments. Boston, 1873. 352 pp. 16° 5616.10

— Rocks ahead; or, the warnings of Cassandra. 2d edition. London, 1874. xli, 233+ pp. Sm. 8°. 5826.6

— *Same.* Boston, 1875. xli, 233+ pp. 16° 1534.12

Contents. — Political rock; Economic rock; Religious rock; Appendix: The mistake of honest democrats; Unionist restrictions on labour; Three men and three eras; United States in recent years.

Note. — In the view of the author the three especial dangers hanging over the future of England are: "The political supremacy of the lower classes; The approaching industrial decline of England; The divorce of the intelligence of the country from its religion."

GREGORIUS *Thaumaturgus, or Neo-Cæsariensis, St.*, and OTHERS. The works of Gregory Thaumaturgus, Dionysius of Alexandria, and Archelaus. Translated by S. D. F. Salmond. Edinburgh, 1871. vi, 429 pp. [Ante-Nicene Christian library.] 8° 6322.4

GREGORIUS VII, *pope* (*Hildebrand*), Life of. Villemain, A. F. London, 1874. 2 v. 8° 5522.6

GREGOROVIUS, Ferdinand. Geschichte der Stadt Rom im Mittelalter. Vom v. bis zum XVI. Jahrhundert. 2te durchgearbeitete Auflage. Stuttgart, 1869–74. 8 v. 8° 5513.6

Shelf. No.

GREGOROVIUS, Ferdinand, *continued.*
— Lucrezia Borgia. Nach Urkunden und Correspondenzen ihrer eigenen Zeit. [*Also* Anhang der Documente.] Band I. Stuttgart, 1874. 329, 140+ pp. Plate. 8° 5733.6
GRENVILLE, George Nugent Temple, *lord Nugent.* Memorials of John Hampden, his party and his times. 4th edition, with a memoir of the writer and a general index. Portraits. London, 1860. lxxv, 420 pp. Sm. 8° 5426.12
GREVILLE, Charles Cavendish Fulke. The Greville memoirs. A journal of the reigns of George IV and William IV. Edited by H. Reeve. 3d edition. London, 1875. 3 v. 8° 5414.6
— *Same.* (*In* Stoddard, R. H. Bric-à-brac series). 1828.5
GREY, *Mrs.* The belle of the family 521.26
— Cousin Harry 534.22
— The duke and the cousin 530.5
— The flirt 521.32
— The gipsy's daughter 521.27
— Good society 521.28
— Hyacinthe 521.29
— Lena Cameron 521.30
— Lion-hearted 521.39
— The little beauty 534.23
— The little wife 521.31
— The manœuvring mother 521.38
— Mary Seaham 521.25
— The old dower house 530.3
— Passion and principle 530.4
— Sybil Lennard 530.2
— The young prima donna 521.34
GRIDIRON, The. Lover, S. (*In* Johnson, (E.) R. Little classics) 529.4.9
GRIER, William. The mechanic's calculator; comprehending principles, rules, and tables in the various departments of mathematics and mechanics. From the 5th Glasgow edition. Philadelphia, 1842. 308 pp. Plates. 12° 1713.5
GRIF. Farjeon, B. L. 521.8
GRIFFIN, Gerald. The collegians 517.7
— The duke of Monmouth 517.8
— The invasion 517.9
— Mr. Tibbot O'Leary, the curious. (*In* Johnson, (E.) R. Little classics) 529.4.5
— The rivals, and Tracy's ambition 517.10
— The swans of Lir. (*In* Johnson, (E.) R. Little classics) 529.4.1
— Tales of the jury room 517.11
— Selections from. *See* HALF hours with Irish authors. New York, 1873. 12° 737.9

Note. — Most of Griffin's novels are illustrative of Irish life and character.

GRIFFITH Gaunt. Reade, C. 527.1
GRIMM, Herman. Life of Michael Angelo. Translated with the author's sanction by F. E. Bunnètt. Boston, 1872. 2 v. Portrait. Sm. 8° .. 1022.2
GRINDON, Leopold H. Phenomena of plant life. Boston, 1866. 93 pp. 12° 1523.13
GRINGO, Harry, *pseud.* *See* WISE, Henry Augustus.
GRINNELL expedition, Second, in search of Sir John Franklin. Kane, E. K. Philadelphia, 1856. 2 v. 8° 422.2
— *Same.* Hartford, 1871. 8° 5912.4

See also Arctic regions.

GRISWOLD, Rufus Wilmot. The female poets of America. With additions by R. H. Stoddard. Revised, enlarged, and continued to the present time. With portraits. New York, 1874. 486+ pp. L. 8° 5212.2
— The poets and poetry of America. With additions by R. H. Stoddard. Revised and enlarged. With portraits. New York, 1873. 666+ pp. L. 8°. 5212.3
GROHMAN, W. A. Baillie. Tyrol and the Tyrolese: the people and the land, in their social, sporting, and mountaineering aspects. London, 1876. xvi, 278 pp. Illustrated. Sm. 8° 5916.12
GROSS, Samuel D., *editor.* Lives of eminent American physicians and surgeons of the 19th century. Philadelphia, 1861. 836 pp. Portrait. 8° ... 6021.6

Shelf. No.

GROTE, George. Aristotle. Edited by A. Bain and G. C. Robertson. London, 1872. 2 v. 8° 6112.1
— History of Greece. New edition. With portrait and plans. London, 1869. 12 v. 16° 5926.1
— Minor works. With critical remarks on his intellectual character, writings, and speeches, by A. Bain. London, 1873. ix, [170] 364 pp. Portrait. 8° 5633.2
— Plato and other companions of Sokrates. 2d edition. London, 1867. 3 v. 8° 6113.2
— Personal history of. Grote, H. London, 1873. 8°. 5333.1
GROTE, Harriet. Personal history of George Grote. 2d edition. London, 1873. xx, 336 pp. Portrait. Fac-simile. 8° 5333.1
GROTESQUE. History of caricature and grotesque in literature and art. Wright, T. London [1864]. Sm. 8° 5923.4
GROVE, William Robert, and OTHERS. The correlation and conservation of forces: a series of expositions. With an introduction and brief biographical notices. By E. L. Youmans. New York, 1873. xliii, 438 pp. 12° 1524.26
GRUEBER, Herbert A. Roman medallions in the British museum. Edited by R. S. Poole. London, 1874. 154 pp. 66 plates. 8° 6131.2
GRUEN, Anastasius, *pseud.* *See* AUERSPERG, Anton Alexander, *Graf* von.
GRUENER, Louis (Emmanuel). The manufacture of steel. Translated from the French by L. Smith. With an appendix on the Bessemer process in the United States, by the translator. Illustrated. New York, 1872. 196 pp. 8° 6631.4
GRUND, Francis J. The Americans in their moral, social, and political relations. Boston, 1837. 423 pp. 12° 1534.1
— Elements of chemistry, with practical exercises, illustrated by engravings. Boston, 1838. xii, 384 pp. 12° 1717.11
GUARDIAN angel, The. [A novel.] Holmes, O. W. Boston, 1872. 16° 526.21
GUERNSEY, Alfred H., and ALDEN, Henry M. Harper's pictorial history of the great rebellion. New York [*cop.* 1866]. 2 v. F° ........*R.R., Desk
GUERNSEY, Clara F. Scrub Hollow Sunday school. 913.33
GUERRAZZI, Francesco Domenico. Beatrice Cenci. [Fiction.] Translated by L. Monti. New York, 1858. 2 v. in 1. Portrait. Sm. 8° 716.5
— Isabella Orsini. Translated by L. Monti. New York, 1859. 330 pp. Portrait. 12° 336.9
— Manfred; or, the battle of Benevento. Translated by L. Monti. New York, 1875. 447 pp. 12° 723.17
GUESSES at truth. [Discussions, apothegms, etc.] Hare, A. W. and J. C. London, 1871. 16° ... 1936.1
GUHL, Ernst, and KONER, Wilhelm. The life of the Greeks and Romans, described from antique monuments. Translated from the 3d German edition by F. Hueffer. With 543 woodcuts. New York [London], 1875. lx, 620+ pp. 8°. 5921.9
GUIDE through the galleries of paintings of the Imperial museum of the Louvre. Paris, 1857. viii, 732 pp. 12° 5527.2
GUIDE to needlework, embroidery and Berlin work. [With] 167 illustrations. Boston [1876]. 7–125 pp. 12° 1515.1
GUILD, Anne Eliza, *joint compiler.* Hymns of the ages. *See* WHITMARSH, Caroline Snowden 1615.5
GUILD, Curtis. Over the ocean; or, sights and scenes in foreign lands. Boston, 1873. viii, 558 pp. Sm. 8° 426.20
GUILLEMIN, Amédée. The forces of nature. Translated by Mrs. N. Lockyer; edited, with additions and notes, by J. N. Lockyer. Illustrated. London, 1872. xxxix, 679 pp. L. 8° 1520.1
— The sun. From the French by A. L. Phipson. With illustrations. New York, 1871. 297+ pp. 12° 1714.10
— Wonders of the moon. Translated by Miss M. G. Mead. Edited, with additions, by Maria Mitchell. Illustrated. New York, 1873. 241 pp. [Illustrated library of wonders.] 12° 1714.29

Shelf. No.

GUILLOTINE, History of the. Croker, J. W. London, 1853. 16° 5528.6
GUILT and innocence. Schwartz, M. S. 531.5
GUINEA. *See* COOMASSIE.
GUISE, Henri de Lorraine, *duc* de. *See* MÉRIMÉE, P. Portraits historiques et littéraires. Paris, 1874. 12° 5527.14
GUIZOT, *Mlle.* *See* WITT, Henriette de.
GUIZOT, *Mlle.* *See* WITT, Pauline de.
GUIZOT, Élisabeth Charlotte Pauline de Meulan. Tales in French. For young persons. 2d edition. Boston, 1835. 163 pp. 12° 2018.1
GUIZOT, François (Pierre Guillaume). Faith and science. (*In* Noyes, G. R. Collection of theological essays) 6325.12
— Great Christians of France: Saint Louis and Calvin. [London, 1869.] vi, 362+ pp. Illustrated. [Sunday library.] Sm. 8° 5937.6
— L'histoire de France, depuis les temps les plus reculés jusqu'en 1789. Illustré. Paris, 1873–76. 5 v. L. 8° 5530.2

Contents. — Vol. I. La Gaule-Charles le Bel, 1328. II. Philippe VI de Valois-Louis XII, 1328-1515. III. François I-Henri IV, 1515-1610. IV. Louis XIII-Louis XIV, 1610-1715. V. Louis XV-Louis XVI, 1715-89.

— History of civilization from the fall of the Roman empire to the French revolution. Translated by William Hazlitt. New York, 1876. 4 v. in 2. 12° 5924.8
— History of France from the earliest times to 1789. Translated by Robert Black. London, 1872. 3 v. Illustrated. 8° 5510.2
GULLIVER's travels. Swift, J. Leipzig 315.8
— *Same.* (*In his* Works.) London 5611.2.1
GUN, rod, and saddle. Personal experiences. Gilmore, P. London, 1869. Sm. 8° 1514.11
GUN-BOAT series, The. *See* FOSDICK, Charles A.
GUNNAR: a tale of Norse life. Boyesen, H. H. 529.3
GUNNERY, Instruction in. Benton, J. G. New York, 1862. 8° 6924.1
GURNEY, John Hampden. Chapters from French history. New edition. London, 1870. xiv, 432 pp. 16° 5517.2
GURNEY, Mary. Mrs. Gurney's apology. In justification of Mrs. ——'s friendship. Philadelphia, 1860. 51+ pp. 8° 1910.3
GUSHINGTON, Angelina, *pseud.* Thoughts on men and things. New York, 1872. 270 pp. 12° .. 1916.4
GUSTAVUS I, VASA, *king of Sweden.* History of. With extracts from his correspondence. London, 1852. xv, 312 pp. Portrait. 8° 5723.3
— Gustavus Vasa; or, king and peasant. Nieritz, (C.) G. Philadelphia, 1872. 16° 537.15
GUSTAVUS II, ADOLPHUS, *king of Sweden.* Gustavus Adolphus in Germany. Trench, R. C. London, 1872. Sm. 8° 5717.2

See also Germany, note on Thirty years' war.

GUTHRIE, Thomas. Autobiography. And memoir by his sons D. K. Guthrie and J. C. Guthrie. New York, 1874, 75. 2 v. 8° 5424.12
— The city: its sins and sorrows. Sermons from Luke xix, 41. And Ragged schools. New York, 1873. 215, 264 pp. 12° 6327.16
GUTZKOW, Carl (Ferdinand). Through night to light. From the German by Mrs. Faber. Leipzig, 1870. 312+ pp. Sq. 16° 312.22
GUTZLAFF, Charles. Journal of two voyages along the coast of China, 1831, 32. New York, 1833. xi, 332 pp. 12° 426.13
GUY Carlton. Wise, D. 932.34
GUY Deverell. Le Fanu, J. S. 314.4
GUY Earlscourt's wife. Fleming, M. A. 522.6
GUY Livingstone. Lawrence, G. A. 315.22
GUY Mannering. Scott, *Sir* W. Boston 523.16
— *Same.* Leipzig 324.13
GUY Rivers. Simms, W. G. 716.28
GUYOT, Arnold. The earth and man: lectures on comparative physical geography, in its relation to the history of mankind. From the French by C. C. Felton. Boston, 1872. 334 pp. Maps. 12° 1523.15
GWENDOLINE's harvest. Payn, J. 312.24

Shelf. No.

GYMNASTICS. Forrest, G. Handbook of. London, 1864. 16° 1519.3
— Howard, J. H. Gymnasts and gymnastics. London, 1873. Sm. 8° 6414.5
GYPSIES. Borrow, G. The Zincali; or, an account of the gypsies of Spain. New York, 1869. 8° 5931.13
— Leland, C. G. The English gypsies and their language. New York, 1873. Sm. 8° 5438.5
GYPSY Breynton. Phelps, E. S. 916.21
GYPSY's cousin Joy. Phelps, E. S. 916.22
GYPSY's sowing and reaping. Phelps, E. S. 916.20
GYPSY's year at the golden crescent. Phelps, E. S. 916.23

H— family, The. Bremer, F. 511.5
HABBERTON, John, *editor.* Select British essays. *Namely:* —
— The spectator. (Selected papers.) By Addison and Steele. New York, 1876. Sq. 16° 1919.3
HABITATIONS, The, of man in all ages. Viollet-le-Duc, E. E. Boston, 1876. 8° 6223.5
HABITS and men. [Sketches, anecdotes, etc.] Doran, J. W. New York, 1865. 12° 1532.3
HACK, Maria. Stories from English history during the middle ages. Revised by D. M. Smith. London, 1872. 264+ pp. Illustrated. 16° .. 5418.2
HACKETT, John. *See* CHRISTOPHERS, S. W. Homes of old English writers. London [1874]. Sm. 8° 5428.16
HACKLAENDER, Friedrich Wilhelm. Behind the counter. From the German by Mary Howitt. Leipzig, 1868. 367+ pp. Sq. 16° 311.11
HACTENUS. Tupper, M. F. Boston, 1848. 16° 1617.5
HADDAD-BEN-AHAB the traveller. Galt, J. (*In* Johnson, (E.) R. Little classics) 529.4.9
HADERMANN, Jeanette R. Against the world 528.3
— Dead men's shoes 533.15
— Forgiven at last 528.10
HADLEY, James. Essays, philological and critical. New York, 1873. vi, 424+ pp. 8° 5214.3
— Introduction to Roman law. New York, 1874. 332+ pp. 16° 6316.2
HAECKEL, Ernst Heinrich. History of creation: or the development of the earth and its inhabitants by the action of natural causes. A popular exposition of the doctrine of evolution. From the German. New York, 1876. 2 v. Illustrated. Folded map. 12° 6615.5
HAENDEL, Georg Friedrich. *See* HANDEL, Georg Friedrich.
HAGARENE. Lawrence, G. A. Leipzig 319.29
— *Same.* New York 711.2
HAGEN, (Ernst) August, *editor.* Künstler-Geschichten. Leipzig, 1833, 40. 4 v. in 3. 12°. 2026.1

Contents. — Vol. [I.] 1, 2. Die Chronik seiner Vaterstadt vom Lorenz Ghiberti. [II.] 3. Die Wunder der Kathrina von Siena. [III.] 4. Leonhard da Vinci in Mailand.

HAHNEMANN, Samuel (Christian Friedrich). Organon of the art of healing. 5th American, translated from the 5th German edition, by C. Wesselhoeft. New York, 1876. 244+ pp. 8° 6022.19
HAIR, Treatise on the. Perry, B. C. New Bedford, 1859. 12° 1525.4
HAKEWELL, George. *See* CHRISTOPHERS, S. W. Homes of old English writers. London [1874]. Sm. 8° 5428.16
HAKLUYT society. Publications. *Namely:* —
— Yule, H., *editor.* Cathay and the way thither; being a collection of medieval notices of China. London, 1866. 2 v. 8° 5923.10
HALE, Edward Everett. (*Col. Frederic Ingham.*) The children of the public. (*In* Johnson, (E.) R. Little classics) 529.4.12
— The good time coming; or, our new crusade 529.7

Note. — A re-issue of "Our new crusade" (published in 1874), with change of title.

— His level best, and other stories 738.2
— How to do it 526.17
— If, yes, and perhaps 526.19
— In His name. A story of the Waldenses, seven hundred years ago. 3d edition. Boston, 1874. 87+ pp. 8° 732.28
— The Ingham papers 526.16

Shelf. No.

HALE, Edward Everett, *continued.*
— Kansas and Nebraska. With map. Boston, 1854. 256 pp. 12° 415.2
— The man without a country. (*In* Johnson, (E.) R. Little classics) 529.4.1
— One hundred years ago. How the [revolutionary] war began. A series of sketches from original authorities. Boston, 1875. 40 pp. 8°. 811.15
— Our new crusade. A temperance story 529.5
— The skeleton in the closet. (*In* Johnson, (E.) R. Little classics) 529.4.5
— A summer vacation. Four sermons. Boston, 1874. 73 pp. 12° 6328.6

Contents.— Worship in Europe; The Vienna exhibition; Pilgrimages; Open air and the Aryan virtues.

— Sybaris and other homes 524.23
— Ups and downs 528.8
— and OTHERS. Tales for travellers. The lost palace, and other tales 720.25

Contents. — The lost palace, by E. E. Hale; Allegro, by Ellis Gray; The last witch, by Clara F. Guernsey; Achsa's possibilities, by Isabella G. Meredith; Jack Maynard's call, by T. M. Osborne; The New England sphinx, by V. G. Smith; Which is the actress? by Lucretia P. Hale; Bombay Shirley's cure.

— — — Nicolette and Aucassin, and other tales 720.24

Contents. — Nicolette and Aucassin; Tom Haliburton's quandary, by K. W. and M. S. S.; A civil servant, by E. E. Hale; They saw a great light, by E. E. Hale.

— — — Spoons in a wherry, and other stories 720.21

Contents. — Devil-puzzlers, by F. B. Perkins; The Pole's story; The improvisatore and the heeler, by F. W. Loring; The two princes, by E. E. Hale; In the wide world, by T. Federhorn; Rebecca's ma, by F. W. Loring; What happened to the khan and the poor man's son; The companion of paradise, by H. A. Miles; A Tartar fairy tale literally translated; Spoons in a wherry, by M. S. Severance; Waveline, the little mermaid, by Annie Moore; A night of terror, by Mrs. S. De Ponte; The housekeeper's story.

— — — Stand and wait, and other tales 720.23

Contents. — Stand and wait: The man-ufactory, by F. B. Perkins; Beatrice's mirror, by Annie D. Perkins; "Against time," by E. Papendick; A contribution to the conscience fund, by R. Scudder; A tress of hair, by Isabella G. Meredith.

— — — Story of the Simplon, and other tales 720.22

Contents. — A tale of the Simplon; Félicie Mordaunt's world, by Lucretia P. Hale; Pilchards, by Mary J. Penwyn; The survivor's story; Two song and dance men, by F. W. Loring.

— — Workingmen's homes. Essays and stories on the homes of men who work in large towns. Boston, 1874. 182+ pp. Illustrated. 16° ... 1516.22
HALE, Nathan. An epitome of universal geography. With maps. Boston, 1830. iv, 404 pp. 12°. 437.3
HALE, Sarah Josepha. Complete dictionary of poetical quotations. Illustrated. Philadelphia, 1872. 576 pp. 8° .... *R.R., F.3.1
— Flora's interpreter, and fortuna flora. Revised edition, with new illustrations. Boston [cop. 1843]. 288 pp. 12° 1625.10
HALES, John. Essays. (*In* Sparks, J. Collection of essays and tracts in theology) 1918.9.5
HALES, John G. Survey of Boston and its vicinity. Boston, 1821. 156 pp. Map. 1 plate. 12° .. 424.21
HALÉVY, Jacques François Fromental Élie. (*In* Ditson, O., and co. Standard opera librettos). 6233.3.1
HALF a million of money. Edwards, A. B. 312.13
HALF-HOURS in the green lanes. Taylor, J. E. London, 1873. 16° 6619.2
HALF hours with Irish authors. Selections from Griffin, Lover, Carleton, and Lever. New York, 1873. 330 pp. Portraits. 12° 737.9
HALF hours with modern scientists. Lectures and essays. With introduction by N. Porter. 1st series. New Haven, 1872. xi, 288 pp. 12° .. 1525.19

Contents. — On the physical basis of life. T. H. Huxley. — Correlation of vital and physical forces. G. F. Barker. — As regards protoplasm. Reply to Huxley. J. H. Stirling. — On the hypothesis of evolution. E. D. Cope. — Scientific addresses: On the methods and tendencies of physical investigation. On haze and dust. On the scientific use of the imagination. J. Tyndall.

HALF-HOURS with the best authors. Knight, C. London [1866]. 4 v. Sm. 8° 5926.4

Shelf. No.

HALIBURTON, Thomas Chandler. (*Sam Slick.*) The clockmaker: sayings and doings of Samuel Slick of Slickville. With illustrations. New York, 1872. xi, 271 pp. 16° 535.12
HALL, Anna Maria. The buccaneer 727.22
— Can wrong be right? 311.8
— The outlaw 727.23
— Sketches of Irish character. With illustrations. London [1875]. 443 pp. 8° 5436.1
— The Whiteboy 521.6
— *joint author.* Ireland: its scenery, character, etc. *See* HALL, Samuel Carter 5431.1
HALL, Basil. Travels in North America, in 1827, 28. Philadelphia, 1829. 2 v. 12° 417.14
HALL, Charles Francis. Arctic researches and life among the Esquimaux: being the narrative of an expedition in search of Sir John Franklin, 1860–62. With maps and illustrations. New York, 1865. 595 pp. 8° 422.4
— Last polar expedition. Hartwig, G. The polar and tropical worlds. Springfield, 1874. 8° ... 1520.7
HALL, Edward Brooks. Memoir of Mary L. Ware. Boston, 1853. vii, 434 pp. Portrait. 12° 1214.4
HALL, Edward H., *compiler.* The national tax law, as amended, with a complete compendium of stamp duties. New York, 1863. 136 pp. 12°. 6927.4
HALL, Herbert Byng. The bric-à-brac hunter; or, chapters on chinamania. Philadelphia [London], 1875. ix, 290 pp. Photograph. Sm. 8°. 6214.4
HALL, James. Legends of the West: sketches illustrative of the habits, occupations, privations, adventures and sports of the pioneers of the West. Cincinnati, 1871. 435 pp. 12° 5036.3
— The romance of Western [United States] history. Cincinnati, 1871. 420 pp. Portrait. 12° 814.2
HALL, John Vine. Autobiography. Edited by Newman Hall. New York [1865]. 264 pp. Portrait. 12° 1226.6
HALL, Louisa Jane. Miriam, and Joanna of Naples, with other pieces in verse and prose. Boston, 1850. 403+ pp. 12° 5216.3
HALL, Robert. Polemical and other miscellanies. And an apology for the freedom of the press. Boston, 1827. 264 pp. 16° 1914.8
— Biography of. Rogers, H. (*In* Macaulay, T. B., *lord*, and others. New biographies of illustrious men) 5428.4
HALL, *Mrs.* Samuel Carter. *See* HALL, Anna Maria.
HALL, Samuel Carter. Book of memories of great men and women of the age, from personal acquaintance. London, 1871. xiv, 488 pp. Illustrated. Portrait. Sm. 4° 1231.1
— *joint author.* The stately homes of England. *See* PRATT, Llewellyn 5434.2
— and Anna Maria. Ireland: its scenery, character, etc. London, 1841–43. 3 v. Illustrated. L. 8° 5431.1
HALL, Theresa Oakey. Her mother's Fancy. A story for juveniles and young old folks. [American homes series] 921.14
HALL, William W. Health by good living. New York, 1872. vi, 285 pp. Sm. 8° 1523.17
— How to live long; or, health maxims, physical, mental, and moral. New York, 1875. 316 pp. 12° 6036.13
— Sleep: or the hygiene of the night. New York, 1871. 357, iv pp. 12° 1523.18
HALLAM, Arthur Henry. Remains in verse and prose. With a preface and memoir. Boston, 1863. 441 pp. 12° 1536.24

Note. — Young Hallam, son of the historian, is commemorated in Tennyson's "In memoriam."

HALLAM, Henry. Constitutional history of England from the accession of Henry VII to the death of George II. New York, 1872. 3 v. Sm. 8° 5416.1
— Introduction to the literature of Europe in the fifteenth, sixteenth, and seventeenth centuries. New York, 1854. 2 v. 8° 1531.2
— View of the state of Europe during the middle ages. New York, 1872. 3 v. Sm. 8° 5916.1

Shelf. No.

HALLECK, Fitz-Greene. Political writings. Edited by J. G. Wilson. New York, 1871. 272 pp. Portrait. Sm. 12° 1618.1
— Life and letters of. Wilson, J. G. New York, 1869. Sm. 8° 5027.1
HALLOCK, Charles. The fishing tourist: angler's guide and reference book. New York, 1873. 239 pp. Illustrated. 16° 1515.12
HALO, The, round the moon. Abbott, J. 917.29
HALPINE, Charles Grahame. (*Miles O'Reilly.*) Poetical works. With a biographical sketch and explanatory notes. Edited by R. B. Roosevelt. New York, 1869. 352 pp. Portrait. 8° 1624.1
HALVES. [Fiction.] Payn, J. Leipzig 334.7
— *Same.* New York 530.14
HAMERSLY, Lewis R. Records of living offices of the U. S. navy and marine corps; with a history of naval operations during the rebellion of 1861–5. Philadelphia, 1870. 350 pp. 8° 5022.41
HAMERTON, Philip Gilbert. Chapters on animals. With etchings. Boston, 1874. 252+ pp. Sm. 4° 6614.9
— Etching and etchers. Illustrated. Boston, 1876. xxx, 459+ pp. 8° 6233.1
— Harry Blount. Passages in a boy's life on land and sea. Boston, 1875. iv, 355+ pp. 1 plate. 16°. 937.31
— The intellectual life. With portrait. Boston, 1873. xix, 455 pp. 16° 1925.1
— A painter's camp. Boston, 1871. xii, 348 pp. 16°. 426.19

Contents. — In England; In Scotland; In France.

— Round my house; notes of rural life in France in peace and war. Boston, 1876. xii, 415 pp. 16°. 5527.16
— Thoughts about art. New edition, revised. Boston, 1871. xv, 385 pp. 16° 1515.3
HAMILTON, Alexander, Life of. Morse, J. T., *jr.* Boston, 1876. 2 v. 16° 5026.7
HAMILTON, Anthony. Mémoires du comte de Grammont. T. I. Paris, 1823. 1 plate. 32° 5528.5
HAMILTON, Celia V., *formerly Miss Dakin.* A crown from the spear 511.28
— Ropes of sand: and other stories 531.21
— Woven of many threads 531.17
HAMILTON, Elizabeth. The cottagers of Glenburnie. A tale 539.5
HAMILTON, Gail, *pseud.* *See* DODGE, Mary Abigail.
HAMILTON, H., *joint author.* The international English and French dictionary. *See* SMITH, Leon. *R.R., D.3.8
HAMILTON, James A. Reminiscences; or, men and events, at home and abroad, during three quarters of a century. New York, 1869. ix, 647 pp. 8° 5022.1
HAMILTON, John William, *editor.* Memorial of Jesse Lee and the old elm. 85th anniversary of Jesse Lee's sermon under the old elm, Boston common, held Sunday evening, July 11, 1875. With a historical sketch of the great tree. Boston, 1875. 55 pp. Illustrated. 12° 617.2
HAMILTON, Thomas. Men and manners in America. 2d American edition. Philadelphia, 1833. 2 v. 16° 416.1
HAMILTON, *Sir* William. Lectures on metaphysics. Edited by H. L. Mansel and J. Veitch. Boston, 1859. 738 pp. 8° 5832.2
HAMILTON, William Gerard. Parliamentary logick: to which are subjoined two speeches, and other pieces. With an appendix, containing considerations on the corn laws, by S. Johnson. London, 1808. xlvi, 253 pp. Portrait. 16° 5416.3
HAMMER and anvil. Spielhagen, F. 512.13
HAMMETT, Samuel A. (*Philip Paxton.*) A stray Yankee in Texas. New York, 1859. 415+ pp. Illustrated. 12° 414.20
HAMMOND, William Alexander. Treatise on hygiene with special reference to the military service. Philadelphia, 1863. 604 pp. Illustrated. 8°. 6022.8
HAMPDEN, John, Memorials of. Grenville, G. N. T., *lord Nugent.* London, 1860. Sm. 8° 5426.12
HANAFORD, Phebe Ann. Abraham Lincoln: his life and public services. Boston, 1865. 216 pp. Portrait. 12° 1214.2

Shelf. No.

HAND, The, its mechanism and vital endowments, as evincing design. Bell, *Sir* C. Philadelphia, 1835. 12° 6036.6
HAND and glove. Edwards, A. B. 312.14
HANDBOOK for immigrants to the United States. Prepared by the American social science association. With maps. New York, 1871. vi, 117 pp. 16° 417.5
HANDEL, *or* HAENDEL, Georg Friedrich. Barnard, C. F., *jr.* Handel and Haydn. Boston, 1871. 16°. 926.22
— Haweis, H. R. Music and morals. New York, 1872. 12° 1513.16

Note. — See Harper's monthly, vol. 15.

HANDIE. Abbott, J. 914.21
HANDSOME is that handsome does. Bradley, M. 935.5
HANDSOME Lawrence. Dudevant, A. L. A. D. 511.17
HANDY Andy: a tale of Irish life. Lover, S. London 536.15
— *Same.* New York 530.15
HANEY, Jesse. Art of training animals. Illustrated. New York [*cop.* 1869]. 210 [200] pp. 12° 1713.3
HANGING, The, of the crane. [Poem.] Longfellow, H. W. Boston, 1875. 16° 1616.14
— *Same.* Boston, 1875. 8° 5214.4
HANNA, William. Wycliffe and the Huguenots; or, sketches of the rise of the reformation in England and of the early history of protestantism in France. Edinburgh, 1860. xv, 276 pp. Sm. 8°. 826.7
HANNAH. Craik, D. (M.) 330.2
HANNAH Thurston. Taylor, (J.) B. 716.35
HANNIBAL. Abbott, J. History of 914.22
— Arnold, T. Life of. New York, 1870. 16° 1028.7

See also Rome, *note.*

HAP-HAZARD. Field, K. Boston, 1873. Sq. 16° 439.1
HAPPY accident, A, at Brighton. Church, F. 337.23
HAPPY boy, The. Björnson, B. 735.25
HAPPY-THOUGHT hall. Burnand, F. C. 533.20
HAPS and mishaps of a tour in Europe. Lippincott, S. J. Boston, 1854. 12° 424.4
HARBINGER, The. [Poems.] Holmes, O. W. Boston, 1833. 12° 1611.2
HARD cash. Reade, C. 316.22
HARD knocks. Clark, W. A. Boston, 1872. 16° 5216.5
HARD-SCRABBLE, The, of Elm island. Kellogg, E. 922.13
HARD times. Dickens, C. (J. H.) Boston 1824.5.2
— *Same.* Leipzig 338.7
HARDEE, William J. Rifle and light infantry tactics. Prepared under the direction of the war department. Philadelphia, 1861. 2 v. Illustrated. Folded plates. 16° 1529.3
HARDENBERG, Friedrich Ludwig von. Henry of Ofterdingen: a romance. From the German of Novalis [*pseud.*]. Cambridge, 1842. 236 pp. 12° 713.10
HARDWICK, Charles. History of the Christian church during the reformation. 4th edition, revised by W. Stubbs. London, 1874. xi, 424 pp. Sm. 8°. 6326.20
— History of the Christian church. Middle age. With maps. 4th edition. Edited by W. Stubbs. London, 1874. xvi, 450 pp. Sm. 8° 6326.21
HARDY, Thomas. Leisure hour series. Desperate remedies 518.22
— — Far from the madding crowd 518.24
— — A pair of blue eyes 539.4
— — Under the greenwood tree. New York 728.4
— Under the greenwood tree. London 728.14
HARE, Augustus John Cuthbert. Cities of northern and central Italy. London, 1876. 3 v. Maps. Illustrations. Sm. 8° 5527.1

Contents. — Vol. I. On the Rivieras, and in Piedmont and Lombardy. II. In Venetia, Parma, the Emilia, the Marche, and northern Tuscany. III. Florence, Siena, and other towns of Tuscany and Umbria.

— Days near Rome. With illustrations. Philadelphia, 1875. 2 v. in 1. 16° 5527.1
— Memorials of a quiet life. 7th edition. London, 1873. 2 v. Portraits. Sm. 8° .... 5427.

Note. — Memorial of the brothers Augustus William and Julius Charles Hare, authors of "Guesses at truth," and of Maria L. Ware.

Shelf. No.

HARE, Augustus John Cuthbert, *continued.*
— Records of a quiet life. Revised for American readers by W. L. Gage. Boston, 1873. xiii, 373+ pp. 12° 5427.3

Note. — An abridgment of the preceding.

— Walks in Rome. 3d American edition. New York, 1873. xxi, 678 pp. 12° 5526.13
— Wanderings in Spain. 3d edition. London, 1873. xxi, 274+ pp. Illustrated. 16° 5934.5
HARE, Augustus William. The Alton sermons. London, 1874. x, 574 pp. Sm. 8° 6325.18
— and Julius Charles. Guesses at truth. New edition. London, 1871. 576 [572] pp. 16° 1936.1
HARE, Francis. Difficulties and discouragements which attend the study of the Scriptures. (*In* Sparks, J. Collection of essays and tracts in theology) 1918.9.2
HARLAND, Marion, *pseud.* *See* TERHUNE, Mary Virginia.
HARNESS, William. Personal reminiscences. (*In* Stoddard, R. H. Bric-à-brac series) 1828.4
— Literary life of. L'Estrange, A. G. London, 1871. 8° 5422.9
HAROLD, the last of the Saxon kings. [Historical romance.] Bulwer-Lytton, E. (G. E.) L. 336.19
HARP of the willows. [Poems.] Perkins, *Mrs.* [E.] Boston, 1859. 16° 1618.2
HARPER establishment. Abbott, J. Harper's story books 936.1.4
HARPER'S bazar. Vol. 6, 7. New York, 1873. 2 v. F° 1430.1
HARPER'S new monthly magazine. Vol. 1–51. New York, 1850–75. 51 v. 8° 1415.1
HARPER'S pictorial history of the great rebellion. Guernsey, A. H., and Alden, H. M. New York [1866]. 2 v. F° .... *R.R. Desk
HARPER'S story books. *See* ABBOTT, Jacob.
HARPER'S weekly. Vol. 16–19. New York, 1872–75. 4 v. F° 1311.1
HARRINGTON, Joseph. Sermons. With a memoir by W. Whiting. Boston, 1854. iv, 276 pp. Portrait. 12° 6325.3
HARRIS, James. Hermes or a philosophical inqviry concerning vniversal grammar. 4th edition. London, 1786. xix, 442+ pp. 1 plate. 8° .. 1734.1
HARRIS, Miriam, *formerly Miss Cole.* Frank Warrington 724.11
— Louie's last term at St. Mary's 724.16
— A perfect Adonis 723.10
— Richard Vandermarck 515.16
— Roundhearts and other stories 724.15
— Rutledge 737.29
— St. Philip's 724.13
— The Sutherlands 724.14
compiler. A rosary for Lent. Original and compiled. New York, 1874. 360 [354] pp. 12°. 1537.18
HARRIS, Thaddeus William. Treatise on some of the insects of New England which are injurious to vegetation. 2d edition. Boston, 1852. viii, 513 pp. 8° 6612.1
HARRIS, *Sir* William Snow. Rudimentary electricity. 6th edition, with additions, including extracts from the Cavendish papers. London, 1872. vi, 200 pp. Illustrated. 12° 1716.20
— Rudimentary magnetism. 2d edition, revised by H. M. Noad. With illustrations. London, 1872. viii, 412 pp. 12° 1715.6
— Rudimentary treatise on galvanism and the general principles of animal and voltaic electricity. New edition, revised, with additions by R. Sabine. With illustrations. London, 1869. xi, 247 pp. 12° 1715.29
HARRIS'S lightning conductors, Papers relative to. Forbes, R. B. Boston, 1853. 8° 1711.3
HARRISON, Agnes. Martin's vineyard 319.14
HARRISON, James Bower. Contamination of water by lead. London, 1852. vii, 196 pp. 16° 6438.7
HARRISON, Robert, *joint author.* Outlines of German literature. *See* GOSTWICK, Joseph 5835.2
HARRY and Lucy. Edgeworth, M. Early lessons. 939.6
HARRY Blount. Hamerton, P. G. 937.31
HARRY Heathcote of Gangoil. Trollope, A. Leipzig. 329.17
— *Same.* New York 732.11
HARRY Lorrequer. Lever, C. (J.) Leipzig 332.2
— *Same.* London 516.12
HART, George. The violin: its famous makers and their imitators. With wood engravings. London, 1875. xiv, 352+ pp. L. 8° 6231.2
HART, James Morgan. German universities: a narrative of personal experience. New York, 1874. vi, 398+ pp. 12° 5836.11
HART, Joseph C. Miriam Coffin, or the whale-fishermen 712.4
HARTE, (Francis) Bret. Condensed novels. [Imitations of celebrated novelists] 524.22
— East and West poems. Boston, 1871. 171 pp. 12°. 1615.13
— Echoes of the foot-hills. [Poems.] Boston, 1875. 146 pp. 12° 1615.8
— The luck of Roaring camp. (*In* Johnson, (E.) R. Little classics) 529.4.4
— *Same.* And other sketches 526.15
— Mrs. Skaggs's husbands, and other sketches 537.17
— The outcasts of Poker Flat. (*In* Johnson, (E.) R. Little classics) 529.4.1
— Poems. Boston, 1873. 152 pp. 12° 1616.9
— Prose and poetry. Leipzig, 1872. 2 v. in 1. Sq. 16° 339.1
— Tales of the Argonauts [California pioneers], and other sketches 728.13
HARTLEY, David. *See* RIBOT, T. English psychology. New York, 1874. 8° 5835.5
HARTT, Charles Frederic. Geology and physical geography of Brazil. With illustrations and maps. Boston, 1870. xxiii, 620 pp. 8° 5033.1
HARTWELL farm, The. Comins, L. B. 912.14
HARTWIG, George. The aerial world: a popular account of the phenomena and life of the atmosphere. With plates, a map, and woodcuts. London, 1874. xviii, 556 pp. 8° 6832.3
— *Same.* New York, 1875. 8° 1520.5
— The polar and tropical worlds. Edited, with additional chapters, by A. H. Guernsey. With illustrations. New edition. With an account of Hall's last expedition, a summary of Arctic explorations, and new maps of the Arctic regions. Springfield, 1874. 811+ pp. 8° 1520.7
— The tropical world: aspects of man and nature in the tropical regions of the globe. With plates and woodcuts. New edition. London, 1873. xix, 556 pp. 8° 6613.5
— The sea and its living wonders. A popular account of the marvels of the deep and of the progress of maritime discovery. 4th edition. With woodcuts and plates. London, 1873. xx, 518 pp. 8° 6633.4
HARVARD college, *Cambridge, Mass.* Eliot, S. A. Sketch of the history of. Boston, 1848. 16° .. 818.4
— Quincy, J. History of. Boston, 1860. 2 v. 8°. 810.7
— Vaille, F. O., and Clark, H. A., *compilers.* The Harvard book. Cambridge, 1875. 2 v. 4° ... 5230.1
HARVARD memorial biographies. Cambridge, 1867. 2 v. Sm. 8° 5025.12

Note. — Memoirs of Harvard students who died in the United States service during the war of 1861–65.

HARVEY, Ellwood. Essay on the American trotting horse [etc.]. *See* WALSH, John Henry 6616.7
HARWOOD, Edward. The causes which conspired to produce our Saviour's agony. (*In* Noyes, G. R. Collection of theological essays) 6325.12
HARWOOD. Coulson, J. G. A. 720.30
HARZ mountains, The. Blackburn, H. London, 1873. Sm. 4° 5733.3
HASHEESH eater, The. Ludlow, F. H. New York [*cop.* 1857]. 12° 737.5
HASSALL, Arthur Hill. Food: its adulterations, and the methods for their detection. Illustrated. London, 1876. viii, 896 pp. Sm. 8° 6035.8
HASSARD, Annie. Floral decorations for the dwelling house: a practical guide to the home arrangement of plants and flowers. With illustrations. London, 1875. vi, 163+ pp. Sm. 8°. 6625.5

Shelf. No.

HASTE and waste. Adams, W. T. 925.2

HASTINGS, Selina, *countess of Huntington*. Lady Huntington and her friends. Knight, H. C. New York [*cop.* 1853]. 12° 1025.2

HASTINGS, Thomas. The mother's nursery songs. [With music.] New York, 1835. 72 pp. 12°. 1625.8

HASTINGS, Warren, Articles of charges, and speeches in the impeachment of. Burke, E. Works. Boston, 1827. 8° ....Vol. 6, 7 of 5634.1

— *Same*. Boston, 1871. Sm. 8° .....Vol. 8–12 of 5635.1

Note.—See Macaulay's Essay [1918.4] and the lives of Sheridan and Burke, and the histories of India.

HASWELL, Charles H. Engineers' and mechanics' pocket-book. 29th edition, revised and enlarged. New York, 1873. 663 pp. 12° 6428.1

HATTON, Joseph. With a show in the North. Reminiscences of Mark Lemon. With Lemon's revised text of Falstaff. London, 1871. 284+ pp. Portrait. 16° 5425.7

HATTON, Thomas. Hints for sketching in water-colour from nature. 10th edition. London, 1869. 64 pp. 16° 6217.4

— Hints for sketching trees from nature in water colours. With illustrations. 3d edition. London, 1869. 61+ pp. 16° 6217.5

HAUFF, Wilhelm. Arabian days' entertainments. From the German by H. P. Curtis 533.6

— Three tales. From the German by M. A. Faber.. 312.21

Contents.—The beggar girl of the Pont des arts; The emperor's picture; The cold heart.

HAUGHTON, Samuel. Principles of animal mechanics. London, 1873. xiv, 495 pp. Illustrated. 8°. 6613.4

HAUNTED crust, The. Saunders, K. (*In* Johnson, (E.) R. Little classics) 529.4.5

HAUNTED hearts. Cummins, M. S. 322.30

HAUNTED homestead, The. Southworth, E. D. E. N. 522.13

HAUNTED house, The 338.3

HAUNTED man, The. Dickens, C. (J. H.) 338.6

HAUNTED ships, The. Cunningham, A. (*In* Johnson, (E.) R. Little classics) 529.4.8

HAUTEVILLE, Paul Daniel Gonzalve Grand d'. Report of the d'Hauteville case: the commonwealth of Pennsylvania, at the suggestion of P. D. G. G. d'Hauteville, *versus* D. Sears, M. C. Sears, and E. S. G. d'Hauteville. Habeas corpus for the custody of an infant child. Philadelphia, 1840. 295 pp. 8° 6313.5

HAVARD, Henry. La Hollande pittoresque, voyage aux villes mortes du Zuiderzée. Illustré. Paris, 1874. 403+ pp. 16° 2016.11

HAVELOCK, *Sir* Henry, Biographical sketch of. Brock, W. Leipzig, 1858. Sq. 16° 1237.3

HAVEN, Alice Bradley. The Coopers 524.20

HAVEN, Gilbert. Our next-door neighbor: a winter in Mexico. New York, 1875. 467 pp. Illustrated. 8° 5032.5

— and RUSSELL, Thomas. Incidents and anecdotes of Edward T. Taylor, for over forty years pastor of the Seamen's bethel, Boston. Boston, 1873. 445 pp. Illustrated. Portrait. 12° 1216.11

HAWEIS, Hugh Reginald. Music and morals. New York, 1872. 478 pp. Illustrated. 12° 1513.16

Contents.—First book. Philosophical: Music, emotion, and morals.—Second book. Biographical: From Ambrose to Handel; Handel; Gluck; Haydn; Schubert; Chopin; The letters of Mozart; The letters of Beethoven; Mendelssohn.—Third book. Instrumental: Violins; Piano-fortes; Bells; Carillons.—Fourth book. Critical: Music in England.

— Pet; or, pastimes and penalties 912.17

HAWKINS, F. W. Life of Edmund Kean. London, 1869. 2 v. 8° ....1221.3 and 5424.2

HAWKS, Francis Lister. Adventures of Captain John Smith, the founder of the colony of Virginia. New York, 1854. 201 pp. 12° 1028.3

— *editor*. Narrative of the expedition of an American squadron to the China seas and Japan, 1852–54. With illustrations. New York, 1856. vii, 624 pp. 8° 421.1

HAWTHORNE, Julian. Bressant 737.13

— Idolatry. A romance 724.10

— Saxon studies. [Mostly Dresden.] Boston, 1876. 452+ pp. 12° 424.5

HAWTHORNE, Nathaniel. The birthmark. (*In* Johnson, (E.) R. Little classics) 529.4.8

— The Blithedale romance. Boston, 1871. 288 pp. 16° 1813.8

— David Swan: a fantasy. (*In* Johnson, (E.) R. Little classics) 529.4.4

— Ethan Brand. (*In* Johnson, (E.) R. Little classics) 529.4.1

— The house of the seven gables [New England life and manners], and The snow image. Boston, 1872. 2 v. in 1. 2 plates. 16° 1813.1

— The marble faun. Boston, 1872. 2 v. in 1. 2 plates. 12° 1813.2

— Mosses from an old manse. [Stories.] Boston, 1872. 2 v. in 1. 2 plates. 16° 1813.3

— Our old home: a series of English sketches. Boston, 1876 [*cop.* 1863]. 380 pp. Sq. 16°. 1839.2 and 5439.1

— Passages from [his] American note-books. Boston, 1872. 2 v. in 1. 2 plates. 12° 1813.6

— Passages from [his] English note-books. Boston, 1871. 2 v. in 1. 2 plates. 12° 1813.4

— *Same*. Leipzig, 1871. 2 v. in 1. Sq. 16° 428.3

— Passages from [his] French and Italian note-books. Boston, 1876 [*cop.* 1871]. 2 v. 16° .. 1839.3

— The scarlet letter. [A tale of early Massachusetts history.] Leipzig, 1852. viii, 311 pp. Sq. 16° 311.7

— The scarlet letter, and The Blithedale romance. Boston, 1873. 2 v. in 1. 2 plates. 16° 1813.11

— Septimius Felton. [Time of Concord fight, etc.] Boston, 1872. 229+ pp. 12° 533.24

— The threefold destiny. (*In* Johnson, (E.) R. Little classics) 529.4.12

— Transformation. Leipzig, 1860. 2 v. in 1. Sq. 16°. 311.6

Note.—This is the same work as "The marble faun," but published under a different title. The scene is in Italy.

— Twice-told tales. Boston, 1871. 2 v. in 1. 2 plates. 12° 1813.7

— Wakefield. (*In* Johnson, (E.) R. Little classics). 529.4.2

— Fields, J. T. Yesterdays with authors. Boston, 1875 [*cop.* 1871]. 12° 6136.13

— Page, H. A. Memoir of. London, 1872. 16° .. 5025.7

— Stephen, L. Hours in a library. London, 1874. 16° 6136.9

Note.—Hawthorne supplies much of autobiographic interest in the introduction to "The scarlet letter," and in his Note-books. He was for a brief season a sojourner with the *Brook farm associates*, whom he is supposed to idealize in his "Blithedale romance;" and in this connection, see the Atlantic monthly, May, 1866, p. 565, etc.; and Dixon's "New America" [418.1].

Fields, in his "Yesterdays with authors," supplies some of his correspondence. G. W. Curtis furnished a paper on Hawthorne, in Harper's monthly, vol. 20 (easy chair), and in the North American review, Oct., 1864. See also Smiles's "Brief biographies" [1024.13]; and the accounts in Griswold, Duyckinck, and Allibone. Dr. Holmes gives an account of his last days, in the Atlantic monthly, July, 1864.

See essays by Longfellow, in his Prose works [1838.9.1], or North American review, July, 1837; by Whipple, in his Essays [1936.2], or Atlantic monthly, May, 1860; by Stoddard, in Harper's monthly, vol. 45; in Atlantic monthly, Sept., 1868; and in Cornhill magazine, 1873.

HAXALL, Robert W. [Boylston prize dissertation.] *See* HOLMES, Oliver Wendell 6023.17

HAY, John. Castilian days. [Spain.] Boston, 1871. 414+ pp. 12° 227.2

— Pike county ballads, and other pieces. Boston, 1871. 167 pp. 16° 1615.14

HAY, Mary Cecil. Old Myddelton's money. A novel 711.5

— The squire's legacy. A novel 530.16

— Victor and vanquished. A novel 530.13

HAY fever. *See* AUTUMNAL catarrh.

HAYDN, Franz Joseph. Barnard, C. F., *jr.* Handel and Haydn. Boston, 1871. 16° 920.22

— Haweis, H. R. Music and morals. New York, 1872. 12° 1513.16

HAYDN, Joseph. Dictionary of dates. [Edited] by B. Vincent. Authorized American edition, with Supplement by G. P. Putnam. New York, 1870. 851, 100+ pp. 1 folded plate. 8° ......*R.R., E.3.8

HAYDON, Benjamin Robert. Life from his autobiography and journals. Edited by T. Taylor. New York, 1853. 2 v. 12° 1224.8

Shelf. No.

HAYES, Albert H. Sexual physiology of woman, and her diseases. Boston [*cop.* 1869]. 345 pp. 12° 1524.25
HAYES, Isaac Israel. An Arctic boat journey, in the autumn of 1854. Boston, 1860. xvii, 375 pp. Maps. 12° 226.1
— Cast away in the cold. Boston, 1872. vi, 263 pp. Illustrated. Sm. 4° 933.7
— The land of desolation: being a personal narrative of observation and adventure in Greenland. Illustrated. New York, 1872. 357 pp. 12° 423.9
— The open polar sea: a narrative of a voyage of discovery towards the North pole, in the schooner "United States." New York, 1867. xxiv, 454 pp. Illustrated. Maps. Portrait. 8° 422.3
HAYLEY, William. The triumphs of temper; a poem. 1st American edition, with plates. Newburyport [1781]. vi, 162 pp. 12° 1617.11
HAYM, R. Die romantische Schule. Ein Beitrag zur Geschichte des deutschen Geistes. Berlin, 1870. xii, 951 pp. 8° 5733.2
HAYNE, Paul H., *editor*. *See* TIMROD, Henry 5617.12
HAYNES, Gideon. Pictures from prison life. An historical sketch of the Massachusetts state prison. With narratives and incidents, and suggestions on discipline. Boston, 1869. 290 pp. 2 plates. 16° 817.16
HAYTI, Santo Domingo, past and present: with a glance at. Hazard, S. New York, 1873. 16°. 5035.4
HAYWARD, Abraham. Biographical and critical essays. 3d series. London, 1874. 411+ pp. 8°. 5833.3
— *editor*. *See* PIOZZI, Esther Lynch 1224.6
HAYWARD, John. The book of religions. Added church and missionary statistics, with biographical sketches. Boston, 1843. 432 pp. 12° 1534.4
— The religious creeds and statistics of every Christian denomination in the United States and British provinces. Boston, 1836. 156 pp. 16°. 5816.20
HAYWARD, John Williams, *joint author*. Health and comfort in house building. *See* DRYSDALE, John (James) 6223.3
HAZARD, Samuel. Santo Domingo, past and present: with a glance at Hayti. Maps and illustrations. New York, 1873. xxix, 511+ pp. 16° 5035.4
HAZARD, Willis P. The library; or, some hints about what books to read, and how to buy them. By an old bookseller. Philadelphia [*cop.* 1870]. 64 pp. 12° 1537.1
HAZEL-BLOSSOMS. [Poems.] Whittier, J. G. Boston, 1875. 16° 1615.24
HAZEN, William Babcock. The school and the army in Germany and France, with a diary of siege life at Versailles. New York, 1872. 408 pp. 8°. 5714.5
HAZLITT, William. Lectures on the English poets. 2d edition. London, 1819. 331+ pp. 8° 5610.6
— Lectures on the English poets, and the English comic writers. New edition, edited by W. C. Hazlitt. London, 1870. 2 v. in 1. Sm. 8° 5616.5
— Personal recollections of. Stoddard, R. H. Bric-à-brac series. New York, 1875. Sq. 16°. 1828.9
HE knew he was right. Trollope, A. 334.11
HEAD, *Sir* Francis Bond. Bubbles from the Brunnen of Nassau. 7th edition. London, 1866. vi, 281+ pp. Illustrated. 12° 425.2

Note. — Minutely descriptive essays on a German watering place.

— A faggot of French sticks; containing sketches of the principal public institutions of Paris, and of the system of instruction of the French army. 3d edition. London, 1855. 2 v. 12°. 5526.11
HEAD, The, of the family. Craik, D. (M.) 323.12
HEADLESS horseman, The. Reid, M. 725.9
HEADLEY, Joel Tyler. The Adirondack; or, life in the woods. New edition, with additional matter. New York, 1875. 461+ pp. Illustrated. Map. 12° 816.8
— The chaplains and clergy of the revolution. New York, 1864. 402 pp. 12° 1014.1
— Farragut and our naval commanders. With portraits and battle scenes. New York, 1867. 609 pp. 8° 5012.4

Shelf. No.

HEADLEY, Joel Tyler, *continued*.
— Mountain adventures. With an introduction and additions. With illustrations. New York, 1872. vi, 356 pp. 16° 1714.4
— Washington and his generals. New York, 1854, 55. 2 v. Portraits. 12° 1216.5
HEADLEY, Phineas Camp. The island of fire; or, a thousand years of the old Northmen's home [Iceland]. 874–1874. Boston, 1875. 339+ pp. Illustrated. 12° 435.3
— Life of Louis Kossuth. With introduction by H. Greeley. Auburn, 1852. 461 pp. Portrait. 16°. 1024.2
HEADS and tails. Lippincott, S. J. 921.15
HEADSMAN, The. Cooper, J. F. 525.25
HEALEY. A romance. Fothergill, J. 721.11
HEALTH. Combe, A. The principles of physiology applied to the preservation of. New York, 1855. 12° 1718.2
— Fothergill, J. M. The maintenance of health. A medical work for lay readers. New York, 1875. 8° 6035.7
— Glover, M. B. Science and health. Boston, 1875. 12° 1733.3
— Hall, W. W. Health by good living. New York, 1872. Sm. 8° 1523.17
— – How to live long; or, health maxims, physical, mental, and moral. New York, 1875. 12° 6036.13
— Hope, G. H. Till the doctor comes, and how to help him. New York, 1871. 12° 1523.16
— Kingsley, C. Health and education. London, 1874. Sm. 8° 5836.10
— Kitchiner, W. Directions for invigorating and prolonging life; or, the invalid's oracle. New York, 1831. 12° 6038.1
— Lewis, D. Five-minute chats with young women on. New York, 1874. 12° 1522.9
— – Our girls. New York, 1871. 12° 1536.3
— Mitchell, S. W. Wear and tear, or hints for the overworked. Philadelphia, 1871. 16° 1537.2
— Mussey, R. D. Health: its friends and its foes. Boston, 1862. 12° 6035.1
— Smith, E. Health. New York, 1875. 12° 6036.11
— Tomes, R. Bazar book of. New York, 1873. 16°. 1538.5
— Warren, J. C. Physical education and the preservation of. Boston, 1846. 12° 1529.6

See also Diet, Digestion, Hygiene, Regimen.

HEALTH and comfort in house building. Drysdale, J. (J.), and Hayward, J. W. London, 1872. 8°. 6223.3
HEALTH reformer, The. Vol. 3–5. Battle Creek, 1868–71. 3 v. 8° 6031.1
HEALTH resorts. On the curative effects of baths and waters. Braun, J. London, 1875. 8° 6032.4
HEALTH trip to the tropics. Willis, N. P. New York, 1853. 12° 426.9
HEALTHY houses. Eassie, W. New York, 1872. 12°. 1525.6 and 6226.7
HEALY, Mary. Lakeville 530.8
HEARD, Franklin Fiske. Curiosities of law reporters. Boston, 1871. 212+ pp. 16° 6317.1
HEART, Practical treatise on the diagnosis, pathology, and treatment of diseases of the. Flint, A. Philadelphia, 1859. 8° 6022.4
HEART, The, of the continent. Ludlow, F. H. New York, 1871. Sm. 8° 413.4

Note. — Travels in the centre of North America.

HEART, The, of Mid-Lothian. Scott, *Sir* W. Boston. 523.6
— *Same*. Leipzig 330.5
HEART-HUNGRY. Westmoreland, M. J. 735.37
HEARTH and home. Vol. 4–7. New York, 1872–75. 4 v. F° 1330.1
HEARTH-STONE, The. Osgood, S. New York, 1854. 12°. 1516.3
HEARTS and faces. Trowbridge, J. T. 929.3
HEARTS and hands. A story. Fisher, F. C. 711.8
HEARTSEASE. Yonge, C. M. 318.3
HEAT. Abbott, J. Science for the young 912.5
— Armour, J. Iron and heat. London, 1871. 12°. 1716.40
— Cazin, A. Phenomena and laws of. New York, 1872. 16° 1714.6
— Lees, W. Elements of. New York [Glasgow], 1873. 16° 1717.10

Shelf. No.

HEAT, *continued.*
— Tyndall, J. Contributions to molecular physics in the domain of radiant heat. New York, 1873. 8° ... 6431.1
— – Heat a mode of motion. New York, 1873. 12°. 1522.5
HEATHER, J. F. Mathematical instruments. London, 1871. 2 v. Illustrated. 12° ... 1716.8

Contents. — Vol. I. Drawing and measuring instruments. II. Optical instruments.

HEATON, *Mrs.* Charles W. *See* HEATON, Mary M.
HEATON, Mary M., and OTHERS. Leonardo da Vinci and his works. London, 1874. xiv, 302+ pp. Illustrated. L. 8° ... 6211.5

Contents. — Life, by Mrs. Charles W. Heaton; Essay on his scientific and literary works by Charles Christopher Black; Account of his most important paintings.

— Life of Albrecht Dürer. With a translation of his letters and journal, and some account of his works. London, 1870. xv, 340 pp. Illustrated. Portrait. 8° ... 6210.5
HEAVEN. Kimball, J. W. Heaven. Boston, 1857. 12° ... 5815.21
— Swedenborg, E. Heaven and its wonders. Boston, 1851. 12° ... 5815.11
— *Same.* New York, 1872. 8° ... 6323.6
— *Same.* Philadelphia, 1873. 8° ... 5812.10
HEBRIDES, Journal of a tour to the. Boswell, J. Life of S. Johnson. London, 1831. 5 v. 8° .. 5423.7
HECKER, Justus Friedrich Carl. Epidemics of the middle ages. Translated by B. G. Babington. London, 1846. xxviii, 380 pp. 8° ... 6013.4
HECKINGTON. Gore, C. G. F. ... 312.25
HEDGE, Frederic Henry. Prose writers of Germany. With portraits. New edition, revised. Philadelphia [*cop.* 1847]. 580 pp. 8° ... 5732.1
— Reason in religion. Boston, 1865. iv, 458 pp. Sm. 8° ... 6325.4
— Recent inquiries in theology, by eminent English churchmen: being "Essays and reviews." Boston, 1860. xii, 480 pp. 12° ... 5814.15

Contents. — Temple, F.: The education of the world; Williams, R.: Bunsen's Biblical researches; Powell, B.: Evidences of Christianity; Wilson, H. B.: The national church; Goodwin, C. W.: On the Mosaic cosmogony; Pattison, M. Tendencies of religious thought in England, 1688-1750; Jowett, B.: On the interpretation of Scripture; Appendix.

— *Same.* 2d edition. With appendix. Boston, 1861. xiv, 498 pp. 12° ... 1526.24

Contents. — Same as preceding, with an additional essay by F. Temple, on The present relations of science to religion.

— *Same.* Leipzig, 1862. Sq. 16°. *See* ESSAYS and reviews ... 1538.3

Contents. — Same as 5814.15, above.

HEDGED in. Phelps, E. S. ... 537.10
HEDGES and evergreens. Warder, J. A. New York, 1858. 12° ... 6626.3
HEDWIG, *queen of Poland,* Love of country, or. Salvandy, N. A., *comte* de. Boston, 1856. 12° ... 916.11
HEIDELBERG. James, G. P. R. ... 327.7

Note. — A novel of the Thirty years' war.

HEIDENMAUER, The. Cooper, J. F. ... 525.31

Note. — A novel of the feudal period in the Vosges mountains.

HEINE, Heinrich. Leisure hour series. Scintillations. Translated from the German by S. A. Stern. New York, 1873. xx, 184+ pp. 16°. 518.14

Contents. — Part I. Florentine nights. II. Excerpts.

— The life work, and opinions of. Stigand, W. London, 1875. 2 v. 8° ... 5721.1
HEINZEN, Carl. [Various publications.] V. P., V. D. PPH. V. 16° ... 6327.4

Contents. — Six letters to a pious man. Indianapolis, 1869. 65 pp. — The true character of Humboldt. Indianapolis, 1869. 18+ pp. — Mankind the criminal. Roxbury [1864]. 24 pp. — What is a real democracy? Answered by an exposition of the constitution of the United States. Indianapolis, 1871. 64 pp.

— Teutscher Radikalismus in Amerika. Ausgewählte Vorträge. N. P., 1867. 364 pp. 16° .. 2025.4
HEIR, The, of Malreward; or, restored. By the author of "Son and heir," etc. ... 732.26

Shelf. No.

HEIR, The, of Redcliffe. Yonge, C. M. ... 318.14
HEIR, The, of Wast-Wayland. Howitt, M. ... 533.23
HEIRESS, The. Stephens, A. S. (W.) ... 522.4
HEIRESS, The, of Haughton. Marsh-Caldwell, A... 313.23
HEISTER, Laurence. General system of surgery. Illustrated. 3d edition. London, 1748. xvi, 338+ pp. 4° ... 6010.1
HELEN and Arthur. Hentz, C. L. ... 534.15
HELEN Ford. Alger, H., *jr.* ... 1115.5
HELEN Gardner's wedding-day. Terhune, M. V.... 727.31
HELL. Swedenborg, E. Boston, 1857. 12° ... 5815.21
— *Same.* New York, 1872. 8° ... 6323.6
— *Same.* Philadelphia, 1873. 8° ... 5812.10
HELLBORN, (Heinrich) Kreissle von. Life of Franz Schubert. From the German by A. D. Coleridge. With an appendix by G. Grove. London, 1869. 2 v. Portrait. 8° ... 5727.1
HELLWALD, Friedrich von. The Russians in Central Asia. A critical examination down to the present time of the geography and history of Central Asia. From the German by T. Wirgman. With a map. London, 1874. xx, 332 pp. Sm. 8° .. 5914.9
HELMHOLTZ, Hermann (Ludwig Ferdinand). Popular lectures on scientific subjects. Translated by E. Atkinson. With an introduction by [J.] Tyndall. London, 1873. xvi, 397 pp. 8° ... 6834.1
— *Same.* New York, 1873. xvi, 397 pp. Sm. 8°. 1522.6
— Théorie physiologique de la musique. Traduit de l'allemand par G. Guéroult. Avec figurés. Paris, 1868. 544 pp. 8° ... 6233.4
HELPER, Hinton Rowan. The impending crisis of the South: how to meet it. New York, 1860. 420 pp. 12° ... 617.1
HELPING hand, A, for town and country. [Receipts, designs, etc.] Draper, L. C., and Croffut, W. A. Cincinnati, 1870. 8° ... 1511.4 and 6422.1
HELPING-HAND series. *See* NOWELL, Harriet P. H.
HELPS, *Sir* Arthur. Casimir Maremma. Boston, 1870. xl, 409 pp. 16° ... 518.12
— Companions of my solitude. Boston, 1870. 276 pp. 16° ... 1914.3
— Conversations on war and general culture. Boston, 1871. 306+ pp. 16° ... 5617.4
— Essays written in the intervals of business. Added an essay on organization in daily life. Boston, 1871. 245 pp. 16° ... 1917.1
— Friends in council. New York [*cop.* 1861]. 2 v. 12° ... 1914.2
— *Same.* Leipzig, 1873. 2 v. in 1. Sq. 16° ... 1538.14
— Ivan de Biron; or, the Russian court in the middle of last century. Boston, 1874. 473+ pp. 16° ... 738.11
— *Same.* Leipzig, 1874. 2 v. in 1. Sq. 16° ... 329.16
— Life and labours of [Thomas] Brassey. 1805–1870. 3d edition. London, 1872. xiv, 386+ pp. Illustrated. Portrait. Maps. Sm. 8° ... 5426.6
— Life of Hernando Cortes. New York, 1871. xiv, 307 pp. Maps. Sm. 8° ... 1025.12

Note. — Drawn chiefly from his "Spanish conquest."

— Realmah. Boston, 1869. x, 499+ pp. 16° ... 524.21
— Social pressure. Boston, 1875. vii, 412 pp. 16°. 5826.5
— Some talk about animals and their masters. London, 1873. 209+ pp. Sm. 8° ... 6617.5
— The Spanish conquest in America. New York, 1836. 4 v. Map. 12° ... 816.6
— Thoughts upon government. London, 1872. viii, 245 pp. Sm. 8° ... 6333.2
HEMANS, Charles Isidore. Historic and monumental Rome. A handbook for the students of classical and Christian antiquity in the Italian capital. London, 1874. iv, 734+ pp. Sm. 8° ... 5517.7
HEMANS, Felicia (Dorothea). Select poetical works. Leipzig, 1865. viii, 342 pp. Sq. 16° ... 1613.22
— The league of the Alps, The siege of Valencia, The vespers of Palermo, and other poems. Boston, 1826. 480+ pp. 8° ... 1621.2
— Memoir of the life and writings of. Hughes, *Mrs.* —. Philadelphia, 1839. 12° ... 1022.4
HEMOPTYSIS as a symptom. Ware, J. (*In* Massachusetts medical society. Publications) ... 6021.4

Shelf. No.

HEMSLEY, W. B. Handbook of hardy trees, shrubs, and herbaceous plants. Based on the French work of Decaisne and Naudin, entitled 'Manuel de l'amateur des jardins,' and including the original woodcuts. With an introduction by E. S. Rand, jr. Boston [London], 1873. viii, v–xliii, 687 pp. 8° 6624.1

HENDERSON, Peter. Gardening for profit. Illustrated. New York [*cop.* 1867]. 243 pp. 12° . 1514.17

HENESS, Theophilus. Introduction to the Leitfaden; a guide for instruction in German without grammar and dictionary. 2d edition. Boston, 1874. 39 pp. 12° 2025.1

HENRIETTA Temple. Disraeli, B. 324.25

HENRY IV, *king of France and Navarre*. Abbott, J. S. C. History of 915.2

— James, G. P. R. Life of. New York, 1855. 2 v. 12° 5525.12

See also France, *note*, and the note in the Bulletin, vol. II, p. 369.

HENRY VIII and his court. An historical romance. Mundt, C. (M.) 531.33

HENRY, Patrick, Sketches of his life and character. Wirt, W. Philadelphia, 1818. 8° 1012.4

HENRY Dunbar. Braddon, M. E. 325.4

HENRY Esmond, History of. Thackeray, W. M. Leipzig 335.10

— *Same.* New York 1820.3

— *Same.* (*In his* Works.) London 513.1.4

HENRY of Guise; or, the states of Blois. James, G. P. R. 722.12

HENRY of Ofterdingen. Hardenberg, F. L. von. Cambridge, 1842. 12° 713.10

HENRY St. John, gentleman. A tale of 1774–75. Cooke, J. E. 524.6

HENRY Smeaton: a Jacobite story of the reign of George I. James, G. P. R. 730.3

HENSLOW, George. The theory of evolution of living things and the application of the principles of evolution to religion. London, 1873. xiv, 220+ pp. 16° 5814.18

HENTZ, Caroline Lee. Aunt Patty's scrap-bag 935.15

— The banished son; and other stories 534.12

— Courtship and marriage 534.13

— Eoline 534.14

— Ernest Linwood 536.12

— Helen and Arthur 534.15

— Linda 536.11

— The lost daughter; and other stories 534.17

— Love after marriage; and other stories 534.18

— Marcus Warland 534.19

— The planter's northern bride 534.20

— Rena 534.16

— Robert Graham. A sequel to "Linda" 534.21

HEPWORTH, George Hughes. The whip, hoe, and sword; or, the gulf-department in '63. Boston, 1864. 294 pp. 12° 414.1

HER dearest foe. Alexander, *Mrs.* 517.21

HER face was her fortune. Robinson, F. W. 731.19

HER lord and master. Church, F. 337.21

HER majesty the queen. A novel. Cooke, J. E. ... 737.15

HER majesty's tower. [London. Historical associations.] Dixon, W. H. Leipzig, 1869. 4 v. in 2. Sq. 16° 838.4

HER mother's Fancy. Hall, T. O. 921.14

HER title of honour. Parr, H. 314.2

HERALD of health. Vol. 55–58. New York, 1873, 74. 4 v. in 2. 8° 1325.1

HERALDRY, ancient and modern. Aveling, S. T. London [1873]. Sm. 4° 5415.7

HÉRAUD, A. Nouveau dictionnaire des plantes médicinales. Avec 261 figures intercalées dans le texte. Paris, 1875. xii, 589 pp. 18° 6627.1

HERBERT, David. Great historical mutinies. London, 1876. 3–607 pp. Wood-cut. Sm. 8° 5924.2

Contents. — The mutiny of the Bounty; The mutiny at Spithead; The mutiny at the Nore; Mutinies in Highland regiments; The Indian mutiny.

HERBERT, George. Poetical works. With a memoir. Boston, 1874. xxxiii, 308 pp. 16° 5628.3

— Life of. Walton, I. London, 1866. 16° 5428.2

Shelf. No.

HERBERT, George Robert Charles, *earl of Pembroke*, and KINGSLEY, George H. South sea bubbles. By the earl and the doctor. Leipzig, 1874. 320 pp. Sq. 16° 310.27

HERBERT, Henry William. (*Frank Forester.*) American game in its seasons. Illustrated. Revised edition. New York, 1873. 343 pp. 12° 1516.14

— The dog. Illustrated. Complete and revised edition. New York [*cop.* 1857]. 663 pp. L. 12°. 1522.3

Contents. — The sportsman's vade mecum, by "Dinks"; Dogs, and their management, by E. Mayhew; Dog breaking, by W. N. Hutchinson.

— The fair puritan. An historical romance of the days of witchcraft. Philadelphia, 1875. 222 pp. 12° 716.1

— Field sports of the United States and British provinces. New edition. With illustrations, and a brief memoir of the author. New York [*cop.* 1848]. 2 v. Portrait. 12° 1514.19

— Fish and fishing of the United States and British provinces. Illustrated. New edition, revised, with an ample supplement by the author, [and] a treatise on fly-fishing by "Dinks." New York, 1866. 512+ pp. L. 12° 1512.1

— Horse and horsemanship of the United States and British provinces. Revised, enlarged, and continued to 1871, by S. D. and B. G. Bruce. With original portraits of celebrated horses. New York, 1871. 2 v. 8° 6612.6

— The Roman traitor: or, the days of Cicero, Cato and Cataline [*sic*]. A true tale of the republic. Philadelphia [*cop.* 1853]. 2 v. in 1. 12° 716.13

HERBERT, *Lady* Mary Elizabeth, A search after sunshine; or, Algeria in 1871. London, 1872. 265+ pp. Illustrated. 8° 5911.2

HERBERT Carter's legacy. Alger, H., *jr* 1115.10

HERCULANEUM, The buried cities of Campania; or. Adams, W. H. D. Boston, 1870. 16° 437.5

HERDER, Johann Gottfried von. Sämmtliche Werke. Stuttgart, 1852, 53. 40 v. in 20. Sq. 16° 5736.1

Contents. — Vol. I [1, 2]. Vom Geist der ebräischen Poesie. II [3, 4]. Salomons Lieder der Liebe; Von der ebräischen Elegie; Aelteste Urkunde des Menschengeschlechts. III [5, 6]. Zusätze du der ältesten Urkunde des Menschengeschlechts; Christliche Reden und Homilien. IV [7, 8]. Erläuterungen zum Neuen Testament; Johannes Offenbarung. V [9, 10]. Vom Studium der Theologie und dem christlichen Predigtamt; Christliche Schriften.

VI [11, 12]. Christliche Schriften; Briefe, das Studium der Theologie betreffend. VII [13, 14]. Gedichte; Der Cid, nach spanischen Romanzen besungen. VIII [15, 16]. Legenden, Dramatische Stücke und Dichtungen; Stimmen der Völker in Liedern. IX [17, 18]. Terpsichore; Fragmente zur deutschen Literatur. X [19, 20]. Fragmente zur deutschen Literatur; Schriften zur römischen Literatur; Schriften zur griechischen Literatur.

XI [21, 22]. Blumenlese aus morgenländischen Dichtern; Früchte aus den sogenannt goldenen Zeiten des achtzehnten Jahrhunderts. XII [23, 24]. Kritische Wälder; Abhandlungen und Briefe über schöne Literatur und Kunst. XIII [25, 26]. Antiquarische Aufsätze; Nachlese zur schönen Literatur und Kunst; Die Vorwelt. XIV [27, 28]. Präludien zur Philosophie der Geschichte der Menschheit; Ideen zur Geschichte der Menschheit. XV [29, 30]. Ideen zur Geschichte der Menschheit; Postscenien zur Geschichte der Menschheit.

XVI [31, 32]. Seele und Gott; Sophron. XVII [33, 34]. Adrastea. XVIII [35, 36]. Briefe zur Beförderung der Humanität; Nachlese historischer Schriften. XIX [37, 38]. Verstand und Erfahrung; Vernunft und Sprache; Kalligone. XX [39, 40]. Erinnerungen aus dem Leben Johann Gottfried von Herders. Gesammelt und beschrieben von Maria Carolina von Herder, geb. Flachsland.

— Reise nach Italien. Briefwechsel mit seiner Gattin, vom August 1788 bis Juli 1789. Herausgegeben von H. Düntzer und F. G. von Herder. Giessen, 1859. xxxii, 416 pp. 16° 1024.1

— Von und an Herder. Ungedruckte Briefe aus Herders Nachlass. Herausgegeben von H. Düntzer und F. G. von Herder. Leipzig, 1861, 62. 3 v. 8° 5735.8

HERESY and Christian doctrine. Pressensé, E. de. London, 1873. 8° 5813.8

HEREWARD the Wake. Kingsley, C. 326.15

Note. — A novel, William the conqueror's time.

HÉRICAULT, Charles d'. Thermidor, Paris en 1794. Paris, 1872. viii, 283 pp. 12° 5516.5

HÉRICOURT, Jenny d'. A woman's philosophy of woman; or woman affranchised. New York, 1864. 317 [315] pp. 12° 1535.8

Shelf. No.

HERMANN Agha. Palgrave, W. G. 537.16

HERMANN and Dorothea. [Poem.] Goethe, J. W. von. Boston, 1870. 16° 1615.16

HERMES or a philosophical inqviry concerning vniversal grammar. Harris, J. London, 1786. 8° 1734.1

HERMITE, L', de la chaussée-d'Antin. Jouy, V. J. É. de. Paris, 1815-18. 5 v. 12° 5518.2

HERMITE, L', en province. Jouy, V. J. É. de. Paris, 1818. 3 v. 12° 5518.4

HERMITS, The. Kingsley, C. [London, 1868.] Sm. 8° 5937.4

Note. — Accounts of famous anchorites, and others.

HERO, A, and a martyr. Reade, C. 710.32

HERO, A, of the pen. Bürstenbinder, E. 521.19

HERO and Leander. Musæus. *See* HOMERUS 6118.11

HERO Carthew. Parr, L. 728.5

HERO Trevelyan. Craik, G. M. 322.4

HERODOTUS. History. A new English version, edited with copious notes and appendices [and a life]. By George Rawlinson, assisted by Sir Henry Rawlinson and Sir J. G. Wilkinson. With maps and illustrations. New York, 1871, 72. 4 v. 8° 6112.2

— Swayne, G. C. Herodotus [outlined and explained]. Edinburgh, 1870. 16° 6116.4

— Wheeler, J. T. Life and travels: an imaginary biography founded on fact. London, 1855. 2 v. Sm. 8° 6117.2

HEROES, The; or, Greek fairy tales. Kingsley, C. 935.25

HEROES, hero-worship and the heroic in history. [Essays.] Carlyle, T. London, 1872. Sq. 16°. 1535.19

HEROLD, Louis Joseph Ferdinand. Zampa. (*In* Ditson, O., and co. Standard opera librettos) . 6233.3.1

HERSEY, George C., Report of the case of, indicted for the murder of B. F. Tirrell. Yerrington, J. M. W. Boston, 1862. 8° 631.6

HERTHA. Bremer, F. 536.8

HERTZ, Henrik. King René's daughter: a Danish lyrical drama. Translated by T. Martin. 3d edition, revised. New York [*cop.* 1866]. xii, 100+ pp. 12° 1615.15

HERVÉ, *pseud.* *See* RONGER, Florimond.

HESEKIEL, John George Louis. Life of Bismarck, private and political; with descriptive notices of his ancestry. Translated and edited by K. R. H. Mackenzie. With illustrations. London, 1870. xxvii, 501 pp. Portraits. 8° 1221.8

— *Same.* New York, 1870. 491 pp. Portraits. 8° 1021.5

HESIODUS. Works and days. *See* HOMERUS 6118.11

— Hesiod [outlined and explained]. Davies, J. Edinburgh, 1873. 16° 6116.16

HESSE, Léopold Auguste Constantin. Bibliothéconomie, ou manuel pour l'arrangement, la conservation et l'administration des bibliothèques. Nouvelle édition, ornée de figures. Paris, 1841. 248+ pp. 24°. [Manuel Roret] 6139.1

HESTER Howard's temptation. Warfield, C. A. 723.24

HESTER Morley's promise. Smith, H. 737.18

HEWITT, Graily. The diagnosis and treatment of diseases of women, including the diagnosis of pregnancy. London, 1863. xiv, 628 pp. 8° .. 6023.7

HEWITT, Mary E. The songs of our land, and other poems. Boston, 1846. 156 pp. 12° 1625.13

HEWITT, Robert, *jr.* Coffee: its history, cultivation, and uses. Illustrated. Map. New York, 1872. 102 pp. 12° 6626.1

HEYSE, Paul (Johann Ludwig). L'Arrabiata and other tales. From the German by M. Wilson .. 311.10

— The dead lake and other tales. From the German by M. Wilson 311.9

— The lonely ones. *See* JOHN, E. Magdelena 710.25

HÉZECQUES, Charles Alexandre François Felix, *comte* d', *baron de Mailly.* Recollections of a page at the court of Louis XVI. Edited, from the French, by Charlotte M. Yonge. London, 1873. xi, 336 pp. 8° 5524.4

HIAWATHA, The song of. Longfellow, H. W. Poetical works. Leipzig, 1856. Sq. 16° 1614.1

Shelf. No.

HIBBERD, James F., *joint author.* Dissertation on the part performed by nature and time in the cure of diseases. *See* EDES, Robert Thaxter 6021.5

HIBBERD, Shirley. The amateur's rose book. New edition. Illustrated. London, 1874. viii, 258 pp. Sm. 8° 6625.3

HIDDEN path, The. Terhune, M. V. 735.14

HIDDEN sin, The. Dupuy, E. A. 735.38

HIDE and seek. Collins, (W.) W. 326.1

HIGGINSON, Thomas Wentworth. Army life in a black regiment. Boston, 1870. iv, 296 pp. 12° 416.5

— Atlantic essays. Boston, 1871. 341+ pp. 12°. 1915.2

— English statesmen. New York, 1875. vi, 363+ pp. [Higginson, T. W., *editor.* Brief biographies of European public men.] 16° 628.7

— Malbone: an Oldport romance. Boston, 1871. iv, 244 pp. 12° 524.24

— Oldport days. With illustrations. Boston, 1873. 268 pp. 16° 5036.2

— Ought women to learn the alphabet? (*In* Woman's suffrage tracts) 1926.5

— Out-door papers. Boston, 1871. 370 pp. 12° . 1915.1

— Young folks' history of the United States. Illustrated. Boston, 1875. vi, 370 pp. Map. Sq. 16°. 618.2

— *editor.* Brief biographies of European public men. New York, 1875. 16°. *Namely:* —

— Higginson, T. W. English statesmen 628.7

— Hinton, R. J. English radical leaders 628.8

HIGGLEDY-PIGGLEDY. Hugessen, E. H. K. 1116.1

HIGH, low, Jack, and the game: a burletta. Planché, J. R., and Dance, C. New York, N. D. 12° ... 1635.5

HIGH mills, The. Saunders, K. 319.28

HIGHER Christian life, The. Boardman, W. E. Boston, 1858. 12° .... 1536.10 and 6325.10

HIGHER law. A romance. Ainslie, H. 737.25

HIGHLAND treason, The: drama. Holland, E. G. Boston, 1852. 12° 1916.9

HIGHLAND widow, The. Scott, *Sir* W. 523.19

HIGHLANDS. *See* SCOTLAND.

HIGINBOTHAM, Josephine M. "Una and her paupers:" memorials of Agnes Elizabeth Jones, by her sister. With an introduction by Florence Nightingale. 3d American edition. With an introductory preface by H. W. Beecher. And a supplementary chapter on hospital nursing and training in the United States, by the author of "Woman's work in the civil war." New York, 1872. Portrait. xlvi, 497 pp. 16° 5427.8

HILA Dart. Mumford, M. E. 1115.3

HILARY St. Ives. Ainsworth, W. H. 322.24

HILDRETH, Richard. Despotism in America; or, an inquiry into the nature and results of the slave-holding system in the United States. Boston, 1840. 186 pp. 12° 816.2

— History of banks: added, a demonstration of the advantages and necessity of free competition in the business of banking. Boston, 1837. 142 pp. 12° 5828.2

— History of the United States, 1497-1789. Revised edition. New York, 1871. 3 v. 8° 5011.10

— - 1788-1821. Revised edition. New York, 1871. 3 v. 8° 5011.11

— Theory of morals. Boston, 1844. xix, 272 pp. 12° 5836.5

HILL, Thomas. Jesus, the interpreter of nature; and other sermons. Boston, 1860. 241 pp. 12°. 6327.18

HILL, Thomas E. Manual of social and business forms: a guide to correct writing. Embracing penmanship, correspondence, legal business forms, etc. Chicago, 1876. 305 pp. Portrait. Illustrations. 4° 5821.3

HILLARD, George Stillman. Life of Captain John Smith. (*In* Sparks, J. Library of American biography) 5028.1.2

— Memoir and correspondence of Jeremiah Mason. Cambridge, 1873. viii, 467 pp. Portrait. 4°. 5020.7

— Six months in Italy. Boston, 1854. 2 v. Sm. 8°. 426.8

HILLER, Ferdinand. Mendelssohn. Letters and recollections. Translated by M. E. von Glehn. London, 1874. xiv, 223+ pp. Portrait. Sm. 8°. 5727.3

Shelf. No.

HILLERN, Wilhelmine von. Geier-Wally. A tale of the Tyrol 521.33
— Only a girl. From the German by Mrs. A. L. Wister 726.27
— A twofold life. Translated by M. S............ 735.19
HILLS, The, of the Shatemuc. Warner, S.......... 331.3
HILLSBORO' farms. Cobb, S. D. 716.9
HILLYARS, The, and the Burtons. Kingsley, H. ... 326.22
HIMALAYA mountains. The Indian Alps and how we crossed them; being a narrative of two years' residence in the eastern Himalaya, etc. London, 1876. L. 8° 5930.6
— Wilson, A. The abode of snow. Observations on a journey from Chinese Tibet to the Indian Caucasus, through the upper valleys of the Himalaya. New York, 1875. Sm. 8° 5933.10
HINDLEY, Charles. Tavern anecdotes and sayings; including the origin of signs, and reminiscences connected with taverns, coffee-houses, clubs, etc. London, 1875. xvi, 414 pp. Sm. 8°..........5616.18

Note. — Partly reprinted from the edition of 1825.

HINDOSTAN. Dandi, S. Hindoo tales. London, 1873. 8° 5936.5
— Gangooly, J. C. Life and religion of the Hindoos. Boston, 1860. 12° ....1025.13 and 5937.2

See also Asia, India.

HINGSTON, Edward P. The genial showman. Being reminiscences of the life of Artemus Ward [*pseud.* for Charles F. Browne] and pictures of a showman's career in the Western world. New York, 1870. 155 pp. 2 plates. 8° 1211.9
HINTON, James, *editor.* Physiology for practical use. With an introduction, by E. L. Youmans. New York, 1874. xi, 507 pp. 12°........... 6035.5
HINTON, Richard J. English radical leaders. New York, 1875. 374 pp. [Higginson, T. W., *editor.* Brief biographies of European public men.] 16° 628.8
HINTS on household taste in furniture, upholstery, and other details. Eastlake, *Sir* C. L. Boston, 1872. Sm. 8°.............................. 6212.1
HINTS to young men, on the true relation of the sexes. Ware, J. Boston, 1850. 16°......... 1528.4
HIPPOLYTUS, *St.* Writings. Translated by S. D. F. Salmond. Edinburgh, 1868, 69. 2 v. [Ante-Nicene Christian library.] 8° .....Vol. 6, 9 of 6322.4

Contents. — Vol. I. The refutation of all heresies, translated by J. H. Macmahon; Fragments from his commentaries on various books of Scripture. II. Extant works and fragments; Fragments of writings [by various authors] of the third century: — *viz.* The epistles of pope Zephyrinus; Fragments of Caius; Extant writings of Julius Africanus; Epistles of pope Callistus; Epistles of pope Urban I; Extant writings of Asterius Urbanus; Epistles of pope Pontianus; Epistle of pope Anterus; Epistles of pope Fabian; Decrees of Fabian; Fragments of the Epistles of Alexander.

Note. — Vol. 2 is bound with IRENÆUS, *St.* Writings. Vol. II.

HIS level best. Hale, E. E. 738.2
HIS natural life. A novel. Clarke, M. 721.24
HIS two wives. Ames, M. C...................... 724.25
HISTOIRE d'une femme. Énault, L. Paris, 1872. 16°.. 5536.6
HISTOLOGY, Pathological. Wedl, C. London, 1855. 8° 6013.18
HISTORICAL and critical essays. De Quincey, T. Boston, 1866. 2 v. 12° 1825.3
HISTORICAL essays. Freeman, E. A. London, 1872, 73. 2 v. 8° 5913.4
HISTORICAL essays, Select. Freeman, E. A. Leipzig, 1873. Sq. 16° 828.9
HISTORICAL sketches. Newman, J. H. London, 1872. Sm. 8°...................825.16 and 5925.5
HISTORY. Abbott, J. Story of ancient history. [Juvenile] 936.1.5
— Allen, W. American biographical and historical dictionary. Boston, 1832. 8° ..........*R.R., D.3.2
— Arnold, T. Introductory lectures on modern history. London, 1871. 8°.................... 5912.1
— Bunsen, C. C. J. von. God in history. London, 1868, 70. 3 v. 8°.........................5813.13
— Butler, F. Sketches of universal history. Hartford, 1821. 12° 817.9
— Freeman, E. A. Outlines of history. New York, 1873. 16°................................ 828.8
— — The unity of history. London, 1873. 8° 5822.10
— Gervinus, G. G. Introduction to the history of the nineteenth century. London, 1866. 16° .. 836.2
— Gilman, A. Seven historic ages. [Juvenile]... 918.30
— Keary, A. The nations around. [London], 1870. Sm. 8°...5937.12
— Michelet, J. A summary of modern history; continued to the present time, by M. C. M. Simpson. London, 1875. Sm. 8° 5528.7
— Mill, J. S. Dissertations and discussions: political, philosophical, and historical. New York, 1874, 75. 8° 5824.4
— Mueller, J. von. An universal history. Boston, 1831. 4 v. 12°.............................. 836.6
— Newman, J. H. Historical sketches. London, 1872, 73. 3 v. Sm. 8°........................ 5925.5
— Rawlinson, G. The five great monarchies of the ancient Eastern world. New York, 1871. 3 v. 8°. 5922.3
— — Manual of ancient history. Oxford, 1869. 8°.5921.10
— Smyth, W. Lectures on modern history. Boston, 1851. 8°....................................5012.10
— *Same.* London, 1854. 2 v. Sm. 8° 5925.7
— Thalheimer, M. E. A manual of mediæval and modern history. Cincinnati [*cop.* 1874]. 8° .. 831.4
— Tytler, A. F. Universal history. Boston, 1840. 2 v. 8° 811.3
— Villemain, A. F. Études d'histoire moderne. Paris, 1862. 12°..............................5537.13
— Whelpley, S. Compend of history, from the earliest times. New York, 1814. 8° 834.1
— Worcester, J. E. Elements of history, ancient and modern. Boston, 1850. 12°............. 836.4

NOTE ON HISTORY.

Study and philosophy of history.

The purpose of Buckle's elaborate and voluminous introduction to his "History of civilization" [5417.1] — his incomplete history not going beyond such introduction — was to study the different principles of action among nations, in those countries where they were most developed, and then to apply the laws of them to English history. His 6th chapter follows the practice of historians through sixteen centuries; and subsequently he traces the progress of historical writing by countries, for the 17th and 18th centuries. Bunsen has traced the manifestations of "God in history," and this same theory lies at the basis of the labors of Niebuhr and Arnold. The peculiarly modern spirit pervades Goldwin Smith's paper [Atlantic monthly, Jan., 1870], who opposes the views of Buckle and Comte; and that on history in Macaulay's Essays [1918.4]. Carl Ritter has unfolded the relations of physical geography to the history of races, and his theory has been illustrated by Guyot, in his "Earth and man" [1523.15]. See also Contemporary review, vol. 5. Draper, in his "History of the American civil war" [811.6], devotes a large portion of the first volume to illustrating his theory of the dependence of events upon physiological causes, arising from race and from the natural conditions of the southern states. Buckle's [in his "History of civilization," 5417.1] necessitarian theory admits more that is spiritual, but he evolves an imperative law of averages to regulate and preserve the character of events. Froude [see his "History of England"] seems to have no theory beyond the wayward forces of a diversified human nature; but he has expressed his views in his essays, "The science of history," and "Scientific method applied to history," in his "Short studies" [1914.5].

Guizot's theory is examined by J. Stuart Mill, in his Dissertations [5824.4.2]; and again by Alison [Essays on Guizot and Michelet, 1531.7], in comparison with the principles of other historians, from the time of Machiavel, "who seems first to have formed a conception of the philosophy of history." Prescott's views are given in his review of Irving's Granada, in his Essays [1537.8; 5237.3]. John Fiske, in the North American review, July, 1869, examines the views of Draper in his "Intellectual development of Europe" [5921.2] and of Maine, in his "Ancient law."

Bishop Dupanloup gives his counsel to young French students on the study of history.

See essays on the study of history by Prof. Seeley [5616.3].

A. Hayward in his "Pearls and mock pearls of history," in his Essays [5833.3], shows how erroneous statements are engrafted upon the historical records.

See essays on the philosophy of history in Emerson's Essays; in Carlyle's Essays [5610.7]; and Harper's monthly, vol. 10, by John Bonner.

See President Porter, on reading history, in his "Books and reading" [6134.2]; and F. W. Newman, on the "Contrasts of ancient and modern history" in Fraser's magazine, 1874.

Universal history.

Probably the best general history of the world is Philip Smith's, which will satisfy the reader of this day by embodying the latest researches, and testing all by that critical spirit which separates myth from fact. He claims, also, to be the only writer in English, since Raleigh, who has traced the story of Divine providence and human progress conjointly. The German work of Mueller gained a good reputation in the early part of this century by a method that brought events together by their affinities, rather than in the order of occurrence. The English work of Tytler dates about the same time, and his plan was to select the successive prominent nations, and make their history the thread of a general narrative.

Bryce's "Holy Roman empire" [5814.19] outlines the cause of civilized history from the time of the Romans. Viollet-le-Duc's "Annals of a fortress" [6223.4], under the guise of fiction, traces the progress of military history during successive ages.

Ancient history.

The most scholarly English edition of the ancient Herodotus is that of the Rawlinsons [6112.2]. J. T. Wheeler's "Life and travels of Herodotus, an imaginary biography" [6117.2], is a good book for the general reader. *See* Herodotus.

Rollin's day of usefulness is past, the science of historical writing having advanced beyond him [5913.1]. Rawlinson, in his Manual, coming down to the fall of the Western empire, has embraced modern research up to 1869.

George Rawlinson's "Five ancient monarchies" [5922.3], covering Assyria, Babylon, Chaldæa, Media, and Persia, is of high standing. Later volumes cover Parthia [5932.6] and the Sassanian empire [5923.11].

Baldwin's "Pre-historic nations" [824.7] traces the origin of the Phœnicians, Chaldæans, Egyptians, etc., to the Cushites of Arabia.

Lord's "Ancient states" [815.8] follows in a compendious way the general plan of Philip Smith's work, and is intended to do for the other ancient nations (Egypt, Assyria, Babylon, Media, Persia, Asia Minor, and Phœnicia) what is usually done for Greece and Rome. Smith's comes down to Alexander's conquest, and avails of both Rawlinson's and Oppert's researches in cuneiform inscriptions.

Plutarch's Lives [5932.5], as gathering the events around the most famous personages, presents an attractive grouping of much of ancient history. F. D. Maurice, in his "Friendship of books" [6136.8], characterizes the chief ancient historians.

See also Assyria, Babylon, Greece, Jews, Persia, Rome, etc.

Modern history.

Dr. Smyth's Lectures are an admirable introduction to the study of modern history, and he gives critical opinions on the authors to be read upon each period, aiming as much to assist as to inform readers. In his own views he is liberal and impartial, and Sparks, who edits the American edition, and adds a list of books on American history, praises Smyth's candor in the lectures devoted to the American revolution. Dr. Arnold's book, which is simply introductory to the study, the American edition of which is edited by Henry Reed, consists of lectures delivered in 1842, and shows the author's own liberal habits of mind and Christian impulses, though he is thought to be somewhat blind to the merits of the side opposed to his sympathies. His treatment is simple and original.

See Disraeli, on the first sources of modern history, in his "Amenities of literature" [1533.13], and also the works of Michelet, Gervinus, and Thalheimer, mentioned above.

History of special countries will be found under their names, as Asia, America, England, Europe, France, Germany, United States, etc.

Shelf. No.

HISTORY of my pets. Lippincott, S. J. Boston, 1871. 16° 933.21

HISTORY of Sandford and Merton. Day, T. 935.4

HISTORY of Tom Jones, a foundling. Fielding, H. 312.20

HITCHCOCK, —. Chronological record of the American civil war. New York, 1868. 106+ pp. Portrait. 8° 5013.4

HITCHCOCK, Edward. Dyspepsy forestalled and resisted: or lectures on diet, regimen, and employment. Amherst, 1831. 452 pp. 12° 6036.7

— Final report on the geology of Massachusetts. *See* MASSACHUSETTS 6630.1

— Report on the geology, mineralogy, botany, and zoology of Massachusetts. *See* MASSACHUSETTS. 6631.1

HITHERTO. Whitney, A. D. T. 735.7

HOADLY, Benjamin. Essays. (*In* Sparks, J. Collection of essays and tracts in theology) 1918.9.1

— Selection from [his] works. Boston, 1823. [No title-page.] 12° 6327.11

HOBART, Aaron. Historical sketch of Abington, Mass. Boston, 1839. 176 pp. 8° 812.1

HOBART family. Thayer, E. Family memorial. Hingham, 1835. 8° 611.2

HOBBS, A. C. The construction of locks. *See* TOMLINSON, Charles 1715.27

HOCQUART, Édouard. La morale en action, ou choix de faits mémorables et instructifs. Nouvelle édition. Nouvelle-Orléans, 1824. 408 pp. Illustrated. 12° 5518.3

HODDER, George. Personal reminiscences. (*In* Stoddard, R. H. Bric-à-brac series) 1828.4

HODGE, Charles. Systematic theology. New York, 1874. 3 v. 8° 5811.10

— What is Darwinism? New York, 1874. iv, 178 pp. 16° 6616.8

HODSON, William Stephen Raikes. Twelve years of a soldier's life in India. Including a personal narrative of the siege of Delhi. Edited by G. H. Hodson. From the 3d and enlarged English edition. Boston, 1860. 444 pp. 12° 426.11

HOEI-SHIN, Narrative of. Leland, C. G. Fusang. London, 1875. 8° 5925.6

Shelf. No.

HOEY, *Mrs.* Cashel. The blossoming of an aloe 711.15

— A golden sorrow 330.21

— Out of court 319.17

HOFFMAN, William. The monitor; or, jottings of a New York merchant during a trip round the globe. With illustrations. New York, 1863. xiv, 448 pp. Portrait. 12° 235.3

HOFFMANN, Ernst Theodor Amadeus (Wilhelm). *See* CARLYLE, T. German romance. Boston, 1841. 2 v. in 1. 12° 5725.2

HOFLAND, Barbara. The young Crusoe; or the shipwrecked boy 918.22

HOGAN, William. Auricular confession and popish nunneries. Boston, 1845. 215 pp. 12° 1538.17

HOGARTH, William. Works: with life and anecdotal descriptions of his pictures. Ireland, J., and Nichols, J. London, N. D. 3 v. Sm. 8° 6214.2

HOGG, John, *editor*. The parlour menagerie. Wherein are exhibited in a descriptive and anecdotal form, the habits, the resources, and the mysterious instincts, of the more interesting portions of animal creation. With wood engravings. London, 1875. 520 pp. Sm. 8° 1522.11

HOLBROOK, James. Ten years among the mail bags: or, notes from the diary of a special agent of the post-office department. With illustrations. Boston, 1856. 432 pp. Portraits. 12° 1216.8

HOLBROOK, Silas Pinckney. Sketches by a traveller. Boston, 1830. 315+ pp. 12° 5914.4

HOLDEN, Charles F. Holden's book on birds. New York, 1873. 82 pp. Portrait. Illustrations. 12° 1519.6

HOLDEN with the cords. Woodruff, J. L. M. 724.9

HOLDSWORTH, Edmund W. H. Deep-sea fishing and fishing boats. An account of the practical working of the various fisheries around the British islands, with illustrations and descriptions of the boats, nets, and other gear in use. London, 1874. xvi, 429 pp. 8° 5932.13

HOLE, Charles. Brief biographical dictionary. With additions and corrections by W. A. Wheeler. New York, 1866. xv, 453+ pp. 16° .... *R.R., F.3.9

Shelf. No.

HOLE, S. Reynolds. The six of spades: a book about the garden and the gardener. Edinburgh, 1872. 236+ pp. Sm. 4° ... 6226.5
HOLIDAYS abroad; or Europe from the West. Kirkland, C. M. New York, 1873. 2 v. in 1. 12°. 427.6
HOLIDAYS at Roselands. Finley, M. ... 926.17
HOLLAND, 3d lord. *See* VASSAL-FOX, Henry Richard.
HOLLAND, Elihu G. Essays: and a drama [The Highland treason]. Boston, 1852. 400+ pp. Portrait. 12° ... 1916.9
HOLLAND, Frederic West. Constantinople. (*In* Many lands and many people) ... 431.3
— Explorations in the peninsula of Sinai. *See* PALESTINE exploration fund ... 5933.1
— Wanderings in Palestine. (*In* Many lands and many people) ... 431.3
HOLLAND, *Sir* Henry. Recollections of past life. New York, 1872. x, 351 pp. 12° ... 5426.1
HOLLAND, Josiah Gilbert. (*Timothy Titcomb.*) Arthur Bonnicastle, an American novel. With illustrations. New York, 1873. 401 pp. 12°.. 536.17
— The bay-path; a tale of New England colonial life. New York, 1872. 418+ pp. 12° ... 536.3
— Bitter-sweet. A poem. 30th edition. New York, 1872. 220 pp. 12° ... 1615.18
— Garnered sheaves: [his] complete poetical works. New York, 1873. 397 pp. Illustrated. Portrait. Sq. 16° ... 1617.2

Contents. — Bitter-sweet; Kathrina; The marble prophecy, and other poems.

— Gold-foil, hammered from popular proverbs. New York, 1859. 358 pp. 12° ... 1535.5
— Kathrina: a poem. 50th edition. New York, 1868. 287 pp. 12° ... 1612.7
— Lessons in life. 15th edition. New York, 1872. 344 pp. 12° ... 1914.4
— Letters to the Joneses. 11th edition. New York, 1872. 347 pp. 12° ... 1934.5
— Letters to young people, single and married. New York, 1872. 235 pp. 12° ... 1928.3
— The marble prophecy, and other poems. New York, 1872. iv, 112 pp. 1 plate. 16° ... 1615.21
— The mistress of the manse. [A poem.] New York, 1874. 245 pp. 12° ... 1625.11
— Sevenoaks. A story of to-day. With illustrations. New York, 1875. viii, 441+ pp. 12°. 536.22
HOLLAND, Saba Smith, *lady.* Memoir of [her father] Sydney Smith. With a selection from his letters, edited by Mrs. Austin. New York [*cop.* 1855]. 2 v. 12° ... 1025.6
HOLLAND. Abbott, J. Rollo in Holland ... 917.21
— Adams, W. T. Dikes and ditches; or, young America in. Boston, 1873. 16° ... 925.9
— Baedeker, C. Handbook for travellers. Coblenz, 1871. 16° ... 5728.5
— Havard, H. La Hollande pittoresque, voyage aux villes mortes du Zuiderzée. Paris, 1874. 16°. 2016.11
— Kampen, N. G. van. History and topography of. London, N. D. 8° ... 5931.19
— Murray, J. Handbook for. London, 1871. 12°. 5915.1

Note. — See also Netherlands, and note annexed; and Harper's monthly, vols. 3, 24 and 44. Also, the "Dutch and their dead cities," in Blackwood's magazine, 1875.

HOLLAND house. Liechtenstein, M., *princess.* London, 1874. 2 v. 8° ... 5434.1

Note. — An account of the associations and celebrated frequenters of a famous English mansion, the seat of the Fox family.

HOLLANDS, The. Townsend, V. F. ... 711.22
HOLLEY, Horace. Discourse on [his] genius and character. Caldwell, C. Boston, 1828. 8° ... 1530.3
HOLLEY, Marietta. My opinions and Betsey Bobbet's. By Josiah Allen's wife ... 724.1
HOLLEY, Mary Austin. Texas. Observations, historical, geographical and descriptive. With an appendix. Baltimore, 1833. 167 pp. Map. 12°. 817.7
HOLM, Saxe, *pseud.* Stories ... 735.30

Contents. — Draxy Miller's dowry; The elder's wife; Whose wife was she? The one-legged dancers; How one woman kept her husband; Esther Wynn's love-letters.

Shelf. No.

HOLMBY house. Melville, G. J. W. ... 321.12
HOLME LEE, *pseud.* *See* PARR, Harriet.
HOLMES, Mary J. The Cameron pride ... 534.9
— Cousin Maude and Rosamond ... 534.2
— Darkness and daylight ... 535.9
— Dora Deane, and Maggie Miller ... 534.3
— Edith Lyle ... 534.26
— Edna Browning ... 535.18
— The English orphans ... 534.4
— Ethelyn's mistake ... 534.5
— The homestead on the hillside, and other tales ... 534.7
— Hugh Worthington ... 534.1
— 'Lena Rivers ... 535.10
— Marian Grey ... 535.8
— Meadow brook ... 535.11
— Millbank; or, Roger Irving's ward ... 534.6
— Rose Mather ... 534.10
— Tempest and sunshine ... 534.8
— West lawn, and The rector of St. Mark's ... 534.25
HOLMES, Oliver Wendell. The autocrat of the breakfast-table. Boston, 1872. viii, 373 pp. Illustrated. 12° ... 1934.3
— Border lines of knowledge in some provinces of medical science. Boston, 1862. 80+ pp. 12°. 1522.14
— Elsie Venner. Boston, 1872. 2 v. in 1. 16°... 526.20
— The guardian angel. Boston, 1872. xii, 420 pp. 16° ... 526.21
— The harbinger; a May-gift. [Poems.] Boston, 1833. vi, 96 pp. 12° ... 1611.2
— Iris. (*In* Johnson, (E.) R. Little classics) ... 529.4.7
— Poems. Boston, 1872. xi, 410 pp. Portrait. 16°. 1616.3
— The poet at the breakfast-table. Boston, 1872. 418 pp. 1 plate. 16° ... 535.16
— The professor at the breakfast-table. Boston, 1872. 410+ pp. 12° ... 1934.4
— Songs in many keys. Boston, 1862. x, 305 pp. 12°. 1612.5
— Soundings from the Atlantic. [Essays from the Atlantic monthly.] Boston, 1866. 468+ pp. 12° ... 1914.1
— A visit to the asylum for aged and decayed punsters. (*In* Johnson, (E.) R. Little classics) .. 529.4.5

Note. — Both of Dr. Holmes's novels are close studies of New England life and character for the ordinary reader; and of curious developments of inherited traits for the psychologist. In "Elsie Venner" "an alien element [rattlesnake characteristics] is introduced into the blood of a human being before that being saw the light." In "The guardian angel" characteristics repeated in successive generations constitute the motive.

— HAXALL, Robert W., and BELL, Luther V. Boylston prize dissertations for 1836. [On the question How far are the external means of exploring the condition of the internal organs to be considered useful and important in medical practice?] Boston, 1836. 288 pp. 8° ... 6023.17
— and OTHERS. Memorial. Bunker hill. June 17th, 1775, 1875. [With illustrations by H. M. Stephenson.] Boston [1875]. 16+ pp. L. 8°.. 810.8

Contents. — Grandmother's story of Bunker-hill battle: as she saw it from the belfry, by O. W. Holmes; Account of the battle, by James M. Bugbee; The crossed swords, by N. L. Frothingham.

HOLY dying. Taylor, J. [Boston, 1864.] 16° ... 5818.4
HOLY grail, The. Tennyson, A. Poetical works. Leipzig, 1860. Sq. 16° ... 1614.10.6
HOLY LAND. Dixon, W. H. The Holy Land. Leipzig, 1865. 2 v. in 1. Sq. 16° ... 428.1
— Maughan, W. C. The Alps of Arabia. Travels in Egypt, Sinai, Arabia, and the Holy Land. London, 1873. 8° ... 5932.10
— Prime, W. C. Tent life in the Holy Land. New York, 1858. 12° ... 425.5
— Thomson, A. In the Holy Land. New York [1875]. 16° ... 436.7
— Thomson, W. M. The Land and the Book. New York, 1871. 2 v. 12° ... 224.5

See also Jerusalem, Palestine.

HOLY living. Taylor, J. [Boston, 1864.] 16° ... 5818.3
HOLY roll and book. *See* SHAKERS ... 5814.8
HOLYOAKE, George Jacob. The history of co-operation in England: its literature and its advocates. Vol. I. London, 1875. Sm. 8° ... 5826.9

Contents. — Vol. I. The pioneer period — 1812 to 1844.

Shelf. No.

HOMAGE aux dames. [In English.] London, 1825. iv, 159, 4, 15+ pp. Illustrated. 24° 539.7
HOMAGE of eminent persons to the Book. Bailey, S. W. New York, 1870. 16° 5819.14
HOMANS, John, *jr.* Pathology and treatment of vaginal cystocele. (*In* Massachusetts medical society. Publications) 6021.4
HOME, Daniel Douglas. Incidents in my life. With an introduction by Judge Edmonds. New York, 1863. 315 pp. 12° 1216.2
HOME, Henry, *lord Kames.* Elements of criticism. Boston, 1796. 2 v. 8° 5834.4
— Sketches of the history of man. Enlarged. Edinburgh, 1788. 4 v. 8° 6614.8
— Memoirs of the life and writings of. Tytler, A. F. Edinburgh, 1807. 2 v. 4° 1020.2
HOME. Sedgwick, C. M. Boston, 1837. 12° 539.6
HOME, The. Stockton, F. R. and M. New York, 1873. 12° 1515.10
HOME and social philosophy; or, chapters on every day topics. From "Household words," edited by C. Dickens. 1st series. New York, 1852. 264 pp. [Putnam's library for the people.] 12°. 1537.22
HOME, The, and the synagogue of the modern Jew. Sketches of modern Jewish life and ceremonies. London [1873]. viii, 243 pp. Illustrated. Sq. 16°. 5818.1
HOME arts for old and young. Smith, C. L. Boston, 1873. 12° 1517.3
HOME as found. Cooper, J. F. 525.20
HOME fairy tales. Macé, J. 933.13
HOME games for old and young. Smith, C. L. Boston, 1873. 12° 1517.2
HOME influence. [Story.] Aguilar, G. 313.1
HOME mission work. Cochrane, T. Edinburgh, 1873. 16° 5819.16
HOME nook. Douglas, A. M. 725.32
HOME pastorals. [Poems.] Taylor, (J.) B. Boston, 1875. 12° 1617.13
HOME scenes and heart studies. Aguilar, G. 533.18
HOME sketches in France, and other papers. Field, H. M. New York, 1875. 12° 837.1
HOMERUS. (*Homer.*) Batrachomyomachia, Hymns and Epigrams. [*Also*] Hesiod's Works and days. Musæus' Hero and Leander. Juvenal's Fifth satire. Translated by G. Chapman. With introduction and notes, by R. Hooper. London, 1858. xxviii, 256 pp. 1 plate. Sq. 16° 6118.11
— The Iliad and Odyssey. Translated by A. Pope. Edited by H. F. Cary. With a biographical notice of the author. London, 1872. viii, 526 pp. 16° 6117.1
— The Iliad. Translated into English blank verse by W. C. Bryant. Boston, 1871. 2 v. 4° 6111.3
— The Iliad, with English notes by F. A. Paley. London, 1866. 2 v. 8° 6114.2
— The first six books of [the] Iliad; with explanatory notes, intended for beginners in the epic dialect. By J. R. Boise. Chicago, 1870. xiv, 235 pp. 12° 6115.1
— The Iliad [outlined and explained]. Collins, W. L. Edinburgh, 1871. 16° 6116.2
— The Iliads. Done according to the Greek by G. Chapman. With introduction and notes, by R. Hooper. 2d edition. London, 1865. 2 v. Portrait. Sq. 16° 6118.9
— The Odyssey. Translated into English blank verse by W. C. Bryant. Boston, 1871. 2 v. 4°. 6111.1
— The Odyssey [outlined and explained]. Collins, W. L. Edinburgh, 1870. 16° 6116.3
— The Odysseys. Translated by G. Chapman. With introduction and notes, by R. Hooper. 2d edition. London, 1874. 2 v. 1 plate. Sq. 16° .. 6118.10
— Blackie, J. S. Biography of. (*In* Macaulay, T. B., *lord,* and others. New biographies of illustrious men) 5428.4
— Gladstone, W. E. Homeric synchronism: an enquiry into the time and place of Homer. London, 1876. Sm. 8° 6117.5

Note. — Gladstone has a paper in the Contemporary review, 1874, on the place of Homer in history; and his "Juventus mundi" [1523.9] is a reproduction of life from the poems, and E. A. Freeman in the second series of his "Historical essays"

HOMERUS, *continued.*

[5913.4.2] examines Gladstone's view. Mahaffy's "Social life in Greece" [5925.1] also gives a section to the Homeric age. See also Mure's Greek literature [6113.5], whose first and second volumes are in large part given to Homer; Felton's Lectures; Smith's "Dictionary of Greek and Roman biography" [E.3.3]; and Froude's "Short studies" [1914.5].

The Wolf theory of authorship is discussed in De Quincey's Essay [1825.3.1] and in Grote's "History of Greece" [5926.1]; and a new view of the Homeric question is taken in the Contemporary review, Jan., 1874; and in vol. 12 there is a paper on the antiquity of the poems. The Legend of Troy is examined in Grote's Greece, chap. 15 [5926.1]. Blackie, in his "Horæ Hellenicæ" [6113.4], has a paper on the theology of Homer. Matthew Arnold's essay [5617.10] pertains to the ways of translating Homer.

Of the translations named above, Chapman's is an early racy English version, with an heroic swing and fitness that has given it great celebrity, which is well commemorated by Keats's sonnet in his poems. Pope's is far from exact or from suiting modern notions of Homer's grandeur, but it is of great repute, and almost becomes an original poem from the infusion of Pope's characteristics. Bryant's version is the latest of all the well-known versions, and shows the quality of his rhythmical skill.

Collins's outline and explanation is the readiest medium for the beginner in Homeric studies to learn the proportions and nature of the subject.

HOMES and haunts of the most eminent British poets. Howitt, W. New York, 1847, 51. 2 v. 12° .. 1225.5
HOMES and how to make them. Gardner, E. C. Boston, 1874. Sq. 16° 1518.6
HOMES of old English writers. Christophers, S. W. London [1874]. Sm. 8° 5428.16
HOMES, The, of other days. Wright, T. London, 1871. 8° 5410.1

Note. — Antiquarian studies of domestic life in England in past times.

HOMES, The, of the New World; impressions of America. Bremer, F. New York, 1853. 2 v. 12° 414.24
HOMESTEAD, The, on the hillside. Holmes, M. J. .. 534.7
HOMEWARD bound. Cooper, J. F. 525.27
HOMME, L', à l'oreille cassée. About, E. (F. V.) Paris, 1862. 16° 2016.7
HONE, William. Every day book. Illustrated. London [1871]. 2 v. Portrait. L. 8° 5621.5
— The table book. With engravings. London [1871]. 870+ pp. L. 8° 5621.6
— The year book of daily recreation and information. With engravings. London, 1832. 856+ pp. 8° 5621.8
HONEY bee, The. London, 1852. 99+ pp. 16° .. 6619.3
HOOD, Thomas. Poetical works. With memoir of the author. New York, 1873. xvi, 583 pp. Sq. 16° 1627.1
— Hood's own; or, laughter from year to year. New edition. London, 1871. 2 v. Illustrated. Portrait. 8° 5612.4
— Tylney hall. [Novel.] Boston, 1865. xii, 479 pp. 12° 515.6
— Up the Rhine. With two steel engravings, and with the author's original illustrations on wood. New York, 1872. 234+ pp. 12° 536.6

Note. — Impressions of scenery, etc., of the Rhine upon different members of an English travelling household, expressed in letters written by the several members of it.

— Whims and oddities. With illustrations. New York, 1872. iv, 270+ pp. Sm. 8° 533.11

Note. — The "Memorials," by his children, is the chief authority, but see also his own reminiscences in "Hood's own"; in S. C. Hall's "Book of memories" [1231.1]; in Atlantic monthly, Nov., 1860; in Whipple's essays [1936.2.2]; in Stedman's "Victorian poets" [1837.1]; in Timb's "Later wits"; in Harper's monthly, vols. 21, 22 (by Thackeray), 26 and 39; and the references in Allibone, Thomas, etc.

HOOD, Thomas, *the younger.* Love and valor 510.3
HOOK, Theodore (Edward). Humorous works. With a new life of the author, portraits by Maclise and D'Orsay, caricatures, and facsimiles. London [1873]. v, 583+ pp. 16° 5616.6

Contents. — Memoir; The Ramsbottom papers; Political songs and squibs; Tentamen, or, an essay towards the history of Whittington, sometime lord mayor of London; Miscellanies in verse and prose; Anecdotes, hoaxes, and jests.

— Theodore Hook: a sketch. 4th edition. 102 pp. London, 1853. 16° 5618.7
HOOKER, Richard, Life of. Walton, I. London, 1866. 16° 5428.2

Shelf. No.

HOOKER, Worthington. Chemistry. Illustrated. New York, 1874. 435 pp. [Science for the school and family.] 12° 6437.4
— Mineralogy and geology. Illustrated. New York, 1872. 360 pp. [Science for the school and family.] 12° 6636.3
— Natural history. Illustrated. New York, 1874. 382+ pp. [Science for the school and family.] 12° 6616.11
— Rational therapeutics. (*In* Massachusetts medical society. Publications) 6021.4
HOOKHAM, Mary Ann. The life and times of Margaret of Anjou, and of her father René "the Good." With memoirs of the houses of Anjou. With portraits and illustrations. London, 1872. 2 v. 8° 5522.10
HOOPER, George. Waterloo: the downfall of the first Napoleon: a history of the campaign of 1815. With map and plans. London, 1862. xii, 344 pp. 8° 5511.2
HOOPER, Samuel. Currency or money; its nature and uses, and the effects of the circulation of bank-notes for currency. Boston, 1855. 112 pp. 8° 5822.4
HOOSAC tunnel, Report of the commissioners upon the. *See* MASSACHUSETTS. *Legislative documents* 6912.4
HOOSIER school-master, The. Eggleston, E. 535.17
HOPE, *Mrs.* —. Conversion of the Teutonic race. Conversion of the Franks and the English. Edited by J. B. Dalgairns. London, 1872. ix, 452 pp. 16° 5735.5
— Sequel to the Conversion of the Teutonic race. S. Boniface and the conversion of Germany. London, 1872. xx, 370 pp. 16° 5735.6
HOPE, Ascott Robert, *pseud.* *See* MONCRIEFF, Ascott Robert Hope.
HOPE, George H. Till the doctor comes, and how to help him. New York, 1871. 99 pp. 12° 1523.16
HOPE, Stanley. A new Godiva 722.17
HOPE and have. Adams, W. T. 925.6
HOPE deferred. Pollard, E. F. 721.8
HOPE Leslie. Sedgwick, C. M. 2 v. 725.21
HOPE Meredith. Tabor, E. 711.13
HOPE on! hope ever! Howitt, M. 937.4
HOPES and fears. Yonge, C. M. 318.5
HOPKINS, Mark. Lectures on the evidences of Christianity. Boston, 1846. 383 pp. 8° 1921.3
— *Same.* Boston, 1861. 383 pp. 8° 1532.7
HOPPER, Isaac Tatem: a true life. Child, L. M. Boston, 1854. 12° 1214.3
HOPPIN, James Mason. Life of Andrew Hull Foote. With a portrait and illustrations. New York, 1874. 411 pp. 8° 1012.3
— Old England: its scenery, art, and people. 4th edition. New York, 1872. iv, 470+ pp. 16° 5438.7
HORACE Templeton, Diary and notes of. Lever, C. (J.) Leipzig, 1848. Sq. 16° 332.9
HORÆ Hellenicæ. [Greek literature, etc.] Blackie, J. S. London, 1874. 8° 6113.4
HORATIUS FLACCUS, Quintus. Opera omnia ex recensione A. J. Macleane. New York, 1860. viii, 211 pp. [Harper's Greek and Latin texts.] 16° 6118.13
— Works. Translated literally into English prose, by C. Smart. Revised, with a copious selection of notes by T. A. Buckley. London, 1872. viii, 325 pp. Portrait. Sm. 8° 6115.15
— Works, with English notes, by A. J. Macleane. Revised and edited by R. H. Chase. Cambridge, 1867. xii, 588 pp. 12° 6117.3
— The odes and epodes of Horace. A metrical translation with introduction and commentaries by Lord Lytton. With Latin text. Leipzig, 1869. 2 v. in 1. Sq. 16° 1613.7
— Martin, T. Biography of. (*In* Macaulay, T. B., *lord*, and others. New biographies of illustrious men) 5428.4
— — Horace [outlined and explained]. Edinburgh, 1870. 16° 6116.7

Shelf. No.

HORDYNSKI, Jozef. History of the late Polish revolution, and the events of the campaign. Boston, 1832. xvi, 406 pp. Plans. 8° 821.3
HORN, John. *See* CHRISTOPHERS, S. W. Homes of old English writers. London [1874]. Sm. 8° .. 5428.16
HORNE, Richard Henry, *editor.* A new spirit of the age. New York, 1844. 365 pp. 18° 1038.1
HORSE. Armitage, G. The horseowner and stableman's companion. London [1871]. Sm. 8° 6616.5
— Herbert, H. W. Horse and horsemanship of the United States and British provinces. New York, 1871. 2 v. 8° 6612.6
— MacClure, R. Every horse owner's cyclopedia. Philadelphia, 1872. 8° 6613.1
— Murray, W. H. H. The perfect horse. Boston, 1873. 8° 6612.7
— Sidney, S. The book of the horse: with hints on horsemanship. London [1875]. 4° 6410.1
— Walsh, J. H. The horse in the stable and the field; his management in health and disease. Philadelphia [*cop.* 1861]. Sm. 8° 6616.7
— Wharton, C. Hand-book on the treatment of the horse in the stable and on the road; or, hints to horse owners. Philadelphia, 1873. 12° 6617.3
— Woodruff, H. The trotting horse of America. New York, 1871. Sm. 8° 6417.2
HORSE-RAILWAYS. Practical treatise on street or horse-power railways. Easton, A. Philadelphia, 1859. 8° 6923.7
HORSE-SHOE Robinson. Kennedy, J. P. 725.15
HORSESHOEING, Practical. Fleming, G. New York, 1872. 12° 1515.11
HORTENSE [mother of Napoleon III], History of. Abbott, J. S. C. 914.32
HORTENSIUS, Quintus. Hortensius: an historical essay on the office and duties of an advocate. Forsyth, W. London, 1874. 8° 6314.3
HORTON, Caroline W. Architecture for general students. With illustrations. New York, 1874. 287 pp. 16° 6227.2
HOSMER, James K. The color-guard: a corporal's notes of military service in the nineteenth army corps. Boston, 1864. 244+ pp. 12° 826.1
HOSPITAL sketches [during the war]. Alcott, L. M. 926.13
HOSPITAL transports. A memoir of the embarkation of the sick and wounded from the peninsula of Virginia in the summer of 1862. Boston, 1863. 167 pp. 16° 5016.16
HOSPITALS, Notes on. Nightingale, F. London, 1863. 4° 6011.7
HOSTAGES to fortune. Braddon, M. E. Leipzig 316.15
— *Same.* New York 521.35
HÔTEL, The, du petit St. Jean. By the author of "Vera" 315.6
HOTTEN, John Camden, *joint author.* The history of signboards. *See* LARWOOD, Jacob 5615.8
— *editor.* The slang dictionary, etymological, historical, and anecdotal. New edition, revised and corrected, with additions. London, 1874. vii, 382+ pp. Sm. 8° 6126.6
HOUDIN, Robert. Ambassador, author, and conjuror. Written by himself. 4th edition. London, N. D. xii, 339 pp. 16° 715.16
HOUGHTON, *Lord.* *See* MILNES, Richard Monckton.
HOUGHTON, William. Sketches of British insects. A handbook for beginners in the study of entomology. Illustrated. London, 1875. vi, 161+ pp. Sm. 8° 6616.13
HOURS in a library. [Essays.] Stephen, L. London, 1874. Sm. 8° 6136.9
HOURS of exercise in the Alps. Tyndall, J. New York, 1873. 12° 223.1
HOUSE and home papers. Stowe, H. (E.) B. Boston, 1869. 12° 1516.8
HOUSE, The, and the brain. Bulwer-Lytton, E. (G. E.) L. (*In* Johnson, (E.) R. Little classics) .. 529.4.2
HOUSE, The, of Elmore. Robinson, F. W. 731.39
HOUSE, The, of the seven gables. Hawthorne, N. Boston, 1872. 2 v. in 1. 16° 1813.1
HOUSE, The, of Yorke. Tincker, M. A. New York, 1872. 8° 531.29

Shelf. No.

HOUSE building. Illustrated homes. Gardner, E. C. Boston, 1875. Sq. 16° 6227.3
HOUSE-PAINTING, Popular treatise on. Masury, J. W. New York, 1872. 12° 6227.1
HOUSEHOLD art. Jones, C. S., and Williams, H. T. Household elegancies. New York, 1875. 8° .. 1512.4
HOUSEHOLD, A, book of English poetry. Trench, R. C. London, 1870. Sq. 16° 5616.4
HOUSEHOLD, The, book of poetry. Dana, C. A. New York, 1873. 8° 1610.2
HOUSEHOLD elegancies. Jones, C. S., and Williams, H. T. New York, 1875. 8° 1512.4
HOUSEHOLD words. Conducted by Charles Dickens. Leipzig, 1851-56. 36 v. in 18. Sq. 16° 320.1
HOUSES. *See* ARCHITECTURE, DWELLING-HOUSES.
HOUSES and housekeeping. Barker, M. A., *lady*. London, 1876. Sm. 8° 6428.8
HOUSSAYE, Arsène. Life in Paris. Letters on art, literature and society. Boston, 1875. 223 pp. Sq. 16° 439.3
HOW, Henry. The mineralogy of Nova Scotia. Report to the provincial government. Halifax, 1869. vi, 217+ pp. 8° 6613.10
How a bride was won. Gerstaecker, F. 521.3
How Charlie Roberts became a man. Thurston, L. M. 1117.18
How Eva Roberts gained her education. Thurston, L. M. 1117.7
How he won her. Southworth, E. D. E. N. 527.12
How I managed my house on £200 a year. Warren, E. Boston, 1866. 12° 1533.1
How Marjory helped. Caroll, M. 915.23
How to be a lady. Newcomb, H. Boston, 1872. 12° 918.17
How to be a man. Newcomb, H. Boston [*cop.* 1847]. 12° 918.16
How to do it. Hale, E. E. 526.17
How to draw. Barry, C. A. Boston, 1871. 12° ... 1516.5
How to live long. Hall, W. W. New York, 1875. 12° 6036.13
How to make a living. Eggleston, G. C. New York, 1875. 12° 1536.20
How to paint. Gardner, F. B. New York, 1872. 16° 6429.1
HOWADJI, The, in Syria. [Travels.] Curtis, G. W. New York, 1856. 12° 425.12
HOWARD, Blanche Willis. One summer 529.8
HOWARD, Clarence J. Book of conundrums and riddles. New York [*cop.* 1869]. 162 pp. 16°. 1518.3
— Drawing-room theatricals. New York [*cop.* 1870]. 178 pp. 16° 1636.2
HOWARD, George William Frederick, *earl of Carlisle*. Diary in Turkish and Greek waters. Edited by C. C. Felton. Boston, 1855. xviii, 299 pp. 12° 825.5
HOWARD, John, Biography of. Dixon, W. H. (*In* Macaulay, T. B., *lord*, and others. New biographies of illustrious men) 5428.4
HOWARD, John H. Gymnasts and gymnastics. New edition. London, 1873. Illustrated. Sm. 8°. 6414.5
HOWE, Henry. Memoirs of the most eminent American mechanics: also, lives of distinguished European mechanics; with anecdotes, descriptions, etc., relating to the mechanic arts. Illustrated. New York [*cop.* 1846]. 482 pp. Portraits. 12°. 1014.2
HOWE, John. *See* CHRISTOPHERS, S. W. Homes of old English writers. London [1874]. Sm. 8° .. 5428.16
HOWE, Julia Ward. From the oak to the olive. A plain record of a pleasant journey [in Europe]. Boston, 1868. vi, 304 pp. 16° 437.2
— A trip to Cuba. Boston, 1860. iv, 251 pp. 12°. 413.9
— *editor*. Sex and education. A reply to Clarke's "Sex in education." Boston, 1874. 203 pp. 16° 1937.4
HOWE, Samuel Gridley. Historical sketch of the Greek revolution. New York, 1828. xxxvi, 452 pp. 8° 821.1
HOWELLS, William Dean. A chance acquaintance. Boston, 1873. 279+ pp. 16° 529.1
— A foregone conclusion. Boston, 1875. 265+ pp. 16° 724.23

Shelf. No.

HOWELLS, William Dean, *continued*.
— Italian journeys. New York, 1872. 320 pp. 16°. 425.20
— A romance of real life. (*In* Johnson, (E.) R. Little classics) 529.4.4
— Their wedding journey. With illustrations. Boston, 1873. 287+ pp. 16° 533.7
— Venetian life. [Essays on Venice.] New and enlarged edition. Boston, 1874. 437 pp. 8°. 227.5
HOWITT, Mary. Alice Franklin 937.6
— The heir of Wast-Wayland 533.23
— Hope on! hope ever! 937.4
— Little coin, much care 937.3
— Love and money 937.2
— My own story 937.1
— My uncle the clockmaker 937.14
— Natural history stories for my juvenile friends. London [1874]. 170 pp. Illustrated. Sm. 4°. 1521.14
— No sense like common sense 937.12
— Pictorial calendar of the seasons, embodying Aikin's Calendar of nature. London, 1862. viii, 567 pp. Sm. 8° 1934.12
— Sowing and reaping 937.5
— Strive and thrive 937.10
— The two apprentices 937.13
— Which is the wiser; or, people abroad 937.9
— Who shall be greatest? 937.7
— Work and wages 937.8

Note. — Mary Howitt's tales suit young readers, who like quiet, truthful stories, not overwrought.

HOWITT, William. The book of the seasons; or the calendar of nature. Philadelphia, 1831. 312 pp. 12° 1838.3
— History of priestcraft in all ages and nations. New York, 1857. 256 [250] pp. 12° 836.5
— Homes and haunts of the most eminent British poets. Illustrated. New York, 1847, 51. 2 v. 12° 1225.5
— Johnny Darbyshire. (*In* Johnson, (E.) R. Little classics) 529.4.9
— The northern heights of London. London, 1869. xxvi, 590 pp. Illustrated. 8° 5423.6

Note. — History and associations of London's northern suburbs.

— Visits to remarkable places. 3d American edition. Philadelphia, 1854. 2 v. 12° 235.2
— Woodburn grange. [Novel.] Philadelphia [1868]. 402 [386] pp. Sm. 8° 534.11
HOWLAND, Edward. With the Count de Beauvoir in Japan and California. (*In* Many lands and many people) 431.3
HOWSHIP, John. Practical remarks on the discrimination and appearances of surgical disease. With appendix. London, 1840. xix, 420 pp. 8° ... 6023.8
HOZIER, Henry M. The seven weeks' war [in Germany, 1866]. Its antecedents and incidents. Philadelphia, 1867. 2 v. Maps. 8° 5922.4
HUBBARD, (Nicolas) Gustave. Histoire de la littérature contemporaine dans les différents états de l'Europe. Histoire de la littérature contemporaine en Espagne. Paris, 1876. 422+ pp. 12° 5536.22
HUC, Évariste Regis. A journey through the Chinese empire. New York, 1855. 2 v. Folded map. 12° 5934.9
HUDSON, C. F. Christ our life. The scriptural argument for immortality through Christ alone. Boston, 1860. viii, 160 pp. 12° 6326.1
HUDSON, Francis, *editor*. Private theatricals for home performance. New York [*cop.* 1870]. 179 pp. 16° 1636.1
HUDSON, Frederic. Journalism in the United States, from 1690 to 1872. New York, 1873. 789+ pp. 8° 5214.2
HUDSON, Henry, Life of. Cleveland, H. R. (*In* Sparks, J. Library of American biography). 5028.1.10
HUDSON, Henry Norman. Shakespeare: his life, art, and characters. With an historical sketch of the origin and growth of the drama in England. Boston, 1872. 2 v. 12° 1024.9

Shelf. No.

HUEBNER, Joseph Alexander von. The life and times of Sixtus the fifth. Translated from the original French by Hubert E. H. Jerningham. London, 1872. 2 v. 8° 5522.11

HUEFFER, Franz. Richard Wagner and the music of the future. History and æsthetics. London, 1874. v, 333+ pp. 8° 6232.6

Note. — Contains also chapters on F. Schubert, R. Schumann, R. Franz, F. Liszt.

HUGESSEN, Edward Hugessen Knatchbull. Higgledy-piggledy: or, stories for everybody and everybody's children 1116.1

— Queer folk. Seven stories 916.30

HUGH Melton. King, K 721.16

HUGH Worthington. Holmes, M. J. 534.1

HUGHES, *Mrs.* —. Memoir of the life and writings of Mrs. Hemans. By her sister. Philadelphia, 1839. 29–317 pp. 12° 1022.4

HUGHES, George E., Memoir of. Hughes, T. Boston, 1873. 12° 1226.20

HUGHES, Samuel. A survey of the metropolitan roads. *See* MALLET, Robert 1716.16

— Treatise on gas works, and the practice of manufacturing and distributing coal gas. 4th edition, with illustrations. Revised by W. Richards. London, 1871. xv, 336 pp. 12° 6438.2

— Treatise on waterworks for the supply of cities and towns. New edition. London, 1872. xiv, 413 pp. Illustrated. 12° 6428.4

HUGHES, Thomas. [Life of] Alfred the great. With map and illustrations. Boston, 1871. 324 pp. 12° 1025.7

— Memoir of a brother. Boston, 1873. xvi [xii], 178 pp. Portrait. 12° 1226.20

— School days at Rugby. Illustrated. Boston, 1872. viii, 405 pp. 12° 922.17

— The scouring of the White Horse. Illustrated. Cambridge, 1859. 244 pp. Sm. 4° 536.1

— Tom Brown at Oxford. Boston, 1871. 2 v. Portrait. 12° 526.14

— Tom Brown's school days. Leipzig, 1858. xviii, 320+ pp. Sq. 16° 311.12

Note. — The books numbered above, 922.17 and 311.12, are the same, and they picture, under the guise of fiction, the school life at Rugby under Dr. Arnold's mastership. "Tom Brown at Oxford" carries the youth to the university.

HUGO, Victor (Marie), *vicomte.* Œuvres. Bruxelles, 1842. 3 v. Illustrated. Portrait. L. 8° 5530.1

Contents. — Vol. I. Bug-Jargel; Han d'Islande; Le dernier jour d'un condamné; Claude Gueux; Notre-dame de Paris; Littérature et philosophie mêlées; Lucrèce Borgia; Angelo; Marie Tudor.

II. Cromwell; Marion de Lorme; Hernani; Le roi s'amuse; Odes et ballades; Les orientales; Les feuilles d'automne; Poésies politiques; Poésies inédites; Les chants du crépuscule; Les voix intérieures.

III. Ruy Blas; Les rayons et les ombres; Les Esmeralda; Le mercure du dix-neuvième siècle; La charité; Le retour de l'empereur; Le Rhin; Les burgraves.

— Actes et paroles, 1870–72. Paris, 1872. 220+ pp. 16° 5536.5

— The hunchback of Notre-Dame. Translated from the French [Notre-Dame de Paris], by H. L. Williams, jr. New York [*cop.* 1862]. 207 [191] pp. 8° 511.27

— The man who laughs. Translated by W. Young. New York, 1869. vi, 351 pp. Portrait. 8° .. 521.2

— Les misérables. Translated by C. E. Wilbour. New York, 1874. 2 v. in 1. 8° 710.19

— Ninety-three. Translated by F. L. Benedict. New York, 1874. 356 pp. 12° 734.18

— The Rhine: a tour from Paris to Mayence by the way of Aix-la-Chapelle. Translated by D. M. Aird. Boston [1874]. xiii, 275 pp. 12° 436.1

— Notre-Dame de Paris. Paris [1832]. 2 v. 12°. 2016.2

— The toilers of the sea. With two engravings from original pictures by G. Doré. New York, 1869. 155 pp. Portrait. L. 8° 510.1

HUGUENOT, The: a tale of the French protestants. James, G. P. R. 722.10

HUGUENOT family, The. Keddie, *Miss* — 735.23

HUGUENOT family, Memoirs of a. Fontaine, J. New York, 1872. 12° 5525.3

Shelf. No.

HUGUENOTS. Hanna, W. Wycliffe and the Huguenots. Edinburgh, 1860. Sm. 8° 826.7

— Smiles, S. The Huguenots: their settlements, churches, and industries in England and Ireland. New York, 1868. Sm. 8° 5514.1

Note. Smiles, after examining the causes which led to the exodus of French protestants after the revocation of the Edict of Nantes, follows their career in England and Ireland, with particular reference to their influence upon the industry of England; and the American edition has an appendix on the Huguenots in America. The "Memoirs of a Huguenot family" [5525.3], compiled from the autobiography of the Rev. James Fontaine, follows the fortunes of an exiled family in Great Britain and America, and an appendix has an English translation of the Edict of Nantes, with documents concerning the revocation.

Parkman's "Pioneers of France in the New World" [5015.5.1] gives an account of the Huguenots in Florida, 1512–74, with a sketch of their colonization in Brazil, and the author enumerates the authorities. White's "Massacre of Saint Bartholomew" follows the religious wars of the latter half of the 16th century, with their culmination in the massacre of Saint Bartholomew, taking protestant ground.

Hanna's is a brief summary for the general reader.

The subject can be further traced in the general histories of Sismondi, Capefigue, Soldan, Ranke, Mignet, Michelet, and in the Mémoires of Castelnau, Conde, Coligni, Tavannes, Montlac, De Nevers, Margaret of Valois, etc., for which see the Bates Hall catalogues and the note on the Huguenots in the Lower Hall Catalogue of history, etc. There is a summary with mention of the chief authorities in McClintock and Strong.

See also France, Ecclesiastical history, and Reformation.

HUGUENOTS, Les. Meyerbeer, G. (*In* Ditson, O., and co. Standard opera librettos) 6233.3.4

HULDA; or, the deliverer. Lewald, F. 727.32

HULDIGUNG, Die, der Künste. Schiller, (J. C.) F. von. Werke. Stuttgart, 1865. 8° 5734.1.6

HULLAH, John. The history of modern music. A course of lectures delivered at the Royal institution of Great Britain. [Added, chronological tables of musical composers.] 2d edition. London, 1875. xi, 210+ pp. Folded sheets. 8°. 6232.8

— *editor.* The song book. London, 1866. 368 pp. 16° 1615.1

HULME, F. Edward, and OTHERS. Art-studies from nature, as applied to design. In four papers by F. E. Hulme; J. Glaisher; S. J. Mackie; Robert Hunt. Reprinted from The art-journal. With illustrations. London, 1872. xii, 212+ pp. Sm. 4° 6222.2

HUMAN body, Wonders of the. Le Pileur, A. New York, 1871. 16° 1714.14

HUMAN longevity. Thoms, W. J. London, 1873. 8°. 6614.5

HUMAN race, The. Figuier, (G.) L. New York, 1872. 8° 6613.2

HUMAN responsibility, The limitations of. Wayland, F. Boston, 1838. 16° 5838.4

HUMANICS. Collins, T. W. New York, 1860. 8°. 1734.2

HUMBERT, Aimé. Japan and the Japanese. Illustrated. Translated by Mrs. Cashel Hoey, and edited by H. W. Bates. New York [London], 1874. xviii, 378+ pp. 4° 5920.5

HUMBOLDT, (Carl) Wilhelm von. Religious thoughts and opinions. Boston, 1851. 171 pp. 16° 5818.10

HUMBOLDT, (Friedrich Heinrich) Alexander, *baron* von. Cosmos: a sketch of a physical description of the universe. From the German, by E. C. Otté. New York, 1871, 72. 5 v. Portrait. 12°. 1523.7

— Personal narrative of travels to the equinoctial regions of America. Translated and edited by Thomasina Ross. London, 1872. 3 v. Sm. 8°. 5036.4

— Travels and researches in the equinoctial regions of America and Asiatic Russia. *See* MACGILLIVRAY, William 438.1

— Views of nature. From the German, by E. C. Otté and H. G. Bohn. With a fac-simile and index. London, 1870. xxx, 452 pp. Sm. 8° ... 1523.19

— Bruhns, C. Life of. London, 1873. 2 v. 8°. 5723.1

— Heinzen, C. The true character of. Indianapolis, 1869. 16° 6327.4

HUME, David. Essays, literary, moral, and political. London, N. D. 552 pp. Sm. 8° 5826.2

— History of England from the invasion of Julius Cæsar to the revolution in 1688. New edition, prefixed a short account of his life, written by himself. Boston, 1868. 6 v. Portrait. 8° ... 5413.2

— Lawrence, E. Lives of the British historians. New York, 1855. 12° 1224.7.2

Shelf. No.

HUME, David, *continued.*

— Rogers, H. Biography of. (*In* Macaulay, T. B., *lord*, and others. New biographies of illustrious men) 5428.4

Note. — The Autobiography is usually prefixed to editions of Hume's History [5413.2], and Burton's Life is authoritative. See also Mrs. Oliphant's "Historical sketches of the reign of George II" [1032.1]. See the authorities given in Thomas's "Biographical dictionary," and Allibone's elaborate collation of the criticisms upon Hume as a historian. Smyth, in his "Lectures on modern history" [5012.10; 5925.7], follows critically the course of Hume's narrative. See also Foster's "Critical essays" [5614.3]; Brougham's "Lives of men of letters of the time of George III" [5614.4.2]; Disraeli's "Amenities of literature" [1533.13]; Life of Sir James Mackintosh [5331.3.2, *sub anno* 1811]; and Contemporary review, vol. 11.

HUMOR. Cox, S. S. Why we laugh. New York, 1876. 12° 1837.2

— Fenn, G. M. The world of humour. London [1872]. L. 8° 5212.4

HUMOROUS poetry of the English language, from Chaucer to Saxe. Parton, J. Boston, 1872. 12°. 1612.31

HUMPHREYS, Andrew Atkinson, and ABBOT, Henry L. Report upon the physics and hydraulics of the Mississippi river; upon the protection of the alluvial region against overflow; and upon the deepening of the mouths. Philadelphia, 1861. 456, cxlvi+ pp. Maps. L. 4° 6920.2

HUMPHRY, Clinker, The expedition of. Smollett, T. (G.) 315.15

HUNCHBACK, The: a play. Knowles, J. S. New York, 1832. 8° 1633.1

HUNCHBACK, The, of Notre-Dame. Hugo, V. (M.), *vicomte.* New York [*cop.* 1862]. 8° 511.27

HUNGARY. Try Cracow and the Carpathians. Hutchinson, A. H. New York [London, 1872]. Sm. 8° 5936.2

HUNNEWELL, James F. The lands of Scott. Boston, 1871. 508+ pp. Folded maps. Portrait. Wood-cut. 16° 5626.10

HUNS. Histoire d'Attila et de ses successeurs. Thierry, A. (S. D.) Paris, 1856. 2 v. 8° 2012.1

HUNT, Freeman. Merchants' magazine, and commercial review. Vol. 1-34. New York, 1840-66. 34 v. 8° 1322.1

— Merchants' magazine year book. 1871. New York [1871]. 452 pp. Portrait. 8° 1322.2

HUNT, Harriot Kesia. Glances and glimpses: or fifty years social, including twenty years professional life [as a physician in Boston]. Boston, 1856. xii, 418 pp. 12° 1214.5

HUNT, Helen (Maria). Bits of talk about home matters. Boston, 1873. 239 pp. Sq. 16° 1939.2

— Bits of travel. Boston, 1872. 304+ pp. Sq. 16°. 428.10

HUNT, (James Henry) Leigh. Autobiography, with reminiscences of friends and contemporaries. New York, 1872. 2 v. Portrait. 12° 1225.20

— Correspondence. Edited by his eldest son [Thornton Hunt]. With portrait. London, 1862. 2 v. Sm. 8° 5614.8

— A day by the fire; and other papers. [Now first collected by J. E. Babson.] Boston, 1870. 368 pp. 12° 5618.4

— Men, women, and books. New edition. London, 1870. xii, 402 pp. 16° 1935.1

— Poetical works. Edited by S. A. Lee. Boston, 1866. 2 v. 16° 1629.1

— The seer; or, common places refreshed. Boston, 1865. 2 v. 12° 1917.8

— The town [London]: its memorable characters and events. With illustrations. New edition. London, 1872. xii, 449 pp. 16° 5437.1

— The wishing-cap papers. Now first collected [by J. E. Babson]. Boston, 1873. 455 pp. 16° .. 1917.2

Note. — The Autobiography is the principal account, the latest edition having an introduction by his son, who also commemorates his father in the article on Shelley in the Atlantic monthly, Feb., 1863. See also S. A. Lee's introduction (with a letter from Hunt) to the American edition of his poems. See sketches in Smiles's "Brief biographies" [1024.13]; in S. C. Hall's "Book of memories" [1231.1]; in Barry Cornwall's Lamb, etc. His correspondence, covering 1803-59, is reviewed in Atlantic monthly, May, 1862. See Harper's monthly, vols. 39 and 40; Howitt's "Homes and haunts of the British poets" [1225.5]; Whipple's Essays [1936.2.2]; and Timb's "Later wits."

"Skimpole," in Dickens's "Bleak house," has been supposed to be drawn from Hunt.

HUNT, Robert. Coal as a reservoir of power. (*In* Estes, D. Half-hour recreations in popular science) 6813.7

HUNTED down. Dickens, C. (J. H.) 338.21

HUNTER and Tom. Abbott, J. 923.2

HUNTER'S, The, feast. Reid, M. 527.7

HUNTINGTON, *Countess of. See* HASTINGS, Selina, *countess of Huntington.*

HUNTINGTON, Daniel. Memories, counsels, and reflections. By an octogenary. Cambridge, 1857. 119 pp. 8° 6322.2

HUNTINGTON, Frederic Dan. Christian believing and living. Sermons. Boston, 1860. v, 528 pp. 12°. 6325.11

— Sermons for the people. Boston, 1856. vii, 468+ pp. 12° 1522.8

HUNTINGTON, Susan. Memoirs, consisting principally of extracts from her journals and letters; with the sermon occasioned by her death. By B. B. Wisner. Boston, 1826. 408 pp. Portrait. 12°. 1217.1

HURRICANE Hurry. Kingston, W. H. G. 912.11

HUSSEY, E. C. National cottage architecture; or, homes for every one. New York, 1874. 24 pp. Illustrated. 4° 6220.2

HUTCHINSON, Alexander H. Try Cracow and the Carpathians. With illustrations. New York [London, 1872]. vi, 256+ pp. Map. Sm. 8°. 5936.2

HUTCHINSON, John, Memoirs of. Hutchinson, L. London, 1863. Sm. 8° 5426.11

HUTCHINSON, Lucy. Memoirs of Colonel Hutchinson. From the original manuscript by Julius Hutchinson. Prefixed the life of Mrs. Hutchinson, written by herself. 10th edition. Added, an account of the siege of Lathom house. London, 1863. xx, 523 pp. Portrait. Sm. 8° 5426.11

HUTCHINSON, Thomas. History of Massachusetts, 1628-1750. 3d edition. Boston, 1795. 2 v. 8°. 813.10

HUTCHINSON, Thomas Joseph. Two years in Peru, with exploration of its antiquities. With a map by Daniel Barrera, and numerous illustrations. London, 1873. 2 v. 8° 5932.9

HUTCHINSON, W. N. Dog breaking. *See* HERBERT, Henry William 1522.3

HUXLEY, Thomas Henry. Critiques and addresses. London, 1873. xiv, 350 pp. 8° 5623.1

— Evidence as to man's place in nature. New York, 1872. 184 pp. Illustrated. 12° 1523.10

— Lay sermons, addresses, and reviews. New York, 1871. xi, 378 pp. Sm. 8° 1922.1

— Manual of the anatomy of vertebrated animals. New York, 1872. 431 pp. Illustrated. 12° .. 1523.12

— On yeast. (*In* Estes, D. Half-hour recreations in popular science) 6813.7

— On protoplasm: being an examination of J. H. Stirling's criticism of [his] views. Ross, J. London, 1874. Sm. 8° 1527.22

HYACINTHE, Père. *See* LOYSON, Charles Jean Marie.

HYACINTHE. Grey, *Mrs.* 521.29

HYDE, Edward, *earl of Clarendon.* History of the rebellion and civil wars in England, to which is added an historical view of the affairs of Ireland. New edition. Boston, 1827. 6 v. 8° 5412.4

— *See* LAWRENCE, E. Lives of the British historians. New York, 1855. 12° 1224.7.1

HYDE PARK, *Mass.* Catalogue of the public library. Hyde Park, 1874. 108+ pp. 8° 6130.3

HYDRAULICS. Burnell, G. R. Rudiments of hydraulic engineering. London, 1868. 12° 1716.10

— Ewbank, T. A descriptive and historical account of hydraulic machines for raising water. New York, 1876 [*cop.* 1863]. 8° 6122.7

HYGIENE. Hammond, W. A. Treatise on. Philadelphia, 1863. 8° 6022.8

— Wilson, G. Handbook of. London, 1873. Sm. 8°. 6036.4

See also Dress, Mental hygiene.

HYMNOLOGY. Baynes, R. H., *editor.* Lyra Anglicana. Hymns and sacred songs. Leipzig, 1868. Sq. 16°. 1613.8

— Christophers, S. W. Hymn-writers and their hymns. London [1866]. 16° 5626.2

— The disciples' hymn book. *See* BOSTON, *Mass. Church of the Disciples* 6323.10

Shelf. No.

HYMNOLOGY, *continued.*
— Juvenile lyre: or hymns and songs set to music for schools. Boston, 1836. 12° 1623.2
— Martineau, J. Hymns for the Christian church and at home. London, 1874. 12° 6328.14
— Putnam, A. P. Singers and songs of the liberal faith. Boston, 1875. Sm. 8° 1513.4
— Whitmarsh, C. S., and Guild, A. E. Hymns of the ages. Boston, 1862–71. 3 v. Sm. 4°..... 1615.5
— Youthful voices: a collection of hymns and tunes for the use of Sunday schools. The music edited by B. J. Lang. Boston [*cop.* 1862]. 12°...... 1625.9
HYPATIA. [Historical novel.] Kingsley, C........ 326.16
HYPERION. Longfellow, H. W. Boston, 1875. 12°. 716.14
— *Same.* (*In his* Prose works.) Boston, 1866 [*cop.* 1857]. 16° 1838.4.2

Note. — Travels in Germany, etc., with a thread of a story.

HYSTERIA. Skey, F. C. New York, 1867. 16°.... 6015.3

I go a-fishing. [Discursive essays.] Prime, W. C. New York, 1873. Sm. 8°...................... 6413.3
ICE. Wonders of the physical world: the glacier, the iceberg, the ice-field, and the avalanche. London, 1875. Sm. 8° 1714.31
ICE-CUTTERS. Lawrence's adventures among the. Trowbridge, J. T............................... 932.20
ICELAND. Blackwood, F. T., *lord Dufferin.* Voyage to, in 1856. Boston, 1859. 12°............ 225.3
— Headley, P. C. The island of fire; or, a thousand years of the old Northmen's home. 874–1874. Boston, 1875. 12°.............................. 435.3
— Taylor, (J.) B. Egypt and Iceland in 1874. New York, 1874. 16°............................ 436.2
ICHTHYOLOGY. The monsters of the deep. Adams, W. H. D. London, 1875. Sm. 8°............ 6617.1
IDA May. Pike, M. H. 312.10
IDALIA. Rame, L. de la............................ 327.19
IDLER, The. [Periodical essays.] Johnson, S. Works. London, 1862. 8°..................... 5422.3
IDOLATRY. A romance. Hawthorne, J............ 724.10
IDYL, An, of work. [Poem.] Larcom, L. Boston, 1875. 12°...................................... 1615.0
IDYLLS of the king. [Arthur.] Tennyson, A. Poetical works. Leipzig, 1860. Sq. 16°........1614.10.1
IERNE. [Irish life.] Trench, W. S. London, 1871. 2 v. Sm. 8° 715.11
IF, yes, and perhaps. Hale, E. E.................... 526.19
IGNATIUS LOYOLA, *St.* Ignatius Loyola and the early Jesuits. Rose, (W.) S. London, 1871. 8°.... 5524.3
IGNORANCE. Foster, J. Essays on the evils of popular ignorance. London, 1865. 16° 5614.2
— – Philosophy of popular ignorance. Boston, 1841. 12°.. 1539.3
IK MARVEL, *pseud. See* MITCHELL, Donald Grant.
IL faut qu'une porte soit ouverte ou fermée; Il ne faut jurer de rien. Musset, (L. C.) A. de. Comédies et proverbes. Paris, 1867. 12° 5534.4.2
'ILÁM-EN-NÁS. Historical tales and anecdotes of the time of the early Khalífahs. Translated from the Arabic and annotated by Mrs. Godfrey Clerk. London, 1873. xvi, 293 pp. Folded sheet. Sm. 8°. 5927.6
ILIAD. Homerus. The Iliad. Translated by A. Pope. London, 1872. 16° 6117.1
— The Iliad. Translated into English blank verse by W. C. Bryant. Boston, 1871. 2 v. 4°.... 6111.3
— The Iliad, with English notes by F. A. Paley. London, 1866. 2 v. 8°........................ 6114.2
— The Iliad [outlined and explained]. Collins, W. L. Edinburgh, 1871. 16° 6116.2
— The first six books of the Iliad; with explanatory notes, by J. R. Boise. Chicago, 1870. 12°..... 6115.1
— The Iliads. Done according to the Greek by G. Chapman. London, 1865. 2 v. Sq. 16°...... 6118.9

See also Homerus.

I'LL try. Baker, H. N. (W.)........................ 934.6
ILL-OMENED marriage, The. Bulwer-Lytton, E. (G. E.) L. 336.15
ILLUMINATED books. Deutsches Leben in Lieb' und Treue. Bremen [1873]. L. 4° 5730.4
— Deutsches Leben in Liedern. Bremen [1873]. L. 4°. 5730.5

Shelf. No.

ILLUSTRATED homes. Gardner, E. C. Boston, 1875. Sq. 16° 6227.3
ILLUSTRATED library of travel, exploration, and adventure. *Namely:* —
— Bacon, G. B. Siam, as it was and as it is 224.10
— Cumming, (W.) G. Wild men and wild beasts; or, scenes in camp and jungle 423.8
— Richardson, J. Wonders of the Yellowstone.... 224.8
— Taylor, (J.) B. Japan, in our day............ 423.7
— – The lake regions of Central Africa........... 224.9
— – Travels in Arabia............................ 224.6
— – Travels in South Africa..................... 224.1
ILLUSTRATED library of wonders. *Namely:* —
— Baile, J. Wonders of electricity 1714.30
— Bernard, F. Wonderful escapes................1714.20
— Cazin, A. Phenomena and laws of heat........ 1714.6
— Depping, G. Wonders of bodily strength and skill 1714.12
— Duplessis, G. G. The wonders of engraving 1714.16
— Flammarion, C. The wonders of the heavens ...1714.13
— Fonvielle, W. de. Thunder and lightning......1714.22
— Guillemin, A. The sun 1714.10
— – Wonders of the moon........................1714.29
— Headley, J. T. Mountain adventures.......... 1714.4
— Lacombe, M. (J.) P. Arms and armour.........1714.15
— Lefèvre, A. Wonders of architecture 1714.2
— Le Pileur, A. Wonders of the human body.....1714.14
— Marion, F. Wonderful balloon ascents 1714.18
— – The wonders of optics 1714.19
— – The wonders of vegetation.................1714.25
— Menault, E. The intelligence of animals....... 1714.5
— Meunier, V. (A.) Adventures on the great hunting grounds of the world......................... 1714.7
— Monnier, M. The wonders of Pompeii.........1714.17
— Radau, R. Wonders of acoustics...............1714.11
— Sauzay, A. Wonders of glass-making in all ages...1714.24
— Sonrel, L. The bottom of the sea 1714.9
— Tissandier, G. Wonders of water.............1714.26
— Tugnot de Lanoye, F. Rameses the great; or, Egypt 3300 years ago 1714.3
— – The sublime in nature........................1714.21
— Viardot, L. Wonders of European art......... 1714.1
— – Wonders of Italian art........................1714.23
— – Wonders of sculpture 1714.28
— Zuercher, F., and Margollé, É. Meteors, aërolites, storms, and atmospheric phenomena........... 1714.8
ILLUSTRATED London news. Vol. 1–55, 58–67. London, 1842–75. 65 v. F° 1410.1
ILLUSTRATION, L'. Tome 49, 51. Paris, 1867, 68. 2 v. F°.. 5321.1
ILLUSTRIOUS stranger, The: a farce. Kenney, F. New York, N. D. 12° 1635.3
ILLUSTRIRTE Zeitung. B. 61–65. Leipzig, 1873–75. 5 v. F°.. 6730.1
IMAGINARY voyages and travels. Clifford, F. S. A romance of perfume lands, or, the search for Capt. Jacob Cole. Boston, 1875. 16°.............. 733.13
— Verne, J. Adventures in the land of the Behemoth [Africa]. Boston, 1874. Sm. 4°........ 713.3
— – Around the world in eighty days. Boston, 1873. Sm. 4°... 725.27
— – The English at the north pole. London, 1875. Sm. 8° 724.27
— – The field of ice. London, 1875. 8°.......... 733.5
— – From the earth to the moon: and a trip round it. New York, 1874. 8°............................. 734.15
— – A journey to the centre of the earth. New York [1871]. 12° 733.7
— – The mysterious island. Part I. Shipwrecked in the air. Boston, 1875. Sm. 4° 724.17
— – – [Part II.] Abandoned. New York, 1875. 16°.. 733.11
— – – [Part III.] The secret of the island. New York, 1876. 16° 733.14
— – Twenty thousand leagues under the seas. Boston, 1873. Sm. 8°.................................. 5535.1
— – A voyage round the world. In search of the castaways. Hartford, 1873. 8°................ 432.1
— – The voyages and adventures of Captain Hatteras. Boston, 1875. 8°.......................... 733.6

Shelf. No.

IMITATION of Christ. Thomas à Kempis. London, N. D. 16° 5819.1
— *Same*. New York [1851]. 12° 1536.16
IMMORTALITY. Canwright, D. M. History of the doctrine of the immortality of the soul. Battle Creek, 1871. 12° 6328.11
— Hudson, C. F. Christ our life. The scriptural argument for immortality through Christ alone. Boston, 1860. 12° 6326.1
— Sears, E. H. Athanasia: or, foregleams of immortality. Boston, 1858. 12° 5816.16

See also Future life.

IMPENDING crisis, The, of the South. Helper, H. R. New York, 1860. 12° 617.1
IMPENDING sword, The. Yates, E. 310.19
IMPHEE, Sorgho and. Olcott, H. S. New York, 1857. 12° 6425.5
IMPROMPTU, L', de Versailles: comédie. Molière, J. B. P. Œuvres. Paris, 1869. 12° 5537.2.1
IMPROMPTU, The, of Versailles: a comedy. Molière, J. B. P. Dramatic works. Edinburgh, 1875. 8°. 5530.3.2
IMPROVISATORE, The. [A tale of Italian life.] Andersen, H. C. 714.25
IN a winter city. A story of the day. Rame, L. de la. 717.13
IN doors and out. Adams, W. T. 714.37
IN exitu Israel. *See* BARING-GOULD, S. Gabrielle André 710.39
IN extremis. Greenough, *Mrs.* R. S. 736.20
IN France with the Germans. Corvin, O. London, 1872. 2 v. Sm. 8° 5715.2
IN His name. Hale, E. E. Boston, 1874. 8° 732.28
IN honor bound. Gibbon, C. 710.34
IN memoriam. Tennyson, A. Poetical works. Leipzig, 1860. Sq. 16° 1614.10.2
IN school and out. Adams, W. T. 925.1
IN search of the castaways. [Fiction.] Verne, J. Hartford, 1873. 8° 432.1
IN silk attire. Black, W. 330.24
IN that state of life. Aïdé, H. 328.24
IN the Camargue. [Fiction.] Bowles, E. 723.6
IN the days of my youth. Edwards, A. B. 339.11
IN the Eastern seas. Kingston, W. H. G. London, 1871. Sm. 8° 921.3
IN the heart of a hill. Payn, J. 312.28
IN the kitchen. Miller, E. S. Boston, 1875. Sm. 4°. 1532.8
IN the ranks. Douglas, A. M. 934.25
IN the year '13: a tale of Mechlenburg life. Reuter, F. Leipzig, 1867. Sq. 16° 316.9
IN trust. Douglas, A. M. 535.6
INA. Washburn, K. S. 531.35
INCIDENTS in my life. Home, D. D. New York, 1863. 12° 1216.2
INCOGNITO, L'. Souvestre, É. Théâtre de la jeunesse. Paris, 1860. 12° 5536.15
INDIA. Allen, D. O. India, ancient and modern. Boston, 1856. 8° 5921.1
— Anderson, R. History of the missions of the American board of commissioners for foreign missions in. Boston, 1874. 8° 5812.4
— Butler, W. The land of the Veda. New York, 1872. 8° 5931.1
— Cooper, T. T. The Mishmee hills. An account of a journey made in an attempt to penetrate Thibet from Assam to open new routes for commerce. London, 1873. Sm. 8° 5933.6
— Cumming, (W.) G. Wild men and wild beasts; or, scenes in camp and jungle. New York, 1872. Sm. 8° 420.0
— Dilke, C. W. Greater Britain: a record of travel in English-speaking countries during 1866 and 1867. New York, 1869. 12° .... 423.13 and 5935.7
— Eastwick, E. B. Handbook for India. London, 1859. 2 v. 12° 5917.7
— Foster, J. Discourse on the communication of Christianity to the people of Hindoostan. London, 1865. 16° 5614.2
— Grant, *Sir* H. Incidents in the Sepoy war. 1857, 58. Edinburgh, 1873. Sm. 8° 5924.6
— Herbert, D. The Indian mutiny. London, 1876. Sm. 8° 5924.2

Shelf. No.

INDIA, *continued.*
— Hodson, W. S. R. Twelve years of a soldier's life in. Boston, 1860. 12° 426.11
— The Indian Alps, and how we crossed them; being a narrative of two years' residence in the eastern Himalaya, and two months' tour into the interior. London, 1876. L. 8° 5930.6
— Johnson, S. Oriental religions and their relation to universal religion. Boston, 1873. 8° 5811.1
— Kaye, *Sir* J. W. History of the Sepoy war in 1857–58. London, 1870, 72. 8° 5922.7
— Law, E., *first earl Ellenborough*. History of the Indian administration of Lord Ellenborough, in his correspondence with the duke of Wellington. London, 1874. 8° 5412.5
— Taylor, (J.) B. Visit to, in 1853. New York, 1864. 12° 425.7
— Vincent, F., *jr*. Thirty thousand miles of travel in. New York, 1876. 12° 436.8

See also Asia, Burmah, Ceylon, Farther India.

Note. — For *ancient* India, consult Robertson [5610.1].

For *British India*, see Macaulay's essays on Clive and Hastings [1918.4], and the speeches of Burke and Sheridan at the trial of Hastings.

For the *religion* of India, and the relations to Christianity, see Johnson's "Oriental religions" [5811.3]; Clarke's "Ten great religions" [1523.2]; Foster's "Critical essays" [5614.3.1]; Müller's "Chips from a German workshop" [5616.1]; McClintock and Strong's Cyclopædia; Fergusson's "Tree and serpent worship;" and the review in Contemporary review, vol. 12.

For *popular* accounts, that of Allen embodies the observations of an American missionary. For the races of men, see Wood's "Natural history of man" [6610.2; 6610.3].

There is some account of the Sepoy revolt, 1856–58, in Butler's "The land of the Veda" [5931.1].

INDIA: the pearl of Pearl river. Southworth, E. D. E. N. 727.8
INDIAN Alps, The, and how we crossed them; being a narrative of two years' residence in the eastern Himalaya, and two months' tour into the interior. By a lady pioneer. Illustrated by herself. London, 1876. xiii, 612+ pp. Map. L. 8° .. 5930.6
INDIAN question, The. Walker, F. A. Boston, 1874. 12° 5016.14
INDIANA. Dudevant, A. L. A. D. 535.3
INDIANS of North America. Bancroft, H. H. The native races of the Pacific states of North America. New York, 1874. 8° 5920.4.1
— Custer, G. A. My life on the plains. Or, personal experiences with Indians. New York, 1874. 8° 412.3
— Marcy, R. B. Thirty years of army life on the border. New York, 1866. 12° 415.16
— Marryat, F. Narrative of the travels and adventures of Monsieur Violet, in California, Sonora, and Western Texas. [Fiction] 337.7
— Parkman, F., *jr*. The conspiracy of Pontiac and the Indian war after the conquest of Canada. Boston, 1870. 2 v. 12° 5015.4
— Stone, W. L. Life of Joseph Brant, including the border wars of the American revolution, and sketches of Indian campaigns and other matters connected with the Indian relations of the United States and Great Britain. Albany, 1865. 2 v. 8° 5022.1
— Thatcher, B. B. Indian biography. New York, 1869. 2 v. 16° 819.2
— – Indian traits. New York, 1865. 2 v. 12° ... 819.1
— Tuttle, E. B. The boy's book about Indians. Philadelphia, 1873. 16° 915.20

Note. — Brinton, in his "Myths of the new world" [5924.7], makes an able and thorough survey, and rejects the Jewish theory of their origin. His introduction discusses the Indian character, and at the end of his first chapter he gives a bibliographical note on his authorities. See also a note in Parkman's "Jesuits" [5015.5.2, p. 88], on the sources of Indian tales. Parkman's histories on France and England in North America [5015.5] treat incidentally of the intercourse of the Jesuits and other early colonists with the Indians; while the same historian's "Pontiac" [5015.4] vividly portrays the last great effort of the Indians to drive Europeans from the continent, in 1763.

Perhaps the best general survey of the Indian character, etc., is found in the introduction to Parkman's "Jesuits" [5015.5.2, or Atlantic monthly, July, 1865, and July, 1866], which is an amplification of the original introduction to his "Pontiac" [5015.4]. Bancroft, in his "History of the United States" [2012.3, ch. 22], confines his descriptions to those east of the Mississippi; and Hildreth, in his "History of the United States" [5011.10], gives his 2d chapter to the subject. See Harper's monthly, vols. 17 and 40; Irving's exculpatory esti-

Shelf. No.

INDIANS of North America, *continued.*

mate of the Indian character in the "Sketch book" [311.13; 715.6; 1815.10]; "What we should do with him," in Harper's monthly, vol. 40; and Lossing, on "Our barbarian brethren," in vol. 40.

For their *origin*, see Brinton, "Myths of the new world" [5924.7], who rejects the Jewish theory. De Vere's "Romance of American history" [5016.1] gives a popular summary. See Baldwin's "Pre-historic nations" [824.7].

On the question of *race*, see Wood's "Natural history of man" [6610.2; 6610.3], etc.

On their *religions*, see McClintock and Strong's Cyclopædia.

New England. Palfrey [5016.2] will be consulted, and the other histories of New England and Massachusetts. See Everett's oration at Bloody Brook [1921.1.1], and Lossing's "Last of the Pequods," in Scribner's monthly, vol. 2.

See a chapter on John Eliot and the Indians, in Yonge's "Pioneers and founders" [5817.5].

New York. The series of biographies written by W. L. Stone covers a century of the history of the great *Iroquois* confederacy, 1735–1838, and can be found in the Bates Hall; perhaps the life of Brant is the most important. Parkman's histories cover much of this confederacy's history.

Western States. For recent descriptions, see Irving's "Tour on the prairies" [417.1]; Dixon's "New America" [418.1] and his "White conquest" [439.4]; Parkman's "Oregon trail" [5015.3]; General Marcy's "Border reminiscences" [413.3] and his "Army life on the border" [415.16]; Harper's monthly, vols. 36 and 39; and Atlantic monthly, "Medicine men," July, 1866.

See papers in Harper's monthly, Comanches, vol. 33; Sioux, vol. 7 and 17; also vols 36 and 39, and further in the Index to the monthly; also vol. 27 for the massacres of 1862. Also "Eight hundred miles in an ambulance," in Lippincott's magazine, July, 1875.

Southern States. See King's "Great South" [5031.6]; Lossing's "War with the Creeks," in Harper's monthly, vol. 28; and for the Cherokees, the article "Sequoyah," in Harper's monthly, vol. 41.

Arizona and New Mexico. The government reports of the explorations for Pacific railroad routes through this region [6611.2.3], by Whipple, etc., contains much valuable information. See also Ross Browne's "Apache country" [415.13]; and papers in Harper's monthly on those of New Mexico, vol. 7; on the Navajos, vol. 8; on the Pimo, vol. 29; on those of the 35th parallel, vol. 17, etc. Also, Harper's monthly, Aug., 1875.

Pacific slope. H. H. Bancroft's "Native races" is an exhaustive collection of data.

Mexico and Peru. See H. H. Bancroft's "Native races," and Prescott's Mexico [5014.2] and Peru [5014.3], and for further references the note on "America before Columbus" in the Bulletin for April, 1876.

In fiction. In novels, the best known delineations are those of Cooper, in his "Leather-stocking tales," and in his "Redskins" [525.2] and "Wyandotte" [525.4], while other novels, like James's "Ticonderoga," which depicts the part of the aborigines in the old French war, give likewise a somewhat conventional and romantic rendering of their character. In poetry, the best known pictures of them are Longfellow's "Hiawatha" [1614.1] and Campbell's "Gertrude of Wyoming."

INDO-CHINA. Carné, L. de. Travels in. London, 1872. 8° 5931.9
— Thomson, J. The straits of Malacca, Indo-China, and China. New York, 1875. 8° 5921.4
INDUSTRIAL biography: iron-workers and tool-makers. Smiles, S. Boston, 1871. 12° 1227.5
INEZ. Wilson, A. J. 725.26
INFANTRY tactics. Casey, S. Infantry tactics. New York, 1862. 3 v. Sm. 12° 1529.1
— Coppée, H. The field manual of evolutions of the line. Philadelphia, 1862. 12° 1529.8
— Hardee, W. J. Rifle and light infantry tactics. Philadelphia, 1861. 2 v. 16° 1529.3
— Infantry tactics. *See* UNITED STATES. *Department of war* 1529.2
— Le Gal, E. School of the guides. New York, 1860. Sq. 16° 1528.3
— Upton, E. Infantry tactics double and single rank. New York, 1876. Sm. 12° 1529.9
INFANTS, Treatise on the diseases of. Billard, C. M. New York, 1839. 8° 6022.10
INFELICE. Wilson, A. J. 723.26
INFIDELITY, The cause and cure of. Nelson, D. New York [*cop.* 1841]. 12° 5815.17
INFLUENZA, Annals of. Thompson, T. London, 1852. 8° 6013.14
INFORMATION for the people. Chambers, W. and R. Philadelphia, N. D. 2 v. 8° .... *R.R., C.2.4
INGELOW, Jean. Complete poems. Boston, 1873. 332 pp. Portrait. 16° 1625.2
— Fated to be free. Boston 717.8
— *Same.* Leipzig 331.19
— Mopsa the fairy 935.23
— Off the Skelligs. Boston 737.7
— *Same.* Leipzig 335.14
— Poems. Leipzig, 1873. 2 v. in 1. Sq. 16° 1628.4
— Stories told to a child 935.21
— — 2d series 935.22
INGHAM, *Col.* Frederic, *pseud.* *See* HALE, Edward Everett.

Shelf. No.

INGHAM papers, The. Hale, E. E. 526.16
INGLEBY, J. T. Facts and cases in obstetric medicine, with observations on some of the most important discoveries incidental to females. London, N. D. viii, 296 pp. 8° 6012.10
INGLIS, Henry David. The new Gil Blas. New edition. London, 1833. 2 v. 12° 5625.2
INGO und Ingraban. Freytag, G. Die Ahnen. Leipzig, 1873. 16° 5733.5.1
INGOLDSBY, Thomas, *pseud.* *See* BARHAM, Richard Harris.
INGOLDSBY legends, The. [Humorous poems.] Barham, R. H. New York, 1872. 2 v. in 1. 12°. 524.9
INGRABAN. Freytag, G. 538.6
INGRAHAM, Joseph Holt. The pillar of fire; or, Israel in bondage. Boston, 1872. 600 pp. 1 plate. Sm. 8° 512.6
— The prince of the house of David. Boston, 1872. 472 pp. Illustrated. 12° 512.5
— The throne of David. Boston, 1872. 603 pp. Illustrated. 12° 512.4
INHERITANCE, The. Ferrier, S. E. 518.19
INITIALS, The. [Novel, German life.] Tautphoeus, J. M., *Baronin* 317.19
INN, The, of the guardian angel. Ségur, S. (R.), *comtesse* de 912.7
INNOCENT. Oliphant, M. (O. W.) 329.10
INNOCENTS, The, abroad. [Humorous travels.] Clemens, S. L. Hartford, 1872. 8° 421.6
INOCULATION, History of, in Massachusetts. Toner, J. M. (*In* Massachusetts medical society. Publications) 6021.4
INSANITY. Fisher, T. W. Plain talk about insanity. Boston, 1872. 8° 6033.1
— Maudsley, H. Responsibility in mental disease. New York, 1874. 12° 6035.4
INSECTIVOROUS plants. Darwin, C. (R.) New York, 1875. 12° 6614.13
INSECTS. Figuier, (G.) L. The insect world; being a popular account of the orders of. London, 1869. 8° 1521.8
— *Same.* London [1872]. Sm. 8° 6615.1
— Harris, T. W. Treatise on some of the insects of New England which are injurious to vegetation. Boston, 1852. 8° 6612.1
— Houghton, W. Sketches of British insects. London, 1875. Sm. 8° 6616.13
— Lubbock, *Sir* J. On the origin and metamorphoses of. London, 1874. Sm. 8° 6617.8
— Michelet, J. The insect. London, 1875. 8° 6612.9
— Packard, A. S., *jr.* Guide to the study of. Salem, 1872. 8° 6613.6
— Wood, J. G. Insects at home. A popular account of insects, their structure, habits, and transformations. New York, 1872. 8° 6612.2

See also Bees.

INSTINCT: its office in the animal kingdom, and its relation to the higher powers in man. Chadbourne, P. A. New York, 1872. Sm. 8° 6617.4
INSTITUTES of Justinian. Justinianus I, *emperor.* London, 1874. 8° 6314.1
INSTITUTIONS, Lectures on the early history of. Maine, *Sir* H. S. New York, 1875. 8° 6313.6
INTELLECTUAL life, The. Hamerton, P. G. Boston, 1873. 16° 1925.1
INTELLECTUAL science. Abercrombie, J. Inquiries concerning the intellectual powers, and the investigation of truth. New York, 1857. 12°. 1529.4
— Porter, N. The human intellect. New York, 1872. 8° 1520.4
— Reid, T. Essays on the intellectual powers of man. Philadelphia, 1861. 12° 1526.23
INTELLIGENCE, The, of animals. Menault, E. New York, 1872. 16° 1714.5
INTEMPERANCE. Burns, D. Christendom and the drink curse: an appeal to the Christian world for efficient action against the causes of. London, 1875. 8° 1912.9
— Macnish, R. Anatomy of drunkenness. (*In* The Alexandrian) 1910.4.2

Shelf. No.

INTERNATIONAL review. Vol. 1. New York [1874]. 8° 6512.1
INTERNATIONAL scientific series. *Namely :* —
— Amos, S. The science of law 6316.3
— Bain, A. Mind and body 6035.2
— Beneden, P. J. van. Animal parasites and messmates 6616.6
— Cooke, J. P., *jr.* The new chemistry 6436.15
— Cooke, M. C. Fungi: their nature and uses 6436.13
— Draper, J. W. History of the conflict between science and religion 5826.4
— Jevons, W. S. Money and the mechanism of exchange 5826.8
— Lommel, E. (C. J.) The nature of light, with a general account of physical optics 6436.17
— Marey, E. J. Animal mechanism 6436.12
— Maudsley, H. Responsibility in mental disease. 6035.4
— Pettigrew, J. B. Animal locomotion, or walking, swimming, and flying 6436.14
— Schmidt, (E.) O. The doctrine of descent and Darwinism 6616.10
— Schuetzenberger, M. P. On fermentation 6436.18
— Smith, E. Foods 6436.6
— Spencer, H. The study of sociology 5826.1
— Stewart, B. The conservation of energy 6436.7
— Vogel, H. The chemistry of light and photography 6436.16
— Whitney, W. D. The life and growth of language 6126.5
INTERNATIONAL series. *Namely :* —
— Bauer, K. At Capri. A story of Italian life ... 714.19
— Feuillet, O. A marriage in high life 722.2
— Keary, A. Castle Daly 714.36
— – Oldbury 714.18
— Moore, *Mrs.* B. H. On dangerous ground 722.1
— Oliphant, M. (O. W.) An odd couple 722.9
— Randolph, *Mrs.* —. Gentianella 714.9
INTEROCEANIC canals. Reports of explorations and surveys to ascertain the practicability of a ship-canal between the Atlantic and Pacific oceans. *See* UNITED STATES. *Department of the navy* ... 5030.6
INTERPRETER, The. Melville, G. J. W. 321.9
INVALIDS, How shall we employ and amuse our. Power, H. London, 1873. 16° 6038.3
INVASION, The. Griffin, G. 517.9
INVASION, The, of France in 1814. [Historical fiction.] Erckmann, É., and Chatrian, A. New York, 1871. 12° 913.23
INVENTIONS. Beckmann, J. History of. London, 1846. 2 v. 16° .... 1526.7 and 6425.1
— Routledge, R. Discoveries and inventions of the nineteenth century. London, 1876. Sm. 8° ... 6425.8
— Timbs, J. Wonderful inventions. London [1867]. Sm. 8° 1525.20
INVENTORS, Stories of. Timbs, J. New York, 1860. 12° 1525.30
INVISIBLE princess, The. O'Conner, F. (*In* Johnson, (E.) R. Little classics) 529.4.8
INVITATION, The, heeded: reasons for a return to catholic unity. Stone, J. K. New York [*cop.* 1870]. 12° 5816.12
IONA. Campbell, G. D., *duke of Argyll.* London, 1870. Sm. 8° 427.9
IONE. Petrella, E. (*In* Ditson, O., and co. Standard opera librettos) 6233.3.6

Shelf. No.

IPHIGÉNIE en Aulide: tragédie. Racine, J. de. Théâtre complet. Paris, 1870. 12° 5537.3
IPHIGENIE in Aulis. Schiller, J. C. F. von. Werke. Stuttgart, 1867. 8° 5734.1.7
IRELAND, John, and NICHOLS, John. Hogarth's works: with life and anecdotal descriptions of his pictures. London, N. D. 3 v. Portraits. Fac-simile. Sm. 8° 6214.2
IRELAND. Adams, W. T. Shamrock and thistle; or, Young America in. Boston, 1871. 16° 916.17
— Barry, M. J., *editor.* The songs of. New York, 1873. 12° 5626.4
— Black, A. and C. Picturesque tourist of. Edinburgh, 1855. Sm. 8° 229.2
— Burke, T. N. English misrule in. New York, 1873. 12° 827.6
— Carleton, W. Traits and stories of the Irish peasantry 524.17
— Conyngham, D. P. Sarsfield; or, the last great struggle for. Boston, 1871. Sq. 16° 828.7
— Cusack, M. F. Illustrated history of. London, 1872. 8° 5412.1
— – The patriot's history of. New York, 1869. 16° 5418.4
— Daunt, W. J. O'N. Ireland and her agitators. Dublin, 1867. 12° 5417.4
— Forbes, R. B. Voyage of the Jamestown on her errand of mercy to. Boston, 1847. 8° 421.4
— Froude, J. A. The English in Ireland in the eighteenth century. New York, 1872, 74. 3 v. 8° 5414.5
— Galibert, L., and Pellé, C. Irlande. Paris, 1844. 8° 5911.7
— Godkin, J. The religious history of. London, 1873. 8° 5412.3
— Hall, A. M. Sketches of Irish character. London [1875]. 8° 5436.1
— Hall, S. C. and A. M. Ireland: its scenery, character, etc. London, 1841–43. 3 v. L. 8°. 5431.1
— Hyde, E., *earl of Clarendon.* An historical view of the affairs of. Boston, 1827. 8° 5412.4.6
— Joyce, R. D. Legends of the wars in. Boston, 1868. 16° 828.6
— Kohl, J. G. Ireland. New York, 1844. 8° ... 431.2
— Lecky, W. E. H. Leaders of public opinion in: Swift — Flood — Grattan — O'Connell. New York, 1872. 12° 1025.9
— MacCarthy, D. F. Book of Irish ballads. New York, 1873. 16° 5626.3
— Mills, A. The literature and the literary men of. New York, 1870. 2 v. 8° 1021.6
— Moore, T. Irish melodies. Leipzig, 1842. Sq. 16° 1614.9.1
— O'Rourke, J. The history of the great Irish famine of 1847, with notices of earlier Irish famines. Dublin, 1875. Sm. 8° 5418.12
— Sheil, R. L. Sketches of the Irish bar. New York [*cop.* 1854]. 2 v. 12° 5417.7
— Smiles, S. The Huguenots: their settlements, churches, and industries in. New York, 1868. Sm. 8° 5514.1
— Street ballads, popular poetry, and household songs of. Boston [1864]. 16° 1615.2
— Trench, W. S. Realities of Irish life. Boston, 1869. Sq. 16° 428.13

NOTE ON IRELAND.

Of general histories, the best for popular use is Cusack's "Illustrated history," of which "The patriot's history" is a condensed summary. See Baldwin's summary [824.7] for pre-historic times. There is an article on the "Ancient Fenians" in Scribner's monthly, vol. 1. Montalembert's "Monks of the West" [5514.5] covers the era of Saint Patrick and the early Christian history. Wright, in his "Middle ages," has a chapter on the Anglo-Norman conquest, and it is treated of in the 2d vol. of Thierry's "Norman conquest" [5417.2]. See also Harper's monthly, vol. 43. There is an account of ancient laws, etc., in Maine's "History of institutions" [6313.6]. Strongbow's invasion in the XIIth century is fully described in Lingard's "History of England" [5417.8], but see Harper's monthly, Oct., 1871. Froude's 2d volume of his "History of England" [826.9] takes up the rebellion of 1534–35; and he also enlarges upon Irish history during the time of Henry VIII and Queen Elizabeth, always, however, with an English leaning. Go to Carlyle's "Cromwell" [1238.1] for the civil war period. The siege of Londonderry in 1689 is graphically described in Macaulay's "History of England" [838.1], who tells the subsequent career of William of Orange in Ireland, and in his 16th chapter describes the *battle of the Boyne*, illustrations of which will be found in Conyngham's "Sarsfield" [828.7] and in Banim's "Boyne water" [517.16].

For the catholic emancipation and other aspects of Irish history of the last century, see Edmund Burke's speeches [5634.1; 5635.1]. Miss Edgeworth's "Castle Rackrent" [514.1.1] pictures the life of the Irish squires.

For the revolution of 1798, see chapters in De Quincey's "Autobiographic sketches" [1825.7]. Sydney Smith, in his essays [1931.1], was exculpatory in his views. Jeffrey, in his essays [5610.8], enforces the argument for legislative union. Lecky has an admirable book on the "Leaders of public opinion in Ireland" [1025.9], chiefly as regards her relations with England, from the days of Swift down, and this can be traced also in the lives of Flood (d. 1791), Emmet (executed 1803), Curran (d. 1817), Grattan (d. 1820), O'Connell (d. 1847), and Shiel (d. 1851). See also Daunt's "Ireland and her agitators" [5417.4]; Sheil's "Sketches of the Irish bar" [5626.3]; and the paper in the North American review, Jan., 1873, on Flood, or Ireland from Swift to O'Connell.

On the *famine of* 1847, beside O'Rourke, who enlarges upon the relations of England and Ireland, see Forbes' "Voyage" [421.4]; Everett's Orations [1921.1.2]; and in fiction A. Trollope's "Castle Richmond" [334.8], and Carleton's "Black prophet."

On the *relations of England and Ireland*, Froude, in his recent history on "The English in Ireland in the 18th century" [5414.5], has been reviewed by Lecky, in Macmillan's magazine, Jan., 1873, and Godkin's "Religious history" and Burke's "English misrule" were in part prepared in refutation of Froude, who covers in a general way the interval 1641-1798. For further on Froude's relations with Ireland, see his two papers "A fortnight in Kerry," in his "Short studies" [1914.5.2]; also Contemporary review, vol. 4. Also, "The Fenian idea," in the Atlantic monthly, May, 1866. McCarthy's "Fair Saxon" [734.8] touches on the Fenian troubles.

Of the present condition of *the tenantry* of Ireland, there is an excellent presentation in Trench's "Realities of Irish life" [428.13]. The vexed *land question* is considered in a paper in Macmillan's magazine, May, 1875.

There are good general descriptions of manners, etc., in Carleton's "Traits and stories of the Irish peasantry" and in the books of Mrs. A. M. Hall.

The three volumes of Mr. and Mrs. S. C. Hall's "Ireland" [5431.1], offer a full descriptive account of Ireland; and there is some good description in Thackeray's "Irish sketch book" [330.29; 513.1.7]. See also Contemporary review, vol. 5; and Harper's monthly, vols. 42, 43, and 47.

S. C. Hall's "Book of memories" [1231.1] touches on modern Irish authors, and there are other books on Irish literature named above.

For illustrations of Irish life and character, see Hall's "Sketches" [5431.1]; Carleton's "Redmond" [518.5] for events of 1696; his "Willy Reilly" [524.3] for the penal laws; Banim's "John Doe" [517.5] for Capt. Rock; A. M. Hall's "Whiteboy" [521.6], time 1822; and generally the following novelists: — Carleton, who, according to Thackeray, is the greatest genius who has depicted Irish character; Banim, who deals chiefly with Leinster peasants in passionate and tragic circumstances; Lever, who places his Irishmen in military and convivial life; Samuel Lover, who tried to divest the Irish peasant of vice and coarseness; Miss Edgeworth, whose "Castle Rackrent" [514.1.1] is not considered a successful representation of Irish peasantry; and whose "Rosanna" [514.1.2] is given to farming life. Gerald Griffin's "Collegians" [517.7] concerns the rural middle class in Munster, and gave rise to the drama of "Colleen bawn." Irish life forms the staple also of some of Anthony Trollope's tales, and an Irish adventurer is drawn in Thackeray's "Barry Lyndon" [333.13.3; 513.1.4].

Shelf. No.

IRENÆUS, *St.* Writings. Translated by A. Roberts and W. H. Rambaut. Edinburgh, 1868, 69. 2 v. [Ante-Nicene Christian library.] 8°. Vol. 5, 9 of 6322.5

IRIS. Holmes, O. W. (*In* Johnson, (E.) R. Little classics) 529.4.7

IRISH brigade, The, and its campaigns [in the civil war, 1861–65]. Conyngham, D. P. Boston, 1869. 12° 824.4

IRISH heirs. Lover, S. 732.20

IRISH sketch-book, The. Thackeray, W. M. Leipzig, 1872. 2 v. in 1. Sq. 16° 330.29

— *Same.* (*In his* Works.) London, 1872. Sm. 8°. 513.1.7

IRISH widow, The: a farce. Garrick, D. New York, N. D. 12° 1635.5

IRON. Armour, J. Iron and heat. London, 1871. 12° 1716.40

— Bauerman, H. Treatise on the metallurgy of. London, 1872. 12° 1716.42

IRON cousin, The. Clarke, M. C. 725.39

IRON hand, The. Dumas, A. (D.) 510.10

IRON mask, The. Dumas, A. (D.) 511.9

Note. — This story concerns the state prisoner of France, who is known by this name, and about whose identity there is much question. The matter will be found treated historically in James's "Life and times of Louis XIV" [5526.5], and in the Encyclopædias.

IRON-MEN, Lawrence's adventures among the. Trowbridge, J. T. 932.20

IRON shroud, The. Mudford, W. (*In* Johnson, (E.) R. Little classics) 529.4.3

IRONTHORPE. Trowbridge, J. T. 929.5

IRVING, David. Biography of James Crichton. (*In* Macaulay, T. B., *lord*, and others. New biographies of illustrious men) 5428.4

IRVING, Pierre M. Life and letters of Washington Irving. New York, 1862–64. 4 v. Portraits. 12° 1214.1

— *Same.* Revised. Philadelphia, 1872. 3 v. Portraits. Sm. 8° 1815.1

IRVING, Theodore. The conquest of Florida, under Hernando de Soto. London, 1850. viii, 280 pp. 16° 826.3

IRVING, Washington. Abbotsford [Walter Scott's home], and Newstead abbey [Byron's home]. London, 1853. iv, 138 pp. 16° 715.5

— Adventures of Captain Bonneville, in the Rocky mountains and the far West. Author's revised edition. London, 1854. x, 280 pp. 16° 826.3

— *Same.* Philadelphia, 1871. 503 pp. Illustrated. Sm. 8° 1815.14

— The Alhambra. New edition, with an historical appendix. London, 1853. 260+ pp. 16° 715.7

— *Same.* Author's revised edition. Philadelphia, 1872. 496 pp. Illustrated. Sm. 8° 1815.15

Note. — Descriptive of this Moorish palace, and associative stories.

Shelf. No.

IRVING, Washington, *continued.*

— Astoria; or, anecdotes of an enterprise beyond the Rocky mountains. Author's revised edition. London, 1850. xii, 340 pp. 1 plate. 16° 417.1

— *Same.* Philadelphia, 1871. xxvi, 649 pp. Illustrated. Sm. 8° 1814.1

— Biography and poetical remains of Margaret Miller Davidson. Philadelphia, 1841. 359 pp. 12° 1217.2

— Biographies and miscellanies. Edited by P. M. Irving. Philadelphia, 1871. 487 pp. Portrait. Sm. 8° 1815.4

— Bracebridge hall. By Geoffrey Crayon [*pseud.*]. Author's revised edition. London, 1850. iv, 320 pp. Portrait. 16° 715.5

— *Same.* Philadelphia, 1871. Illustrated. Sm. 8°. 1814.2

Note. — Sketches of English country life of a past generation.

— Chronicle of the conquest of Granada. From the MSS. of Fray Antonio Agapida. Author's revised edition. Philadelphia, 1871. xxiv, 644 pp. Illustrated. Sm. 8° 1815.6

Note. — Essentially historic, — the MSS. are fictitious.

— *Same.* Added Legends of the conquest of Spain. London, 1850. 2 v. in 1. Sm. 8° 826.4

— Chronicles of Wolfert's Roost and other papers. Leipzig, 1855. vi, 386 pp. Sq. 16° 311.14

Note. — Same as 1815.12.

— The Crayon miscellany. Author's revised edition. Philadelphia, 1872. 441 pp. Sm. 8° 1814.3

— History of New York, from the beginning of the world to the end of the Dutch dynasty. [Comic history.] By Diedrich Knickerbocker [*pseud.*]. Author's revised edition. London, 1854. xxiv, 280 pp. 16° 715.4

— *Same.* Philadelphia, 1872. 528 pp. Illustrated. Sm. 8° 1815.11

— Life and voyages of Christopher Columbus. Author's revised edition. London, 1850. 2 v. Portraits. 16° 1226.7

— *Same.* Added those of his companions. Philadelphia, 1871. 3 v. Illustrated. Portraits. Sm. 8° 1815.2

Note. — These volumes afford the best English account of early Spanish discovery in America, but Prescott's "Ferdinand and Isabella" [5922.5], and Helps's "Spanish conquest" [816.6] may be read in connection.

— Life of George Washington. Leipzig, 1856. 5 v. in 3. Sq. 16° 1238.9

— *Same.* London, 1855–59. 5 v. Portrait. 1 plate. 16° 1216.7

— *Same.* New York, 1855–59. 5 v. Portraits. 1 plate. 8° 1211.3

— *Same.* Philadelphia, 1871. 5 v. Illustrated. Portraits. Sm. 8° 1815.5

Note. — The standard life of Washington, to be compared with Marshall's and Sparks's, if the reader wishes.

Shelf. No.

IRVING, Washington, *continued.*

— Life of Mahomet. Leipzig, 1850. 302+ pp. Sq. 16° 1238.12

— Lives of the successors of Mahomet. Leipzig, 1850. xiv, 404 pp. Sq. 16° 1238.5

— Mahomet and his successors. New York, 1850. 2 v. 12° 1223.4

— *Same.* Philadelphia, 1871. Illustrated. 2 v. Sm. 8° 1815.3

Note. — The best account of the founder of Mohammedanism for English general readers.

— Oliver Goldsmith: a biography. Leipzig, 1850. xiv, 356 pp. Sq. 16° 1238.6

— *Same.* London, 1850. x, 242 pp. 16° 715.6

— *Same.* Philadelphia, 1871. 427 pp. Illustrated. Sm. 8° 1815.13

Note. — The best condensed account of Goldsmith; but Forster's "Life of Goldsmith" must be used for ampler detail.

— Salmagundi. *See* IRVING, William.... 715.4 and 1815.7

— The sketch book. With portrait. Leipzig, 1843. x, 361 pp. Sq. 16° 311.13

— *Same.* London, 1855. vi, 282 pp. Portrait. 16°. 715.6

— *Same.* Author's revised edition. Philadelphia, 1872. 507 pp. Illustrated. Portrait. Sm. 8°. 1815.10

Note. — "The sketch book" gives detached essays and tales, and first gave Irving a reputation.

— Spanish papers and other miscellanies. Edited by P. M. Irving. New York, 1866. 2 v. Portrait. Sm. 8° 1934.1

— *Same.* Philadelphia, 1871. xxiv, 531 pp. 1 plate. Portrait. Sm. 8° 1815.8

Note. — Various biographical sketches and other papers collected after Irving's death.

— Tales of a traveller. London, 1850. viii, 296 pp. 16° 715.7

— *Same.* Author's revised edition. Philadelphia, 1872. 530 pp. Illustrated. Sm. 8° 1815.9

Note. — Various stories.

— Tour on the prairies. London, 1854. v, 137+ pp. 16° 417.1

— Voyages and discoveries of the companions of Columbus. Author's revised edition. With an appendix of historical documents. London, 1850. x, 962 [354] pp. 16° 1226.7.2

— Wolfert's Roost and other papers. Author's revised edition. Philadelphia, 1871. 431+ pp. Illustrated. Fac-simile. Sm. 8° 1815.12

Note. — Same as 311.14.

— Life and letters of. Irving, P. M. New York, 1862–64. 4 v. 12° 1214.1

— *Same.* Philadelphia, 1872. 3 v. Sm. 8° 1815.1

Note. — The life by his nephew is the all-sufficient account, and there is a review by D. G. Mitchell, in Atlantic monthly, June, 1864. Additional biographical memoranda will be found in G. P. Putnam's recollections, in Atlantic monthly, Nov., 1860; in Harper's monthly, vols. 2, 14, 20, 21, 24, and 34 [on Sleepy hollow]. After his death, Bryant [1926.1] commemorated him before the New York historical society; and Everett also in the 4th vol. of his Orations [1921.1]. Thackeray paid him a tribute in his "Roundabout papers" [335.9].

Allibone, in his article, quotes many authorities and gives full references to others, and essays on Irving or his works will be found in Jeffrey's essays [5610.8]; in Prescott's "Miscellanies" [1537.8; 5237.3], etc. See also the literary histories of Duyckinck and Griswold, and the references in Thomas.

IRVING, William, PAULDING, James Kirke, and IRVING, Washington. Salmagundi; or, the whim-whams and opinions of Launcelot Langstaff, Esq., and others. London, 1850. vi, 269 pp. 16° .. 715.4

— *Same.* Preface and notes by E. A. Duyckinck. Philadelphia, 1871. xix, 473 pp. Illustrated. Sm. 8° 1815.7

ISABELLA Orsini. Guerrazzi, F. D. 536.9

ISEULTE. A novel. By the author of "Vera," etc. 720.19

ISLAM. Deutsch, E. (O. M.) Literary remains. New York, 1874. 8° 5733.7

— *Same.* *See* SMITH, R. B. Mohammed and Mohammedanism. New York, 1875. 12° 5816.23

ISHMAEL; or, in the depths. Southworth, E. D. E. N. 522.23

ISLAND, The, of fire. [Iceland.] Headley, P. C. Boston, 1875. 12° 435.3

ISLAND home, The. Keene, *Mrs.* S. F. 923.13

ISLAND pearl, An. Farjeon, B. L. 530.11

Shelf. No.

ISLES OF SHOALS. Jenness, J. S. The Isles of Shoals. New York, 1873. 16° 818.2

— Thaxter, C. Among the Isles of Shoals. Boston, 1873. Sq. 16° 419.1

ISMAILÏA. [Egypt and the upper Nile.] Baker, *Sir* S. W. New York, 1875. 8° 5933.5

ISOMETRIC projection. Davidson, E. A. London [1875]. Sm. 8° 6218.2

ISRAEL Mort, overman. Saunders, J. 319.20

ISTHMIANA. Winthrop, T. 537.19

"IT is never too late to mend." Reade, C. 316.25

IT is the fashion. Auer, A. von 533.21

ITALIAN girl, The. Washburn, K. S. 728.9

ITALIANS, The. [Fiction.] Elliot, F. Leipzig.... 330.16

— *Same.* New York 716.20

ITALY. *Art.*

— Burckhardt, J. The Cicerone: or, art guide to painting in. London, 1873. Sm. 8° 6216.1

— Crowe, J. A., and Cavalcaselle, G. B. History of painting in. London, 1864. 3 v. 8° 6213.2

— – History of painting in North Italy. London, 1871. 2 v. 8° 6213.1

— Jameson, A. (M.) Memoirs of the early Italian painters. Boston, 1875. Sq. 16° 6228.2

— Lanzi, L. History of painting in. London, 1852. 2 v. Sm. 8° 6215.4

— Perkins, C. C. Italian sculptors: a history of sculpture in Northern, Southern, and Eastern Italy. London, 1868. L. 8° 6210.2

— Viardot, L. Wonders of Italian art. New York, 1871. 12° 1714.23

Note. — All general histories of art, architecture, painting, and sculpture necessarily treat largely of art in Italy, and see the notes under those heads, and under Rome, as well as under the names of prominent artists, like Raphael, Buonarotti, etc. Lanzi and Vasari are both native authorities of repute, the latter being contemporary with some of his subjects. Many of Mrs. Jameson's books treat attractively of the subject, and her "Early painters" is a collection of popular lives; while parts of Wornum's "Epochs of painting" [6213.3] and Viardot's "Wonders of Italian art" treat the subject fitly for the general reader; but for the thorough student of painting the new work by Crowe and Cavalcaselle supplies the most satisfactory account.

For Italian *sculpture*, the valuable monograph of Perkins is of the first importance. See also Luebke's "History of sculpture" [6210.3], and for popular use, the "Wonders of sculpture" by Viardot, above named.

For Italian *architecture*, see Fergusson's "History of architecture" [6222.3]. Burckhardt's "Cicerone" is the most important manual.

Geography, description, travel, etc.

— Adams, W. T. Sunny shores; or, young America in. Boston, 1875. 16° 925.12

— Baedeker, C. Handbook for travellers. Coblenz, 1870, 72. 2 v. 16° 5528.2

— – Switzerland, and the adjacent portions of Italy. Handbook for travellers. Coblenz, 1872. 16°. 5718.4

— Castelar, E. Old Rome and new Italy. New York, 1873. 12° 824.11

— Dickens, C. (J. H.) Pictures from Italy. Leipzig, 1846. Sq. 16° 338.18

— *Same.* Boston, 1874. 8° 1824.10

— Elliot, F. Diary of an idle woman in. Leipzig, 1872. 2 v. in 1. Sq. 16° 228.3

— Forsyth, J. Remarks on antiquities, arts, and letters, during an excursion in, 1802, 3. Boston, 1818. 8° 421.3

— Goethe, J. W. von. Travels in. London, 1872. Sm. 8° 1025.5.2

— Hare, A. J. C. Cities of northern and central Italy. London, 1876. 3 v. Sm. 8° 5527.17

Hawthorne, N. Passages from [his] Italian note-books. Boston, 1876 [*cop.* 1871]. 2 v. 16°. 1839.3

— Herder, J. G. von. Reise nach Italien. Giessen, 1859. 16° 1024.1

— Hillard, G. S. Six months in. Boston, 1854. 2 v. Sm. 8° 426.8

— Howells, W. D. Italian journeys. New York, 1872. 16° 425.20

— Itinéraire d'Italie, ou la description des voyages par les routes plus fréquentées aux principales villes d'Italie. Milan, 1817. Sm. 8° 2018.5

— Kemble, F. (A.) A year of consolation. New York, 1847. 12° 426.14

Shelf. No.

ITALY. *Geography, description, travel, etc., continued.*
— Mendelssohn-Bartholdy, F. Letters from Italy. Boston, N. D. 12° 1227.1
— Moens, W. J. C. English travelers and Italian brigands. New York, 1866. 12° 423.16
— Murray, J. Handbook for Central Italy. London, 1867. 12° 5527.5
— – Handbook for Northern Italy. London, 1873. 12° 5527.4
— – Knapsack guide for. London, 1865. 12° 5528.1
— Norton, C. E. Notes of travel and study in. Boston, 1859. 16° 426.12
— Taine, H. A. Italy. London, 1872. 2 v. 8°. 5522.2
— Wallace, *Mrs.* E. D. A woman's experiences in. New York, 1872. 12° 423.11
— Watson, E. H. Child-life in. Boston, 1866. Sm. 8° 931.5
— Willis, N. P. Pencillings by the way. New York, 1844. L. 8° 430.2

NOTE ON ITALIAN TRAVEL, ETC.

The memorials, which give chief or exclusive attention to the *classical associations* of Italy, are Forsyth's reputable work on the antiquities, arts, and letters, and it is reckoned by Hare to be the best book on general Italian travel.

Of modern *traveller's guides*, there are Baedeker, and later editions of Murray.

Of *German travellers*, the most famous is Goethe, and Niebuhr says of him that "he beheld without love."

Of *French travellers*, Taine is the most important of recent ones.

Of *English travellers*, Mrs. Jameson's "Diary" [427.3], though fictitious in form, embodies that lady's fine criticism, particularly upon art and literature. In Dickens, the reader finds shrewd observation during a brief run through the peninsula, with glimpses of character. See also the journals and letters of English authors, who have lived long in Italy, like Byron, Shelley, Landor, etc.; and the descriptive essay by Alison, in his Essays [1531.7].

Hare's "Days near Rome" [5527.15] and his "Cities of northern and central Italy" [5527.17], taking the region farther north up to the Alps, are both works of excellent character.

Of *American travellers*, Hawthorne's Note-books do not, perhaps, embody more observation than was reproduced in his fiction of "The marble faun" [1813.2]. Hillard's book has been widely praised and used with satisfaction, as a scholarly portrayal of fact and feeling regarding what comes naturally within the observation of the visitor, and its concluding chapters give excellent characterizations of preceding writers on Italy from the times of the earliest pilgrims. Howells's books are graceful narratives of personal experience while the author was consul at Venice. Jarves has some close observation in his paper in Harper's monthly, vol. 10. Norton's book is a scholar's jottings, about matters not in the way of every-day observers. Pleasing pictures of life are given in Lowell's "Fireside travels" [426.4]. See the paper on "Peasant life in Northern Italy" in Frazer's magazine, 1875.

Italy is the subject of some well-known works of the imagination, which the reader cannot well omit considering. Madame de Staël's "Corinne" [527.17; in French, 2015.3] connects the aptest pictures of life, manners and scenery, with a romantic love story. Hans Andersen, besides his "Poet's bazaar" [426.18], wrote "The improvisatore" [714.25], which is a very vivid portrayal of the externals of the land. See also the passionate sketches of Byron's "Childe Harold" [1614.13.2], and Rogers's calmer pictures in his "Italy."

Ruffini's "Doctor Antonio" [316.17] and "Lavinia" [316.18] also afford pictures of Italian life and character; as also T. A. Trollope's "Siren" [334.20] and other of his novels. See also the humorous view in De Mille's "Dodge club" [511.22]; in "Mademoiselle Mori" [313.13]; and the Italian characters, which figure in Wilkie Collins's "Woman in white" [326.12], and in Bulwer's "My novel" [336.17].

Of *brigandage* in Italy, besides the book of Moens [see also Harper's monthly, vol. 33], there are other representations in Irving's "Tales of a traveller" [715.7; 1815.9], and in De Mille's "American baron" [511.19].

Shelf. No.

History, etc.

ITALY. Abbott, J. S. C. Italy, and the war for Italian independence. Boston, 1871. 12° 824.15
— Bryce, J. The holy Roman empire. London, 1873. Sm. 8° 5814.19
— Machiavelli, N. History of Florence, with the affairs of. London, 1871. Sm. 8° 5516.8

ITALY. *History, etc., continued.*
— Symonds, J. A. Renaissance in Italy the age of the despots. London, 1875. 8° 5522.8

See also Alps, Corsica, Pompeii, Rome, Savoy, Sicily, Tyrol, Venice.

NOTE ON ITALIAN HISTORY.

For the beginnings of modern Italian history, see the 69th and 70th chapters of Gibbon, in his "Roman empire" [824.9], who leaves the story with the final acquiescence of Rome in the power of the popes; and two chapters in Hallam's "Middle ages" [5916.1].

Much referred to under Rome on the period of its *mediæval history* broadly pertains to Italy, and particularly the work of Gregorovius, of which there is an examination under the title of "The Borgias and their latest historian," in the North British review, 1871. Hallam's "Middle ages" [5916.1] covers Italy for this period.

The period of the *renaissance* may be considered as beginning with the fall of Constantinople in 1453, and ending with the sack of Rome in 1527. Symonds [5522.8] is the latest single authority for this epoch; and for the wars with Spain, see Prescott's "Ferdinand and Isabella" [5922.5], and also the histories of France for Francis I's time.

For the power of *Florence* in Italy there is the well-known history by Machiavelli [5516.8], who, in bringing down the narrative to the death of Lorenzo de' Medici, partly surveyed his own days, and while his reputation is not high for careful research, his manner is animated. Roscoe furnishes, in the "Life of Lorenzo de' Medici," d. 1492 [5525.1], an excellent narrative for the general reader, who can follow it with the same writer's "Life of Leo X," d. 1522 [5526.6], both works of excellent reputation. The lives of Michael Angelo, d. 1564, particularly Grimm's [1022.2, in which, in vol. 1, p. 72, the historical sources are characterized], the autobiography of Cellini, which Roscoe has translated [1225.17], and the lives of other prominent men of the period, afford much illustrative help on the period of Florentine supremacy; while in his "History of the commonwealth of Florence" [5512.3], Trollope has given in some respects the best survey from 1107 to the fall of the republic in 1531, which is available for the English reader, constituting, as it does, a narrative of the political affairs that fitly complements Roscoe's accounts of the æsthetic culture of the Medicean era. Napier's "Florentine history" [5516.2] is a book of good repute, copious in treatment, of adequate research, held to be honest and impartial, and it brings the record down to 1824. See also Symonds's "Renaissance," chapter 3 [5522.8].

For the influence of *Venice* and *Rome* upon Italian history, see those heads.

For the *history of this century*, see the special heads of Sardinia, Florence, Rome, Venice, and Naples; and for the influence of Austria and France upon Italian history, see those countries.

For an account of the recent dissolution of the relations between the state and church, see Fortnightly review, 1872; and Mazzini's article on "The religious side of the Italian question," in Atlantic monthly, July, 1867, or Westminster review, July, 1867. There are several special memoirs on the war of 1859, and the military history of it can be studied in Hamley's "Operations of war" [5910 6]. For the war of 1866, see Germany. See also Harper's monthly, vol. 43, etc.

An examination of the present condition of united Italy is made in the Edinburgh review, Oct., 1875; and Hare's "Cities of northern and central Italy" [5527.17] represents the views of those who find more to disapprove than approve in the present state of affairs.

For the *ecclesiastical history*, see the summary as mapped out in McClintock and Strong's Cyclopædia. Ranke's "History of the popes" [5516.7] covers the 16th and 17th centuries. Macaulay's review, in his Essays [1918.4], is sufficient for the general reader, who may refer to the note under Reformation, for general works touching the convulsion in Italy, and to chapter 11 of Fisher's "Reformation" [5813.7]. For the part borne by Savonarola in preparing for the reformation, see the delineation in George Eliot's "Romola" [310.23], and in Mrs. Stowe's "Agnes of Sorrento" [527.16].

There is an examination of the Italian historians in Disraeli's "Curiosities of literature," second series [5226.6].

Illustrative imaginative literature will be found for the 13th century in Dante's great poem, and in Leigh Hunt's "Story of Rimini." For the 14th century, see Bulwer's "Rienzi" [336.1], and Byron's tragedy of "Marino Faliero" [1614.13.5]. For the 15th century, Byron's tragedy of "The two Foscari" [1614.13.5], Guerrazzi's "Isabella Orsini" [336.9], and Shelley's tragedy of the "Cenci" [1613.11]. Guerrazzi's "Beatrice Cenci" [716.5] is a story of the latter part of the 16th century. For recent history, Charles Albert of Sardinia figures in Mrs. Jenkin's "Who breaks — pays" [313.3]; the revolution of 1848 is commemorated in Mrs. Browning's poem, "Casa Guidi windows" [1612.4.2]; and Garibaldi illustrates modern politics in "The rule of the monk" [521.18].

Shelf. No.

ITALY, *continued.*

Language and literature.

— Ahn, (J.) F. New practical and easy method of learning the Italian language. 1st and 2d course. London, 1861. 12° 2037.1
— Millhouse, J. New English-Italian and Italian-English dictionary. 4th edition. London, 1874. 2 v. Sm. 8° .... *R.R., F.3.11
— Monti, L. Grammar of the Italian language. Boston, 1855. 12° 2035.1
— Ollendorff, H. G. Key to the exercises in the new method of learning a language in six months. Adapted to the Italian. New York, 1849. 12° 2035.3
— – New method of learning the Italian language. New York, 1846. 12° 2034.1
— Prescott, W. H. Italian narrative poetry; Poetry and romance of the Italians. (*In his* Biographical and critical essays) .... 1537.8 and 5237.3
— Villemain, A. F. Tableau de la littérature au moyen âge en Italie. Paris, 1871. 2 v. 12° . 5537.11

Note. — For the 15th, 16th and 17th centuries, see Hallam's "Literature of Europe" [1531.2]. The English reader can have access to an English translation of Sismondi's "Literature of the south of Europe" [5927.10], which, though elegant and pleasing in manner, is sometimes adjudged superficial, though Hallam considers him otherwise. The English reader will find brief summaries in Longfellow's "Poets and poetry of Europe" [5922.1].

ITHACA, *N. Y.*, Scenery of. Spencer, S. Ithaca, 1866. 16° 417.4
ITINÉRAIRE d'Italie, ou la description des voyages par les routes plus fréquentées aux principales villes d'Italie. Avec cartes géographiques. 9e édition Milanoise, augmentée par P. J. V. Milan, 1817. xxxi, 260+ pp. Sm. 8° 2018.5
IVAN de Biron; or, the Russian court in the middle of last century. Helps, *Sir* A. Boston, 1874. Sm. 8° 738.11
— *Same.* Leipzig, 1874. 2 v. in 1. Sq. 16° 329.16
IVANHOE. Scott, *Sir* W. Boston 523.11
— *Same.* Leipzig 324.6
IVAR. Carlén, E. F. 521.16
IVORS. Sewell, E. M. 2 v. 527.22

JACK of all trades. Parker, R. A. 933.15
JACK Arcombe. Bradley, W. I. 913.5
JACK Hazard and his fortunes. Trowbridge, J. T. .. 915.15
JACK Hinton, the guardsman. Lever, C. (J.) Leipzig 332.21
— *Same.* London 516.17
JACK o' Lantern, The. Cooper, J. F. 310.12
JACK Tier. Cooper, J. F. 525.8
JACK's sister. Navers, D. 710.29
JACK's ward. Alger, H., *jr.* 1117.2
JACKSON, Andrew, Life of. Parton, J. New York, 1861. 3 v. 12° 1212.1
JACKSON, James. Another letter to a young physician [on the utility of medicine]: to which are appended some other medical papers. Boston, 1861. xii, 179 pp. 12° .... 6021.5 and 6036.1
— Letters to a young physician. Boston, 1855. iv, 344 pp. 12° 6036.16
— Memoir of James Jackson, jr. With extracts from his letters to his father; and medical cases collected by him. Boston, 1835. 444 pp. 8°. 5022.4
JACKSON, John, and CHATTO, W. A. Treatise on wood engraving, historical and practical. With illustrations. 2d edition. With a chapter on the artists of the present day by H. G. Bohn. London, 1866. xvi, 664 pp. 8° 6211.10
JACKSON, John Barnard Swett. Descriptive catalogue of the anatomical museum of the Boston society for medical improvement. Boston, 1847. xi, 352 pp. Plates. 8° 6022.3
JACKSON, Thomas Jonathan. Life. By an ex-cadet. 2d edition. Richmond, 1864. 196 pp. 16° ... 1013.6
— Stonewall Jackson: a military biography. Cooke, J. E. New York, 1866. Sm. 8° 1214.11
JACKSON family. Thayer, E. Family memorial. Hingham, 1835. 8° 611.2
JACOB Faithful. Marryat, F. 337.2

Shelf. N

JACOX, Francis. Aspects of authorship; or, book marks and book makers. London, 1872. 494+ pp. 16° .... 6136.
— Bible music: being variations, in many keys, on musical themes from Scripture. Boston, 1872. viii, 330 pp. 16° .... 6234.
JACQUEMART, Albert. History of ceramic art. A descriptive and philosophical study of the pottery of all ages and all nations. Woodcuts, engravings [etc.]. Translated by Mrs. Bury Palliser. London, 1873. 627 pp. L. 8° ...... 6231.
JACQUEMONT, Jacques. *See* MÉRIMÉE, P. Portraits historiques et littéraires. Paris, 1874. 12° ... 5527.1
JACQUERIE, The. A novel. James, G. P. R. .... 722.
JACQUES Bonneval; or, the days of the dragonnades. Manning, A. .... 738.
JAEGER, Abraham. Mind and heart in religion; or, Judaism and Christianity. New York, 1873. 295 pp. Sq. 16° 6326.2
JALOUSIE du barbouillé, La: comédie. Molière, J. B. P. Œuvres. Paris, 1869. 12° .... 5537.2.
JAMAICA PLAIN directory for 1873-4. Boston, 1873. 8° .... *R.R., E.2.
JAMES I, *king of England*, Inquiry into the character of. Disraeli, I. New York, 1868. Sm. 8° 1533.1
JAMES, George Payne Rainsford. Agincourt. [Turns on this battle, in Henry V's time] 327.1
— Agnes Sorel. A novel .... 730.
— The ancient régime. A tale 722.1
— Arabella Stuart. [English history, time of James I] 327.1
— Arrah Neil. [Time of the English commonwealth] 327.1
— Beauchamp .... 327.
— The castle of Ehrenstein .... 327.
— The convict .... 327.
— Corse de Leon; or, the brigand. A romance .... 722.
— Darnley: or, the field of the cloth of gold [1520]. 327.1
— The false heir .... 327.
— Forest days. [Robin Hood] 327.1
— The gipsy. [Time of George II] 327.1
— Gowrie; or, the king's plot .... 730.
— Heidelberg. [Thirty years' war in Germany] ... 327.
— Henry of Guise; or, the states of Blois 722.1
— Henry Smeaton: a Jacobite story of the reign of George I .... 730.
— History of Charlemagne. New York, 1860. 408 pp. Portrait. Wood-cuts. Sm. 12° .... 5528.
— History of Richard Cœur-de-Lion, king of England. New edition. London, 1854. 2 v. Portraits. Sm. 8° .... 5526.
— The Huguenot: a tale of the French protestants. 722.1
— The Jacquerie. A novel .... 722.
— Leonora d'Orco. A historical romance .... 730.
— Life and times of Louis XIV. New edition. London, 1851. 2 v. Portraits. Sm. 8° .... 5526.
— Life of Henry the fourth, king of France and Navarre. New York, 1855. 2 v. 12° 5525.1
— Mary of Burgundy; or, the revolt of Ghent 722.1
— Morley Ernstein 327.1
— Philip Augustus; or, the brothers in arms ..... 722.
— Rose d'Albret; or, troublous times. A romance. 730.
— Russell: a tale of the reign of Charles II. [Lord Russell, beheaded 1683] .... 327.
— Sir Theodore Broughton 327.1
— The smuggler .... 327.
— The step-mother .... 327.
— A whim, and its consequences .... 327.

Note. — See E. P. Whipple's review of James's novels [1936.2.1].

JAMES, Henry. Substance and shadow: an essay upon the physics of creation. Boston, 1863. x, 3-539 pp. 8° .... 5834.
JAMES, Henry, *jr.* Roderick Hudson. [Fiction] 723.2
— Transatlantic sketches. Boston, 1875. 401 pp. 12° .... 436.
JAMES, Thomas P. The mystery of Edwin Drood. Part second. *See* DICKENS, C. (J. H.) The mystery of Edwin Drood 732.3
JAMES Montjoy: or, I've been thinking. Roe, A. S. 735.3

Shelf. No.

JAMESON, Anna (Murphy). Diary of an ennuyée. From the last London edition. Boston, 1866. 341 pp. 1 plate. 16° ... 427.3

— Legends of the monastic orders, as represented in the fine arts. Corrected and enlarged edition. Boston, 1866. xv, 489 pp. Portrait. 16° ... 1517.7

— Memoirs of the early Italian painters. Boston, 1875. 352 pp. Portrait. Sq. 16° ... 6228.2

— Memoirs of the loves of the poets. Biographical sketches. From the last London edition. Boston, 1866. 517 pp. 1 plate. 16° ... 5618.2

— Sisters of charity, catholic and protestant. And The communion of labor. Boston, 1857. 302 pp. 12° ... 1538.16

— Sketches of art, literature, and character. Boston, 1866. 502 pp. 1 plate. 16° ... 5618.3

— Studies, stories, and memoirs. Boston, 1866. 408 pp. 1 plate. 16° ... 1916.3

JAMESON, Robert. Mineralogical notes. *See* CUVIER, Georges Léopold Chrétien Frédéric Dagobert, *baron* ... 6633.1

JAMESTOWN, Voyage of the, on her errand of mercy [to Ireland during the famine]. Forbes, R. B. Boston, 1847. 8° ... 421.4

JAN MAYAN, Voyage to, in 1856. Blackwood, F. T., *lord Dufferin*. Boston, 1859. 12° ... 225.3

JANE Eyre. Brontë, C. Leipzig ... 321.23

— *Same.* New York ... 735.29

JANET'S home. Keary, A. ... 717.15

JANET'S love and service. Robertson, M. M. ... 723.7

JAPAN. Adams, F. O. History of. Vol. I. To 1864. London, 1874. 8° ... 5911.6

— Dickson, W. Japan: being a sketch of the history, government and officers of the empire. Edinburgh, 1869. 8° ... 5931.2

— Hawkes, F. L. Narrative of the expedition of an American squadron to, 1852–54. New York, 1856. 8° ... 421.1

— Howland, E. With the Count de Beauvoir in. (*In* Many lands and many people) ... 431.3

— Humbert, A. Japan and the Japanese. New York, 1874. 4° ... 5920.5

— Jarves, J. J. A glimpse at the art of. New York, 1876. 16° ... 6234.7

— Mossman, S. New Japan, the land of the rising sun; its annals during the past twenty years, recording the remarkable progress of the Japanese in western civilization. London, 1873. 8°. 5922.9

— Oliphant, L. Narrative of the Earl of Elgin's mission to, 1857–59. New York, 1860. 8° ... 421.2

— Picture stories from the Japanese. Pictures drawn by native talent; with the stories in English rhyme. London [1874]. 8° ... 5920.3

— Taylor, (J.) B. Japan, in our day. New York, 1872. Sm. 8° ... 423.7

— – Visit to, in 1853. New York, 1864. 12° ... 425.7

JAPANESE, The, in America. Lanman, C. New York, 1872. 12° ... 5925.3

JAPHET in search of a father. Marryat, F. ... 337.6

JARVES, Deming. Reminiscences of glass-making. 2d edition, enlarged. New York, 1865. iv, 116 pp. Folded plate. 8° ... 6425.2

JARVES, James Jackson. Catalogue of [his] collection of early Italian pictures, deposited in the gallery of the Yale school of fine arts. Boston, 1871. 28 pp. 8° ... 6213.7

— Descriptive catalogue of "Old masters," collected by [him] to illustrate the history of painting from 1200 to the best periods of Italian art. Cambridge, 1860. 62 pp. 8° ... 6213.7

— A glimpse at the art of Japan. New York, 1876. 216+ pp. Illustrated. 16° ... 6234.7

JASPER. Abbott, J. Harper's story books ... 936.1.11

JAY, W. M. L., *pseud.* *See* WOODRUFF, Julia Louisa Matilda.

JAY, William. Review of the causes and consequences of the Mexican war. 4th edition. Boston, 1849. 333 pp. 12° ... 5017.2

— A view of the action of the federal government in behalf of slavery. New York, 1839. viii, 217 [205] pp. 12° ... 6316.1

Shelf. No.

JEAFFRESON, John Cordy. Annals of Oxford. London, 1871. 2 v. 8° ... 5433.3

— A book about doctors. Leipzig, 1870. 2 v. in 1. Sq. 16° ... 1238.16

— A book about the table. London, 1875. 2 v. 8°. 6432.3

— Brides and bridals. London, 1872. 2 v. 8° ... 5822.6

— Live it down. A novel ... 732.29

— Lottie Darling. A novel ... 732.15

— Not dead yet. A novel ... 732.25

— Olive Blake's good work. A novel ... 732.24

— A woman in spite of herself ... 311.20

JEAN. Newman, *Mrs.* — ... 720.40

JEAN et Jeannette. Gautier, T. Paris, 1863. 18°. 5536.2

JEANIE'S quiet life. Tabor, E. ... 711.27

JEDDO. Beauvoir, L., *comte* de. London, 1872. 16°. 5935.11

JEFFERSON, Thomas. Parker, T. Historic Americans. Boston, 1871. Sm. 8° ... 5025.4

— Parton, J. Life of. Boston, 1874. 8° ... 1215.1

— Randolph, S. N. The domestic life of. New York, 1872. Sm. 8° ... 5025.3

Note. — Sarah N. Randolph, a great-granddaughter, using family letters and reminiscences, published "The domestic life of Jefferson." For more on his private relations and opinions, see Webster's account of a visit to Monticello, in his "Private correspondence" [5020.2]. See also Harper's monthly, vol. 43. Parton has written the latest and an interesting biography. His political views are reviewed in Brougham's "Statesmen of the time of George III" [5614.4.5]; in Prof. A. D. White's essay on his opinions of slavery, in the Atlantic monthly, Jan., 1862; and in the lives of Washington, Adams, Hamilton, etc., and in Bancroft's "History of the United States." The paper by Theodore Parker is characteristic; and there are references to others in Allibone and Thomas's "Biographical dictionary." Numerous eulogies by Webster [5013.1.1], Everett [1921.1.1], and others will also be found. See also papers in Harper's monthly, vols. 3, 7, 26 and 43; and in vol. 44, on his relations to the University of Virginia.

JEFFREY, Francis, *lord*. Contributions to the Edinburgh review. New York, 1873. 762 pp. Portrait. [Modern British essayists.] 8° ... 5610.8

— Life of. Cockburn, H. T., *lord*. Edinburgh, 1872. Sm. 8° ... 5635.2.1

JENKIN, *Mrs.* C. Leisure hour series. Jupiter's daughters ... 518.21

— – Within an ace ... 539.10

— Madame de Baupré ... 517.15

— Once and again ... 318.2

— A Psyche of to-day ... 518.11

— Skirmishing ... 313.6

— Two French marriages ... 313.5

— "Who breaks — pays" ... 313.3

— Within an ace ... 313.4

JENKIN, Fleming. Electricity and magnetism. London, 1873. xii, 379+ pp. [Text-books of science.] Sm. 8° ... 6438.4

JENKINS, Edward. Ginx's baby, his birth and other misfortunes; [and] Lord Bantam ... 311.21

— Lord Bantam. A satire ... 536.21

Note. — Fiction, constituting satire on local English politics.

JENKINSON, Henry Irwin. Epitome of Lockhart's life of Scott. Edinburgh, 1873. xii, 388 pp. 8°. 5425.10

JENNESS, John Scribner. The Isles of Shoals. An historical sketch. New York, 1873. 182 pp. Illustrated. Portraits. Folded plates. 16° ... 818.2

JERDAN, William. Autobiography. With his literary, political, and social reminiscences and correspondence during the last fifty years. London, 1852, 53. 4 v. Portrait. 1 plate. 16° ... 5425.5

— Men I have known. Illustrated with facsimile autographs. London, 1866. ix, 490 pp. Sm. 8°. 5423.11

— Personal reminiscences. (*In* Stoddard, R. H. Bric-à-brac series) ... 1828.6

JERROLD, Douglas (William). Ambrose Gwinett: a melo-drama. New York, N. D. 35 pp. 12° .. 1635.4

— Fireside saints, Mr. Caudle's breakfast talk, and other papers. Now first collected [by J. E. Babson]. Boston, 1873. 357 pp. 16° ... 728.6

— History of St. Giles and St. James. Leipzig, 1852. 2 v. in 1. Sq. 16° ... 313.9

— Men of character. Leipzig, 1852. 2 v. in 1. Sq. 16° ... 313.8

— Mrs. Caudle's curtain lectures. New York, 1869. xviii, 195 pp. Illustrated. 16° ... 518.9

— Life and remains of. Jerrold, (W.) B. Boston, 1859. 12° ... 1227.3

Shelf. No.

JERROLD, (William) Blanchard. At home in Paris: at peace and at war. London, 1871. 2 v. 16°. 5526.12

— The best of all good company. A day with Charles Dickens. Boston, 1873. 80 pp. Portrait. Fac-simile. 16° 1215.3

— Life and remains of Douglas Jerrold. Boston, 1859. xvi, 450 pp. Portrait. 12° 1227.3

— Life of Napoleon III. Derived from state records, from unpublished family correspondence, and from personal testimony. With portraits and fac-similes of letters. Vol. I, II. London, 1874, 75. 2 v. 8° 5522.3

Contents. — Vol. I. Birth, youth, and education; The Italian insurrection; Arenenberg. II. Between Strasburg and Boulogne; Ham; The revolution of 1848.

JERRY. Simonds, W.......................... 932.27

JERRY Jarvis's wig. Barham, R. H. (*In* Johnson, (E.) R. Little classics)........................ 529.4.4

JERUSALEM. Besant, W., and Palmer, E. H. Jerusalem, the city of Herod and Saladin. London, 1871. 8°.................................. 5924.3

— Creagh, J. A scamper to. London, 1873. 8°. 5931.10

— Warren, I. P. Jerusalem, ancient and modern. Boston [*cop.* 1873]. 8°...................... 821.6

— Wilson, C. W., and others. The recovery of. New York, 1872. 8° 5933.1

See also Palestine.

NOTE ON JERUSALEM.

History. For the ancient period, beside the record of the Bible and Josephus [5923.5], the general reader will find the Old Testament and New Testament histories in Dr. Smith's series of Student's histories the most convenient, for more extended accounts than are given in Smith's "Bible dictionary" and the cyclopædias of McClintock and Strong [elaborate article] and Kitto; in chapter 4 of "Our work in Palestine" [423.10; 5915.6], and others. The story of the siege and destruction by Titus has been told among moderns by Milman, in books 14 and 15 of his "History of the Jews" [5927.1]; and by Merivale, in his Romans, chap. 59 of 6th book [5515.3]. There is an illustrative historical tale in Whyte-Melville's "Gladiators" [321.15]. After the histories of the crusades, of which Tasso's "Jerusalem delivered" [5537.1] is a poetic illustration, Gibbon and the eastern histories come next, in detail. See James's "History of Richard Coeur-de-Lion" [5526.7] for the story in part of the crusading period. Besant's "City of Herod and Saladin" [5924.3] covers the post biblical period, A. D. 33 to our day, and the author "studiously avoids things ecclesiastical;" giving chap. 5 to Christian pilgrimages, and chap. 7 to the Christian kingdom of Jerusalem, A. D. 1099, etc. See also Palestine, *note.*

Topography. Peculiarly in regard to Jerusalem the record of topographical discovery is closely allied with the expansion of our historical knowledge of the city and its vicissitudes. The reader may trace the literature of this subject in the Lower Hall Catalogue of history, etc. The general reader will find a very good summary of antagonistic theories regarding the walls of ancient Jerusalem, and the position of the Holy sepulchre, in Murray's Handbook [5936.1]. Fergusson has advanced peculiar views in identifying Mount Zion with the site of the sepulchre, in an essay which originally appeared in Smith's "Bible dictionary," where, in Hackett and Abbot's edition, he is carefully controverted by Dr. Wolcott. There is a paper on the site of Solomon's temple in Scribner's monthly, Dec., 1875. Porter, the editor of Murray, has a section on Jerusalem, in his "Giant cities of Bashan" [5915.7]. The recent theories about the site of the Temple are stated in chapter 8 of "Our work in Palestine" [423.10; 5915.6]. Ritter's methods of connecting history and geography are given with sufficient exactness for the general reader in Burt's "The land and its story" [421.8], which has a chapter on Jerusalem.

The great promoter of this study in England has been Dean Stanley, who devotes the third chapter of his "Sinai and Palestine," 1853 [5923.1], to Jerusalem; and though his book is too scholarly for the most popular use, its reputation is high with all interested in developing the sacred history by its connection with the sacred geography, while his care for detail makes him very interesting. See references under Stanley in Allibone. A chapter on Jerusalem is given in the 2d volume of Thomson's "Land and the Book" [224.5], who, as a missionary for twenty-five years, had unusual opportunities for studying the manners and customs of the people, and has done much to popularize the subject. The reader will not forget *popular and recent* accounts in Hepworth Dixon's "Holy Land" [428.1]; Thackeray, in his "Cornhill to Cairo" [513.1.7]; Creagh's "Scamper" [5931.10]; W. C. Prime's "Holy city," in Harper's monthly, vol. 14; and E. D. G. Prime's "Round the world" [233.1].

The most elaborate of recent topographical surveys we owe to the Palestine exploration fund of England. The government of Great Britain aided them by detailing engineers to make the most thorough explorations and survey of Jerusalem, and the result is an admirable work, with every advantage of engraving and photography on a large scale, which can be seen in the Bates Hall. The Fund have for some years issued a quarterly statement by which the biblical student could follow the advances of science; and to epitomize results and present the general reader with a complete review of what had been accomplished, they lately (1870) issued "The recovery of Jerusalem" [5933.1, — see Harper's monthly, vol. 43], which is the best summary of existing knowledge that the reader can avail himself of; to be found, however, more condensed in the more recent "Our work in Palestine" [423.10; 5915.6]. See also Blackwood's magazine, under "Explorations," 1873. I. P. Warren's "Jerusalem, ancient and modern" [821.6], is a compact resumé of existing knowledge. Hackett and Abbot's edition of Smith's "Bible dictionary" and McClintock and Strong's Cyclopædia give elaborate summaries of all the topographical data.

Many of the works mentioned under East (The) and Palestine afford sections on Jerusalem.

Shelf. No.

JERUSALEM delivered. [Poem.] Tasso, T. New York, 1871. 12° 5537.1

JERVIS, H. W. The student's France. History of France. From the earliest times to the establishment of the second empire in 1852. Illustrated. New York, 1872 [1862]. xii, 730 pp. [The student's series.] 12° 824.13

JERVIS, William Henley. The Gallican church. A history of the church of France, from the concordat of Bologna, 1516, to the revolution. With portraits. London, 1872. 2 v. 8° 1531.8

JESSAMINE. Terhune, M. V. 735.28

JESSE, John Heneage. London: its celebrated characters and remarkable places. London, 1871. 3 v. Illustrated. Sm. 8°.................. 5435.3

— Memoirs of the pretenders and their adherents. New edition. London, 1860. xii, 564 pp. Portraits. Sm. 8° 5426.14

JESSIE. Simonds, W.......................... 932.25

JESSIE Carlton. Wise, D......................... 932.01

JESSIE Trim. Farjeon, B. L. 710.33

JESSIE's parrot. Mathews, J. H..................1117.31

JESSUP, Henry Harris. Syrian home-life. [Edited] by Isaac Riley. New York [1874]. 366 pp. Illustrated. 12° 5916.10

— The women of the Arabs. With a chapter for children. Edited by C. S. Robinson and Isaac Riley. New York [1873]. x, 372+ pp. Illustrated. 12°............................... 5916.6

JESUITS. The Jesuits in North America in the seventeenth century. Parkman, F., *jr.* Boston, 1872. 12°.....................................5015.5.2

Shelf. No.

JESUITS, *continued.*

Note. — There is a list of books on the Jesuits in Fisher's "Reformation" [5813.7].

The English reader will find chapters in Ranke's "History of the popes" [5516.7] the best for an ordinary purpose, and may compare Macaulay's review [1918.4.3]. Ranke covers the sixteenth and seventeenth centuries only. Martin's "Decline of the French monarchy" covers their suppression in France.

On Loyola and the early Jesuits there is an essay by Stephen [1931.1], also Harper's monthly, vol. 39.

Disraeli, in his "Amenities of literature" [1533.13], has a paper on the first Jesuits in England.

On the labors of the order in America, their own "Relations" have afforded most valuable historical material to Parkman, whose series of monographs on "France and England in North America" [5015.5], are necessary to a thorough comprehension of their career as missionaries and explorers, while the account given by Bancroft, in his "History of the United States" [5012.3], outlines their record with sufficient fulness for the general reader. See Dixon's "White conquest" [439.5] for the order in the West.

See the article in McClintock and Strong's Cyclopædia; and a concise statement from a protestant point of view in book 6 of Robertson's "Charles V" [1226.9]. Catholic authorities favorable to the order can best be looked up in the Bates Hall.

JESUS. *See* CHRIST.

JETTATRICE. Craven, P. 720.5

JEVONS, William Stanley. Money and the mechanism of exchange. New York, 1875. xviii, 349 pp. [International scientific series.] 12°.... 5826.8

JEWELRY. Manuel du bijoutier, du joaillier [etc.]. Fontenelle, J. de. Paris, 1832. 2 v. 24° 6219.2

JEWESS, The. Halévy, J. F. F. É. (*In* Ditson, O., and co. Standard opera librettos) 6233.3.1

JEWETT, *Mrs.* S. W. From fourteen to fourscore ... 714.26

JEWITT, Llewellyn, and HALL, Samuel Carter. The stately homes of England. Illustrated. London, 1874. xi, 399 pp. 4°................... 5434.2

Shelf. No.

JEWS. Adams, H. History of the Jews from the destruction of Jerusalem to the 19th century. Boston, 1812. 2 v. in 1. 12° 828.12
— Aguilar, G. The women of Israel. New York, 1872. 2 v. 12° 1226.19
— Ewald, (G.) H. (A.) History of Israel. London, 1869–74. 5 v. 8° 5813.15
— Frey, J. S. C. F. Judah and Israel: or, the restoration and conversion of the Jews and ten tribes. New York, 1840. 12° 6327.2
— Home, The, and the synagogue of the modern Jew. London [1873]. Sq. 16° 5818.1
— Milman, H. H. History of the. London, 1866. 3 v. 16° 5927.1
— Palfrey, J. G. Academical lectures on the Jewish Scriptures and antiquities. Vol. I. Boston, 1838. 8° 5811.8
— Sharpe, S. History of the Hebrew nation, and its literature. London, 1876. Sm. 8° 5928.3
— Tappan, D. Lectures on Jewish antiquities. Boston, 1807. 8° 1912.7

Note. — Milman's early editions were published over thirty years ago, and his book has maintained a reputation for scholarly candor and accuracy, with picturesque presentation, but he incurred some detraction for his critical examination of the historic truth in the sacred records. His revised edition is enlarged principally in the later periods, and gives the authorities, which of late years have added to our knowledge; and, in a preface, which he thinks will suit neither extreme, the author reaffirms his previous views on the duty of an historian. Both Milman and Stanley acknowledge great indebtedness to Ewald [5813.15], who first brought that critical spirit to the task, which had so rewarded Wolf and Niebuhr in the history of Greece and Rome. Though his conclusions are not always adopted, nor his statements invariably agreed to, his work, for the period before the commencement of the monarchy, B. C. 1095, is the most comprehensive, and his successors only except a certain dogmatism in his opinions from their general praise. Bunsen's "God in history" [5813.13] is written on a speculative, conjectural system, that does not commend itself to sturdy truth-seekers like Milman. Sharpe's "History of the nation and its literature" [5928.3] is the latest English contribution.

The general reader will find Dr. Smith's Old Testament history a sufficient narrative down to about B. C. 400, when Josephus [5923.5] and the Roman historians take up the story. Smith's New Testament history, which substantially closes A. D. 70, is prefaced by a cursory sketch bridging the interval between the old and new record. See Froude's essay on criticism and the gospel history, in his "Short studies" [1914.5.1].

Lessing's "Nathan the wise" [1613.6; 5737.1] was a protest against uncharitable views of the Jewish character; and Disraeli in some of his novels has delineated the Jewish character to disarm prejudice. The same may be said of Miss Sheppard's "Charles Auchester" [532.1] and "Counterparts" [531.19]. There is a paper in Harper's monthly, vol. 49, on "The Jews and their persecutors." Macaulay has an essay [1918.4] on their "Civil disabilities" in England; and Parton, in his "Topics of the time" [1935.3], tells of the "Israelitish Brethren" in America. The story of their expulsion from Spain is told in Prescott's "Ferdinand and Isabella" [5922.5, ch. xvii], and this event is illustrated in Grace Augilar's "Vale of cedars" [533.17].

Judaism. See Baring-Gould's "Origin and development of religious belief," and Clarke's "Ten great religions" [1523.2].

Literature. Sharpe [5928.3] treats of the literature in connection with the history.

Milman praises the article by Cassel in Ersch and Gruber's German encyclopædia; and ordinary readers will very likely be satisfied with the articles in McClintock and Strong, and in Chambers's Encyclopædia.

There are some well-known prose works of the imagination in illustration of Jewish history; W. Ware's "Julian" [736.5], closing with the crucifixion; J. H. Ingraham's "Prince of the house of David" [512.5], presenting Jerusalem under Herod; F. A. Strauss's "Helons Wallfahrt nach Jerusalem," also published as "The glory of the house of Israel" [425 14], depicting the life and manners of the first century before Christ; Whyte-Melville's "Gladiators" [321.15], the fall of Jerusalem. For others, see Chronological list of historical fiction.

JOACHIM, v. Kamern. Nathusius, M. 314.12
JOAN Merryweather. Saunders, K. 339.20
JOAN OF ARC. *See* DARC, Jeanne.
JOANNA of Naples. Hall, L. J. Boston, 1850. 12°. 5216.3
JOCELYN's mistake. Spender, *Mrs.* J. K. 720.17
JOHANNES Olaf. Wille, E. de 737.14
JOHN III (*John Sobieski*), *king of Poland*. Love of country, or Sobieski. Salvandy, N. A., *comte* de. Boston, 1856. 12° 916.11
JOHN, Eugenie. (*E. Marlitt.*) The countess Gisela. From the German by Mrs. A. L. Wister 537.7
— Gold Elsie. From the German by Mrs. A. L. Wister 517.17
— Das Haideprinzesschen. Leipzig, 1872. 2 v. 16° 5736.3
— The old mam'selle's secret. After the German by Mrs. A. L. Wister 517.16
— Over yonder 712.3
— The princess of the moor 319.3

Shelf. No.

JOHN, Eugenie, *continued.*
— Reichsgräfin Gisela. 4te Auflage. Leipzig, 1874. 2 v. 16° 5736.2
— The second wife. From the German by Mrs. A. L. Wister 726.25
— Magdalena. [And] The lonely ones. By Paul Heyse 710.25
JOHN Andross. Davis, R. H. 737.33
JOHN Brent. Winthrop, T. 537.20
JOHN Bull in America; or, the new Munchausen. Paulding, J. K. New York, 1825. 12° 538.11
JOHN Dorrien. Kavanagh, J. Leipzig. 3 v. in 2. 330.19
— *Same.* New York 714.20
JOHN Godfrey's fortunes. Taylor, (J.) B. 716.36
JOHN Godsoe's legacy. Kellogg, E. 922.29
JOHN Halifax, gentleman. Craik, D. (M.) 330.1
JOHN Jago's ghost. Collins, (W.) W. 319.25
JOHN Law, the projector. [Historical romance.] Ainsworth, W. H. 322.14
JOHN Marchmont's legacy. Braddon, M. E. 325.9
JOHN Paul's book. Webb, C. H. Hartford, 1874. 8°. 1531.4
JOHN True. Abbott, J. Harper's story books 936.1.6
JOHN Whopper the newsboy. Clark, T. M. 926.28
JOHN Worthington's name. Benedict, F. L. 731.30
JOHNNY Darbyshire. Howitt, W. (*In* Johnson, (E.) R. Little classics) 529.4.9
JOHNNY Ludlow 329.27
JOHNS, Bennett George. Blind people: their works and ways; with sketches of the lives of some famous blind men. Illustrated. London, 1867. xii, 196 pp. Sm. 8° 5428.7
JOHNSON, Andrew. The great impeachment and trial of Andrew Johnson. With the preliminary proceedings [etc.]. With portraits. Philadelphia [*cop.* 1868]. 289 [281] pp. 8° 5011.14
— Trial on [his] impeachment. *See* UNITED STATES. *Miscellaneous documents* 5010.4
JOHNSON, Anna C. Peasant life in Germany. 4th edition. New York, 1859. 430 pp. 12° 827.9
JOHNSON, (Edwin) Rossiter, *editor.* Little classics. Boston, 1874, 75. 16 v. Sq. 16° 529.4

Contents. — Vol. I. Exile: Ethan Brand, by N. Hawthorne; The swans of Lir, by G. Griffin; A night in a workhouse, by J. Greenwood; The outcasts of Poker Flat, by Bret Harte; The man without a country, by E. E. Hale; Flight of a Tartar tribe, by T. De Quincey.

Vol. II. Intellect: The house and the brain, by E. Bulwer Lytton; D'outre mort, by H. P. Spofford; The fall of the house of Usher, by E. A. Poe; Chops, the dwarf, by C. Dickens; Wakefield, by N. Hawthorne; Murder, considered as one of the fine arts, by T. De Quincey; The captain's story, by R. H. Davis.

Vol. III. Tragedy: The murders in the Rue Morgue, by E. A. Poe; The Lauson tragedy, by J. W. De Forest; The iron shroud, by W. Mudford; The bell-tower, by H. Melville; The Kathayan slave, by E. C. Judson; The story of La Roche, by H. Mackenzie; The vision of sudden death, by T. De Quincey.

Vol. IV. Life: Rab and his friends, by J. Brown, M. D.; A romance of real life, by W. D. Howells, The luck of Roaring camp, by Bret Harte; Jerry Jarvis's wig, by R. H. Barham; Beauty and the beast, by N. P. Willis; David Swan, by N. Hawthorne; Dreamthorp, by A. Smith; A bachelor's revery, by D. G. Mitchell; The grammar of life, by B. F. Taylor; My château, by G. W. Curtis; Dream children, by C. Lamb; The man in the reservoir, by C. F. Hoffman; Westminster abbey, by J. Addison; The puritans, by T. B. Macaulay; Gettysburg, by A. Lincoln.

Vol. V. Laughter: A Christmas carol, by C. Dickens; The haunted crust, by K. Saunders; A dissertation upon roast pig, by C. Lamb; The total depravity of inanimate things, by Mrs. E. A. Walker; The skeleton in the closet, by E. E. Hale; Sandy Wood's sepulchre, by H. Miller; A visit to the asylum for aged and decayed punsters, by O. W. Holmes; Mr. Tibbot O'Leary, the curious, by G. Griffin; Neal Malone, by W. Carleton.

Vol. VI. Love: Love and skates, by T. Winthrop; The maid of Malines, by E. Bulwer Lytton; The story of Ruth, from the Bible; The rise of Iskander, by B. Disraeli.

Vol. VII. Romance: Iris, by O. W. Holmes; The Rosicrucian, by D. M. M. Craik; The South breaker, by H. P. Spofford; The snow-storm, by J. Wilson; The king of the peak, by A. Cunningham.

Vol. VIII. Mystery: The ghost, by W. D. O'Connor; The four-fifteen express, by A. B. Edwards; The signal-man, by C. Dickens; The haunted ships, by A. Cunningham; A raft that no man made, by R. T. S. Lowell; The invisible princess, by F. O'Connor; The advocate's wedding-day, by C. Crowe; The birthmark, by N. Hawthorne.

Vol. IX. Comedy: Barny O'Reirdon the navigator, by S. Lover; Haddad-Ben-Ahab the traveller, by J. Galt; Bluebeard's ghost, by W. M. Thackeray; The picnic party, by H. Smith; Father Tom and the pope, by S. Ferguson; Johnny Darbyshire, by W. Howitt; The gridiron, by S. Lover; The box tunnel, by C. Reade.

Vol. X. Childhood: A dog of Flanders, by L. de la Ramé; The king of the Golden river, by J. Ruskin; The Lady of Shalott, by E. S. Phelps; Marjorie Fleming, by J. Brown, M. D.; Little Jakey, by Mrs. S. H. De Kroyft; The lost child, by H. Kingsley; Goody Gracious! and the forget-me-not, by

Shelf. No.

JOHNSON, (Edwin) Rossiter. Little classics, *cont'd.*

J. Neal; A faded leaf of history, by R. H. Davis; A child's dream of a star, by C. Dickens.

Vol. XI. Heroism: Little Briggs and I, by F. H. Ludlow; Ray, by H. P. Spofford; Three November days, by B. F. Taylor; The forty-seven Rônins, by A. B. Mitford; A chance child, by I. (F.) Mayo; A leaf in the storm, by L. de la Ramé.

Vol. XII. Fortune: The gold-bug, by E. A. Poe; The fairy-finder, by S. Lover; Murad the unlucky, by M. Edgeworth; The children of the public, by E. E. Hale; The rival dreamers, by J. Banim; The threefold destiny, by N. Hawthorne.

Vol. XIII. Poems narrative: The deserted village, by O. Goldsmith; The ancient mariner, by S. T. Coleridge; The prisoner of Chillon, by Lord Byron; Bingen on the Rhine, by C. Norton; O'Connor's child, by T. Campbell; The culprit fay, by J. R. Drake; The sensitive plant, by P. B. Shelley; The eve of St. Agnes, by J. Keats; Paradise and the peri, by T. Moore; The raven, by E. A. Poe; The skeleton in armor, by H. W. Longfellow; The haunted house, by T. Hood; The writing on the image, by W. Morris; Tam O'Shanter, by R. Burns; The forging of the anchor, by S. Ferguson; Morte d'Arthur, by A. Tennyson; Horatius, by T. B. Macaulay.

Vol. XIV. Poems lyrical. XV. Minor poems. XVI. Authors. Biographical sketches of the authors represented in the series. With a general index.

JOHNSON, Elizabeth. Exercises for private devotion. 2d edition. Boston, 1845. 126 pp. 16° 5819.7

JOHNSON, Helen Kendrick. Roddy's reality 1117.15

— Roddy's romance 937.30

JOHNSON, Joseph. Traditions and reminiscences chiefly of the American revolution in the South: including biographical sketches, incidents and anecdotes. Charleston, 1851. viii, 592 pp. Folded plates. Fac-similes. 8° 812.11

JOHNSON, Samuel, *LL. D.* Works. New edition, with an essay on his life and genius, by A. Murphy. London, 1862. 2 v. Portrait. 8°. 5422.3

Contents. — Vol. I. Essay on his life and genius; The rambler; The idler; Lives of the poets. II. Rasselas; Miscellaneous.

— Lives of the English poets. Leipzig, 1858. 2 v. in 1. Sq. 16° 1238.20

Contents. — Cowley; Denham; Milton; Butler; Wilmot; Dillon; Otway; Waller; Pomfret; Sackville; Stepney; J. Philips; Walsh; Dryden; Smith; Duke; King; Sprat; Montague; Parnell; Garth; Rowe; Addison; Hughes; Sheffield; Prior; Congreve; Blackmore; Fenton; Gay; Granville; Yalden; Tickell; Hammond; Somerville; Savage; Swift; Broome; Pope; Pitt; Thomson; Watts; A. Philips; West; Collins; Dyer; Shenstone; Young; Mallet; Akenside; Gray; Lyttleton.

— Boswell, J. Life of. London, 1831. 5 v. 8°. 5423.7

— *Same.* London, N. D. 4 v. 16° 1225.12

- Macaulay, T. B., *lord.* Biography of. (*In his* New biographies of illustrious men) 5428.4

Note. — Boswell's Life is the most famous, and in many respects the best biography in the language, and Croker's edition is the best, notwithstanding the severity with which Macaulay reviewed it in his Essays [1918.4.1]; while the latter's biographical sketch shows the author at his best for brilliant characterization. Carlyle, also, reviews Croker's edition, in his Essays [5610.7], and characterizes Johnson in his "Heroes and hero-worship" [1535.19]. Arthur Murphy's well-known essay on Johnson's life and genius is usually prefixed to the works [5422.3]. Scott's is the best of the briefer lives, in his "Lives of the novelists" [5914.2], and there is a notice in Brougham's "Men of letters" [5614.4.2], and much relating to Johnson in Forster's "Life of Goldsmith" [1022.1]. Also see Hawthorne's "Lichfield and Uttoxeter" in "Our old home" [1839.2; 5439.1]. See Jeaffreson's "Brides and bridals" [5822.6], on his marriage relations; and Harper's monthly, vol. 14. The article in Allibone is elaborate and refers to the principal sources of biography and criticism.

JOHNSON, *Rev.* Samuel. Oriental religions and their relation to universal religion. India. Boston, 1873. vi, 802 pp. 8° 5811.3

JOHNSON, Virginia W. The Calderwood secret. A novel 721.6

— The Catskill fairies. [Juvenile] 910.2

— A sack of gold. A novel 710.20

JOHNSON, *Sir* William, Life and times of. Stone, W. L. Albany, 1865. 2 v. 8° 5022.6

JOHNSON, William, *editor.* The practical draughtsman's book of industrial design, and machinist's and engineer's drawing companion. From the French of [Jacques Eugène] Armengaud, [Charles] Armengaud, and [Jules] Amouroux. Philadelphia, 1873. 200 pp. 54 plates. Illustrated. 4° 6420.2

JOHNSTON, James F. W. The chemistry of common life. Illustrated. 12th edition. New York, 1871. 2 v. 12° 1526.27

Notes on North America. Boston, 1851. 2 v. 16°. 1524.5

Shelf. No.

JOHNSTON, Joseph Eccleston. Narrative of military operations, directed [by him] during the late war between the states. Illustrated. New York, 1874. 602 pp. 8° 813.18

JOINERY. The boy joiner. Davidson, E. A. London [1874]. 4° 1512.3

JOINTS. Brodie, *Sir* B. C. Observations on the diseases of the. Boston, 1842. 8° 6023.16

— Cooper, *Sir* A. (P.) Treatise on dislocations and fractures of the. Boston, 1844. 8° 6021.3

JOLLY good times. Smith, M. P. W. 1117.8

JOLY, Guy, Mémoires de. Gondi, J. F. P. de. Paris, 1817. 12° ....Vol. 5, 6 of 5528.4

JONATHAN. A novel. Tytler, C. C. F. 517.22

JONES, Agnes Elizabeth, Memorials of. Higinbotham, J. M. New York, 1872. Sm. 8° 5427.8

JONES, *Mrs.* C. S., and WILLIAMS, Henry T. Household elegancies. Suggestions in household art and tasteful home decorations. New York, 1875. 300+ pp. Illustrated. 8° 1512.4

— Ladies' fancy work. Hints and helps to home taste and recreations. Vol. 3. Williams' household series. New York, 1876. 300 pp. Illustrated. 8° 1512.6

JONES, Charles H., *editor.* Appletons' Hand-book of American travel. Southern tour. With maps. New York, 1873. 259 pp. 12° 413.5

— *editor and compiler.* Vers de société, selected from recent authors. With illustrated title and vignettes. New York, 1875. xvi, 401 pp. 8°. 5631.3

JONES, Charles Henry. Davault's mills. A novel. 722.4

JONES, Henry. The laws and principles of whist illustrated by hands played completely through. By Cavendish [*pseud.*]. 10th edition. London, 1874. xi, 268 pp. 16° 6418.2

JONES, (Henry) Bence. Life and letters of Faraday. Philadelphia, 1870. 2 v. Illustrated. Portrait. 8° 5423.4

— The Royal institution [of Great Britain]: its founder and its first professors. London, 1871. x, 431 pp. Sm. 8° 5814.10

JONES, (John) Paul. Abbott, J. S. C. Life and adventures of. New York [1874]. 12° 1014.12

— Mackenzie, A. S. Life of. New York [*cop.* 1841]. 2 v. 16° 1228.6

JONES, Joseph S. Life of Jefferson S. Batkins, member from Cranberry centre. Boston [*cop.* 1871]. 496 pp. Portrait. 12° 537.1

JONES, Joseph Seawell. A defence of the revolutionary history of North Carolina from the aspersions of Mr. Jefferson. Boston, 1834. xii, 343 pp. 12° 816.11

JONES, Justin. Virginia Graham 732.21

JONES, Owen. The grammar of ornament. Illustrated by examples from various styles of ornament. 112 plates. London, 1868. 157+ pp. F° 6230.2

JONES, William. The treasures of the earth; or, mines, minerals and metals, with anecdotes of men who have been connected with mining. New York, 1872. xii, 404 pp. Illustrated. 16°. 6635.1

JONSON, Ben. Works. With memoir by William Gifford. New edition. London, 1873. viii, 819 pp. Portrait. 8° 5621.3

JORDAN, William Leighton. The ocean: its tides and currents and their causes. London, 1873. xxiv, 344 pp. 14 plates. 8° 6633.3

JORDAN, The Rob Roy on the. Macgregor, J. New York, 1870. Sm. 8° 423.17

JOSEPH BONAPARTE, *successively king of Naples and of Italy,* History of. Abbott, J. S. C. 914.33

JOSEPH II and his court. Mundt, C. (M.) 531.36

JOSEPH and his friend. Taylor, (J.) B. 736.2

JOSEPH the Jew. The story of an old house. New York, 1874. 131 pp. 12° 732.4

JOSEPHINE, Marie Rose Tascher de la Pagerie, *empress of the French.* Abbott, J. S. C. History of. 914.3

— Le Normand, M. A. Historical and secret memoirs of. Philadelphia, 1852, 54. 2 v. 12°. 1224.

— Memes, J. S. Memoirs of. New York, 1855. 16° 1228.4

Shelf. No.

Josephus, Flavius. Works. With a life written by himself. Translated from the original Greek. Including explanatory notes and observations by William Whiston. With a complete index. New York, 1870. 4 v. Portrait. 12° 5923.5

Josh Billings, his sayings. Shaw, H. W. New York, 1871. 12° 725.16

Joshua Marvel. Farjeon, B. L. 521.9

Journal, The, of a home life. Sewell, E. M. Leipzig, 1867. 2 v. in 1. Sq. 16° 314.19

Journalism in the United States, from 1690 to 1872. Hudson, F. New York, 1873. 8° 5214.2

Journey, A, to the centre of the earth. Verne, J. New York [1871]. 12° 733.7

Jouy, Victor Joseph Étienne de. L'hermite de la chaussée-d'Antin, ou observations sur la mœurs et les usages français au commencement du XIXe siècle. 8e édition, ornée de gravures et vignettes. Paris, 1815–18. 5 v. 12° 5518.2

— L'hermite en province, ou observations sur les mœurs et les usages français au commencement du XIXe siècle. 4e édition, ornée de doux gravures et de vignettes. Paris, 1818. 3 v. 12°. 5518.4

Jowett, Benjamin. Essays. (*In* Noyes, G. R. Collection of theological essays) 6325.12

— On the interpretation of Scripture. (*In* Essays and reviews) 1538.3

— *Same.* (*In* Hedge, F. H. Recent inquiries in theology) ....1526.4 and 5814.15

Joyce, Robert Dwyer. Legends of the wars in Ireland. Boston, 1868. 352 pp. 16° 828.6

Joynson, Francis Herbert. The metals used in construction. Illustrated. Edinburgh, 1868. 124+ pp. 16° 6637.1

Judah and Israel. Frey, J. S. C. F. New York, 1840. 12° 6327.2

Judaism. Mind and heart in religion; or, Judaism and Christianity. Jaeger, A. New York, 1873. Sq. 16° 6326.22

Judd, Sylvester. Margaret............................ 535.13

Judea, Julian; or, scenes in. Ware, W. New York, 1869. 2 v. 12° 736.5

Judge Justin. Abbott, J. Harper's story books.936.1.11

Judson, Adoniram. Page, H. A. Noble workers. London, 1875. Sm. 8° 5936.3

— Wayland, F. Memoir of. Boston, 1853. 2 v. 12° 1214.10

Judson, Emily (Chubbuck). (*Fanny Forrester.*) The Kathayan slave. (*In* Johnson, (E.) R. Little classics) 529.4.3

— My two sisters [Lavinia and Harriet Chubbuck]: a sketch from memory. Boston, 1854. 112 pp. 1 plate. 16° 1216.1

Julian; or, scenes in Judea. Ware, W. New York, 1869. 2 v. 12° 736.5

Julius; or, the street boy out West. Alger, H., *jr.* 934.32

Julius Africanus. *See* Hippolytus, *St.*

Julius Cæsar. *See* Cæsar, Caius Julius.

Jullien, Charles Édouard, and Valerio, Oscar. Nouveau manuel complet du chaudronnier. Orné de figures. Paris, 1846. 304 [299] pp. 24°. [Manuel Roret] 6439.3

Jungfrau, Die, von Orleans. Schiller, (J. C.) F. von. Werke. Stuttgart, 1865. 8° 5734.1.5

Junius, *pseud.* Letters. Added, his confidential correspondence with Mr. Wilkes, and his private letters to H. S. Woodfall. New and enlarged edition. By John Wade. London, 1873. 2 v. Fac-simile. [Bohn's Standard library.] Sm. 8°. 5637.3

Contents. — Vol. I. The entire work as originally published, with illustrative notes. II. Private and miscellaneous letters, and a new essay on the authorship.

Junot, Laure Permon, *duchesse d'Abrantes.* Memoirs of Napoleon, his court and family. With portraits. New York, 1873. 2 v. 8° 5523.5

Jupiter's daughters. Jenkin, *Mrs.* C. 518.21

Justice. Recherches historiques du juste et de l'autorité. Philosophie appliquée. Mailfer, H. C. Paris, 1873. 2 v. 8° 6332.1

Justification, Lectures on the doctrine of. Newman, J. H. New York, 1874. 16° 6326.12

Shelf. No.

Justinianus I, *emperor.* The Institutes of Justinian with English introduction, translation, and notes by T. C. Sandars. 5th edition. London, 1874. lxxiv, 593 pp. 8° 6314.1

Justinus, Nepos, Cornelius, and Eutropius. [Works.] Literally translated, with notes and a general index. By J. S. Watson. London, 1872. xvi, 551 pp. [Bohn's Classical library.] Sm. 8° 6117.10

Justinus *Martyr*, and Athenagoras. Writings. Translated by M. Dods, G. Keith, and B. P. Pratten. Edinburgh, 1867. 465+ pp. [Ante-Nicene Christian library.] 8° 6322.4.2

Jutland series. *See* Kingston, William H. G.

Juvenalis, Decimus Junius. Fifth satire. *See* Homerus 6118.11

— Juvenal [outlined and explained]. Walford, E. Edinburgh, 1872. 16° 6116.15

Juvenile lyre: or hymns and songs set to music for the use of schools. Boston, 1836. 72 pp. 12° 1623.2

Juventis mundi. [Homeric age.] Gladstone, W. E. Boston, 1869. Sm. 8° 1523.9

Kabale und Liebe. Schiller, (J. C.) F. von. Werke. Stuttgart, 1865. 8° 5734.1.2

Kabylia, The Roumi in. (*In* Many lands and many people) 431.3

Kaleidoscope, The, its history, theory, and construction. Brewster, *Sir* D. London, 1870. Sm. 8° 6816.1

Kames, *Lord.* *See* Home, Henry.

Kampen, Nicolas Godfried van. History and topography of Holland and Belgium. Translated by W. G. Fearnside. Illustrated. London, N. D. iv, 204 pp. 8° 5931.19

Kane, Elisha Kent. Arctic explorations: the second Grinnell expedition in search of Sir John Franklin, 1853–55. Illustrated. Philadelphia, 1856. 2 v. 8° 422.2

— *Same.* With a biographical sketch of the author, by C. W. Shields. Illustrated. Hartford, 1871. Portrait. 766 pp. 8° 5912.4

Kangaroo hunters, The. Bowman, A. 938.14

Kansas. Hale, E. E. Kanzas and Nebraska. Boston, 1854. 12° 415.2

— Robinson, S. T. L. Kansas; its interior and exterior life. Boston, 1856. 12° 5035.5

Kant, Immanuel. The metaphysics of ethics. Translated by J. H. Semple. 3d edition. Edited, with introduction, by H. Calderwood. Edinburgh, 1871. xx, 315 pp. Sm. 8° 5836.3

Kapp, Friedrich. Life of Frederick William von Steuben. With an introduction by George Bancroft. New York, 1859. 735 [715] pp. Portrait. 12° 5025.8

— Der Soldatenhandel deutscher Fürsten nach Amerika (1775 bis 1783). Berlin, 1864. xix, 299 pp. 16° 5715.4

Karcher, Théodore, *joint editor.* The graduated course of translation from English into French. *See* Cassal, Charles 5534.7

Karr, (Jean Baptiste) Alphonse. A tour round my garden. Revised and edited by J. G. Wood. New edition. With illustrations. London, [1874]. xii, 332 pp. 4° 6626.4

Kate Carlton. Wise, D. 932.35

Kate Coventry. Melville, G. J. W. 321.13

Kate Kennedy. Newby, C. J. 710.9

Katerfelto: a story of Exmoor. Melville, G. J. W. Leipzig 330.10

— *Same.* Philadelphia 714.14

Katharine Walton. Simms, W. G. 716.30

Kathayan slave, The. Judson, E. (C.) (*In* Johnson, (E.) R. Little classics) 529.4.3

Katherine Earle. Trafton, A. 911.3

Katherine's trial. Parr, H. 339.15

Kathie's aunt Ruth. Douglas, A. M. 934.24

Kathie's harvest days. Douglas, A. M. 934.23

Kathie's soldiers. Douglas, A. M. 934.22

Kathie's stories. *See* Douglas, Amanda M.

Shelf. No.

KATHIE's summer at Cedarwood. Douglas, A. M. .. 934.26
KATHIE's three wishes. Douglas, A. M. 934.27
KATHRINA: a poem. Holland, J. G. New York, 1868. 12° 1612.7
— *Same.* New York, 1873. 16° 1617.2
KATSCH, Adolph Emilie. Under the storks' nest. A romance. From the German, by Emily R. Steinestel 715.22
KAVANAGH, Julia. Adèle 319.1
— Beatrice 323.8
— Daisy Burns 323.10
— Dora 323.4
— English women of letters: biographical sketches. Leipzig, 1862. 330+ pp. Sq. 16° 1238.2

Contents. — Mrs. Aphra Behn; Sarah Fielding; Madame Frances D'Arblay, formerly Miss Burney; Mrs. Charlotte Smith; Mrs. Ann Radcliffe; Mrs. Elizabeth Inchbald; Maria Edgeworth; Jane Austen; Mrs. Amelia Alderson Opie; Sydney Owenson Morgan.

— French women of letters: biographical sketches. Leipzig, 1862. viii, 344 pp. Sq. 16° 1238.3

Contents. — Marie le Jars de Gournay; Madeleine de Scudéry; Marie Madeleine Pioche de la Vergne, comtesse de La Fayette; Claudine Alexandrine Guérin, marquise de Tencin; Marie Jeanne Laboras de Mézières Riccoboni; Stéphanie Félicité, comtesse de Genlis; St. Hyacinthe de Charrière; Julie de Wietinghoff, baroness von Kruedener; Madame Sophie Cottin, formerly Ristaud; Anne Louise Germaine, baronne de Staël-Holstein, née Necker.

— Grace Lee 323.2
— John Dorrien. Leipzig. 3 v. in 2 .... 330.19
— *Same.* New York 714.20
— Nathalie 323.3
— Queen Mab 323.1
— Rachel Gray 323.7
— Seven years, and other tales 323.9
— Silvia 323.5
— A summer and winter in the two Sicilies 428.4
— Sybil's second love 323.6
— Women of Christianity, exemplary for acts of piety and charity. New York, 1860. 384 pp. 12° 1225.6
KAVANAGH. Longfellow, H. W. Prose works. Boston, 1866 [*cop.* 1857]. 16° 1838.4.2
KAYE, *Sir* John William. History of the Sepoy war in India. 1857–58. London, 1870, 72. 2 v. Maps. 8° 5922.7
KEAN, Charles, Life and theatrical times of. Cole, J. W. London, 1859. 2 v. Sm. 8° 5426.3
KEAN, Edmund, Life of. Hawkins, F. W. London, 1869. 2 v. 8° .... 1221.3 and 5424.2

Note. — See also Doran's "Their majesties' servants" [1532.2].

KEARNEY, Philip, Personal and military history of. Peyster, J. W. de. New York, 1869. 8° 5021.6
KEARY, Annie. Castle Daly: the story of an Irish home thirty years ago. Leipzig 321.25
— *Same.* Philadelphia. [International series] 714.36
— Clemency Franklyn 727.33
— Janet's home 717.15
— The nations around. [London], 1870. viii, 331 pp. Illustrated. [Sunday library.] Sm. 8°. 5937.12
— Oldbury. Leipzig 329.23
— *Same.* Philadelphia. [International series] 714.18
KEATS, John. Lowell, J. R. Among my books. Boston, 1876. 16° 1934.8.2
— Masson, D. Wordsworth, Shelley, Keats, and other essays. London, 1874. Sm. 8° 5616.15
— Milnes, R. M. Life and letters of. London, 1867. Sm. 8° 1227.6
KEBLE, John. The Christian year. Thoughts in verse for the Sundays and holidays throughout the year. New York, 1873. 288 pp. 12° 1616.6
— Memoir of. Coleridge, *Sir* J. T. New York, 1869. 2 v. 16° 5426.4
KEDDIE, *Miss* —. (*Sarah Tytler.*) Citoyenne Jacqueline. A woman's lot in the great French revolution. London, 1865. x, 499 pp. Illustrated. 16° 736.14
— Days of yore. London, 1868. 381+ pp. Illustrated. 16° 736.17
— The Huguenot family. New York, 1868. 399 pp. 12° 735.23

Shelf. No.

KEDDIE, *Miss* —, *continued.*
— Lady Bell. A story of last century. With illustrations. Philadelphia, 1874. vi, 442 pp. 12°. 734.14
— Modern painters and their paintings. Boston, 1874. viii, 362 pp. 16° 6216.4
— Musical composers and their works. Boston, 1875. vi, 426 pp. 16° 6237.3
— The old masters and their pictures. London, 1873. 363+ pp. Sm. 8° 1516.21
— *Same.* Boston, 1874. viii, 363 pp. 16° 6216.3
— Sweet counsel. Boston, 1866. 308+ pp. Illustrated. 16° 736.11
KEEL and saddle. [Travel, adventure, etc.] Revere, J. W. Boston, 1872. 12° 5914.3
KEELER, Ralph. Vagabond adventures. [Travels.] Boston, 1870. 274 pp. 12° 1216.3
KEENE, *Mrs.* S. F. The island home; or, the illuminated text 923.13
KEIGHTLEY, Thomas. The mythology of ancient Greece and Italy. 3d edition. Revised and augmented. With 12 plates from the antique. London, 1854. xvi, 512 pp. 8° 5921.8
KELLEY, William Darrah. Speeches, addresses and letters on industrial and financial questions. Added an introduction, with notes and an index. Philadelphia, 1872. xxx, 514 [510] pp. 8° ... 1531.3
KELLOGG, Elijah. Elm island stories. The ark of Elm island 922.16
— – The boy farmers of Elm island 922.12
— – Charlie Bell, the waif of Elm island 922.14
— – The hard-scrabble of Elm island 922.13
— – Lion Ben of Elm island 922.15
— – The young ship-builders of Elm island 922.11
— Forest glen series. Brought to the front 938.10
— – Sowed by the wind 915.17
— – Wolf Run 923.6
— Norman Cline 936.31
— Pleasant cove series. Arthur Brown, the young captain 922.8
— – The child of the island glen 914.42
— – The cruise of the Casco 922.7
— – The fisher boys of Pleasant cove 922.31
— – John Godsoe's legacy 922.29
— – The young deliverers of Pleasant cove 922.6
— Whispering pine series. The sophomores of Radcliffe 922.9
— – The spark of genius 922.10
— – A stout heart 922.30
— – The turning of the tide 922.28
— – The whispering pine 922.27
— – Winning his spurs 914.38
KELLY, Caroline E. Bernice, the farmer's daughter. 928.20
KELLY, Michael. Personal reminiscences. (*In* Stoddard, R. H. Bric-à-brac series) 1828.8
KEMBLE, Frances (Anne). Journal. Philadelphia, 1835. 2 v. in 1. 12° 1937.6
— A year of consolation. New York, 1847. 2 v. in 1. 12° 426.14

Note. — Mrs. Kemble is now printing in the Atlantic monthly, 1876, a series of personal reminiscences, "Old woman's gossip."

KEMBLES, The. Fitzgerald, P. London [1871]. 2 v. Sm. 8° 5425.22

Note. — This work covers the biographies of John Philip, Stephen and Charles Kemble, with their sister, Mrs. Siddons. See also Doran's "Their majesties' servants" [1532.2].

KEMPIS, Thomas à. *See* THOMAS À KEMPIS.
KENDALL, Amos. Autobiography. Edited by W. Stickney. Boston, 1872. ix, 700 pp. Portrait, 1 plate and fac-simile. 8° 5021.5
KENELM Chillingly. Bulwer-Lytton, E. (G. E.) L. Leipzig. 4 v. in 2 .... 319.10
— *Same.* New York 5633.3
KENILWORTH. Scott, *Sir* W. Boston 523.7
— *Same.* Leipzig 324.8
KENILWORTH castle, History of. Adlard, G. London, 1870. 8° 5423.5
KENNAN, George. Tent life in Siberia, and adventures among the Koraks and other tribes in Kamtchatka and Northern Asia. With a map. New York, 1873. ix, 425 pp. 12° 426.22

Shelf. No.

KENNEDY, John Pendleton. Horse-shoe Robinson. [Tories in South Carolina, 1780] 725.15

— Memoirs of William Wirt. Philadelphia, 1849. 2 v. Portrait. Fac-simile. 8° 1011.1

— *Same.* New and revised edition. New York, 1872. 2 v. Portrait. Fac-simile. Sm. 8° ... 5025.5

— Rob of the bowl. [Maryland, Lord Baltimore, etc.] 736.25

— Swallow barn. [Virginia country life about 1800]. 725.13

— Life of. Tuckerman, H. T. New York, 1871. 12° ....1015.7 and 5026.2

Note. — See Appleton's monthly, vol. 10.

KENNETH, my king. A novel. Brock, S. A........ 735.15

KENNEY, F. The illustrious stranger: a farce. New York, N. D. 36 pp. 1 plate. 12°............ 1635.3

KENRICK, Timothy. An exposition of the historical writings of the New Testament. With a memoir of the author. From the 2d London edition. Boston, 1828. 3 v. 8°................ 6324.2

Contents. — Vol. I. Matthew. II. Luke and John. III. Acts of the apostles; Chronological tables, etc.

KER, David. The wild horseman of the Pampas. With illustrations. London, 1876. x, 214+ pp. Sm. 8°................................ 733.16

KERR, Orpheus C., *pseud.* *See* NEWELL, Robert Henry.

KIDD, John. Adaptation of external nature to the physical condition of man. New edition. Philadelphia, 1835. 280 pp. 12°................ 6618.3

KIDD, William. Captain William Kidd and others of the pirates who ravaged America two hundred years ago. Abbott, J. S. C. New York, 1874. 12°..................................1014.11

KIDDER, Daniel Parish, *joint author.* Brazil and the Brazilians. *See* FLETCHER, James Cooley...... 411.5

KIDDER, Frederic. History of the Boston massacre, March 5, 1770. [With] explanatory notes. Albany, 1870. 291+ pp. 1 plate. 8°......... 5011.4

KIDNEYS. Formation and significance of renal casts. Edes, R. T. (*In* Massachusetts medical society. Publications)................................ 6021.4

KIEPERT, Heinrich, and OTHERS. Grosser Hand-Atlas des Himmels und der Erde. Thüringer, 1873. [70 plates.] F° ........................*R.R. Desk

KILMENY. Black, W............................ 319.16

KIMBALL, James William. Heaven. Boston, 1857. 281 pp. 12° 5815.21

KIMBALL, Richard Burleigh. Romance of student life abroad 311.15

— Saint Leger 311.17

— To-day in New York.......................... 311.18

— Was he successful?.......................... 311.16

KINDERGARTEN, The. Douai, A. New York, 1871. 12° 1933.11

KING, Clarence. Mountaineering in the Sierra Nevada. Boston, 1872. 292+ pp. Sm. 8°... 413.1

KING, Edward. The great South. Illustrated. Hartford, 1875. 802 | , iv pp. Map. 8°..... 5031.6

— My Paris. French character sketches. 3d edition. Boston, 1873. 336 pp. 12° 427.7

KING, Katherine. Hugh Melton. A story 721.16

— Off the roll. A novel 521.37

— Our detachment. A novel 711.34

— The queen of the regiment................... 732.33

KING, Thomas Starr. The White hills; their legends, landscape, and poetry. With illustrations. North Conway, N. H. [*cop.* 1859]. xv, 403+ pp. 12°................................ 413.11

— A tribute to. Frothingham, R. Boston, 1865. 16°..1537.10

KING, William Rufus, Addresses on the death of. *See* UNITED STATES. *Miscellaneous documents*.. 1923.3

KING Arthur. [Poem.] Bulwer-Lytton, E. (G. E.) L. Leipzig, 1849. 2 v. in 1. Sq. 16°........... 1614.8

KING, The, of no-land. Farjeon, B. L............. 710.27

KING, The, of the Golden river. Ruskin, J. New York, 1872. 39 pp. 12°..................... 6236.9

Same. (*In* Johnson, (E.) R. Little classics)...529.4.10

KING, The, of the peak. Cunningham, A. (*In* Johnson, (E.) R. Little classics) 529.4.7

Shelf. No.

KING René's daughter: a drama. Hertz, H. New York [1866]. 12°..........................1615.15

KING's cope. A novel.......................... 710.1

KING's, The, own. Marryat, F................... 337.11

KINGLAKE, Alexander William. Eöthen. [Travel in the East.] Leipzig, 1846. xii, 308 pp. Sq. 16°. 228.1

— The invasion of the Crimea: its origin, and an account of its progress down to the death of Lord Raglan. New York, 1875. 3 v. Maps and plans. 8°.................................. 5924.9

Contents. — Vol. I. Transactions which brought on the war; Invasion of the Crimea. II. Invasion of the Crimea. III. Battle of Inkerman.

KINGSFORD, Jane, *pseud.* *See* BARNARD, Charles Francis, *jr.*

KINGSLEY, Charles. Alton Locke. [Chartist movement in England]............................ 326.18

— At last: a Christmas in the West Indies. Leipzig, 1871. 2 v. in 1. Sq. 16°................ 326.17

— Health and education. London, 1874. 411+ pp. Sm. 8°......................................5836.10

— Hereward the Wake.......................... 326.15

Note. — This novel pictures the Norman conquest of England, and may be compared with Bulwer's "Harold" [336.19], which concerns the same events.

— The hermits. [Saints, anchorites, etc.] [London, 1868.] 335+ pp. Illustrated. [Sunday library.] Sm. 8° 5937.4

— The heroes; or, Greek fairy tales 935.25

— Hypatia. [Murdered A. D. 415; Christians at Alexandria]................................ 326.16

— New miscellanies. Boston, 1860. 375 pp. 12°. 1533.8

— Prose idylls, new and old. London, 1873. Sm. 8°. 5616.11

— Sir Walter Raleigh and his time, with other papers. Boston, 1859. 461+ pp. 12°....... 1223.5

— Town geology. [Popular science.] London, 1872. lvi, 239 pp. Sm. 8° ....1526.3 and 6636.2

— Two years ago. [Current political aspects in England] 326.13

— The water-babies: a fairy tale for a land-baby .. 921.4

— Westward ho! or, the voyages and adventures of Sir Amyas Leigh. [Maritime adventures in Queen Elizabeth's time] 326.14

— Yeast. [Current political aspects in England].. 326.19

KINGSLEY, George H., *joint author.* South sea bubbles. *See* HERBERT, George Robert Charles, *earl of Pembroke* 310.27

KINGSLEY, Henry. Austin Elliot. [Corn-laws, Peel, etc.] Boston 724.4

— *Same.* Leipzig 326.24

— The Hillyars and the Burtons 326.22

— Leighton court. [Devonshire life]............ 326.21

— The lost child. (*In* Johnson, (E.) R. Little classics)....................................529.4.10

— Oakshott castle 339.12

— Ravenshoe. [Crimean Oxford war, etc.]........ 336.20

— Reginald Hetherege........................... 310.21

— The recollections of Geoffry Hamlyn 326.23

— Stretton 521,23

— Valentin. A French boy's story of Sedan 330.9

KINGSTON, William H. G. Adventures of Dick Onslow among the red skins 935.26

— Antony Waymouth; or, the gentlemen adventurers 935.27

— Ben Burton; or, born and bred at sea 1118.3

— The boy's own book of boats, with instructions how to make sailing models 1718.1

— Captain Cook: his life, voyages, and discoveries. [London, 1871.] 352 [350] pp. Illustrated. Sq. 16° 215.3

— Charley Laurel: a story of adventure by sea and land...................................... 933.24

— The cruise of the Frolic 737.10

— Digby Heathcote: or, the early days of a country gentleman's son and heir...................... 929.7

— Fred Markham in Russia 936.20

— Hurricane Hurry; or, the adventures of a naval officer afloat and on shore 912.11

— In the Eastern seas 921.3

— Jutland series. Schoolboy days 937.24

— Little Ben Hadden series. Little Ben Hadden; or, do right, whatever comes of it 1117.19

Shelf. No.

KINGSTON, William H. G., *continued.*
— Manco: the Peruvian chief; or, an Englishman's adventures in the country of the Incas 923.14
— Mark Seaworth. A tale of the Indian ocean.... 922.5
— Marmaduke Merry the midshipman 922.3
— My first voyage to Southern seas.............. 937.27
— Old Jack.. 921.7
— On the banks of the Amazon. London, 1872. 512 pp. Illustrated. Sm. 8° 921.6
— Peter the whaler.................................. 922.4
— Ronald Morton; or, the fire-ships.............. 916.15
— Round the world.................................. 922.1
— Salt water 922.2
— The South sea whaler: a story of the loss of the "Champion" and the adventures of her crew .. 921.16
— The three commanders; or, active service afloat in modern days 921.17
— The three lieutenants; or, naval life in the nineteenth century 921.12
— The three midshipmen.......................... 912.24
— True Blue 935.17
— The Western world. Picturesque sketches of nature and natural history in North and South America. London, 1874. 736 pp. Illustrated. 8°.. 434.1
— The wilds of Africa. London, 1872. 560 pp. Illustrated. Sm. 8°........................ 921.2
— Will Weatherhelm: or, the yarn of an old sailor about his life and early adventures............ 934.29

KIP, Leonard. The dead marquise. A romance ... 717.14

KIPPING, Robert. Sails and sail-making. 9th edition enlarged, [and] illustrated. London, 1871. viii, 196 pp. 12°.......................... 1716.4

KIRBY, William. Power, wisdom and goodness of God, as manifested in the creation of animals, and in their history, habits and instincts. Philadelphia, 1836. lxxii, 519 pp. Plates. 8°.... 6613.8

KIRK, John Foster. History of Charles the bold. Philadelphia, 1864. 3 v. Portraits. 8°...... 5511.1

KIRKE, Edmund, *pseud.* *See* GILMORE, James Roberts.

KIRKLAND, Caroline Matilda. The garland of poetry. New York, 1872. 2 v. in 1. 12° 921.1
— Holidays abroad; or Europe from the West. New York, 1873. 2 v. in 1. 12° 427.6

KISSING, The literature of. Bombaugh, C. C. Philadelphia, 1876. 12°............................ 5924.5

KITCHINER, William. The cook's oracle: containing receipts for plain cookery. With an appendix. Boston, 1822. 380 pp. 1 plate. 12° 1516.20
— Directions for invigorating and prolonging life. From the 6th London edition; revised and improved, by T. S. Barrett. New York, 1831. 252 pp. 12° 6038.1

KITTO, John. Popular cyclopædia of biblical literature condensed. Illustrated. Boston, 1871. viii, 800+ pp. 8°.....................*R.R., A.2.2

KITTY's choice. Davis, R. H..................... 731.10

KITTY's class-day. Alcott, L. M.................. 935.20

KNATCHBULL-HUGESSEN, Edward Hugessen. *See* HUGESSEN, Edward Hugessen Knatchbull.

KNICKERBOCKER, Diedrich, *pseud.* *See* IRVING, Washington.

KNIGHT, Charles. Half-hours with the best authors. Including biographical and critical notices. With illustrations. New edition. Revised. London [1866]. 4 v. Portraits. Sm. 8° 5926.4
— History of England. With illustrations. London [1862]. 8 v. Portraits. 8°............ 5413.1
— Knowledge is power: a view of the productive forces of modern society and the results of labor, capital and skill. Revised and edited, with additions, by D. A. Wells. Illustrated. Boston, 1867.. 503 pp. 12° 1524.28
— Passages of a working life during half a century: with a prelude of early reminiscences. Re-issue, with introductory note by James Thorne. London, 1873. 3 v. Portraits. Sm. 8°..........5626.11
— Shadows of the old booksellers. [History of bookselling in London.] London, 1865. xiv, 320+ pp. 16°............................5425.25

Shelf. No.

KNIGHT, Charles, *continued.*
— Studies of Shakspere. London, 1868. 560+ pp. 8° 5621.7

Note. — Drawn mostly from Knight's edition of Shakespeare.

— William Shakspere: a biography. Revised and augmented. London [1865]. Portraits. Fac-similes. Illustrations. 8°.................. 5420.4
— *editor.* English cyclopædia. London, 1866–69. 23 v. 4° ................................*R.R., F.2.1

Contents. — Division I. Geography. 4 v. and Supplement. II. Natural history. 4 v. III. Biography. 6 v. IV. Arts and sciences. 8 v.

— *See* PAGE, H. A. Noble workers. London, 1875. Sm. 8°.. 5936.3

KNIGHT, Cornelia. Personal reminiscences. (*In* Stoddard, R. H. Bric-à-brac series).......... 1828.7

KNIGHT, Frederick. Thorn cottage, or the poet's home. A memorial of Frederick Knight. Boston, 1855. 12°................................. 1013.4

KNIGHT, Helen C. Lady Huntington and her friends. New York [*cop.* 1853]. 292 pp. Portraits. 12°. 1025.2

KNIGHT, Henry Cogswell. Lectures and sermons. Boston, 1831. 2 v. 8°........................ 6325.9

KNIGHT, The, of Gwynne. Lever, C. (J.) Leipzig. 332.18
— *Same.* London.. 516.11

KNIGHTS and their days. Doran, J. W. New York, 1864. Sm. 8° 822.4

KNILL, Richard. Life. Being selections from his reminiscences, journals, and correspondence. By C. M. Birrell. With a review of his character by J. A. James. New York, 1860. 358 pp. Portrait. 12° 1026.2

KNOLLYS, Henry. Incidents in the Sepoy war, 1857, 58. *See* GRANT, *Sir* Hope.................. 5924.6

KNOWLEDGE. Bailey, S. Essays on the progress of. Philadelphia, 1831. 12° 5837.1
— Crabb, G. Dictionary of general knowledge. London, 1830. 12°............................. 1513.6
— Craik, G. L. The pursuit of knowledge under difficulties. Illustrated by anecdotes. New York, 1868. 2 v. 12°......................... 1013.2
— Fichte, J. G. New exposition of the science of. St. Louis, 1869. 8°............................ 1932.4
— Knight, C. Knowledge is power. Boston, 1867. 12° 1524.28

KNOWLES, James Sheridan. The hunchback: a play. New York, 1832. 76 pp. 8°......... 1633.1

KNOX, John, An essay on the portraits of. Carlyle, T. The early kings of Norway. New York, 1875. 12°.. 627.3

KNOX, Vicesimus, *compiler.* Elegant extracts, or useful and entertaining passages, from the best English authors and translations. New edition, with engravings. Prepared by James G. Percival. Vol. 1, 4, 6. Boston, 1842. 3 v. Portraits. 8° 1532.6

KOCK, (Charles) Paul de. Mein Freund Piffard. Deutsch bearbeitet von Heinrich Elsner. 3te Auflage. Stuttgart, 1861. 72 pp. Sq. 16°... 2028.6
— Der Schreckenshund. Deutsch von Anton Langer. Pest, 1857. 2 v. in 1. 16° 2027.5

KOELLIKER, Albert. Manual of human microscopical anatomy. Translated by G. Busk and T. Huxley. Edited, with notes and additions, by J. Da Costa. Illustrated. Philadelphia, 1854. 802 [794] pp. 8°.................................. 6032.3

KOHL, Johann Georg. Ireland. New York, 1844. 115 pp. 8° 431.2

KOHLRAUSCH, Heinrich Friedrich Theodor. History of Germany, from the earliest period to the present time. Translated by J. D. Haas. New York, 1874. 487 pp. 8°.................... 5712.3

KOLDEWEY, Carl. The German arctic expedition of 1869–70, and narrative of the wreck of the "Hansa" in the ice. With illustrations. Translated and abridged by L. Mercier, and edited by H. W. Bates. London, 1874. viii, 583 pp. L. 8° 5722.3

Note. — This volume describes the best organized efforts yet made to reach the north pole by following the coast line of East Greenland, and illustrates the routes by maps on a large scale. See Arctic regions, *note.*

Shelf. No.

KONER, Wilhelm, *joint author.* The life of the Greeks and Romans, described from antique monuments. *See* GUHL, Ernst 5921.9
KORAN, The. Mohammed. Boston, 1862. 16°.... 5815.2
KOSSUTH, Louis, Life of. Headley, P. C. Auburn, 1852. 16°.............................. 1024.2
KROEGER, A. E. The minnesinger of Germany. New York, 1873. 284+ pp. 16° 5735.1
KUECHENMEISTER, Frederich. Animal and vegetable parasites of the human body, a manual of their natural history, diagnosis, and treatment. Translated from the 2d German edition, by E. Lankester. Vol. I. London, 1857. With plates. 8°. 6021.17
KUGLER, Franz Theodor. Handbook of painting. *See* WAAGEN, Gustav Friedrich.............. 6214.1
KURZ, Heinrich. Geschichte der deutschen Literatur. Mit illustrationen. Leipzig, 1873. 4 v. 8°. 5730.2
KUSSMAUL, Adolf, and TENNER, Adolf. Nature and origin of epileptiform convulsions caused by profuse bleeding, and also of those of true epilepsy. Translated by E. Bronner. London, 1859. viii, 380+ pp. 8° 6023.1

LABICHE, Eugène (Marin), and DELACOUR, Alfred (Charlemagne Lartigue). Les petits oiseaux: comédie. With English notes, by F. Bôcher. Boston, 1867. 70 pp. 12° 2015.2
LABOR. Brassey, T. Work and wages practically illustrated. London, 1872. Sm. 8° 6413.2
— *Same.* New York, 1872. Sm. 8°............ 5823.1
— Le Play, (P. G.) F. The organization of. Philadelphia, 1872. 12°........................1526.22
— Ruskin, J. Time and tide, by Weare and Tyne. Letters on the laws of work. New York, 1871. 12°.....................................6236.16
LABOR lost. Abbott, J........................ 917.31
LABORING classes, The, of England. Dod, —. Boston, 1847. 12°........................ 5418.1
LABOULAYE, Édouard (René Lefébvre). Fairy tales of all nations. Translated by M. L. Booth..... 921.5
LACE, History of. Palliser, *Mrs.* B. London, 1869. 8°. 6232.7
LACOMBE, Michel (Jean) Pierre. Arms and armour in antiquity and the middle ages: also a descriptive notice of modern weapons. Translated by C. Boutell. New York, 1871. xvi, 296 pp. Illustrated. 16° 1714.15
LACON. [Apothegms, etc.] Colton, C. C. New York, 1866. 12°..............................1533.12
LACROIX, Paul. Bibliothèque dramatique de monsieur de Soleinne. T. I [and Supplement]. Paris, 1843, 44. 2 v. in 1. 8°............... 5532.1
LACTANTIUS, Lucius Cælius Firmianus. Works. Translated by W. Fletcher. Edinburgh, 1871. 2 v. [Ante-Nicene Christian library.] 8°. Vol. 21, 22 of 6322.4
LACY diamonds, The. Coulson, J. G. A. 721.12
LADIES', The, guide to politeness and perfect manners. Leslie, E. Philadelphia, N. D. Sm. 8°. 1514.2
LADREYT, E. M. Conversational French reader. Boston, 1864. 238+ pp. 16°.............. 2015.1
LADY, The, of Lyons. [Drama.] Bulwer-Lytton, E. (G. E.) L. Leipzig, 1860. Sq. 16°........ 1614.5
— *Same.* New York, N. D. 12°.................1635.21
LADY, The, of Shalott. Phelps, E. S. (*In* Johnson, (E.) R. Little classics) 529.4.10
LADY, The, of the bed-chamber: a farce. New York, N. D. 17 pp. 12°................... 1635.5
LADY, The, of the ice. De Mille, J................ 521.1
LADY, The, of the isle. Southworth, E. D. E. N... 727.20
LADY, The, of the lake. Scott, *Sir* W. Poetical works. Leipzig, 1861. Sq. 16°.............. 1613.5
— *Same.* Dramatized. *See* DIBDEN, Thomas..... 1635.4
LADY, A, of the last century. [Mrs. Montague.] Doran, J. W. London, 1873. 8° 5422.11
LADY Adelaide's oath. Wood, E. P............... 333.9
LADY Anna. Trollope, A. Leipzig 329.15
— *Same.* New York.............................. 732.27
LADY Audley's secret. Braddon, M. E. 325.10
LADY Bell. Keddie, *Miss* —. 734.14
LADY-BIRD. Fullerton, *Lady* G.................. 325.20
LADY Hester. Yonge, C. M........................ 725.33

LADY Judith. MacCarthy, J...................... 531.4
LADY superior, The. Pollard, E. F. 720.20
LADY'S, The, guide to perfect gentility. Thornwell, E. New York, 1856. 12°.................. 1516.2
LADY'S, The, mile. Braddon, M. E. 325.13
LA FAYETTE, Marie Joseph [*not* Jean] Paul Roch Ives Gilbert de Motier, *marquis* de, Life of. Waln, R. Philadelphia, 1825. 8° 5513.2
LA FONTAINE, Jean de. Fables; avec préface, notes et glossaire par P. Jannet. Paris, 1868. 2 v. 16° 5538.2
LAIRD, The, of Norlaw. Oliphant, M. (O. W.) 737.1
LAIRD'S, The, Jock. Scott, *Sir* W. 523.20
LAKE regions, The, of Central Africa. Taylor, (J.) B. New York, 1873. 12° 224.9
LAKE shore series. *See* ADAMS, William T.
LAKEVILLE. Healy, M. 530.8
LAKEY, Charles D. Village and country houses, or cheap homes for all classes, comprising eighty-four pages of designs. New York, 1875. (4) pp. 4°....................................... 6220.8
LALLA Rookh. Moore, T. Poetical works. Leipzig, 1842. Sq. 16° 1614.9.2
LAMARTINE, Alphonse (Marie Louis) de. Confidential disclosures. Translated by E. Plunkett. New York, 1849. 291 pp. 12°.............5536.10
— Fior d'Aliza. Translated by G. Perry. New York, 1868. 240 pp. 16°.................. 517.14
— Geneviève. Translated by A. R. Scoble. New York, 1871. xvii, 80 pp. 8°................ 531.25
— Histoire des Girondins. Paris, 1848. 8 v. Portraits. 8° 2011.1
— History of the French revolution of 1848. Translated from the French. London, 1870. 572 pp. Portrait. Sm. 8°.............................. 827.24
— History of the Girondists. Translated by H. T. Ryde. New York, 1868. 3 v. Portraits. 12°. 827.25
— History of the restoration of monarchy in France. Translated by Captain Rafter. London, 1865. 4 v. Portraits. Sm. 8°.................... 5517.5
— Memoirs of celebrated characters. New York, 1854. 3 v. 12°.............................1025.10
— Memoirs of my youth. New York, N. D. 110 [101] pp. 8° 1021.7
— Raphael; or, pages of the book of life at twenty. New York, 1868. 143 pp. 12° 1935.2
— Recollections. (*In* Stoddard, R. H. Bric-à-brac series).. 1828.1
— Souvenirs, impressions, pensées et paysages pendant un voyage en Orient 1832–33, ou notes d'un voyageur. Paris, 1859. 2 v. 12° 2016.12
— The stone-mason of Saint Point. Translated from the French. New York [1851]. 144 pp. 12°. 512.10
— Twenty-five years of my life and memoirs of my mother. Translated by Lady Herbert. London, 1872. 2 v. Sm. 8°............................ 5525.5
— Lamartine sa vie littéraire et politique. Mazade, C. de. Paris, 1872. 18°.................... 5526.2
LAMB, Charles. Works, with a sketch of his life. By Sir T. N. Talfourd. New York, 1872. 2 v. Portrait. 12°......................1813.5 and 5615.1

Contents. — Vol. I. Life, by T. N. Talfourd; Letters. II. Essays of Elia; Rosamund Gray; Essays; Letters; Mr. H——, a farce; Poems; Sonnets; John Woodvil, a tragedy; The witch; Miscellaneous; The wife's trial.

— A dissertation upon roast pig. (*In* Johnson, (E.) R. Little classics).........................529.4.5
— Elia. [Essays.] New York, 1835. 126+ pp. L. 8°. 1911.4
— Essays of Elia and Eliana. Leipzig, 1869. 371 pp. Sq. 16° 1918.3
— Final memorials; consisting chiefly of his letters not before published, with sketches of some of his companions. By T. N. Talfourd. London, 1848. 2 v. 12°................................ 5625.4
— Fitzgerald, P. Charles Lamb; his friends, his haunts, and his books. London, 1866. Sq. 16°. 5425.8
— Stoddard, R. H. Personal recollections of. New York, 1875. Sq. 16°.......................... 1828.9

Note. — See a full note in the Bulletin, Vol. II, p. 334, and Westminster review, Oct., 1874, on "Charles and Mary Lamb, their editors and biographers."

Shelf. No.

LAMB, Charles and Mary. Poetry for children. Edited and prefaced by R. H. Shepherd. London, 1872. xii, 94 pp. 16° ... 5617.8

— Tales from Shakspeare. With illustrations. London [1866]. viii, 371 pp. 16° ... 935.24

LAMB, Martha J. Spicy ... 530.1

LAMB, Mary and Charles. Poems, letters, and remains: now first collected, with reminiscences and notes. By W. C. Hazlitt. With portrait, fac-similes and illustrations. London, 1874. 307, 31 pp. Sm. 8° ... 5616.13

LAMBERT, James. A hero and a martyr. Reade, C. New York, 1875. 8° ... 710.32

LAMBORN, Robert H. Metallurgy of copper: an introduction to the methods of seeking, mining and assaying copper. 3d edition. London, 1868. vi, 237+ pp. Illustrated. 12° ... 1715.16

— Metallurgy of silver and lead. A description of the ores: their assay and treatment, and valuable constituents. 5th edition. London, 1870. viii, 246 pp. Illustrated. 12° ... 1715.17

LAMON, Ward H. Life of Abraham Lincoln: to his inauguration as president. With illustrations. Boston, 1872. xiv, 547 pp. Portrait. 8° ... 5020.5

LA MOTTE FOUQUÉ, Friedrich (Heinrich Carl), *Freiherr* de. Undine and other tales. Translated by F. E. Bunnett. Leipzig, 1867. 361+ pp. Sq. 16° ... 313.7

Contents. — Undine; The two captains; Aslauga's knight; Sintram and his companions.

— *See* CARLYLE, T. German romance. Boston, 1841. 2 v. in 1. 12° ... 5725.2

LAMPLIGHTER, The. Cummins, M. S. ... 322.28

LANCASTER and York, The houses of. Gairdner, J. New York, 1875. 16° ... 628.4

LANCASHIRE witches, The. Ainsworth, W. H. ... 339.2

LANCES, The, of Lynwood. Yonge, C. M. ... 737.8

LANCEWOOD, Lawrence, *pseud.* *See* WISE, Daniel.

LAND, The, and the Book. [Palestine.] Thomson, W. M. New York, 1871. 2 v. 12° ... 224.5

LAND at last. Yates, E. ... 318.18

LAND, The, of desolation. [Greenland.] Hayes, I. I. New York, 1872. 12° ... 423.9

LAND, The, of Lorne. [In Scotland.] Buchanan, R. London, 1871. 2 v. 12° ... 424.11

LAND, The, of the north wind; or, travels among the Laplanders. Rae, E. London, 1875. Sm. 8°. 5935.5

LAND, The, of the Veda. [India.] Butler, W. New York, 1872. 8° ... 5931.1

LAND, The, of the white elephant. [Asia, etc.] Vincent, F., *jr.* New York, 1874. 8° ... 5923.7

LAND, The, of Thor. [Scandinavia.] Browne, J. R. New York, 1870. 12° ... 424.17

LANDELLS, E. The illustrated paper model maker: containing twelve engravings of the subjects, and descriptive letter-press, with practical diagrams for their construction. New edition. London, N. D. 16 pp. 13 plates. 8° ... 6220.5

LANDER, Sarah West. Spectacles for young eyes. Boston ... 922.20

— – Moscow ... 916.9

— – New York ... 922.19

— – Pekin ... 916.10

— – Rome ... 922.21

— – St. Petersburg ... 922.22

— – Zurich ... 922.18

LANDON, Melville D. Eli Perkins (at large): his sayings and doings. With illustrations. New York, 1875. 218 pp. 12° ... 1536.25

LANDOR, Walter Savage. A biography. Forster, J. Boston, 1869. 8° ... 5423.1

Note. — Forster's is the authoritative life, but the general reader will find it too voluminous; and he may perhaps be better content with such an article as is in vol. 130 of the Edinburgh review, or with Miss Field's account of Landor's last days, in the Atlantic monthly, vol. 17, or with some of the other reviews indicated in Thomas's Biographical dictionary, and in Allibone. See also Contemporary review, vol. 18; and E. C. Stedman's paper, in Scribner's monthly, May, 1873. Also see De Quincey's "Essays on the poets" [1825.4]; Howitt's "Homes and haunts" [1225.5]; Lord Houghton's "Monographs" [5616.7]; Timb's "Later wits;" Emerson's "English traits" [425.4; 1934.6.2]; T. A. Trollope, in Lippincott's magazine, April, 1874; Galaxy, Dec., 1875; Stedman's "Victorian poets" [1837.1]; and H. C. Robinson's "Diary" [5425.3].

Shelf. No.

LANDRIN, H. Manuel du coutelier. Orné de planches. Paris, 1835. xii, 431+ pp. 24°. [Manuel Roret] ... 6429.13

LANDRIOT, Jean François Anne Thomas. Sins of the tongue and jealousy in woman's life. Followed by discourses on rash judgments, patience, and grace. From the French by Helena Lyons. From the 4th London edition. Boston, 1874. 271 pp. 12° ... 1915.7

— The valiant woman: a series of discourses intended for women living in the world. From the French by Helena Lyons. From the 4th London edition. Boston, 1874. 287 pp. 12°. 1915.6

LANDSCAPE gardening. Downing, A. J. Treatise on the theory and practice of. New York, 1844. 8°. 1511.8

— *Same.* New York [*cop.* 1859]. 8° ... 1511.3

— Weidenmann, J. Beautifying country homes. A handbook of. New York [*cop.* 1870]. 4° ... 6220.1

LANDSEER, *Sir* Edwin, Memoirs of. Stephens, F. G. London, 1874. 8° ... 6211.6

LANE, Edward William. Account of the manners and customs of the modern Egyptians. 5th edition. Edited by E. S. Poole. London, 1871. 2 v. Illustrated. 16° ... 5926.2

LANETON parsonage. Sewell, E. M. ... 532.7

LANFREY, Pierre. History of Napoleon the first. London, 1871, 72. 2 v. 8° ... 5522.1

LANG, Benjamin J. Youthful voices: a collection of hymns and tunes for the use of Sunday schools. The music edited by B. J. Lang. Boston [*cop.* 1862]. 12° ... 1625.9

LANG, Fanny Forrester, *aged nine years.* Little poems. Boston, 1858. 24 pp. 12° ... 1618.6

LANG, John Dunmore. An historical and statistical account of New South Wales, from the founding of the colony in 1788 to the present day. 4th edition. The history of the last twenty-five years entirely new. London, 1875. 2 v. Illustrations. Map. 8° ... 5418.9

LANGDON, Mary, *pseud.* *See* PIKE, Mary H.

LANGE, John Peter, and OTHERS. Commentary on the Holy Scriptures. *See* BIBLE ... *R.R., B.2.1

LANGUAGE. Baedeker, C. Traveller's manual of conversation in English, French, German, Italian. Coblenz, 1870. 12° ... 6127.1

— Farrar, F. W. Chapters on. London, 1873. Sm. 8° ... 6127.3

— Mueller, (F.) M. Chips from a German workshop. London, 1875. Sm. 8° ... 5616.1.4

— – Lectures on the science of. New York, 1874. 2 v. Sm. 8° ... 6126.4

— Prendergast, T. Handbook to the mastery series. New York, 1868. 12° ... 1933.1

— Sauveur, L. Introduction to the teaching of living languages without grammar or dictionary. Boston, 1874. 12° ... 1934.14

— Whitney, W. D. Language and the study of language. New York, 1872. Sm. 8° ... 6126.3

— – The life and growth of. New York, 1875. 12°. 6126.5

— – Oriental and linguistic studies. New York, 1873. Sm. 8° ... 6126.2

See also Words, and English, French, German languages, etc.

LANMAN, Charles, *editor.* The Japanese in America. New York, 1872. 352+ pp. Portraits. 12°. 5925.3

LANOYE, Ferdinand Tugnot de. *See* TUGNOT DE LANOYE, Ferdinand.

LANSDOWNE, *Marquis of.* *See* PETTY, Henry.

LANZI, Luigi. History of painting in Italy, from the revival of the fine arts to the end of the 18th century. From the Italian by T. Roscoe. New edition, revised. London, 1852. 2 v. Portraits. Sm. 8° ... 6215.4

LAOCOON. An essay upon the limits of painting and poetry. Lessing, G. E. Boston, 1874. 16° ... 6216.2

LAPLAND. Shairp, T. Up in the North. London, 1872. Sm. 8° ... 5915.4

— Rae, E. The land of the north wind; or, travels among the Laplanders. London, 1875. Sm. 8°. 5935.5

— Taylor, (J.) B. Northern travel: summer and winter pictures of. New York, 1858. 12° ... 426.3

Shelf. No.

LA PLATA. Brazil and La Plata: the personal record of a cruise. Stewart, C. S. New York, 1856. 12° ... 425.18

LAPORTE, Laurent. Sailing on the Nile. Translated by V. Vaughan. Boston, 1872. iv, 291 pp. 16° ... 426.2

LAPSTONE. Abbott, J. Harper's story books ... 936.1.10

LARCOM, Lucy. An idyl of work. [Poem.] Boston, 1875. 183 pp. 12° ... 1615.9

LARDNER, Dionysius. Railway economy; a treatise on the new art of transport. New York, 1850. 442 pp. 12° ... 6424.3

— The steam engine. 11th edition. London, 1871. viii, 135 pp. Illustrated. 12° ... 1716.34

LARWOOD, Jacob, *pseud.* *See* SADLER, L. R.

LA SALLE, Robert Cavelier, *sieur* de. The adventures of. Abbott, J. S. C. New York [1875]. 12° ... 1014.13

LAS CASES, Marin Joseph Emmanuel Augustin Dieudonné. Genealogical, historical, chronological, and geographical atlas. According to the plan of [A.] Le Sage [*pseud.*], greatly improved. By [C. V.] Lavoisne. 3d American edition. Philadelphia, 1821. Unpaged. F°.. 5030.7

LAST baron, The, of Crana. Banim, J. ... 517.5

LAST chronicle, The, of Barset. Trollope, A. ... 334.15

LAST days, The, of Pompeii. [Historical novel.] Bulwer-Lytton, E. (G. E. L.) ... 336.13

LAST house, The, in C—— street. Craik, D. (M.).. 323.27

LAST knight, The. [Translated poem.] Auersperg, A. A., *Graf* von. New York, 1871. Sm. 4°.. 5738.5

LAST, The, of the barons. [An historical tale concerning Warwick, the king-maker.] Bulwer-Lytton, E. (G. E.) L. ... 336.20

LAST, The, of the cavaliers. Yonge, C. M. ... 318.16

LAST, The, of the Mohicans. [Old French war.] Cooper, J. F. ... 525.10

LAST, The, of the Mortimers. Oliphant, M. (O. W.). 328.9

LAST, The, tournament. Tennyson, A. Poetical works. Leipzig, 1872. Sq. 16° ... 1614.10.7

LATE, The, Mrs. Hollingford ... 338.17

LATHE, The, and its uses. 3d edition. London, 1871. iv, 315 pp. Illustrated. 8° ... 6423.5

LATHES and turning. Northcott, W. H. London, 1868. 8° ... 1521.11

LATIMER, John. *See* CHRISTOPHERS, S. W. Homes of old English writers. London [1874]. Sm. 8°. 5428.16

LATIN Christianity, History of. Milman, H. H. London, 1867. 9 v. Sm. 8° ... 5817.11

LATIN language. Andrews, E. A. A copious and critical Latin-English lexicon. New York, 1872. 8° ... *R.R., D.3.5

— – First lessons in Latin. Boston, 1846. Sm. 12°. 1939.4

— Greenwood, J. The London vocabulary, English and Latin. Cambridge, 1816. Sm. 12° ... 6128.1

— Noël, F. (J. M.) Nouveau dictionnaire français-latin [et latin-français]. Paris, 1824, 25. 2 v. 8° ... 6110.1

— White, J. T., and Riddle, J. E. Latin-English dictionary. London, 1872. 2 v. 4° ... *R.R., D.3.13

LATIN literature. History of Roman literature. Teuffel, W. S. London, 1873. 2 v. 8° ... 6111.4

See also Note under Rome, literature.

LATTER-DAY pamphlets. [1850.] Carlyle, T. New York, 1872. Sq. 16° ... 1535.18

LAUSON tragedy, The. De Forest, J. W. (*In* Johnson, (E.) R. Little classics) ... 529.4.3

LAVENGRO; the scholar — the gipsy — the priest. Borrow, G. New York, 1857. 8° ... 511.4

LAVERGNE, Louis (Gabriel Léonce Guilhaud) de. L'agriculture et la population. 2e édition revue et augmentée. Paris, 1865. xii, 468+ pp. 18° ... 5827.1

"LAVINIA." Carlén, E. F. ... 533.9

LAVINIA. [Italian life.] Ruffini, G. ... 316.18

LAW, Edward, *lord Ellenborough.* History of the Indian administration of Lord Ellenborough, in his correspondence with the duke of Wellington. Edited by Lord Colchester. London, 1874. xx, 456 pp. 8° ... 5412.5

Shelf. No.

LAW, Henry. The art of constructing common roads. *See* MALLET, Robert ... 1716.16

— Civil engineering. The section on hydraulic engineering by G. R. Burnell. 5th edition, with notes and illustrations by R. Mallet. With plates and diagrams. London, 1869. 4 v. in 2. 12° ... 1716.37

LAW. Amos, S. The science of law. New York, 1874. 12° ... 6316.3

— Campbell, G. D., *duke of Argyll.* The reign of law. New York [1869]. 16° ... 1525.15

— Vattel, E. de. The law of nations. Dublin, 1792. 8° ... 6315.1

— Ward, R. Foundation and history of the law of nations in Europe. Dublin, 1795. 8° ... 6315.2

See also Civil or Roman law.

LAW, The, and the lady. Collins, (W.) W. Leipzig ... 330.17

— *Same.* New York ... 733.2

LAW reporters, Curiosities of. Heard, F. F. Boston, 1871. 16° ... 6317.1

LAWRENCE, Amos. Extracts from [his] diary and correspondence. Edited by his son, W. R. Lawrence. Boston, 1855. 369+ pp. Portraits. 1 plate. Fac-simile. 8° ... 1211.8

— *Same.* Boston, 1860. 16° ... 1214.9

LAWRENCE, Eugene. Lives of the British historians. New York, 1855. 2 v. 12° ... 1224.7

Contents. — Vol. I. Early historians; Sir Walter Raleigh; William Camden; Edward Hyde, earl of Clarendon; Gilbert Burnet, bishop of Salisbury; Thomas Fuller; Laurence Echard; Robert Brady; John Oldmixon; Thomas Carte; William Robertson; George Lyttleton, lord; Tobias George Smollett; II. David Hume; Paul de Rapen-Thoyras; Catherine Graham, formerly Mrs. Macaulay; James Ralph; James Macpherson; Nathaniel Hooke; Adam Ferguson; Edward Gibbon; Robert Orme; Oliver Goldsmith; Charles James Fox; Fragmentary historians.

LAWRENCE, George Alfred. Anteros ... 315.25

— Barren honour ... 315.21

— Border and Bastille. [The South in the rebellion]. 315.26

— Brakespeare; or, the fortunes of a free lance ... 711.6

— Guy Livingstone ... 315.22

— Hagarene. Leipzig ... 319.29

— *Same.* New York ... 711.2

— Maurice Dering ... 315.27

— Sans merci ... 315.24

— Sword and gown ... 315.23

LAWRENCE, *Sir* Henry. *See* PAGE, H. A. Noble workers. London, 1875. Sm. 8° ... 5936.3

LAWRENCE, William Richards. History of the Boston dispensary. Boston, 1859. xiii, 244+ pp. 2 plates. Portrait. 8° ... 6032.1

LAWRENCE academy, *Groton, Mass.* Catalogue of the library. Lowell, 1850. 206 pp. 1 plate. 8°. 5834.8

— Jubilee, July 12, 1854. [With general catalogue.] New York, 1855. 108 pp. Illustrated. Portraits. 8° ... 5834.8

LAWRENCE's adventures among the ice-cutters, glass-makers, coal-miners, iron-men, and ship-builders. Trowbridge, J. T. ... 832.20

LAWSON, Henry. Manual of popular physiology: being an attempt to explain the science of life in untechnical language. New York [London], 1873. viii, 168 pp. Illustrated. 16° ... 1713.2

LAY, The, of the last minstrel. Scott, *Sir* W. Boston, 1807. 12° ... 1616.13

— *Same.* (*In his* Poetical works.) Leipzig, 1861. Sq. 16° ... 1613.5

LAYARD, Austen Henry. Discoveries in the ruins of Nineveh and Babylon; with travels in Armenia, Kurdistan, and the desert: being the result of a second expedition for the trustees of the British museum. With maps, plans, and illustrations. London, 1853. xxiii, 686+ pp. 8° ... 5912.9

— Nineveh and its remains. 5th edition. London, 1850. 2 v. Illustrated. 8° ... 5912.2

LAYS of ancient Rome. [Ballads of Roman history.] Macaulay, T. B., *lord.* Leipzig, 1851. Sq. 16°. 1614.17

LEAD. Harrison, J. B. Contamination of water by. London, 1852. 16° ... 6438.7

— Lamborn, R. H. Metallurgy of. London, 1870. 12° ... 1715.17

Shelf. No.

Leaf, A, in the storm. Rame, L. de la. Berlin.... 717.1

— *Same.* Leipzig ... 327.23

— *Same.* (*In* Johnson, (E.) R. Little classics). 529.4.11

League, The, of the Alps. [Poem.] Hemans, F. (D.) Boston, 1826. 8° ... 1621.2

Leah: a woman of fashion. Edwards, A. Leipzig. 329.28

— *Same.* New York ... 721.14

Leahy, John. The art of swimming in the Eton style. By "Sargeant" Leahy. Illustrated. London, 1875. ii, 99, xi pp. Sm. 8° ... 6417.3

Lear, A, of the steppe. Turgenef, I. S. ... 528.9

Leared, Arthur. The causes and treatment of imperfect digestion. 6th edition, revised and enlarged. London, 1875. viii, 288 pp. Woodcuts. Sm. 8° ... 6036.13

Leather stocking and silk. Cooke, J. E. ... 524.16

Leather stocking tales. *See* Cooper, James Fenimore.

Lebrun, —. Manuel du mouleur. Nouvelle édition. Paris, 1850. 256+ pp. Folded plate. 24°. [Manuel Roret] ... 6429.11

Lecky, William Edward Hartpole. History of European morals from Augustus to Charlemagne. New York, 1873. 2 v. 8° ... 5914.1

— History of the rise and influence of the spirit of rationalism in Europe. Revised edition. New York, 1872. 2 v. 8° ... 5914.7

— Leaders of public opinion in Ireland: Swift — Flood — Grattan — O'Connell. New York, 1872. xxiv, 320 pp. 12° ... 1025.9

Le Clerc, John. On the choice of our religious opinions. (*In* Sparks, J. Collection of essays and tracts in theology) ... 1918.9.6

Leclercq, Théodore. *See* Mérimée, P. Portraits historiques et littéraires. Paris, 1874. 18°... 5527.14

Le Conte, Joseph. Religion and science. New York, 1874. 324 pp. 12° ... 5817.14

Led astray. Feuillet, O. ... 714.12

Lee, Ann, Biography of. Evans, F. W. Shakers. New York, 1859. 12° ... 5818.19

Lee, Eliza Buckminster. Life of Jean Paul Frederic Richter, compiled from various sources. Preceded by his autobiography. 3d edition. Boston, 1864. xvi, 539 pp. 12° ... 1227.4

— Memoirs of Joseph Buckminster and Joseph Stevens Buckminster. Boston, 1849. x, 486+ pp. Portraits. 12° ... 5025.10

— *Same.* 2d edition. Boston, 1851. x, 492+ pp. 12° ... 1213.2

— Naomi; or Boston, two hundred years ago. Boston, 1848. vii, 448 pp. 16° ... 538.8

— Parthenia: or, the last days of paganism. [Julian the apostate.] 2d edition. Boston, 1858. x, 420 pp. 12° ... 737.11

Lee, Holme, *pseud.* *See* Parr, Harriet.

Lee, Jesse. Memorial of Jesse Lee and the old elm. Hamilton, J. W. Boston, 1875. 12° ... 617.2

Lee, Robert Edward. Cooke, J. E. Life of. New York, 1871. 8° ... 5022.2

— Mason, E. V. Popular life of. Baltimore, 1874. 12° ... 5226.1

Lee, William. Daniel Defoe: his life, and recently discovered writings: extending from 1716 to 1729. London, 1869. 3 v. Illustrated. Portraits. 8° ... 5422.5

Leeds, W. H. Rudimentary architecture. With illustrative engravings. 9th edition, with appendix. London, 1871. viii, 144 pp. 12° ... 1716.22

Lees, William. Elements of acoustics, light, and heat. With illustrations. New York [Glasgow], 1873. 140 pp. 16° ... 1717.10

Le Fanu, Joseph Sheridan. Guy Deverell ... 314.4

— Uncle Silas ... 314.3

Lefèvre, A. Wonders of architecture. From the French. To which is added a chapter on English architecture, by R. Donald. New York, 1872. xii, 264 pp. Illustrated. 16° ... 1714.2

Le Gal, Eugene. School of the guides; designed for the use of the militia of the United States. New York, 1860. 60+ pp. Illustrated. Sq. 16° ... 1528.3

Legaré, J. M. Orta-undis, and other poems. Boston, 1848. viii, 102 pp. 16° ... 1616.19

Legend, The, of Jubal. [Poem.] Lewes, M. Boston, 1874. 16° ... 5617.18

Legend, A, of Montrose. Scott, *Sir* W. Boston... 523.15

— *Same.* Leipzig ... 324.11

Legends, The childhood of religions: embracing a simple account of the birth and growth of. Clodd, E. London, 1875. Sm. 8° ... 6328.21

Legends and lyrics. Procter, A. A. London, 1872. 2 v. 16° ... 5617.11

Legends of Charlemagne. Bulfinch, T. Boston, 1871. Sm. 8° ... 824.2

Legends of the monastic orders, as represented in the fine arts. Jameson, A. (M.) Boston, 1866. 16° ... 1517.7

Legends of the patriarchs and prophets. Baring-Gould, S. New York, 1872. Sm. 8° ... 5814.5

Leger D. Mayne, *pseud.* *See* Dick, William Brisbane.

Legouvé, (Gabriel Jean Baptiste) Ernest (Wilfred), *joint author.* Les doigts de fée: comédie. *See* Scribe, (Augustin) Eugène ... 2015.2

Legros, E., *joint author.* The international English and French dictionary. *See* Smith, Leon. *R.R., D.3.8

Leicester, *Earl of.* *See* Dudley, Robert.

Leicester, *Mass.*, Historical sketches of. Washburn, E. Boston, 1860. 8° ... 5011.7

Leidenschaften, Die. Schwartz, M. S. New York, n. d. 16° ... 2028.5

Leigh, James Edward Austen. *See* Austen-Leigh, James Edward.

Leighton, Robert. Whole works. Prefixed, a life of the author, by J. N. Pearson. New edition. London, 1828. 2 v. Portrait. 8° ... 5612.9

Leighton court. Kingsley, H. ... 326.21

Leila; or, the siege of Granada. Bulwer-Lytton, E. (G. E.) L. ... 532.11

Leisure-day rhymes. Saxe, J. G. Boston, 1875. 12° ... 1616.16

Leisure hour series. *Namely:* —

— Alcestis ... 518.23

— Alexander, *Mrs.* —. Her dearest foe ... 517.21

— — Ralph Wilton's weird ... 518.26

— — Which shall it be? ... 732.12

— — The wooing o't ... 518.18

— Auerbach, B. Black forest village stories ... 926.27

— Butt, B. M. Miss Mollie ... 517.24

— Calverly, C. S. Fly leaves ... 1617.3

— Cherbuliez, V. Count Kostia ... 518.13

— Craven, P. Fleurange ... 518.17

— Droz, G. Babolain ... 518.15

— Erskine, *Mrs.* T. Wyncote ... 518.2

— Freytag, G. Ingraban ... 538.6

— Gift, T. Pretty Miss Bellew ... 529.10

— Hardy, T. Desperate remedies ... 518.22

— — Far from the madding crowd ... 518.24

— — The hand of Ethelberta ... 517.25

— — A pair of blue eyes ... 539.4

— — Under the greenwood tree ... 728.4

— Heine, H. Scintillations ... 518.14

— Jenkin, *Mrs.* C. Jupiter's daughters ... 518.21

— — Within an ace ... 539.10

— Oliphant, M. (O. W.) Whiteladies ... 539.11

— Parr, L. Hero Carthew ... 728.5

— Poynter, *Miss* —. Ersilia ... 517.23

— Richardson, S. Clarissa [Harlowe]; or, the history of a young lady ... 518.27

— Spielhagen, F. What the swallow sang ... 518.16

— Turgenef, I. S. On the eve ... 539.1

— — Smoke ... 537.14

— — Spring floods. A Lear of the steppe ... 528.9

— Tytler, C. C. F. Jonathan ... 517.22

— — Mistress Judith ... 518.25

— Walford, L. B. Mr. Smith ... 518.1

Leitch, Richard Pettigrew. A course of sepia painting. With 24 plates. London [1875]. 32+ pp. Oblong 16° ... 6217.11

— Course of water-colour drawing. With 24 coloured plates. 2d edition. London [1874]. 36+ pp. Oblong 16° ... 6217.9

Shelf. No.

LELAND, Charles Godfrey. The English gipsies and their language. New York, 1873. xiii, 259+ pp. 16° 5438.5

— Meister Karl's sketch-book. Philadelphia [*cop.* 1872]. 287 [271] pp. Sm. 8° 1913.2

— *editor.* Fusang, or the discovery of America by Chinese Buddhist priests in the fifth century. London, 1875. xix, 212 pp. 8° 5925.6

Contents. — The narrative of Hoei-Shin, with comments by C. F. Neumann; Remarks on the text of Neumann; Letter from B. Kennon on the navigation of the North Pacific ocean; Travels of other Buddhist priests from the 4th to the 8th century; American antiquities, with their relations to the old world; The advocates and opponents of the narrative of Hoei-Shin; The latest discussion of Fusang, by T. Simpson and E. Bretschneider.

LEMON, Mark. Falkner Lyle 312.9

— Golden fetters 312.6

— Leyton hall, and other tales 312.5

— Loved at last 312.7

— Wait for the end 312.8

— Reminiscences of, with [his] revised text of Falstaff. Hatton, J. London, 1871. 16° 5425.7

LEMONNYER, J. Les journaux de Paris pendant la commune. Paris [1871]. 94 pp. 12° 5534.2

LENA Cameron. Grey, *Mrs.* 521.30

'LENA Rivers. Holmes, M. J. 535.10

LENNOX, William Pitt, *lord.* My recollections from 1806 to 1873. London, 1874. 2 v. 8° 5633.4

LENOIR, Paul. Le Fayoum, le Sinaï et Pétra. Expédition dans la moyenne Égypte et l'Arabie Pétrée sous la direction de J. L. Gérome. Enrichi de gravures. Paris, 1872. 332+ pp. 18° 5935.10

LE NORMAND, Marie Anne. Historical and secret memoirs of the empress Josephine. Translated by J. M. Howard. New edition. Philadelphia, 1852, 54. 2 v. Portraits. 12° 1224.9

LENORMANT, Amélie (Cyvoct). Madame Récamier and her friends. From the French, by the translator of Madame Récamier's memoirs [Mrs. I. M. Wheelwright]. Boston, 1875. xx, 281 pp. 12° 1226.14

LENORMANT, Charles. *See* MÉRIMÉE, P. Portraits historiques et littéraires. Paris, 1874. 18° 5527.14

LENORMANT, François, and CHEVALLIER, E. The student's manual of oriental history. A manual of the ancient history of the East to the commencement of the Median wars. London, 1869, 70. 2 v. Sm. 8° 5927.8

Contents. — Vol. I. History of the Israelites, Egyptians, Assyrians, and Babylonians. II. Medes and Persians, Phœnicians, and Arabians.

LENT. Orazioni quaresimali ed altre nuove opere. Barbieri, G. Milano, 1836, 37. 2 v. 12° 2038.2

LENZEN, Mario. Not in their set. From the German by MS. 738.14

LEO X, Life of. Roscoe, W. London, 1868. 2 v. Sm. 8° 5526.6

LEOMINSTER, *Mass.*, History of. Wilder, D. Fitchburg, 1853. 12° 817.12

LEONARD, Levi Washburn. History of Dublin, N. H., containing the address by C. Mason, and the proceedings at the centennial celebration, June 17, 1852; with a register of families. Boston, 1855. vi, 433+ pp. Map. Portraits. 8° 5011.3

LEONARD family, A genealogical memoir of the. Deane, W. R. Boston, 1851. 8° 612.4

LEONORA d'Orco. A historical romance. James, G. P. R. 730.5

LEONOWENS, Anna Harriette. The English governess at the Siamese court: being recollections of six years in the royal palace at Bangkok. With illustrations. Boston, 1873. x, 321 pp. Facsimile. Sm. 8° 222.1

— The romance of the harem. Illustrated. Boston, 1873. viii, 277+ pp. Sm. 8° 5933.2

LÉOVILLE-MEILHAN, — , *vicomtesse* de. A chequered life: being [her] memoirs. Edited by the Vicomtesse Solange de Kerkadec. London, 1874. 302+ pp. Sm. 8° 1025.4

Shelf. No.

LE PILEUR, A. Wonders of the human body. Illustrated. New York, 1871. xii, 356 pp. 16° 1714.14

LE PLAY, (Pierre Guillaume) Frederic. The organization of labor in accordance with custom and the law of the decalogue. Translated by G. Emerson. Philadelphia, 1872. 417 pp. 12° 1526.22

LEPPERE, Adam Hamilton. The rainbow creed. A story of the times 532.16

— Where are my horns? Boston, 1873. 35 pp. 16° 6326.8

LEPSIUS, (Carl) Richard. Discoveries in Egypt, Ethiopia, and the peninsula of Sinai, in 1842–45. Edited, with notes, by K. R. H. Mackenzie. 2d edition. London, 1853. Illustrated. Map. 8° 5931.12

LE SAGE, Alain René. The adventures of Gil Blas of Santillane. Translated by T. Smollett. London [1867]. xiv, 442 pp. Illustrated. Sq. 16° 517.18

— Histoire de Gil Blas de Santillane. Paris, 1872. 686+ pp. Portrait. 18° 5536.17

Note. — See account of Le Sage in Scott's "Lives of the novelists" [5914.2].

LESLIE, Charles. Short method with deists. *See* ERSKINE, Thomas 5819.4

LESLIE, Charles Robert. Autobiographical recollections. Edited, with a prefatory essay on Leslie as an artist, and selections from his correspondence, by T. Taylor. With portrait. Boston, 1860. lviii, 363 pp. 8° 1024.10

— and TAYLOR, Tom. Life and times of Sir Joshua Reynolds: with notices of some of his cotemporaries. With portraits and illustrations. London, 1865. 2 v. 8° 5332.6

LESLIE, Eliza. The ladies' guide to true politeness and perfect manners. Philadelphia, N. D. 336 [334] pp. Sm. 8° 1514.2

LESLIE, *Mrs.* Madeline, *pseud.* *See* BAKER, Harriet Newell (Woods).

LESLIE stories, The. *See* BAKER, Harriet Newell (Woods).

LESLIE Tyrrell. Craik, G. M. 322.6

LESSING, Gotthold Ephraim. Laocoon. An essay upon the limits of painting and poetry. Translated by E. Frothingham. Boston, 1874. xi, 245 pp. 16° 6216.2

— Nathan the wise: a dramatic poem. Translated by E. Frothingham. [With] Kuno Fischer's Essay on the poem. 3d edition, revised. New York, 1871. xxviii, 259 pp. 12° 5736.4

— *Same.* Translated by W. Taylor. [And] Emilia Galotti: a tragedy. Translated by C. L. Lewes. Leipzig, 1868. 298 | pp. Sq. 16° 1613.6

— Lowell, J. R. Among my books. Boston, 1873. 16° 1934.8.1

— Stahr, A. The life and works of. New York, 1873. 2 v. 12° 1022.7

Note. — Stahr's Life, in the English translation, is the best account for the general reader; but Lowell's essay is founded on it. See also Hedge's "Prose writers of Germany" [5732.1]; De Quincey's "Essays on philosophical writers;" and Gostwick's "German poets" [5723.5].

LESSONS in life. Holland, J. G. New York, 1872. 12° 1914.4

LESTER, Charles Edwards. The Napoleon dynasty. A history of the Bonaparte family. By the Berkeley men [*pseud.*]. With portraits. New York, 1873. 636 pp. 12° 825.17

LESTER, John Erastus. The Atlantic to the Pacific. What to see and how to see it. Boston, 1873. 365 pp. Map. 12° 417.12

— *Same.* With map and illustrations. London, 1873. xii, 293+ pp. Sm. 8° 417.13

L'ESTRANGE, Alfred Guy (Kingham). Literary life of William Harness. London, 1871. 313+ pp. 8° 5422.9

LETTERING, The art of. Lyford, T. J., and Boyce, A. P. Boston, 1871. Oblong f° 6210.1

LETTERS and social aims. [Essays.] Emerson, R. W. Boston, 1876. 12° 1817.1

Shelf. No.

LETTERS from abroad to kindred at home. Sedgwick, C. M. New York, 1841. 12° 426.15

LETTERS from high latitudes; voyage to Iceland, Jan Mayen, and Spitzbergen, in 1856. Blackwood, F. T., *lord Dufferin.* Boston, 1859. 12°. 225.3

LETTERS from the East. Bryant, W. C. New York, 1869. 12° 424.9

LETTERS from the mountains. Grant, A. Boston, 1809. 2 v. 12° 1918.5

LETTERS of "An Englishman" on Louis Napoleon, the empire, and the coup d'état. Reprinted, with additions, from The times. London, 1852. viii, 134 pp. 16° 1226.12

LETTERS to mothers. Sigourney, L. H. New York, 1839. 12° 5218.2

LETTERS to the Joneses. Holland, J. G. New York, 1872. 12° 1934.5

LETTERS to young people, single and married. Holland, J. G. New York, 1872. 12° 1928.3

LEVER, Charles (James). Arthur O'Leary. Leipzig. 332.27
— *Same.* London 516.21
— Barrington. Leipzig 332.7
— *Same.* London 516.1
— The Bramleighs of Bishop's folly 332.14
— Charles O'Malley. Leipzig 332.1
— *Same.* London 516.13
— Confessions of Con Cregan. Leipzig 332.24
— *Same.* London 516.8
— The Daltons. Leipzig 332.28
— *Same.* London 516.9
— Davenport Dunn. Leipzig 332.4
— *Same.* London 516.7
— A day's ride: a life's romance. Leipzig 332.8
— *Same.* London 516.4
— Diary and notes of Horace Templeton 332.9
— The Dodd family abroad. Leipzig 332.22
— *Same.* London 516.18
— The fortunes of Glencore. Leipzig 332.12
— *Same.* London 516.15
— Gerald Fitzgerald, "the chevalier" 730.4
— Harry Lorrequer. Leipzig 332.2
— *Same.* London 516.12
— Jack Hinton, the guardsman. Leipzig 332.21
— *Same.* London 516.17
— The knight of Gwynne. Leipzig 332.18
— *Same.* London 516.11
— Lord Kilgobbin: a tale of Ireland in our own time. 332.16
— Luttrell of Arran. Leipzig 332.26
— *Same.* London 516.10
— The Martins of Cro' Martin. Leipzig 332.3
— *Same.* London 516.2
— Maurice Tiernay. Leipzig 332.6
— *Same.* London 516.14
— The O'Donoghue. Leipzig 332.17
— *Same.* London 516.16
— One of them. Leipzig 332.20
— *Same.* London 516.6
— A rent in a cloud. Leipzig 332.5
— *Same.* And St. Patrick's eve. London 516.3
— Roland Cashel. Leipzig 332.11
— *Same.* London 516.5
— St. Patrick's eve; Paul Gosslett's confessions 332.13
— Sir Brook Fossbrooke 332.23
— Sir Jasper Carew. Leipzig 332.25
— *Same.* London 516.20
— That boy of Norcott's 332.15
— Tom Burke of "Ours." Leipzig 332.10
— *Same.* London ....516.19 and 5627.3
— Tony Butler 332.19
— Selections from. *See* HALF hours with Irish authors. New York, 1873. 12° 737.9

Note. — Lever's novels are mostly pictures of Irish life and character. "The knight of Gwynne" concerns the bringing about of the union in 1801. The military and convivial Irishman is drawn in "Harry Lorrequer," "Charles O'Malley," and "Jack Hinton." The breaking up of the old families gives plots and character to "The O'Donoghue" and "The Martins of Cro' Martin."
See T. A. Trollope's "Recollections of Lever" in Lippincott's magazine, Dec., 1874.

LÉVY, Daniel. L'Autriche-Hongrie, ses institutions et ses nationalités. Paris, 1871. xxxi, 309+ pp. 2 folded leaves. 18° 627.2

LEWALD, Fanny. Hulda; or, the deliverer. A romance. After the German, by Mrs. A. L. Wister. 727.32

LEWES, George Henry. History of philosophy from Thales to Comte. 4th edition, corrected and partly rewritten. London, 1871. 2 v. 8° 6832.1

Contents. — Vol. I. Ancient philosophy. II. Modern philosophy.

— On actors and the art of acting. Leipzig, 1875. 279 pp. Sq. 16° 1638.1
— *Same.* London, 1875. xiv, 278 pp. Sm. 8° ... 5428.20
— The physiology of common life. With numerous woodcuts. Leipzig, 1860. 2 v. in 1. Sq. 16°. 1528.1
— Problems of life and mind. Vol. I. London, 1874. 8° 5833.4

Contents. — Vol. I. Foundations of a creed.

— Ranthorpe. Leipzig, 1847. xii, 307 pp. Sq. 16°. 312.4
— The story of Goethe's life. London, 1873. vi, 375+ pp. Portrait. 8° 5724.1

LEWES, Marian, *formerly Miss Evans, wife of the preceding.* (*George Eliot.*) Adam Bede. [Ordinary English life] 310.25
— Daniel Deronda. Vol. I 722.20
— Felix Holt 310.24
— The legend of Jubal and other poems. Boston, 1874. 233+ pp. 16° 5617.18
— Middlemarch. [Elaborate picture of provincial town life.] 2 v. ....532.3 and 5636.2
— Romola. [Florence and Savonarola] 310.23
— Scenes of clerical life 310.26
— Silas Marner 310.22
— The Spanish gypsy. A poem. Boston, 1872. 287+ pp. 12° 1625.1
— Wit and wisdom. Boston, 1875. 260+ pp. Sq. 16°. 1839.1
— *See* RIBOT, T. English psychology. New York, 1874. 8° 5835.5

Note. — "George Eliot" is reckoned in the highest sense the greatest of living novelists; but her works require culture in their reader to effect their full power. She shows great insight in the delineation of women, and her stories deal mostly with modern English life. See MacCarthy's "Modern leaders" [5913.6].

LEWIS, Charles B. Goaks and tears. By M. Quad [*pseud.*]. With a centennial calendar, illustrated 713.9

LEWIS, Dioclesian. Five-minute chats with young women, and certain other parties [on health]. New York, 1874. 426 pp. 12° 1522.9
— Our digestion. Philadelphia, 1872. 407 pp. Illustrated. Portrait. 12° 1522.4
— Our girls. New York, 1871. 383 pp. 12° 1536.3
— Weak lungs, and how to make them strong. Illustrated. Boston, 1871. 360 pp. 12° 1536.2

LEWIS, *Sir* George Cornewall. An historical survey of the astronomy of the ancients. London, 1862. viii, 527 pp. 8° 6813.5

LEWIS, Matthew Gregory. Raymond and Agnes: a drama. New York, N. D. 24 pp. 12° 1635.4

LEWIS, Richard. History of the life-boat, and its work. With illustrations. London, 1874. xv, 226 pp. Sm. 8° 5925.3

LEWIS Arundel. Smedley, F. E. 510.11

LEXINGTON, *Mass.*, History of the battle of. Frothingham, R. Boston, 1851. 8° 812.6

Note. — See also the note in the Bulletin for July, 1875.

LEYTON hall. Lemon, M. 312.5

LIBER veritatis. Gelée, C. London, 1872. 3 v. F°. 6220.6

LIBERIA, Documents concerning. *See* AMERICAN colonization society 5222.3

LIBERTY. Mill, J. S. On liberty. New York, 1874. 8° 1733.2
— Stephen, J. F. Liberty, equality, fraternity. London, 1873. 8° 5831.2

LIBERTY bell, The. [Anti-slavery papers.] By friends of freedom. Boston, 1843, 44, 46, 47, 49. 5 v. Portraits. 12° 1417.1

LIBRARIES. Edwards, E. Free town libraries, their formation, management, and history; in Britain, France, Germany, and America. New York, 1869. 8° 6132.2
— — Memoirs of libraries: including a hand-book of library economy. London, 1859. 2 v. 8° 6133.3

Shelf. No.

LIBRARIES, *continued.*

— Hesse, L. A. C. Bibliothéconomie. Paris, 1841. 24°. 6139.1

— Putnam, G. P. The best reading. Hints on the selection of books; on the formation of libraries, etc. New York, 1872. 12° ............*R.R., F.3.5

— *Same.* New York, 1875. 12° 6136.10

LIBRARY of American biography. *See* SPARKS, Jared, *editor* 5028.1

LIDDELL, Henry George, and SCOTT, Robert, *compilers.* A Greek-English lexicon. 6th edition. Oxford, 1869. xvi, 1865 pp. 4° ...............*R.R., D.3.6

LIEBER, Francis. Manual of political ethics. 2d edition, revised. Edited by T. D. Woolsey. Philadelphia, 1875. 2 v. 8° 5833.6

LIEBIG, Justus von. Animal chemistry. Edited by W. Gregory. With additions, notes, and corrections, by Dr. Gregory and J. W. Webster. Cambridge, 1842. xl, 347 pp. 12° 6035.3

— Familiar letters on chemistry. Edited by J. Gardiner. New York, 1856. 180 pp. 12°....... 1525.3

LIECHTENSTEIN, Marie, *princess.* Holland house. With [portraits, fac-similes and] illustrations. 2d edition. London, 1874. 2 v. 8° 5434.1

Note. — The famous seat of the Fox family, with an account of its associations.

LIFE. Beale, L. S. On life and vital action in health and disease. London, 1875. Sm. 8°....6036.14

— Greg, W. R. Enigmas of life. Boston, 1873. 12° ....1534.2 and 6136.5

— Reclus, (J. J.) É. The ocean, atmosphere, and life. New York, 1873. 8°................. 6632.2

LIFE and public services of Major-general George Gordon Meade. Philadelphia [*cop.* 1864]. 80 [62] pp. 8° 1013.5

LIFE, A, for a life. Craik, D. (M.).............. 323.24

LIFE here and there. Willis, N. P. New York, 1850. 12° 714.28

LIFE in Danbury. Bailey, J. M. Boston, 1873. 16°. 538.1

LIFE in the clearings versus the bush. Moodie, S. (S.) New York [1853]. 12°................... 414.8

LIFE in the open air. Winthrop, T. 716.33

LIFE thoughts. Beecher, H. W. Boston, 1858. 12°. 5815.9

— *Same.* New York, 1871. 12° 1533.11

LIFE under glass. [Artificial climates.] Shove, G. A. Boston, 1874. 16°...................... 6837.2

LIFE without and life within. Ossoli, S. M. F., *marchesa* d'. Boston, 1874. 12°................. 1935.7

LIFE'S, A, assize. Riddell, J. H.................. 720.5

LIFE'S lesson. [Fiction.] Thomas, M............ 723.28

LIFE'S, A, lessons. Gore, C. G. F................. 311.2

LIFE'S, A, secret. Wood, E. P. 333.7

LIFE-BOATS. Ballantyne, R. M. The lifeboat..... 934.17

— Gilmore, J. Storm warriors; or life-boat work on the Goodwin sands. London, 1875. Sm. 8°. 5935.6

— Lewis, R. History of the life-boat, and its work. London, 1874. Sm. 8° 5935.3

LIGHT. Abbott, J. Science for the young 912.4

— Lees, W. Elements of. New York [Glasgow], 1873. 16°......................................1717.10

— Lommel, E. (C. J.) The nature of. New York, 1876. 12°......................................6436.17

— Tyndall, J. Light and electricity. New York, 1873. 12°......................................1523.20

— — Six lectures on. London, 1875. Sm. 8°...... 6436.1

— Vogel, H. Chemistry of. New York, 1875. 12°. 6436.16

See also Spectrum analysis.

LIGHT science for leisure hours. Proctor, R. A. New York, 1871. 12° 1527.3

LIGHTFOOT, Joseph Baber, TRENCH, Richard Chenevix, and ELLICOTT, Charles John. The revision of the English version of the New Testament. With an introduction by Philip Schaff. New York, 1873. 3 v. in 1. 8°.....................5814.11

Contents. — Introduction on the revision of the English Bible. By P. Schaff. xlix pp.; On a fresh revision of the English New Testament. By J. B. Lightfoot. 2d edition, revised. 195 pp.; On the authorized version of the New Testament in connection with some recent proposals for its revision. By R. C. Trench. 193 pp.; Considerations on the revision of the English version of the New Testament. By C. J. Ellicott. 178 pp.

Note. — A republication of various English works, of which the one by Trench was published in 1859, those by Ellicott and Lightfoot in 1870 and 1871.

Shelf. No.

LIGHTNING. Fonvielle, W. de. Thunder and lightning. New York, 1872. 16°...............1714.22

— Forbes, R. B. Shipwreck by lightning. Papers relative to Harris's lightning conductors. Boston, 1853. 8°............................... 1711.3

LIGHTNING express. Adams, W. T................ 925.19

LIGHTS and shadows of New York life. MacCabe, J. D. Philadelphia [*cop.* 1872]. 8° 814.9

LIKE father, like son. Payn, J.................... 312.3

LILIAN. Greenough, S. L........................ 716.16

LILIAN Dalzell 732.17

LILLIESLEAF. Oliphant, M. (O. W.).............. 736.13

LILLINGSTONES, The, of Lillingstone. Worboise, E. J. 735.17

LILY, The, and the bee. Warren, S............... 316.10

LILY, The, and the cross. A tale of Acadia. De Mille, J.. 724.12

LILY Norris' enemy. Mathews, J. H..............1117.26

LIMES, Rudimentary treatise on. Burnell, G. R. London, 1872. 12°.............................1716.11

LIMITATIONS, The, of human responsibility. Wayland, F. Boston, 1838. 16°................. 5838.4

LINCOLN, Abraham. Memorial of. *See* BOSTON, *Mass.* 5020.4

— Proceedings of the city council of Boston, April 17, 1865, on occasion of [his] death. *See* BOSTON, *Mass*... 5020.6

— Sermons preached in Boston on [his] death. Together with the funeral services in the east room of the executive mansion at Washington. Boston, 1865. 379 pp. 12° 5027.3

— Bancroft, G. Memorial address on the life and character of. Washington, 1866. 69 pp. 8° . 1212.8

— Carpenter, F. B. The inner life of. Six months at the White house. New York, 1870. 16°... 1216.9

— Hanaford, P. A. Abraham Lincoln: his life and public services. Boston, 1865. 12°.......... 1214.2

— Lamon, W. H. Life of. Boston, 1872. 8° 5020.5

— Thayer, W. M. The pioneer boy, and how he became president. Boston, 1863. 12°........ 916.26

— Welles, G. Lincoln and Seward. New York, 1874. 12°.......................................5027.10

Note. — Confining his narrative to the period before his presidency, Lamon offers by far the amplest account, but the author has little knowledge of book-craft, nor is he very regardful of delicacy or of privacy. While the extent of the book will prevent general familiarity with it, his opportunities have added much of detail, and disclosed something of novelty for the future biographer. Of the shorter tributes, the essay by J. R. Lowell, in "My study windows," may be mentioned. See also North American review, Jan., 1865; and Harper's monthly, vols. 31 and 37.

LINDA. Hentz, C. L............................. 536.11

LINDA di Chamounix. Donizetti, G. (*In* Ditson, O., and co. Standard opera librettos).........6233.3.2

LINDENDALE stories. *See* WISE, Daniel.

LINEAR perspective. Pellegrin, V. New York [London], 1873. 16° 6218.1

LINES in pleasant places. Shillaber, B. P. Chelsea, 1874. 16° 1615.7

LINES left out; or, some of the histories left out in "Line upon line." Mortimer, *Mrs.* —. New York, 1870. 16° 928.8

LINGARD, John. History of England, from the first invasion by the Romans to the accession of William and Mary in 1688. [Catholic view.] 6th edition. London, 1855. 10 v. Illustrated. Portrait. Sm. 8°.................................. 5417.8

LINLEY Rochford. MacCarthy, J................. 710.26

LINTON, Eliza Lynn. Patricia Kemball: a novel. Leipzig.. 330.9

— *Same.* Philadelphia............................ 714.13

— The true history of Joshua Davidson [*i. e.* Joshua (Jesus) David's son], communist. Leipzig, 1873. 254 pp. Sq. 16°.............................. 312.29

— *Same.* Philadelphia, 1873. viii, 279 pp. 12°. 736.22

Note. — "The story of a spiritual-minded young man of the working-class of our own day; beginning his career with the human life of Christ as his absolute ideal, and, in a much too narrow sense, his model, and gradually modifying his conception of it . . . in the course of an unassisted struggle with the principles and machinery of modern society." *The Spectator, March 22, 1873.*

LINWOODS, The. Sedgwick, C. M. 2 v. 737.3

LION Ben of Elm island. Kellogg, E.............. 922.15

LION-HEARTED. Grey, *Mrs.* 521.39

Shelf. No.

LION hunter, The, of South Africa. Cumming, R. G. London, 1870. Sm. 8° 5934.11
LION hunting and sporting life in Algeria. Gérard, (C.) J. (B.) London, 1857. 16° 427.4
LIONEL Lincoln. [Bunker hill, siege of Boston.] Cooper, J. F. 525.9
LIONELLO. Bresciani, A............................ 714.21
LIPPINCOTT, Sara Jane. (*Grace Greenwood.*) Bonnie Scotland. Tales of her history, heroes, and poets. With illustrations. Boston, 1872. 273 pp. 16°. 933.20
— Haps and mishaps of a tour in Europe. Boston, 1854. xii, 437 pp. 12°.................... 424.4
— Heads and tales: studies and stories of pets 921.15
— History of my pets............................ 933.21
— Merrie England. Travels, descriptions, tales and historical sketches. Illustrations. Boston, 1868. 261 pp. 16°.............................. 922.26
— New life in new lands: notes of travel. New York, 1873. 413+ pp. 12° 214.1

Contents. — Chicago as it was; Colorado; Utah; Nevada; California; Homeward journey; Colorado in autumn.

— Recollections of my childhood, and other stories. 922.25
— Stories and legends of travel and history........ 922.23
— Stories from famous ballads 922.24
— Stories of many lands 928.7
LIPPINCOTT's pronouncing gazetteer. *See* THOMAS, Joseph, and BALDWIN, Thomas ..........*R.R., B.3.2
LIPPINCOTT's magazine. Vol. 1-16. Philadelphia, 1868-75. 16 v. 8°........................ 1416.1
LIQUORS, Fermented. Feuchtwanger, L. New York, 1858. 12°.................................. 6826.2
LISBON, Ship and shore, in. Colton, W. New York, 1856. 12° 425.16
LISTON, Robert. Elements of surgery. Philadelphia, 1837. 540 pp. L. 12°........................6023.11
LISZT, Franz. Life of Chopin. From the French by M. W. Cook. Boston, N. D. 4th edition revised. 202 pp. 16° 1227.2
LITERARY and social judgments. Greg, W. R. Boston, 1873. 16°............................5616.10
LITERARY life, Recollections of a. [Mostly selections from authors.] Mitford, M. R. New York, [1851]. 12° 1536.4
LITERARY reminiscences. De Quincey, T. Boston, 1851. 2 v. 12° 1226.1
LITERARY world, The. Vol. 3, 4. Boston [1872-74]. 2 v. 4°.............................. 1434.1
LITERATURE. Arnold, M. Literature and dogma. London, 1873. Sm. 8° 5815.6
— Brande, W. T., and Cox, G. W. Dictionary of. London, 1872. 3 v. 8°................*R.R., E.3.6
— Disraeli, I. Amenities of. New York, 1871. 2 v. 16°.......................................1533.33
— — Curiosities of New York, 1872. 4 v. 16°.... 5626.6
— — The literary character. Literary miscellanies. New York, 1868. 16°..........................1533.14
— Graesse, J. G. T. Lehrbuch einer allgemeinen Literärgeschichte aller bekannten Völker der Welt. Dresden, 1838. 13 v. 8° 6132.1
— Mueller, F. M. Chips from a German workshop. New York, 1872. Sm. 8°.....................5616.1.3
— Purnell, T. Literature and its professors. London [1867]. 16°........................... 5927.3
— Scherer, E. Nouvelles études sur la littérature contemporaine. Paris, 1865. 12°........... 2016.1
— Staël-Holstein, A. L. G. N., *baronne* de. Influence of literature upon society. (*In* The Alexandrian).1910.4.2
— Villemain, A. F. Choix d'études sur la littérature contemporaine. Paris, 1858. 12°........5537.12
— — Études de littérature ancienne et étrangere. Paris, 1870. 12° 5537.17
— Whipple, E. P. Literature and life. Boston, 1871. 16°.............................. 1936.6
— Wright, T. History of caricature and grotesque in. London [1864]. Sm. 4°.................. 5923.4

Note. — For the literature of particular countries and languages, see under their several names.
The history of literature is a department of letters of modern growth. Hallam, in his "Literature of Europe," etc. [1531.2], traces in his preface its rise and progress. Madame de Staël's work on literature in its relations with society is reviewed in Jeffrey's essays [5610.8], and is the earliest extensive work in the modern spirit.

Shelf. No.

LITTELL's living age. Vol. 1-36; 4th series, vol. 26, 27; 5th series, vol. 1-12. Boston, 1844-75. 50 v. 8° 1326.1
LITTELL's museum of foreign literature and science. Vol. 12. Philadelphia, 1828. 8°............ 1712.2
LITTLE, Sophia L. Pentecost. [A poem.] Newport, R. I., 1869. 49 pp. Sq. 16°........... 1617.7
— Thrice through the furnace: a tale of the times of the Iron hoof. Pawtucket, R. I., 1852. 190 pp. 12° 715.18
LITTLE Agnes. Baker, H. N. (W.)................ 934.5
LITTLE beauty, The. Grey, *Mrs*................... 534.23
LITTLE Ben Hadden; or, do right, whatever comes of it. Kingston, W. H. G.........................1117.19
LITTLE Ben Hadden series. *See* KINGSTON, William H. G.
LITTLE Bobtail. Adams, W. T. 923.18
LITTLE Briggs and I. Ludlow, F. H. (*In* Johnson, (E.) R. Little classics)...........................529.4.11
LITTLE by little. Adams, W. T...................... 924.18
LITTLE camp, The, on Eagle hill. Warner, S....... 928.9
LITTLE Canary. Osgood, *Mrs.* M. A.............. 927.17
LITTLE Canary's black Cato. Osgood, *Mrs.* M. A.... 927.19
LITTLE Canary's cousin Eugene. Osgood, *Mrs.* M. A. 927.18
LITTLE Canary's daisy. Osgood, *Mrs.* M. A........ 927.16
LITTLE classics. *See* JOHNSON, (Edwin) Rossiter, *editor*.
LITTLE coin, much care. Howitt, M................. 937.3
LITTLE cricket. Samuels, A. F.................... 918.27
LITTLE Cuba; or, circumstantial evidence. Barclay, G. L.. 710.36
LITTLE Dorrit. Dickens, C. (J. H.) Boston. 2 v...1824.12
— *Same.* Leipzig. 4 v. in 2 .... 338.16
LITTLE flower seekers, The. Mulholland, R........ 912.18
LITTLE folk life. Dodge, M. A...................... 927.21
LITTLE folks astray. Clarke, R. S. 927.9
LITTLE foxes. Stowe, H. (E.) B.................... 537.12
LITTLE grandfather. Clarke, R. S. 939.3
LITTLE Jakey. De Kroyft, S. H. (*In* Johnson, (E.) R. Little classics)..............................529.4.10
LITTLE Joanna, The. Bellamy, *Mrs.* E. W......... 721.21
LITTLE Kate Kirby. Robinson, F. W................. 731.1
LITTLE lame prince, The, and his travelling cloak. Craik, D. (M.) 310.29
LITTLE Louvre. Abbott, J. Harper's story books.. 936.1.2
LITTLE maid, The, of Oxbow. Nowell, H. P. H. ... 936.23
LITTLE men. Alcott, L. M.......................... 926.14
LITTLE merchant, The. Adams, W. T.............. 918.9
LITTLE Paul. Abbott, J. Harper's story books ...936.1.12
LITTLE Prudy. Clarke, R. S. 927.6
LITTLE Prudy series. *See* CLARKE, Rebecca Sophia.
LITTLE Prudy's Flyaway series. *See* CLARKE, Rebecca Sophia.
LITTLE Pussy Willow. Stowe, H. (E.) B. 932.2
LITTLE Spaniard, The. Nowell, H. P. H............ 936.25
LITTLE sunbeams. *See* MATHEWS, Joanna H.
LITTLE wanderers', The, advocate. Vol. 11. Boston, 1875. 8°.. 1335.2
LITTLE wife, The. Grey, *Mrs*...................... 521.31
LITTLE women. Alcott, L. M. 2 v.................. 926.12
LITTLEJOHN, W. H. The constitutional amendment: or the Sunday, the Sabbath, the change, and restitution. A discussion [with] the editor of the Christian statesman. Battle Creek, Mich., 1873. 384 pp. 16°...........................5818.14
LITURGIES and other documents of the ante-Nicene period. Edinburgh, 1872. viii, 186 pp. [Ante-Nicene Christian library.] 8° 6322.4.24
LITURGIES. The Sunday school liturgy. Boston, 1856. 12°.. 5818.6
LIVE and let live. Sedgwick, C. M................. 918.10
LIVE it down. Jeaffreson, J. C.................... 732.29
LIVER. Flint, A., *jr.* Experimental researches into a new excretory function of the. N. P., N. D. 8°.6023.19
— — Recherches expérimentales sur une nouvelle fonction du foie. Paris, 1868. 8° 6023.19
LIVERMORE, Abiel Abbot. The four gospels: with a commentary. Vol. II. Mark, Luke, and John. Boston, 1858. 12°.............................. 1534.6
LIVERMORE, Elizabeth, Sermon on the death of. Ware, J. F. W. Cambridge, 1856. 8°........ 6323.1

Shelf. No.

LIVERMORE, George. Opinions of the founders of the republic on negroes as slaves, as citizens, and as soldiers. Boston, 1862. xiv, 215 pp. 8°. 812.9

LIVERMORE, Nathaniel, Sermon on the death of. Ware, J. F. W. Cambridge, 1856. 8°........ 6323.1

LIVERPOOL. The stranger in Liverpool; or, an historical and descriptive view of the town of Liverpool and its environs. Liverpool [1829]. Sm. 12° 438.5

LIVING link, The. De Mille, J..................... 710.2

LIVINGSTON, Edward. *See* HAYWARD, A. Biographical and critical essays. London, 1873. 8°...5833.3.2

LIVINGSTON, John. Biographical sketches of distinguished Americans. New York, 1853. viii, 504 pp. 8°.............................. 5024.3

LIVINGSTONE, David. Last journals in Central Africa. From 1865 to his death. Continued by a narrative of his last moments and sufferings, obtained from his faithful servants Chuma and Susi, by H. Waller. With portrait, maps, and illustrations. New York, 1875. 541 pp. 8°. 421.10 and 5921.3

— Livingstone and his African explorations: together with a full account of the Young, Stanley, and Dawson search expeditions; chapters on ancient and modern Nile discovery; on the Central African slave trade, etc. New York, 1872. 292 pp. Portrait. Map. 12°........ 5915.2

— Missionary travels and researches in South Africa; including a sketch of sixteen years' residence in the interior of Africa. With portrait, maps, and illustrations. New York, 1858. xxiv [xx], 732 pp. 8°.............................. 422.9

— Perilous adventures and discoveries in the interior of Africa, together with the success and important results of the Herald-Stanley expedition, as furnished by H. M. Stanley. Added a sketch of the diamond diggings. Illustrated. Philadelphia [*cop.* 1872]. xvi, 598 [596] pp. Portraits. 16°.............................. 5915.5

— How I found Livingstone. Stanley, H. M. New York, 1872. 8°..................422.24 and 5931.5

— Travels. *See* ENGLISH explorers. London, 1875. Sm. 8° 5927.9

Note. — There is a summary of Livingstone's explorations in B. Taylor's "South Africa" [224.1]. See Sir Samuel W. Baker's review of Livingstone's "Last journals" in Macmillan's magazine, 1875; also, Sunday magazine, Oct., 1874; and Harper's monthly, vol. 16. See the note under Africa, in this Catalogue, and in that of History, etc., of the Lower Hall of the Central Library.

LIVIUS PATAVINUS, Titus. [*Livy.*] Selections from the first five books. With the 21st and 22nd entire. Chiefly from the text of Alschefski. With English notes. By J. L. Lincoln. With a plan of Rome, and a map of the passage of Hannibal. 10th edition, revised. New York, 1857. vi, 329+ pp. 12°..................1933.15

LIZZIE Leigh. Gaskell, E. C......................... 328.17

LLOYD, William Watkiss. The age of Pericles. A history of the politics and arts of Greece from the Persian to the Peloponnesian war. London, 1875. 2 v. 8°..............................5921.12

LOBDELL, Henry, Life of. Tyler, W. S. Boston [*cop.* 1859]. 12° 1015.4

LOCKE, David Ross. (*Petroleum V. Nasby.*) Eastern fruit on western dishes. The morals of Abou Ben Adhem. Boston, 1875. 231 pp. 12°.1536.22

— Ekkoes from Kentucky. Illustrated. Boston, 1868. 324 pp. 12°.............................. 536.13

— "Swingin round the cirkle." Illustrated. Boston, 1868. 299+ pp. Sm. 8°.............. 536.14

LOCKE, Jane Ermina. The recalled; in voices of the past, and poems of the ideal. Boston, 1854. vii, 246 pp. Portrait. 16°..................1615.10

LOCKE, John. Essay on the human understanding. With a life of the author. New York, 1818. 2 v. in 1. 8° 1912.6

— Essays. (*In* Sparks, J. Collection of essays and tracts in theology) 1918.9.6

— A paraphrase and notes on the epistles of St. Paul. Cambridge, 1832. 455 pp. 8°........ 6322.1

Shelf. No.

LOCKE, John, *continued.*

— and MILTON, John. Some thoughts concerning education, by John Locke; and a treatise of education, by John Milton. With an appendix containing Locke's Memoranda on study. Vol. I. Boston, 1830. 16° 1737.3

LOCKE Amsden. Thompson, D. P................. 734.5

LOCKHART, John Gibson. Ancient Spanish ballads; historical and romantic. New revised edition, with a biographical notice. Boston, 1861. 151 pp. Portrait. Sm. 8° 1616.5

— Memoirs of Sir Walter Scott. New edition. Edinburgh, 1860. xii, 806 pp. Portrait. L. 8°. 1020.1

— — Epitome of. Jenkinson, H. I. Edinburgh, 1873. 8°..............................5425.10

— Valerius. New edition. Edinburgh, 1869. 361+ pp. 16°.............................. 738.7

LOCKS, Construction of. Tomlinson, C. London, N. D. 12° 1715.27

LOCKYER, Joseph Norman. Nature series. The spectroscope and its applications. With coloured plate and illustrations. London, 1873. xii, 117 pp. 16°.............................. 6826.4

LOCOMOTION, Animal mechanism: a treatise on terrestrial and aërial. Marey, É. J. New York, 1874. 12°..............................6436.12

LOCOMOTIVE engine. Dempsey, G. D. Rudimentary treatise on the. London, 1866. 12°.......... 1716.7

— Evers, H. Steam and the. New York [Glasgow], 1873. 16° 1717.3

See also Steam-engine.

LODGE, Edmund. Portraits of illustrious personages of Great Britain. With biographical and historical memoirs of their lives and actions. London, 1849, 50. 8 v. Sm. 8°.................. 5337.6

LOG-BOOK of a fisherman and zoologist. Buckland, F. London, 1875. 8° 6614.12

LOGIC. Mill, J. S. A system of. London, 1872. 2 v. 8° 5833.1

— Swinbourne, A. (J.) Picture logic. London, 1875. Sm. 8°..............................5616.10

See also Parliamentary logick.

LOIS the witch. Gaskell, E. C. 328.14

LOLA MONTEZ, *or* PORRIS Y MONTEZ, Maria Dolores Eliza Rosanna Gilbert. Lectures. Including her autobiography. New York, 1858. 292 pp. 12°. 1024.4

— *Same.* Philadelphia [*cop.* 1858]. 292 pp. 12°. 1225.1

LOMBARD street [London]: a description of the money market. Bagehot, W. New York, 1873. 12°. 5435.8

LOMBARDI, I. Verdi, G. (*In* Ditson, O., and co. Standard opera librettos)..................6233.3.6

LOMMEL, Eugen (Cornelius Joseph). International scientific series. The nature of light, with a general account of physical optics. With illustrations. New York, 1876. xiii, 356 pp. 12°.6436.17

LONDON. Abbott, J. Rollo in London 917.20

— Bagehot, W. Lombard street: a description of the money market. New York, 1873. 12°.... 5435.8

— Becker, B. H. Scientific London. London, 1874. Sm. 8°..............................5616.16

— Davies, C. M. Unorthodox London: or phases of religious life in the metropolis. London, 1873. 8° 5811.4

— Dixon, W. H. Her majesty's tower. Leipzig, 1869. 4 v. in 2. Sq. 16° 838.4

— Grant, J. The great metropolis. New York, 1837. 2 v. in 1. 12°.............................. 827.2

— Great army, The. Sketches of life and character in a Thames-side district. London, 1876. Sm. 8° 1838.2

— Howitt, W. The northern heights of. London, 1869. 8°.............................. 5423.6

— Hunt, (J. H.) L. The town: its memorable characters and events. London, 1872. 16°.... 5437.1

— Jesse, J. H. London: its celebrated characters and remarkable places. London, 1871. 3 v. Sm. 8°.............................. 5435.3

— Mayhew, H., and others. London characters: illustrations of the humour, pathos, and peculiarities of London life. London, 1874. Sm. 8°. 5436.2

Shelf. No.

LONDON, *continued*.
— Meteyard, E. The hallowed spots of ancient London. London, 1870. Sm. 4° 5436.3
— Nadal, E. S. Impressions of London social life. New York, 1875. 16° 436.6
— The national gallery of pictures by the great masters. London, N. D. 4° 6210.9
— Rush, R. Memoranda of a residence at the court of. Philadelphia, 1833. 8° 5433.1
— Thornbury, W. Old and new London. Vol. I. London [1873]. L. 8° 5432.1

Shelf. No.

LONDON, *continued*.
— Timbs, J. Clubs and club life in. London, 1872. Sm. 8° 5417.3
— – Curiosities of. London [1867]. 8° 5435.1
— – London and Westminster. London, 1868. 2 v. 8° 5435.4
— – Romance of. London [1865]. 2 v. Sm. 8°. 5617.15
— Wheatley, H. B. Round about Piccadilly and Pall Mall. London, 1870. 8° 5435.2

See also British museum, City road chapel, Cobden club, Royal institution, Westminster abbey.

NOTE ON LONDON.

There are many books describing the great metropolis, which trace the historical associations connected with its topographical features, and for completeness and purposes of reference the best is probably Cunningham's Handbook, whose alphabetical arrangement makes it, however, somewhat unattractive for the ordinary reader. Its store of information is vast, its accuracy surprising, and great use is made by the author of illustrative citations from past writers, particularly from the old dramatists. As a continuous narrative under different heads, with a great deal of antiquarian lore and interest from associations of all kinds, the general reader will find more enjoyment perhaps from Charles Knight's six royal octavos on London, in which he was assisted by many hands, and of which his Cyclopædia is a convenient abridgment. These books must be sought, however, in the Bates Hall, unless sufficient is gleaned from Grant's "Great metropolis" [827.2], and others to be named. Knight's account is, however, twenty years old, and some of the more recent writers have had the advantage of the later developments, and London has much changed in a score of years. The most fertile and one of the most readable of these is Timbs, who in various books has grouped a great store of curious antiquarian research. The enlarged edition, 1868, of his "Curiosities of London" [5435.1], gives by an alphabetical arrangement the labors of a long life in this field. Of his separate books, his "Club life" [5417.3], describes the life at clubs, coffee-houses and taverns during the 17th-19th centuries, with sketches of characters; his "Romance of London" [5617.15] gives many historic sketches, with accounts of famous duels, highwaymen, crimes, etc.; his "Walks and talks" [in Bates Hall] gives us the historic associations of Vauxhall (of which in its last days we have a picture in Thackeray's "Vanity fair"), Mayfair, the Temple, etc.; while in his "London and Westminster" [5435.4] he develops particularly the changes of metropolitan life. The common highwayman occurrences of Hampstead heath in the last century are described in Howitt's "Northern heights" [5423.6]. One of the most agreeable and compact books is Leigh Hunt's "Town," above named. Jesse is another antiquarian, whose books are well known, his "Literary and historical memorials" being followed by his "London and its celebrities," and the two reappeared amalgamated, with additions, in 1871, in his "London: its celebrated characters and remarkable places" [5435.3]. Another recent book by Miss Meteyard, "Hallowed spots of ancient London" [5436.3], is of moderate compass, and has fresh researches. Thornbury's "Old and new London" [5432.1] depicts the city by successive stages of its growth, as Roman, Saxon, Chaucer's London, with the historic associations of the Temple, St. Paul's, etc. Macaulay [838.1], in his 3d chapter, gives a graphic description of London in 1685.

There are some valuable monographs of confined localities, like Wheatley, on the region about Piccadilly [5435.2], the court end of the town; and William Howitt, on "The northern heights of the metropolis" [5423.6], with full appreciation of their literary memories.

On the *Tower*, there is that by Hepworth Dixon [838.4], who traces its mournful history with much antiquarian zeal, and sections will be found in Jesse's, and other general accounts.

On the *Abbey*, there is Dean Stanley [5414.2], but the chapters in the general accounts will suffice the general reader.

On the *charities* of London, there is much in the "Romance of the streets" [5438.2] on the Ragged schools and City missions; and incidentally in Grant's "Great army."

The subject of *London schools*, which forms so considerable interest in the writings of Coleridge, De Quincey, Leigh Hunt, and others, can be understood from Staunton's "Great schools of England," from Lamb's essay on "Christ's hospital," etc. See also Harper's monthly, vol. 1.

On the *life and manners*, Knight has an instructive chapter about those of the last century, and about the aspects of London in Walpole's day. For the present century, much can be learned in the biographies of prominent Englishmen, and in such special books as Nadal's.

Much has been done to illustrate the *low life* of the metropolis, and by none so extensively as by Henry Mayhew, in his valuable "London labour and the London poor" [in the Bates Hall], embracing those who will, who cannot, and who will not work; but there is an epitome of his labors and others in "London characters;" and much further can be gleaned from Wynter's several books, like "Our social bees," "Curiosities of toil," "Peeps into the human hive" [6436.8], etc. The divertisements of the lower classes at different periods are set forth in Morley's "Bartholomew fair" [5418.8].

The illustration which London and its life has received from fiction should not be passed over. For the period, 1547-49, see Mrs. Manning's "Edward Osborne." Ainsworth's "Tower of London" closes with the execution of Lady Jane Grey, 1553; and see other of his novels. Williams's "Shakespeare and his friends" [531.23] is an elaborate study of life at the Mermaid, etc., in the early part of the seventeenth century, and Knight's "Life of Shakespeare" [5420.4] should be read in the same connection, as also the essay on Shakespeare's London in Rodenberg's England. Scott's "Fortunes of Nigel" [324.12; 523.2] gives us the city in the time of James I. De Foe's book on the plague, 1665 [in the Central Library], is a fiction, but so minutely wrought that it passed for truth for a long time. This epoch, which covers also the period of the great fire of 1666, is also depicted in Mrs. Manning's "Cherry and Violet," and in Ainsworth's "Old Saint Paul's" [712.6]. Thackeray, in his "Henry Esmond" [335.10; 513.1.4], made a very careful study of the life in the time of Queen Anne, a field embraced also, but not so closely studied, by Bulwer, in his "Devereux" [336.3]. Dickens, in his "Barnaby Rudge" [1824.5], has taken the period of the Gordon riots, 1780. Macaulay says Miss Burney's "Evelina" [311.28] depicts the fashionable and vulgar life of the same period with great force.

There are conspicuous examples of the treatment of the low life of the metropolis of our day in Dickens's "Oliver Twist" [338.8; 1824.7] and "Nicholas Nickleby" [338.4; 1824.2]; in Douglas Jerrold's "St. Giles and St. James" [313.9]; and it is carefully studied in Greenwood's "History of a little ragamuffin" [521.5].

Shelf. No.

LONDON quarterly review. Vol. 76. American edition. New York, 1845. 8° 1422.3
LONDON romance, A. Ross, C. H. 316.13
LONDONDERRY, *N. H.* The Londonderry celebration, June 10, 1869. Mack, R. C. Manchester, 1870. Sm. 8° 813.14
LONELY ones, The. Heyse, P. *See* JOHN, Eugenie. 710.25
LONG, George. The decline of the Roman republic. London, 1864-74. 5 v. 8° 5512.2
LONG, Samuel P. Art: its laws, and the reasons for them. Boston, 1871. xxxii, 248 pp. Illustrated. Sm. 8° 1513.7
LONG ISLAND, History of. Thompson, B. F. New York, 1839. 8° 813.20
LONG look ahead, A. Roe, A. S. 715.23
LONGEVITY. Gardner, J. Longevity: the means of prolonging life after middle age. Boston, 1875. 12° 6037.4
— Hall, W. W. How to live long. New York, 1875. 12° 6036.13

Shelf. No.

LONGFELLOW, Henry Wadsworth. Poems. Boston, 1858. 2 v. Portrait. 16° 1612.1

Contents. — Vol. I. Voices of the night; Earlier poems; Translations; Ballads; The children of the Lord's supper, translated from E. Tegnér; Miscellaneous; Poems on slavery; The Spanish student. II. The belfry of Bruges, and other poems; Songs; Sonnets; Translations; Curfew; Evangeline; The seaside and the fireside; Translations.

— Poetical works. With portrait. Leipzig, 1856. 3 v. in 1. Sq. 16° 1014.1

Contents. — Voices of the night; Earlier poems; Translations; Ballads and other poems; The children of the Lord's supper, translated from E. Tegnér; Miscellaneous; Poems on slavery; The Spanish student; The belfry of Bruges and other poems; Songs; Sonnets; Translations; Curfew; Evangeline; The seaside and the fireside; The golden legend; The song of Hiawatha; Tales of a wayside inn; The courtship of Miles Standish; Birds of passage.

— Prose works. Boston, 1866 [*cop.* 1857]. 2 v. Portrait. 16° 1838.4

Contents. — Vol. I. Outre-mer; Driftwood. II. Hyperion; Kavanagh.

Shelf. No.

LONGFELLOW, Henry Wadsworth, *continued.*
— Aftermath. Boston, 1873. iv, 143+ pp. 1 plate. 16° 1615.23

Contents. — Tales of a wayside inn, part third; Birds of passage, flight the third.

— The courtship of Miles Standish [a story of the Plymouth pilgrims], and other poems. Boston, 1859. 215 pp. 16° 1612.3
— The divine tragedy. [Dramatic rendering of Christ's last years.] Leipzig, 1872. 288 pp. Sq. 16° 1614.3
— The hanging of the crane. [Poem.] With illustrations. Boston, 1875. 47 pp. 16° 1616.14
— *Same.* Boston, 1875. 64 pp. 8° 5214.4
— Hyperion. A romance. [Largely travels in Germany.] Revised edition. Boston, 1875. 391 pp. 12° 716.14
— The masque of Pandora and other poems. Boston, 1875. iv, 146 pp. 12° 1617.12

Contents. — The masque of Pandora; The hanging of the crane; Morituri salutamus; Birds of passage, flight the fourth; A book of sonnets.

— The New-England tragedies. Leipzig, 1868. 258+ pp. Sq. 16° 1614.2

Contents. — Endicott; Giles Corey of the Salem farms.

Note. — "Endicott" is a drama of the quaker persecutions, Boston, 1665; and "Giles Corey" of the Salem witchcraft, 1692. See R. H. Allen's historic elucidation of these dramas [817.4].

— The poets and poetry of Europe. New edition, revised and enlarged. Philadelphia, 1871. xxvii, 916 pp. L. 8° 5922.1
— Tales of a wayside inn. Boston, 1863. v, 225 pp. 12° 1612.2

Note. — Stories in verse told of different countries by travellers at the Red Horse inn in Sudbury, Mass., which is described in Appleton's monthly, vol. 11.

— *translator.* The divine comedy of Dante Alighieri. *See* DANTE ALIGHIERI ...... 1614.4 and 5534.1

Note. — See Duyckinck's "Cyclopædia of American literature" [D.3.11]; Griswold's "Poets and poetry of America" [5212.3]; Drake's "Middlesex" [814.4], for the poet's home; Stillman's "Poetic localities of Cambridge" [5231.1], etc. Also Poe's "Literati" [1934.2.3].

LORD, John. Ancient states and empires. New York, 1869. 645 pp. Map. 8° 815.8
— The old Roman world: the grandeur and failure of its civilization. 5th edition. New York, 1873. 605 pp. 8° 826.10
LORD Bantam. A satire. Jenkins, E. Leipzig... 311.21
— *Same.* New York 536.21
LORD Erlistoun. Craik, D. (M.) 323.27
LORD Hope's choice. Stephens, A. S. (W.) 528.6
LORD Kilgobbin. A tale of Ireland. Lever, C. (J.). 332.16
LORD mayor, The, of London. Ainsworth, W. H. .. 322.17
LORD Oakburn's daughters. Wood, E. P. 333.10
LORD of himself. Underwood, F. H. 726.24
LORD, The, of the isles. Scott, *Sir* W. Poetical works. Leipzig, 1861. Sq. 16° 1613.5
LORDS and ladies. Stretton, J. 710.18
LORENZACCIO. Musset, (L. C.) A. de. Comédies et proverbes. Paris, 1867. 12° 5534.4.1
LORENZO Benoni. Ruffini, G. 316.16
LORIMER, George C. Under the evergreens; or, a night with St. Nicholas 916.31
LORING, Francis William, and ATKINSON, Charles Follen. Cotton culture and the South considered with reference to emigration. Boston, 1869. 183 pp. Sm. 8° 6435.3
LORING, Frederick Wadsworth. Two college friends. 515.7
LORING, James Spear. The hundred Boston orators, from 1770 to 1852. 2d edition. Boston, 1853. viii, 716 pp. 8° 5022.9
LORN, *or* LORNE, *Scotland.* The land of Lorne, including the cruise of the "Tern" to the outer Hebrides. Buchanan, R. London, 1871. 2 v. 12°. 424.11
LORNA Doone. Blackmore, R. D. 710.16
LORRAIN, Claude. *See* GELÉE, Claude.
LOS GRINGOS. Wise, H. A. New York, 1849. 12°. 435.4
LOSING to win. Davies, T. 714.8
LOSS and gain: the story of a convert. Newman, J. H. London, 1874. Sm. 8° 5636.6

Shelf. No.

LOSSING, Benson John. Life and times of Philip Schuyler. New York [*cop.* 1872]. 2 v. Portrait. 12° 5023.5
— Outline history of the fine arts. Illustrated. New York, 1857. 330 [328] pp. Portrait. 12°. 1517.1
— Pictorial field-book of the revolution. New York, 1860. 2 v. Portraits. Maps. Fac-similes. 8°. 810.17
— Pictorial field-book of the war of 1812. New York, 1868. 1084+ pp. Portraits. Fac-similes. 8° 810.16
— Pictorial history of the civil war in the United States. Philadelphia, 1866–70. 3 v. Portraits. Maps. Fac-similes. 8° 810.15
LOST and saved. Norton, C. E. S. 314.8
LOST and won. Craik, G. M. 322.7
LOST child, The. Kingsley, H. (*In* Johnson, (E.) R. Little classics) 529.4.10
LOST daughter, The. Hentz, C. L. 534.17
LOST for love. Braddon, M. E. Leipzig 330.8
— *Same.* New York 710.35
LOST heir, The, of Linlithgow. Southworth, E. D. E. N. 727.7
LOST heiress, The. Southworth, E. D. E. N. 522.8
LOST in the fog. De Mille, J. 934.21
LOST in the jungle. Du Chaillu, P. B. 933.6
LOST Lenore. Reid, M. 725.1
LOST manuscript, The. Freytag, G. 521.4
LOST palace, The. Hale, E. E. Tales for travellers 720.25
LOST Sir Massingberd. A romance of real life. Payn, J. 522.25
LOST tales, The, of Miletus. [Poems.] Bulwer-Lytton, E. (G. E.) L. Leipzig, 1866. Sq. 16°. 1614.7
LOST tar, The. Samuels, A. F. 918.25
LOTERIE, La, de Francfort. Souvestre, É. Théâtre de la jeunesse. Paris, 1860. 18° 5536.15
LOTHAIR. [Catholicism in England.] Disraeli, B. Leipzig 324.19
— *Same.* New York 721.3
LOTTIE Darling. Jeaffreson, J. C. 732.15
LOTTIE Eames; or, "Do your best, and leave the rest" 934.34
LOTUS-EATING: a summer book. Curtis, G. W. New York, 1868. 12° 415.14
LOUANDRE, Charles (Léopold), *editor.* Chefs-d'œuvres des conteurs français. Avec une introduction des notes historiques et littéraires et un index. Paris, 1874. 2 v. 18° 5534.3

Contents. — Vol. I. Avant La Fontaine, 1050-1650. II. Contemporaines de La Fontaine, XVIIe siècle.

LOUBAT, J. F. Narrative of the mission to Russia, in 1866, of Gustavus Vasa Fox. Edited by J. D. Champlin, jr. New York, 1873. 444 pp. 1 plate. Portraits. L. 8° 5911.3
LOUDON, Jane Webb. Gardening for ladies; and Companion to the flower-garden. Edited by A. J. Downing. New York, 1847. 430 pp. Illustrated. 12° 6626.9
LOUIE's last term at St. Mary's. Harris, M. 724.16
LOUIS IX, *or St. Louis, king of France.* *See* GUIZOT, F. (P. G.) Great Christians of France. [London, 1869.] Sm. 8° 5937.6
LOUIS XIV, *king of France.* James, G. P. R. Life and times of. London, 1851. 2 v. Sm. 8°... 5526.5
— Pardoe, J. Louis XIV, and the court of France in the seventeenth century. New York, 1847. 2 v. 12° 1223.11

Note. — For Louis, kings of France, see France, *note.*

LOUIS XV and his times; or, the priest and the Huguenot. Bungener, L. L. F. Boston, 1874. 12° 627.4
LOUIS, Pierre Charles Alexandre. Anatomical, pathological and therapeutic researches on the yellow fever of Gibraltar of 1828. Translated by G. C. Shattuck, jr. Boston, 1839. xxiii, 374 pp. 8° 6022.9
— Anatomical, pathological, and therapeutic researches upon gastro-entérite, or typhoid fever. Translated by H. I. Bowditch. Boston, 1836. 2 v. 8° 6021.10

Shelf. No.

LOUIS, Pierre Charles Alexandre, *continued.*
— Researches on phthisis. 2d edition, enlarged. Translated by W. H. Walshe. London, 1846. xxxv, 571+ pp. 8° 6013.6
— Researches on the effects of bloodletting in some inflammatory diseases [etc.]. Translated by C. G. Putnam. With preface and appendix by J. Jackson. Boston, 1836. xxxii, 171 pp. 8° .. 6014.4
LOUIS NAPOLÉON BONAPARTE. *See* NAPOLÉON III.
LOUIS Sinclair. Wise, D. 932.37
LOUISE la Valliere. Dumas, A. (D.) 511.12

Note. — Historical novel; compare Bulwer's play of same name [1614.5].

LOUISIANA. *See* RED river.
LOUVRE, The. *See* PARIS.
LOVE. Michelet, J. New York, 1872. 12° 1934.11
LOVE, Conjugial. Swedenborg, E. New York, 1871. 8° 6323.4
LOVE afloat. Sheppard, F. H. 723.13
LOVE after marriage. Hentz, C. L. 534.18
LOVE and money. Howitt, M. 937.2
LOVE and skates. Winthrop, T. (*In* Johnson, (E.) R. Little classics) 529.4.6
LOVE and valor. Hood, T. 510.3
LOVE at first sight. Curling, H. 710.14
LOVE in the nineteenth century. Preston, H. W. 516.22
LOVE is the best doctor: a comedy. Molière, J. B. P. Dramatic works. Edinburgh, 1876. 8° .. 5530.3.3
"LOVE me little, love me long." Reade, C. 315.2
LOVE of country, or Sobieski and Hedwig. Salvandy, N. A., *comte* de. Boston, 1856. 12° ... 916.11
LOVE or marriage? Black, W. 720.18
LOVE the avenger. A., A. A. 312.2
LOVE, The, that lived. Eiloart, *Mrs.* C. J. 711.12
LOVE-TIFF, The: a comedy. Molière, J. B. P. Dramatic works. Edinburgh, 1875. 8° 5530.3.1
LOVE'S conflict. Church, F. 337.16
LOVE'S labor won. Southworth, E. D. E. N. 727.13
LOVE'S meinie [*i. e.* retinue]. Ruskin, J. New York, 1873. 12° 5236.3
LOVE'S victory. Farjeon, B. L. 711.26
LOVED at last. Lemon, M. 312.7
LOVEL the widower. Thackeray, W. M. Leipzig .. 335.3
— *Same.* (*In his* Works.) London 513.1.11
— *Same.* New York 1820.3
LOVELS, The, of Arden. Braddon, M. E. 325.7
LOVER, Samuel. Barny O'Reirdon the navigator. (*In* Johnson, (E.) R. Little classics) 529.4.9
— The fairy-finder. (*In* Johnson, (E.) R. Little classics) 529.4.12
— The gridiron. (*In* Johnson, (E.) R. Little classics) 529.4.9
— Handy Andy: a tale of Irish life. London 536.15
— *Same.* New York 530.15
— Irish heirs 732.20
— Rory O'More 536.16
— Selections from. *See* Half hours with Irish authors. New York, 1873. 12° 737.9

Note. — Lover's stories are popular pictures of Irish life.

LOVES of the angels. Moore, T. Poetical works. Leipzig, 1842. Sq. 16° 1614.9.2
LOVES of the poets, Memoirs of the. [Biographical sketches.] Jameson, A. (M.) Boston, 1866. 16° 5618.2
LOW, Samuel. Poems. New York, 1800. 2 v. 12° 1617.18
LOW marriage, A. Craik, D. (M.) 330.22
LOWELL, Anna Cabot. Thoughts on the education of girls. Boston, 1853. 72 pp. 16° 1738.2
LOWELL, James Russell. Poetical works. Boston, 1871. 2 v. Portrait. 16° 5228.1

Contents. — Vol. I. Miscellaneous poems; Memorial verses; Sonnets; L'envoi; The vision of Sir Launfal. II. A fable for critics; The Biglow papers; The unhappy lot of Mr. Knott; An oriental apologue.

— Among my books. [1st and] 2d series. Boston, 1873, 76. 2 v. 16° 1934.8

Contents. — Vol. I. Dryden; Witchcraft; Shakespeare once more; New England two centuries ago; Lessing; Rousseau and the sentimentalists. II. Dante; Spenser; Wordsworth; Milton; Keats.

Shelf. No.

LOWELL, James Russell, *continued.*
— The Biglow papers, edited, with an introduction, notes, glossary, and copious index, by Homer Wilbur. 9th edition. Boston, 1871, 72. 2 v. 16°. 5227.1

Note. — These are poems, mostly humorous, but mixed with much powerful satire, written in the Yankee dialect, chiefly of political bearing during the Mexican and the civil war, accompanied by purposely stilted comments of an imaginary editor; while the introduction is of importance in a philological sense as regarding Americanisms.

— A fable for critics. [New York], 1848. 78+ pp. 12° 1622.2

Note. — A satire in easy swinging verse on the prominent American authors.

— Fireside travels. Boston, 1864. 324+ pp. 12°. 464.4

Note. — Experiences at home and abroad.

LOWELL, Robert Traill Spence. Antony Brade 714.5
— A raft that no man made. (*In* Johnson, (E.) R. Little classics) 529.4.8
LOWELL, *Mass.* Appleton, N. Introduction of the power loom, and origin of. Lowell, 1858. 8° . 6434.3
— Miles, H. A. Lowell, as it was and as it is. Lowell, 1847. 12° 5017.5
LOYAL unto death 727.29
LOYAL West, The, in the times of the rebellion; also, before and since. Barber, J. W., and Howe, H. Cincinnati, 1865. 8° 5033.4
LOYSON, Charles Jean Marie, *ecclesiastical name Père Hyacinthe.* Catholic reform. Letters, fragments, discourses, by Father Hyacinthe. Translated by Madame Hyacinthe-Loyson. With a preface by Arthur Penrhyn Stanley. London, 1874. xlv, 234+ pp. Sm. 8° 6326.15
LUBBOCK, *Sir* John. Nature series. On the origin and metamorphoses of insects. With illustrations. London, 1874. xvi, 108 pp. 16° 6617.8
— The origin of civilisation and the primitive condition of man. Mental and social condition of savages. New York, 1871. xvi, 380 pp. Illustrated. 12° 1527.1
LUCE, Stephen B. Seamanship: for the use of the United States naval academy. Illustrated. 5th edition, revised and enlarged. New York, 1873. xv, 667+ pp. 8° 1520.8
LUCIA: her problem. Douglas, A. M. 533.13
LUCIA di Lammermoor. Donizetti, G. (*In* Ditson, O., and co. Standard opera librettos) 6233.3.2
LUCIANUS *Samosatensis.* Lucian [outlined and explained]. Collins, W. L. London, 1873. 16°. 6116.19
LUCILE. [Novel in verse.] Bulwer-Lytton, (E.) R. Boston, 1872. Sq. 16° 1616.2
LUCIUS Davoren. Braddon, M. E. 329.13
LUCK and pluck. Alger, H., *jr.* 935.7
LUCK and pluck series. *See* ALGER, Horatio, *jr.*
LUCK, The, of Roaring camp. Harte, (F.) B. Boston, 1871. 16° 526.15
— *Same.* (*In* Johnson, (E.) R. Little classics) .. 529.4.4
LUCKY disappointment, A. Church, F. 718.6
LUCRETIA: or, the children of night. Bulwer-Lytton, E. (G. E.) L. 336.14
LUCRETIUS CARUS, Titus. On the nature of things. Translated into English verse by C. F. Johnson, with introduction and notes. New York, 1872. 333 pp. Sm. 8° 1526.20
LUCREZIA Borgia. Donizetti, G. (*In* Ditson, O., and co. Standard opera librettos) 6233.3.2
LUCY Crofton. Oliphant, M. (O. W.) 725.20
LUCY Maria. Diaz, A. M. 916.29
LUDLOW, Anna D. Madge Graves. By the author of "Bessie Lovell" 1118.10
LUDLOW, Fitz Hugh. The hasheesh eater: being passages from the life of a Pythagorean. 4th edition. New York [*cop.* 1857]. 371 pp. 12°. 737.5
— The heart of the continent: a record of travel across the plains and in Oregon, with an examination of the Mormon principle. With illustrations. New York, 1871. vi, 568 pp. 16° 413.4
— Little Briggs and I. (*In* Johnson, (E.) R. Little classics) 529.4.11
LUDLOW, Park. Nick Hardy 1115.14
— The red-shanty boys 937.19
LUDWIG der Baier. Uhland, J. L. Gedichte und Dramen. Stuttgart, 1863. 16° 5738.1.3

Shelf. No.

LUEBKE, Wilhelm. History of art. Translated by F. E. Bunnètt. 2d edition. London, 1869. 2 v. Illustrated. 8°.......................... 6210.4

— History of sculpture, from the earliest ages to the present time. Translated by F. E. Bunnètt. With illustrations. London, 1872. 2 v. 8°... 6210.3

Note. — These books are both of good repute.

LUISA Miller. Verdi, G. (*In* Ditson, O., and co. Standard opera librettos).....................6233.3.6

LULEÅ, Notes on a journey from London to. Shairp, T. Up the North. London, 1872. Sm. 8°.... 5915.4

LULU's novel. Polko, E......................... 731.31

LUMBY, Joseph Rawson. The history of the creeds. Cambridge, 1873. xi, 286 pp. Sm. 8°........6326.10

Contents. — Ante-Nicene; Nicene and Constantinopolitan; The Apostolic creed; The Quicunque, commonly called the creed of St. Athanasius.

LUNGS. Fitch, S. S. Six lectures on the uses of the. New York, 1847. 12° 6027.1

— Lewis, D. Weak lungs, and how to make them strong. Boston, 1871. 12°.................. 1536.2

LUNT, George, *editor.* Old New England traits. New York, 1873. v, 244 pp. 16°........... 817.3

LUTFULLAH, Autobiography of. Eastwick, E. B. Leipzig, 1857. Sq. 16°........................ 1238.7

LUTHER, Martin. Life. Written by himself. Collected and arranged by [J.] Michelet. Translated by W. Hazlitt. 2d edition. London, 1862. xv, 471 pp. Sm. 8°.........................1024.12

— Table-talk. Translated by W. Hazlitt. 2d edition. Philadelphia, 1868. xxiv, 464 pp. 12°. 1536.8

— The boyhood of. Mayhew, H. New York, 1864. 16° 937.16

Note. — The life by Michelet is mainly autobiographic, by making Luther's own writings tell the story. Michelet is a catholic, but he is in sympathy with the spirit of the reformer, and he has thoroughly studied his character. From Audin, the chief catholic authority, who is able, but less satisfactory to protestants than Michelet, Hazlitt borrows details of Luther's early years to complete in the translation, in the above list, Michelet's account of that period, and he has also added to other parts of the narrative so as to make it the most complete for the general reader for what is more particularly the personal history of the reformer. The English reader will also consult Carlyle's estimate, in his "Heroes and hero-worship" [1535.19]; Hallam's view in the first volume of his "Literature of Europe" [1531.2] and in his "Middle ages" [5916.1]; the concise and generally just review by Robertson in his "Charles v" [1226.9]; Roscoe's "Leo x" [5526.6], where the tendency is to explain favorably the action of the church authorities, while justice is still done to Luther; Ranke's "History of the popes" [5516.7], who presents the obstacles in the reformer's way; and D'Aubigné's Reformation, a book rather tedious, and at times exaggerated in sentiment. Froude has a paper in his "Short studies" [1914.5] on Luther and Erasmus. See Hedge's "Prose writers of Germany" [5732.1], and the histories of German literature generally; and chap. 4 of Fisher's "Reformation" [5813.7]. What is called the "Table-talk," while generally considered characteristic, is not so established beyond suspicion as authentic, as to make it of the great importance it would seem to be to the understanding of Luther. Archbishop Spaulding, a catholic authority, calls this edition a bad abridgment, with the most objectionable passages carefully left out. See the references in McClintock and Strong's Cyclopædia; and the article on "Luther and Leo" in Harper's monthly, vol. 30.

LUTTRELL of Arran. Lever, (C.) J. Leipzig...... 332.26

— *Same.* London.................................. 516.10

LYELL, *Sir* Charles. Geological evidences of the antiquity of man. With an outline of glacial and post-tertiary geology and remarks on the origin of species, with special reference to man's first appearance on earth. 4th edition. Illustrated. London, 1873. xix, 572 pp. 8°...... 6613.7

— Principles of geology. 11th edition. Illustrated with maps, plates, and woodcuts. New York, 1873. 2 v. 8°................................. 6631.7

— A second visit to the United States. New York, 1849. 2 v. 12°.............................. 415.11

LYFORD, Thomas J., and BOYCE, Allen P. The art of lettering, and sign painter's manual. Boston, 1871. Oblong f°.............................. 6210.1

LYMAN, George Hinckley. History and statistics of ovariotomy. (*In* Massachusetts medical society. Publications)................................ 6021.4

LYMAN family, Genealogy of the. Coleman, L. Albany, 1872. 8° 1211.4

LYNCH, William F. Narrative of the United States' expedition to the river Jordan and the Dead sea. With maps and illustrations. Philadelphia, 1849. 508+ pp. 8°............................ 421.9

Shelf. No.

LYNDON, *pseud.* *See* BRIGHT, Matilda A.

LYNX-HUNTING. Stephens, C. A. 937.25

LYON, George Francis. Brief narrative of an unsuccessful attempt to reach Repulse bay, through Sir Thomas Rowe's "Welcome," in his majesty's ship Griper, in 1824. With a chart and engravings. London, 1825. xvi, 198+ pp. 8°..... 424.1

LYRA Anglicana. Hymns and sacred songs. Baynes, R. H. Leipzig, 1868. Sq. 16°............... 1613.8

LYTTLETON, George, *lord.* *See* LAWRENCE, E. Lives of the British historians. New York, 1855. 12°..1224.7.1

LYTTON, (Edward) Robert (Bulwer). *See* BULWER-LYTTON, (Edward) Robert, *lord Lytton.*

LYTTON, *Lord.* *See* BULWER-LYTTON, Edward (George Earle) Lytton, *lord Lytton.*

M. or N. Melville, G. J. W. 330.6

MABEL Lee. Fisher, F. C.......................... 711.29

MABEL Martin. A harvest idyl. Whittier, J. G. Boston, 1876. 8° 1623.3

MABEL Vaughan. Cummins, M. S. Boston....... 724.7

— *Same.* Leipzig................................ 322.31

MABEL Walton's experiment. Mathews, J. H. 1117.14

MABEL's mistake. Stephens, A. S. (W.) 726.3

MACARIA. Wilson, A. J........................... 725.25

MACAULAY, Thomas Babington, *lord.* Biographical essays. Leipzig, 1857. 296+ pp. Sq. 16°...1238.13

Contents. — Frederic the great; John Bunyan; Oliver Goldsmith; Samuel Johnson; Bertrand Barère.

— Critical and historical essays, contributed to the Edinburgh review. Leipzig, 1850. 5 v. in 3. Sq. 16° 1918.4

— History of England from the accession of James II. [Covering also William III's reign.] Leipzig, 1849–55. 10 v. in 5. Sq. 16°............ 838.1

— Lays of ancient Rome: with "Ivry" and "The Armada." Leipzig, 1851. 240+ pp. 1 plate. Sq. 16°...1614.17

— Life and letters. By his nephew George Otto Trevelyan. London, 1876. 2 v. Portrait. 8°. 5332.7

— *Same.* New York, 1876. 2 v. Portrait. 8°... 1222.4

— Speeches. Leipzig, 1853. 2 v. in 1. Sq. 16°... 1928.2

— William Pitt, [and Francis] Atterbury. Leipzig, 1860. 210+ pp. Sq. 16°.....................1238.18

— ROGERS, Henry, MARTIN, Theodore, and OTHERS. New biographies of illustrious men. Boston, 1857. xxii, 408 pp. 12°....................... 5428.4

Contents. — Joseph Addison, by W. Spalding; Francis Atterbury, by T. B. Macaulay; Francis Bacon, by W. Spalding; Joseph Butler, by H. Rogers; John Howard, by [W.] H. Dixon; John Bunyan, by T. B. Macaulay; Horace, by T. Martin; Robert Hall, by H. Rogers; Sir John Franklin, by Sir J. Richardson; Homer, by J. S. Blackie; Oliver Goldsmith, by T. B. Macaulay; Edward Gibbon, by H. Rogers; Gassendi, by H. Rogers; James Crichton, by D. Irving; Samuel Johnson, by T. B. Macaulay; Sir Humphry Davy, by J. D. Forbes; David Hume, by H. Rogers.

Note. — See the excellent article in Allibone, both under Macaulay and Trevelyan, with the authorities there named, with references to the independent sketches by Dean Milman, Allibone and Hotten. Other illustrative matter can be found in Knight's "Passages of a working life" [5626.11]; Maginn's "Fraserian papers" [1935.5]; Russell's "Life of Thomas Moore;" H. C. Robinson's "Diary" [5425.3]; the "Greville memoirs" [5414.6]; Taine's "English literature" [5613.1.2]; Whipple's Essays [1936.2.1]; W. M. Thackeray, in Harper's magazine, vol. 20; and Bayne's Essays [1226.15.2]. The recent life of Macaulay, by his nephew, is the authoritative record.

Macaulay's "History," a fragment of what he contemplated, is generally accounted the most brilliant piece of historical writing in our day, though it is much criticised on some points. His essays are equally popular, and have done more to entice readers of lighter range than any similar productions. His "Speeches" are lucid, and good examples of the best parliamentary displays. His "Lays" are the best of their kind.

MACAULEY [McAuley], Catherine Elizabeth, (*religious name* Mary Catherine). Life of Catherine McAuley, foundress of the institute of religious sisters of mercy. By a member of the Order of mercy. With an introduction by Richard Baptist O'Brien. New York, 1874 [*cop.* 1866]. 508 pp. Portraits. 12°........................... 5334.1

MACCABE [McCabe], James D. Lights and shadows of New York life; or, the sights and sensations of the great city. Illustrated. Philadelphia [*cop.* 1872]. 850 pp. 8°........................ 814.9

Shelf. No.

MAC-CARTHY, Denis Florence. Shelley's early life from original sources. With curious incidents, letters, and writings, now first published or collected. London [1872]. xxiv, 408 pp. Portraits. Sm. 8° 5426.8
— *editor*. Book of Irish ballads. New York, 1873. 252 pp. 16° 5626.3
MACCARTHY [McCarthy], Justin. Dear Lady Disdain. A novel 721.23
— A fair Saxon. A novel 734.8
— George Sand. Reprinted from "The galaxy" for May, 1870. Boston, 1870. 24 pp. 16° ... 526.23
— Lady Judith 531.4
— Linley Rochford 710.26
— Modern leaders: being a series of biographical sketches. New York, 1872. 243 pp. 8° 5930.2
— My enemy's daughter. A novel 710.38
— Paul Massie. A romance 723.14
— The Waterdale neighbours 313.14
MACCLELLAN [McClellan], George Brinton, *joint author*. Exploration of the Red river of Louisiana, in 1852. *See* MARCY, Randolph B... 5033.2
MACCLINTOCK [M'Clintock], *Sir* Francis Leopold. The voyage of the "Fox" in the Arctic seas. Narrative of the discovery of the fate of Sir John Franklin and his companions. With maps and illustrations. Boston, 1860. xxiii, 375+ pp. 8° 424.7
MACCLINTOCK [M'Clintock], John, and STRONG, James. Cyclopædia of biblical, theological, and ecclesiastical literature. Vol. I–V. New York, 1871–73. 5 v. 8° .... *R.R., A.2.3
MACCLUNG [M'Clung], John Alexander. Sketches of Western adventure: 1775–94. Also additional sketches of adventure, compiled by the publishers, and a biography of J. A. M'Clung, by H. Waller. Covington, Ky., 1872. xxix, 398 [386] pp. Illustrated. Portrait. 8° 5026.4
MACCLURE [McClure], Robert, *editor*. Every horse owners' cyclopedia. With engravings. Philadelphia, 1872. 582 pp. 8° 6613.1

Contents. — Diseases, and how to cure them. By J. H. Walsh. The American trotting horse. By E. Harvey. The turf and trotting horse of America. By J. Elderkin.

MACCOSH [McCosh], James. The Scottish philosophy, from Hutcheson to Hamilton. New York, 1875. vii, 481 pp. 8° 5821.1
MACCRIE [McCrie], Thomas. The story of the Scottish church. From the reformation to the disruption. London, 1875. xv, 576 pp. 8° 5816.22
MACDONALD, George. Adela Cathcart 725.23
— Alec Forbes of Howglen. Leipzig 328.3
— *Same*. New York 720.26
— Annals of a quiet neighbourhood 328.1
— A double story 539.8
— At the back of the north wind 915.16
— David Elginbrod 328.2
— Dealings with the fairies 939.1
— England's antiphon. [London, 1868.] viii, 332 pp. Illustrated. [Sunday library.] Sm. 8° .. 5937.8

Note. — The religious poetry of England, with specimens.

— Malcolm. Leipzig 335.15
— *Same*. Philadelphia 710.31
— Phantastes: a fairie romance for men and women. 512.8
— The portent. [Second sight] 537.3
— The princess and the goblin 936.33
— Ranald Bannerman's boyhood 536.19
— Robert Falconer 512.9
— St. George and St. Michael. A novel. Leipzig. 331.22
— *Same*. New York 714.34
— The seaboard parish. A sequel to "Annals of a quiet neighbourhood" 536.18
— The vicar's daughter 537.23
— Wilfrid Cumbermede 537.4

Note. — MacDonald's novels have many of them a decidedly religious tone; and many of them depict Scottish life.

MACDONELL, Agnes. For the king's dues 532.12
MACDUFF, John Ross. Wells of Baca; or, solaces of the Christian mourner, and other thoughts on bereavement. From the London edition. Boston, 1854. 64 pp. 16° 5819.9

Shelf. No.

MACÉ, Jean. History of a mouthful of bread. Translated from the 8th French edition by Mrs. A. Gatty. New York, 1872. 398 pp. 12° 1527.7
— Home fairy tales. Translated by M. L. Booth .. 933.13
— The servants of the stomach. Reprinted from the London translation, revised and corrected. New York, 1868. 311 pp. 12° 1536.7
MACEDONIANS, Ancient history of the. Rollin, C. Vol. 1–4, 6–8. Boston, 1807. 8° 5913.1
MACFARREN, —. Winning a husband: a burletta. New York, N. D. 34 pp. 12° 1635.3
MACGILLIVRAY, William. Travels and researches of Alexander von Humboldt in the equinoctial regions of America and Asiatic Russia. With map and engravings. New York, 1855. 367 pp. 16° 438.1
MACGREGOR, John. The Rob Roy on the Jordan, Nile, Red sea, and Gennesareth, etc. A canoe cruise in Palestine and Egypt, and the waters of Damascus. With maps and illustrations. New York, 1870. 464 pp. Sm. 8° 423.17
— A thousand miles in the Rob Roy canoe on rivers and lakes of Europe. With illustrations and map. 7th edition. Boston, 1871. viii, 255 pp. 16°. 428.11

Note. — Macgregor was a pioneer in the recent fashion of canoe voyaging, and his books have been very popular.

MACHIAVELLI, Niccolò. The history of Florence, and the affairs of Italy. From the earliest times to the death of Lorenzo the magnificent; together with The prince, and various historical tracts. A new translation. London, 1871. xx, 522 pp. Portrait. Sm. 8° 5516.8
MACHINE construction and drawing. Tomkins, E. New York [Glasgow], 1873. 16° 1717.9
MACHINERY, Elementary principles of. Abel, C. D. London, 1868. 12° 6428.2
MACHINES, Dictionary of. Appleton, D., and co. New York, 1869. 2 v. L. 8° .... *R.R., D.3.3
MACINTOSH [McIntosh], Maria J. Charms and counter-charms 726.32
— Conquest and self-conquest, or, which makes the hero? 718.4
— Emily Herbert; or, the happy home 929.9
— Two lives 735.24
— A year with Maggie and Emma; a true story ... 928.19
MACK, Robert C., *compiler*. The Londonderry celebration, June 10, 1869. Manchester, 1870. 124 pp. Portraits. Sm. 8° 813.14
MACKARNESS, Matilda Anne, *formerly Miss Planché*. A mingled yarn 339.19
— A peerless wife 312.1
— Sunbeam stories 313.18

Contents. — A trap to catch a sunbeam; The cloud with the silver lining; Old Jolliffe; The sequel to Old Jolliffe; The star in the desert; "Only"; A merry Christmas.

MACKEEN [McKeen], Phebe F. Thornton hall 912.16
MACKEEVER [McKeever], Harriet B. Edith's ministry 713.13
— Silver threads 714.31
— Sunshine; or, Kate Vinton 1117.29
— Twice crowned. A story of the days of queen Mary 528.1
— Woodcliff 723.25
— The Woodcliff children. [The Woodcliff library] 1118.6
MACKENZIE, Alexander Slidell. Life of Oliver Hazard Perry. 5th edition. New York [*cop.* 1840]. 2 v. Portrait. 16° 1019.1
— Life of Paul Jones. New York [*cop.* 1841]. 2 v. Portrait. 16° 1020.6
MACKENZIE, C. Five thousand receipts in all the useful and domestic arts. New edition. With additions by an American physician. Philadelphia, 1858. 154 pp. 8° 1531.1
MACKENZIE, Erick. The Roua pass; or, Englishmen in the Highlands. 6th American edition. Boston [1875]. 190 pp. 8° 721.19
MACKENZIE, Henry. Miscellaneous works. 3d edition. New York, 1858. 512 pp. Portrait. 12°. 1935.4
— The story of La Roche. (*In* Johnson, (E.) R. Little classics) 529.4.3

Shelf. No.

MACKENZIE, Robert Shelton. Life of W. Maginn. *See* MAGINN, William 1935.5
MACKENZIE, William. Practical treatise on the diseases of the eye. From the last London edition. Boston, 1833. xii, 719 pp. 8°...... 6011.2
MACKINTOSH, *Sir* James. Memoirs. Edited by his son, Robert James Mackintosh. From the 2d London edition. Boston, 1853. 2 v. Portrait. 8°. 5331.3
— *See* BULWER, *Sir* H. L. (E.) Historical characters. Leipzig, 1868. Sq. 16°...... 1238.14
MACKNIGHT [McKnight], Charles. Captain Jack; or, old Fort Duquesne. A story of Indian adventure. With illustrations. London [1874]. vii, 472 pp. Sm. 8° 923.5
MACLEAR, George Frederick. Apostles of mediæval Europe. [London, 1869.] vi, 332 pp. Illustrated. [Sunday library.] Sm. 8°...... 5937.5
MACLEOD, *Sir* Donald. *See* PAGE, H. A. Noble workers. London, 1875. Sm. 8°...... 5936.3
MACLEOD, Norman. Memoir of Norman Macleod. By his brother, Donald Macleod. London, 1876. Portraits. 2 v. 8°...... 5332.5
— The old lieutenant and his son...... 313.16
MACLISE, Daniel. Gallery of illustrious literary characters. *See* BATES, William, *editor* 5632.2
— Memoir of. O'Driscoll, W. J. London, 1871. Sm. 8°...... 5423.12
MACMILLAN, Hugh. The sabbath of the fields, being a sequel to "Bible teachings in nature." London, 1876. xv, 358 pp. Sm. 8° 6328.23
MACMILLAN'S magazine. Vol. 28–32. London, 1873–75. 5 v. 8° 6527.1
MACNISH, Robert. Anatomy of drunkenness; Philosophy of sleep. (*In* The Alexandrian)...... 1910.4.2
MACPHERSON [McPherson], Edward. Hand-book of politics for 1872, 74. Washington, 1872, 74. 2 v. 8°...... 6924.8
MACQUOID, Katharine S. Diane 337.4
— Miriam's marriage 319.5
— My story. Leipzig 330.14
— *Same.* New York...... 711.14
— Patty 313.15
— Pictures across the channel...... 339.22
— Too soon. Leipzig...... 319.21
— *Same.* New York...... 731.8
MACREADY, William Charles. Reminiscences, and selections from his diaries and letters. Edited by Sir Frederick Pollock. London, 1875. 2 v. Portraits. 8°...... 5623.6
See note in Bulletin, Vol. II, p. 370.
MACTURK, John. Physical geography. New York [Glasgow], 1873. 156 pp. Illustrated. 16°.. 1717.7
MACVICAR, Anne. *See* GRANT, Anne.
MACVICKAR [M'Vickar], John. *See* PAGE, H. A. Noble workers. London, 1875. Sm. 8°...... 5936.3
MAD Dumaresq. Church, F. 2 v...... 329.19
MAD marriage, A. Fleming, M. A. 724.31
MAD Monkton. Collins, (W.) W. 511.25
MADAGASCAR, Twelve months in. Mullens, J. New York, 1875. 16° 5915.11
MADAME de Beaupré. Jenkin, *Mrs.* C...... 517.15
MADAME de Chamblay. Dumas, A. (D.)...... 510.8
MADAME Fontenoy. By the author of "Mademoiselle Mori" 313.12
MADAME Therésè; or, the volunteers of '92. Erckmann, É., and Chatrian, A. New York, 1869. 12° 524.4
MADDEN, Richard Robert. Literary life and correspondence of the countess of Blessington. New York, 1855. 2 v. Portrait. 12° 1223.2
MADEIRA. Colton, W. Ship and shore, in. New York, 1856. 12° 425.16
— Driver, J. Letters from Madeira. London, 1838. 16° 427.1
MADEMOISELLE de la Seiglière: comédie. Sandeau, (L. S.) J. Boston, 1867. 12° 2015.2
MADEMOISELLE Mori; a tale of modern Rome 313.13
MADGE Graves. Ludlow, A. D. 1118.10
MADONNA Mary. Oliphant, M. (O. W.) 328.6
MAFFEI, Giovanni Pietro, *joint author.* Life of St. Francis Xavier. *See* BARTOLI, Daniele 5526.9

Shelf. No.

MAGDALA, *Abyssinia.* Coomassie and Magdala. Stanley, H. M. New York, 1874. 8° 5931.14
MAGDALENA. John, E. 710.25
MAGGIE Miller. Holmes, M. J. 534.3
MAGIC. Brewster, *Sir* D. Letters on natural magic. New York, 1870. 16° 1519.4
— – Nouveau manuel de magie naturelle et amusante. Paris, 1839. 24°...... 6419.2
— Frickel, G. Magic no mystery. London, 1876. Sm. 8° 1515.20
— – The magician's own book. New York [*cop.* 1857]. Sm. 8°...... 1514.18
— – *Same.* New York, 1870. 12° 1514.23
— Parlor magician. New York [*cop.* 1863]. 12°.. 1515.8
— Schele de Vere, M. Modern magic. New York, 1873. 12°...... 1516.16
MAGILL, Edward H. A French grammar. Added a French, English, and Latin vocabulary. 4th edition. Boston, 1867. 287 [285] pp. 12°... 2014.2
— An introductory French reader. 4th edition. Boston, 1868. vi, 451 pp. 12° 2014.1
MAGINN, William. The Fraserian papers. Annotated, with a life of the author, by R. S. Mackenzie. New York, 1857. cx, 358+ pp. Sm. 8°. 1935.5
— Gallery of illustrious literary characters. *See* BATES, William, *editor* 5632.2
MAGNETISM. Farrar, J. Elements of. Cambridge, 1826. 8°...... 6433.1
— Harris, *Sir* W. S. Rudimentary magnetism. London, 1872. 12°...... 1715.6
— Jenkin, F. Electricity and magnetism. London, 1873. Sm. 8°...... 6438.4
See also Electricity, Electro-magnetism, Galvanism.

MAGNIER, M. D. Manuel de l'éclairage au gaz. Orné de planches. Paris, 1849. vi, 312 pp. 24°. [Manuel Roret]...... 6439.7
MAGUIRE, John Francis. Father Mathew: a biography. New York, 1871. xv, 557 pp. Portrait. 12° 5423.14
— Young prince Marigold, and other fairy stories. 928.11
MAGYARS, Poetry of the. Bowring, J. London, 1830. 8°...... 1622.1
MAHAFFY, John Pendleton. Social life in Greece from Homer to Menander. London, 1874. xii, 390 pp. Sm. 8°...... 5925.1
MAHOMET. *See* MOHAMMED.
MAHON, *Lord.* *See* STANHOPE, Philip Henry, *5th earl Stanhope.*
MAID, The, of Killeena. Black, W. Leipzig 330.12
— *Same.* New York 711.9
MAID, The, of Malines. Bulwer-Lytton, E. (G. E.) L. (*In* Johnson, (E.) R. Little classics)...... 529.4.6
MAID, The, of Orleans. *See* DARC, Jeanne.
MAID, The, of Sker. Blackmore, R. D...... 711.20
MAIDEN sisters. By the author of "Still waters".. 313.17
MAIDEN widow, The. Southworth, E. D. E. N. 734.26
MAIDENHOOD series, The. *Namely:* —
— Baker, G. M. Running to waste...... 927.28
— Clarke, R. S. The Asbury twins 1115.15
— – Our Helen...... 933.10
— Douglas, A. M. Seven daughters 913.32
— Townsend, V. F. That queer girl 927.29
MAIL bags, Ten years among the. Holbrook, J. Boston, 1856. 12° 1216.8
MAILFER, H. C. Recherches historiques du juste et de l'autorité. Philosophie appliquée. Paris, 1873. 2 v. 8° 6332.1
MAIN, Robert. Rudimentary astronomy. New and enlarged edition, with appendix on spectrum analysis. London, 1869. xx, 172 pp. Illustrated. 12°...... 1716.38
MAINE, *Sir* Henry Sumner. Lectures on the early history of institutions. New York, 1875. viii, 412 pp. 8° 6313.6
MAINE. *Hydrographic survey.* The water-power of Maine, by Walter Wells, superintendent hydrographic survey of Maine. Augusta, 1869. vii, 526 pp. Map. Illustrations. 8° ....411.2 and 5012.5
— Abbott, J. Marco Paul in the forests of...... 914.3
— Abbott, J. S. C. History of. Boston, 1875. 8°. 813.16

Shelf. No.

MAINE, *continued.*
— Thoreau, H. D. The Maine woods. Boston, 1872. 12° 417.8

See also Castine, Brooksville, Penobscot, Pentagöet.

MAINSTONE's housekeeper. Meteyard, E. 725.37
MAITLAND, Edward. By and by: an historical romance of the future 737.22
MAITLAND, *Sir* Frederick Lewis. Narrative of the surrender of Buonaparte, and of his residence on board H. M. S. Bellerophon; with a detail of the principal events that occurred in that ship, between the 24th of May and the 8th of August, 1815. Boston, 1826. xii, 176 pp. [No title-page.] 12° 827.5
MAÎTRES, Les, mosaistes. Dudevant, A. L. A. D. Paris, 1864. 18° 2016.5
MAKE or break. Adams, W. T. 924.20
MAKE your wills! a farce. Mayhew, E., and Smith, G. New York, N. D. 12° 1635.3
MAKING merry. Thackeray, A. I. Works 512.1.4
MALACCA, The straits of. Thomson, J. New York, 1875. 8° 5921.4
MALADE imaginaire, Le: comédie-ballet. Molière, J. B. P. Œuvres. Paris, 1869. 12° 5537.2.3
MALAY archipelago, The: the land of the orang-utan, and the bird of paradise. Wallace, A. R. New York, 1869. Sm. 8° 5934.1
MALBONE: an Oldport romance. Higginson, T. W. Boston, 1871. 12° 524.24
MALBROOK. A novel 537.24
MALCOLM. MacDonald, G. Leipzig 335.15
— *Same.* Philadelphia 710.31
MALDEN, *Mass.* The bi-centennial book of Malden. Boston, 1850. 251 pp. 12° 5016.4

Contents. — Oration, by James D. Green; Poem, by Gilbert Haven, jr.; The celebration; Historical items; Ancient ministry of Malden; Distinguished citizens; Miscellaneous matters.

MALLARY, Timothy. Narrative. *See* DARNELL, Elias 819.6
MALLET, Paul Heinrich. Northern antiquities; or, an account of the ancient Scandinavians. Translated by Bishop Percy. New edition, revised and enlarged, by I. A. Blackwell. Added, an abstract of the Eyrbyggja Saga, by Sir Walter Scott. London, 1873. 578+ pp. [Bohn's Antiquarian library.] Sm. 8° 5715.5
MALLET, Robert, *editor.* Rudimentary papers on constructing and repairing common roads. 4th edition, with additions. London, 1866. 202+ pp. 12° 1716.16

Contents. — A survey of the metropolitan roads, by S. Hughes; The art of constructing common roads, by H. Law; Remarks on the maintenance of macadamized roads, by Sir J. F. Burgoyne; Note on the true causes of the apparent failure of macadamized roads in certain localities, by R. Mallet.

MALLEVILLE. Abbott, J. 914.15
MALORY, *Sir* Thomas. Morte dArthur. Book of King Arthur and of his noble knights of the Round Table. Original edition of Caxton revised for modern use. With an introduction, by Sir Edward Strachey. London, 1871. xxxvii, 509 pp. Sm. 8° 5618.10
MAMIE's watchword. Mathews, J. H. 1117.32
MAMMALIA. Their various orders and habits popularly illustrated by typical species. Figuier, (G.) L. London, 1870. 8° 1521.2
MAMMON. Gore, C. G. F. 311.3
MAN. Buechner, (F. C. C.) L. Man in the past, present and future. London, 1872. 8° 6613.3
— Campbell, G. D., *duke of Argyll.* Primeval man. London, 1869. 16° 5916.5
— Chalmers, T. The power, wisdom, and goodness of God, as manifested in the adaption of external nature to the moral and intellectual constitution of. Philadelphia, 1835. 12° 6618.2
— Combe, G. The constitution of man, considered in relation to external objects. New York, 1872. 12° 1525.10
— Darwin, C. (R.) The descent of. New York, 1872. 2 v. 12° 1523.5

MAN, *continued.*
— Dawson, J. W. The story of the earth and man. New York, 1873. 12° 1523.22
— Figuier, (G.) L. Primitive man. London, 1870. 8°. 5912.3
— Home, H., *lord Kames.* Sketches of the history of. Edinburgh, 1788. 4 v. 8° 6614.8
— Huxley, T. H. Evidence as to man's place in nature. New York, 1872. 12° 1523.10
— Kidd, J. Adaptation of external nature to the physical condition of. Philadelphia, 1835. 12°. 6618.3
— Lubbock, *Sir* J. The origin of civilisation and the primitive condition of. New York, 1871. 12° 1527.1
— Lyell, *Sir* C. Geological evidences of the antiquity of. London, 1873. 8° 6613.7
— Mivart, St. G. Man and apes. New York, 1874. 16° 6617.6
— Morison, D. The religious history of. London, 1842. Sm. 8° 5816.15
— Pope, A. Essay on. [Poem.] Leipzig, 1848. Sq. 16° 1613.10
— *Same.* London, 1871. 8° 5612.2.2
— Romberg, M. H. Manual of the nervous diseases of. London, 1853. 2 v. 8° 6013.16
— Southall, J. C. Origin of. Philadelphia, 1875. 8°. 6612.8
— Wood, J. G. Man and beast. London, 1874. 2 v. 8° 6614.10
— – The uncivilized races, or natural history of. Hartford, 1870. 2 v. in 1. L. 8° 6610.3
— – *Same.* London, 1870. 2 v. L. 8° 6610.2

See also Anthropology, Civilization, Darwinism, Races.

MAN and nature. Marsh, G. P. New York, 1869. Sm. 8° 6614.6
MAN and wife. Collins, (W.) W. 326.2
MAN, The, in the moon and other people. Raymond, R. W. 912.25
MAN, The, of education: or, beauties of Lord Chesterfield. Stanhope, P. D., *earl of Chesterfield.* Boston, 1801. 12° 1928.6
MAN, A, of honor. Eggleston, G. C. 726.17
MAN, The, of the North, and the man of the South. Bonstetten, C. V. de. New York, 1864. 12° .. 1938.2
MAN, A, of the people. A tale of 1848. Erckmann, É., and Chatrian, A. 2 v. 736.23
MAN on the ocean. A book about boats and ships. Ballantyne, R. M. 1715.30
MAN upon the sea, Remarkable voyages; or. Goodrich, F. B. Philadelphia, 1873. 8° 421.7
MAN, The, who laughs. Hugo, V. (M.), *vicomte* ... 521.2
MAN, The, who was like Shakspeare. Black, W.... 711.9
MAN, The, with the broken ear. About, E. (F. V.). 517.20
MAN, The, without a country. Hale, E. E. (*In* Johnson, (E.) R. Little classics) 529.4.1
MANCHESTER, *N. H.*, History of. Potter, C. E. Manchester, 1856. 8° 812.4
MANCO: the Peruvian chief. Kingston, W. H. G... 913.14
MANDEVILLE, *Sir* John de. Travels. *See* ENGLISH explorers. London, 1875. Sm. 8° 5927.9
MANFRED. [Drama.] Byron, G. G. N., *lord.* Works. Leipzig, 1866. Sq. 16° 1614.13.4
MANFRED; or, the battle of Benevento. Guerrazzi, F. D. 723.17
MANIFESTO, The. Dunlavy, J. New York, 1847. 8°. 5813.3
MANKIND, Types of. Nott, J. C., and Gliddon, G. R. Philadelphia, 1854. 8° 6610.7
MANN, Horace, Life of. Mann, M. Boston, 1865. 8°. 1213.1
MANN, Mary. The flower people. By Mrs. Horace Mann. New and revised edition. Illustrated. Boston, 1875. 170 pp. Sq. 16° 931.9
— Life of Horace Mann. 2d edition. Boston, 1865. 609 [605] pp. 8° 1213.1
MANNERING, May, *pseud.* *See* NOWELL, Harriet P. H.
MANNERS and minor morals. The lady's guide to perfect gentility. Thornwell, E. New York, 1856. 12° 1516.2
MANNING, Anne. Deborah's diary. [Charles II's time]. 738.4
— The household of Sir Thos. More. [Historical fiction.] New edition, with an appendix. New York, 1867. 257 pp. 16° 738.3
— Jacques Bonneval; or, the days of the dragonnades. [Historical fiction, Huguenots] 738.6

Shelf. No.

MANNING, Anne, *continued.*
— The maiden and married life of Mary Powell, afterwards Mistress Milton. [Historical fiction, Milton's household.] 4th edition. London, N. D. 240 pp. 16° 738.1
— Passages in the life of the Faire gospeller, Mistress Anne Askew. [Henry VIII's time.] New York, 1867. 237 pp. 12° 517.19
— The provocations of Madame Palissy [wife of the famous French potter, 16th century] 514.2
— The Spanish barber 738.5
MANNING, Henry Edward, *cardinal.* The Vatican decrees in their bearing on civil allegiance. New York, 1875. 179+ pp. 12° 1916.7

Note. — An answer to the pamphlet of W. E. Gladstone.

MANŒUVRING mother, The. Grey, *Mrs.* 521.38
MANSEL, Henry Longueville. Letters, lectures, and reviews, including the Phrontisterion, or, Oxford in the 19th century. Edited by H. W. Chandler. London, 1873. vii, 408 pp. 8° ... 5612.11
MANSFIELD, Robert Blackford. The log of the Water lily. During two cruises in the summers of 1851-52, on the Rhine, Neckar, Main, Moselle, Danube and other streams of Germany. Leipzig, 1854. xii, 258 pp. Sq. 16° 313.20
MANSFIELD park. Austen, J. 325.25
MANUELS-RORET. *See* RORET, A.
MANUFACTURE, The two paths: being lectures on art, and its application to. Ruskin, J. New York, 1866. 12° 6236.8
MANUFACTURES, Dictionary of. Ure, A. London, 1872. 3 v. 8° 6422.3
"MANY happy returns of the day!" A birth-day book. Clarke, C. and M. C. London [1859]. 16°. 912.8
MANY lands and many people. With illustrations. Philadelphia, 1875. 256 pp. 8° 431.3

Contents. — Searching for the Quinine plant in Peru; Site and antiquities of Athens, by J. L. T. Phillips; The Roumi in Kabylia; Sketches of Eastern travel: I. The Count de Beauvoir in China; II. Batavia, by Fanny R. Feudge; III. Bangkok, by Fannie R. Feudge; At home with the Patagonians, by George Chaworth Musters; A tour in the China seas, by Fannie R. Feudge; In a caravan with Gérôme the painter; With the Count de Beauvoir in Japan and California, by Edward Howland; Constantinople, by F. W. Holland; Wanderings in Palestine, by F. W. Holland.

MAQUET, Auguste, *joint author.* Histoire de la Bastille. *See* Arnould, Auguste 2010.1
MARBLE faun, The, or Transformation. Hawthorne, N. Leipzig, 1860. 2 v. in 1. Sq. 16° 311.6
— *Same.* Boston, 1872. 2 v. in 1. 12° 1813.2
MARBLE prophecy, The. [Poem.] Holland, J. G. New York, 1872. 16° 1615.21
— *Same.* New York, 1873. Sq. 16° 1617.2
MARCH, Charles W. Reminiscences of congress. [A biography of Daniel Webster. With portrait.] 2d edition. New York, 1850. viii, 295 pp. 12°. 1217.3
MARCO Paul's voyages and travels. *See* ABBOTT, Jacob.
MARCO POLO. *See* POLO, Marco.
MARCOY, Paul. Travels in South America from the Pacific ocean to the Atlantic ocean. Illustrated by 525 engravings on wood, drawn by E. Riou, and ten maps from the drawings by the author. [Translated from the French by Elihu Rich.] London, 1875. 2 v. L. 8° 5030.5

Contents. — Vol. I. Ilay; Arequipa; Lampa; Acopia; Cuzco; Echarati; Chulituqui; Tunkini; Paruitcha. II. Tumbuya; Sarayacu; Tierra Blanca; Nauta; Tabatinga; Santa Maria de Belen.

MARCUS. Simonds, W. 932.30
MARCUS Warland. Hentz, C. L. 534.19
MARCY, Randolph B. Border reminiscences. New York, 1872. 396 pp. Illustrated. 12° 413.3
— The prairie traveler. A hand-book for overland expeditions. With maps [and] illustrations. New York, 1859. 340 pp. 16° 417.7
— Thirty years of army life on the border. With illustrations. New York, 1866. 442 [440] pp. 12°. 415.16
— and MACCLELLAN, George Brinton. Exploration of the Red river of Louisiana, in 1852. With illustrations. Washington, 1854. xv, 286 pp. 8° 5033.2

Shelf. No.

MARDI: and a voyage thither. Melville, H. New York, 1864. 2 v. 12° 512.11
MAREY, Étienne Jules. International scientific series. Animal mechanism: a treatise on terrestrial and aërial locomotion. With illustrations. New York, 1874. xvi, 283 pp. 12° .. 6436.12
MAREY-MONGE, Guillaume Stanislas. Memoir on swords, etc. From the French by H. H. Maxwell. Notes and engravings. London, 1860. xii, 90+ pp. 12° 1715.12
MARGARET. [A close study of New England life.] Judd, S. 535.13
MARGARET. Tytler, C. C. F. 735.18
MARGARET of Anjou. Abbott, J. History of. [Juvenile] 914.29
— Hookham, M. A. The life and times of. London, 1872. 2 v. 8° 5522.10
MARGARET Hamilton. Newby, C. J. 710.10
MARGARET Maitland. Oliphant, M. (O. W.) 328.8
MARGARET Percival. Sewell, E. M. 2 v. 532.8
MARGERY Keith. [Juvenile.] Townsend, V. F. ... 1115.16
MARGOLLÉ, É., *joint author.* Meteors, aërolites, storms, and atmospheric phenomena. *See* ZURCHER, F. 1714.8
MARGRET Howth. Davis, R. H. 715.20
MARGUERITE'S journal. A story for girls 532.15
MARIA di Rohan. Donizetti, G. (*In* Ditson, O., and co. Standard opera librettos) 6233.3.2
MARIA Stuart. Schiller, (J. C.) F. von. Werke. Stuttgart, 1865. 8° 5734.1.5
MARIAGE forcé, Le: comédie. Molière, J. B. P. Œuvres. Paris, 1869. 12° 5537.1.1
MARIAN Grey. Holmes, M. J. 535.8
MARIE ANTOINETTE, Josèphe Jeanne de Lorraine, *queen of France.* Abbott, J. S. C. History of. [Juvenile] 913.25
— Hayward, A. Biographical and critical essays. London, 1873. 8° 5833.3.2
MARIE Antoinette and her son. [Historical novel.] Mundt, C. (M.) 531.32
MARIE Derville. A story of a French boarding-school. Witt, H. de 912.6
MARIE STUART. *See* MARY, *queen of Scots.*
MARINE engines and steam vessels, Treatise on. Murray, R. London, 1871. 12° 1716.13
MARINO Faliero. [Drama.] Byron, G. G. N., *lord.* Works. Leipzig, 1866. Sq. 16° 1614.13.5
MARION, Fulgence. Wonderful balloon ascents. From the French. With illustrations. New York, 1871. xvi, 218 pp. 16° 1714.18
— The wonders of optics. From the French, and edited by C. W. Quin. Illustrated. New York, 1871. 276 pp. 16° 1714.19
— The wonders of vegetation. From the French. Edited, with additions, by [M.] Schele de Vere. With illustrations. New York, 1872. 283 pp. 12° 1714.25
MARION Berkley. Comins, L. B. 912.15
MARITANA. Wallace, W. V. (*In* Ditson, O., and co. Standard opera librettos) 6233.3.5
MARITIME adventure, exploration and discovery, History of. Goodrich, F. B. Philadelphia, 1873. 8° 421.7
MARJORIE Daw and other people. Aldrich, T. B. .. 735.27
MARJORIE Fleming. Brown, J. Boston, 1864. 12° 916.32
— *Same.* (*In* Johnson, (E.) R. Little classics) ... 529.4.10
MARJORIE'S quest. Gould, J. T. 723.2
MARK, the match boy. Alger, H., *jr.* 934.16
MARK Seaworth. A tale of the Indian ocean. Kingston, W. H. G. 922.5
MARK Twain's sketches. Clemens, S. L. Hartford, 1875. Sm. 4° 712.8
MARKHAM, Clements R. A general sketch of the history of Persia. London, 1874. xxxvii, 565 pp. Map. 8° 5911.4
MARKET assistant, The. De Voe, T. F. New York, 1867. Sm. 8° 1513.14

Note. — Serves in part as a history of the New York market for provisions, etc.

MARLBOROUGH, *Duke of.* *See* CHURCHILL, John.

Shelf. No.

MARKHAM, Albert Hastings. A whaling cruise to Baffin's bay and the gulf of Boothia. With an account of the rescue of the crew of the "Polaris." With an introduction by S. Osborn. London, 1874. xxiv, 319 pp. Illustrated. Map. 8° 5912.11

Note.—This book is noteworthy as showing how the successful penetration of ice-fields by the Dundee steam whalers confirms Admiral Osborn's expectations in 1850—when he commanded the first screw steamer in these regions—that the use of this power was to reduce the risk of Arctic adventure to a minimum; and in the appendix is given the report to the Royal geographical society on the scientific results yet attained, and the arguments for renewed efforts to penetrate to the pole by the way of Smith's sound, indicated as most likely to give success, from the results of the Polaris expedition, which is made the subject of one of the chapters of the text, the account being chiefly drawn from the information of Dr. Bessels, one of the rescued crew. Capt. Markham's book has a map giving the Polaris's track, and showing the latest configuration of the extreme northern shores of the passage.

See also Arctic regions.

MARLITT, E., *pseud.* *See* John, Eugenie.

MARMADUKE Herbert. Gardiner, M. 310.3

MARMADUKE Merry the midshipman. Kingston, W. H. G. 922.3

MARMION. Scott, *Sir* W. Poetical works. Leipzig, 1861. Sq. 16° 1613.5

MARMONTEL, Jean François. Nouveaux contes moraux. Paris, 1801. 4 v. Portrait. Illustrated. 16°, L. P. 5535.7

MAROON, The. Reid, M. 725.2

MAROON, The. Simms, W. G. 736.24

MAROONER's island. Goulding, F. R. 926.31

MAROT, Clement, and BÈZE, Théodore. Les pseaumes de David. [No title-page.] Unpaged. 16° ... 5819.12

Note.—Contains the psalms set to music, prayers, catechism, etc. Is has been impossible to determine which of the many editions published between 1542 and 1677 this copy is.

MARQUETTE, Jacques, Life of. Sparks, J. (*In* Sparks, J. Library of American biography). 5028.1.10

MARQUIS de Villemer, The. Dudevant, A. L. A. D. 511.18

MARQUIS of Letoriere. From the French [by] Catherine Green Cotting 539.3

MARRIAGE. Ferrier, S. E. 521.21

MARRIAGE. A solemn appeal relative to the abuses and excesses of the marriage relation. White, J. Battle Creek, 1870. 16° 1538.19

MARRIAGE, A, in high life. Feuillet, O. 722.2

MARRIAGE of Figaro. Mozart, J. C. W. A. (*In* Ditson, O., and co. Standard opera librettos). 6233.3.2

MARRIAGE, The, of Moira Fergus. Black, W. 720.38

MARRIED. Newby, C. J. 710.13

MARRIED belle, The. Smith, J. P. 727.27

MARRIED beneath him. Payn, J. 522.21

MARRIED in haste. Stephens, A. S. (W.) 726.2

MARRIED or single? Sedgwick, C. M. 2 v. 725.22

MARRYAT, Florence. *See* CHURCH, Florence.

MARRYAT, Frederick. The children of the New forest. [Charles I's time] 337.8

— Jacob Faithful 337.2

— Japhet in search of a father 337.6

— The king's own. [Mutiny at the Nore, 1797] .. 337.11

— The mission: or, scenes in Africa 337.13

— Mr. Midshipman Easy 337.12

— Narrative of the travels and adventures of Monsieur Violet, in California, Sonora, and Western Texas 337.7

— Newton Forster; or, the merchant service 737.26

— Percival Keene 337.5

— Peter Simple 337.10

— The phantom ship 725.17

— The privateer's-man one hundred years ago 337.22

— The settlers in Canada 337.3

— Snarleyow; or, the dog fiend. [Smuggling, 1700]. 732.5

— Valerie: an autobiography 337.9

— Life and letters of. Church, F. Leipzig, 1872. Sq. 16° 1228.5

— *Same.* London, 1872. 2 v. Sm. 8° 5025.6

Note.—Capt. Marryat's novels are usually spirited, and his tales of life on men-of-war and merchantmen constitute some of the best of nautical stories. They often introduce sea-episodes of the Napoleonic wars.

MARSH, C. C. Theory and practice of bank book-keeping, and joint stock accounts. 4th edition. New York, 1864. 292 pp. 1 plate. L. 4° 1720.1

Shelf. No.

MARSH, George Perkins. The earth as modified by human action. A new edition of Man and nature. New York, 1874. xii, 656 pp. 8° 6831.2

— Man and nature; or, physical geography as modified by human action. New York, 1869. xix, 577 pp. Sm. 8° 6614.6

— Lectures on the English language. 1st series. 4th edition. Revised and enlarged. New York, 1872. viii, 715 pp. Sm. 8° 6123.2

— Origin and history of the English language, and of the early literature it embodies. 3d edition. New York, 1871. xv, 574 pp. Sm. 8° 6123.1

MARSH-CALDWELL, Anne. Aubrey 313.28

— Castle Avon 313.26

— Emilia Wyndham. 2 v. 330.23

— Evelyn Marston 313.27

— The heiress of Haughton 313.23

— Ravenscliffe 313.24

— The rose of Ashurst 313.25

MARSHALL, Edward Chauncey. History of the United States naval academy, with biographical sketches. New York, 1862. 156 pp. Illustrated. 12° 816.9

MARSTONS, The. Aïdé, H. 328.26

MARTHA. Flotow, F. F. A. von. (*In* Ditson, O., and co. Standard opera librettos) 6233.3.5

MARTHA Brown, the heiress. By the author of "Still waters" 313.10

MARTIN, Frances. Angelique Arnauld, abbess of Port Royal. London, 1873. viii, 328 pp. [Sunday library.] Sm. 8° 5937.11

MARTIN, Frederick. Handbook of contemporary biography. London, 1870. 287+ pp. 16°. *R.R., F.3.7

MARTIN, Joseph G. Twenty-one years in the Boston stock market. With notes. Boston, 1856. 80 pp. 8° 1711.1

MARTIN, Theodore. Biography of Horace. (*In* Macaulay, T. B., *lord*, and others. New biographies of illustrious men) 5428.4

— Horace [outlined and explained]. Edinburgh, 1870. 203+ pp. 16°. [Ancient classics for English readers] 6116.7

— Life of the prince consort. With portrait and views. Vol. I. New York, 1875. 420 pp. 12° 1022.3

MARTIN Chuzzlewit. Dickens, C. (J. H.) Boston. 2 v. 1824.3

— *Same.* Leipzig 338.11

MARTIN Merrivale. Trowbridge, J. T. 522.1

MARTIN Paz. Verne, J. 529.6

MARTIN Rattler; or, a boy's adventures in the forests of Brazil. Ballantyne, R. M. 923.10

MARTIN's vineyard. Harrison, A. 319.14

MARTINEAU, Harriet. Deerbrook. A novel 737.21

— Eastern life, present and past. Philadelphia, 1848. ix, 17-523 pp. 8° 232.2

Contents.—Egypt and its faith; Sinai; Palestine; Syria.

— History of the peace: being a history of England from 1816 to 1854. With an introduction, 1800 to 1815. Boston, 1865, 66. 4 v. Sm. 8° 5416.2

MARTINEAU, James. Essays, philosophical and theological. Boston, 1868, 70. 2 v. 8° 5814.14

— Hymns for the Christian church and home. 19th edition. London, 1874. xli, unpaged. 12° ... 6328.14

— Religion as affected by modern materialism. With an introduction by H. W. Bellows. New York, 1875. 68 pp. 16° 5818.2

MARTINGALE, Hawser, *pseud.* *See* SLEEPER, John Sherburne.

MARTINS, The, of Cro' Martin. Lever, C. (J.) Leipzig 332.3

— *Same.* London 516.2

MATIRI, I. Donizetti, G. (*In* Ditson, O., and co. Standard opera librettos) 6233.3.2

MARTYN Ware's temptation. Wood, E. P. 333.13

MARTYRIA. Mountford, W. Boston, 1846. 16° ... 738.8

MARVEL, Ik, *pseud.* *See* MITCHELL, Donald Grant.

MARVELLOUS country, The; or, three years in Arizona and New Mexico. Cozzens, S. W. Boston, 1873. 8° 412.1

Shelf. No.

MARY, *queen of Scots.* Abbott, J. History of.... 915.7
— Bell, H. G. Life of. New York, 1855. 2 v. 12°. 1228.1
— Benger, E. O. Life of. Philadelphia, 1852. 2 v. 12°.................................1224.11
— Petit, J. A. History of. London, 1874. 2 v. 4°. 5410.2
— Raumer, F. (L. G.) von. Die Königinnen Elisabeth und Maria Stuart. Leipzig, 1836. 12° .. 2026.3
— Sainte-Beuve, C. A. English portraits. New York, 1875. 16° 1025.3

Note. — Miss Strickland says that "more books have been written about Mary Stuart than all the queens in the world put together." The views of Buchanan, the earliest of her accusers, have fashioned, perhaps, the predominating opinions, such as are held by Rapin, De Thou, Boyle, Voltaire, Sharon Turner, Dargaud, Raumer, etc.; and the principal cyclopædias, and such writers of history for young readers as Dickens.

In the last century Hume [5413.2] and Robertson [5610.1, less harsh], who shortly followed, were more than strong enough in a literary sense to counteract any sympathy which may have been excited, and Hume, as the ablest and most indulgent of her accusers, has probably done most to establish prevalent views, while Lingard [5417.8] has controverted him in this as in other matters, but without apparently much confidence in her innocence. In 1760, William Tytler's argumentative Inquiry weighed the evidence, and he first critically examined the sonnets and the confession of Paris, and sustained the queen against Hume and Robertson, and his book was reviewed by Dr. Johnson [5422.3.2].

Brougham, in an appendix to his "Statesmen of the time of George III" [5614.4.5], thinks the evidence quite decisive of her guilt, without being such as would convict her in a court of justice. Bell [1228.1] aims to balance the evidence and sides with her vindicators. Miss Benger [1224.11] sides with her defenders, and her life is full upon Mary's residence in France.

Miss Strickland, in her "Queens of Scotland" [5916.4, v. 3 to 6], who has added to our knowledge of Mary's history more than almost any other, has vindicated the queen against the views of Mignet. Sainte Beuve [1025.3] exculpates her.

The latest of her detractors, and called by her friends the most reckless and vituperative, is Froude, in his "History of England" [826.9], who accepts in full faith the authenticity of the Casket letters; and he has provoked much opposition for his laudation of the usurping nobles, and his vindication of Elizabeth. See also Guizot's popular "History of France" [5510.2.4]; Lodge's "Portraits" [5537.6.2]; and Lyman Abbott, in Harper's monthly, Feb., 1873.

The latest of her vindicators is Petit [5410.2], who surveys all that has been written in the controversy, and claims to have completely refuted the various charges against her.

Mary has been almost always pictured with pity, if not with vindication, by writers of the imagination. Scott's famous characterization in "The abbot" [324.10; 523.10] carries her through her escape from Lochleven and the battle of Langside, and where he discusses the question of her guilt in his "History of Scotland," he pronounces the case not proven. See also "The queen's Maries" (her maids in France), by Whyte-Melville [321.17]. Perhaps of the dramas upon her the most famous is Schiller's.

For the bibliography, see Allibone, p. 1826; McClintock and Strong; Hoefer's "Nouvelle biographie générale;" Oettinger; and a full note in the Lower Hall Catalogue of history, etc.

MARY Barton. Gaskell, E. C......................... 328.23
MARY Bell. Abbott, J............................ 914.16
MARY Derwent. Stephens, A. S. (W.)............... 726.14
MARY Erskine. Abbott, J.......................... 914.8
MARY of Burgundy; or, the revolt of Ghent. [Historical novel.] James, G. P. R................ 722.11
MARY Powell, The maiden and married life of. Manning, A. London, N. D. 16° 738.1
MARY Seaham. Grey, *Mrs.* 521.25
MASANIELLO. Auber, D. F. E. (*In* Ditson, O., and co. Standard opera librettos) 6233.3.3
MASHITA, The Persian palace of. Tristram, H. B. New York, 1873. 8°............................. 5933.4
MASKED ball, The. Verdi, G. (*In* Ditson, O., and co. Standard opera librettos) 6233.3.6
MASON, C. Walsh. Rape of the gamp. A novel... 711.36
MASON, Emily V. Popular life of Gen. Robert Edward Lee. Illustrated. 2d revised edition. Baltimore, 1874. 432 pp. Portraits. 12° 5226.1
MASON, George C. Newport illustrated, in a series of pen and pencil sketches. Engravings. New York [*cop.* 1854]. 110 pp. 12°.............. 414.23
MASON, Jeremiah, Memoir and correspondence of. Hillard, G. S. Cambridge, 1873. 4°......... 5020.7
MASON, John. Treatise on self-knowledge. (*In* The Alexandrian)..............................1910.4.2
MASON, Lowell, and WEBB, George James. The psaltery, a new collection of church music. Boston, 1847. 352 pp. Oblong 8°............ 1518.8
MASONIC melodies. Power, T. Boston, 1844. 8° .1518.12
MASONICK melodies. Eastman, T. Boston, 1818. 8°. 1623.1
MASONRY, Rudiments of. Dobson, E. London, 1870. 12°.......................................1716.24

See also Limes.

Shelf. No.

MASQUE, The, of Pandora. [Poem.] Longfellow, H. W. Boston, 1875. 12°...................1617.12
MASQUE, The, of the gods. [Poem.] Taylor, (J.) B. Boston, 1872. 16°........................ 1616.7
MASSACHUSETTS. *Colony and province of Massachusetts bay.*

— Compact, with the charter and laws of the colony of New Plymouth: charter of the council at Plymouth, and the articles of confederation of the United colonies of New England. Boston, 1836. x, 357 pp. 8°.......................... 6313.1
— Records of the colony of New Plymouth in New England. Vol. 1–8. Edited by N. B. Shurtleff. Boston, 1855–57. 8 v. in 6. 4°.............. 6310.1

Contents. — Vol. I–VI. Court orders, 1633–91. VII. Judicial acts, 1636–92. VIII. Miscellaneous records, 1633–89.

— *Same.* Vol. 9–12. Edited by D. Pulsifer. Boston, 1859–61. 4 v. 4° 6310.1

Contents. — Vol. IX, X. Acts of the commissioners of the united colonies of New England, 1643–79. XI. Laws, 1623–82. XII. Deeds, etc. Vol. I. 1620–51. Book of Indian records for their lands.

— Speeches of the governors, from 1765 to 1775; and the answers of the house of representatives; with other papers. Boston, 1818. 424 pp. 8°.................................. 814.10
— As to Roger Williams, and his 'banishment' from the Massachusetts plantation. Dexter, H. M. Boston, 1876. 4° 5011.1

Commonwealth. Constitutions.

— Constitution of Massachusetts, and of the United States [etc.]. Northampton, 1806. 12° 618.1
— Journal of the convention to revise the constitution, 1820, 21. New edition. Boston, 1853. vii, 677+ pp. 8°................................. 610.4

Legislative documents.

— *Acts, laws, etc.* Acts and resolves passed by the general court, in 1872, 73, 75, together with the constitution, messages of the governor, etc. Boston, 1872–75. 3 v. 8° 6311.2
— – Acts and resolves passed by the general court, at a special session of 1872, with the message of the governor. Boston, 1872. 429–474 pp. 8° 6311.3
— – Digest of the militia laws. [Also Supplements 1–3.] Compiled by E. W. Stone. Boston, 1851–54. 4 v. 12°.............................. 6927.9
— – General statutes. With the constitutions of the state and the United States [etc.]. 2d edition, 1873. [With Supplements. 1860–74.] Edited by W. A. Richardson and G. P. Sanger. Boston, 1873 [75]. 4 v. L. 8° 6312.1
— *Adjutant-general.* Annual report, 1862–66. Boston, 1863–67. 5 v. 8° 6916.3
— *Agriculture.* Transactions of the agricultural societies, for 1852. By A. Walker. Boston, 1853. xiv, 783+ pp. 8°.................... 6422.4
— *Board of education.* 37th annual report, 1872–73. Boston, 1874. 229, cxv pp. 8°......... 6913.4
— – The Massachusetts system of common schools; an enlarged and revised edition of the 10th annual report of the first secretary [H. Mann]. Boston, 1849. 212, lxiii, x pp. 8° 813.13
— *Board of health.* 2d–6th annual report. Boston, 1871–75. 5 v. 8° 6913.3
— *Board of State charities.* 6th–10th annual report, 1869–73. Boston, 1870–74. 5 v. 8° 6914.2
— *Board of railroad commissioners.* 4th and 5th annual report, 1872, 73. Boston, 1873, 74. 2 v. 8°.. 6923.8
— *Bureau of statistics of labor.* [1st]–5th annual report. Boston, 1870–74. 5 v. 8° 6913.2
— *Commissioners to the exposition at Vienna,* 1873. Report. February, 1874. Boston, 1874. 91 pp. 8°..5011.15
— – Reports. Edited by H. A. Hill. Boston, 1875. 566+ pp. Illustrated. 8° 6911.3

Shelf. No.

MASSACHUSETTS. *Legislative documents, continued.*

— *Miscellaneous.* Compend of instructions in military tactics, and the manual of percussion arms. Compiled by E. W. Stone. Boston, 1857. 139+ pp. 16°.......... 1528.11

— – Final report on the geology of Massachusetts. By E. Hitchcock. Amherst, 1841. xii, 831 pp. Illustrated. Map. Folded plates. 4°.......... 6630.1

— – Public documents: being the annual reports of various public officers and institutions, for 1871, 73, 74. Boston, 1872–75. 14 v. 8°.......... 6912.2

— – Report on the geology, mineralogy, botany, and zoology of Massachusetts. By E. Hitchcock. Illustrated. Amherst, 1833. xii, 692 pp. 8°. 6631.1

— – Report on the invertebrata of Massachusetts. [By A. A. Gould.] Cambridge, 1841. 373 pp. Plates. 8°.......... 6631.8

— – Report of the commissioners upon the Troy and Greenfield railroad and Hoosac tunnel. Boston, 1863. viii, 229 pp. Folded plates. 8°.......... 6912.4

— – 30th and 31st report relating to the registry and return of births, marriages, and deaths, for 1871, 72. Boston, 1873, [74]. 2 v. 8°... 6923.9

— – Treatise on some of the insects of New England which are injurious to vegetation. By T. W. Harris. 2d edition. Boston, 1852. viii, 513 pp. 8°.......... 6612.1

— Austin, G. L. History of, from the landing of the pilgrims to the present time. Boston, 1876. 8°.......... 813.19

— Barry, J. S. History of. Boston, 1855, 57. 3 v. 8°.......... 812.5

— Bradford, A. History of, 1775–89. Boston, 1825. 8°.......... 811.2

— Emerson, G. B. A report on the trees and shrubs growing naturally in the forests of. Boston, 1875. 2 v. 8°.......... 6621.2

— Freeman, S. The probate directory. Boston, 1803. 12°.......... 6317.2

— Goodwin, N. Genealogical notes of. Hartford, 1856. 8°.......... 5011.8

— Haynes, G. Pictures from prison life. An historical sketch of the Massachusetts state prison. Boston, 1869. 16°.......... 817.16

— Hutchinson, T. History of, 1628–1750. Boston, 1795. 2 v. 8°.......... 813.10

— Peirce, E. W. Contributions biographical, genealogical and historical. Boston, 1874. 8°.... 610.1

— Schouler, W. History of Massachusetts in the civil war. Boston, 1868, 71. 2 v. 8°....... 5012.2

— Walling, H. F., and Gray, O. W. Official topographical atlas of. [Boston], 1871. F°...*R.R. Desk

See also Abington, Brookline, Boston, Cambridge, Cape Cod, Concord, Danvers, Dedham, Dorchester, Framingham, Hyde Park, Leicester, Leominster, Lowell, Malden, Medford, Merrimack river, Middlesex county, Northampton, Plymouth, Salem, Suffolk county, Watertown, Wenham.

Note.—For the discoveries of the coast in the tenth and eleventh centuries by the Northmen, see a note in Bulletin, April, 1876, under "America before Columbus;" and for the early settlement, see Plymouth and New England; histories of the latter title necessarily covering Massachusetts, and like Palfrey's "New England" [5016.2] constituting for the period covered the best history likewise of Massachusetts.

The very important narrative of Governor Winthrop, covering the history of the colony from the sailing of the first colonists in 1630 to Winthrop's death in 1649, and the early documents collected in part or wholly with careful editing in Dr. Young's "Chronicles of Massachusetts" must be sought in the Bates Hall. See Everett's Orations [1921.1.1] on the settlement.

Hutchinson covered originally the period 1628–1749, in a substantial narrative that takes the highest rank among the historical writings of the colonial period, but in continuing his history to 1774, making the 3d volume subsequently published by his grandson, he showed a decided lack of sympathy with the growing political sentiments of the colony. Alden Bradford continued Hutchinson from 1775 to 1789; and subsequently wrote a compendious history, 1620–1820. The latest and most comprehensive history of Massachusetts is by Barry, divided into I, Colonial period, to 1692; II, Provincial period, to 1775; III, Commonwealth period, to 1820. The History by G. L. Austin is a popular narrative bringing the record down to the present time.

For the Witchcraft delusion, see Witchcraft, note. For the Indian wars, see New England, note.

Histories of the United States, like Bancroft's [5012.3], Bryant's [610.5], and Cassell's [810.11], often are full enough for the general reader, particularly upon the early history.

The founders of Massachusetts were puritans, as distinct from the separatists who settled at Plymouth, and this distinction has been much dwelt upon of late. See Plymouth colony, note, and a good discriminating relation of the differences

Shelf. No.

MASSACHUSETTS, *continued.*

between the two colonies by I. N. Tarbox in the Congregational quarterly, vol. 17. See, in this connection, Dr. Bacon's "Genesis of the New England churches" [5812.13] and the note on p. 16 of this Catalogue.

Schouler, who, as adjutant-general of the state, made a contemporary record in his reports, has also in his History given in the first volume a continuous narrative of the part borne by the state in the civil war, and in the second volume has recorded alphabetically, under counties, the part taken by each of the towns.

See the note in the Lower Hall Catalogue of history, etc.

MASSACHUSETTS art teachers' association. The Antefix papers. Papers on art educational subjects, read at the weekly meetings of the association, by members and others connected with the Normal art school. [With a preface by C. C. Perkins.] Boston, 1875. v, 239+ pp. Heliotypes. 8°.......... 6212.3

MASSACHUSETTS charitable mechanic association. Annals. Compiled by J. T. Buckingham. Boston, 1853. viii, 432 pp. 8°.......... 6914.1

— Constitution. Boston, 1871. 98 pp. 16°...... 819.4

MASSACHUSETTS general hospital, History of the. Bowditch, N. I. Boston, 1851. 8°..........6012.25

MASSACHUSETTS historical society. Proceedings. 1855–58. Selected from the records. Boston, 1859. xi, 412+ pp. 8°..........5013.12

— Proceedings of a special meeting, Dec. 16, 1873; being the 100th anniversary of the destruction of the tea in Boston harbor. Boston, 1874. 70 pp. 8°.......... 811.11

MASSACHUSETTS medical society. Publications. Boston, 1860–69. 8°.......... 6021.4

Contents.—History and statistics of ovariotomy, by G. H. Lyman; Rational therapeutics, by W. Hooker; Bronchitis and its consequences, by D. D. Slade; Hemoptysis as a symptom, by J. Ware; Report on spotted fever or cerebro-spinal meningitis in Massachusetts, by L. Parks; History of inoculation in Massachusetts, by J. M. Toner; Cases of trichina spiralis in Springfield, by M. Calkins; Lessons of the war to the medical profession, by G. Derby; Pathology and treatment of vaginal cystocele, by J. Homans, jr.; Myxoma, by A. D. Sinclair; Formation and significance of renal casts, by R. T. Edes; Physiological action of bromide of potassium and ammonium, by R. Amory.

MASSACHUSETTS register, 1862. With a complete account of the Massachusetts volunteers. Serial number, 94. Boston, 1862. 423 pp. 8° 5013.14

MASSACHUSETTS teacher, The. Vol. 10–21. Boston, 1857–68. 12 v. 8°.......... 1324.1

MASSACHUSETTS temperance society. Addresses. Boston, 1861. 98 pp. Illustrated. Portrait. 16°. 1524.2

Contents.—Bishop Potter's address on the drinking-usages of society; Address from members of the clergy of the church of England; Speech of J. B. Gough, in Boston, Sept. 17, 1860; Social clubs; Dr. Warren on the use of tobacco.

— The physiological effects of alcoholic drinks [by John] Forbes; with documents and records of the society. Boston, 1848. xi, 196 pp. 12°..1527.15

MASSINGER, Philip, and FORD, John. Dramatic works. With an introduction by Hartley Coleridge. New edition. London, 1869. 450, 212+ pp. Portrait. 8°.......... 5611.9

MASSON, David. Chatterton: a story of the year 1770. London, 1874. viii, 284 pp. Sm. 8°... 5636.5

— Life of John Milton: with the political, ecclesiastical, and literary history of his time. 1608–49. Vol. 1, Cambridge, 1859; vol. 2, 3, London, 1871, 73. 3 v. Portraits and fac-simile. 8°. 5422.2

— Wordsworth, Shelley, Keats, and other essays. London, 1874. 305 pp. Sm. 8°..........5616.15

MASTER, The, of Greylands. Wood, E. P. Leipzig. 2 v. 329.6

— *Same.* Philadelphia.......... 510.13

MASTER Humphrey's clock. Dickens, C. (J. H.)... 330.3

MASTER-SPIRITS. [Sketches of celebrities.] Buchanan, R. London, 1873. 8°.......... 6134.2

MASTERY series, The. *See* PRENDERGAST, Thomas.

MASURY, John W. How shall we paint our houses? A popular treatise on house-painting: plain and decorative. New York, 1872. 216 pp. 12°.. 6227.1

MATCHES. Manuel pour la fabrication des allumettes chimique. Roussel, T. Paris, 1848. 24°.....6429.12

MATERIA medica. Beck, J. B. Lectures on. New York, 1851. L. 12°..........6022.18

— Wood, G. B. Treatise on therapeutics, and pharmacology or materia medica. Philadelphia, 1856. 2 v. 8°.......... 6011.3

Shelf. No.

MATERIA medica, *continued.*
— Wood, H. C., *jr.* Treatise on therapeutics, comprising materia medica. Philadelphia, 1874. 8°. 6021.7
See also Therapeutics.
MATERIALISM, Religion as affected by modern. Martineau, J. New York, 1875. 16° 5818.2
MATHEMATICAL instruments. Heather, J. F. London, 1871. 2 v. 12° 1716.8
MATHESON, Duncan. *See* PAGE, H. A. Noble workers. London, 1875. Sm. 8° 5936.3
MATHEW, Theobald. Father Mathew: a biography. Maguire, J. F. New York, 1871. 12° 5423.14
MATHEWS, Joanna H. [The Bessie books.] Bessie among the mountains 1117.23
— – Bessie and her friends 1117.22
— – Bessie at school 1117.24
— – Bessie at the sea-side 1117.20
— – Bessie in the city 1117.21
— – Bessie on her travels 1117.25
— [Little sunbeams.] Belle Powers' locket 1117.16
— – Dora's motto 1117.17
— – Jessie's parrot 1117.31
— – Lily Norris' enemy 1117.26
— – Mamie's watchword 1117.32
— – Nellie's housekeeping 1117.33
— [Miss Ashton's girls.] Eleanor's visit 1117.13
— – Elsie's Santa Claus 1117.5
— – Fanny's birthday gift 1115.11
— – Mabel Walton's experiment 1117.14
— – The new scholars 1115.12
— – Rosalie's pet 1115.13
MATHEWS, Lucia Elizabeth. Anecdotes of actors: with other desultory recollections, etc. London, 1844. vii, 430 pp. 8° 5623.7
MATHEWS, William. Getting on in the world; or, hints on success in life. Chicago, 1874. viii, 365 pp. 12° 5836.8
MATTER. Picton, J. A. The mystery of. London, 1873. Sm. 8° 5826.3
— Tice, J. H. The relations between matter and force. (*In* Estes, D. Half-hour recreations in popular science) 6813.7
MATTIE: a stray. Robinson, F. W. 731.14
MATTY Frost. Davis, C. E. 1118.1
MAUD. Tennyson, A. Poetical works. Leipzig, 1860. Sq. 16° 1614.10.1
MAUD or Nina. Melville, G. J. W. 721.2
MAUDSLEY, Henry. Body and mind: an inquiry into their connection and mutual influence, specially in reference to mental disorders: an enlarged and revised edition. Added psychological essays. London, 1873. xii, 342+ pp. 8° 6036.15
— International scientific series. Responsibility in mental disease. New York, 1874. x, 313 pp. 12° 6035.4
— Physiology and pathology of the mind. New York, 1872. xiv, 442 pp. 8° 6011.6
MAUGHAN, William Charles. The Alps of Arabia. Travels in Egypt, Sinai, Arabia, and the Holy Land. London, 1873. xvi, 374 pp. Map. 8°. 5932.10
MAUNSELL, Henry, *joint author.* Practical treatise on the management and diseases of children. *See* EVANSON, R. T. 6012.11
MAUPRAT. Dudevant, A. L. A. D. 526.22
MAUREL, Jules. The duke of Wellington; his character, his actions, and his writings. With a preface by Lord Ellesmere. 3d edition. London, 1853. 143+ pp. 16° 5428.12
MAURICE, *of Saxony, Count, called Marshal Saxe.* *See* HAYWARD, A. Biographical and critical essays. London, 1873. 8° 5833.3.1
MAURICE, (John) Frederick Denison. The friendship of books and other lectures. Edited, with a preface, by T. Hughes. London, 1874. xxxvi, 389 pp. Sm. 8° 6136.8
— Moral and metaphysical philosophy. New edition. London, 1873. 2 v. Portrait. 8° 5833.2
— Sermons preached in country churches. London, 1873. viii, 362 pp. Sm. 8° 6326.5
— Social morality. 21 lectures. London, 1869. xvi, 483 pp. 8° 5833.5

Shelf. No.

MAURICE, Walter, and RICE, James. My little girl .. 731.26
— Ready-Money Mortiboy 732.9
— With harp and crown 721.20
MAURICE Dering. Lawrence, G. A. 315.27
MAURICE Tiernay. Lever, C. (J.) Leipzig 332.6
— *Same.* London 516.14
MAURY, Matthew Fontaine. Physical geography of the sea, and its meteorology. 8th edition, revised and enlarged. New York, 1871. xxxii, 474+ pp. Folded plates. 8° 1520.2
MAX Kromer. Smith, H. 738.12
MAXIMILIAN, Ferdinand Maximilian Joseph, *emperor of Mexico.* Recollections of my life. London, 1868. 3 v. Sm. 8° 5724.3
— The fall of. Chynoweth, W. H. London, 1872. 8°. 5013.2
MAXTON, John. The workman's manual of engineering drawing. With woodcuts and plates. London, 1871. 280+ pp. 12° 1716.28
MAXWELL, William Hamilton. The adventures of Captain Blake 518.8
— The bivouac; or, stories of the peninsular war ... 518.6
— Stories of Waterloo 518.7
MAXWELL Drewitt. Riddell, J. H. 316.2
MAY, John. Journal and letters relative to two journeys to the Ohio country in 1788, 89. With a biographical sketch by R. S. Edes, and illustrative notes by W. M. Darlington. Cincinnati, 1873. 160 pp. 8° 430.1
MAY, Samuel Joseph, Memoir of. Mumford, T. J. Boston, 1873. 16° .... 1016.2 and 5027.6
MAY, Sophie, *pseud.* *See* CLARKE, Rebecca Sophia.
MAY, *Sir* Thomas Erskine. Constitutional history of England, 1760–1860. 3d edition, with a supplementary chapter. London, 1871. 3 v. 16°. 5415.2
MAY. Oliphant, M. (O. W.) Leipzig 339.17
— *Same.* New York 530.9
MAY day and other pieces. [Poems.] Emerson, R. W. Boston, 1874. 16° 1616.15
MAY Martin, and other tales of the Green mountains. Thompson, D. P. 734.3
MAYHEW, Edward. Dogs, and their management. *See* HERBERT, Henry William 1522.3
— and SMITH, George. Make your wills! a farce. New York, N. D. 29 pp. 1 plate. 12° 1635.3
MAYHEW, Henry. The boyhood of Martin Luther. New York, 1864. 372 pp. Illustrated. 16° .. 937.16
— The story of the peasant-boy philosopher [James Ferguson]. New York, 1870. 500 pp. 16° .. 937.15
— Young Benjamin Franklin. With illustrations. London [1860]. xvi, 534 pp. Sm. 8° 916.2
— The wonders of science; or, young Humphry Davy. New York, 1870. 452 pp. Illustrated. 16° .. 936.34
— and OTHERS. London characters: illustrations of the humour, pathos, and peculiarities of London life. With illustrations. London, 1874. lv, 477 pp. Sm. 8° 5436.2
MAYNARD, C. J. The naturalist's guide in collecting and preserving objects of natural history. With illustrations. Boston, 1873. ix, 170 pp. Sm. 8° 1527.6
MAYNE, Leger D., *pseud.* *See* DICK, William Brisbane.
MAYO, Amory Dwight, and VICKERS, Thomas. The Bible in the public schools. Addresses. New York, 1870. 223 pp. 24° 5819.2
MAYO, Isabella Fivy. (*Edward Garrett.*) By still waters 724.8
— A chance child. (*In* Johnson, (E.) R. Little classics) 529.4.11
— The dead sin and other stories 524.18
— Doing and dreaming 714.22
— Gold and dross 734.17
— The occupations of a retired life 723.16
MAYO, William Starbuck. The Berber; or the mountaineer of the Atlas. A tale of Morocco .. 532.13
— Never again 724.5
MAZADE, Charles de. Lamartine sa vie littéraire et politique. Paris, 1872. xxxv, 207+ pp. 18°. 5526.2
MAZZINI, Giuseppe. Joseph Mazzini: his life, writings, and political principles. With an introduction by W. L. Garrison. New York, 1872. xxxii, 366 pp. Portrait. Sm. 8° 5525.4

Shelf. No.

MEADE, George Gordon, Life and public services of. Philadelphia [*cop.* 1864]. 80 [73] pp. 8° 1013.5

MEADE, Herbert. Hot springs in New Zealand. (*In* Estes, D. Half-hour recreations in popular science) 6813.7

MEADOW brook. Holmes, M. J. 535.11

MEADOWS, Thomas Taylor. The Chinese and their rebellions, viewed in connection with their national philosophy, ethics, legislation, and administration. Added, an essay on civilization and its present state in the East and West. London, 1856. lx, 656 pp. Maps. 8° 5921.13

MEASLES, Treatise on. Abú Becr Mohammed Ibn Zacaríyá Ar-rází. London, 1848. 8° 6013.10

MECCAH, Personal narrative of a pilgrimage to. Burton, R. F. Boston, 1858. 12° 423.14

— *Same.* Leipzig, 1874. 3 v. in 1. Sq. 16° 428.5

See also Arabia, Mahomet.

MECHANICS. Appleton, D., and co. Dictionary of. New York, 1869. 2 v. L. 8° .... *R.R., D.3.3

— Baker, T. Elements of practical mechanism and machine tools. London, 1871. 12° 1716.14

— Brown, H. T. Five hundred and seven mechanical movements. New York, 1871. Sm. 4° 1525.16

— Burn, R. S. Self-aid cyclopædia. London, N. D. 8° 6223.2

— Ewbank, T. A descriptive and historical account of hydraulic and other machines; with observations on the mechanic arts. New York, 1876 [*cop.* 1863]. 8° 6422.7

— Goodeve, T. M. Elements of mechanism. London, 1871. 16° 6817.2

— Howe, H. Memoirs of the most eminent mechanics. New York [*cop.* 1846]. 12° 1014.2

— Tomlinson, C. Rudimentary mechanics. London, 1872. 12° 1716.33

— The young mechanic. New York, 1871. Sm. 4°. 6426.3

See also Drawing.

MECHANIC's, The, calculator. Grier, W. Philadelphia, 1842. 12° 1713.5

MECHANICS' magazine. Vol. 1–6, 19, 22. London, 1830–35. 8 v. 8° 6421.1

MECHANICS' magazine. Vol. 5–9. New York, 1835–37. 5 v. in 4. 8° 6421.2

MEDBERY, James K. Men and mysteries of Wall street. [New York money market.] With illustrations. Boston, 1870. 344+ pp. Sm. 4° ... 413.2

MÉDECIN, Le, malgré lui: comédie. Molière, J. B. P. Œuvres. Paris, 1869. 12° 5537.2.2

MÉDECIN, Le, volant: comédie. Molière, J. B. P. Œuvres. Paris, 1869. 12° 5537.2.1

MEDFORD, *Mass.*, History of. Brooks, C. Boston, 1855. 8° 5013.16

MEDHURST, Walter Henry. The foreigner in far Cathay. New York, 1873. 204+ pp. Map. 12° 424.19

MEDIA. Rawlinson, G. The five great monarchies of the ancient Eastern world; or, the history, geography, and antiquities of. London, 1871. 3 v. 8° 5922.3

— Rollin, C. Ancient history of the Medes and Persians. Vol. 1–4, 6–8. Boston, 1807. 8° ... 5913.1

See also Asia, Persia, etc.

MEDICAL and physiological studies. Paine, M. New York, 1840. 2 v. 8° 6012.5

MEDICAL botany. Nouveau dictionnaire des plantes médicinales. Avec 261 figures intercalées dans le texte. Héraud, A. Paris, 1875. 18° 6627.1

MEDICAL electricity. Cavallo, T. Essay on the theory and practice of. London, 1781. 8° 6014.3

— Garratt, A. C. Medical electricity. Philadelphia, 1866. 8 .... 6012.2

— Meyer, M. Electricity in its relations to practical medicine. New York, 1869. 8° 6022.5

— Smee, A. Manuel d'électricité médicale. Paris, 1850. 24° 6019.1

MEDICAL jurisprudence, Manual of. Taylor, A. S. Philadelphia, 1873. 8° 6021.18

MEDICAL logic. Oesterlen, F. London, 1855. 8°. 6013.19

Shelf. No.

MEDICAL psychology, Principles of. Feuchtersleben, E., *Freiherr* von. London, 1847. 8° 6013.8

MEDICI, Lorenzo de', Life of. Roscoe, W. London, 1862. 16° 5525.1

Note. — Roscoe's book is of high repute, and much the best. See also Macchiavelli's "History of Florence" [5516.8]; Sismondi's "History of the Italian republics;" Grimm's "Life of Michael Angelo" [1022.2]; and Longfellow's "Poets and poetry of Europe" [5922.1]. See Italy, *note.*

MEDICINE. Bigelow, J. Brief expositions of rational medicine. Boston, 1858. 12° 6037.1

— Braithwaite, W. and J., *editors.* Retrospect of practical medicine and surgery. Part 1–4, 6–54, 63–66. New York, 1843–73. 33 v. 8° 6010.2

— Buchan, W. Domestic medicine. Boston, 1809. 8° 6034.2

— Cotting, B. E. Medical addresses. Boston, 1875. 12° 6015.5

— Dictionnaire des sciences médicales. Paris, 1812–22. 60 v. 8° 6026.1

— Dunglison, R. A dictionary of medical science. Philadelphia, 1874. 8° 6021.13

— Flint, A. Treatise on the principles and practice of. Philadelphia, 1866. 8° 6021.1

— Garnier, P. Dictionnaire annuel des progrès des sciences et institutiones médicales. Paris, 1867. 12° 6016.1

— Gross, S. D., *editor.* Lives of eminent American physicians and surgeons of the 19th century. Philadelphia, 1861. 8° 6021.6

— Hahnemann, S. (C. F.) Organon of the art of healing. New York, 1876. 8° 6022.19

— Jackson, J. Letters to a young physician. Boston, 1855. 12° 6036.16

— – Another letter. Boston, 1861. 12°. 6021.5 and 6036.1

— Neligan, J. M. Medicine, their uses and mode of administration. New York, 1844. 8° 6022.2

— Niemeyer, F. von. Text-book of practical medicine. New York, 1872. 2 v. 8° 6013.3

— Paine, M. Institutes of. New York, 1870. 8°. 6012.1

— Parsons, U. Boylston prize dissertations. Boston, 1839. 8° 6013.1

— Sydenham, T. Opera omnia. Londoni, 1846. 8°. 6013.5

— Ruppaner, A. Hypodermic injections in the treatment of neuralgia, rheumatism, gout, and other diseases. Boston, 1865. 16° 6015.2

See also Anatomy, Bioplasm, Epidemics, Health, Hygiene, Materia medica, Midwifery, Nerves, Pathology, Physiology, Therapeutics.

MEDINA. *See* EL-MEDINAH.

MEDITATION, Essay on divine. Bates, W. *See* BURDER, George. Village sermons 6327.7.4

MEDITERRANEAN sea. Bennet, J. H. Winter and spring on the shore of the Mediterranean. London, 1875. Sm. 8° 436.3

— Colton, W. Ship and shore, in the Mediterranean. New York, 1856. 12° 425.16

— Willis, N. P. Summer cruise in the Mediterranean, on board an American frigate. New York, 1854. 12° 424.12

MEDLEY, Julius George. An autumn tour in the United States and Canada. London, 1873. 180+ pp. Sm. 8° 5036.6

MEDULLA oblongata, Structure and functions of the. Schroder van der Kolk, J. L. C. London, 1859. 8° 6023.2

MEDUSA, and other tales. Sartoris, A. (K.) 732.6

MEILLE, J. P. General Beckwith: his life and labours among the Waldenses of Piedmont. With an introductory notice by W. Arnot. London, 1873. 312 pp. 16° 5338.1

MEIN Freund Piffard. Kock, (C.) P. de. Stuttgart, 1861. Sq. 16° 2028.6

MEINHOLD, (Johann) Wilhelm. Sidonia the sorceress. New York, N. D. 230 [221] pp. 8° 531.1

MEISTER Karl's sketch-book. Leland, C. G. Philadelphia [*cop.* 1872]. Sm. 8° 1913.2

MELBOURNE house. Warner, S. 724.24

MÉLICERTE: pastorale héroïque. Molière, J. B. P. Œuvres. Paris, 1869. 12° 5537.2.2

MELINDA the caboceer; or, sport in Ashanti. Skertchly, J. A. 433.3

Shelf. No.

MELLICHAMPE. Simms, W. G. 716.24
MELVILLE, George John Whyte. The Brookes of Bridlemere. [London and country life] 321.19
— Cerise 321.10
— Contraband 321.18
— Digby Grand 321.14
— The gladiators. [Time of Vespasian] 321.15
— Good for nothing 321.11
— Holmby house. [Cromwellian period] 321.12
— The interpreter. [Crimean war, etc.] 321.9
— Kate Coventry 321.13
— Katerfelto: a story of Exmoor. [Gypsies.] Leipzig 330.10
— *Same.* Philadelphia 714.14
— M. or N. 330.6
— Maud or Nina 721.2
— The queen's Maries. [Mary, queen of Scots and her ladies] 321.17
— Sarchedon: a legend of the great queen. [Semiramis, 13th century B. C.] 321.8
— Sister Louise, or, the story of a woman's repentance 321.26
— Uncle John 319.12
— The white rose. Leipzig 321.16
— *Same.* New York 532.5
MELVILLE, Herman. Battle-pieces and aspects of the [civil] war. [Poems.] New York, 1866. 272 pp. 12° 1624.3
— The bell-tower. (*In* Johnson, (E.) R. Little classics) 529.4.3
— Mardi: and a voyage thither. New York, 1864. 2 v. 12° 512.11
— Moby-Dick; or, the whale. New York, 1871. xxiii, 634+ pp. 12° 512.12
— Omoo: a narrative of adventures in the South seas. 6th edition. New York, 1868. 389 pp. Map. 12° 425.23

Note. — A sequel to Typee, — partly autobiographical, partly fictitious.

— Typee: a peep at Polynesian life, during a four months' residence in a valley of the Marquesas. Revised edition, with a sequel. New York, 1871. xiv, 307 pp. Map. 12° 737.4
— White-jacket; or, the world in a man-of-war. New York [*cop.* 1850]. 465 pp. 12° 725.12
MEMBER for Paris, The. Murray, G. 316.7
MEMES, John S. Memoirs of the empress Josephine. New York, 1855. 396 [394] pp. Portraits. 16°. 1228.4
MEMOIRS of a femme de chambre. Gardiner, M. 310.4
MEMOIRS of a New England village choir. Gilman, S. Boston, 1829. Sm. 12° 1238.22
MEMOIRS of a physician. Dumas, A. (D.) 511.11
MEMOIRS of Mr. C. J. Yellowplush. Thackeray, W. M. Miscellanies. Leipzig 335.13.2
— *Same.* (*In his* Works.) London 513.1.8
MEMOIRS of my youth. Lamartine, A. (M. L.) de. New York, N. D. 8° 1021.7
MEMOR, *pseud.* *See* GRAMONT, Antoine Agénor Alfred, *duc* de.
MEMORABILIA of Socrates. Xenophon. London, 1872. Sm. 8° 6115.12
MEMORABLE women of the puritan times. Anderson, J. London, 1872. 2 v. Sm. 8° 5427.6
MEMORIALS, and other papers. De Quincey, T. Boston, 1868. 2 v. 12° 1825.8
MEMORIALS of a quiet life. Hare, A. J. C. London, 1873. 2 v. Sm. 8° 5427.1
MEMORIES, counsels, and reflections. Huntington, D. Cambridge, 1857. 8° 6322.2
MEN and manners in America. Hamilton, T. Philadelphia, 1833. 2 v. 16° 416.1
MEN and mysteries of Wall street. Medbery, J. K. Boston, 1870. Sm. 4° 413.2
MEN and things. Baker, J. L. Boston, 1858. 12°. 5216.4
MEN I have known. Jerdan, W. London, 1866. Sm. 8° 5423.11
MEN of character. Jerrold, D. (W.) Leipzig, 1852. 2 v. in 1. Sq. 16° 313.8
MEN of letters of the time of George III. [Brief biographies, etc.] Brougham, H., *lord.* Works. Edinburgh, 1872. 16° 5614.4.2

Shelf. No.

MEN of our times, or leading patriots of the day. Stowe, H. (E.) B. Hartford, 1869. 8° 5023.9
MEN, The, of the third republic; or, the present leaders of France. Philadelphia, 1873. 384+ pp. Sm. 8° 5517.1

Note. — This has been attributed to W. F. Rae, editor of the London Daily news.

MEN, women, and books. [Papers.] Hunt, (J. H.) L. London, 1870. 16° 1935.1
MEN, women, and ghosts. Phelps, E. S. 537.8
MENAULT, Ernest. The intelligence of animals. From the French. With illustrations. [New York] 1872. xvi, 368 pp. 16° 1714.5
MENCIUS, *joint author.* Chinese classics. *See* CONFUCIUS 5923.2
MENDELSSOHN-BARTHOLDY, Carl. Goethe and Mendelssohn. (1821-1831.) Translated, with additions, by M. E. von Glehn. With portraits and facsimile, and letters by [Felix] Mendelssohn of later date. 2d edition, with additional letters. London, 1874. xviii, 198 pp. Sm. 8° 5726.4
MENDELSSOHN-BARTHOLDY, Felix. Letters from Italy and Switzerland. Translated by Lady Wallace. With a biographical notice by J. de Marguerittes. Boston, N. D. 12° 1227.1
— Barnard, C. F., *jr.* Mozart and Mendelssohn. Boston, 1870. 16° 926.23
— Devrient, (P.) E. My recollections of. London, 1869. 8° 5727.2
— Hiller, F. Mendelssohn. Letters and recollections. London, 1874. Sm. 8° 5727.3
— Mendelssohn-Bartholdy, C. Goethe and Mendelssohn. (1821-1831.) London, 1874. Sm. 8°. 5726.4

Note. — See note on Music in the Bulletin for Jan., 1876. Miss Sheppard's "Charles Auchester" [532.1] contains a delineation of Mendelssohn.

MENSCHENFEIND, Der. Schiller, (J. C.) F. von. Werke. Stuttgart, 1865. 8° 5734.1.3
MENTAL-CURE, The. Evans, W. F. Boston [*cop.* 1869]. 12° 1525.8
MENTAL disease, Responsibility in. Maudsley, H. New York, 1874. 12° 6035.4
MENTAL hygiene. Ray, I. Boston, 1863. 16° 6036.5
MENTAL philosophy. Edwards, J. Enquiry into the modern prevailing notions of that freedom of will which is essential to moral agency. Boston, 1754. 16° 1524.12
— Locke, J. Essay on the human understanding. New York, 1818. 8° 1912.6
— Stewart, D. Philosophy of the human mind. Cambridge, 1829. 3 v. 8° 5832.4

See also Intellectual science, Mind.

MENZEL, Wolfgang. History of Germany, from the earliest period to the present time. Translated from the German by Mrs. George Horrocks. London, 1871. 3 v. Portraits. 8° 5715.3
MERCADANTE, Saverio. Il giuramento. (*In* Ditson, O., and co. Standard opera librettos) 6233.3.1
MERCEDES of Castile. [Spain and Columbus.] Cooper, J. F. 525.14
MERCERSBURG theology inconsistent with protestant reformed doctrine. Schenck, B. S. Philadelphia, 1874. 12° 6326.14
MERCHANTS' magazine, and commercial review. *See* HUNT, Freeman 1322.1
MERCY Gliddon's work. Phelps, E. S. Boston [*cop.* 1865]. 16° 916.25
MEREDITH, George. Beauchamp's career 331.24
— The ordeal of Richard Feverel. A history of father and son 331.13
MEREDITH, Owen, *pseud.* *See* BULWER-LYTTON (Edward) Robert, *lord Lytton.*
MEREDITH. Gardiner, M. 330.25
MERIDIANA. Verne, J. London, 1873. Sm. 4° 713.1
MÉRIMÉE, Prosper. Letters to an incognita. (*In* Stoddard, R. H. Bric-à-brac series) 1828.1
— Portraits historiques et littéraires. Paris, 1874. 357+ pp. 18° 5527.14

Contents. — Cervantes; Victor Jacquemont; Henri de Guise; Charles Nodier; J. J. Ampère; Henri Beyle (Stendhal); Théodore Leclercq; Alexis de Valon; Alexandre du Sommerard; Froissart; Branthôme; Charles Lenormant; Edmond Ellice; Alexandre Pouchkine; Ivan Tourguénef.

Shelf. No.

MERIVALE, Charles. A general history of Rome, from the foundation of the city to the fall of Augustulus, B. C. 753 — A. D. 476. 2d edition. London, 1875. xxiii, 708+ pp. Folded maps. 8°. 5517.8

— History of the Romans under the empire. From the 4th London edition. With a copious analytical index. New York, 1866. 7 v. 6 maps. 8°. 5515.3

MERRIE England. [Sketches for youth.] Lippincott, S. J. Boston, 1868. 16° ... 922.26

MERRIMACK river, *Mass.*, A week on the. Thoreau, H. D. Boston, 1868. 12° ... 215.1

MERRY England: or, nobles and serfs. [Fiction.] Ainsworth, W. H. ... 319.18

MERVYN Clitheroe. Ainsworth, W. H. ... 322.22

MERVYN Clitheroe's Leben und Abenteuer. Ainsworth, W. H. Pest, 1859. 4 v. in 1. 16° ... 2026.2

MÉRY, Joseph, *joint author*. The cross of Berny. *See* GIRARDIN, Delphine Gay de ... 725.30

MESSAGE, A, from the sea ... 338.3

META's faith. Tabor, E. ... 711.19

METALLURGY. Bauerman, H. Treatise on the metallurgy of iron. London, 1872. 12° ... 1716.42

— Joynson, F. H. The metals used in construction. Edinburgh, 1868. 16° ... 6637.1

— Lamborn, R. H. Metallurgy of copper. London, 1868. 12° ... 1715.16

— - Metallurgy of silver and lead. London, 1870. 12° ... 1715.17

— Percy, J. Metallurgy: the art of extracting metals from their ores. London, 1875. 8° ... 6631.10

See also Electro-metallurgy.

METAMORPHOSES, Comic. Valentine, W. New York [*cop.* 1856]. 12° ... 1516.18

METAPHYSICS. Hamilton, *Sir* W. Lectures on. Boston, 1859. 8° ... 5832.2

— Kant, I. The metaphysics of ethics. Edinburgh, 1871. Sm. 8° ... 5836.3

METCALFE, Samuel L. Caloric: its mechanical, chemical and vital agencies in the phenomena of nature. Philadelphia, 1869. 2 v. 8° ... 5832.1

METEOROLOGY considered with reference to natural theology. Prout, W. London, 1855. Sm. 8° ... 6436.10

METEORS, aërolites, storms, and atmospheric phenomena. Zuercher, F., and Margollé, É. New York, 1871. 12° ... 1714.8

METEYARD, Eliza. A group of Englishmen (1795 to 1815), being records of the younger Wedgwoods and their friends, embracing the history of the discovery of photography and a facsimile of the first photograph. London, 1871. xxii, 416 pp. 1 plate. 8° ... 5424.4

— The hallowed spots of ancient London. New edition. London, 1870. xii, 291 pp. Illustrated. Sm. 4° ... 5436.3

— Life of Josiah Wedgwood. With an introductory sketch of the art of pottery in England. With illustrations. London, 1865, 66. Portraits. 2 v. 8° ... 6231.3

— Mainstone's housekeeper ... 725.37

METHODISM. Stevenson, G. J. City road chapel, London, and its associations. London [1872]. 8°. 5414.1

— Tyerman, L. The Oxford methodists. New York, 1873. 8° ... 5424.5

Note. — Biographies of the Arminian Wesley and the Calvinistic Whitefield necessarily detail the history of the rise and progress of the two schools of methodism; — see the notes under those names, and the note on Wesley in the Bulletin for Oct., 1875, p. 428. The literature of the subject is large. Stevens's "History of English methodism" [in the Bates Hall], his first volume closing with the death of Whitefield, and his second coming down to the death of Wesley, an American book, was very favorably received in England, and it is the best comprehensive history of the movement, which began under Wesley. It is treated by Stevens in a broader view than that of a sectarian growth. The general reader will be, perhaps, content with an excellent chapter of Earl Stanhope's [Mahon's] "History of England" [838.3]. See also a summary in the first vol. of J. H. Newman's Essays [5614.5]. The recent Bampton lectures by Curteis give a section to the history of the relations of methodism to the established church [5816.11]. A recent monograph by Stevenson [5414.1] on the "City road chapel, London," which was the head-quarters of Wesley's followers, detailing its associations, has a good deal of interest for the reader of antiquarian zeal. Also see Harper's monthly, Feb., 1874. See the "Rise of methodism in America," in Harper's magazine, vol. 33, given in a sketch of Bishop Asbury. The present state and subdivisions of the methodist church are explained in the first chapter of Tyerman's Wesley [5423.2].

Shelf. No.

METHODIST quarterly review. Vol. 55, 56. New York, 1873, 74. 2 v. 8° ... 6727.1

METHODIUS, *bishop of Tyre*, and OTHERS. The writings of Methodius, Alexander of Lycopolis, Peter of Alexandria, and several fragments. Edinburgh, 1869. 471+ pp. [Ante-Nicene Christian library.] 8° ... 6322.4.14

Note. — The treatises in this volume, from page 1 to page 230, are translated by W. R. Clark; from page 233 to 363, by J. B. H. Hawkins; from page 365 to 395 by B. L. [P.] Pratten; and from page 396 to 455, by S. D. F. Salmond.

MEUNIER, Victor (Amédée). Adventures on the great hunting grounds of the world. Illustrated. New York, 1872. vii, 297 pp. 16° ... 1714.7

MEXICAN war. *See* UNITED STATES.

MEXICO. Haven, G. Our next-door neighbor: a winter in. New York, 1875. 8° ... 5032.5

— Prescott, W. H. History of the conquest of, with a preliminary view of the ancient Mexican civilization. Philadelphia, 1873. 3 v. 8° ... 5014.2

— *Same.* Philadelphia, 1875. 3 v. 12° ... 815.6

— Taylor, (J.) B. Eldorado; or, adventures in the path of empire. New York, 1864. 12° ... 425.6

— Thompson, W. Recollections of. New York, 1847. 16° ... 816.3

— Wise, H. A. Los Gringos; or, an inside view of. New York, 1849. 12° ... 435.4

See also Chiapas, Yucatan.

Note. — For the ancient *Aztec civilization*, read the introductory portion of Prescott, and his inquiry into the origin of it, in his appendix to his third volume, where his conclusion that it was a peculiar indigenous civilization, having a very remote connection with Eastern Asia, was reached independently of, and is the same with, that of Stephens [422.5]. See also Bancroft's "Native races" [5920.4] and Baldwin's "Ancient America" [5027.5]. For the symbolism and mythology of the Aztecs, see Brinton's "Myths of the new world" [5924.7]. See the note on "America before Columbus" in the Bulletin, April, 1876; and Lew Wallace's "Fair god" [737.16; 5014.10] is a novel depicting this early Mexican life.

For the *Spanish conquest* under Cortés, the English historian Robertson [1226.9] prefixes his authorities, and treats the theme with his accustomed dignity; and Smyth, in his 21st lecture on "Modern history" [5012.10; 5925.7] points out his value. The first choice on this subject, however, will necessarily be Prescott's graphic history, in which the narrative is carried down to the death of Cortés, and the reader is instructed at intervals with his clear estimates of his chief authorities. He added much to previous knowledge of the subject, and Allibone gives a full list of critiques on his book, with a collation of the important ones. Arthur Helps, in the second volume of his "Spanish conquest" [816.6]. has told the story over again, with the special aim of tracing the results of the conquest in the rise of slavery and the founding of colonial governments. The general reader will find a popular narrative of the conquest in Harper's monthly, vol. 12.

For the *war with the United States*, see United States, History.

For the *French invasion and the career of Maximilian*, see under Maximilian, and the Atlantic monthly, July, 1864.

Books descriptive of modern Mexico are numerous. Madame Calderon de la Barca's book is well-known, and was reviewed by Prescott in his Miscellanies [1537.8; 5237.3]. Harper's monthly has illustrated papers on the Indians, vol. 19; on Popocatepetl, vol. 31; and on Modern Mexico, vols. 17 and 49.

MEYER, Heinrich August Wilhelm. Critical and exegetical commentary on the New Testament. From the German [by J. C. Moore]. The translation revised and edited by W. P. Dickson. Part IV. Edinburgh, 1873. xl, 324 pp. 8° ... 5810.2

Contents. — Part IV, vol. 1. Romans.

MEYER, Moritz. Electricity in its relations to practical medicine. Translated from the 3d German edition, with notes and additions, by W. A. Hammond. New York, 1869. xxi, 497 pp. Illustrated. 8° ... 6022.5

MEYERBEER, Giacomo. L'Africaine; Dinorah; L'étoile du nord; Les Huguenots; Le prophète; Robert le diable. (*In* Ditson, O., and co. Standard opera librettos) ... 6233.3.4

MICE at play. Floyd, C. ... 1117.11

MICHAEL Rudolph. Dupuy, E. A. ... 522.20

MICHAUX, André. Flora Boreali-Americana. Paris, 1803. 2 v. Illustrated. 8° ... 6624.2

MICHEL-ANGELO. *See* BUONARROTI, Michel-Angelo.

MICHELET, Jules. The bird. With illustrations. New edition, revised. London, 1870. 349+ pp. 8° ... 6612.5

— Historical view of the French revolution. From the earliest indications to 1791. Translated by C. Cocks. New edition. With general index. London, 1864. xxiv, 621 pp. 1 plate. Sm. 8°. 5517.3

Shelf. No.

MICHELET, Jules, *continued.*

— History of France. Translated by G. H. Smith. New York, 1869. 2 v. 8° 811.7

— History of the Roman republic. Translated by W. Hazlitt. London, 1863. 466+ pp. 16° .. 826.11

— The insect. With illustrations by Giacomelli. London, 1875. 368 pp. 8° 6612.9

— Jeanne d'Arc. 1412–32. 3e édition. Paris, 1873. xvi, 152 pp. Sm. 8° 2016.8

— Joan of Arc: or, the maid of Orleans. From [his] History of France. [By O. W. Wight.] New York, 1870. 238 pp. 16° 1029.2

— Love. Translated from the 4th Paris edition, by J. W. Palmer. New York, 1872. xviii, 342 pp. 12° 1934.11

— Nature; or, the poetry of earth and sea. From the French. With 200 designs by Giacomelli. London, 1872. xxxi, 431 pp. 8° 6830.2

— The sea. Translated from the latest Paris edition. New York, 1861. 405 pp. 12° 1934.13

— A summary of modern history. Translated from the French, and continued to the present time, by M. C. M. Simpson. London, 1875. xx, 376 pp. Sm. 8° 5528.7

— The women of the French revolution [of 1789]. Philadelphia, 1855. 371 pp. 12° 1226.3

MICROSCOPE. Beale, L. S. How to work with the. London, 1868. 8° 6822.1

— Carpenter, W. B. The microscope and its revelations. London, 1868. 16° 6827.1

— Gosse, P. H. Evenings at the. New York, 1872. 12° 1523.11

— Somerville, M. On molecular and microscopic science. London, 1869. 2 v. Sm. 8° 6816.2

MIDDLE ages. Baring-Gould, S. Curious myths of the. London, 1872. 16° 716.2

— Cutts, E. L. Scenes and characters of the. London, 1872. Sm. 4° 5913.7

— Hallam, H. View of the state of Europe during the. New York, 1872. 3 v. Sm. 8° 5916.1

— Viollet-le-Duc, E. E. An essay on the military architecture of the. Oxford, 1860. 8° 6221.5

Note.—The middle ages are generally considered to embrace the period from the fall of Rome, A. D. 476, to the overthrow of the Eastern empire in 1453, or perhaps to the time of the reformation. The causes and effects of the overthrow of Rome are traced in Guizot's "History of civilization" [5924.8], and there is a summary in Alison's essay on Guizot [1531.7]. Hallam's book, above named, is the chief English authority; but Gibbon's great work on the "Decline and fall of the Roman empire" [824.9] covers A. D. 100-1420, and is the grand authority for all the relations of that empire during this period. The reader will do well to examine Smyth's third and fourth lectures in his "Modern history" [5012.10; 5925.7].

The view of the progress of society, which Robertson prefixed to his "Charles V" [1226.9], has been praised as the greatest step yet made in the philosophy of history. A recent authority of high repute is Lecky, on the "History of morals from the times of Augustus to Charlemagne" [5914.1].

The military history of the epoch will be studied in connection with the Crusades, and in the lives of such heroes as Richard Cœur-de-Lion and Philip Augustus, and collaterally in Viollet-le-Duc's "Military architecture of the middle ages," above named.

For the religious element of the latest era, there is the protestant Ranke's "History of the popes" [5516.7]. Mrs. Oliphant's "Francis of Assisi" [5937.10] gives a good picture of the religious life at the beginning of the 13th century.

For the popular myths, see Baring-Gould [716.2], which covers such subjects as the Wandering Jew, Prester John, etc.

Accounts of the *Revival of learning* can be found in Hallam's "Literature of Europe" [1531.2] and in his "Middle ages" [5916.1]; in Gibbon's 53d and 66th chapters of the "Roman empire" [824.9]; in Roscoe's "Lorenzo de' Medici" [5525.1] and "Leo X" [5526.6]; in Robertson's introduction to his "Charles V" [1226.9], and in Pater's "Renaissance" [5925.2].

See this period under Europe and the several countries of Europe; Crusades; Feudal system, etc., in this and the Bates Hall catalogues.

MIDDLEMARCH. Lewes, M. 2 v. .... 532.3 and 5636.2

MIDDLESEX county, *Mass.* Historic fields and mansions of Middlesex. Drake, S. A. Boston, 1874. 8° 814.4

MIDDLETON, Conyers. Life of M. Tullius Cicero. New edition. London, 1837. 739 pp. Portrait. 8° 5521.2

MIDSHIPMAN Easy, Mr. Marryat, F. 337.12

MIDWIFERY. Cazeaux, P. Theoretical and practical treatise on. Philadelphia, 1866. 8° 6012.23

— Churchill, F. Theory and practice of. Philadelphia, 1855. 8° 6022.17

Shelf. No.

MIDWIFERY, *continued.*

— Collins, R. Practical treatise on. Boston, 1841. 8°. 6023.15

— Ingleby, J. T. Facts and cases in obstetric medicine. London, N. D. 8° 6012.10

— Pasta, A. Traité des pertes de sang chez les femmes enceintes. Paris, 1797. 2 v. 8° 6014.2

— Simpson, *Sir* J. Y. Obstetric memoirs and contributions. Philadelphia, 1855, 56. 2 v. 8°. 6011.5

MIGNET, François Auguste (Marie). History of the French revolution, 1789–1814. London, 1868. xi, 424 pp. Portrait. Sm. 8° 5517.4

MIGNON. Thomas, (C.) A. (*In* Ditson, O., and co. Standard opera librettos) 6233.3.1

MIKE Howe, the bushranger of Van Dieman's land. Bonwick, J. 725.28

MILBURN, William Henry. Ten years of preacher-life: chapters from an autobiography. New York, 1859. 363 pp. Portrait. 12° 1015.1

MILDRED. Craik, G. M. 322.1

MILDRED Arkell. Wood, E. P. 333.15

MILDRED's wedding. Notley, *Mrs.* — 711.37

MILES, Henry Adolphus. Lowell, as it was, and as it is. 2d edition. Lowell, 1847. 234 pp. Folded plan. 12° 5017.5

— *editor.* The altar at home: prayers for the family and the closet. 4th edition. Boston, 1855. 350 pp. 16° 6327.8

— *Same.* 10th edition. Boston, 1859. 350 pp. 16°. 6327.19

MILES, Leonidas Clint. Water-colour painting; with the art of sketching from nature. With illustrations. London, N. D. 88 pp. 16° 6216.5

MILES Wallingford. Cooper, J. F. 525.17

MILETUS, The lost tales of. [Poems.] Bulwer-Lytton, E. (G. E.) L. Leipzig, 1866. Sq. 16°. 1614.7

MILITARY architecture. An essay on the military architecture of the middle ages. Viollet-le-Duc, E. E. Oxford, 1860. 8° 6221.5

MILITARY art and science. Andrews, C. C. Hints to company officers on their military duties. New York, 1863. 24° 6927.7

— Hamley, E. B. The operations of war explained and illustrated. Edinburgh, 1872. 4° 5910.6

— Praissac, —. [A short method for the easy resolving of any military question, propounded; translated by John Cruso. Cambridge, 1639.] Sm. 8° 5918.2

— Revised regulations for the army of the United States. 1861. *See* UNITED STATES. *Department of war* 1521.12

See also Infantry tactics.

MILITARY biography. Chesney, C. C. Essays in modern military biography. London, 1874. 8°. 5922.8

— Shanks, W. F. G. Personal recollections of distinguished generals. New York, 1866. 12° ... 1015.5

MILITARY education. The school and the army in Germany and France. Hazen, W. B. New York, 1872. 8° 5714.5

MILITARY service. *See* HYGIENE.

MILL, James. *See* RIBOT, T. English psychology. New York, 1874. 8° 5835.5

MILL, John Stuart. Autobiography. New York, 1874. vi, 313 pp. 8° 5424.7

— Dissertations and discussions: political, philosophical, and historical. New York, 1874, 75. 5 v. 8° 5824.4

Contents.—Vol. I. The contest in America; State interference with corporation and church property; The currency juggle; Observations on the French revolution; Poetry and its varieties; Professor Sedgwick's discourse; Civilization; Aphorisms; Armand Carrel; A prophecy; Alfred de Vigny; Bentham; Appendix. II. Coleridge; De Tocqueville on Democracy in America; Bailey on Berkeley's Theory of vision; Michelet's History of France; The claims of labor; Guizot's essays and lectures on history; Early Grecian history and legend. III. Vindication of the French revolution of 1848; Enfranchisement of women; Dr. Whewell on moral philosophy; Grote's History of Greece; A few words on non-intervention; The slave power; Utilitarianism. IV. Thoughts on parliamentary reform; Recent writers on reform; Bain's psychology; Austin on jurisprudence; Plato; Inaugural address [at St. Andrews, Feb. 1, 1867]. V. Endowments; Thornton on labour and its claims; Leslie on the land question; Taine, De l'intelligence; Treaty obligations; Maine on Village communities; Grote's Aristotle; L'avere e l'imposta; Papers on land tenure: Programme of the Land tenure reform association; Speeches on land tenure reform, May 15, 1871, March 18, 1873; Advice to land reformers; The right of property in land.

Shelf. No.

MILL, John Stuart, *continued.*

— On liberty. The subjection of women. New York, 1874. 394 pp. 8°.................... 1733.2

— Principles of political economy, with some of their applications to social philosophy. From the 5th London edition. New York, 1872. 2 v. 8°... 5822.3

— Suffrage for women. (*In* Woman's suffrage tracts). 1926.5

— A system of logic, ratiocinative and inductive. 8th edition. London, 1872. 2 v. 8°......... 5833.1

— Three essays on religion. [Added an essay on Berkeley's life and writings.] New York, 1874. xi, 302 pp. 8°............................ 6325.7

— Ribot, T. English psychology. New York, 1874. 8°. 5835.5

— Spencer, H., and others. John Stuart Mill: his life and works. Boston, 1873. 12°..........5427.10

MILLBANK; or, Roger Irving's ward. Holmes, M. J. 534.6

MILLE, Les, et une nuits. Contes Arabes. Traduits par Galland. Nouvelle édition. Paris, 1842. 2 v. Sm. 8°.............................. 5537.5

MILLER, Cincinnatus Hiner. (*Joaquin Miller.*) First fam'lies of the Sierras. [Fiction]........ 717.12

— Songs of the Sierras. Boston, 1873. 299+ pp. 16°. 1615.20

— The one fair woman........................... 522.22

— The ship in the desert. [Poem.] Boston, 1875. xi, 205 pp. 12°..........................1617.14

MILLER, Elizabeth S. In the kitchen. [Receipts.] Boston, 1875. 568 pp. Sm. 4°............. 1532.8

MILLER, Hugh. An autobiography. My schools and schoolmasters. Boston, 1872. 551 pp. Portrait. 12°.............................1025.11

— First impressions of England and its people. Boston, 1853. 430 pp. Portrait. 12°........ 425.13

— The foot-prints of the Creator. [Geology.] With a memoir of the author by L. Agassiz. Boston, 1859. 337+ pp. Portrait. Illustrated. 12°. 1526.16

— The old red sandstone; or, new walks in an old field. [Geology.] Illustrated. Boston, 1857. xxiv, 288 pp. 1 plate. 12°................1524.20

— Popular geology: a series of lectures read before the philosophical institution of Edinburgh. With Descriptive sketches from a geologist's portfolio. With an introductory résumé of the progress of geological science within the last two years, by Mrs. Miller. Boston, 1859. 423+ pp. 12°...................................1524.19

— Sandy Wood's sepulchre. (*In* Johnson, (E.) R. Little classics)............................529.4.5

— The testimony of the rocks; or, geology in its bearings on the two theologies, natural and revealed. With memorials of the death and character of the author. Boston, 1872. xiv, 502 [500] pp. Illustrated. 12°............... 1527.2

— Life and letters of. Bayne, P. Boston, 1871. 2 v. 12°.................................1225.16

Note. — Bayne's Life is the authoritative one; and there are brief sketches by Smiles, in his "Brief biographies" [1024.13], and by Agassiz [1526.16]. See also P. Bayne's "Essays" [1226.15].

MILLER, James. The practice of surgery. 3d American edition. Edited, with additions, by F. W. Sargent. Illustrated. Philadelphia, 1853. 720+ pp. 8°.............................6022.16

MILLER, Joaquin, *pseud.* *See* MILLER, Cincinnatus Hiner.

MILLER, Samuel. Life of Jonathan Edwards. (*In* Sparks, J. Library of American biography)..5028.1.8

MILLER, William. Evidence from Scripture and history of the second coming of Christ, about 1843. Boston, 1842. 300, 1 pp. Folded sheet. 12° 5818.11

MILLER, William Allen. Elements of chemistry: theoretical and practical. Vol. 1, 5th edition; vol. 3, 4, 4th edition, with additions. London, 1868–72. 3 v. Illustrated. 8°............. 6432.2

Contents. — Vol. I. Chemical physics. II. Inorganic chemistry. III. Organic chemistry.

MILLER, The, of Angibault. Dudevant, A. L. A. D. 526.5

MILLHOUSE, John. New English-Italian and Italian-English dictionary. 4th edition. With additions by Ferdinand Bracciforti. London, 1874. 2 v. Sm. 8°..........................*R.R., F.3.11

Contents. — Vol. I. English and Italian. II. Italian and English.

Shelf. No.

MILLS, Abraham. The literature and the literary men of Great Britain and Ireland. New York, 1870. 2 v. 8°................................ 1021.6

MILLS, The, of the gods. Twells, J. H............ 714.15

MILLS, The, of Tuxbury. Townsend, V. F......... 711.23

MILLY; or, the hidden cross. Guernsey, L. E...... 1114.3

MILMAN, Henry Hart. History of Christianity. New and revised edition. London, 1867. 3 v. 16°... 5817.1

— History of Latin Christianity; including that of the popes to the pontificate of Nicolas v. 4th and revised edition. London, 1867. 9 v. Sm. 8°.5817.11

— History of the Jews; from the earliest period down to modern times. 4th edition, revised and extended. London, 1866. 3 v. 16°......... 5927.1

MILNER, H. M. The gambler's fate: a drama. New York, N. D. 37 pp. 12°................... 1635.4

MILNES, Richard Monckton, *lord Houghton.* Life and letters of John Keats. New edition. London, 1867. 363+ pp. Portrait. Sm. 8°......... 1227.6

— Monographs, personal and social. [Essays, etc.] New York, 1873. v, 328+ pp. Portraits. 12°. 5616.7

— Selection from [his] works. London, 1867. viii, 236 pp. Portrait. Sq. 16°.................. 5618.1

MILTON, John. Poetical works. Leipzig, 1850. vi, 358 pp. Sq. 16°........................1614.12

Contents. — Paradise lost; Paradise regained.

— Prose [and poetical] works. With an introductory review by R. Fletcher. London, 1866. 2 v. in 1. Portrait. L. 8°................. 5610.2

— Paradise lost. A poem. Boston, 1825. 294 pp. Sm. 12°.. 1618.4

— Lowell, J. R. Among my books. Boston, 1876. 16°...1934.8.2

— Masson, D. Life of. Vol. I–III. Vol. 1, Cambridge, 1859; vol. 2, 3, London, 1871, 73. 3 v. 8°. 5422.2

Note. — Preliminary to reading about Milton, consult Allibone's elaborate article, where he has given the authorities with copious citations upon the chief phases of Milton's life and writings. Also see McClintock and Strong. It has been the fault of most of the subsequent lives, that they have been partisan, either in respect to politics or religion, but the general reader will find more than enough for his purpose in Masson's elaborate "Life of Milton." It tells the story in connection with his times, of which the first volume covers 1608–39, the second 1638–43, and the third 1643–49.

Of the lesser lives, Johnson's, in his "Lives of the poets" [1238 20], shows a tory's and high churchman's estimates of a republican and a puritan, and is by general concession prejudiced and unwise, though of value for its critical discernment and for its statements of the literary defects of Paradise lost. Of the briefer memoirs and essays, the following may be named: Channing's, in his "Works" [1525.1.1]; Macaulay's, in his essays [1918.4]; Hume's, in chapter 52 of his "History of England" [5413.2]; Essays on his poetry by Coleridge; by Seeley, in his "Roman imperialism" [5613.3], etc.; and one, on Milton as a schoolmaster, in F. D. Maurice's "Friendship of books" [6136.8]. Also Hazlitt's "Table talk," on his sonnets; Howitt's "Homes of the poets" [1225.5], etc.

See also the general literary histories by Hallam and Taine. In historical fiction we have Mrs. Manning's "Mary Powell," a tale of Milton's courtship [738.1].

MIND. Bain, A. Mind and body. The theories of their relation. New York, 1873. 12°........ 6035.2

— Evans, W. F. The mental-cure, illustrating the influence of the mind on the body, both in health and disease. Boston [*cop.* 1869]. 12° .. 1525.8

— Jaeger, A. Mind and heart in religion. New York, 1873. 16°..........................6326.22

— Maudsley, H. Physiology and pathology of the. New York, 1872. 8°....................... 6011.6

— Reid, T. An inquiry into the human mind, on the principles of common sense. London, 1775. 8°.. 5834.9

— Stewart, D. Elements of the philosophy of the. Brattleborough, 1808. 8°........................ 1522.1

See also Insanity, Intellectual science, Mental philosophy, Metaphysics, Philosophy, Psychology.

MINER, Alonzo Ames. Bible exercises, or, the Sunday school one class. Boston, 1863. 166 pp. Illustrated. 12°..................................1538.10

MINERALOGY. Collins, J. H. The first book of. New York [Glasgow], 1873. 16°.............. 1717.8

— Dana, J. D., and Brush, G. J. A system of. New York, 1875. 8°.............................. 6630.2

— Hooker, W. Mineralogy. New York, 1872. 12°. 6636.3

— Jameson, R. Mineralogical notes. *See* CUVIER, G. L. C. F. D., *baron*.............................. 6633.1

Shelf. No.

MINERALOGY, *continued.*
— Jones, W. The treasures of the earth. New York, 1872. 16° 6635.1
— Ramsay, A. Rudiments of. London, 1868. 12°. 1715.21

See also Coal, Crystallisation, Geology, Metallurgy, Mines, Natural history.

MINES and mining. Jones, W. The treasures of the earth. New York, 1872. 16° 6635.1
— Raymond, R. W. Statistics of mines and mining west of the Rocky mountains. Washington, 1873. 8° 5035.8
— Ure, A. Dictionary of mines. London, 1872. 3 v. 8° 6422.3

See also Metallurgy.

MINGLED yarn, A. Mackarness, M. A. 339.19
MINIFIE, William. A text book of geometrical drawing for the use of mechanics and schools. Illustrated with steel plates. Revised by the author. New York, 1873. 162+ pp. L. 8° 6420.3
MINIGO. Abbott, J. Harper's story books 936.1.11
MINISTER'S, The, story. Roe, A. S. 735.34
MINISTER'S, The, wife. Oliphant, M. (O. W.) 328.4
MINISTER'S, The, wooing. Stowe, H. (E.) B. 314.24
MINNESINGER, The, of Germany. Kroeger, A. E. New York, 1873. 16° 5735.1
MINNESOTA and Dacotah, in 1856. Andrews, C. C. Washington, 1857. 12° 415.3
MINTO, *Earl of.* *See* ELLIOT, *Sir* Gilbert.
MIRACLES. Mountford, W. Miracles past and present. Boston, 1870. 16° 1536.6
— Wallace, A. R. Miracles and modern spiritualism. London, 1875. Sm. 8° 6328.24
MIRÈIO. A Provençal poem. Mistral, F. Boston, 1874. Sm. 4° 5533.3
MIRIAM. [Poem.] Hall, L. J. Boston, 1850. 12°. 5216.3
MIRIAM Coffin, or the whale-fishermen. Hart, J. C. 712.4
MIRIAM'S marriage. Macquoid, K. S. 319.5
MIRIAM'S memoirs. Warfield, C. A. 723.34
MISANTHROPE, Le: comédie. Molière, J. B. P. Œuvres. Paris, 1869. 12° 5537.2.2
MISANTHROPE, The: a comedy. Molière, J. B. P. Dramatic works. Edinburgh, 1876. 8° 5530.3.3
MISCHIEF'S Thanksgiving. Woolsey, S. C. 933.11
MISÉRABLES, Les. Hugo, V. (M.), *vicomte.* New York, 1874. 2 v. in 1. 8° 710.19
MISER'S, The, daughter. Ainsworth, W. H. 721.22
MISHMEE hills, The. Cooper, T. T. London, 1873. Sm. 8° 5933.6
MISS Angel. [Angelica Kaufmann, the artist.] Thackeray, A. I. Leipzig 311.27
— *Same.* New York 720.28
MISS Carew. Edwards, A. B. 312.11
MISS Dorothy's charge. Benedict, F. L. 731.9
MISS Forrester. Edwards, A. 732.2
MISS Hitchcock's wedding dress. [Fiction] 717.11
MISS Marjoribanks. Oliphant, M. (O. W.) 328.13
MISS Molly. Butt, B. M. 517.24
MISS Moore. Craik, G. M. 937.27
MISS or Mrs.? Collins, (W.) W. 326.9
MISS Ravenel's conversion from secession to loyalty. De Forest, J. W. 535.5
MISS Rovel. Cherbuliez, V. 711.32
MISS Thistledown. Clarke, R. S. 927.26
MISS Tiller's vegetable garden and the money she made by it. Warner, A. B. New York [1873]. 12° 1518.2
MISS Van Kortland. Benedict, F. L. 710.5
MISSALE Romanum. *See* ROMAN catholic church 5816.15
MISSING bride, The. Southworth, E. D. E. N. 727.15
MISSION, The: or, scenes in Africa. Marryat, F. 337.13
MISSIONS. Anderson, R. Foreign missions: thei relations and claims. New York, 1869. 8° 5812.16
— – History of the missions of the American board of commissioners for foreign missions in India. Boston, 1874. 8° 5812.4
— – History of the missions of the American board of commissioners for foreign missions to the Oriental churches. Boston, 1872. 2 v. 8° 5812.1
— – History of the Sandwich Islands mission. Boston, 1870. 8° 5812.15

Shelf. No.

MISSIONS, *continued.*
— Cochrane, T. Home mission work. Edinburgh, 1873. 16° 5819.16
— Yonge, C. M. Pioneers and founders; or, recent [English and American] workers in the mission field. [London, 1871.] 16° 5817.5

Note. — Parkman's histories largely illustrate the missions of the Jesuits to North America in the 17th and 18th centuries.

MISSISSIPPI river, Report upon the physics and hydraulics of the. Humphreys, A. A., and Abbot, H. L. Philadelphia, 1861. L. 4° 6920.2
MR. and Mrs. Faulconbridge. Aïdé, H. 720.14
MR. Midshipman Easy. Marryat, F. 337.12
MR. Pendleton's cup. Bradley, W. I. 913.10
MR. Rutherford's children. Warner, A. B. 932.22
MR. Smith. [Fiction.] Walford, L. P. Leipzig 335.19
— *Same.* New York 518.1
MR. Stewart's intentions. Robinson, F. W. 731.15
MR. Tibbot O'Leary, the curious. Griffin, G. (*In* Johnson, (E.) R. Little classics) 529.4.5
MR. Vaughan's heir. Benedict, F. L. 721.4
MISTRAL, Frédéric. Mirèio. A Provençal poem. Translated by Harriet W. Preston. Boston, 1872. xvii, 249 pp. Sm. 4° 5533.3
MISTRESS and maid. Craik, D. (M.) 323.11
MRS. Armington's maid. Wright, D. T. 714.1
MRS. Caudle's curtain lecture, dramatized from D. Jerrold. Stirling, E. New York, N. D. 12° .. 1635.5
MRS. Caudle's curtain lectures. Jerrold, D. (W.) New York, 1869. 16° 518.9
MRS. Gerald's niece. Fullerton, *Lady* G. 325.15
MRS. Gurney's apology. Gurney, M. Philadelphia, 1860. 8° 1910.3
MRS. Halliburton's troubles. Wood, E. P. 333.5
MISTRESS Judith. Tytler, C. C. F. 518.25
MRS. Limber's raffle. Butler, W. A. 718.5
MRS. Lirriper's legacy. Dickens, C. (J. H.), and others 338.2
MRS. Lirriper's lodgings. Dickens, C. (J. H.), and others 338.2
MISTRESS, The, of the manse. [A poem.] Holland, J. G. New York, 1874. 12° 1625.11
MRS. Skaggs's husbands. Harte, (F.) B. 537.17
MISUNDERSTOOD. Montgomery, F. 313.21
MITCHELL, Donald Grant. (*Ik Marvel.*) A bachelor's revery. (*In* Johnson, (E.) R. Little classics) .. 529.4.4
— Dream life. New York, 1872. xvi, 263 pp. 12° .. 1934.10
— My farm of Edgewood. New York, 1864. x, 319+ pp. 12° 715.2
— Reveries of a bachelor. New edition. New York, 1873. 280 pp. 12° 1934.9
— Rural studies. New York, 1867. viii, 295+ pp. 12° 6226.1
— Seven stories, with basement and attic. New York, 1864. viii, 314 pp. 12° 715.3
MITCHELL, Ormsby MacKnight. The planetary and stellar worlds: a popular exposition of the great discoveries and theories of modern astronomy. With additions by J. Glaisher. London [1860]. 240 pp. Illustrated. 16° 1526.14
MITCHELL, S. Weir. Wear and tear, or hints for the overworked. Philadelphia, 1871. 59 pp. 16°. 1537.2
MITCHELL, Samuel Augustus. A system of modern geography. Illustrated. Philadelphia, 1846. 336 pp. 16° 437.4
— *publisher.* Accompaniment to Mitchell's new map of Texas, Oregon, and California, with the regions adjoining. [Also the map.] Philadelphia, 1846. 38 pp. Sm. 12° 418.7
MITCHELL, Samuel Latham. Observations on the geology of North America. *See* CUVIER, Georges Léopold Chrétien Frédéric Dagobert, *baron* 6633.1
MITFORD, A. Bertram. The forty-seven Rōnins. (*In* Johnson, (E.) R. Little classics) 529.4.11
MITFORD, Mary Russell. Letters. 2d series. Edited by H. Chorley. London, 1872. 2 v. Sm. 8°. 5626.7
— Letters. *See* BONER, Charles 5426.2
— Life. Told by herself in letters to her friends. Edited by A. G. K. L'Estrange. New York, 1870. 2 v. 12° 1226.16

Shelf. No.

MITFORD, Mary Russell, *continued.*

— Our village. New edition. London, 1865, 71. Illustrated. 2 v. Sm. 8° 527.19

Note. — Pictures of English village life, admirably portrayed.

— Recollections of a literary life; or, books, places, and people. New York [1851]. xii, 558 pp. 12° 1536.4

— *See* FIELDS, J. T. Yesterdays with authors. Boston, 1875 [*cop.* 1871]. 12° 6136.13

Note. — The chief life is that of L'Estrange [1226.16], but there is an additional volume of her letters, edited by Chorley [5626.7], and her letters to Charles Boner [5426.2], beside those contained in Fields's book. The "Recollections of a literary life" contains but sparse biographical memoranda, and is mostly a selection of prose passages and short poems, which have pleased her. See also Allibone's article; Taylor's "At home and abroad" [234.1]; and Harper's monthly, vols. 39 and 40.

MITHRIDATE: tragédie. Racine, J. de. Théâtre complet. Paris, 1870. 12° 5537.3

MIVART, St. George. Man and apes, an exposition of structural resemblances and differences bearing upon questions of affinity and origin. New York, 1874. vi, 200+ pp. Illustrated. 16°. 6617.6

— On the genesis of species. With illustrations. 2d edition. London, 1871. xv, 342 pp. Sm. 8°. 1536.5

See also Darwinism, *note.*

MOAB, The land of. Tristram, H. B. New York, 1873. 8° 5933.4

MOABITE stone, Lectures on the. Colenso, J. W. London, 1873. 8° 5811.5

Note. — See also Scribner's monthly, vol. 2.

MOBY-DICK; or, the whale. Melville, H. New York, 1871. 12° 512.12

MODERN inquiries: classical, professional, and miscellaneous. Bigelow, J. Boston, 1870. Sm. 8°.. 5216.1

MODERN leaders: being a series of biographical sketches. MacCarthy, J. New York, 1872. 8°. 5930.2

MODERN magic. Schele de Vere, M. New York, 1873. 12° 1516.16

MODERN painters. [Criticism and theories.] Ruskin, J. New York, 1872. 5 v. 12° 6236.18

MODERN playmate, The. Wood, J. G. London [1870]. Sq. 16° 6414.3

— *Same.* London [1875]. Sm. 8° 6414.6

MODERN workshop practice. Winton, J. G. London, 1870. 12° 1715.2

MOENS, W. J. C. English travelers and Italian brigands. With map and illustrations. New York, 1866. 355 pp. Portrait. 12° 423.16

MOHAMMED, *or* MAHOMET. The Koran. Translated from the Arabic; by G. Sale. Prefixed a Life of Mohammed. Boston, 1862. 472 pp. 16°.. 5815.2

— Irving, W. Life of. Leipzig, 1850. Sq. 16°...1238.12

— – Lives of the successors of. Leipzig, 1850. Sq. 16° 1238.5

— – Mahomet and his successors. New York, 1850. 2 v. 12° 1223.4

— – *Same.* Philadelphia, 1871. 2 v. Sm. 8° 1815.3

— Smith, R. B. Mohammed and Mohammedanism. New York, 1875. 12° 5816.23

Note. — The best popular account of Mohammed is Irving's, which makes no pretence to original investigation, and the same may be said of his account of the successors of Mohammed to the invasion of Spain, A. D. 710. Smyth's third lecture on "Modern history" [5012.10; 5925.7] will indicate the old authorities. The 50th chapter of Gibbon's Rome [824.9] shows that historian at the best, and is perhaps the strongest vindication that Mahommed has received from a European. Carlyle, in his "Heroes and hero worship" [1505.10], has also taken the palliative side, and he is followed by Kingsley, in his "Alexandria and her schools" [1223.5], who agrees to Carlyle's "true and just description of a much calumniated man." Mahommed's career necessarily is covered in Milman's "Latin Christianity" [5817.11]. Sale's English version of the Koran [5815.2] has a dissertation prefixed forming one of the best of the descriptive and historical surveys. See also Clarke's account in his "Ten great religions" [1523.2], or Atlantic monthly, vol. 24. In many travels [see Arabia] the condition and history of this faith is dwelt upon; and Warburton gives a chapter to it in his "Crescent and the cross" [317.8]. See an illustrated article on "Mecca and Medina," in Harper's monthly, vol. 14, and Taylor's "Lands of the Saracen" [424.13].

The two lives which probably present the greatest research are those by Sir William Muir, 1858, in English; and that in German, by Sprenger, 1861, neither of which are in this Branch, but may be found in Bates Hall.

See also F. W. Newman, in Fraser's magazine, Aug., 1873; and Clodd's "Childhood of religions" [6328.21]. R. B.

Shelf. No.

MOHAMMED, *or* MAHOMET, *continued.*

Smith's book [5816.23] is a recent reputable survey, which has Emanuel Deutsch's article on "Islam" for an appendix, and this article can also be found in Deutsch's "Literary remains" [5733.7]. There are fuller references to the literature of the subject in Milman's "Latin Christianity" [5817.11.1], and in the notes in the Lower Hall Catalogue of history, etc. See also McClintock and Strong's Cyclopædia. Draper's "Conflict between religion and science" [5826.4] views Mohammedanism as an earlier reformation.

MOHAMMED Ali and his house. [Historical fiction.] Mundt, C. (M.) 531.28

MOLECULAR physics in the domain of radiant heat, Contributions to. Tyndall, J. New York, 1873. 8° 6431.1

MOLECULAR science. Somerville, M. London, 1869. 2 v. Sm. 8° 6816.2

MOLESWORTH, William Nassau. History of England from 1830. London, 1871–73. 3 v. 8° 5413.3

— *Same.* New edition. London, 1874. 3 v. Sm. 8°. 5415.1

MOLIÈRE, Jean Baptiste Poquelin, *called.* Œuvres complètes. Édition variorum. [Avec] notes [etc.]. Par C. Louandre. Portrait. Paris, 1869. 3 v. 12 .... 5537.2

Contents. — Vol. I. Précis de l'histoire du théâtre en France; Vie de Molière; La jalousie du barbouillé; Le médecin volant; L'étourdi; Le dépit amoureux; Les précieuses ridicules; Sganarelle, ou le cocu imaginaire; Don Garcie de Navarre; L'école des maris; Les fâcheux; L'école des femmes; La critique de L'école des femmes; L'impromptu de Versailles; Le mariage forcé. II. La princesse d'Élide; Don Juan, ou le festin de Pierre: L'amour médecin; Le misanthrope; Le médecin malgré lui; Mélicerte; Pastorale comique; Le Sicilien; Le Tartuffe; Amphitryon; George Dandin; Fête de Versailles; Appendice. III. L'avare; Monsieur de Pourceaugnac; Les amants magnifiques; Le bourgeois gentilhomme; Psyché; Les fourberies de Scapin; La comtesse d'Escarbagnas; Les femmes savantes; Le malade imaginaire; Poésies diverses.

— Dramatic works. Rendered into English by Henri Van Laun. With a prefatory memoir, introductory notices, appendices and notes. Vol. I–III. Edinburgh, 1875, 76. 3 v. Portrait. Etchings. 8° 5530.3

Contents. — Vol. I. Preface; Prefatory memoir; The blunderer; The love-tiff; The pretentious young ladies; Sganarelle; Don Garcia of Navarre. II. The school for husbands; The bores; The school for wives; The school for wives criticised; The impromptu of Versailles; The forced marriage. III. The princess of Elis; Don Juan, or the feast with the statue; Love is the best doctor; The misanthrope; The physician in spite of himself.

— *See* PRESCOTT, W. H. Biographical and critical essays. London, 1856. 16° 1537.8

— *Same.* Philadelphia, 1875. 12°............... 5237.3

MOLLOY, Gerald. The passion play at Ober-Ammergau, in the summer of 1871. 2d edition. Boston, 1872. 120 pp. 12 photographs. 4° 5735.9

MOLLUSCA, Manual of the. Woodward, S. P. London, 1871. 12° 1715.9

MOLTKE, Helmuth Carl Bernhard von. Histoire de la campagne de 1866. Traduite de l'allemand par F. Raynaud. Paris, 1868. 226+ pp. 8°. 5712.1

MOMMSEN, Theodor. History of Rome. Translated by W. P. Dickson. With a preface by L. Schmitz. New edition. New York, 1872. 4 v. 12°.... 5516.1

MONARCH, The, of Mincing-Lane. Black, W....... 720.13

MONARCHS retired from business [after abdication]. Doran, J. W. New York, 1865. 2 v. 12°.... 1223.1

MONASTERY, The. Scott, *Sir* W. Boston 523.9

— *Same.* Leipzig 330.4

MONASTIC orders, Legends of the. Jameson, A. (M.) Boston, 1866. 16° 1517.7

MONCKTON, James H. The national builder, a work on constructive carpentry. With a glossary. New York [*cop.* 1872]. 22 pp. 92 plates, with accompanying text. 4° 6420.1

MONCRIEFF, Ascott Robert Hope. (*Ascott Robert Hope.*) A book about boys. Boston, 1869. xii, 247 pp. 16° 926.24

— Book about dominies. Boston, 1869. 265 pp. 16°. 1535.9

— The day after the holidays. With illustrations. New York [Edinburgh, 1875]. 203+ pp. [Hope's annual.] Sm. 8° 1115.8

— My schoolboy friends: a story of Whitminster grammar school. Edinburgh, 1870. 354+ pp. 8° 912.2

— Stories of French school life. Edinburgh, 1871. xviii, 446 pp. Illustrated. 16°............. 715.17

Shelf. No.

MONCRIEFF, W. T. Monsieur Tonson: a farce. New York, N. D. 40 pp. 12° 1635.3

— Tom and Jerry: a burletta. New York, N. D. 28 pp. 12° 1635.5

MONDE illustré, Le. Vol. 23, 24, 25, 27, 28, 32, 33. Paris, 1868–73. 7 v. F° 5320.1

MONEY: a comedy. Bulwer-Lytton, E. (G. E.) L. Dramatic works. Leipzig, 1860. Sq. 16° 1614.5

MONEY. Eggleston, G. C. How to make a living. Suggestions upon the art of making, saving, and using money. New York, 1875. 12° 1536.20

— Jevons, W. S. Money and the mechanism of exchange. New York, 1875. 12° 5826.8

— Tables of money, weight, and measure. *See* WEBSTER, N. Dictionary of the English language [Counting-house edition], pp. 550–608 ..................................*R.R., A.2.5

See also Currency.

MONEY-MAKER. Adams, W. T. 923.17

MONFORT Hall. Warfield, C. A. 723.32

MONIKINS, The. Cooper, J. F. 525.21

MONKS, The, of the West. Montalembert, C. F. de Tryon, *comte* de. Boston, 1872. 2 v. 8° 5514.5

Note. — Voluminous record of this life and its results in Western Europe.

MONNIER, Marc. The wonders of Pompeii. From the French. New York, 1872. 250 pp. Illustrated. 12° 1714.17

MONOGRAPHS, personal and social. [Essays, etc.] Milnes, R. M. New York, 1873. 12° 5616.7

MONROE, Lewis Baxter, *editor*. Public and parlor readings. Dialogues and dramas. Boston, 1873. vi, 341 pp. 12° 1516.15

— — Humorous. Boston, 1874. viii, 326 pp. 12°.1515.18

— — Miscellaneous. Boston, 1875. viii, 352 pp. 12° 1515.14

MONSIEUR de Pourceaugnac: comédie-ballet. Molière, J. B. P. Œuvres. Paris, 1869. 12°...5537.2.3

MONSIEUR Sylvestre. Dudevant, A. L. A. D....... 526.3

MONSIEUR Tonson: a farce. Moncrieff, W. T. New York, N. D. 12° 1635.3

MONSIEUR Violet, Narrative of the travels and adventures of. Marryat, F. 337.7

MONSTERS, The, of the deep. Adams, W. H. D. London, 1875. Sm. 8° 6617.1

MONTAGU, Elizabeth. A [English] lady of the last century: illustrated in her unpublished letters. Doran, J. W. London, 1873. 8° 5422.11

MONTAGU, Mary Wortley, *lady*. Letters and works. Edited by Lord Wharncliffe. 3d edition, with a new memoir by W. May Thomas. London, 1861, 66. 2 v. Portraits. 8° 5623.3

Note. — See Mrs. Oliphant's sketch, in her "George II" [1032.1]; Leigh Hunt's "Men, women, and books" [1935.1]; and Allibone and his references.

MONTAIGNE, Michel Eyquem de. Works. Comprising his essays, journey into Italy, and letters, with notes from all the commentators, biographical and bibliographical notices, etc. By W. Hazlitt. New and revised edition. Edited by O. W. Wight. New York, 1872. 4 v. Portrait. Sm. 8° 5536.8

Note. — The old English translation with a life is Charles Cotton's, but successive editors have modified the text, and Hazlitt's, with his summarized life, is now usually met with, but in this edition will be found, in the third volume, a bibliography of the essays, and in the fourth volume a full collection of titles of lives and commentaries, as well as an abridgment of St. John's latest and best life of Montaigne, 1858, who enumerates in an appendix the principal sources of information. Estimates of Montaigne will be found in Emerson's "Representative men" [1916.6; 1934.6.2]; Hallam's "Literature" [1531.2], and in the histories of Martin and Michelet.

MONTALEMBERT, Charles Forbes de Tryon, *comte* de. Des intérêts catholiques au XIXe siècle. 3e édition. Paris, 1852. 251+ pp. 18° 2018.4

— Letters to a schoolfellow, 1827–30. From the French by C. F. Audley. London, 1874. xx, 267 pp. Portrait. Sq. 16° 5527.12

— The monks of the West. Boston, 1872. 2 v. 8°. 5514.5

— Memoir of. Oliphant, M. (O. W.) Leipzig, 1872. 2 v. in 1. Sq. 16° 1237.2

Shelf. No.

MONTEPIN, Xavier Aymon de, *joint author*. The Corsican brothers. *See* BASTÉ, Eugène Pierre. 1635.3

MONTEZ, Lola. *See* LOLA MONTEZ.

MONTGOMERY, Florence. Misunderstood........... 313.21

Thrown together 313.22

— Wild Mike and his victim 313.29

MONTGOMERY, James. Poems. Added a memoir of the author. New edition, with illustrations. Boston, 1873. xxxvi, 362 pp. 16° 1628.2

MONTGOMERY, Richard, Life of. Armstrong, J. (*In* Sparks, J. Library of American biography).5028.1.1

MONTGOMERY, Robert. A universal prayer; Death; A vision of heaven, etc. [Poems.] From the second London edition. Boston, 1829. xviii, 9–132 pp. Portrait. 12° 1616.18

Note. — See Macaulay's caustic review in his Essays [1918.4].

MONTHLY miscellany, The, of religion and letters. Vol. 1–9. Boston, 1839–43. 9 v. in 5. 8°.... 6536.1

MONTHLY religious magazine and theological review. *See* RELIGIOUS magazine and monthly review... 6725.1

MONTI, Luigi. Grammar of the Italian language. Boston, 1855. xii, 252 pp. 12° 2035.1

MONTOLIEU, Jeanne Isabelle Pauline de Bottens, *baronne* de, *joint author*. The Swiss family Robinson. *See* WYSS, Johann Rudolf.......733.8 and 735.6

MONTPELIER, *Vermont*, History of. Thompson, D. P. Montpelier, 1860. 8° 813.11

MOODIE, Susanna (Strickland). Life in the clearings versus the bush. New York [1853]. 300 pp. 12°. 414.8

— Roughing it in the bush; or, life in Canada. New York, 1852. 2 v. 12° 414.12

— *Same.* 2 v. in 1 .... 414.9

MOODS. Alcott, L. M. 517.3

MOON. Guillemin, A. Wonders of the. New York, 1873. 12° 1714.29

— Proctor, R. A. The moon. New York, 1873. 16°.6814.2

MOONFOLK. Austin, J. G. 912.22

MOONSTONE, The. Collins, (W.) W. 326.10

MOORE, Clara Jessup. On dangerous ground. A romance of American society. By Mrs. Bloomfield H. Moore. [International series] 722.1

MOORE, Charles H. What to read, and how to read. New York, 1871. 152 [148] pp. 12° 1537.3

MOORE, Frank. Memorial services at the graves of our soldiers, May 30, 1868. *See* UNITED STATES. *History. Civil war* 5013.13

MOORE, Jacob Bailey, *joint editor*. Collections, historical and miscellaneous; and monthly literary journal. *See* FARMER, John 1912.5

— Collections, topographical, historical and biographical, relating principally to New-Hampshire. *See* FARMER, John 612.1

MOORE, John Weeks. Complete encyclopædia of music. Boston [*cop.* 1852]. 1004 pp. L. 8°. *R.R., E.2.3

MOORE, Thomas. Poetical works. With portrait. Leipzig, 1842. 5 v. in 3. Sq. 16° 1614.9

Contents. — Vol. [I.] 1, 2. Odes of Anacreon, translated, with notes; Epigrams from the Anthologia; Juvenile poems; Poems relating to America; Corruption, and intolerance; The sceptic; Twopenny post-bag; Intercepted letters, etc.; Satirical and humorous poems; Irish melodies; National airs; Sacred songs. [II.] 3, 4. Evenings in Greece; Legendary ballads; Set of glees; Ballads, songs, miscellaneous poems, etc.; Songs from the Greek anthology; Unpublished songs, etc.; Lalla Rookh; Political and satirical poems; The Fudge family in Paris; Fables for the holy alliance; Rhymes on the road; Miscellaneous poems; The loves of the angels; Satirical and humorous poems. [III.] 5. Satirical and humorous poems; The Fudges in England; Songs from M. P., or the blue stocking; Miscellaneous poems; The epicurean; Alciphron.

— Memoirs of Richard Brinsley Sheridan. New York, 1853. 2 v. Portrait. 12° 1223.8

— Personal reminiscences. (*In* Stoddard, R. H. Bric-à-brac series) 1828.6

Note. — See Mrs. Hall's "Recollections," in the Atlantic monthly, Jan., 1865; Howitt's "Homes of the British poets" [1225.5]; Maginn's "Fraserian papers" [1935.5]; Leigh Hunt's "Autobiography" [1225.20]; H. C. Robinson's "Diary" [5425.3]; the "Greville journals" [5414.6]; Madden's "Blessington" [1223.2]; Willis's "Pencillings by the way" [430.2]; and the appendix to vol. 4 of the life of Washington Irving [1214.1].

MOORLAND cottage, The. Gaskell, E. C. 526.13

MOPSA the fairy. Ingelow, J. 935.23

MORAL philosophy. *See* ETHICS.

Shelf. No.

MORAL science, First principles of. Birks, T. R. London, 1873. Sm. 8° 5836.2
MORALE, La, en action. Hocquart, É. Nouvelle-Orléans, 1824. 12° 5518.3
MORALS. Hildreth, R. Theory of. Boston, 1844. 12°. 5836.5
— Spencer, H. Recent discussions in. New York, 1873. 12° 6835.2

See also Ethics.

MORALS, The, of Abou Ben Adhem. Locke, D. R. Boston, 1875. 12° 1536.22
MORALS and mysteries. Aidé, H. 328.27
MORAVIAN historical society, *Bethlehem, Pa.* A memorial of the dedication of monuments erected to mark the sites of ancient missionary stations in New York and Connecticut. Reichel, W. C., *editor.* New York, 1860. 8° 831.3
MORBID anatomy, An introduction to. Green, T. H. Philadelphia, 1871. 8° 6021.9
MORE, Hannah, Memoirs of the life and correspondence of. Roberts, W. New York, 1834. 2 v. 12° 1025.1
MORE, *Sir* Thomas. Utopia. Translated into English by Ralph Robinson. His second and revised edition, 1556: preceded by the title and epistle of his first edition, 1551. Edited by Edward Arber. London, 1869. 168 pp. [English reprints.] Sm. 8° 5618.8
— Manning, A. The household of. New York, 1867. 16° 738.3
— Seebohm, T. The Oxford reformers. London, 1869. 8° 5811.12

Note. — The general historians like Hume, Hallam and Lingard have viewed his character much according to their own impulses, till Mackintosh, in his Essays, did much to defend his subject, relying largely upon More's own apology, which earlier writers had neglected. Disraeli inclines to the unfavorable side in his "Psychological character of Sir Thomas More," in his "Amenities of literature" [1533.13]. A fresh attack was made by Froude, in his History [826.9]. See also Campbell's "Lord chancellors" [5427.9]; Mrs. Hall's Pilgrimage to his home, in Harper's monthly, vol. 1; Foster's "Critical essays" [5614.3.1]; Lodge's "Portraits" [5337.6.1]. Allibone has a full article.

Mrs. Manning's fictitious reproduction of More's domestic life, in her "Household of Sir Thomas More" is of good repute.

MOREAS, Francisco de. Palmerin of England. London, 1807. 4 v. 16° 5928.2
MOREAU, Henry. La politique française en Amérique 1861–64. Paris, 1864. 176 pp. 8° 831.1
MOREAU DE SAINT MÉRY, Médéric Louis Élie. Topographical and political description of the Spanish part of Saint-Domingo. Translated from the French, by William Cobbett. Philadelphia, 1798. 2 v. in 1. 8° 1913.3
MORETTI's campanula. Thackeray, A. I. Works. 512.1.4
MORFIT, Campbell, and MUCKLÉ, Alexander. Chemical and pharmaceutic manipulations. With illustrations. Philadelphia, 1849. 482 [476] pp. 12° 6433.3
MORGAN, Henry. Ned Nevins, the news boy. Illustrated. Boston, 1869. 418+ pp. 16° 936.32
MORGAN, John Ed. University oars, being a critical enquiry into the after health of the men who rowed in the Oxford and Cambridge boat-race, 1829–69. London, 1873. xvi, 397 pp. 16° ... 6416.1
MORGAN, Sydney Owenson, *lady.* Memoirs: autobiography, diaries and correspondence. Leipzig, 1863. 3 v. in 1. Sq. 16° 1238.10
MORISON, David. The religious history of man. 2d edition. London, 1842. x, 384+ pp. Sm. 8°. 5816.15
MORISON, James Cotter. The life and times of Saint Bernard, abbot of Clairvaux. A. D. 1091–1153. New edition. London, 1868. x, 448+ pp. Sm. 8° 5525.9
MORLEY, Henry. English writers. Vol. 1, 2, part 1. London, 1867. 2 v. in 3. 8° 5622.1

Contents. — Vol. I, Part 1. Celts and Anglo-Saxons; with an introductory sketch of the four periods of English literature. Part 2. From the conquest to Chaucer. II. Chaucer to Dunbar.

— Memoirs of Bartholomew fair. With facsimile drawings, engraved upon wood. A verbatim reprint of the original edition. London [1874]. xvi, 404 pp. Sm. 8° 5418.8

Shelf. No.

MORLEY, John. Edmund Burke: a historical study. London, 1867. xv, 312 pp. 8° 5613.3
— On compromise. London, 1874. x, 214 pp. 8°. 5823.4
— Rousseau. London, 1873. 2 v. 8° 5523.4
— Voltaire. London, 1872. xiii, 346 pp. 8°. 1221.2 and 5523.2
MORLEY, Susan. Aileen Ferrers 710.30
— Throstlethwaite 723.33
MORLEY Ernstein. James, G. P. R. 327.10
MORMONISM. Ludlow, F. H. Examination of the Mormon principle. New York, 1871. 16° 413.4
— Rae, W. F. A visit to the Mormons. Leipzig, 1874. Sq. 16° 438.3
— Stenhouse, T. B. H. The Rocky mountain saints: a full and complete history of the Mormons. New York, 1873. 8° 5933.9

See also Great Salt Lake city, Utah.

Note. — See also travels, like Dixon's "New America" [418.1]; Ludlow's "Heart of the continent" [413.4]; Rae's "Westward by rail" [438.3]; Dilke's "Greater Britain" [423.13; 5935.7]; and also Dixon's "Spiritual wives" [1538.2] and his "White conquest" [439.4]. There are articles on the Utah war in the Atlantic monthly, vol. 3; also a paper by Lossing, in Harper's monthly, vol. 6.

MORNING-GLORIES. Alcott, L. M. 926.10
MORPHY, Paul, the chess-champion, The exploits and triumphs, in Europe, of. Edge, F. M. New York, 1859. 12° 1516.25
MORRIS, Edmund. Farming for boys. With illustrations. Boston, 1872. ix, 286+ pp. Sm. 4°. 932.1
MORRIS, Edward E., *editor.* Epochs of history. *Namely:* —
— Cox, G. W. The crusades. New York, 1874. 16°. 628.1
— Gairdner, J. The houses of Lancaster and York. New York, 1874. 16° 628.4
— Gardiner, S. R. The thirty years' war. London, 1874. 16° 628.2
— Morris, W. O'C. The French revolution and first empire. New York [1875]. 16° 628.5
— Seebohm, F. The era of the protestant revolution. London, 1874. 16° 628.3
— Warburton, W. P. Edward III. London, 1875. 16° 628.6
MORRIS, Thomas. A house for the suburbs, socially and architecturally sketched. 3d edition, with illustrative designs. London, 1870. vi, 191+ pp. Sm. 8° 6223.1
MORRIS, William. The earthly paradise. A poem. Boston, 1871. 3 v. Sm. 8° 1625.3
MORRIS, William O'Connor. The French revolution and first empire: an historical sketch. With an appendix upon the bibliography of the subject and a course of study by A. D. White. New York [1875]. xxvii, 306+ pp. 2 folded maps. [Morris, E. E., *editor.* Epochs of history.] 16° 628.5
MORSE, Jedidiah. American universal geography. With maps. 5th edition. Boston, 1805. 2 v. 8°. 432.2
— and PARISH, Elijah. New gazetteer of the Eastern continent. With maps. Charlestown, 1802. Unpaged. 8° 432.4
MORSE, John Torrey, *jr.* Life of Alexander Hamilton. Boston, 1876. 2 v. 16° 5026.7
MORSE, Samuel Finley Breese. Paris exposition, 1867. Reports of the United States commissioners. Examination of the telegraphic apparatus and processes of telegraphy. Washington, 1869. 166 pp. 8° 6822.3
— Memorial of. *See* BOSTON, *Mass.* .... 1211.5 and 5023.3
— Prime, S. I. Life of. New York, 1875. 8° 5331.1
MORTARS, Rudimentary treatise on. Burnell, G. R. London, 1872. 12° 1710.11
MORTIMER, *Mrs.* —. Lines left out; or, some of the histories left out in "Line upon line." New York, 1870. xiv, 339 pp. Illustrated. 16° ... 928.8
MORTE dArthur. Malory, *Sir* T. London, 1871. Sm. 8° 5618.10
MORTIMER, Grace, *pseud.* *See* STUART, M. B.
MORTOMLEY's estate. A novel. Riddell, J. H. 319.31
MORTON, John Madison. Box and Cox: [a comedy]. New York, N. D. 24 [22] pp. 12° 1635.4
MORTON, Thomas. The children in the wood: an opera. New York, N. D. 28 pp. 12° 1635.3

Shelf. No.

MORTON, William Thomas Green. Statements on his claim to the discovery of the anæsthetic properties of ether. *See* UNITED STATES. *Miscellaneous documents* 6812.3
— Trials of a public benefactor, as illustrated in the discovery of etherization. Rice, N. P. New York, 1859. 12° 6826.1
MORTON house. Fisher, F. C. 711.30
MOSAIC cosmogony. Goodwin, C. W. (*In* Essays and reviews) 1538.3
— *Same.* (*In* Hedge, F. H. Recent inquiries in theology) .... 1526.24 and 5814.15
MOSBY, John Singleton, Partisan life with. [Civil war, 1861-65.] Scott, J. New York, 1867. 8°. 811.14
MOSCHELES, Charlotte. Life of Moscheles, with selections from his diaries and correspondence. Adapted from the German by A. D. Coleridge. London, 1873. 2 v. Portrait. 8° 5525.6
MOSCHELES, Ignaz. Recent music and musicians, as described in [his] diaries and correspondence. Edited by his wife. And adapted from the original German by A. D. Coleridge. New York, 1873. xviii, 434 pp. 12° 6234.4
— Life, with selections from his diaries and correspondence. Moscheles, C. London, 1873. 2 v. 8°. 5525.6
MOSCHUS. Idylls. *See* THEOCRITUS 6115.17
MOSCOW. Spectacles for young eyes. Lander, S. W. 916.9
MOSE Evans. Baker, W. M. 726.23
MOSELEY, Joseph. What is contraband of war and what is not. London, 1861. xi, 114 pp. 12°. 6927.6
MOSSES from an old manse. [Short stories.] Hawthorne, N. Boston, 1872. 2 v. in 1. 16° 1813.3
MOSSMAN, Samuel. New Japan, the land of the rising sun; its annals during the past twenty years, recording the remarkable progress of the Japanese in western civilization. With map. London, 1873. vii, 484 pp. 8° 5922.9
MOTHER goose for grown folks. [Verse.] Whitney, A. D. T. 1625.5
MOTHER-IN-LAW, The. Southworth, E. D. E. N. .. 727.9
MOTHER'S, The, nursery songs. Hastings, T. New York, 1835. 12° 1625.8
MOTHER'S, The, recompense. Aguilar, G. 313.2
MOTHERLY talks with young housekeepers. Beecher, E. W. New York, 1873. 12° 1515.13
MOTION, Power in. Armour, J. London, 1871. 12° 1716.41
MOTLEY, John Lothrop. History of the United Netherlands: 1584-1609. With portraits. New York, 1868-71. 4 v. 8° 5912.1
— Life and death of John of Barneveld; with a view of the primary causes and movements of the Thirty years' war. With illustrations. New York, 1874. 2 v. 8° 5713.3
— The rise of the Dutch republic. New York, 1856. 3 v. 8° 822.2

Note. — Motley's histories follow in this order. — 1. Dutch republic; 2. United Netherlands; 3. John of Barneveld. See Netherlands, *note.*

MOULDING. Manuel du mouleur. Lebrun, —. Paris, 1850. 24° 6429.11
MOULTON, Louise Chandler. Bed-time stories 927.24
— Some women's hearts 714.2
MOUNSEY, Augustus H. Journey through the Caucasus and the interior of Persia. With a map. London, 1872. xi, 336 pp. 8° 5931.7
MOUNT AUBURN, Guide through. Dearborn, N. S. Boston, 1857. 12° 413.8
MT. HOLYOKE female seminary. 25th anniversary. Memorial. South Hadley, 1862. 174 pp. Plate. 12° 1813.9
MOUNT VERNON papers, The. Everett, E. New York, 1860. 12° 1534.13
MOUNTAIN adventures. Headley, J. T. New York, 1872. 16° 1714.4
MOUNTAINEERING in the Sierra Nevada. King, C. Boston, 1872. Sm. 8° 413.1
MOUNTFORD, William. Euthanasy; or, happy talk towards the end of life. Boston, 1874. xviii, 511 pp. 16° 5836.7

Shelf. No.

MOUNTFORD, William, *continued.*
— Martyria: a legend of the reign of Edward sixth. With an introduction. Boston, 1846. xx, 328 pp. 16° 738.8
— Miracles past and present. Boston, 1870. viii, 512 pp. 16° 1536.6
— Thorpe, a quiet English town, and human life therein. Boston, 1852. 390 pp. 16° 715.9
MOUSTACHE, Vieux, *pseud.* *See* GORDON, Clarence.
MOVEMENT-CURE, An exposition of the Swedish. Taylor, G. H. New York, 1860. 12° 6036.12
MOWATT, Anna Cora. *See* RITCHIE, Anna Cora.
MOZART, Johann Chrysostom Wolfgang Amadeus. Don Giovanni; Il flauto magico; Marriage of Figaro. (*In* Ditson, O., and co. Standard opera librettos) 6233.3.2
— Letters. 1769-91. Translated by Lady Wallace. With a portrait and facsimile. New York, 1866. 2 v. 16° 1024.11
— Mozart and Mendelssohn. Barnard, C. F., *jr.* Boston, 1870. 16° 926.23

Note. — See the note on music in the Bulletin, Jan., 1876.

MUCKLÉ, Alexander, *joint author.* Chemical and pharmaceutic manipulations. *See* MORFIT, Campbell 6433.3
MUDDOCK, J. E. A wingless angel. A novel 535.21
MUDFORD, William. The iron shroud. (*In* Johnson, (E.) R. Little classics) 529.4.3
MUEHLBACH, Louise, *pseud.* *See* MUNDT, Clara (Mueller).
MUELLER, Carl Otfried. History of the literature of ancient Greece. Continued after the author's death by John W. Donaldson. London [1858]. 3 v. Portrait. 8° 6113.3
MUELLER, (Friedrich) Max. Chips from a German workshop. New York, 1871-75. 4 v. Sm. 8°. 5616.1

Contents. — Vol. I. The science of religion. II. Mythology, traditions, and customs. III. Literature, biography, and antiquities. IV. Essays chiefly on the science of language, with index to vol. III and IV.

— Lectures on the science of language. New York, 1874. 2 v. Sm. 8° 6126.4
— Lectures on the science of religion; with a paper on Buddhist nihilism, and a translation of the Dhammapada or "Path of virtue." New York, 1872. iv, 300 pp. Sm. 8° 5616.2
MUELLER, George. The life of trust: a narrative of the Lord's dealings with G. Müller, by himself. Edited by H. L. Wayland. With an introduction by F. Wayland. Boston, 1863. 490 pp. Illustrated. 12° 5815.8

Note. — Effects of prayer in supporting a charitable institution.

MUELLER, Johann von. An universal history. Translated from the German. Boston, 1831. 4 v. 12°. 836.6
MUGBY junction. Dickens, C., and others 338.9
MULHOLLAND, Rosa. The little flower seekers, being adventures of Trot and Daisy in a wonderful garden, by moonlight 912.18
MULLENS, Joseph. Twelve months in Madagascar. New York, 1875. xiii, 334+ pp. Illustrated. 16° 5915.11
MULLER, Christine, *pseud.* *See* WALRÉE, E. C. W.
MULOCK, Dinah (Maria). *See* CRAIK, Dinah (Maria).
MUMFORD, Mary E. Hila Dart 1115.3
MUMFORD, Thomas J. Memoir of Samuel Joseph May. Boston, 1873. 297+ pp. Portrait. 16°. 1016.2 and 5027.6
MUNCHAUSEN, *Baron*, Adventures of. Raspe, R. E. London [1869]. 4° 5731.1
MUNDT, Clara (Mueller). (*Louise Muehlbach.*) Andreas Hofer 531.37
— Berlin and Sans-souci 531.15
— The daughter of an empress 531.3
— The empress Josephine 531.11
— Frederick the great and his court 531.16
— Frederick the great and his family 510.4
— Henry the eighth and his court 531.33
— Joseph II and his court 531.36
— Marie Antoinette and her son 531.32

Shelf. No.

MUNDT, Clara (Mueller), *continued.*
— Mohammed Ali and his house 531.28
— Prince Eugene and his times 531.2
— The story of a millionnaire 533.22

Note. — The Muehlbach novels, originally German, are all historical, but of doubtful value as delineations of character and events.

MUNERA pulveris. Ruskin, J. New York, 1872. 12°. 6236.7
MUNK, Salomon. Palestine. Paris, 1845. 704+ pp. 68 plates. Maps. [L'Univers.] 8°..... 5911.9
MUNN, B. The practical land drainer. Illustrated. New York, 1855. 190 pp. 12° 1524.23
MUNSELL, Joel. A chronology of paper and paper-making. 4th edition. Albany, 1870. vii, 226 pp. Illustrated. 8° 6423.2
MURAD the unlucky. Edgeworth, M. (*In* Johnson, (E.) R. Little classics) 529.4.12
MURCHISON, *Sir* Roderick Impey, Life of. Geikie, A. London, 1875. 2 v. 8°................ 5333.3
MURDER, considered as one of the fine arts. De Quincey, T. (*In* Johnson, (E.) R. Little classics) 529.4.2
MURDERS, The, in the Rue Morgue. Poe, E. A. (*In* Johnson, (E.) R. Little classics)......... 529.4.3
MURE, William. Critical history of the language and literature of antient Greece. 2d edition. London, 1854–67. 5 v. 8°................. 6113.5
MURPHY, Joseph John. The scientific bases of faith. London, 1873. xliv, 474 pp. 8° 5812.5
MURPHY's master. Payn, J...................... 339.14
MURRAY, Alexander S. Manual of mythology. With plates. London, 1873. viii, 399 pp. 16°. 5927.2
MURRAY, J. Clark. The ballads and songs of Scotland, in view of their influence on the character of the people. London, 1874. xvi, 205 pp. Sm. 8° 5626.5
MURRAY, Grenville. (*Trois-Étoiles.*) The boudoir cabal. 3 v. in 2............................314.11
— The member for Paris 316.7
— Young Brown 319.24
MURRAY, Hugh. Historical account of discoveries and travels in Africa, from the earliest ages to the present time; including the substance of the late Dr. Leydon's work on that subject. 2d edition, corrected and enlarged. Edinburgh, 1818. 2 v. Maps. 8° 423.3
MURRAY, *Rev.* John, *of Boston.* Letters and sketches of sermons. Boston, 1812. 3 v. 8°..........5814.12

Note. — Two portraits of Mr. Murray are fastened on to fly leaves of the first and second volumes.

MURRAY, John, *publisher.* Handbook for Corsica and Sardinia. With maps. London, 1868. 12°. 5917.3
— Handbook for Denmark, Norway, and Sweden. 3d edition, revised. With maps and plans. London, 1871. xxiii, 207+ pp. 12°........ 5716.3
— Handbook for Egypt. 4th edition, revised. London, 1873. xx, 505 pp. 12° 5917.8
— Handbook for Southern Germany. 11th edition, revised. London, 1871. xii, 635 pp. 12°.... 5716.2
— Handbook for Greece. With map, plans, and views. London, 1872. xiii, 505 pp. 12°.....5917.10
— Handbook for Holland, Belgium, Prussia, Northern Germany, and the Rhine from Holland to Switzerland. With map and plans. 17th edition, corrected. London, 1871. xl, 606 pp. 12°... 5915.1
— Handbook for India. *See* EASTWICK, Edward Backhouse 5917.7
— Handbook for Central Italy. 7th edition, revised. With maps and plans. London, 1867. xi, 480 pp. 12°.. 5527.5
— Handbook for Northern Italy. 12th edition, revised. With map and plans. London, 1873. xxxv, 620 pp. 12° 5527.4
— Handbook for Paris. 5th edition, revised. With clue map and plans. London, 1872. iv, 266+ pp. 12°.. 5527.6
— Handbook for Portugal. 3d edition, revised. With map. London, 1864. lxiv, 216 pp. 12°. 5917.2
— Handbook for Russia, Poland, and Finland. 2d revised edition. With map and plans. London, 1868. x, 400 pp. 12°....................... 5917.5

Shelf. No.

MURRAY, John, *publisher, continued.*
— Handbook for Sicily. With map and plans. London, 1864. lvi, 524 pp. 12° 5917.4
— Handbook for Spain. *See* FORD, Richard....... 5917.1
— Handbook for Switzerland, and the Alps of Savoy and Piedmont. 3d edition, corrected and augmented. London, 1846. lxxii, 420 pp. Folded maps. 2 folded plates. 12°................. 227.3
— Handbook for Syria and Palestine. Maps and plans. New and revised edition. London, 1868. 2 v. 12° 5936.1
— Handbook for Turkey in Asia. New edition, revised. With maps and plans. London, N. D. xii, 492 pp. 12° 5917.9
— Handbook of Rome and its environs. 11th edition, revised. With plan[s] and map. London, 1872. lviii, 498 pp. 16°.................... 5526.4
— Knapsack guide for Italy. With maps and plans of towns, galleries, etc. 2d edition, revised. London, 1865. xxviii, 639 pp. 12°.......... 5528.1
— Knapsack guide for Switzerland. New edition, revised. With clue maps, plans, and mountain outlines. London, 1867. xl, 602 pp. 12°.... 5717.3
— Knapsack guide for Tyrol and the Eastern Alps. With maps and plans. London, 1867. xl, 636 columns. 16°.................................. 5527.8
— Knapsack guide to Norway. New edition. With map. London, 1872. 207 pp. 12° 5716.4

Note. — These Murray Handbooks are the favorite manuals of American and English tourists, though they are often complained of for insufficient and dilatory revision. They, however, contain much full and reliable information on the history and art of the places treated of. Baedeker's series is preferred by some; but they are much less full in this respect. On the other hand, as regards the practical details expected in a guide-book the information given is minute, precise, and carefully revised to the latest date. Murray and Baedeker admirably supplement each other.

MURRAY, Robert. Treatise on marine engines and steam vessels. 5th edition, revised. London, 1871. xv, 272 pp. Illustrated. 12°.........1716.13
MURRAY, William Henry Harrison. Adventures in the wilderness; or, camp-life in the Adirondacks. With illustrations. Boston, 1869. 236 pp. 12°...................................... 414.13
— Deacons. [A lecture.] Boston, 1875. 82 pp. Illustrated. Sq. 12° 724.6
— Music-hall sermons. 2d series. Boston, 1873. iv, 207 pp. 12°...................................5816.13
— The perfect horse. With an introduction by H. W. Beecher; and a treatise on agriculture and the horse by G. B. Loring. [With] illustrations. Boston, 1873. xi, 480 pp. 8° 6612.7
MUSÆUS. Hero and Leander. *See* HOMERUS......6118.11
MUSAEUS, (Johann Carl) August. *See* CARLYLE, T. German romance. Boston, 1841. 2 v. in 1. 12° 5725.2
MUSARD ball, The: an extravaganza. Brougham, J. New York, N. D. 12° 1635.5
MUSEUM, The. Abbott, J. Harper's story books...936.1.6
MUSIC. Chappell, W. The history of. Vol. I. London [1874]. 8°........................... 6232.5
— Haweis, H. R. Music and morals. New York, 1872. 12°...1513.16
— Helmholtz, H. (L. F.) Théorie physiologique de la musique. Paris, 1868. 8°................ 6233.4
— Hueffer, F. Richard Wagner and the music of the future. London, 1874. 8°............... 6232.6
— Hullah, J. The history of modern music. London, 1875. 8°.............................. 6232.8
— Jacox, F. Bible music. Boston, 1872. 16°.... 6234.2
Koddio, *Miss* —. Musical composers and their works. Boston, 1875. 16° 6237.3
— Moore, J. W. Complete encyclopædia of. Boston [*cop.* 1852]. L. 8°......................*R.R., E.2.3
— Moscheles, I. Recent music and musicians. New York, 1873. 12°......................... 6234.4
— Ritter, F. L. History of. Boston, 1870, 74. 2 v. 16°.. 6237.2
— Rousseau, J. J. Dictionnaire de musique. Paris, 1768. 8°....................................... 5535.5
— Spencer, C. C. Rudimentary and practical treatise on. London, 1866. 12°.................1716.35

Shelf. No.

MUSIC, *continued*.

— Wagner, (W.) R. Art life and theories. New York, 1875. 12° 6234.3

— Wieck, J. G. F. Piano and song. Boston, 1875. 12° 6234.5

See also Church music, German music, Sacred music.

Note. — See also the extensive note in the Bulletin, Jan., 1876.

MUSIC-HALL sermons. Murray, W. H. H. 2d series. Boston, 1873. 12° 5816.13

MUSICAL recollections of the last half-century. London, 1872. 2 v. 8° 6232.4

MUSINGS over the "Christian year" and "Lyra innocentium." Yonge, C. M. New York, 1871. 12° 1538.15

MUSSET, (Louis Charles) Alfred de. Comédies et proverbes. Paris, 1867. 2 v. 12° 5534.4

Contents. — Vol. I. André del Sarto; Lorenzaccio; Les caprices de Marianne; Fantasio; On ne badine pas avec l'amour; La nuit vénitienne; Barberine. II. Le chandelier; Il ne faut jurer de rien; Un caprice; Il faut qu'une porte soit ouverte ou fermée; Louison; On ne saurait penser à tout; Carmosine; Bettine.

MUSSEY, Reuben Dimond. Health: its friends and its foes. Boston, 1862. 368 pp. Portrait. 12°. 6035.1

MUSTERS, George Chaworth. At home with the Patagonians. 2d edition. With maps and illustrations. London, 1873. xix, 340 pp. Sm. 8°. 5036.5

MUTINEERS, The, of the Bounty. Belcher, *Lady* D. London, 1870. Sm. 8° 1224.4

— *Same.* New York, 1871. 12° 435.2

MUTINIES, Great historical. Herbert, D. London, 1876. Sm. 8° 5924.2

MY Apingi kingdom. [Africa.] Du Chaillu, P. B. New York, 1872. 12° 933.2

MY aunt Margaret's mirror. Scott, *Sir* W. 523.20

MY boys. Alcott, L. M. Aunt Jo's scrap-bag 926.15.1

MY brother's keeper. Warner, A. B. 736.3

MY châteaux. Curtis, G. W. (*In* Johnson, (E.) R. Little classics) 529.4.4

MY darling's album 912.27

MY daughter Elinor. Benedict, F. L. 710.4

MY days and nights on the battle-field. [Civil war, 1861–65.] Coffin, C. C. Boston, 1872. 12° ... 913.18

MY diary North and South. [Early in civil war, 1861–62.] Russell, W. H. Boston, 1863. 12°. 413.6

MY enemy's daughter. MacCarthy, J. 710.38

MY Kalulu: a story of Central Africa. Stanley, H. M. New York, 1874. Sm. 8° 921.9

MY farm of Edgewood. [Rural affairs.] Mitchell, D. G. New York, 1864. 12° 715.2

MY first voyage to Southern seas. Kingston, W. H. G. 937.27

MY lady Ludlow. Gaskell, E. C. 521.17

MY life on the plains. Or, personal experiences with Indians. Custer, G. A. New York, 1874. 8°. 412.3

MY little girl. Maurice, W., and Rice, J. 731.26

MY little lady. Poynter, *Miss* — 313.11

MY married life at Hillside. Coffin, R. B. 720.29

MY mother and I. Craik, D. (M.) Leipzig 310.18

— *Same.* New York 726.22

MY novel. Bulwer-Lytton, E. (G. E.) L. 4 v. in 2. 336.17

MY opinions and Betsey Bobbet's. Holley, M. 724.1

MY own story. Howitt, M. 937.1

MY Paris. French character sketches. King, E. Boston, 1873. 12° 427.7

MY recollections from 1806 to 1873. Lennox, W. P., *lord*. London, 1874. 2 v. 8° 5633.4

MY schoolboy friends. Moncrieff, A. R. H. Edinburgh, 1870. 8° 912.2

MY schools and schoolmasters. Miller, H. Boston, 1872. 12° 1025.11

MY sister Jeannie. Dudevant, A. L. A. D. 717.5

MY Southern friends. Gilmore, J. R. New York, 1863. 12° 715.21

MY story. Macquoid, K. S. Leipzig 330.14

— *Same.* New York 711.14

MY summer in a garden. Warner, C. D. Boston, 1875. 16° 1527.16

MY two sisters. Judson, E. (C.) Boston, 1854. 16°. 1216.1

MY uncle the clockmaker. Howitt, M. 937.14

MY wife and I. Stowe, H. (E.) B. 725.14

Shelf. No.

MY wife's husband: a farce. Challis, F. New York, N. D. 12° 1635.3

MY young Alcides. [Fiction.] Yonge, C. M. Leipzig. 318.25

— *Same.* New York 733.18

MYDDELTON, *Sir* Hugh, Life of. Smiles, S. Lives of the engineers. London, 1861. 8° 5421.4.1

MYDDLETON Pomfret. Ainsworth, W. H. 322.16

MYER, Albert J. Manual of signals. New edition, illustrated. New York, 1866. xiv, 398 pp. 12°. 6927.1

MYRA Sherwood's cross and how she bore it 933.26

MYSTERIOUS guest, The. Dupuy, E. A. 522.5

MYSTERIOUS island, The. Part I. Verne, J. Boston, 1875. Sm. 4° 724.17

— *Same.* Part II. New York, 1875. 16° 733.11

— *Same.* Part III. New York, 1876. 16° 733.14

MYSTERY, The, of Dark hollow. Southworth, E. D. E. N. 522.18

MYSTERY, The, of Edwin Drood. Dickens, C. (J. H.) Boston 1824.18

— *Same.* Leipzig 338.5

— *Same.* [*Added*, Part second. By the spirit-pen of C. Dickens, through a medium, Thomas P. James] 732.31

MYSTERY, The, of matter. Picton, J. A. London, 1873. Sm. 8° 5826.3

MYSTERY, The, of Metropolisville. Eggleston, E. .. 528.5

MYTHOLOGY. Arundell, J. F., *baron of Wardaur*. Tradition, principally with reference to. London, 1872. 8° 6333.1

— Brinton, D. G. The myths of the new world. New York, 1876. 8° 5924.7

— Bulfinch, T. Age of fable; or, beauties of. Boston, 1871. 12° 1523.3

— Clement, C. E. Handbook of legendary and mythological art. New York, 1872. Sm. 8° .. 1513.15

— Clodd, E. The childhood of religions: embracing a simple account of the birth and growth of myths and legends. London, 1875. Sm. 8° ... 6328.21

— Dillaway, C. K. Roman antiquities, and ancient mythology. Boston, 1857 [*cop.* 1833]. 16° 5516.3

— Keightley, T. The mythology of ancient Greece and Italy. London, 1854. 8° 5921.8

— Mueller, F. M. Chips from a German workshop. New York, 1872. Sm. 8° 5616.1.2

— Murray, A. S. Manual of. London, 1873. 16°. 5927.2

— Noël, F. (J. M.) Dictionnaire de la fable. Paris, 1803. 2 v. 8° 5517.6

— Ruskin, J. The queen of the air: being a study of the Greek myths of cloud and storm. New York, 1872. 12° 6236.17

— Smith, W. Dictionary of Greek and Roman mythology. London, 1870. 3 v. 8° .... *R.R., E.3.3

— Thomas, J. Universal pronouncing dictionary of. Philadelphia, 1871. 2 v. 8° .... *R.R., A.3.5

Note. — For ancient mythologies of all nations, the reader will find Dr. Thomas's "Dictionary of biography and mythology" an excellent source of information, particularly on the Norse and Hindoo mythologies, which are not in most reference books so fully treated as those of Greece and Rome. Bulfinch's "Age of fable" is a popular compilation, showing particularly the use of mythological references in literature; while Mrs. Clement's "Handbook" shows the use in art. Leigh Hunt's "Day by the fire" [5618.4] has a chapter on the popular view of the heathen mythology. See Max Müller on Comparative mythology in his "Chips" [5616.1.2], and his article in the Contemporary review on the Philosophy of mythology. See also Fiske's "Myths and myth makers" [5924.1] and Baring Gould's "Curious myths of the middle ages" [716.2].

Greek and Roman. Keightley [5921.8] is very painstaking and his book is the fullest and best for general readers; but British writers will not compare with Germans in investigating the interpretations of the myths. Grote's review, however, in the early volumes of his "History of Greece" [5926.1], may be said to be a clear exposition of importance, in which chap. XVI concerns myths as felt by the Greeks, and chap. XVII compares them with those of modern Europe. Max Müller has an important article in English, in his "Chips" [5616.1.2]. For reference, use Smith's Dictionary; Thomas's Dictionary; and for popular uses, Bulfinch will suffice. See Clarke's "Ten great religions" [1523.2], and Gladstone's "Juventus mundi" [1523.9]. Hawthorne's "Tanglewood tales" are an illustration of myths. See the notes under Greece and Rome.

Norse. The Germans here are very strong. Mallet's "Northern antiquities" [5715.5] is the readiest source in English; and in Wright's "Middle ages" there is a review of Grimm's "German mythology." See also Carlyle's "Heroes and hero-worship" [1535.19].

American aborigines. See Brinton [5924.7] and the notes at the end of his first chapter; and treatises on the Indians generally, together with accounts of the Mexican and Peruvian civilizations.

Cox's Mythology of the Aryan nations is reviewed in W. D. Whitney's "Oriental studies" [6126 2].

Shelf. No.

MYTHS, The, of the new world. Brinton, D. G. New York, 1876. 8° 5924.7

MYTHS and myth-makers. Fiske, J. Boston, 1873. 16° 5924.1

MYTTON, John, Life of. Apperley, C. J. London [1871]. Sm. 8° 5427.2

MYXOMA. Sinclair, A. D. (*In* Massachusetts medical society. Publications) 6021.4

NADAL, Ehrman Syme. Impressions of London social life, with other papers suggested by an English residence. New York, 1875. x, 223 pp. 16°. 436.6

NANCY. Broughton, R. Leipzig. 2 v. 329.14

— *Same.* New York 725.34

NAOMI; or Boston, two hundred years ago. Lee, E. B. Boston, 1848. 16° 538.8

NAPIER, Charles Ottley Groom. Tommy Try and what he did in science. With illustrations. London, 1869. vii, 303 pp. Sm. 8° 1524.24

NAPIER, Henry Edward. Florentine history, from the earliest authentic records to the accession of Ferdinand III. London, 1846, 47. 6 v. 16°. 5516.2

NAPIER, Mark. Memorials and letters illustrative of the life and times of John Graham of Claverhouse, viscount Dundee. Edinburgh, 1859, 62. 3 v. Portraits. 8° 5331.2

NAPIER, *Sir* William Francis Patrick. English battles and sieges in the peninsula. Extracted from his "Peninsular war." New edition. With portrait. London, 1873. vii, 469 pp. Sm. 8° 5916.9

— History of the war in the peninsula, and in the south of France; 1807-14. New York, 1853. 792+ pp. L. 8° 5920.1

NAPLES, Rollo in. Abbott, J. 917.24

NAPOLÉON I. (*Napoléon Bonaparte.*) Confidential correspondence with his brother Joseph. New York, 1856. 2 v. Portraits. 12° 1223.9

— Abbott, J. S. C. History of Napoleon Bonaparte. New York, 1870. 2 v. 8° 1021.1

— The campaigns of Napoleon Buonaparte, from the siege of Toulon to his death. Boston, 1840. 8°. 825.7

— The court and camp of Bonaparte. New York, 1832. 16° 1028.4

— Denon, (D.) V., *baron.* Travels in upper and lower Egypt, during the campaigns of Bonaparte in that country. New York, 1803. 2 v. 8° 222.3

— Hooper, G. Waterloo: the downfall of the first Napoleon. London, 1862. 8° 5511.2

— Junot, L. P., *duchesse d'Abrantes.* Memoirs of Napoleon, his court and family. New York, 1873. 2 v. 8° 5523.5

— Lanfrey, P. History of Napoleon the first. London, 1871, 72. 2 v. 8° 5522.1

— Maitland, *Sir* F. L. Narrative of the surrender of Buonaparte, and of his residence on board H. M. S. Bellerophon. Boston, 1826. 12° 627.5

— Scott, *Sir* W. Life of Napoleon Buonaparte. Exeter, 1828. 2 v. 8° 1223.12

— *Same.* Philadelphia, 1858. 8° 1221.5

Note.—There had been editions of Napoleon's "Correspondance" before an edition was undertaken by Napoleon III, the first fifteen volumes of which, covering Oct. 1793-Aug. 1809, being printed under directions "to make no alteration or suppression," when a new commission continued the work through the 28th volume, inserting "only what the emperor would have printed," and bringing the record down to the embarkation for St. Helena. The disclosures of the first fifteen volumes afforded much assistance to Lanfrey in his unfavorable estimate of Napoleon; and they gave rise to a review in Parton's "Topics of the time" [1935.3].

Lives in French. The highest military authority is that of Jomini, one of Napoleon's generals, who after 1813 went over to the Russian service, and who makes Napoleon in elysium rehearse the story of his career to Alexander, Cæsar, and Frederick the great, who finally agree that he surpassed them all. A large part of the success of Thiers's "Consulate and empire" has been owing to his championship of Napoleon, but he is accused of concealing the bad traits of his character and of finding scapegoats for his mistakes.

The reaction from Thiers, represented by several episodical writers, has found, since the publication of the last edition of the Correspondance threw such new light on Napoleon's character, emphatic utterance in Lanfrey's work, in which the sympathies are rather republican than revolutionary, and which is not yet completed. It is reviewed in Hayward's "Biographical and critical essays" [5833.3.3].

Lamartine, in the first volume of his "Restoration" [5517.5], makes an eloquent imprecation against Napoleon.

Lives in English. Scott's was the view of an English tory, and consequently unsatisfactory to the admirers of Napoleon.

NAPOLÉON I, *continued.*

Alison, who complains that Scott did not comprehend the continental spirit, made a record in his Europe [5913.6] quite as much tinctured with English aristocratic dislike. Abbott's life is supremely laudatory. Channing's estimate, in his Works [1525.1.1], is deprecatory; and Emerson, in his "Representative men" [1916.6; 1934.6.2], views him as a man of the world. See also Bayne's Essays [1226.15.2]; Brougham's "Statesmen of the time of George III" [5614.4.5]; Alison's Essay [1531.7]; and Thackeray's "Paris sketch book" [339.21].

Battles. See Hamley's "Operations of war" [5910.6] and Chesney's "Essays in military biography" [5922.8]. The narratives in the histories and larger lives may be supplemented in fiction by Miss Young's "Kenneth," for the retreat from Moscow; and by several of Erckmann-Chatrian's novels. See France, note.

At Elba. See the account in Lamartine's "History of the restoration" [5517.5]; and Lossing's "Spectre from Elba," in Harper's monthly, vol. 43.

Hundred days and Waterloo. Hooper's [5511.2] is the best single comprehensive account of this period, and there is a paper on the hundred days in the Atlantic monthly, vol. 1; but the curious reader may consult an extended note on the Waterloo campaign in the Library Bulletin, for Oct., 1875.

At St. Helena. See Scott's life, and Abbott's, and the latter's article in Harper's monthly, vol. 10.

Private and court life. The memoirs of the duchess of Abrantes [5523.5] is a picture of his domestic and private life, and Alison's Essay [1531.7] is based upon it.

Thackeray has described the second funeral at Paris [335.13.1; 513.1.10]. Louis Napoleon's "Des idées napoléoniennes" [825.3] is of interest as the views of his successor on the purposes of the emperor.

NAPOLÉON III. (*Louis Napoléon Bonaparte.*) History of Julius Cæsar. New York, 1866. 2 v. 8°. 5521.1

— Napoleonic ideas. Des idées napoléoniennes, par le prince Napoléon-Louis Bonaparte. Brussels: 1839. Translated by J. A. Dorr. New York, 1859. 154 pp. 12° 825.3

— Abbott, J. S. C. History of. Boston, 1870. 8°. 1021.2

— Jerrold, (W.) B. Life of. Vol. I, II. London, 1874, 75. 2 v. 8° 5522.7

— Letters of "An Englishman" on Louis Napoleon, the empire, and the coup d'état. London, 1852. 16° 1226.12

Note.—Abbott's "History" is the work of a warm partisan, and comes down to 1868. His career previous to the Crimean war is characterized unsparingly in Kinglake's 14th chapter of his "Invasion of the Crimea" [5924.9]; also see Harper's monthly, vol. 26. See Alison's "History of Europe" for his public career down to 1854. An article by C. C. Hazewell, in the Atlantic monthly, June, 1861, reviews his career up to that time somewhat favorably. His "Napoleonic ideas" sets forth his own theory of government, which, under color of a life of the Roman conqueror, he has enforced in his "History of Cæsar."

See also MacCarthy's "Modern leaders" [5930.2] and Adams's "Democracy and monarchy in France" [5515.4].

NAPOLEON dynasty. A history of the Bonaparte family. Lester, C. E. New York, 1873. 12°. 825.17

NARBONNE, Louis, *comte* de. *See* VILLEMAIN, A. F. Souvenirs contemporains d'histoire et de littérature. Paris, 1874. 12° 5537.18.1

NARRATIVE and miscellaneous papers. De Quincey, T. Boston, 1871. 2 v. 12° 1825.1

NARROW escape, A. Cudlip, A. 317.23

NASBY, Petroleum Vesuvius, *pseud.* *See* LOCKE, David Ross.

NASH, James Adams. The progressive farmer: a scientific treatise on agricultural chemistry, the geology of agriculture; on plants, animals, manures, and soils. Applied to practical agriculture. New York, 1856. 254 pp. Sm. 8° 1524.10

NASON, Elias. Sir Charles Henry Frankland, baronet: or, Boston in the colonial times. Albany, 1865. 129 pp. 8° 5013.15

— and RUSSELL, Thomas. The life and public services of Henry Wilson. Boston, 1876. 452 pp. Portrait. Illustrations. 12° 1016.4

NASSAU, Bubbles from the Brunnen of. [Life at a German watering place.] Head, *Sir* F. B. London, 1866. 12° 425.2

NAST, Thomas. Illustrated almanac for 1873. 80 illustrations. New York, 1872. 48 pp. 8° ... 1816.2

NAT the navigator. Life of Nathaniel Bowditch. Bowditch, H. I. Boston, 1870. 16° 913.20

NATHALIE. Kavanagh, J. 323.3

NATHAN the wise: a dramatic poem. Lessing, G. E. Leipzig, 1868. Sq. 16° 1613.6

— *Same.* New York, 1871. 12° 5736.4

NATHUSIUS, Maria. Joachim v. Kamern; Diary of a poor young lady. From the German by Miss Thompson. Leipzig, 1869. 333+ pp. Sq. 16°. 314.12

Shelf. No.

NATION, The. Vol. 4-11, 13-21. New York, 1867-75. 17 v. 4°.......................... 1312.1
NATIONAL almanac and annual record for 1864. Philadelphia, 1864. 641 pp. 16°..........5016.13
NATIONAL association of wool manufacturers, *Boston*. Bulletin. 1869-71. Edited by J. L. Hayes. Boston, 1869, 71. 2 v. 8°.................... 6432.1
NATIONAL board of trade. Proceedings of the third annual meeting, 1870. Boston, 1871. xiii, 338+ pp. 8°.......................... 5222.1
NATIONAL builder, The. Monckton, J. H. New York [*cop.* 1872]. 4°.................. 6620.1
NATIONAL gallery [in London] of pictures by the great masters. London, N. D. Unpaged. 4°.. 6210.9
NATIONAL songs, Essay on. Salisbury, S. Worcester, 1873. 8°..........................5010.16
NATIVE races, The, of the Pacific states of North America. Bancroft, H. H. New York, 1874-76. 5 v. 8°.......................... 5920.4
NATURAL history. Adams, W. H. D. Animal life throughout the globe. An illustrated book of. London, 1876. Sm. 8°....................1523.25
— Agassiz, L. (J. R.) Methods of study in. Boston, 1873. 12°..........................1525.11
— Annals of the Lyceum of natural history of New York. Vol. II. New York, 1828. 8°........ 6614.1
— Biart, L. Adventures of a young naturalist. New York, 1872. 12°.................... 912.9
— Buckland, F. Log-book of a fisherman and zoologist. London, 1875. 8°..............6614.12
— Child, G. C. Benedicite; illustrations of the power, wisdom, and goodness of God, as manifested in his works. New York, 1872. 8°.... 6615.4
— Darwin, C. (R.) Journal of researches into the natural history of the countries visited during the voyage of the Beagle round the world. New York, 1871. 2 v. 16°....................1526.11
— Gosse, P. H. The romance of. Boston [1860]. Sm. 8°..........................1523.14
— Harris, T. M. The natural history of the Bible. Boston, 1820. 8°..........................6323.11
— Hogg, J. The parlour menagerie. London, 1875. Sm. 8°..........................1522.11
— Hooker, W. Natural history. New York, 1874. 12°..........................6616.11
— Howitt, M. Natural history stories [in verse]. London [1874]. Sm. 4°....................1521.14
— Knight, C. Natural history; or, second division of "The English cyclopædia." London, 1866, 67. 4 v. 4°....................*R.R., F.2.1
— Maynard, C. A. The naturalist's guide in collecting and preserving objects of. Boston, 1873. Sm. 8°.......................... 1527.6
— Pouchet, F. A. The universe: or, the infinitely great and the infinitely little. London, 1871. L. 8°.......................... 6830.1
— *Same.* New York, 1873. 8°.................... 1520.6
— Taylor, J. E. Half-hours in the green lanes. London, 1873. 16°.................... 6619.2
— Ware, J. The philosophy of. Boston, 1861. 12°.1522.10
— Wood, J. G. Homes without hands. New York, 1866. 8°.......................... 6612.3
— — Illustrated natural history. London, 1867-74. 3 v. L. 8°.................... 6610.4
— — Out of doors. London, 1874. Sm. 8°........ 6616.9
— — The popular natural history. London, 1876. Sm. 8°..........................6616.12

See also America, Animals, Birds, Botany, Chemistry, Darwinism, Geology, Insects, Meteorology, Mineralogy, Nature, Ornithology, Philosophy, Physical geography, Sea, Zoology.

NATURAL phenomena, The unity of. Saigey, É. Boston, 1873. 16°..........................1526.21
NATURAL philosophy. *See* PHYSICS.
NATURAL science, A short history of. Buckley, A. B. New York, 1876. 12°.................... 6835.4
NATURAL selection, Contributions to the theory of. Wallace, A. R. London, 1871. 16°.......... 6616.4
— *Same.* New York, 1871. 16°.................... 6836.1

See also Darwinism, *note*.

NATURAL theology. *See* THEOLOGY.

NATURALIST, The, on the river Amazons. Bates, H. W. London, 1873. Sm. 8°.................... 5935.2
NATURE. A weekly illustrated journal of science. Vol. 8-12. London, 1873-75. 5 v. L. 8°.... 6733.1
NATURE. Chalmers, T. The power, wisdom, and goodness of God, as manifested in the adaptation of external nature to the moral and intellectual constitution of man. Philadelphia, 1835. 12°. 6618.2
— Collyer, R. Nature and life: sermons. Boston, 1872. 12°.......................... 1537.4
— Emerson, R. W. Nature. Boston, 1836. 12°. 5218.5
— Good, J. M. The book of. Boston, 1826. 2 v. 8°.......................... 6833.1
— Humboldt, (F. H.) A., *baron* von. Views of. London, 1870. Sm. 8°....................1523.19
— Kidd, J. Adaptation of external nature to the physical condition of man. Philadelphia, 1835. 12°.......................... 6618.3
— Lucretius Carus, T. On the nature of things. New York, 1872. Sm. 8°....................1526.29
— Michelet, J. Nature; or, the poetry of earth and sea. London, 1872. 8°.................... 6830.2
— Papillon, F. Nature and life. New York, 1875. 12°.......................... 1735.6
— Saint-Pierre, J. H. B. de. Studies of. Worcester, 1797. 3 v. 8°.................... 6833.2
— Tugnot de Lanoye, F. The sublime in. New York, 1872. 16°..........................1714.21
NATURE series. *Namely:* —
— Lockyer, J. N. The spectroscope and its applications.......................... 6826.4
— Lubbock, *Sir* J. On the origin and metamorphoses of insects.......................... 6617.8
NAUDIN, Charles Victor. Handbook of hardy trees, shrubs, and herbaceous plants. *See* HEMSLEY, W. B.......................... 6624.1
NAUTICAL astronomy, in theory and practice. Young, J. R. London, N. D. 12°....................1715.22
NAVAL science: a quarterly magazine. Vol. 1-4. London, 1872-75. 4 v. 8°.................... 6714.1

Note. — Vol. 1 and 4, imperfect.

NAVAL text-book and dictionary. Totten, B. J. New York, 1864. 12°....................1527.21
NAVERS, Dora. Jack's sister.................... 710.29
NAVIGATION. Greenwood, J. Rudimentary treatise on. London, 1870. 12°....................1715.11
— Young, J. R. Navigation, in theory and practice. London, N. D. 12°....................1715.22
NEAL, Daniel. History of the puritans, or protestant nonconformists; 1517 to 1688. Reprinted from the text of [Joshua] Toulmin's edition: with his life of the author and account of his writings. Revised, corrected, and enlarged, with additional notes, by John O. Choules. With 9 portraits. New York, 1871. 2 v. 8°. 5411.1
NEAL, John. Goody Gracious! and the forget-me-not. (*In* Johnson, (E.) R. Little classics)...529.4.10
NEAL Malone. Carleton, W. (*In* Johnson, (E.) R. Little classics).................... 529.4.5
NEAVES, Charles, *lord Neaves*. The Greek anthology [outlined and explained]. Philadelphia, 1874. 210+ pp. 16°. [Ancient classics for English readers]....................6116.21
NEBRASKA, Kanzas and. Hale, E. E. Boston, 1854. 12°.......................... 415.2
NECKER DE SAUSSURE, Albertine Adrienne. Notice sur la vie et les ouvrages de Madame de Staël. *See* STAËL-HOLSTEIN, Anne Louise Germaine Necker, *baronne* de....................5527.11
NED Nevins, the news boy. Morgan, H.......... 936.32
NEEDLEWORK, Guide to. Boston [1876]. 12°..... 1515.1
NEELE, Henry. The romance of history. England. With illustrations. London, N. D. viii, 598 pp. 16°.......................... 827.27
NEFFE, Der, als Onkel. Aus dem Französischen des Picard. Schiller, J. C. F. von. Werke. Stuttgart, 1867. 8°..........................5734.1.7
NEGROES. Brown, W. W. The rising son; or the antecedents and advancement of the colored race. Boston, 1874. 8°.................... 814.6

Shelf. No.

Negroes, *continued.*
— Campbell, J. Negro-mania: being an examination of the falsely assumed equality of the various races of men. Philadelphia, 1851. 12°.... 6614.7
Neighbor Jackwood. [New England life.] Trowbridge, J. T. 735.21
Neighbors' wives. Trowbridge, J. T. 735.20
Neighbours, The. Bremer, F. 716.3
Neily, Kate J. The proverb series. Actions speak louder than words 938.20
— – Fine feathers do not make fine birds.......... 936.28
— – One good turn deserves another.............. 938.21
Neligan, J. Moore. Medicines, their uses and mode of administration. With notes and additions by D. M. Reese. New York, 1844. 453 pp. 8°. 6022.2
Nellie Warren. Wise, D. 932.40
Nellie's housekeeping. Mathews, J. H...........1117.33
Nelly Brooke. Church, F. 337.14
Nelson, David. The cause and cure of infidelity. 2d edition. New York [*cop.* 1841]. 399 pp. Portrait. 12°............................5815.17
Nelson, Horatio, *viscount*, Life of. Southey, R. New York, 1857. 16°...................... 1228.3

Note. — For fiction, see Cooper's "Wing-and-wing" [525.3]; also Allen's "Battles of the British navy" [5417.5]; and Lodge's "Portraits" [5337.6.8].

Nepos, Cornelius. [Works.] *See* Justinus. London, 1872. Sm. 8°..........................6117.10
Neptune's defeat: a comedy. Brougham, J. New York, n. d. 12°.......................... 1635.5
Nero, History of. Abbott, J. 914.27
Nero: an historical play. Story, W. W. Edinburgh, 1875. Sm. 8°........................ 1637.1
Nerves. Brown-Séquard, C. É. Lectures on the physiology and pathology of the central nervous system. Philadelphia, 1860. 8°..............6022.14
— Campbell, H. Nervous exhaustion and the diseases induced by it. With observations on the origin and nature of nervous force. London, 1873. Sm. 8° 6036.8
— Prochaska, G. Dissertation on the functions of the nervous system. London, 1851. 8°.......6013.15
— Romberg, M. H. Manual of the nervous diseases of man. London, 1853. 2 v. 8°...........6013.16
— Warren, J. C. Comparative view of the sensorial and nervous systems. Boston, 1822. 12° 6012.8
Nest, Das, der Zaunkönige. Freytag, G. Die Ahnen. Leipzig, 1874. 16° 5733.5.2
Netherlands. Motley, J. L. History of the United Netherlands: 1584–1609. New York, 1868–71. 4 v. 8° 5912.1
— Schiller, (J. C.) F. von. Geschichte des Abfalls der vereinigten Niederlande. Stuttgart, 1867. 8°.5734.1.8
— – History of the revolt of the. New York, 1847. 12°.. 826.5
— – – Continued. (*In his* Works.) New York, 1872. Sm. 8°................................ 827.26
— Taine, H. A. Art in the. New York, 1871. 16°. 6217.1
— Waring, G. E., *jr.* A farmer's vacation. Boston, 1876. 8°...................................5933.11

Note. — Book 1 of Schiller's "Revolt of the Netherlands" traces the history previous to the 16th century; and there is a summary from the Roman period down in the introduction to Motley's "Dutch republic" [822.2].

For the rise and early progress of the reformation, see general histories of Charles V and Philip II, and Fisher's "Reformation," ch. 9 [5813.7]. The well-known works of Motley are of the first importance, as using much unprinted material, not before availed of. The "Dutch republic" comes first in order, then its sequel, the "United Netherlands," and next his "John of Barneveld" [5713.3] covers the causes of the Thirty years' war, and of this conflict the reader can pursue the history in Schiller's monograph [826.2]. Schiller's book recounts the stirring episode of the sixteenth century, and this and the volume, 827.26, contains also his paper on the "Trial of Counts Egmont and Horn," and that on "The siege of Antwerp" in 1584–85. For a summary during the time of William and Mary of England, see Macaulay's "History of England" [838.1].

On the later periods of the French revolution and the Napoleonic war, see the general histories.

For *Dutch literature*, see Longfellow's "Poets and poetry of Europe" [5922.1].

For *Dutch art*, see Taine's monograph. See Painting, note.

For *travels, descriptions, etc.*, see Murray's and Baedeker's guide-books.

Neumann, Carl Friedrich. Narrative of Hoei-Shin, with comments by C. F. Neumann. (*In* Leland, C. G. Fusang, etc.) 5925.6

Shelf. No.

Nevada, Notes on the silver regions of. Browne, J. R. New York, 1871. 12°.................. 415.13
Never again. Mayo, W. S. 724.5
Never give up. Baker, H. N. (W.).............. 926.5
Nevins, William. Thoughts on popery. New York [*cop.* 1836]. 216 pp. 16°.......................1538.20
Nevius, John L. China and the Chinese. With map and illustrations. New York, 1872. 456 pp. 12°. 423.15
New America. Dixon, W. H. Leipzig, 1867. 2 v. in 1. Sq. 16°.......................... 418.1
New American cyclopædia. Edited by G. Ripley and C. A. Dana. New York, 1872. 16 v. 8°. *R.R., B.3.1
New and old. [Poems.] n. p., 1851. v, 151 pp. Sm. 8°..1612.12
New church independent and monthly review. Vol. 22. Chicago, 1874. 8°................ 1323.1
New-church magazine. Vol. 1, 2. Boston, 1873, 74. 2 v. 8° 1333.1
New day, The. [Poem.] Gilder, R. W. New York, 1876. Sq. 16°...................................1617.16
New Gil Blas, The. Inglis, H. D. London, 1833. 2 v. 12° 5625.2
New Godiva, A. [Fiction.] Hope, S. 722.17
New homes. Braim, T. H. London, 1870. 12°...5934.10
New homes for the old country. Powell, G. S. B. London, 1872. 8° 5931.6
New Hyperion, The. Shinn, E. Philadelphia, 1875. 8°.. 5722.4
New life in new lands. Lippincott, S. J. New York, 1873. 12° 214.1
New Magdalen, The. Collins, (W.) W. Leipzig... 339.18
— *Same.* New York.............................. 731.2
New monthly magazine and literary journal. Vol. 1, 2. Philadelphia, 1821, 22. 2 v. 8°....... 1435.1
New scholars, The. Mathews, J. H...............1115.12
New, A, spirit of the age. Horne, R. H, *editor.* New York, 1844. 18° 1038.1
New Timon, The. A poetical romance [and satire]. Bulwer-Lytton, E. (G. E.) L. Leipzig, 1860. Sq. 16° 1614.6
New Timothy, The. Baker, W. M. 535.1
New way, A, to win a fortune. Dupuy, E. A...... 522.19
New year's day, a winter's tale. Gore, C. G. F..... 938.7
New Brunswick. Field and forest rambles, with notes and observations on the natural history of eastern Canada. Adams, A. L. London, 1873. 8°.6613.11
Newby, C. J. Common sense...................... 314.10
— Kate Kennedy.................................. 710.9
— Margaret Hamilton 710.10
— Married 710.13
— Only temper.................................... 710.12
— Right and left.................................. 710.6
— Sunshine and shadow 710.3
— Trodden down 710.11
— Wondrous strange.............................. 710.8
Newcastle, *Duke and duchess of.* *See* Cavendish, William and Margaret.
Newcomb, Harvey. Anecdotes for boys. Boston, 1869. 144 pp. Illustrated. 12° 918.21
— Anecdotes for girls. Boston, 1870. 144 pp. Illustrated. 12° 918.18
— How to be a lady. 15th edition. Boston, 1872. 224 pp. 12° 918.17
— How to be a man. Boston [*cop.* 1847]. 224 pp. 12°. 918.16
Newcome, William. Observations on our Lord's conduct as a divine instructor. Charlestown, 1810. xii, 516+ pp. 8° 5813.1
— Our Lord's fortitude. (*In* Noyes, G. R. Collection of theological essays) 6325.12
Newcomes, The. Thackeray, W. M. Leipzig. 4 v. in 2.. 335.4
— *Same.* (*In his* Works.) London............... 513.1.3
— *Same.* New York............................. 1820.2
Newell, Robert Henry. (*Orpheus C. Kerr.*) The Orpheus C. Kerr papers: being a complete contemporaneous military history of the mackerel brigade. New York, 1871. 525 pp. 12° 1936.7
New England: a handbook for travellers. With maps and plans. Boston, 1873. xvi, 399 pp. 16°. 5038.2
— *Same.* New edition. Boston, 1874. 431 pp. 12°. 5038.2

Shelf. No.

NEW ENGLAND. Adams, H. An abridgement of the history of. Boston, 1805. 12° 818.7

— Bacon, L. The genesis of the New England churches. New York, 1874. 8° 5812.13

— Bartlett, W. H. The pilgrim fathers; or, the founders of New England in the reign of James I. London, 1853. 8° 5021.4

— Bradford, A. Biographical notices of distinguished men in. Boston, 1842. 12° 1015.3

— - New England chronology, 1497–1820. Boston, 1843. 12° 817.6

— Carter, R. A summer cruise on the coast of. Boston [*cop.* 1864]. 12° 415.15

— Chauncy, C. Seasonable thoughts on the state of religion in. Boston, 1743. 8° 1926.3

— Drake, S. A. Nooks and corners of the New England coast. New York, 1875. Sq. 8° 411.4

— Felt, J. B. Ecclesiastical history of. Boston, 1855. 2 v. 8° 5811.2

— Fitton, J. Sketches of the establishment of the [Roman catholic] church in. Boston, 1872. Sm. 8° 5816.5

— Flagg, W. The birds and seasons of. Boston, 1875. 8° 6614.11

— - The woods and by-ways of. Boston, 1872. Sm. 8° 5035.2

NEW ENGLAND, *continued.*

— Frothingham, O. B. Transcendentalism in. New York, 1876. 16° 6325.21

— Harris, T. W. Treatise on some of the insects of New England which are injurious to vegetation. Boston, 1852. 8° 6612.1

— Lowell, J. R. New England two centuries ago. (*In his* Among my books) 1934.8.1

— Lunt, G. Old New England traits. New York, 1873. 16° 817.3

— Palfrey, J. G. Compendious history of New England from the accession of George II to the first general congress of the Anglo-American colonies. Boston, 1873. 16° 5016.3

— - History of. Boston, 1870–76 [*cop.* 1858–64]. 4 v. 8° 5014.7

— - History of New England, from the discovery by Europeans to the revolution of the seventeenth century. New York, 1866. 2 v. Sm. 8°. 5016.2

— Samuels, E. A. The birds of. Boston, 1872. 8°. 6612.4

— Savage, J. Genealogical dictionary of the first settlers of. Boston, 1862. 4 v. 8°......*R.R., C.2.2

— Thayer, E. Genealogy of fourteen families of the early settlers of. Hingham, 1835. 8°..... 611.2

— Winthrop, J. History of. Boston, 1825, 26. 2 v. 8° 814.7

NOTE ON NEW ENGLAND.

Full particulars of the literature of New England history can be found in the Lower Hall Catalogue of history, etc. See Webster's [5013.1] and Everett's [1921.1] Orations on the first settlements. For Plymouth colony, see Plymouth, *note.* See also the several states.

The later historians of New England find the earliest authority in Winthrop's Journal [814.7]. After Dr. Robertson's death, his "Summary of the history of New England to 1652," which was not originally included in his history of America, was published in 1796 [5610.1]. The Rev. George E. Ellis, D. D., in his lecture of the Historical society's course, has learnedly traced the relations of the colonists to the baptists and quakers. Longfellow, in his "New England tragedies," has rendered the story of quaker persecution dramatically, and R. H. Allen has supplied the historical basis of the poem in a popular compilation [817.4]. See also Salem witchcraft, *note.*

Palfrey left little to be desired in his scholarly and circumspect work, and it must be awarded by far the highest place yet attained by a history of New England. He has since abridged, for the general reader, the narrative of this larger work, which ends with the revolution of 1688; and has recently continued the narrative in the same abridged shape to 1727, which abridgments are far better compends for the period covered than Bradford's Chronology, 1497–1820, or Hannah Adams's History. There are of course chapters in Bancroft's, and in Hildreth's United States, and also in Cassell's, and in Bryant's.

In church affairs, see Felt's "Ecclesiastical history" [5811.2] and Bacon's "Genesis of the New England churches" [5812.13]. Also "Pulpit wits" in Harper's monthly, vol. 14.

For the genealogies of New England, see Savage's Dictionary, who has traced three generations of those who came before May, 1692, and the New England historical and genealogical register [611.1] is rich in material of this kind.

For the associations of places, in connection with revolutionary history, see Lossing's "Field-book of the revolution" [810.17]; while S. A. Drake's "Middlesex" [814.4] and "Nooks and corners" [411.4] treat similarly the coast and our inland country by describing their associations with the entire course of New England history.

For the rural aspects of the country, Flagg's books, above named, are the results of long and close observation. See also Porte Crayon's "Summer in New England," in Harper's monthly, vol 27.

Fiction. The phases of the earliest period are studied in Mrs. Lee's "Naomi" [538.8], where the scene is at Boston; in Dr. Holland's "Bay-path" [536.3], which touches early religious dissensions in the back country; in Cooper's "Wept of Wish-ton-wish" [525.12], at the time of the regicides, who were concealed by the colonists; in Mrs. Sedgwick's "Hope Leslie" [725.21], scene in the western part of the state, with Indians as characters; in Hawthorne's "Scarlet letter" [311.7; 1813.11], Boston in Governor Bellingham's time, and in several of his "Twice-told tales" [1813.7]; and in Whittier's "Margaret Smith's journal" [1937.1.1] date, 1678.

The slave trade of Newport in the last century is touched upon in Cooper's "Red Rover" [525.21], and in connection with Hopkinsianism in Mrs. Stowe's "Minister's wooing" [314.24]. Newport of a later time is depicted in Higginson's "Malbone" [524.24] and "Oldport days" [5036.2]. The Calvinistic and Arminian controversy which once racked the social circles of New England is graphically drawn in Mrs. Stowe's "Oldtown folks" [314.22].

Manners of a period somewhat gone by are drawn in D. G. Mitchell's "Doctor Johns;" in Edmund Quincy's "Wensley;" in Miss Sedgwick's "Redwood;" in Gilman's "Village choir" [1238.22]; and in Hawthorne's "House of the seven gables" [1813.1].

Traces of the peculiar New England quality of life, not so apparent now, except in remoter sections, are cunningly portrayed in Dr. Holmes' "Elsie Venner" [526.20] and "Guardian angel" [526.21]; and with quiet precision in Longfellow's "Kavanagh," [1838.4.2]. There is another delineation of the Yankee schoolmaster in D. P. Thompson's "Locke Amsden" [734.5]. Cooper, in "The pilot" [525.29], depicts in Long Tom Coffin the Nantucket whaleman.

Life on the coast of Maine is drawn in Mrs. Stowe's "Pearl of Orr's island" [527.20]; factory life in Miss Phelps's "Silent partner" [537.11]; and there is some sharp characterization of every day life in Mrs. A. D. T. Whitney's books. Other traits of New England character can be found in Judd's "Margaret" [535.13]; in Trowbridge's "Neighbor Jackwood" [735.21]; in Beecher's "Norwood" [524.5]; and in Cummins's "Lamplighter" [322.28], a realistic picture of humble town life. Haliburton's "Sayings and doings of Sam Slick" [535.12] is a somewhat conventional and amusing presentation of the Yankee character.

Shelf. No.

NEW ENGLAND historical and genealogical register. Vol. 1–20. Boston, 1847–66. 20 v. 8°...... 611.1

NEW-ENGLAND legends. Spofford, H. E. Boston, 1871. 8° 531.13

NEW-ENGLAND, The, magazine. Vol. 1–9. Boston, 1831–35. 9 v. 8° 1436.1

NEW-ENGLAND primer, The. Impoved [*sic*] for the more easy attaining the true reading of English. Added The assembly of divines, and Mr. Cotton's Catechism. Boston, 1777. Unpaged. Reprint. Sq. 32° 5819.5

NEW-ENGLAND tragedies, The. Longfellow, H. W. Leipzig, 1868. Sq. 16° 1614.2

NEW-ENGLAND tragedies, The, in prose. Allen, R. H. Boston, 1869. 12° 817.4

Note. — A prose historical parallel on the preceding dramas.

NEW ENGLAND village choir, Memoirs of a. Gilman, S. Boston, 1829. Sm. 12° 1238.22

NEW HAMPSHIRE, Collections, topographical, historical and biographical, relating principally to. Farmer, J., and Moore, J. B. Concord, 1822, 23. 2 v. 8° 612.1

Shelf. No.

NEW HAMPSHIRE, *continued.*
— Sons of. Festival of the sons of New Hampshire, in Boston, Nov. 7, 1849. Phonographic report by J. W. Stone. Boston, 1850. 178 pp. Portraits. 8° 1811.1
— – Second, Nov. 2, 1853, including proceedings in Boston commemorative of the death of Daniel Webster. Phonographic report by A. C. Felton. Boston, 1854. 229 pp. Portraits. 8° 1920.1

See also Dublin, Londonderry, Manchester, Portsmouth, White mountains.

NEW HAVEN colony historical society. Papers. Vol. I. New Haven, 1865. 8° 812.12

Contents. — Vol. I. Organization of the society; The New Haven colony, by H. White; Civil government in New Haven colony, by L. Bacon; History of the Cutler lot, by H. White; History of Trinity church, New Haven, by F. Croswell; History of Long wharf in New Haven, by T. R. Trowbridge; The parsonage of "the blue meeting house," by E. E. Beardsley; The governor Gilbert lot, by E. L. Cleaveland; Notice of the early pomologists in New Haven, by N. A. Bacon; Correspondence between president Jefferson and Abraham Bishop; Bishop Berkeley's gifts to Yale college, by D. C. Gilman; Historical account of Connecticut currency, etc., by H. Bronson.

NEW JERUSALEM, Church of the. [Various tracts.] V. P., V. D. 12° 6327.13

Contents. — Emanuel Swedenborg, as a philosopher, metaphysician, and theologian, by G. B. Porteous. [*Also*,] Sermon on redemption, by Abiel Silver. New York, 1874. 36, x pp. 12°. — The spiritual world as the world of life and cause, by Robert Jobson. New York, 1875. 24 pp. 12°. — The church of the New Jerusalem, a new dispensation of divine truth, by Chauncy Giles. Philadelphia, N. D. 32 pp. 8°. — Perpetual existence, by Jabez Fox. London, 1874. 16 pp. Sm. 8°.

— Bayley, J. Great truths on great subjects. London, 1874. Sm. 8° 6328.17
— Bush, G. Statement of reasons for embracing the doctrines and disclosures of Emanuel Swedenborg. New York, 1875. 12° 6328.18
— Fernald, W. M. A new age for the New church. Boston, 1860. 8° 1530.6
— Swedenborg, E. Doctrines of the New Jerusalem. New York, 1873. 12° 5814.20
— – The four leading doctrines of the New church. New York, 1873. 8° 6323.8
— – The true Christian religion, containing the entire theology of the New church. Philadelphia, 1869. 2 v. 8° 5812.9
— – The true Christian religion, containing the universal theology of the New church. New York, 1871. 8° 6323.7

See also Swedenborg.

NEW JERUSALEM messenger. Vol. 28. New York, 1875. F° 1432.5
NEWMAN, *Mrs.* —. Jean. A novel 720.40
NEWMAN, Francis William. Miscellanies; chiefly addresses, academical and historical. London, 1869. 356+ pp. 8° 5612.10
— Phases of faith: or, passages from the history of my creed. 3d edition. London, 1853. vi, 201+ pp. 12° 1526.29
— The soul, her sorrows and her aspirations. London, 1849. vii, 222 pp. 12° 5814.17
— *Same.* 3d edition. London, 1852. xi, 162+ pp. 12° 1534.5
NEWMAN, John Henry. Callista; a sketch of the third century. Leipzig, 1869. 334 pp. Sq. 16°. 319.9
— Characteristics from [his] writings. Being selections from his works. Arranged by W. S. Lilly, with the author's approval. London, 1875. xvi, 447 pp. Portrait. Sm. 8° 6325.15
— Discourses addressed to mixed congregations. 4th edition. London, 1871. viii, 380 pp. Sm. 8° 6325.20
— Discussions and arguments on various subjects. London, 1872. viii, 398 pp. Sm. 8° 5815.10
— Essays critical and historical. London, 1871. 2 v. Sm. 8° 5614.5
— Historical sketches. London, 1872, 73. 3 v. Sm. 8° 5925.5

Contents. — Vol. I. Rise and progress of universities; Northmen and Normans in England and Ireland; Medieval Oxford; Convocation of Canterbury. II. The Turks in their relation to Europe; Marcus Tullius Cicero; Apollonius of

Shelf. No.

NEWMAN, John Henry. Historical sketches, *continued.*

Tyana; Primitive Christianity. III. The church of the fathers; St. Chrysostom; Theodoret; Mission of St. Benedict; Benedictine schools.

— *Same.* Vol. I. London, 1872. 421+ pp. Sm. 8°. 825.16
— The idea of a university defined and illustrated. 3d edition. London, 1873. xxii, 527+ pp. Sm. 8° 5836.9
— Lectures on the doctrine of justification. 3d edition. New York, 1874. xvi, 404 pp. Sm. 8°. 6326.12
— Loss and gain: the story of a convert. 6th edition. London, 1874. x, 432 pp. Sm. 8° 5636.6
— Parochial and plain sermons. New edition. London, 1875. 8 v. Sm. 8° 6326.19
— Sermons preached on various occasions. 4th edition. London, 1874. xi, 337 pp. Sm. 8° 6326.16
NEWMAN, Samuel Phillips. A practical system of rhetoric. 7th edition. Andover, 1839. 311 pp. 12° 1537.15
NEW MEXICO, The marvellous country; or, three years in. Cozzens, S. W. Boston, 1873. 8° .. 412.1
NEW ORLEANS, *La.* Reports on the New Orleans riots. *See* UNITED STATES. *Miscellaneous documents* 6922.2
NEWPORT, *R. I.* Fuller, H. Belle Brittan on a tour at. New York, 1858. 12° 413.7
— Mason, G. C. Newport illustrated. New York [*cop.* 1854]. 12° 414.23

Note. — See also Note under New England, *fiction;* and vol. 9 of Harper's monthly.

NEW SOUTH WALES, An historical and statistical account of, from 1788. Lang, J. D. London, 1875. 2 v. 8° 5418.9
NEWSPAPER literature, Specimens of. Buckingham, J. T. Boston, 1850. 2 v. 12° 1913.1

See also Note in Bulletin, Oct., 1875.

NEWSTEAD abbey. [Byron's residence.] Irving, W. London, 1853. 16° 715.5
NEW Sydenham society, *London.* Publications. *Namely:* —
— Diday, P. Treatise on syphilis in new-born children and infants at the breast 6023.3
— Gooch, B. On some of the most important diseases peculiar to women; with other papers ... 6023.4
— Graefe, A. von. Three memoirs on iridectomy in certain forms of iritis, choroiditis and glaucoma. 6023.1
— Kussmaul, A., and Tenner, A. Nature and origin of epileptiform convulsions caused by profuse bleeding, and also of those of true epilepsy. 6023.1
— Schroeder van der Kolk, J. C. L. Structure and functions of the spinal cord and medulla oblongata. And on the proximate and rational treatment of epilepsy 6023.2
— Semple, R. H. Memoirs on diphtheria 6023.5
— Wagner, A. Process of repair after resection and extirpation of bones 5023.1

See also Sydenham society.

NEWTON, *Sir* Isaac. Historical account of two corruptions of Scripture. (*In* Sparks, J. Collection of essays and tracts in theology) 1918.9.2
— Life of. Brewster, *Sir* D. New York [1831]. 16°. 1028.1
NEWTON, John. Review of ecclesiastical history. [No title-page.] London [1770]. xviii, 320 [318] pp. 12° 1538.7
NEWTON Forster. Marryat, F. 737.26
NEW YORK, *City.* Report of the council of hygiene and public health of the citizens' association of New York upon the sanitary condition of the city. New York, 1865. cxliii, 360 pp. Illustrated. Maps. 8° 5033.3
— Abbott, J. Marco Polo in New York 914.6
— Brace, C. L. The dangerous classes of. New York, 1872. 12° 5824.1
— Crapsey, E. The nether side of. New York, 1872. 8° 5013.6
— Dawson, H. B. The sons of liberty in. [New York] 1859. 8° 811.12
— Fairfield, F. G. The clubs of. New York, 1873. 12° 5036.1
— Lander, S. W. Spectacles for young eyes 922.19

Shelf. No.

NEW YORK, *City, continued.*
— MacCabe, J. D. Lights and shadows of. Philadelphia [*cop.* 1872]. 8° 814.9
— Medbery, J. K. Men and mysteries of Wall street. Boston, 1870. Sm. 4° 413.2
— Stone, W. L. History of. New York, 1872. 8°. 5010.8
— Train, G. F. Young America in Wall-street. New York, 1857. 12° 414.3
— Wallys, P. About New York. New York, 1857. 12° 414.19
— *Astor library.* Catalogue [and Supplement]. New York, 1857–66. 5 v. L. 8° 6130.2

Contents. — Vol. I–IV. Authors and books. 1. A–E. 2. F–L. 3. M–P. 4. Q–Z. V. Supplement; Index of subjects.

— *Mercantile library.* Second supplement to the catalogue. New York, 1872. 29 pp. 8°...*R.R., D.2.12

Note. — Stone must be taken for a general history, but see Lossing's paper on "The Dutch in Manhattan" in Harper's monthly, vol. 9.

For the externals of the city, see T. A. Richards's paper in Harper's monthly, vol. 23. Central Park is well delineated in another of Richards's papers in the same volume; and also see Scribner's monthly, Oct., 1873.

For phases of life in Wall street, Medbery's book is an entertaining exposure, and in this connection read Adams's "Chapter of Erie" [1916.1], and Parton's Life of Vanderbilt [1214.14], etc. The "Ring government" is exposed in Parton's "Topics" [1935.3] and in the North American review, Jan., 1875. See "The story of Tammany," in Harper's monthly, vol. 44. Crapsey's "Nether side of New York" [5013.6] depicts the humble and depraved life; see also Brace's "Dangerous classes" [5824.1] and McCabe's "Lights and shadows," [814.9].

For the growth and magnitude of the city, see Fitz Hugh Ludlow's article in the Atlantic monthly, Jan., 1865. The same magazine has for Dec., 1866, a paper by H. T. Tuckerman, "Through Broadway;" for May, 1867, "Germany in New York," by C. D. Shanley, who writes in the November number, 1867, on "The Bowery by night." The "flat system" of homes is described in the Galaxy, May, 1874. The Croton aqueduct is described in Harper's monthly, vol. 22; Blackwell island institutions, in vols. 32 and 33; Broadway, in vol. 25; Castle Garden emigrants, in vol. 42, etc.

NEW YORK, *Colony and province.* Documentary history [1609–1833] of the state of New York. Arranged by E. B. O'Callaghan. Albany, 1849–51. 4 v. 8° 6917.1
NEW YORK, *State. Metropolitan board of health.* Annual report, 1866–68. New York, 1867, 68. With illustrations. 3 v. 8° 5012.7
— Second report of the commissioners appointed to revise the laws for the assessment and collection of taxes, in 1872. *See* COBDEN club, *London*... 5828.5
— Edwards, C. Pleasantries about courts and lawyers of. New York, 1867. 8° 5023.1
— Irving, W. History of. London, 1854. 16°... 715.4
— *Same.* Philadelphia, 1872. Sm. 8° 1815.11
— *Lyceum of natural history.* Annals. Vol. 2. [Synopsis of the birds of the United States.] New York, 1828. 480+ pp. 8° 6614.1

See also Adirondacks, Cayuga lake, Ithaca.

Note. — Irving's book is the humorous and satirical account of the Dutch rule, known as Knickerbocker's history, and the Bates Hall must be consulted for the regular histories of the state.

NEW ZEALAND. Barker, M. A., *lady.* Station amusements in. Leipzig, 1874. Sq. 16° 319.5
— – Station life in. Leipzig, 1874. Sq. 16° 438.4
— Braim, T. H. New homes: the rise, progress, present position, and future prospects of. London, 1870. 12° 5934.10
— Meade, H. Hot springs in. (*In* Estes, D. Half-hour recreations in popular science) 6813.7
— Powell, G. S. B. New homes for the old country. A personal experience in. London, 1872. 8°. 5931.6
— Tinne, J. E. The wonderland of the antipodes; and other sketches of travel in the north island of. London, 1873. L. 8° 5930.4
— Trollope, A. Australia and New Zealand. Leipzig, 1873. 3 v. in 1. Sq. 16° 418.5
NEXT of kin, Index to. Chambers, R. London, 1872. 8° 5415.3
NIAGARA. A poem. Bulkley, C. H. A. New York, 1848. 12° 1625.14
NICCOLINI, Giovanni Battista. Opere. Edizione ordinata e revista dall' autore. Terza impressione. Firenze, 1852. 3 v. 12° 2036.1
NICHOLAS Nickleby. Dickens, C. (J. H.) Boston. 2 v. 1824.2
— *Same.* Leipzig 338.4

Shelf. No.

NICHOLS, George Ward. The sanctuary: a story of the civil war. With illustrations. New York, 1866. 286 [284] pp. 12° 716.11
— Story of the great march [Sherman's]. With map and illustrations. 26th edition. New York, 1866. 456 pp. 12° 815.7
NICHOLS, James R. Fireside science. A series of popular scientific essays upon subjects connected with every-day life. New York, 1872. vi, 283 pp. Sm. 8° 1525.9
NICHOLS, John, *joint author.* Hogarth's works. *See* IRELAND, John 6214.2
NICHOLS, Thomas. Handbook for readers at the British museum. London, 1866. xvi, 166 pp. 16°. 6136.4
NICK Hardy. Ludlow, P. 1115.14
NICK of the woods. Bird, R. M. 536.4
NICOLETTE and Aucassin. *See* HALE, E. E., and others. Tales for travellers 720.24
NIEBUHR, Barthold Georg. Lectures on the history of Rome, from the earliest times to the fall of the Western empire. Edited by L. Schmitz. 3d edition. London, 1853. 3 v. Portrait. 8°. 5514.6
— Life and letters. With essays on his character and influence, by the Chevalier Bunsen, and Professors Brandis and Lorbell. New York, 1854. 363 pp. 12° 5724.2
NIEMANN, A. The French campaign, 1870–71. Military description. With maps and plans. Translated by E. Newdigate. London, 1872. 420 pp. 8° 5515.1
NIEMEYER, Felix von. Text-book of practical medicine, with particular reference to physiology and pathological anatomy. Translated by G. H. Humphreys and C. E. Hackley. Revised edition. New York, 1872. 2 v. 8° 6013.3
NIERITZ, (Carl) Gustavus. Gustavus Vasa; or, king and peasant. From the German. By J. F. Smith. With a historic sketch and notes, by A. L. Guss. Philadelphia, 1872. 258 pp. Illustrated. 16° 537.15
NIGHT, A, in a workhouse. Greenwood, J. (*In* Johnson, (E.) R. Little classics) 529.4.1
NIGHT, A, on the borders of the Black forest. Edwards, A. B. 329.20
NIGHT and morning. Bulwer-Lytton, E. (G. E.) L. 336.8
NIGHT-WALK, The, over the mill stream. Wood, E. P. 333.13
NIGHTINGALE, Florence. Notes on hospitals. 3d edition, enlarged. London, 1863. ix, 187+ pp. Folded plates. 4° 6011.7
— Notes on nursing: what it is and what it is not. New York, 1860. 140 pp. 12° 6035.6
NILE. Appleton, T. G. A Nile journal. Boston [London], 1876. 16° 436.9
— Baker, *Sir* S. W. The Albert N'yanza great basin of the Nile, and explorations of the Nile sources. London, 1872. Sm. 8° 5936.4
— – The Nile tributaries of Abyssinia. London, 1871. Sm. 8° 425.3
— – *Same.* With a supplement. By W. L. Gage. Hartford, 1871. 8° 5932.1
— Curtis, G. W. Nile notes of a howadji. New York, 1857. 12° 424.15
— Eden, F. The Nile without a dragoman. London, 1871. Sm. 8° 5934.3
— Laporte, L. Sailing on the. Boston, 1872. 16°. 426.2
— Macgregor, J. The Rob Roy on the. New York, 1870. Sm. 8° 423.17
— Smith, A. C. The Nile and its banks. London, 1868. 2 v. Sm. 8° 425.1
— Speke, J. A. Journal of the discovery of the source of the. New York, 1864. 8° 5932.2

See also Africa, East (The), Egypt, etc.

Note. — Recent discovery has settled the question of the sources of the Nile as follows: Bruce, in 1768–73, traced the sources of the Blue Nile, or the Eastern tributary of the main stream, which with the other tributaries have been more fully explored by Baker, in his "Nile tributaries of Abyssinia," who establishes that in this region the rainfall takes place that causes the yearly inundation of the lower Nile. The main source of the constant stream, which for fifteen hundred miles sweeps without a tributary to the Mediterranean, comes from the great lake sources of the White Nile in Central Africa, one of which, the Victoria N'yanza, which is the easterly, Speke discovered in 1858, and revisited with Capt. Grant in 1861, and

Shelf. No.

NILE, *continued.*

the other, the Albert N'yanza, the westerly, Baker discovered in 1864, and writes further on it in his "Ismailïa" [5933.5]. See Speke, J. H., in Allibone, vol. 2, p. 2195.

Among the books of modern travel and description, see Eden's "Nile without a dragoman," disclosing the expedients of an economical tourist; and Macgregor's "Rob Roy" canoe experiences.

See papers in Harper's monthly, vols. 14 and 28; and the article, Nile, in Smith's Bible dictionary; also, the "Tour of the Nile" in Scribner's monthly, Dec., 1875; and a paper on the cataracts, in the Atlantic monthly, July, 1875.

There are summaries of Nilotic discovery in chap. I of "Livingstone and his African explorations" [5915.2]; and in Bayard Taylor's "South Africa" [224.1].

NILES, Willys. Five hundred majority; or, the days of Tammany. New York, 1872. 200 pp. 8°. 521.12

NIMROD, *pseud.* *See* APPERLEY, Charles James.

NIMROD of the sea. Davis, W. M. ... 726.28

NINA Balatka, the story of a maiden of Prague ... 316.12

NINA'S atonement. Fisher, F. C. ... 732.3

NINE-DAYS' wonder, A. Aïdé, H. Boston ... 720.27

— *Same.* Leipzig ... 331.15

NINE little goslings. Woolsey, S. C. ... 1115.6

NINETY-THREE. [A tale of the French revolution.] Hugo, V. (M.), *vicomte* ... 734.18

NINEVEH. Layard, A. H. Discoveries in the ruins of. London, 1853. 8° ... 5912.9

— – Nineveh and its remains. London, 1850. 2 v. 8° ... 5912.2

— Smith, G. Assyrian discoveries; an account of explorations and discoveries on the site of, 1873, 74. London, 1875. 8° ... 5932.12

Note. — Layard, to whom we owe most, begun his work in 1845, and published his "Nineveh and its remains" in 1849; and in 1851 his popular abridgment. In 1852, he produced further results in his "Discoveries in the ruins," which he also abridged; and again, in 1853, his additional Discoveries, and in the same year another large work in illustration of the sculptures, etc. The latest publication is Smith's [5932.12], who made his exploration in 1873–74, but his book is mostly filled with translations of cuneiform inscriptions. He gives a brief summary of previous explorations, and a bibliography. See an article in Blackwood, 1874, and Sayce's lecture in Fraser's magazine, 1874. The most elaborate historical use of these results has been made by George Rawlinson, in the section on Assyria in his "Five ancient monarchies," 1862 [5922.3]; but a briefer summary will be found in Philip Smith's "Students' ancient history," book 2. See also Rawlinson's "Manual of ancient history" [5921.10].

The art aspect of the remains can be studied in Lübke's "Sculpture" [6210.3], and in Fergusson's "History of architecture" [6222.3].

See reference in Allibone under Layard; the article in Smith's Bible dictionary, Hackett and Abbot's edition.

NISBET, James, *joint author.* Annals of San Francisco. *See* SOULÉ, Frank ... 810.3

No alternative. Cudlip, A. ... 714.10

No church. Robinson, F. W. ... 314.6

No intentions. Church, F. ... 310.28

No man's friend. Robinson, F. W. ... 731.17

No moss. Fosdick, C. A. ... 934.8

No name. Collins, (W.) W. ... 326.3

No sense like common sense. Howitt, M. ... 937.12

No thoroughfare. Dickens, C. (J. H.), and Collins, (W.) W. [Boston] ... 730.1

— *Same.* Leipzig ... 338.17

NOBLE life, A. Craik, D. (M.) ... 323.15

NOBLE lord, A. Southworth, E. D. E. N. ... 734.21

NOBLE sister, A. Denison, M. A. ... 1117.27

NOBLE woman, A. Stephens, A. S. (W.) ... 726.7

NOBLE workers. Page, H. A. London, 1875. Sm. 8°. 5936.3

NOBODY'S fortune. Yates, E. ... 318.21

NOCTES ambrosianæ, The, of "Blackwood." Wilson, J. Philadelphia, 1843. 4 v. Sm. 8° ... 515.15

Note. — Dialogues on life and literature.

NODIER, Charles. *See* MÉRIMÉE, P. Portraits historiques et littéraires. Paris, 1874. 18° ... 5527.14

NOEHDEN, George Henry. Grammar of the German language. From the 8th London edition. With alterations and additions, by B. Sears. Andover, 1842. viii, 452 pp. 1 folded plate. 12° ... 1933.8

NOEL, *Lady* Augusta. Owen Gwynne's great work. A novel ... 530.12

NOËL, François (Joseph Michael). Dictionnaire de la fable. Nouvelle édition. Paris, 1803. 2 v. 8°. 5517.6

— Nouveau dictionnaire français-latin [et latin-français]. Nouvelle édition. Paris, 1824, 25. 2 v. 8° ... 6110.1

NOOKS and corners of the New England coast. Drake, S. A. New York, 1875. Sq. 8° ... 411.4

Shelf. No.

NORDHOFF, Charles. California: for health, pleasure, and residence. New York, 1873. 255 [251] pp. Illustrated. Maps. Portraits. 4° ... 5031.2

— Cape Cod and all along shore. New York, 1868. 235 pp. 12° ... 536.27

— The communistic societies of the United States; from personal visit and observation: including detailed accounts of the Economists, Zoarites, Shakers [etc.], and other existing societies, their religious creeds, social practices, numbers, industries, and present condition. With illustrations. New York, 1875. 439 pp. 8° ... 5821.2

— Northern California, Oregon, and the Sandwich Islands. New York, 1874. 256 pp. Illustrated. Portraits. Maps. 8° ... 432.5

— Politics for young Americans. New York, 1875. 259 pp. 12° ... 5826.10

— Whaling and fishing. Cincinnati, 1856. 383 pp. Illustrated. 16° ... 936.2

NORE, The mutiny at the. Herbert, D. Great historical mutinies. London, 1876. Sm. 8° ... 5924.2

NORFOLK argus, The. Vol. I, no. 1–28. Roxbury, 1837. F° ... 6730.36

NORFOLK democrat, The. Vol. I, II. Dedham, 1839–41. 2 v. in 1. F° ... 6730.35

NORFOLK island. Belcher, *Lady* D. The mutineers of the Bounty and their descendants in Pitcairn and Norfolk islands. London, 1870. Sm. 8° .. 1224.4

— *Same.* New York, 1871. 12° ... 435.2

NORINE'S revenge. Fleming, M. A. ... 723.22

NORMA. Bellini, V. (*In* Ditson, O., and co. Standard opera librettos) ... 6233.3.4

NORMAN Cline. Kellogg, E. ... 936.31

NORMANDY, *France.* Blackburn, H. Normandy picturesque. Boston, 1873. Sq. 16° ... 5528.3

— Waring, G. E., *jr.* A farmer's vacation. Boston, 1876. 8° ... 5933.11

NORRIS, Thaddeus. The American angler's book: embracing the natural history of sporting fish, and the art of taking them. To which is added, [descriptions of] noted fishing-places. New edition, with a supplement. Illustrated. Philadelphia, 1865. 701 pp. 8° ... 1511.5

NORSE-FOLK, The. Brace, C. L. New York, 1857. 12°. 426.21

NORSEMAN'S, A, pilgrimage. Boyesen, H. H. ... 728.12

NORSEMEN, The, in the West. Ballantyne, R. M. .. 914.37

NORTH, Christopher, *pseud.* *See* WILSON, John.

NORTH America. Trollope, A. Leipzig, 1862. 3 v. Sq. 16° ... 418.4

— *Same.* 3 v. in 1. Sq. 16° ... 418.3

— *Same.* New York, 1862. 12° ... 414.5

— *Same.* Philadelphia, 1862. 2 v. in 1. 12° ... 415.10

NORTH American review. Vol. 10, 12–106, 108–114, 116–121. Boston, 1820–75. 108 v. 8° ... 5117.1

NORTH and South. Gaskell, E. C. Leipzig, 1855. Sq. 16° ... 328.16

NORTHAMPTON, *Mass.*, Inscriptions on the grave stones of. With brief annals of. Bridgman, T. Northampton, 1850. 12° ... 5016.6

NORTHANGER abbey. Austen, J. ... 325.24

NORTH CAROLINA. A defence of the revolutionary history of North Carolina from the aspersions of Mr. Jefferson. Jones, J. S. Boston, 1834. 12°. 816.11

NORTHCOTT, W. Henry. Treatise on lathes and turning, simple, mechanical, and ornamental. With illustrations. London, 1868. xiv, 298 pp. 8°. 1521.11

NORTHEND, Charles. A book of epitaphs: being light readings on grave subjects. New York, 1871. 171 pp. 12° ... 1535.2

— The teacher's assistant. Boston, 1860. 358 pp. 1 plate. 12° ... 1533.3

NORTHERN antiquities. Mallet, P. H. London, 1873. Sm. 8° ... 5715.5

NORTHERN courts, The; containing memoirs of the sovereigns of Sweden and Denmark, since 1766. Brown, J. London, 1818. 2 v. 8° ... 5713.1

NORTHERN lands; or, Young America in Russia and Prussia. Adams, W. T. Boston, 1872. 16°. 925.7

NORTHERN lights. Stories from Swedish and Finnish authors. Translated by Selma Borg and Marie A. Brown ... 912.13

Shelf. No.

Northmen.

Note. — See a note on their discovery of America in Bulletin, April, 1876, under "America before Columbus."

North-west passage, The, by land. Fitzwilliam, W. W., *viscount Milton*, and Cheadle, W. B. London, 1866. 8° 5931.15

Norton, Caroline Elizabeth Sarah. Lost and saved. 314.8

— Old Sir Douglas 314.9

— Stuart of Dunleath 314.7

Norton, Charles Eliot. Notes of travel and study in Italy. Boston, 1859. ix, 320+ pp. 16° ... 426.12

Norton, John Pitkin. Elements of scientific agriculture. New York, 1855. x, 208 pp. 12° ... 1524.17

Norway. Adams, W. T. Up the Baltic; or, Young America in. Boston, 1873. 16° 925.8

— Brace, C. L. The Norse-folk; or, a visit to the homes of. New York, 1857. 12° 426.21

— Carlyle, T. The early kings of. New York, 1875. 12° 627.3

— Murray, J. Handbook for. London, 1871. 12°. 5716.3

— – Knapsack guide to. London, 1872. 12° 5716.4

— Smith, H. Tent life with English gipsies in. London, 1873. 8° 5722.1

Norwood. Beecher, H. W. New York, 1868. 12°. 524.5

Not bread alone; or, Miss Helen's neighbors. Drinkwater, J. M. 1118.8

Not dead yet. Jeaffreson, J. C. 732.25

Not easily jealous 330.27

Not in their set. Lenzen, M. 738.14

Not so bad as we seem. Bulwer-Lytton, E. (G. E.) L. Dramatic works. Leipzig, 1860. Sq. 16°. 1614.5

Not wisely, but too well. Broughton, R. 310.2

Not without thorns. Graham, E. 731.5

Not wooed but won. Payn, J. 314.5

Notes and queries. Vol. 4; 3d series, vol. 9–12; 4th series, vol. 1, 2. London, 1852, 66–68. 7 v. Sm. 4° 6735.1

Notes on North America. Johnston, J. F. W. Boston, 1851. 2 v. 16° 1524.5

Notes on Paris. Taine, H. A. New York, 1875. 12° 5533.2

"Nothing to nobody." Brenda, *pseud.* 1118.2

Notley, *Mrs.* —. (*Francis Derrick.*) Mildred's wedding 711.37

— Olive Varcoe 720.4

Notre-Dame de Paris. [Historical novel.] Hugo, V. (M.), *vicomte*. Paris [1832]. 2 v. 12° ... 2016.2

Nott, Josiah Clark, and Gliddon, George R. Types of mankind. Illustrated by selections from S. G. Morton, L. Agassiz [and others]. Philadelphia, 1854. lxxvi, 49–738 pp. Map. Portrait. Illustrations. 8° 6610.7

Nova Scotia, The mineralogy of. How, H. Halifax, 1869. 8° 6613.10

Novalis, *pseud.* *See* Hardenberg, Friedrich Ludwig von.

Nouveau lundis. Sainte-Beuve, C. A. Paris, 1870. 13 v. 12° 5538.5

Nouvelle Héloise, La. Rousseau, J. J. Neuchatel, 1864. 4 v. 8° 5535.4

Novelists, Lives of the. Scott, *Sir* W. New York, 1872. 12° 5914.2

Novels and novelists, The, of the eighteenth century, in illustration of the manners and morals of the age. Forsyth, W. London, 1871. Sm. 8°. 6136.1

Novels and tales reprinted from Household words. Conducted by Charles Dickens. Leipzig, 1856–58. 11 v. in 6. Sq. 16° 337.1

Contents. — Vol. [I.] 1. An ordeal; Nemesis; Two college friends; A rogue's life; My country town. 2. The ninth of June; Bond and free; My blind sister; Eric Walderthorn; The diary of Anne Rodway; My little ward; On 'change in Paris; Dick Dallington; Black and blue; Salome and I.

[II.] 3. A day of reckoning; Kester's evil eye; The poor clare; My brother Robert; The Frenchman of two wives; The forbidden fruit; Left, and never called for; The wreck of the Golden Mary. 4. The dead secret, by (W.) W. Collins.

[III.] 5. The dead secret, continued; The murder of the archbishop of Paris; The new boy at Styles's; How the old love fared; Helena Mathewson; Agnes Lee; The yellow tiger; My window; A queen's revenge; The Amphlett love-match. 6. Eleanor Clare's journal for ten years; Romantic breach of promise; The brave coucou driver; Mrs. Badgery; Our family picture; The lazy tour of two idle apprentices.

[IV.] 7. The perils of certain English prisoners, and their treasure in women, children, silver and jewels; Lyndon hall; Marie Courtenay; My lost home; Number five, Hanbury ter-

Shelf. No.

Novels and tales reprinted from Household words, *continued.*

race; Two in a legion; Old Saint Ann's gateway; Max and his companions; The legend of my native town; The little Huguenot; Famine abroad; The Patagonian brothers. 8. Well authenticated rappings; "A gude conceit o' oursels"; The apparition of Monsieur Bodry; Mr. Pearson; Shadowless men; Little Constancy's birthday; A tale of an old man's youth; Years and years ago; Lost Alice; The Balcombe street mystery; The six giants of Lehon; The Devil's mark; Boscobel; The blood of the Sundons; History of a miracle; The end of the Fordyce, brothers.

[V.] 9. My lady Ludlow [by E. C. Gaskell]; The reverend Alfred Hoblush's statement; Truth in irons; A princess royal; What Mr. Burleigh could not see. 10. A house to let; The canon's clock; Her face; The poisoned meal; Tried friendship; The heir of Hardington; Lina Fernie; The sin of a father.

[VI.] 11. The Fleur de Lys; Saving little, wasting much; Her first appearance; The Gringe family; Home again! A gipsy king; A new mind; Ground and lofty tumbling; The clergyman's wife; The Smallchange family; Miss Cicely's portrait; Douglas Jerrold; My two partners; Dishonoured; The Chetwyndes; The lucky leg; From first to last.

Now and then. Warren, S. 317.4

Now or never. Adams, W. T. 924.13

Nowell, Harriet P. H. (*May Mannering.*) Helping-hand series. Billy Grimes' favorite 936.26

— – Climbing the rope 936.21

— – The cruise of the Dashaway 936.22

— – The little maid of Oxbow 936.23

— – The little Spaniard 936.25

— – Salt-water Dick 936.24

Noyes, George Rapall, *editor*. Collection of theological essays from various authors. With an introduction. Boston, 1856. xlvi, 512+ pp. 12° 6325.12

Contents. — Introduction, by G. R. Noyes; Faith and science, by F. P. G. Guizot; The law and the gospel, by Baden Powell; The doctrine of inspiration, by F. A. D. Tholuck; Holy Scripture, Servants of God speaking as moved by the Holy Ghost, The spirit and the letter, or the truth and the Book, by R. Williams; The causes which conspired to produce our Saviour's agony, by E. Harwood; Our Lord's fortitude, by W. Newcome; The atonement, Righteousness by faith, Imputation of the sin of Adam, Conversion and changes of character, Casuistry, Connection of immorality and idolatry, The Old Testament, Quotations from the Old Testament in the New, Character of St. Paul, St. Paul and the twelve, Evils in the church of the apostolical age, Belief in the coming of Christ in the apostolical age, by B. Jowett; The death of Christ, a sacrifice, by J. Foster; The epistles to the Corinthians, in relation to the gospel history, Apostolical worship, The eucharist, Unity and variety of spiritual gifts, The gift of tongues and the gift of prophesying, Love, the greatest of gifts, The resurrection of Christ, The resurrection of the dead, by A. P. Stanley; The credibility of miracles, by T. Brown.

Nubia, Boat life in. Prime, W. C. New York, 1858. 12° 424.6

Nugent, *Lord*. *See* Grenville, George Nugent Temple.

Nuit vénitienne, La. Musset, (L. C.) A. de. Comédies et proverbes. Paris, 1867. 12° 5534.4

Numa Pompilius, second roi de Rome. Florian, J. P. C. de. Paris, 1812. Sm. 12° 2019.1

Numismatics. Roman medallions in the British museum. Grueber, H. A. London, 1874. 8°. 6131.2

Nurse and spy in the union army. Edmonds, S. E. E. Hartford, 1865. 8° 813.1

Nursery songs. Elliott, J. W. National nursery rhymes and songs. London, 1872. 8° 1510.1

— Hastings, T. The mother's nursery songs. [With music.] New York, 1835. 12° 1625.8

Nurses and nursing. Child, L. M. The family nurse. Boston, 1837. 16° 1525.31

— Nightingale, F. Notes on nursing: what it is and what it is not. New York, 1860. 12° 6035.6

Nutt, David, and Truebner and co. Catalogue of theological books in foreign languages on sale by [them]. London, 1857. viii, 600 pp. 8°. 6132.5

O. T. A Danish romance. Andersen, H. C. 524.14

Oak-openings, The. [Early Michigan life.] Cooper, J. F. 525.19

Oakes, William. Scenery of the White mountains: with 16 plates from the drawings of Isaac Sprague. Boston [*cop.* 1848]. Unpaged. F°. 5030.4

Oakridge. Smith, J. E. 723.11

Oakshott castle. Kingsley, H. 339.12

"Oars and sculls," and how to use them. Woodgate, W. B. London, 1875. Sm. 8° 6418.3

Object lessons, Primary. Calkins, N. A. New York, 1862. 12° 1535.4

Shelf. No.

O'BRIEN, Fitzjames. A gentlemen from Ireland: a comedy. New York, N. D. 20 pp. 12°....... 1635.5
OBSERVATIONS on the Bible, for the use of young persons. Boston, 1842. 203 pp. 12°........5818.20
OBSTRETRICS. *See* MIDWIFERY.
OCCIDENTI, Maria del, *pseud.* *See* BROOKS, Maria Gowen.
OCCUPATIONS, The, of a retired life. Mayo, I. F.... 723.16
OCEAN. Adams, W. H. D. The monsters of the deep: and curiosities of ocean life. London, 1875. Sm. 8°........................... 6617.1
— Figuier, (G.) L. The ocean world: being a description of the sea, and its living inhabitants. London, 1869. 8°........................ 1521.5
— Jordan, W. L. The ocean: its tides and currents and their causes. London, 1873. 8°.......... 6633.3
— Reclus, (J. J.) É. The ocean, atmosphere, and life. New York, 1873. 8°................. 6632.2
OCEAN-BORN; or, the cruise of the clubs. Adams, W. T..................................... 923.20
OCEAN life series. *See* THOMES, William H.
OCEANICA, Thirty thousand miles of travel in. Vincent, F., *jr.* New York, 1876. 12°.......... 436.8
O'CONNELL, Daniel. Cusack, M. F. The liberator, his life and times. London, 1872. 4°........ 5420.1
— Lecky, W. E. H. Leaders of public opinion in Ireland. New York, 1872. 12°.............. 1025.9

See also Ireland, *note.*

O'CONNOR, Francis. The invisible princess. (*In* Johnson, (E.) R. Little classics).................529.4.8
O'CONNOR, William D. The ghost. (*In* Johnson, (E.) R. Little classics).......................529.4.8
ODD couple, An. Oliphant, M. (O. W.)........... 722.9
ODD people. Reid, M............................ 923.32
ODD trump, The. Coulson, J. G. A............... 720.1
O'DONOGHUE, The. Lever, C. (J.) Leipzig....... 332.17
— *Same.* London................................ 516.16
O'DRISCOLL, W. Justin. Memoir of Daniel Maclise. London, 1871. xiv, 264 pp. Portrait. Sm. 8°. 5423.12
ODYSSEY, The. Homerus. Translated into English blank verse by W. C. Bryant. Boston, 1871. 2 v. 4°.................................... 6111.1
— *Same.* Translated by A. Pope. London, 1872. 16°... 6117.1
— The Odyssey [outlined and explained]. Collins, W. L. Edinburgh, 1870. 16°................ 6116.3
— The Odysseys. Translated by G. Chapman. London, 1874. 2 v. Sq. 16°....................6118.10

See also Homerus.

ŒCUMENICAL council, Five letters on the. Deutsch, E. (O. M.) Literary remains. New York, 1874. 8°. 5733.7
OESTERLIN, F. Medical logic. Translated and edited by G. Whitley. London, 1855. xii, 437 pp. 8°......................................6013.19
OFF the roll. A novel. King, K.................. 521.37
OFF the Skelligs. Ingelow, J. Boston........... 737.7
— *Same.* Leipzig............................... 335.14
OFFENBACH, Jacques. Barbe-bleue; La belle Hélène; Geneviève de Brabant; Grand duchess of Gerolstein; "Orpheus;" La perichole. (*In* Ditson, O., and co. Standard opera librettos)....6233.3.5
OGILVIES, The. Craik, D. (M.).................. 323.17
OHIO country, Journals and letters relative to two journeys to the, in 1788, 89. May, J. Cincinnati, 1873. 8°............................. 430.1
O'KEEFE, John. Personal reminiscences. (*In* Stoddard, R. H. Bric-à-brac series)............. 1828.8
OLCOTT, Henry Steele. Sorgho and imphee, the Chinese and African sugar canes. A treatise upon their origin, varieties and culture. Illustrated. New York, 1857. 350 pp. 12°.............. 6425.5
OLD and new. Vol. 1-11. Boston, 1870-75. 11 v. 8°. 1426.1
OLD-BATTLE ground, The. Trowbridge, J. T....... 929.4
OLD countess, The. Stephens, A. S. (W.)......... 734.9
OLD court. Ainsworth, W. H...................... 322.26
OLD court life in France. Elliot, F. Leipzig, 1873. 2 v. in 1. Sq. 16°........................ 329.4
OLD curiosity shop, The. Dickens, C. (J. H.) 2 v. 1824.4
OLD dower house, The. Grey, *Mrs*................ 530.3

Shelf. No.

OLD-ENGLISH history. Freeman, E. A. London, 1873. Sm. 8°..............................5418.11
OLD faith, The, and the new. Strauss, D. F. New York, 1873. 12°.........................5815.22
OLD-FASHIONED boy, An. Finley, M.............. 926.24
OLD-FASHIONED girl, An. Alcott, L. M........... 926.9
OLD helmet, The. Warner, S..................... 317.11
OLD homestead, The. Stephens, A. S. (W.)....... 726.4
OLD Jack. Kingston, W. H. G.................... 921.7
OLD Kensington. Thackeray, A. I. Leipzig...... 339.5
— *Same.* (*In her* Works.) London.............512.1.1
— *Same.* New York.............................. 731.3
OLD lieutenant, The, and his son. Macleod, N..... 313.16
OLD mam'selle's, The, secret. John, E.......... 517.16
OLD man's, An, prayer. [Poem.] Baker, G. M. Boston, 1868. Sq. 16°........................1617.17
OLD masters, The, and their pictures. Keddie, *Miss* —. London, 1873. Sm. 8°...................1516.21
— *Same.* Boston, 1874. 16°..................... 6216.3
OLD Mortality. Scott, *Sir* W. Boston........... 523.13
— *Same.* Leipzig............................... 324.15
OLD Myddelton's money. Hay, M. C.............. 711.5
OLD red sandstone, The. [Geology.] Miller, H. Boston, 1857. 12°..........................1524.20
OLD Rome and new Italy. Castelar, E. New York, 1873. 12°.............................. 824.11
OLD Saint Paul's. [Historical novel.] Ainsworth, W. H...................................... 712.6
OLD Sir Douglas. Norton, C. E. S................ 314.9
OLD woman, The, who lived in a shoe. Douglas, A. M...................................... 933.9
OLD world, The, in its new face. Impressions of Europe in 1867, 68. Bellows, H. W. New York, 1870. 2 v. 12°........................ 423.6
OLDBURY. Keary, A. Leipzig..................... 329.23
— *Same.* Philadelphia.......................... 714.18
OLDEST, The, of the old world. Eckley, S. M. London, 1860. 12°............................ 224.7
OLDPORT days. Higginson, T. W. Boston, 1873. 16°. 5036.2
OLDTOWN folks. Stowe, H. (E. B.) Boston....... 723.21
— *Same.* Leipzig............................... 314.22
OLIPHANT, Lawrence. Narrative of the Earl of Elgin's mission to China and Japan, 1857-59. New York, 1860. 645 pp. Illustrated. 8°... 421.2
OLIPHANT, Margaret (O. Wilson). Agnes......... 328.5
— Agnes Hopetoun's schools and holidays......... 936.27
— At his gates.................................. 510.5
— Brownlows..................................... 531.27
— Chronicles of Carlingford...................... 521.40
— - Miss Majoribanks............................ 328.13
— - The perpetual curate........................ 328.12
— - The rector and the doctor's family.......... 328.7
— - Salem chapel................................ 328.10
— The curate in charge. Leipzig................. 331.23
— *Same.* New York.............................. 721.25
— The days of my life. An autobiography. New York, 1868. 428+ pp. 12°................... 512.7
— For love and life. Leipzig.................... 328.30
— *Same.* New York.............................. 731.36
— Francis of Assisi. [A biography.] [London, 1871.] xxiv [xvi], 304 pp. Portrait. 1 plate. [Sunday library.] Sm. 8°....................5937.10
— Historical sketches of the reign of George II. [Biographies.] Boston, N. D. 243 pp. 8°.... 1032.1
— Innocent...................................... 329.10
— The laird of Norlaw. A Scottish story......... 737.1
— The last of the Mortimers..................... 328.9
— Leisure hour series. Whiteladies. New York...539.11
— Lilliesleaf................................... 730.10
— Lucy Crofton.................................. 725.20
— Madonna Mary.................................. 328.6
— Margaret Maitland............................. 328.8
— May. [Coast of Scotland.] Leipzig............ 339.17
— *Same.* New York.............................. 530.9
— Memoir of Count de Montalembert. Leipzig, 1872. 2 v. in 1. Sq. 16°........................ 1237.2
— The minister's wife........................... 328.4
— An odd couple. [International series]........ 722.9
— Ombra... 328.11
— A rose in June. Boston........................ 711.1
— *Same.* Leipzig............................... 319.22

Shelf. No.

OLIPHANT, Margaret (O. W. Wilson), *continued.*
— A son of the soil 536.20
— Squire Arden 710.17
— The story of Valentine and his brother. Leipzig. 331.6
— *Same.* New York 711.25
— Whiteladies. Leipzig 331.20
— Zaidee: a romance 721.10

Note.— Mrs. Oliphant ranks among the best of the second-class novelists. She is Scotch, and many of her novels show her nationality.

OLIVE. Craik, D. (M.) 323.18
OLIVE Blake's good work. Jeaffreson, J. C. 732.24
OLIVE Varcoe. Notley, *Mrs.* — 720.4
OLIVER OPTIC, *pseud.* *See* ADAMS, William T.
OLIVER OPTIC'S magazine. Our boys and girls. Vol. 11, 12. Boston, 1872, 73. 2 v. Illustrated. 8°. 1431.1
OLIVER Twist. Dickens, C. (J. H.) Boston 1824.7
— *Same.* Leipzig 338.8
OLLENDORFF, Henri Godefroy. Key to the exercises in the new method of learning a language in six months. Adapted to the Italian. Edited by Felix Forresti. New York, 1849. 183 pp. 12°. 2035.3
— New method of learning the German language. Added a systematic outline of German grammar, by G. J. Adler. New York, 1852. xii, 510 pp. 12° 2025.3
— New method of learning the Italian language. With additions and corrections by Felix Foresti. New York, 1846. xii, 533 pp. 12° 2034.1
— New method of learning the Spanish language: with an appendix [etc.]. By M. Velazquez and T. Simonné. New York, 1850. 558 pp. 1 folded sheet. 12° 2035.2
OLLIER, Edmund. Cassell's History of the United States. Vol. I. Illustrated. London [1875]. Maps. L. 8° 810.11

Contents. — Vol. I. 1584–1762.

OLMSTEAD, Dwight Hinckley. A lecture on the protestant faith. New York, 1874. 71 [69] pp. 12°. 6328.15
OLMSTED, Denison. A compendium of natural philosophy. New Haven, 1833. xvi, 336 pp. 8°. 6434.2
OLMSTED, Frederick Law. Journey in the back country. New York, 1860. xvi, 492 [482] pp. 12°. 414.6
— Journey in the seaboard slave states, with remarks on their economy. New York, 1859. 723 pp. 12°. 414.7
— Journey through Texas. New York, 1857. xxxiv, 516 pp. 1 plate. Map. 12° 414.4
OLYNTHIAC, The. Demosthenes. London, 1871. Sm. 8° 6115.19
OMBRA. Oliphant, M. (O. W.) 328.11
OMOO: a narrative of adventures in the South seas. Melville, H. New York, 1868. 12° 425.23
ON both sides of the sea. [English Commonwealth period.] Charles, E. 321.7
ON dangerous ground. Moore, C. J. 722.1
ON guard. Cudlip, A. 317.17
ON ne badine pas avec l'amour. Musset, (L. C.) A. de. Comédies et proverbes. Paris, 1867. 12°. 5534.4.1
ON ne saurait penser à tout. Musset, (L. C.) A. de. Comédies et proverbes. Paris, 1867. 12° 5534.4.2
ON the Amazons. Stephens, C. A. 916.28
ON the edge of the storm. By the author of "Mademoiselle Mori" 315.19
ON the eve. Turgenef, I. S. 539.1
ON the heights. Auerbach, B. Boston 517.2
— *Same.* Leipzig 311.22
ON the wave. Samuels, A. F. 918.26
ON the wing. A book for sportsmen. Bumstead, J. Boston, 1871. 16° 1516.4
ON the wing. Eyster, N. 938.3
ON time. Adams, W. T. 925.15
ONCE and again. Jenkin, *Mrs.* C. 318.2
ONE and twenty. Robinson, F. W. 731.22
ONE fair woman, The. Miller, C. H. 522.22
ONE good turn deserves another. Neily, K. J. 938.21
ONE hundred choice selections in poetry and prose. Philadelphia, 1872. 4 v. in 2. 16° 1537.9
ONE hundred years ago. Hale, E. E. Boston, 1875. 8° 811.15

Note. — Sketches of Concord, Lexington, and the siege of Boston.

ONE night's mystery. Fleming, M. A. 723.37
ONE of them. Lever, C. (J.) Leipzig 332.20
— *Same.* London 516.6
ONE summer. Howard, B. W. 529.8
ONE woman's two lovers. Townsend, V. F. 723.1
ONE year. Peard, F. M. 314.15
ONE year at a boarding-school. Phelps, A. 1114.2
ONLY a butterfly. Craik, G. M. 319.13
ONLY a clod. Braddon, M. E. 325.1
ONLY a fiddler. A Danish romance. Andersen, H. C. 524.13
ONLY a girl. Hillern, W. von 726.27
ONLY girls. Townsend, V. F. 931.2
ONLY herself. Cudlip, A. 317.16
ONLY sister, An. Witt, P. de 928.2
ONLY temper. Newby, C. J. 710.12
OPEN question, An. De Mille, J. 520.1
OPEN! Sesame! Church, F. 720.35
OPENING a chestnut burr. Roe, E. P. 714.6
OPERA. Art life and theories. Wagner, (W.) R. New York, 1875. 12° 6234.3
OPIUM-EATER, The confessions of an English. [Autobiographic.] De Quincey, T. Boston, 1872. 16°. 1825.5
OPIUM habit, The. Day, H. New York, 1868. 12°. 1525.17
OPPOSITE the jail. Denison, M. A. 926.20
OPTIC, Oliver, *pseud.* *See* ADAMS, William T.
OPTICS. Guillemin, A. La lumière et les couleurs. Paris, 1874. 16° 2015.8
— Lommel, E. (C. J.) The nature of light, with a general account of physical optics. New York, 1876. 12° 6436.17
— Marion, F. The wonders of. New York, 1871. 16° 1714.19
ORATORY. Quintilianus, M. F. De institutione oratoria. Philadelphiæ [*cop.* 1844]. Sm. 12° 6118.5
— Tacitus, C. C. De oratoribus dialogus. Philadelphia, 1849. Sm. 12° 6118.6
ORAZIONI quaresimali ed altre nuove opere. Barbieri, G. Milano, 1836, 37. 2 v. 12° 2038.2
ORDEAL, The, for wives. A novel. Edwards, A. 724.28
ORDEAL, The, of Richard Feverel. Meredith, G. 331.13
ORDNANCE, Instruction in. Benton, J. G. New York, 1862. 8° 6924.1
OREGON. Frémont, J. C. The exploring expedition to. Auburn, 1854. 12° 414.14
— Greenhow, R. History of. Boston, 1845. 8°.. 810.2
— Ludlow, F. H. The heart of the continent: a record of travel across the plains and in. New York, 1871. 16° 413.4
— Marcy, R. B. The prairie traveler. A hand-book for overland expeditions. New York, 1859. 16°. 417.7
— Mitchell, S. A. Map, etc., of. Philadelphia, 1846. Sm. 12° 418.7
— Nordhoff, C. Northern California, Oregon, and the Sandwich Islands. New York, 1874. 8°... 402.5
OREGON trail, The. Parkman, F., *jr.* Boston, 1872. 12° 5015.3
O'REILLY, Eleanor Grace. Giles's minority; or, scenes at the Red house. By Mrs. Robert O'Reilly 928.10
O'REILLY, Miles, *pseud.* *See* HALPINE, Charles Graham.
O'REILLY, *Mrs.* Robert. *See* O'REILLY, Eleanor Grace.
ORFORD, *4th earl of.* *See* WALPOLE, Horace.
ORIENT, The. *See* EAST, The.
ORIENTAL and linguistic studies. Whitney, W. D. New York, 1873. Sm. 8° 6126.2
ORIENTAL religions and their relation to universal religion. Johnson, S. Boston, 1873. 8° 5811.3
ORIGENES. Writings. Translated by Frederick Crombie. Edinburgh, 1869, 72. 2 v. [Ante-Nicene Christian library.] 8°.... Vol. 10, 23 of 6322.4
ORIGIN of civilisation. Lubbock, *Sir* J. New York, 1871. 12° 1527.1
ORIGINAL sin, Doctrine of, defended. Edwards, J. Worcester [1757]. 8° 6325.1
ORKNEY. Abbott, J. Harper's story books 936.1.10
ORLEY farm. Trollope, A. 334.17
ORLIAC, *Mme.* J. M. S. History of the Society of Jesus. Translated from the French of J. M. S. Daurignac [*pseud.*], by J. Clements. Cincinnati, 1865. 2 v. 12° 5817.6

Shelf. No.

ORNAMENT. Bourgoin, J. Théorie de l'ornement. Paris, 1873. 8° ... 6220.4
— Brigham, W. T. Cast catalogue of antique sculpture. With an introduction to the study of. Boston, 1874. 4° ... 6210.7
— Jones, O. The grammar of. London, 1868. F°. 6230.2
— Wornum, R. N. Analysis of. London, 1873. 8°. 6211.9

Note. — See note in Bulletin, vol. II, p. 389.

ORNAMENTAL art. Self-aid cyclopædia. Burn, R. S. London, N. D. 8° ... 6223.2
ORNITHOLOGY, Field. Coues, E. Salem, 1874. 8°. 6613.12

See also Birds.

O'ROURKE, John. The history of the great Irish famine of 1847, with notices of earlier Irish famines. Dublin, 1875. xxiv, 559 pp. Sm. 8°. 5418.12
ORPHAN, An, of the Old dominion. Silvervale, L. .. 735.16
ORPHAN Anne. Denison, M. A. ... 928.18
ORPHEUS. Offenbach, J. (*In* Ditson, O., and co. Standard opera librettos) ... 6233.3.5
ORPHEUS C. KERR, *pseud.* *See* NEWELL, Robert Henry.
ORTA-UNDIS, and other poems. Legaré, J. M. Boston, 1848. 16° ... 1616.19
ORTHOGRAPHIC projection. Davidson, E. A. London [1875]. Sm. 8° ... 6218.2
ORTHOPEDY. Bauer, L. Lectures on orthopædic surgery. New York, 1868. 8° ... 6022.13
— Bigelow, H. J. Manual of orthopedic surgery. Boston, 1845. 8° ... 6011.10
ORTON, James. The Andes and the Amazon; or, across the continent of South America. With map and illustrations. New York, 1871. 356 pp. 16°. 5933.13
ORVILLE college. Wood, E. P. ... 333.6
OSCAR. Simonds, W. ... 932.28
OSCEOLA the Seminole. Reid, M. ... 725.11
OSGOOD, John Felt. Notes of travel; or, recollections of Majunga, Zanzibar, Muscat, Aden, Mocha, and other Eastern ports. Salem, 1854. x, 253 pp. 12° ... 5915.8
OSGOOD, *Mrs.* M. A. Little Canary series. Little Canary ... 927.17
— – Little Canary's black Cato ... 927.19
— – Little Canary's cousin Eugene ... 927.18
— – Little Canary's daisy ... 927.16
OSGOOD, Samuel. The hearth-stone: thoughts upon home-life in our cities. 4th edition. New York, 1854. 290 pp. 12° ... 1516.3
OSSIAN. Poems. Translated by J. Macpherson. With dissertations on the æra and poems of Ossian; and Dr. Blair's critical dissertation. Leipzig, 1847. vi, 382 pp. Sq. 16° ... 1613.19
OSSOLI, Sarah Margaret Fuller, *marchesa* d'. Life without and life within; or, reviews, narratives, essays, and poems. Edited by A. B. Fuller. Boston, 1874. 424 pp. 12° ... 1935.7
— Memoirs. Edited by R. W. Emerson, W. H. Channing, and J. F. Clarke. With a portrait and an appendix. Boston, 1875 [*cop.* 1859]. 2 v. 12° ... 1215.4
— Woman in the nineteenth century. New York, 1845. 201 pp. 12° ... 1736.9
OSWALD Cray. Wood, E. P. ... 333.14
OTELLO. Rossini, G. (*In* Ditson, O., and co. Standard opera librettos) ... 6233.3.3
OTHER girls, The. Whitney, A. D. T. ... 734.7
OTHER people's money. Gaboriau, É. ... 711.4
OTHER worlds than ours. [Astronomy.] Proctor, R. A. New York, 1871. 12° ... 1527.4
OTIS, James, Life of. Tudor, W. Boston, 1823. 8°. 1012.2
OTTLEY, Drewry, *editor and translator.* Observations on surgical diseases of the head and neck. Selected from the memoirs of the Royal academy of surgery of France. London, 1848. x, 293 pp. 8° ... 6013.9
OTTO, Emil. German conversation-grammar. 15th edition. New York, 1868. viii, 440 pp. Sm. 8°. 1933.5
OUGHT we to visit her? Edwards, A. ... 312.17
OUIDA, *pseud.* *See* RAME, Louise de la.
OUR bishops and deans. [Church of England.] Arnold, F. London, 1875. 2 v. 8° ... 5810.6

Shelf. No.

OUR boys and girls. *See* OLIVER OPTIC's magazine.
OUR boys and girls album. Adams, W. T. ... 911.1
OUR campaigns. Woodward, E. M. Philadelphia, 1865. 16° ... 817.14
OUR detachment. King, K. ... 711.34
OUR digestion. Lewis, D. Philadelphia, 1872. 12°. 1522.4
OUR Father and his family union. Porter, W. H. Boston, 1861. 16° ... 5818.5
OUR Fred. Finley, M. ... 926.19
OUR girls. Lewis, D. New York, 1871. 12° ... 1536.3
OUR Helen. Clarke, R. S. ... 933.10
OUR mutual friend. Dickens, C. (J. H.) Boston. 2 v. 1824.16
— *Same.* Leipzig. 4 v. in 2 ... 338.13
— *Same.* New York. 2 v. ... 731.27
OUR new crusade. Hale, E. E. ... 529.5
OUR new masters. Wright, T. London, 1873. 8°. 5415.9
OUR new way round the world. [Travels.] Coffin, C. C. Boston [*cop.* 1869]. 8° ... 433.1
OUR next-door neighbor: a winter in Mexico. Haven, G. New York, 1875. 8° ... 5032.5
OUR old home: a series of English sketches. Hawthorne, N. Boston, 1876 [*cop.* 1863]. Sq. 16°. 1839.2 and 5439.1
OUR place among infinities. [Astronomy.] Proctor, R. A. London, 1875. Sm. 8° ... 6815.2
OUR standard-bearer; or, the life of U. S. Grant. Adams, W. T. Boston, 1868. 16° ... 916.14
OUR summer at Hillside farm. Barrett, M. ... 1118.9
OUR village. [Sketches of English rural life.] Mitford, M. R. London, 1865, 71. 2 v. Sm. 8°. 527.19
OUR wasted resources; the missing link in the temperance reform. Hargreaves, W. New York, 1876. 12° ... 5835.8
OUR young folks. Vol. 8, 9. Boston, 1872, 73. 2 v. 8° ... 1433.1
OUT-DOOR papers. Higginson, T. W. Boston, 1871. 12° ... 1915.1
OUT of court. Hoey, *Mrs.* C. ... 319.17
OUT of doors. Wood, J. G. London, 1874. Sm. 8°. 6616.9
OUT-OF-DOORS: a handbook of games for the playground. Elliott, A. London, 1872. 12° ... 1517.8
OUT of prison. Denison, M. A. ... 1118.4
OUT of the deep. Wood, E. P. ... 521.11
OUT of the hurly-burly; or, life in an odd corner. Clark, C. H. ... 723.5
OUT of the world. Thackeray, A. I. Works ... 512.14
OUT of town. Coffin, R. B. ... 724.29
OUTBREAK, The, of the great French revolution. [Historical novel.] Erckmann, É., and Chatrian, A. London, 1871. 3 v. 16° ... 825.2
OUTCASTS, The, of Poker Flat. Harte, (F.) B. (*In* Johnson, (E.) R. Little classics) ... 529.4.1
OUTLAW, The. Hall, A. M. ... 727.23
OUTRE-MER. [European travel.] Longfellow, H. W. Prose works. Boston, 1866 [*cop.* 1857]. 16° ... 1838.4.1
OUTWARD bound; or, Young America afloat. Adams, W. T. Boston, 1873. 16° ... 925.13
OVARIOTOMY, History and statistics of. Lyman, G. H. (*In* Massachusetts medical society. Publications) ... 6021.4
OVER the ocean; or, sights and scenes in foreign lands. Guild, C. Boston, 1873. Sm. 8° ... 426.20
OVER the river. Thayer, T. B. Boston, 1867. 16°. 1526.1
OVER yonder. John, E. ... 712.3
OVERDALE. Worboise, E. J. ... 536.23
OVERLAND. De Forest, J. W. ... 531.24
OVERLAND monthly. Vol. 9–15. San Francisco, 1872–75. 7 v. 8° ... 1316.1
OVINGDEAN grange: a tale of the South Downs. Ainsworth, W. H. ... 322.13
OWEN, Richard. Key to the geology of the globe. Illustrated by maps and diagrams. Boston, 1857. 256 pp. 8° ... 6631.9
OWEN, Robert Dale. The debatable land between this world and the next. New York, 1872. 542 pp. 12° ... 1526.28
— Footfalls on the boundary of another world. Philadelphia, 1872. 528 pp. 12° ... 1533.7
— Threading my way. [An autobiography.] New York, 1874. 360 pp. 12° ... 5427.6

Shelf. No.

OWEN: — a waif. Robinson, F. W. 318.1
OWEN Gwynne's great work. Noel, *Lady* A. 530.12
OWEN MEREDITH, *pseud.* *See* BULWER-LYTTON, (Edward) Robert, *lord Lytton.*
OXFORD, *England.* Arnold, F. Oxford and Cambridge: their colleges, memories, and associations. London [1874]. Sm. 4° 5433.2
— Jeaffreson, J. C. Annals of Oxford. London, 1871. 2 v. 8° 5433.3
— Tyerman, L. The Oxford methodists. New York, 1873. 8° 5424.5
OXLEY. Bright, M. A. 528.4
OZONE and antozone, their history and nature. Fox, C. B. London, 1873. 8° 6433.8

PACIFIC states. Bancroft, H. H. The native races of the Pacific states of North America. New York, 1874–76. 5 v. 8° 5920.4
— Bates, *Mrs.* D. B. Incidents on land and water, or four years on the Pacific coast. Boston, 1858. 12° 235.1
— Exploration of the Colorado river of the West. *See* SMITHSONIAN institution, *Washington, D. C.* Washington, 1875. 4° 230.1
PACINI, Giovanni. Saffo. (*In* Ditson, O., and co. Standard opera librettos) 6233.3.1
PACKARD, Alpheus Spring, *jr.* Guide to the study of insects, and a treatise on those injurious and beneficial to crops. With plates and wood-cuts. 3d edition. Salem, 1872. viii, 715+ pp. 8° 6613.6
PAEZ, Ramon. Travels and adventures in South and Central America. First series: life in the Llanos of Venezuela. New York, 1868. xlviii, 473+ pp. Map. Illustrations. 12° 427.8
PAGE, H. A. Memoir of Nathaniel Hawthorne. With stories now first published in this country. London, 1872. xi, 301+ pp. 16° 5025.7
— Noble workers. A book of examples for young men. London, 1875. 411+ pp. Portraits. Sm. 8° 5936.3

Contents. — John Coleridge Patteson; Charles Knight; Robert Chambers; Duncan Matheson; John M'Vickar; Arthur Tappan; Charles Cullis; Adoniram Judson; Sir Donald Macleod; Henry Alford; Sir James Y. Simpson; Sir Henry Lawrence; James D. Forbes; Thomas Adams.

PAGET, James. Lectures on surgical pathology. Philadelphia, 1854. 699 pp. Illustrated. 8°. 6012.3
PAINE, Martyn. Institutes of medicine. 9th edition. New York, 1870. xvi, 1151 pp. Portrait. 8° 6012.1
— Medical and physiological commentaries. New York, 1840. 2 v. 8° 6012.5
— Physiology of the soul and instinct, as distinguished from materialism. New York, 1872. 707 pp. Portrait. 8° 5831.1
PAINE, Robert Troup. Memoir. By his parents. New York, 1852. viii, 524 pp. Portraits. 1 plate. 4° 5020.3
PAINE family. Thayer, E. Family memorials. Hingham, 1835. 8° 611.2

Shelf. No.

PAINTERS. Clement, C. E. Painters, and their works. New York, 1874. 16° 1513.17
— Crowe, J. A., and Cavalcaselle, G. B. The early Flemish painters. London, 1872. Sm. 8° 6215.3
— Keddie, *Miss* —. Modern painters and their paintings. Boston, 1874. 16° 6216.4
— — The old masters and their pictures. London, 1873. Sm. 8° 1516.21
— — *Same.* Boston, 1874. 16° 6216.3
— Ruskin, J. Frondes agrestes. Readings in 'Modern painters.' Orpington, Kent, 1875. Sm. 8° 6236.21
— — Modern painters. New York, 1872. 5 v. 12°. 6236.18
— Shedd, J. A. Famous painters and paintings. Boston, 1876. 8° 6212.4
— Stephens, F. G. Flemish and French pictures, with notes concerning the painters and their works. London, 1875. 4° 6211.8
— Vasari, G. Lives of the most eminent painters. London, 1855. 5 v. Sm. 8° 6215.6
PAINTING. Arsenne, L. C. Manuel du peintre. Paris, 1833. 2 v. 24° 6219.1
— Blanc, (A. A. P.) C. Grammar of. New York, 1874. L. 8° 6212.2
— Burckhardt, J. The Cicerone: or, art guide to painting in Italy. London, 1873. Sm. 8° 6216.1
— Crowe, J. A., and Cavalcaselle, G. B. History of painting in Italy from the second to the fourteenth century. London, 1864. 3 v. 8° 6213.2
— — History of painting in North Italy. London, 1871. 2 v. 8° 6213.1
— Field, G. Grammar of colouring. London, N. D. 12° 1715.3
— Fromberg, E. O. Rudimentary essay on the art of painting on glass. London, 1857. 12° 1716.23
— Gardner, F. B. How to paint. New York, 1872. 16° 6429.1
— Jarves, J. J. Catalogue of [his] collection of early Italian pictures. Boston, 1871. 8° 6213.7
— — Descriptive catalogue of "Old masters," collected by [him] to illustrate the history of painting from 1200 to the best periods of Italian art. Cambridge, 1860. 8° 6213.7
— Lanzi, L. History of painting in Italy, from the revival of the fine arts to the end of the 18th century. London, 1852. 2 v. Sm. 8° 6215.4
— Riffault, J. R. D., and Vernaud, A. R. Manuel du peintre en bâtiments, vitrier, doreur, argenteur et vernisseur. Paris, 1851. 24° 6429.3
— Ruskin, J. Lectures on. New York, 1872. 12°. 6236.12
— Shedd, J. A. Famous painters and paintings. Boston, 1876. 8° 6212.4
— Turner, M. The young ladies' assistant in drawing and painting. Cincinnati, 1833. 16° 1517.4
— Tyrwhitt, R. St. J. A handbook of pictorial art. Oxford, 1875. 8° 6213.12
— Waagen, G. F. Handbook of painting. German, Flemish and Dutch schools. London, 1860. 2 v. 8° 6214.1
— Wornum, R. N. The epochs of. London, 1864. 8°. 6213.3

See also Sepia painting, Water color painting.

NOTE ON PAINTING.

General histories. The general reader will probably find Wornum's "Epochs" the most useful survey of the whole field, the edition of 1864 [6213.3] being much improved over previous ones. It does not, however, include living painters. The notes make a very useful bibliographical record. Miss Tytler's "Old masters and their pictures" [1516.21; 6216.3] covers the various national schools, and is a concise popular statement, and she has also a similar handbook on "Modern painters" [6216.4]. The recent popular German work by Luebke, of which there is an English translation [6210.4], is a very comprehensive introduction to all phases of the subject. See Lossing's popular outline sketch [1517.1]. Ruskin's "Modern painters" [6236.18] contains little of biography, but is chiefly confined to criticism of modern principles, as compared with those of the older schools; and is in considerable portions a comparison of Turner, the English landscape painter, with Claude Lorraine. Lessing's "Laocoon" [6216.2] is a search for the limits of poetry and painting. Sir Joshua Reynolds's Lectures [6230.1] are deemed sound criticism, but they have a tendency to the Academic principles, not so much in vogue now as in Sir Joshua's day. Tyrwhitt's Handbook [6213.12] is a convenient manual.

Ancient painting. Digby Wyatt's "Fine art" [6232.2] has a summarized sketch of ancient art. The material for its history among the ancient nations is necessarily scant, but chapters in Wornum [6213.3] will probably suffice the general reader regarding the painting among the Aztecs, the Asian peoples, Japanese, etc.; but he may desire the fuller accounts of *Egyptian* painting to be found in Wilkinson's "Manners and customs of the ancient Egyptians" [5926.3]. And so of *Greece*, to which Wornum devotes three chapters (he also wrote the article "Painting" in Smith's "Dictionary of Greek and Roman antiquities"), the reader may find in Taine [6217.2], who is chiefly dependent, however, on the remains of sculpture, an exposition of climatic and ethnological theories, while Winckelmann, in his "Ancient art" [6211.1], is not to be forgotten by the student, and is reviewed in the Atlantic monthly, April, 1873. See also Van Brunt's papers on the principles of Greek art in the Atlantic monthly, June, 1861, etc. There are chapters on Greek art in Grote's "History of Greece" [5926.1], and in Felton's Lectures. Also see chap. 22 of Lloyd's "Age of Pericles" [5921.12]. Greenough's "Apelles and his contemporaries" [536.10] is a novel. There is a chapter on Greek landscape in vol. 3 of Ruskin's "Modern painters" [6236.18]. Max Müller's "Chips" [5616.1.1] has a paper on the art use of their mythology. For *Roman* painting, we are largely dependent on the discoveries at Pompeii, which see. See also chapters in histories of Rome like Mommsen's [5516.1], and popular compends like Lord's "Roman world" [826.10].

Early Christian art forms a section of Milman's "Latin Christianity" [5817.11], and several of Mrs. Jameson's books point out the connection of the religious sentiment with its artistic treatment. See the *note* on the Catacombs in the Library Bulletin, vol. II, p. 289.

Italian painting. The English translation of Vasari's Lives, above-named, will supply the general reader with all that he wants. The failure of Lanzi, in his "History of painting" [6215.4], to recognize sufficiently the claims of the earlier Italian painters, led Kugler to write his history of the Italian schools from the time of Constantine down, which, under the editing of Sir Charles Eastlake, became one of Murray's handbooks, prefixed to which will be found a list of authorities. See Mrs. Jameson's brief memoirs of the earlier artists, and the historical surveys of Taine in his "Italy" [5522.2]. See also the biographies of Da Vinci, Michel-Angelo, Raphael; of the later eclectic school, Carracci, Domenichino, Correggio, Guido; of the Venetian school, Titian, Tintoretto, Paul Veronese; of the naturalists, Caravaggio, Spagnoletto, Salvator Rosa, and of Cellini in this and in the Bates Hall catalogues. There is a paper on the Venetian school in the Westminster review, 1873; and much of interest in Pater's "Renaissance" [5925.2]. Roscoe's "Lorenzo de' Medici" [5525.1] and "Leo x" [5526.6] deal largely with the artistic aspects of that period.

Beside chapters (16, 17) in Wornum, the general reader will find a popular review in Viardot's "Wonders of Italian art" [1714.23]; while the student will seek the new and elaborate history by Crowe and Cavalcaselle [6213.2]. See also Goethe's "Winckelmann und sein Jahrhundert," in his Werke [5737.1.13]; and an excellent guide in Burckhardt's "Cicerone" [6216.1]. Travels in Italy almost always cover more or less the art-sights, like Hillard's "Six months in Italy" [426.8]; Jameson's "Diary of an ennuyée" [427.3], etc. Art novels, like Greenough's "Ernest Carroll" [737.28] and Allston's "Monaldi," will be found of interest.

German painting. The general reader will find a concise account of the art of illumination in book 2 of Wornum [6213.3]; but see in this connection the note in the Library Bulletin for April, 1876.

Murray's Handbook for the German school, which was originally issued as a translation of Kugler, with notes by Sir Edmund Head, 1846, was reissued, so nearly re-written by Dr. Waagen, 1864 [6214.1], as to make a new work, in the preface of which he has given a careful account of the sources of the history. See also the lives of Dürer, Holbein, etc.

For later German painting, see the pleasing experiences in Mrs. Jameson's "Sketches" [5618.3], and Miss Howitt's "Art-student in Munich." See the summary in the concluding chapter of Grimm's "Life of Michael Angelo" [1022.2].

Flemish and Dutch painting. For the earlier art, see chap. 30 of Wornum [6213.3, where, on p. 459, will be found an enumeration of authorities]; Waagen's "Handbook" [6214.1]; but probably the best special treatise is that by Crowe and Cavalcaselle on "The early Flemish painters" [6215.3]. Taine's Essay [6217.1] represents the philosophizing element in modern critical history. Stephen's monograph [6211.8] is the latest contribution.

See also in this and in Bates Hall catalogues for the Flemish school (catholic Brabant), the biographies of Rubens, Vandyck, Teniers, Snyders, etc.; and for the Dutch school (protestant Holland), those of Rembrandt, Vanderhelst, Cuyp, Terburg, Ostade, Wouvermans, etc.

French painting. Kugler gave small space to France in his Handbook, and so Sir E. Head prepared a special manual for Murray's series, in which he recapitulates the authorities. Chapter 32 of Wornum is devoted to France, and he gives on p. 490 the principal authorities. There is a chapter in Guizot's "History of France" [5010.2] on the art of Louis XIV's time. See Hamerton [426.19] for contemporary painters, and Stigand's Heine [5721.1].

The principal biographies illustrative of French painting are those of Poussin, Claude Lorraine, Watteau, Greuze, David (who revived the classical school during the first empire), Prudhon, Delaroche, Vernet, Scheffer, Delacroix, Ingres, etc., most of which must be searched for in the Bates Hall catalogues. On Frere and the artists of this day, see Harper's monthly, vol. 43; Thackeray's "Paris sketch book" [339.21], and the Atlantic monthly, Sept., 1875.

Spanish painting. Besides Head's Handbook, the general manual on Spain by Ford [5917.1], and chapter 29 in Wornum [6213.3, who gives the chief authorities on p. 395], constitute in English a full survey. Hay, in his "Castilian days" [227.2], has a chapter on the galleries of Madrid. See also general travels in Spain.

English painting. The lives of Holbein, Rubens, Vandyck, and Kneller, who carried foreign taste into England, indicate rather the patronage of art in that country, since there could hardly be said to be a native school, until Hogarth. Walpole's "Anecdotes of painting" refer to this pre-Hogarthian period. Wornum [6213.3], in his closing chapters, gives a summary.

The history of British painting can be well traced in the following lives: — Hogarth, Reynolds, George Romney, West, Richard Wilson, Gainsborough, William Blake, Fuseli, Opie, Haydon, David Scott, William Etty, Turner, Constable, William Collins, Lawrence, Stothard, Wilkie, and Leslie. Most of the material on these artists must be sought for in the Bates Hall catalogues.

There is a paper on recent art in Bayne's "Essays" [1226.15]; "State of English painting," in Quarterly review, 1873. Wilkie Collins's "Hide and seek" [326.1] concerns in part recent artists' life.

Painting in the United States. Tuckerman's "Book of the artists," 1867 [1511.6], is the best work, including the fullest memoir yet published of Allston, and covering also the careers of such Americans as achieved or increased their reputation in England, like West, Copley, and Leslie.

There are reminiscences of painters by John Neal, in the Atlantic monthly for Dec., 1868, and March, 1869. See "First American art academy" in Lippincott's magazine, vol. 9; Bryant's address on Cole, in his Orations [1926.1]; "American artists in Italy," in Harper's monthly, vol. 41.

Biographical dictionaries. Spooner's is an extensive compilation, and on the whole the best for general use. Biographies of artists will, however, be found in Brande and Cox's Cyclopædia, in Appleton's, in Chambers's, and in Thomas's Biographical dictionary; and for the ancients, in Smith's "Dictionary of Greek and Roman biography;" and in the case of English or American artists, who have also been writers, in Allibone.

See further the *note* under Painting in the Lower Hall Catalogue of history, etc.

	Shelf. No.
PAIR, A, of blue eyes. Hardy, T.	539.4
PALACE and cottage; or, Young America in France and Switzerland. Adams, W. T. Boston, 1873. 16°	925.10
PALACE of truth, The: a comedy. Gilbert, W. S. Original plays. New York, 1876. 12°	1634.1
PALEONTOLOGY. Nouveau manuel complet de paléontologie. Serres, M. de. Paris, 1846. 2 v. With atlas. 24°	6639.1
PALESTINE. Burt, N. C. The land and its story; or, the sacred historical geography of. New York, 1869. Sm. 4°	421.8
— Holland, F. W. Wanderings in. (*In* Many lands and many people)	431.3
— Lynch, W. F. Narrative of the United States' expedition to the river Jordan and the Dead sea. Philadelphia, 1849. 8°	421.9
— Munk, S. Palestine. Paris, 1845. 8°	5911.9
— Murray, J. Handbook for Palestine. London, 1868. 12°	5936.1
— Robinson, E., and Smith, E. Biblical researches in. Boston, 1841. 3 v. 8°	5810.5
— Stanley, A. P. Sinai and Palestine. New York, 1870. 8°	5923.1
— Strauss, (G.) F. (A.) The glory of the house of Israel; comprising a picture of Judaism in the century which preceded the advent of our Saviour. Philadelphia, 1859. 12°	425.14
PALESTINE, *continued.*	
— Taylor, (J.) B. The lands of the Saracen; or, pictures of. New York, 1857. 12°	424.13

See also Bashan, East (The), Holy Land, Jerusalem, Jews, Sinai, Syria.

Note. — The second chapter of the second volume of Gage's "Life of Ritter" [1024.8] reviews the list of authorities from the Gentile writers before Christ down to our day, including important articles in periodicals; and in the third appendix to the same volume will be found a summary of the literature on Palestine, by Tobler, the first living authority. A similar review is given by Robinson [5810.5]; and also in the introduction to "Our work in Palestine" [423.10]. See also Smith's "Bible dictionary," and the Cyclopædia of Kitto, where a list of the most important works is given, in vol. 2, p. 465. The article on Palestine in Smith's Dictionary is by George Grove, and is one of the best summaries.

For historical accounts, see note under Jerusalem.

The modern scientific explorations began in 1805-7. In 1838, Robinson made his remarkable advance, as an explorer, and his books [5810.5, etc.], after thirty years, are still the most valuable on the geography, and with their ignoring of legendry, have found their firmest admirer in Ritter, and have instigated the later researches of Schultz, Krafft, Tobler, and Gadow. Within a few years after this, two English travellers gave vivid and popular accounts of Palestine, — Kinglake, in his "Eothen" [228.1], in 1838; and Warburton, in his "Crescent and cross," in 1843 [317.8]. Ten years later, 1852, the United States government aided science by the publication of Lynch's expedition to the Jordan and the Dead sea [421.9], the standard authority on this region; and in the next year, 1853, biblical scholars received the most important contribution in English since Robinson in Dean Stanley's book [5923.1]. Macgregor's "Rob Roy on the Jordan" [423.17] gives some new views on the site of Capernaum. See further, Porter's "Giant cities of Bashan" [5915.7]; Dixon's "Holy Land" [428.1]; Prime's "Tent life" [425.1]; Thackeray's "From Cornhill to Cairo" [513.1.7]; and Thomson's "Land and the book" [224.5].

Shelf. No.

PALESTINE, *continued.*

Beside Robinson and Kitto on the physical geography, there is in English the valuable work of Tristram, 2d edition, 1866 [in Bates Hall]; but the great German authority is Ritter, 1850; and Gage's English adaptation retains all of the original that illustrates the Bible. Ritter's views and methods, with the advantage of the latest researches, have been presented for popular appreciation by Burt [421.8]. The brilliant enthusiasm of Chateaubriand [5532.3.5] is well-known, but he is of no value as an authority; while the equally famous "Souvenirs" of Lamartine, by his own acknowledgment, have nothing either of science, history, geography, or manners.

What has been done by the Palestine exploration fund of England has been mentioned in the note under Jerusalem, and will be found epitomized in "Our work in Palestine" [423.10], including Capt. Warren's explorations east of the Jordan, in Lebanon, etc., abridged from the detail of the quarterly statements.

For guide books, that of Murray [5936.1] is admirable, receiving the praise of Tobler, and the English reader can hardly find anything better for a single survey, and it has a special summary of the divisions into sects of the modern inhabitants, with enumeration of authorities. In Kitto, the principal authorities on the subdivisions of the subject will be found grouped together, pointing out chapters in more general works.

For maps, there is in Gage's "Life of Ritter," vol. 2, ch. 2 [1024.8], a sketch of the rise and progress of the chartography; but the general reader will find the maps in the work by Stanley, and Murray's "Handbook," generally corrected up to date of publication.

In the 6th vol. of Merivale's "History of the Romans" [5515.3] there is a map of Palestine in the 1st century.

For views, see the list in Smith's "Bible dictionary," and in Gage's "Life of Ritter," vol. 2, ch. 2.

See illustrated papers in Harper's monthly, vols. 5, 6, 8, 36; a paper on "Galilee in the time of Christ," in the Bibliotheca sacra, Jan., 1874; and one on "The Arabs in Palestine" in Macmillan, Aug., 1875.

See further in the note in the Lower Hall Catalogue of history, etc.

Moabite stone. — See the article in Contemporary review, v. 15; "Recovery of Jerusalem" [5933.1]; chap. 12 of "Our work in Palestine" [423.10], with references; Burton and Drake's "Unexplored Syria" [5933.3]; Palmer's "Desert of the Exodus" [222.2], for the Arab quarrels over it; Grove's article "Moab" in Smith's "Dictionary of the Bible," etc. Tristram's "Land of Moab" [5933.4] gives an account of the place where it was found.

In fiction. — Ware's "Julian" [736.5] is a picture of the time of Christ; and so is Ingraham's "Prince of the house of David" [512.5]; and Strauss's "Glory of the house of Israel" [425.14].

PALESTINE exploration fund. Our work in Palestine: being an account of the different expeditions sent out to the Holy Land by the committee since the establishment of the fund in 1865. London, 1873. iv, 343+ pp. Illustrated. Maps. 16°.... 423.10

— *Same.* New York, 1873. Sm. 8°.... 5915.6

— The recovery of Jerusalem. A narrative of exploration and discovery in the city and the Holy Land. By (C. W.) Wilson [and others]. With an introduction by A. P. Stanley. Edited by W. Morrison. [Also Explorations in the peninsula of Sinai. By F. W. Holland.] New York, 1872. xxiv, 435 pp. Illustrated. Maps. 8°.... 5933.1

PALEY, William. Works. With a memoir of his life, by G. W. Meadley. Boston, 1810–12. 5 v. Portrait. 8°.... 6324.5

Contents. — Vol. I. Natural theology. II. Evidences of Christianity. III. Principles of moral and political philosophy. IV. Sermons and tracts. V. Horæ Paulinæ; The young Christian instructed; Clergyman's companion, etc.

— Principles of moral and political philosophy. 10th edition. London, 1794. 2 v. 8°.... 5823.3

— *Same.* Boston, 1830. 2 v. 1 plate. Portrait. Sm. 12°.... 1538.6

— Sermons on various subjects. Originally published by Edmund Paley. 1st American edition. Boston, 1827. xv, 438 pp. 8°.... 5810.8

— View of the evidences of Christianity. Hallowell, 1826. 310 pp. 12°.... 5816.8

PALFREY, John Gorham. Academical lectures on the Jewish Scriptures and antiquities. Vol. I. Boston, 1838. 8°.... 5811.8

Contents. — Vol. I. Last four books of the Pentateuch.

— Compendious history of New England from the accession of George II to the first general congress of the Anglo-American colonies. Boston, 1873. xii, 439 pp. 16°.... 5016.3

— History of New England. Boston, 1870–76 [*cop.* 1858–64]. 4 v. Maps. Illustrations. 8°.... 5014.7

Contents. — Vol. I–III. During the Stuart dynasty. IV. From the revolution of the seventeenth century.

Shelf. No.

PALFREY, John Gorham, *continued.*

— History of New England, from the discovery by Europeans to the revolution of the seventeenth century, being an abridgment of his "History of New England during the Stuart dynasty." New York, 1866. 2 v. Sm. 8°.... 5016.2

— Sermons on duties belonging to some of the conditions and relations of private life. Boston, 1834. x, 368 pp. 8°.... 5811.9

PALGRAVE, Francis Turner, *editor.* The golden treasury of the best songs and lyrical poems in the English language. London, 1874. 332 pp. Sm. 8°.... 1627.4

PALGRAVE, William Gifford. Essays on Eastern questions. London, 1872. vi, 349+ pp. 8°. 6135.1

— Leisure hour series. Hermann Agha: an Eastern narrative. New York, 1872. vi, 281 pp. 16°. 537.16

— Personal narrative of a year's journey through central and eastern Arabia (1862–63). 6th edition. London, 1871. vi, 427+ pp. Folded plans. 1 folded map. Sm. 8°.... 5916.7

PALISSY, Madame, The provocations of. Manning, A.... 514.2

PALISSY the Huguenot potter. Boston, 1859. 239 pp. 16°.... 538.4

PALL MALL budget. A weekly collection of articles printed in the Pall Mall gazette from day to day. Vol. 10–14. London, 1874, 75. 5 v. F°. 6720.1

PALLISTER, *Mrs.* Berry. History of lace. 2d edition. London, 1869. viii, 442 pp. Illustrated. Portraits. 8°.... 6232.7

PALM land; or, Dick Travers in the Chagos islands. Samuels, A. F.... 918.24

PALMER, E. H. The desert of the Exodus. With maps and illustrations. New York, 1872. 470+ pp. Sm. 8°.... 222.2

— *joint author.* Jerusalem, the city of Herod and Saladin. *See* BESANT, Walter.... 5924.2

PALMER, Ray. Earnest words on true success in life. New York, 1873. 295+ pp. 8°.... 6136.7

PALMERIN of England. Moreas, F. de. London, 1807. 4 v. 16°.... 5928.2

PALMERSTON, *Lord.* *See* TEMPLE, Henry John.

PALMERSTON, *Viscountess.* *See* TEMPLE, Amelia.

PALMETTO-LEAVES. [Florida.] Stowe, H. (E.) B. Boston, 1873. Sq. 16°.... 417.10

PAMPAS, The, and Andes. Bishop, N. H. Boston, 1872. 16°.... 934.1

PANDURANG HÀRì, or, memoirs of a Hindoo. With an introductory preface by Sir H. B. E. Frere. London, 1873. 2 v. Sm. 8°.... 5934.7

PANTOMIMES, The book of shadow. Frost, S. A. New York [*cop.* 1869]. 12°.... 1518.1

PAPACY. Life of Gregory VII. Preceded by a sketch of papacy to the 11th century. Villemain, A. F. London, 1874. 2 v. 8°.... 5522.6

See also Popery, Popes, Roman catholic church.

PAPAL infallibility. Gladstone, W. E. The Vatican decrees in their bearing on civil allegiance. New York, 1875. 8°.... 1911.1

— — Vaticanism: an answer to Reproofs and replies. New York, 1875. 8°.... 1911.2

— Manning, H. E., *cardinal.* The Vatican decrees in their bearing on civil allegiance. New York, 1875. 12°.... 1916.7

PAPER and paper-making, A chronology of. Munsell, J. Albany, 1870. 8°.... 6423.2

PAPER model maker, The illustrated. Landells, E. London, N. D. 8°.... 6220.5

PAPILLON, Fernand. Nature and life. Facts and doctrines relating to the constitution of matter, the new dynamics, and the philosophy of nature. From the 2d French edition, by A. R. Macdonough. New York, 1875. v, 363+ pp. 12°.. 1735.6

PARADISE, The, of doctors. Bigelow, J. Boston, 1858. 12°.... 6037.1

PARADISE lost. [A poem.] Milton, J. Boston, 1825. Sm. 12°.... 1618.4

— *Same.* (*In his* Poetical works.) Leipzig, 1850. Sq. 16°.... 1614.12

Shelf. No.

PARADISE regained. [A poem.] Milton, J. Poetical works. Leipzig, 1850. Sq. 16° 1614.12

PARASIT, Der. Schiller, (J. C.) F. von. Werke. Stuttgart, 1867. 8° 5734.1.7

PARASITES, Animal. Benedin, P. J. van. New York, 1876. 12° 6616.6

PARDOE, Julia. Louis XIV, and the court of France in the seventeenth century. New York, 1847. 2 v. Illustrated. Portrait. 12° 1223.11

PARDON, George Frederick. Handbook of whist. On the text of Hoyle. New edition. London, 1863. 94 pp. 16° 1519.2

PARIS, Louis Philippe Albert d'Orléans, *comte* de. History of the civil war in America. Translated, with the approval of the author, by Louis F. Tasistro. Edited by Henry Coppée. Vol. I, II. Philadelphia, 1875, 76. 2 v. Folded maps. 8° 813.17

— Les associations ouvrières en Angleterre. (Trades-unions.) Paris, 1869. viii, 338 pp. 12° 5827.2

PARIS. Abbott, J. Rollo in Paris 917.22

— An American family in. New York, 1870. 16°. 911.4

— Baedeker, C. Handbook for Paris. Coblenz, 1872. 16° 5527.7

— Fetridge, W. P. Rise and fall of the Paris commune in 1871. New York, 1871. 12° 824.8

— Head, *Sir* F. B. A faggot of French sticks; containing a series of sketches of the principal public institutions of. London, 1855. 2 v. 12°. 5526.11

— Houssaye, A. Life in. Boston, 1875. Sq. 16°. 439.3

— Jerrold, (W.) B. At home in Paris: at peace and at war. London, 1871. 2 v. 16° 5526.12

— King, E. My Paris: French character sketches. Boston, 1873. 12° 427.7

— Lemonnyer, J. Les journaux de Paris pendant la commune. Paris [1871]. 12° 5534.2

— Murray, J. Handbook for Paris. London, 1872. 12° 5527.6

— Sheppard, N. Shut up in. [Siege of Paris.] Leipzig, 1871. Sq. 16° 315.13

— Taine, H. A. Notes on. New York, 1875. 12°. 5533.2

— *Galleries, museums, etc.* Guide through the galleries of paintings of the Imperial museum of the Louvre. Paris, 1857. 12° 5527.2

Note. — See the note in the Lower Hall Catalogue of history, etc.

For the architecture of modern Paris, see Fergusson's "Modern architecture" [6212.3], and the description of the new opera house in Scribner's monthly, May, 1875.

For the varied phases of life in Paris, beside the book by Head (curious in its researches), and others named above, see Jarves's papers in Harper's monthly, vols. 5 to 8; other papers in Appleton's monthly, vol. 11; Scribner's monthly, vols. 4 and 10 (the Latin quarter); A. Hayward's Essays [5833.3.2]; and E. A. Freeman's Essays [5913.4] on the early sieges.

PARIS exposition, 1867. Examination of the telegraphic apparatus, and the processes of telegraphy. Morse, S. F. B. Washington, 1869. 8°. 6822.3

PARIS sketch book, The. Thackeray, W. M. Leipzig, 1873. 2 v. in 1. Sq. 16° 339.21

— *Same.* (*In his* Works.) London, 1872. Sm. 8°. 513.1.7

PARISIANS, The. Bulwer-Lytton, E. (G. E.) L. Leipzig. 4 v. in 2 .... 329.21

— *Same.* New York .... 734.16 and 5533.1

PARK, Mungo. Travels. *See* ENGLISH explorers. London, 1875. Sm. 8° 5927.9

PARKER, Joseph. Ecce Deus: essays on the life and doctrine of Jesus Christ. With controversial notes on "Ecce Homo." Boston, 1867. 363 [361] pp. 12° 1526.4

PARKER, Richard Green. Sketch of the history of the grammar school, in the easterly part of Roxbury. Roxbury, 1826. 36 pp. 8° 817.11

— A tribute to the life and character of Jonas Chickering. "By one who knew him well." Boston, 1854. 162 pp. Portrait. Woodcut. 12° 1016.3

PARKER, Rosa Abbott. Rosa Abbott stories. Alexis the runaway 933.14

— – Jack of all trades 933.15

— – The pinks and blues 933.16

— – Tommy Hickup 933.19

— – Upside down 933.18

— – The young detective 933.17

Shelf. No.

PARKER, Theodore. [Works.] Boston, 1871. 9 v. 12° 5237.1

Contents. — Vol. I-V. Speeches. addresses, and occasional sermons. VI. Discourse of matters pertaining to religion. VII. Historic Americans. VIII, IX. Sermons on theism, and popular theology.

— Experience as a minister, with some account of his early life, and education for the ministry. Boston, 1859. 182 pp. 12° 5217.3

— Historic Americans. 2d edition. Boston, 1871. 312 pp. Sm. 8° 5025.4

Contents. — Franklin; Washington; John Adams; Thomas Jefferson,

— Prayers. Boston, 1862. 200 pp. Portrait. 16°. 1526.6

— Frothingham, O. B. Theodore Parker: a biography. Boston, 1874. 12° 5025.11

— Weiss, J. Life and correspondence of. New York, 1864. 2 v. 8° 5021.2

Note. — There are autobiographic materials in his works, and in his own "Experience as a minister," which is also in the appendix of Weiss. Weiss is the authoritative biographer, but Frothingham's is a more compact narrative. See T. W. Higginson's paper on his death, in the Atlantic monthly, Oct., 1860. There are full references in Allibone.

PARKHURST, John Lucas. Elements of moral philosophy. 2d edition. Boston, 1832. 216 pp. 12°. 1537.14

PARKMAN, Francis, *D.D.*, *compiler*. Offering of sympathy to parents bereaved of their children, and to others under affliction. Boston, 1830. xvii, 224+ pp. 18° .... 1538.4 and 5819.19

PARKMAN, Francis, *jr.* The conspiracy of Pontiac and the Indian war after the conquest of Canada. 6th edition, revised, with additions. Boston, 1870. 2 v. Maps. 12° 5015.4

— France and England in North America. Boston, 1871–74. 4 v. 12° 5015.5

Contents. — Vol. I. Pioneers of France in the New World. II. The Jesuits in North America in the seventeenth century. III. The discovery of the Great West. IV. The old régime in Canada.

Note. — Parkman's histories constitute the best narrative of events connected with the French settlements of North America, and England's forcible wresting of them from France. When this series of histories is complete, and the final end of French power on this continent portrayed, the reader will find the "Conspiracy of Pontiac" a proper sequel, which in its introduction epitomizes the preceding series, and then in its text narrates the last great effort of the Indians east of the Mississippi to rid themselves of the yoke put upon them by the Europeans and the colonists.

— The Oregon trail: sketches of prairie and Rocky-mountain life. 4th edition, revised. Boston, 1872. xii, 381 pp. 12° 5015.3

PARKMAN, George. Bemis, G. Report of the case of John W. Webster, indicted for the murder of. Boston, 1850. 8° 1530.1

— Stone, J. W. Report of the trial of J. W. Webster, indicted for the murder of. Boston, 1850. 8° 631.5

PARKS, Luther. Report on spotted fever or cerebro-spinal miningitis in Massachusetts. (*In* Massachusetts medical society. Publications) 6021.4

PARKWATER; or, told in the twilight. Wood, E. P. Leipzig 333.22.1

— *Same.* Philadelphia 521.13

PARLIAMENTARY logick. Hamilton, W. G. London, 1808. 16° 5416.3

PARLIAMENTARY practice, Manual of. Cushing, L. S. Boston, 1868. 16° 1929.1

PARLOA, Marie. The Appledore cook book. Boston [*cop.* 1872]. 204 pp. 16° 6426.2

PARLOR amusements for the young folks. Bartlett, G. B. Boston, 1875. 16° 1517.5

PARLOR magician, The. Illustrated. New York [*cop.* 1863]. 126 pp. 12° 1515.8

PARLOR tricks with cards. With 70 engravings. New York [*cop.* 1863]. 130 [118] pp. 16° .. 1516.23

PARLOUR menagerie, The. Hogg, J. London, 1875. Sm. 8° 1522.11

PARNASSUS. [Poems by various authors.] Emerson, R. W., *editor*. Boston, 1875. 8° 5214.5

PARR, Harriet. (*Holme Lee.*) Basil Godfrey's caprice 314.1

— The beautiful Miss Barrington 315.28

— Ben Milner's wooing 327.26

Shelf. No.

PARR, Harriet, *continued.*
— For richer, for poorer........................ 315.29
— Her title of honour 314.2
— Katharine's trial............................. 339.15
— Life and death of Jeanne d'Arc, called *the maid.* London, 1866. 2 v. Portrait. Sm. 8° 1225.8
— Sylvan Holt's daughter........................ 733.12
— The vicissitudes of Bessie Fairfax. Leipzig 329.24
— *Same.* Philadelphia.......................... 726.26
PARR, Louisa. Dorothy Fox 314.13
— The Gosau smithy and other stories 335.18
— Leisure hour series. Hero Carthew 728.5
— The Prescotts of Pamphillon.................. 329.22
PARRA Sastha. Carleton, W. 518.4
PARSONS, Benjamin. The Christian layman: or, the doctrine of the trinity fully considered, and adjudged according to the Bible. Mobile, 1840. vii, 271 pp. 12°..........................5815.16
— Christian views: discourses. Boston, 1848. 300 pp. 12°...................................1524.16
PARSONS, Theophilus, *the younger.* Memoir of Theophilus Parsons, chief justice of Massachusetts; with notices of some of his contemporaries. Boston, 1859. viii, 476 pp. Sm. 8° 1031.1
PARSONS, Usher. Boylston prize dissertations. Boston, 1839. 248+ pp. 8°...................6011.12

Contents. — Inflammation of the periosteum; Eneuresis irritata; Cutaneous diseases; Cancer of the breast; Remarks on malaria.

PARTHIA, The sixth great oriental monarchy; or, the geography, history, and antiquities of. Rawlinson, G. London, 1873. 8°................ 5932.6
PARTINGTONIAN patchwork. [Humorous miscellany.] Shillaber, B. P. Boston, 1873. 12°.......... 736.28
PARTISAN, The. Simms, W. G...................... 716.23
PARTON, James. Famous Americans of recent times. Boston, 1871. 473 pp. Portrait. 8° 1214.14

Contents. — H. Clay; D. Webster; J. C. Calhoun; J. Randolph; S. Girard and his college; J. G. Bennett and the New York herald; C. Goodyear; H. W. Beecher and his church; C. Vanderbilt; T. Durr; J. J. Astor.

— General Butler in New Orleans. History of the administration of the department of the Gulf in 1862. 10th edition. New York, 1864. 661 [659] pp. Portraits. 12° 815.2
— The humorous poetry of the English language, from Chaucer to Saxe. 11th edition. Boston, 1872. 689 pp. Portraits. 12°..............1612.31
— Life and times of Aaron Burr. 14th edition. New York, 1861. 706 pp. Portraits. 12°...1223.10
— Life and times of Benjamin Franklin. New York, 1864. 2 v. Portraits. 12° 1212.2
— Life of Andrew Jackson. New York, 1861. 3 v. Portraits. 12°................................ 1212.1
— Life of Horace Greeley. Boston, 1869. 598 pp. Portraits. 12° 5023.6
— Life of Thomas Jefferson. Boston, 1874. vi, 764 pp. Portrait. 8° 1215.1
— Topics of the time. Boston, 1871. 401 pp. 12°. 1935.3
PARTON, Sara Payson. (*Fanny Fern.*) Folly as it flies; hit at. New York, 1872. 355 pp. 12°. 524.19
PASCAL, Blaise. Provincial letters. A new translation with historical introduction and notes. By Thomas M'Crie. Preceded by a life of Pascal, a critical essay, and a biographical notice. Edited by O. W. Wight. New York, 1872. 470 pp. 12° 5536.9
PASCAL, Jaqueline. Cousin, V., and others. New York, 1854. 12°..........................1226.10
PASCARÈL. Rame, L. de la. Leipzig............. 329.7
— *Same.* Philadelphia.......................... 528.7
PASSAGES from the diary of a late physician. [Novel.] Warren, S. Leipzig, 1844. 2 v. in 1. Sq. 16° 317.3
PASSAVANT, Johann David. Raphael of Urbino and his father Giovanni Santi. Illustrated. London, 1872. x, 313 pp. L. 8°................. 6211.2
PASSING the portal; or, a girl's struggle. An autobiography. Victor, M. V. New York, 1876. 12° 532.19
PASSION and principle. Grey, *Mrs*................ 530.4

PASSION play, The, at Ober-Ammergau, in the summer of 1871. Molloy, G. Boston, 1872. 4° .. 5735.9

Note. — Dramatic representations of the events of Passion week as held at Ober-Ammergau every tenth year, in fulfilment of a vow by the villagers. Beside the book above named, see Andersen's "Pictures of travel" [426.17]; Harper's monthly, vol. 42; and the description in the novel "Quits" [317.21]. Also Contemporary review, vol. 18.

PASTA, André. Traité des pertes de sang chez les femmes enceintes. Traduit de l'Italien avec des notes; par J. L. Alibert. Paris, 1797. 2 v. 8° 6014.2
PASTOR'S, A, sketches. Spencer, I. S. New York, 1857. 12°..................................1535.17
PATAGONIA. At home with the Patagonians. Musters, G. C. London, 1873. Sm. 8°........... 5036.5
PATENTS. *See* UNITED STATES.
PATER, Walter H. Studies in the history of the renaissance. London, 1873. xiv, 213+ pp. Sm. 8°...................................... 5925.2
PATER mundi. Burr, E. F. Boston, 1872, 73. 2 v. Sm. 8°......................................1527.11
PARTHENIA: or, the last days of paganism. [Julian the apostate.] Lee, E. B. Boston, 1858. 12°. 737.11
PATHETISM. Sunderland, L. R. New York, 1843. 12°.. 1536.9
PATHFINDER, The. Cooper, J. F. 525.5
PATHOLOGICAL histology, Rudiments of. Wedl, C. London, 1855. 8° 6013.18
PATHOLOGY. Billard, C. M. Treatise on the diseases of infants. New York, 1839. 8° 6022.10
— Green, T. H. An introduction to. Philadelphia, 1871. 8°...................................... 6021.9
— Paget, J. Lectures on surgical pathology. Philadelphia, 1854. 8° 6012.3

See also Anatomy, Disease, Ear, Eye, Hygiene, Nerves, Surgery, Venereal diseases.

PATIENCE of hope, The. Greenwell, D. Boston, 1862. Sm. 8°.............................. 1535.7
PATIENCE Hathaway. Bradley, W. I.............. 913.8
PATIENCE Strong's outings. Whitney, A. D. T..... 734.6
PATMORE, Coventry (Kearsey Dighton). The angel in the house. Boston, 1856. 2 v. 16° 1612.10

Contents. — Vol. I. The betrothal. II. The espousals.

— The victories of love. Boston, 1862. 96 pp. 16°. 1612.6
PATRIARCHS and prophets, Legends of the. Baring-Gould, S. New York, 1872. Sm. 8°.......... 5814.5
PATRICIA Kemball. Linton, E. L. Leipzig 330.9
— *Same.* Philadelphia............................ 714.13
PATRICIUS, *St., of Ireland.* Life of Saint Patrick. Cusack, M. F. New York, 1870. 4° 5420.2
PATTERSON, Lawson B. Twelve years in the mines of California. Cambridge, 1862. 108 pp. 12°. 417.3
PATTERSON, Robert. A narrative of the campaign in the Shenandoah, in 1861. Philadelphia, 1865. 128, 194+ pp. Portrait. Map. 8° ..5013.20
PATTESON, John Coleridge. Page, H. A. Noble workers. London, 1875. Sm. 8°............. 5936.3
— Yonge, C. M. Life of. London, 1875. 2 v. 8°. 5337.5
PATTISON, Mark. Tendencies of religious thought in England, 1688-1750. (*In* Essays and reviews)... 1538.3
— *Same.* (*In* Hedge, F. H. Recent inquiries in theology)....................1526.24 and 5814.15
PATTY. Macquoid, K. S.......................... 313.15
PAUL, *St.* St. Paul and protestantism. Arnold, M. London, 1870. Sm. 8°........................5815.24
PAUL the peddler. Alger, H., *jr*.................. 934.10
PAUL Clifford. Bulwer-Lytton, E. (G. E.) L....... 336.2
PAUL Ferroll. Clive, C........................... 310.7
PAUL Gosslett's confessions. Lever, C. (J.)........ 332.13
PAUL Massie. MacCarthy, J...................... 723.14
PAUL Prescott's charge. Alger, H., *jr*............. 924.25
PAULDING, James Kirke. John Bull in America; or, the new Munchausen. 2d edition. New York, 1825. xviii, 228 pp. 12° 538.11
— *joint author.* Salmagundi. *See* IRVING, William. 715.4 and 1815.7
PAULE Méré. Cherbuliez, V. Paris, 1865. 18° ..5536.16

Shelf. No.

PAULI, Reinhold. Life of Alfred the great. From the German. Appended Alfred's Anglo-Saxon version of Orosius. With a literal English translation, and an Anglo-Saxon alphabet and glossary. By B. Thorpe. London, 1857. ix, 582 pp. 1 plate. Sm. 8° 5427.5
PAUSANIAS the Spartan. An unfinished historical romance. Bulwer-Lytton, E. (G. E.) L. Leipzig 336.22
— *Same.* New York 733.19
PAUTET, J. F. Jules. Manuel d'économie politique. Paris, 1835. 252 pp. 24°. [Manuel Roret] .. 5829.1
PAXTON, Philip, *pseud.* *See* HAMMETT, Samuel A.
PAYN, James. At her mercy. Leipzig 319.19
— *Same.* New York 732.30
— The best of husbands. Leipzig 319.27
— *Same.* New York 731.35
— Cecil's tryst 310.10
— The Clyffards of Clyffe 522.24
— Found dead 312.19
— Gwendoline's harvest 312.24
— Halves. Leipzig 334.2
— *Same.* New York 530.14
— In the heart of a hill and other stories 312.28
— Like father, like son 312.3
— Lost Sir Massingberd. A romance of real life ... 522.25
— Married beneath him 522.21
— Murphy's master 339.14
— Not wooed, but won 314.5
— Walter's word. Leipzig 331.12
— *Same.* New York 720.10
PAYNE, A. M. Mitchell. Rhoda's corner. [Juvenile] 1118.7
PEABODY, Andrew Preston. Christianity and science. A series of lectures. New York, 1874. viii, 287 pp. 12° 6326.17
— Lectures on Christian doctrine. Boston, 1844. 227+ pp. 12° 5815.20
— Sermons connected with the re-opening of the church of the South parish, in Portsmouth, N. H. Portsmouth, 1859. 112 pp. 16° 5818.7
PEABODY, Elizabeth Palmer. Record of Mr. Alcott's school, exemplifying the principles and methods of moral culture. 3d edition, revised. Boston, 1874. 297 pp. Wood-cut. 16° 1937.3
PEABODY, Ephraim. Christian days and thoughts. Boston, 1858. 304 pp. 16° 6328.13
PEABODY, George. Account of the proceedings at the dinner given by [him] to the Americans connected with the Great exhibition. Stevens, H. London, 1851. 8° 1923.2
— Proceedings at the reception and dinner in honor of, Oct. 9, 1856. *See* DANVERS, *Mass.* 612.6
— Proceedings in relation to the donation of. *See* DANVERS, *Mass.* 5222.2
PEABODY, Oliver William Bourn. Life of Israel Putnam. (*In* Sparks, J. Library of American biography) 5028.1.7
PEABODY, William Bourn Oliver. Life of Alexander Wilson. (*In* Sparks, J. Library of American biography) 5028.1.2
— Life of David Brainerd. (*In* Sparks, J. Library of American biography) 5028.1.8
— Literary remains. Edited by E. Peabody. Boston, 1850. 448 pp. Portrait. 12° 1813.10
— Sermons. With a memoir, by his brother. Boston, 1849. cxli, 259+ pp. 12° 6326.7
PEACOCK, George. Life of Thomas Young. London, 1855. xi, 514+ pp. Portrait. 8° 5421.3
PEAKE, Richard Brinsley. Amateurs and actors: a musical farce. New York, N. D. 25 pp. 12° . 1635.5
PEAKS, passes and glaciers. A series of excursions by members of the Alpine club. Ball, J., *editor.* London, 1860. Sm. 8° 5717.1
PEARD, Francis Mary. One year 314.15
— The rose-garden 314.14
— Thorpe Regis. Boston 727.28
— *Same.* Leipzig 329.26
— Unawares 331.1
PEARL, The, of Orr's island. [Coast of Maine story.] Stowe, H. (E.) B. 527.20

Shelf.

PEARSON, C. H. Frontier series. The cabin on the prairie 937
— - The young pioneers of the North-west 937
PEARSON, Hugh. Life and writings of Claudius Buchanan. Boston, 1818. 444+ pp. 12° 122
PEARSON, John. Principles of surgery. Boston, 1832. 263 pp. 8° 601
PEASANT life in Germany. Johnson, A. C. New York, 1859. 12° 82
PEASE, Giles. Ninetieth birthday gathering of Rev. Charles Cleveland, June 21, 1862. Boston, 1862. 64 pp. 1 plate. Portrait. 16° ... 101
PECK, Jesse T. The true woman; or, life and happiness at home and abroad. New York [*cop.* 1857]. 400 pp. 16° 173
PÉDRONI, P. M. Manuel des falsifications des drogues simples et composées. Orné de figures. Paris, 1848. vi, 296 pp. 24°. [Manuel Roret] 643
PEELE, George. Dramatic and poetical works. *See* GREENE, Robert 562
PEEP o' day, The. Banim, J. 51
PEEPS into the human hive. [London.] Wynter, A. London, 1874. 2 v. Sm. 8° 643
PEERLESS, A, wife. Mackarness, M. A. 31
PEET, Stephen. History of the presbyterian and congregational churches and ministers in Wisconsin. Milwaukee, 1851. 208 pp. Sm. 12°. 153
PEG Woffington. Reade, C. Boston 52
— *Same.* Leipzig .... 316.

Note.— Theatrical story, time of Colley Cibber.

PEIRCE, Benjamin. Elementary treatise on sound. Boston, 1836. lvi, 220 pp. Folded plate. 8°. 643
PEIRCE, Ebenezer Weaver. Contributions biographical, genealogical and historical. Boston, 1874. ix, 443 pp. Illustrations. 8° .... 61(

Note.— Contains genealogies of the following families:— Barnaby, Bartlett, Booth, Brownell, Caswell, Gardiner, Godfrey, Harlow, Haskins, Howland, Macomber, Pearce, Richmond, Rogers, Rounsevill, Sheffield, Shelley, Warren, Weaver, and Williams.

— The Peirce family of the Old Colony: or the lineal descendants of Abraham Peirce. Boston, 1870. xx, 490 pp. 8° .... 61(
PEKIN. Beauvoir, L., *comte* de. Pekin, Jeddo, and San Francisco. London, 1872. 16° .... 5935.
— Lander, S. W. Spectacles for young eyes .... 916.
PELHAM. Bulwer-Lytton, E. (G. E.) L. .... 33(
PELLÉ, Clément, *joint author.* Angleterre, Écosse et Irelande. *See* GALIBERT, Léon 5911
PELLEGRIN, V. Theory and practice of linear perspective. From the French. New York [London], 1873. vii, 51 pp. 1 folded plate. 16° .. 6218
PELOPONNESIAN war, History of the. Thucydides. London, 1868, 70. 2 v. Sm. 8° 6115
PELOPONNESUS, An excursion in the. Wyse, *Sir* T. London, 1865. 2 v. 8° 5930
PEMBROKE, *Earl of.* *See* HERBERT, George Robert Charles.
PENCILLINGS by the way. Willis, N. P. New York, 1844. L. 8° .... 43(

Note.— Travels, with sketches of foreign society.

PENDENNIS, History of. Thackeray, W. M. Leipzig. 335
— *Same.* (*In his* Works.) London 513.1
— *Same.* New York .... 182(
PENINSULAR war. History of the war in the peninsula, 1807–14. Napier, *Sir* W. F. P. New York, 1853. L. 8° 5920

See also Spain.

PENMANSHIP. Manual of social and business forms: a guide to correct writing. Hill, T. E. Chicago, 1876. 4° 5821
PENN, William. Creeds should be expressed in the language of Scripture; The sandy foundation shaken. (*In* Sparks, J. Collection of essays and tracts in theology) 1918.9
PENNINGTON, Arthur Robert. The life and character of Erasmus. London, 1875. xvi, 383 pp. Portrait. 8° 5726
PENNOT, *Rev.* Peter, *pseud.* *See* ROUND, William M. F.

Shelf. No.

PENNSYLVANIA pilgrim, The. [Poem.] Whittier, J. G. Boston, 1872. 16° 1616.10

PENNY cyclopædia, The. *See* SOCIETY for the diffusion of useful knowledge, *London*. London, 1833–36. 5 v. L. 8° ....................*R.R., F.2.2

PENOBSCOT, *Maine*, History of. Wheeler, G. A. Bangor, 1875. 8° 813.2

PENRUDDOCKE. Aidé, H. Leipzig, 1873. 2 v. in 1. Sq. 16° 329.2

PENTAGÖET, *Maine*, History of. Wheeler, G. A. Bangor, 1875. 8° 813.2

PENTECOST. [A poem.] Little, S. L. Newport, R. I., 1869. Sq. 16° 1617.7

PEOPLE's, The, magazine. Vol. 1, 2. [Boston], 1833–35. 2 v. in 1. L. 8° 1432.2

PEPPER, John Henry. The boy's playbook of science. New edition. Illustrated. London [1861]. vii, 440 pp. Sm. 8° 1524.18

PEPYS, Samuel. Diary and correspondence. The diary deciphered by J. Smith from the original shorthand MS. With a life and notes by Richard lord Braybrooke. New edition. London, 1869. 4 v. Portraits. Sm. 8° 5627.1

PERCIVAL, James Gates. Poems. New York, 1823. 396+ pp. 8° 1611.4

PERCIVAL Keene. Marryat, F. 337.5

PERCY, John. Metallurgy: the art of extracting metals from their ores. Introduction, refractory materials, and fuel. Revised and enlarged edition. With illustrations. London, 1875. xii, 596 pp. 8° 6631.10

PERCY, Sholto and Reuben, *pseud.* *See* BYERLEY, Thomas, and ROBERTSON, James Cragie.

PERCY, Thomas. Reliques of ancient English poetry; together with some few of later date. Leipzig, 1866. 3 v. in 1. Sq. 16° 1613.12

PEREGRINE Pickle, The adventures of. Smollett, T. (G.) 315.17

PERFECT Adonis, A. Harris, M. 723.10

PERFECT love casteth out fear. Washburn, K. S. ... 723.9

PERFUMERY. Clifford, F. S. A romance of perfume lands. With facts about perfumes and articles used in the toilet. Boston, 1875. 16° 733.13

— Cooley, A. J. Hand-book of perfumes, cosmetics and other toilet articles. Philadelphia, 1873. Sm. 8° 1514.13

PERICHOLE, La. Offenbach, J. (*In* Ditson, O., and co. Standard opera librettos) 6233.3.5

PERILS, The, of orphanhood. Robertson, M. M. ... 714.33

PERIODICALS. The academy. Vol. 5–8. London, 1874, 75. 4 v. 4° 6721.1

— The Aldine. Vol. 6–8. New York, 1873–75. 3 v. F° 6520.1

— All the year round. Conducted by Charles Dickens. New series. Vol. 6. London, 1871. 8°. 1334.1

— The American agriculturist. Vol. 31, 32. New York, 1872, 73. 2 v. in 1. 4° 1432.3

— American annual cyclopædia and register of important events. 1861–72. New York, 1872. 12 v. 8° ....................*R.R., C.3.1

— The American naturalist. Vol. 4, 7–9. Salem, 1871–75. 4 v. 8° 6523.1

— The American protestant magazine. Vol. 1–4. New York [1845–48]. 4 v. 8° 1336.2

— The analectic magazine. Vol. 1–4. Philadelphia, 1813, 14. 4 v. 8° 1336.1

— Annual of scientific discovery: or, year-book of facts in science and art, 1850–59. Boston, 1850–59. 10 v. 12° 1524.6

— Appletons' journal of literature, science, and art. Vol. 9–14. New York, 1873–75. 6 v. 4° 1332.1

— Appletons' juvenile annual for 1871. New York, 1871. 12° 933.8

— Army and navy official gazette. Vol. 1. 1863–64. Washington, 1864. 4° 6910.4

— L'art. Revue hebdomadaire illustrée. Tome 1, 3. Paris, 1875. 2 v. F° 5310.1

— The art-journal. New series. Vol. 12–14. London, 1873–75. 3 v. 4° 6521.1

— The athenæum. Vol. 1–6. London, 1873–75. 6 v. 4° 6732.1

Shelf. No.

PERIODICALS, *continued*.

— Atlantic monthly. Vol. 1–36. Boston, 1857–75. 36 v. 8° 1425.1

— Ballou's monthly magazine. Vol. 36–42. Boston, 1872–75. 7 v. 8° 1433.2

— The Bay state democrat. August 24—Nov. 9, 1838. Boston, 1838. 4° 6730.38

— Bibliotheca sacra, and theological eclectic. Vol. 30–32. Andover, 1873–75. 3 v. 8° 6736.1

— The Boston pearl and galaxy. Vol. 21. Boston, 1838. F° 6730.34

— Carey's library of choice literature. The literary chronicle. Part 1, 2. Philadelphia, 1836. 2 v. in 1. 8° 6730.42

— The catholic world. Vol. 16–22. New York, 1873–75. 7 v. 8° 6715.1

— Christian disciple. Vol. 1–4; new series, vol. 1, 2. Boston, 1813–20. 6 v. 8° 6324.3

— Christian examiner and theological review. Vol. 36–41. Boston, 1844–46. 6 v. in 3. 8° 6324.4

— The Christian monitor. Vol. 1–10. Boston, 1806–11. 10 v. 12° 1327.1

— Common school journal. Vol. 1–6, 8–11. Boston, 1839–49. 10 v. 8° 1335.1

— Congregational quarterly. Vol. 15–17. Boston, 1873–75. 3 v. 8° 6716.1

— The contemporary review. Vol. 22–26. London, 1873–75. 5 v. 8° 6511.1

— Cornhill magazine. Vol. 1–32. London, 1860–75. 32 v. 8° 6534.1

— Deutsche Rundschau. Vol. 1–4. Berlin, 1874, 75. 4 v. 8° 1422.5

— Dexter Smith's musical, literary, dramatic and art paper. Vol. 3–6. Boston, 1873, 74. 4 v. in 2. 4°. 1331.1

— Dublin review. New series. Vol. 20–25. London, 1873–75. 6 v. 8° 6517.1

— Dublin university magazine. Vol. 81–86. Dublin, 1873–75. 6 v. 8° 6537.1

— Eclectic magazine of foreign literature, science, and art. New series. Vol. 16–22. New York, 1872–75. 7 v. 8° 1314.1

— Englishwoman's domestic magazine. Vol. 15–19. London, 1873–75. 5 v. 4° 6532.1

— The essayist. Vol. 2. Boston, 1830. 4° 6730.39

— Every Saturday. Vol. 1, 3, 6, 7; new series, vol. 1–4; new series, vol. 1, 2. Boston, 1866–74. 10 v. 4° 1313.1

— The extra globe. Vol. 6, 7. Washington, 1840, 41. 2 v. 4° 6730.40

— The folio. Vol. 12. Boston, 1875. 4° 1331.2

— Fortnightly review. New series. Vol. 13–18. London, 1873–75. 6 v. 8° 6713.1

— Fraser's magazine. Vol. 7–12. London, 1873–75. 6 v. 8° 6718.1

— The galaxy. Vol. 1, 2, 5–12, 14–20. New York, 1866–75. 17 v. 8° 1428.1

— Die Gartenlaube. 1873. Leipzig, 1873. L. 4°. 1330.2

— Gazette des beaux-arts. Vol. 11, 12. Paris, 1875. 2 v. L. 8° 5322.1

— Die Gegenwart. Vol. 7, 8. Berlin, 1875. 2 v. in 1. 4° 6722.1

— Godey's lady's book. Vol. 85–91. Philadelphia, 1872–75. 7 v. 8° 1412.1

— Good words. Vol. 14, 15. London, 1873, 74. 2 v. 8° 1338.1

— The graphic. Vol. 8–12. London, 1873–75. 5 v. F°. 6710.1

— Harper's bazar. Vol. 6–8. New York, 1873, 74. 3 v. F° 1430.1

— Harper's new monthly magazine. Vol. 1–51. New York, 1850–75. 51 v. 8° 1415.1

— Harper's weekly. Vol. 16–19. New York, 1872–75. 4 v. F° 1311.1

— The health reformer. Vol. 3–5. Battle Creek, 1868–71. 3 v. 8° 6031.1

— Hearth and home. Vol. 4–7. New York, 1872–75. 4 v. F° 1330.1

— Herald of health. Vol. 55–60. New York, 1873–75. 6 v. in 3. 8° 1325.1

— Hunt's merchants' magazine, and commercial review. Vol. 1–34, 41–43. New York, 1840–60. 37 v. 8° 1322.1

Shelf. No.

PERIODICALS, *continued*.
— Hunt's merchants' magazine year-book. 1871. New York [1871]. 8° 1322.2
— Illustrated London news. Vol. 1-67. London, 1842-75. 67 v. F° 5134.1
— *Same*. Vol. 28, 31. London, 1856, 57. 2 v. F°. 1410.1
— L'illustration. Tome 49, 51, 66. Paris, 1867, 68, 75. 3 v. F° 5321.1
— Illustrirte Zeitung. B. 61-65. Leipzig, 1873-75. 5 v. F° 6730.1
— International review. Vol. 1. New York [1874]. 8° 6512.1
— Lippincott's magazine. Vol. 1-16. Philadelphia, 1868-75. 16 v. 8° 1416.1
— The literary world. Vol. 3, 4. Boston [1872-74]. 2 v. 4° 1434.1
— Littell's living age. Vol. 1-36; 4th series, vol. 26, 27; 5th series, vol. 1-12. Boston, 1844-75. 50 v. 8° 1326.1
— The little wanderers' advocate. Vol. 8, 10, 11. Boston, 1872-75. 3 v. 8° 1335.2
— London quarterly review. Vol. 76. American edition. New York, 1845. 8° 1422.3
— Macmillan's magazine. Vol. 28-32. London, 1873-75. 5 v. 8° 6527.1
— The Massachusetts teacher. Vol. 10-21. Boston, 1857-68. 12 v. 8° 1324.1
— Mechanics' magazine. Vol. 1-6, 19, 22. London, 1830-35. 8 v. 8° 6421.1
— Mechanics' magazine. Vol. 5-9. New York, 1835-37. 5 v. in 4. 8° 6421.2
— Methodist quarterly review. Vol. 31, 41, 44, 45, 55-57. New York, 1857-75. 7 v. 8° 6727.1
— Le monde illustré. Vol. 23, 24, 25, 27, 28, 32, 33. Paris, 1868-73. 7 v. F° 5320.1
— The monthly miscellany of religion and letters. Vol. 1-9. Boston, 1839-43. 9 v. in 5. 8° 6536.1
— The nation. Vol. 4-11, 13-21. New York, 1867-75. 17 v. 4° 1312.1
— Nature. A weekly illustrated journal of science. Vol. 8-12. London, 1873-75. 5 v. L. 8° 6733.1
— Naval science. Vol. 1-4. London, 1872-75. 4 v. 8°. 6714.1
— New church independent and monthly review. Vol. 22. Chicago, 1874. 8° 1323.1
— New-church magazine. Vol. 1, 2. Boston, 1873, 74. 2 v. 8° 1333.1
— New England historical and genealogical register. Vol. 1-20. Boston, 1847-66. 20 v. 8° 611.1
— The New-England magazine. Vol. 1-9. Boston, 1831-35. 9 v. 8° 1436.1
— New Jerusalem messenger. Vol. 28. New York, 1875. F° 1432.5
— New monthly magazine and literary journal. Vol. 1, 2. Philadelphia, 1821, 22. 2 v. 8° ... 1435.1
— The Norfolk argus. Vol. 1, no. 1-28. Roxbury, 1837. F° 6730.36
— The Norfolk democrat. Vol. 1, 2. Dedham, 1839-41. 2 v. in 1. F° 6730.35
— North American review. Vol. 10, 12-106, 108-114, 116-121. Boston, 1820-75. 109 v. 8° .. 5117.1
— Notes and queries. Vol. 4; 3d series, vol. 9-12; 4th series, vol. 1, 2. London, 1852, 66-68. 7 v. Sm. 4° 6735.1
— Official gazette of the United States patent office. Vol. 2-8. Washington, 1872-75. 6 v. 4° 6930.1
— Old and new. Vol. 1-11. Boston, 1870-75. 11 v. 8° 1426.1
— Oliver Optic's magazine. Our boys and girls. Vol. 11, 12. Boston, 1872, 73. 2 v. 8° 1431.1
— Our young folks. Vol. 8, 9. Boston, 1872, 73. 2 v. 8° 1433.1
— Overland monthly. Vol. 9-15. San Francisco, 1872-75. 7 v. 8° 1316.1
— Pall Mall budget. Vol. 10-14. London, 1874, 75. 5 v. F° 6720.1
— The people's magazine. Vol. 1, 2. [Boston], 1833-35. 2 v. in 1. L. 8° 1432.2
— The polyanthos enlarged. Vol. 1-4. Boston, 1812-14. 4 v. 8° 1317.1
— Popular science monthly. Vol. 3-7. New York, 1873-75. 5 v. 8° 6516.1

Shelf. No.

PERIODICALS, *continued*.
— The portfolio. Conducted by Oliver Oldschool [*pseud.* of Joseph Dennie]. New series, vol. 1-5; new [2d] series, vol. 1-6. Philadelphia, 1806-11. 11 v. 8° 1435.2
— Practical magazine. Vol. 1-5. London, 1873-75. 5 v. 4° 6510.1
— Practical mechanic and engineer's magazine. Vol. 1-4; 2d series, vol. 1, 2. Glasgow, 1842-50. 6 v. 4° 6420.5
— Practical mechanic's journal. Vol. 1-8; 2d series, vol. 1, 2. 10 v. 4° 6420.4
— Punch. Vol. 64-68. London, 1873-75. 5 v. 4°. 6531.1
— Putnam's monthly magazine. Vol. 1, 3-[10]; new series, vol. 1-6. New York, 1853-70. 15 v. 8°. 5127.1
— Quarterly review. Vol. 57, 59, 119, 134-138. London, 1836, 37, 66, 73-75. 8 v. 8° 6717.1
— Religious magazine and monthly review. Vol. 49, 50, 51, no. 1, 2. Boston, 1873, 74. 3 v. 8°. 6738.1
— Revue des deux mondes. Tome 3, 4; Seconde période, Tome 10, 49-54, 64-72, 105-108; Troisième période, Tome 1-13. Paris, 1853-76. 35 v. in 39. 8° 5315.1
— Saint Nicholas. Vol. 1. New York [1874]. 8°. 1315.1
— Salem mercury. Vol. 1-3. Salem, 1831-33. 3 v. in 1. F° 6730.37
— Saturday review. Vol. 6, 35-40. London, 1858, 73-75. 7 v. Sm. f° 6712.1
— The science record, for 1876. New York, 1876. 12° 6836.5
— Scientific American. Vol. 27, 28-33. New York, 1872-75. 7 v. F° 1320.1
— Scribner's monthly. Vol. 4-10. New York, 1872-75. 7 v. 8° 1438.1
— The spectator. Vol. 23, 24, 39, 46-48. [London], 1850, 51, 73-75. 6 v. Sm. f° 6731.1
— The spirit of the pilgrims. Vol. 1-6. Boston [1828-33]. 6 v. 8° 1321.1
— United States army and navy journal and official gazette of the regular and volunteer forces. Vol. 1, 11. New York, 1863-64, 73-74. 2 v. F°. 6530.1
— United States literary gazette. Vol. 1, 2. Boston, 1825. 2 v. 1 v. 4°; 1 v. 8° 1432.1
— Waldie's select circulating library. Vol. 10. Philadelphia, 1837. 4° 6730.41
— Westminster review. Vol. 43, no. 85; vol. 44, no. 86, 87; vol. 45, no. 88; new series, vol. 43-47. London, 1845, 46, 73-75. 6 v. 8° 6737.1
— Youth's companion. Vol. 1-3, 5, 7-14, 16-19, 23-29, 32, 46. Boston, 1827-73. 25 v. 4° ... 1420.1

PERKINS, Charles C. Italian sculptors: a history of sculpture in Northern, Southern, and Eastern Italy. With engravings. London, 1868. 326+ pp. L. 8° 6210.2
PERKINS, *Mrs.* [Elvira?]. Harp of the willows. [Poems.] Boston, 1859. 152 pp. Illustrated. 16° 1618.2
PERKINS, Frederic Beecher. Scrope; or, the lost library. A novel of New York and Hartford. 732.34
PERKINS, Thomas Handasyd, Memoir of. Cary, T. G. Boston, 1856. 8° 5021.12
PERPETUAL curate, The. Oliphant, M. (O. W.) 328.12
PERRIER, Amelia. A good match 725.31
PERROT, A. M. Manuel du graveur. Nouvelle édition très-augmentée, par F. Malepeyre. Paris, 1844. ix, 270+ pp. Folded plates. 24°. [Manuel Roret] 6439.4
PERRY, Arthur Latham. Elements of political economy. 13th edition, revised. New York, 1876. xxiv, 543 pp. 8° 5824.3
PERRY, Bela C. Treatise on the human hair and its diseases. New Bedford, 1859. xi, 192 pp. 12°. 1525.4
PERRY, Nora. Bessie's trials at boarding-school 1115.18
PERRY, Oliver Hazard, Life of. Mackenzie, A. S. New York [*cop.* 1840]. 2 v. 16° 1019.1
PERSIA. Cunynghame, *Sir* A. T. Travels on the frontiers of. London, 1872. 8° 5931.8
— Markham, C. R. A general sketch of the history of. London, 1874. 8° 5911.4
— Mounsey, A. H. Journey through the Caucasus and the interior of. London, 1872. 8° 5931.7

Shelf. No.

PERSIA, *continued.*

— Rawlinson, G. The five great monarchies of the ancient Eastern world; or, the history, geography, and antiquities of. London, 1871. 3 v. 8°. 5922.3

— – The seventh great oriental monarchy; or, the geography, history, and antiquities of the Sassanian or new Persian empire. London, 1876. 8°. 5923.11

— Rawlinson, *Sir* H. (C.) England and Russia in the East. A series of papers on the political and geographical condition of Central Asia. London, 1875. 8° ... 5921.5

— Rollin, C. Ancient history of the Medes and Persians. Vol. 1–4, 6–8. Boston, 1807. 8°... 5913.1

PERSPECTIVE. Pyne, G. Perspective for beginners. London, 1870. 12° ... 1716.29

— Ruskin, J. Elements of. New York, 1871. 12°. 6236.14

See also Linear perspective.

PERSUASION. Austen, J. Boston ... 515.5

— *Same.* Leipzig ... 325.24

PERU. Hutchinson, T. J. Two years in, with exploration of its antiquities. London, 1873. 2 v. 8°. 5932.9

— Prescott, W. H. History of the conquest of. Philadelphia, 1873. 2 v. 8° ... 5914.3

— Searching for the quinine plant in Peru. (*In* Many lands and many people) ... 431.3

— Wise, H. A. Los Gringos; or, wanderings in. New York, 1849. 12° ... 435.4

Note. — For the authorities on the ancient civilization of Peru, see the Library Bulletin for April, 1876.

PET; or, pastimes and penalties. Haweis, H. R.... 912.17

PETER, *St., the apostle.* Rodrigues-Henriques, J. H. Saint Pierre. Paris, 1871. 8° ... 5813.10

PETER I, *Alexiowitsch, the great, emperor of Russia.* Abbott, J. History of ... 915.4

— Barrow, *Sir* J. Life of. New York, 1856. 16°. 1228.8

See also Russia.

PETER Clinton. Wise, D. ... 932.41

PETER Simple. Marryat, F. ... 337.10

PETER the whaler. Kingston, W. H. G. ... 922.4

PETIT, J. A. History of Mary Stuart, queen of Scots. From the original unpublished manuscript by Charles De Flandre. London, 1874. 2 v. Portraits. 4° ... 5410.2

Note. — The author's sympathies are with Mary Stuart, whose innocence he asserts. See *note* under Mary, queen of Scots.

PETITS oiseaux, Les: comédie. Labiche, E. (M.), and Delacour, A. (C. L.) Boston, 1867. 12°. 2015.2

PÉTRA, Le. Lenoir, P. Paris, 1872. 18° ... 5935.10

PETRELLA, Enrico. Carnival of Venice; Ione. (*In* Ditson, O., and co. Standard opera librettos).. 6233.3.6

PETRONEL. Church, F. ... 337.15

PETS, Heads and tails: studies and stories of. Lippincott, S. J. ... 921.15

PETTIGREW, A. The handy book of bees: being a practical treatise on their profitable management. 2d edition, revised. Edinburgh, 1875. xiv, 162 pp. Illustrated. Sm. 8° ... 6619.4

PETTIGREW, James Bell. International scientific series. Animal locomotion, or walking, swimming, and flying, with a dissertation on aëronautics. Illustrated. New York, 1874. xiii, 264+ pp. 12° ... 6436.14

PETTY, Henry, *marquis of Lansdowne.* *See* HAYWARD, A. Biographical and critical essays. London, 1873. 8° ... 5833.3.2

PEVERIL of the Peak. Scott, *Sir* W. Boston ... 523.1

— *Same.* Leipzig ... 324.17

PEYSTER, John Watts de. Personal and military history of Philip Kearney. New York, 1869. 512+ pp. Portrait. 8° ... 5021.6

PHANTASTES. MacDonald, G. ... 512.8

PHANTOM ship, The. Marryat, F. ... 725.17

PHARMACOPŒIA of the United States. Philadelphia, 1851. xxiii, 317 pp. 8° ... 6021.8

PHARMACY. Chemical and pharmaceutic manipulations. Morfit, C., and Mucklé, A. Philadelphia, 1849. 12° ... 6433.3

PHASES of faith. Newman, F. W. London, 1853. 12° ... 1526.29

Shelf. No.

PHÈDRE: tragédie. Racine, J. de. Théâtre complet. Paris, 1870. 12° ... 5537.3

— Phädra. Schiller, (J. C.) F. von. Werke. Stuttgart, 1867. 8° ... 5734.1.7

PHELPS, Agnes. One year at our boarding-school... 1114.2

PHELPS, Almira Hart, *formerly Miss Lincoln.* Botany for beginners. Hartford, 1833. 256 pp. 12°. 6627.3

— *Same.* 3d edition. New York, 1838. 216 pp. Illustrated. 12° ... 1528.5

PHELPS, Austin. The still hour; or, communion with God. Boston, 1860. 136 pp. 16° ... 6328.5

PHELPS, Elizabeth Stuart. The gates ajar ... 537.9

— The gypsy series. Gypsy Breynton ... 916.21

— – Gypsy's cousin Joy ... 916.22

— – Gypsy's sowing and reaping ... 916.20

— – Gypsy's year at the golden crescent ... 916.23

— Hedged in ... 537.10

— The lady of Shalott. (*In* Johnson, (E.) R. Little classics) ... 529.4.10

— Men, women, and ghosts ... 537.8

— Mercy Gliddon's work ... 916.25

— Poetic studies. Boston, 1875. 141 pp. Sq. 16°. 1617.9

— The silent partner ... 537.11

— The Trotty book ... 932.13

— Trotty's wedding tour, and story-book ... 913.27

— What to wear. Boston, 1873. 92 pp. 12° ... 1537.7

PHEMIE Frost's experiences. Stephens, A. S. (W.). 734.22

PHENOMENA and laws of heat. Cazin, A. New York, 1872. 16° ... 1714.6

PHIL, the fiddler. Alger, H., *jr.* ... 934.30

PHILIP II, *king of Spain.* Prescott, W. H. History of the reign of. Boston, 1855, 59. 3 v. 8°... 1222.1

— Watson, R. History of. New York, 1818. 8°. 823.3

See also Spain.

PHILIP, *chief of the Wampanoags,* History of. Abbott, J. S. C. ... 914.31

Note. — The events of King Philip's war, 1675, the great uprising by the natives of New England against the English colonists, are narrated in Palfrey's "History of New England" [5016.2]; in Barry's "History of Massachusetts" [812.5]; in Austin's "History of Massachusetts" [813.19]; and they form the subject of Cooper's "Wept of Wish-ton-Wish" [525.12]. Irving delineates King Philip in his "Sketch book" [311.13; 715.6; 1815.10].

PHILIP, George, and SON, *publishers.* Philip's atlas of the counties of England, reduced from the ordnance survey. By Edward Weller. New edition, with a complete consulting index, by John Bartholomew. London, 1875. 106+ pp. 48 maps. F° ... *R.R. Desk

PHILIP, The adventures of. Thackeray, W. M. Leipzig ... 335.5

— *Same.* (*In his* Works.) London ... 513.1.6

— *Same.* New York ... 1820.2

PHILIP Augustus; or, the brothers in arms. [French history, — novel.] James, G. P. R. ... 722.7

PHILIP Earnscliffe. Edwards, A. B. ... 520.2

PHILLIPS, John L. Thomas. Site and antiquities of Athens. (*In* Many lands and many people) ... 431.3

PHILLIPS, Lawrence B. Dictionary of biographical reference. London, 1871. x, 1020+ pp. 8°. *R.R., E.3.2

PHILLIPS, Samuel March. Famous cases of circumstantial evidence. With an introduction on the theory of presumptive proof. Boston, 1873. xxxix, 153 pp. 8° ... 6313.2

PHILLIPS, Watts. For a woman's sake ... 721.5 and 731.6

PHILLIPS, Willard. Manual of political economy. Boston, 1828. 278 pp. 8° ... 5822.8

— Propositions concerning protection and free trade. Boston, 1850. xv, 233 pp. 12° ... 6435.2

PHILOJUVENIS, *pseud.* Edda; or, the tales of a grandmother. History of Denmark, from the earliest ages to the accession of the Oldenburg dynasty, A. D. 1448. London, 1875. 398+ pp. Illustrated. L. 8° ... 5712.2

PHILOSOPHERS, Lives of, of the time of George III. Brougham, H., *lord.* Edinburgh, 1872. 16°... 5614.4.1

PHILOSOPHY. Fiske, J. Outlines of cosmic philosophy, based on the doctrine of evolution, with criticisms on the positive philosophy. Boston, 1875. 2 v. 8° ... 5824.2

— Lewes, G. H. History of philosophy from Thales to Comte. London, 1871. 2 v. 8° ... 6832.1

Shelf. No.

PHILOSOPHY, *continued.*
— MacCosh, J. The Scottish philosophy, from Hutcheson to Hamilton. New York, 1875. 8°. 5821.1
— Martineau, J. Essays, philosophical and theological. Boston, 1868, 70. 2 v. 8° 5814.14
— Maurice, (J.) F. D. Moral and metaphysical philosophy. London, 1873. 2 v. 8° 5833.2
— Mill, J. S. Dissertations and discussions: political, philosophical, and historical. New York, 1874, 75. 5 v. 8° 5824.4
— Paley, W. Principles of moral and political philosophy. London, 1794. 2 v. 8° 5823.3
— Shairp, J. C. Studies in poetry and philosophy. New York, 1872. 16° 1535.14
— Spencer, H. First principles of a new system of. New York, 1873. 12° 6835.1
— – Recent discussions in. New York, 1873. 12°. 6835.2

See also Intellectual science, Moral philosophy, Physics, Political philosophy.

PHILOSOPHY, The, of eating. Bellows, A. J. New York, 1872. 16° 1523.4
PHILOSOPHY of English literature. Bascom, J. New York, 1874. 12° 5216.8
PHILOSOPHY of rhetoric. Bascom, J. Boston, 1870. 12° 1535.12
PHILOSOPHY of style. Spencer, H. New York, 1872. 12° 6126.1
PHILOTHEA. Child, L. M. 515.1
PHINEAS Finn, the Irish member. Trollope, A. 334.6
PHINEAS redux. Trollope, A. 732.14
PHIPS, *Sir* William, Life of. Bowen, F. (*In* Sparks, J. Library of American biography) 5028.1.7
PHIPSON, T. L. Phosphorescence; or, the emission of light by minerals, plants, and animals. London, 1870. xv, 210 pp. Illustrated. 16°. 6637.3
PHŒNIX, John, *pseud.* *See* DERBY, George Horatio.
PHŒNIXIANA. [Humors of California life, etc.] Derby, G. H. New York, 1869. 12° 535.14
PHONIC primer and reader. Zachos, J. C. Boston, 1864. 12° 1736.3
PHOSPHORESCENCE; or, the emission of light by minerals, plants, and animals. Phipson, T. L. London, 1870. 16° 6637.3
PHOTOGRAPHY. Ayers, G. B. How to paint photographs in water colors. Philadelphia, 1870. 12°. 6217.8
— Meteyard, E. A group of Englishmen, embracing the history of the discovery of. London, 1871. 8°. 5424.4
— Van Monckhoven, D. Popular treatise on. London, 1867. 12° 1716.19
— Vogel, H. Chemistry of. New York, 1875. 12°. 6436.16
PHRASES. Dictionary of phrase and fable. Brewer, E. C. London [1875]. 8° .........*R.R., F.3.13
PHRENOLOGY. Spurzheim, (J.) G. Outlines of. Boston, 1832. 12° 1528.10
— Wells, S. R. How to read character: a new illustrated hand-book of. New York, 1875. 12°..1525.22
PHTHISIS. Louis, P. C. A. Researches on. London, 1846. 8° 6013.6
— Rohden, L. Treatment of phthisis by baths and climate. (*In* Braun, J. On the curative effects of baths and waters) 6032.4
PHYSICAL exercises, Manual of. Wood, W. New York, 1870. 12° 1516.7
PHYSICAL geography. Abbott, J. Water and land. [Juvenile] 912.3
— Guyot, A. The earth and man: lectures on comparative physical geography, in its relation to the history of mankind. Boston, 1872. 12° 1523.15
— Macturk, J. Physical geography. New York [Glasgow], 1873. 16° 1717.7
— Marsh, G. P. The earth as modified by human action. New York, 1874. 8° 6831.2
— Maury, M. F. Physical geography of the sea. New York, 1871. 8° 1520.2
— Somerville, M. Physical geography. London, 1870. Sm. 8° 6836.2
— Wallace, A. R. The Malay archipelago: the land of the orang-utan, and the bird of paradise. New York, 1869. Sm. 8° 5934.1

See also Earth, Geography, Geology, Meteors, Physics, Volcanoes.

Shelf. No.

PHYSICIAN, The, in spite of himself: a comedy. Molière, J. B. P. Dramatic works. Edinburgh, 1876. 8° 5530.3.3
PHYSICIAN'S, A, holiday. Forbes, *Sir* J. London, 1849. 12° 226.2
PHYSICIAN'S, A, problems. [Essays.] Elam, C. Boston, 1869. 12° 1535.21
PHYSICIAN'S, A, vacation; or, a summer in Europe. Channing, W. Boston, 1856. 12° 422.21
PHYSICIAN'S, The, wife. Spangler, H. K. 723.23
PHYSICIANS. Jackson, J. Letters to a young physician. Boston, 1855. 12° .... 6021.5 and 6036.1
— – Another letter. Boston, 1861. 12° 6036.1
PHYSICS. Bagehot, W. Physics and politics. London, 1872. Sm. 8° 1526.25
— *Same.* New York, 1873. 12° 6436.2
— Blair, D. A grammar of natural and experimental philosophy. Hartford, 1824. 12° 1538.22
— Blake, J. L. Conversations on natural philosophy. Boston, 1837. 12° 1526.30
— Fontenelle, J. de. Nouveau manuel complet de physique amusante. Paris, 1850. 24° 6439.5
— Olmsted, D. A compendium of natural philosophy. New Haven, 1833. 8° 6434.2
— Quackenbos, G. P. Natural philosophy. New York, 1864. 12° 6436.5
— Rolfe, W. J., and Gillet, J. A. Natural philosophy. Boston, 1869. 12° 6436.9
— Stewart, B. Lessons in elementary physics. London, 1873. 16° 6438.6
— Tomlinson, C. Introduction to the study of natural philosophy. London, 1851. 12° 1526.17
— *Same.* London, 1870. 12° 1716.30
— Whewell, W. Astronomy and general physics considered with reference to natural theology. Philadelphia, 1833. 12° 6438.5

See also Astronomy, Electricity, Force, Heat, Molecular physics, Physical geography, Science, Sound.

PHYSIOGNOMY. Darwin, C. (R.) The expression of the emotions in man and animals. New York, 1873. Sm. 8° 6615.2
— Redfield, J. W. Comparative physiognomy. New York, 1852. 8° 1521.15
— Wells, S. R. How to read character: a new illustrated hand-book of. New York, 1875. 12°... 1525.22
— – New physiognomy, or, signs of character. New York, 1874. 12° 1521.13
PHYSIOLOGY. Beecher, C. E. Physiology and calisthenics. New York, 1858. 16° 6038.2
— Bichat, (M. F.) X. Physiological researches upon life and death. Philadelphia, 1809. 8°. 6023.10
— Carpenter, W. B. Principles of human physiology. Philadelphia, 1868. 8° 6012.6
— Combe, A. The principles of physiology applied to the preservation of health, and to the improvement of physical and mental education. New York, 1855. 12° 1718.2
— Cutter, C. Anatomy and physiology. Boston, 1847. 12° 6037.3
— Edwards, H. M. Outlines of. Boston, 1841. 8°. 6021.15
— Flint, A., *jr.* The physiology of man. New York, 1873. 4 v. 8° 6011.4
— Hinton, J. Physiology for practical use. New York, 1874. 12° 6035.5
— Lawson, H. Manual of popular physiology. New York [London], 1873. 16° 1713.2
— Le Pileur, A. Wonders of the human body. New York, 1871. 10° 1714.14
— Lewes, G. H. The physiology of common life. Leipzig, 1860. 2 v. in 1. Sq. 16° 1528.1
— Macé, J. The servants of the stomach. New York, 1868. 16° 1536.7
— Paine, M. Medical and physiological commentaries. New York, 1840. 2 v. 8° 6012.5
— Roget, P. M. Animal and vegetable physiology considered with reference to natural theology. Philadelphia, 1836. 2 v. 8° 6032.2
— Unzer, J. A. Principles of. London, 1851. 8° 6013.15

See also Anatomy, Bioplasm, Eye, Medicine, Nerves, Pathology.

Shelf. No.

PIANO and song. Wieck, J. G. F. Boston, 1875. 12° ... 6234.5

PIANO-FORTE, Rudiments of the art of playing the. Spencer, C. C. London, 1870. 12° ... 1716.36

PICARD, Louis Benoît. Der Neffe als Onkel. *See* SCHILLER, (J. C.) F. von. Werke. Stuttgart, 1867. 8° ... 5734.1.7

PICCIOLA. Saintine, (J.) X. B. New York, 1858. 12° ... 2015.4

PICCOLOMINI, Die. Schiller, (J. C.) F. von. Boston, 1865. 12° ... 5735.3

— *Same.* (*In his* Works.) London, 1872. Sm. 8°. 827.26

— *Same.* (*In his* Werke.) Stuttgart, 1865. 8° .. 5734.1.4

— *Same.* (*In* Coleridge, S. T. Works) ... 1611.5

PICKED up adrift. De Mille, J. ... 914.39

PICKERING, John. A vocabulary, or collection of words and phrases peculiar to the United States. Boston, 1816. 206+ pp. 8° ... 6121.1

PICKERING, Octavius, and UPHAM, Charles Wentworth. Life of Timothy Pickering. Boston, 1867, 73. 4 v. 2 portraits. 2 plates. 8° ... 5021.1

Note. — The 1st volume is by O. Pickering, the remaining volumes by C. W. Upham.

PICKERING, Timothy, Life of. Pickering, O., and Upham, C. W. Boston, 1867, 73. 4 v. 8° ... 5021.1

PICKWICK papers. Dickens, C. (J. H.) Boston. 2 v. ... 1824.1

— *Same.* Leipzig ... 338.1

PICNIC party, The. Adams, W. T. ... 918.6

PICNIC party, The. Smith, H. (*In* Johnson, (E.) R. Little classics) ... 529.4.9

PICTON, J. Allanson. The mystery of matter and other essays. London, 1873. xii, 492 pp. Sm. 8° ... 5826.3

PICTURE logic. Swinbourne, A. (J.) London, 1875. 8° ... 5616.19

PICTURE stories from the Japanese. Pictures drawn by native talent; with the stories in English rhyme. London [1874]. Unpaged. 8° ... 5920.3

PICTURES across the channel. Macquoid, K. S. ... 339.22

PICTURES from Italy. [Travels.] Dickens, C. (J. H.) Boston, 1874. 16° ... 1824.10

— *Same.* Leipzig, 1846. Sq. 16° ... 338.18

PICTURES from prison life. An historical sketch of the Massachusetts state prison. Haynes, G. Boston, 1869. 16° ... 817.16

PICTURESQUE America; or, the land we live in. Bryant, W. C., *editor*. New York [1872, 73]. 2 v. 4° ... 5030.9

PIEDMONT, Handbook for. Murray, J. London, 1846. 12° ... 227.3

PIERCE, Abraham P. The revelator: being an account of the twenty-one days' entrancement of A. P. Pierce, together with a sketch of his life. 2d edition. Boston, 1870. 88 pp. 12° ... 1538.10

PIERCE, Gilbert A. The Dickens dictionary. A key to the characters and principal incidents in the tales of Charles Dickens. With additions by W. A. Wheeler. Illustrated. Boston, 1872. xv, 573 pp. Portrait. 12° ... *R.R., F.3.3

PIERPONT, John. Airs of Palestine. A poem. Baltimore, 1816. xxvi, 56 pp. 8° ... 1611.3

PIERS, Experimental essays on the principles of construction in. Bland, W. London, 1867. 12° .. 1716.6

PIERSON, Helen Wall. Edith Vaughan's victory ... 1118.11

PIETY, Exercises of. Zollikofer, G. J. Boston, 1855. 12° ... 1535.24

PIKE, Albert. Prose sketches and poems, written in the Western country. Boston, 1834. 200 pp. Sm. 8° ... 1612.11

PIKE, Francis West Atherton. Safely married! A novel ... 721.7

PIKE, James S. The prostrate state: South Carolina under negro government. New York, 1874. 279 pp. 12° ... 5017.4

PIKE, Luke Owen. History of crime in England. Vol. I. London, 1873. 8° ... 5412.2

Contents. — Vol. I. From the Roman invasion to the accession of Henry VII.

PIKE, Mary H. Ida May. By Mary Langdon [*pseud.*] ... 312.10

Shelf. No.

PIKE, Nicolas. New and complete system of arithmetick. 7th edition, revised and improved by N. Lord. Boston, 1809. 300 pp. 12° ... 1933.16

PIKE county ballads. Hay, J. Boston, 1871. 16°. 1615.14

PILGRIM, The, and the shrine. Ainslie, H. London, 1871. 8° ... 5626.8

PILGRIM fathers, The. Bartlett, W. H. London, 1853. 8° ... 5021.4

See also Plymouth.

PILGRIM society, *Plymouth, Mass.* Proceedings at the 250th anniversary of the landing of the pilgrims. Cambridge, 1871. 208 pp. 8° ... 1920.2

PILGRIM'S, The, progress. Bunyan, J. Leipzig, 1855. Sq. 16° ... 315.18

PILGRIMS, Guide to Plymouth, and recollections of the. Russell, W. S. Boston, 1846. 12° ... 5017.1

PILGRIMS, The, of the Rhine. Bulwer-Lytton, E. (G. E.) L. ... 336.15

PILLAR of fire, The; or, Israel in bondage. Ingraham, J. H. Boston, 1872. Sm. 8° ... 512.6

PILLARS, The, of the house. Yonge, C. M. Leipzig. 4 v. in 2 ... 339.16

— *Same.* London. 2 v. ... 734.12

PILOT, The. [Paul Jones, etc.] Cooper, J. F. ... 525.29

PINK and white tyranny. Stowe, H. (E.) B. ... 537.6

PINKNEY, William, Life of. Wheaton, H. (*In* Sparks, J. Library of American biography) ... 5028.1.6

PINKS, The, and blues. Parker, R. A. ... 933.16

PINNEY, Norman, and ARNOULT, Émile. French grammar. New York, 1861. 520 pp. 12° ... 2013.1

PIONEER boy [A. Lincoln], The, and how he became president. Thayer, W. M. Boston, 1863. 16°. 916.26

PIONEERS, The. [Novel, Indian life.] Cooper, J. F. 525.28

PIONEERS and founders; or, recent workers in the mission field. Yonge, C. M. [London, 1871.] 16° ... 5817.5

PIONEERS of France in the New World. Parkman, F., *jr.* Boston, 1871. 12° ... 5015.5.1

PIOZZI, Esther Lynch. (*Mrs. Thrale.*) Autobiography, letters and literary remains. Edited, with notes, and an introductory account of her life and writings by A. Hayward. Boston, 1861. vi, 531 pp. 12° ... 1224.6

PIQUE ... 725.38

PIRATA, Il. Bellini, V. (*In* Ditson, O., and co. Standard opera librettos) ... 6233.3.4

PIRATE, The. Scott, *Sir* W. Boston ... 523.8

— *Same.* Leipzig ... 324.9

PIRATE city, The. An Algerine tale. Ballantyne, R. M. ... 927.30

PIRATES. Captain William Kidd, and others of the pirates who ravaged America two hundred years ago. Abbott, J. S. C. New York, 1874. 12° ... 1014.11

PISA. Descrizione delle pitture del Campo Santo di Pisa. Rosini, G. Pisa, 1829. 16° ... 2038.1

PITCAIRN island. The mutineers of the Bounty and their descendants in Pitcairn and Norfolk islands. Belcher, *Lady* D. New York, 1870. Sm. 8° ... 1224.4

— *Same.* New York, 1871. 12° ... 435.2

PITT, William, *the younger*. Macaulay, T. B., *lord*. William Pitt. Leipzig, 1860. Sq. 16° ... 1238.18

— Stanhope, P. H., *earl*. Life of. London, 1867. 4 v. Sm. 8° ... 5424.11

Note. — The latest and by far the best life is the moderate tory view by Earl Stanhope, who had the advantages, given to a kinsman, in the use of private papers.

The most brilliant of the lesser sketches is Macaulay's, from a moderate whig point of view, which originally appeared in the Encyclopædia Britannica, in which he continues the political history of George III's time, begun in his two Essays on Chatham. See also Bulwer's paper on "Pitt and Fox," in his "Miscellanies" [336.5.1]; Macaulay's sketch, in Harper's monthly, vol. 19; Lodge's "Portraits" [5337.6.8]; Brougham's sketch, in his "Statesmen" [5614.4.3]; Goldwin Smith's political history of Pitt's time, in his "Three English statesmen" [5425.1]; Alison's Europe [5913.6], particularly for his financial theories; the lives of contemporaries Fox, Canning, Moore, and Sheridan; and the full references in Allibone.

PITZMAROON; or, the magic hammer. Beach, C. A. 912.12

PIUS IX, *pope*, Speeches of. Gladstone, W. E. Leipzig, 1875. Sq. 16° ... 1918.12

— *Same.* New York, 1875. 8° ... 1911.3

Shelf. No.

PIZARRO: a tragedy. Sheridan, R. B. Dramatic works. London, 1848. 16° ... 1635.2
— *Same.* Leipzig, 1869. Sq. 16° ... 1614.11
— *Same.* London, 1875. Sm. 8° ... 5626.9
PLACE, A, in thy memory. De Kroyft, S. H. New York, 1851. 12° ... 5218.7
PLACENTA prævia; its history and treatment. Read, W. Philadelphia, 1861. 8° ... 6021.5
PLAIDEURS, Les: comédie. Racine, J. de. Théâtre complet. Paris, 1870. 12° ... 5537.3
PLANCHÉ, James Robinson. The brigand: a drama. New York, N. D. 35 pp. 1 plate. 12° ... 1635.4
— History of British costume, from the earliest period to the close of the 18th century. With illustrations. 3d edition. London, 1874. xxiv, 416 pp. Sm. 8° ... 6235.3
— Personal reminiscences. (*In* Stoddard, R. H. Bric-à-brac series) ... 1828.2
— Promotion: a vaudeville. New York, N. D. 17 pp. 12° ... 1635.5
— Recollections and reflections. A professional autobiography. London, 1872. 2 v. Illustrated. Folded plate. 8° ... 5524.2
— and DANCE, Charles. High, low, Jack, and the game: a burletta. New York, N. D. 16 pp. 12° ... 1635.5
PLANCHÉ, Matilda Anne. *See* MACKARNESS, Matilda Anne.
PLANE and plank. Adams, W. T. ... 924.12
PLANETARY and stellar worlds, The. Mitchell, O. M. London [1860]. 16° ... 1526.14
PLANT hunters, The. Reid, M. ... 923.29
PLANT life, Phenomena of. Grindon, L. H. Boston, 1866. 12° ... 1523.13
PLANTER'S, The, northern bride. Hentz, C. L. ... 534.20
PLANTS. Hassard, A. Floral decorations for the dwelling house: a practical guide to the home arrangement of plants and flowers. London, 1875. Sm. 8° ... 6625.5
— Hemsley, W. B. Handbook of herbaceous plants. Boston [London], 1873. 8° ... 6624.1

See also Climbing plants, Flowers.

PLANTZ, Tobias A. Effectual prayer. [And] Prayer. By F. Sewall. New York, 1874. 24 pp. 12°. 6328.19
PLATO. Dialogues. Translated, with analyses and introductions, by B. Jowett. Oxford, 1871. 4 v. 8° ... 6111.2

Contents. — Vol. I. Charmides; Lysis; Laches; Protagoras; Euthydemus; Ion; Meno; Euthyphro; Apology; Crito; Phaedo; Symposium; Phaedrus; Cratylus.
II. The republic; Timaeus; Critias.
III. Gorgias; Philebus; Parmenides; Theaetetus; The sophist; The statesman.
IV. Laws; Appendix; Lesser Hippias; First Alcibiades; Menexenus; Index.

— Collins, C. W. Plato [outlined and explained]. Philadelphia, 1874. 16° ... 6116.20
— Grote, G. Plato and other companions of Sokrates. London, 1867. 3 v. 8° ... 6113.2

Note. — The interest in Plato centres largely in his teachings, and all treatises on philosophy embody more or less biographical illustrations. Grote's "Plato and other companions of Sokrates" takes a somewhat utilitarian view, which is opposed by Jowett, with an idealistic view, in the introductions to his edition of the "Dialogues." Compare Lewes's "Biographical history of philosophy" [6832.1.1]; two chapters in Dr. Cocker's "Christianity and Greek philosophy" [5814.4]; James Martineau's "Essays" [5814.14]; Felton's "Lectures on Greece;" Macaulay's comparison of Plato and Bacon, in his Essay on Bacon [1918.4], which is in part controverted in Peter Bayne's Essay on Plato [1226.15.2]; Emerson's "Representative men" [1916.6; 1934.6.2]; De Quincey's "Historical essays" [1825.3]; Bunsen's "God in history" [5813.13]; and Grote's "History of Greece" [5926.1].

See the articles in Smith's "Dictionary of Greek and Roman biography;" Anthon's "Classical dictionary;" and the references in Abbot's "Bibliography of a future life" [5831.3].

PLAUTUS, Titus Maccius. Amphitruo et Aulularia. Accidunt notæ Anglicæ. Cura C. K. Dillaway. Philadelphiæ [*cop.* 1842]. 211 pp. Sm. 12° .. 6118.4
— Plautus [outlined and explained]. Collins, W. L. Edinburgh, 1873. 16° ... 6116.17
PLAY and profit in my garden. Roe, E. P. New York [*cop.* 1873]. Sm. 8° ... 1516.13
PLAY and study. Baker, H. N. (W.) ... 935.6
PLAYED out. Cudlip, A. ... 317.13
PLAYGROUND, The, of Europe. [Switzerland.] Stephen, L. London, 1871. 16° ... 5935.8
PLAYING the mischief. De Forest, J. W. ... 720.29
PLEASANT cove series. *See* KELLOGG, Elijah.
PLEASANT memories of pleasant lands. Sigourney, L. H. Boston, 1842. Sm. 8° ... 1537.12
PLÉBISCITE, Histoire du. Erckmann, É., and Chatrian, A. Paris, 1872. 18° ... 5516.4
PLÉBISCITE, The story of the. Erckmann, É., and Chatrian, A. London, 1872. 16° ... 524.25
PLINIUS CÆCILIUS SECUNDUS, Caius. Pliny's letters [outlined and explained]. Church, A., and Brodribb, W. J. Edinburgh, 1872. 16° ... 6116.12
PLOT, A, in private life. Collins, (W.) W. ... 326.8
PLUCKED from the burning. Church, F. ... 337.23
PLUMMER, John Isaac. Introduction to astronomy. New York [Glasgow], 1873. 174 pp. Illustrated. 16° ... 1717.6
PLURALITY of worlds. *See* WORLDS, Plurality of.
PLUTARCHUS. Lives [of ancient Greeks and Romans]. The translation called Dryden's. Corrected from the Greek and revised by A. H. Clough. Boston, 1872. 5 v. 8° ... 5932.5
— *Same.* Translated, with notes, and a life of Plutarch. By J. and W. Langhorne. New edition. London, 1828. 748 pp. Portrait. 8° .. 5932.7
— Morals. Translated from the Greek by several hands. Corrected and revised by W. W. Goodwin. With an introduction by R. W. Emerson. Boston, 1871. 5 v. 8° ... 6113.1
— Plutarch, his life and his morals. Trench, R. C. London, 1873. Sm. 8° ... 6118.7
PLYMOUTH, *Mass.* Russell, W. S. Guide to. Boston, 1846. 12° ... 5017.1
— Thacher, J. History of. Boston, 1832. 12° ... 817.9
PLYMOUTH colony. Compact, with the charter and laws of. *See* MASSACHUSETTS ... 6313.1
— Records of the. *See* MASSACHUSETTS ... 6310.1

Note. — A chapter in vol. 2 of Masson's "Life of Milton" [5422.2] is devoted to the rise and progress of English independency, and other authorities on English ecclesiastical history traces the course of the separatist movement; and it can be studied also in Bacon's "Genesis of the New England churches" [5812.13], pointing out wherein the Plymouth churches differed from those of Massachusetts bay.

The reader who wishes to examine carefully the sources of Pilgrim history will find them given in the note under Plymouth in the Lower Hall Catalogue of history, etc.

The story has been told by Bancroft in his "History of the United States" [5012.3]; by Palfrey, in his "History of New England" [5016.2]; and by Barry, in his "History of Massachusetts" [812.5]. The history of the town of Plymouth, by Thacher [817.9], and Russell's "Guide" [5017.1], necessarily preserve much of the record; while Bartlett has been a follower on their track with pen and pencil, both in England, in Holland, and in the old colony [5021.4]. The records of the colony have been edited by Shurtleff [6310.1], as also the charter, laws, etc. [6313.1], edited by William Brigham, whose lecture in the series delivered by members of the Massachusetts historical society, discussed the relations of the two colonies. Webster's [5013.1], Everett's [1921.1] and Winthrop's [1920.2] orations also summarize the history; also a popular narrative by Abbott, in his "Miles Standish" [1014.6]. See C. W. Philleo's article on Plymouth, in Harper's monthly, vol. 8, and Drake's "Nooks and corners of the New England coast" [411.4].

PLYMPTON, George W. A system of instruction in the practical use of the blowpipe. 2d edition. With an appendix and a copious index. New York, 1868. 288 pp. 12° ... 6436.3
PNEUMATICS for beginners. Tomlinson, C. London, 1866. 12° ... 1716.32
POE, Edgar Allan. Works. New York, 1866. 4 v. 16° ... 1934.2

Contents. — Vol. I. Notices of his life and genius, by J. R. Lowell and N. P. Willis; Memoir by R. W. Griswold; Tales. II. Poems; Eureka; Tales. III. The literati; Marginalia; Fifty suggestions. IV. Arthur Gordon Pym; Miscellaneous.

— Prose tales. 1st series. New York [*cop.* 1849]. vi, 483 pp. 16° ... 526.9
— – 2d series. New York, 1867. vi, 498 [496] pp. 12° ... 526.18
— The fall of the house of Usher. (*In* Johnson, (E.) R. Little classics) ... 529.4.2
— The gold-bug. (*In* Johnson, (E.) R. Little classics) ... 529.4.12
— The murders in the Rue Morgue. (*In* Johnson, (E.) R. Little classics) ... 529.4.3
POET, The, at the breakfast-table. Holmes, O. W. Boston, 1872. 16° ... 535.16

Shelf. No.

POETIC studies. Phelps, E. S. Boston, 1875. Sq. 16°. 1617.9

POETICAL quotations, Complete dictionary of. Hale, S. J. Philadelphia, 1872. 8° ..........*R.R., F.3.1

POETRY. Beeton, S. O. Great book of. London [1871]. 8° 5631.1

— Griswold, R. W. The poets and poetry of America. New York, 1873. L. 8° 5212.3

— Lamb, C. and M. Poetry for children. London, 1872. 16° 5617.8

— Shairp, J. C. Studies in. New York, 1872. 16°. 1535.14

Note. — See also the titles on literature under the names of countries.

POET'S, A, bazaar. [Travels.] Andersen, H. C. New York, 1871. Sm. 8° 426.18

POETS. De Quincey, T. Essays on the. Boston, 1871. 16° 1825.4

— Stedman, E. C. Victorian poets. Boston, 1876. 12° 1837.1

POISON of asps, The. Church, F. 337.23

POITOU, Eugène (Louis). Spain and its people. A record of recent travel. From the French [by W. H. D. Adams]. With illustrations. London, 1873. 497+ pp. Sm. 8° 5914.8

POLAND. Hordynski, J. History of the late Polish revolution. Boston, 1832. 8° 821.3

— Murray, J. Handbook for Poland. London, 1868. 12° 5927.5

See also Cracow.

POLAR, The, and tropical worlds. Hartwig, G. Springfield, 1874. 8° 1520.7

POLAR sea, The open. Hayes, I. I. New York, 1867. 8° 422.3

POLARIS expedition. Blake, E. V. Arctic experiences: containing a history of the. New York, 1874. 8° 5911.15

— Markham, A. H. Account of the rescue of the crew of the "Polaris." London, 1874. 8° 5912.11

POLICE records and recollections; or, Boston by daylight and gaslight for two hundred and forty years. Savage, E. H. Boston, 1873. 8° 5013.8

POLITICAL economy. Bastiat, F. Essays on. London, 1872. 16° 5828.1

— *Same.* 4th edition. London [1875]. 16° 5828.3

— Cobden club, *London.* Essays, 2d series, 1871–2. London, 1872. 8° 5822.1

— Du Mesnil-Marigny, J. Histoire de l'économie politique des anciens peuples de l'Inde, de l'Égypte, de la Judée et de la Grèce. Paris, 1872. 2 v. 8° 5823.2

— Fawcett, M. G. Tales in. London, 1874. Sm. 8°. 5827.4

— Greeley, H. Essays designed to elucidate the science of. Boston, 1871. 12° 1525.18

— Mill, J. S. Dissertations and discussions: political, philosophical, and historical. New York, 1874, 75. 5 v. 8° 5824.4

— – Principles of. New York, 1872. 2 v. 8° ... 5822.3

— Pautet, J. F. J. Manuel d'économie politique. Paris, 1835. 24° 5829.1

— Perry, A. L. Elements of. New York, 1875. 8°. 5824.3

— Phillips, W. Manual of. Boston, 1828. 8° ... 5822.8

— Rae, J. Statement of some new principles of. Boston, 1834. 8° 5822.7

— Ruskin, J. Munera pulveris. Six essays on the elements of. New York, 1872. 12° 6236.7

— – The political economy of art. New York, 1866. 12° 6236.8

— – "Unto this last:" four essays on the first principles of. New York, 1866. 12° 6236.4

— Smith, A. An inquiry into the nature and causes of the wealth of nations. Oxford, 1869. 2 v. 8°. 5822.9

POLITICAL philosophy, Principles of. Paley, W. London, 1794. 2 v. 8° 5823.3

— *Same.* Boston, 1830. 2 v. Sm. 12° 1538.6

POLITICAL science. Freeman, E. A. Comparative politics. London, 1873. 8° 5822.10

— MacPherson, E. Hand-book of politics for 1872, 74. Washington, 1872, 74. 2 v. 8° 6924.8

— Mill, J. S. Dissertations and discussions: political, philosophical, and historical. New York, 1874, 75. 5 v. 8° 5824.4

Shelf. No.

POLITICAL science, *continued.*

— Nordhoff, C. Politics for young Americans. New York, 1875. 12° 5826.10

POLKO, Elise. Lulu's novel. [And Alessandro Stradella.] From the German 731.31

POLLARD, Edward A. Black diamonds gathered in the darkey homes of the South. New York, 1859. 12° 1915.8

— Life of Jefferson Davis, with a secret history of the Southern confederacy. Philadelphia [*cop.* 1869]. viii, 536 pp. Portrait. 8° 5013.3

— Southern history of the war. New York, 1864, 66. 3 v. Portraits. 8° 5013.17

POLLARD, Eliza F. Hope deferred 721.8

— The lady superior. A novel 720.20

POLLEN, John Hungerford. Ancient and modern furniture and woodwork. *See* SOUTH KENSINGTON museum, *London.* [London, 1875.] 8° ... 6214.5

POLO, Marco. The book of Ser Marco Polo the Venetian, concerning the kingdoms and marvels of the East. Newly translated and edited with notes, maps [fac-similes] and illustrations. By Henry Yule. 2d edition. London, 1875. 2 v. Engraved title-pages. 8° 5933.7

See also Note in Bulletin, vol. II, p. 374.

POLYANTHOS, The, enlarged. Vol. 1–4. Illustrated. Portraits. Boston, 1812–14. 4 v. 8° 1317.1

POLYNESIAN life, Typee: a peep at. [A story.] Melville, H. New York, 1871. 12° 737.4

POLYNIA, The gateway to the. Wells, J. C. London, 1873. 8° 5911.14

POMPEII. Adams, W. H. D. The buried cities of Campania; or. Boston, 1870. 16° 437.5

— Bulwer-Lytton, E. (G. E.) L. The last days of. [Historical fiction] 336.13

— Dyer, T. H. Pompeii. Its history, buildings, and antiquity. London, 1871. 8° 5513.1

— Monnier, M. The wonders of. New York, 1872. 12° 1714.17

Note. — The best account in English for the general reader is Dyer's book. It is illustrated, and in his preface he gives a recapitulation of his authorities. For the present condition the reader may find Murray's "Handbook of Southern Italy" the readiest manual. The English translation, "The wonders of Pompeii" [1714.17], of Monnier's "Pompéi et les Pompéiens," is an entertaining popular view of the subject, with cuts, and so is Adams's "Buried cities" [437.5]. The sumptuous works which are so necessary aids to the study of Pompeii are named in the note in the Lower Hall Catalogue of history, etc. On the general subject of Pompeiian art, the reader will find chapters in Dyer, and a brief summary in Taine's "Italy" [5522.2].

There are popular sketches in the books of travellers, like Hillard's "Six months in Italy" [426.8]. See Jarves's illustrated paper in Harper's monthly, vol. II. Bulwer's novel, "The last days of Pompeii" [336.13], is a tale of life and manners at that time.

PONTIAC, The conspiracy of. Parkman, F., *jr.* Boston, 1870. 2 v. 12° 5015.4

PONTIANUS, *pope.* *See* HIPPOLYTUS, *St.*

POOR, Henry V. Manual of the railroads of the United States, 1871, 72. With an appendix. 4th series. New York, 1871. xxxiv, 592 pp. 8°. 6923.10

POOR and proud. Adams, W. T. 924.16

POOR humanity. Robinson, F. W. 731.11

POOR Miss Finch. Collins, (W.) W. 326.6

POOR, The, of New York: a drama. New York, N. D. 45 pp. 12° 1635.4

POOR rich man, The, and the rich poor man. Sedgwick, C. M. 918.15

POPE, Alexander. Works. New edition. Collected in part by J. W. Croker. With introduction and notes, by W. Elwin. With portraits and other illustrations. Vol. 1, 2, 6–8. London, 1871, 72. 5 v. 8° 5612.2

Contents. — Vol. I, II. Poetry. (1.) Translations; January and May, from Chaucer; The wife of Bath, from Chaucer; The temple of fame; Pastorals; Messiah; Windsor forest. (2.) Essay on criticism; Rape of the lock; Eloisa to Abelard; Essay on man. VI–VIII. Letters.

— Select poetical works. With life and portrait of the author. Leipzig, 1848. vi, 305 pp. Sq. 16°. 1613.10

Contents. — Life; Pastorals; Messiah; Windsor forest; Ode on St. Cecilia's day; Odes; Essay on criticism; Rape of the lock; Eloisa to Abelard; Temple of fame; January and May, from Chaucer; The wife of Bath, from Chaucer; Imitations; Essay on man; Moral essays; Miscellanies; Epitaphs.

Shelf. No.

POPE, Alexander, *continued.*
— Ruffhead, O. Life of. London, 1869. Sm. 8°. 1222.1
— Saint-Beuve, C. A. English portraits. New York, 1875. 16° 1025.3
— Stephen, L. Hours in a library. London, 1874. Sm. 8° 6136.9

Note.—The reader will get a good preliminary survey in Allibone's long and elaborate article; and find a full list of authorities in Bohn's Lowndes; while for a comprehensive life he will find Carruther's the latest and best; while Ruffhead's earlier one, 1767, shows a still less extent of information, and is desultory in treatment and imperfect in detail. Johnson's life, in his "Lives of the English poets" [1238.20], is a characteristic specimen of that writer's powers, while Disraeli, in his "Curiosities of literature" [5626.6], has given the indications of the way in which Johnson shaped it; but see also De Quincey, consulting his Note-book and "Theological essays." See Disraeli's "Quarrels of authors" [1537.17]; Jameson's "Loves of the poets" [5618.2]; Howitt's "Homes and haunts of the British poets" [1225.5]; Lowell's "My study windows;" F. W. Robertson's lecture; Kingsley's "New miscellanies" [1533.8], comparing him with the modern school of poets; W. B. O. Peabody's "Literary remains," where his relations with Addison are particularly examined; Fields's "Yesterdays with authors" [6136.13]; Mrs. Oliphant's "Historical sketches of the reign of George II" [1032.1]; Thackeray's "Humourists" [1238.8]; and Leigh Hunt's "Men, women, and books" [1935.1].

The latest information is given in the valuable introductions to the new edition of Pope's works, begun by the late J. W. Croker, and in progress by Elwin [5612.2]. See also as the best authority on Pope's private life, Spence's "Anecdotes" [5617.19]; and for a thorough study of the subject, the investigator will need to consult Lady Montagu's "Letters and works" [5623.3]; and Walpole's.

POPE, Frank L. The modern practice of the electric telegraph. A handbook for electricians and operators. 8th edition. New York, 1873. 160 pp. Illustrated. 8° 6825.1
POPERY. Gavin, A. The great red dragon; or the master-key to. Boston, 1854. 12° 1226.21
— Nevins, W. Thoughts on. New York [*cop.* 1836]. 16° 1538.20

See also Papacy, Roman catholic church.

POPES. Doellinger, J. J. I. von. Fables respecting the popes of the middle ages. London, 1871. 8° 5813.5
— *Same.* New York, 1872. 12° 5816.10
— Ranke, (F.) L. History of the. London, 1871. 3 v. Sm. 8° 5516.7
POPKIN, John Snelling. A memorial. Edited [with a biographical sketch] by C. C. Felton. Cambridge, 1852. lxxxviii, 392 pp. Portrait. 16°. 6326.4
POPULAR ignorance, Essay on the evils of. Foster, J. London, 1865. 16° 5614.2
POPULAR science monthly. Vol. 3–7. New York, 1873–75. 5 v. 8° 6516.1
POPULATION. L'agriculture et la population. Lavergne, L. (G. L. G.) de. Paris, 1865. 18°... 5827.1
PORCELAIN. Boyer, —. Nouveau manuel complet du porcelainier. Paris, 1846. 2 v. 24° 6439.8
— Treadwell, J. H. Manual of. New York, 1872. 8° .... 1512.2 and 6211.4
PORT folio, The. Conducted by Oliver Oldschool [*pseud.* of Joseph Dennie]. New series, vol. 1–5; New [2d] series, vol. 1–6. Philadelphia, 1806–11. 11 v. 8° 1435.2
PORTE CRAYON, *pseud.* *See* STROTHER, David H.
PORTENT, The. MacDonald, G. 537.3
PORTER, David, Memoir of. Porter, D. D. Albany, 1876. 8° 5022.18
PORTER, David Dixon. Memoir of Commodore David Porter of the United States navy. With portrait and heliotypes. Albany, 1875. ix, 427+ pp. 8° 5022.18
PORTER, Edward Griffin, and STEPHENSON, Harris Marshall. Souvenir of 1775. Lexington. 1775–1875. [Boston, 1875.] 16 pp. Illustrated. 4°. 810.5

Note.—The text by E. G. Porter, the illustrations by H. M. Stephenson.

PORTER, Jane. The Scottish chiefs 1225.19

Note.—A tale of the days of Wallace, but not considered a close study of those times.

— Thaddeus of Warsaw 734.10

Note.—Kosciusko—Poland, 1791, etc.

PORTER, John Leech. The giant cities of Bashan; and Syria's holy places. New York, 1871. 377+ pp. Illustrated. 12° 5915.7

Shelf. No.

PORTER, Noah. The American colleges and the American public. New Haven, 1870. 285 pp. 12° 1934.7
— Books and reading; or, what books shall I read and how shall I read them? 4th edition, with an index. New York, 1873. viii, 394 pp. Sm. 8° 6134.1
— The human intellect: with an introduction upon psychology and the soul. 4th edition. New York, 1872. xxvii, 673 [669] pp. 8° 1520.4
PORTER, Rose. Summer drift-wood for the winter fire 718.2
— The years that are told 717.9
PORTER, William Henry. Our Father and his family union. [Religious discourses, etc.] Boston, 1861. 302 pp. 16° 5818.5
PORTER, William Trotter, Life of. Brinley, F. New York, 1860. 12° 1215.2
PORTLOCK, Joseph Ellison. Rudiments of geology. With illustrations. 5th edition. London, N. D. viii, 202 pp. 12° 1716.3
PORTRAITS of celebrated women. Sainte-Beuve, C. A. Boston, 1868. 16° 1226.5
PORTRAITS of illustrious personages of Great Britain. Lodge, E. London, 1849, 50. 8 v. Sm. 8°... 5337.6
PORT ROYAL, *France.* Sainte-Beuve, C. A. Port-Royal. Paris, 1867. 7 v. 12° 5538.6
— *Convent of.* Martin, F. Angelique Arnauld, abbess of Port Royal. London, 1873. Sm. 8°. 5937.11
PORTSMOUTH, *N. H.* *South parish.* Sermons connected with the re-opening of the church. Peabody, A. P. Portsmouth, 1859. 16° 5818.7
PORTUGAL. Andersen, H. C. In Spain and a visit to. New York, 1870. Sm. 8° 426.16
— Denis, (J.) F. Portugal. Paris, 1846. 8°.... 5911.10
— Murray, J. Handbook for Portugal. London, 1864. 12° 5917.2
POSITIVE philosophy, Outlines of cosmic philosophy, based on the doctrine of evolution, with criticisms on the. Fiske, J. Boston, 1875. 2 v. 8°. 5824.2
POTASSIUM. *See* BROMIDE of potassium.
POTIPHAR papers. Curtis, G. W. 526.2
POTOMAC, Army of the, Engineer and artillery operations of the. Barnard, J. G., and Barry, W. F. New York, 1863. 8° 6924.2
POTTER, Alonzo. Address on the drinking usages of society. *See* MASSACHUSETTS temperance society 1524.2
POTTER, Chandler E. History of Manchester, N. H. Manchester, 1856. xiii, 763 pp. Illustrated. 8°. 812.4
POTTER, Henry C. Sisterhoods and deaconesses at home and abroad. New York, 1873. 358 pp. 16° 1535.23
POTTERY. Boyer, —. Nouveau manuel complet du potier de terre. Paris, 1846. 2 v. 24° 6439.8
— Hall, H. B. The bric-à-brac hunter; or, chapters on chinamania. Philadelphia [London], 1875. Sm. 8° 6214.4
— Jacquemart, A. History of ceramic art. A descriptive and philosophical study of the pottery of all ages and all nations. London, 1873. L. 8°. 6231.1
— Meteyard, E. Life of Josiah Wedgwood. With an introductory sketch of the art of pottery in England. London, 1865, 66. 2 v. 8° 6231.3
— Treadwell, J. H. Manual of. New York, 1872. 8° .... 1512.2 and 6211.4

Note.—See also Palissy the Huguenot potter [538.4].

POUCHET, Félix Archimède. The universe; or, the infinitely great and the infinitely little. [Translated from the French.] New edition. Illustrated. London, 1871. xx, 818 pp. L. 8°.... 6830.1
— *Same.* With an introduction by A. Guyot. Illustrated. New York, 1873. xxiv, 818 pp. 8°. 1520.6
POUCHKINE, Alexandre. *See* MÉRIMÉE, P. Portraits historiques et littéraires. Paris, 1874. 18°. 5527.14
POUQUEVILLE, François Charles Hugues Laurent. Grèce. Paris, 1843. 447+ pp. 112 plates. Map. [L'Univers.] 8° 5911.8
POULTRY, Illustrated book of. Wright, L. London [1873]. 4° 6610.5

Shelf. No.

POWDER and gold. Schucking, L. 538.3
POWELL, Baden. The law and the gospel. (*In* Noyes, G. R. Collection of theological essays). 6325.12
— The study of the evidences of Christianity. (*In* Essays and reviews) 1538.3
— *Same.* (*In* Hedge, F. H. Recent inquiries in theology) .... 1526.24 and 5814.15
— The unity of worlds and of nature: three essays. 2d edition. London, 1856. xix, 556 pp. Sm. 8°. 6836.1
POWELL, George Smyth Baden. New homes for the old country. A personal experience of Australia and New Zealand. With illustrations. London, 1872. xx, 512 pp. Maps. 8° 5931.6
POWELL, Warington Baden. Canoe travelling: log of a cruise on the Baltic, and practical hints on building and fitting canoes. With illustrations and a map. London, 1871. xiii, 172+ pp. Sm. 8° 5934.8
POWER, Harriet. How shall we employ and amuse our invalids? London, 1873. 89+ pp. 16°.. 6038.3
POWER, Thomas. Masonic melodies: adapted to the ceremonies and festivals of the fraternity. Boston, 1844. 105 pp. 8° 1518.12
POWER in motion. Armour, J. London, 1871. 12° 1716.41
POWERS, *Mrs.* S. D. The ugly-girl papers; or, hints for the toilet. New York, 1875. 283 pp. 16°. 1528.13
POYNTER, *Miss* —. Ersilia. Leipzig 331.25
— *Same.* Leisure hour series. New York 517.23
— My little lady 313.11
PRACTICAL evangelism. Cheever, W. M. Boston, 1856. 12° 1536.15
PRACTICAL magazine. Vol. 1-5. Illustrated. London, 1873-75. 5 v. 4° 6510.1
PRACTICAL mechanic and engineer's magazine. Vol. 1-4; 2d series, vol. 1, 2. Glasgow, 1842-50. 6 v. 4° 6420.5
PRACTICAL mechanic's journal. Vol. 1-8; 2d series, vol. 1, 2. Glasgow and London, 1848-58. 10 v. 4° 6420.4
PRAED, Winthrop Mackworth. Poems. Revised and enlarged edition. With a memoir by D. Coleridge. New York, 1865. 2 v. Portrait. 12° 5616.12
PRAIRIE, The. Cooper, J. F. 525.22
PRAIRIE traveler, The. A hand-book for overland expeditions. Marcy, R. B. New York, 1859. 16°. 417.7
PRAIRIES, Tour on the. Irving, W. London, 1854. 16° 417.1
PRAISSAC, —. [A short method for the easy resolving of any military question, propounded; translated by John Cruso. Cambridge, 1639. Title-page gone.] 202+ pp. Illustrated. Sm. 8°. 5918.2
PRANK. Abbott, J. Harper's story books 936.1.2
PRATT, Mary E. Rhoda Thornton's girlhood 934.33
PRAYER. Answers to prayer; or, Dorothea Trüdel. Boston, N. D. 12° 1026.3
— Brooks, C. Family prayer book. Boston, 1853. 12° 5815.18
— Miles, H. A. The altar at home: prayers for the family and the closet. Boston, 1855. 16° 6327.8
— *Same.* Boston, 1859. 16° 6327.19
— Plantz, T. A. Effectual prayer. New York, 1874. 12° 6328.19
— Rossetti, C. G. Annus Domini: a prayer for each day of the year, founded on a text of Holy Scripture. Oxford, 1874. Sq. 16° 5819.15
— Sewall, F. Prayer. New York, 1874. 12° 6328.19
PREACHER, The [Bourdaloue], and the king [Louis XIV]. Bungener, L. L. F. Boston, 1855. 12°.. 716.4
PREBLE, George Henry. Our flag. Origin and progress of the flag of the United States. With an introductory account of the symbols, standards, banners and flags of ancient and modern nations. Albany, 1872. 535+ pp. Illustrated. 8° ... 5013.5
PRECAUTION. Cooper, J. F. 525.32
PRECIOUS stones, Diamonds and. Emanuel, H. New York, 1873. Sm. 8° 6635.3
PREECE, William Henry, and SIVEWRIGHT, J. Telegraphy. London, 1876. 300 pp. Illustrated. [Text-books of science.] Sm. 8° 6826.6

Shelf. No.

PRE-HISTORIC man. Rau, C. Early man in Europe. New York, 1876. 8° 6612.10
— Southall, J. C. The recent origin of man. Philadelphia, 1875. 8° 6612.8
— Wilson, D. Researches into the origin of civilisation in the old and new world. London, 1876. 2 v. 8° 6613.13

Note. — See also the note on Pre-historic archæology in the Library Bulletin, vol. II, p. 298.

PRE-HISTORIC nations. Baldwin, J. D. New York, 1872. 12° 824.7
PRENDERGAST, Thomas. Handbook to the mastery series. New York, 1868. 92 pp. 12° 1933.1
— The mastery series. French. New York, 1868. 115 pp. 12° 1933.2
— — German. New York, 1868. 98 pp. 12° 1933.3
PRENTICE *or* PRENTISS family, History and genealogy of the. Binney, C. J. F. Boston, 1852. 8°. 612.2
PRENTISS, Elizabeth. Aunt Jane's hero 737.2
— The flower of the family 728.10
— Fred, and Maria, and me 717.2
— Stepping heavenward 537.2
— The story Lizzie told 736.30
PRE-RAPHAELITISM. Ruskin, J. New York, 1872. 12°. 6236.9
PRESCOTT, George B. History, theory, and practice of the electric telegraph. 5th edition, revised and enlarged. Boston, 1871. xiii, 508 pp. Illustrated. Sm. 8° 1527.5
PRESCOTT, Harriet Elizabeth. *See* SPOFFORD, Harriet Elizabeth.
PRESCOTT, William Hickling. Biographical and critical essays. London, 1856. 347+ pp. 16°. 1537.8

Contents. — Charles Brockden Brown, the American novelist; Asylum for the blind; Irving's Conquest of Granada; Cervantes; Sir Walter Scott; Chateaubriand's English literature; Bancroft's United States; Madame Calderon's Life in Mexico; Molière; Italian narrative poetry; Poetry and romance of the Italians; Scottish song; Da Ponte's Observations.

— Biographical and critical miscellanies. New edition. Philadelphia, 1875. 682+ pp. Portrait. 12° 5237.3

Contents. — Same as the preceding, with an additional essay on Ticknor's History of Spanish literature.

— History of the conquest of Mexico, with a preliminary view of the ancient Mexican civilization, and the life of the conqueror, Hernando Cortez. Philadelphia, 1873. 3 v. Portraits. Map. 8° 5014.2
— *Same.* New and revised edition, by J. F. Kirk. Philadelphia, 1875. 3 v. Fac-simile. Portraits. 12° 815.6
— History of the conquest of Peru; with a preliminary view of the civilization of the Incas. Philadelphia, 1873. 2 v. Portraits. Map. 8°. 5014.3
— History of the reign of Ferdinand and Isabella the catholic. Philadelphia, 1873. 3 v. Portraits. Fac-similes. 8° 5922.5
— History of the reign of Philip II, king of Spain. Boston, 1855, 59. 3 v. Portraits. 8° 1222.1
— Life of Charles V, after his abdication. *See* ROBERTSON, William 1226.9.2
— Life of Charles Brockden Brown. [Sparks, J. Library of American biography] 5028.1.1
— Life of. Ticknor, G. Boston, 1864. 12° 1223.7
— Review of a part of [his] 'History of Ferdinand and Isabella.' *See* REVIEWS, etc. 1536.23

Note. — Prescott's histories follow in this order: — 1st, his "Ferdinand and Isabella," which includes the discovery of America; 2d, Cortés's subsequent conquest of Mexico; 3d, Pizarro's later conquest of Peru; 4th, the old standard history of the emperor Charles V (Charles I of Spain), to which Prescott only contributed the concluding sketch of that monarch's "Life, after his abdication," this work being used to fill the gap between his "Ferdinand and Isabella;" and 5th, his "History of Philip II," which he did not live to complete.

PRESCOTTS, The, of Pamphillon. Parr, L. 329.22
PRESIDENT'S, The, daughters. Bremer, F. 511.3
PRESSENSÉ, Edmond de. The early years of Christianity. Translated by A. Harwood. The martyrs and apologists. New York, 1871. viii, 654 pp. 12° 5816.2
— Heresy and Christian doctrine. Translated by A. Harwood. London, 1873. viii, 479 pp. 8°... 5813.8

Shelf. No.

PRESTON, Harriet Waters. Aspendale............. 718.3
— Love in the nineteenth century.............. 516.22
PRESTON fight; or, the insurrection of 1715. A tale. Ainsworth, W. H.......................... 331.16
PRETENDERS, Memoirs of the. Jesse, J. H. London, 1860. Sm. 8°......................5426.14
PRETENTIOUS young ladies, The: a comedy. Molière, J. B. P. Dramatic works. Edinburgh, 1875. 8°..............................5530.3.1
PRETTY Miss Bellew. Gift, T................. 529.10
PRETTY Mrs. Gaston. Cooke, J. E.............. 736.29
PRETTY widow, The. Ross, C. H................ 316.14
PREY, The, of the gods. Church, F............. 337.20
PRICE, Joseph M. Tables of sterling exchange. 3d edition. New York, 1852. 105 pp. L. 8°.... 1721.1
PRICHARD, Sarah J. Aunt Saidee's cow........... 928.23
PRIDE and prejudice. Austen, J................ 325.23
PRIDEAUX, T. Symes. The economy of fuel, with reference to reverberatory furnaces for the manufacture of iron, and to steam boilers. London, N. D. xvi, 128 pp. Illustrated. 12°.........1715.13
PRIESTCRAFT, History of. Howitt, W. New York, 1857. 12°.............................. 836.5
PRIESTLEY, Joseph. Views of Christian truth, piety, and morality, selected from [his] writings. With a memoir of his life, by H. Ware, jr. Cambridge, 1834. lxxx, 207 pp. 16°....... 6326.6
PRIESTLEY, Joseph, *jr.* Memoirs of Joseph Priestley. With observations on his writings by T. Cooper and W. Christie. London, 1806. 2 v. 8°.... 5424.3
PRIME, Edward Dorr Griffin. Around the world: sketches of travel. With illustrations. New York, 1873. 455 pp. Illustrated. 8°....... 233.1
PRIME, Samuel Irenæus. The Alhambra and the Kremlin. The south and the north of Europe. New York [1873]. xxiv, 482 pp. Illustrated. 8°. 5914.6
— Life of Samuel F. B. Morse, inventor of the electro-magnetic recording telegraph. New York, 1875. xii, 776+ pp. Portraits. Illustrations. 8°.................................... 5331.1
PRIME, William Cowper. Boat life in Egypt and Nubia. New York, 1858. 498 pp. 12°...... 424.6
— I go a-fishing. New York, 1873. 365 pp. Sm. 8°.................................... 6413.3

Contents. — Why Peter went a-fishing; At the Rookery; Iskander Effendi; Morning trout; Sunday morning and evening; An exploring expedition; The St. Regis waters; Connecticut streams; Among the Franconia mountains; On a mountain brook; On Echo lake; Three bottles of claret; What flies to cast on a Sunday; In northern New Hampshire; At the Ferns; Going home.

— Tent life in the Holy Land. New York, 1858. 498 pp. Illustrated. 12°.................. 425.5
PRIME minister, The. Trollope, A. Vol. I, II. Leipzig. 331.26
— *Same.* New York.......................... 730.13
PRIMITIVE culture. Tylor, E. B. London, 1871. 2 v. 8°.................................. 5922.6
PRIMITIVE man. Figuier, (G.) L. London, 1870. 8°. 5912.3
PRINCE, Nancy. Narrative of [her] life and travels. Written by herself. 2d edition. Boston, 1853. 89 pp. 16°............................... 418.6
PRINCE, The, and the page. Yonge, C. M......... 318.7
PRINCE, The, of darkness. Southworth, E. D. E. N. 527.14
PRINCE, The, of the house of David. [Novel, scene in Jerusalem.] Ingraham, J. H. Boston, 1872. 12°.................................... 512.5
PRINCE Eugene and his times. [Historical novel.] Mundt, C. (M.)......................... 531.2
PRINCESS, The. Tennyson, A. Poetical works. Leipzig, 1860. Sq. 16°...................1614.10.2
PRINCESS, The: comedy. Gilbert, W. S. Original plays. New York, 1876. 12°............. 1634.1
PRINCESS, The, and the goblin. MacDonald, G.... 936.33
PRINCESS, The, of Brunswick-Wolfenbüttel. Zschokke, (J.) H. (D.) Leipzig, 1867. Sq. 16°. 316.11
PRINCESS, The, of Elis: comedy-ballet. Molière, J. B. P. Dramatic works. Edinburgh, 1876. 8°.5530.3.3
PRINCESS, The, of the moor. John, E............ 319.3
PRINCESS, A, of Thule. Black, W. Leipzig...... 328.28
— *Same.* New York.......................... 732.10
PRINCESSE, La, d'Élide: comédie-ballet. Molière, J. B. P. Œuvres. Paris, 1869. 12°........5537.2.2

PRINTING, American encyclopædia of. Ringwalt, J. L. Philadelphia, 1871. L. 8°........*R.R., A.3.4
PRIOR, James. Life and character of Edmund Burke: with specimens of his poetry and letters, and an estimate of his genius and talents compared with those of his contemporaries. Philadelphia, 1825. 5071 pp. Portrait. 8°....... 5424.6
PRISON discipline society, *Boston.* Reports. 1826–54. Boston, 1855. 3 v. 8°................ 6912.1
PRISON of Weltevreden, The. Gibson, W. M. New York, 1855. 12°......................... 424.3
PRIVATE theatricals. Baker, G. M. The social stage. Boston, 1875 [*cop.* 1870]. 16°........ 1635.7
PRIVATEER'S-MAN, The. Marryat, F. 337.22
PROBLEMATIC characters. Spielhagen, F.......... 736.16
PROBLEMS of life and mind. Lewes, G. H. Vol. I. London, 1874. 8°......................... 5833.4
PROBUS. *See* AURELIAN.
PROCHASKA, George. Dissertation on the functions of the nervous system. *See* UNZER, John Augustus.................................6013.15
PROCTER, Adelaide Anne. Legends and lyrics. With an introduction by C. Dickens. 14th edition. London, 1872. 2 v. Portrait. 16°..........5617.11
PROCTER, Bryan Waller. Barry Cornwall and some of his friends. Fields, J. T. Boston, 1876. 16°. 1829.1
PROCTOR, Edna Dean. A Russian journey. Boston, 1872. 324 pp. Sm. 8°.................... 428.12
PROCTOR, Richard Anthony. The borderland of science. With portrait. London, 1873. vii, 438+ pp. Sm. 8°.......................... 6814.3
— Essays on astronomy. Preceded by a sketch of the life and work of Sir John Herschel. With plates and drawings on wood. London, 1872. xiv, 401 pp. 8°...................1521.4 and 6813.1
— The expanse of heaven: a series of essays on the wonders of the firmament. London, 1873. 305 pp. Sm. 8°.............................. 6815.1
— Half-hours with the stars: a plain and easy guide to the knowledge of the constellations. Maps. 3d edition. London, 1871. 22 pp. 4°....... 6810.1
— Half-hours with the telescope; being a popular guide to [its] use. With illustrations. New York [London], 1873. viii, 109 pp. 16°..... 1713.1
— Light science for leisure hours. New York, 1871. 343 pp. 12°............................. 1527.3
— The moon: her motions, aspect, scenery, and physical condition. With 3 lunar photographs. New York, 1873. xx, 394+ pp. 16°........ 6814.2
— Other worlds than ours: the plurality of worlds studied under the light of recent scientific researches. New York, 1871. 334 pp. Illustrated. 12°............................. 1527.4
— Our place among infinities. Essays contrasting our little abode in space and time with the infinities around us. Added Essays on astrology and the Jewish Sabbath. London, 1875. 323+ pp. Sm. 8°.............................. 6815.2
— Recent solar researches. (*In* Estes, D. Half-hour recreations in popular science).......... 6813.7
— Saturn and its system. Illustrated. London, 1865. xvi, 252+ pp. 8°.................. 6813.3
— Science byways: familiar dissertations on life in other worlds; comets and the sun; the north pole; rain; danger from lightning; growth and decay of mind; the brain and mental feats; automata, &c. Appended an essay entitled Money for science. Portrait. Philadelphia [London], 1876. xiv, 422+ pp. Sm. 8°..... 6836.4
— Strange discoveries respecting the aurora. (*In* Estes, D. Half-hour recreations in popular science)................................ 6813.7
— The sun. With plates and drawings on wood. 2d edition. London, 1872. xxviii, 503 pp. Sm. 8°................................... 6814.1
— Transits of Venus. A popular account of past and coming transits, from 1639 to 2012. With plates and woodcuts. London, 1874. xiv, 236 pp. Sm. 8°.............................. 6814.4
— The universe and the coming transits. London, 1874. Woodcuts. xiv, 303 pp. 22 plates. 8°. 6813.4

Shelf. No.

PROFESSOR, The. Brontë, C. 321.20
PROFESSOR, The, at the breakfast-table. Holmes, O. W. Boston, 1872. 12° 1934.4
PROGRÈS, Le. About, E. (F. V.) Paris, 1865. 18°. 5536.3
PROGRESS and prejudice. Gore, C. G. F. 311.4
PROMOTION: a vaudeville. Planché, J. R. New York, N. D. 12° 1635.5
PROPHÈTE, Le. Meyerbeer, G. (*In* Ditson, O., and co. Standard opera librettos) 6233.3.4
PROPHETIC voices concerning America. Sumner, C. Boston, 1874. 16° 833.1
PROPIAC, Catherine Joseph Ferdinand Girard de. Beautés de l'histoire de la Suisse. Orné de gravures. Paris, 1817. 435 pp. 12° 5728.6
PROSE and poetry. Harte, (F.) B. Leipzig, 1872. 2 v. in 1. Sq. 16° 339.1
PROSE idylls, new and old. Kingsley, C. London, 1873. Sm. 8° 5616.11
PROSE sketches and poems. Pike, A. Boston, 1834. Sm. 8° 1612.11
PROSE writers of Germany. Hedge, F. H. Philadelphia [*cop.* 1847]. 8° 5732.1
PROSTRATE state, The: South Carolina under negro government. Pike, J. S. New York, 1874. 12°. 5017.4
PROTESTANT episcopal church in America, History of the. Wilberforce, S. London, 1846. 16° 6328.3
PROTESTANT faith, A lecture on the. Olmstead, D. H. New York, 1874. 12° 6328.15
PROTESTANTISM. Arnold, M. St. Paul and protestantism. London, 1870. Sm. 8° 5815.2
— Weninger, F. X. Protestantism and infidelity. New York, 1862. 16° 1538.9

See also Reformation.

PROTOPLASM. Huxley, T. H. On yeast. (*In* Estes, D. Half-hour recreations in popular science) .. 6813.7
— Ross, J. On protoplasm: being an examination of J. H. Stirling's criticism of Prof. Huxley's views. London, 1874. Sm. 8° 1527.22
PROUD and lazy. Adams, W. T. 918.10
PROUDHON, Pierre Joseph. Sa vie et sa correspondance, 1838–48. Sainte-Beuve, C. A. Paris, 1872. 12° 5538.10
PROUT, William. Chemistry, meteorology, and the function of digestion, considered with reference to natural theology. 4th edition. Edited by J. W. Griffith. London, 1855. xxviii, 419 pp. Plate. [Bridgewater treatises.] Sm. 8° 6436.10
PROVERB series. *Namely:* —
— Bradley, M. Birds of a feather 936.30
— – Handsome is that handsome does 934.5
— – A wrong confessed is half redressed 945.4
— Neily, K. J. Actions speak louder than words .. 938.20
— – Fine feathers do not make fine birds 936.28
— – One good turn deserves another 938.21
PROVERBIAL philosophy. [Poem.] Tupper, M. F. New York, 1845. 2 v. in 1. Sm. 8° 5616.8
PROVOCATIONS of Madame Palissy, The. Manning, A. 514.2
PROVOST, The. Galt, J. 526.24
PRUDENCE Palfrey. Aldrich, T. B. 738.13
PRUDY keeping house. Clarke, R. S. 927.7
PRUE and I. Curtis, G. W. 526.1
PRUSSIA. Adams, W. T. Northern lands; or, Young America in. Boston, 1872. 16° 925.7
— Murray, J. Handbook for Prussia. London, 1871. 12° 5915.1

See also Germany.

PSALMODY. The psaltery. Mason, L., and Webb, G. J. Boston, 1847. Oblong 8° 1518.8
PSYCHÉ: tragédie-ballet. Molière, J. B. P. Œuvres. Paris, 1869. 12° 5537.2.3
PSYCHE, A, of to-day. Jenkin, *Mrs.* C. 518.11
PSYCHE's art. Alcott, L. M. 935.20
PSYCHOLOGY. Feuchterleben, E., *Freiherr* von. Principles of medical psychology. London, 1847. 8° 6013.8
— Follen, C. (T. C.) Fragment of a work on. Boston, 1842. 12° 5735.4.3
— Maudsley, H. Body and mind. Added psychological essays. London, 1873. 8° 6036.15

PSYCHOLOGY, *continued.*
— Porter, N. Psychology and the soul. New York, 1872. 8° 1520.4
— Spencer, H. Principles of. New York, 1871, 73. 2 v. 12° 6615.3
PUBLIC and parlor readings. *See* MONROE, Lewis Baxter.
PUBLIC libraries. *See* AMERICAN social science association. Free lending libraries. By W. W. Greenough. Cambridge, 1874. 8° 1932.2
PUBLICANS and sinners. Braddon, M. E. Leipzig. 3 v. in 2 .... 329.13
— *Same.* New York 732.13
PUCK. Rame, L. de la 327.24
PUDDLEFORD papers, The. Riley, H. H. 723.3
PULLEN, Henry William. Modern Christianity, a civilized heathenism. Boston, 1875. 167 pp 12° 6325.6
PULSZKY, Ferencz (Aurel) and Terezia. White, red, black. Sketches of American society in the United States. New York, 1853. 2 v. 12° ... 414.17
PUMPELLY, Raphael. Across America and Asia. Notes of a five years' journey around the world and of residence in Arizona, Japan and China. 5th edition, revised. New York, 1871. xvi, 454 pp. Maps. Folded plate. Illustrations. 8°. 5916.2
PUMPS, Treatise on. Swindell, J. G. London, N. D. 12° 1715.14
PUNCH. Vol. 64–68. London, 1873–75. 5 v. 4°. 6531.1
PUPILS, The, of St. John the divine. Yonge, C. M. [London, 1868.] Sm. 8° 5937.9
PURITANI, I. Bellini, V. (*In* Ditson, O., and co. Sandard opera librettos) 6233.3.3
PURITANISM, Essay on. Arnold, M. London, 1870. Sm. 8° 5815.24
PURITANS, History of the; 1517 to 1688. Neal, D. New York, 1871. 2 v. 8° 5411.1

Note. — Neal is a defender of the puritans, and he is reviewed in Whipple's Essays [1936.2.1], where there is a glowing tribute to their influence in New England history; and Higginson, in his "Atlantic essays" [1915.2, from the Atlantic monthly, Sept., 1863], depicts the life of the puritan minister in New England. Palfrey's delineation of the puritan character, in his "History of New England" [5010.2], is a moderate and generally just one, as opposed to the stronger light and shade of Macaulay in his "Essay on Milton" [5422.2], and of Bancroft in his "History of the United States" [5012.3]. The historical relations of the established church to the schools of independents, which grew out of puritanism, is shown from a churchman's point of view, in Curteis's Bampton lectures [5816.11]. Johnson gives, though briefly, the views of a tory in his Life of Butler [1238.20]. M. Arnold's "St. Paul and protestantism" [5815.24] has an introduction on the relations of puritanism to the church of England. Parton, in Harper's monthly, May, 1875, has a paper on the "Caricatures of the puritan times."

Works like Masson's Milton [see note under Milton] will afford much illustrative detail on one side or the other. Kingsley's essay [1223.5] has a popular defence of the puritan character, and instances the habits of our own day as justifying their views. Also see Carlyle's "Heroes and hero-worship" [1535.19] and Jeffreason's "Book about the clergy" [6320.6].

Histories of Massachusetts, New England, and Plymouth colony embrace the general subject, and particularly the phases of the movement on American soil; but the distinction should be borne in mind that the settlers of Massachusetts were the proper puritans, who would purify within the church, while those of Plymouth were seekers of that reform on an independent basis. See in this connection Bacon's "Genesis of the New England churches" [5212.13].

PURNELL, Thomas. Literature and its professors. London [1867]. xi, 292 pp. 16° 5927.3
PURSUIT, The, of knowledge under difficulties. Illustrated by anecdotes. Craik, G. L. New York, 1868. 2 v. 12° 1013.2
PUSSY Tip-toes' family. Sanford, *Mrs.* D. P. 912.26
PUT yourself in his place. Reade, C. 315.3
PUTLITZ, Gustav (Heinrich Gans) zu. Forest voices. Translated from the German. C. A. Smith, editor. Albany, 1866. 102 pp. 16° 1538.23
PUTNAM, Alfred Porter, *editor.* Singers and songs of the liberal faith. With biographical sketches of the writers and with historical and illustrative notes. Boston, 1875. xxiii, 556 pp. Sm. 8°. 1513.4
PUTNAM, Allen. Agassiz and spiritualism. Boston [1874]. 70+ pp. 16° 1538.12
— Bible marvel workers. Boston, 1873. 238 pp. 16° ....1536.18 and 5815.25
PUTNAM, E. Receipt book. New York, 1872. xxiii, 322 pp. Illustrated. 12° 1515.7

Shelf. No.

PUTNAM, George. Sermons, etc. V. P., V. D. PPH. V. 8° ... 1932.1

Contents.— The signs of the times. Boston, 1836. 24 pp.; Oration delivered before the Phi Beta Kappa society. Boston, 1844. 36 pp.; Discourse delivered at the installation of David Fosdick. Boston, 1846. vi, 72 pp.; Address delivered at the consecration of the cemetery at Forest hills, June 28, 1848. Roxbury, 1848. 28 pp.; Address on the life and character of H. A. S. Dearborn. Roxbury, 1851. 22 pp.

PUTNAM, George Palmer. The best reading. Hints on the selection of books; on the formation of libraries; on courses of reading, etc. With a classified bibliography. New York, 1872. 255 pp. 12° ... *R.R., F.3.5
— *Same.* Revised, enlarged, and continued to December, 1874. New York, 1875. 345 pp. [Putnam's handy-book series.] 12° ... 6136.10
PUTNAM, Israel. Drake, S. A. General Israel Putnam, the commander at Bunker hill. Boston, 1875. 8° ... 1011.8
— Peabody, O. W. B. Life of. (*In* Sparks, J. Library of American biography) ... 5028.1.7
— Tarbox, I. N. Life of. Boston, 1876. 8° ... 1012.7

Note.— For the authorities on the controversy as to General Putnam's share in the battle of Bunker hill, see the note in the Library Bulletin on Centennial reading, July, 1875.

PUTNAM'S handy-book series. *Namely:* —
— Eggleston, G. C. How to make a living ... 1536.20
— Putnam, G. P. The best reading ... 6136.10
PUTNAM'S monthly magazine. Vol. 1, 3–[10]; new series, vol. 1–6. New York, 1853–70. 15 v. 8°. 5127.1

Note.— In October, 1857, united with Emerson's United States magazine, and published under the double title of Emerson's magazine and Putnam's monthly until November, 1858, when it was discontinued. In 1868 a new series was begun by the original publishers under the original name, and was continued until November, 1870, when the work was merged in Scribner's monthly.

PYGMALION and Galatea: comedy. Gilbert, W. S. Original plays. New York, 1876. 12° ... 1634.1
PYM, John. *See* SMITH, G. Three English statesmen. New York, 1867. 12° ... 5425.1
PYNE, George. Perspective for beginners. 10th edition, with illustrations. London, 1870. iv, 168+ pp. Folded plates. 12° ... 1716.29
PYRAMIDS of Ghizeh. Découverte de l'âge et de la véritable destination des quatre pyramides de Gizeh. Dufeu, A. Paris, 1873. 8° ... 5932.11
PYRENEES. Blackburn, H. The Pyrenees: a description of summer life at French watering places. London, 1867. 8° ... 5522.3
— Taine, H. A. A tour through the. New York, 1874. 8° ... 423.18
PYRRHUS, History of. Abbott, J. ... 915.12

QUACKENBOS, George Payne. Natural philosophy. New York, 1864. 450 pp. 12° ... 6436.5
QUAD, M., *pseud.* *See* LEWIS, Charles B.
QUADROON, The. Reid, M. ... 725.7
QUARRELS of authors. Disraeli, I. New York, 1814. 2 v. 12° ... 1537.17
QUARRYING of stone, Treatise on the. Burgoyne, *Sir* J. F. London, N. D. 12° ... 1716.15
QUARTERLY review. Vol. 57, 59, 119, 134–138. London, 1836, 37, 66, 73–75. 8 v. 8° ... 6717.1
QUARTREMÈRE DE QUINCY, Antoine Chrysostome. Life and works of Raphael. *See* DUPPA, Richard ... 6217.3
QUEECHY. Warner, S. ... 317.12
QUEEN, The, of Connaught. A story ... 721.15
QUEEN, The, of hearts. Collins, (W.) W. ... 524.8
QUEEN, The, of the Adriatic; or, Venice, past and present. Adams, W. H. D. Boston, 1869. 16°. 227.4
QUEEN, The, of the regiment. King, K. ... 732.33
QUEEN Mab. Kavanagh, J. ... 323.1
QUEEN Mary. ["Bloody Mary" of England.] A drama. Tennyson, A. Boston, 1875. 16° ... 1617.10
— *Same.* Leipzig, 1876. Sq. 16° ... 1618.8
QUEEN Tita's wager. Black, W. Leipzig ... 330.12
— *Same.* New York ... 711.9
QUEEN'S, The, Maries. [Mary, queen of Scots, and her maids.] Melville, G. J. W. ... 321.17
QUEEN'S, The, necklace. Dumas, A. (D.) ... 511.6
QUEEN'S, The, revenge. Collins, (W.) W. ... 511.2

Shelf. No.

QUEENS. Emery, E. B. ... 931.3
QUEENS of Scotland, Lives of the. Strickland, A. New York, 1859–73. 8 v. 12° ... 627.1
QUEENS, The, of society. [Biographies.] Thomson, K. and J. C. New York, 1861. 12° ... 1216.17
QUEENS of song. [Biographies.] Clayton, E. C. London, 1863. 2 v. 8° ... 1221.4
QUEER bonnets. Tuthill, L. C. ... 933.27
QUEER folk. Hugessen, E. H. K. ... 916.30
QUEER little people. Stowe, H. (E.) B. ... 933.22
QUENTIN Durward. Scott, *Sir* W. Boston ... 523.4
— *Same.* Leipzig ... 324.2
QUESTION, A, of honor. Fisher, F. C. ... 713.8
QUIET nook, A, in the Jura. Ruffini, G. ... 316.20
QUINCY, Edmund. Life of Josiah Quincy. Boston, 1869. xii, 560 pp. Portraits. 8° ... 5025.2
QUINCY, Josiah, *jr.*, *b.* 1744, *d.* 1775, Life of. Quincy, J. Boston, 1825. 8° ... 5021.9
— *Same.* 2d edition. Boston, 1874. 8° ... 5022.16
QUINCY, Josiah, *b.* 1772, *d.* 1864. Essays on the soiling of cattle, and an address containing suggestions which may be useful to farmers. Boston, 1859. 64 pp. 8° ... 6614.4
— History of Harvard university. Boston, 1860. 2 v. Illustrated. 8° ... 810.7
— Life of Josiah Quincy, jun. Boston, 1825. viii, 498 pp. 8° ... 5021.9
— *Same.* 2d edition. [Edited with some additions by Eliza Susan Quincy. Added a reprint of Observations on the act of parliament commonly called the Boston port-bill; with thoughts on civil society and standing armies. Boston, 1774. Also an appendix.] Boston, 1874. Fac-similes. 8° ... 5022.16
— Municipal history of Boston, 1630–1830. Boston, 1852. xi, 444 pp. 1 plate. Plan. 8° ... 5011.5
— History of the Boston athenæum, with biographical notices of its deceased founders. Cambridge, 1851. xii, 263, 104+ pp. 8° ... 811.4
— Life of. Quincy, E. Boston, 1869. 8° ... 5025.2
QUINCY, Josiah Phillips. Charicles: a dramatic poem. Boston, 1856. 106 pp. 16° ... 1615.17
QUININE plant, Searching for the, in Peru. (*In* Many lands and many people) ... 431.3
QUINTILIANUS, Marcus Fabius. De institutione oratoria libri duo. Accedunt notæ Anglicæ. Cura C. K. Dillaway. Philadelphiæ [*cop.* 1844]. 207 pp. Sm. 12° ... 6118.5
QUINTUS Smyrnæus. Étude sur Quintus de Smyrna. Sainte-Beuve, C. A. Paris, 1870. 12° ... 5538.11
QUITS. Tautphoeus, J. M., *Baronin* ... 317.21
QUOTATIONS. Ballou, M. M. Treasury of thought. Forming an encyclopædia of quotations from ancient and modern authors. Boston, 1873. 8°. *R.R., E.2.4
— Bartlett, J. Familiar quotations. 6th edition. Boston, 1872. 16° ... *R.R., F.3.8
— *Same.* 7th edition. Boston, 1875. 16° .. *R.R., F.3.10
— Hale, S. J. Complete dictionary of poetical quotations. Philadelphia, 1872. 8° ... *R.R., F.3.1

Note.— Bartlett's book is of a distinct character from other books of quotations, in that only *familiar* excerpts are admitted, and a verbal index enables the user to trace the quotation to its source.

RAB [a dog] and his friends. Brown, J. Leipzig, 1862. Sq. 16° ... 311.29
— *Same.* (*In* Johnson, (E.) R. Little classics) ... 529.4.4
RABBIT fancier, The. Bement, C. N. New York, 1855. 12° ... 1524.3
RACE, The, for wealth. Riddell, J. H. ... 316.4
RACES, The, of the old world. Brace, C. L. New York, 1870. 12° ... 1523.1
RACHEL Gray. Kavanagh, J. ... 323.7
RACHEL Ray. Trollope, A. ... 319.4
RACINE, Jean de. Théâtre complet. Édition variorum. Par C. Louandre. Paris, 1870. 750+ pp. 12° ... 5537.3

Contents.— La Thébaïde; Alexandre le grand; Andromaque; Les plaideurs; Britannicus; Bérénice; Bajazet; Mithridate; Iphigénie; Phèdre; Esther; Athalie.

— Phädra. *See* SCHILLER, (J. C.) F. von. Werke. Stuttgart, 1867. 8° ... 5734.1.7

Shelf. No.

RADAU, Rodolphe. Wonders of acoustics. From the French. The English revised by R. Ball. With illustrations. New York, 1870. viii, 267 pp. 16°....1714.11

RADICAL problems. Bartol, C. A. Boston, 1873. 16°. 1525.14

RADICALISM. Teutscher Radikalismus in Amerika. Heinzen, C. N. P., 1867. 16°.... 2025.4

RAE, Edward. The land of the north wind; or, travels among the Laplanders and the Samoyedes. London, 1875. xvi, 352+ pp. Illustrations. Map. Sm. 8°.... 5935.5

RAE, John. Statement of some new principles of political economy. Boston, 1834. xvi, 414 pp. 8°.... 5822.7

RAE, W. Fraser. Westward by rail: a journey to San Francisco and back and a visit to the Mormons. With a map. Leipzig, 1874. 326 pp. Sq. 16°.... 438.3

— *editor.* Wilkes, Sheridan, Fox: the opposition under George III. New York, 1874. viii, 462 pp. 16°.... 5415.8

RAFFAELLO SANTI, *or* SANZIO DA URBINO. *See* SANTI, *or* SANZIO, Raffaello (Raphael) da Urbino.

RAFT, A, that no man made. Lowell, R. T. S. (*In* Johnson, (E.) R. Little classics).... 529.4.8

RAGGED Dick. Alger, H., *jr*.... 934.13

RAGGED Dick series. *See* ALGER, Horatio, *jr.*

RAGGED schools. Guthrie, T. New York, 1873. 12°. 6327.16

RAIKES, Thomas. Personal reminiscences. (*In* Stoddard, R. H. Bric-à-brac series).... 1828.7

RAILROAD jubilee, Sept. 17–19, 1851. *See* BOSTON, *Mass.*....811.5 and 6923.3

RAILROADS. Lardner, D. Railway economy; a treatise on the new art of transport. New York, 1850. 12°.... 6424.3

— Poor, H. V. Manual of the railroads of the United States, 1871–72. New York, 1871. 8°. 6923.10

— Stephenson, *Sir* R. M. The science of railway construction. London, 1869. 12°....1715.23

— Taylor, J. A fast life on the modern highway; being a glance into the railroad world from a new point of view. New York, 1874. 12°.... 735.35

— Vose, G. L. Handbook of railroad construction. Boston, 1857. 8°.... 6422.5

— – Manual for railroad engineers. Boston, 1873. 2 v. 8°.... 6424.1

RAINBOW and Lucky, Stories of. *See* ABBOTT, Jacob.

RAINBOW creed, The. Leppere, A. H.... 532.16

RAINBOW's journey. Abbott, J.... 914.19

RAINFORD series. *See* BRADLEY, Warren Ives.

RALEIGH, *Sir* Walter. Kingsley, C. Sir Walter Raleigh and his time. Boston, 1859. 12°.... 1223.5

— Lawrence, E. Lives of the British historians. New York, 1855. 12°....1224.7.1

— St. John, J. A. Life of. London, 1869. Sm. 8°. 5423.10

Note.—The best life for the general reader is that by St. John, 1868, based on the fullest information; Hume brought forward his accusations in the 45th and 48th chapters of his "History of England" [5413.2]. Kingsley's essay is based upon Tytler and other authorities, and is readable. There are beside an essay in Whipple's "Age of Elizabeth" [1936.5]; Lodge's "Portraits" [5337.6.3]; a "Secret history" in Disraeli's "Curiosities of literature" [5626.6]; a "psychological" study by Disraeli, in his "Amenities of literature" [1533.13]; and some new material by S. G. Drake, in the Genealogical register, April, 1862. See also the full account in Allibone. Raleigh figures in Scott's "Kenilworth" [324.8; 523.7].

RALPH Somerville. Eden, C. H....1115.19

RALPH the heir. Trollope, A.... 334.4

RALPH Wilton's weird. Alexander, *Mrs.* —.... 518.26

RALSTON, William Ralston Shedden. Russian folktales. London, 1873. xvi, 382 pp. 8°.... 5923.8

RAMBLER, The. [Periodic essays.] Johnson, S. Works. London, 1862. 8°....5422.3.1

RAMBLES and adventures of our school field-club. Davies, G. C. London, 1875. Sm. 8°....1115.15

RAMBLES of an archæologist among old books and old places. Fairholt, F. W. London, 1871. Sm. 4°.... 6232.3

RAMBLING story, A. Clarke, M. C.... 718.1

RAMBOSSON, J. Astronomy. Translated by C. B. Pitman. With wood engravings, maps, and coloured plates. London, 1875. xvii, 385+ pp. 8°.... 6812.1

Shelf. No.

RAME, Louise de la. (*Ouida.*) Bébée; or, two little wooden shoes.... 913.30

— Cecil Castlemaine's gage, and other novelettes... 331.5

— Chandos.... 327.21

— A dog of Flanders. (*In* Johnson, (E.) R. Little classics)....529.4.10

— Folle-Farine.... 327.22

— Idalia.... 327.19

— In a winter city. A story of the day.... 717.13

— A leaf in the storm. (*In* Johnson, (E.) R. Little classics)....529.4.11

— A leaf in the storm and other stories. Berlin... 717.1

— *Same.* Leipzig.... 327.23

— Pascarèl. Leipzig.... 329.7

— *Same.* Philadelphia.... 528.7

— Puck.... 327.24

— Signa. Leipzig.... 331.11

— *Same.* Philadelphia.... 723.15

— Strathmore.... 327.18

— Tricotrin.... 327.20

— Two little wooden shoes.... 329.18

— Under two flags.... 327.25

RAMESES the great; or, Egypt 3300 years ago. Tugnot de Lanoye, F. New York, 1872. 16°.... 1714.3

RAMROD, The, broken; or, the Bible, history, and common sense in favor of the moderate use of good spirituous liquors. Boston, 1859. 300 pp. Wood-cut. 12°.... 1915.9

RAMSAY, Allan. Works. With life by G. Chalmers; an essay on his genius and writings by Lord Woodhouselee; and an appendix relative to his life and posthumous reputation. Edinburgh [1852]. 3 v. Portrait. Illustrations. 12°... 5618.9

RAMSAY, Alexander. Rudiments of mineralogy. London, 1868. viii, 330 pp. Illustrated. Folded plate. 12°....1715.21

RAMSAY, Edward Bannerman. Reminiscences of Scottish life and character. [16th edition.] Edinburgh, 1867. xxviii, 280 pp. Portrait. 16°.... 5637.2

RAN away to sea. Reid, M.... 923.28

RANALD Bannerman's boyhood. MacDonald, G.... 536.19

RAND, Edward Sprague, *jr.* Flowers for the parlor and garden. Illustrations. Boston, 1870. 411 pp. 12°.... 1515.6

— Popular flowers, and how to cultivate them. Boston, 1873. 208 [206] pp. Illustrated. Sm. 4°....1516.17

— The window gardener. Boston, 1872. 132+ pp. Illustrated. 16°.... 6626.5

RANDOLPH, *Mrs.* —. Gentianella.... 714.9

— Wild hyacinth.... 714.32

RANDOLPH, John. *See* PARTON, J. Famous Americans of recent times. Boston, 1871. 8°....1214.14

RANDOLPH, Sarah N. The domestic life of Thomas Jefferson. Compiled from family letters and reminiscences. New York, 1872. 432 pp. Portraits. Illustrated. Sm. 8°.... 5025.3

RANGERS, The. [American historical novel.] Thompson, D. P. 2 v.... 734.2

RANGERS and regulators, The, of the Tanaha. A tale of the republic of Texas. Reid, M.... 527.18

RANKE, (Franz) Leopold von. A history of England principally in the seventeenth century. Oxford, 1875. 6 v. 8°.... 5412.6

Contents.—Vol. I. Crises in the early history, 1603-1629. II. 1629-1649. III. 1649-1674. IV. 1675-1691. V. 1690-1760; Appendix: [Extracts] from original documents. VI. Appendix: Criticisms of the historians; The war in Ireland, 1689, 90; Extracts from the reports of F. Bonnet; Extracts from the correspondence of William III; Index.

— History of the popes, their church and state, and especially of their conflicts with protestantism in the 16th and 17th centuries. Translated by E. Foster. London, 1871. 3 v. Portraits. Sm. 8°. 5516.7

RANTHORPE. Lewes, G. H.... 312.4

RAPE of the gamp. Mason, C. W.... 711.36

RAPE of the lock, The. [Poem.] Pope, A. Select poetical works. Leipzig, 1848. Sq. 16°....1613.10

— *Same.* (*In his* Works.) London, 1871. 8°....5612.2.5

RAPHAEL. *See* SANTI, *or* SANZIO, Raffaello (Raphael) da Urbino.

Shelf. No.

RAPHAEL; or, pages of the book of life at twenty. Lamartine, A. (M. L.) de. New York, 1868. 12°. 1935.2

RAPIDS, The, of Niagara. Warner, S. New York, 1876. 16°.............................. 1117.6

RASPE, Rodolph Eric. The adventures of Baron Munchausen. New and revised edition. With an introduction by T. Teignmouth Shore. Illustrated by Gustave Doré. 3d edition. London [1869]. 4°.............................. 5731.1

RASSELAS. [An Eastern tale.] Johnson, S. Works. London, 1862. 8°..........................5422.3.2

RATIONALISM. History of the rise and influence of the spirit of rationalism in Europe. Lecky, W. E. H. New York, 1872. 2 v. 8°............ 5914.7

RAU, Charles. Early man in Europe. Illustrated. New York, 1876. 162 pp. 8°..............6612.10

RÄUBER, Die. Schiller, (J. C.) F. von. Werke. Stuttgart, 1865. 8°.........................5734.1.2

RAUMER, Friedrich (Ludwig Georg) von. Die Königinnen Elisabeth und Maria Stuart. Mit dem Bildness der Maria Stuart. Leipzig, 1836. xvi, 630 pp. 12°.............................. 2026.3

RAVENSCLIFFE. Marsh-Caldwell, A.............. 313.24

RAVENSHOE. [Novel, Crimean war.] Kingsley, H. 326.20

RAWLINSON, George. The five great monarchies of the ancient Eastern world; or, the history, geography, and antiquities of Chaldæa, Assyria, Babylon, Media, and Persia. 2d edition. With maps and illustrations. London, 1871. 3 v. 8°. 5922.3

— A manual of ancient history from the earlier times to the fall of the Western empire. Oxford, 1869. xii, 580 pp. 8°......................5921.10

— The sixth great oriental monarchy; or the geography, history, and antiquities of Parthia. London, 1873. xiii, 458 pp. Maps. Illustrations. 8°.............................. 5932.6

— The seventh great oriental monarchy; or, the geography, history, and antiquities of the Sassanian or new Persian empire. Collected and illustrated from ancient and modern sources. London, 1876. xxi, 691 pp. Folded map. 8°....5923.11

RAWLINSON, *Sir* Henry (Creswicke). England and Russia in the East. A series of papers on the political and geographical condition of Central Asia. With map. London, 1875. xvi, 393 pp. 8°. 5921.5

RAY, Isaac. Mental hygiene. Boston, 1863. xi, 338 pp. 16°.............................. 6036.5

RAY. Spofford, H. E. (*In* Johnson, (E.) R. Little classics)..................................529.4.11

RAYMOND, Rossiter Worthington. The man in the moon and other people.......................... 912.25

— Silver and gold: an account of the mining and metallurgical industry of the United States, with reference chiefly to the precious metals. New York, 1873. 566 [564] pp. Illustrated. 8°.............................. 6631.5

— Statistics of mines and mining in the states and territories west of the Rocky mountains. 4th annual report. *See* UNITED STATES. *Department of the treasury*.............................. 5035.8

RAYMOND and Agnes: a drama. Lewis, M. G. New York, N. D. 12°.............................. 1635.4

RAYNOUARD, François Juste Marie. Lexique roman ou dictionnaire de la langue des troubadours, comparée avec les autres langues de l'Europe latine. Paris, 1838–44. 6 v. 8°............ 5531.1

Contents. — Vol. I. Recherches philologiques sur la langue romane; Résumé de la grammaire romane; Roman de Flamenca; Roman de Jaufre; Roman de Gérard de Rossillon; Chronique des Albigeois, poème de Guillaume de Tudèle; Roman de Fierabras; Roman de Blandin de Cornouailles; Pièces diverses; Breviari d'amor, par Matfre Ermengaud de Beziers; Le libre de Senequa: La vie de Sainte Énimie; Les quatre vertus cardinales, par Deudes de Prades; Vies de SS. Trophime, Honorat, Alexis; Évangile de Nicodème; Évangile de l'enfance II. Introduction au dictionnaire; A–C. III. D–K. IV. L–P. V. Q–Z. VI. Appendice; Vocabulaire alphabétique des mots disposés par familles dans le lexique.

READ, Harriette Fanning. Dramatic poems. Boston, 1848. vi, 297+ pp. 8°.............................. 1631.1

Contents. — Medea; Erminia; The new world.

READ, William. Placenta prævia; its history and treatment. Philadelphia, 1861. 340 pp. 8°.. 6021.5

Shelf. No.

READE, Charles. The box tunnel. (*In* Johnson, (E.) R. Little classics)..............................529.4.9

— Christie Johnstone. Leipzig.............................. 339.23

— The cloister and hearth. [15th century on the continent].............................. 316.24

— The eighth commandment.............................. 716.6

— A good fight, and other tales.............................. 538.2

— Griffith Gaunt.............................. 527.1

— Hard cash. [Private insane asylums].............. 316.22

— A hero and a martyr [James Lambert]: a true narrative. With portrait. New York, 1875. 8°. 710.32

— "It is never too late to mend".............. 316.25

Note. — Prison life in England; sheep raising in Australia.

— "Love me little, love me long".............. 315.2

— Peg Woffington, and other stories. Boston...... 527.3

Contents. — Peg Woffington; Christie Johnstone; Clouds and sunshine; Art; Propria quæ maribus; The box tunnel; Jack of all trades.

— Peg Woffington. [Theatrical life, Colley Cibber's time.] Leipzig.............................. 316.23

— Put yourself in his place. [Trade unions]..... 315.3

— A simpleton. Leipzig.............................. 328.29

— *Same.* New York.............................. 531.30

— A terrible temptation. Leipzig.............. 315.1

— *Same.* New York.............................. 531.34

— The wandering heir. Leipzig.............. 335.16

— *Same.* New York.............................. 531.14

— White lies. [Napoleonic times].............. 527.2

— and BOUCICAULT, Dion (L.) Foul play........ 724.18

READE, (William) Winwood. The African sketch-book. With maps and illustrations. London, 1873. 2 v. 8°.............................. 5925.4

READING. What to read, and how to read. Moore, C. H. New York, 1871. 12°.............. 1537.3

READING club, The. Baker, G. M. Boston, 1875, 76. 3 v. 12°..............................1538.1

READY-MONEY Mortiboy. Maurice, W., and Rice, J. 732.

READY reckoner, American. Day, B. H. New York [*cop.* 1866]. 16°.............................. 1938.

REAL folks. Whitney, A. D. T.............................. 735.1

REALM, The, of the ice king. By the author of "Saved from the wreck." London [1874]. 318 pp. Map. Illustrations. Sq. 16°..............5934.1

REALMAH. Helps, *Sir* A. Boston, 1869. 16°.... 524.2

REASON and redemption, or the Gospel as it attests itself. White, R. B. Philadelphia, 1873. 8°. 1532.

REASON in religion. Hedge, F. H. Boston, 1865. Sm. 8°.............................. 6325.

REBEL'S, A, recollections. Eggleston, G. C. New York, 1875. 16°..............................5016.1

RÉCAMIER, Jeanne Françoise Julie Adelaide Bernard. Memoirs and correspondence. Translated and edited by I. M. Luyster. 2d edition. Boston, 1867. xxii, 408 pp. Portrait. 12°.......... 1226.

— Madame Récamier and her friends. Lenormant, A. (C.) Boston, 1875. 12°..............1226.1

RECEIPTS. Benjamin, P. Wrinkles and recipes. New York [1875]. 12°..............................1717.

— Kitchiner, W. The cook's oracle: containing receipts for plain cookery. Boston, 1822. 12°...1516.

— Mackenzie, C. Five thousand receipts in all the useful and domestic arts. Philadelphia, 1858. 8°. 1531

— Miller, E. S. In the kitchen. Boston, 1875. Sm. 4°.............................. 153

— Putnam, E. Receipt book. New York, 1872. 12°. 151

— Woodman, M. S. Choice receipts. Boston, 1875. 12°.............................. 642

RECLUS, (Jean Jacques) Élisée. The earth; a descriptive history of the phenomena of the life of the globe. Translated by B. B. Woodward, and edited by H. Woodward. Illustrated by maps. New York, 1872. 573 pp. 8°.............. 663

— The ocean, atmosphere, and life. Being the second series of a descriptive history of the life of the globe. Illustrated. Maps. New York, 1873. 534 [528] pp. 8°.............................. 663

RECOLLECTIONS and reflections. Planché, J. R. London, 1872. 2 v. 8°.............................. 552

RECOLLECTIONS of a busy life. Greeley, H. New York, 1873. 8°.............................. 502

Shelf. No.

RECOLLECTIONS of a literary life. Mitford, M. R. New York [1851]. 12° 1536.4

Note. — Mostly citations of favorite writings.

RECOLLECTIONS of a page at the court of Louis XVI. Hézecques, C. A. F. F., *comte* d', *baron de Mailly*. London, 1873. 8° 5524.4
RECOLLECTIONS of my childhood. Lippincott, S. J. 922.25
RECOLLECTIONS of past life. Holland, *Sir* H. New York, 1872. 12° 5426.1
RECOLLECTIONS of seventy years. Farrar, E. W. Boston, 1866. 12° 1225.2
"RECOMMENDED to mercy" 315.4
RECREATIONS of a country parson. [Essays.] Boyd, A. K. H. Boston, 1862. 2 v. 16° 1535.16
RECREATIONS of Christopher North. [Essays.] Wilson, J. New York, 1871. 8° 1531.7
RECREATIVE arts. Bartlett, G. B. Parlor amusements for the young folks. Boston, 1875. 12°. 1517.5
— Bellew, F. The art of amusing. London, N. D. Sm. 8° 1518.10
— Boy's own book: a complete encyclopædia of outdoor and indoor exercises and diversions 916.5
— Cremer, W. H. The secret out; or, one thousand tricks in drawing-room or white magic. London, N. D. 16° 1516.11
— Dick, W. B., Frost, S. A., and Taylor, W. What shall we do to-night? or social amusements for evening parties. New York [1873]. 12° 1516.19
— Elliott, A. Out-of-doors: a handbook of games for the playground. London, 1872. 12°...... 1517.8
— — Within-doors: a book of games and pastimes for the drawing-room. London, 1872. 16° 916.19
— Frickell, G. Magic no mystery, etc. London, 1876. Sm. 8° 1515.20
— — The secret out; or, one thousand tricks with cards, and other recreations. New York [*cop.* 1869]. 12° 1515.15
— — The sociable; or, 1001 home amusements. New York [*cop.* 1858]. 12° 1514.6
— Routledge, E., *editor*. Every boy's book: a complete encyclopædia of sports and amusements. London, 1863. 16° 916.4
— *Same.* London [1868]. 16° 6414.2
— Smith, C. L. Home arts for young and old. Boston, 1873. 12° 1517.3
— Strutt, J. The sports and pastimes of the people of England. London, 1876. Sm. 8° 6414.4
— Wood, J. G. The modern playmate. London [1870]. Sq. 16° 6414.3
— *Same.* London [1875]. Sm. 8° 6414.6

See also Billiards, Cards, Charades, Chess, Fish and fishing, Games, Magic, Magician, Skating, Sports and sporting, Swimming, Whist.

RECTOR, The, and the doctor's family. Oliphant, M. (O. W.) 328.7
RECTOR, The, of St. Mark's. Holmes, M. J........ 534.25
RED as a rose is she. Broughton, R............... 310.1
RED cotton night-cap country. [Poems.] Browning, R. Boston, 1873. 12° 1617.4
RED court farm, The. Wood, E. P................. 333.12
RED cross; or, Young America in England and Wales. Adams, W. T. Boston, 1871. 16° ... 916.18
RED-JACKET. *See* SA-GO-YE-WAT-HA.
RED river, *Louisiana*, Exploration of the, in 1852. Marcy, R. B., and MacClellan, G. B. Washington, 1854. 8° 5033.2
RED Rover, The. Cooper, J. F. 525.24
RED sea, The Rob Roy on the. [Canoe voyage.] Macgregor, J. New York, 1870. Sm. 8°..... 423.17
RED-SHANTY boys, The. Ludlow, P............... 937.19
REDFIELD, James W. Comparative physiognomy; or, resemblances between men and animals. Illustrated. New York, 1852. 334 pp. 8°...1521.15
REDGAUNTLET. Scott, *Sir* W..................... 523.5
REDMOND, count O'Hanlon, the Irish rapparee. Carleton, W.. 518.5
REDSKINS, The. Cooper, J. F..................... 525.2
REED, Rebecca Theresa. Six months in a convent. Boston, 1835. 192 pp. 16° 1539.2
REED, A, shaken with the wind. Faithful, E. 737.12

Shelf. No.

REEMELIN, Charles. The vine-dresser's manual, an illustrated treatise on vineyards and wine-making. New York, 1855. 103 pp. 12°......... 6426.4
REFLECTION, Aids to. Coleridge, S. T. London, 1867. 16° 5818.11
REFORMATION, The. Burnet, G. The history of the reformation of the church of England. Oxford, 1865. 7 v. 8° 6320.5
— Fisher, G. P. The reformation. New York, 1873. 8° 5813.7
— Hardwick, C. History of the Christian church during the. London, 1874. Sm. 8° 6326.20
— Seebohm, F. The era of the protestant revolution. London, 1874. Sq. 16° 628.3

Note. — For the preliminaries of the general movement, see Newman's "Essays" [5614.5.2] for that of the 11th century; the English church histories and lives of Wickliff with Milman's "Latin Christianity" [5817.11] for that in England in the 14th century. Lives of Huss cover that in Bohemia in the 15th century. The struggle of the Waldenses is told in Milman's "Latin Christianity" [5817.11]. Robertson's "History of the Christian church" [6327.10] comes down to the beginning of the German movement under Luther.

In general. The general reader will find Prof. Fisher's book [5813.7] ample, and derive aid from his references and list of books. If a more condensed account is wanted use Seebohm. Hardwick, who takes a church of England standpoint, may be read in connection, and will be found a convenient manual, with foot note references, and in chapter 5 he names the different sects and heresies accompanying the movement. If further study is needed, see the note in the Lower Hall Catalogue of history. D'Aubigné is reviewed in Sir James Stephen's Essays [1931.1].

In England and Scotland. See England, ecclesiastical history, note. The general historians Hume and Robertson on the protestant side, and Lingard on the catholic side, will give a general view. See lives of principal English reformers, and Bacon's "Genesis of the New England churches" [5812.13]; and Froude's History [826.9] for the part of Henry VIII and Wolsey in the movement, and several papers in his "Short studies" [1914.5], having in part relation to the movement in Scotland, concerning which lives of Knox should be consulted, and the general histories of Scotland. Neal's "Puritans" [5411.1] elucidates the events from the puritan point of view.

In Germany. See Germany, ecclesiastical history, note; Luther, note; and Melanchthon, note. Fisher's general history will ordinarily suffice. Döllinger has a chapter in his "Reunion of the churches" [5816.6]; and Robertson's "Charles V" [5610.1] necessarily concerns it. Macaulay's Essays [1918.4] on Ranke and Hallam relate in part to the reformation.

In France, etc. See France, ecclesiastical history, note; Switzerland, note; Calvin, note; also Froude on Calvinism, in his "Short studies" [1914.5.1]; and Huguenots, note. Also, D'Aumale's "Princes of Condé" [5522.9] and White's Saint Bartholomew.

In the Netherlands. Motley's "Dutch republic" [822.2] and Prescott's "Philip II" [1222.1].

In Spain. Beside Fisher and the general accounts, see Prescott's "Philip II" [1222.1] and Ticknor's "Spanish literature" [5922.2].

See also Coxe's "House of Austria" [5715.1]; Roscoe's "Leo X" [5526.6]; Robertson's "Charles V" [5610.1]; Gibbon's 54th chapter [824.9]; Smyth's 9th and 10th lecture [5012.10; 5925.7]; Hallam's literature [1531.2]; Prescott's "Ferdinand and Isabella" [5922.5]; Ranke's "Lives of the popes" [5516.7]; and Guizot's "History of civilization" [5924.8]. Parton, in Harper's monthly, April, 1875, has a paper on the caricatures of the reformation period.

Also, Ecclesiastical history, Protestantism.

In Fiction. In England, Holt's "Isoult Barry of Wynscote" and "Robin Tremayne," time of Mary I. In Scotland, Mrs. Oliphant's "Magdalen Hepburn." In France, James's "Huguenot" [722.10], and Bungener's "Bourdaloue and Louis XIV" [716.4] and "Priest and Huguenot" [627.4], time of Louis XV. In Germany, Mrs. Charles's "Schönberg-Cotta family" [321.3]; and Mrs. Manning's "Good old times." In Spain, Mrs. Charles's "Martyrs of Spain." For Savonarola's agency in Italy, see George Eliot's "Romola" [310.23].

REGIMEN, Lectures on. Willich, A. F. M. Boston, 1800. 2 v. 12° 6015.1
REGINALD Hastings. Warburton, E. (B. G.) 531.18
REGINALD Hetherege. Kingsley, H............... 310.21
REICHEL, William C., *editor*. A memorial of the dedication of monuments erected by the Moravian historical society to mark the sites of ancient missionary stations in New York and Connecticut. New York, 1860. viii, 5–184+ pp. Illustrated. 8° 831.3
REICHSGRÄFIN Gisela. John, E. Leipzig, 1874. 2 v. 16° 5736.2
REID, Christian, *pseud.* *See* FISHER, Frances C.
REID, Mayne. The boy hunters 932.14
— The boy slaves 931.1
— The boy tar 923.26
— Bruin: the grand bear hunt 937.22
— The bush-boys 923.27
— The castaways: a story of adventure in the wilds of Borneo 937.23
— The child wife 527.5

Shelf. No.

Reid, Mayne, *continued.*
— The cliff-climbers; or, the lone home in the Himalayas.................................. 923.31
— The English family Robinson. The desert home. 937.21
— The flag of distress: a tale of the South sea 921.18
— The headless horseman 725.9
— The hunter's feast.................................. 527.7
— Lost Lenore... 725.1
— The maroon: or planter life in Jamaica......... 725.2
— Odd people. A popular description of singular races of man 923.32
— Osceola the Seminole 725.11
— The plant hunters; or, adventures among the Himalaya mountains 923.29
— The quadroon 725.7
— Ran away to sea...................................... 923.28
— The rangers and regulators of the Tanaha: or, life among the lawless. A tale of the republic of Texas.. 527.18
— The rifle-rangers; or, adventures in Southern Mexico 527.6
— The scalp-hunters.................................... 725.5
— The tiger-hunter...................................... 725.4
— The war-trail.. 725.10
— The white chief. A legend of North Mexico ... 713.14
— The white gauntlet 527.4
— The wild huntress 725.6
— Wild life; or, adventures on the frontier 725.3
— The wood-rangers; or, the trappers of Sonora... 725.8
— The young voyageurs 923.33
— The young yägers, or a narrative of hunting adventures in Southern Africa.................. 923.30
Reid, Thomas. Essays on the intellectual powers of man. Abridged. With notes and illustrations from Sir W. Hamilton and others. Edited by J. Walker. 10th edition. Philadelphia, 1861. xv, 492 pp. 12° 1526.23
— An inquiry into the human mind, on the principles of common sense. 4th edition. London, 1775. xvi, 488 pp. 8° 5834.9
Reign of law, The, [in natural science]. Campbell, G. D., *duke of Argyll.* New York [1869]. 16° 1525.15
Rejected addresses, and other poems. Smith, J. and H. New York, 1871. 12° 1624.2

Note.—At the opening of the new Drury Lane theatre in 1812, there was a competition of poets for the opening address, and these rejected addresses are the supposed unsuccessful ones, being capital imitations of the well-known poets of the day.

Rejected wife, The. Stephens, A. S. (W.)........ 727.14
Religio medici. Browne, *Sir* T. Boston, 1872. 16°.5617.16
Religion, The, of Rome described by a Roman. Authorised translation [with an introduction]. By W. Howitt. London, 1873. xxii, 374 pp. Sm. 8° 5817.6
Religion. The Bremen lectures on fundamental, living, religious questions. Boston, 1871. 12°.1536.11
— Brinton, D. G. The religious sentiment, its source and aim. A contribution to the science and philosophy of. New York, 1876. 16° 5815.27
— Clarke, J. F. Common-sense in. Boston, 1874. 12° 5817.7
— Dewey, O. Discourses on the nature of. New York, 1847. 3 v. 12°........................ 5237.2
— Doddridge, P. The rise and progress of religion in the soul. Exeter, 1794. 12° 6327.9
— Draper, J. W. History of the conflict between science and religion. New York, 1875. 12°... 5826.4
— Foster, J. Essay on the importance of considering the subject of. Boston, 1828. 12° 1916.8
— Frothingham, O. B. The religion of humanity. New York, 1873. 12° 1537.6
— Hedge, F. H. Reason in. Boston, 1865. Sm. 8°. 6325.4
— Humboldt, (C.) W. von. Religious thoughts and opinions. Boston, 1851. 16°...................5818.10
— Johnson, S. Oriental religions and their relation to universal religion. Boston, 1873. 8° 5811.3
— Le Conte, J. Religion and science. New York, 1874. 12° 5817.14
— Martineau, J. Religion as affected by modern materialism. New York, 1875. 16°.......... 5818.2

Religion, *continued.*
— Mill, J. S. Three essays on. New York, 1874. 8°. 6325.7
— Morison, D. The religious history of man. London, 1842. Sm. 8°..................................5816.15
— Mueller, (F.) M. Lectures on the science of. New York, 1872. Sm. 8° 5616.2
— Temple, F. The present relations of science to. (*In* Hedge, F. H. Recent inquiries in theology).1526.24
— Ware, H. Inquiry into the foundation, evidences, and truths of. Cambridge, 1842. 2 v. 12°. 5815.1
— Weiss, J. American religion. Boston, 1871. 12°. 1537.5

See also Christianity, Evidences, Sects, Theology.

Religions. Adams, H. Dictionary of all religions and religious denominations, ancient and modern. Boston, 1817. 8° 5812.3
— – A view of. Boston, 1801. 8° .....1530.4 and 5814.7
— Hayward, J. The book of. Boston, 1843. 12°. 1534.4
Religious magazine and monthly review. Vol. 49, 50, 51, no. 1, 2. Boston, 1873, 74. 3 v. 8°.. 6738.1

Note.—In vol. 51, the title is changed to "Monthly religious magazine and theological review."

Rémusat, Charles (François Marie), *comte* de. Bacon, sa vie, son temps, sa philosophie, et de son influence jusqu'à nos jours. 2e édition. Paris, 1858. xv, 464+ pp. 18° 2016.9
Rena. Hentz, C. L.. 534.16
Renaissance. Pater, W. H. Studies in the history of the. London, 1873. Sm 8°........... 5925.2
— Symonds, J. A. Renaissance. London, 1875. 8°. 5522.8

Note.—Symonds's book so far as published does not touch the artistic development of this period. Pater covers the chief manifestations of this many-sided movement, which is commonly defined as the revival in the 15th century of the feelings of classic antiquity. See notes under Italy and the Middle ages.

Renan, (Joseph) Ernest. The apostles. From the original French. London, 1869. 288+ pp. 8°. 5812.8
— Life of Jesus. From the French by C. E. Wilbour. New York, 1865. 376 pp. 12°...... 1525.2
Rendezvous, The: an operetta. Ayton, R. New York, n. d. 12° 1635.3
René of Anjou, *king of Sicily, Naples, and Jerusalem,* Life and times of. Hookham, M. A. London, 1872. 8°..5522.10
Rennie, John, Life of. Smiles, S. Lives of the engineers. London, 1861. 8°......................5421.4.2
Rent, A, in a cloud. Lever, C. (J.) Leipzig..... 332.5
— *Same.* London.. 516.3
Renwick, James. Life of David Rittenhouse. (*In* Sparks, J. Library of American biography) .. 528.1.7
— Life of Robert Fulton. (*In* Sparks, J. Library of American biography).........................528.1.10
Representative men. [Essays on different celebrated characters.] Emerson, R. W. Boston, 1875. 12° 1916.6
— *Same.* (*In his* Prose works.) Boston, 1873. 12°.1934.6.2
Reptiles and birds. Figuier, (G.) L. London [1869]. 8° 1521.3
Republic, The, of letters. Vol. 2–4. Whitelaw, A. Glasgow, 1833. 3 v. 16°......................... 5618.6
Repulse bay, Brief narrative of an unsuccessful attempt to reach, in 1824. Lyon, G. F. London, 1825. 8° 424.1
Responsibility, The limitations of human. Wayland, F. Boston, 1838. 16°....................... 5838.4
Retina, Treatise upon the nature and treatment of morbid sensibility of the. Dix, J. H. Boston, 1849. 12°... 6015.7
Retribution. Southworth, E. D. E. N. 727.12
Retz, *Cardinal de.* *See* Gondi, Jean François Paul de.
Reumont, Alfred von. Römische Briefe. 1837, 38. Leipzig, 1840. 2 v. 12°.......................... 2027.3
— Neue römische briefe. Leipzig, 1844. 2 v. 12°.2027.4
Reuter, Fritz. In the year '13: a tale of Mecklenburg life. Translated by C. L. Lewes........... 316.9
Revealed religion. *See* Supernatural religion.
Revelator, The. Pierce, A. P. Boston, 1870. 12°.1538.18
Revere, Joseph Warren. Kool and saddle: a retrospect of forty years of military and naval service. Boston, 1872. xiii, 360 pp. 12° 5914.3

Shelf. No.

REVERIES of a bachelor. Mitchell, D. G. New York, 1873. 12° 1934.9

REVIEW of a part of Prescott's 'History of Ferdinand and Isabella,' and of Campbell's 'Lectures on poetry.' Boston, 1841. 199 pp. 12° 1536.23

REVUE des deux mondes. Tome 3, 4; Seconde période, Tome 10, 49-54, 64-72; 105-108; Troisième période, Tome 1-13. Paris, 1853-76. 35 v. in 39. 8° 5315.1

— Table générale 1831-1874. Paris, 1875. viii, 477+ pp. 8° 5315.2

REYNOLDS, Frederick. Life and times. Written by himself. London, 1826. 2 v. Portrait. 8° 1222.3

REYNOLDS, George W. M. The rye-house plot 510.12

REYNOLDS, *Sir* Joshua. Discourses. [With] notes and plates by J. Burnet. London, 1842. iv, 279+ pp. 4° 6230.1

— Literary works. Prefixed a memoir, with remarks on his professional character, illustrative of his principles and practice. By Henry W. Beechy. New edition. London, 1855. 2 v. Portrait. 12° 6215.8

Life and times of. Leslie, C. R., and Taylor, T. London, 1865. 2 v. 8° 5332.6

Note. — The life begun by Leslie and finished by Tom Taylor is the fullest and most elaborate account, and it was originally undertaken because Leslie was dissatisfied with Cunningham's life. The memoir by Beechy, prefixed to his edition of Reynold's "Discourses" is compact. See references in Allibone, and lives of his contemporaries, like Boswell's Johnson [1225.12; 5423.7], Forster's Goldsmith [1022.1], etc. Also, note under Painting, English school.

RHAZES. *See* ABÚ BECR MOHAMMED IBN ZACARÍYÁ AR-RÁZÍ.

RHETORIC. Abbott, E. A., and Seeley, J. R. English lessons for English people. London, 1871. Sm. 8° 1531.5

— Bascom, J. Philosophy of. Boston, 1870. 12° 1535.12

— Blair, H. Lectures on. Brooklyn, 1807. 2 v. 8° 1912.2

— *Same.* Abridged. Windsor, 1809. 12° 1918.6

— Campbell, G. The philosophy of. New York, 1868. 12° 1533.5

RHEUMATISM, Treatise on the nature and cure of. Scudamore, C. Philadelphia, 1819. 8° 6023.14

RHINE, The. Abbott, J. Rollo on the Rhine 917.17

— Baedeker, C. Handbook for travellers. Coblenz, 1870. 16° 5718.3

— Hood, T. Up the Rhine. New York, 1872. 12° 536.6

— Hugo, V. (M.), *vicomte.* The Rhine. Boston [1874]. 12° 436.1

— Murray, J. Handbook for the Rhine from Holland to Switzerland. London, 1871. 12° 5915.1

Note. — Murray's "Handbook," and for more condensed information, Baedeker's, form the most convenient manuals. Hood's book humorously chronicles the impressions of the Rhine scenery, etc., on different members of a London Cockney family, who, with their servants, record their sentiments in letters sent home. See general travels in Europe, Germany, etc.

RHODA Thornton's girlhood. Pratt, M. E. 934.33

RHODA'S corner. [Juvenile.] Payne, A. M. M. 1118.7

RHODES, Albert. The French at home. With illustrations. New York [1875]. 256 pp. Sq. 16° 5528.8

RIBOT, Th. English psychology. Translated from the French. New York, 1874. viii, 328 pp. 8° 5835.5

Contents. — Hartley; James Mill; Herbert Spencer; A. Bain; G. H. Lewes; Samuel Bailey; John Stuart Mill.

RICCI, Frederico and Luigi. Crispino e la comare. (*In* Ditson, O., and co. Standard opera librettos) 6233.3.1

RICE, James, *joint author.* My little girl. *See* MAURICE, Walter 731.26

— Ready-Money Mortiboy. *See* MAURICE, Walter 732.9

— With harp and crown. *See* MAURICE, Walter 721.20

RICE, Nathan P. Trials of a public benefactor, as illustrated in the discovery of etherization. New York, 1859. 460+ pp. Illustrated. Portraits. 12° 6826.1

RICH and humble. Adams, W. T. 925.5

RICH Medway's two loves. Gardner, C. E. 714.24

RICHARD I (*Cœur de Lion*), *of England.* Abbott, J. History of. [Juvenile] 915.13

— James, G. P. R. History of. London, 1854. 2 v. Sm. 8° 5526.7

RICHARD II, *of England,* History of. Abbott, J. [Juvenile] 915.6

RICHARD III, *of England.* Abbott, J. History of. [Juvenile] 915.5

— Hayward, A. Biographical and critical essays. London, 1873. 8° 5833.3.2

RICHARD Hurdis. Simms, W. G. 716.32

RICHARD the fearless. Yonge, C. M. 927.20

RICHARD Vandermarck. Harris, M. 515.16

RICHARDSON, Abby Sage. The history of our country from its discovery by Columbus to the celebration of the centennial anniversary of its declaration of independence. Illustrated. Boston, 1875. 600 pp. Maps. Fac-similes. 8° 812.3

RICHARDSON, Albert Deane. A personal history of Ulysses S. Grant. Illustrated by engravings, fac-similes, and maps. With a portrait and sketch of Schuyler Colfax. Hartford, 1868. 560 pp. 8° 1210.2

— The secret service, the field, the dungeon, and the escape. Hartford, 1866. 512 pp. Portraits. Illustrations. Fac-simile. 8° 813.15

RICHARDSON, Charles J. House-building, from a cottage to a mansion. 2d edition, corrected and enlarged with illustrations. New York, 1873. viii, 504 pp. Sm. 8° 6226.3

RICHARDSON, James. Wonders of the Yellowstone. New edition, with map[s] and illustrations. New York, 1873. xii, 256 pp. 12° 224.8

RICHARDSON, *Sir* John. Biography of Sir John Franklin. (*In* Macaulay, T. B., and others. New biographies of illustrious men) 5428.4

RICHARDSON, Samuel. Clarissa [Harlowe]. Leipzig. 4 v. in 2 .... 316.21

— *Same.* Leisure hour series. Condensed by C. H. Jones. New York 518.27

— Richardson's novels. Stephen, L. Hours in a library. London, 1874. Sm. 8° 6136.9

RICHARDSON, T. A. Art of architectural modelling in paper. With illustrations. London, 1859. 109+ pp. 12° 1716.5

RICHELIEU: a play. Bulwer-Lytton, E. (G. E.) L. Dramatic works. Leipzig, 1860. Sq. 16° 1614.5

Note. — May be compared with James's novel of "Richelieu" [722.22], and De Vigny's "Cinq-mars" [537.21], touching on the same era and characters.

RICHELIEU. A tale of France. James, G. P. R. 722.22

RICHTER, Jean Paul Friedrich. Flower, fruit and thorn pieces. Translated from the German by E. H. Noel. Leipzig, 1871. 2 v. in 1. Sq. 16° 316.8

— Carlyle, T. German romance. Boston, 1841. 2 v. in 1. 12° 5725.2

— Lee, E. B. Life of. Boston, 1864. 12° 1227.4

Note. — The best English account of considerable extent is Mrs. Lee's, who translates Richter's autobiography, and continues the narrative, drawing aid from the German continuation by Förster and others. For French estimates, see Madame de Staël's "Germany" [5726.1]. Carlyle has done much to familiarize the English reader with Richter, — see his Essays [5610.7] and his "German romance" [5725.2]. See also Hedge's "Prose writers of Germany" [5732.1], and De Quincey's "Philosophical writers." See Germany, literature, *note.*

RICORD, Frederick William. History of Rome. New York, 1859. 315 pp. Illustrated. 12° 826.8

RIDDELL, J. H. (*F. G. Trafford.*) Above suspicion. 730.17

— The earl's promise. 2 v. 329.5

— Far above rubies 316.3

— George Geith of Fen court 316.1

— A life's assize 720.5

— Maxwell Drewitt 316.2

— Mortomley's estate 319.31

— The race for wealth 316.4

— Too much alone 720.7

RIDDLE, Albert G. Alice Brand. A romance of the capital 713.6

RIDDLE, Joseph Esmond, *joint author.* Latin-English dictionary. *See* WHITE, John Tahourdin. *R.R., D.3.13

RIDER, Jane C., Account of. Belden, L. W. Springfield, 1834. 12° 1928.4

RIDGELY, David, *editor.* Annals of Annapolis, 1649-1812: with incidents in the history of Maryland. Baltimore, 1841. 283+ pp. Plate. 12° 817.15

Shelf. No.

RIDGWAY, R., *joint author.* History of North American birds. *See* BAIRD, Spencer Fullerton 6611.1
RIENZI. [Historical novel, Italian events.] Bulwer-Lytton, E. (G. E.) L. Leipzig 336.1
— *Same.* New York 5536.11
RIFFAULT, Jean René Denis, and VERGNAUD, Amand. Manuel du peintre en bâtiments, vitrier, doreur, argenteur et vernisseur. Nouvelle édition, entièrement refondue et ornée de figures. Paris, 1851. viii, 386 pp. 24°. [Manuel Roret] 6429.3
RIFLE, The, and the hound in Ceylon. Baker, *Sir* S. W. Philadelphia, 1871. 16° 1515.2
RIFLE-RANGERS, The. Reid, M. 527.6
RIGHT one, The. Schwartz, M. S. 531.7
RIGHTED at last. Fuller, M. 521.10
RIGOLETTO. Verdi, G. (*In* Ditson, O., and co. Standard opera librettos) 6233.3.6
RILEY, Henry Hopkins. The Puddleford papers; or, humors of the West. With illustrations. Boston, 1875. 386 [384] pp. 16° 723.3
RINGWALT, J. Luther, *editor.* American encyclopædia of printing. Philadelphia, 1871. 512 pp. Illustrated. L. 8° .... *R.R., A.3.4
RIO, A. F. Poetry of Christian art. From the French. London, 1854. xi, 417 pp. 1 plate. 12° 6234.1
RISE, The, of great families. Burke, *Sir* (J.) B. London, 1873. Sm. 8° 5611.8
RISE, The, of Iskander. Disraeli, B. (*In* Johnson, (E.) R. Little classics) 529.4.6
RISEN from the ranks. Alger, H., *jr.* 935.32
RISING faith, The. Bartol, C. A. Boston, 1874. 16°. 5817.12
RISING son, The; or the antecedents and advancement of the colored race. Brown, W. W. Boston, 1874. 8° 814.6
RITA: an autobiography. Aïdé, H. 311.19
RITCHIE, Anna Cora, *formerly Mrs. Mowatt.* Autobiography of an actress. Boston, 1854. 448 pp. Portrait. Sm. 8° 1216.6
— The clergyman's wife and other sketches 723.30
— Fairy fingers. A novel 723.19
— Plays. New and revised edition. Boston, 1855. 2 v. in 1. 12° 1635.1

Contents. — Armand; Fashion.

RITCHIE, Leitch. The romance of history. France. With illustrations. London, N. D. 560+ pp. 16°. 828.11
RITTENHOUSE, David, Life of. Renwick, J. (*In* Sparks, J. Library of American biography) .. 5028.1.7
RITTER, Carl, Life of. Gage, W. L. New York, 1867. Sm. 8° 1024.8
RITTER, Frederic Louis. History of music, in the form of lectures. Boston, 1870, 74. 2 v. 16°. 6237.2
RITUALISM. The ritual reason why. Walker, C. London [1868]. 16° 6328.10
RIVAL dreamers, The. Banim, J. (*In* Johnson, (E.) R. Little classics) 529.4.12
RIVALS, The. Griffin, G. 517.10
RIVALS, The: a comedy. Sheridan, R. B. Dramatic works. London, 1848. 16° 1635.2
— *Same.* Leipzig, 1869. Sq. 16° 1614.11
— *Same.* London, 1875. Sm. 8° 5626.9
RIVERDALE books. *See* ADAMS, William T.
RIVER-SIDE visitor, The. The great army. London, 1876. Sm. 8° 1838.2
RIVERS and torrents, Treatise on. Frisi, P. London, N. D. 12° 1715.20
RIVERS of ice. A tale illustrative of Alpine adventure and glacier action. Ballantyne, R. M. 931.11
ROADS, Rudimentary papers on constructing and repairing common. Mallet, R. London, 1866. 12° 1716.16
ROAST pig, A dissertation upon. Lamb, C. (*In* Johnson, (E.) R. Little classics) 529.4.5
ROB of the bowl. Kennedy, J. P. 736.25
ROBERT Falconer. MacDonald, G. 512.9
ROBERT Graham. Hentz, C. L. 534.21
ROBERT le diable. Meyerbeer, G. (*In* Ditson, O., and co. Standard opera librettos) 6233.3.4
ROBERTS, William. Memoirs of the life and correspondence of Hannah More. New York, 1834. 2 v. 12° 1025.1

Shelf. No.

ROBERTSON, Frederick William. Life and letters. Edited by S. A. Brooke. Boston, 1865. 2 v. Portrait. 12° 1225.7
— Sermons preached at Trinity chapel, Brighton. Leipzig, 1861. 4 v. in 2. Sq. 16° 1538.1
ROBERTSON, James Craigie. Becket, archbishop of Canterbury. A biography. London, 1859. xi, 360 pp. Illustrated. Sm. 8° 5424.13
— History of the Christian church from the apostolic age to the reformation. New and revised edition. Vol. I–IV. London, 1874. 4 v. Sm. 8°. 6327.10
— Percy anecdotes. *See* BYERLEY, Thomas 1231.3
ROBERTSON, Margaret Murray. Janet's love and service 723.7
— The perils of orphanhood; or, Frederica and her guardians 714.33
ROBERTSON, William. Works. Prefixed an account of his life and writings by D. Stewart. With portrait. London, 1840. lviii, 1184, 30 pp. 8°. 5610.1

Contents. — The situation of the world at the time of Christ's appearance: a sermon; History of Scotland; History of the reign of Charles V; History of America; Historical disquisition concerning ancient India.

— History of the reign of Charles V. With an account of the emperor's life after his abdication, by W. H. Prescott. London, 1857. 2 v. 16°. 1226.9
— *See* LAWRENCE, E. Lives of the British historians. New York, 1855. 12° 1224.7.1
ROBINSON, Edward, and SMITH, Eli. Biblical researches in Palestine, Mount Sinai and Arabia Petræa. With maps and plans. Boston, 1841. 3 v. Atlas. 8° 5810.5
ROBINSON, Frederick William. Anne Judge, spinster. 731.25
— Carry's confession 731.18
— Christie's faith 716.8
— A girl's romance, and other tales 731.37
— Grandmother's money 731.23
— Her face was her fortune 731.19
— The house of Elmore 731.39
— Little Kate Kirby 731.1
— Mattie: a stray 731.14
— Mr. Stewart's intentions 731.15
— No church 314.6
— No man's friend 731.17
— One and twenty 731.22
— Owen: — a waif 318.1
— Poor humanity 731.11
— Second-cousin Sarah 732.32
— Slaves of the ring 731.33
— Stern necessity 731.13
— Sweet nineteen 731.40
— True to herself 731.12
— Under the spell 731.24
— Wildflower 731.38
— A woman's ransom 734.19
ROBINSON, Henry Crabb. Diary, reminiscences, and correspondence. Selected and edited by T. Sadler. Boston, 1871. 2 v. 12° 5425.3
ROBINSON, J. R. Explosions of steam boilers: how they are caused, and how they may be prevented. Boston, 1870. 96 pp. 12° 1713.4
ROBINSON, Robert. Essays. (*In* Sparks, J. Collection of essays and tracts in theology) 1918.9.3
ROBINSON, Sara T. L. Kansas; its interior and exterior life. 3d edition. Boston, 1856. ix, 366 pp. 1 plate. 12° 5035.5
ROBINSON, Therese Albertina Louise von Jakob. Fifteen years. A picture from the last century. By Talvi [*pseud.*]. New York, 1871. 315 pp. 12° 714.27
ROBINSON, W. Hardy flowers. Description and directions for their arrangement, culture, etc. New edition. London, 1872. viii, 341 pp. 1 plate. Sq. 16° 6626.2
ROBINSON Crusoe. De Foe, D. Leipzig, 1845. Sq. 16° 310.14
— *Same.* London, 1868. Sq. 16° 916.13
— *Same.* New York, 1874. 16° 733.9
ROBINSON Crusoe, jr. Adams, W. T. 918.7
ROB Roy. Scott, *Sir* W. Boston 523.14
— *Same.* Leipzig 324.7

Shelf. No.

ROB Roy, *yawl*. Macgregor, J. The Rob Roy on the Jordan, Nile, Red sea, and Gennesareth, etc. New York, 1870. Sm. 8° 423.17
— - A thousand miles in the Rob Roy, on rivers and lakes of Europe. Boston, 1871. 16° 428.11
ROBSART, Amye, and the earl of Leycester. Adlard, G. London, 1870. 8° 5423.5
ROCHE, Regina Maria. The children of the abbey.. 527.15
ROCK, Daniel. Textile fabrics. *See* SOUTH KENSINGTON museum, *London*. [London, 1875.] 8°. 6214.6
ROCK, The, ahead. Yates, E. 317.1
ROCK of ages, The. Bickersteth, E. H. Boston, 1860. 12° ....1524.7 and 5816.24
ROCKS ahead. Greg, W. R. London, 1874. Sm. 8°. 5826.6
— *Same*. Boston, 1875. 16° 1534.12
ROCKY mountains. Burton, R. F. The city of the saints, and across the Rocky mountains to California. New York, 1862. 8° 412.2
— Carnegie, J., *earl of Southesk*. Saskatchewan and the. Edinburgh, 1875. 8° 5931.16
— Frémont, J. C. The exploring expedition to the. Auburn, 1854. 12° 414.14
— Irving, W. Adventures of Captain Bonneville in the. London, 1854. 16° 826.3
— *Same*. Philadelphia, 1871. Sm. 8° 1815.14
— Marcy, R. B. Thirty years of army life on the border. New York, 1866. 12° 415.16
— Parkman, F., *jr*. The Oregon trail: sketches of prairie and Rocky-mountain life. Boston, 1872. 12° 5015.3
ROCKY mountain series. *See* FOSDICK, Charles A.
RODDY'S reality. Johnson, H. K. 1117.15
RODDY'S romance. Johnson, H. K. 937.30
RODENBOUGH, Theophilus Francis. From everglade to cañon with the 2d dragoons (2d United States cavalry). An authentic account of service in Florida, Mexico, Virginia, and the Indian country, including the personal recollections of prominent officers. With an appendix. 1836–75. Illustrated. New York, 1875. 561 pp. 8°. 5032.6
RODERICK Hudson. James, H., *jr*. 723.27
RODERICK Random, The adventures of. Smollett, T. (G.) 315.16
RODOLPHUS. Abbott, J. 914.9
RODRIGUES-HENRIQUES, Jacob Hippolyte. Saint Pierre. Paris, 1871. xxxvii, 366 pp. 8° 5813.10
ROE, Azel Stephens. The cloud on the heart 723.31
— James Montjoy: or, I've been thinking 735.32
— A long look ahead; or, the first stroke and the last 715.23
— To love and to be loved, and The minister's story. 735.34
ROE, Edward Payson. Barriers burned away 724.21
— From jest to earnest 723.20
— Opening a chestnut burr 714.6
— Play and profit in my garden. New York [*cop*. 1873]. 349 pp. Sm. 8° 1516.13
— What can she do? 737.24
ROGERS, Henry. Biographies of David Hume, Edward Gibbon, Gassendi, Joseph Butler, and Robert Hall. (*In* Macaulay, T. B., *lord*, and others. New biographies of illustrious men) 5428.4
ROGERS, Henry Darwin, and JOHNSTON, Alexander Keith. Atlas of the United States of North America, Canada, New Brunswick, Nova Scotia, Newfoundland, Mexico, Central America, Cuba, and Jamaica. From the most recent state documents, marine surveys, and unpublished materials. With plans of the principal cities and sea-ports, and an introductory essay on the physical geography, products, and resources of North America. London, 1857. 20 pp. 29 maps. F° 5030.1
ROGERS, James E. Thorold. Social economy. Revised for American readers. New York, 1872. 167 pp. 12° 1525.23
ROGERS, Samuel. Poetical works. With a memoir by E. Bell. [Aldine edition.] London, 1875. xlvi, 392 pp. Portrait. Sm. 8° 5617.15

Note.— See also R. S. Mackenzie's "Recollections," in Harper's monthly, vols. 12 and 14; S. C. Hall's "Book of memories" [1231.1]; Hayward's Essays [5833.3]; Reviews in Jeffrey's Essays [5610.8], etc.; and full references in Allibone.

Shelf. No.

ROGET, Peter Mark. Animal and vegetable physiology considered with reference to natural theology. Philadelphia, 1836. 2 v. Illustrated. 8°. 6032.2
ROHDEN, Ludwig. Treatment of phthisis by baths and climate. (*In* Braun, J. On the curative effects of baths and waters) 6032.4
ROI, Le, des montagnes. [Brigandage in Greece.] About, E. (F. V.) Paris, 1863. 18° 5536.13
ROKEBY. Scott, *Sir* W. Poetical works. Leipzig, 1861. Sq. 16° 1613.5
ROLAND, Marie Jeanne Phlipon, History of. Abbott, J. S. C. 915.9
ROLAND Cashel. Lever, C. (J.) Leipzig 332.11
— *Same*. London 516.5
ROLAND Yorke. Wood, E. P. 333.17
ROLFE, William James, and GILLET, Joseph Antony. Natural philosophy. Boston, 1869. viii, 405 pp. Illustrated. 12° 6436.9
ROLLIN, Charles. Ancient history of the Egyptians, Carthaginians, Assyrians, Babylonians, Medes and Persians, Macedonians, and Grecians. Translated from the French. Vol. 1–4, 6–8. Boston, 1807. 7 v. Portrait. 8° 5913.1
ROLLING stone, A. Dudevant, A. L. A. D. 511.16
ROLLO at play. Abbott, J. 917.6
ROLLO at school. Abbott, J. 917.11
ROLLO at work. Abbott, J. 917.3
ROLLO in Geneva. Abbott, J. 917.18
ROLLO in Holland. Abbott, J. 917.21
ROLLO in London. Abbott, J. 917.20
ROLLO in Naples. Abbott, J. 917.24
ROLLO in Paris. Abbott, J. 917.22
ROLLO in Rome. Abbott, J. 915.14
ROLLO in Scotland. Abbott, J. 917.19
ROLLO in Switzerland. Abbott, J. 917.23
ROLLO in the woods. Abbott, J. 917.30
ROLLO learning to read. Abbott, J. 917.15
ROLLO learning to talk. Abbott, J. 917.8
ROLLO on the Atlantic. Abbott, J. 917.16
ROLLO on the Rhine. Abbott, J. 917.17
ROLLO series, The. *See* ABBOTT, Jacob.
ROLLO story books, The. *See* ABBOTT, Jacob.
ROLLO'S correspondence. Abbott, J. 917.5
ROLLO'S experiments. Abbott, J. 917.12
ROLLO'S garden. Abbott, J. 917.32
ROLLO'S museum. Abbott, J. 917.4
ROLLO'S philosophy. Air. Abbott, J. 917.14
— Fire. Abbott, J. 917.10
— Sky. Abbott, J. 917.9
— Water. Abbott, J. 917.13
ROLLO'S tour in Europe. *See* ABBOTT, Jacob.
ROLLO'S travels. Abbott, J. 917.7
ROLLO'S vacation. Abbott, J. 917.2
ROMAN, Le, d'un jeune homme pauvre: comédie. Feuillet, O. Boston, 1867. 12° 2015.2
ROMAN catholic church. Missale Romanum ex decreto sacrosancti concilii Tridentini restitutum. Mechliniæ, 1870. lxxii, 520, clxxx pp. 12°.5816.14
— Clarke, R. H. Lives of the deceased bishops of the catholic church in the United States. New York, 1872. 2 v. 8° 5811.1
— Czechowski, M. B. Thrilling and instructive developments: an experience of fifteen years as Roman catholic clergyman and priest. Boston, 1862. 12° 1226.11
— Derby, E. H. The catholic. Letters addressed by a jurist to a young kinsman proposing to join the church of Rome. Boston, 1856. 12°.1524.22
— Fitton, J. Sketches of the establishment of the [Roman catholic] church in New England. Boston, 1872. Sm. 8° 5816.5
— Hogan, W. Auricular confession and popish nunneries. Boston, 1845. 12° 1538.17
— Loyson, C. J. M., *ecclesiastical name Père Hyacinthe*. Catholic reform. Letters, fragments, discourses. London, 1874. Sm. 8° 6326.15
— Montalembert, C. F. de Tryon, *comte* de. Des intérêts catholiques au XIXe siècle. Paris, 1852. 18° 2018.4
— Reed, R. T. Six months in a convent. Boston, 1835. 16° 1539.2

Shelf. No.

ROMAN catholic church, *continued.*

— Spalding, M. J. Lectures on the evidences of catholicity. Baltimore, 1870. 8° 5811.6

— Stone, J. K. The invitation heeded: reasons for a return to catholic unity. New York [*cop.* 1870]. 12° 5816.12

— Tondini, C. The pope of Rome and the popes of the oriental orthodox church. London, 1871. Sm. 8° 5816.1

See also Christianity, Ecclesiastical history, France, Jesuits, Popes, Reformation.

ROMAN law. *See* CIVIL *or* Roman law.

ROMAN literature. *See* LATIN literature; ROME, Note, *literature.*

ROMAN traitor, The: or, the days of Cicero, Cato and Catiline. A true tale of the republic. Herbert, H. W. Philadelphia [*cop.* 1853]. 2 v. in 1. 12° 716.13

ROMANCE after marriage: a comedy. Goodrich, F. B., and Warden, F. L. New York, N. D. 12°. 1635.4

ROMANCE and humor of the rail. Smith, S. New York, 1873. 12° 534.24

ROMANCE of American history. [Essays on special points.] Schele de Vere, M. New York, 1872. 12° 5016.1

ROMANCE, The, of an honest woman. Cherbuliez, V. 728.11

ROMANCE, The, of history. [Historical tales.] England. Neele, H. London, N. D. 16° 827.27

— France. Ritchie, L. London, N. D. 16° 828.11

ROMANCE of old court-life in France. Elliot, F. New York, 1874. L. 8° 5510.1

ROMANCE, A, of perfume lands. Clifford, F. S. Boston, 1875. 16° 733.13

ROMANCE, A, of real life. Howells, W. D. (*In* Johnson, (E.) R. Little classics) 529.4.4

ROMANCE of student life abroad. Kimball, R. B.... 311.15

ROMANCE, The, of the age; or, the discovery of gold in California. Dunbar, E. E. New York, 1867. 12° 815.9

ROMANCE. The, of the association. Dall, C. (W.) H. Cambridge, 1875. 16° 1534.11

ROMANCE, The, of the English stage. Fitzgerald, P. London, 1874. 2 v. 8° 5622.4

Note. — Sketches of theatrical life, actresses marrying peers, etc.

ROMANCE, The, of the harem. Leonowens, A. H. Boston, 1873. Sm. 8° 5933.2

ROMANCE, A, of the republic. [Political novel.] Child, L. M. Boston, 1871. 12° 526.7

ROMANCE, The, of the streets. By a London rambler. London, 1872. 310+ pp. Sq. 16° 5438.2

Note. — An account of the ragged-schools and city missions of London.

ROMANCES. Disraeli, I. New York, 1803. 12°... 1918.8

ROMANTIC tales. Craik, D. (M.) 323.25

ROMANY Rye. [Gipsies.] Borrow, G. 511.21

ROMBERG, Moritz Heinrich. Manual of the nervous diseases of man. Translated and edited by E. H. Sieveking. London, 1853. 2 v. 8° 6013.16

ROME. Abbott, J. Rollo in Rome 915.14

— Ammianus Marcellinus. Roman history during the reigns of the emperors Constantius, Julian, Jovianus, Valentinian, and Valens. London, 1862. Sm. 8° 6117.9

— Arnold, T. History of. New York, 1872. 8°. 821.5

— Becker, W. A. Gallus, or Roman scenes of the time of Augustus. London, 1873. Sm. 8° 6117.14

— Boissier, M. L. G. L'opposition sous les Césars. Paris, 1875. 8° 5513.7

— Bonner, J. Child's history of. New York, 1870. 2 v. 16° 926.1

— Brun, F. (S. C.) Römisches Leben. Leipzig, 1833. 2 v. 16° 2027.2

— Cæsar, C. J. Commentaries on the Gallic and civil wars. London, 1872. Sm. 8° 6115.5

— Castelar, E. Old Rome and new Italy. New York, 1873. 12° 824.11

— De Mille, J. The seven hills 914.41

— Dillaway, C. K. Roman antiquities, and ancient mythology. Boston, 1857 [*cop.* 1833]. 16° 5516.3

Shelf. No.

ROME, *continued.*

— Dyer, T. H. History of the city of Rome: its structures and monuments. From its foundation to the end of the middle ages. London, 1865. 8°. 5512.5

— – History of the kings of. London, 1868. 8° .. 5512.6

— Eaton, C. A. Rome in the 19th century. London, 1860. 2 v. Sm. 8° 5516.6

— Fairholt, F. W. Rambles in. London, 1873. Sm. 4° 6213.6

— Fustel de Coulanges, M. D. The ancient city: a study on the religion, laws, and institutions of. Boston, 1874. Sm. 8° 5923.6

— Gibbon, E. History of the decline and fall of the Roman empire. Philadelphia [1845]. 6 v. 12°. 824.9

— Gladstone, W. E. Rome and the newest fashions in religion. Leipzig, 1875. Sq. 16° 1918.12

— Gregorovius, F. Geschichte der Stadt Rom im Mittelalter. Vom V. bis zum XVI. Jahrhundert. Stuttgart, 1869–74. 8 v. 8° 5513.6

— Grueber, H. A. Roman medallions in the British museum. London, 1874. 8° 6131.2

— Guhl, E., and Koner, W. The life of the Greeks and Romans, described from antique monuments. New York [London], 1875. 8° 5921.9

— Hare, A. J. C. Days near Rome. Philadelphia, 1875. 2 v. in 1. 16° 5527.15

— – Walks in. New York, 1873. 12° 5526.13

— Hemans, C. I. Historic and monumental Rome. London, 1874. Sm. 8° 5517.7

— Justinus, Nepos, C., and Eutropius. [Works.] London, 1872. Sm. 8° 6117.10

— Lander, S. W. Spectacles for young eyes 922.21

— Livius Patavinus, T. The history of. The first eight books. London, 1875. 4 v. Sm. 8° 6117.11

— *Same.* Books I–X. Oxford, 1874. 8° 6112.3

— *Same.* *See* COLLINS, W. L. Livy [outlined and explained]. Philadelphia, 1876. 16° 6116.22

— Long, G. The decline of the Roman republic. London, 1864–74. 5 v. 8° 5512.2

— Lord, J. The old Roman world: the grandeur and failure of its civilization. New York, 1873. 8° 826.10

— Macaulay, T. B., *lord.* Lays of ancient Rome. Leipzig, 1851. Sq. 16° 1614.17

— Merivale, C. A general history of Rome, from the foundation of the city to the fall of Augustulus, B. C. 753 — A. D. 476. London, 1875. Sm. 8°. 5517.8

— – History of the Romans under the empire. New York, 1866. 7 v. 8° 5515.3

— Michelet, J. History of the Roman republic. London, 1863. 16° 826.11

— Mommsen, T. History of. New York, 1872. 4 v. 12° 5516.1

— Murray, J. Handbook of. London, 1872. 16°. 5526.4

— Niebuhr, B. G. Lectures on the history of, from the earliest times to the fall of the Western empire. London, 1853. 3 v. 8° 5514.6

— Religion, The, of Rome described by a Roman. London, 1873. Sm. 8° 5817.6

— Reumont, A. von. Römische Briefe, 1837, 38. Leipzig, 1840. 2 v. 12° 2027.3

— – Neue römische Briefe. Leipzig, 1844. 2 v. 12°. 2027.4

— Ricord, F. W. History of. New York, 1859. 12°. 826.8

— Sallustius Crispus, C., Florus, L. A., and Velleius Paterculus, C. [Works.] London, 1872. Sm. 8°. 6117.7

— Seeley, J. R. Roman imperialism. Boston, 1871. 12° 5616.3

— Smith, W. Dictionary of Greek and Roman antiquities. London, 1872. 8° .... *R.R., E.3.5

— – Dictionary of Greek and Roman biography and mythology. London, 1870. 3 v. 8° .... *R.R., E.3.3

— – Dictionary of Greek and Roman geography. London, 1872. 2 v. 8° .... *R.R., E.3.4

— Story, W. W. Roba di Roma. London, 1871. 8°. 5524.1

— Suetonius Tranquillus, C. Lives of the twelve Cæsars; added, lives of the grammarians, rhetoricians, and poets. London, 1872. Sm. 8° 6117.8

— Taine, H. A. Italy. Rome and Naples. New York, 1872. 8° 5522.2.1

— Wey, F. (A.) Rome. London, 1872. 4° 5520.1

— *Same.* New York, 1875. 4° 5520.2

NOTE ON ROME.

Antiquities, manners, etc.

See full list of authorities in the note in the Lower Hall Catalogue of history, etc.; but Smith's Dictionary will ordinarily suffice. Gibbon's "Roman empire" [824.9], chap. 71, is devoted to the topography and monuments; and there is a summary of the antiquities in Lord's "Old Roman world" [826.10], compiled from Dyer's "History of the city" [5512.5].

Becker's "Gallus" [6117.14] has a thread of fiction, but is a close study of manners. See also the illustrated papers on the old Romans at home in Harper's monthly, 1872; and the article "Laurentium," based on Pliny's letters, in Lippincott's magazine, Oct., 1873. Guhl and Koner [5921.9] are of assistance in this connection.

Catacombs. See the note in the Library Bulletin, vol. II, p. 289; but a general survey of the subject may be found in McClintock and Strong's Cyclopædia. Murray's Rome gives a good general survey. See an illustrated paper in Harper's monthly, vols. 10 and 15, and April, 1865, and a chapter in Castelar's "Old Rome and new Italy" [824.11]. Cardinal Wiseman's historical tale "Fabiola" [736.19] caused a great increase of interest on the subject.

Mrs. Jameson's "Sacred and legendary art" will be useful in this connection of the early Christian art and antiquities.

Hemans's "Historic and monumental Rome" [5517.7] answers for much investigation, and shows what has been done of recent years; and E. A. Freeman has summarized the later discoveries in a paper in Macmillan's magazine, 1874.

General history, etc., modern authorities.

Book V of Rawlinson's "Manual of ancient history" [5921.10] maps out the subject best for a reader intending to make the history of Rome a subject for study.

The note in the Lower Hall Catalogue of history traces the rise of the disbelief in the legendary history, down to Niebuhr, who first advanced his views in a lecture, then published the first edition of his history in 1811, his enlarged edition with somewhat modified views in 1827, while his lectures, published after his death from notes taken by his scholars, bring the narrative down to A. D. 476, and present his more matured views, beside giving a particular review of the sources of his own history. With indisputable learning, he united a dogmatism, and a boldness in pulling down and building up, that have produced much opposition in particulars, while his general results have been in good part accepted. His theory of the existence of early narrative ballads, upon which the later Roman historians based their accounts, was first brought to the attention of English readers by Dr. Arnold, and in his subsequent history [821.5] he lucidly arranged Niebuhr's material, whom he reverently followed; and he had brought his narrative down to the second Punic war, B. C. 218, when he died. Arnold's sympathies were democratic. See Alison's "Miscellaneous essays" [1531.7].

The clearest exposition of Niebuhr's ballad theory is perhaps to be found in Macaulay's preface to his "Lays of ancient Rome" [1614.17]. It has been controverted by Dyer, in the introduction to his "History of the city" [5512.5] and in his "History of the kings" [5512.6].

There has been in more recent writers a reaction in a greater or less degree from Niebuhr's iconoclastic views. Dyer, in his "History of the kings," 1868, has aimed to preserve as much as possible of the received history, maintaining that exaggerations by the ancient historians do not invalidate the main outline of truth, and defending Livy, making a translation of him the text of his book, upon which he strings critical inquiries. Dyer, in his "History of the kings," has a dissertation on the sources of early Roman history, and on the internal evidences of their credibility, and Michelet, who follows Niebuhr nearly, in an appendix to his "Roman commonwealth" discusses this question, while in his introduction he traces the rise of this critical doubt. See Seeley's edition of Livy, Clarendon press series [6112.3], for latest conclusions, the editor giving a clear exposition of his disbelief in the legends.

The most recent histories are German. Mommsen [5516.1] follows Niebuhr with caution, and continues the history to the establishment of the military monarchy, but is hardly read to advantage except by those somewhat advanced in their knowledge of Roman history. He is reviewed in E. A. Freeman's Essays [5913.4.2]. Mommsen thinks there is no authentic history till Hannibal's time.

For the decline of the republic, Long's history [5512.2] extends from the destruction of Carthage to Cæsar's campaigns in Gaul, and he gives his authorities.

Merivale's "History of the Romans" has foot note references to his authorities, and he bridges the gap between Arnold and Gibbon, B. C. 100 to A. D. 180, and his 1st and 2d volumes cover the interval from the first triumvirate to the death of Cæsar; the 3d brings the narrative to Augustus; the 4th and 5th to Claudius; the 6th to the destruction of Jerusalem, A. D. 70; and the 7th to Commodus, where Gibbon's "Decline and fall of the Roman empire" [824.9] begins A. D. 180, coming down to A. D. 1420, and leaving the popes in temporal power. Seeley's "Roman imperialism" [5616.3] is a rapid review of the progress and fall of the empire.

On the *military history*, beside the ancients, Polybius, Livy, Cæsar, etc., see Gibbon's first chapter; Ramsay's article "Exercitus" in Smith's Dictionary; Napoleon's Cæsar, and the lives of other Roman generals; and on their military engineering, see Viollet-le-Duc's "Annals of a fortress" [6223.4]. The account of Josephus [5923.5] on the siege of Jerusalem is instructive in this respect.

General history of the city.

The *city* itself is the subject of a history by Dyer, 1865, recording its vicissitudes, without entering into the political causes, down to the end of the middle ages, which is an enlargement of the excellent and very thorough article, "Roma," by the same author, in Smith's Dictionary. Dyer makes good use of the German histories of Rome in the middle ages by Gregorovius, 1851, which begins with the reign of Honorius and the siege by Alaric in the 5th century and ends with the 16th [5513.6], and by Papencordt, 1857. In chapter 24 of Conybeare and Howson's "Life of St. Paul" there is a good account of the city at that time, and in Huebner's "Life of Sixtus V" [5522.11], particularly in part 6, there are accounts of feudal Rome and Rome of the Renaissance under Gregory XIII and Sixtus V. For the middle age period, see a chapter in Bryce's "Holy Roman empire" [5814.19].

Maps of the city. See maps in Burn, Merivale, Murray, and other books.

History. By periods.

I. *B. C. 753 to 508. Regal period.* Livy [outlined 6116.22] is the most copious; but Plutarch's Lives [5932.5; 5932.7] of Romulus, Numa, and Poplicola, may be read in connection. It is the value of these authorities that has given rise to the Niebuhr controversy, as explained above in the section on "Modern authorities." There is a summary of this period in Philip Smith's "Ancient history," ch. 20. Florian's "Numa Pompilius" [2019.1] is a novel, whose action lies in that king's reign.

Burn's "Rome and the Campagna" is a most elaborate survey to establish the legends of the regal period by physical geography. The sources of the early history are examined in chapter 2 of Hemans's "Historical and monumental Rome" [5517.7].

II. *B. C. 508 to 340. Commonwealth.* Livy, Book 2 to 7 [6116.22] and Plutarch's Lives [5932.5; 5932.7] of Poplicola, Coriolanus, and Camillus, are still the most accessible of the ancient authorities. Of the moderns Mommsen [5516.1] is scanty; but Niebuhr [5514.6] and Arnold [821.5] are copious. A general summary of the entire Commonwealth period will be found in Book I of Napoleon's "Cæsar" [5521.1]. Michelet's "Roman republic" [826.11] covers this period and continues to the founding of the Empire.

There fall within this period the "Defence of the bridge by Horatius Cocles," the "Battle of Lake Regillus," and the well-known story of "Virginia," all of which are celebrated in Macaulay's "Lays" [1614.17]. Coriolanus is the subject of one of Shakespeare's tragedies.

III. *B. C. 340 to 264. Roman supremacy, etc.* Livy [6116.22], and Plutarch's Life [5932.5; 5932.7] of Pyrrhus may be compared with Mommsen and Arnold, as before.

IV. *B. C. 264 to 133. Punic wars, etc.* Polybius is the preferable authority, but Livy [6116.22] will do in part, supplemented by Plutarch's Lives [5932.5; 5932.7] of Fabius Maximus, Paulus Æmilius, Marcellus, Marcus Cato, and Flaminius, with Nepos on Hannibal. Mommsen [5516.1], book 3, chap. 11 and 12, is particularly strong on the internal condition of Rome at this time; and Arnold's Rome [821.5] is remarkably helpful on the second Punic war, and Hannibal.

V. *B. C. 133 to 30. Foreign and civil wars.* For the early part of the period Plutarch, in his Lives [5932.5; 5932.7] of the Gracchi, Marius, Sylla, Lucullus, Crassus, and Sertorius, with Sallust on the war with Jugurtha, makes the chief source of a study. For the latter part, Plutarch again in his Lives [5932.5; 5932.7] of Cicero, Pompey, Cæsar, Cato the younger, Brutus, and Antonius, must be supplemented by Cicero's speeches and letters; by Cæsar's "Commentaries" [6115.5]; by Sallust, on the "Conspiracy of Catiline," and by Suetonius, in his "Lives of the Cæsars" [6117.8], for Julius and Octavius.

Mommsen, Michelet, and Merivale are the chief modern authorities; and for illustration read Addison's tragedy of "Cato," and Shakespeare's "Julius Cæsar" and "Antony and Cleopatra." The conspiracy of Catiline gives a plot to Herbert's "Roman traitor" [716.13].

See also Napoleon's "Cæsar" [5521.1] and Forsyth's "Cicero" [5932.8].

Philip Smith's "Ancient history" gives a good summary of this period in his 7th book.

VI. *B. C. 31 to A. D. 192. Empire.* Tacitus, Annals and History [6115.7] extend from the closing years of Augustus to the death of Domitian. Merivale thinks the History more trustworthy than the Annals. Suetonius in his "Cæsars" [6117.8] is considered not always trustworthy. Plutarch's Lives [5932.5; 5932.7] of Galba and Otho, and Josephus's Antiquities and Jewish war make up the essential authorities.

The chief modern authority in English is Merivale's "Romans under the empire" [5515.3], of which the last chapter is on the general condition of the empire at this time. Lecky's "History of morals" [5914.1] shows the moral effects of Christianity, and gives an account of the persecution of the Christians, while a further account of their relations to the empire can be found in Milman's "History of Christianity" [5817.1]. Lives of Augustus, Nero, Trajan, and Hadrian, necessarily illustrate the period. Gibbon begins his "Decline and fall" [824.9] with Commodus, the last emperor of this epoch. De Quincey's "Cæsars" [1825.10] is a cursory sketch of the line of emperors down to Dioclesian, touching on their less known doings; and something of interest will be found in the paper on the barbarism of the empire in De Quincey's "Historical essays" [1825.3].

There is a summary of this period in Book 8 of Philip Smith's "Ancient history."

Illustrations of the life of the period will be found in Whyte-Melville's "Gladiators" [321.15], time A. D. 69; and in Bulwer's "Last days of Pompeii" [336.13], time A. D. 79.

VII. *A. D.* 193 *to* 284. *Empire, continued.* The writers known as the Augustan historians are the chief source of our knowledge, and De Quincey bases his "Cæsars" [1825.10] largely upon them; and Rawlinson, in his "Manual of ancient history" [5921.10], points out the details. Gibbon's Rome [824.9], however, supplies the best narrative.

Pictures of the life of the early Christians, and their persecutions during this time, can be found in Newman's "Callista" [319.9]; in Mrs. Charles's "Victory of the vanquished" [321.6], and in W. Ware's "Aurelian" [512.14].

VIII. *A. D.* 284 *to* 395, *when the Empire was divided.* Ammianus Marcellinus [6117.9] may be followed for a portion of the time; but Gibbon [824.9], in chapters 13 to 28, will suffice the general reader. Constantine the great and Julian the apostate are the central figures, and books regarding them may be consulted. Mrs. Lee's "Parthenia" [737.11] concerns the apostate.

IX. *A. D.* 395 *to* 476, *when the Empire fell.* This is the period of Alaric, Attila and Genseric, and the general reader will find enough in Gibbon's Rome [824.9], chapters 29 to 38, and in Milman's "Latin Christianity" [5817.11].

For fiction, see Wilkie Collins's "Antonina" [326.4].

Lecky says, "There is much curious information about the growth of Roman luxury in Pliny's 'Natural history,' lib. xxxvi; and the movement of decomposition has been lately fully traced by Mommsen in his 'History of Rome' [5516.1]; by Döllinger in his 'First ages of Christianity' [5813.4]; by Pressensé in his 'History of the early centuries of Christianity' [5816.2]; and in the beautiful closing chapters of Renan's 'Apostles' [5812.8]." There is an essay on the Flavian Cæsars in E. A. Freeman's "Essays" [5913.4.2].

A summary of the period of decline constitutes Book 9 of Philip Smith's "Ancient history;" and in Merivale's "Roman empire" [5515.3], chap. 33, there is an estimate of the sources of the history of the imperial period. See also in this connection Smith's "Dictionary of biography," under Tacitus.

Later periods must be followed under Italy.

Abridged, compendious, and juvenile histories.

For the period B. C. 753 to A. D. 476, Merivale's "General history" [5517.8] is perhaps the best. Lord's "Old Roman world" [826.10] is a treatment by topics and phases, and he enumerates authorities at the end of his chapters. Book 3 of his "Ancient states and empires" [815.8] is a compendious history of Rome; and so is Book 5 of Rawlinson's "Manual of ancient history" [5921.10]. See also Bonner and Ricord in the above list, which come down to A. D. 476.

Literature.

In the English translations of Niebuhr and Mommsen, and in Arnold's History, there are chapters on the literature of Rome; in the biographies of authors in Smith's Dictionary there will be found ample references. A summary of the literature is given in Lord's "Old Roman world" [826.10], and the 64th chapter of Merivale's "Romans under the empire" [5515.3] is upon the literature of Trajan's time. Hallam, in his literary history [1531.2], traces the fortunes of Latin literature in the 15th, 16th, and 17th centuries.

There is a general survey of Latin literature in Blackwood, 1874.

Mythology.

For a concise account of the religion of Rome, see Clarke's "Ten great religions" [1523.2]; Coulanges' "Ancient city" [5923.6]; also the chapters in Mommsen [5516.1]; and Smith's "Dictionary of biography and mythology." For a popular account, see Bulfinch's "Age of fable" [1523.3.] See also Myths, *note.*

Travels, description, etc.

The literature of Roman travel is examined in chap. 1 of Hemans's "Historical and monumental Rome" [5517.1]. The most convenient general descriptions are Murray's [5526.4] and Baedeker's [5528.2.2]. Eaton's "Rome in the 19th century" [5516.6] is a popular descriptive volume, with illustrations, but the most elaborate pictorial helps, beside those mentioned under the head of antiquities, are Burn's "Rome and the Campagna," with maps and plans, presenting the latest archæological and topographical investigations, and rendered particularly useful to the classical scholar by its index to passages in the ancient writers, 1871, and Wey's "Rome" [5520.1; 5520.2], rambling and unsystematic, but devoted to both the ancient and modern city, and it has 346 excellent wood engravings. The sumptuous French history of the recent Ecumenical council in the Bates Hall offers admirable illustrations of the religious ceremonics of modern Rome; see also a popular paper on Holy week in Harper's monthly, vol. 9, and another on the church ceremonies, by L. Abbott, in vol. 45.

Story's "Roba di Roma" is an excellent miscellany of information regarding the modern city; and Taine [5522.2.1] and Norton's "Travel and study" [426.12] offer the observations of scholarly minds. Among general books of Italian travels, there may be named as characteristic: Hare's "Walks in Rome," 1871 [5526.13]; Strother's pictorial narrative in Harper's monthly, vol. 15; the "Eternal city" in vol. 44; the "Rome of to-day" in Atlantic monthly, April, 1859; "Rome in midsummer," in Longfellow's "Outre-mer" [1838.4.1]; Hawthorne's "Marble faun" [1813.2] and "Italian note-books" [1839.3].

See also general travels in Italy, like Hillard's "Six months" [426.8], etc.; and a paper on present social life in Rome by T. A. Trollope, in Lippincott's magazine, June, 1874. Hare's "Days near Rome" [5527.15] pertains particularly to the hilly country seen from the city.

	Shelf. No.
ROMILLY, *Sir* Samuel. Life, written by himself. With a selection from his correspondence. Edited by his sons. 3d edition. London, 1842. 2 v. Portrait. 16°	5428.9
ROMOLA. [Florence, time of Savonarola, historical novel.] Lewes, M.	310.23
RONALD Morton; or, the fire-ships. Kingston, W. H. G.	916.15
RONGER, Florimond. (*Hervé.*) Fleur-de-thé. (*In* Ditson, O., and co. Standard opera librettos).	6233.3.1
ROOKWOOD. A romance. Ainsworth, W. H.	712.9
ROPE. Nouveau manuel du cordier. Boitard, P. Paris, 1839. 24°	6429.8
ROPES of sand. Hamilton, C. V.	531.21
RORET, A. Manuels-Roret. Paris, v. D. 24°. *Namely:* —	
— Artois, V. d'. Manuel du fabricant de gants	6439.2
— Bayle-Mouillard, E. Manuel des dames, ou l'art de l'élégance	6229.1
— – Nouveau manuel d'économie domestique	6429.6
— Boitard, P. Nouveau manuel du cordier	6429.8

	Shelf. No.
RORET, A. Manuels-Roret, *continued.*	
— Boyer, —. Nouveau manuel complet du porcelainier, du faïencier, du potier de terre, du briquetier, du tuilier. 2 v.	6439.8
— Brewster, *Sir* D. Nouveau manuel de magie naturelle et amusante	6419.2
— Duval, H., and others. Manuel du limonadier du glacier, du chocolatier et du confiseur	6429.7
— Fontenelle, J. de. Manuel du bijoutier, du joaillier, de l'orfèvre, du graveur sur métaux et du changeur	6219.1
— – Nouveau manuel complet de physique amusante.	6439.5
— Hesse, L. A. C. Bibliothéconomie, ou manuel pour l'arrangement, la conservation et l'administration des bibliothèques	6139.1
— Jullien, C. É., and Valerio, O. Nouveau manuel complet du chaudronnier	6439.3
— Landrin, H. Manuel du coutelier	6429.13
— Lebrun, —. Manuel du mouleur	6429.11
— Magnier, M. D. Manuel de l'éclairage du gaz	6439.7
— Pautet, J. F. J. Manuel d'économie politique	5829.1

Shelf. No.

ROBET, A. Manuels-Roret, *continued.*
— Pédroni, P. M. Manuel des falsifications des drogues simples et composées 6439.6
— Perrot, A. M. Manuel du graveur 6439.4
— Riffault, J. R. D., and Vergnaud, A. Manuel du peintre en bâtiments, vitrier, doreur, argenteur et vernisseur 6429.3
— Roussel, T. Manuel pour la fabrication des allumettes chimiques, du coton et papier-poudre des poudres et amorces fulminantes 6429.12
— Serres, M. de. Nouveau manuel complet de paléontologie. With atlas. 3 v. 6639.1
— Smee, A. Manuel d'électricité médicale 6019.1
— Trémery, F. Nouveau manuel complet du teneur de livres 6819.1
— Valicourt, E. de. Manuel de dorure et d'argenture par la méthode électro-chimique et par simple immersion 6429.10
— Vandael, —. Manuel théorique et pratique du tailleur 6429.5
— Walker, C. V. Nouveau manuel complet de la télégraphie électrique 6829.1
RORY O'More. Lover, S. 536.16
ROSA Abbott stories. *See* PARKER, Rosa Abbott.
ROSALIE's pet. Mathews, J. H. 1115.13
ROSARY, A, for Lent. Harris, M. New York, 1874. 12° 1537.18
ROSCOE, *Mrs.* Henry. Vittoria Colonna: her life and poems. London, 1868. x, 371+ pp. Portraits. Sm. 8° 5525.11
ROSCOE, William. Life and pontificate of Leo x. 7th edition, revised by T. Roscoe. London, 1868. 2 v. Portraits. Sm. 8° 5526.6
— Life of Lorenzo de' Medici. 10th edition, revised. London, 1862. 564 pp. Portrait. 16°. 5525.1
ROSE, Hugh James. Untrodden Spain, and her Black country; being sketches of the life and character of the Spaniards of the interior. 2d edition. London, 1875. 2 v. 8° 5921.6
ROSE, (William) Stewart. Ignatius Loyola and the early Jesuits. 2d edition. London, 1871. ix, 548+ pp. Portrait. 8° 5524.3
ROSE d'Albret; or, troublous times. A romance. James, G. P. R. 730.7
ROSE-GARDEN, The. Peard, F. M. Leipzig, 1872. Sq. 16° 314.14
ROSE, A, in June. Oliphant, M. (O. W.) Boston. 711.1
— *Same.* Leipzig 319.22
ROSE Mather. Holmes, M. J. 534.10
ROSE, The, of Ashurst. Marsh-Caldwell, A. 313.25
ROSE of Castile. Balfe, M. W. (*In* Ditson, O., and co. Standard opera librettos) 6233.3.3
ROSE, The, of Disentis. Zschokke, (J.) H. (D.) ... 737.27
ROSENGARTEN, A. A handbook of architectural styles. Translated from the German by W. Collett-Sandars. With 639 illustrations. New York, 1876. xxii, 501 pp. 8° 6222.4
ROSES. The amateur's rose book. Hibberd, S. London, 1874. Sm. 8° 6625.2
ROSICRUCIAN, The. Craik, D. (M.) (*In* Johnson, (E.) R. Little classics) 529.4.7
ROSINI, Giovanni. Descrizione delle pitture del Campo Santo di Pisa. Terza edizione. Pisa, 1829. vi, 223+ pp. Plates. 16° 2038.1
ROSS, Charles H. A London romance 316.13
— The pretty widow 316.14
ROSS, James. On protoplasm: being an examination of James H. Stirling's criticism of Professor Huxley's views. London, 1874. 125+ pp. Sm. 8°. 1527.22
ROSSETTI, Christina G. Annus Domini; a prayer for each day of the year, founded on a text of Holy Scripture. Oxford, 1874. xii, 366 pp. Sq. 16°. 5819.15
— Speaking likenesses. With pictures thereof by Arthur Hughes. Boston, 1875. viii, 96 pp. 16°. 912.23
ROSSETTI, Dante Gabriel. Poems. With a memoir by F. Hüffer. Leipzig, 1873. xxvi, 282+ pp. Sq. 16° 1614.14
ROSSETTI, Maria Francesca. A shadow of Dante: being an essay towards studying himself, his world and his pilgrimage. Boston [London], 1872. 296+ pp. Folded plates. Portrait. 16°. 5536.1

Shelf. No.

ROSSINI, Giovacchino. Il barbiere de Siviglia; Cinderella; La gazza ladra; Otello; Semiramide; William Tell. (*In* Ditson, O., and co. Standard opera librettos) 6233.3.2
— Life of. Edwards, H. S. London, 1869. 8° ... 5523.4
ROUA pass, The; or, Englishmen in the Highlands. Mackenzie, E. Boston [1875]. 8° 721.19
ROUGH and ready. Alger, H., *jr.* 934.15
ROUGHING it. Clemens, S. L. Hartford, 1872. 8°. 212.2
ROUGHING it in the bush; or, life in Canada. Moodie, S. (S.) New York, 1852. 2 v. 12°. 414.12
— *Same.* 2 v. in 1 .... 414.9
ROUND, William M. F. Achsah: a New England life-study. By Rev. Peter Pennot [*pseud.*] 532.20
ROUND about Piccadilly and Pall Mall. Wheatley, H. B. London, 1870. 8° 5435.2
ROUND my house; notes of rural life in France in peace and war. Hamerton, P. G. Boston, 1876. 16° .... 827.4 and 5527.16
ROUND the moon. Verne, J. London, 1876. Sm. 8° 715.29
ROUND the world. Kingston, W. H. G. 922.1
ROUNDABOUT papers. Thackeray, W. M. Leipzig. 335.9
— *Same.* (*In his* Works.) London 513.1.10
ROUNDHEARTS and other stories. Harris, M. 724.15
ROUSSEAU, Jean Jacques. Œuvres [diverses]. Nouvelle édition. Neuchatel, 1764-69. 10 v. Portrait. Folded plate. 8° 5535.2
— Dictionnaire de musique. Paris, 1768. xiv, 547+, 4 pp. 8° 5535.5
— Émile, ou de l'éducation. La Haye, 1762. 4 v. 8° 5535.6
— Esprit, maximes, et principes. Neuchatel, 1764. xxiv, 444 pp. 8° 5535.3
— La nouvelle Héloise, ou lettres de deux amans. Nouvelle édition. Neuchatel, 1764. 4 v. Plates. 8° 5535.4
— Lowell, J. R. Rousseau and the sentimentalists. (*In his* Among my books) 1934.8.1
— Morley, J. Rousseau. London, 1873. 2 v. 8°. 5523.3
ROUSSEL, Théophile. Manuel pour la fabrication des allumettes chimiques, du coton et papier poudre, des poudres et amorces fulminantes. Orné de figures. Paris, 1848. viii, 174 pp. 24°. [Manuel Roret] 6429.12
ROUTLEDGE, Edmund, *editor.* Every boy's annual. London [1875]. iv, 668+ pp. Sm. 4° 930.1
— Every boy's book: a complete encyclopædia of sports and amusements. With illustrations. New edition. London, 1863. 630+ pp. 16° .. 916.4
— *Same.* London [1868]. xvi, 816 pp. 16° 6414.2
ROUTLEDGE, Robert. Discoveries and inventions of the nineteenth century. With illustrations. New edition, revised. London, 1876. xiii, 594+ pp. Sm. 8° .... 1522.17 and 6425.8
ROWING. Oars and sculls, and how to use them. Woodgate, W. B. London, 1875. 16° 6418.3
ROXBURY, *Mass.* City documents. Roxbury, 1846-67. 21 v. 8° 6925.1
— Directory, 1856, 58, 64. Roxbury, 1856, 58, 64. 3 v. 16° 5017.3
— Dillaway, C. K. History of the grammar school, or, "The free schoole of 1645 in Roxburie." Roxbury, 1860. 12° 5016.10
— Parker, R. G. Sketch of the history of the grammar school in the easterly part of. Roxbury, 1826. 8° 817.11
— *First church.* Chants, sentences and anthems sung at the introduction and close of public worship. N. P., 1855. 51 pp. 12° 5819.8
— *Lincoln freedmen's aid society.* 1st-9th annual report. Boston [1864-73]. 8° 5014.4
ROYAL geographical society, *London.* Arctic geography and ethnology. A selection of papers reprinted, and presented to the Arctic expedition of 1875. London, 1875. xii, 292 pp. Illustrations. 8° 5923.9
ROYAL institution of Great Britain, *London.* Its founder and its first professors. Jones, (H.) B. London, 1871. Sm. 8° 5814.10
RUBY Gray's strategy. Stephens, A. S. (W.) 726.8

Shelf. No.

RUECKERT, Friedrich. Gesammelte poetische Werke. Frankfurt, 1868, 69. 12 v. Portraits. 16° .. 5738.2

Contents. — Vol. I-VIII. Lyrische Gedichte. IX, X. Dramatische Gedichte. XI, XII. Epische Gedichte.

RUFFHEAD, Owen. Life of Alexander Pope, compiled from original manuscripts; with a critical essay on his writings. London, 1769. 578+ pp. 1 plate. Sm. 8° 1222.2

RUFFINI, Giovanni. Doctor Antonio 316.17

— Lavinia 316.18

— Lorenzo Benoni 316.16

— A quiet nook in the Jura 316.20

— Vincenzo 316.19

Note. — These novels are in good part well-drawn pictures of Italian life.

RUFUS and Rose. Alger, H., *jr* 934.14

RULE of the monk, The; or, Rome in the nineteenth century. Garibaldi, G. New York, 1870. 8°. 521.18

RUMFORD, *Count.* *See* THOMPSON, Benjamin.

"RUMFORD," *pseud.* The claims of classical learning examined and refuted by argument, and by the confessions of scholars. Boston, 1824. 140 pp. 8°. 5834.7

RUMOR. Sheppard, E. S 530.10

RUN to earth. Braddon, M. E 325.6

RUNNING the blockade. Thomes, W. H. 712.5

RUNNING to waste. Baker, G. M 927.28

RUPERT Godwin. Braddon, M. E 325.8

RUPPANER, Antoine. Hypodermic injections in the treatment of neuralgia, rheumatism, gout, and other diseases. Boston, 1865. 160 pp. 16° ... 6015.2

RURAL homes. Wheeler, G. New York, 1852. 12°. 1513.2

RURAL sports. Blaine, D. P. An encyclopædia of. London, 1870. 8° 6412.2

— Daniel, W. B. Rural sports. [London, 1801.] 2 v. in 3. 8° 6412.1

RURAL studies. Mitchell, D. G. New York, 1867. 12° 6226.1

RURAL tales, ballads, and songs. Bloomfield, R. London, 1802. 16° 1628.3

RUSH, Richard. Memoranda of a residence at the court of London. Philadelphia, 1833. 460 pp. 8° 5433.1

RUSKIN, John. Arata pentelici. Six lectures on the elements of sculpture. New York, 1872. xi, 181 pp. Illustrated. 12° 6236.2

— The crown of wild olive. Three lectures on work, traffic, and war. New York, 1872. xxi, 127+ pp. 12° 6236.6

— The eagle's nest. Ten lectures on the relation of natural science to art. New York, 1873. vi, 203 pp. 12° 6236.5

— Elements of drawing. With illustrations. New York, 1872. 234 pp. 12° 6236.11

— Elements of perspective. New York, 1871. xii, 144 pp. Illustrated. 12° 6236.14

— The ethics of the dust. Ten lectures to little housewives on the elements of crystallisation. New York, 1866. 250 pp. 12° 6236.4

— Fors clavigera. Letters to the workmen and labourers of Great Britain. New York, 1871, 72. 2 v. 1 plate. 12° 6236.10

— Frondes agrestes. Readings in 'Modern painters,' chosen by the author's friend, the younger lady of the Thwaite, Coniston. Orpington, Kent, 1875. vii, 184 pp. Sm. 8° 6236.21

— Inquiry into some of the conditions at present affecting "the study of architecture" in our schools. New York, 1872. 29 pp. 12° 6236.12

— The king of the Golden river. A legend of Stiria. New York, 1872. 39 pp. 12° 6236.9

— *Same.* (*In* Johnson, (E.) R. Little classics). 529.4.10

— Lectures on architecture and painting. With illustrations. New York, 1872. 189 pp. 12°. 6236.12

— Lectures on art. New York, 1872. 202 pp. 12°. 6236.13

— Love's meinie [*i. e.* retinue]. Lectures on Greek and English birds. New York, 1873. 74 pp. 12°. 6236.20

— Modern painters. New York, 1872. 5 v. Illustrated. 12° 6236.18

Contents. — Vol. I. Of general principles and truth. II. Of the imaginative and theoretic faculties. III. Of many things. IV. Of mountain beauty. V. Of leaf beauty; Of cloud beauty; Of ideas of relation.

RUSKIN, John, *continued.*

— Munera pulveris. Six essays on the elements of political economy. New York, 1872. xxvii, 164 pp. 12° 6236.7

— Notes on the construction of sheepfolds [*i. e.* church architecture]. New York, 1872. 40 pp. 12° 6236.9

— The poetry of architecture: cottage, villa, etc. To which is added suggestions on works of art. With illustrations. New York, 1873. 246+ pp. 12° 6236.19

— The political economy of art. New York, 1866. 125 pp. 12° 6236.8

— Pre-Raphaelitism. New York, 1872. 56 pp. 12°. 6236.9

Note. — This rather vague designation in modern art criticism is supposed to embody the trustful, somewhat ungraceful and homely rendering of nature, which is thought to characterize the painters before Raphael.

— The queen of the air: being a study of the Greek myths of cloud and storm. New York, 1872. vii, 178 pp. 12° 6236.17

— Sesame and lilies. Two lectures. 1. Of kings' treasuries. [Books and reading, ostensibly.] 2. Of queens' gardens. [Power of women.] New York, 1872. xvi, 119 [115] pp. 12° 6236.15

— The seven lamps of architecture [*i. e.* seven fundamental principles]. With illustrations. New York, 1871. viii, 186+ pp. 12° 6236.3

— The stones of Venice. [Venetian architecture.] With illustrations. New York, 1872. 3 v. 12°. 6236.1

Contents. — Vol. I. The foundations. II. The sea-stories. III. The fall.

— Time and tide, by Weare and Tyne. Letters on the laws of work. New York, 1871. x, 210 pp. 12° 6236.16

— The two paths: being lectures on art, and its application to decoration and manufacture. With plates and cuts. New York, 1866. 217 pp. 12°. 6236.8

— "Unto this last:" four essays on the first principles of political economy. [Labor and its relation to capital.] New York, 1866. 138 pp. 12° 6236.4

Note. — In 1843, Ruskin published the first volume of his "Modern painters," mainly to defend Turner, the landscapist, from current detraction, but the work gradually expanded into an exposition of art and nature in many bearings, and its fifth volume was issued in 1860. It is understood that the author now discards much of these volumes, which gave him his reputation. Their fine perceptions and imaginative rendering of nature, given with enthusiasm and with a superb radiancy of style, will doubtless retain the reputation for him which they made. By his paradoxes, Mr. Ruskin has gained the disfavor of many critics; and a certain wayward impulse in his later writings — which have run into political economy and other various matters — have done much to make his readers distrust his thinking. See a paper by Leslie Stephen on his recent writings in Fraser's magazine, 1874. Allibone gives full references to reviews of his several books. See also McCarthy's "Modern leaders" [5930.2]; Peter Bayne's "Essays" [1226.15]; Eastlake's "Gothic revival" [6121.2], etc.

RUSSEL, Alexander. The salmon. Edinburgh, 1864. viii, 248 pp. 8° .... 1521.

RUSSELL, John, *earl.* Essays on the history of the Christian religion. New edition. London, 1873. xvi, 336 pp. 16° 6238.8

— Life and times of Charles James Fox. London, 1866. 3 v. Portrait. Sm. 8° 5337.1

— Life of William, lord Russell. 4th edition. London, 1853. xxii, 470+ pp. Portrait. Sm. 8°. 5425.1

— Recollections and suggestions, 1813-1873. London, 1875. x, 475 pp. 8° .... 5332.

RUSSELL, Michael. Life of Oliver Cromwell. New York, 1856. 2 v. Portrait. 12° .... 1228.

RUSSELL, Thomas, *joint author.* Incidents and anecdotes of Edward T. Taylor. *See* HAVEN, Gilbert 1216.1

— The life and public services of Henry Wilson. *See* NASON, Elias .... 1016.

RUSSELL, W. Clark. The book of authors. A collection of criticisms, ana, môts, personal descriptions, etc. New edition. London [1871]. iv, 516 pp. 1 plate of portraits. Sm. 8° ...... 5638.

— Representative actors. A collection of criticisms, anecdotes, personal descriptions, etc. From the 16th to the present century. London [1872]. xv, 496 pp. 1 plate of portraits. Sm. 8° .... 5638.

Shelf. No.

RUSSELL, William, *lord*, Life of. Russell, J., *earl*. London, 1853. Sm. 8° 5425.11

RUSSELL, *Prof.* William. Rudiments of gesture, comprising illustrations of faults in attitude and action. With engravings. Boston, 1830. viii, 48 pp. 12° 1517.9

RUSSELL, William, *Scotch historian*. History of modern Europe. New edition, continued to the present time. London, 1850. 4 v. 8° 5913.3

RUSSELL, William Howard. General Todleben's History of the defence of Sebastopol. 1854–5. A review. London, 1865. xii, 321 pp. 8° ... 5923.3

— My diary North and South. Boston, 1863. xxii, 602 pp. 12° 413.6

RUSSELL, William S. Guide to Plymouth, and recollections of the pilgrims. Boston, 1846. xii, 306, 76, xx pp. Illustrated. Map. 12° 5017.1

RUSSELL: a tale of the reign of Charles II. James, G. P. R. 327.6

RUSSIA. Adams, W. T. Northern lands; or, Young America in. Boston, 1872. 16° 925.7

— Cobden, R. Russia and the Eastern question. Boston, 1854. 12° 827.3

— Distinguished persons in Russian society. London, 1873. Sm. 8° 5924.4

— Dixon, W. H. Free Russia. New York, 1870. Sm. 8° 422.22

— Gautier, T. A winter in. New York, 1874. 12°. 824.5 and 5915.10

— Hellwald, F. von. The Russians in Central Asia. London, 1874. Sm. 8° 5914.9

— Kingston, W. H. G. Fred Markham in. [Juvenile] 936.20

— Loubat, J. F. Narrative of the mission to Russia, in 1866, of Gustavus Vasa Fox. New York, 1873. L. 8° 5911.3

— Murray, J. Handbook for Russia. London, 1868. 12° 5917.5

— Ralston, W. R. S. Russian folk-tales. London, 1873. 8° 5923.8

— Rawlinson, *Sir* H. (C.) England and Russia in the East. London, 1875. 8° 5921.5

— Sala, G. A. A journey due North; being notes of a residence in. Boston, 1858. 12° 426.7

— Taylor, (J.) B. Travels in. New York, 1872. 12°. 224.3

— Tondini, C. The pope of Rome and the popes of the oriental orthodox church, with special reference to. London, 1871. Sm. 8° 5816.1

See also Daghestan, Moscow, St. Petersburg.

Note. — Gibbon's "Roman empire" [824.9], chap. 55, traces the origin of the Russian monarchy. The principal history by Karamsin is epitomized in Alison's Essays [1531.7], while in the latter historian's Europe [5913.6.1] there is a description of the Russian army. See also the opening chapters of Kinglake's "Crimean war" [837.2]; and a paper on "The traditional policy of Russia," in the Atlantic monthly, Nov., 1868.

For Peter the great's time, see that name; and Voltaire's account of his struggle with Charles XII of Sweden, in his "History of Charles XII" [5726.6], is well-known. See "House of Romanoff," in Harper's monthly, vol. 10.

Madame Swetchine's "Life and letters" [1226.2] give pictures of court life under Paul, Alexander, and Nicholas. On the emancipation of the serfs, beside Dixon's "Free Russia," see a chapter in J. Ross Browne's "Land of Thor" [424.17]; papers in the Atlantic monthly, July, 1861, and Nov., 1862; and the paper on "Self-government in Russia," in Macmillan's magazine, Aug., 1875. On Russia in the East, see Froude's "Short studies" [1914.5.2]; Atlantic monthly, July, 1875; beside Rawlinson's book [5921.5].

For additional descriptions, see Murray, last edition; Browne's "Land of Thor" [424.17]; Channing's "Physician's vacation" [422.21]; see also Harper's monthly, Feb., 1869; Miss Proctor's paper in Scribner's monthly, Nov., 1872; and papers in the Atlantic monthly on Lake Ladoga, May, 1864; on a journey from Moscow to Nijni-Novogorod, Jan., 1865; and on Winter life in St. Petersburg, July, 1865, and a paper by Delmar in Appleton's monthly, vol. 11.

Turgenef's novels give pictures of Russian life. Also see Muehlbach's "Daughter of an empress" [531.3].

RUSSIAN journey, A. Proctor, E. D. Boston, 1872. Sm. 8° 428.12

RUTH. Gaskell, E. C. 328.15

RUTH Margerie: a romance of the revolt of 1689. Denison, M. A. 539.9

RUTH Maxwell. Blake, *Lady* —.................. 731.4

RUTHERFORD, John. The troubadours: their loves and their lyrics; with remarks on their influence, social and literary. London, 1873. x, 356 pp. 8° 5525.10

RUTLEDGE. Harris, M. 737.29

Shelf. No.

RYE-HOUSE plot, The. Reynolds, G. W. M. 510.12

RYLAND, John E., *editor*. Life and correspondence of John Foster. With notices of Mr. Foster as a preacher and a companion, by J. Sheppard. London, 1861. 2 v. 16° 5426.5

SABBATH, The. Andrews, J. N. Sermons on the Sabbath and law. Battle Creek, 1870. 16° 6328.2

— Gilfillan, J. The Sabbath viewed in the light of reason, of revelation, and history, with sketches of its literature. New York [1862]. 16° 1534.3

— Littlejohn, W. H. The constitutional amendment: or the Sunday, the Sabbath, the change, and restitution. Battle Creek, 1873. 16° 5818.14

— Macmillan, H. The sabbath of the fields. London, 1876. Sm. 8° 6328.23

— Permanent Sabbath documents of the American and foreign Sabbath union. Boston, 1851. 12°.1536.17

SABINE, Lorenzo. Biographical sketches of loyalists of the American revolution, with an historical essay. Boston, 1864. 2 v. 12° 1211.1

— Report on the principal fisheries of the American seas. *See* UNITED STATES. *Department of the treasury* 811.9

SABINE, Robert. History and progress of the electric telegraph. 2d edition. New York, 1869. xiv, 280 pp. Illustrated. 12° 6826.3

— *Same.* 3d edition. London, 1872. xiv, 280 pp. Illustrated. 12° 1716.39

SACK, A, of gold. Johnson, V. W................ 710.20

SACRED allegories. Adams, W. Leipzig, 1864. Sq. 16° 311.23

SACRED anthology, The. Conway, M. D. London, 1874. 8° 5813.14

SACRED music. Ancient harmony revived; being a selection of choice music for divine worship, taken from old and approved authors. Boston, 1857. Oblong 8° 1518.7

SADLER, L. R. (*Jacob Larwood*), and HOTTEN, John Camden. The history of signboards, from the earliest times to the present day. With 100 illustrations in fac-simile, by J. Larwood. 6th edition. London [1875]. x, 536 pp. 1 colored plate. Sm. 8° 5615.8

SAFELY married! Pike, F. W. A. 721.7

SAFES, Locks and. Tomlinson, C. London, N. D. 12°.1715.27

SAFFELL, W. T. R The Bonaparte-Patterson marriage in 1803, and the secret correspondence never before made public. Philadelphia, 1873. 254 [244] pp. 2 portraits. Sm. 8° 825.4

SAFFO. Pacini, C. (*In* Ditson, O., and co. Standard opera librettos)..........................6233.3.1

SA-GO-YE-WAT-HA, *or* RED JACKET, Life and times of. Stone, W. L. Albany, 1866. 8° 5022.5

SAHARA, My Apingi kingdom: with life in the great. DuChaillu, P. B. New York, 1872. 12° 933.2

SAIGEY, Émile. The unity of natural phenomena. From the French. With an introduction and notes by T. F. Moses. Boston, 1873. 253+ pp. 16° 1526.21

SAILING on the Nile. Laporte, L. Boston, 1872. 16°. 426.2

SAILOR boy, The. Adams, W. T. 924.4

SAILS and sail-making. Kipping, R. London, 1871. 12° 1716.4

SAINT DOMINGO, Topographical and political description of the Spanish part of. Moreau de Saint Méry, M. L. É. Philadelphia, 1798. 2 v. in 1. 8°. 1913.3

ST. Elmo. Wilson, A. J. 725.24

ST. George and St. Michael. A novel. MacDonald, G. Leipzig 331.22

— *Same.* New York 714.34

ST. Giles and St. James, History of. [London low life.] Jerrold, D. (W.) Leipzig, 1852. 2 v. in 1. Sq. 16° 313.9

SAINT James's; or, the court of Queen Anne. [Historical tale.] Ainsworth, W. H. 322.18

SAINT JOHN, *the apostle*. The pupils of St. John the divine. Yonge, C. M. [London, 1868.] Sm. 8°. 5937.9

ST. JOHN, James Augustus. Life of Sir Walter Raleigh. 1552–1618. New edition. London, 1869. x, 381 pp. Sm. 8° 5423.10

Shelf. No.

SAINT Leger. Kimball, R. B. 311.17
ST. Martin's eve. Wood, E. P. 333.11
ST. MAUR, *or* SEYMOUR, Edward Adolphus, *duke of Somerset*. Christian theology and modern skepticism. New York, 1872. 182 pp. 12° 5817.2
SAINT Nicholas: Scribner's illustrated magazine for girls and boys. Conducted by Mary Mapes Dodge. Vol. 1. New York [1874]. 8° 1315.1
ST. Olave's. Tabor, E. 711.21
ST. Patrick's day: a farce. Sheridan, R. B. Dramatic works. London, 1848. 16° 1635.2
— *Same*. Leipzig, 1869. Sq. 16° 1614.11
— *Same*. London, 1875. Sm. 8° 5626.9
ST. Patrick's eve. Lever, C. (J.) Leipzig 332.13
— *Same*. London 516.3
ST. PETERSBURG. Spectacles for young eyes. Lander, S. W. 922.22

See also travels in Russia.

ST. Philip's. Harris, M. 724.13
SAINT-PIERRE, Jacques Henri Bernardin de. Studies of nature. Translated by H. Hunter. Worcester, 1797. 3 v. Illustrated. 8° 6833.2
ST. Ronan's well. Scott, *Sir* W. 523.3
SAINT-SIMON, Louis de Rouvroi, *duc* de. Le duc de Saint-Simon, son cabinet et l'historique de ses manuscrits. Baschat, A. Paris, 1874. 8°, l. p. 5531.2
ST. Simon's niece. Benedict, F. L. 720.39
ST. Stephen's. A poem. Bulwer-Lytton, E. (G. E.) L. Leipzig, 1860. Sq. 16° 1614.6
SAINTE-BEUVE, Charles Augustin. Causeries du lundi. 4e édition. Paris [1873]. 15 v. 12°. 5538.4
— English portraits. Selected and translated from "Causeries du lundi," with an introductory chapter on Sainte-Beuve's life and writings [by W. F. Rae]. New York, 1875. cxiii, 301 pp. 16° 1025.3

Contents. — Sainte-Beuve's life and writings; Mary, queen of Scots; Lord Chesterfield; Benjamin Franklin; Edward Gibbon; William Cowper; English literature, by H. Taine; Pope as a poet.

— Étude sur Virgile, suivie d'une étude sur Quintus de Smyrne. 2e édition. Paris, 1870. 444+ pp. 12° 5538.11
— Lettres à la princesse. 3e édition. Paris, 1873. iii, 367+ pp. 12° 5538.14
— Memoirs of Madame Desbordes-Valmore. With a selection from her poems. Translated by H. W. Preston. Boston, 1873. viii, 227 pp. 16°. 5527.3
— Nouveaux lundis. 3e édition. Paris, 1870. 13 v. 12° 5538.5
— P. J. Proudhon, sa vie et sa correspondance, 1838–48. Paris, 1872. 352 pp. 12° 5538.10
— Poésies complètes. Édition revue et augmentée. Paris, 1869. 476+ pp. 12° 5538.13
— Portraits contemporains. Nouvelle édition. Paris, 1870. 5 v. 12° 5538.7
— Portraits de femmes. Paris, 1870. 542+ pp. 12°. 5538.17
— Portraits of celebrated women. Translated by H. W. Preston. Boston, 1868. 384+ pp. Portrait. 16° 1226.5
— Port-Royal. 3e édition. Paris, 1867. 7 v. 12°. 5538.6
— Souvenirs et indiscrétions. Publiés par son dernier secrétaire [J. Troubat]. Paris, 1872. 354 pp. 12° 5538.16
— Tableau historique et critique de la poésie française et du théâtre française au XVIe siècle. Nouvelle édition, suivie de portraits particuliers des principaux poëtes. Paris, 1869. 499+ pp. 12° 5538.15
— Volupté. 7e édition. Paris, 1872. 416+ pp. 12° 5538.12
SAINTINE, (Joseph) Xavier Boniface, *called*. Picciola, précédé de quelques recherches sur l'emploi du temps dans les prisons d'état, par Paul L. Jacob. Nouvelle édition, revue et corrigée. New York, 1858. 252 pp. 12° 2015.4
SAINTS, The lives of the. Baring-Gould, S. London, 1872, 73. 5 v. 16° 5937.1
SALA, George Augustus. A journey due North; being notes of a residence in Russia. Boston, 1858. viii, 459 pp. 12° 426.7

Shelf. No.

SALA, George Augustus, *continued*.
— The seven sons of mammon. Leipzig, 1869. 2 v. in 1. Sq. 16° 315.10
— Under the sun: essays mainly written in hot countries. London, 1872. xix, 395 pp. 8° 5611.3
SALAD for the solitary and the social. [Essays.] Saunders, F. New York, 1872. 8° 5213.1
SALATHIEL, the immortal. [The wandering Jew.] Croly, G. London [1858]. 16° 517.13
SALEM, *Mass.*, Annals of. Felt, J. B. Salem, 1845, 49. 2 v. Sm. 8° 5016.7
SALEM chapel. Oliphant, M. (O. W.) 328.10
SALEM mercury. Vol. 1–3. Salem, 1831–33. 3 v. in 1. F° 6730.37

Note. — Vol. I, no. 3, repeated, and nos. 2, 4, 44–49, missing. Vol. II, no. 25–52, missing.

SALEM witchcraft. Upham, C. W. Boston, 1867. 2 v. Sm. 8° 5015.2

Note. — See Palfrey's "History of New England" [5016.2]; Barry's "History of Massachusetts" [812.5]; Austin's "History of Massachusetts" [813.19]; and Cassell's "History of the United States" [810.11]. Upham, in 1831, first issued his lectures, which have since been greatly enlarged, giving a picture of old Salem and a history of opinion regarding witchcraft [5015.2]. This book was reviewed by Lowell, in North American review, Jan., 1868, also in his "Among my books" [1934.8], which last is, however, chiefly upon the general subject of witchcraft; in which connection, see Lecky's chapter in his "Rationalism" [5933.5].

See Everett's anecdotes of early local history, in his Orations [1921.1.2]; R. H. Allen's exposition of the historical evidences [817.4], upon which Longfellow based his tragedy, "Giles Corey of the Salem farms" [1614.2]. Also Drake's "Nooks and corners of the New England coast" [411.4].

SALISBURY, Stephen. Essay on the star spangled banner and national songs. Worcester, 1873. 24 pp. 8° 5010.16
SALLUSTIUS CRISPUS, Caius, FLORUS, Lucius Annæus, and VELLEIUS PATERCULUS, Caius. [Works.] Literally translated, with copious notes and a general index. By J. S. Watson. London, 1872. xvi, 560 pp. [Bohn's Classical library.] Sm. 8° 6117.7
SALLY Williams, the mountain girl. Cheney, E. D. 915.21
SALMAGUNDI. Irving, William, Paulding, J. K., and Irving, Washington. London, 1850. 16° 715.4
— *Same*. Philadelphia, 1871. Sm. 8° 1815.7
SALMON, The. Russell, A. Edinburgh, 1864. 8°. 1521.9
SALMONIA; or, days of fly fishing. Davy, *Sir* H. Boston, 1870. 16° 1515.4
SALT water. Kingston, W. H. G. 922.2
SALT water bubbles. Sleeper, J. S. 716.10
SALT-WATER Dick. Nowell, H. P. H. 936.24
SALVANDY, Narcisse Achille, *comte* de. Love of country, or Sobieski and Hedwig. Compiled and translated from the French, by Trauermantel. Boston, 1856. vi, 260 pp. Illustrated. 12°. 916.11
SALZKAMMERGUT, *Austria*. The Bavarian highlands and the Salzkammergut. Schmid, H., and Stieler, C. London, 1874. 8° 5720.1
SAM Lawson's Oldtown fireside stories. Stowe, H. (E.) B. 736.10
SAM SLICK, *pseud*. *See* Haliburton, Thomas Chandler.
SAM'S chance. Alger, H., *jr*. 933.28
SAMOIEDE country. The land of the north wind; or, travels among the Laplanders and the Samoyedes. Rae, E. London, 1875. Sm. 8° 5935.5
SAMPSON, Henry. History of advertising from the earliest times. Illustrated by anecdotes, curious specimens, and biographical notes. With illustrations and facsimiles. London, 1874. x, 616 pp. Sm. 8° 6136.12
SAMUEL Slick, Sayings and doings of. Haliburton, T. C. New York, 1872. 16° 535.12
SAMUELS, Adelaide F. Dick Travers abroad. Little cricket; or, Dick Travers in London 918.27
— – The lost tar; or, Dick Travers in Africa 918.25
— – On the wave; or, Dick Travers aboard the "Happy Jack" 918.26
— – Palm land; or, Dick Travers in the Chagos islands 918.24
SAMUELS, Edward A. The birds of New England and adjacent states. With illustrations. With appendix. 6th edition, revised and enlarged. Boston, 1872. vii, 591 pp. 8° 6612.4

Shelf. No.

SANCTUARY, The: a story of the civil war. Nichols, G. W. New York, 1866. 12° 716.11

SAND, George, *pseud.* *See* DUDEVANT, Amantine Lucile Aurore Dupin.

SANDEAU, (Léonard Sylvain) Jules. Mademoiselle de la Seiglière: comédie. With English notes, by F. Bôcher. Boston, 1867. 99 pp. 12°.... 2015.2

— *joint author.* The cross of Berny. *See* GIRARDIN, Delphine Gay de.

SANDERSON, Robert, Life of. Walton, I. London, 1866. 16°.............................. 5428.2

SANDFORD and Merton, History of. Day, T. London [1850]. 16° 935.4

SANDHAM, *Mrs.* —. The twin sisters.............. 929.11

SANDWICH ISLANDS. Anderson, R. History of the Sandwich Islands mission. Boston, 1870. 8°..5812.15

— Nordhoff, C. Northern California, Oregon, and the Sandwich Islands. New York, 1874. 8°.. 432.5

SANDY Wood's sepulchre. Miller, H. (*In* Johnson, (E.) R. Little classics)...................529.4.5

SANFORD, *Mrs.* D. P. Pussy Tip-toes' family 912.26

SAN FRANCISCO. Beauvoir, L., *comte* de. Pekin, Jeddo, and San Francisco. London, 1872. 16°.5935.11

— Soulé, F., Gihon, J. H., and Nisbet, J. Annals of. New York, 1855. 8° 810.3

See also California.

[SANITARY tracts.] N. P., N. D. 16° 939.4

Contents. — The power of soap and water, a dream that came true; The mischief of bad air: or what "bad air" really is; Health of mothers; Croaking Kate and chirping Jane; The influence of wholesome drink; Washing the children; Sowing the seed; The value of good food; Whose fault is it? or, how to make a happy home; Is it too late?

SANS merci. Lawrence, G. A...................... 315.24

SANS-SOUCI series. *See* STODDARD, Richard Henry, *editor.*

SANTA Claus land. Douglas, A. M................ 928.12

SANTI, *or* SANZIO, Raffaello (Raphael) da Urbino. A series of studies: designed and engraved after five paintings by Raphael. With historical and critical notes, [translated from] T. B. Éméric-David. American edition, reproduced by the heliotype process. Boston, 1875. 61 pp. L. 4°. 6210.10

Note. — The very rare work, of which this is a translation, consists of crayon studies (about three times the size of these heliotypes) from five paintings in the Madrid gallery. A copy may be found in the Tosti collection of the Boston Public library.

— Passavant, J. D. Raphael of Urbino and his father Giovanni Santi. London, 1872. 8°..... 6211.2

— Quatremère de Quincy, A. C. Life of. London, 1870. 16°.............................. 6217.3

Note. — The most complete account of Raphael yet produced is Passavant's, and in the preface there is a characterization of the authorities. Quatremère de Quincy's was the most important of earlier lives.

The most accessible memoirs in English are the accounts in the English versions of Vasari [6215.6]; Lanzi [6215.4]; some chapters in Grimm's "Michael Angelo" [1022.2]; a paper in Fairholt's "Rambles in Rome" [6213.6]; Jameson's "Lives of the early painters" [6228.2]; Tytler's [i. e. Keddie's] "Old masters" [1510.21; 6210.3]; Roscoe's "Leo X" [5526.6]; and Tyrwhitt's "Christian art" [1514.14; 6235.1]. See also Painting, *note.*

SANTO DOMINGO. *See* HAYTI.

SAPPHIRE, The. [Selections.] Sargent, E. Boston, 1867. 16°.............................. 715.15

SARACEN, The lands of the. Taylor, (J.) B. New York, 1857. 12° 424.13

SARATOGA, *New York*, An analysis of the mineral waters of. Steel, J. H. Saratoga Springs, 1838. 12° 417.15

SARCHEDON. Melville, G. J. W.................. 321.8

SARDANAPALUS: a tragedy. Byron, G. G. N., *lord.* Works. Leipzig, 1866. Sq. 16°...........1614.13.5

SARDINIA, Handbook for. Murray, J. London, 1868. 12° 5917.3

SARGENT, Epes. Arctic adventure by sea and land. With maps and illustrations. Boston, 1857. 480 pp. Portraits. 12°.................. 426.10

— [Gem series.] The emerald. Boston, 1866. 316 [314] pp. 12° 715.14

— — The sapphire. [Selections.] Boston, 1867. 319 pp. 16°.............................. 715.15

— Songs of the sea, with other poems. Boston, 1847. 208 pp. 16° 1612.9

SARGENT, Epes, *continued.*

— The standard fourth reader for public and private schools. Boston, 1861. 336 pp. 12°......... 1735.4

— The standard speaker; containing exercises in prose and poetry for declamation. 60th edition. Philadelphia, 1873. 558 pp. 8°.............1933.12

SARGENT, Fitz William. England, the United States, and the Southern confederacy. 2d edition. London, 1864. viii, 184 pp. 8°............. 812.7

SARGENT, Henry Jackson. Feathers from a moulting muse. [Poems.] Boston, 1854. vii, 270 pp. 16°. 1615.4

SARGENT, Lucius Manlius. Dealings with the dead. [Reminiscences, — chiefly of Boston.] By a sexton of the old school. Boston, 1856. 2 v. 12° 1816.1

SARGENT, Nathan. Public men and events from the commencement of Munroe's administration, in 1817, to the close of Fillmore's administration, in 1853. Philadelphia, 1875. 2 v. 8°....... 5223.1

SARGENT, Winthrop. Life and career of Major John André. Boston, 1861. xiv, 471 pp. Portrait. Sm. 8° 5426.9

SARMIENTO, Ferdinand L. Life of Pauline Cushman. The celebrated union spy and scout. Philadelphia [*cop.* 1865]. 374 pp. Portrait. 16°.. 1015.6

SARSFIELD; or, the last great struggle for Ireland. [Historical novel.] Conyngham, D. P. Boston, 1871. Sq. 16° 828.7

SARTOR resartus. Carlyle, T. London [1831]. Sm. 8°. 5838.6

SARTORIS, Adelaide (Kemble). A week in a French country-house, Medusa, and other tales........ 732.6

SASKATCHEWAN, *river.* Saskatchewan and the Rocky mountains. Carnegie, J., *earl of Southesk.* Edinburgh, 1875. 8° 5931.16

SATANSTOE. Cooper, J. F........................ 525.6

SATCHEL guide for the vacation tourist in Europe. New York, 1872. xxxii, 188 pp. 16°........ 427.2

SATCHEL series, The. Stories, poems, essays, and sketches. Vol. I. Illustrated. Boston, 1875. 102 pp. 8° 713.7

Contents. — Vol. I. Old Rudderford Hall, by M. E. Braddon; Bringing home the May, by A. H. B.; Going somewhere, by M. Quad [*pseud. of* Charles B. Lewis]; A strange warning, by A. H. W.; The ladies of one hundred years ago; Holy wells and Druid relics, by Wilkie Collins; Last words, by Owen Meredith [*pseud. of* E. R. Bulwer-Lytton, *lord Lytton*].

SATURDAY review. Vol. 6, 35–40. London, 1858, 73–75. 7 v. Sm. f°........................ 6712.1

SATURN and its system. Proctor, R. A. London, 1865. 8°.................................. 6813.3

SAUNDERS, Frederick. Salad for the solitary and the social: by an epicure. [Essays.] Illustrated. New York, 1872. 526 pp. 8°.................. 5213.1

SAUNDERS, John. Israel Mort, overman 319.20

SAUNDERS, Katharine. Gideon's rock and other tales. 339.24

— The haunted crust. (*In* Johnson, (E.) R. Little classics) 529.4.5

— The high mills 319.28

— Joan Merryweather and other tales 339.20

SAUNTERINGS. Warner, C. D. Boston, 1872. Sq. 16°. 229.1

SAUVEUR, Lambert. Causeries avec mes élèves. Boston, 1874. 220 pp. 16°.................. 2015.5

— Introduction to the teaching of living languages without grammar or dictionary. Boston, 1874. 76 pp. 12°..................................1934.14

SAUZAY, A. Marvels of glass-making in all ages. Illustrated. London [1869]. xx, 272 pp. Sm. 8°. 6425.3

— Wonders of glass-making in all ages. Illustrated. New York, 1871. 325 pp. 16°..............1714.24

Note. — This is the same work as the preceding, with a changed title.

SAVAGE, Edward H. Chronological history of the Boston watch and police, 1861–65; with recollections of a Boston police officer. Boston, 1865. 396 pp. 12°.................................. 5010.7

— Police records and recollections; or, Boston by daylight and gaslight for two hundred and forty years. Boston, 1873. 400+ pp. Illustrated. Portrait. 8°.................................. 5013.8

SAVAGE, James. Genealogical dictionary of the first settlers of New England. Boston, 1860, 62. 4 v. 8°.............................*R.R., C.2.2

Shelf. No.

SAVAGE, Marmion W. The bachelor of the Albany. 535.19

SAVOY. Baedeker, C. Handbook for travellers. Coblenz, 1872. 16° 5718.4

— Murray, J. Handbook for the Alps of. London, 1846. 12° 227.3

SAWYER, George A. Fret-sawing and wood-carving for amateurs. Illustrated. Boston, 1875. 63 pp. Sm. 4° 1515.91

SAXE, John Godfrey. Leisure-day rhymes. Boston, 1875. 268+ pp. 12° 1616.16

— Poems. Boston, 1858. 192 pp. Portrait. 16°. 5217.5

— *Same.* Highgate edition. Boston, 1871. xii, 491 pp. 12° 1615.19

SAXE, *Marshal.* *See* MAURICE OF SAXONY, *Count.*

SAXE HOLM's stories. *See* HOLM, Saxe, *pseud.*

SAXON studies. [Dresden, etc.] Hawthorne, J. Boston, 1876. 12° 424.5

SAY and seal. Warner, S. and A. B. 317.10

SCALP hunters, The. Reid, M. 725.5

SCANDINAVIA. Browne, J. R. The land of Thor. New York, 1870. 12° 424.17

— Mallet, P. H. Northern antiquities; or, an account of the ancient Scandinavians. London, 1873. Sm. 8° 5715.5

SCARLET letter, The. Hawthorne, N. Leipzig, 1852. Sq. 16° 311.7

— *Same.* Boston, 1873. 16° 1813.11

SCENES from the life of Jesus. Boston, 1858. 137 pp. 16° 918.2

SCENES of clerical life. Lewes, M. 310.26

SCEPTRES and crowns. Warner, S. 927.27

SCHAFF, Philip. History of the Vatican council. (*In* Gladstone, W. E. The Vatican decrees, etc.). 1911.1

— The revision of the English version of the New Testament. *See* LIGHTFOOT, Joseph Baber 5814.11

SCHEFER, Leopold. The artist's married life; being that of Albert Dürer. Translated by Mrs. J. R. Stodart. Revised edition, with memoir. New York, 1871. xxvii, 204 pp. 16° 1027.3

SCHEFFEL, Joseph Victor. Ekkehard. A tale of the tenth century. Translated by S. Delffs 315.9

SCHELE DE VERE, Maximilian. Americanisms; the English of the New World. New York, 1872. 685 pp. 12° 6124.1

— Modern magic. New York, 1873. 466 pp. 12°. 1516.16

— Romance of American history. Early annals. New York, 1872. 254+ pp. 12° 5016.1

— Studies in English; or, glimpses of the inner life of our language. 3d edition. New York, 1868. vi, 365 pp. Sm. 8° 1533.4

SCHELLEN, H. Spectrum analysis in its application to terrestrial substances, and the physical constitution of the heavenly bodies. Translated from the 2d German edition by J. and C. Lassell. Edited, with notes by W. Huggins. With wood-cuts, coloured plates and Ångström's and Kirchhoff's maps. London, 1872. xxvi, 662 pp. 8° 6822.2

— and OTHERS. Spectrum analysis explained, and its uses to science illustrated; Spectrum analysis discoveries. (*In* Estes, D. Half-hour recreations in popular science) 6813.7

SHERER, Edmond. Nouvelles études sur la littérature contemporaine. Paris, 1865. 420+pp. 12°. 2016.1

SCHILLER, (Johann Christoph) Friedrich von. Werke. Stuttgart, 1865, 67. 12 v. 8° 5734.1

Contents.—Vol. I. Leben; Gedichte; Semele. II. Die Räuber; Die Verschwörung des Fiesco zu Genua; Kabale und Liebe. III. Don Carlos; Der Menschenfeind. IV. Wallensteins Lager; Die Piccolomini; Wallensteins Tod. V. Maria Stuart; Die Jungfrau von Orleans. VI. Wilhelm Tell; Die Huldigung der Künste; Die Braut von Messina.
VII. Iphigenie in Aulis; Scenen aus den Phönizierinnen; Macbeth; Turandot; Der Parasit; Der Neffe als Onkel; Phädra. VIII. Geschichte des Abfalls der vereinigten Niederlande. IX. Geschichte des dreissigjährigen Kriegs. X. Prosaische Schriften. XI, XII. Kleine Schriften vermischten Inhalts.

— Works. Historical and dramatic. From the German. London, 1872. iv, 553 pp. Portrait. Sm. 8° 827.26

Contents.—Revolt of the Netherlands, continued, book iv; Trial of Counts Egmont and Horn; The siege of Antwerp; Wallenstein's camp; The Piccolomini; Death of Wallenstein; Wilhelm Tell.

SCHILLER, (Johann Christoph) Friedrich von, *cont'd.*

— Death of Wallenstein; The Piccolomini. *See* COLERIDGE, S. T. Works 1611.5

— Die Piccolomini. With English notes by E. C. F. Krauss. Boston, 1865. 139 pp. 12° 5735.3

— History of the revolt of the Netherlands; Trial and execution of Counts Egmont and Horn; and The siege of Antwerp. Translated by A. J. W. Morrison. New York, 1847. 333 pp. 12° 826.5

— History of the thirty years' war. Translated by A. J. W. Morrison. New York, 1846. iv, 370 pp. 12° 826.2

— Poems and ballads. Translated by Sir E. Bulwer-Lytton. With a brief sketch of the author's life. Leipzig, 1844. civ, 284+ pp. Sq. 16°. 1613.4

— Wallenstein's Tod. With English notes by E. C. F. Krauss. Boston, 1865. 210 pp. 12° 5735.3

— Wilhelm Tell. With English notes by E. C. F. Krauss. Boston, 1868. 171 pp. 12° 5735.2

— Carlyle, T. Life of: comprehending an examination of his works. Leipzig, 1869. Sq. 16° .. 1238.19

— Follen, C. (T. C.) Schiller's life and dramas. Boston, 1842. 12° 5735.4.4

Note.—In English, Bulwer's memoir [1613.4], is perhaps the best, though Carlyle's is a characteristic sketch [1238.19], and he has further comments in his Essays [5610.7].
There is also an essay by Max Müller, in his "Chips" [5616.1.3]; something in Lewes's "Life of Goethe" [5724.1]; a section in De Staël's "Germany" [5726.1]; and one in Longfellow's "Poets and poetry of Europe" [5922.1].
See also De Quincey's "Biographical essays" [1825.6]; Hedge's "Prose writers of Germany" [5732.1]; Mrs. Jameson's "Studies" [1916.3]; Bryant's "Orations" [1926.1]; H. C. Robinson's "Diary" [5425.3]; and Gostwick's "German poets" [5723.5].

SCHLEGEL, August Wilhelm von. Lectures on dramatic art and literature. Translated by J. Black. Revised, according to the last German edition, by A. J. W. Morrison. London, 1871. viii [vi], 535 pp. Portrait. 16° 6136.2

SCHLIEMANN, Heinrich. Troy and its remains; a narrative of researches and discoveries made on the site of Ilium, and in the Trojan plain. Translated [by L. Dora Schmitz]. Edited by P. Smith. London, 1875. With maps, plans, views, and cuts. lv, 392 pp. 8° 5933.8

See also Bulletin, vol. II, p. 342.

SCHMID, Herman, and STIELER, Carl. The Bavarian highlands and the Salzkammergut. Illustrated by G. Gloss, and others. With an account of the habits and manners of the hunters, poachers, and peasantry of these districts. London, 1874. viii, 205+ pp. 4° 5720.1

SCHMIDT, (Eduard) Oscar. International scientific series. The doctrine of descent and Darwinism. With 26 woodcuts. New York, 1875. viii, 334+ pp. 12° 6616.10

SCHNECK, Benjamin S. Mercersburg theology inconsistent with protestant and reformed doctrine. Philadelphia, 1874. 188+ pp. 12° 6326.14

SCHÖNBERG-COTTA family, Chronicles of the. [Luther and the reformation.] Charles, E. 321.3

SCHOOL, The, and the army in Germany and France. Hazen, W. B. New York, 1872. 8° 5714.5

SCHOOL days at Rugby. [Vivid picture of school life under Dr. Arnold.] Hughes, T. Boston, 1872. 12° 922.17

SCHOOL field-club, Rambles and adventures of our. Davies, G. C. London, 1875. Sm. 8° 1115.15

SCHOOL, The, for husbands: a comedy. Molière, J. B. P. Dramatic works. Edinburgh, 1875. 8° 5530.3.2

SCHOOL, The, for scandal: a comedy. Sheridan, R. B. Dramatic works. London, 1848. 16° 1635.2

— *Same.* Leipzig, 1869. Sq. 16° 1614.11

— *Same.* London, 1875. Sm. 8° 5626.9

SCHOOL, The, for wives: a comedy. Molière, J. B. P. Dramatic works. Edinburgh, 1875. 8° .. 5530.3.2

SCHOOL, The, for wives criticised: a comedy. Molière, J. B. P. Dramatic works. Edinburgh, 1875. 8° 5530.3.2

SCHOOL of the guides. Le Gal, E. New York, 1860. Sq. 16° 1528.3

Shelf. No.

SCHOOLBOY days. Kingston, W. H. G. 937.24
SCHOOLMASTER'S, The, stories. Eggleston, E. 921.13
SCHOOLMASTER'S, The, trunk. Diaz, A. M. 714.4
SCHOONER Mary Ann, The. Abbott, J. 923.3
SCHOULER, William. History of Massachusetts in the civil war. Boston, 1868, 71. 2 v. Portrait. Map. 8° 5012.2
SCHRECKENSHUND, Der. Kock, (C.) P. de. Pest, 1857. 2 v. in 1. 16° 2027.5
SCHROEDER VAN DER KOLK, J. C. L. Structure and functions of the spinal cord and medulla oblongata. And on the proximate cause and rational treatment of epilepsy. Translated by W. D. Moore. London, 1859. ix, 291+ pp. 8° 6023.2
SCHUBERT, Franz. Austin, G. L. Life of. Boston, 1873. 12° 1228.7
— Hellborn, (H.) K. von. Life of. London, 1869. 2 v. 8° 5727.1
SCHUBERT, Franz Ludwig. Die Blechinstrumente der Musik. Ihre Geschichte, Natur, Handhabung und Verwendung in der Instrumental-, Gesangs-, Militair- und Tanzmusik. Leipzig, 1866. vii, 112 pp. Sq. 16° 2028.2
SCHUCKING, Levin. The Puck novels. Powder and gold. A story of the Franco-Prussian war. Translated from the German by M. S. 538.5
SCHUETZENBERGER, M. Paul. International scientific series. On fermentation. With 28 illustrations. New York, 1876. viii, 331 pp. 12° 6436.18
SCHUMANN, Robert, Life of. Wasielewski, J. W. von. Boston [*cop.* 1871]. 16° 5728.1
SCHUTZLOSEN, Die. Schwartz, M. S. New-York, N. D. 16° 2028.4
SCHUYLER, Philip, Life and times of. Lossing, B. J. New York [*cop.* 1872]. 2 v. 12° 5023.5
SCHWARTZ, Marie Sophie. Birth and education. From the Swedish, by S. Borg and M. A. Brown. 531.6
— Gerda; or, the children of work. From the Swedish, by S. Borg and M. A. Brown 735.36
— Gold and name. From the Swedish, by S. Borg and M. A. Brown 531.10
— Gold und Name. Aus dem Schwedischen von Dr. Otto, gen. Reventlow. New-York, N. D. 2 v. 16° 2028.3
— Guilt and innocence. From the Swedish, by S. Borg and M. A. Brown 531.5
— Die Leidenschaften. Aus dem Schwedischen von Dr. Otto, gen. Reventlow. New-York, N. D. 299 [297] pp. 16° 2628.5
— The right one. From the Swedish, by S. Borg and M. A. Brown 531.7
— Die Schutzlosen. Aus dem Swedischen von Dr. Otto, gen. Reventlow. New-York, N. D. 249 [247] pp. 16° 2028.4
— Two family mothers. From the Swedish, by S. Borg and M. A. Brown 531.8
— The wife of a vain man. From the Swedish, by S. Borg and M. A. Brown. [Also, A reminiscence of Kreuznach] 531.9
SCHWEINFURTH, Georg A. The heart of Africa. Three years' travels and adventures. From 1868 to 1871. Translated by Ellen E. Frewer, with an introduction by Winwood Reade. With maps and illustrations. 2d edition. New York, 1874. 2 v. 8° 5911.12
SCIENCE. Abbott, J. Science for the young.......912.3-5
— Annual of scientific discovery: or, year-book of facts in science and art, 1850-59. Boston, 1850-59. 10 v. 12° 1524.6
— Brande, W. T., and Cox, G. W. Dictionary of. London, 1872. 3 v. 8° ...................*R.R., E.3.6
— Burr, E. F. Pater mundi; or, modern science testifying to the Heavenly Father. Boston, 1872. Sm. 8° 1527.11.1
— Draper, J. C., *editor*. Year-book of nature and popular science for 1872. New York, 1873. 12° 1525.21
— Draper, J. W. History of the conflict between science and religion. New York, 1875. 12°... 5826.4
— Estes, D., *editor*. Half-hour recreations in popular science. 1st series. Boston [1874]. 8°... 6813.7

Shelf. No.

SCIENCE, *continued*.
— Glover, M. B. Science and health. Boston, 1875. 12° 1733.3
— Half hours with modern scientists. 1st series. New Haven, 1872. 12° 1525.19
— Helmholtz, H. (L. F.) Popular lectures on scientific subjects. London, 1873. 8° 6834.1
— *Same*. New York, 1873. Sm. 8° 1522.6
— Knight, C. Arts and sciences, or fourth division of "The English cyclopædia." London, 1866-68. 8 v. 4° ........................*R.R., F.2.1
— Le Conte, J. Religion and science. New York, 1874. 12° 5817.14
— Napier, C. O. G. Tommy Try and what he did in. London, 1869. Sm. 8° 1524.24
— Peabody, A. P. Christianity and science. New York, 1874. 12° 6326.17
— Pepper, J. H. The boy's playbook of. London [1861]. Sm. 8° 1524.18
— Proctor, R. A. The borderland of. London, 1873. Sm. 8° 6814.3
— - Light science for leisure hours. New York, 1871. 12° 1527.3
— - Science byways. Philadelphia [London], 1876. Sm. 8° 6836.4
— Spencer, H. Recent discussions in. New York, 1873. 12° 6835.2
— Temple, F. The present relations of science to religion. (*In* Hedge, F. H. Recent inquiries in theology) 1526.24
— Timbs, J. The year-book of facts in science and art. London, 1866. Sm. 8° 1527.12
— Tyndall, J. Fragments of science for unscientific people. New York, 1872. Sm. 8° 1524.27
— Wells, D. A. The science of common things. New York, 1872. 12° 1527.9
— Winchell, A. Sketches of creation. A popular view of some of the grand conclusions of the sciences in reference to the history of matter and of life. New York, 1874. 12° 1523.23

See also Molecular science. Social science, and the names of special sciences, like Astronomy, etc.

SCIENCE record, The, for 1866. With illustrations. Edited by Alfred E. Beach. New York, 1876. 597 pp. 12° 6836.5
SCIENTIFIC American. Vol. 27-33. New York, 1872-75. Illustrated. 7 v. F° 1320.1
SCIENTIFIC, The, bases of faith. Murphy, J. J. London, 1873. 8° 5812.5
SCIENTIFIC London. Becker, B. H. London, 1874. Sm. 8° 5616.16
SCOTLAND. Abbott, J. Rollo in Scotland 917.19
— - A summer in. New York, 1848. 12° 425.11
— Adams, W. T. Shamrock and thistle; or, Young America in. Boston, 1871. 16° 916.17
— Burton, J. H. History of Scotland from Agricola's invasion to the extinction of the last Jacobite insurrection. Edinburgh, 1874. 8 v. Sm. 8° 5418.6
— Chambers, R. The songs of Scotland prior to Burns. With the tunes. Edinburgh [1873]. Sq. 16° 5637.1
— Dodds, J. The fifty years' struggle of the Scottish covenanters, 1638 to 1688. London [1868]. Sm. 8° 5417.9
— Galibert, L., and Pellé, C. Angleterre, Écosse et Irlande. Paris, 1844. 8° 5911.7
— Hamerton, P. G. A painter's camp in. Boston, 1871. 16° 426.19
— Herbert, D. Mutinies in Highland regiments. London, 1876. Sm. 8° 5924.2
— Lippincott, S. J. Bonnie Scotland. Tales of her history, heroes, and poets. [Juvenile.] Boston, 1872. 16° 933.20
— Murray, J. Handbook for Scotland. London, 1875. 12° 5437.3
— Murray, J. C. The ballads and songs of Scotland, in view of their influence on the character of the people. London, 1874. Sm. 8° 5626.5
— Ramsay, E. B. Reminiscences of Scottish life and character. Edinburgh, 1867. 16° 5637.2

Shelf. No.

SCOTLAND, *continued.*
— Robertson, W. History of. London, 1840. 8°. 5610.1
— Scott, *Sir* W. Tales of a grandfather; being stories taken from Scottish history. New York, 1828. 2 v. 16° 939.5
— Strickland, A. Lives of the queens of. New York, 1859–73. 8 v. 12° 627.1

Shelf. No.

SCOTLAND, *continued.*
— Victoria, A., *queen of England.* Leaves from the journal of our life in the Highlands, from 1848 to 1861. New York, 1868. 12° 225.1
— Wordsworth, D. Recollections of a tour made in, 1803. Edinburgh, 1874. 8° 5435.5
See also Lorn, Skye.

NOTE ON SCOTLAND.

Popular histories are those of Scott, both in the "Tales of a grandfather," and in the "History of Scotland." The former is an abridged history from Macbeth down, selecting picturesque episodes and prominent points; the latter gives attention chiefly to the elucidation of principles, but Palgrave says that having exhausted his pleasurable stores in the tales, Scott thus ruined his history.

The *latest and most elaborate general* history is that by Burton [5418.6]. He is a thorough antiquarian, but as a historian he possesses the modern skeptical view regarding the early unchronicled periods, and finds the dawn of true history in Malcolm Canmore's reign, 1057-93. His narrative of the Roman and unrecorded ages of heathen belief is ample. His treatment of the St. Columba period may be contrasted with the reverent belief of Montalembert, in his "Monks of the West" [5514.5]. See also in this connection the Duke of Argyle's "Iona" [427.9]. See also Palgrave's "Normandy and England," on the beginning of Scottish history in Malcolm's time.

There are three phases to the earliest history of Scotland. First, a fulness of fabulous detail. Second, a confounding of the Picts and Scots. Third, an obscurity attending everything like authentic detail. The third century is the Ossian period, and the literature of that subject yields discussions more or less historical. See McPherson's Ossian [1613.19] and its dissertations.

For the Norwegian invasion, 1264, see the translation of the old Saga of Haco in Buchanan's "Land of Lorne" [424.11], chapter 14.

The long interval of the contest with England will be found illustrated in Freeman's "History of the Norman conquest in England" [5014.4], and it forms the distinctive feature of Burton's third volume. For illustrations of the period of Wallace and Bruce, see the note under Scott. Miss Porter's "Scottish chiefs" [1225.19] pertains to this epoch, but though a favorite novel, it is not considered trustworthy as a guide to the understanding of the times. In a later period, the captivity of King James I in England, Miss Yonge has found a subject for her "Caged lion" [318.12]. Robertson's well-known history, while it is introduced by a cursory examination of antecedent Scottish history, is confined to the reign of Mary, and down to James VI's accession to the English throne in 1603. Buckle says of Robertson that he is still valuable because of his broad views, and that he made wonderful use of the material he had in his time. See the note under Mary, queen of Scots. Miss Strickland's "Lives of the queens" [627.1] will be found a companionable commentary.

Stanhope's Queen Anne, chap. viii, and Smyth's 25th lecture, are on the union in Queen Anne's time, and in Smyth will be found the general characteristics of its history and historians. For the subsequent rebellions, see Jesse's "Memoirs of the pretenders" [5426.14], and for that of 1745, see the excellent account in Stanhope's "History of England" [838.3].

For the manners, of which the traits are gone or just lingering, nothing is better than Dean Ramsay's book [5637.2].

For estimates of the Scottish character, see Macaulay's third volume [838.1] and Froude's third volume [826.9].

Church history. The history of the church of Scotland is closely connected with that of the state, but it can be distinctively traced for a general review, dwelling upon prominent points, in Stanley's Lectures [5812.6], or in particular chapters of Burton, and in MacCrie's "Story of the Scottish church" [5816.22].

Dividing the record into epochs, we refer for the *early Celtic period* to Montalembert's "Monks of the West" [5514.5].

For the *Reformation period,* see lives of Knox; Burton's 4th volume; chapters in Froude's History [826.9], and his essay on "The influence of the reformation on the Scottish character," in his "Short studies" [1914.5.1], in which he rebuts Buckle's chapter on the Scotch, and in his "History of civilization" [5417.1]. See the note under Reformation, and the list of authorities in Fisher's "Reformation" [5813.7, p. 587].

For the period of the *Covenanters,* from the first banding against enforced episcopacy in 1638, to the revolution of 1688, Dodd's book, "Fifty years struggle of the Scottish covenanters" [5417.9], is a useful popular sketch. See also Burnet's "Own time" [5410.4]; and Macaulay's History [838.1]; a paper in Harper's monthly, vol. 46; and Peter Bayne's article in the Contemporary review, 1875, on the Covenanters, Charles II, and Argyle.

There is much in the 2d volume of Buckle's "History of civilization" [5417.1] on the condition of Scotland from the 14th century, and on the characteristics of the Scottish intellect.

Literature and art.

David Irving's is the most considerable history of Scottish poetry, 1861, covering the interval from Ossian to Lady Wardlaw. For dissertations upon Scottish songs and ballads, see the prefaces and introductions to such collections as Murray's [5626.5]; Chambers's "Songs of Scotland prior to Burns" [5637.1]; Percy's "Reliques" [1613.12]; Scott's "Minstrelsy of the border," in which he runs over the labor of his predecessors in preserving these records. See a bibliography of this department in Child's "Ballads" [5628.5.1]; and articles in Prescott's essays [1537.8; 5237.3]; and in Kingsley's essays on "Burns and his school" [1223.5].

For the influence on English literature in the founding of the Edinburgh review and Blackwood's magazine, see the lives of Jeffrey [5635.2.1]; Sydney Smith [1025.6]; John Wilson [1024.7]; and "Noctes ambrosianæ" [515.15]. Also see Curwen's "History of booksellers" [5426.16]; a chapter in Archibald Constable's life [5424.10]; and the statement in Brougham's "Autobiography" [5425.2] contradicting Sydney Smith's account of the beginning of the Edinburgh review.

Travels, description, etc.

The best itineraries are those by Murray and Black; but Hunnewell's "Lands of Scott" [5626.10] will be of interest to such as have derived their chief knowledge of its scenery and history from Sir Walter Scott. See also portions of Mrs. Hawthorne's Notes, and Mrs. Stowe's "Sunny memories" [426.6].

For the Hebrides, see Johnson's famous Tour [5423.7]; Buchanan's "Land of Lorne" [424.11]; Alexander Smith's "Summer in Skye" [426.1]; and the articles on Mull in the Atlantic monthly, July and August, 1865.

See the note under Scott, *Sir* Walter, on the Waverley novels, etc., for a chronological commentary of authorities and illustrative imaginary renderings of many events and periods in Scottish history.

Other delineations of Scottish life will be found in Galt's novels; in several of Mrs. Oliphant's; in many of George MacDonald's, and particularly "The portent" [537.3] for second-sight; in Mrs. Craik's [Muloch] "Head of the family" [323.12] and "A noble life" [323.15]; in Black's "Princess of Thule" [328.28; 732.10] for life in the Hebrides; in Charles Reade's "Christie Johnstone" [339.23; 527.3]; and in H. Kingsley's "Austin Elliot" [326.24; 724.4] for the famine period.

Shelf. No.

SCOTLAND, *Church of.* MacCrie, T. The story of the Scottish church. London, 1875. 8° 5816.22
Stanley, A. P. Lectures on the history of the New York, 1872. 8° 5812.6

SCOTT, Genio C. Fishing in American waters. New edition. With illustrations. New York, 1875. 539 pp. 8° 6412.4

SCOTT, John. Partisan life with John S. Mosby. With portraits and engravings. New York, 1867. 492 pp. Map. Fac-simile. 8° 811.14

SCOTT, *Sir* Walter. Poetical works. Leipzig, 1861. 2 v. in 1. Sq. 16° 1613.5

Contents. — The lay of the last minstrel; Marmion; The lady of the lake; The vision of Don Roderick; Rokeby; The lord of the isles; Songs; Lyrical pieces; Miscellaneous poems; Ballads.

Shelf. No.

SCOTT, *Sir* Walter, *continued.*
— The abbot. Boston 523.10
— *Same.* Leipzig 324.10
— Anne of Geierstein. Boston 533.1
— *Same.* Leipzig 324.1
— The antiquary. Boston 523.17
— *Same.* Leipzig 324.4
— Ballads and lyrical pieces. Baltimore, 1811. 215 pp. 16° 1618.5
— The betrothed. The highland widow 523.19
— The black dwarf. A legend of Montrose. Boston. 523.15
— *Same.* Leipzig 324.11
— The bride of Lammermoor. Boston 523.12
— *Same.* Leipzig 324.16
— Count Robert of Paris 533.4

	Shelf. No.
SCOTT, *Sir* Walter, *continued.*	
— The fair maid of Perth. Boston	533.2
— *Same.* Leipzig	324.14
— The fortunes of Nigel. Boston	523.2
— *Same.* Leipzig	324.12
— Guy Mannering. Boston	523.16
— *Same.* Leipzig	324.13
— The heart of Mid-Lothian. Boston	523.6
— *Same.* Leipzig	330.5
— Ivanhoe. Boston	523.11
— *Same.* Leipzig	324.6
— Kenilworth. Boston	523.7
— *Same.* Leipzig	324.8
— The lay of the last minstrel, a poem. Boston, 1807. 252 pp. 12°	1616.13
— Life of Napoleon Buonaparte. With a preliminary view of the French revolution. Exeter, 1828. 2 v. 8°	1223.12
— *Same.* Philadelphia, 1858. 2 v. in 1. Illustrated. 8°	1221.5
— Lives of the novelists. With notes. New York, 1872. 436 pp. 12°	5914.2
— The monastery. Boston	523.9
— *Same.* Leipzig	330.4
— Old Mortality. Boston	523.13
— *Same.* Leipzig	324.15
— Peveril of the Peak. Boston	523.1
— *Same.* Leipzig	324.17
— The pirate. Boston	523.8
— *Same.* Leipzig	324.9

	Shelf. No.
SCOTT, *Sir* Walter, *continued.*	
— Quentin Durward. Boston	523.4
— *Same.* Leipzig	324.2
— Redgauntlet	523.5
— Rob Roy. Boston	523.14
— *Same.* Leipzig	324.7
— St. Ronan's well	523.3
— The surgeon's daughter; Castle Dangerous	533.5
— Tales of a grandfather; being stories taken from Scottish history. 2 v.	939.5
— The talisman; The two drovers; My aunt Margaret's mirror; The tapestried chamber; The laird's Jock	523.20
— Waverley. Boston	523.18
— *Same.* Leipzig	324.3
— Woodstock. Boston	533.3
— *Same.* Leipzig	324.5
— Chambers, R. Life of. Edinburgh, 1871. 16°.	5425.9
— Hunnewell, J. F. The lands of Scott. Boston, 1871. 16°	5626.10
— Jenkinson, H. I. Epitome of Lockhart's life of Scott. Edinburgh, 1873. 8°	5425.10
— Lockhart, J. G. Memoirs of. Edinburgh, 1860. L. 8°	1020.1
— Prescott, W. H. Biographical and critical essays. London, 1856. 16°	1537.8
— - Biographical and critical miscellanies. Philadelphia, 1875. 12°	5237.3
— Stephen, L. Some words about Sir Walter Scott. (*In his* Hours in a library)	6136.9

SCOTT'S NOVELS AND POEMS,

ARRANGED CHRONOLOGICALLY BY THEIR SUBJECTS.

Hunnewell's "Lands of Scott" [5626.10] is a convenient key to the scenery of Scott's novels and poems; and a sample of the criticism with which they were received can be found in Jeffrey's Essays [5610.8]. See other references later under LIVES, etc.

Count Robert of Paris, A. D. 1090. This novel is a general study of the times of the first crusade, rather than a close correspondence to the historical events of that period. The scene is in and about Constantinople at the time when the army of the crusaders had reached that city on their way to the Holy Land. So far as the events are historical, they can be cursorily surveyed in Cox's "Crusades" [628.1]; but for more extended study, see chapters 48, 49 and 50 of Gibbon's "Roman empire" [824.9] and Milman's "Latin Christianity" [5817.11].

The betrothed, A. D. 1187, *etc.* A tale of the warfare on the Welsh border at the time when the third crusade was in contemplation, and efforts were making to turn the warring propensities of the age against the infidel. Scott himself says, "The war between the Welsh and the Norman lords of the marches is a period when all freedom might be taken with the strict truth of history without encountering any well-known fact which might render the narrative improbable." The general histories of England covering the reign of Henry II will elucidate the historical bearing of the events.

The talisman, A. D. 1193. This story of the third crusade, with the scenes in Palestine, contrasts strongly the characters of Richard Cœur-de-Lion and Saladin. The personages are historical, but the action is chiefly fictitious. As far as the events have a relation to history, they can be compared with the summaries regarding the third crusade in Gibbon's 59th chapter [824.9]; in Hume's [5413.2]; Lingard's [5417.8], and Knight's England [5413.1] under the reign of Richard I; the account given in James's "History of Richard Cœur-de-Lion" [5526.7]; and the narrative in Guizot's "History of France" [5510.2] during the time of Philip Augustus, who appears in "The talisman;" but a more particular delineation of this rival of Richard can be found in James's novel, "Philip Augustus" [722.7]. An account of this crusade will be found in Palmer and Besant's "City of Herod and Saladin" [5924.2]. It may be of interest to compare Scott's delineation of Saladin with that of Lessing in his "Nathan the wise," a drama [5736.4].

Ivanhoe, A. D. 1194. This novel, in some respects Scott's best, and his first attempt outside of Scottish history, introduces Cœur-de-Lion in disguise as a knight, and it is an interesting study of a period in English history, when the subjugated Saxons had not yet lost their characteristics under the rule of the Normans. Other well-known characters are Friar Tuck, Robin Hood, Isaac of York, a representative of the Jews in England at this time, and his daughter Rebecca, the Jewish maiden.

Robin Hood appears in Ivanhoe, and he is also a character in James's "Forest days" [327.14]. The historical standing of this semi-mythical hero is explained in Prof. Child's introduction to vol. v of his "English and Scottish ballads" [5628.5.5], also in Atlantic monthly, Dec., 1859; and in Thierry's Norman conquest [5417.2.2]. See also Timbs's "Abbeys, castles, etc." [5138.1].

Castle Dangerous, A. D. 1306–7. This novel has its scenes in the time of Bruce of Scotland, and pictures the efforts of Lord Douglas, "Black Douglas," one of Bruce's adherents, to advance the Scottish attempts to wrest Scotland from the rule of Edward of England. Considerable liberty is taken with historical events.

The lord of the isles, A. D. 1307–14. The historic interest of this poem centres in Bruce and Bannockburn, which conflict is described in the last canto. Scott's "Tales of a grandfather" [939.5] may be read in connection, and other histories of Scotland, particularly Burton's [5418.6.2], and histories of England covering the reign of Edward I. Grace Aguilar's "Days of Bruce" [533.19] is another imaginative portrayal of this epoch.

The fair maid of Perth, A. D. 1402. Time of King Robert III of Scotland. Illustrates the wild mediæval manners; the wager of battle between leaders of rival Highland clans; and the haughty power of the Douglas, beside the throne.

Quentin Durward, A. D. 1470. This novel was the first of Scott's ventures on a continental theme, and it shows the period of the decay of chivalry in France, under Louis XI, who with Charles the bold of Burgundy is the leading hero. The French king is depicted with detestable characteristics; and his nature is closely analyzed in Scott's introduction to the novel. Charles is painted somewhat grosser than Kirk, in his "Charles the bold" [5811.1], admits to be true; but see E. A. Freeman's Essays [5913.4]. Guizot's "History of France" [5510.2] will suffice for the general reader concerning the historical bearings of this novel. For comparison, Victor Hugo's "Hunchback of Notre-Dame" [511.27] affords another study of Louis's character; and an altogether different kind of delineation of these times will be found in Charles Reade's "Cloister and the hearth" [316.24].

Anne of Geierstein, A. D. 1474–77. The story turns in its historical data on the union of the Swiss with Louis XI of France to defeat Charles the bold, and some of the same characters appear, as in "Quentin Durward." The novelist has turned the historic events pretty freely to his own uses, and he wrote of Swiss scenery without personal knowledge of it. The reader will follow events to his satisfaction in Zschokke's "History of Switzerland" [5914.5] and Froissart's "Chronicles" [5920.2], beside the general histories of France. Scott, in his introduction, gives elucidatory explanations of the Vehmgerichte, the famous tribunal of Westphalia, which makes a feature of this novel, as it had before in his dramatic sketch of "The house of Aspen," and in his translation of Goethe's "Goetz von Berlichingen."

Marmion, A. D. 1513. This poem shows the adventures of a fictitious personage, but they are given an historical bearing as connected with the causes of the battle of Flodden Field, and with the battle itself, when the Earl of Surrey for Henry the Eighth of England defeated King James IV of Scotland. The English historians, like Hume [5413.2], Lingard [5417.8], and Froude [826.9], touch almost wholly on the political aspects attending Flodden Field, and more details of the conflict must be sought in Burton's Scotland [5418.6] and Scott's "Tales of a grandfather" [939.5]. There is an account of the locality in Howitt's "Visits to remarkable places" [235.2].

The lady of the lake, A. D. about 1540. This poem, perhaps the most popular of Scott's poems, depicts Highland manners and customs in contrast with those of the Lowlands; has its scene about Loch Katrine, and turns in good part upon highland irruptions into the lowlands, and a personal conflict of the Scottish king with a Highland leader.

The lay of the last minstrel, A. D. about 1550. This poem, told in cantos by a minstrel, depicts the manners and customs of the Scotch and English border, more particularly in warfare, and with a mixture of Scottish popular demonology.

The monastery, A. D. 1559-68. As in "The lay of the last minstrel," the scenery is laid at Melrose abbey; and in his introduction Scott points out his variations from the geography of the neighborhood. The ecclesiastical life of the abbey is, however, at a different stage, for its existence is threatened, and the story turns upon the contrasts of two enthusiasts, one catholic and the other reformed, and upon the rivalries between the vassals of the church and the lay barons. The machinery of the plot is derived from the "White lady of Avenel," and presents a view of Scottish superstitions. Public events, though not a part of its tale, are made to shape its development; and Burton's Scotland [5418.6.4] will afford the historical commentary, and a likeness of Murray the regent, can be found in Lodge's "Portraits" [5337.6.2].

The abbot, A. D. 1568. This novel, partly a continuation of the preceding, includes the imprisonment of Mary, queen of Scots, in Lochleven castle, her escape from it, and the battle of Langside, which decided her future. The note under Mary, queen of Scots, will give the historical parallels, and indicate other delineations of her character in imaginative works.

Kenilworth, A. D. 1575. This novel turns upon the death of Amy Robsart, the countess of Leicester, leaving the ambitious earl more at liberty to gain the favor of Queen Elizabeth, with a possibility of sharing her throne; and it exemplifies his flattery in the splendid reception accorded to the queen at his Castle of Kenilworth. There is an examination of Amy Robsart's real career and a history of Kenilworth by Adlard [5423.5], pointing out divergencies from Scott's tale; but, except as a picture of the time, public events other than as stated, do not much concern the progress of this story. Beside the Queen and Leicester (see Lodge's "Portraits" [5337.6], vol. 2), the best known of the other historical personages represented is Sir Walter Raleigh, at an earlier age than he appears on a different theatre in Kingsley's "Sir Amyas Leigh" [326.14]. The mysterious element of the story centres in Wayland Smith.

The fortunes of Nigel, A. D. 1620. The hero of this novel (besides Nigel himself, the lover) is Heriot, the king's goldsmith, of Edinboro', who accompanied James VI of Scotland to London, when he became James I of England, and the tale was an attempt by Scott to invest a man without the conventional attributes of heroism, with importance in a story. See the accounts of Heriot in chap. X of Fox Bourne's "English merchants." The tale, however, depicts the king in a masterly manner, and it is one of Scott's most famous delineations. The reader who wishes to see how such a monarch may be defended, can compare Disraeli's "Character of James" [1533.14]. In delineating London life of this period, Scott has shown his familiarity with the dramatists of the period, particularly in the wild existence of Alsatia or Whitefriars. The story is without much historical bearing; but Knight and the other general histories will throw light upon "Steenie," the Duke of Buckingham, and other historical characters which figure in it.

Rokeby, A. D. 1644. The scenes of this poem are in Yorkshire, just subsequent to the battle of Marston Moor, and the character of its personages depends largely upon the troublesome state of the times, and the events have no connection with the actual occurrences of the civil war, though typical Cavaliers and Roundheads make up the scenes; but they are not considered in Scott's handling to have marked characteristics of the times, owing partly perhaps to Scott's want of sympathy with the puritans, in whose nature he saw little of the poetical, which Kingsley claims for them in his "Plays and puritans" [1223.5].

A legend of Montrose, A. D. 1645-46. The scene is near the Trosachs, and on the west coast of Scotland. The central historical event of this tale is the murder of Lord Kilpont in Montrose's camp by Ardvoirlich, who fled to the Covenanters. Montrose's career is traced from his escape to the Highlands, in disguise, to raise the Highlanders in King Charles's behalf, and the story carries him through much of his year's victorious career, by which he sought to save the English royalists by forcing the withdrawal to their own territory of the army which the Covenanters had lent the parliamentarians. The tragedy is enlivened by the humors of Capt. Dalgetty, a soldier of fortune. A contrast of characters is drawn in Montrose and Argyle, or "McCallum More," the Covenanters' leader, and sketches of these heroes are in Lodge's "Portraits" [5337.6], volumes 4 and 5 respectively. The historical parallels can best be read in Clarendon's Rebellion [5412.4] and in Burton's Scotland [5418.6.7], chap. 73. See also Contemporary review, 1873, by Peter Bayne.

Woodstock, A. D. 1652-60. The scene of this novel is mostly at the old royal lodge of Woodstock (in what is now the domain of Blenheim), and the time extends from just after the battle of Worcester, when Charles II as a fugitive finds shelter there, to that monarch's restoration. The machinery of the tale comes from some witchcraft tricks played by a crafty royalist, which are explained at length in the introduction. The important historical characters are Cromwell and Charles II, and the public events of the period can be studied in the general histories of Knight [5413.1], Hume [5413.2], Lingard [5417.8], and Clarendon's Rebellion [5412.4]. Further study may be given to the biography of Cromwell by Carlyle [1238.1], and the more condensed one by Southey [5428.6], and to the paper on his character as a ruler by Goldwin Smith [5425.1]. The apt characterizations of this period by Macaulay can be found in his "History of England" [838.1.1], and his essays on Hallam, on Milton, and on Hampden [1918.4]. Some chapters in Masson's "Life of Milton" [5422.2] will be of use for further study. Cromwell and the king are sketched respectively in Lodge's "Portraits" [5337.6], vol. 5 and 6.

For other imaginative delineations of this period, see Horace Smith's "Brambletye house," James's "Cavalier," and "Arrah Neil" [327.11]; Ainsworth's "Ovingdean grange" [322.13] and "Boscobel" [339.10]; Mrs. Charles's "Draytons and Davenants" [329.1] and its sequel "On both sides of the sea" [321.7]; and Miss Yonge's "Pigeon pie." See also De Foe's "Memoirs of a cavalier" and "History of Col. Jack;" and for contemporary satire Butler's "Hudibras."

Peveril of the Peak, A. D. 1660-80. This novel, which opens just after the restoration of Charles II, and extends in its action over a score of years, describes the contrasts of society at that time, in the jovial cavalier (Scott is thought to lean by preference to this side of the contest) and the soberer puritan, and the hero and heroine of this story evince these respective sympathies. The scene is partly in Derbyshire, partly in London, and for a while in the Isle of Man, where the countess of Derby had judicially executed a Manxman for siding with the parliamentarians in the late civil war, and is now pursued for this assumption of feudal right. The famous "Popish plot" of 1678-80 comes incidentally into the thread of the story, which is carried in one place to the metropolis, and presents a picture of the dissolute court of Charles II. The general histories covering his reign give all the public events by which the plot is surrounded, while the "Diary" of Pepys [5627.1] forms an interesting commentary on the manners of the day.

Old Mortality, A. D. 1679-90. This is a tale of the west country Covenanters and their defeats by and their victories over the royal troops under Claverhouse, with the actions at Drumclog and Bothwell Bridge. It is a vivid picture of the passions and manners of the two parties in politics and church, while the revolution of 1688 was impending. The friends of the Covenanters may claim that Balfour of Burley, their leader, is drawn in darker colors, and Claverhouse with more indulgences, than the records warrant. Burton's "History of Scotland" [5418.6.7], chap. 79, will give sufficient of the historical parallel; and a sketch of Claverhouse is given in Lodge's "Portraits" [5337.6.6]. The histories of the Covenanters necessarily cover many of the historic events.

"Old Mortality," an aged religious wanderer, who cleans gravestones of their mosses, is represented as furnishing the material of the story.

The characters of the Covenanters are also drawn in Hogg's "Brownie of Bodsbeck;" in Wilson's "Covenanter's marriage day," etc.

The pirate, A. D. about 1700. This story has no historical basis; but is a picture of life in the Orkneys and northern parts of Scotland, about the beginning of the last century, and is developed largely through the author's imagination from observation of what he saw in this region in 1814.

The bride of Lammermoor, A. D. about 1700. This is another private family story, placed at about the same period as the last, but having no reference to public events.

The black dwarf, A. D. 1708. This short story uses a dwarf, whom the author had known, for a prototype, placing the incidents along the Midland Border, at a period when the Jacobites were planning a rising, which did not take shape in rebellion, till as portrayed in "Rob Roy."

Rob Roy, A. D. 1715. This novel contrasts the wild Highland life with that of the town (Glasgow), and shows the marauding exploits of Rob Roy, the outlawed McGregor, at the time of the first attempt to make head in rebellion for the Pretender. Beside Rob Roy, much of whose historic career is told in the long introduction, no actual characters of this era appear with any prominence; but the historic names of Argyle and Mar were borne by the opposing commanders of the forces. The serious interest of the plot rests in Rob Roy and Diana Vernon; and the comic in Bailie Nicol Jarvie and Andrew Fairservice. The events of this rebellion are also somewhat interwoven in James's "Henry Smeaton" [750.3].

The historic rendering of the events of these years can be followed in Scott's "Tales of a grandfather" [939.5]; in Stanhope's "History of England" [5418.5], chap. 6; in Jesse's "Pretenders" [5426 14]; and in Burton's Scotland, 1689-1748 [5418.6.2], chap. 19.

Wordsworth's poem on "Rob Roy's grave" expresses the common estimation of the wild outlaw.

The heart of Mid-Lothian, A. D. 1736-51. This novel, of which the scene is mostly in Edinburgh, with an episode in London, opens with the famous Porteous mob, which lynched an officer of that name for hanging smugglers. The story is otherwise a domestic one, with little dependence upon historical events, but some well-known characters figure in it, like John, Duke of Argyle, who is sketched in Lodge's "Portraits" [5337.6.7]; and Queen Caroline, the wife of George II, who is portrayed in Mrs. Oliphant's "Sketches of the reign of George II" [1032.1]. The pathetic interest of a touching story is developed in the characters of Jeanie and Effie Deans; its mysterious element lies in the personage known in the opening as Madge Wildfire; and its grotesqueness in the Laird of Dumbiedykes. Its descriptions of the Edinburgh of a century and more ago lend interest to the localities of the modern town.

Waverley, A. D. 1745. This picture of the life and manners of Scotland, at a time when the old feudal feeling and the Covenanter's fanaticism had not wholly died out, though their equivalents had long since disappeared in the southern country, accompanies the historical events of the rebellion of the chevalier Charles Edward, the battle of Preston Pans, the "race to Derby," and the Pretender's court in Holyrood Castle, Edinburgh.

The events of a public nature which it covers can be studied in Stanhope's "History of England" [5418.3], chap. 26; in his separate monograph "The Forty-five" [5418.7]; in Burton's Scotland, 1689-1748 [5418.6.2], chap. 21, etc.; in Jesse's "Pretenders" [5426.14], and in Scott's "Tales of a grandfather" [939.5]. Ainsworth's novel "Good old times" [329.11] concerns the same period.

Guy Mannering, A. D. 1750-70. This tale gives the southern coast of Scotland and its manners in the last century, with the life of smugglers and gypsies — Meg Merrilies being of the last, — and with the portrait of a devoted old family tutor in Dominie Sampson. Guy Mannering himself has been said to greatly resemble Scott in the traits of a high-minded gentleman.

Redgauntlet, A. D. 1770. This novel has less of historical interest than Waverley, to which it is in some sort a sequel, pertaining to the last attempt of the chevalier Charles Edward, when an old man, to head a Jacobite rising in the north. The scene is laid in large part on both sides of Solway Frith, and in the old town of Edinburgh, and the narrative derives more perhaps from Scott's own reminiscences than any other of his novels. The introduction sketches the history of the Pretender from the rebellion of 1745-46, where Waverley leaves him, till he comes again on the scene in this novel.

The antiquary, A. D. 1798. This picture of Scottish manners during the last ten years of the last century, has little to connect it with public events, except an episode of the alarm felt along the coast through fear of a French invasion, the historical bearing of which may be read of in Alison's "History of Europe" [5913.6], and in Knight's "Popular history of England" [5413.1]. The chief characters of interest are Jonathan Oldbuck, the Laird of Monkbarns, and Edie Ochiltree, a Scottish mendicant of the privileged Blue-Gown order.

St. Ronan's well, A. D. 1800. A tale of life at a Scottish watering-place in Scott's own day.

Chronicles of the Canongate. This is a series of short stories, published after Scott had dropped his incognito, and in the introduction he makes the first printed acknowledgment of his authorship of the Waverley novels, with some details of their composition. The Chronicles themselves have pleasant prefatory matter representing an imaginary editor, Mr. Croftangry. The two series of this name contained: —

The Highland widow (A. D. 1755).
The two drovers (A. D. 1765).
The surgeon's daughter (A. D. 1750-70).
My aunt Margaret's mirror (A. D. 1700).
The tapestried chamber (A. D. 1780).
The laird's Jock (A. D. 1600).

Lives of Scott, etc.

The biography by his son-in-law, Lockhart, is the principal and authoritative life, and the epitome by Jenkinson is a popular summary. Chambers's is also a briefer narrative. See also Irving's account of Abbotsford [715.5]; the Essays by Prescott [1537.8; 5237.3]; by Jeffrey [5610.8]; and the accounts of Allibone and Thomas.

Also see Masson's "English novelists;" John Brown's "Spare hours," second series [537.5.2], for Scott's diversions with a pet child; Bryant's "Orations" [1926.1], for his address at the unveiling of a statue of Scott in Central Park, New York; illustrated papers in Harper's monthly, vols. 26, 36, 43, and 44; Carlyle's Essays [5610.7], for a review of Lockhart; Jerdan's "Men I have known" [5423.11]; C. R. Leslie's "Autobiographical recollections" [1024.10]; Lodge's "Portraits" [5337.6.8]; Maginn's "Fraserian papers" [1935.5]; Hugh Miller's "Abbotsford baronetcy," in his Essays; an account of a visit to Scott in Moscheles's "Recent music" [6234.4]; Forsyth's "Novels and novelists" [6136.1]; and Howitt's "Homes and haunts of the British poets" [1225.5].

The English magazines, in 1871, had numerous articles on Scott, that year being the centenary of his birth.

The 3d volume of the memoirs of Archibald Constable [5424.10] wholly pertains to Scott and his relations with the Edinburgh publisher, and a concise account of this connection is given in Curwen's "Booksellers" [5426.16]. The lives of Scott's contemporaries necessarily throw much light on his career, like Russell's life of Thomas Moore; the life of Irving [1214.1; 1815.1]; the life of George Ticknor [1012.5; 5023.10]; Moore's life of Byron [5631.4]; and Miss Ferrier's "Recollections of Scott at home" in Temple bar, 1874. Allibone's article has letters of reminiscences from Edward Everett and George Ticknor.

Everett also gives nos. 13 and 15 of his "Mount Vernon papers" [1534.13] to reminiscences of Scott.

Principal Shairp has a paper on the Homeric element in Scott's poetry, in Good words, 1875; and Eastlake notes the effect of the novels on the revival of mediæval architecture in his "Gothic revival" [6221.2].

Shelf. No.

SCOTT, William Bell. Albert Durer: his life and works. Including autobiographical papers and complete catalogues. With six etchings by the author and other illustrations. London, 1869. xiv, 324+ pp. Portrait. 8° ... 6213.10

SCOTT, Winfield. Infantry tactics; or, rules for the exercise and manœuvres of the United States infantry. New edition. New York, 1852. 3 v. 16° ... 1529.7

Contents. — Vol. I. Schools of the soldier and company. II. The battalion, and instruction for light infantry or rifle. III. Evolutions of the line.

— Memoirs. Written by himself. New York, 1864. 2 v. Portraits. 12° ... 1214.8

SCOTTISH chiefs, The. [Wallace, etc.] Porter, J... 1225.19

SCOTTISH philosophy, The, from Hutcheson to Hamilton. MacCosh, J. New York, 1875. 8° ... 5821.1

SCOURING, The, of the White Horse. Hughes, T. Cambridge, 1859. Sm. 4° ... 536.1

SCOUT, The. Simms, W. G. ... 716.22

SCRIBE, (Augustin) Eugène, and LEGOUVÉ, (Gabriel Jean Baptiste) Ernest (Wilfred). Les doigts de fée: comédie. With English notes, by F. Bôcher. Boston, 1867. 105 pp. 12° ... 2015.2

SCRIBNER'S monthly. An illustrated magazine for the people. Vol. 4-10. New York, 1872-75. 7 v. 8° ... 1438.1

SCRIPTURE lessons; being a selection from the Old and New Testament, for the use of schools. Boston, 1823. 242 [240] pp. 12° ... 1537.16

SCROPE, George Poulett. Volcanoes. The character of their phenomena [etc.]. 2d edition, revised and enlarged. With a map, frontispiece, woodcuts, etc. London, 1872. xi, 23, 490+ pp. 8°. 6631.2

SCROPE; or, the lost library. A novel of New York and Hartford. Perkins, F. B. ... 732.34

SCRUB Hollow Sunday-school. Guernsey, C. F. ... 913.33

SCUDAMORE, Charles. Treatise on the nature and cure of gout and rheumatism, including general considerations on morbid states of the digestive organs. 1st American, from the 2d London edition. Philadelphia, 1819. xix, 335 pp. 8°. 6023.14

Shelf. No.

SCUDDER, Horace Elisha. Doings of the Bodley family in town and country ... 910.1

— Dream children ... 938.1

— The dwellers in Five-sisters court ... 717.18

— Seven little people and their friends ... 938.6

— Stories from my attic ... 728.2

SCULPTORS. Clement, C. E. Sculptors, and their works. New York, 1874. 16° ... 1513.17

— Perkins, C. C. Italian sculptors. London, 1868. L. 8° ... 6210.2

— Vasari, G. Lives of the most eminent sculptors. London, 1855. 5 v. Sm. 8° ... 6215.6

SCULPTURE. Arsenne, L. C. Manuel du peintre et du sculpteur. Paris, 1833. 2 v. 24° ... 6219.1

— Brigham, W. T. Cast catalogue of antique sculpture. Boston, 1874. 4° ... 6210.7

— Flaxman, J. Lectures on. London, 1865. Sm. 8°. 6215.5

— Luebke, W. History of. London, 1872. 2 v. 8°. 6210.3

— Perkins, C. C. Italian sculptors: a history of sculpture in Northern, Southern and Eastern Italy. London, 1868. L. 8° ... 6210.2

— Ruskin, J. Aratra pentelici. Six lectures on the elements of. New York, 1872. 12° ... 6236.2

— Viardot, L. Wonders of. New York, 1873. 16°. 1714.28

Note. — Luebke's is the first comprehensive general history of the plastic art ever written and ranks well. A condensed history will be found in the 5th lecture of Digby Wyatt's "Fine art" [6232.2]; and popular summaries are given in Clement and Viardot. Flaxman's "Lectures" also cover much historical elucidation. Of the sculpture of the ancients, see the lives of sculptors in Smith's "Dictionary of Greek and Roman biography" [R.R., E.3.3] and Winckelmann's "History of ancient art" [6211.1], beside the specimens in Brigham's "Cast catalogue." Vasari and Perkins will do much for Italian sculpture. For English sculpture, see Lady Eastlake's "Life of Gibson" [5423.13]. Tuckerman's "Book of the artists" [1511.6] gives memoirs of the American sculptors, Greenough, Crawford, Powers, and others. Modern travels in Italy often give accounts of the studios of sculptors in Florence and Rome. Channing's "Physician's vacation" [422.21] gives an account of Thorwaldsen. There is a paper by Harriet Hosmer on the processes of sculpture, in the Atlantic monthly, vol. 14; see also Scribner's monthly, vol. 4.

SEA. Figuier, (G.) L. Earth and sea. London, 1870. 8° ... 6631.3

— Hartwig, G. The sea and its living wonders. London, 1873. 8° ... 6633.4

Shelf. No.

SEA, *continued*.

— Maury, M. F. Physical geography of the sea, and its meteorology. New York, 1871. 8° ... 1520.2

— Michelet, J. The sea. New York, 1861. 12°. 1934.13

— Sonrel, L. The bottom of the. New York, 1872. 16° ... 1714.9

— Thomson, C. W. The depths of the. London, 1872. 8° ... 6632.3

See also Ocean.

SEA and shore. Adams, W. T. ... 924.9

SEA and shore. Warfield, C. A. ... 723.35

SEA-KINGS and naval heroes. Edgar, J. G. New York, 1868. 16° ... 913.16

SEA lions, The. Cooper, J. F. ... 525.11

SEABOARD parish, The. MacDonald, G. ... 536.18

SEAMANSHIP. Luce, S. B. New York, 1873. 8° .. 1520.8

SEARCH, A, after sunshine; or, Algeria in 1871. Herbert, *Lady* M. E. London, 1872. 8° ... 5911.2

SEARS, Edmund Hamilton. Athanasia: or, foregleams of immortality. Boston, 1858. xii, 340 pp. 12° ... 5816.16

— The fourth gospel the heart of Christ. Boston, 1872. viii, 551 pp. Sm. 8° ... 6326.9

SEASONS. Howitt, M. Pictorial calendar of the. London, 1862. Sm. 8° ... 1394.12

— Howitt, W. The book of the. Philadelphia, 1831. 12° ... 1838.3

— Thomson, J. The seasons. Leipzig, 1853. Sq. 16° ... 1613.9

SEAT, The, of empire. Coffin, C. C. Boston, 1870. 12° ... 425.15

SEATON, *Sir* Thomas. Manual of fret cutting and wood carving. With diagrams. London, 1875. viii, 152 pp. Sm. 8° ... 6425.7

SEAVER family, The. A genealogy of Robert Seaver of Roxbury, Mass., and some of his descendants. Trask, W. B. Boston, 1872. Sm. 4° ... 5013.10

SEBASTOPOL. Creagh, S. A scamper to, in 1867. London, 1873. 8° ... 5931.10

— Russell, W. H. General Todleben's History of the defence of. 1854–5. London, 1865. 8° ... 5923.3

See also Crimea.

SECESSION, Sketches of the history, progress, and decline of. Brownlow, W. G. Philadelphia, 1862. 12° ... 815.3

SECOND-COUSIN Sarah. Robinson, F. W. ... 732.32

SECOND wife, The. John, E. ... 726.25

SECRET, The, of success. Baker, H. N. (W.) ... 926.6

SECRET, The, of the island. Verne, J. New York, 1876. 16° ... 733.14

SECRET, The, out; or, one thousand tricks with cards, and other recreations. Frickell, G. New York [*cop.* 1869]. 12° ... 1515.15

SECRET passion, The. [Shakespeare novel.] Williams, R. F. ... 531.23

SECRET service, The. Richardson, A. D. Hartford, 1866. 8° ... 813.15

SECTS. Hayward, J. The book of religions. Boston, 1843. 12° ... 1534.4

— — The religious creeds and statistics of every Christian denomination in the United States and British provinces. Boston, 1836. 16° ... 5816.20

See also Religions.

SEDGWICK, Catherine Maria. Facts and fancies for school-day reading ... 929.6

— Home. Boston, 1837. 158 pp. 12° ... 539.6

— Hope Leslie. 2 v. ... 725.21

— Letters from abroad to kindred at home. New York, 1841. 2 v. 12° ... 426.15

— Life and letters. Edited by M. E. Dewey. New York, 1871. 446 [442] pp. 1 plate. Portraits. 12° ... 1224.12

— The Linwoods. 2 v. ... 737.3

— Live and let live ... 918.19

— Married or single? 2 v. ... 725.22

— Memoir of Lucretia Maria Davidson. (*In* Sparks, J. Library of American biography) ... 5028.1.7

— The poor rich man, and the rich poor man ... 918.15

— Stories for young persons ... 918.20

Shelf. No.

SEEBOHM, Friedrich. The era of the protestant revolution. With maps. New York, 1874. xv, 242 pp. 16°. [Morris, E. E., *editor*. Epochs of history] ... 628.3

— The Oxford reformers, John Colet, Erasmus, and Thomas More; being a history of their fellow-work. 2d edition, revised and enlarged. London, 1869. xiv, 551 pp. 8° ... 5811.12

SEED-TIME and harvest. Tweedie, W. K. ... 916.6

SEEK and find. Adams, W. T. ... 924.19

SEEKERS after God. Farrar, F. W. London, 1875. Sm. 8° ... 5937.7

SEEKING his fortune, and other dialogues. Alger, H., *jr.*, and Cheney, O. A. Boston [1875]. 16°. 1518.11

SEELEY, John Robert. Ecce Homo: a survey of the life and work of Jesus Christ. Boston, 1866. 355 pp. 12° ... 1526.5

— Roman imperialism, and other lectures and essays. Boston, 1871. 335 pp. 12° ... 5616.3

— *joint author*. English lessons for English people. *See* ABBOTT, Edwin Abbott ... 1535.1

SEEN and unseen. A novel. Algatchie, *pseud.* ... 532.21

SEER, The; or, common places refreshed. [Essays.] Hunt, (J. H.) L. Boston, 1865. 2 v. 12° ... 1917.8

SÉGUR, Philippe Paul, *comte* de. Histoire et mémoires. Paris, 1873. 7 v. 8° ... 5513.4

— Mélanges. Paris, 1873. 528+ pp. 8° ... 5513.5

SÉGUR, Sophie (Rostopchine), *comtesse* de. The inn of the guardian angel. [A novel.] From the French by Miss H. I. Adams ... 912.7

SELBORNE, *England*, Natural history of. White, G. Boston, 1866. 32° ... 1539.1

SELDEN, John. Table-talk. With a biographical preface and notes by S. W. Singer. 3d edition. London, 1860. 270 pp. Portrait. 16° ... 5617.17

SELECT British essays. *See* HABBERTON, John, *editor*.

SELECT historical essays. Freeman, E. A. Leipzig, 1873. Sq. 16° ... 828.9

SELECTION, A, of patriotic addresses, to [John Adams], the president of the United States. With the president's answers. Boston, 1798. 360 pp. 12°. 1917.4

SELF-AID cyclopædia for self-taught students. Burn, R. S. London, N. D. 8° ... 6223.2

SELF-CULTURE, On. Blackie, J. S. Edinburgh, 1874. 16° ... 5838.5

SELF-EDUCATION. Gerando, J. M., *baron* de. Boston, 1860. 16° ... 1536.13

SELF-HELP. Smiles, S. Boston, 1861. 12° ... 1535.3

— *Same*. New York [1870]. 12° ... 1534.9

SELF-KNOWLEDGE, Treatise on. Mason, J. (*In* The Alexandrian) ... 1910.4.2

SELF-RAISED; or, from the depths. Southworth, E. D. E. N. ... 522.26

SELFRIDGE, Thomas Oliver. Reports of explorations and surveys to ascertain the practicability of a ship-canal between the Atlantic and Pacific oceans by the way of the isthmus of Darien. *See* UNITED STATES. *Department of the navy* ... 5030.6

SELLING Lucky. Abbott, J. ... 914.20

SEMIRAMIDE. Rossini, G. (*In* Ditson, O., and co. Standard opera librettos) ... 6233.3.3

SEMPLE, Robert Hunter, *editor and translator*. Memoirs on diphtheria. From the writings of Bretonneau [and others]. With a biographical appendix, by J. Chatto. London, 1859. 407 pp. 8° ... 6023.5

SENECA, Lucius Annæus. *See* FARRAR, F. W. Seekers after God. London, 1875. Sm. 8° ... 5937.7

SENIOR, Nassau William. Historical and philosophical essays. London, 1865. 2 v. Sm. 8° ... 5825.2

SENSE and sensibility. Austen, J. Boston ... 515.5

— *Same*. Leipzig ... 325.22

SENSORIAL and nervous systems, Comparative view of the. Warren, J. C. Boston, 1822. 12° ... 6012.8

SENTIMENTAL journal through France and Italy. Sterne, L. Leipzig, 1861. Sq. 16° ... 428.2

SEPIA painting, A course of. Leitch, R. P. London [1875]. Oblong 8° ... 6217.11

SEPOY war. *See* INDIA.

SEPTIMIUS Felton. [Time of Concord fight, etc.] Hawthorne, N. Boston, 1872. 12° ... 533.24

Shelf. No.

SERMONS. Andrews, J. N. Sermons on the Sabbath and law. Battle Creek, 1870. 16° 6328.2
— Bartol, C. A. Discourses on the Christian spirit and life. Boston, 1850. 12° .....5815.19 and 6325.14
— Beecher, H. W. A summer parish: Sabbath discourses at the "Twin mountain house," White mountains, 1874. New York, 1875. 8° 6325.8
— Blair, H. Sermons. London, 1783. 2 v. 8°. 5814.1
— Briggs, G. W. The bow in the cloud. Fifteen discourses. Boston, 1846. 12° 5818.9
— Brooke, S. A. Christ in modern life. Sermons. New York, 1872. Sm. 8° 5814.9
— - Freedom in the church of England. Sermons suggested by the Voysey judgment. London, 1871. 16° 5816.9
— - Sermons preached in St. James's chapel, York street, London. Boston, 1869. Sm. 8° 5815.4
— Brooks, F. Sermons. Boston, 1876. 16° 6325.16
— Buckminster, J. S. Sermons. Boston, 1829. 8°. 6322.3
— Burgess, E. Dedham pulpit. Boston, 1840. 8°.5813.11
— Burnap, G. W. Discourses on the rectitude of human nature. Boston, 1850. 12° 1522.7
— Candlish, R. S. Sermons. New York, 1874. 16°.6326.23
— Chauncy, C. Twelve sermons. Boston, 1765. 8°. 1922.3
— Clarke, J. F. The hour which cometh and now is: sermons. Boston, 1864. 16° 6326.3
— Clarke, J. Sermons. Boston, 1799. 8° 5814.3
— Codman, J. Sermons, with addresses. Boston, 1834. 8° 5813.9
— Collyer, R. Nature and life: sermons. Boston, 1872. 12° 1537.4
— Dewey, O. Discourses on human nature, human life, and the nature of religion. New York, 1847. 3 v. 12° 5237.2
— - Discourses on various subjects. New York, 1835. 12° 5815.26
— Fox, W. J. Christ and Christianity. Sermons on the mission, character, and doctrine, of Jesus of Nazareth. Boston, 1833. 2 v. 12° 5815.12
— - Christian morality. Sermons. Boston, 1833. 12°.5815.13
— Frothingham, N. L. Sermons, in the order of a twelvemonth. Boston, 1852. 12° 1525.7
— Goodwin, E. S. Sermons. Boston, 1834. 12°.5816.19
— Greenwood, F. W. P. Sermons of consolation. Boston, 1844. 16° 5817.10
— Guthrie, T. The city: its sins and sorrows. Sermons from Luke xix, 41. New York, 1873. 12°.6327.16
— Hare, A. W. The Alton sermons. London, 1874. Sm. 8° 6325.18
— Harrington, J. Sermons. Boston, 1854. 12°.. 6325.3
— Hill, T. Jesus, the interpreter of nature; and other sermons. Boston, 1860. 12° 6327.18
— Huntington, F. D. Christian believing and living. Sermons. Boston, 1860. 12° 6325.11
— - Sermons for the people. Boston, 1856. 12°. 1522.8
— Knight, H. C. Lectures and sermons. Boston, 1831 2 v. 8° 6325.9
— Maurice, (J.) F. D. Sermons preached in country churches. London, 1873. Sm. 8° 6326.5
— Murray, W. H. H. Music-hall sermons. 2d series. Boston, 1873. 12° 5816.13
— Newman, J. H. Discourses addressed to mixed congregations. London, 1871. Sm. 8° 6325.20
— - Parochial and plain sermons. London, 1875. 8 v. Sm. 8° 6326.19
— - Sermons preached on various occasions. London, 1874. Sm. 8° 6326.16
— Paley, W. Sermons on various subjects. Boston, 1827. 8° 5810.8
— Palfrey, J. G. Sermons on duties belonging to some of the conditions and relations of private life. Boston, 1834. 8° 5811.9
— Parsons, B. Christian views: discourses. Boston, 1848. 12° 1524.16
— Peabody, W. B. O. Sermons. Boston, 1849. 12°. 6326.7
— Tappan, D. Sermons on important subjects. Cambridge, 1807. 8° 5812.2
— Thacher, S. C. Sermons. Boston, 1824. 8° ... 5814.6
— Uhlhorn, G. The modern representations of the life of Jesus. Four discourses. Boston, 1868. 16° 6328.7

Shelf. No.

SERMONS, *continued.*
— Walker, J. Sermons preached in the chapel of Harvard college. Boston, 1861. 12° 1524.4
— Ware, H., *jr.* Discourses on the life and character of Jesus Christ. Boston, 1825. Sm. 8° 5814.2
— Welles, —. "Things new and old:" sermons. Portland, 1845. 8° 1533.9
SERMONS out of church. Craik, D. (M.) Leipzig, 1875. Sq. 16° 1928.5
— *Same.* New York, 1875. 12° 6327.15
SERMONS to the clergy. Dodge, M. A. Boston, 1876. 12° 1926.4
SERRES, Marcel de. Nouveau manuel complet de paléontologie. Paris, 1846. With atlas. 3 v. 24° [Manuel Roret] 6639.1
SERVANTS, The, of the stomach. Macé, J. New York, 1868. 12° 1536.7
SERVITUDE et grandeur militaires. Vigny, A. (V.), *comte* de. Paris, 1872. 18° 5536.20
SESAME and lilies. Ruskin, J. New York, 1872. 12°.6236.15
SETTLERS, The, in Canada. Marryat, F. 337.3
SEVEN daughters. Douglas, A. M. 913.32
SEVEN hills, The [*i. e.* Rome]. De Mille, J........ 914.41
SEVEN historic ages. Gilman, A. [Juvenile] 918.30
SEVEN lamps, The, of architecture. Ruskin, J. New York, 1871. 12° 6236.3
SEVEN little people and their friends. Scudder, H. E. 938.6
SEVEN little sisters, The, who live on the round ball that floats in the air. Andrew, J. 928.5
SEVEN sons, The, of mammon. Sala, G. A. Leipzig, 1869. 2 v. in 1. Sq. 16° 315.10
SEVEN stories, with basement and attic. Mitchell, D. G. New York, 1864. 12° 715.3
SEVEN weeks' war, The. [Prussia and Austria, 1866.] Hozier, H. M. Philadelphia, 1867. 2 v. 8°. 5922.4
SEVEN years. Kavanagh, J. 323.9
SEVENOAKS. Holland, J. G. New York, 1875. 12°. 536.22
SEVENTH-DAY adventists. Littlejohn, W. H. The constitutional amendment: or the Sunday, the Sabbath, the change, and restitution. A discussion [with] the editor of the Christian statesman. Battle Creek, 1873. 16° 5818.14
— White, J. Life incidents, in connection with the great advent movement. Battle Creek, 1868. 12° ....1537.11 and 6328.4
SEWALL, Samuel E. The legal condition of women in Massachusetts. (*In* Woman's suffrage tracts). 1926.5
SEWARD, William Henry. Travels around the world. Edited by O. R. Seward. With illustrations. New York, 1873. xii, 788 pp. Portrait. Map. 8° ....431.1 and 5910.1
— Lincoln and Seward. Remarks upon the memorial address of C. F. Adams, on. Welles, G. New York, 1874. 12° 5027.10
SEWELL, Elizabeth Mary. After life 314.18
Cleve hall 532.6
— The earl's daughter 738.10
— The experience of life; or, aunt Sarah 319.23
— A first history of Greece. New York, 1869. 358 pp. 12° 828.13
— Gertrude. Edited by W. Sewell 527.21
— A glimpse of the world 314.17
— Ivors. 2 v. 527.22
— The journal of a home life. Leipzig, 1867. 2 v. in 1. Sq. 16° 314.19
— Laneton parsonage. Edited by W. Sewell. 3 v. 532.7
— Margaret Percival. Edited by W. Sewell. 2 v. 532.8
— Ursula 314.16
— and YONGE, Charlotte Mary, *editors.* European history, narrated in a series of historical selections from the best authorities. [Vol. I, 3d edition; vol. II, 2d edition.] London, 1872, 73. 2 v. Sm. 8° 5927.7

Contents. — Vol. I. 1003-1154. II. 1088-1228.

SEX in education. Clarke, E. H. Boston, 1873. 16°. 1937.2 and 5838.1
— - A reply to. *See* HOWE, Julia Ward 1937.4
SEX in industry. Ames, A., *jr.* Boston, 1875. 16°. 1937.5
SEXES, The, throughout nature. Blackwell, A. B. New York, 1875. 12° 5837.5

Shelf. No.

SEXUAL physiology of woman. Hayes, A. H. Boston [*cop.* 1869]. 12° 1524.25

SGANARELLE: comédie. Molière, J. B. P. Œuvres. Paris, 1869. 12° 5537.2.1

SGANARELLE: a comedy. Molière, J. B. P. Dramatic works. Edinburgh, 1875. 8° 5530.3.1

SHABBY genteel story, A. Thackeray, W. M. Miscellanies. Leipzig 335.13.4

— *Same.* (*In his* Works.) London 513.1.6

SHADOW, The, of Ashlydyat. Wood, E. P. 3 v.... 330.28

SHADOW, A, of Dante. Rossetti, M. F. Boston, 1872. Sm. 8° 5536.1

SHADOW, The, of Moloch mountain. Austin, J. G. 511.1

SHADOWS of the old booksellers. [Reminiscences.] Knight, C. London, 1865. 16° 5425.25

SHAIRP, John Campbell. Culture and religion in some of their relations. New York, 1872. 197+ pp. 16° 5617.3

— Studies in poetry and philosophy. New York, 1872. xvii, 340 pp. 16° 1535.14

— TAIT, Peter Guthrie, and ADAMS-REILLY, A. Life and letters of James David Forbes. With portraits, map, and illustrations. London, 1873. xiii, 577 pp. 8° 5332.4

SHAIRP, Thomas. Up in the North. Notes on a journey from London to Luleå and into Lapland. London, 1872. x, 244 pp. Illustrated. Map. Sm. 8° 5915.4

SHAKERS. Holy roll and book; from the Lord God of heaven, to the inhabitants of earth. Printed in the United society, Canterbury, N. H., 1843. vii, 402+ pp. 8° 5814.8

— Compendium of the origin, history, principles, and doctrines of the United society of believers in Christ's second appearing. Evans, F. W. New York, 1859. 12° 5818.19

SHAKESPEARE, William. Works. From the text of A. Dyce's 2d edition. Leipzig, 1868. 7 v. Portrait. Sq. 16° 1613.1

Contents. — Vol. I. Measure for measure; The comedy of errors; Much ado about nothing; Love's labour's lost; A midsummer-night's dream; The merchant of Venice; As you like it. II. The taming of the shrew; All's well that ends well; Twelfth-night; The winter's tale; King John; Richard II. III. Henry IV, parts 1 and 2; Henry V; Henry VI, parts 1 and 2. IV. Henry VI, part 3; Richard III; Henry VIII; Troilus and Cressida; Titus Andronicus. V. Coriolanus; Romeo and Juliet; Timon of Athens; Julius Cæsar; Macbeth. VI. Hamlet; King Lear; Othello; Antony and Cleopatra; Cymbeline. VII. Pericles; The tempest; The two gentlemen of Verona; The merry wives of Windsor; Poems; Venus and Adonis; Lucrece; Sonnets; A lover's complaint; The passionate pilgrim; Life; Glossary.

— Works. The plays edited from the folio of 1623, with various readings from all the editions, notes [etc.], by R. G. White. Boston, 1872. 12 v. Portrait. Illustrated. 12° 5615.4

Contents. — Vol. I. Preface; Supplementary notes and corrections; Memoirs of Shakespeare; Shakespeare's will; Chronological tables of Shakespeare's works; Notes on the portraits and autograph signatures of Shakespeare; An account of the rise and progress of the English drama to the time of Shakespeare; Essay on Shakespeare's genius; Historical sketch of the text of Shakespeare; Poems; Venus and Adonis; Lucrece; The passionate pilgrim; Sonnets; A lover's complaint; Attributed verses. II. Preliminary matter to the folio of 1623; The tempest; The two gentlemen of Verona; The merry wives of Windsor. III. Measure for measure; The comedy of errors; Much ado about nothing; Love's labour's lost. IV. Midsummer-night's dream; Merchant of Venice; As you like it; Taming of the shrew. V. All's well that ends well; Twelfth night, or what you will; The winter's tale. VI. King John; Richard II; Henry IV, parts 1 and 2. VII. Henry V; Henry VI, parts 1 and 2; Essay on the authorship of Henry VI. VIII. Henry VI, part 3; Richard III; Henry VIII. IX. Troilus and Cressida; Coriolanus; Titus Andronicus. X. Romeo and Juliet; Timon of Athens; Julius Cæsar; Macbeth. XI. Hamlet; King Lear; Othello. XII. Antony and Cleopatra; Cymbeline; Pericles; Appendix.

— Plays prepared for use in schools, clubs, classes, and families. With introduction and notes. By H. N. Hudson. Vol. I, II. Boston, 1872. 2 v. 12° 5615.3

Contents. — Vol. I. Life; State and sources of the text; As you like it; Merchant of Venice; Twelfth night; Henry IV; Julius Cæsar; Hamlet. II. The tempest; Winter's tale; Henry V; Richard III; King Lear; Macbeth; Antony and Cleopatra.

— [Works.] New variorum edition. Edited by H. H. Furness. Vol. I, II. Philadelphia, 1871, 73. 2 v. 8° 5621.1

Contents. — Vol. I. Romeo and Juliet. II. Macbeth.

Shelf. No.

SHAKESPEARE, William, *continued.*

— Doubtful plays. Leipzig, 1869. 352+ pp. 16°. 1613.2

— Macbeth. *See* SCHILLER, (J. C.) F. von. Werke. 5734.1.7

— The merchant of Venice. The text from the folio of 1623; with notices of the known editions preuiously issued. London, 1862. 22+ pp. 4°. 5621.9

— The tragedie of Hamlet, prince of Denmarke. The text from the folio of 1623; with notices of the known editions preuiously issued. London, 1864. iv, 31 pp. 4° 5621.10

— Abbott, E. A. A Shakespearian grammar. London, 1872. 16° 5617.7

— Boydell, J. The gallery of illustrations for Shakespeare's dramatic works, reduced and re-engraved by the heliotype process. With selections from the text. Philadelphia, 1874. 4°... 5620.2

— Clarke, M. C. The complete concordance to Shakspere. Boston [London], 1873. 8° 5611.5

— Craik, G. L. The English of Shakespeare; illustrated in a philological commentary on his Julius Cæsar. Boston, 1871. 16° 5626.1

— Elze, C. (F.) Essays on. London, 1874. 8°.... 5623.5

— Gervinus, G. G. Shakespeare commentaries. London, 1875. 8° 5610.5

— Hudson, H. N. Shakespeare: his life, art, and characters. Boston, 1872. 2 v. 12° 1024.9

— Knight, C. Studies of. London, 1868. 8° 5621.7

— – William Shakspere: a biography. London [1865]. 8° 5420.4

— Lamb, C. and M. Tales from Shakspeare. London [1866]. 16° 935.24

— Lemon, M. Revised text of Falstaff. London, 1871. 16° 5425.7

— Lowell, J. R. Among my books. Boston, 1873. 16° 1934.8.1

— Williams, R. F. Shakspeare and his friends. [Fiction.] Philadelphia, N. D. 8° 531.23

— – The youth of. [Fiction.] Philadelphia, N. D. 8°. 531.23

Note. — The readiest reference to learn the very great extent of English literature pertaining to Shakespeare, with samples of the diversified criticisms upon him, is the elaborate article in Allibone, which, coming down to 1869, covers a wider range chronologically than any of the other bibliographies.

The progress of Shakespearian criticism in England is traced with care in Knight's "Studies" [5621.7] and in Whipple's Essays [1936.3].

So little is absolutely known of the personal history of Shakespeare, that the voluminous lives are largely made up of the customs and manners of his time, as allusions may be found to them in his works.

There are two excellent American lives, that by R. G. White enlarged upon the memoir prefixed to his edition of the works [5615.4.1]; and that by Hudson [1024.9], accompanied by an essay on his art, his contemporaries, the drama, and his characters, recast from his original memoir, and also his memoir prefixed to his abridged plays [5615.3.1]. See also Emerson's essay in his "Representative men" [1916.6; 1934.6.2]; and those by Whipple [1936.3] and Lowell [1934.8.1]; also see Whipple, in Atlantic monthly, vol. 20; and his "Age of Elizabeth" [1936.5].

Of the briefer accounts in English, see also De Quincey's "Biographical essays" [1825.6], and Conway's paper in Harper's monthly, vol. 29.

Attempts have also been made independently by W. H. Smith, an Englishman, and by Delia Bacon, an American, to prove that the real author of Shakespeare's plays was Lord Bacon, and while there have been, perhaps, needless refutations of the theory, Judge Holmes has summarized all the evidence, chiefly internal, with skill, apparently as a critical and logical venture. See also Hawthorne's "Our old home" [1839.2; 5439.1], or Atlantic monthly, vol. 11. The latest summary of the Baconian theory is in Fraser's magazine, 1874.

Concerning Shakespeare's connection with Stratford, see Howitt's "Remarkable places" [235.2]; Beecher's "Star papers" [1924.2]; Wilson's papers in Harper's monthly, vol. 23; also Howitt's "Homes and haunts" [1225.5] and Irving's "Sketch book" [311.13; 715.6; 1815.10].

For accounts of the progress of Shakespearian criticism in Germany, see Knight's "Studies" [5621.7]. Goethe's celebrated criticism on Hamlet will be found in his "Wilhelm Meister" [529.9; 819.4]. See also Schlegel's "Lectures on the dramatic art and literature" [6136.2], and the appendix to Furness's Macbeth [5621.1.2].

See also Taine and the other general histories of English literature, and Ward's "History of English dramatic literature" [5624.3.]

Further elucidation find in Bryant's "Orations" [1926.1]; Carlyle's "Hero and hero-worship" [1535.19]; Disraeli's "Amenities of literature" [1533.13]; and for the portraits of Shakespeare, in Scribner's monthly, vols. 8 and 10. Wilkie Collins's "Stolen mask" relates to a cast from Shakespeare's bust.

SHAKESPEARE'S dream: an historic pageant. Brougham, J. New York, N. D. 12° 1635.5

SHAMROCK and thistle; or, Young America in Ireland and Scotland. Adams, W. T. Boston, 1871. 16° 916.17

Shelf. No.

SHANKS, William Franklin Gore. Personal recollections of distinguished generals. New York, 1866. 352 pp. Portraits. 12° 1015.5

SHARPE, Samuel. History of the Hebrew nation, and its literature; 3d edition enlarged; with an appendix on the journeys and epistles of the apostle Paul. London, 1876. xxix, 449 pp. Sm. 8° 5928.3

SHATTUCK, George Cheyne. Three dissertations on Boylston prize questions for 1806 and 1807. Boston, 1808. 192+ pp. 8° 6023.9

SHATTUCK, Lemuel. Memorials of the descendants of William Shattuck. Boston, 1855. 414 pp. Portrait. 8° 612.7

SHATTUCK family. Memorials of the descendants of William Shattuck. Shattuck, L. Boston, 1855. 8°. 612.7

SHAW, Henry W. (*Josh Billings.*) Josh Billings, his sayings. With illustrations. New York, 1871. 232 pp. 12° 725.16

SHAW, Samuel. Journals. With a life of the author by Josiah Quincy. Boston, 1847. xiii, 360 pp. Portrait. 8° 1211.10

SHAW, William Smith, Memorials of. Felt, J. B. Boston, 1852. 12° 5027.7

SHAWL-STRAPS. Alcott, L. M. Aunt Jo's scrap-bag. 926.15.2

SHE stoops to conquer: a comedy. Goldsmith, O. Select works. Leipzig, 1842. Sq. 16° 312.23

— *Same.* (*In his* Works.) London, 1854. 8° ... 5612.1.1

SHEAF, A, of papers. Appleton, T. G. Boston, 1875. 12° 1537.23

SHEDD, Julia Ann. Famous painters and paintings. Illustrated with heliotypes of engravings. Boston, 1876. vi, 326 pp. 8° 6212.4

SHEEPFOLDS [*i. e.* church architecture], Notes on the construction of. Ruskin, J. New York, 1872. 12° 6236.9

SHEIL, Richard Lalor. Sketches of the Irish bar. With memoir and notes by R. S. Mackenzie. New York [*cop.* 1854]. 2 v. 12° 5417.7

SHELLEY, C. P. B. Workshop appliances. New York [London], 1873. ix, 312 pp. Sm. 8° 6427.1

SHELLEY, Jane, *lady*. Shelley memorials: from authentic sources. To which is added an Essay on Christianity, by P. B. Shelley. Boston, 1859. 308 pp. 12° 1225.10

SHELLEY, Percy Bysshe. Essay on Christianity. *See* SHELLEY, Jane, *lady* 1225.10

— Poetical works. [Added, Essays, Letters from abroad, etc.] Edited by Mrs. Shelley. New edition. London, 1869. 3631, 1641 pp. Portrait. L. 8° 5610.4

— Selections from [his] poems. Edited with a memoir by M. Blind. Leipzig, 1872. xl, 334 pp. Sq. 16° 1613.11

— Mac-Carthy, D. F. Shelley's early life. London, 1872. Sm. 8° 5426.8

— Masson, D. Wordsworth, Shelley, Keats, and other essays. London, 1874. Sm. 8° 5616.15

Note. — The only regular life of full extent is that in W. M. Rossetti's edition of his works, but a brief continuous memoir by M. Blind is given in the Tauchnitz edition of selected works [1613.11]. Mrs. Shelley's contributions are of course authoritative in the edition of her husband's letters, etc. [5610.4], and in the notices appended to the different sections of her chronological arrangement of the poems. Beside some articles by T. L. Peacock, in Fraser's magazine for 1858 and 1860, there have been some monographs, of value towards the full elucidation of Shelley's career, like Lady Shelley's "Shelley memorials" [1225.10]. The "Autobiography" of Leigh Hunt [1225.20] affords much material. There is a long list of authorities given in Allibone's article. Mac-Carthy's book, above named, has new particulars on his early life.

See also Howitt's "Homes and haunts" [1225.5]; De Quincey's "Essays on the poets" [1825.4]; Masson's Essay [5616.15]; and Moore's "Life of Byron" [5631.4].

SHELLS, Beautiful. Adams, H. G. London, 1871. 16°. 6636.1

SHENANDOAH, Narrative of the campaign in the valley of the, in 1861. Patterson, R. Philadelphia, 1865. 8° 5013.20

SHEPPARD, Elizabeth Sara. (*E. Berger.*) Charles Auchester 532.1

— Counterparts 531.19

— Rumor 530.10

Note. — These novels are delineations of musical art-life; Mendelssohn appearing as Seraphael in "Charles Auchester," and Beethoven in "Rumor."

Shelf. No.

SHEPPARD, Francis Henry. Love afloat. A story of the American navy 723.13

SHEPPARD, Nathan. Shut up in Paris. Leipzig, 1871. 302 pp. Sq. 16° 315.13

SHERBURNE, Andrew. Memoirs. Written by himself. 2d edition, enlarged and improved. Providence, 1831. 312 pp. 12° 5027.2

SHERIDAN, Richard Brinsley. Works. With a memoir of the author, a collection of ana, and 10 chalk drawings. Edited by F. Stainforth. London, 1875. viii, 656 pp. Sm. 8° 5626.9

Contents. — Life; Plays: The rivals; St. Patrick's day; The duenna; The school for scandal; The critic; A trip to Scarborough; Pizarro; Poems; Unfinished plays and poems; Speeches; Ana.

— Dramatic works. With life, by G. G. S[igmund]. London, 1848. viii, 563 pp. Portrait. 16° ... 1635.2

Contents. — Life; The rivals; St. Patrick's day: The duenna; The school for scandal; The critic; Trip to Scarborough; Pizarro; Verses to the memory of Garrick.

— *Same.* Leipzig, 1869. 440 pp. Sq. 16° 1614.11

Contents. — The rivals; St. Patrick's day; The duenna; The school for scandal; The critic; Trip to Scarborough; Pizarro; Verses to the memory of Garrick.

— Moore, T. Memoirs of. New York, 1853. 2 v. 12° 1223.8

— Rae, W. F. Wilkes, Sheridan, Fox: the opposition under George III. New York, 1874. 16°. 5415.8

Note. — Allibone has a full article with references. Thomas Moore's Memoirs was based upon ample knowledge, except perhaps of the man, but his panegyrics of Fox were distasteful to Sheridan's friends, who claim that Sheridan is wilfully belittled. A briefer compact life is that by Sigmund (based in good measure on a suppressed memoir by Prof. Smyth) [1635.2]. See also Stainforth's life [5626.9]. See also Brougham's "Statesmen" [5614.4.3]; Whipple's Essays [1936.2.2]; Jerdan's "Men I have known" [5423.11]; Thomson's "Wits and beaux" [1216.18]; and Maginn's "Fraserian papers" [1935.5]; Thomas's Biographical dictionary and its references; and the lives of his contemporaries Burke, Pitt, Fox, with Macaulay's Essay on Hastings.

SHERMAN, William Tecumseh. Memoirs. By himself. New York, 1875. 2 v. Folded map. 8°. 1212.3 and 5024.4

Contents. — Vol. I. 1846 — February, 1864. II. March, 1864 — May, 1865.

— Sherman's historical raid. Boynton, H. V. N. Cincinnati, 1875. 8° 5024.5

See also United States, *Civil war.*

SHERWIN, Thomas, Address on the life and character of. Waterston, R. C. Boston, 1870. L. 12° .. 1011.2

SHIFTING winds. Ballantyne, R. M. 926.33

SHIFTLESS folks. Smith, F. N. 714.17

SHILLABER, Benjamin Penhallow. Lines in pleasant places. [Poems.] Chelsea, 1874. 305 pp. Portrait. 16° 1615.7

— Partingtonian patchwork. Boston, 1873. 360 pp. Illustrated. 16° 736.28

SHILOH; or, without and within. Woodruff, J. L. M. 716.12

SHINN, Earl. The new Hyperion. From Paris to Marly by way of the Rhine. By Edward Strahan [*pseud.*]. With illustrations by Gustave Doré and others. Philadelphia, 1875. 271+ pp. 8° 5722.4

Note. — The illustrations in this book are borrowed from "Le chemin des écoliers. Par F. B. Saintine [*pseud.* of Joseph Xavier Boniface]. Paris, 1861." The text is in large measure drawn from the same source.

"SHIP ahoy!" A yarn in thirty-six cable lengths. 732.18

SHIP and shore, in Madeira, Lisbon, and the Mediterranean. Colton, W. New York, 1856. 12°. 425.16

SHIP, The, in the desert. [Poem.] Miller, C. H. Boston, 1875. 12° 1617.14

SHIP-BUILDERS, Lawrence's adventures among the. Trowbridge, J. T. 932.20

SHIPS. Ballantyne, R. M. Man on the ocean. A book about boats and ships 1715.30

— Bland, W. Forms of ships and boats. London, 1868. 12° 1715.10

SHIPWRECK by lightning. Forbes, R. B. Boston, 1853. 8° 1711.3

SHIRLEY. Brontë, C. Leipzig 321.22

— *Same.* London 728.8

SHORT studies on great subjects. Froude, J. A. New York, 1872, 73. 2 v. Sm. 8° 1914.5

Shelf. No.

SHOVE, George A. Life under glass. Containing suggestions toward the formation of artificial climates. Boston, 1874. 111 pp. 16° 6837.2

Note.—The author sets forth a plan for modifying the severity of the northern climate by means of buildings constructed of glass.

SHRUBS, Handbook of. Hemsley, W. B. Boston [London], 1873. 8° 6624.1
SHURTLEFF, Nathaniel Bradstreet. Topographical and historical description of Boston. Boston, 1871. ix, 720 pp. Folded plates. 8° 5010.1
SHUT up in Paris. Sheppard, N. Leipzig, 1871. Sq. 16° 315.13
SIAM. Bacon, G. B. Siam, as it was and is. New York, 1873. 12° 224.10
— Leonowens, A. H. The English governess at the Siamese court. Boston, 1873. Sm. 8° 222.1
— – The romance of the harem. Boston, 1873. Sm. 8° 5933.2
— Vincent, F., *jr.* The land of the white elephant. New York, 1874. 8° 5923.7
SIBERIA, Tent life in. Kennan, G. New York, 1873. 12° 426.22
SICHEL, Julius. Spectacles: their uses and abuses in long and short sightedness. From the French by H. W. Williams. Boston, 1850. 202+ pp. 8°. 6011.11
SICILIAN vespers. Verdi, G. (*In* Ditson, O., and co. Standard opera librettos) 6223.3.6
SICILIEN, Le: comédie-ballet. Molière, J. B. P. Œuvres. Paris, 1869. 12° 5537.2.2
SICILY. Kavanagh, J. A summer and winter in the two Sicilies. Leipzig, 1858. 2 v. in 1. Sq. 16°. 428.4
— Murray, J. Handbook for Sicily. London, 1864. 12° 5917.4
— Taylor, (J.) B. The lands of the Saracen; or, pictures of. New York, 1857. 12° 424.13

See also Italy, general travels.

SIDDONS, Sarah Kemble, Life of. Fitzgerald, P. The Kembles, etc. London [1871]. 2 v. Sm. 8°. 5425.22

Note.—See Doran's "Their majesties' servants" [1532.2], etc.

SIDNEY, Algernon. Discourses on government. Added, an account of the author's life, and a copious index. New York, 1805. 3 v. 8° 1923.1
SIDNEY, *Sir* Philip, Life and times of. Davis, *Mrs.* S. M. Boston, 1859. 16° 1225.11
— *Same.* New York, 1875. 16° 5337.4
SIDNEY, Samuel. The book of the horse: saddle and harness, British and foreign, with hints on horsemanship [etc.]. Illustrations. London [1875]. 604+ pp. 4° 6410.1
SIDNEY De Grey. Wise, D 932.38
SIDONIA the sorceress. Meinhold, (J.) W. New York, N. D. 8° 531.1
SIEBE, Henry. The conquest of the sea. A book about divers and diving. With illustrations. London [1874]. xi, 299 pp. Sm. 8° 6418.4
SIEGE, The, of Valencia. [Poem.] Hemans, F. (D.) Boston, 1826. 8° 1621.2
SIERRA NEVADA, Mountaineering in the. King, C. Boston, 1872. Sm. 8° 413.1
SIERRAS, Songs of the. Miller, C. H. Boston, 1873. 16° 1615.20
SIGHTS a-foot. Collins, (W.) W. 511.24
SIGHTS and insights. [Fiction.] Whitney, A. D. T. 2 v. 722.3
SIGNA. Rame, L. de la. Leipzig 331.1
— *Same.* Philadelphia 723.15
SIGNAL-MAN, The. Dickens, C. (J. H.) (*In* Johnson, (E.) R. Little classics) 529.4.8
SIGNALS, Manual of. Myer, A. J. New York, 1866. 12° 6927.1
SIGNBOARDS, The history of. Sadler, L. R., and Hotten, J. C. London [1875]. Sm. 8° 5615.8
SIGOURNEY, Henry Howell Williams. Genealogy of the Sigourney family. Boston, 1857. 31 pp. 8°. 5022.10
SIGOURNEY, Lydia Howard, *formerly Miss Huntley.* Letters to mothers. 2d edition. New York, 1839. 297 pp. 12° 5218.2
— Pleasant memories of pleasant lands. Boston, 1842. viii, 368 pp. 1 plate. 16° 1537.12

Shelf. No.

SIGOURNEY, Lydia Howard, *continued.*
— and OTHERS. The young lady's offering; or, gems of prose and poetry. Illustrated. Boston, 1858. 264 pp. 12° 5216.2
SIGOURNEY family, Genealogy of the. Sigourney, H. H. W. Boston, 1857. 8° 5022.10
SILAS Marner. Lewes, M. 310.22
SILENT partner, The. Phelps, E. S. 537.11
SILENT struggles. Stephens, A. S. (W.) 527.13
SILENT Tom. Edson, N. I. 928.4
SILENT witness, The. Yates, E. Boston 720.32
— *Same.* Leipzig 316.24
SILVER, Metallurgy of. Lamborn, R. H. London, 1870. 12° 1715.17
SILVER and gold. Raymond, R. W. New York, 1873. 8° 6631.5
SILVER cord, The. Brooks, (C.) S. 310.6
SILVER lake. Ballantyne, R. M. 935.14
SILVER pitchers. [Fiction.] Alcott, L. M. 718.9
SILVER threads. MacKeever, H. B. 714.31
SILVERVALE, Lumina, *pseud.* An orphan of the Old dominion 735.16
SILVIA. Kavanagh, J. 323.5
SIMMS, William Gilmore. Poems. New York, 1853. 2 v. Portrait. 12° 1625.6

Contents.—Vol. I. Norman Maurice; Atalantis; Tales and traditions of the South; The city of the silent. II. Southern passages and pictures; Historical and dramatic sketches; Scripture legends; Francesca da Rimini.

— Beauchampe; or, the Kentucky tragedy. Sequel to Charlemont 725.18
— Border beagles: a tale of [the first settlers of] Mississippi 716.27
— Charlemont; or, the pride of the village: a tale of [the first settlers of] Kentucky 725.19
— Confession; or, the blind heart 716.25
— Eutaw; a tale of the revolution 716.29
— The forayers 716.26
— Guy Rivers: a tale of [the first settlers of] Georgia. 716.28
— Katharine Walton 716.30
— The maroon, and other tales 736.24
— Mellichampe: a legend of the Santee 716.24
— The partisan 716.23
— Richard Hurdis: a tale of [the first settlers of] Alabama 716.32
— The scout 716.22
— Southward ho! 716.31
— Woodcraft; or, hawks about the dovecote. A story of the South at the close of the revolution. 733.10
— The Yemassee. [Indian conspiracy, 1715] 716.21

Note.—The following of the above tales form a connected series of revolutionary romances concerning the struggle in South Carolina:—1. The partisan (from fall of Charleston to Gates's defeat at Camden). 2. Mellichampe (from Camden to Green's arrival). 3. The scout, called originally The kinsman (siege of ninety-six and Green's career). 4. Katharine Walton (waning fortunes of the British). 5. The forayers. 6. Eutaw.

SIMONDE DE SISMONDI, Jean Charles Léonard. Historical view of the literature of the south of Europe. Translated from the original, with notes, and a life of the author, by Thomas Roscoe. 4th edition. London, 1872. 2 v. Portraits. [Bohn's Standard library.] Sm. 8° 5927.10
SIMONDS, William. (*Walter Aimwell.*) Aimwell stories. Clinton 932.29
— – Ella 932.39
— – Jerry. Added a memoir of the author, with a likeness 932.27
— – Jessie 932.25
— – Marcus 932.30
— – Oscar 932.28
— – Whistler 932.26
SIMPLETON, A. Reade, C. Leipzig 328.29
— *Same.* New York 531.30
SIMPLICITY and fascination. Beale, A. 535.4
SIMPSON, *Sir* James Young. Obstetric memoirs and contributions. Edited by W. O. Priestley and H. R. Storer. Philadelphia, 1855, 56. 2 v. Illustrated. 8° 6011.5
— *See* PAGE, H. A. Noble workers. London, 1875. Sm. 8° 5936.3

Shelf. No.

SINAI. Holland, F. W. Explorations in the peninsula of. *See* PALESTINE exploration fund 5933.1
— Lenoir, P. Le Sinaï. Paris, 1872. 18° 5935.10
— Lepsius, (C.) R. Discoveries in Egypt. Ethiopia, and the peninsula of Sinai, in 1842–45. London, 1853. 8° 5931.12
— Maughan, W. C. The Alps of Arabia. Travels in Egypt, Sinai, Arabia, and the Holy Land. London, 1873. 8° 5932.10
— Palmer, E. H. The desert of the Exodus. New York, 1872. Sm. 8° 222.2
— Robinson, E., and Smith, E. Biblical researches in Palestine, Mount Sinai and Arabia Petræa. Boston, 1841. 3 v. 8° 5810.5
— Stanley, A. P. Sinai and Palestine in connection with their history. New York, 1870. 8° 5933.1

See also Note under Palestine.

SINCLAIR, Alexander Doall. Myxoma. (*In* Massachusetts medical society. Publications) 6021.4
SINCLAIR, Catherine. Beatrice; or, the unknown relatives 714.29
SINGERS and songs of the liberal faith. [Unitarian.] Putnam, A. P. Boston, 1875. Sm. 8° 1513.4
SINGULAR creatures, and how they were found. Cupples, A. J. 913.19
SINK or swim. Alger, H., *jr.* 935.8
SINS of the tongue and jealousy in woman's life. Landriot, J. F. A. T. Boston, 1874. 12° 1915.7
SINTRAM and his companions. La Motte Fouque, F. (H. C.), *Freiherr* de 313.7
SIR Andrew Wylie of that ilk. Galt, J. 515.10
SIR Brook Fossbrooke. Lever, C. (J.) 332.23
SIR Harry Hotspur of Humblethwaite. Trollope, A. 334.18
SIR Jasper Carew. Lever, C. (J.) Leipzig 332.25
— *Same.* London 516.20
SIR Jasper's tenant. Braddon, M. E. 325.5
SIR Noel's heir. Fleming, M. A. 723.22
SIR Rohan's ghost. Spofford, H. E. 537.22
SIR Theodore Broughton. James, G. P. R. 327.15
SIREN, A. Trollope, T. A. 334.20
SISTER Louise. Melville, G. J. W. 321.26
SISTER Susy. Clarke, R. S. 927.5
SISTERHOODS and deaconesses at home and abroad. Potter, H. C. New York, 1873. 16° 1535.23
SISTERS of charity, catholic and protestant. Jameson, A. (M.) Boston, 1857. 12° 1538.16
SIVEWRIGHT, J., *joint author.* Telegraphy. *See* PREECE, William Henry 6826.6
SIX in all. Townsend, V. F. 713.5
SIX months at the White house. Carpenter, F. B. New York, 1870. 12° 1216.9
SIX months in a convent. Reed, R. T. Boston, 1835. 8° 1539.2
SIX months in Italy. Hillard, G. S. Boston, 1854. 2 v. Sm. 8° 426.8
SIX, The, of spades: a book about the garden and the gardener. Hole, S. R. Edinburgh, 1872. Sm. 4° 6226.5
SIX to sixteen. Ewing, J. H. 1117.10
SIX years later. Dumas, A. (D.) 511.14
SIXTUS V, *pope*, The life and times of. Huebner, J. A. von. London, 1872. 2 v. 8° 5522.11
SKATING, Handbook of. Forrest, G. London, 1863. 16° 1519.1
SKELETON, The, in the closet. Hale, E. E. (*In* Johnson, (E.) R. Little classics) 529.4.5
SKEPTICISM, Christian theology and modern. St. Maur, *or* Seymour, E. A., *duke of Somerset.* New York, 1872. 12° 5817.2
SKERTCHLY, J. A. Melinda the caboceer; or, sport in Ashanti. A tale of the Gold coast. With illustrations. New York [London], 1876. x, 358+pp. 16° 433.3
SKETCH book, The. Irving, W. Leipzig, 1843. Sq. 16° 311.13
— *Same.* London, 1855. 16° 715.6
— *Same.* Philadelphia, 1872. Sm. 8° 1815.10
SKETCHES. Dickens, C. (J. H.) 338.22
SKETCHES abroad with pen and pencil. Darley, F. O. C. New York, 1869. Sm. 4° 433.2

Shelf. No.

SKETCHES by a traveller. Holbrook, S. P. Boston, 1830. 12° 5914.4
SKETCHES of creation. [Popular natural history.] Winchell, A. New York, 1874. 12° 1523.32
SKETCHES of Germany and the Germans. Spencer, E. London, 1836. 2 v. 8° 422.6
SKETCHES of scenery and manners in the United States. By the author of the "Northern traveler." New York, 1829. 188+ pp. Illustrated. 12° 413.12
SKETCHING. Hatton, T. Hints for sketching in water-colour from nature. London, 1869. 16°. 6217.4
— – Hints for sketching trees from nature in water colours. London, 1869. 16° 6217.5
SKEY, Frederic C. Hysteria. New York, 1867. viii, 103 pp. 16° 6015.3
SKILLINGS, D. N., and FLINT, D. B. Illustrated catalogue of portable sectional buildings. New York [*cop.* 1862]. 53 pp. 4° 6222.1
SKIN, Practical compendium of the diseases of the. Green, J. Boston, 1839. 8° 6012.9
SKIRMISHING. Jenkin, *Mrs.* C. 313.6
SKYE, *Scotland*, A summer in. Smith, A. Boston, 1865. 12° 426.1
SLACK, J. H. Practical trout culture. [With a chapter on the bibliography of fish-culture.] New York, 1872. 143 pp. Illustrated. 12°.. 6616.2
SLADE, Daniel Denison. Bronchitis and its consequences. (*In* Massachusetts medical society. Publications) 6021.4
SLANG dictionary, The. Hotten, J. C. London, 1874. Sm. 8° 6126.6
SLAVER'S, A, adventures. Thomes, W. H. Boston, 1873. Sm. 8° 735.2
SLAVERY. Adam, W. The law and custom of slavery in British India, in a series of letters to T. F. Buxton. Boston, 1840. 12° 1915.4
— Channing, W. E. Slavery. Boston, 1835. 16°. 818.5
— Helper, H. R. The impending crisis of the South: how to meet it. New York, 1860. 12°. 617.1
— Wilson, H. History of the rise and fall of the slave power in America. Boston, 1874. 8° 5012.9
SLEEP. Hall, W. W. Sleep: or the hygiene of the night. New York, 1871. 12° 1523.18
— Macnish, R. Philosophy of. (*In* the Alexandrian) 1910.4.2
SLEEPER, John Sherburne. Salt water bubbles. By Hawser Martingale, *pseud.* With illustrations. Boston, 1854. xii, 408 pp. 12° 716.10
SLICK, Sam, *pseud.* *See* HALIBURTON, Thomas Chandler.
SMALL house, The, at Allington. Trollope, A. 334.9
SMALL-POX, Treatise on. Abú Beer Mohammed Ibn Zacaríyá Ar rází. London, 1848. 8° 6013.10
SMEATON, John, Life of. Smiles, S. Lives of the engineers. London, 1861. 8° 5421.4
SMEDLEY, Francis Edward. Frank Fairlegh 315.11
— Lewis Arundel 510.11
SMEE, Alfred. Manuel d'électricité médicale. Orné de figures. Paris, 1850. x, 304 pp. 24°. [Manuel Roret] 6019.1
SMELLIE, William. The philosophy of natural history. *See* WARE, John 1522.10
SMILES, Samuel. Brief biographies. Boston, 1873. vi, 517 pp. 16° 1024.13
— Character. New York, 1872. 387 [383] pp. 12° 1935.41
— The Huguenots: their settlements, churches, and industries in England and Ireland. With an appendix relating to the Huguenots in America. New York, 1868. 448 [446] pp. Sm. 8° 5514.1
— Industrial biography: iron-workers and toolmakers. Boston, 1871. 410 pp. 12° 1227.5
— Life of George Stephenson and of his son Robert; also a history of the invention of the railway locomotive. With portraits and illustrations. New York, 1868. 501 pp. 8° 5422.1
— Lives of Boulton and Watt. Comprising also a history of the invention and introduction of the steam-engine. London, 1865. xv, 521+ pp. Illustrated. Portraits. 8° 5421.5

Shelf. No.

SMILES, Samuel, *continued.*
— Lives of the engineers, with an account of their principal works; comprising also a history of inland communication in Britain. With portraits and illustrations. London, 1861. 2 v. 8°. 5421.4

Contents. — Vol. I. Early works of embanking and draining; Life of Sir Hugh Myddelton; Early roads and modes of travelling; Bridges, harbours, and ferries; Life of James Brindley. II. Life of John Smeaton; Life of John Rennie; Life of Thomas Telfourd.

— Self-help; with illustrations of character and conduct. Revised and enlarged edition. Boston, 1861. 430 pp. Portrait. 12° 1535.3
— *Same.* New edition. New York [1870]. 383+ pp. Portraits. 12° 1534.9
— Thrift. New York, 1876. 404 pp. 12° 5826.11
SMITH, Adam. An inquiry into the nature and causes of the wealth of nations. Edited by James E. Thorold Rogers. Oxford, 1869. 2 v. Portrait. 8°. 5822.9
SMITH, Alexander. Dreamthorp. (*In* Johnson, (E.) R. Little classics) 529.4.4
— A summer in Skye. Boston, 1865. iv, 423 pp. 12° 426.1
SMITH, Alfred Charles. The Nile and its banks: a journal of travels in Egypt and Nubia. With illustrations. London, 1868. 2 v. Sm. 8° 425.1
SMITH, Caroline Lombard. Home arts for old and young. Illustrated. Boston, 1873. 198 pp. 12°. 1517.3
— Home games for old and young. Illustrated. Boston, 1873. vi, 190 [188] pp. 12° 1517.2
SMITH, Edward. Foods. New York, 1873. xvi, 485 pp. Illustrated. [International scientific series.] 12°. 6436.6
— Health: a handbook for households and schools. New York, 1875. viii, 198+ pp. Illustrated. 12°. 6036.11
SMITH, Eli, *joint author.* Biblical researches in Palestine, Mount Sinai and Arabia Petræa. *See* ROBINSON, Edward 5810.5
SMITH, Fannie N. Shiftless folks. An undiluted love story. By Christabel Goldsmith [*pseud.*]. 714.17
SMITH, George, *of the British museum.* Assyrian discoveries; an account of explorations and discoveries on the site of Nineveh, during 1873 and 1874. With illustrations. London, 1875. xvi, 461 pp. Map. 8° 5932.12

Note. — This volume is occupied in part with an account of the author's explorations at Nineveh in 1873 and 1874, in search for tablets with cuneiform inscriptions, so as to complete the records in this character preserved in the British museum, giving an account of the deluge, etc., translations of which fill the greater part of the volume, which contains also a brief recapitulation of former discoveries, and a bibliography of the subject.

— The Chaldean account of Genesis. Containing the description of the creation, the fall of man, the deluge, the tower of Babel [etc.]; from the cuneiform inscriptions. With illustrations. New York [London], 1876. xvi, 319 pp. 8° .. 6320.4
SMITH, George, *joint author.* Make your wills! a farce. *See* MAYHEW, Edward 1635.3
SMITH, Goldwin. Three English statesmen [Pym, Cromwell, Pitt]: lectures on the political history of England. New York, 1867. 298 [296] pp. 12° 5425.1
SMITH, Hannah. (*Hesba Stretton.*) Alone in London. 1128.1
— Bede's charity 737.34
— The crew of the Dolphin 529.11
— The doctor's dilemma 530.6
— Hester Morley's promise 737.18
— Jessica's first prayer 1128.3
— Little Meg's children 1128.2
— Max Kromer: a story of the siege of Strasburg .. 730.12
— Nelly's dark days 1118.14
SMITH, Horace. The picnic party. (*In* Johnson, (E.) R. Little classics) 529.4.9
— *joint author.* Rejected addresses, and other poems. *See* SMITH, James 1624.2
SMITH, Hubert. Tent life with English gipsies in Norway. With illustrations and map. London, 1873. xxii, 540+ pp. Portrait. 8° 5722.1
SMITH, J. Frederick. Woman's love; or, like and unlike 711.38
SMITH, James. The temperance reformation and its claims upon the Christian church. A prize essay. London, 1875. x, 403 pp. 8° 1912.8

Shelf. No.

SMITH, James and Horace. Rejected addresses, and other poems. With a biographical sketch. Edited by E. Sargent. New York, 1871. xxiii, 414 pp. 12° 1624.2
SMITH, Jepson Huband. Notes and marginalia, illustrative of the public life and works of Alfred Tennyson. London [1874]. xix, 202 pp. Sm. 8°. 5337.2
SMITH, *Capt.* John. Hawks, F. L. Adventures of. New York, 1854. 12° 1028.3
— Hillard, G. S. Life of. (*In* Sparks, J. Library of American biography) 5028.1.2
SMITH, Joseph Emerson. Oakridge: an old-time story. 723.11
SMITH, Julie P. Chris and Otho 727.26
— Courting and farming; or, which is the gentleman? 724.32
— The married belle 727.27
— Ten old maids: and five of them were wise and five of them were foolish. A novel 727.35
— Widow Goldsmith's daughter 727.24
— The widower 727.25
SMITH, Leon, HAMILTON, H., and LEGROS, E. The international English and French dictionary. London, 1873. 2 v. 8° ..........*R.R., D.3.8
SMITH, Mary P. Wells. Jolly good times; or childlife on a farm. By P. Thorne [*pseud.*] 1117.8
SMITH, Philip. The student's ancient history. The ancient history of the East. From the earliest times to the conquest by Alexander the great. Illustrated. London, 1871. xiv, 594 pp. 12°. 5916.14
SMITH, Philip Vernon. History of the English institutions. Philadelphia, 1874. xiv, 303+ pp. 16° 5418.5
SMITH, Reginald Bosworth. Mohammed and Mohammedanism. Appendix containing Emanuel Deutsch's article on "Islam." New York, 1875. 388 pp. 12° 5816.23
SMITH, S. Compton. Chile con carne; or, the camp and the field. New York, 1857. xvi, 404 pp. Illustrated. 12° 515.2
SMITH, Southwood. Treatise on fever. Boston, 1831. xvi, 262 pp. 8° 6011.9
SMITH, Stephen, *editor.* Romance and humor of the rail. New York, 1873. 343 pp. Illustrated. 12°. 534.24
SMITH, Sydney. Works. New York, 1871. 480 pp. Portrait. 8° 1931.1
— Memoir of. With a selection from his letters. Holland, S. S., *lady.* New York [*cop.* 1855]. 2 v. 12° .... 1025.
SMITH, T. Roger. Acoustics in relation to architecture and building: the laws of sound as applied to the arrangement of buildings. New edition, with illustrations. London, N. D. vi, 165 pp. 12° 1715.1
SMITH, Thomas Southwood. Illustrations of the divine government. Boston, 1831. 347 pp. 12°. 5814.1
SMITH, Uriah. The state of the dead and the destiny of the wicked. Battle Creek, 1873. 368 pp. 16°. 6327.
SMITH, Walter. Art education, scholastic and industrial. With illustrations. Boston, 1872. x, 398 pp. 8° .... 6211.
— Teachers' manual of free-hand drawing and designing, and guide to self-instruction. Boston, 1873. vi, 156 pp. Illustrated. L. 8° .... 6210.
— *Same.* Boston, 1875. vi, 156 pp. L. 8° 6210.1
SMITH, William. Dictionary of Greek and Roman antiquities. Illustrated. London, 1872. xii, 1293 pp. 8° ..........*R.R., E.3.
— Dictionary of Greek and Roman biography and mythology. Illustrated. London, 1870. 3 v. 8° ..........*R.R., E.3.
— Dictionary of Greek and Roman geography. Illustrated. London, 1872. 2 v. 8° ....*R.R., E.3.
— Dictionary of the Bible. Revised and edited by H. B. Hackett and E. Abbot. New York, 1872. Illustrated. 4 v. 8° ..........*R.R. B.2.
— History of Greece, from the earliest times to the Roman conquest. With supplementary chapters on the history of literature and art. Revised, with an appendix, by George W. Greene. Illustrated. New York, 1875. 704 pp. [The student's series.] 12° 5916.1

Shelf. No.

SMITH, William, *continued.*
— Memoir of J. G. Fichte. *See* FICHTE, J. G. Popular works. London, 1873. 8° 5723.4
— The student's Scripture history. The Old Testament history. From the creation to the return of the Jews from captivity. With maps and woodcuts. New edition. London, 1874. xii, 619 pp. Sm. 8° 6325.22
— — The New Testament history. With an introduction, connecting the history of the Old and New Testaments. With maps and woodcuts. New edition. London, 1873. xii, 675 pp. Sm. 8° 6325.23
SMITHSONIAN institution, *Washington, D. C.* Annual report of the board of regents, 1873, 74. Washington, 1874, 75. 2 v. 8° 6914.3
— Exploration of the Colorado river of the West and its tributaries. Explored in 1869–72, under the direction of the secretary of the Smithsonian institution [by J. W. Powell]. Washington, 1875. xi, 291 pp. Illustrations. Maps. 4° .. 230.1
SMOKE. Turgenef, I. S. New York, 1872. 12° ... 537.14
SMOKE, Prevention of. Williams, C. W. London, 1858. 12° 1715.19
SMOLLETT, Tobias (George). The adventures of Peregrine Pickle 315.17
— The adventures of Roderick Random. London .. 513.13
— *Same.* With the life of the author. Leipzig ... 315.16
— The expedition of Humphry Clinker 315.15
— *See* LAWRENCE, E. Lives of the British historians. New York, 1855. 12° 1224.7.1
SMUGGLER, The. James, G. P. R. 327.4
SMYTH, William. Lectures on modern history, from the irruption of the north nations to the close of the American revolution. 3d American edition. With preface, and a list of books on American history, by J. Sparks. Boston, 1851. xxii, 738 pp. 8° 5012.10
— *Same.* New edition. London, 1854. 2 v. [Bohn's Standard library.] Sm. 8° 5925.7
— Lectures on the history of the French revolution. New edition. London, 1860. 2 v. [Bohn's Standard library.] Sm. 8° 5517.10
SNARLEYOW; or, the dog fiend. Marryat, F. 732.5
SNOW, Samuel Sheffield. The voice of Elias; or, prophecy restored. Being a complete and truthful exposition of the visions of the prophet Daniel and the book of the Revelation. New York, 1863. 395 pp. Portrait. 12° 1524.9
SNOW image, The. Hawthorne, N. Boston, 1872. 16° 1813.1
SNOW man, The. Dudevant, A. L. A. D. 526.6
SNOW-STORM, The. Wilson, J. (*In* Johnson, (E.) R. Little classics) 529.4.7
SNOWDEN, Richard. History of North and South America, from its discovery to the death of Washington. Philadelphia, 1818. 2 v. in 1. Maps. 12° 818.8
SOBIESKI, John. *See* JOHN III, *king of Poland.*
SOCIABLE, The; or, 1001 home amusements. Frickell, G. New York [*cop.* 1858]. 12° 1514.6
SOCIAL economy. About, E. (F. V.) Handbook of. New York, 1873. 12° 1528.9
— Rogers, J. E. T. Social economy. New York, 1872. 12° 1525.23
SOCIAL gleanings. Boyd, M. London, 1875. Sm. 8°. 5613.7
SOCIAL morality. Maurice, (J.) F. D. London, 1869. 8° 5833.5
SOCIAL pressure. Helps, *Sir* A. Boston, 1875. 16° 5826.5
SOCIAL science. About, E. (F. V.) Le progrès. Paris, 1865. 18° 5536.3
— Considerations on some recent social theories. Boston, 1853. 16° 5827.3
— Knight, C. Knowledge is power: a view of the productive forces of modern society and the results of labor, capital and skill. Boston, 1867. 12° 1524.24
— Nordhoff, C. The communistic societies of the United States. New York, 1875. 8° 5821.2

See also Ethics, Labor, Temperance.

Shelf. No.

SOCIAL stage, The: original dramas, etc. Baker, G. M. Boston, 1875 [*cop.* 1870]. 16° 1635.7
SOCIAL statics. Spencer, H. New York, 1872. 12°. 5825.1
SOCIETY and solitude. [Essays.] Emerson, R. W. Boston, 1875. 16° 1537.21
SOCIETY for the diffusion of useful knowledge, *London.* The penny cyclopædia. Vol. I–V. London, 1833–36. 5 v. L. 8° .... *R.R., F.2.2

Contents. — Vol. I. A—Andes. II. Andocides—Athanagilde. III. Athanaric—Bassano. IV. Bassantin—Bloemaart. V. Buffalo.

SOCIETY of Jesus [Jesuits], History of the. Orliac, *Mme.* J. M. S. Cincinnati, 1865. 2 v. 12° ... 5817.6
SOCIOLOGY, The study of. Spencer, H. New York, 1874. 12° 5826.1
SOCRATES. Grote, G. Plato and other companions of. London, 1867. 3 v. 8° 6113.2
— Xenophon. Memorabilia of. London, 1872. Sm. 8° 6115.12
SOCRATES SCHOLASTICUS. Ecclesiastical history. Translated from the Greek: with some account of the author, and notes selected from Valesius. London, 1853. xx, 449 pp. 16° 5815.3
SOLA. Thackeray, A. I. Works 512.1.4
SOLDIER boy, The. Adams, W. T. 924.5
SOLDIER'S, The, orphans. Stephens, A. S. (W.) 726.1
SOLDIERING and scribbling. A series of sketches. Forbes, A. Leipzig, 1872. Sq. 16° 319.7
SOLEINNE, — de. Bibliothèque dramatique. Catalogue rédigé par P. L. Jacob [*pseud. of Paul Lacroix*]. T. I. Paris, 1843. 8° 5532.1
SOLITARY vice, A solemn appeal relative to. White, J. Battle Creek, 1870. 16° 1538.19
SOLITUDES, The, of nature and of man. Alger, W. R. Boston, 1871. 16° 1535.22
SOLL und Haben. Freytag, G. Leipzig, 1874. 2 v. Sq. 16° 5738.3
SOLLY, N. Neal. Memoir of David Cox. With selections from his correspondence, and some account of his works. Illustrated. London, 1873. xii, 339 pp. 2 portraits. L. 8° 5420.3
SOME women's hearts. Moulton, L. C. 714.2
SOMEBODY'S luggage. Dickens, C. (J. H.), and others. 338.2
SOMERSET, G. A. Day after the fair: a burletta. New York, N. D. 33 pp. Illustrated. 12° ... 1635.3
SOMERSET, *Duke of. See* ST. MAUR, *or* SEYMOUR, Edward Adolphus.
SOMERVILLE, Mary. On molecular and microscopic science. With illustrations. London, 1869. 2 v. Sm. 8° 6816.2
— Personal recollections. With selections from her correspondence. By her daughter, Martha Somerville. London, 1873. vi, 377 pp. Portrait. Sm. 8° 5424.9
— *Same.* Boston, 1874. vi, 377 pp. Portrait. Sm. 8° .... 1223.13 and 5424.15
— Physical geography. 6th edition, revised by H. W. Bates. With portrait. London, 1870. xvi, 564 pp. Sm. 8° 6856.2
SOMERVILLE, William C. Letters from Paris on the causes and consequences of the French revolution. Baltimore, 1822. 390+ pp. 8° 5512.1
SOMNAMBULISM. Account of Jane C. Rider, the Springfield somnambulist. Belden, L. W. Springfield, 1834. 12° 1928.4
SON, A, of the soil. Oliphant, M. (O. W.) 536.20
SONG, The, of Hiawatha. Longfellow, H. W. Poetical works. Leipzig, 1856. Sq. 16° 1614.1
SONGS in the night: or, hymns for the sick and suffering. Boston, 1845. xvi, 271 pp. 16° 5816.17
SONGS. Chambers, R. The songs of Scotland prior to Burns. With the tunes. Edinburgh [1873]. Sq. 16° 5637.1
— Deutsches Leben in Liedern. Bremen [1873]. L. 4° 5730.5
— Hewitt, M. E. The songs of our land, and other poems. Boston, 1846. 12° 1625.13
— Holmes, O. W. Songs in many keys. Boston, 1862. 12° 1612.5
— Hullah, J. The song book. London, 1866. 16° 1615.1

Shelf. No.

SONGS, *continued.*

— Juvenile lyre: or hymns and songs set to music for the use of schools. Boston, 1836. 12°..... 1623.2

— Miller, C. H. Songs of the Sierras. Boston, 1873. 16°.................................1615.20

— Murray, J. C. The ballads and songs of Scotland. London, 1874. Sm. 8°...................... 5626.5

— Sargent, E. Songs of the sea. Boston, 1847. 16°. 1612.9

SONNAMBULA, La. Bellini, V. (*In* Ditson, O., and co. Standard opera librettos)...............6233.3.4

SONORA. Browne, J. R. A tour through Sonora. New York, 1871. 12°.............................. 415.13

— Marryat, F. Narrative of the travels and adventures of Monsieur Violet, in. [Fiction]....... 337.7

SONREL, L. The bottom of the sea. Translated and edited by E. Rich. New York, 1872. xix, 402 pp. Illustrated. 16°..................... 1714.9

SOONER or later. Brooks, (C.) S................. 310.5

SOPHOCLES. Tragedies: in English prose. The Oxford translation. New edition. London, 1873. xvi, 339 pp. Portrait. Sm. 8°.............6115.20

— Sophocles [outlined and explained]. Collins, C. W. Edinburgh, 1871. 16°.................6116.11

SOPHOCLES, Evangelinus Apostolides. A glossary of later and Byzantine Greek. [Memoirs of the American academy, vol. VII, new series. Cambridge, 1860. Title-page missing.] 624+ pp. 4°. 6110.2

SOPHOMORES, The, of Radcliffe. Kellogg, E....... 922.9

SORET, Frédéric, Conversations of Goethe with. *See* GOETHE, Johann Wolfgang von...............5735.11

SORGHO. Olcott, H. S. New York, 1857. 12°.... 6425.5

SOTO, Ferdinand de, the discoverer of the Mississippi. Abbott, J. S. C. New York, 1873. 12°....... 923.34

SOUL. Feuchtersleben, E., *Freiherr* von. The dietetics of the. New York, 1854. 12°.........1527.18

— Newman, F. W. The soul, her sorrows and her aspirations. London, 1849. 12°.............5814.17

— *Same.* London, 1852. 12°.................. 1534.5

SOULÉ, Frank, GIHON, John H., and NISBET, James. Annals of San Francisco; containing a summary of the history of California. Illustrated. New York, 1855. 824 pp. Maps. Portraits. 8°.. 810.3

SOULE, Richard. Dictionary of English synonymes. Boston, 1871. vi, 456+ pp. 16°.......*R.R., F.3.2

SOULT, Nicolas Jean de Dieu, *marshal of France.* Extracts from [his] journal, addressed to a friend. Newburyport, 1817. 141 pp. 12°.... 1917.7

SOUND. Peirce, B. Elementary treatise on. Boston, 1836. 8°................................ 6434.1

— Tyndall, J. Sound. New York, 1874. 8° 1914.11

See also Acoustics.

SOUNDINGS from the Atlantic. [Essays.] Holmes, O. W. Boston, 1866. 12°................. 1914.1

SOUTH, The, *or,* Southern States of the United States. Helper, H. R. The impending crisis of the South: how to meet it. New York, 1860. 12°. 617.1

— Jones, C. H. Appletons' Hand-book of American travel. Southern tour. New York, 1873. 12°. 413.5

— King, E. The great South. [Illustrated descriptions since the war.] Hartford, 1875. 8°. 5031.6

— Loring, F. W., and Atkinson, C. F. Cotton culture and the South considered with reference to emigration. Boston, 1869. Sm. 8°.......... 6435.3

— Pollard, E. A. Black diamonds gathered in the darkey homes of the South. New York, 1859. 12°. 1915.8

SOUTH breaker, The. Spofford, H. E. (*In* Johnson, (E.) R. Little classics)...................529.4.7

SOUTH CAROLINA. The prostrate state: South Carolina under negro government. Pike, J. S. New York, 1874. 12°......................... 5017.4

Note. — See under Simms for novels founded on the history of South Carolina in the American revolution.

SOUTH KENSINGTON museum, *London,* [Art handbooks. Edited by William Maskell, No. 1.] Textile fabrics. By Daniel Rock. With woodcuts. [London] 1876. 116+ pp. 8°....... 6214.6

— - No. 3. Ancient and modern furniture and woodwork. By John Hungerford Pollen. With numerous woodcuts. [London, 1875.] vii, 143 pp. 8°................................ 6214.5

SOUTH-SEA bubble, The. A tale of the year 1720. Ainsworth, W. H........................... 322.20

SOUTH sea bubbles. [Travels.] Herbert, G. R. C., and Kingsley, G. H. Leipzig, 1874. Sq. 16°. 310.27

SOUTH sea whaler, The. Kingston, W. H. G....... 921.16

SOUTH seas. Melville, H. Omoo: a narrative of adventures in the. New York, 1868. 12°.... 425.23

— Stewart, C. S. Visit to the. New York, 1833. 2 v. 12°................................ 225.4

SOUTHALL, James C. The recent origin of man, as illustrated by geology and the modern science of pre-historic archæology. Illustrated. Philadelphia, 1875. 606 pp. 8°................. 6612.8

SOUTHESK, *Earl of.* *See* CARNEGIE, James.

SOUTHEY, Robert. Common-place book. Edited by his son-in-law, J. W. Warter. London, 1850. 4 v. 8°................................ 5624.1

— The doctor, etc. New York, 1860. 2 v. in 1. 12°.1534.10

— *Same.* New York, 1872. 2 v. in 1. 12°...... 5617.9

— Life and correspondence. Edited by his son, C. C. Southey. New York, 1851. 579 pp. 8°... 1221.1

— Life of Nelson. New York, 1857. 309 [301] pp. Portrait. 16°.............................. 1228.3

— Poems. Boston, 1799. 125 pp. 12°.......... 1618.7

— Select lives of Cromwell and Bunyan. New edition. London, 1861. viii, 180 pp. Sm. 8° ... 5428.6

— Selections from [his] letters. Edited by J. W. Warter. London, 1856. 4 v. Sm. 8°........5425.23

Note. — The full, authoritative life is that edited by his son. "Selections from his letters" [5425.23] was published by his family. See the full references in Allibone. The lives of Scott, Moore, Byron, Wordsworth, Coleridge, Sara Coleridge, Lamb, De Quincey's "Autobiographic sketches," etc., illustrate many parts of Southey's life.

There are papers on Southey in the Cornhill magazine, 1873, and in Temple bar, 1874.

See also Macaulay's Essays [1918.4]; Howitt's "Homes and haunts" [1225.5]; Jerdan's "Men I have known" [5423.11]; Coleridge's "Biographia literaria," chap. 3 [1611.5]; S. C. Hall's "Book of memories" [1231.1]; and H. C. Robinson's "Diary" [5425.3].

SOUTHWARD ho! Simms, W. G..................... 716.31

SOUTHWORTH, Emma Dorothy Eliza Nevitte. Allworth abbey.................................. 727.5

— A beautiful fiend.............................. 726.19

— The bridal eve................................ 727.10

— The bride of Llewellyn........................ 727.2

— The bride's fate.............................. 727.16

— The changed brides........................... 727.4

— Cruel as the grave............................ 726.10

— The curse of Clifton.......................... 527.8

— The deserted wife............................. 527.10

— The discarded daughter....................... 727.3

— Fair play..................................... 737.6

— Fallen pride.................................. 727.1

Note. — This work is the same as that published under the title "The curse of Clifton."

— The family doom.............................. 734.25

— The fatal marriage............................ 727.21

— The fortune seeker........................... 727.6

— The gipsy's prophecy......................... 527.11

— The haunted homestead; and other novellettes. With an autobiography....................... 522.13

— How he won her.............................. 527.12

— India: the pearl of Pearl river................ 727.8

— Ishmael; or, in the depths.................... 522.23

— The lady of the isle.......................... 727.20

— The lost heir of Linlithgow................... 727.7

— The lost heiress.............................. 522.8

— Love's labor won............................. 727.13

— The maiden widow............................. 734.26

— The missing bride............................. 727.15

— The mother-in-law............................ 727.9

— A noble lord.................................. 734.21

— The prince of darkness........................ 527.14

— Retribution.................................. 727.12

— Self-raised; or, from the depths. A sequel to Ishmael...................................... 522.26

— The three beauties........................... 527.9

— Tried for her life............................ 522.10

— The two sisters.............................. 727.18

— Victor's triumph............................. 734.20

— Vivia.. 727.19

— The widow's son.............................. 727.11

Shelf. No.

SOUTHWORTH, Emma Dorothy Eliza Nevitte, *cont'd.*
— The wife's victory; and other novelettes........ 727.17
— *editor.* The mystery of Dark hollow........... 522.18
— and BADEN, Frances Henshaw. The Christmas guest.................................... 522.9
— – The spectre lover by E. D. E. N. Southworth, and other stories by F. H. Baden 522.11

Note. — The story by Mrs. Southworth is contained in pp. 23-47.

SOUVENIR of 1775. [Lexington fight.] Porter, E. G., and Stephenson, H. M. [Boston, 1875.] 4°. 810.5
SOUVENIRS et indiscrétions. Sainte-Beuve, C. A. Paris, 1872. 12°..........................5538.16
SOUVESTRE, Émile. Théâtre de la jeunesse. Paris, 1860. 256+ pp. 18°......................5536.15

Contents. — La loterie de Francfort; Le testament de Madame Patural; Comme on fait son lit on se couche; La vielle cousine; L'incognito; Le cousin Pierre.

— An attic philosopher in Paris. New York, 1873. 144 pp. 12°.............................. 532.9
SOWED by the wind. Kellogg, E.................. 715.17
SOWERBY, George Brettingham. A conchological manual. With illustrations. London, 1852. vi, 337+ pp. 2 folded sheets. 8°........... 6632.4
SOWING and reaping. Howitt, M.................. 937.5
SPAIN. *History, travel, etc.*
— Abbott, J. S. C. Romance of Spanish history. New York, 1869. 12° 824.3
— Andersen, H. C. In Spain. New York, 1870. Sm. 8° 426.16
— Borrow, G. The Bible in. New York, 1869. 8°.5931.13
— – The Zincali; or, an account of the gypsies of. New York, 1869. 8°.......................5931.13
— Davillier, (J.) C., *baron.* L'Espagne. Paris, 1874. L. 4° 5910.5
— Field, K. Ten days in. Boston, 1875. Sq. 16°. 428.7
— Ford, R. Handbook for Spain. London, 1869. 2 v. 16° 5917.1
— Froissart, *Sir* J. Chronicles of. London, 1868. 2 v. L. 8°................................ 5920.2
— Hare, A. J. C. Wanderings in. London, 1873. 16°. 5934.5

Shelf. No.

SPAIN. *History, travel, etc., continued.*
— Hay, J. Castilian days. Boston, 1871. 12°... 227.2
— Helps, *Sir* A. The Spanish conquest in America. New York, 1856. 4 v. 12°................. 816.6
— Irving, W. Legends of the conquest of. London, 1850. Sm. 8°.............................. 826.4
— – Spanish papers and other miscellanies. New York, 1866. 2 v. Sm. 8°.................. 1934.1
— – *Same.* Philadelphia, 1871. Sm. 8°......... 1815.8
— Napier, *Sir* W. F. P. English battles and sieges in the peninsula. London, 1873. Sm. 8° 5916.9
— Poitou, E. (L.) Spain and its people. A record of recent travel. London, 1873. Sm. 8° 5914.8
— Rose, H. J. Untrodden Spain, and her Black country; being sketches of the life and character of the Spaniards of the interior. London, 1875. 2 v. 8° 5921.6
— Stone, J. B. A tour with Cook through Spain. London, 1873. Sm. 8° 5916.8
— Taylor, (J.) B. The lands of the Saracen; or, pictures of. New York, 1857. 12° 424.13
— Thiéblin, N. L. Spain and the Spaniards. Boston, 1875. 16° 427.5
— Tollemache, *Mrs.* W. A. Spanish towns and Spanish pictures. A guide to the galleries of. London [1872]. Sm. 8°..................... 5916.3
— Wylie, J. A. Daybreak in Spain; or, sketches of Spain and its new reformation. London [1870]. Sm. 8° 227.1

See also Peninsular war.

Language and literature.

— Hubbard, (N.) G. Histoire de la littérature contemporaine en Espagne. Paris, 1876. 12°. 5536.22
— Ollendorff, H. G. New method of learning the Spanish language. New York, 1850. 12° 2035.2
— Ticknor, G. History of Spanish literature. Boston, 1872. 3 v. 8° 5922.2
— Villemain, A. F. Tableau de la littérature au moyen âge en Espagne. Paris, 1871. 2 v. 12° 5437.11

NOTE ON SPAIN.

The history of Spain is singularly well illustrated by books in English, though there is no elaborate general history in English; but Abbott's "Romance of Spanish history" is a popular account of principal events.

Ford calls Buckle's account in his "History of civilization" [5417.1] "an excellent if rather violent commentary on Spanish history." See Smyth's estimate of her early history in his 8th lecture on "Modern history" [5012.10; 5925.7].

Arabs and Moors. See Gibbon's 51st chapter of his "Decline and fall of the Roman empire" [824.9]. Much of this early legendary history of the 8th and 9th century is told by Irving in his "Spanish papers" [1815.8; 1934.1], particularly for the union of Castile and Leon in the 13th century. For the conquests of the French, see Guizot's "History of France" [5510.2].

Granada, A. D. 1238-1492. The general reader can depend upon Irving's "Conquest of Granada" [826.4; 1815.6], and consult Irving's own explanation of the real nature of the work and its claim to historic truth in his "Spanish papers" [1815.8; 1934.1], and the review in Prescott's Essays [5237.3], which pronounces it "substantially an authentic record." See also Prescott's "Ferdinand and Isabella" [5922.5] and Hallam's "Middle ages" [5916.1].

Christian Spain. Prescott introduces his "Ferdinand and Isabella" [5922.5] with a summary of the previous history of the several monarchies, then united under one crown, but for the episodes of the Spanish discovery and conquest in America, see Columbus, Cortés, Mexico, Peru, etc. Robertson's "History of Charles the fifth," 1515-56 [1226.9], follows next; but see note under Charles V.

The reign of Philip II, 1556-98, had already been illustrated by Watson, in a work of little research, and confined chiefly to the War in the Netherlands (in which he has been superseded by Motley; see Netherlands, *note*), when Prescott, to continue Robertson's "History of Charles the fifth" [1226.9], begun his Philip II, which he left unfinished [1222.1]. Motley's histories may be read by parallel courses with Prescott's Philip II. Froude's "History of England" [826.9], covering the reigns of Henry VIII and Elizabeth, concerns constantly the relations of that kingdom with Spain, and in his last volume he describes the overthrow of the Spanish armada, sent to invade England, as does Motley in his "United Netherlands" [5912.1].

Later come the wars of the succession, 1700-14, upon which Earl Stanhope has a special monograph, confining his narrative as much as possible to what occurred in Spain, which has been reviewed by Macaulay, in his Essays [1918.4]. See also Smyth's 23d lecture on "Modern history" [5012.10; 5925.7], and English history under Queen Anne, and the paper on the Bourbons in Spain in Harper's monthly, vol. 10.

On the peninsular war, see the well-known work of Napier [5920.1, — also see the English battles and sieges, above-named] and the lives of Wellington, beside Hamley's "Operations of war" [5910.6]. Its political aspects can be studied in such books as Brougham's autobiography [5425.2]; Alison's "History of Europe" [5913.5], and Knight's "History of England" [5413.1]. See also papers in Alison's Essays [1531.7] on the revolution of 1820 and the Carlist struggle. Thiéblin's "Spain and the Spaniards" is made up of the letters of a newspaper correspondent, during the late revolutions. For this period, see also Lippincott's magazine, Aug., 1875; and a paper on Don Carlos in Fraser's magazine, 1873.

Literature and art.

Literature. Buckle, in his "History of civilization" [5417.1.1, chap. 1], outlines the history of the Spanish intellect from the fifth century down. The old history of Spanish literature by Sismondi in his "Literature of the south of Europe" [5927.10] has been surpassed by Ticknor, who is reviewed in Prescott's essays [5237.3], with references in Allibone. See also the Life of George Ticknor [1012.5; 5023.10]. There is a brief sketch with references in Longfellow's "Poets of Europe" [5922.1], and a chapter in his "Outre-mer" [1838.4.1] on the devotional poetry. See also Lockhart, on the ballad literature [1616.5]; Schlegel, on the drama, in his "Dramatic literature" [6136.2]. See also Villemain's "Moyen âge;" the chapters on literature in Prescott's "Ferdinand and Isabella" [5922.5]; those on Spain in Hallam's "Literature of Europe" [1531.2], and the lives of Cervantes, Lope de Vega, etc.

Art. There is a recent guide to the galleries of Spain by Tollemache [5916.3], but see Painting, *note*, and also chap. 13 of Poitou's "Spain and its people." Fergusson's "History of architecture" [6999.6] covers that art.

Travels, etc.

Ford's Handbook in Murray's series is of excellent reputation, and the fourth edition, 1869 [5917.1], is considerably recast in the first part to make the routes conform to the railway routes, lately introduced into Spain; and in the second part is put a variety of most valuable matter illustrative of Spanish history, manners, etc., with references to authorities. Buckle's unfavorable estimate of Ford pertained to the earlier editions. Borrow's books have had great success. He resided in Spain, trying to introduce the protestant Scriptures. Irving's "Alhambra" [715.7; 1815.15] is a graceful semi-fiction of manners. Davillier has Doré's illustrations. See Bayard Taylor's article in the Atlantic monthly, March, 1868, and a paper in Harper's monthly, vol. 36. Hay's book is a series of essays on present experiences (also Atlantic monthly, vol. 27 and 28), and the titles of others above explain themselves, to which may be added Prime's "Alhambra and Kremlin" [5914.6]; Revere's "Keel and saddle" [5914.3], etc.

Of modern manners there are delineations in Rose's "Untrodden Spain," and in a paper in Macmillan's magazine, 1873.

In Fiction.

For the period of the Goths in the 8th century, see Southey's poem, "Roderick, the last of the Goths." Bulfinch's "Age of chivalry" [824.1] illustrates the period of Charlemagne and his Paladins in the same century; and in this connection, see Lockhart's "Spanish ballads" [1616.5], which have also much concerning the Cid in the 11th century. For the 15th century and the Jews, see Grace Aguilar's "Vale of cedars" [533.17]; and for the era of Columbus, from the marriage of Ferdinand and Isabella, 1469-92, Cooper's "Mercedes of Castile" [525.14]. Prescott says "Don Quixote" [5927.4] gives a far better view of the Spanish manners of the middle ages than the monkish chronicles. "Gil Blas" [517.18] may also be read for its illustration of Spanish manners and character. For the siege of Granada, see Bulwer's "Leila" [532.11]; and for the time of Philip III, see "Bulwer's "Calderon, the courtier" [5618.5]. A favorite story of gypsy life, started by Cervantes, has reappeared in various forms, particularly in Victor Hugo's "Hunchback of Notre-Dame" [511.27] and in Longfellow's drama, "The Spanish student" [1612.1.1; 1614.1]. Mrs. Manning's "Spanish barber" [738.5] is a tale of colporteurs in Spain, and in this connection, see Borrow's "Bible in Spain" [5931.13]. Byron's "Childe Harold," first canto [1614.12.2], illustrates the poetic associations of the country. Scott's poem, "The vision of Don Roderick" [1613.5], pictures the Moorish invasion, the height of Spanish power, and the peninsular war.

Shelf. No.

SPALDING, Martin John. Lectures on the evidences of catholicity. Baltimore, 1870. 440 pp. 8°. 5811.6

SPALDING, William. Biography of Joseph Addison and Francis Bacon. (*In* Macaulay, T. B., *lord*, and others. New biographies of illustrious men). 5428.4

— History of English literature; with an outline of the origin and growth of the English language. 12th edition. Edinburgh, 1873. 446+ pp. Sm. 8°. 6127.2

SPANGLER, Helen King. The physician's wife 723.23

SPANISH ballads, Ancient. Lockhart, J. G. Boston, 1861. Sm. 8° 1616.5

SPANISH barber, The. Manning, A. 738.5

SPANISH gypsy, The. A poem. Lewes, M. Boston, 1872. 12° 1625.1

SPANISH match, The; or, Charles Stuart at Madrid. Ainsworth, W. H. 322.23

SPANISH student, The. [Drama.] Longfellow, H. W. Poetical works. Leipzig, 1856. Sq. 16°. 1614.1

— *Same.* (*In his* Poems.) Boston, 1858. 16°....1612.1.1

SPARE, John, *joint author.* Dissertation on the part performed by nature and time in the cure of diseases. *See* EDES, Robert Thaxter 6021.5

SPARE hours. [Essays and tales.] Brown, J. Boston, 1873. 2 v. Sm. 8° 537.5

SPARK, The, of genius. Kellogg, E. 922.10

SPARKS, Jared. Life and treason of Benedict Arnold. (*In his* Library of American biography).5028.1.3

— Life of Ethan Allen. (*In his* Library of American biography) 5028.1.1

— Life of Father Marquette. (*In his* Library of American biography)........5028.1.10

— *editor.* Collection of essays and tracts in theology, from various authors, with biographical and critical notices. Boston, 1823–26. 6 v. 12°.. 1918.9

Contents. — Vol. I. Turretin, J. A.: Fundamentals in religion; Abauzit, F.: Essays; Blackburne, F.: Confessions of faith; Hoadly, B.: Essays. II. Whitby, D.: Last thoughts; Hare, F.: Difficulties and discouragements which attend the study of the Scriptures; Newton, Sir I.: Historical account of two corruptions of Scripture; Butler, C.: Historical outline of the controversy respecting the text of the three heavenly witnesses. III. Robinson, R.: Essays; Cogan, T.: Letters to Wilberforce on total depravity. IV. Penn, W.: The sandy foundation shaken; Creeds should be expressed in the language of Scripture; Sykes, A. A.: The innocency of involuntary error asserted and vindicated; Benson, G.: Essay on the belief of things above reason; Emlyn, T.: Humble inquiry into the Scripture account of Jesus Christ; Barbauld, A. L.: Thoughts on public worship. V. Hales, J.: Essays; Foster, J.: Essays. VI. Taylor, J.: Essays; Locke, J.: Essays; Clayton, R.: Speech before the Irish house of lords on subscription to articles and creeds; Watts, I.: Causes of uncharitableness; Le Clerc, J.: On the choice of our religious opinions.

— — Library of American biography. New York [*cop.*1834–]65. 10 v. Fac-similes. Portraits. 16°. 5028.1

Contents. — Vol. I. J. Stark, by E. Everett; C. B. Brown, by W. H. Prescott; R. Montgomery, by J. Armstrong; E. Allen, by J. Sparks. II. A. Wilson, by W. B. O. Peabody; Capt. J. Smith, by G. S. Hillard. III. Life and treason of B. Arnold, by J. Sparks. IV. A. Wayne, by J. Armstrong; Sir H. Vane, by C. W. Upham. V. J. Eliot, by C. Francis. VI. W. Pinkney, by H. Wheaton; W. Ellery, by E. T. Channing; C. Mather, by W. B. O. Peabody. VII. Sir W. Phips, by F. Bowen; I. Putnam, by O. W. B. Peabody; Memoir of L. M. Davidson, by C. M. Sedgwick; D. Rittenhouse, by J. Renwick. VIII. J. Edwards, by S. Miller; D. Brainerd, by W. B. O. Peabody. IX. Baron Steuben, by F. Bowen; S. Cabot, by C. Hayward, jr.; W. Eaton, by C. C. Felton. X. R. Fulton, by J. Renwick; J. Warren, by A. H. Everett; H. Hudson, by H. R. Cleveland; Father Marquette, by J. Sparks.

Shelf. No.

SPAS of Europe, On the curative effects of baths and waters, being a handbook to the. Braun, J. London, 1875. 8° 6032.4

SPEAKER. *See* ELOCUTION.

SPEAKING likenesses. Rossetti, C. (G.) Boston, 1875. 16° 912.23

SPECIES. Darwin, C. (R.) Origin of species by means of natural selection. New York, 1873. 12° 1523.6

— Mivart, St. G. On the genesis of. London, 1871. Sm. 8° 1536.5

See also Darwinism.

SPECTACLES: their uses and abuses. Sichel, J. Boston, 1850. 8°........6011.11

SPECTACLES for young eyes. *See* LANDER, Sarah West.

SPECTATOR, The. New edition. With prefaces, historical and biographical. By A. Chalmers. New York, 1864. 6 v. 8° 5611.4

— (Selected papers.) By Addison and Steele. With introductory essay and biographical sketches by J. Habberton. New York, 1876. xxix, 279+ pp. [Habberton, J. Select British essays.] Sq. 16° 1919.3

SPECTATOR, The. Vol. 23, 24, 39, 46–48. [London], 1850, 51, 73–75. 6 v. Sm. f° 6731.1

SPECTRE lover, The. Southworth, E. D. E. N. 522.11

SPECTROSCOPE, The, and its applications. Lockyer, J. N. London, 1873. 16° 6826.4

SPECTRUM analysis. Schellen, H. Spectrum analysis in its application to terrestrial substances, and the physical constitution of the heavenly bodies. London, 1872. 8° 6822.2

— — and OTHERS. Spectrum analysis explained, and its uses to science illustrated; Spectrum analysis discoveries. (*In* Estes, D. Half-hour recreations in popular science) 6813.7

— Watts, W. M. Index of spectra. London, 1872. 8° 6813.6

SPEIGHT, T. W. Under lock and key 528.2

SPEKE, John Hanning. Journal of the discovery of the source of the Nile. With map and portraits, and illustrations. New York, 1864. 590 [588] pp. 8° 5932.2

SPENCE, Joseph. Anecdotes, observations, and characters, of books and men. Collected from the conversation of Pope, and other eminent persons of his time. With notes, and a life of the author. By S. W. Singer. 2d edition. London, 1858. xxxii, 396 pp. Portrait. [Library of old authors.] Sm. 8°........5617.19

SPENCER, Charles Child. Rudimentary and practical treatise on music. 7th edition. London, 1866. 2 v. in 1. 12°........1716.35

— Rudiments of the art of playing the pianoforte. London, 1870. v, 136+ pp. 12°........1716.36

SPENCER, Edmund. Sketches of Germany and the Germans, with a glance at Poland, Hungary, and Switzerland, 1834–36. London, 1836. 2 v. Illustrated. 8° 422.6

Shelf. No.

SPENCER, Herbert. Education: intellectual, moral, and physical. New York, 1873. 283 pp. 12°. 5835.3

— First principles of a new system of philosophy. 2d edition. New York, 1873. xx, 566 pp. 12° 6835.1

— Illustrations of universal progress; a series of discussions. New York, 1872. xxiv, 451 pp. 12° 5215.1

— Philosophy of style. An essay. With notes by the editor [B. A.]. New York, 1872. 55 pp. 12° 6126.1

— Principles of biology. New York, 1868, 73. 2 v. 12° 6635.2

— Principles of psychology. New York, 1871, 73. 2 v. 12° 6615.3

— Recent discussions in science, philosophy, and morals. New and enlarged edition. New York, 1873. 349 pp. 12° 6835.2

— Social statics; or, the conditions essential to human happiness specified, and the first of them developed. With a notice of the author. New York, 1872. xviii, 523 [513] pp. 12° 5825.1

— The study of sociology. New York, 1874. xiv, 423 pp. 12° 5826.1

— and OTHERS. John Stuart Mill: his life and works. Twelve sketches. Boston, 1873. 96 pp. 12° 5427.10

— *See* RIBOT, T. English psychology. New York, 1874. 8° 5835.5

SPENCER, Ichabod Smith. A pastor's sketches: or, conversations respecting the way of salvation. New York, 1857. x, 414 pp. 12° 1535.17

SPENCER, Jesse Ames. A course of English reading. Based on the manual of J. Pycroft. New York, 1873. 299 pp. 16° 1537.13

SPENCER, Spence, *publisher*. The scenery of Ithaca and the head waters of Cayuga lake, as portrayed by different writers. Ithaca, N. Y., 1866. 150+ pp. Illustrated. 16° 417.4

SPENDER, *Mrs.* John Kent. Jocelyn's mistake 720.17

SPENDTHRIFT, The. Ainsworth, W. H. 322.15

SPENSER, Edmund. Poetical works. The text carefully revised, and illustrated with notes, original and selected, by F. J. Child. Boston, 1871. 5 v. Portrait. 16° 5628.4

Contents. — Vol. I-IV. The fairie queen. IV, V. Miscellaneous.

— *See* LOWELL, J. R. Among my books. Boston, 1876. 16° 1934.8.2

SPICY. Lamb, M. J. 530.1

SPIELHAGEN, Friedrich. Sämmtliche Werke. Neue, vom Verfasser revidirte Ausgabe. Leipzig, 1872, 74. 6 v. 16° 5734.2

Contents. — Vol. I, II. Problematische Naturen. III. Auf der Düne; Röschen vom Hofe; Clara Vere; In der Zwölften Stunde. IV. Die von Hohenstein. V, VI. In Reih' und Glied.

— Deutsche Pioniere. Berlin, 1871. 364+ pp. 16° 5735.10

— Hammer and anvil. From the German by W. H. Browne 512.13

— Leisure hour series. What the swallow sang. From the German by MS. 518.16

— Problematic characters. From the German by [M.] Schele de Vere 736.16

— Through night to light. From the German by [M.] Schele de Vere 518.10

SPIERS, Alexandre, and SURENNE, Gabriel. French and English [and English and French] pronouncing dictionary. Revised and enlarged by G. P. Quackenbos. New York, 1872. xxii, 651+ pp. 8° .... *R.R., D.3.12

SPINAL cord, Minute structure and functions of the. Schroeder van der Kolk, J. L. C. London, 1859. 8° 6023.2

SPIRIT of the age, A new. Horne, R. H. New York, 1844. 12° 1038.1

SPIRIT, The, of the pilgrims. [Religious periodical.] Vol. 1–6. Boston [1828–33]. 6 v. 8° 1321.1

SPIRITUAL wives. [Communistic societies, etc.] Dixon, W. H. Leipzig, 1868. 2 v. in 1. Sq. 16°. 1538.2

Shelf. No.

SPIRITUALISM, *or* Spiritism. De Morgan, C. From matter to spirit. The result of ten years' experience in spirit manifestations. London, 1863. Sm. 8° 6325.19

— Dods, J. B. Spirit manifestations examined and explained. Judge Edmonds refuted. New York [*cop.* 1854]. 12° 1926.2

— Faber, F. W. Spiritual conferences. Baltimore, N. D. 12° 6327.17

— Owen, R. D. The debatable land between this world and the next. New York, 1872. 12° ... 1526.28

— – Footfalls on the boundary of another world. Philadelphia, 1872. 12° 1533.7

— Pierce, A. P. The revelator: being an account of the twenty-one days' entrancement of A. P. Pierce, together with a sketch of his life. Boston, 1870. 12° 1538.18

— Putnam, A. Agassiz and spiritualism. Boston [1874]. 16° 1538.12

— Wallace, A. R. Miracles and modern spiritualism. London, 1875. Sm. 8° 6328.24

— Watson, S. The clock struck three. Showing the harmony between Christianity, science, and spiritualism. Chicago, 1874. 16° 6325.17

SPITHEAD, The mutiny at. Herbert, D. Great historical mutinies. London, 1876. Sm. 8° 5924.2

SPITZBERGEN. Blackwood, F. T., *lord Dufferin*. Voyage to, in 1856. Boston, 1859. 12° 225.3

— Wells, J. C. The gateway to the Polynia. A voyage to. London, 1873. 8° 5911.14

SPOFFORD, Harriet Elizabeth, *formerly Miss Prescott*. The amber gods and other stories 538.3

— Azarian 728.1

— D'outre mort. (*In* Johnson, (E.) R. Little classics) 529.4.2

— New England legends. With illustrations. Boston, 1871. 40 pp. 8° 531.13

— Ray. (*In* Johnson, (E.) R. Little classics) 529.4.11

— Sir Rohan's ghost 537.22

— The South breaker. (*In* Johnson, (E.) R. Little classics) 529.4.7

— The thief in the night 736.15

SPOONER, Thomas. Memorial of William Spooner, 1637, and of his descendants to the third generation; of his great-grandson, Elnathan Spooner, and of his descendants, to 1871. Cincinnati, 1871. 242 pp. 8° 1011.5

SPOONER, William, Memorial of. Spooner, T. Cincinnati, 1871. 8° 1011.5

SPOONS in a wherry. *See* HALE, E. E., and others. Tales for travellers 720.21

SPORTS and sporting. Bumstead, J. On the wing. A book for sportsmen. Boston, 1871. 16° 1516.4

— Daniel, W. B. Rural sports. [London, 1801.] 2 v. in 3. 8° 6412.1

— Gilmore, P. Accessible field sports. London, 1869. Sm. 8° 1514.10

— – Gun, rod, and saddle. Personal experiences. London, 1869. Sm. 8° 1514.11

— – Prairie and forest: a description of the game of North America, with personal adventures in their pursuit. New York, 1874. 12° 6415.1

— Greenwood, J. Wild sports of the world. New York, 1870. 8° 1514.21

— Herbert, H. W. American game in its seasons. New York, 1873. 12° 1516.14

— – Field sports of the United States and British provinces. New York [*cop.* 1848]. 2 v. 12°. 1514.19

— Meunier, V. (A.) Adventures on the great hunting grounds of the world. New York, 1872. 16° 1714.7

— Strutt, J. Sports and pastimes of the people of England. London, 1876. Sm. 8° 6414.4

— Walsh, J. H. British rural sports. London, 1872. Sq. 16° 6414.1

See also Dog, Fish and fishing, Recreative arts, Rural sports.

SPORTSMAN'S, The, club afloat. Fosdick, C. A. 913.34

SPORTSMAN'S, The, club among the trappers. Fosdick, C. A. 913.36

SPORTSMAN'S, The, club in the saddle. Fosdick, C. A. 913.35

Shelf. No.

SPRING floods. Turgenef, I. S. 528.9

SPRINGER, Anton Heinrich. Handbuch der Kunstgeschichte. Mit einem Vorwort von F. T. Vischer. Mit illustrationen. Stuttgart, 1855. xii, 386 pp. 8° 1513.1

SPRINGFIELD armory, Marco Paul at the. Abbott, J. 914.4

SPRUNER, Carl von. Atlas antiquus. Edidit T. Menke. Gothæ, 1865. 17 pp. 31 maps. 4°.*R.R., Desk

SPURZHEIM, (Johann) Gasper. Outlines of phrenology. Boston, 1832. iv, 96+ pp. 12° 1528.10

— Memoir of the life and philosophy of. Carmichael, A. Boston, 1833. 12° 1227.9

SPY, The. Cooper, J. F. Leipzig 310.11

— *Same.* New York 525.26

SQUIRE Arden. Oliphant, M. (O. W.) 710.17

SQUIRE'S, The, legacy. Hay, M. C. 530.16

STAËL-HOLSTEIN, Anne Louise Germaine Necker, *baronne* de. De l'Allemagne. Nouvelle édition. Paris, 1869. 628 pp. 18° 5536.21

— Corinne; or, Italy. Translated by Isabel Hill; with metrical versions of the odes by L. E. Landon. New York, 1873. xxvii, 396 pp. 12° .. 527.17

— Corinne ou l'Italie. Nouvelle édition. Précédée d'une notice par Mme M. N. de Saussure. New York, 1873. 422+ pp. 12° 2015.3

— Germany. With notes and appendix by O. W. Wight. New York, 1871. 2 v. in 1. 12° 5726.1

— Influence of literature upon society. (*In* The Alexandrian) 1910.4.2

— Mémoires (dix années d'exil). Ouvrage posthume publié en 1818 par M. le duc de Broglie et M. le baron de Staël. Nouvelle édition précédée d'une notice sur la vie et les ouvrages de Madame de Staël par Mme Necker de Saussure. Paris, 1861. 483 pp. 18° 5527.11

— Reflections on suicide. (*In* The Alexandrian)..1910.4.2

STAGE, The mimic. Baker, G. M. Boston, 1871. 12° 1635.23

See also Actors and acting, English stage.

STAGE-COACHES. Annals of the road, or notes on mail and stage coaching in Great Britain. Malet, H. E. London, 1876. 8° 5433.4

STAGE-STRUCK Yankee, The: a farce. Durivage, O. E. New York, N. D. 12° 1635.4

STAHR, Adolf. The life and works of Gotthold Ephraim Lessing. From the German, by E. P. Evans. New York, 1873. 2 v. 12° 1022.7

STAND and wait. *See* HALE, E. E., and others. Tales for travellers 720.23

STANDISH, Miles. Abbott, J. S. C. Miles Standish, the puritan captain. New York, 1872. 12°... 1014.6

— Longfellow, H. W. The courtship of. [Poem.] Leipzig, 1856. Sq. 16° 1614.1

— *Same.* Boston, 1859. 16° 1612.3

See also Plymouth, *note.*

STANHOPE, Philip Dormer, *earl of Chesterfield.* Letters to his son. Edited, with a biographical notice, by C. S. Carey. London, 1872. 2 v. Portrait. Sm. 8° 5615.6

— The man of education: or, beauties of Lord Chesterfield. Selections. Boston, 1801. 300 pp. 12°. 1928.6

— *See* SAINTE-BEUVE, C. A. English portraits. New York, 1875. 16° 1025.3

STANHOPE, Philip Henry, *5th earl Stanhope, formerly lord Mahon.* The "forty-five." Being the narrative of the insurrection of 1745 extracted from Lord Mahon's History of England. Added, Letters of prince Charles Stuart. New edition. London, 1869. viii, 160 pp. Sm. 8°. 5418.7

— History of England, comprising the reign of Queen Anne, until the peace of Utrecht, 1701-13. 4th edition. London, 1872. 2 v. Portrait. Sm. 8° 5418.3

— History of England, from the peace of Utrecht to the peace of Versailles. 1713-83. Leipzig, 1853, 54. 7 v. in 4. Sq. 16° 838.3

— Life of Louis prince of Condé. New edition. London, 1861. viii, 308 pp. Sm. 8° 5527.10

— Life of William Pitt. London, 1867. 4 v. Portraits. Fac-simile. Sm. 8° 5424.11

STANLEY, Arthur Penrhyn. Historical memorials of Westminster abbey. 3d and revised edition. With illustrations. London, 1869. liv, 704+ pp. 8° 5414.2

— Lectures on the history of the church of Scotland. New York, 1872. xiv, 207 pp. 8° 5812.6

— Life and correspondence of Thomas Arnold. 9th American edition. Boston, 1872. 2 v. in 1. Portrait. 12° 1225.14

— Sinai and Palestine. In connection with their history. New edition, with maps and plans. New York, 1870. lv, 535 pp. 8° 5923.1

— Theological essays. (*In* Noyes, G. R. Collection of theological essays) 6325.12

STANLEY, Henry Morton. Coomassie and Magdala: the story of two British campaigns in Africa. With illustrations and two maps. New York, 1874. xiv, 510 pp. 8° 5931.14

— How I found Livingstone: travels, adventures and discoveries in Central Africa. With maps and illustrations. New York, 1872. xxiii, 736 pp. 8° ....422.24 and 5931.5

— My Kalulu, prince, king, and slave: a story of Central Africa. With illustrations. New York, 1874. xiv, 436+ pp. Sm. 8° 921.9

STANLEY Thorn. Cockton, H. 717.4

STAR, A, and a heart. [Fiction.] Church, F. Boston. 730.10

— *Same.* Leipzig 334.7

STAR-CHAMBER, The. [James I's time.] Ainsworth, W. H. 322.9

STAR papers; or, experiences of art and nature. Beecher, H. W. New York, 1855. 12° 1924.2

— *Same.* New edition, with additional articles. New York, 1873. 12° 1924.4

STAR spangled banner, Essay on the. Salisbury, S. Worcester, 1873. 8° 5010.16

STARK, John, Life of. Everett, E. (*In* Sparks, J. Library of American biography) 5028.1.1

STARRY flag, The. Adams, W. T. 924.23

STARRY flag series. *See* ADAMS, William T.

STARS. Proctor, R. A. Half-hours with the. London, 1871. 4° 6810.1

— Winchell, A. Geology of the. (*In* Estes, D. Half-hour recreations in popular science) 6813.7

See also Astronomy.

STARS and stripes, The, in rebeldom. A series of papers written by federal prisoners (privates) in Richmond [etc.]. Boston, 1862. 137 pp. 12°. 817.2

STATESMEN of the time of George III and IV. Brougham, H., *lord.* Works. Edinburgh, 1872. 16°.5614.4.3-5

STAUNTON, Howard. The chess-player's handbook. Illustrated. 2d edition, revised. London, 1858. viii, 518 pp. 16° 1514.3

— The great schools of England. New edition, revised and corrected; with an appendix, containing notices of the endowed grammar schools of England and Wales. London, 1869. xlv, 596+ pp. Sm. 8° 5416.5

STEAM, An elementary treatise on. Clark, D. K. London, 1875. 12° 6428.7

STEAM boilers. Prideaux, T. S. The economy of fuel, with reference to. London, N. D. 12°...1715.13

— Robinson, J. R. Explosions of: how they are caused, and how they may be prevented. Boston, 1870. 12° 1713.4

STEAM-ENGINE. Baker, T. Mathematical theory of the. London, 1870. 12° 1716.1

— Bourne, J. Catechism of the. New York, 1854. 12° 1526.13

— Burn, R. S. Self-aid cyclopædia for self-taught students. London, N. D. 8° 6223.2

— Clark, D. K. An elementary treatise on steam and the steam-engine, stationary and portable. London, 1875. 12° 6428.7

— Evers, H. Steam and the steam engine: land and marine. New York [Glasgow], 1873. 16°. 1717.5

— Ewbank, T. A descriptive and historical account of hydraulic and other machines; with observations on the. New York, 1876 [*cop.* 1863]. 8°. 6422.7

— Lardner, D. The steam engine. London, 1871. 12° 1716.34

Shelf. No.

STEAM-ENGINE, *continued.*

— Murray, R. Treatise on marine engines and steam vessels. London, 1871. 12° 1716.13

— Smiles, S. Lives of Boulton and Watt. Comprising also a history of the invention and introduction of the. London, 1865. 8° 5421.5

See also Locomotive engine.

STEARNS, Edward Josiah. A practical guide to English pronunciation. Boston, 1857. lxxx, 55 [51] pp. 12° 1737.2

STEDMAN, Edmund Clarence. Victorian poets. Boston, 1876. xxiii, 441 pp. 12° 1837.1

Contents. — Walter Savage Landor; Thomas Hood; Matthew Arnold; Bryan Waller Procter; Elizabeth Barrett Browning; Alfred Tennyson; Tennyson and Theocritus; Robert Browning; Robert Buchanan; Dante Gabriel Rossetti; William Morris; Algernon Charles Swinburne, etc.

STEEDMAN, Charles. A manual of swimming. London, 1873. xvi, 270 pp. Illustrated. Sm. 8°. 6418.1

STEEL, John H. An analysis of the mineral waters of Saratoga and Ballston. 2d edition. Saratoga Springs, 1838. 203 pp. 12° 417.15

STEEL, The manufacture of. Gruener, L. (E.). New York, 1872. 8° 6631.4

STEELE, Anne. Works. Boston, 1808. 300 pp. 12°. 5218.1

STEELE, *Sir* Richard. *See* FORSTER, J. Biographical essays. London, 1860. Sm. 8° 5425.12

See also Spectator.

STEEPLE trap, The. Abbott, J. 917.33

STEFFENS, Heinrich. The story of my career, as student at Freiburg and Jena, and as professor at Halle, Breslau and Berlin. Translated by W. L. Gage. Boston, 1863. 284 pp. 16° 1025.8

STELLO. Vigny, A. (V.), *comte* de. Paris, 1873. 18° 5536.18

STENHOUSE, T. B. H. The Rocky mountain saints: a full and complete history of the Mormons, including the colonization and development of the mineral wealth of Utah. Illustrated. New York, 1873. xxiv, 761 pp. 8° 5933.9

STEP-MOTHER, The. James, G. P. R. 327.9

STEPHEN, *Sir* James. Critical and miscellaneous essays. New York, 1871. 158 pp. 8° 1931.1

— Lectures on the history of France. 3d edition. London, 1857. 2 v. 8° 5514.8

STEPHEN, James Fitzjames. Liberty, equality, fraternity. London, 1873. vi, 350+ pp. 8° 5831.2

STEPHEN, Leslie. Essays on freethinking and plainspeaking. London, 1873. 362+ pp. Sm. 8°. 5838.3

— Hours in a library. New York, 1874. 392+ pp. 12° 6136.9

Contents. — De Foe's novels; Richardson's novels; Pope as a moralist; Mr. Elwin's edition of Pope; Some words about Sir Walter Scott, Nathaniel Hawthorne; Balzac's novels; De Quincey.

— The playground of Europe. [Switzerland.] London, 1871. x, 321+ pp. Illustrated. 12° ... 5025.8

STEPHEN Dane. Douglas, A. M. 533.14

STEPHENS, Ann Sophia (Winterbotham). Bellehood and bondage 734.11

— Bertha's engagement 522.17

— The curse of gold 726.11

— Doubly false 726.13

— Fashion and famine 726.5

— The gold brick 726.12

— The heiress 522.4

— Lord Hope's choice 528.6

— Mabel's mistake 726.3

— Married in haste 726.2

— Mary Derwent 726.14

— A noble woman 726.7

— The old countess 734.9

— The old homestead 726.4

— Phemie Frost's experiences 734.22

— The rejected wife 727.14

— Ruby Gray's strategy 726.8

— Silent struggles 527.13

— The soldier's orphans 726.1

— The wife's secret 726.9

— Wives and widows 726.6

Shelf. No.

STEPHENS, Charles Asbury. [American homes series.] The young moose hunters, a backwoods-boy's story 921.11

— The camping-out series. Vol. I. Camping out; as recorded by "Kit" 1127.1

— — Vol. III. Off to the geysers; or, the young yachters in Iceland. As recorded by "Wade". 1127.2

— — Vol. IV. Lynx-hunting: from notes by the author of "Camping out" 937.25

— — Vol. V. Fox-hunting, as recorded by Raed ... 927.25

— — Vol. VI. On the Amazons; or, the cruise of "The rambler." As recorded by Wash 916.28

STEPHENS, Frederic G. Flemish and French pictures, with notes concerning the painters and their works. London, 1875. x, 280+ pp. Illustrated by 20 etchings. 4° 6211.8

— Memoir of Sir Edwin Landseer. A sketch of [his] life. Illustrated. Being a new edition of "The early works of Sir Edwin Landseer." London, 1874. xv, 184 pp. L. 8° 6211.6

STEPHENS, John Lloyd. Incidents of travel in Central America, Chiapas, and Yucatan. Illustrated. 12th edition. New York, 1856. 2 v. 8° 422.5

— Incidents of travel in Yucatan. Illustrated. New York, 1843. 2 v. 8° 5930.5

STEPHENS, William Richard Wood. Saint Chrysostom: his life and times. With a portrait. London, 1872. xiv, 474+ pp. 8° 5813.6

STEPHENSON, George, Life of. Smiles, S. New York, 1868. 8° 5422.1

STEPHENSON, Harris Marshall. Souvenir of 1775. *See* PORTER, Edward Griffin 810.5

STEPHENSON, Robert, Life of. Smiles, S. New York, 1868. 8° 5422.1

STEPHENSON, *Sir* Rowland Macdonald. Elementary and practical instructions on the science of railway construction. 4th edition, revised by E. Nugent. With illustrations. London, 1869. viii, 262 pp. 1 folded plate. 12° 1715.23

STEPPING heavenward. Prentiss, E. 537.2

STERLING exchange, Tables of. Price, J. M. New York, 1852. L. 8° 1721.1

STERN necessity. Robinson, F. W. 731.13

STERNE, Laurence. Life and opinions of Tristram Shandy. Leipzig, 1849. 502+ pp. Sq. 16°. 315.14

— A sentimental journey through France and Italy. Added the letters and a life of the author. With portrait. Leipzig, 1861. viii, 347 pp. Sq. 16°. 428.2

— Life of. Fitzgerald, P. London, 1864. 2 v. Sm. 8° 1224.1

Note. — The first and only full memoir of Sterne is Fitzgerald's, 1864, who presents a more favorable view of his character than that of the popular notion, derived largely from Thackeray's lecture in his "English humourists" [1238.8]. Sterne wrote a brief autobiography, which is usually prefixed to his works. Scott reprints it, and adds to it, in his "Lives of the novelists" [5914.2]. See also Disraeli's "Literary miscellanies" [1533.4], and references in Allibone; besides articles in Macmillan's magazine, 1873, and Fraser's magazine, 1874.

STETSON, Charles B. Technical education: what it is, and what American public schools should teach. Boston, 1874. iv, 284 pp. 12° 5837.2

STEUBEN, Friedrich Wilhelm August Heinrich Ferdinand, *baron* von. Regulations for the order and discipline of the troops of the United States. Part I. 10th edition. Added, the manual exercise, and evolutions of the cavalry: as practised in the late American army. New York, 1794. 95 pp. Plates. Sm. 12° 6928.2

— Bowen, F. Life of. (*In* Sparks, J. Library of American biography) 5028.1.9

— Kapp, F. Life of. New York, 1859. 12° 5025.8

STEVEN Lawrence, yeoman. Edwards, A. 312.16

STEVENS, Edward T. Flint chips. A guide to prehistoric archæology, as illustrated by the collection in the Blackmore museum, Salisbury. London, 1870. xxxviii, 593+ pp. Illustrated. 8° 5913.7

STEVENS, Henry. Account of the proceedings at the dinner given by George Peabody to the Americans connected with the Great exhibition. London, 1851. 114 pp. 8° 1923.2

Shelf. No.

STEVENS, Isaac Ingalls. Campaigns of the Rio Grande and of Mexico. With notices of the recent work of Major Ripley. New York, 1851. 108 pp. 8° ... 612.3
STEVENSON, David. Sketch of civil engineering in North America. 2d edition. London, 1859. x, 218 pp. 12° ... 6428.3
STEVENSON, George J. City road chapel, London, and its associations. With engravings. London [1872]. 624 pp. 8° ... 5414.1

Note. — The head-quarters of the Wesleyan methodists of Great Britain; built in 1778 by John Wesley and his followers.

STEVENSON, Sarah Hackett. Boys and girls in biology; or, simple studies of the lower forms of life, based upon the latest lectures of T. H. Huxley. Illustrated. New York, 1875. 186 pp. 12° ... 1527.17
STEWART, Balfour. International scientific series. The conservation of energy. New York, 1874. viii, 236+ pp. 12° ... 6436.7
— Lessons in elementary physics. New edition. London, 1873. x, 376 pp. Illustrated. 16° ... 6438.6
— *joint author.* The unseen universe or physical speculations on a future state. *See* TAIT, Peter Guthrie ... 5834.6
STEWART, Charles Samuel. Brazil and La Plata: the personal record of a cruise. New York, 1856. xi, 428 pp. Illustrated. 12° ... 425.18
— A visit to the South seas, in the U. S. ship Vincennes, in 1829, 30. New York, 1833. 2 v. 12° ... 225.4
STEWART, Dugald. Works. Vol. I–III. Cambridge, 1829. 3 v. 8° ... 5832.4

Contents. — Vol. I-III. Elements of the philosophy of the human mind.

— Elements of the philosophy of the human mind. Brattleborough, 1808. 496 pp. 8° ... 1522.1
STIELER, Carl, *joint author.* The Bavarian highlands and the Salzkammergut. *See* SCHMID, Herman. 5720.1
STIGAND, William. The life work, and opinions of Heinrich Heine. London, 1875. 2 v. Portrait. 8° ... 5721.1
STILL hour, The; or, communion with God. Phelps, A. Boston, 1860. 16° ... 6328.5
STILL waters ... 315.12
STILLÉ, Charles Janeway. Memorial of the Great central fair for the United States sanitary commission, held at Philadelphia, June, 1864. Philadelphia, 1864. 211 pp. Illustrated. 4° ... 6910.1
STILLMAN, William J., *editor.* Poetic localities of Cambridge. Illustrated with heliotypes from nature. Boston, 1876. 41 pp. Sm. 4° ... 5231.1
STIRLING, Edward. Mrs. Caudle's curtain lecture. [Dramatized from D. Jerrold.] New York, N. D. 8 pp. 12° ... 1635.5
— The young scamp: a farce. New York, N. D. 17 pp. 12° ... 1635.4
STIRLING, James Hutchinson. On protoplasm: being an examination of [his] criticism of Professor Huxley's views. Ross, J. London, 1874. Sm. 8° ... 1527.22
STIRLING, William. Cloister life of Charles V. Boston, 1853. xxv, 322 pp. Portrait. 12° ... 1223.6

Note. — Compare the continuation by Prescott to Robertson's "Charles V" [1226.9].

STOCK market, Twenty-one years in the Boston. Martin, J. G. Boston, 1856. 8° ... 1711.1
STOCKMAR, Christian Friedrich, *baron*, Memoirs of. Stockmar, E., *baron* von. London, 1873. 2 v. Sm. 8° ... 5725.1
STOCKMAR, Ernst, *baron* von. Memoirs of Baron Stockmar. Translated from the German by G. A. M[üller]. Edited by F. Max Müller. London, 1873. 2 v. Sm. 8° ... 5725.1
STOCKTON, Frank R. and Marian. Putnam's handy-book series. The home: where it should be and what to put in it. New York, 1873. 182 pp. 12° ... 1515.10

STODDARD, Richard Henry, *editor.* Bric-à-brac series. Anecdote biographies of Thackeray and Dickens. New York, 1874. xxiv, 305 pp. Sq. 16° ... 1828.3
— – The Greville memoirs. A journal of the reigns of George IV and William IV. By Charles C. F. Greville. New York, 1875. xi, 346 pp. Sq. 16° ... 1828.5
— – Personal recollections of Lamb, Hazlitt [Campbell, and Countess of Blessington]. New York, 1875. xxii, 322 pp. Portraits. Fac-simile. Sq. 16° ... 1828.9
— – Personal reminiscences by Barham, Harness, and Hodder. New York, 1875. 335 pp. Sq. 16°. 1828.4
— – Personal reminiscences by Chorley, Planché, and Young. New York, 1874. xxiii, 297 pp. Sq. 16°. 1828.2
— – Personal reminiscences by Constable and Gillies. New York, 1876. 336 pp. Portraits. Sq. 16°. 1828.10
— – Personal reminiscences by Cornelia Knight and Thomas Raikes. New York, 1875. xvi, 339+ pp. Portraits. Sq. 16° ... 1828.7
— – Personal reminiscences by Moore and Jerdan. New York, 1875. 293 pp. Portraits. Sq. 16°. 1828.6
— – Personal reminiscences by O'Keeffe, Kelly, and Taylor. New York, 1875. xxi, 341 pp. Illustrations. Sq. 16° ... 1828.8
— – Prosper Mérimée's Letters to an incognita. With recollections by Lamartine and George Sand. New York, 1874. 350+ pp. Sq. 16° .. 1828.1
— Sans-souci series. Men and manners in America one hundred years ago. Edited by H. E. Scudder. New York, 1876. 320 pp. Illustrated. 16°. 1827.1
— The treasure-trove series. *See* WALSH, William Shepard ... 538.10
STOECKHARDT, Julius Adolphus. Chemical field lectures for agriculturists. Translated from the German. Edited, with notes, by J. E. Teschemacher. New York, 1854. xii, 242+ pp. 12°. 1525.29
STOKESLEY secret, The. Yonge, C. M. ... 918.23
STOLEN waters. [Poem.] Gardner, C. E. New York, 1875. 12° ... 1625.12
STONE, Ebenezer W., *compiler.* Compend of instructions in military tactics, and the manual of percussion arms. *See* MASSACHUSETTS. *Legislative documents. Miscellaneous* ... 1528.11
— Digest of the militia laws of Massachusetts. *See* MASSACHUSETTS. *Acts, laws, etc.* ... 6927.9
STONE, J. B. A tour with Cook through Spain: being a series of descriptive letters of ancient cities and scenery of Spain, and of life, manners, and customs of Spaniards. Illustrated. London, 1873. vi, 229+ pp. Sm. 8° ... 5916.8

Note. — The Mr. Cook mentioned in the title has organized a system for conducting tourist parties over the world.

STONE, James Kent. The invitation heeded: reasons for a return to catholic unity. 7th edition. New York [*cop.* 1870]. 341 pp. 12° ... 5816.12
STONE, James W. Report of the trial of J. W. Webster, indicted for the murder of G. Parkman. Boston, 1850. vi, 314 pp. 8° ... 631.5
STONE, Livingston. Domesticated trout. How to breed and grow them. [Appendix, Books on fish culture, pp. 336–342.] Boston, 1872. x, 347 pp. Illustrated. 16° ... 6616.3
STONE, William Leete. Border wars of the American revolution. New York, 1857. 2 v. 16° ... 818.1
— History of New York city from the discovery to the present day. New York, 1872. xx, 658, 136+ pp. Illustrated. Portraits. 8° ... 5010.8
— Life and times of Sa-go-ye-wat ha, or Red Jacket. With a memoir of the author, by his son. Albany, 1866. 509 pp. Portraits. 8° ... 5022.5
— Life and times of Sir William Johnson. Albany, 1865. 2 v. Portrait. 8° ... 5022.6
— Life of Joseph Brant (Thayendanegea), including the border wars of the American revolution [etc.]. Albany, 1865. 2 v. Portraits. 8° ... 5022.4

Note. — These biographies, in this order, Johnson, Brant, Red Jacket, form a history of the great Iroquois confederacy, 1735-1838.

STONE, Treatise on the blasting and quarrying of. Burgoyne, *Sir* J. F. London, N. D. 12° ... 1716.15

Shelf. No.

STONE age, The. (*In* Estes, D. Half-hour recreations in popular science) ... 6813.7

See also Pre-historic man.

STONECUTTING, Rudiments of masonry and. Dobson, E. London, 1870. 12° ... 1716.24

STONEHENGE, *pseud.* *See* WALSH, John Henry.

STONE-MASON, The, of Saint Point. Lamartine, A. (M. L.) de. New York [1851]. 12° ... 512.10

STONES of the temple. Field, W. London, 1873. Sm. 8° ... 5815.7

STONES of Venice, The. [Venetian architecture.] Ruskin, J. New York, 1872. 3 v. 12° ... 6236.1

STORER, Francis Humphreys, *joint author.* A compendious manual of qualitative chemical analysis. *See* ELIOT, Charles William ... 6436.4

STORIES and legends of travel and history. Lippincott, S. J. ... 922.23

STORIES and tales. Andersen, H. C. ... 923.25

STORIES for children. By eleven sophomores ... 928.17

Note. — Written as themes, in the spring of 1874, by eleven sophomores of Harvard college.

STORIES for young persons. Sedgwick, C. M. ... 918.20

STORIES from famous ballads. Lippincott, S. J. ... 922.24

STORIES from my attic. Scudder, H. E. ... 728.2

STORIES of a grandfather about American history. Dodge, N. S. Boston, 1874. Sq. 16° ... 913.29

STORIES of bird life. Berthoud, H. London, 1875. Sm. 8° ... 6617.9

STORIES of French school life. Moncrieff, A. R. H. 715.17

STORIES of infinity. Flammarion, C. Boston, 1873. 16°. 6837.1

STORIES of many lands. Lippincott, S. J. ... 928.7

STORIES of the gorilla country. [Africa.] Du Chaillu, P. B. New York, 1870. 12° ... 933.5

STORIES of the prairie. Cooper, J. F. ... 515.13

STORIES of the sea. Cooper, J. F. ... 515.12

STORIES of the woods. Cooper, J. F. ... 515.14

Note. — These three books by Cooper consist of extracts from his novels.

STORIES told to a child. Ingelow, J. ... 935.21

— - 2d series ... 935.22

STORM warriors; or, life-boat work on the Goodwin sands. Gilmore, J. London, 1875. Sm. 8° ... 5935.6

STORMY life, A. Fullerton, *Lady* G. ... 325.16

STORY, James P. Choisy ... 521.20

STORY, Joseph. Commentaries on the constitution of the United States. Abridged. Boston, 1833. xliii, 736 pp. L. 8° ... 5030.2

— Life and letters. Edited by his son, W. W. Story. Boston, 1851. 2 v. Portrait. 8° ... 5021.3

STORY, William Wetmore. Nero: an historical play. Edinburgh, 1875. viii, 275 pp. Sm. 8° ... 1637.1

— Roba di Roma. 6th edition, with additions. London, 1871. x, 594 pp. Portrait. 8° ... 5524.1

STORY, The, Lizzie told. Prentiss, E. ... 736.30

STORY of a bad boy. Aldrich, T. B. ... 923.23

STORY of a genius. By the author of "How to win love," etc. ... 937.11

STORY, The, of a house. [History of building a house.] Viollet-le-Duc, E. E. Boston, 1874. 8°. 1513.3

STORY, The, of a millionnaire. Mundt, C. (M.) ... 533.22

STORY, The, of a trooper. Adams, F. C. New York, 1865. 12° ... 816.10

STORY, The, of Elizabeth. Thackeray, A. I. ... 335.12

STORY, The, of La Roche. Mackenzie, H. (*In* Johnson, (E.) R. Little classics) ... 529.4.3

STORY, The, of my career. [Biography.] Steffens, H. Boston, 1863. 16° ... 1025.8

STORY, The, of my life. Andersen, H. C. ... 1225.18

STORY of the great march [Sherman's]. Nichols, G. W. New York, 1866. 12° ... 815.7

STORY, The, of the guard: a chronicle of the [civil] war. Frémont, J. B. ... 815.5

STORY, The, of the peasant-boy philosopher [James Ferguson]. Mayhew, H. New York, 1870. 16°. 937.15

STORY of the Simplon. *See* HALE, E. E., and others. Tales for travellers ... 720.22

STORY, A, of three sisters. Maxwell, C. ... 517.26

STORY, The, of Valentine and his brother. Oliphant, M. (O. W.) Leipzig ... 331.6

— *Same.* New York ... 711.25

STORY-BOOK, A, for the children. Diaz, A. M. ... 1115.9

30

Shelf. No.

STOTHARD, Thomas, Life of. Bray, A. E. London, 1851. 4° ... 6213.8

STOUT heart, A. Kellogg, E. ... 922.30

STOWE, Harriet (Elizabeth) Beecher. (*Christopher Crowfield.*) Agnes of Sorrento ... 527.16

Note. — This is a story of Italy, Savonarola, etc.; and for parallel reading compare George Eliot's "Romola" [310.23].

— Betty's bright idea. Also, Deacon Pitkin's farm, and The first Christmas of New England ... 715.24

— The chimney-corner. [Essays] ... 1535.15

— Dred ... 314.23

Note. — Sometimes known as "Nina Gordon"; it is a tale of slavery and the Dismal swamp.

— House and home papers. Boston, 1869. 333 pp. 12° ... 1516.8

— Key to Uncle Tom's cabin ... 314.21

— Little foxes ... 537.12

Note. — Papers and short tales illustrating fault-finding and other minor vices.

— Little Pussy Willow. [Juvenile] ... 932.2

— Men of our times; or leading patriots of the day. With portraits. Hartford, 1869. xiv, 575 [565] pp. 8° ... 5023.9

— The minister's wooing ... 314.24

Note. — A story of Newport in the last century, when Hopkinsianism was rife and the slave-trade was still conducted by Newport merchants.

— My wife and I ... 725.14

— Oldtown folks. Boston ... 723.21

— *Same.* Leipzig ... 314.22

Note. — A tale of New England manners.

— Palmetto-leaves ... 417.10

— The pearl of Orr's island. [Coast of Maine story]. 527.20

— Pink and white tyranny ... 537.6

— Queer little people ... 933.22

— Sam Lawson's Oldtown fireside stories ... 736.10

— Sunny memories of foreign lands. Illustrated. Boston, 1854. 2 v. 12° ... 426.6

— Uncle Tom's cabin. Boston ... 733.4

— *Same.* Leipzig ... 314.20

Note. — A tale of Southern slavery, and of fugitives to the North.

— We and our neighbors; or, the records of an unfashionable street. (Sequel to "My wife and I.") A novel ... 723.12

— Woman in sacred history: a series of sketches. With 16 chromo-lithographs. New York, 1874. Unpaged. L. 8° ... 6320.1

— *joint author.* The new housekeeper's manual. *See* BEECHER, Catharine Esther ... 1723.8

STRAFFORD, *Earl of.* *See* WENTWORTH, Thomas.

STRAHAN, Edward, *pseud.* *See* SHINN, *Earl.*

STRAIT gate, The. Abbott, J. Harper's story books. 936.1.1

STRANGE adventures, The, of a phaeton. Black, W. 319.6

STRANGE horse, The, of loch Suainbhal. Black, W. 331.28

STRANGE story, A. Bulwer-Lytton, E. (G. E.) L. ... 336.12

STRANGE world, A. Braddon, M. E. Leipzig ... 330.18

— *Same.* New York ... 711.11

STRANGER, The, in Liverpool; or, an historical and descriptive view of the town of Liverpool and its environs. Liverpool [1829]. 280+ pp. Map. Illustrations. Sm. 12° ... 438.5

STRANGERS and pilgrims. Braddon, M. E. Leipzig. 330.13

— *Same.* New York ... 731.7

STRATHERN. Gardiner, M. 2 v. ... 330.26

STRATHMORE. Rame, L. de la ... 327.18

STRAUSS, David Friedrich. The old faith and the new. A confession. Authorized translation, from the 6th edition. By Mathilde Blind. American edition. The translation revised and partly rewritten. New York, 1874. 2 v. in 1. 12°. 5815.22

Contents. — 1. Are we still Christians? 2. Have we still a religion? 3. What is our conception of the universe? 4. What is our rule of life? Appendix. Of our great poets. Of our great composers.

STRAUSS, (Gerhard) Friedrich (Abram). The glory of the house of Israel: comprising a picture of Judaism in the century which preceded the advent of our Saviour. Philadelphia, 1859. 480 pp. Illustrated. 12° ... 425.14

Note. — This book was originally published under the title of "Helon's pilgrimage to Jerusalem."

Shelf. No.

STRAY Yankee, A, in Texas. Hammett, S. A. New York, 1859. 12° 414.20

STREET ballads, popular poetry, and household songs of Ireland. Boston [1864]. 312 pp. 16° 1615.2

STRETTON, Hesba, *pseud.* *See* SMITH, Hannah.

STRETTON, Julia. Lords and ladies 710.18

STRETTON. Kingsley, H. 521.23

STRICKLAND, Agnes. Lives of the queens of England, from the Norman conquest. London, 1840–48. 12 v. Illustrated. Portraits. 12° 5416.4

Contents. — Vol. I. Matilda of Flanders, A. D. 1066; Matilda of Scotland, 1100; Adelicia of Louvaine, 1120; Matilda of Boulogne, 1136; Eleanora of Aquitaine, 1154. II. Berengaria of Navarre, 1191; Isabella of Angoulême, 1200; Eleanora of Provence, 1236; Eleanor of Castile, 1273; Marguerite of France, 1299; Isabella of France, 1308; Philippa of Hainault, 1327; Anne of Bohemia, 1380. III. Isabella of Valois, 1397; Joanna of Navarre, 1402; Katherine of Valois, 1402; Margaret of Anjou, 1444; Elizabeth Woodville, 1464; Anne of Warwick, 1473. IV. Elizabeth of York, 1486; Katherine of Aragon, 1509; Anne Boleyn, 1533; Jane Seymour, 1536; Anne of Cleves, 1539; Katherine Howard, 1540. V. Katharine Parr, 1543; Mary I, 1553. VI. Elizabeth, 1558. VII. Elizabeth, continued; Anne of Denmark, 1603. VIII. Henrietta Maria, 1628; Catharine of Braganza, 1661. IX, X. Mary Beatrice of Modena, 1685; Mary II, 1688. XI. Mary II, continued; Anne, 1702. XII. Anne, continued.

— Lives of the queens of Scotland and English princesses connected with the regal succession of Great Britain. New York, 1859–73. 8 v. 12° 627.1

Contents.—Vol. I. Margaret Tudor, queen of James IV; Magdalene of France, 1st queen of James V; Mary of Lorraine, 2d queen of James V. II. Mary of Lorraine; Lady Margaret Douglas, countess of Lennox. III–VII. Mary Stuart, queen of Scots. VIII. Elizabeth Stuart, 1st princess-royal of Great Britain.

STRIVE and succeed. Alger, H., *jr.* 935.28

STRIVE and thrive. Howitt, M. 937.10

STRONG, James, *joint author.* Cyclopædia of biblical, theological, and ecclesiastical literature. *See* MACCLINTOCK, John .... *R.R., A.2.3

STRONG and steady. Alger, H., *jr.* 935.9

STROTHER, David H. (*Porte Crayon.*) Virginia illustrated: containing A visit to the Virginia Canaan, and The adventures of Porte Crayon and his cousins. Illustrated from drawings by Porte Crayon [*pseud.*]. New York, 1871. 300 pp. L. 8° .... 531.12 and 5031.3

STRUGGLE, The, for existence. A romance. Bayer, C. R. 728.7

STRUTT, Joseph. The sports and pastimes of the people of England; from the earliest period to the present time. Edited by William Hone. Illustrated. London, 1876. xii, 530+ pp. Sm. 8° 6414.4

STUART, Charles B. Lives and works of civil and military engineers of America. New York, 1871. 343 pp. Portraits. Illustrations. 8°. 1012.6

STUART, M. B. The two Barbaras. A novel. By Grace Mortimer [*pseud.*] 532.17

STUART of Dunleath. Norton, C. E. S. 314.7

STUDENT-LIFE, The, of Germany. Howitt, W. London, 1841. 8° 5712.4

STUDENT's ancient history. *Namely:* —

— Smith, P. Ancient history of the East. London, 1871. 12° 5916.14

STUDENT's France, The. History of France. Jervis, H. W. New York, 1872 [1862]. 12° 824.13

STUDENT's manual of oriental history, The. Lenormant, F., and Chevallier, E. London, 1869, 70. Sm. 8° 5927.8

STUDENT's Scripture history. *See* SMITH, William, *editor.*

STUDENT's series, The. *Namely:* —

— Jervis, H. W. The student's France. History of France. New York, 1872 [1862]. 12° 824.13

STUDIES from life. Craik, D. (M.) 323.16

STUDIES in English; or, glimpses of the inner life of our language. Schele de Vere, M. New York, 1868. Sm. 8 .... 1533.4

STUDIES in the history of the renaissance. Pater, W. H. London, 1873. Sm. 8° 5925.2

STUDIES, stories, and memoirs. Jameson, A. (M.) Boston, 1866. 16° 1916.3

STUDIO, The. Abbott, J. Harper's story books 936.1.4

Shelf. No.

STURTEVANT, Edward Lewis and Joseph N. The dairy cow. A monograph on the Ayrshire breed of cattle. With an appendix on Ayrshire, Jersey, and Dutch milks. Boston, 1875. 252 pp. Illustrated. 12° 1522.12

STUYVESANT, Peter, the last Dutch governor of New Amsterdam. Abbott, J. S. C. New York, 1873. 12° 1014.14

STUYVESANT. Abbott, J. 914.12

SUBJECTION, The, of women. Mill, J. S. New York, 1874. 8° 1733.2

SUBLIME and beautiful, Inquiry into the origin of our ideas of the. Burke, E. Works. Boston, 1826. 8° 5634.1.1

— *Same.* Boston, 1871. Sm. 8° 5635.1.1

SUBLIME, The, in nature. Tugnot de Lanoye, F. New York, 1872. 16° 1714.21

SUBSTANCE and shadow. James, H. Boston, 1863. 8°. 5834.1

SUCCESS and its conditions. [Essays.] Whipple, E. P. Boston, 1871. 16° 1936.4

SUE, Eugène, *pseud.* *See* SUE, Marie Joseph.

SUE, Marie Joseph, *called* Eugène. Der Admiral Levacher. Achilles fillias. Deutsch von Anton Langer. Pest, 1852. 200 [198] pp. 16° 2027.7

— Les mystères de Paris. Nouvelle édition, conformée à l'édition in-8° corrigée par l'auteur en 1851. Paris, 1869. 4 v. 18° 2016.4

— The wandering Jew. London [1845]. 2 v. in 1. Sm. 8° 725.35

SUETONIUS TRANQUILLUS, Caius. Lives of the twelve Cæsars; added, lives of the grammarians, rhetoricians, and poets. The translation of Alexander Thomson. Revised and corrected by T. Forester. London, 1872. vii, 557+ pp. [Bohn's Classical library.] Sm. 8° 6117.8

SUFFOLK county, *Mass.* Atlas. Vol. II. Roxbury. Philadelphia, 1873. 77 pp. F° .... *R.R. Desk

SUFFOLK surnames. Bowditch, N. I. Boston, 1857. 8°. 5022.11

— *Same.* Boston, 1858. 8° 5022.17

SUICIDE, Reflections on. Staël-Holstein, A. L. G. N., *baronne* de. (*In* The Alexandrian) 1910.4.2

SULLY, Maximilian de Béthune, *duc* de. Memoirs. Translated from the French [by C. Lennox]. New edition, with an historical introduction, attributed to Sir Walter Scott. London, 1856. 4 v. Portraits. Sm. 8° 5526.8

SUMMER, A, in Leslie Goldthwaite's life. Whitney, A. D. T. 735.12

SUMMER cruise, A, on the coast of New England. Carter, R. Boston [*cop.* 1864]. 12° 415.15

SUMMER drift-wood for the winter fire. Porter, R... 718.2

SUMMER parish, A: Sabbath discourses and service of prayer, at the "Twin mountain house." Beecher, H. W. New York, 1875. 8° 6325.8

SUMMER vacation, A. Four sermons. Hale, E. E. Boston, 1874. 12° 6328.6

SUMNER, Charles. Works. Vol. I–XI. Boston, 1870–75. 11 v. Portrait. 8° 5234.1

— Prophetic voices concerning America. A monograph. Boston, 1874. 176+ pp. Portrait. 16°. 833.1

— Memorial addresses on his life and character. *See* UNITED STATES. *Miscellaneous documents* 5020.8

SUMNER, Increase, Memoir of. Sumner, W. H. Boston, 1854. 8° 5022.15

SUMNER, William Hyslop. Memoir of Increase Sumner. With a genealogy of the Sumner family. Boston, 1854. 70 pp. Portrait. 8° 5022.15

SUN, The. Guillemin, A. The sun. New York, 1871. 12° 1714.10

— Proctor, R. A. Recent solar researches. (*In* Eston, D. Half-hour recreations in popular science) .. 6813.7

— – The sun. London, 1872. Sm. 8° 6814.1

SUNBEAM stories. Mackarness, M. A. 313.18

SUNDAY. *See* SABBATH.

SUNDAY echoes in weekday hours. Brock, *Mrs.* C. London, 1868. Sm. 8° 911.2

SUNDAY library. 10 v. *Namely:* —

— Church, R. W. Saint Anselm 5937.3

— Farrar, F. W. Seekers after God 5937.7

— Guizot, F. (P. G.) Great Christians of France: Saint Louis and Calvin 5937.6

Shelf. No.

SUNDAY library, *continued.*
— Keary, A. The nations around................5937.12
— Kingsley, C. The hermits.................... 5937.4
— MacDonald, G. England's antiphon........... 5937.8
— Maclear, G. F. Apostles of mediæval Europe.. 5937.5
— Martin, F. Angelique Arnauld, abbess of Port Royal..5937.11
— Oliphant, M. (O. W.) Francis of Assisi........5937.10
— Yonge, C. M. The pupils of St. John the divine. 5937.9
SUNDAY pleasure book, The. Containing gospel and other stories told to children. Illustrated. London [1875]. xiii, 240+ pp. Sm. 4°...... 910.5
SUNDAY school liturgy, The. Boston, 1856. x, 260 pp. 12°.................................... 5818.6
SUNDERLAND, La Roy. Pathetism; with practical instructions. New York, 1843. xvi, 247 pp. 12°. 1536.9
SUNNY hour stories. *See* EYSTER, Nellie.
SUNNY memories of foreign lands. Stowe, H. (E.) B. Boston, 1854. 2 v. 12°.................... 426.6
SUNNY shores; or, Young America in Italy and Austria. Adams, W. T. Boston, 1875. 16°.. 925.12
SUNNYBANK. A novel. Terhune, M. V........... 722.25
SUNSHINE; or, Kate Vinton. MacKeever, H. B. ...1117.29
SUNSHINE and shadow. Newby, C. J............. 710.3
SUPERNATURAL religion; an inquiry into the reality of divine revelation. 3d edition. London, 1874. 2 v. 8°....................................5812.14
SURENNE, Gabrielle, *joint author.* French and English [and English and French] pronouncing dictionary. *See* SPIERS, Alexandre.....*R.R., D.3.12
SURETTE, Louis A. By-laws [etc.] of Corinthian lodge, of ancient, free and accepted masons, of Concord, Mass. Added an historical sketch of masonry. Concord, 1859. 191 pp. Portraits. 12°. 817.13
SURGEON'S, The, daughter. Scott, *Sir* W......... 533.5
SURGERY. Bell, B. A system of. Edinburgh, 1801. 7 v. 12°.................................... 6023.6
— Braithwaite, W. and J. Retrospect of practical medicine and surgery. Part 1-4, 6-54, 63-66. New York, 1843-73. 33 v. 8°.............. 6010.2
— Dupuytren, G., *baron.* Lesions of the vascular system, diseases of the rectum, and other surgical complaints. London, 1854. 8°...........6013.17
— Erichson, J. The science and art of. Philadelphia, 1854. 8°.............................6022.15
— Green, H. Surgical treatment of polypi of the larynx, and œdema of the glottis. New York, 1852. 8°...................................6023.12
— Heister, L. General system of. London, 1748. 4°. 6010.1
— Howship, J. Practical remarks on the discrimination and appearances of surgical disease. London, 1840. 8°.......................... 6023.8
— Liston, R. Elements of. Philadelphia, 1837. L. 12°....................................6023.11
— Miller, J. The practice of. Philadelphia, 1853. 8°.6022.16
— Ottley, D. Observations on surgical diseases of the head and neck. London, 1848. 8°....... 6013.9
— Pearson, J. Principles of. Boston, 1832. 8°. 6011.8

See also Orthopedy, Pathology.

SUSAN Fielding. Edwards, A.................... 710.37
SUSPIRIA de profundis. De Quincey, T. Boston, 1872. 16°.................................. 1825.5
SUTHERLANDS, The. Harris, M.................. 724.14
SVETCHINE, Sophie Soymonof. *See* SWETCHINE, Sophie Soymonof.
SWALLOW barn. Kennedy, J. P.................. 725.13
SWANS, The, of Lir. Griffin, G. (*In* Johnson, (E.) R. Little classics)............................529.4.1
SWAYNE, George C. Herodotus [outlined and explained]. Edinburgh, 1870. 180+ pp. 16°. [Ancient classics for English readers]......... 6116.4
SWEAT, Margaret Jane Mussey. The novels of George Sand. Boston, 1870. 23 pp. Sm. 8°. 526.23
SWEDEN. Adams, W. T. Up the Baltic; or, Young America in. Boston, 1873. 16°............. 925.8
— Brace, C. L. The Norse-folk; or, a visit to the homes of. New York, 1857. 12°........... 426.21
— Brown, J. The Northern courts; containing memoirs of the sovereigns of, since 1766. London, 1818. 2 v. 8°............................. 5713.1

Shelf. No.

SWEDEN, *continued.*
— Murray, J. Handbook for Sweden. London, 1871. 12°................................ 5716.3
— Shairp, T. Up in the North. London, 1872. Sm. 8°...................................... 5915.4
— Taylor, (J.) B. Northern travel: summer and winter pictures of. New York, 1858. 12°.... 426.3
— Whitelocke, B. A journal of the Swedish embassy in 1653 and 1654. London, 1855. 2 v. 8°. 822.3
SWEDENBORG, *or* SVEDENBORG, *originally* Swedberg, *or* Svedberg, Emmanuel. Miscellaneous theological works. New York, 1873. 526+ pp. 8°. 6323.5
— Angelic wisdom concerning the divine love and wisdom. Translated from the Latin. From the last London edition. New York, 1872. xii, 199 pp. 8°...................................... 6323.9
— Angelic wisdom concerning the divine providence. Translated from the Latin. From the last London edition. New York, 1873. xiii, 308 pp. 8°.6323.10
— The Apocalypse revealed, wherein are disclosed the arcana there foretold which have heretofore remained concealed. New edition. New York, 1873. 2 v. 8°.......................... 6323.3
— Arcana cœlestia. The heavenly arcana contained in the Holy Scriptures unfolded. Translated from the Latin. New York, 1870-73. 10 v. 8°. 6323.2
— Concerning heaven and its wonders, and hell. Boston, 1851. 361 pp. Portrait. 12°.......5815.11
— Conjugial love and its chaste delights; also, adulterous love and its sinful pleasures. New York, 1871. 472 pp. 8°.......................... 6323.4
— Doctrines of the New Jerusalem. Translated from the Latin. New York, 1873. 7 v. in 1. 12°. 5814.20

Contents. — The four leading doctrines; The New Jerusalem and its heavenly doctrine; Intercourse between the soul and the body; Charity.

— The earths in our solar system, which are called planets, and the earths in the starry heavens; with an account of their inhabitants, and also of the spirits and angels there; from what has been seen and heard. Boston, 1851. 94 pp. 8°. 6831.1
— The four leading doctrines of the New church. New York, 1873. 4 v. in 1. 8°............. 6323.8

Contents. — Concerning the Lord. — Respecting the Sacred Scripture. — The doctrine of faith. — The doctrine of life.

— Heaven and its wonders, the world of spirits, and hell: from things heard and seen. Translated from the Latin. By Samuel Noble. New York, 1872. xxxvi, 375 pp. 8°.................. 6323.6
— *Same.* Philadelphia, 1873. 453 pp. 8°......5812.10
— The true Christian religion, containing the entire theology of the New church. From the Latin. Translated by R. N. Foster. Philadelphia, 1869. 2 v. Portrait. 8°.................. 5812.9
— The true Christian religion, containing the universal theology of the New church. Translated from the Latin. New York, 1871. xviii, 982+ pp. 8°...................................... 632.37

Note. — See Emerson's "Representative men" [1916.6; 1934.6.2] and Alger's "Future life" [5831.3]. James's "Substance and shadow" [5834.1] treats Swedenborg as a philosopher, not as a seer. See also De Quincey's "Literary reminiscences" [1226.1]; Atlantic monthly, June, 1869; Fraser's magazine, vol. 55; and Thomas's Dictionary.

SWEET and twenty. Collins, M.................. 331.21
SWEET counsel. Keddie, *Miss* —. Boston, 1866. 16°. 736.11
SWEET nineteen. Robinson, F. W................ 731.40
SWEETSER, Charles Humphreys. Tourists' and invalids' guide to the Northwest. New York, 1868. 64+ pp. Illustrated. Folded map. 8°..... 432.3
SWEETSER, Moses Foster. Europe for $2 a day. Notes for the assistance of tourists of moderate means, with some reminiscences of travel. Boston, 1875. 128 pp. Sq. 16°................ 428.8
— The White mountains: a handbook for travellers. A guide to the White mountains of New Hampshire; the lakes and mountains of western Maine; also, Lake Winnepesaukee, and the upper Connecticut valley. With maps and panoramas. Boston, 1876. xiv, 436+ pp. 16°.......... 418.9
SWEETSER, William. Treatise on digestion. Boston, 1837. 359 pp. 16°.......................... 1525.5

Shelf. No.

SWETCHINE, *or* SVETCHINE, Sophia Soymonof. Writings. Edited by Count de Falloux. Translated by H. W. Preston. Boston, 1869. viii, 255 pp. 12° 5537.8

— Life and letters of. Falloux, F. A. P., *vicomte* de. Boston, 1868. 16° 1226.2

SWETT, John Appleton. A treatise on the diseases of the chest. New York, 1852. 585+ pp. Plates. 8° 6021.14

SWIFT, Jonathan. Works. With memoir, by T. Roscoe; portrait and autograph. London, 1856. 2 v. 8° 5611.2

Contents. — Vol. I. Life; Travels of Lemuel Gulliver; Tale of a tub; The battle of the books; Miscellaneous. II. The Drapier's letters; Miscellaneous; Miscellanies in prose and verse by Swift and Sheridan.

— Gulliver's travels. With a sketch of his life. Leipzig, 1844. x, 341 pp. Sq. 16° 315.8

— Forster, J. Life of. Vol. I. New York, 1876. 8°. 5333.6

— Lecky, W. E. H. Leaders of public opinion in Ireland. New York, 1872. 12° 1025.9

Note. — The most considerable and latest life of Swift is that by John Forster, but the author did not live to publish more than the first volume, ending 1711.

Dr. Johnson showed in his "Lives of the English poets" [1238.20] his evident dislike for his subject. Scott found the popular view of Swift's character very derogatory, when he undertook to palliate his weaknesses, but he was taken to task for it by Jeffrey, in his Essays [5610.8], and this opposition of view is commented on in Lockhart's "Memoirs of Scott" [1020.1]. Thackeray's lectures on the Humourists [1238.8] and his delineation in "Henry Esmond" [325.10; 1820.1] are very unfavorable. See the lives of Dryden, Addison, Pope, etc., and the references in Allibone, beside the accounts or estimates by Roscoe [5611.2]; Lecky, in his "Leaders of public opinion" [1025.9]; Taine, in his "English literature" [5613.1]; the account in Howitt's "Homes and haunts" [1225.5]; Jameson's "Loves of the poets" [5618.2] for Stella and Vanessa, and in the same connection Lawrence's "Days of Queen Anne," in Harper's monthly, vol. 44. Forster calls the "Journal to Stella" the most important of all illustrations of Swift's life, and for the bibliography of it, see Forster's "Life of Swift" [5333.6.1, p. 405–409]. See also Temple bar, Feb., 1876; Forsyth's "Novelists" [6136.1], and the references in Allibone, vol. 2.

SWIMMING. Forrest, G. Handbook of. London, 1863. 16° 1519.1

— Leahy, J. The art of swimming in the Eton style. London, 1875. Sm. 8° 6417.3

— Steedman, C. A manual of. London, 1873. Sm. 8° 6418.1

SWINBOURNE, Alfred (James). Picture logic; or, the grave made gay. An attempt to popularize the science of reasoning by the combination of humorous pictures. With illustrations. London, 1875. xii, 166 pp. Sm. 8° 5616.19

SWINDELL, John G. Wells and pumps: a treatise on well-digging and boring, and the various ways of raising water. With illustrations. New edition, revised and enlarged, by G. R. Burnell. London, N. D. viii, 112 pp. 12° 1715.14

"SWINGIN round the cirkle." Locke, D. R. Boston, 1868. Sm. 8° 536.14

SWINTON, William. The twelve decisive battles of the war: a history of the Eastern and Western campaigns, in relation to the actions that decided their issue. New York, 1873 [*cop.* 1867]. 520 pp. Maps. Plans. Portraits. 8° 812.13

SWISS family Robinson, The. Wyss, J. R., and Montolieu, J. I. P. de Bottens, *baronne* de. Boston. 733.8

— *Same.* Philadelphia 735.6

SWITCH off. Adams, W. T. 925.20

SWITZERLAND. Abbott, J. Rollo in Switzerland... 917.23

— Adams, W. T. Palace and cottage; or, Young America in. Boston, 1873. 16° 925.10

— Andersen, H. C. Pictures of travel in. New York, 1871. Sm. 8° 426.17

— Baedeker, C. Handbook for travellers. Coblenz, 1872. 16° 5718.4

— Forbes, *Sir* J. A physician's holiday; or, a month in. London, 1849. 12° 226.2

— Goethe, J. W. von. Letters from Switzerland. London, 1872. Sm. 8° 1025.5.2

— Mendelssohn-Bartholdy, F. Letters from Switzerland. Boston, N. D. 12° 1227.1

— Murray, J. Handbook for Switzerland. London, 1846. 12° 227.3

— – Knapsack guide for Switzerland. London, 1867. 12° 5717.3

Shelf. No.

SWITZERLAND, *continued.*

— Propiac, C. J. F. G. de. Beautés de l'histoire de la Suisse. Paris, 1817. 12° 5728.6

— Zschokke, (J.) H. (D.) History of. New York, 1860. 12° 5914.5

See also Alps.

Note. — Zschokke's is the most useful manual for the general reader, and the English translation is brought down to 1848. For primeval life in Switzerland, see Edinburgh review, Jan., 1874. Coxe's "House of Austria" [5715.1], which covers 1218–1792, and Kirk's "Charles the bold" [5511.1], covering the Swiss war of 1477, wherein Scott places the scenes of his "Anne of Geierstein" [324.1; 533.1]. can be read collaterally. For the events in which Tell was so prominent an actor, see H. J. Warner's article on the "Men of Schwyz," in the Atlantic monthly, March, 1861, and the note under Tell.

For the reformation period, see Reformation, *note*, and the lives of Calvin, Zwingli, etc. Also chap. v of Fisher's "Reformation" [5813.7] and references there.

Alison's "History of Europe" [5913.6], well covers the revolutionary period, 1797–1803.

See Smyth's 8th lecture in his "Modern history" [5012.10; 5925.7].

Travels, description, manners, etc.

For additional descriptive works, see Dixon's "Switzers" [5931.3]; Mrs. Stowe's "Sunny memories" [426.6]; and a chapter in Prime's "Alhambra and Kremlin" [5914.6].

Alpine description. See the enumeration of titles under the heading of Alps in this and in the Bates Hall catalogues. See the illustrated papers in Harper's magazine by B. Taylor, in vol. 24; by Prime, in vol. 14; by Lyman Abbott, on the "Monarch of mountains," Mont Blanc, in vol. 42; and a paper on "Lake Geneva" in vol. 48. The 4th volume of Ruskin's "Modern painters" [6236.18] can be usefully read in this connection, as well as the third canto of Byron's "Childe Harold" [1614.13.2]

Alpine exploration. Stephen, in his "Playground of Europe," 1871 [5935.8], which is made up of articles originally appearing in Fraser's magazine, the Alpine journal and the Cornhill, traces historically the growth of the modern appreciation of mountain scenery, and the habit of "mountaineering," which he thinks began about 1760, with the first efforts of Saussure, while the ascents of Auldjo, Brockedon, Forbes, and others, had ostensibly at least the object of science, up to about 1851, when Albert Smith set the fashion of Alpine climbing as a recreation, which has since been followed with a spirit of rivalry to the accomplishments, which a multitude of books have recorded. Wills's "Wanderings among the high Alps," 1856, was among the most important of the early books. before the formation of the English Alpine club in 1857 (since followed, in 1862, by an Austrian, and in 1863 by an Italian and by a Swiss club), under whose auspices a journal was published from March, 1863, through 1866, and two series of "Peaks, passes and glaciers," by members of the club [1st series, edited by Ball, 5717.1]. Since then the most important English contributions have been Tyndall's Glaciers, 1860, which has both narrative and scientific sections, while his occasional papers for the next ten years have been collected in his "Hours of exercise in the Alps" [223.1]. Whymper's beautiful "Scrambles" [5932.3] is of interest. The Bates Hall catalogues should be consulted further on this subject.

Guide books. For general use, both Murray [227.3 and 5717.3] and Baedeker [5718.2 and 4] are excellent; but the climber and student of science will prize Ball's "Alpine guide" [5936.6] accompanied by a general introduction, which enumerates the comprehensive and geological authorities, while the special local authorities are given in connection with each part.

SWITZERS, The. Dixon, W. H. London, 1872. 8°. 5931.3

SWORD and gown. Lawrence, G. A. 315.23

SWORDS, Memoir on. Marey-Monge, G. S. London, 1860. 12° 1715.12

SYBARIS and other homes. Hale, E. E. 524.23

SYBEL, Heinrich (Carl Ludolf) von. History of the French revolution. Translated from the 3d edition of the original German work, by W. C. Perry. London, 1867, 69. 4 v. 8° 5514.2

— The history and literature of the crusades. From the German. Edited by Lady Duff Gordon. London, 1861. viii, 356+ pp. 8° 5924.11

SYBIL. Disraeli, B. 324.24

SYBIL Lennard. Grey, *Mrs.* 530.2

SYBIL's second love. Kavanagh, J. 323.6

SYDENHAM, Thomas. Opera omnia. Edidit G. A. Greenhill. Editio altera. Londini, 1846. xxx, 667+ pp. 8° 6013.5

— Works. Translated from the Latin edition of Dr. Greenhill, with a life of the author by R. G. Latham. London, 1848, 50. 2 v. 8° 6013.12

— Works, on acute and chronic diseases; with their histories and modes of cure. With notes, by B. Rush. Philadelphia, 1809. xl, 473+ pp. 8°. 6014.1

SYDENHAM society, *London.* Publications. *Namely:* —.

— Abú Becr Mohammed Ibn Zacaríyá Ar-rází. Treatise on small-pox and measles 6013.10

— Aretæus, the Cappadocian. Extant works. [Greek and English] 6013.20

— Churchill, F. Essays on the puerperal fever and other diseases peculiar to women 6013.13

Shelf. No.

SYDENHAM society, *London*. Publications, *continued*.
— Dupuytren, G., *baron*. Injuries and diseases of bones 6013.7
— – Lesions of the vascular system, diseases of the rectum, and other surgical complaints 6013.17
— Feuchtersleben, E., *Freiherr* von. Principles of medical psychology 6013.8
— Hecker, J. F. C. Epidemics of the middle ages. 6013.4
— Louis, P. C. A. Researches on phthisis 6013.6
— Oesterlen, F. Medical logic 6013.19
— Ottley, D. Observations on surgical diseases of the head and neck 6013.9
— Romberg, M. H. Manual of the nervous diseases of man 6013.16
— Sydenham, T. Opera omnia 6013.5
— – Works 6013.12
— Thompson, T. Annals of influenza; or, epidemic catarrhal fever in Great Britain from 1510 to 1837 .... 6013.14
— Unzer, J. A. Principles of physiology; and A dissertation on the functions of the nervous system, by G. Prochaska 6013.15
— Velpeau, A. A. L. M. Treatise on the diseases of the breast and mammary region 6013.21
— Wedl, C. Rudiments of pathological histology .. 6013.18

See also New Sydenham society.

SYDNEY, Algernon, Life and times of. Ewald, A. C. London, 1873. 2 v. 8° 5422.10
SYDNIE Adriance. Douglas, A. M. 726.16
SYKES, Arthur Ashley. The innocency of involuntary error asserted and vindicated. (*In* Sparks, J. Collection of essays and tracts in theology) . 1918.9.4
SYLVAN Holt's daughter. Parr, H. 733.12
SYLVAN year, The. Hamerton, P. G. Boston, 1876. 16° 5527.18
SYLVESTER Sound; the somnambulist. Cockton, H. 521.41
SYLVESTRES, The. Edwards, M. de B. 312.27
SYLVIA's choice. Craik, G. M. Leipzig 335.17
— *Same*. New York 710.15
SYLVIA's lovers. Gaskell, E. C. 328.20
SYMBOLISM. Brinton, D. G. The myths of the new world. New York, 1870. 8° 5924.7
SYMONDS, John Addington. Renaissance in Italy the age of the despots. London, 1875. xvi, 574 pp. 8° 5522.8
SYNONYMES, Dictionary of English. Soule, R. Boston, 1871. 16° .... *R.R., F.3.2
SYPHILIS in new-born children and infants at the breast, Treatise on. Diday, P. London, 1859. 8° 6023.3
SYRIA. Burton, R. F., and Drake, C. F. T. Unexplored Syria. London, 1872. 2 v. 8° 5933.3
— Curtis, G. W. The howadji in. New York, 1856. 12° 425.12
— Jessup, H. H. Syrian home-life. New York [1874]. 12° 5916.10
— Murray, J. Handbook for Syria. London, 1868. 2 v. 12° 5936.1
— Porter, J. L. The giant cities of Bashan; and Syria's holy places. New York, 1871. 12° 5915.7

See also Palestine, *note*.

SYRIAC documents attributed to the first three centuries. Translated by B. P. Pratten. Edinburgh, 1871. [*With* GREGORIUS *Thaumaturgus, St.*, and others. Works. Ante-Nicene Christian library.] 8° 6322.4.20

TABER, Sarah W. Early piety; or, recollections of Harriet B[ird]. 2d edition. Boston, 1857. 68 pp. Sm. 12° 5819.20
TABLE, A book about the. Jeaffreson, J. C. London, 1875. 2 v. 8° 6432.3
TABLE book, The. Hone, W. London [1871]. L. 8°. 5621.6
TABLE-TALK. Coleridge, S. T. Specimens of [his] table talk. London, 1870. 16° 5617.1
— Luther, M. Table-talk. Philadelphia, 1868. 12°. 1536.8
— Selden, J. Table-talk. London, 1860. 16° 5617.17
TABLE traits with something on them. Doran, J. W. New York, 1865. L. 12° 1532.4

Shelf. No.

TABLEAUX, The book of. Frost, S. A. New York [*cop.* 1869]. 12° 1518.1
TABOR, Eliza. The blue ribbon 732.19
— Eglantine 720.37
— Hope Meredith 711.13
— Jeanie's quiet life 711.27
— Meta's faith 711.19
— St. Olave's 711.21
TACITUS, Caius Cornelius. Works. The Oxford translation revised. With notes. London, 1871, 72. 2 v. Sm. 8° 6115.7

Contents. — Vol. I. The annals. II. The history; Germany; Agricola; Dialogue on orators.

— Germania, Agricola, et De oratoribus dialogus. Accedunt notæ Anglicæ. Cura C. K. Dillaway. Philadelphia, 1849. 180 pp. Sm. 12° 6118.6
— Tacitus [outlined and explained]. Donne, W. B. Philadelphia, 1873. 16° 6116.18

See also Rome, *history*.

TACTICS. Regulations for the order and discipline of the troops of the United States. Added, the manual exercise, and evolutions of the cavalry, etc. Steuben, F. W. A. H. F., *baron* von. New York, 1794. Sm. 12° 6928.2

See also Infantry tactics, United States.

TAILORING. Manuel théorique et pratique du tailleur. Vandael, —. Paris, 1833. 24° 6429.5
TAINE, Hippolyte Adolphe. History of English literature. Translated by H. Van Laun. With a preface prepared expressly for this translation by the author. New York, 1872. 2 v. 8° 5613.1
— – *See* SAINTE-BEUVE, C. A. English portraits. New York, 1875. 16° 1025.3
— *Same*. Abridged, and edited with chronological table, notes, and index by J. Fiske. New York, 1872. 502 pp. Sm. 8° 5614.7
— Italy. From the French by J. Durand. 4th edition, with corrections and an index. New York, 1872. 2 v. 8° 5522.2

Contents. — Vol. I. Rome and Naples. II. Florence and Venice.

— Notes on England. Translated, with an introductory chapter, by W. F. Rae. With a portrait. New York, 1874. lix, 377 pp. 8° 5435.7
— Notes on Paris. [The life and opinions of Frederic Thomas Graindorge, doctor of philosophy at the University of Jena, special partner in the house of Graindorge and co., oils and salt pork, Cincinnati, U. S. A. Collected and published by H. Taine, executor.] Translated with notes by J. A. Stevens. New York, 1875. ix, 372 pp. 12° 5533.2

Note. — The original French edition was published, Paris, 1868.

— The philosophy of art. Art in Greece. Translated by J. Durand. New York, 1872. vi, 188 pp. 12° 6217.2
— – Art in the Netherlands. Translated by J. Durand. New York, 1871. 190 pp. 12° 6217.1
— A tour through the Pyrenees. Translated by J. S. Fiske. New York, 1874. vi, 349 pp. 12°. 423.18
TAIT, Peter Guthrie, and STEWART, Balfour. The unseen universe, or physical speculations on a future state. 3d edition. London, 1875. xxiv, 211 pp. 8° 5834.6
— *joint author*. Life and letters of J. D. Forbes. *See* SHAIRP, John Campbell 5332.4
TAKE a peep. Cobden, P. 934.35
TAKE care of little Charley: a farce. Brougham, J. New York, N. D. 12° 1635.5
TAKEN at the flood. Braddon, M. E. Leipzig 329.25
— *Same*. New York 731.34
TALBOT, Frederick. Through fire and water 732.22
TALBOT Harland. A tale of the days of Charles II. Ainsworth, W. H. 322.10
TALCOTT, H. D., *formerly Mrs. Goodwin*. The fortunes of Miss Follen 722.23
TALE of a tub. Swift, J. Works 5611.2.1

Shelf. No.

TALE, A, of two cities. [Paris and London,— French revolution.] Dickens, C. (J. H.) Boston. 1824.14
— *Same.* Leipzig 338.20
TALES for Christmas eve. Broughton, R. 319.8
TALES for the marines. Wise, H. A. 716.18
TALES for travellers. *See* HALE, Edward Everett, and others.
TALES from Shakspeare. Lamb, C. and M. London [1866]. 16° 935.24

Note.— These tales give the stories of some of Shakespeare's principal plays in a manner suited to young readers.

TALES of a grandfather; being stories taken from Scottish history. Scott, *Sir* W. 2 v. 939.5
TALES of a traveller. Irving, W. London, 1850. 16°. 715.7
— *Same.* Philadelphia, 1872. Sm. 8° 1815.9
TALES of a wayside inn. Longfellow, H. W. Boston, 1863. 12° 1612.2

Note.— Narratives in verse, supposed to be told by travellers at the Red Horse inn in Sudbury, Mass.

TALES of adventure. Ballantyne, R. M. 933.25
TALES of adventure on the coast. Ballantyne, R. M. 1115.4
TALES of the Argonauts. [California pioneers.] Harte, (F.) B. 728.13
TALES of the borders. Wilson, J. M., and others. New York, 1851. 5 v. in 3. 8° 5631.5
TALES of the jury room. Griffin, G. 517.11
TALFOURD, *Sir* Thomas Noon. Critical and miscellaneous writings. 3d American edition. New York, 1871. 176 pp. Portrait. 8° 1931.1
TALISMAN, The. Scott, *Sir* W. 523.30
TALLEYRAND-PÉRIGORD, Charles Maurice de. *See* BULWER, *Sir* H. L. (E.) Historical characters. Leipzig, 1868. Sq. 16° 1238.14
TALMUD, The. Deutsch, E. (O. M.) Literary remains. New York, 1874. 8° 5733.7
TALVI, *pseud.* *See* ROBINSON, Therese Albertine Louise von Jakob.
TANGLED skein, A. Fonblanque, A., *jr.* 720.8
TAPESTRIED chamber, The. Scott, *Sir* W. 523.20
TAPPAN, Arthur. *See* PAGE, H. A. Noble workers. London, 1875. Sm. 8° 5936.3
TAPPAN, David. Lectures on Jewish antiquities. Boston, 1807. 364+ pp. 8° 1912.7
— Sermons on important subjects. Prefixed a biographical sketch of the author; and a sermon preached at his funeral by Dr. Holmes. Cambridge, 1807. 334 pp. 8° 5812.2
TARA: a Mahratta tale. Taylor, M. 316.6
TARBOX, Increase Niles. Life of Israel Putnam ("Old Put"), major-general in the continental army. With map and illustrations. Boston, 1876. 389 pp. Portrait. 8° 1012.7
— Tyre and Alexandria: the chief commercial cities of Scripture times. Boston [*cop.* 1865]. 362 pp. Illustrated. 16° 426.5
TARGUMS, On the. Deutsch, E. (O. M.) Literary remains. New York, 1874. 8° 5733.7
TARTARY, Travels in, 1844–6. Huc, É. R. London [1852]. 2 v. 16° 5935.12
TARTUFFE, Le: comédie. Molière, J. B. P. Œuvres. Paris, 1869. 12° 5537.2.2
TASSO, Torquato. Jerusalem delivered. Translated into English Spenserian verse, with a life of the author, by J. H. Wiffin. 3d American from the last English edition. New York, 1871. 624 pp. Portrait. Illustrated. 12° 5537.1
TASTE. Inquiry into the origin of our ideas of the sublime and beautiful. Burke, E. Works. Boston, 1826. 8° 5634.1.1
— *Same.* Boston, 1871. Sm. 8° 5635.1.1
TATE, Ralph. Rudimentary treatise on geology. [Partly based on Major-Gen. Portlock's Rudiments of geology.] With illustrations and an index. London, 1871. 2 v. 12° 1715.7

Contents.— Vol. I. Physical geology. II. Historical geology.

TATIANUS, and OTHERS. The writings of Tatian and Theophilus; and The Clementine recognitions. Translated by B. P. Pratten, Marcus Dods, and Thomas Smith. Edinburgh, 1867. 485 pp. [Ante-Nicene Christian library.] 8° 6322.4.3

TATTERED Tom. Alger, H., *jr.* 934.9
TATTERED Tom series. *See* ALGER, Horatio, *jr.*
TAUCHNITZ, Christian Bernhard, *baron* von. Five centuries of the English language and literature. Leipzig, 1860. 429 pp. Sq. 16° 1918.1
TAUTPHOEUS, Jemima Montgomery, *Baronin.* At odds 317.22
— Cyrilla 317.20
— The initials 317.19
— Quits 317.21

Note.— These novels contain vivid descriptions of German scenery and afford good pictures of German habits and life.

TAVERN anecdotes and sayings. Hindley, C. London, 1875. Sm. 8° 5616.18
TAXATION. The national tax law, as amended. Hall, E. H. New York, 1863. 12° 6927.4
TAXIDERMY. Field ornithology. Comprising a manual of instruction for procuring, preparing, and preserving birds. Coues, E. Salem, 1874. 8° 6613.12
TAYLOR, Alfred Swaine. Manual of medical jurisprudence. 7th American edition, revised and edited by John J. Reese. With illustrations. Philadelphia, 1873. 879 pp. 8° 6021.18
TAYLOR, Benjamin F. Three November days. (*In* Johnson, (E.) R. Little classics) 529.4.11
TAYLOR, Edward T. [*Father Taylor, of Boston*], Incidents and anecdotes of. Haven, G., and Russell, T. Boston, 1873. 12° 1216.11
TAYLOR, George H. An exposition of the Swedish movement-cure. New York, 1860. 396 pp. 12°. 6036.12
TAYLOR, Isaac. Etruscan researches. London, 1874. 388+ pp. 1 plate. 8° 6124.2
TAYLOR, J. E. Geological stories: a series of autobiographies in chronological order. London, 1873. xviii, 301 pp. Illustrated. 16° 6637.2
— Half-hours in the green lanes; a book for a country stroll. London, 1873. viii, 328 pp. Illustrated. 16° 6619.2

Note.— Describes objects in natural history to be seen in an ordinary country walk.

TAYLOR, (James) Bayard. At home and abroad: a sketch-book of life, scenery, and men. Household edition. New York, 1870, 72. 2 v. Illustrated. 12° 234.1
— By-ways of Europe. Household edition. New York, 1872. 470 pp. Illustrated. Sm. 8° ... 224.4
— Cyclopædia of modern travel. Illustrated. Maps. Cincinnati, 1869. 956 pp. Portraits. 8° 5930.3
— Egypt and Iceland in 1874. New York, 1874. 282 pp. 16° 436.2
— Eldorado; or, adventures in the path of empire. 18th edition. New York, 1864. xiv, 444 pp. 12°. 425.6
— Hannah Thurston 716.35
— Home pastorals, ballads and lyrics. Boston, 1875. viii, 214 pp. 12° 1617.13
— Illustrated library of travel, exploration, and adventure. Japan, in our day. New York, 1872. xvi, 280 pp. Illustrated. Map. Sm. 8° 423.7
— - The lake regions of Central Africa. With map and illustrations. New York, 1873. 397+ pp. 12° 224.9
— - Travels in Arabia. New York, 1872. iv, 325+ pp. Illustrated. Map. 12° 224.6
— - Travels in South Africa. New York, 1872. 336+ pp. Map and illustrations. Portrait. Sm. 8° 224.1
— John Godfrey's fortunes 716.36
— Joseph and his friend 730.2
— Journey to Central Africa; or, life and landscapes from Egypt to the negro kingdoms of the White Nile. With map and illustrations. 10th edition. New York, 1857. 522+ pp. 12° 425.8
— The lands of the Saracen; or, pictures of Palestine, Asia Minor, Sicily, and Spain. New York, 1857. 451 pp. 1 plate. Map. 12° 424.13
— The masque of the gods. [Poem.] Boston, 1872. 47+ pp. 16° 1616.7
— Northern travel: summer and winter pictures of Sweden, Denmark and Lapland. New York, 1858. 436+ pp. 12° 426.3

Shelf. No.

TAYLOR, (James) Bayard, *continued.*
— Travels in Greece and Russia; with an excursion to Crete. Household edition. New York, 1872. vii, 426 pp. Illustrated. 12° 224.3
— Views a-foot; or, Europe seen with knapsack and staff. 20th edition, revised. New York, 1856. 506 pp. 12° 425.22
— Visit to India, China, and Japan, in 1853. 16th edition. New York, 1864. 530+ pp. 1 plate. 12° 425.7
TAYLOR, James W. Report on the mineral resources east of the Rocky mountains. *See* UNITED STATES. *Department of the treasury* 6631.6
TAYLOR, Jeremy. The rule and exercises of holy dying. [Boston, 1864.] xxvii, 373 pp. 16°. 5818.4
— The rule and exercises of holy living. [Boston, 1864.] xix, 451 pp. 16° 5818.3
— Theological essays. (*In* Sparks, J. Collection of essays and tracts in theology) 1918.9.6
TAYLOR, John, *D. D., of Norwich, b.* 1694, *d.* 1761. The Scripture doctrine of atonement examined. Boston, 1809. 298 pp. 12°................ 6328.1
TAYLOR, John, *an English writer, d.* 1832. Personal reminiscences. (*In* Stoddard, R. H. Bric-à-brac series)........................... 1828.8
TAYLOR, Joseph. A fast life on the modern highway; being a glance into the railroad world from a new point of view. With illustrations. New York, 1874. 220 pp. 12° 735.35
TAYLOR, Meadows. Tara: a Mahratta tale........ 316.6
TAYLOR, Owen M., *editor.* History of Annapolis, Md. With a history and description of the United States naval academy. Baltimore, 1872. 54 pp. 8° 813.9
TAYLOR, Tom. Victims: an original comedy. New York, N. D. 44 pp. 12°.................... 1635.4
— *joint author.* Life and times of Sir Joshua Reynolds. *See* LESLIE, Charles Robert.......... 5332.6
TEACHER'S, The, assistant. Northend, C. Boston, 1865. 12°.............................. 1533.3
TECHNICAL education. Stetson, C. B. Boston, 1874. 12° 5837.2
TECHNOLOGY. *See* CHEMICAL technology.
TELEGRAPH. Bond, R. Handbook of the. London, 1870. 12°..................................... 1715.4
— Culley, R. S. A handbook of practical telegraphy. London, 1871. 8°................. 6813.2
— Douglas, J. C. A manual of telegraph construction: the mechanical elements of electric telegraph engineering. London, 1875. Sm. 8° ... 6826.5
— Morse, S. F. B. Paris exposition, 1867. Reports of the United States commissioners. Examination of the telegraphic apparatus and the processes in telegraphy. Washington, 1869. 8°. 6822.3
— Pope, F. L. The modern practice of the electric telegraph. New York, 1873. 8° 6825.1
— Preece, W. H., and Sivewright, J. Telegraphy. London, 1876. Sm. 8° 6820.6
— Prescott, G. B. History, theory, and practice of the electric telegraph. Boston, 1871. Sm. 8°. 1527.5
— Sabine, R. History and progress of the electric telegraph. New York, 1869. 12° 6826.3
— *Same.* London, 1872. 12° 1716.39
— Villefranche, J. M. La télégraphie française. Paris, 1870. 18° 6817.3
— Walker, C. V. Nouveau manuel complet de la télégraphie électrique. Paris, 1851. 24°..... 6829.1
TELEMACHUS. Fénelon, F. (de S. de La Mothe). Adventures of. New York, 1872. 12° 1534.8
— – Aventures de Télémaque. Paris, 1853. 12°. 2016.6
— – *Same.* Paris, 1873. 12° 5526.10
TELESCOPE, Half-hours with the. Proctor, R. A. New York [London], 1873. 16°............. 1713.1
TELFOURD, Thomas, Life of. Smiles, S. Lives of the engineers. London, 1861. 8°...............5421.4.2
TELL, Wilhelm. Guillaume Tell, au la Suisse libre. Florian, J. P. C. de. Boston, 1849. Sm. 12°.. 2019.2

Note. — The main points of the popular story of Tell are derived from the old chroniclers, Russ and Etterling (15th century) repeated by Tschudi (16th century); but within the same century it was first questioned as mythical, though not generally disputed till Freudenberger, 1760, traced its resemblance to a story told by Saxo Grammaticus as connected with Danish

TELL, Wilhelm, *continued.*

legendry. During the same century the legend was defended by Balthazar (1760), Zurlauben (1767), and others. Haller, Grimm, Kopp, and others have pronounced Tell mythical. Numerous books have since been written in a critical spirit, more or less tending to confirm the doubt. Writers like Lamartine [1025.10.3], in whom sentiment prevails, usually accept the truth of the story, which has its strongest ground in the early instituting of a festival and the building of a chapel in Tell's honor. For more recent discussions, see H. J. Warner's "Men of Schwyz," in Atlantic monthly, March, 1861, where the evidences are balanced; Baring-Gould's "Myths of the middle ages" [716.2], where Tell is pronounced fabulous. Also see Fiske's "Myths and myth-makers" [5924.1]; and the paper in Harper's magazine, vol. 14.

See Child's "English and Scottish ballads" [5628.5, under "Wyllyam of Cloudeslé"] for the legend in England and the North.

Beside Florian's tale, see the drama by Schiller [5735:2].

TELL me a story. Graham, E. 1117.28
TEMPERANCE. Channing, W. E. Address on. Boston, 1837. 12° 5834.5
— *Same.* (*In his* Works.) Boston, 1848. 12°...1525.1.2
— Edwards, J. The temperance manual. New York [1847]. 16°.......................... 1919.2
— Hargreaves, W. Our wasted resources; the missing link in the temperance reform. New York, 1876. 12° 5835.8
— Permanent documents of the American temperance society. Boston, 1835. 12° 5834.2
— The ramrod broken; or, the Bible, history, and common sense in favor of the moderate use of good spirituous liquors. Boston, 1859. 12° ... 1915.9
— Smith, J. The temperance reformation and its claims upon the Christian church. London, 1875. 8°................................ 1912.8

See also Massachusetts temperance society.

TEMPERANCE drama, The. Baker, G. M. Boston, 1874. 16°.................................. 1636.5
TEMPEST and sunshine. Holmes, M. J. 534.8
TEMPEST-TOSSED. Tilton, T......................... 724.2
TEMPLE, Amelia, *viscountess Palmerston. See* HAYWARD, A. Biographical and critical essays. London, 1873. 8°.........................5833.3.2
TEMPLE, Charlotte. *See* STANLEY, Charlotte.
TEMPLE, Daniel. Life and letters. By his son Daniel H. Temple. With an introductory notice by R. S. Storrs. Boston, 1855. xii, 492 pp. Portrait. 12° 6325.2
TEMPLE, Frederick. The education of the world. (*In* Essays and reviews) 1538.3
— *Same.* (*In* Hedge, F. H. Recent inquiries in theology).......................1526.24 and 5814.15
— The present relations of science to religion. (*In* Hedge, F. H. Recent inquiries in theology)...1526.24
TEMPLE, Henry John, *viscount Palmerston,* Life of. Bulwer, *Sir* H. L. (E.) Leipzig, 1871, 74. 3 v. in 2. Sq. 16° 1238.15
TEN BROOK, Andrew. American state universities, their origin and progress. Cincinnati, 1875. viii, 410+ pp. 8° 5831.4
TEN days in Spain. Field, K. Boston, 1875. Sq. 16°. 428.7
TEN great religions. Clarke, J. F. Boston, 1872. 8°. 1523.2
TEN-MINUTE talks on all sorts of topics. Burritt, E. Boston, 1874. 16°............................ 5238.1
TEN old maids. Smith, J. P. 727.35
TEN thousand a year. Warren, S.................. 317.5
TEN years among the mail bags. Holbrook, J. Boston, 1856. 12°............................ 1216.8
TEN years in Washington. Ames, M. C. Hartford, 1875. 8° 612.8
TEN years of preacher life. Milburn, W. H. New York, 1859. 12° 1015.1
TENANT, The, of Wildfell hall. Brontë, A. 738.9
TENNER, Adolph, *joint author.* Nature and origin of epileptiform convulsions caused by profuse bleeding, and also of those of true epilepsy. *See* KUSSMAUL, Adolf 6023.1
TENNYSON, Alfred. Poetical works. Leipzig, 1860–72. 7 v. in 4. Sq. 16° 1614.10

Contents. — Vol. [I.] 1. Idylls of the king [Arthur]; Maud. 2. In memoriam [Arthur Hallam]; The princess. [II.] 3, 4. Miscellaneous poems. [III.] 5. Enoch Arden. 6. The holy grail and other poems. [IV.] 7. Gareth and Lynette; The last tournament.

— Enoch Arden [and other poems]. Boston, 1864. 204 pp. 12° 1612.8

Shelf. No.

TENNYSON, Alfred, *continued.*

— Gareth and Lynette. With illustrations. Boston, 1872. 96 pp. 16° 5617.6

— Queen Mary. A drama. [" Bloody Mary" — historical.] Boston, 1875. 284 pp. 16° 1617.10

— *Same.* Leipzig, 1876. 256 pp. Sq. 16° 1618.8

— Notes and marginalia, illustrative of the public life and works of. Smith, J. H. London [1874]. Sm. 8° 5337.2

Note. — See Taine's " English literature " [5613.1] and references in Allibone, vol. 3; and papers in Bayne's " Essays " [1226.15.1]; in Horne's " New spirit of the age " [1038.1]; in Buchanan's " Master-spirits " [6134.2]; in Kingsley's " Sir Walter Raleigh, and other papers " [1223.5]; in Stedman's " Victorian poets " [1837.1, or Scribner's monthly, 1874]; in the Atlantic monthly, 1871, and Fortnightly review, 1874. For local associations, see Howitt's " Homes and haunts " [1225.5], and a paper in Macmillan's magazine, 1873, on Lincolnshire scenery.

TENT life with the English gipsies in Norway. Smith, H. London, 1873. 8° 5722.1

TERENTIUS AFER, Publius. Andria Adelphique. Ex editione Westerhoviana. Accedunt notæ Anglicæ. Cura C. K. Dillaway. Philadelphiæ, 1843. 186 pp. Sm. 12° 6118.14

— Terence [outlined and explained]. Collins, W. L. Edinburgh, 1873. 16° 6116.17

TERHUNE, Mary Virginia, *formerly Miss Hawes.* (*Marian Harland.*) Alone 724.3

— Common sense in the household: a manual of practical housewifery. New York, 1871. 12°. 1533.6

— " Common sense in the household " series. Breakfast, luncheon and tea. New York, 1875. 459+ pp. 12° 1533.2

— From my youth up 724.22

— Helen Gardner's wedding-day. [Also] A battle summer 727.31

— The hidden path 735.14

— Jessamine 735.28

— Miriam 722.24

— Moss-side 722.28

— Ruby's husband 722.29

— Sunnybank 722.25

— True as steel 735.13

TERRIBLE secret, A. Fleming, M. A. 724.19

TERRIBLE temptation, A. Reade, C. Leipzig 315.1

— *Same.* New York 531.34

TERTULLIANUS, Quintus Septimius Florens. Writings. [Translated, vol. I, by S. Thelwall and P. Holmes; vol. II, by P. Holmes; vol. III, by S. Thelwall and R. E. Wallis.] Edinburgh, 1869, 70. 3 v. [Ante-Nicene Christian library.] 8° .... Vol. 11, 15, 18 of 6322.4

Note. — Vol. 3 contains also the Extant works of Victorinus and Commodianus.

— The five books against Marcion. Translated by Peter Holmes. Edinburgh, 1868. xx, 496 pp. [Ante-Nicene Christian library.] 8° 6322.4.7

TESTAMENT, Le, de Madame Patural. Souvestre, É. Théâtre de la jeunesse. Paris, 1860. 12° 5536.15

TESTAMENTS, The, of the twelve patriarchs [translated by Robert Sinker], and Fragments of the second and third centuries [translated by B. P. P[ratten]]. Edinburgh, 1871. 223 pp. [With LACTANTIUS, L. C. F. Works. Vol. II. Ante-Nicene Christian library.] 8° 6322.4.22

TESTED. Gardner, C. E. 714.7

TESTIMONY, The, of the rocks; or, geology in its bearings on the two theologies, natural and revealed. Miller, H. Boston, 1872. 12° 1527.2

TEUFFEL, W. S. History of Roman literature. Translated by Wilhelm Wagner. London, 1873. 2 v. 8° 6111.4

Contents. — Vol. I. The republican period. II. The imperial period.

TEXAS. Hammett, S. A. A stray Yankee in. New York, 1859. 12° 414.20

— Holley, M. A. Texas. Observations, historical, geographical and descriptive. Baltimore, 1833. 12° 817.7

— Marryat, F. Narrative of the travels and adventures of Monsieur Violet, in Western Texas. [Fiction] 337.7

Shelf. No.

TEXAS, *continued.*

— Mitchell, S. A. Map, etc., of. Philadelphia, 1846. Sm. 12° 418.7

— Olmsted, F. L. Journey through Texas. New York, 1857. 12° 414.4

TEXT-BOOKS of science. *Namely:* —

— Jenkin, F. Electricity and magnetism 6438.4

— Preece, W. H., and Sivewright, J. Telegraphy. 6826.6

— Shelley, C. P. B. Workshop appliances 6427.1

TEXTILE fabrics. Rock, D. [London] 1876. 8° 6214.6

THACHER, James. History of the town of Plymouth; from its first settlement in 1620, to 1832. Boston, 1832. 382 pp. 1 plate. Folded map. 12°. 817.9

THACHER, Samuel Cooper. Sermons. With a memoir by F. W. P. Greenwood. Boston, 1824. lxix, 335+ pp. 8° 5814.6

THACKERAY, Anne Isabella. Works. Vol. 1-4. London, 1875, 76. 4 v. 8° 512.1

Contents. — Vol. I. Old Kensington. II. The village on the cliff. III. Five old friends; A young prince. IV. To Esther; Out of the world; Making merry; Sola; Moretti's campanula.

— Bluebeard's keys and other stories. Leipzig 330.20

Contents. — Bluebeard's keys; Riquet à la houppe; Jack and the bean-stalk.

— *Same.* New York 720.11

Contents. — Bluebeard's keys; Riquet à la houppe; Jack and the bean-stalk; The white cat.

— Five old friends. Leipzig 331.7

Contents. — The sleeping beauty in the wood; Cinderella; Beauty and the beast; Little Red Riding Hood; Jack the giant-killer.

— Miss Angel. [Angelica Kauffmann.] Leipzig 311.27

— *Same.* New York 720.28

— Old Kensington. Leipzig 339.13

— *Same.* New York 731.3

— The story of Elizabeth 335.12

— The village on the cliff. Leipzig 335.11

THACKERAY, William Makepeace. (*Michael Angelo Titmarsh.*) Miscellanies. Leipzig, 1849, 56, 57. 8 v. in 4. Sq. 16° 335.13

Contents. — Vol. [I.] 1, 2. History of Samuel Titmarsh and The great Hoggarty diamond; The book of snobs; The Kickleburys abroad; A legend of the Rhine; Rebecca and Rowena; The second funeral of Napoleon; The chronicle of the drum. [II.] 3, 4. The tremendous adventures of Major Gahagan; The fatal boots; Ballads; Love songs made easy; Four German ditties; Imitation of Horace; An old friend with a new face; Lyra Hybernica; The ballads of policeman X; Memoirs of Mr. Charles J. Yellowplush; The diary of C. Jeames de La Pluche, esq.; Cox's diary. [III.] 5, 6. Sketches and travels in London; Novels by eminent hands; Character sketches; Memoirs of Barry Lyndon, esq. [IV.] 7, 8. A little dinner at Timmins's; The Bedford-row conspiracy; The Fitz-Boodle papers; A shabby genteel story; Men's wives.

— Works. London, 1871, 72. 12 v. Illustrated. Portrait. Sm. 8° 513.1

Contents. — Vol. I. Vanity fair. II. Pendennis. III. The Newcomes. IV. History of Henry Esmond, esq.; Memoirs of Barry Lyndon, esq. V. The Virginians. VI. The adventures of Philip; A shabby genteel story. VII. The Paris sketch book; The Irish sketch book; Notes of a journey from Cornhill to Grand Cairo. VIII. History of Samuel Titmarsh and The great Hoggarty diamond; Memoirs of Mr. C. J. Yellowplush; Burlesques. IX. The book of snobs; Sketches of life and character, etc. X. Roundabout papers; The four Georges; The English humourists; Second funeral of Napoleon. XI. Catherine; Lovel the widower; Denis Duval; Ballads, etc. XII. Christmas books.

— The adventures of Philip. Leipzig 335.5

— *Same.* New York 1820.2

— Bluebeard's ghost. (*In* Johnson, (E.) R. Little classics) 529.4.9

— Catherine. Leipzig 335.8

— Denis Duval. Leipzig 335.1

— Early and late papers hitherto uncollected. Boston, 1867. vi, 407+ pp. Portrait. 16° 715.13

— The English humourists of the eighteenth century. A series of lectures. Leipzig, 1853. 309+ pp. Sq. 16° 1238.8

Contents. — J. Swift; W. Congreve; J. Addison; Sir R. Steele; M. Prior; J. Gay; A. Pope; W. Hogarth; T. G. Smollett; H. Fielding; L. Sterne; O. Goldsmith.

— The four Georges; Lovel the widower. Leipzig. 335.3

— History of Henry Esmond, esq. Leipzig 335.10

— *Same.* New York 1820.3

— History of Pendennis. Leipzig 335.2

— *Same.* New York 1820.1

Shelf. No.

THACKERAY, William Makepeace, *continued.*
— The Irish sketch-book. Leipzig, 1872. 2 v. in 1. Sq. 16° 330.29
— Lovel the widower. New York 1820.3
— The Newcomes. Leipzig. 4 v. in 2 .... 335.4
— *Same.* New York 1820.2
— The Paris sketch book. With portrait. Leipzig, 1873. 2 v. in 1. Sq. 16° 339.21
— Roundabout papers. Leipzig, 1861. 326+ pp. Sq. 16° 335.9
— Thackerayana: notes and anecdotes. Illustrated by Thackeray. New York [London], 1875. xx, 494 pp. Sm. 8° 513.2
— Vanity fair. Leipzig 335.7
— *Same.* New York 1820.1
— The Virginians. A tale of the last century. Leipzig. 4 v. in 2 .... 335.6
— *Same.* New York 1820.3
— Fields, J. T. Yesterdays with authors. Boston, 1875 [*cop.* 1871]. 12° 6136.13
— Stoddard, R. H. Anecdote biography of. Bric-à-brac series. New York, 1874. Sq. 16° 1828.3

Note. — Stoddard's "Anecdote biography" and the "Thackerayana," which is a running sketch of his life and readings with fac-similes of his off-hand drawings found on the margins of his books, take the place at present of a regular biography, and may be supplemented with Dickens's tribute in Harper's monthly, vol. 28, and other recollections in vols. 41 and 49. See also B. Taylor's paper, in the Atlantic monthly, vol. 13. Beside the references in Allibone, vol. 3, see Bayne's "Essays" [1226 15.1]; Brown's "Spare hours" [537.5.2]; Whipple's "Character and characteristic men" [1936.3]; chapters in Taine's "English literature" [5613.1]; and a paper in the Edinburgh review, Jan., 1873.

As a novelist, Thackeray's strength lies in his probing of individual character, rather than in any dramatic rendering, and in his marvellous style. His novels are mostly corrective satires on contemporary life; but he has essayed historical relations in his "Henry Esmond," which pertains to Queen Anne's time, its manners and literature; and in his "Virginians," which gives us scenes in London and in the Old Dominion between 1756 and 1780. His "Catherine" is a covert satire on those novels which convert criminals into heroes. "Vanity fair" was his earliest and perhaps remains his most famous novel.

THADDEUS of Warsaw. [London and the Polish struggle with Russia.] Porter, J. 734.10
THALHEIMER, Mary Elsie. A manual of mediæval and modern history. Cincinnati [*cop.* 1874]. 480 pp. Maps. 8° 831.4
THAT boy of Norcott's. Lever, C. (J.) 332.15
THAT good old time. Gordon, C. 916.34
THAT queer girl. Townsend, V. F. 927.29
THATCHER, Benjamin Bussey. Indian biography. New York, 1869. 2 v. 1 plate. 16° 819.2
— Indian traits. New York, 1865. 2 v. Illustrated. 12° 819.1
THAXTER, Celia. Among the Isles of Shoals. With illustrations. Boston, 1873. 184 pp. Sq. 16°. 419.1
— Poems. New York, 1874. 188 pp. Sq. 16° ... 1627.2
THAYENDANEGEA, *Mohawk chief.* *See* BRANT, Joseph.
THAYER, Elisha. Family memorial. Hingham, 1835. 2 v. in 1. 8° 611.2

Contents. — Part I. Genealogy of fourteen families of the early settlers of New-England, of the names of Alden, Adams, Arnold, Bass, Billings, Capen, Copeland, French, Hobart, Jackson, Paine, Thayer, Wales and White. II. Genealogy of Ephraim and Sarah Thayer; with their fourteen children.

THAYER, Thomas Baldwin. Over the river; or, pleasant thoughts into the valley of shadows, and beyond. Boston, 1867. 272 pp. 16° 1526.1
THAYER, William Makepeace. The bobbin boy [N. P. Banks]; or, how Nat got his learning. Boston, 1860. xiii, 310 pp. 16° 916.8
— The pioneer boy [Abraham Lincoln], and how he became president. Boston, 1863. 310 pp. Illustrated. 16° 916.26
THAYER family. Thayer, E. Family memorials. Hingham, 1835. 8° 611.2
THEATRE. Howard, C. J. Drawing-room theatricals. New York [*cop.* 1870]. 16° 1636.2
— Hudson, F. Private theatricals for home performance. New York [*cop.* 1870]. 16° 1636.1

See also English stage, Stage.

THÉBAÏDE, La: tragédie. Racine, J. de. Théâtre complet. Paris, 1870. 12° 5537.3

Shelf. No.

THEIR wedding journey. Howells, W. D. Boston, 1873. 16° 533.7
THEOCRITUS, BION, and MOSCHUS. Idylls. And the war-songs of Tyrtæus. Literally translated into English prose, by J. Banks, with metrical versions, by J. M. Chapman. London, 1870. xxiv, 343 pp. Portrait. Sm. 8° 6115.17
THEOGNIS [outlined and explained]. Davies, J. Edinburgh, 1873. 16° 6116.16
THEOLOGY. Abbott, L. A dictionary of religious knowledge. New York, 1875. 8° 6320.2
— Beecher, E. The conflict of ages; or, the moral relations of God and man. Boston, 1854. 12°. 1524.21
— Beecher, L. Views in. Cincinnati, 1836. 12°. 6328.20
— Clarke, J. F. Ten great religions: an essay in comparative theology. Boston, 1872. 8° 1523.2
— Dunlavy, J. The manifesto, or a declaration of the doctrine and practice of the church of Christ. New York, 1847. 8° 5813.3
— Farley, S. Discourses and essays on theological and speculative topics. Boston, 1851. 12° 5815.23
— Greg, W. R. The creed of Christendom: its foundations contrasted with its superstructure. London, 1874. 2 v. Sm. 8° 5816.21
— Hedge, F. H. Recent inquiries in theology, by eminent English churchmen. Boston, 1860. 12° 5814.15
— *Same.* Boston, 1861. 12° 1526.24
— *Same.* Leipzig, 1862. Sq. 16°. *See* ESSAYS and reviews 1538.3
— Hodge, C. Systematic theology. New York, 1874. 3 v. 8° 5811.10
— MacClintock, J., and Strong, J. Cyclopædia of biblical, theological, and ecclesiastical literature. Vol. 1-5. New York, 1871-73. 5 v. 8°. *R.R., A.2.3
— Martineau, J. Essays, philosophical and theological. Boston, 1868, 70. 2 v. 8° 5814.14
— Mueller, (F.) M. Chips from a German workshop. New York, 1871-75. 4 v. Sm. 8° 5616.1
— Murphy, J. J. The scientific bases of faith. London, 1873. 8° 5012.5
— Prout, W. Chemistry, meteorology, and the function of digestion, considered with reference to natural theology. London, 1855. Sm. 8° 6436.10
— Roget, P. M. Animal and vegetable physiology, considered with reference to natural theology. Philadelphia, 1836. 2 v. 8° 6032.2
— St. Maur, *or* Seymour, E. A., *duke of Somerset.* Christian theology and modern skepticism. New York, 1872. 12° 5817.2
— Sparks, J. Collection of essays and tracts in. Boston, 1823-26. 5 v. 12° 1918.9
— Whewell, W. Astronomy and general physics considered with reference to natural theology. Philadelphia, 1833. 12° 6438.5

See also Christ, Christianity, Deism, Mercersburg theology, Religion.

THEOPHILUS, *of Antioch.* Writings. *See* TATIANUS, and OTHERS 6322.6
THEOPHILUS and others. Dodge, M. M. 713.15
THEOPHRASTUS. Les caractères [de Théophraste, avec les mœurs de ce siècle]. Bruyère, J. de la. Paris, 1816. 2 v. 12° 5537.7
THERAPEUTICS. Hooker, W. Rational therapeutics. (*In* Massachusetts medical society. Publications) 6021.4
— Wood, G. B. Treatise on. Philadelphia, 1856. 2 v. 8° 6011.3
— Wood, H. C., *jr.* Treatise on. Philadelphia, 1874. 8° 6021.7
THERESA. Craik, G. M. 335.17
THIBET, Travels in, 1844-6. Huc, É. R. London [1852]. 2 v. 16° 5935.12
THIÉBLIN, N. L. Spain and the Spaniards. Boston, 1875. 404 pp. Sm. 8° 427.5
THIEF, The, in the night. Spofford, H. E. 736.15
THIERRY, Amédée (Simon Dominique). Histoire d'Attila et de ses successeurs. Paris, 1856. 2 v. 8° 2012.1

Shelf. No.

THIERRY, (Jacques Nicolas) Augustin. The formation and progress of the tiers état, or third estate in France. Translated by Francis B. Wells. London, 1859. 2 v. in 1. [Bohn's Standard library.] Sm. 8° 5517.9
— History of the conquest of England by the Normans. Translated from the 7th Paris edition, by W. Hazlitt. London, 1869. 2 v. Portrait. Sm. 8° 5417.2
THIERS, Louis (Adolphe). History of the French revolution. Translated, with notes and illustrations from the most authentic sources, by Frederick Shoberl. With engravings. New York, 1874. 4 v. in 2. 8° 5511.3
— M. Thiers et les Napoléon (Jérôme). Lettres et documents inedits 1837 à 1848. Paris, 1873. 141 pp. 8° 5515.2
"THINGS new and old:" sermons. Welles, —. Portland, 1845. 8° 1533.9
THINGS not generally known. Wells, D. A. New York, 1873. 12° 1714.27
THIRTY years of army life on the border. Marcy, R. B. New York, 1866. 12° 415.16
THIRTY years' war. Gardiner, S. R. The thirty years' war. London, 1874. 16° 628.2
— Schiller, (J. C.) F. von. History of the. New York, 1846. 12° 826.6
THOLUCK, Friedrich August Gottreu. The doctrine of inspiration. (*In* Noyes, G. R. Collection of theological essays) 6325.12
THOMAS À BECKET. Becket, archbishop of Canterbury. A biography. Robertson, J. C. London, 1859. Sm. 8° 5424.14
THOMAS À KEMPIS. Imitation of Christ. New edition. London, N. D. xiii, 207+ pp. 16° 5819.1
— *Same*. From the Latin by J. Payne. With an introductory essay by T. Chalmers. New York [1851]. 307 pp. 12° 1536.16
THOMAS, Annie. *See* CUDLIP, Annie.
THOMAS, (Charles) Ambrose. Mignon. (*In* Ditson, O., and co. Standard opera librettos) 6233.3.1
THOMAS, Benjamin Franklin. Speeches in the 2d and 3d sessions of the 37th congress, and in the vacation. Boston, 1863. vi, 217+ pp. 8° ... 1921.2
THOMAS, George Henry. *See* BROCKETT, L. P. Our great captains. New York, 1865. 12° 1015.8
THOMAS, Joseph. Universal pronouncing dictionary of biography and mythology. Philadelphia, 1871. 2 v. 8° .... *R.R., A.3.5
— and BALDWIN, Thomas. Lippincott's pronouncing gazetteer. Revised edition, with appendix containing 10,000 new notices and the census of 1870. Philadelphia, 1874. xx, 2336 [2328] pp. 8° .... *R.R., B.3.2
THOMAS, M. Life's lesson. A tale 723.28
THOMAS Wingfold, curate. MacDonald, G. 536.24
THOMES, William H. The gold hunter's library. The bushrangers. A Yankee's adventures during his second visit to Australia. Boston, 1873. 480 pp. Illustrated. 12° 735.4
— – The gold hunters in Europe; or, the dead alive. Boston, 1873. 284 pp. Illustrated. Sm. 8°. 735.4
— – The gold hunters' adventures; or, life in Australia. Boston, 1873. 564 pp. Illustrated. 12°. 735.3
— The ocean life series. Life in the East Indies. Illustrated. Boston, 1873. 354 pp. Sm. 8° .. 535.15
— – A slaver's adventures on land and sea. Illustrated. Boston, 1873. 406 pp. Sm. 8° 735.2
— – The whaleman's adventures in the Sandwich Islands and California. Illustrated. Boston, 1873. 444 pp. Sm. 8° 735.1
— Running the blockade; or, U. S. secret service adventures. Boston, 1875. 474 pp. 8° 712.5
THOMPSON, *Sir* Benjamin, *count Rumford*, Memoir of. Ellis, G. E. *See* AMERICAN academy of arts and sciences 5022.3
THOMPSON, Benjamin F. History of Long Island; containing an account of the discovery and settlement; with other important and interesting matters to the present time. New York, 1839. 536 pp. Illustrated. 8° 813.20

Shelf. No.

THOMPSON, Daniel Pierce. The Green mountain boys: a historical tale of the early settlement of Vermont 734.1
— History of Montpelier, 1781–1860. Montpelier, 1860. 312 pp. Portrait. 8° 813.11
— Locke Amsden 734.5
— May Martin, and other tales of the Green mountains 734.3
— The rangers. A tale, illustrative of the revolutionary history of Vermont, and the Northern campaign of 1777. 2 v. 734.2
THOMPSON, Ella W. Beaten paths; or, a woman's vacation. Boston, 1874. 274 pp. 16° 437.6
THOMPSON, Theophilus. Annals of influenza; or, epidemic catarrhal fever in Great Britain from 1510 to 1837. London, 1852. xvi, 406 pp. 8°. 6013.14
THOMPSON, Waddy. Recollections of Mexico. New York, 1846. x, 304 pp. 16° 816.3
THOMS, William John. Human longevity, its facts and its fictions. London, 1873. xii, 320 pp. 8°. 6614.5
THOMSON, Andrew. In the Holy Land. New York [1875]. 364 pp. Illustrated. 16° 436.7
THOMSON, C. Wyville. The depths of the sea. An account of the general results of the dredging cruises of H. M. SS. 'Porcupine' and 'Lightning,' 1868–70, under the direction of Dr. Carpenter [and others]. With illustrations and maps. London, 1873. xx, 527+ pp. 8° 6623.3
THOMSON, David. Handy book of fruit culture under glass. Edinburgh, 1873. x, 316 pp. Sm. 8° 6625.6
THOMSON, James. Poetical works. With portrait. Leipzig, 1853. 402+ pp. Sq. 16° 1613.9

Contents. — The seasons; Poems; Songs; Britannia; Liberty.

THOMSON, John. The straits of Malacca, Indo-China, and China; or, ten years' travels, adventures, and residence abroad. Illustrated. New York, 1875. xv, 546 pp. Maps. 8° 5921.4
THOMSON, John Cockburn, *joint author*. The queens of society. *See* THOMSON, Katherine 1216.17
— The wits and beaux of society. *See* THOMSON, Katherine 1216.18
THOMSON, Katherine and John Cockburn. The queens of society. By Grace and Philip Wharton [*pseud.*]. Illustrated. New York, 1861. 488 pp. 12° 1216.17
— The wits and beaux of society. By Grace and Philip Wharton [*pseud.*]. With illustrations. New York, 1861. 481 pp. 12° 1216.18
THOMSON, Mortimer. (*Q. K. Philander Doesticks.*) Doesticks' letters: and what he says. Philadelphia [*cop.* 1855]. 330 pp. Illustrated. 12° .. 736.1
THOMSON, Robert Dundas. Experimental researches on the food of animals, and the fattening of cattle. With remarks on the food of man. From the last London edition. New York, 1856. 172 pp. Illustrated. 12° 1524.13
THOMSON, William M. The Land and the Book; or, biblical illustrations drawn from the manners and customs, the scenes and scenery of the Holy Land. Maps, engravings, etc. New York, 1871. 2 v. 12° 224.5
THOR, The land of. Browne, J. R. New York, 1870. 12° 424.17
THORBURN, Grant. Forty years' residence in America: or the doctrine of a particular Providence exemplified in [his] life. Written by himself. Boston, 1834. 264 pp. Portrait. 12° 1216.12
THOREAU, Henry David. Cape Cod. Boston, 1873. 252+ pp. 16° 215.2
— Excursions. Boston, 1866. 319 pp. Portrait. 16° 417.9
— The Maine woods. Boston, 1872. 328 pp. 12°. 417.8
— Walden; or, life in the woods. Boston, 1854. 357 pp. 16° 417.2
— A week on the Concord and Merrimack rivers. New and revised edition. Boston, 1868. 415 pp. 12° 215.1
— A Yankee in Canada, with anti-slavery and reform papers. Boston, 1872. 286+ pp. 12°. 225.2

Shelf. No.

THOREAU, Henry David, *continued.*

— Thoreau; the poet-naturalist. Channing, W. E. Boston, 1873. 12° .... 1227.7 and 5027.8

Note. — Most of Thoreau's writings, beside his Letters, as embodying personal feelings, are largely autobiographical in their character. The only memoirs of him are by Channing [1227.7 : 5027.8]; by Emerson [417.9, also see Atlantic monthly, Aug., 1862], but there are sketches in Alger's "Solitudes of nature and of man" [1535.22]; in Lowell's "My study windows"; in Alcott's "Concord days" [5217.1]; in the North American review, Oct., 1863, by J. H. Ward; in the Atlantic monthly, Sept. 1863, by Louisa M. Alcott; and in Fraser's magazine, April, 1866.

Also see Flagg's "Woods and by-ways of New England" [5035.2], and Harper's monthly, vol. 51.

THORNBURY, Walter. British artists from Hogarth to Turner. London, 1861. 2 v. Portraits. Sm. 8°. 6214.3

— Old and new London. Vol. I. Illustrated. London [1873]. Portraits. L. 8° 5432.1

THORNE, P., *pseud.* *See* SMITH, Mary P. Wells.

THORNICROFT's model. Beaumont, A. 319.26

THORNTON, John Wingate. The first records of Anglo-American colonization: their history. Boston, 1859. 12 pp. 8° 612.5

— The pulpit of the American revolution: or, the political sermons of the period of 1776. With a historical introduction, notes, and illustrations. 2d edition. Boston [1876]. 537 pp. 8° 1921.4

THORNTON hall. MacKeen, P. F. 912.16

THORNWELL, Emily. The lady's guide to perfect gentility. New York, 1856. 226+ pp. 1 plate. 12° 1516.2

THORPE, Kamba, *pseud.* *See* BELLAMY, *Mrs.* E. W.

THORPE, a quiet English town, and human life therein. Mountford, W. Boston, 1852. 16°.. 715.9

THORPE Regis. Peard, F. M. Boston 727.28

— *Same.* Leipzig 329.26

THOUGHTS about art. Hamerton, P. G. Boston, 1871. 16° 1515.3

THOUGHTS on the administration of God's moral government over our fallen world. By a plain man. New-Haven, 1860. 142+ pp. Sm. 12°. 5828.4

THOUSAND and one nights, or the Arabian nights entertainments 928.14

THRALE, *Mrs.* *See* PIOZZI, Esther Lynch.

THREADING my way. [An autobiography.] Owen, R. D. New York, 1874. 12° 5427.6

THREADS of knowledge, drawn from a cambric handkerchief; a Brussels carpet; a print dress; a kid glove; a sheet of paper. Carey, A. London [1872]. Sq. 16° 6438.1

THREE beauties, The. Southworth, E. D. E. N..... 527.9

THREE clerks, The. Trollope, A. 724.6

THREE commanders, The. Kingston, W. H. G. 921.17

THREE dissertations on Boylston prize questions for 1806 and 1807. Shattuck, G. C. Boston, 1808. 8°. 6023.9

THREE feathers. Black, W. Leipzig 331.0

— *Same.* New York 720.2

THREE gold dollars. Abbott, J. Harper's story books 936.1.7

THREE guardsmen, The. Dumas, A. (D.) 511.10

THREE lieutenants, The. Kingston, W. H. G. 921.12

THREE little spades. Warner, A. B. 932.24

THREE midshipmen, The. Kingston, W. H. G. 912.24

THREE November days. Taylor, B. F. (*In* Johnson, (E.) R. Little classics) 529.4.11

THREE pines, The. Abbott, J. 914.17

THREE proverb stories. Alcott, L. M. 935.20

THREE scouts, The. Trowbridge, J. T. 734.4

THREE successful girls. Crouch, J. 714.23

THREE tales. Hauff, W. 312.21

THREEfold destiny, The. Hawthorne, N. (*In* Johnson, (E.) R. Little classics) 529.4.12

THRICE through the furnace. Little, S. L. 715.18

THRIFT. Smiles, S. New York, 1876. 12° 5826.11

THRILLING and instructive developments: an experience of fifteen years as Roman catholic clergyman and priest. Czechowski, M. B. Boston, 1862. 12° 1226.11

THRONE, The, of David. Ingraham, J. H. Boston, 1872. 12° 512.4

THROOP, Montgomery H. The future: a political essay. New York, 1864. 343+ pp. 12° 1914.9

THROSTLETHWAITE. Morley, S. 723.33

Shelf. No.

THROUGH and through the tropics. Vincent, F., *jr.* New York, 1876. 12° 436.8

THROUGH by daylight. Adams, W. T. 925.16

THROUGH fire and water. Talbot, F. 732.22

THROUGH night to light. Gutzkow, C. (F.) 312.22

THROUGH night to light. Spielhagen, F. 518.10

THROUGH the air. [Ballooning.] Wise, J. Philadelphia, 1873. 8° 1520.3

THROUGH the looking-glass, and what Alice found there. Dodgson, C. L. 912.21

THROWN together. Montgomery, F. 313.22

THUCYDIDES. History of the Peloponnesian war. A literal version, by H. Dale. London, 1868, 70. 2 v. Portrait. Sm. 8° 6115.8

THUDICHUM, John Louis William, and DUPRÉ, August. Treatise on the origin, nature, and varieties of wine. London, 1872. xxiv, 760 pp. Illustrated. 8° 6423.4

THUNDER and lightning. Fonvielle, W. de. New York, 1872. 16° 1714.22

THURSTON, Louise M. Charley Roberts series. Charley and Eva Roberts' home in the West. 1117.9

— – The children of Amity court 1117.12

— – How Charley Roberts became a man 1117.18

— – How Eva Roberts gained her education 1117.7

TICE, John H. The relations between matter and force. (*In* Estes, D. Half-hour recreations in popular science) 6813.7

TICKNOR, George. History of Spanish literature. 4th edition, corrected and enlarged. Boston, 1872. 3 v. 8° 5922.2

— – *See* PRESCOTT, W. H. Biographical and critical miscellanies. Philadelphia, 1875. 12° 5237.3

— Life, letters, and journals. Boston, 1876. 2 v. Plate. Portraits. 8° .... 1012.5 and 5023.10

Note. — The first ten chapters were edited by G. S. Hillard, and the remainder by Mrs. Ticknor and her eldest daughter.

— Life of William Hickling Prescott. Boston, 1864. xii, 458 pp. Portrait. 12° 1223.7

TIECK, (Johann) Ludwig. *See* CARLYLE, T. German romance. Boston, 1841. 12° 5725.2

TIGER, The. The royal tiger of Bengal, his life and death. Fayrer, J. London, 1875. Sm. 8° 5935.9

TIGER-HUNTER, The. Reid, M. 725.4

TILES. Boyer, —. Nouveau manuel complet du tuilier. Paris, 1846. 24° 6439.8.2

— Dobson, E. Treatise on the manufacture of. London, 1868. 12° 1716.25

TILL the doctor comes, and how to help him. Hope, G. H. New York, 1871. 12° 1523.16

TILTON, Theodore. Memorial of Elizabeth Barrett Browning. New York, 1862. 16° 1612.4.4

— Tempest-tossed. A romance 724.2

TIMBERLAKE, Henry. Memoirs. London, 1765. 16°. 1218.3

Note. — Map and all pages after 128 wanting.

TIMBOO and Fanny. Abbott, J. Harper's story books 936.1.3

TIMBOO and Joliba. Abbott, J. Harper's story books 936.1.3

TIMBS, John. Abbeys, castles, and ancient halls of England and Wales; their legendary lore and popular history. Re-edited, revised, and enlarged by A. Gunn. London [1870]. 3 v. Illustrated. 16° 5438.1

Contents. — Vol. I. South. II. Midland. III. North.

— Clubs and club life in London. With anecdotes of its famous coffee houses, hostelries, and taverns, from the seventeenth century to the present time. With illustrations. London [1872]. xiv, 544+ pp. Sm. 8° 5417.3

— Curiosities of London. New edition. London [1867]. vii, 871+ pp. Portrait. Illustrated. 8°. 5435.1

— English eccentrics and eccentricities. With illustrations. London, 1875. xvi, 578 pp. Portraits. Sm. 8° 5617.20

— London and Westminster: city and suburb. Strange events, characteristics, and changes, of metropolitan life. London, 1868. 2 v. 8° ... 5435.4

— Romance of London. London [1865]. 2 v. Illustrated. Sm. 8° 5617.15

Shelf. No.

TIMBS, John, *continued.*
— School-days of eminent men: or, early lives of celebrated British authors, philosophers, poets, inventors [etc.]; with sketches of the progress of education in England, the foundation of public schools, etc. With illustrations. New edition, revised, enlarged, and partly re-written. London [1876]. x, 312 pp. Portraits. Sm. 8°. 5428.10
— Stories of inventors and discoverers in science and the useful arts. With illustrations. New York, 1860. 473 pp. 12° 1525.30
— Wonderful inventions: from the mariner's compass to the electric telegraph cable. With engravings. London [1867]. xvi, 400 pp. Sm. 8°. 1525.20
— The year-book of facts in science and art. London, 1866. 288 pp. Portraits. Sm. 8° 1527.12
TIME and tide, by Weare and Tyne. Letters on the laws of work. Ruskin, J. New York, 1871. 12° 6236.16
TIMROD, Henry. Poems. Edited, with a sketch of the poet's life, by P. H. Hayne. New revised edition. New York, 1873. 232+ pp. 12° ... 5617.12
TINCKER, Mary Agnes. Grapes and thorns 720.12
— The house of Yorke. New York, 1872. 261 pp. Illustrated. 8° 531.29
TINNE, John Ernest. The wonderland of the antipodes; and other sketches of travel in the north island of New Zealand. With illustrations. London, 1873. 124+ pp. L. 8° 5930.4
TIRRELL, Betsy Frances, Report of the case of G. C. Hersey, indicted for the murder of. Yerrington, J. M. W. Boston, 1862. 8° 631.6
TISCHENDORF, (Lobegott Friedrich) Constantine. The New Testament: the authorized English version; with introduction, and various readings from the three most celebrated manuscripts of the original Greek text. Leipzig, 1869. 414+ pp. 1 plate. Sq. 16° 1528.2
TISSANDIER, Gaston. The wonders of water. From the French. Edited, with additions, by [M.] Schele de Vere. With illustrations. New York, 1872. x, 350+ pp. 12° 1714.26
— *joint author.* Travels in the air. *See* GLAISHER, James 5911.1
TITCOMB, Timothy, *pseud.* *See* HOLLAND, Josiah Gilbert.
To Buddlecombe and back. Burnand, F. C. 539.12
To Esther. Thackeray, A. .I Works 312.1.4
To love and to be loved. Roe, A. S. 735.34
To the bitter end. Braddon, M. E. 532.10
TOBACCO: its history and associations. Fairholt, F. W. London, 1876. Sm. 8° 6425.6
TOBEY, Edward Silas. The Boston hydraulic protector against fire. Boston, 1873. 27 pp. 12°. 1712.1
TOCQUEVILLE, Alexis (Charles Henri Clerel) de. De la démocratie en Amérique. Orné d'une carte. 5e édition, revue et corrigée. Paris, 1836. 2 v. 12° 2018.6
— Democracy in America. Translated by Henry Reeve. Edited, with notes, by Francis Bowen. Boston, 1873. 2 v. Sm. 8° 5015.1
— On the state of society in France before the revolution of 1789, and on the causes which led to that event. Translated by Henry Reeve. 2d edition. London, 1873. xxiii, 416 pp. 8° ... 5514.9
TO-DAY in New York. Kimball, R. B. 311.18
TODD, John. The story of his life. Told mainly by himself. Compiled and edited by John E. Todd. New York, 1876. 529 pp. Portrait. Illustrations. 16° 5025.15
TOILERS, The, of the sea. Hugo, V. (M.), *vicomte.* New York, 1869. L. 8° 510.1
TOILET. Bayle-Mouillard, E. Manuel des dames, ou l'art de l'élégance. Paris, 1833. 24° 6229.1
— Cooley, A. J. The toilet in ancient and modern times. Philadelphia, 1873. Sm. 8° 1514.12
— Powers, S. D. The ugly-girl papers; or, hints for the. New York, 1875. Sq. 16° 1528.13

See also Perfumery.

TOLD in the twilight. Wood, E. P. Leipzig 333.22
— *Same.* Philadelphia 521.13

Shelf. No.

TOLLEMACHE, *Mrs.* W. A. Spanish towns and Spanish pictures. A guide to the galleries of Spain. London [1872]. xxiv, 318 pp. Illustrated. Portraits. Sm. 8° 5916.3
TOM and Jerry: a burletta. Moncrieff, W. T. New York, N. D. 12° 1635.5
TOM and the crocodiles. Bowman, A. 938.16
TOM Brown at Oxford. Hughes, T. Boston, 1871. 2 v. 12° 526.14
TOM Brown's school days. Hughes, T. Leipzig, 1858. Sq. 16° 311.12
TOM Burke of "Ours." Lever, C. (J.) Leipzig .. 332.10
— *Same.* London ..... 516.19 and 5627.3
TOM Harding and his friends. Eyster, N. 938.2
TOM Jones, History of. Fielding, H. Leipzig 312.20
— *Same.* (*In his* Works.) London 5611.2
TOM Newcombe. Fosdick, C. A. 923.7
TOM Tiddler's ground 338.3
TOMES, Robert. The bazar book of health. New York, 1873. 280 pp. 16° 1538.5
— The bazar book of the household. New York, 1875. 266 pp. 16° 1518.9
TOMKINS, Edward. Machine construction and drawing. New York [Glasgow], 1873. 141 pp. Illustrated. 16° 1717.9
TOMLINSON, Charles. Cyclopædia of useful arts, mechanical and chemical, manufactures, mining, and engineering. Illustrated. London, 1866–68. 3 v. L. 8° ..... *R.R., A.3.3
— Experimental essays. Illustrated. London, 1863. 123+ pp. 12° 1716.31

Contents. — I. On the motion of camphor on water. II. On the motion of camphor towards the light. III. History of the modern theory of dew.

— Introduction to the study of natural philosophy. London, 1851. vi, 162 pp. Illustrated. 12° .. 1526.17
— *Same.* 8th edition. London, 1870. vi, 164 pp. Illustrated. 12° 1716.30
— Locks and safes. The construction of locks; compiled from the papers of A. C. Hobbs. To which is added a description of J. Beverley Fenby's patent locks, and a note upon iron safes. By R. Mallet. London, N. D. vi, 212+ pp. Illustrated. 12° 1715.27
— Pneumatics; for the use of beginners. 3d edition, enlarged. London, 1866. iv, 162 pp. Illustrated. 12° 1716.32
— Rudimentary mechanics. 10th edition, corrected. London, 1872. viii, 176 pp. Illustrated. 12°. 1716.33
— Rudimentary treatise on warming and ventilation. 6th edition. London, 1869. xi, 339 pp. Illustrated. Folded plate. 12° 1715.26
— Winter in the Arctic regions and summer in the Antarctic regions. London [1872]. viii, 368 pp. Maps and illustrations. Sm. 8° 5915.3
TOMMY Hickup. Parker, R. A. 933.19
TOMMY Try and what he did in science. Napier, C. O. G. London, 1869. Sm. 8° 1524.24
TONDINI, Cæsarius. The pope of Rome and the popes of the oriental orthodox church: an essay on monarchy in the church, with special reference to Russia, from original documents, Russian and Greek. London, 1871. xiii, 183 pp. Sm. 8° 5816.1
TONE masters, The. *See* BARNARD, Charles Francis, *jr.*
TONER, Joseph M. History of inoculation in Massachusetts. (*In* Massachusetts medical society. Publications) 6021.4
TONY Butler. Lever, C. (J.) 332.19
Too much alone. Riddell, J. H. 720.7
Too soon. Macquoid, K. S. Leipzig 319.21
— *Same.* New York 731.8
Too strange not to be true. Fullerton, *Lady* G. 325.18
TOPICS of the time. [Essays.] Parton, J. Boston, 1871. 12° 1935.3
TORREY, Joseph. A theory of fine art. New York, 1874. 290 pp. 16° 6237.1
TOTAL depravity, The, of inanimate things. Walker, *Mrs.* E. A. (*In* Johnson, (E.) R. Little classics) 529.4.5

Shelf. No.

TOTTEN, Benjamin J. Naval text-book, and dictionary for the use of the midshipmen of the U. S. navy. New edition. New York, 1864. 449 pp. 12° 1527.21
TOUR du monde, Le, en quatre-vingts jours. Verne, J. Paris [1873]. 8° 5818.1
TOUR of the world, The, in eighty days. [Fiction.] Verne, J. Boston, 1873. Sq. 16° 239.1
TOUR on the prairies. Irving, W. London, 1854. 16°. 417.1
TOUR, A, round my garden. Karr, (J. B.) A. London [1874]. 4° 6626.4
TOURGUÉNEF, Ivan Sergievitch. *See* TURGENEF, Ivan Sergievitch.
TOWER hill. [Henry VIII's time.] Ainsworth, W. H. 322.12
TOWN, The [London]: its memorable characters and events. Hunt, (J. H.) L. London, 1872. 16°. 5437.1
TOWN geology. [Popular science.] Kingsley, C. London, 1872. Sm. 8° .... 1526.3 and 6636.2
TOWNSEND, Luther Tracy. The arena and the throne. Boston, 1874. 264 pp. 1 plate. 16° 1527.14
— Credo. [Theological essays.] Boston, 1875 [*cop.* 1869]. 444 pp. 16° 1917.6
TOWNSEND, Virginia Frances. The Deerings of Medbury 711.24
— The Hollands 711.22
— The maidenhood series. That queer girl 927.29
— Margery Keith 1115.16
— The mills of Tuxbury 711.23
— One woman's two lovers; or, Jacqueline Thayne's choice 723.1
— Only girls 931.2
— Six in all 713.5
TOWNSHEND, Frederick Trench. Wild life in Florida, with a visit to Cuba. London, 1875. xiv, 319 pp. Map. Wood-cut. 8° 5932.14
TOXICOLOGY, Treatise on therapeutics, comprising. Wood, H. C., *jr.* Philadelphia, 1874. 8° 6021.7
TRACY's ambition. Griffin, G. 517.10
TRADE circular. annual for 1871, including the American catalogue of books published in 1870; also, a list of the principal books published in England; a publishers', manufacturers', and importers' directory, and miscellaneous literary and trade information. [By F. Leypoldt.] New York, 1871. Portraits. Folded plate. 8° 6130.4
TRADES-UNIONS. Les associations ouvrières en Angleterre. Paris, L. P. d'Orleans, *comte* de. Paris, 1869. 12° 5827.2
TRADITION, principally with reference to mythology and the law of nations. Arundell, J. F., *baron of Wardour.* London, 1872. 8° 6333.1
TRAFFIC. The crown of wild olive. Three lectures on work, traffic, and war. Ruskin, J. New York, 1872. 12° 6236.6
TRAFFORD, F. G. *See* RIDDELL, J. H.
TRAFTON, Adeline. An American girl abroad. Illustrated. Boston, 1873. 245 pp. 16° 736.12
— Katherine Earle 911.3
TRAIN, George Francis. Young America in Wall-street. New York, 1857. 406 pp. 12° 414.3
TRAITS and stories of the Irish peasantry. Carleton, W. 524.17
TRÄLINNAN. Bremer, F. 511.5
TRANSATLANTIC sketches. James, H., *jr.* Boston, 1875. 12° 436.4
TRANSCENDENTALISM in New England. Frothingham, O. B. New York, 1876. 12° 6325.21
TRANSFORMATION. Hawthorne, N. Leipzig, 1860. 2 v. in 1. Sq. 16° 311.6
— *Same.* Boston, 1872. 2 v. in 1. 12° 1813.2

Note. — This is the same as "The marble faun."

TRANSITS of Venus. Proctor, R. A. London, 1874. Sm. 8° 6814.4
TRASK, William Blake. The Seaver family. A genealogy of Robert Seaver of Roxbury, Mass., and some of his descendants. Boston, 1872. 52 pp. Sm. 4° 5013.10
TRAVEL, The art of. Galton, F. London, 1867. 16° 5918.1

Shelf. No.

TRAVELLER, The. [Poem.] Goldsmith, O. Works. Leipzig, 1842. Sq. 16° 312.23
— *Same.* London, 1854. 8° 5612.1.1
TRAVELLER's manual of conversation in English, French, German, Italian. Baedeker, C. Coblenz, 1870. 12° 6127.1
TRAVELLING bachelor, The; or, notions of the Americans. Cooper, J. F. 536.7
TRAVELS in the air. Glaisher, J., and others. Philadelphia [London], 1871. 8° 5911.1
TRAVIATA, La. Verdi, G. (*In* Ditson, O., and co. Standard opera librettos) 6233.3.6
TREADWELL, John H. Manual of pottery and porcelain for American collectors. New York, 1872. 161 pp. Illustrated. 8° .... 1512.2 and 6211.4
TREADWELL, Seymour B. American liberties and American slavery morally and physically illustrated. New York, 1838. 466 pp. 12° 817.10
TREASON at home. Greenough, S. D. 522.3
TREASURE, The, of the seas. De Mille, J. 928.6
TREASURE hunters, The. Fenn, G. M. 710.28
TREASURE-TROVE series. *See* WALSH, William Shepard 538.10
TREASURES, The, of the earth. Jones, W. New York, 1872. 16° 6635.1
TREASURY of thought. [Extracts.] Ballou, M. M. Boston, 1873. 8° .... *R.R., E.2.4
TREATY of Washington, The. Cushing, C. New York, 1873. Sm. 8° 816.1
TREES. Emerson, G. B. A report on the trees and shrubs growing naturally in the forests of Massachusetts. Boston, 1875. 2 v. 8° 6621.2
— Hemsley, W. B. Handbook of hardy trees. Boston [London], 1873. 8° 6624.1
TRÉMERY, F. Nouveau manuel complet du teneur de livres. Nouvelle édition, corrigée, et augmentée. Paris, N. D. x, 347+ pp. 24°. [Manuel Roret] 6819.1
TRENCH, Richard Chenevix. English, past and present. 7th edition, revised. New York, 1871. vi, 352+ pp. 12° 1735.3
— Gustavus Adolphus in Germany, and other lectures on the thirty years' war. 2d edition. London, 1872. x, 194+ pp. Sm. 8° 5717.2
— A household book of English poetry. 2d edition, revised. London, 1870. xii, 238 pp. Sq. 16°. 5616.4
— Plutarch, his life and his morals. Four lectures. London, 1873. 131+ pp. Sm. 8° 6118.7
— On the study of words. 25th American from the 9th English edition, revised. New York [1851]. 248 pp. 12° 1735.2
— The revision of the English version of the New Testament. *See* LIGHTFOOT, Joseph Baber 5814.11
TRENCH, W. Steuart. Ierne. [Irish life.] London, 1871. 2 v. Sm. 8° 715.11
— Realities of Irish life. Boston, 1869. x, 297 pp. Sq. 16° 428.13
TREVLYN hold. Wood, E. P. 333.19
TRIAL, The. Yonge, C. M. 318.8
TRIAL by jury; a dramatic cantata. Gilbert, W. S. Original plays. New York, 1876. 12° 1634.1
TRIALS. Memories of Westminster hall. Foss, E. Boston, 1874. 2 v. 8° 5421.2
TRICHINA spiralis, Cases of, in Springfield. Calkins, M. (*In* Massachusetts medical society. Publications) 6021.4
TRICKS. Magic no mystery: conjuring tricks, etc. Frickell, G. London, 1876. Sm. 8° 1515.20
TRICOTRIN. Rame, L. de la 327.20
TRIED for her life. Southworth, E. D. E. N. 522.10
TRINITY. Bickersteth, E. H. The Rock of ages; or Scripture testimony to the one eternal Godhead of the Father, and of the Son, and of the Holy Ghost. Boston, 1860. 12° ... 1524.7 and 5816.24
— Norton, A. A statement of reasons for not believing the doctrines of trinitarians. Cambridge, 1833. 12° 5816.25
— Parsons, B. The Christian layman; or, the doctrine of the trinity fully considered, and adjudged according to the Bible. Mobile, 1840. 12° 5815.16

Shelf. No.

TRIP, A, to Scarborough: a comedy. Sheridan, R. B. Dramatic works. London, 1848. 16° 1635.2
— *Same.* Leipzig, 1869. Sq. 16° 1614.11
— *Same.* London, 1875. Sm. 8° 5626.9
TRISTRAM, Henry Baker. The land of Moab: travels and discoveries on the east side of the Dead sea and the Jordan. With a chapter on the Persian palace of Mashita, by J. Fergusson. With map and illustrations. New York, 1873. 416 pp. 8°. 5933.4
TRISTRAM Shandy, Life and opinions of. Sterne, L. Leipzig, 1849. Sq. 16° 315.14
TRIUMPHS, The, of temper; a poem. Hayley, W. Newburyport [1781]. 12° 1617.11
TRODDEN down. Newby, C. J. 710.11
TROELTSCH, Anton von. Treatise on the diseases of the ear, including the anatomy of the organ. Translated and edited by D. B. St. J. Roosa. 2d American, from the 4th German edition. New York, 1869. xx, 565+ pp. Illustrated. 8°.. 6022.11
TROIS-ÉTOILES, *pseud.* *See* MURRAY, Grenville.
TROLLOPE, Anthony. Australia and New Zealand. Leipzig, 1873. 3 v. in 1. Sq. 16° 418.5
— Barchester towers 334.10
— The Belton estate 334.16
— The Bertrams 334.14
— Can you forgive her? 330.7
— Castle Richmond 334.8
— The Claverings 334.1
— The commentaries of Cæsar [outlined and explained]. Edinburgh, 1870. vi, 182 pp. 16°. [Ancient classics for English readers] 6116.5
— Doctor Thorne 334.5
— The Eustace diamonds 720.33
— Framley parsonage 334.12
— The golden lion of Granpere 334.19
— Harry Heathcote of Gangoil. Leipzig 329.17
— *Same.* New York 732.11
— He knew he was right 334.11
— Lady Anna. Leipzig 329.15
— *Same.* New York 732.27
— The last chronicle of Barset 334.15
— North America. Leipzig, 1862. 3 v. Sq. 16°. 418.4
— *Same.* 3 v. in 1. Sq. 16° 418.3
— *Same.* New York, 1862. vii, 623 pp. 12° 414.5
— *Same.* Philadelphia, 1862. 2 v. in 1. 12° 415.10
— Orley farm 334.17
— Phineas Finn, the Irish member 334.6
— Phineas redux 732.14
— The prime minister. Leipzig. Vol. I, II 331.26
— *Same.* New York 730.13
— Rachel Ray 319.4
— Ralph the heir 334.4
— Sir Harry Hotspur of Humblethwaite 334.18
— The small house at Allington 334.9
— The three clerks 724.6
— The vicar of Bullhampton 334.3
— The warden 334.13
— The way we live now. Leipzig. 4 v. in 2 ..... 331.8
— *Same.* New York 720.34
— The West Indies and the Spanish main. Leipzig, 1860. 320+ pp. Sq. 16° 228.2

Note. — Trollope ranks among the better and most popular English novelists, describing mostly the better classes of English society.

TROLLOPE, Thomas Adolphus. Diamond cut diamond: a story of Tuscan life 725.36
— Durnton abbey 711.16
— The Garstangs of Garstang grange 334.21
— History of the commonwealth of Florence, from the earliest independence of the commune to the fall of the republic in 1531. London, 1865. 4 v. 8° 5512.3
— A siren 334.20
TRÖLTSCH, Anton von. *See* TROELTSCH, Anton von.
TROPICS. Hartwig, G. The polar and tropical worlds. Springfield, 1874. 8° 1520.7
— — The tropical world. London, 1873. 8° 6613.5
— Willis, N. P. Health trip to the. New York, 1853. 12° 426.9
TROTTY book, The. Phelps, E. S. 932.13
TROTTY's wedding tour. Phelps, E. S. 913.27

Shelf. No.

TROUBADOURS. Raynouard, F. J. M. Lexique roman ou dictionnaire de la langue des troubadours. Paris, 1838–44. 6 v. 8° .... 5531.
— Rutherford, J. The troubadours: their loves and their lyrics. London, 1873. 8° 5525.1

Note. — See Longfellow's "Poets and poetry of Europe" [5922.1].

TROUBLE on the mountain. Abbott, J. 917.3
TROUT. Slack, J. H. Practical trout culture. New York, 1871. 12° .... 6616.
— Stone, L. Domesticated trout. How to breed and grow them. Boston, 1872. 16° .... 6616.
TROVATORE, Il. Verdi, G. (*In* Ditson, O., and co. Standard opera librettos) .... 6233.3.
TROWBRIDGE, John Townsend. (*Paul Creyton.*) Burcliff: its sunshine and its clouds .... 929.
— A chance for himself 925.2
— Coupon bonds, and other stories .... 522.
— Cudjo's cave 735.2
— Doing his best 916.2
— The drummer boy .... 931.
— The emigrant's story, and other poems. Boston, 1875. vi, 170+ pp. Wood-cut. 12° 1615.2
— Fast friends 921.1
— Father Brighthopes .... 929.
— Hearts and faces .... 929.
— Ironthorpe 929.5
— Jack Hazard and his fortunes 915.1
— Lawrence's adventures among the ice-cutters, glass-makers, coal-miners, iron-men, and shipbuilders 932.2
— Martin Merrivale .... 522.
— Neighbor Jackwood 735.2
— Neighbors' wives 735.2
— The old battle-ground .... 929.
— The three scouts .... 734.
— The young surveyor; or, Jack on the prairies ... 1115.
TROY and its remains. Schliemann, H. London, 1875. 8° .... 5933.
TRUE as steel. Terhune, M. V. 735.1
TRUE Blue. Kingston, W. H. G. 935.1
TRUE history, The, of a little ragamuffin. Greenwood, J. .... 521.
TRUE history, The, of Joshua Davidson, communist. Linton, E. L. Leipzig, 1873. Sq. 16° 312.2
— *Same.* Philadelphia, 1873. 12° 736.2
TRUE legend, The, of a billiard club. Black, W. Leipzig 330.1
— *Same.* New York .... 711.
TRUE Robinson Crusoes, The. Denis, (J.) F., and Chauvin, V. .... 938.
TRUE to herself. Robinson, F. W. 731.1
TRUE woman, The; or, life and happiness at home and abroad. Peck, J. T. New York [*cop.* 1857]. 16° .... 1736.
TRUEDEL, Dorothea. Answers to prayer; or, Dorothea Trüdel. Boston, N. D. 16° .... 1026.
TRUMBULL, Henry. History of the discovery of America, of the landing of our forefathers, at Plymouth, and their engagements with the Indians in New-England, 1620–79. Boston, 1819. 256 pp. 8° .... 814.
TRUMBULL, John. Poetical works. Hartford, 1820. 2 v. Illustrated. Portrait. 8° .... 1610.

Contents. — Vol. I. Memoir; M'Fingal. II. The progress of dulness; The genius of America; Lines to Dwight and Barlow; Ode to sleep; A fable; Orpheus and Eurydice; The prophecy of Balaam; Fable; The future glory of America; Elegy; Advice to ladies; Characters; Elegy; Babylon; Elegy on the times.

"TRUMPS," *pseud.* *See* DICK, William Brisbane.
TRUMPS. Curtis, G. W. 524.1
TRUTH. Bailey, S. Essays on the pursuit of. Philadelphia, 1831. 12° .... 5837.
— Catlin, J. A compendium of the system of divine truth. Boston, 1851. 12° .... 5817.
TRUTH's advocate and monthly anti-Jackson expositor. [Jan. to Oct., 1828.] By an association of individuals. Cincinnati, 1828. 400+ pp. 8°. 6535.
TRY again. Adams, W. T. 924.1
TRY and trust. Alger, H., *jr.* .... 928.

Shelf. No.

TRY Cracow and the Carpathians. Hutchinson, A. H. New York [London, 1872]. Sm. 8° ... 5936.2
TUBERCULOSIS: its nature, cause, and treatment. Dobell, H. [London] 1866. 16° 6015.4
TUCKERMAN, Henry Theodore. America and her commentators. With a critical sketch of travel in the United States. New York, 1864. viii, 460 pp. 8° 5033.5
— Book of the artists. American artist life. With an appendix containing an account of notable pictures and private collections. New York, 1870. 639+ pp. Portrait. 8° 1511.6
— Life of John Pendleton Kennedy. New York, 1871. 490 pp. Portrait. 1 plate. Fac-simile. 12° ....1015.7 and 5026.2
TUDOR, William. Gebel Teir. [A political allegory.] Boston, 1829. viii, 13–158 pp. 12° 532.4
— Letters on the Eastern states. New York, 1820. vi, 356 [352] pp. 12°..................... 1915.5
— Life of James Otis, of Massachusetts: containing also, notices of some contemporary characters and events from 1760 to 1775. Boston, 1823. xx, 508 pp. Portrait. Illustrated. 8°...... 1012.2
TUGNOT DE LANOYE, Ferdinand. Rameses the great; or, Egypt 3300 years ago. From the French. With wood-cuts. New York, 1872. 296+ pp. Portrait. 16°.............................. 1714.3
— The sublime in nature. With additions. New York, 1872. 344 pp. Illustrated. 16° 1714.21
TUPPER, Martin Farquhar. Hactenus: more droppings from the pen that wrote "Proverbial philosophy." Boston, 1848. 106 pp. Portrait. 16° 1617.5
— Proverbial philosophy. 1st [and] 2d series. New York, 1845. 2 v. in 1. Sm. 8° 5616.8
TURANDOT. Ein tragikomisches Mährchen nach Gozzi. *See* SCHILLER, (J. C.) F. von. Werke.5734.1.7
TURGENEF, Ivan Sergievitch. Leisure hour series. On the eve. A tale. Translated from the Russian by C. E. Turner 539.1
— — Smoke. A Russian novel. Translated from the author's French version by W. F. West 537.14
— — Spring floods. Translated from the Russian by Sophie Mitchell Butts. A Lear of the steppe. Translated from the French by William Hand Browne 528.9
— *See* MÉRIMÉE, P. Portraits historiques et littéraires. Paris, 1874. 18°.........................5527.14
TURKEY. Adams, W. T. Cross and crescent; or, Young America in. Boston, 1874. 16°....... 925.11
— Cunynghame, *Sir* A. T. Travels on the frontiers of, 1871. London, 1872. 8° 5931.8
— Howard, G. W. F., *7th earl of Carlisle.* Diary in Turkish and Greek waters. Boston, 1855. 12° 825.5
— Murray, J. Handbook for Turkey. London, N. D. 12° 5917.9
— Willis, N. P. Pencillings by the way. New York, 1844. L. 8° 430.2

See also Assyria, Babylon, Black sea, East (The), Palestine, Red sea, Syria.

TURNER, Maria. The young ladies' assistant in drawing and painting. Cincinnati, 1833. 71 pp. 16°..1517.4
TURNER, Sharon. Sacred history of the world. New York, 1858. 3 v. 12°........................ 828.3
TURNING, Treatise on lathes and. Northcott, W. H. London, 1868. 8°...............................1521.11
TURNING, The, of the tide. Kellogg, E. 922.28
TURNING-POINTS in life. Arnold, F. New York, 1873. 12°...1536.12
TURNING wheel, The. Cobden, P. 1115.2
TURRETIN, John Alphonsus. Fundamentals in religion. (*In* Sparks, J. Collection of essays and tracts in theology) 1918.9.1
TUSCULAN questions. Cicero, M. T. Philadelphia, 1849. 2 v. Sm. 12° 6118.3
TUTHILL, Louisa Caroline. Braggadocio. A book for boys 915.24
— Queer bonnets; or, truthfulness and generosity. 933.27

Shelf. No.

TUTTLE, Edward B. The boy's book about Indians. Philadelphia, 1873. 207 pp. Illustrated. 16°. 915.20
TUTTLE, Herbert. German political leaders. New York, 1876. viii, 264+ pp. [Higginson, T. W., *editor*. Brief biographies of European public men.] 16°..................................... 628.9
TWAIN, Mark, *pseud.* *See* CLEMENS, Samuel Langhorne.
TWEEDIE, Alexander. Clinical illustrations of fever. Boston, 1831. 412 [150] pp. 8° 6011.9
TWEEDIE, William K. The early choice. London, 1856. 320 pp. 16°.............................. 916.7
— Seed-time and harvest; or, sow well and reap well. Boston, 1854. 248 pp. 1 plate. 12° .. 916.6
TWELFTH-NIGHT at the century club, January 6, 1858. New York, 1858. 93 pp. 4° 817.1
TWELLS, Julia Helen. The mills of the gods. A novel 714.15
TWELVE miles from a lemon. Dodge, M. A. New York, 1874. 12°.............................1536.19
TWELVE nights in the hunters' camp. Barrows, W. 934.2
TWENTY-ONE years in the Boston stock market. Martin, J. G. Boston, 1856. 8°............. 1711.1
TWENTY thousand leagues under the sea. Verne, J. Boston, 1873. Sm. 8°.......................... 5535.1
— *Same.* London, 1876. Sm. 8°................ 715.27
TWENTY years after. Dumas, A. (D.) 511.31
TWICE crowned. MacKeever, H. B. 528.1
TWICE-TOLD tales. Hawthorne, N. Boston, 1871. 2 v. in 1. 12° 1813.7
TWICKENHAM, Memorials of. Cobbett, R. S. London, 1872. 8°.. 5424.1
TWIN lieutenants, The. Dumas, A. (D.) 511.26
TWIN sisters, The; a tale for youths. Sandham, *Mrs.* —... 929.11
TWITCHELL, Amos, Memoir of. Bowditch, H. I. Boston, 1851. 12°.................................1216.13
Two admirals, The. Cooper, J. F. Leipzig....... 310.13
— *Same.* New York 525.16
Two apprentices, The. Howitt, M................ 937.13
Two aristocracies, The. Gore, C. G. F............. 312.26
Two Barbaras, The. A novel. Stuart, M. B. 532.17
Two baronesses, The. Andersen, H. C. 524.15
Two, by tricks. Yates, E. 330.15
Two captains, The. La Motte Fouqué, F. (H. C.), *Freiherr* de 313.7
Two college friends. Loring, F. W. 515.7
Two Cosmos, The 316.5
Two drovers, The. Scott, *Sir* W. 523.20
Two family mothers. Schwartz, M. S............. 531.8
Two Foscari, The. [Drama.] Byron, G. G. N., *lord.* Works. Leipzig, 1866. Sq. 16°......1614.13.5
Two French marriages. Jenkin, *Mrs.* C. 313.5
Two guardians, The. Yonge, C. M. 318.13
Two homes, The. Baker, H. N. (W.) 926.4
Two little wooden shoes. Rame, L. de la 329.18
Two lives. MacIntosh, M. J. 735.24
Two marriages. Craik, D. (M.) 323.21
Two paths, The: being lectures on art, and its application to decoration and manufacture. Ruskin, J. New York, 1866. 12°........................ 6236.8
Two sisters, The. Southworth, E. D. E. N. 727.18
Two wheelbarrows, The. Abbott, J. 917.36
Two years ago. Kingsley, C........................ 326.13
Two years before the mast. [Sea experiences round Cape Horn to California.] Dana, R. H., *jr.* New York, 1840. 12° ....918.1 and 5037.1
TWOFOLD life, A. Hillern, W. von................ 735.19
TYERMAN, Luke. Life and times of John Wesley. New York, 1872. 3 v. Portraits. 8°........ 5423.2
— The Oxford methodists. New York, 1873. viii, 413 pp. Portraits. 8° 5424.5

Contents. — The first of the Oxford methodists: Robert Kirkham; William Morgan; Charles Morgan; Rev. John Clayton; Rev. Benjamin Ingham; Rev. John Gambold; Rev. James Hervey; Rev. Thomas Broughton; Other Oxford methodists.

TYLER, William Seymour. Memoir of Henry Lobdell. Including the early history of the Assyrian mission. Boston [*cop.* 1859]. 414 pp. Portrait. 12°.. 1015.4
TYLNEY hall. [Novel.] Hood, T. 515.6

Shelf. No.

TYLOR, Edward Burnett. Primitive culture. London, 1871. 2 v. 8° 5922.6
— Researches into the early history of mankind and the development of civilization. 2d edition. London, 1870. vi, 386 pp. Illustrated. 8°... 5912.8
— The stone age, past and present. (*In* Estes, D. Half-hour recreations in popular science)...... 6813.7
TYNDALL, John. Contributions to molecular physics in the domain of radiant heat. New York, 1873. xiv, 446+ pp. Illustrated. 1 folded plate. 8° 6431.1
— Faraday as a discoverer. New York, 1868. viii, 171 pp. Portrait. 12° 1224.14
— *Same.* New York, 1873. viii, 171 pp. 12° ...1523.21
— The forms of water in clouds and rivers, ice and glaciers. With illustrations. New York, 1872. xiii, 192+ pp. Portrait. 12° 6436.11
— Fragments of science for unscientific people. New York, 1872. 422+ pp. Sm. 8° 1524.27
— Heat a mode of motion. From the 4th English edition. New York, 1873. xx, 532 pp. Illustrated. 12° 1522.5
— Hours of exercise in the Alps. New York, 1873. x, 473+ pp. Illustrated. 12° 223.1
— Light and electricity. New York, 1873. 194 pp. 12° 1523.20
— Six lectures on light, delivered in America in 1872–73. 2d edition. London, 1875. xvii, 272+ pp. Illustrated. Sm. 8° 6436.1
— Sound. New York, 1873. xiii, 335 pp. Illustrated. 12° 1914.11
TYPEE: a peep at Polynesian life, during a four months' residence in a valley of the Marquesas. Melville, H. New York, 1871. 12° 737.4
TYPHOID fever, Anatomical, pathological, and therapeutic researches upon gastro-entérite, or. Louis, P. C. A. Boston, 1836. 2 v. 8° 6021.10
TYRE and Alexandria. Tarbox, I. N. Boston [*cop.* 1865]. 16° 426.5
TYROL. Baedeker, C. Handbook for travellers. Coblenz, 1872. 16° 5718.4
— Grohman, W. A. B. Tyrol and the Tyrolese. London, 1876. Sm. 8° 5916.12
— Murray, J. Knapsack guide for Tyrol. London, 1867. 16° 5527.8
TYRTÆUS. War-songs. *See* THEOCRITUS 6115.17
TYRWHITT, Richard St. John. The art teaching of the primitive church; with an index of subjects, historical and emblematic. London [1875]. x, 381+ pp. Illustrated. Sm. 8° 6234.6
— Christian art and symbolism, with hints on the study of landscape. With illustrations. London, 1872. xii, 292 pp. 1 folded sheet. 16°.1514.14 and 6235.1
— A handbook of pictorial art. With a chapter on perspective. By A. Macdonald. 2d edition. Oxford, 1875. x, 384+ pp. Illustrated. 8°.6213.12
TYSON, George E. Wonderful drift on the ice-floe. (*In* Blake, E. V., *editor.* Arctic experiences)..5911.15
TYTLER, Alexander Fraser, *lord Woodhouselee.* Memoirs of the life and writings of Henry Home of Kames. Edinburgh, 1807. 2 v. 4° 1020.2
— Universal history, from the creation of the world to the beginning of the eighteenth century. Boston, 1840. 2 v. 8° 811.3
TYTLER, Christina C. Fraser. Jasmine Leigh 717.19
— Leisure hour series. Jonathan. A novel....... 517.22
— – Mistress Judith. A Cambridgeshire story.... 518.25
— Margaret 735.18
TYTLER, Sarah, *pseud.* *See* KEDDIE, *Miss*

UBIQUE, *pseud.* *See* GILMORE, Parker.
UGLY-GIRL papers, The; or, hints for the toilet. Powers, *Mrs.* S. D. New York, 1875. 16°....1528.13
UHLAND, Johann Ludwig. Gedichte und Dramen. Volksausgabe. Stuttgart, 1863. 3 v. Sq. 16°. 5738.1

Contents.—Vol. I, II. Gedichte. III. Dramen.

UHLHORN, Gerhard. The modern representations of the life of Jesus. Four discourses. From the 3d German edition, by C. E. Grinnell. Boston, 1868. x, 164+ pp. 16° 6328.7

Shelf. No.

"UNA and her paupers:" memorials of Agnes Elizabeth Jones. Higinbotham, J. M. New York, 1872. 16° 5427.8
UNAWARES. Peard, F. M. 331.1
UNCIVILIZED races, The. Wood, J. G. Hartford, 1870. 2 v. in 1. L. 8° 6610.3
— *Same.* London, 1870. 2 v. L. 8° 6610.2
UNCLAIMED. By an English woman 726.21
UNCLE Ben. Adams, W. T. 918.5
UNCLE John. Melville, G. J. W. 319.12
UNCLE Ralph. By the author of "Still waters"... 315.7
UNCLE Silas. Le Fanu, J. S. 314.3
UNCLE Tom's cabin. Stowe, H. (E.) B. Boston ... 733.4
— *Same.* Leipzig 314.20
— Key to. Stowe, H. (E.) B. 314.21
UNCOMMERCIAL traveller, The. Dickens, C. (J. H.) Boston 1824.17
— *Same.* Leipzig 338.21
UNDER lock and key. Speight, T. W. 528.2
UNDER the evergreens. Lorimer, G. C. 916.31
UNDER the greenwood tree. Hardy, T. London ... 728.14
— *Same.* New York 728.4
UNDER the limes. Archer, E. M., *pseud.* 713.11
UNDER the spell. Robinson, F. W. 731.24
UNDER the storks' nest. Katsch, A. E. 715.22
UNDER the sun. Sala, G. A. London, 1872. 8°... 5611.3
UNDER two flags. Rame, L. de la 327.25
UNDERSTANDING, Essay on the human. Locke, J. New York, 1818. 2 v. in 1. 8° 1912.6
UNDERWOOD, Francis Henry. Cloud-pictures. Boston, 1872. vi, 166+ pp. 16° 537.18

Contents.—The exile of von Adelstein's soul; Topankalon; Herr Regenbogen's concert; A great-organ prelude.

— Handbook of English literature. American authors. Boston, 1873. xlviii, 640 pp. Sm. 8°. 5214.1
— – British authors. Boston, 1875. xxxviii, 608 pp. Sm. 8° 5613.6
— Lord of himself. Boston, 1874. 512 pp. 16°. 726.24
UNDERWOOD, Michael. Treatise on the diseases of children; with directions for the management of infants. From the 9th English edition, with notes by S. Merriman, M. Hall, and J. Bell. Philadelphia, 1842. 368 pp. 8° 6023.13
UNDINE. La Motte Fouqué, F. (H. C.), *Freiherr* de. 313.7
UNGAVA: a tale of Esquimaux-land. Ballantyne, R. M. 923.12
UNITED STATES. *Acts, laws, etc.* The commercial laws of the states. New York, 1870. 328 pp. 8°. 6332.2
— *Constitutions.* The constitution of Massachusetts, and of the United States; the declaration of independence, with Washington's farewell address. Northampton, 1806. 12° 618.1
— – The constitutions of the sixteen states which compose the confederated republic of America. Prefixed, the declaration of independence; articles of confederation; the definitive treaty of peace with Great Britain; and the constitution of the United States. Boston, 1797. 12° 818.3
— – What is real democracy? Answered by an exposition of the constitution of the United States. Heinzen, C. Indianapolis, 1871. 16° 6327.4
— *Congressional documents. Journals, reports, etc.* Report of the committee appointed to inquire into the late invasion and seizure of public property at Harper's ferry. [No title-page.] Washington, 1860. 255+ pp. 8° 5013.19
— — – Report of the joint committee on the conduct of the war. Washington, 1863. 3 v. 8° 6916.1
— — – Report of the select committee on the New Orleans riots. Washington, 1867. 596 pp. 8°. 6922.2
— — – Report of the special committee to investigate the troubles in Kansas; with the views of the minority. Washington, 1856. vii, 1206 pp. 8° 6917.2
— — – Supplemental report of the joint committee on the conduct of the war. Washington, 1866. 2 v. 8° 6916.2
— – *Miscellaneous.* Congressional globe. Debates and proceedings, 1st session of 23d congress to 1st session of 41st congress. Washington, 1834–69. 86 v. 4° ....Case 65

Shelf. No.

UNITED STATES. *Congressional documents, cont'd.*

— — *Miscellaneous.* Memorial addresses on the life and character of Charles Sumner, in the senate and house of representatives, April 27, 1874. With other congressional tributes of respect. Washington, 1874. 112 pp. Portrait. 8°.... 5020.8

— — — Message from the president [and accompanying documents regarding the Mexican war], at the 1st session of the 30th congress. [With appendix.] Washington, 1847. 1367, 249 pp. Folded map. Folded sheet. 8°.............5011.13

— — — Message of the president, and accompanying documents. Washington, 1864–69. 8 v. 8°.. 6926.1

— — — Obituary addresses on the occasion of the death of William R. King, in the senate and house of representatives, 8th of Dec., 1853. Washington, 1854. 77 pp. Portrait. 8°..... 1923.3

— — — Papers relating to foreign affairs, accompanying the annual message of the president [1862–67]. Washington, 1864–68. 8 v. 8°........ 6915.1

— *Department of agriculture.* Report of the commissioner, 1865–68, 71. Washington, 1866–72. 5 v. 8°. 6422.2

— — Report of the commissioner on the diseases of cattle. Washington, 1871. 205+ pp. 7 colored plates. 4°.......................... 6610.1

— *Department of education.* Report of the commissioner, 1870, 72, 74. Washington, 1870, 72, 75. 3 v. 8°.................................. 6913.1

— — Special report of the commissioner on the condition and improvement of public schools in the District of Columbia. Washington, 1871. 912 pp. 8°.................................. 6913.7

— *Department of the interior. Census bureau.* Seventh census. Compendium. Washington, 1854. 400 pp. 8°.................................. 6923.4

— — — Eighth census. Preliminary report. 1860. By J. C. G. Kennedy. Washington, 1862. xvi, 294 pp. 8°.............................. 6923.6

— — — — Agriculture of the United States in 1860; compiled from the original returns of the eighth census, by J. C. G. Kennedy. Washington, 1864. clxxii, 292 pp. 4°.................. 6910.2

— — — Ninth census. Compendium. By F. A. Walker. Washington, 1872. vii, 942 pp. 8°. 5010.12

— — — — Statistics of population. Tables 1–8. Washington, 1872. 391+ pp. 4°........... 5010.9

Contents. — Table I. Population, 1870–1790, by states and territories, as white, free colored, slave, Chinese, and Indian. II. 1870–1790. By counties, as white, free colored, etc. III. 1870–1850. By civil divisions less than counties, as white and colored; native and foreign (1870). IV. Nativity (general), 1870–1850, foreign parentage, 1870, by states and territories. V. Nativity (general), 1870–1860, foreign parentage, 1860, in each state, by counties. VI. Nativity (special), 1870, by states and territories. VII. Nativity (selected special), 1870, in each state, by counties. VIII. Nativity (special), 1870, fifty principal cities.

— — — — Statistics of the population [etc.]. Compiled, from the original returns of the ninth census, 1870, by F. A. Walker. Washington, 1872. 3 v. Maps. 4°.......................... 5010.2

Contents. — Vol. I. Population and social statistics. II. Vital statistics. III. Industry and wealth.

— — *Patent office.* Catalogue of curiosities in the national institute. [And] List of patented models. Washington, 1859. 38+, 68 pp. 8°. 6937.1

— — — General index of the Official gazette and monthly volumes of patents. 1872–74. Washington, 1873–75. 3 v. 4°................ 6930.2

— — — Official gazette. Vol. 2–8. Washington, 1872–76. 6 v. Illustrated. 4°............. 6930.1

— — — Report of the commissioner. Washington, 1845, 47–71. 70 v. 8°.................... 6935.1

— *Department of the navy.* Register of the officers of the navy, including officers of the marine corps, and others, to Jan. 1, 1874. Washington, 1874. 176 pp. 8°........................ 6924.7

— — Reports of explorations and surveys to ascertain the practicability of a ship-canal between the Atlantic and Pacific oceans by the way of the isthmus of Darien. By T. O. Selfridge. Washington, 1874. 268+ pp. Illustrated. 17 folded plates. 4°.......................... 5030.6

UNITED STATES. *Department of the navy, continued.*

— — *Naval observatory.* Appendix II. Reports on observations of the total eclipse of the sun, August 7, 1869. Conducted under the direction of B. F. Sands. Washington, 1869. v, 214+ pp. 12 plates. 4°.............................. 6910.3

— *Department of state.* The case of Great Britain as laid before the tribunal of arbitration, convened at Geneva. Washington, 1872. 3 v. 8°..... 5011.2

— — The case of the United States, to be laid before the tribunal of arbitration, to be convened at Geneva. Washington, 1872. 204 pp. 8°.... 5010.6

— — The counter case of Great Britain, as laid before the tribunal of arbitration, convened at Geneva. With volumes 5–7 of Appendix to the British case. Washington, 1872. 1105+ pp. 8°.... 5011.9

— — Correspondence concerning claims against Great Britain. Washington, 1869–71. 7 v. 8°..... 6911.1

Contents. — Vol. I. Recognition of rebel belligerency. I, II. Enforcement of neutrality. II, III. Rebel cruisers. III. Negotiations concerning claims convention. IV, V. General appendix; Parliamentary and judicial appendix. VI. Most important documents rearranged. VII. List of claims; General index.

— — Papers relating to foreign affairs, 1863, 70, 71. Washington, 1864, 70, 71. 5 v. 8°.......... 6915.1

— — Papers relating to the foreign relations of the United States. Washington, 1870, 71. 2 v. 8°. 6911.2

— *Department of the treasury.* Manual of the direct and excise tax system of the United States. By G. S. Boutwell. Washington, 1863. x, 500 pp. 8°.............................. 6923.5

— — Report on the principal fisheries of the American seas. By L. Sabine. Washington, 1853. 317 pp. 8°.................................. 811.9

— — [Reports on the mineral resources.] Washington, 1868. 684+, 71+ pp. 8°............ 6631.6

Contents. — Report of J. Ross Browne on the mineral resources of the states and territories west of the Rocky mountains; Report of J. W. Taylor on the mineral resources east of the Rocky mountains.

— — *Coast survey.* Report of the superintendent, showing the progress of the survey, 1851–57, 59–64, 66. Washington, 1852–69. Plates. 1 v. 8°; 15 v. 4°.......................... 6920.1

— — *Commissioner of fish and fisheries.* Report on the condition of the sea fisheries of the south coast of New England, 1871–73. By S. F. Baird. Part I, II. With supplementary papers. Washington, 1873, 74. 2 v. Maps. Plates. 8°...6923.12

— — *Commissioner of mining statistics.* Statistics of mines and mining in the states and territories west of the Rocky mountains; being the fourth annual report of R. W. Raymond. Washington, 1873. 566 pp. 8°........................ 5035.8

— — *Supervising surgeon's office.* The cholera epidemic of 1873 in the United States. Washington, 1875. 28, vi, 1025+ pp. Illustrations. Maps. 8°.................................. 6030.1

— *Department of war.* Digest of the laws relating to the military establishment of the United States. By A. Mordecai. Washington, 1833. 134 pp. 12°. 6927.5

— — Infantry tactics. 1861. Philadelphia, 1863. 450 pp. Illustrated. 1 folded plate. Sm. 12°. 1529.2

— — Notes of military reconnoissance[s]. Washington, 1848. 614 pp. Illustrated. Maps. 8°.. 5032.1

Contents. — Notes of a military reconnoissance, from Missouri to California. By William H. Emory; Report of James J. Abert, of his examination of New Mexico; Report of Philip St. George Cooke of his march from New Mexico to Upper California; Journal of Abraham R. Johnston.

— — Regulations for the army, 1857. New York [1857]. xxv, 457, 21 pp. 12°.............. 6927.8

— — Report of the chief engineer of the U. S. army, for the year ending June 30, 1865. [No title-page. Washington, 1865.] 81 pp. Maps. 8°. 6422.6

— — Report on the art of war in Europe in 1854–56; by R. Delafield. Washington, 1861. xxiv, 277 pp. Illustrated. Maps. Plans. 4°..... 5910.3

— — Reports of explorations and surveys, to ascertain the most practicable and economical route for a railroad from the Mississippi river to the Pacific ocean. Vol. 1–12. Maps and plates. Washington, 1855–66. 12 v. in 13. 4°...... 6611.2

Shelf. No.

UNITED STATES. *Department of war, continued.*

— - Revised regulations for the army, 1861. Philadelphia [1861]. 559 pp. 12° 6921.1
— - *Same.* Philadelphia, 1862. 559 pp. 12° ... 1521.12
— - *Same.* With appendix containing changes to June, 1863. Washington, 1863. 594 pp. 12°. 6921.2
— - *Adjutant general's office.* General orders, 1861–63. Washington, 1861–63. 5 v. 16°........ 5016.9
— - - Military laws and rules and regulations for the armies. [Washington, 1813.] xix, 271+ pp. Sm. 12° 6928.1
— - *Bureau of engineers.* Northwestern Georgia (with portions of Tennessee and Alabama), being part of the department of the Cumberland, 1863. Corrections and additions from Capt. W. E. Merrill's map of "Northern Georgia," in 1864. [Washington, 1864.] Size, 38¼ × 33 in. Scale, 1: 350,000 .... 5030.10
— - - Portions of the military departments of the Cumberland, of the South, and of the Gulf. Compiled Jan., 1863, by Dennis Callahan. [Washington, 1863.] Size, 66 × 50½ in. Scale, 5.524 m. to 1 in.......................... 5030.10
— - - Report of a reconnaissance of the Black hills of Dakota, made in the summer of 1874. By William Ludlow. Washington, 1875. 121 pp. Plate. Folded maps. 4° 630.1
— - - Report upon the reconnaissance of Northwestern Wyoming, including Yellowstone national park, made in 1873 by William A. Jones. With appendix. Washington, 1875. vi, 331 pp. Maps. Illustrations. 8°.............. 6924.9
— - *Bureau of topographical engineers.* Report upon the physics and hydraulics of the Mississippi river; upon the protection of the alluvial region against overflow; and upon the deepening of the mouths. By A. A. Humphreys and H. L. Abbot. Philadelphia, 1861. xxiv, 17–456, cxlv pp. Maps. 4° 6920.2
— - *Office of the chief signal officer.* Circular. The practical use of meteorological reports and weather-maps. Washington, 1871. 79 pp. Illustrated. 8° 6924.4
— - *Ordnance department.* Ordnance memoranda. No. 17. Report of the board of officers on Gatling guns of large caliber for flank-defence. Washington, 1874. 50+ pp. Plates. 4° 6910.7
— - - Reports of experiments on the properties of metals for cannon, and the qualities of cannon powder. By T. J. Rodman. Boston, 1861. xii, 308+ pp. Plates. 4°...................... 6910.6
— - - Reports of experiments on the strength and other properties of metals for cannon. Philadelphia, 1856. xx, 428 pp. Plates. 4°...... 6910.5
— - *Provost marshal general's office.* Circular 1–106. Washington, 1863. [No title-page.] 16°..... 5016.8
— *Miscellaneous documents.* Statements, supported by evidence, of W. T. G. Morton on his claim to the discovery of the anæsthetic properties of ether, submitted to the select committee appointed by the senate of the United States. Washington, 1853. 582, 135 pp. 8°......... 6812.3
— - Trial of Andrew Johnson, before the senate of the United States, on impeachment by the house of representatives for high crimes and misdemeanors. Washington, 1868. 3 v. 8°....... 5010.4

Biography.

— Allen, W. American biographical and historical dictionary. Boston, 1832. 8°...........*R.R., D.3.2
— Bungay, G. W. Crayon sketches and off-hand takings, of distinguished American statesmen, orators, divines, essayists, editors, poets, and philanthropists. Boston, 1852. 16°.......... 1516.24
— Clarke, R. H. Lives of the deceased bishops of the catholic church in the. New York, 1872. 2 v. 8°.................................. 5811.1
— Drake, F. S. Dictionary of American biography, including men of the time. Boston, 1872. 8°. *R.R., E.1.3

Shelf. No.

UNITED STATES. *Biography, continued.*

— Durrie, D. S. Bibliographia genealogica Americana: an alphabetical index to American genealogies and pedigrees. Albany, 1868. 8° 5022.8
— Goodrich, C. A. Lives of the signers to the declaration of independence. Boston, 1834. 12°.. 1014.7
— Griswold, R. W. The female poets of America. New York, 1874. L. 8° 5212.2
— - The poets and poetry of America. New York, 1873. L. 8° 5212.3
— Lanman, C. Biographical annals of the civil government of the United States during its first century. Washington, 1876. 8° ........*R.R., C.3.2
— Livingston, J. Biographical sketches of distinguished Americans. New York, 1853. 8°.. 5024.3
— Parker, T. Historic Americans. [Franklin, Washington, Adams, and Jefferson.] Boston, 1871. Sm. 8° 5025.4
— Parton, J. Famous Americans of recent times. Boston, 1871. 8° 1214.14
— Sargent, N. Public men and events from the commencement of Munroe's administration, in 1817, to the close of Fillmore's administration, in 1853. Philadelphia, 1875. 2 v. 8° 5223.1
— Shanks, W. F. G. Personal recollections of distinguished generals [in the civil war]. New York, 1866. 12° 1015.5
— Sparks, J. Library of American biography. New York [*cop.* 1834–]65. 10 v. 16°....... 5028.1
— Stowe, H. (E.) B. Men of our times; or leading patriots of the day. Hartford, 1869. 8°...... 5023.9

Geography, description, travel, etc.

— Alden, J. The science of government in connection with American institutions. New York [*cop.* 1866]. 12° 6336.1
— Appleton, D., and co. Hand-book of American travel. Northern and Eastern tour. New York, 1872. 12° 425.17
— - Southern tour. *See* Jones, Charles H......... 413.5
— Asher, J. R., and Adams, G. H. New commercial, topographical, and statistical atlas and gazetteer of the. New York [1873]. F°..*R.R. Desk
— Bachelder, J. B. Illustrated tourist's guide of the. Boston, 1873. Sm. 8° 413.10
— Blake, S. J. A visit to some American schools and colleges. London, 1867. Sm. 8° 1736.7
— Bogen, F. W. The German in America. Boston, 1851. 12° 1939.3
— Bowles, S. Across the continent: a summer's journey to the Rocky mountains, the Mormons, and the Pacific states. Springfield, 1868. 16°. 417.6
— Bremer, F. The homes of the New World; impressions of America. New York, 1853. 2 v. 12° 414.24
— Bryant, W. C. Picturesque America; or, the land we live in. New York [*cop.* 1872, 73]. 2 v. 4° 5030.9
— Coffin, C. C. The seat of empire. Boston, 1870. 12° 425.15
— Darby, W. Tour from the city of New York to Detroit, in the Michigan territory. New York, 1819. 8° 411.1
— Dickens, C. (J. H.) American notes. Boston, 1874. 16°.............................. 1824.10
— *Same.* Leipzig, 1842. Sq. 16° 418.2
— *Same.* Philadelphia, N. D. 8° 732.37
— Dixon, W. H. New America. Leipzig, 1867. 2 v. in 1. Sq. 16° 418.1
— - White conquest. Leipzig, 1876. 2 v. in 1. Sq. 16° 439.4
— Grund, F. J. The Americans in their moral, social, and political relations. Boston, 1837. 12° 1534.1
— Hamilton, T. Men and manners in America. Philadelphia, 1833. 2 v. 16°............... 416.1
— Handbook for immigrants to the. New York, 1871. 16° 417.5
— Johnston, J. F. W. Notes on North America. Boston, 1851. 2 v. 16° 1524.5

Shelf. No.

UNITED STATES. *Geography, description, travel, etc., continued.*
— Kelley, W. D. Speeches, addresses and letters on industrial and financial questions. Philadelphia, 1872. 8° 1531.3
— Lester, J. E. The Atlantic to the Pacific. What to see and how to see it. Boston, 1873. 12° ... 417.12
— *Same.* London, 1873. Sm. 8° 417.13
— Lyell, *Sir* C. A second visit to the. New York, 1849. 2 v. 12° 415.11
— Map of the United States, the British provinces, Mexico, the West Indies and Central America, with a part of New Granada and Venezuela. New York, 1849. Size: 2 ft. 4 in. × 3 ft. 3 in. 5032.4
— Medley, J. G. An autumn tour in the. London, 1873. Sm. 8° 5036.6
— Nordhoff, C. The communistic societies of the. New York, 1875. 8° 5821.2
— — Politics for young Americans. New York, 1875. 12° 5826.10
— Olmsted, F. L. Journey in the back country. New York, 1860. 12° 414.6
— — Journey in the seaboard slave states. New York, 1859. 12° 414.7
— Pulszky, F. (A.) and T. White, red, black. Sketches of American society in the. New York, 1853. 2 v. 12° 414.17
— Rae, W. F. Westward by rail: a journey to San Francisco and back. Leipzig, 1874. Sq. 16° .. 438.3
— Sketches of scenery and manners in the. New York, 1829. 12° 413.12
— Stoddard, R. H., *editor.* Sans-souci series. Men and manners in America one hundred years ago. Edited by H. E. Scudder. New York, 1876. 16°. 1827.1
— Trollope, A. North America. Leipzig, 1862. 3 v. Sq. 16° 418.4
— Tuckerman, H. T. America and her commentators. With a critical sketch of travel in the. New York, 1864. 8° 5033.5
— Wilkes, C. Narrative of the United States exploring expedition, 1838–42. London, 1852. 2 v. Sm. 8° 414.21

History, etc.

— Abbott, J. Story of American history 936.1.5
— Bancroft, G. History of the, from the discovery of the continent. Boston, 1872–74. 10 v. 8° .. 5012.3
— — *Same.* Thoroughly revised edition. Vol. I–VI. Boston, 1876. [Centenary edition.] 6 v. 16°. 815.4
— — History of the colonization of the. Abridged. Boston, 1841. 16° 5016.11
— Bancroft, H. H. The native races of the Pacific states of North America. New York, 1874–76. 5 v. 8° 5920.4
— Benton, T. H. Thirty years' view; or, a history of the American government, 1820–50. New York, 1854, 56. 2 v. 8° 812.2
— Bonner, J. Child's history of the. New York, 1870. 3 v. 16° 926.3
— Bradford, A. History of the federal government, for fifty years: from March, 1789, to March, 1839. Boston, 1840. 8° 5010.13
— Bryant, W. C., and Gay, S. H. A popular history of the United States, from the first discovery of the western hemisphere by the Northmen, to the end of the first century of the union of the states. Vol. I. New York, 1876. 8° 610.5
— Butler, F. Complete history of the, to 1820. Hartford, 1821. 3 v. 8° 812.9
— Dodge, N. S. Stories of a grandfather about American history. Boston, 1874. Sq. 16° 913.29
— Doyle, J. A. History of the. New York, 1876. 16° 618.4
— Goodrich, C. A. History of the. Boston, 1827. 12°. 818.6
— *Same.* Boston, 1858. 12° 615.1
— Greeley, H., and others. The great industries of the. Hartford, 1872. 8° 1511.1
— Hall, J. The romance of Western history. Cincinnati, 1871. 12° 814.2
— Higginson, T. W. Young folks' history of the. Boston, 1875. Sq. 16° 618.2

Shelf. No.

UNITED STATES. *History, etc., continued.*
— Hildreth, R. History of the, 1497–1789. New York, 1871. 3 v. 8° 5011.10
— — 1788–1821. New York, 1871. 3 v. 8° 5011.11
— Hopkins, L. A comic history of the. New York, 1870. 12° 617.3
— Hudson, F. Journalism in the, from 1690 to 1872. New York, 1873. 8° 5214.2
— MacPherson, E. Hand-book of politics for 1872, 74. Washington, 1872, 74. 2 v. 8° 6924.8
— Ollier, E. Cassell's History of the United States. Vol. I. London [1875]. L. 8° 810.11
— Preble, G. H. Our flag. Origin and progress of the flag of the. Albany, 1872. 8° 5013.5
— Richardson, A. S. The history of our country from its discovery by Columbus to the celebration of the centennial anniversary of its declaration of independence. Boston, 1875. 8° 812.3
— Story, J. Commentaries on the constitution of the. Boston, 1833. L. 8° 1530.2
— Tocqueville, A. (C. H. C.) de. De la démocratie en Amérique. Paris, 1836. 2 v. 12° 2018.6
— — Democracy in America. Boston, 1873. 2 v. Sm. 8° 5015.1
— Trumbull, H. History of the discovery of America, of the landing of our forefathers, at Plymouth, and their engagements with the Indians, in New-England, 1620–79. Boston, 1819. 8° 814.5
— Walker, F. A. The Indian question. Boston, 1874. 12° 5016.14

See also the names of the several states and other divisions of the country, as New England, the West, etc.

History. Colonial period.

— Frothingham, R. The rise of the republic of the. Boston, 1872. 8° 5010.5
— Parkman, F., *jr.* The conspiracy of Pontiac and the Indian war after the conquest of Canada. Boston, 1870. 2 v. 12° 5015.4
— — France and England in North America. Boston, 1871–74. 4 v. 12° 5015.5
— Schele de Vere, M. Romance of American history. Early annals. New York, 1872. 12° 5016.1
— Walsh, R. An appeal from the judgments of Great Britain, respecting the. Philadelphia, 1819. 8° 811.10
— Whitmore, W. H. The cavalier dismounted: an essay on the origin and founders of the thirteen colonies. Salem, 1864. 8° 5014.6

History. Revolution, and preceding controversy.

— Etting, F. M. An historical account of the old state house of Pennsylvania now known as the Hall of independence. Boston, 1876. Sm. 4° .. 5220.1
— Goodrich, C. A. Lives of the signers to the declaration of independence. Boston, 1834. 12° 1014.7
— Hale, E. E. One hundred years ago. How the war began. Boston, 1875. 8° 811.15
— Headley, J. T. The chaplains and clergy of the revolution. New York, 1864. 12° 1014.1
— — Washington and his generals. New York, 1854, 55. 2 v. 12° 1216.5
— Johnson, J. Traditions and reminiscences chiefly of the American revolution in the South. Charleston, 1851. 8° 812.11
— Kapp, F. Der Soldatenhandel deutscher Fürsten nach Amerika (1775 bis 1783). Berlin, 1864. 16° 5715.4
— Lossing, B. J. Pictorial field-book of the revolution. New York, 1860. 2 v. 8° 810.17
— Ludlow, J. M. The war of American independence. London, 1876. 16° 5018.1
— Porter, E. G., and Stephenson, H. M. Souvenir of 1775. Lexington. 1775–1875. [Boston, 1875.] 4° 810.5
— Sabine, L. Biographical sketches of loyalists of the American revolution, with an historical essay. Boston, 1864. 2 v. 12° 1211.1

Shelf. No.

UNITED STATES. *History. Revolution, etc., cont'd.*
— Stone, W. L. Border wars of the American revolution. New York, 1857. 2 v. 16° 818.1
— – Life of Joseph Brant, including the border wars of the American revolution. Albany, 1865. 2 v. 8° 5022.4
— Thornton, J. W. The pulpit of the American revolution: or, the political sermons of the period of 1776. Boston [1876]. 8° 1921.4
— Watson, E. Men and times of the revolution. New York, 1856. 8° 1214.15
— Watson, H. C. Camp-fires of the revolution. New York, 1869. 8° 811.8
See also Bunker hill.

History. War of 1812–15.

— Darnell, E. Journal containing an account of those Kentucky volunteers and regulars, commanded by General Winchester, 1812–13. Philadelphia, 1854. Sm. 12° 819.6
— Lossing, B. J. Pictorial field-book of the war of 1812. New York, 1868. 8° 810.16

History. War with Mexico, 1845–47.

— Jay, W. Review of the causes and consequences of the Mexican war. Boston, 1849. 12° 5017.2
— Smith, S. C. Chile con carne; or, the camp and the field. New York, 1857. 12° 515.2
— Stevens, I. I. Campaigns of the Rio Grande and of Mexico. With notices of the recent work of Major Ripley. New York, 1851. 8°. 612.3

History. Civil war, 1861–65.

— Adams, F. C. The story of a trooper. New York, 1865. 12° 816.10
— Alcott, L. M. Hospital sketches, and Camp and fireside stories 926.13
— Boynton, C. B. History of the navy during the rebellion. New York, 1867. 2 v. 8° 5012.1
— Boynton, H. V. N. Sherman's historical raid. The memoirs in the light of the record. Cincinnati, 1875. 8° 5024.5
— Brownlow, W. G. Sketches of the rise, progress, and decline of secession. Philadelphia, 1862. 12°. 815.3
— Buchanan, J. Mr. Buchanan's administration on the eve of the rebellion. New York, 1866. 8°. 813.8
— Coffin, C. C. Following the flag. From August, 1861, to November, 1862, with the army of the Potomac. Boston, 1865. 12° 913.17
— – Four years of fighting, from the battle of Bull Run to the fall of Richmond. Boston, 1866. 8°. 813.7
— – My days and nights on the battle-field. Boston, 1872. 12° 913.18
— Conyngham, D. P. The Irish brigade and its campaigns. Boston, 1869. 12° 824.4
— Draper, J. W. History of the American civil war. New York, 1868, 70. 3 v. 8° 811.6
— Edmonds, S. E. E. Nurse and spy in the union army. Hartford, 1865. 8° 813.1
— Eggleston, G. C. A rebel's recollections. New York, 1875. 16° 5016.15
— Ellis, D. Thrilling adventures of the great union guide of East Tennessee during the Southern rebellion. New York, 1867. 12° 816.7
— Frémont, J. B. The story of the guard: a chronicle of the war. Boston, 1863. 16° 815.5
— Gasparin, A. (É.), *comte* de. The uprising of a great people: the United States in 1861. London, 1861. Sm. 8° 817.5
— Gilmor, H. Four years in the saddle. New York, 1866. 12° 817.17
— Gilmore, J. R. Among the pines: or, South in secession-time. New York, 1862. 12° 916.3
— Greeley, H. The American conflict, 1860–65. Hartford, 1865, 67. 2 v. 8° 810.1
— Guernsey, A. H., and Alden, H. M. Harper's pictorial history of the great rebellion. New York [*cop.* 1866]. 2 v. F° ..............*R.R. Desk
— Hamersly, L. R. Records of living officers of the U. S. navy and marine corps; with a history of naval operations during the rebellion of 1861–5. Philadelphia, 1870. 8° 5022.14

UNITED STATES. *History. Civil war, continued.*
— Harvard memorial biographies. Cambridge, 1867. 2 v. Sm. 8° 5025.12
— Hepworth, G. H. The whip, hoe, and sword; or, the gulf-department in '63. Boston, 1864. 12°. 414.1
— Higginson, T. W. Army life in a black regiment. Boston, 1870. 12° 416.5
— Hitchcock, —. Chronological record of the American civil war. New York, 1868. 8° 5013.4
— Hosmer, J. K. The color-guard: a corporal's notes of military service in the nineteenth army corps. Boston, 1864. 12° 826.1
— Hospital transports. A memoir of the embarkation of the sick and wounded from the peninsula of Virginia in the summer of 1862. Boston, 1863. 16° 5016.16
— Johnson, A. The great impeachment and trial of Andrew Johnson. Philadelphia [*cop.* 1868]. 8°.5011.14
— Johnston, J. E. Narrative of military operations, during the late war between the states. New York, 1874. 8° 813.18
— Lossing, B. J. Pictorial history of the civil war in the. Philadelphia, 1866–70. 3 v. 8° 810.15
— Maps relating to the war. V. P., V. D. F°.*R.R. Desk
— Melville, H. Battle-pieces and aspects of the war. [Poems.] New York, 1866. 12° 1624.3
— Memorial ceremonies at the graves of our soldiers, May 30, 1868. By Frank Moore. Washington city, 1869. 736+ pp. 8° 5013.13
— Moreau, H. La politique française en Amérique. Paris, 1864. 8° 831.1
— Nichols, G. W. Story of the great march [Sherman's]. New York, 1866. 12° 815.7
— Paris, L. P. A. d'Orleans, *comte* de. History of the civil war in America. Vol. I, II. Philadelphia, 1875, 76. 2 v. 8° 813.17
— Parton, J. General Butler in New Orleans. History of the administration of the department of the Gulf in 1862. New York, 1864. 12° 815.2
— Patterson, R. Narrative of the campaign in the valley of the Shenandoah, in 1861. Philadelphia, 1865. 8° 5013.20
— Pollard, E. A. Life of Jefferson Davis, with a secret history of the Southern confederacy. Philadelphia [*cop.* 1869]. 8° 5013.3
— – Southern history of the war. New York, 1864, 66. 3 v. 8° 5013.17
— Richardson, A. D. The secret service, the field, the dungeon, and the escape. Hartford, 1866. 8° 813.15
— Russell, W. H. My diary North and South. Boston, 1863. 12° 413.6
— Sargent, F. W. England, the United States, and the Southern confederacy. London, 1864. 8°. 812.7
— Scott, J. Partisan life with John S. Mosby. New York, 1867. 8° 811.14
— Shanks, W. F. G. Personal recollections of distinguished generals. New York, 1866. 12° ... 1015.5
— Sherman, W. T. Memoirs. By himself. New York, 1875. 2 v. 8° ....1212.3 and 5024.4
— Stars and stripes, The, in rebeldom. A series of papers written by federal prisoners [privates] in Richmond [etc.]. Boston, 1862. 12° 817.2
— Swinton, W. The twelve decisive battles of the war. New York, 1873 [*cop.* 1867]. 8° 812.13
— Whiting, W. War powers under the constitution of the United States. Boston, 1871. 8° 5013.18
— Woodward, E. M. Our campaigns. Philadelphia, 1865. 16° 817.14

History. Civil war. Maps.

— *Department of the Cumberland.* Northwestern Georgia (with portions of Tennessee and Alabama), being part of the department of the Cumberland, 1863. [Washington, 1864.] *See* UNITED STATES. *Department of war. Bureau of engineers* 5030.10
— – Portions of the military departments of the Cumberland, of the South, and of the Gulf. [Washington, 1863.] *See* UNITED STATES. *Department of war. Bureau of engineers* 5030.10

Shelf. No.

UNITED STATES, *continued.*

Literature.

— Allibone, S. A. Critical dictionary of English literature and British and American authors. Philadelphia, 1871. 3 v. 8° .... *R.R., A.3.6
— American publishers' circular and literary gazette. Vol. I–IV. Philadelphia, 1863–65. 4 v. in 2. 8° 1422.4
— Cheever, G. B., *editor.* The American commonplace book of poetry. Philadelphia, 1841. 12°. 1534.14
— Duyckinck, E. A. and G. L. Cyclopædia of American literature. Philadelphia, 1875. 2 v. 4° .... *R.R., D.3.11
— Griswold, R. W. The poets and poetry of America. New York, 1873. L. 8° 5212.3
— Smyth, W. Lectures on modern history. With a list of books on American history, by J. Sparks. Boston, 1851. 8° 5012.10
— Underwood, F. H. Hand-book of English literature. American authors. Boston, 1873. Sm. 8°. 5214.1
— Van Rhyn, G. A. F. What and how to read; containing a list of the best books published in America during the past five years. New York, 1875. 12° 6136.11
— Whipple, E. P. Essays and reviews. Boston, 1871. 2 v. 16° 1936.2

See also Americanisms.

Military and naval institutions and affairs.

— Boynton, C. B. History of the navy during the rebellion. New York, 1867. 2 v. 8° 5012.1
— Brackett, A. G. History of the United States cavalry. New York, 1865. 12° 816.5
— Cooper, J. F. History of the navy of the, 1607 to 1853. New York, 1853. 3 v. in 1. 8° 813.4
— — Continued to 1860. New York, 1866. 3 v. in 1. 8° 813.5
— Marshall, E. C. History of the United States naval academy. New York, 1862. 12° 816.9
— Rodenbough, T. F. From everglade to cañon with the 2d dragoons (2d United States cavalry). 1836–75. New York, 1875. 8° 5032.6
— Scott, W. Infantry tactics; or, rules for the exercise and manœuvres of the United States infantry. New York, 1852. 3 v. 16° 1529.7
— Steuben, F. W. A. H. F., *baron* von. Regulations for the order and discipline of the troops of the United States. New York, 1794. Sm. 12°. 6928.2
— Taylor, O. M. History and description of the United States naval academy. Baltimore, 1872. 8° 813.9

Shelf. No.

UNITED STATES, *continued.*

Slavery question.

— Adams, N. A south-side view of slavery; or, three months at the South, in 1854. Boston, 1854. 16° 817.8
— The anti-slavery examiner. No. 10. American slavery as it is. New York, 1869. 8° 812.10
— Hildreth, R. Despotism in America; or, an inquiry into the nature and results of the slave-holding system in the. Boston, 1840. 12° 816.2
— Jay, W. A view of the action of the federal government in behalf of slavery. New York, 1839. 12° 6316.1
— Livermore, G. Opinions of the founders of the republic on negroes as slaves, as citizens, and as soldiers. Boston, 1862. 8° 812.8
— Treadwell, S. B. American liberties and American slavery morally and physically illustrated. New York, 1838. 12° 817.10
— Wilson, H. History of the rise and fall of the slave power in America. Boston, 1874, 75. 2 v. 8° 5012.9

Miscellaneous.

— Baird, S. F., Brewer, T. M., and Ridgway, R. History of North American birds. Vol. I, II. Boston, 1874. 2 v. L. 8° 6611.1
— Batchelder, S. Introduction and early progress of cotton manufacture in the. Boston, 1863. 16° 6435.4
— Colton, C. Thoughts on the religious state of the country; with reasons for preferring episcopacy. New York, 1836. 12° 6326.13
— The commercial laws of the states. New York, 1870. 8° 6332.2
— Hayward, J. The religious creeds and statistics of every Christian denomination in the. Boston, 1836. 16° 5816.20
— Pharmacopœia of the. Philadelphia, 1851. 8°. 6021.8
— Poor, H. V. Manual of the railroads of the, 1871, 72. New York, 1871. 8° 6923.10
— Sumner, C. Prophetic voices concerning America. Boston, 1874. 16° 833.1
— Ten Brook, A. American state universities, their origin and progress. Cincinnati, 1875. 8° 5831.4
— Washington, G. Letters, containing an account of his husbandry, with his opinions on various questions in agriculture; and many particulars of the rural economy of the. Alexandria, 1803. 8° 1912.1

NOTE ON THE UNITED STATES.

The centennial period has given occasion to many reviews of the progress of the country during the past hundred years, and in vol. 50 and vol. 51 of Harper's monthly particularly there is a series called "The first century of the republic."

Art.

Tuckerman's "Book of the artists" [1511.6] constitutes much the best, and the only considerable, history of American art. For architecture, see Fergusson's "Modern styles of architecture" [6212.3]. For sculpture, see the translation of Viardot [1714.28]; and see also the paper on "American artists in Italy," in Harper's monthly, vol. 41.

The paper in Harper's monthly, April, 1876, is on the "Progress of the fine arts" during the century. Miss Tytler's "Modern painters" [6216.4] give a concise sketch from Allston down.

See also the note under Painting.

Biography.

The most recent and most comprehensive biographical dictionary of Americans is F. S. Drake's; but Allibone, Griswold, and Duyckinck for such as are writers; Tuckerman [1511.6] for such as are artists; the Biographical dictionary of Thomas and Appleton's Cyclopædia will often supplement or expand the information. The titles of the other books under this head will sufficiently explain them.

HISTORY.

Comprehensive works.

The only general history of established reputation and considerable extent, coming down into this century, is Hildreth's [5011.10 and 11]. He is painstaking and judicial, but often curt in his judgments, and held by some to be prejudiced, particularly where his federal sympathies find play. Lossing's Pictorial field-books of the revolution [810.17] and of the war of 1812 [810.16], with the introduction to the former and the connecting links, prefixed to the latter, make a history covering nearly the same interval, but in the earlier work it hardly has the shape of a regular historical narrative.

Cassell's History [810.11], when completed, with its profusion of illustrations, is the best popular general history of extended character written abroad, but at the time of writing this note only the first volume of the native History by Bryant and Gay [610.5] is before the public. The reader who desires further examination will find Sparks's list of authorities, as given in his edition of Smyth's "Lectures on modern history" [5012.10], of use; as also the more popular selection made by Col. Higginson, in his condensed "Young folks' history" [618.2], which is perhaps the best of minor narratives.

Colonial period.

Bancroft has the leading reputation, his history as yet coming down only through the revolution. His research is laborious, but a somewhat declamatory style, with strong contrasts, and the marked democratic sentiments of the author, with characteristic adhesion to his opinions, have opened his work to criticism. The recent centenary edition [815.4] is revised and somewhat condensed from his original issue [5012.3]. His early volumes are reviewed in Prescott's "Miscellanies" [1537.8; 5237.3]. His narrative can often be compared with Hildreth's [5011.10] with advantage. Frothingham [5010.5] has a specific purpose in tracing the rise of the union sentiment till its culmination under the constitution. Robertson's well-known general history of the discovery and settlement of America has sections upon the English colonies.

For local aspects, see the notes under the heads of New England, Massachusetts, Plymouth, New York, Pennsylvania, Virginia, etc.

The *French colonization* is graphically traced by Parkman, in his series called "France and England in North America" [5015.5]. Part 1, "Pioneers of France," contains an account of the Huguenots in Florida, and of Champlain and his associates in Canada, and along the northern line [see Atlantic monthly, Oct., 1865]; in part 2, he traces the experiences of the Jesuits, while in part 3 [reviewed in North American review, April, 1870] he recounts "The discovery of the great West," by La Salle; and in part 4, "The old régime in Canada," he traces the growth and downfall of the French power. Chapter 2d of Tuckerman's "America and her commentators" [5033.5] enumerates the early French discoverers.

Old French war, 1755-62. The English accounts may be read in Stanhope and the other general histories of England. See further accounts in Bancroft (vols. 3 and 4), Hildreth, Cassell, and popularly in Palfrey's abridged "History of New England," and in vol. II of Barry's "History of Massachusetts" [812.5], etc. For Braddock's expedition, see the appendix in vol. 2d of Sparks's "Life of Washington," and the account in Irving's "Life of Washington" [1211.2, etc.]; and in the opening parts of Parkman's "Conspiracy of Pontiac" [5015.4]. Everett has an oration on this war as the school of the revolution [1921.1.1], and the Comte de Paris, in his "History of the civil war" [813.17], treats it in the same way.

In fiction for this period, there are Cooper's "Last of the Mohicans" [523.10] and James's "Ticonderoga."

Parkman, in the opening chapters of his "Conspiracy of Pontiac" [5015.4], recapitulates the history of the relations of the French and English down to the close of the war in 1762, and then takes up the history of the war between the Indians and the English, carrying the story down to the death of Pontiac, 1769.

Draper, in his "History of the civil war" [811.6], gives a general summary of the character of the colonial period.

The revolution and preceding controversy.

General histories. The earliest American accounts of value are the history of Gordon, an English clergyman, resident through the war in America, who is little more than an annalist; that of Ramsay, a South Carolinian member of congress, who had access to official papers, and whose account is concise and candid; and the life of Washington by Marshall. The chief English accounts, written at a like early period, are the somewhat arbitrary history of George III's reign by Adolphus, who sides with the king's ministers, and Belsham, who favors the colonists. The principal military historian on the royal side is Stedman, who throws much blame on Sir William Howe, and is strongly opinionated in his views. We have further on the same side Sir William Howe's own narrative, and Clinton's account of the campaign of 1781. Andrews's History of the war, 1775-83, in Europe and America, is chiefly a compilation from the public prints and the debates. It was principally upon the authorities already mentioned that Smyth based the closing lectures of his well-known "Lectures on modern history" [5012.10; 5925.7], in which he has with great candor discussed both sides of the preceding controversy, and the conduct of the succeeding war. Sabine's "American loyalists" [1211.1] gives the Tory side of the question, and Chesney, in his "Military biographies" [5922.8], has a paper on a "Carolina loyalist." The reader, beside the treatment of the more recent general historians of the war, will find much illustrative matter on the rise of the controversy in Frothingham's "Life and times of Joseph Warren" [1010.6], in his articles in the Atlantic monthly, June and Aug., 1862, and Nov., 1863, on the "Sam Adams regiments," and in his recent "Rise of the republic" [5010.5]. See also for this formative period, Loring's "Hundred orators" [5022.9]; Tudor's "Life of Otis" [1012.2]; Quincy's "Life of Quincy" [5021.9; 5022.16]; Life and writings, including diary of John Adams; and the Letters to his wife; Wells's "Life of Samuel Adams" [5021.7]; the Autobiography and writings of Franklin [1012.3; 1213.3; 5025.13]; and Wirt's "Life of Patrick Henry" [1012.4]. A full guide to the beginnings of the revolution in Massachusetts will be found in the Library Bulletin for July, 1875, under "Centennial reading," which account, without the shelf-numbers of the Central Library copies, is repeated in the Memorial of Bunker hill [810.10] published by the city of Boston.

Of the later histories of the war, the most important American account is perhaps that contained in Bancroft, who begins the history of the revolution proper in his seventh volume, with 1774. He is thought to extol Washington's military capacity by disparagement of others. Hildreth treats the subject concisely, giving about half of his third volume to it [5011.10.3]. The lives of Washington by Sparks and Irving are also important contributions. Lossing's "Field-book" [810.17] is a very valuable gathering of the scattered traditions and other minor details of the conflict, arranged in the course of an itinerary, covering all the important localities associated with the contest.

Allen's "Battles of the British navy" [5417.5] gives the English side, and Cooper's "History of the American navy" [813.4; 813.5] the American side, of the warfare on the ocean. There are English accounts in Knight's "History of England" [5413.1], etc.; but the narrative of Earl Stanhope (Lord Mahon), in his "History of England" [838.3], is considered very temperate and fair.

In closer illustration of the period, reference may be made, for the *political aspects*, to the lives of John Adams; Samuel Adams; Thomas Jefferson; John Jay; George Read; Madison, by Rives, which contains the fullest account of congress, 1780-83; Franklin; Patrick Henry; Hamilton; Morris, for the finances, etc.; while, for the *military events*, see the lives of Arnold; Ethan Allen; De Kalb; Gates; Greene; Heath; La Fayette; Lincoln; Lee; Marion; Montgomery; Pickering; Putnam; Steuben, by Kapp, elaborate; Schuyler, by Lossing; Sullivan, by Amory; and Stark. Some of these books must be sought for in the Bates Hall. The literature of the first year of the war, 1776, is elucidated in the Library Bulletin for Jan., 1876.

See the titles and note under Military and naval history in this article.

For elucidation of the part played by the *French auxiliaries*, see chap. 3 of Tuckerman's "America and her commentators" [5033.5].

Hessians. Beside Kapp [above, in German], see Bancroft [5012.3.8] and G. W. Green's paper in the Atlantic monthly, Feb., 1875.

Headley has commemorated the clergy of the epoch [1014.1]. The "Life of Brant," by Stone [5022.1], pictures the border warfare with the Indians.

Harper's monthly contains various articles on revolutionary episodes, chiefly by Lossing,— "Our national anniversary," in vol. 3; on General Putnam, in vol. 12; on Marion, in vol. 17; on Bennington and King's mountain, in vol. 21; on Cowpens, in vol. 22; and on Continental money, in vol. 26.

There is a paper on the "Caricature of the revolutionary period," in Harper's monthly, July, 1875.

There is a history of the United States flag by Preble, 1872 [5013.5]; and a popular account of the chief military careers in Headley's "Washington and his generals" [1216.5].

In fiction. For the early days of the struggle in and around Boston, see Hawthorne's "Septimius Felton" [533.24] and Cooper's "Lionel Lincoln" [525.9]. Cooper's "Spy" [310.11; 525.26] covers the events of the neutral ground, between the British in New York and the Americans on the Hudson in 1780. D. P. Thompson's "Green mountain boys" [734.1] for the opening scenes, and his "Rangers" [734.2] covers the campaign in northern New York and Vermont of 1777. W. G. Simms [see his name] has a series of romances covering the events of the struggle in South Carolina. J. P. Kennedy's "Horseshoe Robinson" [725.15] relates to the tories of South Carolina in 1780.

This period is also delineated in Cooper's "Chainbearer" [525.18] and in Miss Sedgwick's "Linwoods" [737.3].

The events on the ocean find a chronicle in Cooper's "Pilot" [525.29] for Paul Jones, and also in Hermann Melville's "Israel Potter."

General political history, 1789-1875.

The general histories of Hildreth and Higginson will give ample accounts for the ordinary reader; but the closer student will consult the lives of the presidents, and of the leading public characters like Burr, by Parton; Pinkney, by Wheaton; Wirt, by Kennedy; Clinton; Livingston, by Hunt; Calhoun; Clay, by Colton; Webster, by Curtis; Crittenden, by his daughter; Taney; Greeley's "Recollections"; and Benton's "Thirty years' view." Wilson's "History of the slave power" [5012.9] is unfinished.

For the effects of newspapers, see Hudson's "History of journalism" [5214.2].

Some of these books must be sought in the Bates Hall.

War of 1812-15.

The best and most elaborate history is Lossing's "Field-book" [810.16], portions of which appeared originally in Harper's monthly, namely: Cruise of the Essex, vol. 19; The navy, vol. 24; Scott in the war, vol. 26; Scenes, vols. 26-30. See Cooper's and other naval histories for the war on the ocean. Alison, in his "History of Europe" [5913.5], on the English side, allows Cooper's Naval history [813.4; 813.5] to be fair. See Porter's "Memoir of Commodore Porter" [5022.18]. Parton's "Life of Jackson" [1212.1] necessarily covers portions of the struggle. Also see the autobiography of General Winfield Scott [1214.8].

See also Hildreth's second series [5011.11]. See also titles and note under Military and naval history in this article.

War with Mexico, 1845–47.

The most considerable separate history is that of Major Ripley, who is controverted in part by Stevens [612.3].

See also Harper's monthly, vol. 11, for the battles under Scott and Taylor, and the lives of generals Scott [1214.8] and Frémont [1214.6], as well as histories of the United States covering this period.

For the political bearings, see Webster's Speeches [5013.1.5]; Benton's "Thirty years' view" [812.2], etc.

Civil war, 1861–65.

General histories. Draper's "Civil war in America" [811.6], in three large volumes, is the chief elaborate history, in which philosophical suggestions hold prominence. His first volume is given to tracing the rise and progress of the antagonistic feeling between the North and South in ethnological and climatic causes, and this gives the book its character, for it is not esteemed of marked importance either as a history of politics or of the military operations, but its interest consists rather in his efforts to place the reader from time to time at the point of view assumed respectively by the opposing leaders. Wilson's "History of the slave power" [5012.9] necessarily covers the causes of the war. The chief value of Horace Greeley's "American conflict" [810.1] rests upon it as a narrative of the causes of the war and of the history of politics by a strong anti-slavery man; for the military parts, though reasonably well done, generally impartial and accurate, lack the spirit that makes a military record become the fitting reflex of history. Swinton's "Twelve decisive battles" [812.13] is perhaps upon the whole the best general view of the military operations. He selects Bull Run, Donelson, Shiloh, Antietam, Murfreesboro', the Monitor and the Merrimac, Vicksburg, Gettysburg, Wilderness, Atlanta, Nashville, and Five Forks, giving the prelude and the results of each, as the most indicative conflicts; and the chief mistakes of the book arise naturally from his too positively connecting subordinate events with his chosen crises.

Pollard's "Southern history of the war" [5013.17] is the only important general record on the Southern side, and it is characterized by a strong aversion to the North, and an almost equal dislike of Jefferson Davis, which is likewise the case with his "Secret history of the Southern confederacy" [5013.3]. The Comte de Paris's History is mentioned under Foreign views.

The various popular histories of the war have their distinctive merits. Lossing's [810.15] is very readable, and the narrative is helped by many excellent wood-cuts. Guernsey's, known as Harper's, preserves on large pages the contemporary wood-cuts which accompanied the progress of the war in a weekly journal.

There are numerous personal narratives of officers or camp followers, covering large portions of the entire field, like Carleton Coffin's "Four years of fighting" [813.7]; Strother's "Personal recollections," in Harper's monthly, vols. 33-36. See also Abbott's "Heroic deeds of heroic men," in vols. 30-34.

See also the lives of Lincoln, Grant, Jackson, Sherman, etc., and in the only volume of Badeau's "Life of Grant" yet published, there is one of the best accounts of the military operations participated in by that general down to the spring of 1864.

Chesney's "Military biographies" [5922.8] contains the criticism of a distinguished English officer on some of the leaders and events of the war.

Chapter 48 of Hudson's "Journalism" [5414.2] is given to the newspaper correspondents of the war.

The Army of the Potomac. Perhaps the best general history is Swinton's, but it is alleged that in his desire to be impartial, he sometimes under-estimates the forces of the confederates. See the general histories of the war, and the lives of Grant, Lee, etc.; special regimental histories; Conyngham's "Irish brigade" [824.4]; Shank's "Distinguished generals" [1015.15], etc. On the confederate side, beside Pollard's History, see Cooke, above-mentioned, and Gorman on Lee's last campaign, in Bates Hall.

Of Bull Run, there is a special account by Barnard, beside the official reports; and the narrative of Dr. Russell, the London Times' correspondent [413.6]. Sherman's Memoirs [1212.3; 5024.4] has a chapter. Patterson [5013.20] covers the preceding movements in the Shenandoah.

Of the Peninsular campaign, there are sufficient accounts in the general histories, particularly in that by the Comte de Paris [813.17], who was on McClellan's staff at the time. That general's Report and Barnard's criticism of it can be found in the Bates Hall. J. S. C. Abbott's paper on the Chickahominy campaign is in Harper's monthly, vol. 30. Hamley examines the military aspects in his "Operations of war" [5910.6].

Of General Pope's campaign, see that general's Report; Mill's comment on it, and the testimony in the court martial of General Porter.

Of Hooker's campaign, the most valuable monograph is Hotchkiss and Allan's account of the battle of Chancellorsville — a very clear and impartial narrative by two of General Jackson's staff-officers, who furnish excellent maps, and who are rarely inaccurate, but in matters necessarily beyond their knowledge.

General Custer's paper on the battle of the Wilderness is in The galaxy, May, 1876; and an article, "After the battle of the Wilderness," is in the Atlantic monthly, May, 1876.

Of the final campaign under Grant, Newhall's "With General Sheridan in Lee's last campaign" is a vivid portrayal of the closing scenes. See also the lives of Grant.

The Virginia and Maryland campaigns have also been reviewed by Lieut.-Col. Chesney, 1863, who is reputed the chief of the English military critics, in two valuable and entertaining little volumes, not including, however, the closing campaign. His political sympathies are with the confederates.

See Harper's monthly, "In and around Richmond," vol. 32.

Western campaigns. For Sherman's campaign, see Nichols, Conyngham, etc., beside the general histories, and lives of Sherman, Lyon, Grant, Foote, etc. See Harper's monthly, for Sherman's march, vol. 31; for Chattanooga, vol. 36; and for Lookout mountain, vol. 37.

The chief interest of late has rested in Sherman's own account in his Memoirs [1212.3; 5024.4], and in Boynton's criticism [5024.5]. General W. F. Smith gives an account of the battle of Chickamauga in the Galaxy, Nov., 1875.

The Vicksburg campaign is examined in chap. XII of Sherman's Memoirs [1212.3; 5024.4], which may be compared with Badeau's "Life of Grant" [5021.8], the best of the single accounts.

Southern campaigns. Beside the general histories, see Parton's "Butler in New Orleans" [815.2]; and Hepworth, Hosmer, etc., mentioned above.

States, regiments, etc., in the war. Numerous records of this kind are given in the note in the Lower Hall Catalogue of history, etc., and much more will be found in the Bates Ball catalogues.

Hospital and sanitary service, etc. Adequate records have been made in the histories of the Sanitary commission [in Bates Hall; see reviews in North American, Jan., 1867, and in the Atlantic monthly, April, 1867] and of the Christian commission [in Bates Hall; see Lippincott's magazine, Feb., 1868; and no. 1269 of Living age], while there are numerous personal records, like Miss Alcott's, etc. See article on "The military hospitals at Fortress Monroe," in Harper's monthly, vol. 29. See Eudora Clark's "Hospital memories" in the Atlantic monthly, Aug. and Sept., 1867.

There is a paper on the "National cemeteries" in Harper's monthly, vol. 33.

Prison experience. See numerous records in the Bates Hall catalogues. Also Harper's monthly, vol. 31. The "Pleasant side of rebel prisons" is given in "Old and new," April, 1875.

Confederate narratives. Beside General Johnstone's "Narrative" [813.18], the general narrative of Pollard, his "Life of Jefferson Davis" [5013.3], and the official despatches, see in the list above, Gilmor [817.17]; Scott's "Partisan life with Mosby" [811.14]; Eggleston's "Rebel's recollections" [5016.15, — see Atlantic monthly, June, 1874], and many others to be found in the Bates Hall.

Political aspects. For the causes, beside the general histories, particularly Greeley's and Draper's, see Fowler's "Sectional controversy" [in Bates Hall], which traces the development of sectionalism from colonial days; Greeley's "Recollections of a busy life" [5023.8]; Olmsted's "Seaboard states" [414.7]; Helper's "Impending crisis" [617.1]; and Lamon's "Life of Lincoln" [5020.5].

Botts's "Great rebellion" traces its rise and progress, and his book is the author's personal vindication as a unionist of the South. Stephens, the vice-president of the confederacy, has put forth his "Constitutional view" of the war, and has published a reply to his reviewers. These and others are to be found in the Bates Hall. Pollard's "Life of Jefferson Davis" [5013.3] covers the secret history of the confederacy, as told by an actor on that side. President Buchanan has published since the war a defence of his "administration on the eve of the rebellion" [813.8], tracing also the history of the anti-slavery agitation, and the right of secession. See Towle's paper on "Secession leaders" in vol. 26 of Harper's monthly. There are chapters on foreign relations in Draper's "Civil war" [811.6] and Carleton's "Four years of fighting" [813.7].

Secret service. Richardson [813.15] represents the books of this class.

Naval history. Boynton's [5012.1] is the only considerable history; but there is an outline of naval operations in Hamersly's "Records of living officers" [5022.14] and a popular view in Headley's "Farragut and our naval commanders" [5012.4]. Chesney's "Military biographies" [5922.8] criticises the exploits of Farragut and Porter.

Swinton's "Decisive battles" [812.13] contains an account of the battle between the Monitor and Merrimac.

See Harper's monthly, on ironclads, vol. 25; on the first cruise of the Passaic, vol. 27; and on the cruise of the Sassacus, vol. 29. The daring exploits of Lieut. W. B. Cushing are narrated in "One of many" in Harper's monthly, July, 1874.

Foreign views. The writings of J. S. Mill, Cairnes, Newman, Bright, and Cobden among Englishmen; and Cochin, Laugel, Lecomte, Laboulaye, and Gasparin are favorable to the North in the political aspect. These and others may be found in the Bates Hall.

See Lowell's "My study windows," for his paper on a "Certain condescension in foreigners."

Of the military operations, Trollope offered the earliest English account, followed by Russell [413.6], while the English officers, Fletcher, Frazier, and Chesney, already mentioned, are opposed in sympathy to the North. See also the French accounts of Pisani, Prince Napoleon's aide-de-camp; of the Prince de Joinville; of Chanal; of Cortambert and De Tranaltos; and of Vigo-Roussillon; and the German Von Borcke. The "History of the war" by the Comte de Paris [813.17] is taking rank as showing the observations of a close student of military science, and will perhaps be considered among the best of the military histories.

Military and naval history.

Cooper's "History of the navy" [813.4; 813.5], with Boynton's [5012.1] for the civil war, make a continuous record in effect; while Allen's "British navy" [5417.5] gives the English side.

Hamersly's "Records of living officers of the navy," 1870 [5022.14], contains brief memoirs, arranged by seniority with alphabetical index, and a concise narrative of naval operations in the civil war, and lists of all officers engaged.

There is a "History of the cavalry" [816.5] by Brackett.

The general histories necessarily cover this aspect, and also particular histories of periods, as mentioned under preceding sections.

Constitutional history, etc.

The history of the ideas of local self-government, and of a spirit of union which resulted in the American constitution, is ably and elaborately traced in Frothingham's "Rise of the republic" [5010.5]; while Curtis, in his "History of the constitution," is more closely concerned with the effort to fashion the sentiment of union and local independency into the written charter. Towle also traces the historical antecedents in the earlier confederacies. The debates that preceded the adoption can be studied in Elliot, and in Rives's Madison; and the Federalist, chiefly by Hamilton, was written to commend the constitution to general favor. See Everett's oration on American constitutions [1921.1.1], and Judge Story's "Commentaries" [1530.2]. The history of the formation and of the powers of the constitution is popularly told in Alden's "Science of government" [6336.1]; a comparison with those of Athens, Lacedæmon and Carthage is given in President Monroe's posthumous "The people the sovereign." The works of John Adams [vols. 4, 5, and 6] unfold the ideas of a prominent actor in the events from 1775 down to the full operation of the constitution. Hildreth [5011.10.3, chapter 47] traces the history of the formation of the constitution. Diverse views of the workings of the constitution and of its powers may be studied in Story; in Bowen; in Farrar; in Pomeroy; in Mulford; in Brownson; in Jennings, who is an alarmist, etc. The histories of parties, like Van Buren's, and Gillet's Democracy, and records of political action, like Benton's "Thirty years' view," and the speeches of Webster, will afford additional light. J. A. Hamilton's "Reminiscences" [5022.1] is in part a reply to Van Buren's "Political parties."

Among foreign comments the chief in importance is De Tocqueville, 1830 "Democracy in America" [5015.1], and he is reviewed by J. S. Mill and others. See also the observations of Martineau, Thornton, Gurowski, Anthony Trollope, Chevalier, etc.

A full study of these and other authorities can only be had by using the Bates Hall catalogues.

Ecclesiastical history.

The general histories necessarily trace the introduction and progress of sects, and the accompaniments of the religious fervor which in different sections of the country was connected with the founding of the colonies. For New England, see the headings New England, Massachusetts, Plymouth, Puritans, etc. For the Jesuits of the North-west, see Parkman's histories. There is a recent sketch by Fitton [5816.5] of the establishment of the catholic church in New England. For the Huguenots in Florida, see Parkman's "Pioneers" [5015.5.1]. Lives of Whitefield cover the rise of methodism. Sprague's "Annals of the American pulpit" [in Bates Hall] surveys the field comprehensively, coming down to a recent date. Vols. 1 and 2 are given to Trinitarian congregationalists; vols. 3 and 4, to Presbyterians; vol. 5, to Episcopalians; vol. 6, to Baptists; vol. 7, to Methodists; vol. 8, to Unitarians. Each series has a compendious historical sketch of the sect, prefixed, with indications of authorities.

For the peculiar socialistic sects, see Nordhoff's "Communistic societies" [5821.2]; Dixon's "Spiritual wives" [1538.2] and his "New America" [418.1]; Robert Dale Owen's "Threading my way" [5427.6], and chapters in Greeley's "Recollections of a busy life" [5023.8]. The shakers are also described by Lossing in vol. 15 of Harper's monthly. See Mormonism, *note.*

The Bates Hall catalogues will enlarge, in many directions, the field of this investigation.

Literature.

The best account will be found in Duyckinck's Cyclopædia, which traces the progress of letters in America from the earliest days to our time, giving extracts. It may be supplemented by various classified collections of extracts, with biographical and critical addenda, like Dr. Griswold's [5212.3]; his Female authors [5212.2], etc. Underwood's American authors [5214.1] has a historical introduction. Whipple wrote the review of the last century of American literature in Harper's monthly, Feb., 1876.

Among separate papers the following may be designated: Everett's address on "The circumstances favorable to the progress of literature in America," in his Orations [1921.1.1]; Emerson's "American scholar," in his Miscellanies [1934.6]; Higginson's "Americanism in literature," in his "Atlantic essays" [1915.2, or Atlantic monthly, Jan., 1870]. There is a recent history of "Journalism in the United States, from 1690 to 1873," by Hudson [5414.2].

For the *drama*, see Dunlap's "History of the American theatre," 1832 [in Bates Hall]; Mrs. Mowatt's "Autobiography of an actress" [1216.6], etc. See also the biographies of Kean, Cooke, Matthews and other English actors who have performed in the United States.

Allibone will of course be consulted for particular writers. The lives of Irving, Percival, Paulding, George Ticknor, Prescott, and Fitz-Green Halleck of course afford parallel illustrations of the history of literature in their day. See English literature, *note.*

The educational progress of the country during the last century is traced in Harper's monthly, Nov., 1875.

Manners, customs, etc.

De Tocqueville [5015.1] viewed American society and institutions with favor, and with a discernment that made him philosophical and critical.

Lamon's "Life of Lincoln" [5020.5] affords pictures of western life in the early part of this century.

Dixon [chap. 59 of his "New America," 418.1] gives a later aspect.

For frontier life, see Parton's "Life of Jackson" [1212.1], and authorities there given; also Marcy's "Border reminiscences" [413.3] and "Thirty years of army life on the border" [415.16]. See also note under Travels.

See also "Society in America," in the Cornhill, 1873, or Living age, Feb. 1, 1873.

Travels in America, and numerous other works in the Bates Hall, some of which are mentioned in the notes in the Lower Hall Catalogue of history, etc., afford additional light on this aspect.

Travels, description, etc.

The history of travel in the United States has been well traced by Tuckerman in his "America and her commentators" [5033.5]; and a somewhat extended chronological arrangement of travellers is given in the note in the Lower Hall Catalogue of history, etc.

Much misrepresentation by English writers led to Irving's kind remonstrance with the English writers on America, in his "Sketch book" [311.13; 715.6; 1815.10], and Walsh's "Appeal from the judgment of Great Britain respecting the United States," was kindly reviewed by Jeffrey, in his Essays [5610.8]. Sidney Smith, in his Essays, also rebuked some of the vilifiers of America. Tuckerman gives a chapter to English abuse of America. A good deal of just satire was also dealt out by Cooper, in his "Homeward bound" [525.27] and in his "Home as found" [525.20].

De Tocqueville, in 1830, made the observations that led to his famous book [5015.1], the most important work that a foreigner had up to that time written upon American institutions. [See Constitutional history, *note.*]

The "Picturesque America" [5030.9] is a sumptuous illustrated description of the country at large.

The West. See the titles under West.

The mountain region of Kentucky and Tennessee is described in "A strange land and a peculiar people," in Lippincott's magazine, Oct., 1873. Also Irving's "Tour on the prairies" [417.1], and for frontier life, see note under Manners.

Of the remoter West, beside Dixon and Bowles, see Coffin's "Seat of empire" [425.15], with the best map of the country between the 36th and 55th parallels.

The government reports of explorations in the West and South-west are of importance, like that for a Pacific railroad route [6611.2]; that of Dacotah [630.1]; and that of Wyoming [6924.9]. See also Arizona.

Browne's "Resources of the Pacific slope" [6631.6] is the fullest work on that region. H. H. Bancroft's "Native races" [5920.4] pertains at full length to the Indian antiquities, etc. of this region. See also California, Oregon, etc.

The South. See Virginia and the names of the other Southern states. King's "Great South" [5031.6] is the chief descriptive work, with illustrations, part of which originally appeared in Scribner's monthly in 1873-74. See also Slavery, and Olmsted's books.

Guides. Appleton's is the principal one [425.17]. There are also numerous local guides, for which see their respective heads, in states, cities, etc.

The commercial progress of the country during the last century is followed in Harper's monthly, July, 1875.

Shelf. No.

UNITED STATES, The, in the light of prophecy; or, an exposition of Rev. 13: 11–17. Battle Creek, Mich., 1872. 160 pp. 16° 6327.5

UNITED STATES army and navy journal and official gazette of the regular and volunteer forces. Vol. 1, 11. New York, 1863–64, 73–74. 2 v. F°. 6530.1

UNITED STATES literary gazette. Vol. 1, 2. Boston, 1825. 2 v. 1 v. 4°; 1 v. 8° 1432.1

UNITED STATES register, or blue book, for 1862. Compiled by J. Disturnell. New York [1861]. 94+ pp. 12° 6927.3

UNITED STATES sanitary commission. Narrative of privations and sufferings of United States officers and soldiers while prisoners in the hands of the rebel authorities. With an appendix containing the testimony. Philadelphia, 1864. 283 pp. 8°. 813.12

— A sketch of its purposes and its work. Compiled from documents and private papers. Boston, 1863. xii, 299 pp. 16° 815.1

— Memorial of the Great central fair for the, held at Philadelphia, June, 1864. Stillé, C. J. Philadelphia, 1864. 4° 6910.1

UNITY of worlds, The, and of nature. Powell, B. London, 1856. Sm. 8° 6836.1

UNIVERS, L'. Histoire et description des tous les peuples. 5 v. 8°. *Namely:* —

— Denis, (J.) F. Portugal. Paris, 1846 .... 5911.10

— Eyriès, J. B. B. Danemark. Continué par M. Chopin. Paris, 1846 .... 5911.11

— Galibert, L., and Pellé, C. Angleterre, Écosse et Irlande. Paris, 1844 .... 5911.7

— Munk, S. Palestine. Paris, 1845 .... 5911.9

— Pouqueville, F. C. H. L. Grèce. Paris, 1843 .. 5911.8

UNIVERSAL history. Tytler, A. F. Boston, 1840. 2 v. 8° 811.3

UNIVERSAL progress, Illustrations of. Spencer, H. New York, 1872. 12° 6835.3

UNIVERSE, The. Pouchet, F. A. The universe; or, the infinitely great and the infinitely little. London, 1871. L. 8° 6830.1

— *Same.* New York, 1873. 8° 1520.6

— Proctor, R. A. The universe and the coming transits. London, 1874. 8° 6813.4

UNIVERSITIES. Newman, J. H. The idea of a university defined and illustrated. London, 1873. Sm. 8° 5836.9

— Ten Brook, A. American state universities, their origin and progress. Cincinnati, 1875. 8° 5831.4

UNIVERSITY oars. Morgan, J. E. London, 1873. 16°. 6416.1

UNKIND word, The. Craik, D. (M.) 323.22

UNKNOWN river, The. Hamerton, P. G. Boston, 1876. 16° 5527.18

UNSEEN universe, The, or physical speculations on a future state. Tait, P. G., and Stewart, B. London, 1875. 8° 5834.6

UNSEEN world, The. Fiske, J. Boston, 1876. 12°. 5836.1

"UNTO this last:" four essays on the first principles of political economy. Ruskin, J. New York, 1866. 12° 6236.4

UNTRODDEN Spain. Rose, H. J. London, 1875. 2 v. 8° 5921.6

UNZER, Johann August. Principles of physiology; and A dissertation on the functions of the nervous system, by George Prochaska. Translated and edited by T. Laycock. London, 1851. xii, xv, 463 pp. 8° 6013.15

UP the Baltic; or, Young America in Norway, Sweden, and Denmark. Adams, W. T. Boston, 1873. 16° 925.8

Shelf. No.

UP the ladder. Baker, H. N. (W.) 926.8

UP the Rhine. Hood, T. New York, 1872. 12° .. 536.6

UP the river. Abbott, J. 914.18

UPHAM, Charles Wentworth. Life, explorations and public services of John Charles Frémont. With illustrations. Boston, 1856. 366 pp. Portrait. 12° 1214.6

— Life of Sir Henry Vane. (*In* Sparks, J. Library of American biography) 5028.1.4

— Salem witchcraft; with an account of Salem village, and a history of opinions on witchcraft and kindred subjects. Boston, 1867. 2 v. Illustrated. Fac-similes. Sm. 8° 5015.2

— *joint author.* Life of Timothy Pickering. *See* PICKERING, Octavius 5021.1

UPS and downs. Hale, E. E. 528.8

UPSIDE down. Parker, R. A. 933.18

UPTON, Emory. Infantry tactics double and single rank. Adapted to American topography and improved fire-arms. Revised edition. New York, 1876. 445+ pp. Illustrated. Sm. 12°. 1529.9

UPWARD and onward series. *See* ADAMS, William T.

URBANUS I, *pope.* *See* HIPPOLYTUS, *St.*

URBINO, Lavinia Buoncore, DAY, Henry, and OTHERS. Art recreations. With valuable receipts for preparing materials. Illustrated. Boston, 1873. 344 pp. 12° 1515.9

URE, Andrew. Dictionary of arts, manufactures, and mines. Edited by Robert Hunt. Illustrated. 6th edition. London, 1872. 3 v. 8°. 6422.3

URSULA. Sewell, E. M. 314.16

USEFUL arts. Bigelow, J. The useful arts, considered in connexion with the applications of science. New York, 1851. 2 v. 12° 1514.1

— Tomlinson, C. Cyclopædia of. London, 1868. 3 v. 8° .... *R.R., A.3.3

See also Agriculture, Assaying, Bricks, Building, Chemistry, Crockery, Domestic economy, Engineering, Glass, Gloves, Metallurgy, Photography, Porcelain, Printing, Pottery, Tiles.

UTAH. The Rocky mountain saints: a full and complete history of the Mormons, including the colonization and development of the mineral wealth of Utah. Stenhouse, T. B. H. New York, 1873. 8° 5033.0

See also Great Salt Lake city.

UTOPIA. More, *Sir* T. London, 1869. Sm. 8° 5618.8

UTTER impossibility, An. [Fiction.] Church, F... 334.7

VAGABOND heroine, A. Edwards, A. Leipzig 319.11

— *Same.* New York 725.29

VAGINA. Pathology and treatment of vaginal cystocele. Homans, J., *jr.* (*In* Massachusetts medical society. Publications) 6021.4

VAILLE, Frederic Ozni, and CLARK, Henry Alden, *compilers.* The Harvard book. A series of historical, biographical, and descriptive sketches. By various authors. Illustrated with views and portraits. Cambridge, 1875. 2 v. 4° 5230.1

VALE of cedars, The. [Jews in Spain, 15th century.] Aguilar, G. 533.17

VALENTIN. Kingsley, H. 339.9

VALENTINE, W. Comic metamorphoses. With portraits. New York [*cop.* 1856]. 280 pp. 12°. 1516.18

VALENTINE, the countess. Bauer, K. 723.4

VALENTINE VOX, the ventriloquist, Life and adventures of. Cockton, H. 712.2

VALERIE; an autobiography. Marryat, F. 337.9

Shelf. No.

VALERIE Aylmer. Fisher, F. C. 711.31
VALERIO, Katherine. *See* WASHBURN, Katherine Sedgwick.
VALERIUS. [Persecution of Christians, time of Trajan.] Lockhart, J. G. 738.7
VALIANT woman, The. A series of discourses. Landriot, J. F. A. T. Boston, 1874. 12°..... 1915.6
VALICOURT, E. de. Manuel de dorure et d'argenture par la méthode électro-chimique, et par simple immersion. Paris, 1845. xii, 173 pp. 24°. [Manuel Roret]..........6429.10
VALMORE-DESBORDES, *Madame*, Memoir of. Sainte-Beuve, C. A. Boston, 1873. 16° 5527.3
VALON, Alexis de. *See* MÉRIMÉE, P. Portraits historiques et littéraires. Paris, 1874. 18°...5527.14
VANBRUGH, *Sir* John. Dramatic works. *See* WYCHERLEY, William 5611.6
VANDAEL, —. Manuel théorique et pratique du tailleur. Paris, 1833. 236+ pp. Folded plates. 24°. [Manuel Roret] 6429.5
VANDERBILT, Cornelius. *See* PARTON, J. Famous Americans of recent times. Boston, 1871. 8°.1214.14
VANDERDECKEN, *pseud.* *See* COOPER, William.
VANE, *Sir* Henry, Life of. Upham, C. W. (*In* Sparks, J. Library of American biography)..5028.1.4
VANESSA. By the author of "Still waters," etc.... 319.30
VANITY fair. Thackeray, W. M. Leipzig......... 335.7
— *Same.* (*In his* Works.) London.............. 513.1.1
— *Same.* New York.............................. 1820.1
VAN MONCKHOVEN, D. Popular treatise on photography. Translated by W. H. Thornthwaite. Illustrated. 2d edition, revised. London, 1867. 141+ pp. 12°..............................1716.19
VAN RHYN, G. A. F. What and how to read: a guide to recent English literature, containing a minutely classified list of the best books published in England and America during the past five years. New York, 1875. xxx, 221 pp. 12°.6136.11
VAPEREAU, Guillaume. Dictionnaire universel des contemporains. 4e édition. [*Added*, Supplément.] Paris, 1870, 73. iv, 1888+, iv, 181+ pp. L. 8°.............................*R.R., E.2.10
VASA, Gustavus. *See* GUSTAVUS I, VASA, *king of Sweden.*
VASARI, Giorgio. Lives of the most eminent painters, sculptors, and architects. From the Italian, with notes and illustrations, chiefly selected from various commentators. By Mrs. Jonathan Foster. London, 1855. 5 v. Portrait. Sm. 8°. 6215.6
VASHTI. Wilson, A. J. 737.20
VASSAL-FOX, Henry Richard, *3d lord Holland.* Foreign reminiscences. Edited by his son. London, 1851. viii, 360 pp. Fac-simile. Sm. 8° 5435.6
— Memoirs of the whig party during my time. Edited by his son. London, 1852. 2 v. Sm. 8°. 5415.6
VATHEK. Beckford, W. New York, 1869. Sq. 16°. 518.3
VATICAN council, History of the. Schaff, P. (*In* Gladstone, W. E. The Vatican decrees, etc.).. 1911.1
VATICAN decrees. Gladstone, W. E. The Vatican decrees in their bearing on civil allegiance. Leipzig, 1875. Sq. 16°.....................1918.12
— *Same.* New York, 1875. 8° 1911.1
— Manning, H. E., *cardinal.* The Vatican decrees in their bearing on civil allegiance. New York, 1875. 12°.................................. 1916.7

Note. — An answer to the preceding.

VATICANISM: an answer to Reproofs and replies. Gladstone, W. E. Leipzig, 1875. Sq. 16°.....1918.12
— *Same.* New York, 1875. 8° 1911.2

See also Roman catholic church.

VATTEL, Emmerich de. The law of nations; or, principles of the law of nature applied to the conduct and affairs of nations and sovereigns. From the French. Dublin, 1792. lxxii, 728 pp. 8°.................................. 6315.1
VAUX, Calvert. Villas and cottages. A series of designs prepared for execution in the United States. Illustrated. New York, 1872. 348 pp. 8° 6221.1

VEGETATION. Figuier, (G.) F. The vegetable world. London, 1868. 8° 1521.6
— Harris, T. W. Treatise on some of the insects of New England which are injurious to. Boston, 1852. 8°..................................... 6612.1
— Marion, F. The wonders of. New York, 1872. 12° 1714.25
VELLEIUS PATERCULUS, Caius. [Works.] *See* SALLUSTIUS CRISPUS, Caius. London, 1872. Sm. 8°. 6117.7
VELOCIPEDE, The; its history, varieties, and practice. Goddard, J. T. New York, 1869. 16°. 1514.5
VELPEAU, Alfred Armand Louis Marie. Treatise on the diseases of the breast and mammary region. Translated by M. Henry. London, 1856. xxxii, 608 pp. 8°..............................6013.21
VENEREAL diseases, The pathology and treatment of. Bumstead, F. J. Philadelphia, 1861. 8°. 6022.7
VENETIA. Disraeli, B.................................. 324.20
VENEZUELA, Los Gringos; or, wanderings in. Wise, H. A. New York, 1849. 12° 435.4
VENICE. Adams, W. H. D. The queen of the Adriatic; or, Venice, past and present. Boston, 1869. 16° 227.4
— Howells, W. D. Venetian life. Boston, 1874. 16° 227.5
— Ruskin, J. The stones of. New York, 1872. 3 v. 12° 6236.1

Note. — Daru's history, 1819 [in Bates Hall], was for many years the chief authority, and his hostility to the republic has been transmitted to the many books that have been based upon his researches, particularly as regards the inquisitors of state, the documents he cites concerning which are alleged to be spurious by Hazlitt [in Bates Hall], whose history, 1860, extending from 409 to 1457, is the most considerable and authoritative account in English, though the ordinary reader may be satisfied with the mingled history and description including art, literature, and manners, in Davenport Adams's "Queen of the Adriatic," mentioned above.

Further illustration of Venetian history will be found in Gibbon's "Roman empire" [824.9]; Hallam's "Middle ages" [5916.1], and Sismondi's "Italian republics."

The closing days of the Venetian republic are told by Alison in his "History of Europe" [5913.5]. See the paper on the Rise and fall of the republic of Venice, in London Quarterly review, Oct., 1874.

For Venetian art, see Painting, *note*, and some chapters in Taine [5522.2.2]. Ruskin's "Stones of Venice" [6236.1; for reviews, see references in Allibone] illustrates her history by her architecture, which can be further studied in general works like Fergusson, Luebke, etc.

A very successful delineation of modern Venice is Howell's "Venetian life" [227.5]. See also Taine [5522.2.2]; Hillard's "Six months in Italy" [426.6, chapters 2 and 3]; Longfellow's "Outre-mer" [1838.4.1]; Harper's monthly, Sept., 1872; a chapter in Castelar's "Old Rome and new Italy" [824.11]; Hare's "Cities of Northern Italy" [5527.17]; and the illustrated paper in the Art-journal, Dec., 1875.

The chief literary associations with Venice and her history come from Shakespeare's Merchant of Venice, and Othello; Schiller's Fiesco; Byron's "Childe Harold" [1614.13.2]; Beppo [1614.13.2]; "Marino Faliero" [1614.13.5]; and "The two Foscari" [1614.13.5]; Cooper's "Bravo" [525.30]; Rogers's "Italy" [5515.5]; and Schiller's "Ghost-seer."

VENTILATION. Drysdale, J. (J.), and Hayward, J. W. Health and comfort in house building. London, 1872. 8° .... 6223.
— Tomlinson, C. Rudimentary treatise on warming and ventilation. London, 1869. 12° 1715.2
VENUS, *the planet.* Proctor, R. A. Transits of Venus. London, 1874. Sm. 8° .... 6814.
— — The universe and the coming transits. London, 1874. 8° .... 6813.
VÉRA. Leipzig, 1871. 303 pp. Sq. 16°........... 315.
VERDI, Guiseppe. Don Carlos; Ernani; I Lombardi; Luisa Miller; The masked ball; Rigoletto; Sicilian vespers; La traviata; Il trovatore. (*In* Ditson, O., and co. Standard opera librettos)..6233.3.
VERGNAUD, Amand, *joint author.* Manuel du peintre en bâtiments, vitrier, doreur, argenteur et vernisseur. *See* RIFFAULT, Jean René Denis . 6429.
VERLORENE Handschrift, Die. Freytag, G. Leipzig, 1873. 8°...................................... 5733.
VERMONT, Marco Paul in. Abbott, J. .... 914.

See also Montpelier.

VERNE, Jules. Adventures in the land of the Behemoth [Africa]. Illustrated. Boston, 1874. 190 pp. Sm. 4° .... 713.
— The adventures of three Englishmen and three Russians in South Africa. Translated by Ellen E. Frewer. Illustrated. London, 1876. 191 pp. Sm. 8°.. 715.3

Shelf. No.

VERNE, Jules, *continued.*
— Around the world in eighty days. Translated by G. M. Towle. Boston, 1873. xvi, 315 pp. Illustrated. Sm. 4° 725.27
— The blockade runners. From the French. Illustrated. London, 1876. 120+ pp. Portrait. Sm. 8° 715.31
— Doctor Ox, and other stories. Translated by G. M. Towle. Boston, 1874. vi, 292 pp. Sq. 16° ... 529.2

Contents. — Doctor Ox's experiment; Master Zacharius; A drama in the air; A winter in the ice; The fortieth French ascension of Mont Blanc.

— Dr. Ox's experiment, and Master Zacharius. From the French. Illustrated edition. London, 1876. 190 pp. Sm. 8° 715.36
— The English at the north pole. With illustrations. London, 1875. iv, 314+ pp. Sm. 8°.. 724.27

Note.— This is identical with "A journey to the north pole." It is a translation of "Les Anglais au pole nord, aventures du capitaine Hatteras." Paris [1872].

— The field of ice. With illustrations. London, 1875. iv, 296 pp. 8° 733.5
— Five weeks in a balloon. A voyage of exploration and discovery in Central Africa. From the French. Illustrated. London, 1876. 190 pp. Sm. 8° 715.30
— Five weeks in a balloon; or, journeys and discoveries in Africa by three Englishmen. Done into English by "William Lackland." New York, 1869. 345+ pp. Illustrated. 8° 735.26
— A floating city. From the French. Illustrated. London, 1876. 208 pp. Sm. 8° 715.26
— A floating city, and The blockade runners. From the French. New York, 1874. iv, 286 pp. Illustrated. 8° 713.4
— From the earth to the moon direct in 97 hours 20 minutes: and a trip round it. Translated by Louis Mercier and Eleanor E. King. With illustrations. New York, 1874. viii, 323 pp. 8°.... 734.15
— *Same.* London, 1876. 160 pp. Sm. 8° 715.28
— The fur country; or, 70 degrees north latitude. Translated by N. d'Anvers. With illustrations. Boston, 1874. xiii, 334+ pp. 8° 713.2
— A journey to the centre of the earth. From the French. With illustrations. New York [1871]. 305+ pp. 12° 733.7
— Martin Paz. Translated by Ellen E. Frewer. Illustrated edition. London, 1876. 126 pp. Sm. 8°. 715.34
— Meridiana: the adventures of three Englishmen and three Russians in South Africa. From the French. With illustrations. London, 1873. viii, 232 pp. Sm. 4° 713.1
— The mysterious island. Part I. Shipwrecked in the air. From the French. With illustrations. Boston, 1875. 202 pp. Sm. 4° 724.17
— – [Part II.] Abandoned. Translated by W. H. G. Kingston. New York, 1875. viii, 304 pp. Illustrated. 16° 733.11
— – [Part III.] The secret of the island. Translated by W. H. G. Kingston. New York, 1876. viii, 299 pp. Illustrated. 16° 733.14
— Round the moon: a sequel to "From the earth to the moon." Translated by Louis Mercier and Eleanor E. King. With illustrations. London, 1876. 192 pp. Sm. 8° 715.29
— *Le tour du monde en quatre-vingts jours.* Paris [1873]. 308+ pp. 18° 5518.1
— The tour of the world in eighty days. Boston, 1873. 291 pp. 1 plate. Sq. 16° 239.1
— Twenty thousand leagues under the seas. From the French. [With] illustrations. Boston, 1873. viii, 303 pp. Sm. 8° 5535.1
— *Same.* London, 1876. 302 pp. Sm. 8° 715.27
— A voyage around the world. In search of the castaways. Illustrated. Hartford, 1873. 620 pp. 8° 432.1
— The voyages and adventures of Captain Hatteras. From the French. With illustrations. Boston, 1875. xxv, 440 pp. 8° 733.6

Note. — This is identical with "A journey to the north pole." It is a translation of "Les Anglais au pole nord, aventures du capitaine Hatteras." Paris [1872].

Shelf. No.

VERNE, Jules, *continued.*
— A winter amid the ice, and other stories. From the French. Illustrated edition. London, 1876. 192 pp. Sm. 8° 715.35

Contents. — A winter amid the ice; A drama in the air; Ascent of Mont Blanc.

— The wreck of the Chancellor. [*Also,* Martin Paz.] Translated by G. M. Towle. Boston, 1875. 285 pp. Sq. 16° 529.6
VERNER's pride. Wood, E. P. 333.20
VERNON. Abbott, J. Harper's story books........ 936.1.9
VÉRONIQUE. Church, F. 337.19
VERS de société. Jones, C. H. New York, 1875. 8° 5631.3
VERSCHWÖRUNG, Die, des Fiesco zu Genua. Schiller, (J. C.) F. von. Werke. Stuttgart, 1865. 8°. 5734.1.2
VERTEBRATED animals, Manual of the anatomy of. Huxley, T. H. New York, 1872. 12° 1523.12
VESPERS, The, of Palermo. [Poem.] Hemans, F. (D.) Boston, 1826. 8° 1621.2
VEST-POCKET series. *Namely:* —
— Fields, J. T. Old acquaintance. Barry Cornwall and some of his friends 1829.1
VESTIGES of the natural history of creation. Chambers, R. New York, 1846. 12° 1515.17

See also Darwinism.

VIARDOT, Louis. Wonders of European art. Illustrated. New York, 1871. vi, 335+ pp. 16°. 1714.1
— Wonders of Italian art. Illustrated. New York, 1871. 343 pp. 16° 1714.23
— Wonders of sculpture. Illustrated. 2d edition. New York, 1873. xii, 403 pp. 16° 1714.28
VICAR, The, of Bullhampton. Trollope, A. 334.3
VICAR, The, of Wakefield. Goldsmith, O. London, N. D. Sm. 4° 515.3
— *Same.* (*In his* Select works.) Leipzig, 1842. Sq. 16° 312.23
— *Same.* (*In his* Works.) London, 1854. 8°.. 5612.1.1
VICAR's, The, daughter. MacDonald, G. 537.23
VICISSITUDES, The, of Bessie Fairfax. Parr, H. Leipzig 329.24
— *Same.* Philadelphia 726.26
VICKERS, Thomas, *joint author.* The Bible in the public schools. *See* MAYO, Amory Dwight 5819.2
VICTIMS: a comedy. Taylor, T. New York, N. D. 12° 1635.4
VICTOR, Metta V. Passing the portal; or, a girl's struggle. An autobiography. New York, 1876. 408 pp. 12° 532.19
VICTOR and vanquished. A novel. Hay, M. C. 530.13
VICTOR La Tourette. A novel. Warriner, E. A. ... 738.15
VICTOR Lescar. Grant, *Miss* — 331.18
VICTOR's triumph. Southworth, E. D. E. N. 734.20
VICTORIA, Alexandrina, *queen of England.* The early years of the prince consort. Compiled by C. Grey. New York, 1867. 371 pp. Portrait. 12°. 1224.13
— *Same.* New York, 1868. 371 pp. Portrait. 12°. 1022.5
— Leaves from the journal of our life in the Highlands, from 1848 to 1861. Edited by A. Helps. New York, 1868. 287 pp. Illustrated. 12°.. 225.1
VICTORIA, Glimpses of life in. By a resident. Edinburgh, 1872. 8° 5931.11
VICTORIAN poets. Stedman, E. C. Boston, 1876. 12° 1837.1
VICTORIES and defeats. Anderson, R. P. London, 1873. 8° 5922.10
VICTORIES, The, of love. Patmore, C. (K. D.) Boston, 1862. 16° 1612.6
VICTORY, The, of the vanquished. Charles, E. 321.6
VIELLE cousine, La. Souvestre, É. Théâtre de la jeunesse. Paris, 1860. 12° 5536.15
VIENNA. Plan of Vienna and its exhibition. *See* AUSTRIA 5730.3
— Report of the commissioners [of Massachusetts] to the exposition. *See* MASSACHUSETTS. *Legislative documents* .... 5011.15 and 6911.3
VIEUX MOUSTACHE, *pseud.* *See* GORDON, Clarence.
VIEWS a-foot; or, Europe seen with knapsack and staff. Taylor, (J.) B. New York, 1856. 12°. 425.22
VIEWS of nature. Humboldt, (F. H.) A., *baron* von. London, 1870. Sm. 8° 1523.19

Shelf. No.

VIGNY, Alfred (Victor), *comte* de. Cinq-Mars: or a conspiracy under Louis XIII. Translated by W. Hazlitt. London, 1860. xvii, 397 pp. Portrait. Sm. 8° 537.21
— Cinq-Mars ou une conjuration sous Louis XIII. 29e édition. Précédée de Reflexions sur la vérité dans l'art. Accompagnée de documents historiques. Paris, 1873. 496+ pp. Fac-similes. 18° 5536.19
— Servitude et grandeur militaires. 12e édition. Paris, 1872. 355+ pp. 18° 5536.20

Contents. — Laurette ou le cachet rouge; La veillée de Vincennes; La canne de jonc.

— Stello. 11e édition. Paris, 1873. 351+ pp. 18°.5536.18
VILLA Eden. Auerbach, B. 511.20
VILLAGE and country houses. Lakey, C. D. New York, 1875. 4° 6220.8
VILLAGE lawyer, The: a farce. New York, N. D. 16 pp. 12° 1635.5
VILLAGE, The, on the cliff. Thackeray, A. I. Leipzig 335.11
— *Same.* (*In her* Works.) London 512.1.3
VILLAGE sermons. Burder, G. Philadelphia, 1821. 4 v. 12° 6327.7
VILLAS and cottages. Vaux, C. New York, 1872. 8°. 6221.1
VILLEFRANCHE, J. M. La télégraphie française. Avec figures suivie d'un guide-tarif à l'usage des expéditeurs des télégrammes. Paris, 1870. viii, 348+ pp. 18° 6817.3
VILLEMAIN, Abel François. Choix d'études sur la littérature contemporaine. Paris, 1858. xi, 462 pp. 12° 5537.12
— Cours de littérature française. Tableau de la littérature au XVIIIe siècle. Nouvelle édition. Paris, 1873. 4 v. 12° 5537.10
— Cours de littérature française. Tableau de la littérature au moyen âge en France, en Italie, en Espagne et en Angleterre. Nouvelle édition. Paris, 1871. 2 v. 12° 5537.11
— Discours et mélanges littéraires. Nouvelle édition. Paris, 1873. 403+ pp. 12° 5537.15
— Études de littérature ancienne et étrangère. Nouvelle édition. Paris, 1870. 395+ pp. 12°.5537.17
— Études d'histoire moderne. Nouvelle édition. Paris, 1862. xvi, 420 pp. 12° 5537.13
— Histoire de Cromwell d'après les mémoires du temps et les recueils parlementaires. Bruxelles, 1851. 437 pp. 12° 2015.7
— Life of Gregory VII. Preceded by a sketch of the history of the papacy to the eleventh century. Translated by J. B. Brockley. London, 1874. 2 v. 8° 5522.6
— Souvenirs contemporains d'histoire et de littérature. 9e édition. Paris, 1874. 2 v. 18°....5537.18
— Tableau de l'éloquence chrétienne au IVe siècle. Nouvelle édition. Paris, 1865. 537+ pp. 12°.5537.14
VILLETTE. Brontë, C. 321.21
VILMAR, August Friedrich Christian. Geschichte der deutschen National-Literatur. 15te Auflage. Marburg, 1873. 631 pp. 8° 5733.1
VINCENNES, *France.* Le donjon de Vincennes. Alboize du Pujol, É., and Maquet, A. *See* ARNOULD, Auguste ....Vol. 7, 8 of 2010.1
VINCENT, Frank, *jr.* The land of the white elephant: sights and scenes in south-eastern Asia. With map, plans, and illustrations. New York, 1874. xix, 316 pp. 8° 5923.7
— Through and through the tropics. Thirty thousand miles of travel in Oceanica, Australasia, and India. New York, 1876. 304 pp. 12°... 436.8
VINCENZO. Ruffini, G. 316.19
VINCI, Lionardo da. Hagen, (E.) A. Leonhard da Vinci in Mailand. Leipzig, 1833. 12° 2026.1.3
— Heaton, M. M., and others. Leonardo da Vinci and his works. London, 1874. L. 8° 6211.5
VINE-DRESSER'S manual, The. Reemelin, C. New York, 1855. 12° 6426.4
VINET, Alexandre (Rudolphe). History of French literature in the 18th century. From the French by J. Bryce. Edinburgh, 1854. x, 484 pp. 8°. 6132.3
VIOLA and Arno. Abbott, J. Harper's story books.936.1.12

Shelf. No.

VIOLIN, The: its famous makers and their imitators. Hart, G. London, 1875. L. 8° 6231.2
VIOLLET-LE-DUC, Eugène Emmanuel. Annals of a fortress. Translated by B. Bucknall. Boston, 1876. xv, 390 pp. Map. Plans. Illustrations. 8° 6223.4
— Discourses on architecture. Translated, with an introductory essay, by Henry Van Brunt. Illustrated. Boston, 1875. xx, 517+ pp. L. 8°. 6220.9
— An essay on the military architecture of the middle ages. Translated from the French by M. Macdermott. With engravings. Oxford, 1860. xvi, 274 pp. 8° 6221.5
— The habitations of man in all ages. Translated by B. Bucknall. With illustrations. Boston, 1876. xvi, 394 pp. 8° 6223.5
— The story of [the building of] a house. Translated from the French by G. M. Towle. Illustrated. Boston, 1874. vi, 284 pp. 8° 1513.3
VIRCHOW, Rudolph. The cranial affinities of man and the ape. (*In* Estes, D. Half-hour recreations in popular science) 6813.7
VIRGILIUS MARO, Publius. Works, translated into English verse, by J. Dryden. Baltimore, 1814. 2 v. Illustrated. 18° 6118.1
— L'Énéide, traduite par Jacques Delille. [Latin and French.] Paris, 1804. 4 v. Plates. 12°. 2018.7
— Aeneid: with explanatory notes. By Henry S. Frieze. New York, 1864. xviii, 598 pp. Illustrated. Portrait. 12° 1933.14
— The Æneids of Virgil. Done into English verse by William Morris. Boston [London], 1876. 382+ pp. Sm. 8° 6117.4
— Eclogues and Georgics, with notes by H. Andrews. Boston, 1862. vi, 336+ pp. 12° 1933.13
— Collins, W. L. Virgil [outlined and explained]. Edinburgh, 1870. 16° 6116.6
— Sainte-Beuve, C. A. Étude sur Virgile. Paris, 1870. 12° 5538.11
VIRGINIA. "Surveys for military defences." Map of north eastern Virginia and vicinity of Washington. Compiled at division head quarters of General Irvin McDowell, Arlington, Jan. 1, 1862. N. P., N. D. Size 5 ft. 8 in. × 4 ft. 1½ in. 5035.7
VIRGINIA. Abbott, J. Harper's story books 936.1.3
VIRGINIA Graham. Jones, J. 732.21
VIRGINIA illustrated. Strother, D. H. New York, 1871. L. 8° ....531.12 and 5031.3
VIRGINIANS, The. Thackeray, W. M. Leipzig. 4 v. in 2 .... 335.6
— *Same.* (*In his* Works.) London 513.1.5
— *Same.* New York 1820.3
VISION, The, of Don Roderick. Scott, *Sir* W. Poetical works. Leipzig, 1861. Sq. 16° 1613.5
VISION, The, of sudden death. De Quincey, T. (*In* Johnson, (E.) R. Little classics) 529.4.3
VISIT, A, to the asylum for aged and decayed punsters. Holmes, O. W. (*In* Johnson, (E.) R. Little classics) 529.4.5
VISITS to remarkable places. Howitt, W. Philadelphia, 1854. 2 v. 12° 235.2
VITALITY. On life and vital action in health and disease. Beale, L. S. London, 1875. Sm. 8°...6036.14
VITICULTURE. Treatise on the origin, nature, and varieties of wine. Thudichum, J. L. W., and Dupré, A. London, 1872. 8° 6423.4
VIVIA. Southworth, E. D. E. N. 727.19
VIVIAN Grey. Disraeli, B. 324.21
VOGEL, Hermann. International scientific series. The chemistry of light and photography. With illustrations. New York, 1875. xi, 288+ pp. 12° 6436.16
VOICE, The, of Elias. Snow, S. S. New York, 1863. 12° 1524.9
VOICES of the night. Longfellow, H. W. Poetical works. Leipzig, 1856. Sq. 16° 1614.1
— *Same.* (*In his* Poems.) Boston, 1858. 16°....1612.1.1
VOLCANOES. The character of their phenomena [etc.]. Scrope, G. P. London, 1872. 8° 6631.2
VOLCKHAUSEN, Ad. von. Why did he not die? After the German by Mrs. A. L. Wister 726.31

Shelf. No.

VOLTAIRE, François Marie Arouet, *called* de. History of Charles XII, king of Sweden. Edinburgh, 1873. xxiv, 369 pp. Folded map. Portraits. Sm. 8° 5726.6

— Zadig; or, the book of fate. Translated by F. Ashmore. London, 1784. 41 pp. 8° 513.13

— Voltaire. Morley, J. London, 1872. 8°.1221.2 and 5523.2

Note. — Compare also the general and literary histories covering the age of Louis XV.

Regarding the *early life* of Voltaire, see Carlyle's "Frederick the great" [1237.1.2].

On his *private life*, see Mrs. Jameson's "Loves of the poets" [5618.2].

His *relations with Frederick the great* are fully discussed in Carlyle's "Life of Frederick the great" [1237.1], and they are also elucidated in Lewes's Goethe [5724.1]; in Stahr's "Life of Lessing" [1022.7]; and generally in the German literary histories covering that period. See also Grimm's Correspondence, reviewed in Jeffrey's Essays [5610.8].

The English reader, if he has a fair knowledge of Voltaire's career and character, will find help from Morley's "Voltaire," as being rather critical than biographical, and altogether a high estimate. There are essays on Voltaire, one by Carlyle, who put adroitness as his prime characteristic, in his Essays [5610.7]; and the other is in Brougham's "Men of letters of the time of George III" [5614.4.2].

There are also views of his character and influence in Buckle's "Civilization" [5417.1]; in Lamartine's "Girondists" [827.25]; in Lecky's "Rationalism" [5933.5]; and in Martin's "Decline of the French monarchy." See summary of his life in Quarterly review, 1873.

Voltaire is one of the characters in Mühlbach's "Berlin and Sans-souci" [531.15]; and Bungener's "Priest and Huguenot" [627.4] and "Preacher and the king" [716.4].

VOLUPTÉ. Sainte-Beuve, C. A. Paris, 1872. 12°.5538.12

VOSE, George Leonard. Handbook of railroad construction; for the use of American engineers. With illustrations. Boston, 1857. xx, 480 pp. 8° 6422.5

— Manual for railroad engineers and engineering students. With woodcuts and plates. Boston, 1873. 2 v. 8° 6424.1

Contents. — Vol. I. Text. II. Plates.

VOYAGES and adventures, The, of Captain Hatteras. Verne, J. Boston, 1875. 8° 733.6

VOYAGES round the world. Brooks, J. A seven months' run, up, and down, and around the world. New York, 1873. Sm. 8° 423.12

— Delano, A. Narrative of voyages and travels in the northern and southern hemispheres, comprising three voyages round the world. Boston, 1817. 8° 432.6

— Hoffman, W. The monitor; or, jottings of a New York merchant during a trip round the globe. New York, 1863. 12° 235.3

— Seward, W. H. Travels around the world. New York, 1873. 8° ....431.1 and 5910.1

— Verne, J. A voyage around the world. In search of the castaways. [Fiction.] Hartford, 1873. 8°. 432.1

W., H. Ellen Clinton; or, the influence of a loving spirit 532.18

WAAGEN, Gustav Friedrich. Handbook of painting. German, Flemish, and Dutch schools. Based on the handbook of Kugler. Enlarged and for the most part re-written. With illustrations. London, 1860. 2 v. 8° 6214.1

WACHENHUSEN, Hans. For a woman's sake, or, the mysteries of the castle. From the German by MS. 721.5

WADDINGTON, John. Congregational history, 1200–1700. London, 1869, 74. 2 v. 8° 5810.1

Contents. — Vol. I. 1200–1567. II. 1567–1700.

WAGES, The, of sin. Yates, E. 721.17

WAGNER, Albrecht. Process of repair after resection and extirpation of bones. Translated, with an appendix of cases, by T. Holmes. London, 1859. 111–245 pp. 8° 6023.1

WAGNER, Rudolf (Johannes). Handbook of chemical technology. Translated and edited from the 8th German edition, with extensive additions, by W. Crookes. With illustrations. New York, 1872. xvi, 745, xvi pp. 8° 6431.2

WAGNER, (Wilhelm) Richard. Amateur series. Art life and theories. Selected from his writings and translated by E. L. Burlingame. With a preface, a catalogue of Wagner's published works and drawings of the Bayreuth opera house. New York, 1875. xiii, 305 pp. 12° 6234.3

Shelf. No.

WAGNER, (Wilhelm) Richard, *continued.*

— Richard Wagner and the music of the future. Hueffer, F. London, 1874. 8° 6232.6

WAIBLINGER, William (Friedrich). Gesammelte Werke, mit Leben von H. v. Canitz. 2te rechtmässige Gesammtausgabe. Mit Kupfern. Hamburg, 1842. 9 v. in 5. Sq. 16° 2028.1

Contents. — Vol. [I.] 1. Leben; Die Britten in Rom. 2. Francesco Spina; Die Britten in Rom. Schluss; Das Abenteuer von der Sohle. [II.] 3. Das Märchen von der blauen Grotte; Das Blumenfest; Friedrich Hölderlin's Leben, Dichtung und Wahnsinn. 4. Die heilege Woche; Drei Tage in der Unterwelt; Rosa Taddei; Aus Waiblinger's Tagebuch. [III.] 5. Anna Bullen; Die Nacht in St. Peter; Sinngedichte und Epigramme. 6. Erzählungen aus der Geschicte des jetzigen Griechenlands [1826]. [IV.] 7. Lied der Weihe 1827; Rom und Umgegend; Neapel die Stadt und das Land; Inseln; Lieder der Sehnsucht und Liebe; Vermischte Gedichte. [V.] 8. Der Frühling in den Gebirgen Latiums 1827; Wanderung ins Sabinerland 1827; Aus einem Tagebuch in Olevano 1827; Wanderung von Olevano nach Rom 1827; Sommerausflug nach Olevano 1828; Skizze eines Wegweisers durch die Umgebungen Roms 1830. 9. Keisen in die Abruzzen und an den Fucinersee 1828; Ausflug von Neapel nach Pästum 1828; Briefe aus der Insel Capri 1828; Ueber das St. Carlinotheater in Neapel 1828; Der Vesur im Jahre 1829; Briefe über Benevent und Avellino 1829; Briefe über Pompeii 1829; Briefe aus Palermo 1829.

WAIT for the end. Lemon, M. 312.8

WAITING race, A. Yates, E. 2 v. 331.2

WAKEFIELD. Hawthorne, N. (*In* Johnson, (E.) R. Little classics) 529.4.2

WAKE-ROBIN. [On birds.] Burroughs, J. New York, 1871. 16° 1525.12

WAKEFIELD, Priscilla. An introduction to botany, with illustrative engravings. Added a catalogue of American plants, and a glossary of botanical terms. Philadelphia, 1818. xii, 215 pp. Sm. 8° 6626.8

WALDEN, Treadwell. Our English Bible and its ancestors. Philadelphia [*cop.* 1871]. 231 pp. 16° 5818.13

WALDEN; or, life in the woods. Thoreau, H. D. Boston, 1854. 16° 417.2

WALDIE's select circulating library. Vol. x. Philadelphia, 1837. 4° 6730.41

WALDFRIED. A novel. Auerbach, B. 734.24

WALES, Abby L. Reminiscences of the Boston female asylum. Boston, 1844. 88 pp. 16° 5835.6

WALES. Adams, W. T. Red cross; or, Young America in. Boston, 1871. 16° 916.18

— Black, A. and C., *publishers.* Black's guide to. Edinburgh, 1874. Sm. 8° 5437.2

— Borrow, G. Wild Wales: its people, language, and scenery. London, 1872. Sm. 8° 5438.6

— Timbs, J. Abbeys, castles, and ancient halls of. London [1870]. 3 v. 16° 5438.1

WALES family. Thayer, E. Family memorial. Hingham, 1835. 8° 611.2

WALFORD, Edward. Juvenal [outlined and explained]. Edinburgh, 1872. 169+ pp. 16°. [Ancient classics for English readers] 6116.15

WALFORD, L. B. Mr. Smith. A part of his life. Leipzig 335.19

— *Same.* Leisure hour series. New York........ 518.1

WALK, A, from London to Lands end and back, with notes by the way. Burritt, E. London, 1868. Sq. 16° 5438.4

WALKER, Amasa. Transactions of the agricultural societies of Massachusetts, for 1852. *See* MASSACHUSETTS. *Legislative documents. Agriculture.* 6422.4

WALKER, Charles, *editor.* The ritual reason why. London [1868. 2d edition]. 263 pp. 16°....6328.10

WALKER, Charles V. Nouveau manuel complet de la télégraphie électrique. Traduit de l'anglais par D. Magnier. Suivi d'un appendice. Ouvrage orné de figures. Paris, 1851. 197 pp. 24°. [Manuel Roret] 6829.1

WALKER, Francis Amasa. Compendium, etc. of the ninth census. *See* UNITED STATES. *Department of the interior. Census bureau* 5010.2, 12

— The Indian question. Boston, 1874. 268 pp. Folded map. 12° 5016.14

WALKER, James. Sermons preached in the chapel of Harvard college. Boston, 1861. v, 307 pp. 12° 1524.4

WALKER, Mary Spring. Both sides of the street... 913.28

Shelf. No.

WALKER, *Mrs.* Edward Ashley. The total depravity of inanimate things. (*In* Johnson, (E.) R. Little classics) 529.4.5

WALKS in Rome. Hare, A. J. C. New York, 1873. 12° 5526.13

WALLACE, Alfred Russel. Contributions to the theory of natural selection. 2d edition. London, 1871. xvi, 384 pp. 16° 6616.4

— *Same.* New York, 1871. xvi, 384 pp. 16° ... 6836.1

See Darwinism, *note.*

— The Malay archipelago: the land of the orang-utan, and the bird of paradise. New York, 1869. 638 pp. Maps. Illustrations. Sm. 8°. 5934.1

— Miracles and modern spiritualism. Three essays. London, 1875. viii, 236 pp. Sm. 8° 6328.24

WALLACE, *Mrs.* E. D. A woman's experiences in Europe. Including England, France, Germany, and Italy. New York, 1872. 315 pp. 12°... 423.11

WALLACE, Lewis. The fair god; or, the last of the 'tzins. Boston, 1873. xiv, 586 pp. 12°. 737.16 and 5014.10

WALLACE, William Vincent. Maritana. (*In* Ditson, O., and co. Standard opera librettos) 6233.3.5

WALLACE. Abbott, J. 914.11

WALLENSTEIN, Death of. Schiller, (J. C.) F. von. Works. London, 1872. Sm. 8° 827.26

— — *See* COLERIDGE, S. T. Works 1611.5

WALLENSTEIN'S Lager. Schiller, (J. C.) F. von. Werke. Stuttgart, 1865. 8° 5734.1.4

WALLENSTEIN'S Tod. Schiller, (J. C.) F. von. Boston, 1865. 12° 5735.3

— *Same.* (*In his* Werke.) Stuttgart, 1865. 8°. 5734.1.4

WALLING, H. F., and GRAY, O. W., *compilers.* Official topographical atlas of Massachusetts. [Boston] 1871. F° .... *R.R.Desk

WALLYS, Philip. About New York: an account of what a boy saw in his visit to the city. Illustrated. New York, 1857. 102+ pp. 12°.... 414.19

WALMSLEY, Hugh Mulleneux. Wild sports and savage life in Zulu land. With illustrations. London [1872]. viii, 374 pp. 16° 5928.1

WALN, Robert. Life of the marquis de La Fayette. Philadelphia, 1825. 505 [501] pp. Portrait. 8° 5513.2

WALPOLE, Horace, *4th earl of Oxford.* Anecdotes of painting in England. Reprint. London, 1871. viii, 532 pp. 16° 6215.7

— Letters. Edited by Peter Cunningham. Now first chronologically arranged. London, 1857. 9 v. Portraits. 8° 5623.2

Note. — The reader will do well at first to survey the subject as mapped out in Allibone, and to note his references. Walpole's own autobiography is merely a matter of dates; but his long series of Letters shows his times and their writer equally well. After successive issues by instalments, they have been consolidated in one chronological sequence by Peter Cunningham, in nine volumes, embracing 2665 letters, covering 1735-97. Of similar value in studying the author and his times, are his Reminiscences of the court of George I and George II; his memoirs of the last ten years of George II, 1751-60; of George III, 1760-71, followed by Journals, 1771-83, the whole forming, with the Letters, an unmatched contribution to the political and social history of England for the greater part of the last century. All but the Letters must be sought in the Bates Hall.

For accounts of Strawberry hill, his residence, see Cobbett's "Memorials of Twickenham" [5424.1] and Eastlake's "History of the Gothic revival" [6221.2]. Also Wharton's "Wits and beaux" [1216.18].

The only memoir of Walpole of regular proportions is that edited by Eliot Warburton. Of the lesser accounts, Scott's, in his "Lives of the novelists" [5914.2], is the earliest, and that of Lord Dover, prefixed to his letters, is meagre, but it gave occasion to Macaulay's review, in his Essays [1918.4], whose unfavorable estimate of Walpole's character probably prevails against the higher one of Croker. Cunningham holds Walpole's character to be between the estimates of Macaulay and Croker. Disraeli, in his paper "Pains of fastidious egotism" [" Calamities of authors "], takes a low view. Also the sketch in Lodge's "Portraits" [5337.6.8].

WALRÉE, E. C. W. van. The burgomaster's family. By Christine Muller [*pseud.*]. From the Dutch by Sir John Shaw Lefevre 731.20

WALSH, John Henry. (*Stonehenge.*) British rural sports. Illustrated. 9th edition, with additions. London, 1871. xx, 872 pp. Portrait. Sq. 16°. 6414.1

— The dog in health and disease. 2d edition. London, 1872. xvi, 470 pp. Illustrated. 8°. 6614.3

Shelf. No.

WALSH, John Henry, *continued.*

— The horse in the stable and the field; his management in health and disease. From the last London edition. With notes and additions. By R. McClure. And an essay on the American trotting horse [etc.]. By E. Harvey. Illustrated. Philadelphia [*cop.* 1871]. 540 pp. Sm. 8° 6616.7

WALSH, Michael. A new system of mercantile arithmetic, adapted to the commerce of the United States. 2d edition. Newburyport, 1803. 264 pp. 12° 1933.17

WALSH, Robert. An appeal from the judgments of Great Britain respecting the United States of America. 2d edition. Philadelphia, 1819. lvi, 512 pp. 8° 811.10

WALSH, William Shepard, *compiler.* The treasure-trove series. Edited by R. H. Stoddard. [Vol. I.] Burlesque. Boston, 1875. 224 pp. 16°.. 538.10

Contents. — Vol. I. The noble savage, by C. Dickens; Our new livery, and other things, by G. W. Curtis; Mrs. Battle's opinion on cards, by C. Lamb; The parish revolution, by T. Hood; A day in the academy, by F. C. Burnand; Mrs. Brown at the play, by A. Sketchley; The will of a virtuoso, by J. Addison; The golden age of New York, by W. Irving; The insanity of Cain, by M. M. Dodge; An encounter with an interviewer, by Mark Twain; The painter's bargain, by W. M. Thackeray; The lady Rohesia, by R. H. Barham.

WALTER Goring. Cudlip, A. 317.18

WALTER Sherwood. Wise, D. 932.32

WALTER'S word. Payn, J. Leipzig 331.12

— *Same.* New York 720.10

WALTON, Izaak. The lives of John Donne; Sir Henry Wotton; Richard Hooker; George Herbert; and Robert Sanderson. London, 1866. xii, 403+ pp. Portrait. 16° 5428.2

— and COTTON, Charles. The complete angler, or the contemplative man's recreation. With lives of the authors, and notes. Edited by E. Jesse. Added papers on fishing-tackle, etc. By H. G. Bohn. London, 1861. xix, 496 pp. Illustrated. Portraits. Sm. 8° 6416.2

WANDERING heir, The. Reade, C. Leipzig 335.16

— *Same.* New York 531.14

WANDERING Jew, The. Sue, M. J. London [1845]. 2 v. in 1. Sm. 8° 725.35

WANTED — a pedigree. Finley, M. 736.27

WAR. Graham, J. J. Elementary history of the progress of the art of. London, 1858. 12°.... 6927.2

— Hamley, E. B. The operations of war explained and illustrated. Edinburgh, 1872. 4° 5910.6

— Helps, *Sir* A. Conversations on war and general culture. Boston, 1871. 16° 5617.4

— Ruskin, J. The crown of wild olive. Three lectures on work, traffic, and war. New York, 1872. 12° 6236.6

— Whiting, W. War powers under the constitution of the United States. Boston, 1871. 8°.. 5013.18

WAR-TRAIL, The. Reid, M. 725.10

WARBURTON, Eliot (Bartholomew George). The crescent and the cross; or, romance and realities of Eastern travel. Leipzig, 1852. 2 v. in 1. Sq. 16° 317.8

— Darien. A historical romance 317.7

— Reginald Hastings 531.18

WARBURTON, William P. Edward III. With maps. London, 1875. x, 266 pp. Folded sheets. [Morris, E. E., *editor.* Epochs of history.] 16°.... 628.6

WARD, Adolphus William. History of English dramatic literature to the death of Queen Anne. London, 1875. 2 v. 8° 5624.3

WARD, Artemus, *pseud.* *See* BROWNE, Charles Farrar.

WARD, James. The world in its workshops. London, N. D. 138+ pp. 2 plates. 16° 6428.5

WARD, John. Experiences of a diplomatist, being recollections of Germany, 1840-70. London, 1872. viii, 278 pp. 8° 5714.6

WARD, Robert. An enquiry into the foundation and history of the law of nations in Europe, from the time of the Greeks and Romans to the age of Grotius. Dublin, 1795. 2 v. in 1. 8°.... 6315.2

WARD or wife? A romance 720.31

Shelf. No.

WARDEN, Frank L., *joint author.* Romance after marriage: a comedy. *See* GOODRICH, Frank Boot. 1635.4
WARDEN, The. Trollope, A. 334.13
WARDER, John A. Hedges and evergreens. A complete manual for the cultivation of all plants suitable for American hedging. Illustrated. New York, 1858. 291 pp. 12° 6626.3
WARE, Henry. Inquiry into the foundation, evidences, and truths of religion. Cambridge, 1842. 2 v. 12° 5815.1
WARE, Henry, *jr.* Discourses on the life and character of Jesus Christ. Boston, 1825. 217+ pp. Sm. 8° 5814.2
— Of the formation of the Christian character. 3d edition. Cambridge, 1831. viii, 176 pp. Sm. 12° 5819.13
— Memoir of. Ware, J. Boston, 1846. 12° 1215.5
WARE, John. Hemoptysis as a symptom. (*In* Massachusetts medical society. Publications) 6021.4
— Hints to young men, on the true relation of the sexes. Boston, 1850. 64 pp. 16° 1528.4
— Memoir of Henry Ware, jr. Boston, 1846. xii, 484 pp. Portrait. 12° 1215.5
— The philosophy of natural history. Prepared on the plan, and retaining portions, of the work of William Smellie. Boston, 1861. viii, 448 pp. Illustrated. 12° 1522.10
WARE, John Fothergill Waterhouse. Sermon on the death of Elizabeth Livermore. Cambridge, 1856. 20 pp. Portrait. 8° 6323.1
— Sermon on the death of Nathaniel Livermore. Cambridge, 1862. 24 pp. Portrait. 8° 6323.1
WARE, Mary Greene (Chandler). Death and life. Boston, 1864. 174 pp. 12° 1526.10
WARE, Mary Lovell, Memoir of. Hall, E. B. Boston, 1853. 12° 1214.4
WARE, William. Aurelian; or, Rome in the third century. 5th edition. New York, 1869. 2 v. 12° 512.14

Note. — This work was originally published under the title of Probus.

— Julian; or, scenes in Judea. 2d edition. New York, 1869. 2 v. 12° 736.5
— Sketches of European capitals. [London, Rome, Naples, etc.] Boston, 1851. 320+ pp. 12°. 236.1
— Zenobia: or, the fall of Palmyra. [Historical novel.] 9th edition. New York, 1869. 2 v. 12° 726.15
WARFIELD, Catharine Anne. A double wedding; or, how she was won 723.18
— Hester Howard's temptation. A soul's story 723.24
— Miriam's memoirs. A sequel to "Monfort Hall." Being a romance of the House of Beauseincourt. 723.34
— Monfort Hall. A novel 723.32
— Sea and shore. A sequel to "Miriam's memoirs." 723.35
WARING, George Edwin, *jr.* The elements of agriculture. New York, 1854. 288+ pp. 12° ... 1527.19
— A farmer's vacation. Reprinted (with additions) from Scribner's monthly. Illustrated. Boston, 1876. 251 pp. 8° 5933.11

Note. — Notes of a trip made in 1873, through some of the Netherland provinces, parts of Normandy, Brittany, and the Channel islands.

— Whip and spur. Boston, 1875. 245 pp. Sq. 16°. 439.2
WARING, J. B. Ceramic art in remote ages; with essays on the symbols of the circle, the cross and circle [etc.], showing their relation to the primitive forms of solar and nature worship. London, 1874. ii, 127+ pp. Illuminated title-page. 55 plates. F° 6231.1
WARMING buildings. Rudimentary treatise on warming. Tomlinson, C. London, 1869. 12°. 1715.26
WARNER, Anna B. [Ellen Montgomery's book shelf.] Mr. Rutherford's children 932.22
— Dollars and cents 736.9
— Gardening by myself. New York, 1872. 223 pp. Illustrated. 12° 6627.2
— Miss Tiller's vegetable garden and the money she made by it. New York [*cop.* 1873]. 140 pp. 12° 1518.2
— My brother's keeper 736.3

Shelf. No.

WARNER, Anna B., *continued.*
— Three little spades 932.24
— *joint author.* Say and seal. *See* WARNER, Susan. 317.10
— - Wych Hazel. *See* WARNER, Susan 722.15
WARNER, Charles Dudley. Backlog studies. With illustrations. Boston, 1873. 281+ pp. 16°. 928.1
— Baddeck, and that sort of thing. [Nova Scotia.] Boston, 1874. 191 pp. 16° 418.8
— My summer in a garden. Boston, 1875. 186+ pp. 16° 1527.16
— Saunterings. Boston, 1872. xii, 289 pp. 12°. 229.1
— *joint author.* The gilded age. *See* CLEMENS, Samuel Langhorne 712.1
WARNER, Susan. (*Elizabeth Wetherell.*) Bread and oranges 1117.4
— Daisy 722.19
— The hills of the Shatemuc 331.3
— The little camp on Eagle hill 928.9
— Melbourne house 724.24
— The old helmet 317.11
— Queechy 317.12
— The rapids of Niagara 1117.6
— Sceptres and crowns 927.27
— "What she could" 932.21
— The wide, wide world 737.31
— Willow brook 913.31
— and Anna B. Say and seal 317.10
— - Wych Hazel 722.15
WARREN, Edward. Life of John Warren, M. D. Boston, 1874. xv, 568 pp. Portrait. 8° 5024.1
WARREN, Elizabeth. Comfort for small incomes. Boston, 1866. 94 pp. 12° 1533.16
— How I managed my house on £200 a year. 7th edition. Boston, 1866. 95 pp. 12° 1533.1
WARREN, Israel Perkins. Jerusalem, ancient and modern. Boston [*cop.* 1873]. 60 pp. 8° 821.6
WARREN, John, Life of. Warren, E. Boston, 1874. 8°. 5024.1
WARREN, John Collins. Address to the Boston society of natural history. Boston, 1853. 48 pp. 8° 6613.9
— Comparative view of the sensorial and nervous systems in men and animals. Boston, 1822. 159 pp. Folded plates. 12° 6012.8
— Etherization; with surgical remarks. Boston, 1848. 100+ pp. 12° 6036.3
— Physical education and the preservation of health. Boston, 1846. 90 pp. 12° 1529.6
— The great tree on Boston common. Boston, 1855. 20 pp. 1 plate. Map. 8° 411.1
WARREN, Joseph. Everett, A. H. Life of. (*In* Sparks, J. Library of American biography). 5028.1.10
— Frothingham, R. Life and times of. Boston, 1865. 8° 1010.6
— Inauguration of the statue of. *See* BUNKER-HILL monument association 1211.3
WARREN, Samuel. The lily and the bee 316.10
— Now and then 317.4
— Passages from the diary of a late physician. Leipzig, 1844. 2 v. in 1. Sq. 16° 317.4
— Ten thousand a-year 317.5
WARRENIANA: with notes critical and explanatory. Boston, 1851. 192 pp. 12° 1625.7

Note. — "A jeu d'esprit in verse after the manner of Rejected addresses. It contains puffs of Robert Warren's blacking, in imitation of the styles of W. Gifford, Wordsworth, Hogg, Southey, Byron, Coleridge, Sir W. Scott, and others." — *Bohn's edition of Lowndes's Bibliographer's manual.*

WARRINER, Edward A. Victor La Tourette. A novel. By a broad churchman 738.15
WARS, The, of the roses; or, stories of the struggle of York and Lancaster. Edgar, J. G. New York, 1859. 16° 913.15
WARTENSLEBEN, Hermann (Ludwig Wilhelm Carl Alexander Friedrich), *Graf* von. The campaign of 1870–71. Operations of the south army in January and February, 1871. Translated by C. H. von Wright. London, 1872. viii, 136 pp. Maps. Sm. 8° 5514.3
WARTON, Thomas. The history of English poetry, from the eleventh to the seventeenth century. Reprint of edition, London, 1778, 1781. London [1870]. 1032 pp. Sm. 8° 5627.5

Shelf. No.

WASHINGTON, George. Writings; with life, notes and illustrations. By J. Sparks. New York, 1847-52. 12 v. Portraits. Maps. 8° 1031.2

WAs he successful? Kimball, R. B. 311.16

WASHBURN, Emory. Commencement address, July 30, 1873. *See* WORCESTER county free institute of industrial science 5013.11

— Historical sketches of the town of Leicester, Mass. Boston, 1860. Map, illustrations, portraits. 467+ pp. 8° 5011.7

WASHBURN, Katherine Sedgwick, *formerly Mrs. Valerio.* Ina 531.35

— The Italian girl 728.9

— Perfect love casteth out fear 723.9

WASHBURN, William Tucker. Fair Harvard: a story of American college life 533.12

WASHINGTON, George. Writings; with life, notes and illustrations. By J. Sparks. New York, 1847-52. 12 v. Portraits. Maps. 8° 1031.2

Contents. — Vol. I. Life, by J. Sparks. II. Letters before the American revolution, March, 1754, to May, 1755. III. Correspondence and papers relating to the American revolution, June, 1775, to July, 1776. IV. Correspondence, July, 1776, to July, 1777. V. Correspondence, July, 1777, to July, 1778. VI. Correspondence, July, 1778, to March, 1780. VII. Correspondence, March, 1780, to April, 1781. VIII. Correspondence, April, 1781, to Dec., 1783. IX. Correspondence, Dec., 1783, to April, 1789. X. Correspondence, May, 1789, to Nov., 1794. XI. Correspondence, Nov., 1794, to Dec., 1799. XII. Speeches and messages to congress; Proclamations; Addresses; Appendix; Indexes.

— Farewell address to the people of the United States. With a German translation, by F. W. Bogen. New York, 1852. 71 pp. 12° 1918.7

— *Same. See* CONSTITUTION, The, of Massachusetts, etc. Northampton, 1806. 12° 618.1

— *Same. See* DECLARATION, The, of independence of the United States, 1776. Boston, 1876. 4°. 1920.3

— Letters, containing an account of his husbandry, with his opinions on various questions in agriculture; and many particulars of the rural economy of the United States. Alexandria, 1803. 128 pp. 8° 1912.1

— Political legacies. Annexed an appendix, containing an account of his illness, death, and the national tributes of respect paid to his memory, with a biographical outline of his life and character. Boston, 1800. 208 pp. 8° 814.3

— Abbott, J. S. C. George Washington; or, life in America one hundred years ago. New York [1875]. 12° 1014.16

— Bancroft, A. Essay on the life of. Worcester, 1807. 8° 5024.2

— Custis, G. W. P. Recollections and private memoirs of. Philadelphia [*cop.* 1859]. 8° 1011.6

— Everett, E. Life of. New York, 1860. 12° ... 1214.7

— Fox, C. [History] of a portrait of. Boston, 1851. L. 8° 1010.1

— Headley, J. T. Washington and his generals. New York, 1854, 55. 2 v. 12° 1216.5

— Irving, W. Life of. Leipzig, 1856. 5 v. in 3. Sq. 16° 1238.9

— *Same.* London, 1855-59. 5 v. 16° 1216.7

— *Same.* New York, 1855-59. 5 v. 8° 1211.2

— *Same.* Philadelphia, 1871. 5 v. Sm. 8° 1815.5

— Parker, T. Historic Americans. Boston, 1871. Sm. 8° 5025.4

— *Same.* (*In his* Works) 5237.1.7

Note. — The life by chief justice Marshall [in Bates Hall], which is the earliest of the important biographies, will always maintain its value for its calm, judicial character, and as being the only one by a biographer who knew his subject personally. Sparks, who first edited a collected edition of the Writings and correspondence [1031.2], themselves of biographical importance, accompanied the series with a lucid and painstaking memoir [1031.2.1]. Irving has supplied what must remain for a long time the most popular of the extended lives. Its chief merit is its graceful narrative, though its research is respectable. See also Allibone, under Irving. Of the lesser lives, Everett's was written for the Encyclopædia Britannica, and is founded on the three authorities already named, and gives, in an appendix, Dr. Jackson's paper on Washington's death and Mrs. Washington's will, all printed for the first time. Abbott's paper in Harper's monthly, vol. 12, is an illustrated popular narrative.

Among the essays on his life and character there may be mentioned those by Brougham, in his "Statesmen of the time of George III" [5614.4.5]. Of a rhetorical character are the addresses by Webster [5013.1.1]; by Everett [in vols. 1, 3 and 4 of 1921.1]; by Winthrop [5212.8]; and by Whipple, in his "Character and characteristic men" [1936.3].

For monographs on special episodes of his life or phases of his character, see Custis's "Recollections" [1011.6]; Lossing's "Home of Washington," in Harper's monthly, vol. 18; papers in Harper's monthly, vols. 7 (Arlington house), 12 and 18 (Morristown); and Everett's "Mount Vernon papers"

Shelf. No.

WASHINGTON, George, *continued.*

[1534.13]. There is much in Drake's "Middlesex" [814.4] relative to his career while in command at Cambridge.

Of his presidency, see the general histories of Hildreth and Higginson, and the estimate of his dealing with men in Van Buren's "History of political parties."

Beside the enumeration of authorities in Allibone, etc., see general histories of the revolution and of the United States, and the lives of his chief contemporaries, like Adams, Jefferson, Hamilton, etc.

In Thackeray's "Virginians" [335.6; 1820.3] Washington is introduced in his younger days; and in Cooper's "Spy" [310.11] he appears during his revolutionary career.

WASHOE, Sketches of adventure in. Browne, J. R. New York, 1872. 12° 415.12

WASIELEWSKI, Joseph Wilhelm von. Life of Robert Schumann. Translated by A. L. Alger. Boston [*cop.* 1871]. 275 pp. 16° 5728.1

WATCH and wait. Adams, W. T. 925.3

WATCHES, Rudimentary treatise on. Denison, E. B. London, 1868. 12° 1716.12

WATER. Abbott, J. Science for the young 912.3

— Dove, H. W. The circulation of the waters on the surface of the earth. (*In* Estes, D. Half-hour recreations in popular science) 6813.7

— Tissandier, G. The wonders of. New York, 1872. 12° 1714.26

— Tyndall, J. The forms of water in clouds and rivers, ice and glaciers. New York, 1872. 12°. 6436.11

WATER-BABIES, The: a fairy tale for a land-baby. Kingsley, C. 921.4

WATER-COLOR painting. Ayers, G. B. How to paint photographs in water colors. Philadelphia, 1870. 12° 6217.8

— Miles, L. C. Water-colour painting; with the art of sketching from nature. London, N. D. 16° 6216.5

WATER-COLOUR drawing, Course of. Leitch, R. P. London [1874]. Oblong 16° 6217.9

WATER-WITCH, The. Cooper, J. F. 525.23

WATER-WORKS, Treatise on. Hughes, S. London, 1872. 12° 6428.4

WATERDALE neighbours, The. MacCarthy, J. 313.14

WATERLOO. Chesney, C. C. Waterloo lectures: a study of the campaign of 1815. London, 1874. 8° 5513.3

— Erckmann, É., and Chatrian, A. Waterloo. New York, 1872. 12° 913.24

— Gleig, G. R. Story of the battle of. London, 1861. Sm. 8° 5927.5

— Hooper, G. Waterloo: the downfall of the first Napoleon: a history of the campaign of 1815. London, 1862. 8° 5511.2

— Maxwell, W. H. Stories of 518.7

Note. — See a note on the literature of the Waterloo campaign in the Library Bulletin, Oct., 1875. Hooper's is the best general account in English; Chesney's is a military critique.

WATERSTON, Robert Cassie. Address on the life and character of Thomas Sherwin. Boston, 1870. 74+ pp. Portrait. L. 12° 1011.2

WATERTOWN, *Mass.*, Historical sketch of. Francis, C. Cambridge, 1830. 12° 5014.5

WATSON, Elkanah. Men and times of the revolution; or, memoirs of Elkanah Watson, including journals of travel in Europe and America, from 1777 to 1842, with his correspondence with public men and reminiscences and incidents of the revolution. Edited by W. C. Watson. New York, 1856. 460 pp. 8° 1214.15

WATSON, Emily H. Child-life in Italy; a story of six years abroad. Boston, 1866. 363+ pp. 16°. 931.5

— Fairies of our garden. Boston, 1867. 377 pp. 16°. 931.6

WATSON, Henry C. Camp-fires of the revolution. With illustrations. New York, 1869. 447 pp. 8°. 811.8

WATSON, Richard. An apology for Christianity. In a series of letters to Edward Gibbon. Providence, 1794. viii, 155 pp. 16° 1925.2

WATSON, Robert. History of the reign of Philip II, king of Spain. New York, 1818. 448 pp. 8°. 823.3

WATSON, Samuel. The clock struck three, being a review of Clock struck one, and a reply to it. Part II. Showing the harmony between Christianity, science, and spiritualism. Chicago, 1874. 352 pp. Portrait. 16° 6325.17

Shelf. No.

WATT, Alexander. Electro-metallurgy. 4th edition. London, 1871. viii [vi], 152 pp. Illustrated. 12° 1715.18

WATT, James, Life of. Smiles, S. London, 1865. 8°. 5421.5

WATTS, Henry. Dictionary of chemistry and the allied branches of other sciences. London, 1868–72. 6 v. Illustrated. 8° .... *R.R., C.2.1

WATTS, Isaac. The beauties of Watts: containing passages in [his] works. Added, the life of the author. Newburyport, 1797. 239 pp. 12° ... 1737.4

— Causes of uncharitableness. (*In* Sparks, J. Collection of essays and tracts in theology) 1918.9.6

WATTS, W. Marshall. Index of spectra. With a preface by H. E. Roscoe. London, 1872. xvi, 74 pp. 9 plates. 8° 6813.6

WAVERLEY. Scott, *Sir* W. Boston 523.18

— *Same.* Leipzig 324.3

WAY, The, to do good. Abbott, J. Boston, 1836. 12° 5836.4

WAY, The, we live now. Trollope, A. Leipzig. 4 v. in 2 .... 331.8

— *Same.* New York 720.34

WAYLAND, Francis. Elements of moral science. 3d edition. Boston, 1836. 402+ pp. 12° 5826.7

— *Same.* Abridged. Boston, 1850. 212 pp. Sm. 12° 1528.7

— The limitations of human responsibility. Boston, 1838. 188 pp. 16° 5838.4

— Memoir of Adoniram Judson. Boston, 1853. 2 v. Portrait. 12° 1214.10

WAYNE, Anthony, Life of. Armstrong, J. (*In* Sparks, J. Library of American biography) .. 5028.1.4

WAYS, The, of the hour. Cooper, J. F. 525.13

WE and our neighbors. Stowe, H. (E.) B. 733.12

WE girls. Whitney, A. D. T. 735.11

WEAK lungs, and how to make them strong. Lewis, D. Boston, 1871. 12° 1536.2

WEALE's rudimentary series. *Namely:* —

— Clark, D. K. An elementary treatise on steam and the steam-engine, stationary and portable .. 6428.7

WEALTH. An inquiry into the nature and causes of the wealth of nations. Smith, A. Oxford, 1869. 2 v. 8° 5822.9

WEAR and tear, or hints for the overworked. Mitchell, S. W. Philadelphia, 1871. 16° 1537.2

WEBB, Charles Henry. John Paul's book: moral and instructive: consisting of travels, tales, poetry, and like fabrications. By John Paul [*pseud.*]. With portrait and engravings. Hartford, 1874. 621 pp. 8° 1531.4

WEBB, W. E. Buffalo land: an authentic account of the discoveries, adventures, and mishaps of a scientific and sporting party in the wild West. Illustrated. Cincinnati, 1872. 503 pp. 8° ... 5032.2

WEBER, Carl Maria Friedrich Ernst, *baron* von. Der Freyschütz. (*In* Ditson, O., and co. Standard opera librettos) 6233.3.1

WEBSTER, *Mrs.* A. L. The improved housewife, or book of receipts; with engravings for marketing and carving. By a married lady. 12th edition, revised; with supplement. Hartford, 1850. 233 pp. 12° 1533.17

WEBSTER, Daniel. Works. 16th edition. Boston, 1872. 6 v. Portrait. 8° 5013.1

Contents. — Vol. I. Biographical memoir, by E. Everett. I, II. Speeches on various public occasions. III. Speeches in the convention to amend the constitution of Massachusetts. III, IV. Speeches in congress. V, VI. Legal arguments. VI. Diplomatic and official papers.

— Private correspondence. Edited by F. Webster. Boston, 1857. 2 v. Portraits. L. 8° 5020.2

— Curtis, G. T. Life of. New York, 1872. 2 v. 8° 1225.3

— March, C. W. Reminiscences of congress. A biography of. New York, 1850. 12° 1217.3

— Memorial of. *See* BOSTON, *Mass.* 1011.4

— Parton, J. Famous Americans of recent times. Boston, 1871. 8° 1214.14

— Proceedings in Boston commemorative of the death of. *See* NEW HAMPSHIRE, Sons of. Second festival. Boston, 1854. 8° 1920.1

Shelf. No.

WEBSTER, Daniel, *continued.*

Note. — March's "Reminiscences of congress," devoted chiefly to Webster and his career to 1835 [1217.3], had already appeared, when Everett prefixed to the final edition of Webster's Speeches, the only authoritative regular memoir [5013.1] which appeared in Webster's lifetime. Upon his death, in 1852, there were a large number of eulogies, which will be found in the Bates Hall catalogues; chief among them may be named Everett, in his Orations [1921.1.3]. A few years after his death, Fletcher Webster printed the "Private correspondence" of his father [5020.2], and the collection was rendered more valuable for an autobiography, ending 1817, which it contained, and some personal recollections of his student days, by those who knew him. In 1869, with the approbation of his literary executors, George T. Curtis issued his elaborate and authoritative life [1225.3]. The unfriendly view of Webster will be found vigorously expressed in Parton's sketch [1214.14].

Beside the references in Allibone, see Van Buren's "History of political parties"; Whipple's essay, in his "Essays and reviews" [1936.2.1]; Benton's "Thirty years' view" [812.2]; Loring's "Boston orators" [5022.9]; Greeley's "Recollections of a busy life" [5023.8]; Miss Mitford's "Recollections of a literary life" [1536.4]; and Everett's vindication of the statue by Powers, in his Orations [1921.1.4].

See Charles Hale's paper on Webster's literary efforts in college, in "Old and new," July, 1873; and a paper on his "Social hours," in Harper's monthly, vol. 13. There are letters from him in Hillard's "Memoir of Jeremiah Mason" [5020.7]. See also Allibone, vol. 3.

WEBSTER, John White. Bemis, G. Report of the case of. Boston, 1850. 8° 1530.1

— Stone, J. W. Report of the trial of. Boston, 1850. 8° 631.5

WEBSTER, Noah. American dictionary of the English language. Revised and improved by C. A. Goodrich and N. Porter. Springfield, 1873. lxxii, 1768 pp. Illustrated. Portraits. 4°. *R.R., A.3.1

— Dictionary of the English language. With an appendix containing tables [of money, weight, and measure, etc.]. Abridged from the latest edition of the quarto dictionary, by W. G. Webster and W. A. Wheeler. Illustrated. [Counting-house edition.] New York, 1872. xxxii, 832+ pp. Sm. 4° .... *R.R., A.2.5

WEDDING day, The, in all ages and countries. Wood, E. J. New York, 1869. 12° 1527.8

WEDGWOOD, Hensleigh. A dictionary of English etymology. 2d edition, revised and enlarged; with an introduction on the origin of language. London, 1872. lxix, 744+ pp. 8° ..... *R.R., D.3.10

WEDGWOOD, Josiah, Life of. Meteyard, E. London, 1865, 66. 2 v. 8° 6231.3

WEDGWOODS, The. A group of Englishmen, being records of the younger Wedgwoods. Meteyard, E. London, 1871. 8° 5424.4

WEDL, Carl. Rudiments of pathological histology. With illustrations. Translated and edited by G. Busk. London, 1855. xxvi, 637 pp. 8° .. 6013.18

WEEK, A, in a French country-house. Sartoris, A. (K.) 732.6

WEEKS, John M. A manual: or, an easy method of managing bees. With an appendix, by W. A. Flanders. New York, 1855. 119 pp. Illustrations. 12° 1524.14

WEIDENMANN, J. Beautifying country homes. A handbook of landscape gardening. Illustrated by plans of places already improved. New York [*cop.* 1870]. 40+ pp. 4° 6220.1

WEIGALL, Rose, *lady.* Brief memoir of the princess Charlotte of Wales. With portrait. London, 1874. x, 169 pp. Sm. 8° 5427.7

WEIGHTS and measures. *See* WEBSTER, N. Dictionary of the English language [Counting-house edition], pp. 550–608 .... *R.R., A.2.5

WEISS, John. American religion. Boston, 1871. 326 pp. 12° 1537.5

— Life and correspondence of Theodore Parker. New York, 1864. 2 v. Portraits. Illustrations. 8° 5021.2

WELCOME home. A choice collection of piano-forte music. Boston [*cop.* 1874]. 224 pp. 4° 1510.2

WELLES, —. "Things new and old:" sermons. Portland, 1845. 261 pp. 8° 1533.9

WELLES, Gideon. Lincoln and Seward. Remarks upon the memorial address of Chas. Francis Adams, on the late Wm. H. Seward. New York, 1874. 215+ pp. 12° 5027.10

Shelf. No.

WELLESLEY, Arthur, *duke of Wellington*. Gleig, G. R. Life of. London, 1871. Sm. 8°..........5426.13

— Maurel, J. The duke of Wellington: his character, his actions, and his writings. London, 1853. 16°..............................5428.12

WELLINGTON, *Duke of*. *See* WELLESLEY, Arthur.

Note. — There will be found in Allibone a full list of memoirs of the duke, with other references of use to the inquirer. In 1858, Gleig translated and enlarged the very just French life by Brialmont, an officer of the Belgian staff, who is a skilful military critic, and ranks Wellington next to Napoleon as a soldier, and what is known as Gleig's "Life of Wellington" [5426.13], is a condensation of this extended work of Brialmont, with additional matter based upon the "Supplemental despatches." In 1860, C. D. Yonge published a life [in Bates Hall], in two volumes octavo, which derives importance from new matter, has plans of battles, including a fac-simile of a plan of the field of Waterloo surveyed for the duke, just before the battle, and showing his pencil tracings, and in the appendix there is Wellington's commentary on Clausewitz's account of Waterloo.

Among the lesser English accounts, see Bayne's Essays [1226.15.2] and Lodge's "Portraits" [5337.6.8]. See also Harper's monthly, vols. 5, 26, and 31.

For French views, besides Brialmont, see Maurel, which is brief, closing with Waterloo, and introduced in the translation [5428.12] by the earl of Ellesmere.

Students will find it necessary to examine the "Despatches" and particularly the "Supplemental despatches," printed since his death, and throwing much light on his character and his relations to his contemporaries, while analyses of them will be found in the various reviews mentioned by Allibone, and the series themselves in the Bates Hall.

For further study of his military career, see works mentioned under India; Peninsular war; France, history; Waterloo, etc.

For the Waterloo campaign, see the note in the Library Bulletin for Oct., 1875. There is much concerning him in the "Greville journals" [5914.6]; in Jerdan's "Autobiography" [5425.5]; and in Madden's Lady Blessington [1223.2].

WELLINGTON mills, *London*. Duke of Wellington's biography. Mining and manufacture of emery. [Boston, 1876.] 48 pp. Portraits. Illustrations. 8°.............................. 1711.4

WELLS, David Ames. The science of common things; a familiar explanation of the first principles of physical science. Illustrated. New York, 1872. 323+ pp. 12°.............................. 1527.9

— Things not generally known: in literature, history, and science. New York, 1873. 432 pp. 12°....................................1714.27

WELLS, John C. The gateway to the Polynia. A voyage to Spitzbergen. With illustrations. London, 1873. 355+ pp. 8°...............5911.14

WELLS, Samuel Roberts. How to read character: a new illustrated hand-book of phrenology and physiognomy; with a descriptive chart. New York, 1875. 191 pp. 12° 1525.22

— New physiognomy, or, signs of character. With illustrations. New York, 1874. 768 pp. 12°.1521.13

WELLS, Walter. The water-power of Maine. *See* MAINE. *Hydrographic survey*........411.2 and 5012.5

WELLS, William Harvey. A graded course of instruction for public schools: with copious practical directions to teachers. New York, 1862. 200 pp. 12°.............................1535.11

WELLS, William Vincent. Life and public services of Samuel Adams. Boston, 1865. 3 v. Portraits. Fac-similes. 8°..................... 5021.7

WELLS and pumps: a treatise on well-digging and boring, and the various ways of raising water. Swindell, J. G. London, N. D. 12° 1715.14

WELLS of Baca. Macduff, J. R. Boston, 1854. 16°. 5819.9

WELTEVREDEN, The prison of. Gibson, W. M. New York, 1855. 12° 424.3

WENHAM, *Mass.*, History of. Allen, M. O. Boston, 1860. 12°.............................. 816.4

WENNINGER, F. X. Protestantism and infidelity. New York, 1862. xv, 329 pp. 16°........... 1538.9

WENTWORTH, Thomas, *earl of Strafford*, Life of. Cooper, E. London, 1874. 2 v. 8° 5333.5

WEPT of Wish-ton-Wish, The. Cooper, J. F. 525.12

WERNER, Ernst. At the altar. From the German. By J. S. L. 727.24

— Broken chains. Translated by Frances A. Shaw. 732.36

— "Good luck!" Translated by Frances A. Shaw. 731.29

WESLEY, John. Stevenson, G. J. City road chapel, London, and its associations. London [1872]. 8° 5414.1

— Tyermann, L. Life and times of. New York, 1872. 3 v. 8° 5423.2

WEST, The. Barber, J. W., and Howe, H. The loyal West in the times of the rebellion; also, before and since. Cincinnati, 1865. 8°....... 5033.4

— Gerstaecker, F. Wild sports in the far West. Boston, 1861. 12°.......................... 416.1

— Hall, J. Legends of the West: sketches illustrative of the habits, occupations, privations, adventures and sports of the pioneers of the West. Cincinnati, 1871. 12° 5036.3

— – The romance of Western history. Cincinnati, 1871. 12°.................................. 814.2

— Irving, W. Adventures of Captain Bonneville in the far West. London, 1854. 16° 826.3

— *Same.* Philadelphia, 1871. Sm. 8°...........1815.14

— Lippincott, S. J. New life in new lands: notes of travel. New York, 1873. 12° 214.1

— MacClung, J. A. Sketches of Western adventure: 1775–94. Covington, Ky., 1872. 8° 5026.4

— Marcy, R. B. Thirty years of army life on the border. New York, 1866. 12° 415.16

— Parkman, F., *jr.* The discovery of the great West. Boston, 1872. 12°........................5015.5.3

— Sweetser, C. H. Tourists' and invalids' guide to the Northwest. New York, 1868. 8° 432.3

— Webb, W. E. Buffalo land: an authentic account of the discoveries, adventures, and mishaps of a scientific and sporting party in the wild West. Cincinnati, 1872. 8° 5032.2

See also America, California, Oregon, Prairies, United States, and the note.

WEST INDIES. Kingsley, C. At last: a Christmas in the. Leipzig, 1871. 2 v. in 1. Sq. 16°.... 326.17

— Trollope, A. The West Indies and the Spanish main. Leipzig, 1860. Sq. 16° 228.2

WEST lawn. Holmes, M. J. 534.25

WESTMINSTER, London and. Timbs, J. London, 1868. 2 v. 8° 5435.4

WESTMINSTER abbey, Historical memorials of. Stanley, A. P. London, 1869. 8° 5414.2

WESTMINSTER hall, *London, Eng.*, Memories of. Foss, E. New York, 1874. 2 v. 8°......... 5421.2

WESTMINSTER review. Vol. 43, no. 85; vol. 44, no. 86, 87; vol. 45, no. 88; new series, vol. 43–48. New York, 1845, 46, 73–75. 7 v. 8°......... 6737.1

WESTMORELAND, Maria Jourdan. Heart-hungry ... 735.37

WEST Roxbury directory for 1873, 74. Boston, 1873. 8°...*R.R., E.2.9

WESTWARD by rail: a journey to San Francisco and back and a visit to the Mormons. Rae, W. F. Leipzig, 1874. Sq. 16°...................... 438.3

WESTWARD ho! or, the voyages and adventures of Sir Amyas Leigh. [Maritime adventures in Queen Elizabeth's time.] Kingsley, C......... 326.14

WETHEREL affair, The. De Forest, J. W............ 732.8

WETHERELL, Elizabeth, *pseud.* *See* WARNER, Susan.

WEY, Francis (Adolphe). Rome. Containing 345 engravings on wood and a plan of Rome. With an introduction by W. W. Story. London, 1872. xxiii, 552 pp. 4° 5520.1

— *Same.* New York, 1875. xxi, 339 pp. 4° 5520.2

WEYER, Jean Sylvain van de. *See* HAYWARD, A. Biographical and critical essays. London, 1873. 8°......................................5833.3.1

WHALE, Moby-Dick; or, the. Melville, H. New York, 1871. 12° 512.12

WHALEMAN'S, The, adventures in the Sandwich Islands and California. Thomes, W. H. Boston, 1873. Sm. 8°.............................. 735.1

WHALING and fishing. Nordhoff, C. Cincinnati, 1856. 16°................................ 936.2

WHALING cruise, A, to Baffin's bay and the gulf of Boothia. Markham, A. H. London, 1874. 8°.5912.11

WHARTON, Charles. Hand-book on the treatment of the horse in the stable and on the road; or, hints to horse owners. With illustrations. Philadelphia, 1873. 137 pp. 12° 6617.3

WHARTON, Eliza, The romance of the association; or, one last glimpse of. Dall, C. (W.) H. Cambridge, 1875. 16°...............................1534.11

WHARTON, Grace and Philip, *pseud.* *See* THOMSON, Katherine and John Cockburn.

Shelf. No.

WHAT a boy! Willis, J. A. 931.7
WHAT a house should be, *versus* death in the house. Bardwell, W. London [1873]. 8° 6221.4
WHAT and how to read. Van Rhyn, G. A. F. New York, 1875. 12° 6136.11
WHAT answer? Dickinson, A. E. 515.8
WHAT can she do? Roe, E. P. 737.24
WHAT Katy did. Woolsey, S. C. 925.29
WHAT Katy did at school. Woolsey, S. C. 925.28
WHAT shall we do to-night? or social amusements for evening parties. Dick, W. B., Frost, S. A., and Taylor, W. New York [1873]. 12° 1516.19
"WHAT she could." Warner, S. 932.21
WHAT the swallow sang. Spielhagen, F. 518.16
WHAT to read, and how to read. Moore, C. H. New York, 1871. 12° 1537.3
WHAT to wear? Phelps, E. S. Boston, 1873. 12°. 1537.7
WHAT will he do with it? Bulwer-Lytton, E. (G. E.) L. 4 v. in 2 .... 336.21
WHATELY, Richard. Life and correspondence, by E. Jane Whately. New edition. London, 1875. xvi, 495 pp. Portrait. Sm. 8° 5337.3
WHEATLEY, Henry B. Round about Piccadilly and Pall Mall. London, 1870. xi, 405+ pp. Illustrated. 8° 5435.2
WHEATON, Henry. Life of William Pinkney. (*In* Sparks, J. Library of American biography) .. 5028.1.6
WHEATON, Robert. Memoir, with selections from his writings. Boston, 1854. 385 pp. Sm. 8° .. 1216.10
WHEELER, George Augustus. History of Castine, Penobscot, and Brooksville, Maine; including the ancient settlement of Pentagöet. Bangor, 1875. 401 pp. Illustrations. Maps. Portraits. 8° 813.2
WHEELER, Gervase. The choice of a dwelling. A practical handbook of useful information on all points connected with hiring, buying, or building a house, with its stables and garden-outbuildings. With plans and views. 2d edition, revised. London, 1872. xii, 305 pp. Sm. 8°. 6226.2
— Rural homes; or, sketches of houses suited to American country life. With original plans, designs, etc. New York, 1852. 298 pp. 12°. 1513.2
WHEELER, J. Talboys. Life and travels of Herodotus in the fifth century before Christ: an imaginary biography founded on fact. London, 1855. 2 v. Sm. 8° 6117.2
WHEELER, William Adolphus. Dictionary of the noted names of fiction. Boston, 1872. xxxii, 410+ pp. 16° .... *R.R., F.3.6
WHEILDON, William Willder. Memoir of Solomon Willard. [Boston] 1865. 272 pp. Plates. 8°. 1011.5
— New history of the battle of Bunker hill. Reprinted from "The Boston daily herald." Revised and enlarged. 2d edition. Boston, 1875. 56+ pp. Folded map. 8° 811.17
— Siege and evacuation of Boston and Charlestown, with a brief account of pre-revolutionary public buildings. With illustrations and map. Boston, 1876. 64 pp. Portrait. 8° 811.19
WHELPLEY, Samuel. Compend of history, from the earliest times. New York, 1814. 2 v. in 1. 1 plate. 8° 834.1
WHERE are my horns? Leppere, A. H. Boston, 1873. 16° 6326.8
WHEWELL, William. Astronomy and general physics considered with reference to natural theology. Philadelphia, 1833. 284 pp. 12° 6438.5
WHICH is the wiser; or, people abroad. Howitt, M. 937.9
WHICH shall it be? Alexander, *Mrs.* — 732.12
WHIG party, Memoirs of the. Vassal-Fox, H. R., 3d *lord Holland*. London, 1852. 2 v. Sm. 8° 5435.5
WHIM, A, and its consequences. James, G. P. R. .. 327.5
WHIMS and oddities. Hood, T. New York, 1872. Sm. 8° 533.11
WHIP, The, hoe, and sword; or, the gulf-department in '63. Hepworth, G. H. Boston, 1864. 12° 414.1
WHIP and spur. Waring, G. E., *jr.* Boston, 1875. Sq. 16° 439.2

Shelf. No.

WHIPPLE, Edwin Percy. Character and characteristic men. [Essays.] Boston, 1871. vi, 324+ pp. 16°. 1936.3
— Essays and reviews. 5th edition. Boston, 1871. 2 v. 16° 1936.2
— Literature and life. Enlarged edition. Boston, 1871. 344 pp. 16° 1936.6
— The literature of the age of Elizabeth. Boston, 1871. 364 pp. 16° 1936.5
— Success and its conditions. [Essays.] Boston, 1871. iv, 333+ pp. 16° 1936.4
WHISPERING pine, The. Kellogg, E. 922.27
WHISPERING pine series. *See* KELLOGG, Elijah.
WHIST. Jones, H. The laws and principles of whist illustrated by hands played completely through. London, 1874. 16° 6418.2
— Pardon, G. F. Handbook of whist. On the text of Hoyle. London, 1863. 16° 1519.2
WHISTLER. Simonds, W. 932.26
WHITBY, Daniel. Last thoughts. (*In* Sparks, J. Collection of essays and tracts in theology) ... 1918.9.2
WHITE, Gilbert. Natural history of Selborne. Boston, 1866. vi, 430 pp. 32° 1539.1
WHITE, Henry Kirke. Remains; with an account of his life, by Robert Southey. Boston, 1815. 2 v. Portrait. Plate. 16° 1619.3
WHITE, James. Life incidents, in connection with the great advent movement, as illustrated by the three angels of Revelation XIV. Battle Creek, 1868. 373 pp. 12° .... 1537.11 and 6328.4
— *editor.* A solemn appeal relative to solitary vice, and the abuses and excesses of the marriage relation. Battle Creek, 1870. 272 pp. 16° .. 1538.19
WHITE, John Tahourdin, and RIDDLE, Joseph Esmond. Latin-English dictionary. 4th edition. London, 1872. 2 v. 4° .... *R.R., D.3.13
WHITE, Richard Grant. Words and their uses, past and present. A study of the English language. New York, 1870. 437 pp. Sm. 8° 1735.5
— *Same.* New edition, revised. New York, 1872. vii, 461+ pp. Sm. 8° 1735.1
WHITE, Robert Baker. Reason and redemption, or the Gospel as it attests itself. Philadelphia, 1873. 351 pp. 8° 1532.5
WHITE chief, The. Reid, M. 713.14
WHITE conquest. Dixon, W. H. Leipzig, 1876. 2 v. in 1. Sq. 16° 439.4

Note.— Sketches of travel in the United States in 1875.

WHITE gauntlet, The. Reid, M. 527.4
WHITE Horse, The scouring of the. Hughes, T. Cambridge, 1859. Sm. 4° 536.1
WHITE-JACKET; or, the world in a man-of-war. Melville, H. New York [*cop.* 1850]. 12° 725.12
WHITE lies. [Napoleonic times.] Reade, C 527.2
WHITE mountains, *N. H.* King, T. S. The White hills; their legends, landscape, and poetry. North Conway, N. H. [*cop.* 1859]. 12° 413.11
— Oakes, W. Scenery of the. Boston [*cop.* 1848]. F°. 5030.4
— Sweetser, M. F. The White mountains: a handbook for travellers. Boston, 1876. 16° 418.9
WHITE, red, black. Sketches of American society in the United States. Pulszky, F. (A.) and T. New York, 1853. 2 v. 12° 414.17
WHITE rose, The. Melville, G. J. W. Leipzig 321.16
— *Same.* New York 532.5
WHITEBOY, The. Hall, A. M. 521.6
WHITEHURST, Felix M. Court and social life in France under Napoleon III. London, 1873. 2 v. 8° 5514.4
WHITELADIES. Oliphant, M. (O. W.) Leipzig 331.20
— *Same.* New York 539.11
WHITELAW, Alexander. The republic of letters, a selection, in poetry and prose, from the works of the most eminent writers, with many original pieces. With engravings. Vol. II–IV. Glasgow, 1833. 3 v. 16° 5618.6
WHITELOCKE, Bulstrode. A journal of the Swedish embassy in 1653 and 1654. First published from the original manuscript by Charles Morton. New edition, revised by Henry Reeve. London, 1855. 2 v. 8° 822.3

Shelf. No.

WHITING, William. [Addresses, arguments, etc.] PPH. V. V. P., V. D. 8° 6924.5

Contents. — Argument in the case, Boston gas light company vs. W. Gault. Boston, 1848. — Report of the committee in favor of the union of Boston and Roxbury. Boston, 1851. — Military arrests in time of war. Washington, 1863. — The return of the rebellious states to the union. Letter, July 28, 1863. Philadelphia, 1864. — Same. Broadside. — War claims against the United States. Boston, 1866. — Address before the Boston Highlands Grant club, Aug. 5, 1868. Boston, 1868. — City of Chicago vs. G. T. Bigelow, adm'r, etc. Argument in behalf of the appellee. Boston, 1869. — Argument in behalf of P. S. Crowell, in the case of interfering applications of Crowell vs. Sim and Hutchinson. Boston, 1869. — Address, 22d of July, 1872, before the combined literary societies of Colby university. Boston, 1872.

— [Destruction of Boston harbor.] Speech before [a] joint legislative committee, April 17, 1851, [against an application for leave to fill up flats in Mystic river]. Boston, 1851. 80 pp. Folded map. 8° 6923.2

— Memoir of Samuel Whiting, and of his wife, Elizabeth St. John; with references to some of their English ancestors and American descendants. 2d edition. Boston, 1873. 334 pp. 1 plate. 2 folded sheets. 8°, l. p. 5022.13

— Twenty years' war against the railroads. [Argument in the supreme court of the United States. No title-page.] N. P. [1860]. 116 pp. 8° 6313.4

— Union sugar refinery *vs.* Continental sugar refinery. Closing argument for respondents. Boston, 1867. 190 pp. 8° 6313.3

— War powers under the constitution of the United States. 43d edition. Boston, 1871. xxviii, 695 pp. 8° 5013.18

WHITMARSH, Caroline Snowden, and GUILD, Anne Eliza, *compilers.* Hymns of the ages. With an introduction by F. D. Huntington. Boston, 1862–71. 3 v. 2 plates. Sm. 4° 1615.5

WHITMORE, William Henry. The American genealogist. A catalogue of family histories [etc.]. Albany, 1868. 287 pp. 8° 5022.7

— The cavalier dismounted: an essay on the origin of the founders of the thirteen colonies. Salem, 1864. 48+ pp. 8° 5014.6

WHITNEY, Adelaide Dutton Train. Boys at Chequasset 932.23

— Faith Gartney's girlhood 735.9

— The Gayworthys 735.8

— Hitherto 735.7

— Mother Goose for grown folks. New edition. Illustrated. Boston [*cop.* 1870]. iv, 144 pp. 12° 1625.5

— The other girls 734.7

— Patience Strong's outings 734.6

— Real folks 735.10

— Sights and insights: Patience Strong's story over the way [Europe]. 2 v. 722.3

— A summer in Leslie Goldthwaite's life 735.12

— We girls 735.11

— Zerub Throop's experiment 537.13

WHITNEY, Josiah D. Geological survey of California. *See* CALIFORNIA 5039.1

WHITNEY, William Dwight. A compendious German grammar. New York, 1869. xvi, 248 pp. 12° 1933.6

— The international scientific series. The life and growth of language: an outline of linguistic science. New York, 1875. vii, 326+ pp. 12°. 6126.5

— Language and the study of language. 5th edition. New York, 1872. xi, 505+ pp. Sm. 8°. 6126.3

— Oriental and linguistic studies. New York, 1873. vii, 416+ pp. Sm. 8° 6126.2

WHITTEMORE, Thomas. Life of Hosea Ballou; and sketches of his seniors and contemporaries in the universalist ministry. Boston, 1854. 2 v. Portrait. 12° 5026.6

WHITTIER, John Greenleaf. Poetical works. Boston, 1872. 2 v. Portrait. 16° 1616.8

Contents. — Vol. I. The bridal of Pennacook; Mogg Megone; Legendary; Voices of freedom; Miscellaneous; In war time; Home ballads; Occasional poems. II. Songs of labor; Miscellaneous; The chapel of the hermits; The panorama; Ballads; Later poems; Home ballads; Poems and lyrics; Among the hills; Miscellaneous; Miriam; Poems.

Shelf. No.

WHITTIER, John Greenleaf, *continued.*

— Prose works. Boston, 1866. 2 v. Portrait. 16°. 1937.1

Contents. — Vol. I. Margaret Smith's journal; Old portraits and modern sketches. II. Literary recreations and miscellanies.

— Hazel-blossoms. [Poems.] Boston, 1875. 133 pp. 1 plate. 16° 1615.24

— Mabel Martin. A harvest idyl. With illustrations. Boston, 1876. 72 pp. 8° 1623.3

Note. — First published under the title of "The witch's daughter." It is now reproduced with additions.

— The Pennsylvania pilgrim, and other poems. Boston, 1872. 129 pp. Illustrated. 16° 1616.10

— Poems written during the progress of the abolition question in the United States, 1830–38. Boston, 1837. 103 pp. Illustrated. 16° 1617.1

— *editor.* Child life: a collection of poems. With illustrations. Boston, 1875. xiii, 263 pp. Sm. 4° 1624.4

— Child life in prose. Illustrated. Boston, 1874. 301 pp. Sm. 4° 912.10

"WHO breaks — pays." Jenkin, *Mrs.* C. 313.3

WHO shall be greatest? Howitt, M. 937.7

WHO shall be victor? Dupuy, E. A. 522.15

WHO will win? Cobden, P. 934.36

WHY did he not die? Volckhausen, A. von 736.31

WHY did he marry her? Dupuy, E. A. 522.14

WHY Paul Ferroll killed his wife. Clive, C. 310.8

WHY we laugh. Cox, S. S. New York, 1876. 12°. 1837.2

WHYMPER, Edward. Scrambles amongst the Alps, 1860–69. With illustrations. Philadelphia, 1873. 164 pp. 8° 5932.3

WHYMPER, Frederick. Travels and adventures in Alaska, and other parts of the North Pacific. With map and illustrations. New York, 1869. 353 [348] pp. 8° 5035.1

WHYTE-MELVILLE, George John. *See* MELVILLE, George John Whyte.

WICHERT, Ernst. The green gate. A romance. Translated from the German by Mrs. A. L. Wister 714.16

WICKED world, The: a comedy. Gilbert, W. S. Original plays. New York, 1876. 12° 1634.1

WICKETS in the West; or, the twelve in America. Fitzgerald, R. A. London, 1873. Sm. 8° 5035.6

WIDDEMER, Irene. Daisy Brentwell 723.36

WIDE, wide world, The. Warner, S. 737.31

WIDOW Goldsmith's daughter. Smith, J. P. 727.24

WIDOW Lerouge, The. Gaboriau, E. 530.7

WIDOW'S, The, son. Southworth, E. D. E. N. 727.11

WIDOWER, The. Smith, J. P. 727.25

WIECK, Johann Gottlob Friedrich. Piano and song: how to teach, how to learn, and how to form a judgment of musical performances. Translated from the German [by Mary P. Nichols]. Boston, 1875. x, 189+ pp. 12° 6234.5

WIFE, The, of a vain man. Schwartz, M. S. 531.9

WIFE'S, The, secret. Stephens, A. S. (W.) 726.9

WIFE'S, The, trial. Lamb, C. Works..1813.5.2 and 5615.1.2

WIFE'S, The, victory. Southworth, E. D. E. N. 727.17

WIGHTMAN, Joseph M., *compiler.* Annals of the Boston primary school committee, 1818–55. Boston, 1860. 8, 305 pp. 8° 5010.3

WILBERFORCE, Samuel. History of the protestant episcopal church in America. 2d edition. London, 1846. xvi, 462 [458] pp. Map. Folded sheet. 16° 6328.3

— Life of William Wilberforce. Revised and condensed edition. London, 1872. xiv, 452+ pp. Portrait. Sm. 8° 5424.1

WILBERFORCE, William, Life of. Wilberforce, S. London, 1872. Sm. 8° 5424.1

WILD horseman, The, of the Pampas. Ker, D. London, 1876. Sm. 8° 733.1

WILD huntress, The. Reid, M. .... 725.

WILD Hyacinth. A novel. Randolph, *Mrs.* — 714.3

WILD life; or, adventures on the frontier. Reid, M. 725.

WILD life under the equator. Du Chaillu, P. B. ... 933.

WILD man, The, of the West. Ballantyne, R. M. .. 926.3

WILD men and wild beasts. Cumming, (W.) G. .... 423.

WILD Mike and his victim. Montgomery, F. 313.2

Shelf. No.

WILD north land, The. Butler, W. F. London, 1874. 8° 5032.3
WILD oats. Wraxall, *Sir* (F. C.) L. 317.9
WILD sports of the world. Greenwood, J. New York, 1870. 8° 1514.21
WILD Wales: its people, language, and scenery. Borrow, G. London, 1872. Sm. 8° 5438.6
WILDENHAHN, Karl August. The blind girl of Wittenberg. From the German by J. G. Morris... 722.27
WILDER, David. History of Leominster. Fitchburg, 1853. 263+ pp. 12° 817.12
WILDFLOWER. Robinson, F. W. 731.38
WILDMOOR. A novel. Burckett, F. 532.2
WILDS, The, of Africa. Kingston, W. H. G. London, 1872. Sm. 8° 921.2
WILFRID Cumbermede. MacDonald, G. 537.4
WILHEIM Meister's apprenticeship. Goethe, J. W. von 329.9
WILHELM Meister's apprenticeship and travels. Goethe, J. W. von. 2 v. 515.4
WILHELM Tell. Schiller, J. (C. F.) Boston, 1868. 12°. 5735.2
— *Same.* (*In his* Werke.) Stuttgart, 1865. 8°. 5734.1.6
— *Same.* (*In his* Works.) London, 1872. Sm. 8°. 827.26

See also Tell, Wilhelm.

WILKES, Charles. Narrative of the United States exploring expedition, 1838–42. London, 1852. 2 v. Portraits. Sm. 8° 414.21
WILKES, John. Wilkes, Sheridan, Fox: the opposition under George III. Rae, W. F. New York, 1874. 16° 5415.8
WILKINS, Edward G. P. Young New York: a comedy. New York, N. D. 36 pp. 12° 1635.4
WILKINSON, *Sir* John Gardner. Popular account of the ancient Egyptians. Illustrated. New edition. London, 1871. 2 v. Sm. 8° 5926.3
WILKS, Thomas Egerton. The captain's not a-miss: a farce. New York, N. D. 16 pp. 12° 1635.5
WILL Rood's friendship. Bradley, W. I. 913.7
WILL Weatherhelm. Kingston, W. H. G. 934.29
WILLARD, Joseph. Willard memoir; or, life and times of Major Simon Willard. With engravings. Boston, 1858. xiii, 470+ pp. 8° 1211.7
WILLARD, Simon, Life and times of. Willard, J. Boston, 1858. 8° 1211.7
WILLARD, Solomon, Memoir of. Wheildon, W. W. [Boston] 1865. 8° 1011.5
WILLE, Elizabeth de. Johannes Olaf. From the German by F. E. Bunnètt 737.14
WILLIAM the conqueror, History of. Abbott, J. 914.24

Note. — Bulwer's "Harold" [336.19] and Kingsley's "Hereward" [326.15] are novels on the conquest of England, presenting the conqueror's times.

WILLIAM Henry and his friends. Diaz, A. M. 935.19
WILLIAM Henry letters, The. Diaz, A. M. 935.1
WILLIAM Tell. Rossini, G. (*In* Ditson, O., and co. Standard opera librettos) 6233.3.3

See also Tell, Wilhelm.

WILLIAMS, Charles Wye. Elementary treatise on the combustion of coal and the prevention of smoke. With an appendix. London, 1858. xvi, 252 pp. Illustrated. Folded plates. 12°. 1715.19
WILLIAMS, Francis Stanton. English into French. A book of practice in French conversation. 10th edition. New York [*cop.* 1860]. viii, 206, 122 pp. Sm. 8° 2015.6
WILLIAMS, Henry T., *editor.* Window gardening. Devoted especially to the culture of flowers and ornamental plants, for in door use and parlor decoration. 12th edition. New York, 1876. 300+ pp. Illustrated. 8° 1512.5
— *joint author.* Household elegancies. *See* JONES, *Mrs.* C. S. 1512.4
— – Ladies' fancy work. *See* JONES, *Mrs.* C. S. ... 1512.6
WILLIAMS, Henry Willard. A practical guide to the study of the diseases of the eye: their medical and surgical treatment. Boston, 1862. xii, 317 pp. 8° 6015.6
WILLIAMS, Robert Folkstone. [The Shakespeare novels.] Philadelphia, N. D. 3 v. in 1. 8° ... 531.23

Contents. — The secret passion; The youth of Shakspeare; Shakspeare and his friends.

WILLIAMS, Roger. As to Roger Williams and his 'banishment' from the Massachusetts plantation. Dexter, H. M. Boston, 1876. 4° 5011.1
WILLIAMS, Rowland. Bunsen's Biblical researches. (*In* Essays and reviews) 1538.3
— *Same.* (*In* Hedge, F. H. Recent inquiries in theology) .... 1526.24 and 5814.15
— Holy Scripture, etc. (*In* Noyes, G. R. Collection of theological essays) 6325.12
WILLICH, A. F. M. Lectures on diet and regimen. Boston, 1800. 2 v. 12° 6015.1
WILLIE and the mortgage. Abbott, J. Harper's story books 936.1.1
WILLIE Russell's temptation 931.13
WILLIS, Julia A. What a boy! What shall we do with him? What will he do with himself? Who is to blame for the consequences? 931.7
WILLIS, Nathaniel Parker. Beauty and the beast. (*In* Johnson, (E.) R. Little classics) 529.4.4
— Health trip to the tropics. New York, 1853. 421, xxiii+ pp. 12° 426.9
— Life here and there: or sketches of society and adventure. New York, 1850. vii, 377 pp. 12°. 714.28
— Pencillings by the way: written during some years of residence and travel in France, Italy, Greece, Asia Minor, Turkey, and England. New York, 1844. vii, 216 pp. L. 8° 430.2
— Summer cruise in the Mediterranean, on board an American frigate. New York, 1854. 396 pp. 12°. 424.12
WILLOW brook. Warner, S. 913.31
WILLY Reilly, and his dear Coleen bawn. Carleton, W. 524.3
WILSON, Alexander, Life of. Peabody, W. B. O. (*In* Sparks, J. Library of American biography) 5028.1.2
WILSON, Andrew. The abode of snow. Observations on a tour from Chinese Tibet to the Indian Caucasus, through the upper valleys of the Himalaya. (Reprinted from "Blackwood's magazine.") New York, 1875. xviii, 380 pp. Plate. Folded map. Sm. 8° 5933.10
WILSON, Augusta J., *formerly Miss Evans.* Beulah. 737.32
— Inez 725.26
— Infelice 723.26
— Macaria 725.25
— St. Elmo 725.24
— Vashti 737.20
WILSON, Charles W. The recovery of Jerusalem. *See* PALESTINE oriental fund 5933.1
WILSON, Daniel. Caliban: the missing link. London, 1873. xvi, 274+ pp. 8° 1533.15
— Chatterton: a biographical study. London, 1869. xvi, 328 pp. Sm. 8° 5425.6
— Prehistoric man. Researches into the origin of civilization in the old and the new world. 3d edition, revised and enlarged, with illustrations. London, 1876. 2 v. 8° 6613.13
WILSON, George. Handbook of hygiene. London, 1873. xxviii, 380 pp. Sm. 8° 6036.4
WILSON, Henry. History of the rise and fall of the slave power in America. [Vol. I, 4th edition.] Boston, 1874, 75. 2 v. 8° 5012.9
WILSON, Henry Bristow. Séances historiques de Genève. The national church. (*In* Essays and reviews) 1538.3
— *Same.* (*In* Hedge, F. H. Recent inquiries in theology) .... 1526.24 and 5814.15
WILSON, James Grant. Life and letters of Fitz-Greene Halleck. New York, 1869. 607 pp. Portrait. 1 plate. Sm. 8° 5027.1
WILSON, John. (*Christopher North.*) Noctes ambrosianæ of "Blackwood." Philadelphia, 1843. 4 v. Sm. 8° 515.15
— Recreations of Christopher North. New York, 1871. 307 pp. 1 plate. 8° 1531.7
— The snow-storm. (*In* Johnson, (E.) R. Little classics) 529.4.7
— Memoir of. Gordon, M. New York, 1866. 12°. 1024.7
WILSON, John, *printer.* Treatise on English punctuation. 2d edition. Boston, 1850. xi, 204 pp. Folded sheet. 12° 1736.4

Shelf. No.

Wilson, John Mackay, and others. Historical, traditionary, and imaginative tales of the borders, and of Scotland, with a glossary of Scotch words. New York, 1851. 5 v. in 3. Portraits. 3 v. 8° 5631.5
Winchell, Alexander. The doctrine of evolution. New York, 1874. 148 pp. 12° 6836.3
— Geology of the stars. (*In* Estes, D. Half-hour recreations in popular science) 6813.7
— Sketches of creation. With illustrations. New York, 1874. 459 pp. 12° 1523.23
Winckelmann, Johann (Joachim). History of ancient art, translated from the German, by G. H. Lodge. Boston, 1872, 73. 4 v. Illustrated. L. 8°. 6211.1
Window gardener, The. Rand, E. S., *jr.* Boston, 1872. 16° 6626.5
Window gardening. Williams, H. T. New York, 1876. 8° 1512.5
Windsor castle. [Henry VIII's time.] Ainsworth, W. H. 322.11
Wine. Reemelin, C. The vine-dresser's manual, an illustrated treatise on vineyards and wine-making. New York, 1855. 12° 6426.4
— Thudichum, J. L. W., and Dupré, A. Treatise on the origin, nature, and varieties of. London, 1872. 8° 6423.4
Wing-and-wing, The. Cooper, J. F. 525.3
Wingless angel, A. A novel. Muddock, J. E. ... 535.21
Winifred Bertram. Charles, E. 321.5
Winifred's wooing. Craik, G. M. 322.2
Winning a husband: a burletta. Macfarren, —. New York, N. D. 12° 1635.3
Winning his spurs. Kellogg, E. 914.38
Winning his way. Coffin, C. C. 929.8
Winter, A, amid the ice. Verne, J. London, 1876. Sm. 8° 715.35
Winter and spring on the shores of the Mediterranean. Bennet, J. H. London, 1875. Sm. 8°. 436.3
Winter and summer, A, at Burton hall. Greene, R. J. 926.29
Winter fire, The. Porter, R. 717.22
Winter story, A. Peard, F. M. 331.27
Winthrop, John. History of New England from 1630 to 1649. From his original manuscripts. With notes. By James Savage. Boston, 1825, 26. 2 v. Portrait. Fac-simile. 8° 814.7
Winthrop, Robert Charles. Addresses and speeches. Boston, 1867. 2 v. 8° 5212.8
Winthrop, Theodore. The canoe and the saddle; and Isthmiana 537.19
— Cecil Dreeme 736.7
— Edwin Brothertoft 736.8
— John Brent 537.20
— Life in the open air, and other papers 716.33
— Love and skates. (*In* Johnson, (E.) R. Little classics) 529.4.6
Winton, John G. Modern workshop practice as applied to marine, land, and locomotive engines, floating docks, dredging machines, bridges, ship building, cranes, etc. London, 1870. xii, 300 pp. Illustrated. 12° 1715.2
Wirt, William. Sketches of the life and character of Patrick Henry. 3d edition. Philadelphia, 1818. xv, 427, xii pp. Portrait. 8° 1012.4
— Memoirs of. Kennedy, J. P. Philadelphia, 1849. 2 v. 8° 1011.1
— *Same.* New York, 1872. 2 v. Sm. 8° 5025.5
Wisconsin, History of the presbyterian and congregational churches and ministers in. Peet, S. Milwaukee, 1851. Sm. 12° 1538.8
Wise, Daniel. (*Francis Forrester; Lawrence Lancewood.*) Glen Morris stories. Dick Duncan 932.33
— - Guy Carlton 932.34
— - Jessie Carlton 932.31
— - Kate Carlton 932.35
— Lindendale stories. Cousin Clara 932.36
— - Louis Sinclair 932.37
— - Nellie Warren 932.40
— - Peter Clinton 932.41
— - Sidney De Grey 932.38
— - Walter Sherwood 932.32
Wise, Henry Augustus. (*Harry Gringo.*) Captain Brand, of the "Centipede" 720.6
— Los Gringos; or, an inside view of Mexico and California, with wanderings in Peru, Chili, and Polynesia. New York, 1849. xvi, 453 pp. 12°. 435.4
— Tales for the marines 716.18
Wise, John. Through the air: a narrative of forty years' experience as an aëronaut. Illustrated. Philadelphia, 1873. 650 pp. 8° 1520.3
Wiseman, Nicholas (Patrice Stephen). Fabiola; or, the church of the catacombs. [Fiction.] New York, 1872. xii, 385 pp. 1 plate. Sm. 8° ... 736.19
Wishing-cap papers, The. Hunt, (J. H.) L. Boston, 1873. 16° 1917.2
Wisner, Benjamin Blydenburg, *compiler.* Memoirs of Mrs. Susan Huntington. *See* Huntington, Susan 1217.1
Wit. The world of wit and humour. Fenn, G. M. London [1872]. L. 8° 5212.4
Witchcraft. Lowell, J. R. Among my books. Boston, 1873. 16° 1934.8.1
— Upham, C. W. Salem witchcraft; with an account of Salem village, and a history of opinions on witchcraft and kindred subjects. Boston, 1867. 2 v. Sm. 8° 5015.2
With a show in the North. Hatton, J. London, 1871. 16° 5425.7
With fate against him. Douglas, A. M. 735.31
With harp and crown. [Fiction.] Maurice, W., and Rice, J. 721.20
Witherspoon, John. Sermon on Christian magnanimity, and an address to his senior class. *See* Amator Virtutis, *pseud.* 1919.1
Within an ace. Jenkin, *Mrs.* C. Leipzig 313.4
— *Same.* New York 539.10
Within an inch of his life. Gaboriau, É. 732.35
Within the maze. Wood, E. P. 730.25
Within-doors: a book of games and pastimes for the drawing-room. Elliott, A. London, 1872. 16° 916.19
Withington, Hiram. Memoir, with selections from his sermons and correspondence. Boston, 1849. 190+ pp. Sm. 8° 5027.9
Without kith or kin. Craik, G. M. 2 v. 331.4
Wits, The, and beaux of society. Thomson, K. and J. C. New York, 1861. 12° 1216.18
Witt, Henriette de, *formerly Mlle Guizot.* Marie Derville. A story of a French boarding-school. From the French. By M. G. Wells 912.6
Witt, Pauline de, *formerly Mlle. Guizot.* [Stories for girls.] An only sister 928.2
Wives and daughters. Gaskell, E. C. 328.19
Wives and widows. Stephens, A. S. (W.) 726.6
Wives, The, of England. Ellis, S. (S.) New York, 1843. 12° 1935.6
Wolf, Joseph. The life and habits of wild animals illustrated by [his] designs. Engraved by J. W. and Edward Whymper. With descriptive letter-press by Daniel Giraud Elliott. London, 1874. 72 pp. 20 plates. 4° 6610.6
Wolf Run. Kellogg, E. 923.6
Wolfert's Roost, Chronicles of. Irving, W. Leipzig, 1855. Sq. 16° 311.14
— *Same.* Philadelphia, 1871. Sm. 8° 1815.12
Wolff, Joseph. Narrative of a mission to Bokara, in 1843–45, to ascertain the fate of Colonel Stoddard and Captain Connolly. New York, 1845. 384 pp. Illustrated. 8° 821.4
Woman against woman. Church, F. 710.21
Woman, The, I loved, and the woman who loved me: a Tuscan wedding. Blagden, I. 339.5
Woman, A, in spite of herself. Jeaffreson, J. C. ... 311.20
Woman, The, in white. Collins, (W.) W. 326.12
Woman, The, of honor; or, false friendships in society. Énault, L. Philadelphia [1875]. 8°. 721.1
Woman's, A, experiences in Europe. Wallace, *Mrs.* E. D. New York, 1872. 12° 423.11
Woman's friendship. Aguilar, G. 533.16
Woman's, The, kingdom. Craik, D. (M.) 323.28
Woman's love. Smith, J. F. 711.38
Woman's, A, ransom. Robinson, F. W. 734.19

Shelf. No.

WOMAN's suffrage tracts. No. 1–5. Boston, 1869. 12° 1926.5

Contents. — Woman's influence in politics. Address by H. W. Beecher at New York, Feb. 2, 1860. 17 pp.; Equal rights for women. Speech by G. W. Curtis, in the Constitutional convention of New York, at Albany, July 19, 1867. 24 pp.; Suffrage for women. Speech by J. S. Mill, in the British parliament, May 20, 1867. 14 pp.; Ought women to learn the alphabet? By T. W. Higginson. 20 pp.; The legal condition of women in Massachusetts. By S. E. Sewall. 15 pp.

WOMAN's, A, thoughts about women. Craik, D. (M.) Leipzig 323.26
— *Same.* New York 1535.13
WOMAN's, A, vengeance. Payn, J. 730.23
WOMAN's worth and worthlessness. Dodge, M. A. New York, 1872. 12° 1736.11
WOMEN. Aguilar, G. The women of Israel. New York, 1872. 2 v. 12° 1226.19
— "Alex," *pseud.* As it should be. Philadelphia, 1874. 16° 1736.5

Note. — An essay on the condition of women.

— – As she would have it. Philadelphia, 1873. 16°. 1736.6

Note. — An essay on woman's rights.

— Ames, A., *jr.* Sex in industry: a plea for the working-girl. Boston, 1875. 16° 1937.5
— Anderson, J. Memorable women of the puritan times. London, 1872. 2 v. Sm. 8° 5427.6
— Clayton, E. C. Queens of song: being memoirs of some of the most celebrated female vocalists. London, 1863. 2 v. 8° 1221.4
— Dall, C. (W.) H. The college, the market, and the court; or, woman's relation to education, labor, and law. Boston, 1867. 8° 1733.1
— – "Woman's right to labor;" or, low wages and hard work. Boston, 1860. 16° 1737.1
— Dodge, M. A. Woman's wrongs: a counter-irritant. Boston, 1868. 16° 1535.10
— Héricourt, J. d'. A woman's philosophy of woman; or woman affranchised. New York, 1864. 12° 1535.8
— Kavanagh, J. English women of letters: biographical sketches. Leipzig, 1862. Sq. 16° ... 1238.2
— – French women of letters: biographical sketches. Leipzig, 1862. Sq. 16° 1238.3
— – Women of Christianity, exemplary for acts of piety and charity. New York, 1860. 12° 1225.6
— Landriot, J. F. A. T. Sins of the tongue and jealousy in woman's life. Boston, 1874. 12° .. 1915.7
— – The valiant woman. Boston, 1874. 12° 1915.6
— Michelet, J. The women of the French revolution [of 1789]. Philadelphia, 1855. 12° 1226.3
— Mill, J. S. The subjection of. New York, 1874. 8° 1733.2
— Ossoli, S. M. F., *marchesa* d'. Woman in the nineteenth century. New York, 1845. 12° ... 1736.9
— Peck, J. T. The true woman; or, life and happiness at home and abroad. New York [*cop.* 1857]. 16° 1736.8
— Sainte-Beuve, C. A. Portraits of celebrated women. Boston, 1868. 16° 1226.5
— Stowe, H. (E.) B. Woman in sacred history. New York, 1874. 8° 6320.1
— Thomson, K. and J. C. The queens of society. New York, 1861. 12° 1216.17
— Woman's suffrage tracts. No. 1–5. Boston, 1869. 12° 1926.5
— Woolson, A. G. Woman in American society. Boston, 1873. 16° 417.11

Diseases of.

— Ashwell, S. A practical treatise on the diseases peculiar to women, illustrated by cases. Boston, 1843. 8° 6021.11
— Churchill, F. The diseases of females. Philadelphia, 1850. 8° 6012.4
— – Essays on the puerperal fever and other diseases peculiar to women. London, 1849. 8° 6013.13
— Gooch, B. On some of the most important diseases peculiar to women. London, 1859. 8° .. 6023.4
— Hayes, A. H. Sexual physiology of woman, and her diseases. Boston [*cop.* 1869]. 12° 1524.25

See also Breast, Midwifery.

WONDER stories told for children. Andersen, H. C. 923.24
WONDERFUL balloon ascents. Marion, F. New York, 1871. 16° 1714.18
WONDERFUL escapes. Bernard, F. New York, 1871. 16° 1714.20
WONDERFUL inventions. Timbs, J. London [1867]. Sm. 8° 1525.20
WONDERFUL woman, A. Fleming, M. A. 737.19
WONDERLAND, The, of the antipodes. Tinne, J. E. London, 1873. L. 8° 5930.4
WONDERS, The, of science; or, Young Humphry Davy. Mayhew, H. New York, 1870. 16° .. 936.34
WONDERS of the physical world: the glacier, the iceberg, the ice-field, and the avalanche. London, 1875. 314 pp. Illustrated. Sm. 8° 1714.31
WONDROUS strange. Newby, C. J. 710.8
WOOD, Edward J. The wedding day in all ages and countries. New York, 1869. xi, 299 pp. 12°. 1527.8
WOOD, Ella Price. Adam Grainger 333.23
— Anne Hereford 333.8
— Bessy Rane 333.2
— The Channings 333.1
— Dene hollow 333.16
— East Lynne. Leipzig 333.4
— *Same.* New York 521.36
— Elster's folly 333.18
— The foggy night at Offord; Martyn Ware's temptation; The night-walk over the mill stream 333.13
— Frances Hildyard 720.16
— George Canterbury's will 333.3
— Lady Adelaide's oath 333.9
— A life's secret 333.7
— Lord Oakburn's daughters 333.10
— The master of Greylands. Leipzig. 2 v. 329.6
— *Same.* Philadelphia 510.13
— Mildred Arkell 333.15
— Mrs. Halliburton's troubles 333.5
— Orville college 333.6
— Oswald Cray 333.14
— Out of the deep 521.11
— Parkwater; or, told in the twilight. Philadelphia. 521.13

Note. — The English and Tauchnitz editions were published under the title "Told in the twilight."

— The Red court farm 333.12
— Roland Yorke 333.17
— St. Martin's eve 333.11
— The shadow of Ashlydyat. 3 v. 330.28
— Told in the twilight. Leipzig 333.22

Contents. — Vol. I. Parkwater. II. All Souls' eve; The dream of Gertrude Lisle; Cyrilla Maude; The self-convicted; Mr. North's dream; My cousin Caroline's wedding; An incident in the life of Lord Byron; Feathers and spangles.

— Trevlyn hold 333.19
— Verner's pride 333.20
— Within the maze 730.25
WOOD, George B. Historical and biographical memoirs, essays, addresses, etc. Philadelphia, 1872. viii, 576 pp. Illustrated. 8° 1231.2
— Treatise on therapeutics, and pharmacology or materia medica. Philadelphia, 1856. 2 v. 8°. 6011.3
WOOD, *Mrs.* Henry. *See* WOOD, Ella Price.
WOOD, Horatio C., *jr.* Treatise on therapeutics, comprising materia medica and toxicology. Philadelphia, 1874. 578 pp. 8° 6021.7
WOOD, John George. Common objects of the microscope. With upwards of 400 illustrations. London [1866]. iv, 127+ pp. 12 colored plates. Sm. 8° 1528.14
— Homes without hands. A description of the habitations of animals, classed according to their principle of construction. With new designs. New York, 1866. 651 pp. 8° 6612.3
— Illustrated natural history. With new designs. London, 1867, 72, 74. 3 v. L. 8° 6610.4

Contents. — Vol. I. Reptiles, Fishes, Molluscs, etc. II. Mammalia. III. Birds.

— Insects at home. A popular account of insects, their structure, habits, and transformations. With upwards of 700 figures. New York, 1872. xx, 670 pp. 8° 6612.2

Shelf. No.

WOOD, John George, *continued.*
— Man and beast, here and hereafter. Illustrated by more than three hundred original anecdotes. London, 1874. 2 v. 8° 6614.10
— The modern playmate: a book of games, sports, and diversions for boys of all ages. With illustrations. London [1870]. x, 883+ pp. Sq. 16°. 6414.3
— *Same.* Revised edition. London [1875]. Sm. 8°. 6414.6
— Out of doors: a selection of original articles on practical natural history. London, 1874. vi, 342+ pp. Illustrated. Sm. 8° 6616.9
— The popular natural history. With illustrations. London, 1876. 596+ pp. Sm. 8° 6616.12
— The uncivilized races, or natural history of man. With a description of the races of Alaska and Siberia, by an eminent American traveller. With illustrations. Hartford, 1870. 2 v. in 1. L. 8°. 6610.3
— *Same.* London, 1870. 2 v. L. 8° 6610.2
WOOD, William. Manual of physical exercises. With illustrations. 2d edition, enlarged. New York, 1870. 343 pp. Portrait. 12° 1516.7
WOOD-CARVING. Sawyer, G. A. Wood-carving. Boston, 1875. Sm. 4° 1515.19
— Seaton, *Sir* T. Manual of. London, 1875. Sm. 8° 6425.7
WOOD engraving, Treatise on. Jackson, J., and Chatto, W. A. London, 1866. 8° 6211.10
WOOD-RANGERS, The. Reid, M. 725.8
WOODBURN grange. Howitt, W. 534.11
WOODCLIFF. MacKeever, H. B. 723.25
WOODCLIFF children, The. MacKeever, H. B. 1118.6
WOODCLIFF library, The. *See* MACKEEVER, Harriet B.
WOODCRAFT. [A story of the South at the close of the revolution.] Simms, W. G. 733.10
WOODGATE, Walter Bradford. "Oars and sculls," and how to use them. London, 1875. vi, 171+ pp. Sm. 8° 6418.3
WOODHOUSELEE, *Lord.* *See* TYTLER, Alexander Fraser.
WOODMAN, M. S. Choice receipts. Boston, 1875. 200+ pp. 12° 6427.2
WOODRUFF, Hiram. The trotting horse of America. Edited by C. J. Foster. Including an introductory notice by G. Wilkes, and a biographical sketch by the editor. New York, 1871. 412 pp. Portrait. Sm. 8° 6417.2
WOODRUFF, Julia Louisa Matilda. (*W. M. L. Jay.*) Holden with the cords 724.9
— Shiloh; or, without and within 716.12
WOODS, The, and by-ways of New England. Flagg, W. Boston, 1872. Sm. 8° 5035.2
WOODSTOCK. Scott, *Sir* W. Boston 533.3
— *Same.* Leipzig 324.5
WOODVILLE series. *See* ADAMS, William T.
WOODWARD, Bernard Bolingbroke, and CATES, William L. R. Encyclopædia of chronology, historical and biographical. London, 1872. viii, 1487 pp. 8° .... *R.R., E.3.7
WOODWARD, Evan M. Our campaigns. Philadelphia, 1865. 362 pp. 16° 817.14
WOODWARD, Samuel P. Manual of the mollusca: a treatise on recent and fossil shells. 2d edition, with an appendix of discoveries to the present time by R. Tate. With illustrations. London, 1871. xiv, 542, 86+ pp. Map. 12° 1715.9
WOODWORK, Ancient and modern. Pollen, J. H. [London, 1875.] 8° 6214.5
WOOED and married. Carey, R. N. 733.17
WOOING o't, The. Alexander, *Mrs.* — 518.18
WOOL. Bulletin of the national association of wool manufacturers. 1869–71. Boston, 1869, 71. 2 v. 8° 6432.1
WOOLSEY, Sarah Chauncey. (*Susan Coolidge.*) For summer afternoons 539.13
— Mischief's Thanksgiving, and other stories 933.11
— Nine little goslings 1115.6
— What Katy did 925.29
— What Katy did at school 925.28
WOOLSON, Abba Goold. Woman in American society. Boston, 1873. 271 pp. 16° 417.11

Shelf. No.

WOOLSON, Abba Gould, *continued.*
— *editor.* Dress-reform: lectures on dress as it affects the health of women. With illustrations. Boston, 1874. xviii, 263+ pp. 16° 1537.19

Contents. — Lecture 1. By Mary J. Safford Blake. 2. By Caroline E. Hastings. 3. By Mercy B. Jackson. 4. By Arvilla B. Haynes. 5. By Abba Goold Woolson.

WORBOISE, Emma Jane. The Lillingstones of Lillingstone 735.17
— Overdale; or, the story of a pervert 536.23
WORCESTER, Joseph Emerson. Dictionary of the English language. Boston, 1873. lxviii, 1786 pp. Illustrated. Portrait. 4° .... *R.R., A.3.2
— Elements of history, ancient and modern. New edition. Boston, 1850. x, 408 pp. Folded map. 12° 836.4
— Pocket dictionary of the English language. Compiled from the quarto and school dictionaries, by L. J. Campbell. With illustrations and tables. Boston, 1872. 310 pp. 32° 1719.1
WORCESTER county free institute of industrial science, *Worcester, Mass.* Commencement, July 30, 1873. Commencement address by Emory Washburn. Address of the trustees by Seth Sweetser. Privately printed. Worcester, 1873. 15 pp. 8° 5013.11
WORD, The, of the Spirit to the church. Bartol, C. A. Boston, 1859. 16° 6321.1
WORDS. Mathews, W. Words; their use and abuse. Chicago, 1876. 12° 1736.10
— Trench, R. C. On the study of. New York [1851]. 12° 1735.2
— White, R. G. Words and their uses, past and present. New York, 1870. Sm. 8° 1735.5
— *Same.* New York, 1872. Sm. 8° 1735.1
WORDSWORTH, Christopher. Social life at the English universities in the 18th century. Cambridge, 1874. xxxvi, 727+ pp. Sm. 8° 5835.7
WORDSWORTH, Dorothy. Recollections of a tour made [with Coleridge and W. Wordsworth] in Scotland, 1803. Edited by J. C. Shairp. 2d edition. Edinburgh, 1874. l, 316+ pp. Sm. 8°. 5435.5
WORDSWORTH, William. Complete poetical works. London, 1869. xxiv, 704 pp. Portrait. L. 8°. 5610.3
— Prose works. For the first time collected, with additions from unpublished manuscripts. Edited, with preface, notes and illustrations, by Alexander B. Grosart. London, 1876. 3 v. 8° 5624.2

Contents. — Vol. I. Political and ethical. II. Æsthetical and literary. III. Critical and ethical.

— Select poetical works. Leipzig, 1864. 2 v. in 1. Sq. 16° 1613.14
— Fields, J. T. Yesterdays with authors. Boston, 1875 [*cop.* 1871]. 12° 6136.13
— Lowell, J. R. Among my books. Boston, 1876. 16° 1934.8.2
— Masson, D. Wordsworth, Shelley, Keats, and other essays. London, 1874. Sm. 8° 5616.15

Note. — The principal life is that by Christopher Wordsworth. Illustrative matter will be found in Coleridge's "Biographia literaria" [1611.5]; in De Quincey's "Literary reminiscences" [1226.1] and in his "Essays on the poets" [1825.4]; in Miss Mitford's "Life" [1226.16]; in Chorley's Reminiscences [5616.14]; in Hall's "Book of memories" [1231.1]; and in the lives of Lamb and Southey; with additional commentary in Grosart's preface to the "Prose works" [5624.2].

Essays on his life and poems will be found in Jeffrey [5610.8, adverse]; in Talfourd [1931.1]; in Masson [5616.15]; in Whipple's "Essays and reviews" [1936.2.1] and "Literature and life" [1936.6]; in Lowell's "Among my books" [1934.8.2]; in Shairp's "Studies" [1535.14]; in Alger's "Solitudes" [1535.22], in Macmillan's magazine, Aug., 1873, and in the Fortnightly review, April, 1874.

Visits to the poet and the associations of the lake region are described in Fields's "Yesterdays with authors" [6136.13]; in Emerson's "English traits" [425.4; 1934.6.2]; and in Hawthorne's "English note-books" [428.3; 1813.4, or Atlantic monthly, July, 1867]. See further Jerdan's "Men I have known" [5423.11]; Howitt's "Homes and haunts" [1225.5]; and Horne's "New spirit of the age" [1038.1]. There are full references in Allibone.

WORK. Alcott, L. M. 918.28
WORK. Ruskin, J. The crown of wild olive. Three lectures on work, traffic, and war. New York, 1872. 12° 6236.6
— — Time and tide, by Weare and Tyne. Letters on the laws of. New York, 1871. 12° 6236.1

Shelf. No.

WORK and wages. Howitt, M. 937.8
WORK and wages practically illustrated. Brassey, T. London, 1872. Sm. 8° 6413.2
— *Same.* New York, 1872. Sm. 8°.............. 5823.1
WORK and win. Adams, W. T. 925.4
WORKINGMEN'S homes. Hale, E. E., and others. Boston, 1874. 16° 1516.22
WORKSHOP appliances. Shelley, C. P. B. New York [London], 1873. Sm. 8° 6427.1
WORLD, Sacred history of the. Turner, S. New York, 1858. 3 v. 12°...................... 828.3
WORLD, The, before the deluge. Figuier, (G.) L. London [1866]. 8°.................1521.1 and 6617.2
WORLD, A, without souls. Cunningham, J. W. Baltimore, 1810. 12°......................1538.11
WORLDS, The unity of. Powell, B. London, 1856. Sm. 8° 6836.1
WORNUM, Ralph Nicholson. Analysis of ornament. The characteristics of styles: an introduction to the study of the history of ornamental art. 4th edition. London, 1873. vi, 138 pp. Illustrated. 8°.. 6211.9
— The epochs of painting. A biographical and critical essay on painting and painters. London, 1864. xv, 583 pp. Illustrated. Portraits. 8°. 6213.3
WORTH and wealth. Baker, H. N. (W.).......... 926.7
WORTHINGTON, Erastus. History of Dedham, from the beginning of its settlement, 1635, to 1827. Boston, 1827. 146 pp. 8° 811.18
WOTTON, *Sir* Henry, Life of. Walton, I. London, 1866. 16°.. 5428.2
WOVEN of many threads. Hamilton, C. V......... 531.17
WRAXALL, *Sir* (Frederick Charles) Lascelles. The backwoodsman; or, life on the Indian frontier.. 735.39
— The black panther; or, a boy's adventures among the redskins.. 931.10
— Wild oats.. 717.9
WRAXALL, *Sir* Nathaniel William. Memoirs. Philadelphia, 1836, 37. 2 v. 8° 5812.7

Contents. — Vol. I. Historical memoirs of my own time. 1772-84. II. Posthumous memoirs of his own time.

WRECK, The, of the Chancellor. Verne, J. Boston, 1875. Sq. 16°.................................. 529.6
WRECKED in port. Yates, E. 317.2
WRIGHT, A. S. Wright's book of 3000 practical receipts, or complete book of reference, containing valuable and important receipts for medicine, cookery [etc.]. New York [1852]. 359 pp. 12°. 1533.10
WRIGHT, Daniel Thew. Mrs. Armington's ward; or, the inferior sex. [A novel]................... 714.1
WRIGHT, Lewis. Illustrated book of poultry. With 50 coloured portraits of prize birds. London [1873]. viii, 591 pp. 4° 6610.5
WRIGHT, Thomas. Caricature history of the Georges. With illustrations. London [1867]. xiii, 639+ pp. Sm. 8°.. 5415.5
— History of caricature and grotesque in literature and art. With illustrations. London [1864]. xvi, 494 pp. Sm. 4°................................ 5923.4
— The homes of other days. A history of domestic manners and sentiments in England. London, 1871. xv, 511 pp. Illustrated. L. 8° 5410.1
— Our new masters. London, 1873. viii, 392+ pp. 8° 5415.9

Note. — "A book dealing with the working classes and their views, as they stand in these latter days, when those classes are, potentially at any rate, the New Masters of the political and social situation." — *Preface.*

— Works of James Gillray, the caricaturist; with the history of his life and times. With illustrations. London [1873]. 376+ pp. 4° 5632.1
WRINKLES and recipes. Benjamin, P. New York [1875]. 12°......................................1717.12
WRITINGS, The, of the apostolic fathers. Translated by [A.] Roberts, [J.] Donaldson, and F. Crombie. Edinburgh, 1867. viii, 506 pp. [Ante-Nicene Christian library.] 8°...............6322.4.1

Contents. — First epistle of Clement to the Corinthians; Second epistle of Clement; Epistle of Polycarp to the Philippians; Martyrdom of Polycarp; Epistle of Barnabas; Epistles of Ignatius; Martyrdom of Ignatius; Epistle to Diognetus; The pastor of Hermas; Fragments of Papias; Spurious epistles of Ignatius.

Shelf. No.

WRONG, A, confessed is half redressed. Bradley, M.. 934.4
WROTTESLEY, George. Life and correspondence of Sir John Burgoyne. London, 1873. 2 v. Portrait. Fac-simile. 8° 5333.2
WUTHERING heights. Brontë, E. (J.) 321.24
WYANDOTTÉ. Cooper, J. F.......................... 525.4
WYATT, Matthew Digby. Fine art. A sketch of its history, theory, practice, and application to industry. London, 1870. viii, 375 pp. 8°... 6232.2
WYCH Hazel. Warner, S. and A. 722.15
WYCHERLEY, William, CONGREVE, William, VANBRUGH, *Sir* John, and FARQUHAR, George. Dramatic works. With biographical and critical notices. By Leigh Hunt. New edition. London, 1871. lxxxiv, 368 pp. Portrait and plate. 8°.. 5611.6
WYCLIFFE, John. Wycliffe and the Huguenots. Hanna, W. Edinburgh, 1860. Sm. 8°........ 826.7
WYLIE, James Aitken. Daybreak in Spain; or, sketches of Spain and its new reformation. London [1870]. viii, 424 pp. Illustrated. Sm. 8°. 227.1
WYMAN, Morrill. Autumnal catarrh (hay fever). With maps. New York, 1872. xi, 173 pp. Sm. 8°.. 6012.7
WYNCOTE. Erskine, *Mrs.* T......................... 518.2
WYNTER, Andrew. Peeps into the human hive. London, 1874. 2 v. Sm. 8°................. 6436.8

Note. — A collection of miscellaneous essays which first appeared in the Quarterly and Edinburgh reviews, the Times, Graphic, etc.

WYSE, *Sir* Thomas. An excursion in the Peloponnesus in 1858. Edited by W. M. Wyse. With illustrations. London, 1865. 2 v. 8°........ 5930.1
— Impressions of Greece. With an introduction by Miss Wyse, and Letters from Greece to friends at home by A. P. Stanley. London, 1871. vii, 332+ pp. 8°.. 5931.4
WYSS, Johann Rudolf, and MONTOLIEU, Jeanne Isabelle Pauline de Bottens, *baronne* de. The Swiss family Robinson. With map and illustrations. Philadelphia, N. D. 394 pp. 12°...... 735.6
— *Same.* Boston, 1875. 383 pp. 12°........... 733.8

XAVIER, *St.*, Francisco, Life of. Bartoli, D., and Maffei, G. P. Baltimore, 1872. 12° 5526.9
XENOPHON. The Anabasis, and the Memorabilia of Socrates. Literally translated by J. S. Watson. With a geographical commentary by W. F. Ainsworth. London, 1872. vi, 518+ pp. Portrait. Sm. 8°..6115.12
— The Cyropædia. And the Hellenics. Literally translated by J. S. Watson and H. Dale. London, 1872. xvi, 579 pp. Sm. 8°.............. 6115.4
— Minor works. Literally translated, with notes and illustrations, by J. S. Watson. London, 1857. 384+ pp. Sm. 8°........................6115.13
— Xenophon [outlined and explained]. Grant, *Sir* A. Edinburgh, 1871. 16°.................. 6116.9

YACHT club, The. Adams, W. T.................. 923.16
YACHT club series. *See* ADAMS, William T.
YACHTS and yachting. Cooper, W. The yacht sailor. London, 1874. 8° 6412.3
— - Yachts and yachting. London, 1873. 8°..... 6412.5
YALE lectures on preaching. Beecher, H. W. New York, 1872. 12° 1914.7
YANKEE, A, in Canada. Thoreau, H. D. Boston, 1872. 12°.. 225.2
YANKEE middy, The. Adams, W. T. 924.1
YATES, Edmund. Black sheep.................... 318.22
— Broken to harness 318.19
— Castaway 318.24
— A dangerous game................................. 731.32
— Dr. Wainwright's patient 318.20
— The forlorn hope.................................. 318.23
— The impending sword.............................. 310.19
— Land at last...................................... 318.18
— Nobody's fortune 318.21
— The rock ahead.................................... 317.1
— A silent witness. Leipzig......................... 317.24

Shelf. No.

YATES, Edmund, *continued.*
— The silent witness. Boston.................... 730.32
— Two, by tricks 330.15
— The wages of sin.............................. 721.17
— A waiting race. 2 v........................... 331.2
— Wrecked in port............................... 317.2
— The yellow flag. Boston 531.31
— *Same.* Leipzig 333.21
YEAR after year. Clive, C....................... 310.9
YEAR book, The, of daily recreation and information. Hone, W. London, 1832. 8° 5621.8
YEAR-BOOK, The, of facts in science and art. Timbs, J. London, 1866. Sm. 8° 1527.12
YEAR-BOOK of nature and popular science for 1872. Edited by J. C. Draper. New York, 1873. x, 333+ pp. 12° 1525.21
YEAR, A, of consolation. Kemble, F. (A.) New York, 1847. 2 v. in 1. 12°.................426.14
YEAR, A, with Maggie and Emma. MacIntosh, M. J. 928.19
YEARS, The, that are told. Porter, R............ 717.9
YEAST, On. Huxley, T. H. (*In* Estes, D. Half-hour recreations in popular science) 6813.7
YEAST. Kingsley, C.............................. 326.19
YEATS, John. Growth and vicissitudes of commerce from B. C. 1500 to A. D. 1789. London, 1872. xxix, 19, 396 pp. 1 folded plate. Map. 16°. 6437.3
— Manual of recent and existing commerce from 1789 to 1872. London, 1872. xxv, 409 pp. 16°. 6437.2
YELLOW fever of Gibraltar of 1828, Anatomical, pathological and therapeutic researches on the. Louis, P. C. A. Boston, 1839. 8° 6022.9
YELLOW flag, The. Yates, E. Boston 531.31
— *Same.* Leipzig 333.21
YELLOW frigate, The. Grant, J................... 517.12
YELLOWSTONE, Wonders of the. Richardson, J. New York, 1873. 12° 224.8
YEMASSEE, The. Simms, W. G...................... 716.21
YERRINGTON, James M. W. Report of the case of G. C. Hersey, indicted for the murder of B. F. Tirrell. Boston, 1862. 267 pp. 8°.......... 631.6
YESTERDAYS with authors. Fields, J. T. Boston, 1875 [*cop.* 1871]. 12° 6136.13
YONGE, Charles Duke. History of the British navy, from the earliest period to the present time. 2d edition. London, 1866. 3 v. Folded plans. 8° 5412.7
— Three centuries of English literature. New York, 1872. xxi, 649 pp. 12° 1536.1
YONGE, Charlotte Mary. Beechcroft.............. 736.4
— A book of golden deeds. London, 1870. x, 454 pp. 1 plate. 16°.......................... 1939.1
— The caged lion 318.12

Note. — Captivity of James I of Scotland in England, reign of Henry V.

— Cameos from English history. London, 1869. 2 v. 16° 826.12

Contents. — Vol. I. From Rollo to Edward II. II. The wars in France.

— The chaplet of pearls. [Time of Henry II of France.] Leipzig 318.4
— *Same.* New York.............................. 531.20
— The clever woman of the family................ 318.9
— Countess Kate 1116.2
— The daisy chain. [Home circles in middle classes]. 318.6
— The Danvers papers; The prince and the page... 318.7
— The dove in the eagle's nest. [Baronial life, Thirty years' war] 318.17
— Dynevor terrace 318.11
— The gain of a loss............................ 318.15
— Heartsease. [Distinctions of rank]............ 318.3
— The heir of Redclyffe. [English high church, domestic life of upper classes]............... 318.14
— Hopes and fears 318.5
— Lady Hester; or, Ursula's narrative........... 725.33
— The lances of Lynwood. [Time of Edward III, 14th century] 737.8
— The last of the cavaliers. [James II's time] 318.16
— Life of John Coleridge Patteson. 5th edition. London, 1875. 2 v. Portraits. 8° 5337.5

Shelf. No.

YONGE, Charlotte Mary, *continued.*
— Musings over the "Christian year" and "Lyra innocentium;" together with a few gleanings of recollections of Rev. John Keble. New York, 1871. 431 pp. 12°...................1538.15
— My young Alcides. A faded photograph. Leipzig. 318.25
— *Same.* New York............................... 733.18
— The pillars of the house. [English high church.] Leipzig. 4 v. in 2.......................... 339.16
— *Same.* London. 2 v. 734.12
— Pioneers and founders; or, recent workers in the mission field. [London, 1871.] xvi [x], 316 pp. 1 plate. Portrait. 16° 5817.5
— The pupils of St. John the divine. [London, 1868.] xvi, 320 pp. Illustrated. [Sunday library.] Sm. 8°............................. 5937.9
— Richard the fearless. [Richard Sans Peur, Normandy, 10th century]........................ 927.20
— The Stokesley secret 918.23
— The trial: more links of The daisy chain 318.8
— The two guardians 318.13
— The young step-mother.......................... 318.10
— *joint editor.* European history. *See* SEWELL, Elizabeth Mary 5927.7

Note. — Miss Yonge's novels, so far as they picture contemporary life, are perhaps the most popular representations of English home life which we have. She also excels in delineations of life in the higher classes.

YORKSHIRE, *England.* Yorkshire oddities, incidents, and strange events. Baring-Gould, S. London, 1875. 2 v. Sm. 8° 5616.17
YOSEMITE, The, guide-book [pocket edition]. *See* CALIFORNIA. Geological survey 5039.1
YOUMANS, Edward Livingstone, *editor.* The culture demanded by modern life; addresses and arguments on the claims of scientific education. New York, 1872. x, 473+ pp. 12°...............5835.4

Contents. — Youmans, E. L.: Mental discipline in education; Tyndall, J.: Importance of the study of physics; Henfrey, A.: Educational claims of botanical science; Huxley, T. H.: Methods of studying zoology; Paget, J.: Importance of the study of physiology; Faraday, M.: Observations on the education of the judgment; Whewell, W.: Influence of the history of science upon intellectual education; Hodgson, W. B.: Importance of the study of economic science; Spencer, H.: Political education; Barnard, F. A. P.: Early mental training and the studies best fitted for it; Liebig, J. von: The development of ideas in physical science; Youmans, E. L.: Observations on the scientific study of human nature; Appendix.

YOUNG, Charles Frederick T. Fires, fire engines, and fire brigades: with a history of manual and steam fire engines. With illustrations. London, 1866. viii, 534 pp. 8°.....................1521.10
YOUNG, Charles Mayne, Memoir of. Young, J. C. London, 1871. 2 v. Sm. 8°................. 5425.4
YOUNG, John Radford. Navigation and nautical astronomy, in theory and practice. New edition, with index. London, N. D. 282 pp. 12°.....1715.22
YOUNG, Julian Charles. Memoir of Charles Mayne Young, with extracts from [the] journal [of J. C. Young]. London, 1871. 2 v. Illustrated. Portraits. Sm. 8° 5425.4
— Personal reminiscences. (*In* Stoddard, R. H. Bric-à-brac series)............................ 1828.2
YOUNG, Thomas. Miscellaneous works. London, 1855. 3 v. Portrait. Illustrated. Folded plates. 8°.................................... 5612.3
— Life of. Peacock, G. London, 1855. 8° 5421.3
YOUNG America abroad. *See* ADAMS, William T.
YOUNG America in Wall-street. Train, G. F. New York, 1857. 12° 414.3
YOUNG Brown. Murray, G. 310.24
YOUNG Crusoe, The. Hofland, B.................. 918.22
YOUNG deliverers, The, of Pleasant cove. Kellogg, E. 922.6
YOUNG detective, The. Parker, R. A. 933.17
YOUNG Dodge club series, The. *See* DE MILLE, James.
YOUNG duke, The. Disraeli, B.................... 721.18
YOUNG exiles, The. Bowman, A.................... 1118.5
YOUNG folks' history of the United States. Higginson, T. W. Boston, 1875. Sq. 16°........... 618.2
YOUNG lady's offering, The; or, gems of prose and poetry. Sigourney, L. H., and others. Boston, 1858. 12°.................................. 5216.2

Shelf. No.

YOUNG lieutenant, The. Adams, W. T. 924.2

YOUNG marooners, The, on the Florida coast; or, Robert and Harold. Goulding, F. R. 1127.5

YOUNG mechanic, The. Containing directions for the use of all kinds of tools, and for the construction of steam engines and mechanical models, including the art of turning in wood and metal. By the author of "The lathe and its uses," etc. From the English edition, with corrections. New York, 1872. iv, 346+ pp. Illustrated. Sm. 4° 6426.3

YOUNG middy, The. Armstrong, F. C. 931.8

YOUNG moose hunters, The. Stephens, C. A. 921.11

YOUNG New York: a comedy. Wilkins, E. G. P. New York, N. D. 12° 1635.4

YOUNG outlaw, The. Alger, H., *jr.* 933.12

YOUNG pioneers, The, of the North-west. Pearson, C. H. 937.17

YOUNG prima donna, The. Grey, *Mrs.* 521.34

YOUNG prince, A. Thackeray, A. I. Works 512.1.3

YOUNG prince Marigold. Maguire, J. F. 928.11

YOUNG scamp, The: a farce. Stirling, E. New York, N. D. 12° 1635.4

YOUNG ship-builders, The, of Elm island. Kellogg, E. 922.11

YOUNG step-mother, The. Yonge, C. M. 318.10

YOUNG surveyor, The. Trowbridge, J. T. 1115.7

YOUNG voyagers, The. Adams, W. T. 918.3

YOUNG voyageurs, The. Reid, M. 923.33

YOUNG yachtsmen, The. Bowman, A. 938.17

YOUNG yägers, The. Reid, M. 923.30

YOUTH'S companion. Vol. 1–3, 5, 7–14, 16–19, 23–29, 32, 46. Boston, 1827–73. 25 v. 4° 1420.1

YOUTH'S companion, The; or a safe guide to eminence. Amator Virtutis, *pseud.* Andover, 1820. Sm. 12° 1919.1

YOUTHFUL voices: a collection of hymns and tunes, for the use of Sunday schools. The music edited by B. J. Lang. Boston [*cop.* 1862]. 120 pp. 12° 1625.9

YUCATAN, Incidents of travel in. Stephens, J. L. New York, 1843. 2 v. 8° 5030.5

— *Same.* New York, 1856. 2 v. 8° 422.5

YULE, Henry, *editor.* Cathay and the way thither; being a collection of medieval notices of China. With a preliminary essay on the intercourse between China and the western nations previous to the discovery of the Cape route. London, 1866. 2 v. Wood-cuts. Folded maps. 8° 5923.10

ZACHOS, John C. Phonic primer and reader: a rational method of teaching reading by the sounds of the letters, without altering the orthography. Boston, 1864. x, 75 pp. 12° 1736.3

ZADIG; or, the book of fate. Voltaire, F. M. A. de. London, 1784. 8° 513.13

ZAIDEE: a romance. Oliphant, M. (O. W.) 721.10

ZAMPA. Herold, L. J. F. (*In* Ditson, O., and co. Standard opera librettos) 6233.3.1

ZANONI. Bulwer-Lytton, E. (G. E.) L. 336.6

ZELDA'S fortune. Francillon, R. E. 731.28

ZENOBIA: or, the fall of Palmyra. [Historical novel.] Ware, W. New York, 1869. 2 v. 12° 726.15

ZEPHYRINUS, *pope.* *See* HIPPOLYTUS, *St.*

Shelf. No.

ZERUB Throop's experiment. Whitney, A. D. T. 537.13

ZEUNER, Ch. The ancient lyre, a collection of old, new, and original church music. 11th edition. Boston, 1840. xv, 363+ pp. Oblong 8° 1518.5

ZINCALI, The; or, an account of the gypsies of Spain. Borrow, G. New York, 1869. 8° 5931.13

ZINCKE, Foster Barham. Egypt of the Pharaohs and of the Khedivé. 2d edition. With a map. London, 1873. xii, 546 pp. 8° 5911.13

ZOE'S 'brand.' By the author of "Recommended to mercy" 317.6

ZOLLIKOFER, Georg Joachim. Exercises of piety: or, meditations on the principal doctrines and duties of religion. Translated from the French edition, by J. Manning. Abridged by T. M. Harris. Boston, 1855. xii, 186 pp. 12° 1535.24

ZOOLOGY. Carpenter, W. B. London, 1857. 2 v. 16°. 6616.1

See also Animals.

ZOONOMIA; or, the laws of organic life. Darwin, E. London, 1801. 2 v. 8° 6614.2

ZÓPHIËL; or, the bride of seven. [Poem.] Brooks, M. G. Boston, 1833. 16° 1618.3

ZSCHOKKE, (Johann) Heinrich (Daniel). Novellen und Dichtungen. Zehnte vermehrte Ausgabe. Aarau, 1865. 17 v. in 8. Sq. 16° 5738.4

Contents.—[Vol. I.] 1. Sehnsucht nach dem Schauen des Unsichtbaren; Alamontade; Harmonius; Der Eros, oder über die Liebe; Die Herrnhuter-Familie. 2. Diocletian in Salona; Blätter aus dem Tagebuch des armen Pfarr-Vikars von Wiltshire; Die Verklärungen; Kleine Ursachen; Jonathan Frock. [II.] 3. Ein Narr des neunzehnten Jahrhunderts; Die weiblichen Stufenjahre; Der Millionär; Der todte Gaft; Der Fürstenblick; Das Loch im Aermel. 4. Addrich im Moos. [III.] 5. Der Freihof von Aarau. 6. Der Flüchtling im Jura; Die Gründung von Maryland; Die Irrfahrt des Philhelenen; Florette; Maryam in der Wüste. [IV.] 7. Die Prinzessen von Wolfenbüttel; Agathokles; Der Pflanzer in Cuba; Hermingarde. 8. Der Pascha von Buda; Der Creole; Der Feldweibel; Das blaue Wunder. [V.] 9. Das Abenteuer der Neujahrsnacht; Die Walpurgisnacht; Der Blondin von Namur; Kriegerische Abenteuer eines Friedfertigen; Die Bohne; Die Nacht in Brczwezmcisl; Das Bein; Es ist sehr möglich! Erzählungen im Nebel; Die isländischen Briefe. 10. Rückwirkungen, oder wer regiert denn? Der zerbrochene Krug; Herrn Quints Verlobung; Hans Dampf in allen Gassen; Tantchen Rosemarin, oder Alles verkehrt; Die Reise wider Willen; Der Abend vor der Hochzeit; Das Wirthshaus zu Cransac. [VI.] 11. Die Rose von Disentis; Die Liebe der Ausgewanderten; Schulze von Celle und Cäcilie. 12. Lyonel Harlington; Die Lampe des Anaxagoras und die russische Fürstin; An Euphrasien über den Nachruhm; Der König von Akim; An Rosais. [VII.] 13. Genfer Novellen. 14. Bilder aus dem häuslichen Leben; Schweizer-Skizzen; Olavides, der neue Belisar; Der Besuch im Marienbade. [VIII.] 15. Wie man lieben muss; Abellino; Gedichte. 16. Das Goldmacherdorf; Meister Jordan, oder Handwerk hat goldenen Boden; Die Branntweinpest. 17. Spruch und Schwank des Schweizerboten.

— History of Switzerland. With a continuation to 1848 by E. Zschokke. Translated by F. G. Shaw. New York, 1860. xi, 405 pp. Map. 12° 5914.5

— The princess of Brunswick-Wolfenbüttel and other tales. From the German by M. A. Faber. 316.11

— The rose of Disentis. A novel. From the German by J. J. D. Trenor 737.27

ZUERCHER, F., and MARGOLLÉ, É. Meteors, aërolites, storms, and atmospheric phenomena. From the French. By W. Lackland. Illustrated. New York, 1871. 324 pp. 12° 1714.8

ZULU land, Wild sports and savage life in. Walmsley, H. M. London [1872]. 16° 5928.1

ZURICH. Spectacles for young eyes. Lander, S. W. 922.18

ZUYDER-ZEE, *Holland.* La Hollande pittoresque, voyage aux villes mortes du Zuiderzée. Havard, H. Paris, 1874. 16° 2016.11

ADDITIONS

MADE DURING THE PRINTING OF THE CATALOGUE.

Note. — As far as practicable, entries of these books, either by main titles or cross-references, have been made in the foregoing list; and the entries here, whether of main titles or cross-references, are supplemental to such in the preceding list, except in cases where the entire record is made here. Several titles from the preceding list are here repeated to include corrections since made.

Shelf. No.

ABBOT, Henry L., *joint author*. Report upon the physics and hydraulics of the Mississippi river, etc. *See* HUMPHREYS, Andrew Atkinson...... 6920.2

ABBOTT, John Stevens Cabot. American pioneers and patriots. Benjamin Franklin. A picture of the struggles of our infant nation, one hundred years ago. Illustrated. New York [1876]. 373+ pp. 12°.......................... 1014.17

ABOUT, Edmond (François Valentin). The man with the broken ear. Translated by H. Holt... 517.20

ABOVE suspicion. Riddell, J. H.................. 730.17

ACHSAH: a New England life-study. Round, W. M. F. 532.20

ACTIONS speak louder than words. Neily, K. J. ... 938.20

ADAM Grainger. Wood, E. P. 333.23

ADAMS, Abigail. Familiar letters during the revolution. *See* ADAMS, John.................. 5026.8

ADAMS, Charles Kendall. Democracy and monarchy in France from the inception of the great revolution to the overthrow of the second empire. 2d edition, revised. New York, 1875. viii, 544 pp. 12°.............................. 5515.4

ADAMS, Harriet A. Dawn........................ 722.18

ADAMS, John and Abigail. Familiar letters during the revolution. With a memoir of Mrs. Adams. By Charles Francis Adams. New York, 1876. xxxii, 424 pp. Portrait. 16° 5026.8

ADAMS, John Quincy. Memoirs. Edited by Charles Francis Adams. Vol. x. Philadelphia, 1876. 8°. 5021.10

ADAMS, William T. Young America abroad. Red cross; or, Young America in England and Wales. Boston, 1871. 336 pp. Illustrated. 16°. 916.18

ADELPHI. *See* TERENTIUS.

ADRIFT in a boat. Kingston, W. H. G............ 931.12

ADRIFT in Dixie; or, a Yankee officer among the rebels. Estabrooks, H. L. New York, 1866. 16°. 715.33

AFRICA. Verne, J. The adventures of three Englishmen and three Russians in South Africa. [Fiction.] London, 1876. Sm. 8°........... 715.32

— – Five weeks in a balloon. A voyage of exploration and discovery in Central Africa. [Burlesque.] London, 1876. Sm. 8° 715.30

AGNES Sorel. A novel. James, G. P. R. 730.6

AGRICULTURE. The New-England farmer; or georgical dictionary. Deane, S. Boston, 1822. 8°. 6423.3

AINSWORTH, William Harrison. Crichton 722.13

ALBANY, Louise, *countess of*. *See* HAYWARD, A. Biographical and critical essays. London, 1873. 8°.................................. 5833.3.2

ALBEMARLE, 6*th earl of*. *See* KEPPEL, George Thomas.

ALCOTT, Louisa May. Little women. 2 v......... 926.12

— Silver pitchers: and Independence, a centennial love story................................ 718.9

ALDRICH, Thomas Bailey. Daisy's necklace: and what came of it. (A literary episode) 115.2

Shelf. No.

ALFIERI, Vittorio. *See* HAYWARD, A. Biographical and critical essays. London, 1873. 8°.... 5833.3.2

ALFORD, Henry. Poetical works. Boston, 1853. 424+ pp. 16°............................ 1624.5

ALGATCHIE, *pseud.* Seen and unseen. A novel 532.21

ALGER, Horatio, *jr.* Sam's chance; and how he improved it. [Tattered Tom series. 2d series]... 933.28

— Timothy Crump's ward......................... 1126.1

ALONE in London. Smith, H...................... 1128.1

ALPS. Alpine guides. Pennine Alps, including Mont Blanc and Monte Rosa. Ball, J. London, 1873. 16° 5936.6

ALWYN's first wife. Craik, D. (M.) Leipzig...... 323.27

— *Same.* New York............................ 530.23

AMELIA, History of. [Fiction.] Fielding, H...... 722.21

AMERICAN angler's guide, The. Brown, J. J. New York, 1876. 8°........................... 6413.4

AMERICAN homes series. *Namely:* —

— Stephens, C. A. The young moose hunters, a backwoods-boy's story 921.11

AMMIANUS MARCELLINUS. Roman history, during the reigns of the emperors Constantius, Julian, Jovianus, Valentinian, and Valens. Translated by C. D. Yonge. With a general index. London, 1862. vii, 646 pp. [Bohn's Classical library.] Sm. 8°........................... 6117.9

ANASTASIUS, M. Craik, D. (M.)................. 530.23

ANCIENT régime, The. A tale. James, G. P. R.... 722.14

ANDREWS, Fanny. A family secret. A novel 730.11

ANDRIA. *See* TERENTIUS.

ANECDOTES. Hindley, C. Tavern anecdotes and sayings. London, 1875. Sm. 8° 5616.18

— Spence, J. Anecdotes, observations, and characters, of books and men. London, 1858. Sm. 8°. 5617.19

— Timbs, J. English eccentrics and eccentricities. London, 1875. Sm. 8° 5617.20

ANGLING. *See* FISH and fishing.

ANIMAL magnetism; or psycodunamy. Leger, T. New York, 1846. 12° 1522.16

ANNALS, The, of England. Foote, W. E.? Oxford, 1876. 8°............................ 5413.4

ANNALS of the road. Malet, H. E. London, 1876. 8°. 5433.4

ANNE Judge, spinster. Robinson, F. W.......... 731.25

APPERLEY, Charles James. Essays on the road. *See* MALET, Harold Esdaile 5433.4

APPLETON, Thomas Gold. A Nile journal. Illustrated. Boston [London], 1876. 307+ pp. 16°. 436.9

APPLETON's journal of literature, science, and art. Vol. 14. New York, 1875. 8°.............. 1332.1

ARBLAY, Frances d', *formerly Miss Burney*. Diary and letters. Edited by her niece, Charlotte Barrett. New edition, revised, with portraits. London, 1876. 4 v. Fac-simile. 8°......... 5333.7

Contents. — Vol. I. 1778 to 1784. II. 1785 to 1788. III. 1788 to 1796. IV. 1797 to 1840.

ARCHER, E. M., *pseud.* Under the limes 713.11

Shelf. No.

ARMY and navy journal. Vol. 12. New York, 1874–75. F° 6530.1
ARNOLD, Matthew. New poems. Boston, 1867. viii, 208 pp. 16° 1616.20
ART, L'. Revue hebdomadaire illustrée. Tome 1, 3, 4. Paris, 1875, 76. 3 v. F° 5310.1
ART-JOURNAL, The. New series. Vol. 14. London, 1875. 4° 6521.1
ART-STUDENT, An, in Munich. Howitt, A. M. London, 1853. 2 v. in 1. Sm. 8° 6215.1
ARTHUR. *See* MORTE dArthur.
ARTIST'S, The, love. Southworth, E. D. E. N. 522.28
ARTISTS, The, of America. Lester, C. E. New York, 1846. 8° 1012.8
ATONEMENT, The, of Leam Dundas. [Fiction.] Linton, E. L. 730.19
AUNT Saidee's cow. Prichard, S. J. 928.23
AUTOBIOGRAPHY, The, of a seaman. Cochrane, T. London, 1860. 2 v. 8° 5334.2
AUTUMN leaves. [Juvenile.] Denison, E. F. 938.12

BADEN, Frances Henshaw. Stories. *See* SOUTHWORTH, Emma Dorothy Eliza Nevitte 522.28
BAKER, George Melville. An old man's prayer. [Poem.] Illustrated. Boston, 1868. 57+ pp. Sq. 16° 1617.17
— The social stage: original dramas, comedies, burlesques, and entertainments for home recreation, schools, and public exhibitions. Boston, 1875 [*cop.* 1870]. Illustrated. 16° 1635.7
— The temperance drama: a series of dramas, comedies, and farces, for temperance exhibitions, and home and school entertainment. Boston, 1874. 230 pp. 16° 1636.5
BALLADS, English and Scottish. Child, F. J., *editor*. Boston, 1871. 8 v. 16° 5628.5
BALLOU'S monthly magazine. Vol. 41, 42. Boston, 1875. 2 v. 8° 1433.2
BALLSTON, *New York*, An analysis of the mineral waters of. Steel, J. H. Saratoga Springs, 1838. 12° 417.15
BANCROFT, George. History of the United States of America, from the discovery of the continent. Vol. I–VI. Thoroughly revised edition. Boston, 1876. [Centenary edition.] 6 v. 16° 815.4
BARNES, Albert. Notes on the gospels. *See* BIBLE. *New Testament. Gospels* 6327.23
BARRETT, Mary. Our summer at Hillside farm 1118.9
BATH-CHAIR man's, The, story. Church, F. 337.23
BAVARIAN highlands, The. Schmid, H., and Stieler, C. London, 1874. 4° 5720.1
BEADLE, Erastus F. Beadle's dime book of dreams: their romance and mystery; with a complete interpretation dictionary. Compiled from the most accredited sources. New York [*cop.* 1863]. 80 pp. 12° 1518.14
BEAR hunters, The, of the Rocky mountains. Bowman, A. 938.18
BEAUCHAMP'S career. Meredith, G. 331.24
BEAUMARCHAIS, Pierre Augustin Caron de. Loménie, L. L. de. Beaumarchais and his times. London, 1856. 4 v. Sm. 8° 5527.19
BECKER, Wilhelm Adolf. Charicles, or illustrations of the private life of the ancient Greeks. With notes and excursuses. From the German. Translated by F. Metcalfe. 4th edition. London, 1874. xxi, 512 pp. Illustrated. Sm. 8° 6117.15
— Gallus, or Roman scenes of the time of Augustus. With notes and excursuses illustrative of the manners and customs of the Romans. Translated by F. Metcalfe. 4th edition. London, 1873. xxi, 535 pp. Illustrated. Sm. 8° 6117.14
BEECHER, Henry Ward. Woman's influence in politics. (*In* Woman's suffrage tracts) 1926.5
BEN Milner's wooing. Parr, H. 327.26
BENEDEN, Pierre Joseph van. International scientific series. Animal parasites and messmates. With illustrations. New York, 1876. xxviii, 274 pp. 12°. 6010.6
BÉRANGER, Pierre Jean de. Memoirs. Written by himself. 2d edition, with additional anecdotes and notes. London, 1858. 390+ pp. Portrait. 8°. 5523.6

Shelf. No.

BERNARD, Charles de. *See* DU GRAIL DE LA VILLETTE, Charles Bernard.
BESSIE Lovell; or, the power of a loving child 1118.15
BIBLE. Harris, T. M. The natural history of the Bible. Boston, 1820. 8° 6323.11
— Smith, W. The student's Scripture history. The Old Testament history. From the creation to the return of the Jews from captivity. London, 1874. Sm. 8° 6325.22
— *New Testament*. The student's Scripture history. The New Testament history. Smith, W. London, 1873. Sm. 8° 6325.23
— – *German*. Protestanten-Bibel. Neuen Testamentes. Herausgegeben von P. W. Schmidt und Franz von Holtzendorff. 2te revidirte Auflage. Leipzig, 1874. xxxi, 1055 pp. 8° 5733.8
— – *Gospels*. Notes, explanatory and practical, on the gospels. By Albert Barnes. 17th edition. Revised and corrected, with an index, a chronological table, etc. New York, 1841. 2 v. Folded map and plan. Illustrations. 12° 6327.23
BIBLIOTHECA sacra, and theological eclectic. Vol. 32. Andover, 1875. 8° 6736.1
BICKERSTETH, Edward Henry. The Rock of ages; or Scripture testimony to the one eternal Godhead of the Father, and of the Son, and of the Holy Ghost. With an introduction by F. D. Huntington. Boston, 1860. 214 pp. 12°. 1524.7 and 5816.24
BIOGRAPHY. Hayward, A. Biographical and critical essays. London, 1873, 74. 3 v. 8° 5833.3
— Timbs, J. English eccentrics and eccentricities. London, 1875. Sm. 8° 5617.20
BLACK, Adam and Charles, *publishers*. Black's guide to England and Wales. Containing plans of the principal cities, charts, maps, and views, and a list of hotels. 11th edition. Edinburgh, 1874. xxiv, 544 pp. Folded maps. Illustrations. Sm. 8° 5437.2
BLACK, William. Lady Silverdale's sweetheart, and other stories. Leipzig 331.28

Contents. — Lady Silverdale's sweetheart; The marriage of Moira Fergus; The man who was like Shakspeare; The Highlands of the city; The strange horse of Loch Suainabhal.

BLACKMORE, Richard Doddridge. Cradock Nowell: a tale of the New forest 730.14
— Cripps, the carrier. A woodland tale 530.24
BLIND girl, The, of Wittenberg. Wildenhahn, K. A. 722.27
BLOCKADE runners, The. Verne, J. New York, 1874. 8° 713.4
— *Same*. London, 1876. Sm. 8° 715.31
BLUE jackets; or, the adventures of J. Thompson among "the heathen Chinee." Greey, E. 730.22
BOATS, Forms of ships and. Bland, W. London, 1868. 12° 1715.10
BOHN'S Antiquarian library. *Namely*: —
— Mallet, P. H. Northern antiquities 5715.5
BOHN'S Classical library. *Namely*: —
— Ammianus Marcellinus. Roman history, during the reigns of the emperors Constantius, Julian, Jovianus, Valentinian, and Valens 6117.9
— Cicero, M. T. Orations. 4 v. 6117.6
— Justinus, Nepos, C., and Eutropius. [Works] 6117.10
— Livius Patavinus, T. The history of Rome 6117.11
— Sallustius Crispus, C., Florus, L. A., and Velleius Paterculus, C. [Works] 6117.7
— Suetonius Tranquillus, C. Lives of the twelve Cæsars; added, lives of the grammarians, rhetoricians, and poets 6117.8
BOHN'S Standard library. *Namely*: —
— Junius, *pseud*. Letters 5637.3
— Smyth, W. Lectures on modern history. 2 v. 5925.7
— – Lectures on the history of the French revolution. 2 v. 5517.10
— Thierry, (J. N.) A. The formation and progress of the tiers état, or third estate in France 5517.9
BOISSIER, Marie Louis Gaston. L'opposition sous les Césars. Paris, 1875. 372+ pp. 8° 5513.7
BOSSUET, Jacques Bénigne. Bossuet and his contemporaries. Farrer, H. L. London, 1874. Sm. 8°. 5526.14

Shelf. No.

BOSTON, *Mass. Municipal government.* March 17th, 1876. Celebration of the centennial anniversary of the evacuation of Boston by the British army, March 17th, 1776. Reception of the Washington medal. Oration delivered in Music hall, and a chronicle of the siege of Boston. By George E. Ellis. Boston, 1876. 199 pp. Maps. Folded plan. Illustrations. L. 8° 810.12
— – Second report of the board of commissioners [T. J. Coolidge, W. Gray, jr., C. H. Dalton] of the department of parks, 1876. Boston, 1876. 42 pp. Folded maps and plans. 8° 6926.3
— *Baldwin Place home for little wanderers.* The little wanderers' advocate. Vol. 8, 10, 11. Boston, 1872-75. 3 v. 8° 1335.2
BOSTON directory for 1876. Boston [1876]. 8°. *R.R., E.2.5
BOTANY. A dictionary of botanical terms. Henslow, J. S. London [1861]. Sm. 8° 6627.4
BOWMAN, Anne. The bear hunters of the Rocky mountains 938.18
— The boy voyagers; or, the pirates of the East ... 938.15
— Clarissa; or, the Mervyn inheritance. A book for young ladies 938.19
— Esperanza; or, the home of the wanderers 938.13
— The kangaroo hunters; or, adventures in the bush 938.14
— Tom and the crocodiles 938.16
— The young yachtsmen 938.17
BOY voyagers, The; or, the pirates of the East. Bowman, A. 938.15
BRADDON, Mary Elizabeth. Dead men's shoes. Leipzig 321.27
— *Same.* New York 730.9
— My sister's confession and other stories 730.24

Contents. — My sister's confession; Old Rudderford hall; At Chrighton abbey; Colonel Benyon's entanglement; The scene-painter's wife; The dreaded guest.

BRADLEY, Mary E. Douglass farm; a juvenile story of life in Virginia 1118.12
BRAY, Anna Eliza. The good St. Louis and his times. London, 1870. xvi, 392 pp. Portrait. Sm. 8° 5937.13
BREMER, Fredrika. The home: or, family cares and family joys. Translated from the Swedish, by Mary Howitt 730.20
BRINTON, Daniel Garrison. The religious sentiment, its source and aim. A contribution to the science and philosophy of religion. New York, 1876. iv, 284+ pp. 16° 5815.27
BROCKETT, Linus P. Our great captains. Grant, Sherman, Thomas, Sheridan, and Farragut. New York, 1865. 251 pp. Portraits. 12° 1015.8
BROOKE, Stopford Augustus. English literature. New York, 1876. 167+ pp. [Green, J. R., *editor.* Literature primers.] 16° 1738.3
BROWN, John J. The American angler's guide; or, complete fisher's manual, for the United States. 5th edition. Illustrated. New York, 1876. 428+ pp. 8° 6413.4
BRYANT, William Cullen, and GAY, Sydney Howard. A popular history of the United States, from the first discovery of the western hemisphere by the Northmen, to the end of the first century of the union of the states. Preceded by a sketch of the pre-historic period and the age of the mound builders. Vol. I. New York, 1876. Maps. Portraits. Fac-similes. Illustrations. 8° 610.5
BUCKLEY, Arabella B. A short history of natural science and of the progress of discovery from the time of the Greeks to the present day. With illustrations. New York, 1876. xxiii, 467 pp. 12° 6835.4
BULWER, *Sir* Henry Lytton Earle, *baron Dalling and Bulwer. See* HAYWARD, A. Biographical and critical essays. London, 1873. 8° 5833.3.2
BULWER-LYTTON, Edward (George Earle) Lytton, *lord Lytton.* Pausanias the Spartan. An unfinished historical romance. Edited by his son. Leipzig 336.22
BUONARROTI, Michelangelo, *or* Michel Agnolo, Life and works of. Wilson, C. H. London, 1876. 8°. 6211.11

Shelf. No.

BURCKETT, Florence. Wildmoor. A novel 532.2
BURNAND, Francis Cowley. To Buddlecombe and back 539.12
BURNET, Gilbert. The history of the reformation of the church of England. New edition, revised, and the records collated with the originals, by N. Pocock. Oxford, 1865. 7 v. 8° 6320.5
BURNS, Dawson. Christendom and the drink curse: an appeal to the Christian world for efficient action against the causes of intemperance. London, 1875. xii, 333 pp. 8° 1912.9
BURTON, John Hill. History of Scotland from Agricola's invasion to the extinction of the last Jacobite insurrection. 2d edition. Edinburgh, 1874. 8 v. Sm. 8° 5418.6
BUTLER, William Allen. Poems. Boston, 1871. vi, 263 pp. 12° 1626.1
BUTT, Beatrice May. Leisure hour series. Miss Molly 517.24
BYRON, George Gordon Noel, *lord.* Works. 2d edition. With portrait. Leipzig, 1866. 5 v. Sq. 16° 1614.13

Note. — For contents, see page 36.

— Life of. Castelar, E. New York, 1876. 12° ... 1236.1

CADELL, H. M. Leisure hour series. Ida Craven .. 517.27
CÆSARS. Boissier, M. L. G. L'opposition sous les Césars. Paris, 1875. 8° 5513.7
— Suetonius Tranquillus, C. Lives of the twelve Cæsars. London, 1872. Sm. 8° 6117.8
CAMP-FIRES of the revolution. Watson, H. C. New York, 1869. 8° 811.8
CAMPING out. Stephens, C. A. 1127.1
CANNING, George. George Canning as a man of letters. Hayward, A. Biographical and critical essays. London, 1873. 8° 5833.3.1
CARLYLE, Thomas. German romance: specimens of its chief authors; with biographical and critical notices. Boston, 1841. 2 v. in 1. 12° 5725.2

Contents. — (Johann Carl) August Musaeus; Friedrich (Heinrich Carl) de La Motte Fouqué; (Johann) Ludwig Tieck; Ernst Theodor Amadeus (Wilhelm) Hoffmann; Jean Paul Friedrich Richter.

CARMICHAEL, Andrew. Memoir of the life and philosophy of Spurzheim. 1st American edition, with notes. Boston, 1833. vi, 96 pp. 12° 1227.9
CARRIE Allison; or, in the vineyard. Davis, C. E... 929.10
CASH-BOY'S, The, trust. Mitchell, A. M. 1127.13
CASTELAR, Emilio. Life of Lord Byron and other sketches. Translated by Mrs. Arthur Arnold. New York, 1876. xii, 347 pp. 12° 1236.1

Contents. — Lord Byron; Victor Hugo; Alexander Dumas; Emile Girardin; Daniel Manin; Adolphe Thiers.

CATHOLIC world, The. Vol. 22. New York, 1875. 8°. 6715.1
CENTENNIAL commissioner, A, in Europe, 1874-76. Forney, J. W. Philadelphia, 1876. 12° 436.10
CENTENNIALS. Boston, *Mass. Municipal government.* March 17th, 1876. Celebration of the centennial anniversary of the evacuation of Boston by the British army, March 17th, 1776. Boston, 1876. L. 8° 810.12
CHANNING, William Ellery. A selection from [his] works. Boston, 1855. v, 480+ pp. 12° 1915.11
CHANTREY, *Sir* Francis, Memorials of. Holland, J. London [1851]. Sm. 8° 5338.2
CHAPPAQUA, *N. Y.* Story of a summer [at Horace Greeley's home]; or, journal leaves from Chappaqua. Cleveland, O. New York, 1874. Sq. 16° 1019.2
CHARICLES, or illustrations of the private life of the ancient Greeks. Becker, W. A. London, 1874. Sm. 8° 6117.15
CHARLES I, *of England,* Commentaries on the life and reign of. Disraeli, I. London, 1851. 2 v. 8°. 5421.6
CHARLES XII, *of Sweden,* History of. Voltaire, F. M. A. de. Edinburgh, 1873. Sm. 8° 5726.6
CHARLESWORTH, Maria Louisa. Oliver of the mill. A tale 722.26
CHEEVER, George Barrell, *editor.* The American common-place book of poetry, with occasional notes. Philadelphia, 1841. 405 pp. 12° 1534.14

Shelf. No.

CHERBULIEZ, Victor. Meta Holdenis. [Fiction.] 3e édition. Paris, 1875. 271+ pp. 16°.....2016.13

— Paule Méré. Paris, 1865. 352+ pp. 18°....5536.16

CHESNEY, George. The dilemma. A novel........ 730.12

CHICOT, the jester. An historical romance. Dumas, A. (D.).. 718.8

CHIKAMATSU Monzayemon. Chiushingura; or, the loyal league. A Japanese romance. Translated by F. V. Dickins. With introduction by Hoffman Atkinson. [*Added* Appendix.] New York, 1876. 213+ pp. Fac-similes. Illustrations. Oblong 4°.. 5928.4

Note. — The appendix contains a metrical version of parts of the story. The illustrations were "drawn and engraved by Japanese artists, and printed by Japanese printers." The binding is of bark paper made by the Japanese.

CHILD, The, of the wreck; or, the loss of the Royal George. Kingston, W. H. G.................1118.13

CHINA, Travels in, 1844-6. Huc, É. R. London [1852]. 2 v. 16°........................5935.12

CHIUSHINGURA; or, the loyal league. A Japanese romance. Chikamatsu Monzayemon. New York, 1876. Oblong 4°...................... 5928.4

CHRONICLE of events, discoveries, and improvements, for the popular diffusion of useful knowledge, with an authentic record of facts. Illustrated with maps and drawings. Boston [1841, 42]. 2 v. in 1. 8°.............................. 1317.2

Note. — The Monthly chronicle, Vol. 2, 3 (1841, 42), with a new title, and some changes.

CHRYSOSTOMUS, Joannes, *St.* Macgilvray, W. John of the golden mouth. London, 1871. Sm. 8°.5937.14

CHURCH, Florence, *formerly Miss Marryat.* The girls of Feversham.............................. 530.21

— A lucky disappointment and other stories. Leipzig.. 331.31

Contents. — A lucky disappointment; The little Gordon; Sir Marcus's choice; Meg Hartley's cure.

— The poison of asps and other stories............ 337.23

Contents. — The poison of asps; The bath-chair man's story; Plucked from the burning; A happy accident at Brighton.

— A star and a heart. Boston.................. 730.10

— "Too good for him"............................ 530.22

CHURCHILL, Charles. *See* FORSTER, J. Biographical essays. London, 1860. Sm. 8°...........5425.12

CHURCHILL, Fleetwood. Essays on the puerperal fever and other diseases peculiar to women. Selected from the writings of British authors previous to the close of the eighteenth century. London, 1849. viii, 552 pp. 8°.............6013.13

CICERO, Marcus Tullius. Orations. Literally translated by C. D. Yonge. London, 1871, 72. 4 v. [Bohn's Classical library.] Sm. 8°........... 6117.6

Contents. — Vol. I. For P. Quintius, Sextus Roscius, Quintus Roscius; against Quintus Cæcilius, and Verres. II. For M. Tullius, M. Fonteius, A. Cæcina, A. Cluentius, C. Cornelius, C. Rabirius, L. Murena, P. Sylla, A. L. Archias, L. Flaccus, M. E. Scaurus; in defence of the proposed Manilian law; against C. Antonius, L. Catilini, P. Clodius, C. Curio; concerning the Agrarian law; after his return. III. For his House; respecting the answers of the soothsayers; for C. Plancius, P. Sextius, M. Cœlius, L. C. Balbus, T. A. Milo, C. R. Postumus, M. C. Marcellus, Q. Ligarius, King Deiotarus; against P. Vatinius, L. C. Piso; on the consular provinces. IV. Philippics; Treatise on rhetorical invention; The orator; On topics; Dialogue concerning oratorical partitions; Treatise on the best style of orators.

— De natura Deorum. Libri tres. Accedunt notæ Anglicæ. Cura C. K. Dillaway. Philadelphiæ [*cop.* 1846]. 2 v. Sm. 12°.............6118.16

— Ad Quintum fratrem dialogi tres de oratore. Ex editionibus Oliveti et Ernesti. Accedunt notæ Anglicæ. Cura C. K. Dillaway. Philadelphia, 1849. 2 v. Sm. 12°.......................6118.17

— De senectute et de amicitia. Ex editionibus Oliveti et Ernesti. Accedunt notæ Anglicæ. Cura C. K. Dillaway. Editio tertia. Philadelphiæ, 1842. 156 pp. Sm. 12°.............6118.15

CLARISSA; or, the Mervyn inheritance. Bowman, A. 938.19

CLARK, Thomas March. John Whopper the newsboy.. 926.28

CLERGY, A book about the. Jeaffreson, J. C. London, 1870. 2 v. 8°...............1231.4 and 6320.6

Shelf. No.

CLYFFARDS, The, of Clyffe. Payn, J..............

COCHRANE, Thomas, 10*th earl of Dundonald.* The autobiography of a seaman. London, 1860. 2 v. Charts. 8°.......................... 522.24 5334.2

COLET, John. *See* SEEBOHM, F. The Oxford reformers. London, 1869. 8°.................5811.12

COLLECTION, A, of psalms and hymns, for social and private worship. 3d edition. Boston, 1832. 422 pp. 12°..................................6328.26

COLLINS, William Lucas. Livy [outlined and explained]. Philadelphia, 1876. 186+ pp. Folded map. [Ancient classics for English readers.] 16° 6116.22

COLORS. La lumière et les couleurs. Guillemin, A. Paris, 1874. 16°...................... 2015.8

COMIC history, A, of the United States. Hopkins, L. New York, 1876. 12°.................. 617.3

CONANT farm. By the author of "Squire Downing's heirs" [etc.].............................. 1127.9

CONSPIRATORS, The; or, the chevalier d'Harmental. Dumas, A. (D.)............................ 718.7

CORNELIUS NEPOS. *See* NEPOS, Cornelius.

CORNWALL, Barry, *pseud.* *See* PROCTER, Bryan Waller.

CORNWALL, C. M., *pseud.* Free, yet forging their own chains. [Fiction]...................... 722.16

CORTÉS, Hernando, History of the conquest of Mexico, and the life of. Prescott, W. H. Philadelphia, 1873. 3 v. 8°................ 5014.2

— *Same.* Philadelphia, 1875. 3 v. 12°........ 815.6

COUNTESS Kate. Yonge, C. M.................. 1116.2

COUSIN Clara. Wise, D........................ 932.36

COVENANTERS. Dodds, J. The fifty years' struggle of the Scottish covenanters, 1638 to 1688. London [1868]. Sm. 8°..................... 5417.9

— Napier, M. Montrose and the covenanters, their characters and conduct. London, 1838. 2 v. 8°. 5411.2

CRADOCK Nowell: a tale of the New forest. Blackmore, R. D............................ 730.14

CRAIK, Dinah (Maria), *formerly Miss Muloch.* Nothing new. Tales. New York............ 530.23

Contents. — Lord Erlistoun; Alwyn's first wife; M. Anastasius; The water cure; The last house in C—— street; A family in love; A low marriage; The double house.

CREW, The, of the Dolphin. Smith, H........... 529.11

CRIMEAN war, 1853-56. The invasion of the Crimea: its origin, and an account of its progress down to the death of Lord Raglan. Kinglake, A. W. Leipzig, 1863-75. 10 v. in 4. Sq. 16°........ 837.2

CRIPPS, the carrier. A woodland tale. Blackmore, R. D.. 530.24

CROMWELL, Oliver. Forster, J. Biographical essays. London, 1860. Sm. 8°......................5425.12

— Villemain, A. F. Histoire de Cromwell d'après les mémoires du temps et les recueils parlementaires. Bruxelles, 1851. 12°............... 2015.7

CRUSADES, The history and literature of the. Sybel, H. (C. L.) von. London, 1861. 8°...........5924.11

CRUST, The, and the cake. Mayo, I. F............ 115.1

CUDLIP, Annie, *formerly Miss Thomas.* A narrow escape. Boston.............................. 730.16

— *Same.* Leipzig............................ 317.23

CUMMING, (W.) Gordon. Wild men and wild beasts; or, scenes in camp and jungle. New York, 1872. xiv, 372+ pp. Illustrated. Sm. 8°......... 423.8

CURATE, The, in charge. Oliphant, M. (O. W.) Leipzig.. 331.23

— *Same.* New York............................ 721.25

CURTIS, George William. Equal rights for women. (*In* Woman's suffrage tracts)................ 1926.5

DAISY. Warner, S............................. 722.19

DAISY'S necklace: and what came of it. (A literary episode.) Aldrich, T. B....................... 115.2

DANIEL Deronda. Lewes, M. Vol. I............. 722.20

DAVIS, Caroline E., *formerly Miss Kelly.* Carrie Allison; or, in the vineyard.................. 929.10

DAWN. [Fiction.] Adams, H. A.................. 722.18

DEACON Pitkin's farm. Stowe, H. (E.) B.......... 715.24

DEAD marquise, The. A romance. Kip, L......... 717.14

DEAD men's shoes. Braddon, M. E. Leipzig...... 321.27

— *Same.* New York............................ 730.9

Shelf. No.

DEANE, Samuel. The New-England farmer; or georgical dictionary. 3d edition. Boston, 1822. xi, 532 pp. 8° 6423.3

DEAR Lady Disdain. MacCarthy, J. Leipzig..... 331.29

— *Same.* New York 721.23

DECLARATION, The, of independence of the United States of America, 1776; and Washington's Farewell address to the people of the United States, 1796. Boston, 1876. 57 pp. Plate. Fac-similes. 4° 1920.3

DE FOE, Daniel. Forster, J. Biographical essays. London, 1860. Sm. 8° 5425.12

— Lee, W. Daniel Defoe: his life, and recently discovered writings: extending from 1716 to 1729. London, 1869. 3 v. 8° 5422.5

DELANY, Mary Granville. Autobiography and correspondence: with interesting reminiscences of George the third and Queen Charlotte. Edited by Lady Llanover. London, 1861. 3 v. Woodcuts. Portraits. 8° 5624.4

DEUTSCHE Rundschau. Band 5, 6. Berlin, 1875, 76. 2 v. 8° 6513.1

DEXTER, Henry Martyn. As to Roger Williams, and his 'banishment' from the Massachusetts plantation; with a few further words concerning the baptists, the quakers, and religious liberty: a monograph. Boston, 1876. vi, 146 pp. 4°... 5011.1

DEXTER SMITH's musical, literary, dramatic and art paper. Vol. 7. Boston, 1875. 4° 1331.1

DICK Duncan. Wise, D. 932.33

DILEMMA, The. A novel. Chesney, G. 730.12

DILLAWAY, Charles Knapp. Roman antiquities, and ancient mythology; for classical schools. 9th edition. Boston, 1857 [*cop.* 1833]. 144 pp. Illustrated. 16° 5516.3

DISCOVERIES and inventions of the nineteenth century. Routledge, R. London, 1876. Sm. 8°.1522.17

DISRAELI, Isaac. Commentaries on the life and reign of Charles the first, king of England. New edition, revised by the author, and edited by his son. London, 1851. 2 v. 8° 5421.6

DR. Ox's experiment. Verne, J. Boston 529.2

— *Same.* London 715.36

DODDS, James. The fifty years' struggle of the Scottish covenanters, 1638 to 1688. London [1868]. xii, 388 pp. Sm. 8° 5417.9

DODGE, Mary Abigail. Woman's worth and worthlessness. The complement to "A new atmosphere." By Gail Hamilton [*pseud.*]. New York, 1872. 291 pp. 12° 1736.11

DODGE, Mary Mapes. Theophilus and others 713.15

DOLLIVER romance, The. Hawthorne, N. Boston, 1876. 12° 1813.13

DORAN, John Wilberforce. Saints and sinners; or, in church and about it. London, 1868. 2 v. in 1. Sm. 8° 6325.24

DOUBLE house, The. Craik, D. (M.) Leipzig 330.22

— *Same.* New York 530.23

DOUGLAS, Marian, *pseud.* *See* GREENE, Annie D.

DOUGLASS farm; a juvenile story of life in Virginia. Bradley, M. E. 1118.12

DRAMA, The temperance. Baker, G. M. Boston, 1874. 16° 1636.5

DREAMS. The other world; or, glimpses of the supernatural. Being facts, records, and traditions relating to dreams, etc. Lee, F. G. London, 1875. 2 v. Sm. 8° 6327.24

DRINKWATER, Jennie M. Not bread alone; or, Miss Helen's neighbors 1118.8

DUMAS, Alexandre (Davy). Chicot, the jester. An historical romance 718.8

— The conspirators; or, the chevalier d'Harmental 718.7

— *See* HAYWARD, A. Biographical and critical essays. London, 1873. 8° 5833.3.1

DUNDONALD, 10*th earl of.* *See* COCHRANE, Thomas.

DUPRÉ, August, *joint author.* Treatise on the origin, nature, and varieties of wine. *See* THUDICHUM, John Louis William 6423.4

DWELLERS, The, in Five-sisters court. Scudder, H. E. 717.18

Shelf. No.

DYER, Thomas Henry. History of the city of Rome: its structures and monuments. From its foundation to the end of the middle ages. London, 1865. lxxii, 415 pp. Folded maps. 8° 5512.5

— History of the kings of Rome. With a prefatory dissertation on its sources and evidence. London, 1868. cxxxx, 440 pp. 8° 5512.6

EARLY man in Europe. Rau, C. New York, 1876. 8°.6612.10

EASSIE, William. Sanitary arrangements for dwellings. London, 1874. ix, 188 pp. Illustrated. 16°. 6226.8

ECCENTRICITIES, English eccentrics and. Timbs, J. London, 1875. Sm. 8° 5617.20

ECHO club, The. Taylor, (J.) B. Boston, 1876. 16°. 1539.4

EDGEWORTH, Maria: her life and writings. Hayward, A. Biographical and critical essays. London, 1873. 8° 5833.3.1

EDITH Lyle. Holmes, M. J. 534.26

EDITH Vaughan's victory. Pierson, H. W. 1118.11

EDWARDS, Edward. Memoirs of libraries: including a hand-book of library economy. London, 1859. 2 v. Plates. Wood-cuts. Folded sheets. 8°.. 6133.3

EGYPT. A Nile journal. Appleton, T. G. Boston [London], 1876. 16° 436.9

ELAM, Charles. A physician's problems. [Essays.] Boston, 1869. vi, 400 pp. 12° 1535.21

ELLERSLIE house. A book for boys. Leslie, E. 939.7

ELLIOTT, Charles Wyllys. The book of American interiors. From existing houses, with preliminary essays and letterpress descriptions. Illustrated in heliotype. Boston, 1876. 135 pp. 22 plates. 4° 6230.4

ELLIS, George Edward. Celebration of the centennial anniversary of the evacuation of Boston by the British army, March 17th, 1776. Oration, and a chronicle of the siege of Boston. *See* BOSTON, *Mass.* *Municipal government.* March 17th, 1876 .... 810.12

EMILY Herbert. MacIntosh, M. J. 929.9

ENGLAND. Black, A. and C. Black's guide to. Edinburgh, 1874. Sm. 8° 5437.2

— Foote, W. E.? The annals of: an epitome of English history. Oxford, 1876. 8° 5413.4

— Gardiner, S. R. The first two Stuarts and the puritan revolution, 1603–1660. London, 1876. 16° 5419.2

— Hale, E. The fall of the Stuarts and Western Europe from 1678 to 1697. London, 1876. 16°. 5419.1

— Hoppin, J. M. Old England: its scenery, art, and people. New York, 1872. 16° 5438.7

— Ranke, (F.) L. von. A history of England principally in the seventeenth century. Oxford, 1875. 6 v. 8° 5412.6

— Staunton, H. The great schools of. London, 1869. Sm. 8° 5416.5

— Timbs, J. English eccentrics and eccentricities. London, 1875. Sm. 8° 5617.20

— – School-days of eminent men; or, early lives of celebrated British authors, philosophers, poets, inventors, etc. London [1876]. Sm. 8° 5428.10

ENGLAND, Church of, The history of the reformation of the. Burnet, G. Oxford, 1865. 7 v. 8°.. 6320.5

ENGLISH language. Mathews, W. Words; their use and abuse. Chicago, 1876. 12° 1736.10

— Wedgwood, H. A dictionary of English etymology. London, 1872. 8° ...........*R.R., D.3.10

— Worcester, J. E. Pocket dictionary of the. Boston, 1872. 32° 1719.1

ENGLISH literature. Brooke, S. A. English literature. New York, 1876. 16° 1738.3

— Sigourney, L. H., and others. The young lady's offering; or, gems of prose and poetry. Boston, 1858. 12° 5216.2

— Taylor, (J.) B. The Echo club, and other literary diversions. Boston, 1876. 16° 1539.4

— Ward, A. W. History of English dramatic literature to the death of Queen Anne. London, 1875. 2 v. 8° 5624.3

— Warton, T. The history of English poetry, from the eleventh to the seventeenth century. London [1870]. Sm. 8° 5627.5

Shelf. No.

ENGLISHWOMAN'S domestic magazine. Vol. 18, 19. London, 1875. 2 v. 4° 6532.1
ENOCH Arden. Tennyson, A. Poetical works. Leipzig, 1860. Sq. 16° 1614.10.3
EPOCHS of modern history. *See* MORRIS, Edward E., and PHILLPOTTS, James Surtees, *editors*.
ERASMUS, Desiderius. Colloquies, with a vocabulary. For classical schools. Edited by C. K. Dillaway. Boston, 1833. 211 pp. Portrait. 12°. 6117.16
ESPERANZA; or, the home of the wanderers. Bowman, A. 938.13
ESTABROOKS, Henry L. Adrift in Dixie; or, a Yankee officer among the rebels. With an introduction by Edmund Kirke [*pseud.*]. New York, 1866. 224 pp. 16° 715.33
ETTING, Frank M. An historical account of the old state house of Pennsylvania, now known as the Hall of independence. With illustrations. Boston, 1876. ix, 204+ pp. Portraits. Facsimiles. Sm. 4° 5220.1
EUROPE. Forney, J. W. A centennial commissioner in. 1874–76. Philadelphia, 1876. 12°. 436.10
— Lecky, W. E. H. History of the rise and influence of the spirit of rationalism in. New York, 1872. 2 v. 8° 5914.7
EUTROPIUS. [Works.] *See* JUSTINUS. London, 1872. Sm. 8° 6117.10
EVERETT, Edward. The Mount Vernon papers. New York, 1860. xxi, 490 pp. 12° 1534.13
EVERY boy's book: a complete encyclopædia of sports and amusements. Routledge, E., *editor*. London, 1863. 16° 916.4
— *Same*. London [1868]. 16° 6414.2
EVERY Saturday. Vol. 1, 3, 6, 7; new series, vol. 1–4; new series, vol. 1, 2. Boston, 1866–74. 10 v. 4°. 1313.1
EWALD, (Georg) Heinrich (August). The antiquities of Israel. Translated from the German by Henry Shaen Solly. London, 1876. xii, 386 pp. Plan. 8° 5811.13

FAMILIAR talks to boys. Hall, J. New York [1876]. 12°. 1916.10
FAMILY, A, in love. Craik, D. (M.) Leipzig 330.22
— *Same*. New York 530.23
FAMILY secret, A. A novel. Andrews, F. 730.11
FAMILY tree, A. [Fiction.] Fonblanque, A., *jr.* .. 730.18
FANSHAWE. Hawthorne, N. Boston, 1876. 12° .. 1813.12
FARRAGUT, David Glascoe. *See* BROCKETT, L. P. Our great captains. New York, 1865. 12° ... 1015.8
FERMENTATION, On. Schuetzenberger, M. P. New York, 1876. 12° 6436.18
FIELDING, Henry. History of Amelia. [Fiction.] With illustrations by George Cruikshank 722.21
FIELDS, James Thomas. Old acquaintance. Barry Cornwall and some of his friends. Boston, 1876. 121 pp. Portraits. [Vest-pocket series.] 16° .. 1829.1
FINE arts. The arts in the middle ages and at the period of the renaissance. Lacroix, P. London, 1875. L. 8° 6230.5
FIRE and flame. Schucking, L. 520.5
FIRST Christmas, The, of New England. Stowe, H. (E.) B. 715.24
FISH and fishing. The American angler's guide; or, complete fisher's manual, for the United States. Brown, J. J. New York, 1876. 8° 6413.4
FISHER, Frances C. "The land of the sky"; or, adventures in mountain by-ways. By Christian Reid [*pseud.*] 730.15
FIVE weeks in a balloon. A voyage of exploration and discovery in Central Africa. [Burlesque.] Verne, J. London, 1876. Sm. 8° 715.30
FLINT, D. B. Illustrated catalogue of portable sectional buildings. *See* SKILLINGS, D. N. 6222.1
FLOATING city, A. Verne, J. London, 1876. Sm. 8°. 715.26
FLORIDA, Wild life in. Townshend, F. T. London, 1875. 8° 5932.14
FLOWERS. Garden flowers: how to cultivate them. Rand, E. S., *jr.* New York, 1876 [*cop.* 1866]. 16°. 6625.7
FOLIO. Vol. 12. Boston, 1875. 4° 1331.2
FONBLANQUE, Albany, *jr.* A family tree. [Fiction]. 730.18
FOOTE, Samuel. *See* FORSTER, J. Biographical essays. London, 1860. Sm. 8° 5425.12

Shelf. No.

FOOTE, W. E.? The annals of England: an epitome of English history, from contemporary writers, the rolls of parliament, and other public records. Library edition. Oxford, 1876. xi, 643+ pp. Illustrated. 8° 5413.4

Note. — The Annals close with the death of Queen Anne, 1714. The appendix contains bibliographical lists of works on English history, historical publications by the government, and societies, the Record reports, etc., and an index of statutes.

FOR a woman's sake, or, the mysteries of the castle. Wachenhusen, H. 721.5
FOR summer afternoons. Woolsey, S. C. 539.13
FORNEY, John Weiss. A centennial commissioner in Europe. 1874–76. Philadelphia, 1876. 412 pp. 12° 436.10
FORRESTER, *Mrs.* —. My hero 522.27
FORSTER, John. Biographical essays. 3d edition. London, 1860. xxxi, 487+ pp. Sm. 8° 5425.12

Contents. — Oliver Cromwell; Daniel De Foe; Sir Richard Steele; Charles Churchill; Samuel Foote.

FORTNIGHTLY review. New series. Vol. 17, 18. London, 1875. 2 v. 6713.1
FORTUNE hunter, The: a novel of New York society. Ritchie, A. C. 530.20
FORTUNES, The, of Miss Follen. Talcott, H. B. 722.23
FOX-HUNTING. Stephens, C. A. 927.25
FRAMLEY parsonage. Trollope, A. 334.12
FRANCE. Freer, M. W. Henry III, king of France and Poland: his court and times. London, 1858. 3 v. Sm. 8° 5525.13
— Hamerton, P. G. Round my house; notes of rural life in France in peace and war. Boston, 1876. 16° 827.4
— Lacroix, P. The XVIIIth century. Its institutions, customs, and costumes. France, 1700–1789. London, 1876. L. 8° 5510.3
— Loménie, L. L. de. Beaumarchais and his times. Sketches of French society in the 18th century. London, 1856. 4 v. Sm. 8° 5527.19
FRANCIS I, *king of France*, The court and reign of. Pardoe, J. London, 1849. 2 v. 8° 5511.5
FRANK Mildmay; or, the naval officer. Marryat, F. 520.6
FRANKLIN, Benjamin. Abbott, J. S. C. New York [1876]. 12° 1014.17
FREER, Martha Walker. Henry III, king of France and Poland: his court and times. London, 1858. 3 v. Portraits. Sm. 8° 5525.13
— Life of Marguerite d'Angoulême, queen of Navarre, duchesse d'Alençon and de Berry, sister of Francis I, king of France. From numerous unpublished sources, etc. London, 1854. 2 v. Portraits. Sm. 8° 5527.20
FROM the earth to the moon. Verne, J. London, 1876. Sm. 8° 715.28
FROTHINGHAM, Octavius Brooks. Transcendentalism in New England. A history. New York, 1876. ix, 395 pp. Portrait. 12° 6325.21
FUTURE life, The unseen universe, or physical speculations on a. Tait, P. G., and Stewart, B. London, 1875. 8° 5834.6

GALLUS, or Roman scenes of the time of Augustus. Becker, W. A. London, 1873. Sm. 8° 6117.14
GARDINER, Samuel Rawson. The first two Stuarts and the puritan revolution, 1603–1660. With four maps. London, 1876. xxi, 215+ pp. [Morris, E. E., and Phillpotts, J. S., *editors*. Epochs of modern history.] 16° 5419.2
GARETH and Lynette. Tennyson, A. Poetical works. Leipzig, 1872. Sq. 16° 1614.10.4
GARTENLAUBE, Die. 1856. Leipzig, 1856. L. 4°. 1330.2
GAY, Sydney Howard, *joint author*. A popular history of the United States. *See* BRYANT, William Cullen 610.5
GAZETTE des beaux-arts. Tome 11, 12. Paris, 1875. 2 v. Illustrated. L. 8° 5322.1
GEGENWART, Die. Band 7, 8. Berlin, 1875. 2 v. in 1. 4°. 6722.1
GENEALOGIES. Keppel, G. T. Fifty years of my life. London, 1876. 2 v. 8° 5333.8
— Whitmore, W. H. The American genealogist. Albany, 1868. 8° 5022.7

Shelf. No.

GENTZ, Friedrich von. *See* HAYWARD, A. Biographical and critical essays. London, 1873. 8° 5833.3.1

GEORGE III, *king of England.* Correspondence with Lord North from 1768 to 1783. Edited from the originals at Windsor, with an introduction and notes, by W. Bodham Donne. London, 1867. 2 v. 8° 5624.5

— Journal of the reign of, from 1771 to 1783. Walpole, H. London, 1859. 2 v. 8° 5624.6

GERMANY. Howitt, W. The student-life of. London, 1841. 8° 5712.4

— Tuttle, H. German political leaders. New York, 1876. 16° 628.9

GIANNETTO. Majendie, *Lady* M. (E.) 117.1

GIRLS of Feversham, The. Church, F. 530.21

GLADSTONE, *Mrs.* George. Tom Gillies; the knots he tied and untied. [*Also,* Willie Russell's temptation. *Anon.*] 931.13

GLIMPSES of the supernatural, The other world; or. Lee, F. G. London, 1875. 2 v. Sm. 8° 6327.24

GOLD und Name. Schwartz, M. S. New-York, N. D. 2 v. 16° 2028.3

GOLDEN robin, The. [Music.] Perkins, W. O. Boston [*cop.* 1863]. Oblong 12° 1518.15

GOLDSMITH, Christabel, *pseud.* *See* SMITH, Fannie N.

GONNEVILLE, Aymar Olivier Le Harivel de. Recollections. Published by his daughter, the countess of Mirabeau, with an introductory sketch by general baron Ambert. Edited from the French, by Charlotte M. Yonge. London, 1875. 2 v. Sm. 8° 5525.14

GOODRICH, Charles Augustus. History of the United States. Illustrated. Added, the Constitution of the United States, and the Declaration of independence. Revised from former editions. Boston, 1858. 433 pp. 12° 615.1

GOODWIN, *Mrs.* H. B. *See* TALCOTT, H. B.

GOULDING, F. R. The young marooners, on the Florida coast; or, Robert and Harold 1127.5

GRAHAM, James, *1st marquis of Montrose.* Montrose and the covenanters. Napier, M. London, 1838. 2 v. 8° 5411.2

GRANDFATHER'S Nell; or, what happened at the toll-gate. By the author of "Squire Downing's heirs" [etc.] 1127.8

GRANT, Ulysses Simpson. *See* BROCKETT, L. P. Our great captains. New York, 1865. 12° 1015.8

GREAT BRITAIN. Commentaries on the life and reign of Charles the first, king of England. Disraeli, I. London, 1851. 2 v. 8° 5421.6

GREECE. Charicles, or illustrations of the private life of the Greeks. Becker, W. A. London, 1874. Sm. 8°. 6117.15

GREEN, John Richard, *editor.* Literature primers. *Namely:* —

— Brooke, S. A. English literature 1738.3

GREENE, Annie D. Peter and Polly, or home-life in New England a hundred years ago. By Marian Douglas [*pseud.*] 119.1

GREENWELL, Dora. The patience of hope. Boston, 1862. 171 pp. Sm. 8° 1535.7

GREEY, Edward. Blue jackets; or, the adventures of J. Thompson among "the heathen Chinee." A nautical novel 730.22

GUERNSEY, Lucy Ellen. Irish Amy 929.12

— Milly; or, the hidden cross 1114.3

GUILLEMIN, Amédée. Petite encyclopédie populaire. La lumière et les couleurs. Illustré de figures sur bois. Paris, 1874. viii, 302 pp. 16° 2015.8

GUIZOT, François (Pierre Guillaume). Memoirs to illustrate the history of my time. Translated by J. W. Cole. London, 1858–61. 4 v. 8° 5512.4

HADERMANN, Jeanette R. Heavy yokes 530.19

HAIDEPRINZESSCHEN, Das. John, E. Leipzig, 1872. 2 v. 16° 5736.3

HALE, Edward. The fall of the Stuarts and Western Europe from 1678 to 1697. With maps and plans. London, 1876. xi, 240+ pp. [Morris, E. E., and Phillpotts, J. S., *editors.* Epochs of modern history.] 16° 5419.1

Shelf. No.

HALL, John. Familiar talks to boys. New York [1876]. 98 pp. 12° 1916.10

HALVES. [Fiction.] Payn, J. Leipzig 334.2

HAMERSLY, Lewis R. Records of living officers of the U. S. navy and marine corps; with a history of naval operations during the rebellion of 1861–5. Philadelphia, 1870. 350 pp. 8° 5022.14

HAMERTON, Philip Gilbert. Round my house; notes of rural life in France in peace and war. Boston, 1876. xii, 415 pp. 16° 827.4

— The sylvan year. Leaves from the note-book of Raoul Dubois. [*Also,* The unknown river. An etcher's voyage of discovery.] Boston, 1876. 2 v. in 1. Portrait. 16° 5527.18

HAMLEY, Edward Bruce. The operations of war explained and illustrated. 3d edition. Edinburgh, 1872. xxv, 479 pp. Folded maps and plans. 4° 5910.6

HAND, The, of Ethelberta. Hardy, T. 517.25

HARDY, Thomas. Leisure hour series. The hand of Ethelberta. A comedy in chapters 517.25

HARE, Augustus John Cuthbert. Memorials of a quiet life. Supplementary volume [III]. With 57 photographs. London, 1876. vi, 263 pp. Sm. 8° 5427.1.3

HARGREAVES, William. Our wasted resources; the missing link in the temperance reform. New York, 1876. 201 pp. 12° 5835.8

HARPER'S bazar. Vol. 8. New York, 1875. F°. .. 1430.1

HARRIS, Thaddeus Mason. The natural history of the Bible. Boston, 1820. xl, 476 pp. 8° 6323.11

HAWTHORNE, Nathaniel. The Dolliver romance and other pieces. Boston, 1876. 213 pp. 12° 1813.13

— Fanshawe and other pieces. Boston, 1876. 243 pp. 12° 1813.12

Contents. — Fanshawe; Biographical sketches: Mrs. Hutchinson; Sir William Phips; Sir William Pepperell; Thomas Green Fessenden; Jonathan Cilley.

— A study of Hawthorne. Lathrop, G. P. Boston, 1876. Sq. 16° 1839.4

HAY, Mary Cecil. Hidden perils. A novel 530.18

HAYWARD, Abraham. Biographical and critical essays. Reprinted from reviews, with additions and corrections. Vol. 1, 2, 2d edition. London, 1873, 74. 3 v. 8° 5833.3

Contents. — Vol. I. The pearls and mock pearls of history; Frederic von Gentz; Maria Edgeworth: her life and writings; George Canning as a man of letters; Marshal Saxe; Sylvain Van de Weyer; Alexander Dumas; Salons; Whist and whist-players. II. Varieties of history and art; Edward Livingston; Richard the third; Marie Antoinette; The countess of Albany and Alfieri; Sir Henry Holland's Recollections; Lady Palmerston; Lord Lansdowne; Lord Dalling and Bulwer; More about Junius. III. The British parliament: its history and eloquence; Curiosities of German archives; England and France: their national qualities, manners, morals, and society; Lanfrey's Napoleon; Vicissitudes of families: English, Scotch, Irish, and continental nobility; Lives of the Lord chancellors of Ireland; The second Armada; The purchase system.

HEAVENWARD — EARTHWARD. MacKeever, H. B. .. 1127.11

HEAVY yokes. Hadermann, J. R. 530.19

HELEN Erskine. Robinson, *Mrs.* M. H. 116.3

HELPS, *Sir* Arthur. The Spanish conquest in America. New York, 1856. 4 v. Map. 12°. 816.6

HENRY III, *king of France and Poland.* His court and times. Freer, M. W. London, 1858. 3 v. Sm. 8° 5525.13

HENSLOW, John Stevens. A dictionary of botanical terms. New edition. Illustrated. London [1861]. 218+ pp. Sm. 8° 6627.4

HEPWORTH, George Hughes. Starboard and port: the "Nettie" along shore. New York, 1876. 237 pp. Map. Illustrations. 12° 435.5

HERALD of health. Vol. 59, 60. New York, 1875. 2 v. in 1. 8° 1325.1

HIDDEN perils. A novel. Hay, M. C. 530.18

HIGGINSON, Thomas Wentworth, *editor.* Brief biographies of European public men. *Namely:* —

— Tuttle, H. German political leaders. New York, 1876. 16° 628.9

HIGHLANDS, The, of the city. Black, W. 331.28

HOLLAND, *Sir* Henry. Recollections. *See* HAYWARD, A. Biographical and critical essays. London, 1873. 8° 5833.3.2

Shelf. No.

HOLLAND, John, *editor*. Memorials of Sir Francis Chantrey, sculptor, in Hallamshire and elsewhere. London [1851]. 364+ pp. Woodcut. Sm. 8° 5338.2
HOME, The. [Fiction.] Bremer, F. 730.20
HOPKINS, Ellice. Rose Turquand 530.25
HOPKINS, Livingston. A comic history of the United States. New York, 1876. 223 pp. Illustrated. 12° 617.3
HOUSE, The, on the heights. MacKeever, H. B. ... 717.17
HOUSEHOLD art. The book of American interiors. Elliott, C. W. Boston, 1876. 4° 6230.4
HOWITT, Anna Mary. An art-student in Munich. London, 1853. 2 v. in 1. Sm. 8° 6215.1
HOWITT, William. The student-life of Germany: from the unpublished MS. of Dr. Cornelius. Containing nearly forty of the most famous student songs, with the original music, adapted to the piano-forte, by Winkelmeyer. Illustrated. London, 1841. xviii, 484 pp. 8° 5712.4
HUC, Évariste Régis. Travels in Tartary, Thibet, and China, 1844–6. Translated from the French by W. Hazlitt. Illustrated. London [1852]. 2 v. Folded map. 16° 5935.12
HUDSON, Elizabeth Harriet. The life and times of Louisa, queen of Prussia. With an introductory sketch of Prussian history. 2d edition. London, 1876. 2 v. Portrait. Sm. 8° 5726.5
HUNT'S merchants' magazine, and commercial review. Vol. 1–34, 41–43. New York, 1840–60. 37 v. 8° 1322.1
HYMNOLOGY. A collection of psalms and hymns, for social and private worship. 3d edition. Boston, 1832. 12° 6328.26

IDA Craven. Cadell, H. M. 517.27
ILLUSTRATED London news. Vol. 1–67. London, 1842–75. 67 v. F° 5134.1
— *Same*. Vol. 28, 31. London, 1856, 57. 2 v. F° 1410.1
ILLUSTRATION, L'. Tome 66. Paris, 1875. F° 5321.1
IMAGINARY voyages. Verne, J. Five weeks in a balloon. New York, 1869. 8° 735.26
— – *Same*. London, 1876. Sm. 8° 715.30
— – From the earth to the moon direct in 97 hours 20 minutes: and a trip round it. New York, 1874. 8° 734.15
— – *Same*. London, 1876. Sm. 8° 715.28
— – Round the moon. London, 1876. Sm. 8° 715.29
— – Twenty thousand leagues under the seas. London, 1876. Sm. 8° 715.27
IMMORTALITY. The unseen universe, or physical speculations on a future state. Tait, P. G., and Stewart, B. London, 1875. 8° 5834.6
IN a winter city. A sketch. Rame, L. de la. Leipzig 331.30
INDEPENDENCE, a centennial love story. Alcott, L. M. 718.9
INDEPENDENCE hall, *Philadelphia, Pa*. An historical account of the old state house of Pennsylvania. Etting, F. M. Boston, 1876. Sm. 4° 5220.1
INDUSTRIAL arts. Lacroix, P. The arts in the middle ages and at the period of the renaissance. London, 1875. L. 8° 6230.5
— *See* SOUTH KENSINGTON museum, *London*. [London, 1876.] 8° 6423.6
INFANTRY tactics; or, rules for the exercise and manœuvres of the United States infantry. Scott, W. New York, 1852. 3 v. 16° 1529.7
INVENTIONS. Discoveries and inventions of the nineteenth century. Routledge, R. London, 1876. Sm. 8° 1522.17
IRISH Amy. Guernsey, L. E. 929.12
ITALY, a poem. Rogers, S. London, 1842. 8° 5515.5

JAMES, George Payne Rainsford. Richelieu. A tale of France 722.22
JASMINE Leigh. Tytler, C. C. F. 717.19
JEAFFRESON, John Cordy. A book about the clergy. London, 1870. 2 v. 8° .... 1231.4 and 6320.6
JESSICA'S first prayer. Smith, H. 1128.3

Shelf. No.

JEWS. The antiquities of Israel. Ewald, (G.) H. (A.) London, 1876. 8° 5811.13
JUNIUS, *pseud*. More about Junius. Hayward, A. Biographical and critical essays. London, 1873. 8° 5833.3.2

KAVANAGH, Julia. A summer and winter in the two Sicilies. Leipzig, 1858. 2 v. in 1. Sq. 16° ... 428.4
KENNEDY, W. R. Sporting adventures in the Pacific, whilst in command of the "Reindeer." London, 1876. 303+ pp. Illustrated. 8° 5912.6
KEPPEL, George Thomas, *6th earl of Albemarle*. Fifty years of my life. 2d edition, enlarged. London, 1876. 2 v. Portrait. Folded sheet. 8° 5333.8
KINGLAKE, Alexander William. The invasion of the Crimea: its origin, and an account of its progress down to the death of Lord Raglan. With all the plans, maps and emendations of the 3d London edition. Vol. I–X. Leipzig, 1863–75. 10 v. in 4. Sq. 16° 837.2

Contents. — Vol. I, II. Transactions which brought on the war. III–VIII. Invasion of the Crimea. IX, X. Battle of Inkerman.

KINGSLEY, Henry. Ravenshoe 326.20
KINGSTON, William H. G. Adrift in a boat 931.12
— The child of the wreck; or, the loss of the Royal George 1118.13
KNOWLES, James Sheridan. Dramatic works. London [1858]. 2 v. in 1. Portrait. Sm. 8° 5626.12

LACROIX, Paul. The arts in the middle ages and at the period of the renaissance. Illustrated with 10 chromolithographic prints and upwards of 400 engravings on wood. London, 1875. xix, 520 pp. L. 8° 6230.5
— Manners, customs, and dress during the middle ages, and during the renaissance period. Illustrated with 19 chromolithographic prints and upwards of 400 engravings on wood. London, 1876. xviii, 554 pp. L. 8° 6230.6
— The XVIIIth century. Its institutions, customs, and costumes. France, 1700–1789. [From the French.] Illustrated with 21 chromolithographs and 351 wood engravings. London, 1876. xvi, 489 pp. L. 8° 5510.3
LADY Silverdale's sweetheart. Black, W. 331.28
"LAND, The, of the sky." Fisher, F. C. 730.15
LANETON parsonage. Sewell, E. M. 3 v. 532.7
LANGDON, Mary, *pseud*. *See* PIKE, Mary Hayden.
LANMAN, Charles. Biographical annals of the civil government of the United States during its first century. From original and official sources. Washington, 1876. 6, 676 pp. 8° .... *R.R., C.3.2
LAST house, The, on C—— street. Craik, D. (M.) Leipzig 323.27
— *Same*. New York 530.23
LATHROP, George Parsons. A study of Hawthorne. Boston, 1876. 350 pp. Wood-cut. Sq. 16° ... 1839.4
LAWRENCE'S adventures among the ice-cutters, glass-makers, coal-miners, iron-men, and ship-builders. Trowbridge, J. T. 932.20
LEE, Frederick George, *editor*. The other world; or, glimpses of the supernatural. Being facts, records, and traditions relating to dreams, omens, miraculous occurrences, etc. London, 1875. 2 v. Sm. 8° 6327.24
LEFT-HANDED Elsa. [Reprinted from Blackwood's magazine] 717.16
LEGER, Theodor. Animal magnetism; or psycodunamy. New York, 1846. 402 pp. 12° 1522.16
LEISURE hour series. *Namely* : —
— Cadell, H. M. Ida Craven 517.27
— Majendie, *Lady* M. (E.) Giannetto 117.1
— Maxwell, C. A story of three sisters 517.26
LESLIE, Emma. Ellerslie house. A book for boys. 939.7
LESTER, Charles Edwards. The artists of America: a series of biographical sketches of American artists; with portraits and designs on steel. New York, 1846. vi, 257+ pp. 8° 1012.8
LESTRANGE family, The. A true story. Wilmer, M. E. 1127.7

Shelf. No.

LETO, Pomponio, *pseud.* The Vatican council. Eight months at Rome during the Vatican council. Impressions of a contemporary. Translated from the original. London, 1876. xx, 340 pp. 8°. 5511.4

LIE, Jonas. A Norse love story. The pilot and his wife. Translated by Mrs. Ole Bull 116.1

LIFE, Nature and. Papillon, F. New York, 1875. 12° 1735.6

LIFE, The, and death of Jason. A poem. Morris, W. London, 1872. Sm. 8° 6114.5

LIGHT. La lumière et les couleurs. Guillemin, A. Paris, 1874. 16° 2015.8

LINTON, Eliza Lynn. The atonement of Leam Dundas. [Fiction] 730.19

LITERATURE primers. *Namely:* —

— Brooke, S. A. English literature 1738.3

LITTLE Gordon, The. Church, F. 331.31

LITTLE Meg's children. Smith, H. 1128.2

LITTLE wanderers', The, advocate. Vol. 8, 10. Boston, 1872, 74. 2 v. 8° 1335.2

LIVERMORE, Nathaniel, Sermon on the death of. Ware, J. F. W. Cambridge, 1862. 8° 6323.1

LIVIUS PATAVINUS, Titus. The history of Rome. The first eight books. Literally translated, with notes and illustrations, by D. Spillan. London, 1875. 4 v. [Bohn's Classical library.] Sm. 8°. 6117.11

— *Same.* Books I–X. With introduction, historical examination, and notes. By J. R. Seeley. Book I, 2d edition. Oxford, 1874. [Clarendon press series.] 8° 6112.3

— Livy [outlined and explained]. Collins, W. L. Philadelphia, 1876. 16° 6116.22

LOMÉNIE, Louis Léonard de. Beaumarchais and his times. Sketches of French society in the 18th century from unpublished documents. Translated by Henry S. Edwards. London, 1856. 4 v. Sm. 8° 5527.19

LONDON illustrated news. Extra supplements. PPH. v. London [etc.], [1873–75]. 69 plates. F°. *R.R. Desk

Note. — Several from The graphic and other illustrated papers.

LORD Erlistoun. Craik, D. (M.) Leipzig 323.27

— *Same.* New York 530.23

LOUIS IX, *or St. Louis, king of France.* The good St. Louis and his times. Bray, A. E. London, 1870. Sm. 8° 5937.13

LOUISE AUGUSTA WILHELMINE AMÉLIE, *queen of Prussia*, The life and times of. Hudson, E. H. London, 1876. 2 v. Sm. 8° 5726.5

LOW marriage, A. Craik, D. (M.) Leipzig 330.22

— *Same.* New York 530.23

LUCKY disappointment, A. Church, F. Boston 718.6

— *Same.* Leipzig 331.31

LUDLOW, John Malcolm. The war of American independence, 1775–1783. With four maps. London, 1876. xviii, 246+ pp. [Morris, E. E., and Phillpotts, J. S., *editors.* Epochs of modern history.] 16° 5018.1

MACAULAY, Thomas Babington, *lord.* Life and letters. By his nephew George Otto Trevelyan. With portrait. Leipzig, 1876. 4 v. in 2. Sq. 16°. 1237.4

— *Same.* New York, 1876. 2 v. Portrait. 8° .. 5332.8

MACCARTHY [McCarthy], Justin. Dear Lady Disdain. Leipzig 331.29

— *Same.* New York 721.23

MACDONALD [McDonald], Flora. The autobiography of Flora McDonald, being the home life of a heroine. Edited by her grand-daughter. Edinburgh, 1870. 2 v. in 1. Portrait. Sm. 8°. 5338.3

MACDONALD, George. Thomas Wingfold, curate ... 536.24

MACGILVRAY, Walter. John of the golden mouth; preacher of Antioch, and primate of Constantinople. London, 1871. xvi, 358 pp. Sm. 8°. 5937.14

MACKEEVER [McKeever], Harriet B. Heavenward — earthward 1127.11

— The house on the heights 717.17

MACMILLAN's magazine. Vol. 33. London, 1876. 8°. 6527.1

MAJENDIE, *Lady* Margaret (Elizabeth). Leisure hour series. Giannetto 117.1

MALET, Harold Esdaile. Annals of the road, or notes on mail and stage coaching in Great Britain. To which are added essays on the road, by Nimrod [*pseud.* of C. J. Apperley]. London, 1876. xiii, 403+ pp. Colored plates. 8° 5433.4

MAN, The, who was like Shakspeare. Black, W. Leipzig 331.28

— *Same.* New York 711.9

MANNERS and minor morals. Familiar talks to boys. Hall, J. New York [1876]. 12° 1916.10

MARGUERITE D'ANGOULÊME, *queen of Navarre*, Life of. Freer, M. W. London, 1854. 2 v. Sm. 8°. 5527.20

MARRIAGE, The, of Moira Fergus. Black, W. Boston. 720.30

— *Same.* Leipzig 331.28

MARRYAT, Frederick. Frank Mildmay; or, the naval officer 520.6

— Rattlin, the reefer 520.7

MARTIN, W. S. Our school days. Edited by C. S. Harington 1127.10

MARTIN Paz. Verne, J. Boston 529.6

— *Same.* London 715.34

MASSACHUSETTS. *Legislative documents. Board of agriculture.* 18th–23d annual report of the secretary. Boston, 1871–76. 6 v. Illustrated. 8°. 6921.3

— — *Board of health.* 7th annual report. Boston, 1876. xxii, 551 pp. Charts. Plans. Plates. Diagrams. Folded maps. 8° 6913.3

MASTER Zacharius. Verne, J. Boston 529.2

— *Same.* London 715.36

MATHEWS, William. Words; their use and abuse. Chicago, 1876. 384 pp. 12° 1736.10

MAXWELL, Cecil. Leisure hour series. A story of three sisters 517.26

MAYO, Isabella Fivy. The crust and the cake. By Edward Garrett [*pseud.*] 115.1

MEG Hartley's cure. Church, F. 331.31

MEMORIALS of a quiet life. Supplementary volume. Hare, A. J. C. London, 1876. Sm. 8° 5427.1.3

MERCERSBURG theology inconsistent with protestant and reformed doctrine. Schneck, B. S. Philadelphia, 1874. 12° 6326.14

META Holdenis. Cherbuliez, V. Paris, 1875. 16°. 2016.13

METHODIST quarterly review. Vol. 31, 41, 44, 45, 57. New York, 1857–75. 5 v. 8° 6727.1

MICROSCOPE, Common objects of the. Wood, J. G. London [1866]. Sm. 8° 1528.14

MIDDLE ages. Lacroix, P. The arts in the. London, 1875. L. 8° 6230.5

— — Manners, customs, and dress during the. London, 1876. L. 8° 6230.6

MIRIAM. Terhune, M. V. 722.24

MISSALE Romanum. *See* ROMAN catholic church ... 5816.14

MRS. Armington's ward; or, the inferior sex. [A novel.] Wright, D. T. 714.1

MITCHELL, Anne M. The cash-boy's trust 1127.13

MONDE illustré, Le. Tome 36, 37. Paris, 1875. 2 v. F° 5320.1

MONTROSE, *Earl of. See* GRAHAM, James, *1st marquis of Montrose.*

MOODY Mike; or, the power of love. A Christmas story. Sewall, F. 1128.4

MORRIS, Edward E., and PHILLPOTTS, James Surtees, *editors.* Epochs of modern history. *Namely:* —

— Gardiner, S. R. The first two Stuarts and the puritan revolution, 1603–1660. London, 1876. 16° 5419.2

— Hale, E. The fall of the Stuarts and Western Europe from 1678 to 1697. London, 1876. 16°. 5419.1

— Ludlow, J. M. The war of American independence, 1775–1783. London, 1876. 16° 5018.1

MORRIS, William. The life and death of Jason. A poem. 6th edition. London, 1872. 367+ pp. Sm. 8° 6114.5

MOSS-SIDE. Terhune, M. V. 722.28

MUNICH, An art-student in. Howitt, A. M. London, 1853. 2 v. in 1. Sm. 8° 6215.1

MURRAY, John, *publisher.* Handbook for Scotland. 4th edition, revised. With travelling maps and plans. London, 1875. 478 pp. 12° 5437.3

MY hero. Forrester, *Mrs.* — 522.27

MY sister's confession. Braddon, M. E. 730.24

Shelf. No.

NAPIER, Mark. Montrose and the covenanters, their characters and conduct, illustrated from private letters and other documents hitherto unpublished, embracing the times of Charles the first, from the rise of the troubles in Scotland, to the death of Montrose. London, 1838. 2 v. Facsimile. 8° 5411.2
NARROW escape, A. Cudlip, A. Boston 730.16
— *Same.* Leipzig 317.23
NATURE. Vol. 13. London, 1876. L. 8° 6733.1
NELLY'S dark days. Smith, H. 1118.14
NEW-ENGLAND farmer, The, or, georgical dictionary. Deane, S. Boston, 1822. 8° 6423.3
NEW YORK, *State.* Pioneer history of the Holland purchase of western New York. Turner, O. Buffalo, 1849. 8° 612.9
NORTH, Frederick, *2d earl of Guilford, called lord North,* Correspondence of George the third with, from 1768 to 1783. *See* GEORGE III, *king of England* 5624.5
NORTON, Andrews. A statement of reasons for not believing the doctrines of trinitarians, concerning the nature of God, and the person of Christ. Cambridge, 1833. xxxix, 331 pp. 12° 5816.25
NOTHING new. Tales. Craik, D. (M.) 530.23

ŒCUMENICAL council, 1869, 70. Leto, P., *pseud.* The Vatican council. London, 1876. 8° 5511.4
OFF to the Geysers. Stephens, C. A. 1127.2
OLD Kensington. Thackeray, A. I. Leipzig 339.13
OLIVER of the mill. A tale. Charlesworth, M. L. 722.26
ONE poor girl: the story of thousands. Sikes, W. 116.4
OTHER world, The; or, glimpses of the supernatural. Lee, F. G., London, 1875. 2 v. Sm. 8° 6327.24
OUR great captains. Brockett, L. P. New York, 1865. 12° 1015.8
OUR school days. Martin, W. S. 1127.10

PACIFIC ocean. Sporting adventures in the Pacific, whilst in command of the "Reindeer." Kennedy, W. R. London, 1876. 8° 5912.6
PALL MALL budget. Vol. 15. London, 1875. F°. 6720.1
PARDOE, Julia. The court and reign of Francis the first, king of France. London, 1849. 2 v. Portraits. 8° 5511.5
PAYN, James. A woman's vengeance 730.23
PEARD, Frances Mary. A winter story 331.27
PERIODICALS. Army and navy journal. Vol. 12. New York, 1874-75. F° 6530.1
— L'art. Revue hebdomadaire illustrée. Tome 1, 3, 4. Paris, 1875, 76. 3 v. F° 5310.1
— Deutsche Rundschau. Band 5, 6. Berlin, 1875, 76. 2 v. 8° 6513.1
— Dexter Smith's musical, literary, dramatic and art paper. Vol. 7. Boston, 1875. 4° 1331.1
— Die Gartenlaube. 1856. Leipzig, 1856. L. 4°. 1330.2
— Macmillan's magazine. Vol. 33. London, 1876. 8°. 6527.1
— Le monde illustré. Tome 36, 37. Paris, 1875. 2 v. F° 5320.1
— Nature. Vol. 13. London, 1876. L. 8° 6733.1
— Pall Mall budget. Vol. 15. London, 1875. F°. 6720.1
— Popular science monthly. Vol. 8. New York, 1876. 8° 6516.1
— Quarterly review. Vol. 139. London, 1875. 8°. 6717.1
— Revue des deux mondes. Troisième période, Tome 14. Paris, 1876. 8° 5315.1
— Westminster review. Vol. 48. London, 1875. 8°. 6737.1
PERKINS, William O. The golden robin, for the use of juvenile classes, public schools, and seminaries. Boston [*cop.* 1863]. 223+ pp. Oblong 12°. 1518.15
PETER and Polly, or home-life in New England a hundred years ago. Greene, A. D. 119.1
PHILADELPHIA, *Pa.* An historical account of the old state house of Pennsylvania. Etting, F. M. Boston, 1876. Sm. 4° 5220.1
PHILLPOTTS, James Surtees, *joint editor.* Epochs of modern history. *See* MORRIS, Edward E.
PHOTOGRAPHY. The silver sunbeam: a practical and theoretical text-book on sun drawing and photographic printing. Towler, J. New York, 1864. 12° 1713.6
PIANO-FORTE music, A choice collection of. *See* WELCOME home. Boston [*cop.* 1874]. 4° 1510.2
PIKE, Mary Hayden. (*Mary Langdon.*) Safely married! A novel 721.7
PILOT, The, and his wife. A Norse love story. Lie, J. 116.1
POLYNESIA, Los Gringos; or, wanderings in. Wise, H. A. New York, 1849. 12° 435.4
POPULAR science monthly. Vol. 8. New York, 1876. 8° 6516.1
PORTER, Rose. The winter fire. A sequel to "Summer drift-wood" 717.22
PRITCHARD, Sarah J. Rose Marbury 1127.3
PULPIT, The, of the American revolution: or, the political sermons of the period of 1776. Thornton, J. W. Boston [1876]. 8° 1921.4
PUTNAM'S handy-book series. *Namely:* —
— Stockton, F. R. and M. The home: where it should be and what to put in it 1515.10

QUARTERLY review. Vol. 139. London, 1875. 8°. 6717.1

RAME, Louise de la. In a winter city. A sketch. By Ouida [*pseud.*]. Leipzig 331.30
RAND, Edward Sprague, *jr.* Garden flowers: how to cultivate them. A treatise on the culture of hardy ornamental trees, shrubs, annuals [etc.]. New York, 1876 [*cop.* 1866]. 384 pp. 16° 6625.7
RANDOLPH, *Mrs.* —. Wild Hyacinth. A novel 714.32
RATTLIN, the reefer. Marryat, F. 520.7
REASON why, The: general science. A careful collection of reasons for things which, though generally believed, are imperfectly understood. A book of condensed scientific knowledge for the million. By the author of "Inquire within" [etc.]. New York [*cop.* 1869]. 346 pp. Illustrated. 12° 1527.23
RECEIPTS. Webster, *Mrs.* A. L. The improved housewife, or book of. Hartford, 1850. 12° ... 1533.17
— Wright, A. S. Wright's book of 3000 practical receipts. New York [1852]. 12° 1533.10
RENAISSANCE, The arts at the period of the. Lacroix, P. London, 1875. L. 8° 6230.5
REVUE des deux mondes. Troisième période, Tome 14. Paris, 1876. 8° 5315.1
RITCHIE, Anna Cora, *formerly Mrs. Mowatt.* The fortune hunter: a novel of New York society 530.20
ROBINSON, *Mrs.* M. Harrison. Helen Erskine 116.3
ROGERS, Samuel. Italy, a poem. London, 1842. vii, 320 pp. Illustrated. 8° 5515.5
ROMANTIC Belinda. Tuthill, L. C. 1127.12
ROSE Marbury. Pritchard, S. J. 1127.3
ROSE Turquand. Hopkins, E. 530.25
RUBY'S husband. Terhune, M. V. 722.29

SAFELY married! A novel. Pike, M. H. 721.7
SAINTS and sinners; or, in church and about it. Doran, J. W. London, 1868. 2 v. in 1. Sm. 8°. 6325.24
SANITARY arrangements for dwellings. Eassie, W. London, 1874. 16° 6226.8
SAWYER, George A. Fret-sawing and wood-carving for amateurs. Illustrated. Boston, 1875. 63 pp. Sm. 4° 1515.19
SCHUCKING, Levin. Fire and flame. From the German. Translated by Eva M. Johnson 520.5
SCIENCE. Reason why, The: general science. New York [*cop.* 1869]. 12° 1527.23
SERMONS. The pulpit of the American revolution: or, the political sermons of the period of 1776. Thornton, J. W. Boston [1876]. 8° 1921.4
SEWALL, Frank. Moody Mike; or, the power of love. A Christmas story 1128.4
SHERIDAN, Philip Henry. *See* BROCKETT, L. P. Our great captains. New York, 1865. 12° 1015.8
SHERMAN, William Tecumseh. *See* BROCKETT, L. P. Our great captains. New York, 1865. 12° 1015.8
SIKES, Wirt. One poor girl: the story of thousands. 116.4
SILENT witness, A. Yates, E. Leipzig 317.24
SILVER sunbeam, The. Towler, J. New York, 1864. 12° 1713.6
SIR Marcus's choice. Church, F. 331.31

Shelf. No.

SOUTH KENSINGTON museum, *London*. The industrial arts. Historical sketches with numerous illustrations. [Edited by William Maskell.] Published for the committee of council on education. [London, 1876.] xiv, 276 pp. 8° 6423.6

Contents. — Gold and silver work; Bronze, copper, and iron; Enamels; Ivories; Pottery and porcelain; Maiolica; Glass; Mosaics; Arms and armour; Textile fabrics; Lace.

SOUTHWORTH, Emma Dorothy Eliza Nevitte. The artist's love. And stories by Frances Henshaw Baden 522.28

SPENCER, Herbert. Illustrations of universal progress; a series of discussions. New York, 1872. xxiv, 451 pp. 12° 6835.3

SPIRITUALISM, *or* Spiritism. The other world; or, glimpses of the supernatural. Lee, F. G. London, 1875. 2 v. Sm. 8° 6327.24

SPORTING adventures in the Pacific. Kennedy, W. R. London, 1876. 8° 5912.6

STARBOARD and port: the "Nettie" along shore. Hepworth, G. H. New York, 1876. 12° 435.5

STRANGE horse, The, of Loch Suainabhal. Black, W. 331.28

SUPERNATURAL, The other world; or, glimpses of the. Lee, F. G. London, 1875. 2 v. Sm. 8° 6327.24

TAYLOR, (James) Bayard. The Echo club, and other literary diversions. Boston, 1876. 187 pp. 16° 1539.4

THIRTY years' war, Gustavus Adolphus in Germany, and other lectures on the. Trench, R. C. London, 1872. Sm. 8° 5717.2

TIMOTHY Crump's ward. Alger, H., *jr*. 1126.1

TOM Gillies; the knots he tied and untied. Gladstone, *Mrs.* G. 931.13

"Too good for him." Church, F. 530.22

Shelf. No.

TOWLER, John. The silver sunbeam: a practical and theoretical text-book on sun drawing and photographic printing: comprehending all the wet and dry processes at present known; as also heliographic engraving, photolithography [etc.]. 3d edition, enlarged. New York, 1864. 373+ pp. 12° 1713.6

TURNER, O. Pioneer history of the Holland purchase of western New York: embracing some account of the ancient remains; a brief history of the confederated Iroquois, and a history of pioneer settlement under the Holland company; including reminiscences of the war of 1812; Erie canal, etc. Buffalo, 1849. 666 pp. Maps. Portraits. Illustrations. 8° 612.9

TUTHILL, Louisa Caroline. Romantic Belinda 1127.12

UNITED STATES. *History. Civil war*, 1861–65. Adrift in Dixie; or, a Yankee officer among the rebels. Estabrooks, H. L. New York, 1866. 16° 715.33

VOSS, Sophie Wilhelmine Charlotte Marie, *Gräfinn* von. Sixty-nine years at the court of Prussia, from the recollections of the mistress of the household. Translated from the German by Emily and Agnes Stephenson. London, 1876. 2 v. Portrait. Sm. 8° 5727.5

WALPOLE, Horace. Journal of the reign of George the third, from 1771 to 1783. Edited, with notes, by Dr. Doran. London, 1859. 2 v. Portraits. 8°. 5624.6

WATER cure, The. Craik, D. (M.) Leipzig 323.27

— *Same*. New York 530.23

WILMER, Margaret E. The Lestrange family. A true story 1127.7

WILSON, Charles Heath. Life and works of Michelangelo Buonarroti. The life partly compiled from that by Aurelio Gotti. London, 1876. xliii, 567 pp. Portrait. Illustrations. Folded sheet. Fac-simile. 8° 6211.11

PERIODICALS

CURRENTLY RECEIVED IN THE READING ROOM.

The titles with an asterisk prefixed are furnished by the Fellowes Athenæum. After the figures denoting the size of a periodical, indication is given of the frequency of publication; *m.* signifying monthly, ½*m.* semi-monthly, *q.* quarterly, *w.* weekly, ⅓*w.* tri-weekly.

Box no.			
68	*Academy, The. London. [*Literature, science, and art*]	4°	*w.*
49	*Aldine, The. New York. [*Illustrated*]	F°	*m.*
23	*American naturalist. Salem	8°	*m.*
30	Appleton's journal of literature, science, and art. New York	4°	*w.*
44	*Army and navy journal. New York	F°	*w.*
72	*Art, L'. Revue hebdomadaire illustrée. Paris	F°	*w.*
1	*Art-journal, The. London. [*Illustrated*]	4°	*m.*
2	*Athenæum, The. London. [*Literary criticism, etc.*]	4°	*w.*
9	Atlantic monthly. Boston. [*Literary*]	8°	*m.*
10	Ballou's monthly magazine. Boston. [*Literary*]	8°	*m.*
75	Bee-hive, The. London. [*Labor organ*]	F°	*w.*
80	*Boston daily advertiser. Boston	F°	*d.*
62	*Bibliotheca sacra. Andover. [*Congregational trinitarian*]	8°	*q.*
63	*Catholic world. New York	8°	*m.*
57	*Church and state. New York and Boston. [*Episcopal*]	F°	*w.*
60	*Contemporary review. London. [*Literary*]	8°	*m.*
3	*Cornhill magazine. London. [*Literary*]	8°	*m.*
7	Daily graphic. New York. [*Illustrated.*]	F°	*w.*
67	*Deutsche Rundschau. Berlin. [*Literary*]	8°	*m.*
47	Dexter Smith's musical, literary, dramatic and art paper. Boston	4°	*m.*
4	*Dublin review. London. [*Catholic*]	8°	*q.*
17	*Dublin university magazine. Dublin. [*Literary*]	8°	*m.*
25	*Dwight's journal of music. Boston	4°	½*m.*
12	Eclectic magazine. New York. [*Literary compilation*]	8°	*m.*
51	*Englishwoman's domestic magazine. London. [*Fashion*]	4°	*m.*
79	Every boy's magazine. London	L. 8°	*m.*
58	Folio. Boston. [*Musical*]	4°	*m.*
18	*Fortnightly review. London. [*Literary*]	8°	*m.*
48	Frank Leslie's illustrated newspaper. New York	F°	*w.*
19	*Fraser's magazine. London. [*Literary and critical*]	8°	*m.*
8	Galaxy, The. New York. [*Literary*]	8°	*m.*
74	*Gazette des beaux-arts. Paris	L. 8°	*m.*
14	*Gegenwart, Die. Berlin. [*Literary*]	4°	*w.*
31	Godey's lady's book. Philadelphia. [*Fashion*]	8°	*m.*
77	Golden rule, The. Boston. [*Religious and literary*]	F°	*w.*
45	Good words. London. [*Literary*]	8°	*m.*
20	*Graphic, The. London. [*Illustrated, literary, etc.*]	F°	*w.*
27	Harper's bazar. New York. [*Fashion*]	F°	*w.*
13	Harper's new monthly magazine. New York. [*Illustrated, literary, etc.*]	8°	*m.*
6	Harper's weekly. New York. [*Illustrated, literary, etc.*]	F°	*w.*
55	Herald of health. New York. [*Hygienic*]	8°	*m.*
21	*Illustrated London news. London	F°	*w.*
73	*Illustration, L', journal universel. Paris. [*News, etc.*]	F°	*w.*

Box. no.			
54	*Illustrirte Zeitung. Leipzig. [*News, etc.*]	F°	*w.*
64	*International review. New York	8°	$\frac{1}{2}$*m.*
15	Lippincott's magazine. Philadelphia. [*Literary*]	8°	*m.*
43	Literary world. Boston. [*Critical*]	4°	*m.*
46	Littell's living age. Boston. [*Eclectic*]	8°	*w.*
52	*Macmillan's magazine. London. [*Literary*]	8°	*m.*
69	*Mail, The. London. [*News*]	F°	$\frac{1}{3}$*w.*
40	*Methodist quarterly review. New York	8°	*q.*
38	*Monde, Le, illustré. Paris. [*Literary, illustrated*]	F°	*w.*
59	Nation, The. New York. [*News, criticism, etc.*]	4°	*w.*
53	*Nature. London. [*Science and art*]	L. 8°	*w.*
76	New church independent and monthly review. Chicago	8°	*m.*
11	New-England journal of education. Boston	4°	*w.*
78	New Jerusalem messenger. New York	F°	*w.*
28	*North American review. Boston. [*Literary, critical*]	8°	*m.*
50	Official gazette of the United States patent office. Washington	4°	*w.*
42	Our dumb animals. Boston	4°	*m.*
33	*Pall Mall budget. London. [*News*]	F°	*w.*
5	*Popular science monthly. New York	8°	*m.*
41	*Practical magazine. London and Boston. [*Technological*]	F°	*m.*
34	*Punch. London. [*Comic*]	4°	*w.*
35	*Quarterly review. London. [*Literary, critical, conservative*]	8°	*q.*
39	*Revue des deux mondes. Paris. [*Literary*]	8°	$\frac{1}{2}$*m.*
16	St. Nicholas. New York. [*Juvenile*]	8°	*m.*
36	*Saturday review. London. [*Literary and critical*]	Sm. f°	*w.*
22	Scientific American. New York. [*Technological*]	F°	*w.*
22a	Scientific American Supplement. New York	F°	*w.*
26	Scribner's monthly. New York. [*Literary, illustrated*]	8°	*m.*
61	*Spectator, The. London. [*Literary and critical*]	Sm. f°	*w.*
40	*Ueber Land und Meer. Stuttgart. [*Illustrated, literary*]	F°	*w.*
56	*Unitarian review, and religious magazine. Boston. [*Conservative*]	8°	*m.*
37	*Westminster review. London. [*Literary and liberal*]	8°	*q.*
66	Woman's journal. Boston and Chicago	F°	*w.*
29	Youth's companion. Boston	F°	*w.*

Made in United States
Orlando, FL
21 October 2026

89529438R00162